(see back endpap

Here's t

Argentina

SXXX

ASIA 56–57

82–83

76–77

68–69

80–81

65

66–67

70–71

58–59

78–79

74–75

64

72–73

62–63

60–61

THE TIMES
ATLAS
OF THE
WORLD

COMPACT EDITION

Times Books, 77-85 Fulham Palace Road,
London W6 8JB

The Times is a registered trademark of
Times Newspapers Ltd

First published 1994
Second Edition 2000
Third Edition 2004
Reprinted 2005

Printed in Thailand

British Library Cataloguing in Publication Data.
A catalogue record for this book is
available from the British Library.

ISBN 0 00 715723 1

QH11452 Imp 002

All mapping in this atlas is generated from Collins Bartholomew digital databases.
Collins Bartholomew, the UK's leading independent geographical information supplier,
can provide a digital, custom, and premium mapping service to a variety of markets.
For further information:
Tel: +44 (0) 141 306 3752
e-mail: collinsbartholomew@harpercollins.co.uk

or visit our website at: www.collinsbartholomew.com

www.harpercollins.co.uk
visit the book lover's website

THE 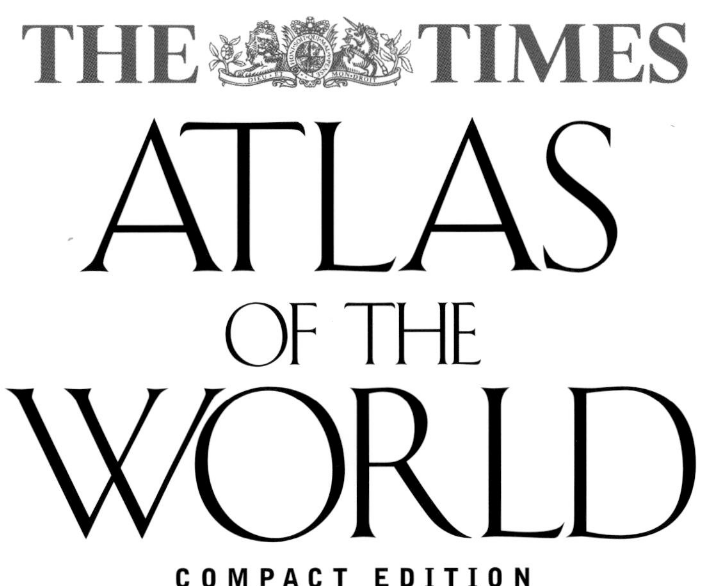 TIMES
ATLAS
OF THE
WORLD

COMPACT EDITION

TIMES BOOKS
London

Pages	Title	Scale

THE WORLD TODAY

Pages	Title
6–29	STATES AND TERRITORIES OF THE WORLD
30–33	CONTINENTS AND OCEANS
34–35	CLIMATE
36–37	ENVIRONMENT
38–39	POPULATION AND CITIES
40–41	TELECOMMUNICATIONS

ATLAS OF THE WORLD

Pages	Title
42–43	INTRODUCTION TO ATLAS OF THE WORLD
44–45	**WORLD** PHYSICAL FEATURES
46–47	**WORLD** COUNTRIES

Pages	Title	Scale
48–49	**OCEANIA**	**1:50 000 000**
50–51	AUSTRALIA	1:20 000 000
52–53	AUSTRALIA Southeast	1:7 500 000
54	NEW ZEALAND	1:7 500 000
55	ANTARCTICA	1:45 000 000
56–57	**ASIA**	**1:55 000 000**
58–59	SOUTHEAST ASIA	1:25 000 000

Pages	Title	Scale
60–61	MALAYSIA AND INDONESIA West	1:12 000 000
62–63	CONTINENTAL SOUTHEAST ASIA	1:12 000 000
64	PHILIPPINES	1:12 000 000
65	NORTH KOREA AND SOUTH KOREA	1:6 500 000
66–67	JAPAN	1:7 500 000
68–69	CHINA AND MONGOLIA	1:25 000 000
70–71	CHINA Central	1:12 000 000
72–73	SOUTH ASIA	1:15 000 000
74–75	PAKISTAN, INDIA North AND BANGLADESH	1:12 000 000
76–77	CENTRAL ASIA	1:15 000 000
78–79	ARABIAN PENINSULA	1:12 000 000
80–81	EAST MEDITERRANEAN	1:12 000 000
82–83	RUSSIAN FEDERATION	1:30 000 000
84–85	**EUROPE**	**1:25 000 000**
86–87	EUROPEAN RUSSIAN FEDERATION	1:15 000 000
88–89	NORTHEAST EUROPE	1:6 000 000
90–91	UKRAINE AND MOLDOVA	1:6 000 000
92–93	SCANDINAVIA AND ICELAND	1:7 500 000
94–95	BRITISH ISLES	1:6 000 000

Pages	Title	Scale
96	SCOTLAND	1:3 000 000
97	IRELAND	1:3 000 000
98–99	ENGLAND AND WALES	1:3 000 000
100–101	NORTHWEST EUROPE	1:3 000 000
102–103	CENTRAL EUROPE	1:6 000 000
104–105	FRANCE AND SWITZERLAND	1:6 000 000
106–107	SPAIN AND PORTUGAL	1:6 000 000
108–109	ITALY AND THE BALKANS	1:6 000 000
110–111	SOUTHEAST EUROPE	1:6 000 000
112–113	**AFRICA**	**1:45 000 000**
114–115	NORTHWEST AFRICA	1:20 000 000
116–117	NORTHEAST AFRICA	1:20 000 000
118–119	CENTRAL AFRICA	1:15 000 000
120–121	SOUTHERN AFRICA	1:15 000 000
122–123	REPUBLIC OF SOUTH AFRICA	1:7 500 000
124–125	**NORTH AMERICA**	**1:40 000 000**
126–127	CANADA	1:25 000 000
128–129	CANADA West	1:12 000 000
130–131	CANADA East	1:12 000 000
132–133	UNITED STATES OF AMERICA	1:20 000 000
134–135	USA West	1:8 000 000
136–137	USA North Central	1:8 000 000
138–139	USA Northeast	1:8 000 000
140–141	USA Southeast	1:8 000 000
142–143	USA South Central	1:8 000 000
144–145	MEXICO	1:12 000 000
146–147	CENTRAL AMERICA AND THE CARIBBEAN	1:15 000 000
148–149	**SOUTH AMERICA**	**1:35 000 000**
150–151	SOUTH AMERICA North	1:20 000 000
152–153	SOUTH AMERICA South	1:20 000 000
154–155	BRAZIL Southeast	1:7 500 000
OCEANS		
156–157	PACIFIC OCEAN	1:90 000 000
158	ATLANTIC OCEAN	1:90 000 000
159	INDIAN OCEAN	1:90 000 000
160	ARCTIC OCEAN	1:45 000 000
161–240	**INDEX**	

All independent countries and populated dependent and disputed territories are included in this list of the states and territories of the world; the list is arranged in alphabetical order by the conventional name form. For independent states, the full name is given below the conventional name, if this is different; for territories, the status is given. The capital city name is the same form as shown on the reference maps.

The statistics used for the area and population are the latest available and include estimates. The information on languages and religions is based on the latest information on 'de facto' speakers of the language or 'de facto' adherents to the religion. The information available on languages and religions varies greatly from country to country. Some countries include questions in censuses, others do not, in which case best estimates are used. The order of the languages and religions reflect their relative importance within the country; generally, languages or religions are included when more than one per cent of the population are estimated to be speakers or adherents.

Membership of selected international organizations is shown for each independent country. Territories are not shown as having separate memberships of these organizations.

ABBREVIATIONS

Currencies

| CFA | Communauté Financière Africaine |
| CFP | Comptoirs Français du Pacifique |

Organizations

APEC	Asia-Pacific Economic Cooperation
ASEAN	Association of Southeast Asian Nations
CARICOM	Caribbean Community
CIS	Commonwealth of Independent States
Comm.	The Commonwealth
EU	European Union
OECD	Organization of Economic Cooperation and Development
OPEC	Organization of Petroleum Exporting Countries
SADC	Southern African Development Community
UN	United Nations

AFGHANISTAN
Islamic State of Afghanistan

Area Sq Km	652 225	Religions	Sunni Muslim, Shi'a Muslim
Area Sq Miles	251 825		
Population	23 897 000	Currency	Afghani
Capital	Kābul	Organizations	UN
Languages	Dari, Pushtu, Uzbek,Turkmen	Map page	76–77

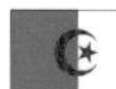

ALBANIA
Republic of Albania

Area Sq Km	28 748	Religions	Sunni Muslim, Albanian Orthodox, Roman Catholic
Area Sq Miles	11 100		
Population	3 166 000		
Capital	Tirana (Tiranë)	Currency	Lek
Languages	Albanian, Greek	Organizations	UN
		Map page	109

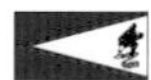

ALGERIA
People's Democratic Republic of Algeria

Area Sq Km	2 381 741	Religions	Sunni Muslim
Area Sq Miles	919 595	Currency	Algerian dinar
Population	31 800 000	Organizations	OPEC, UN
Capital	Algiers (Alger)	Map page	114–115
Languages	Arabic, French, Berber		

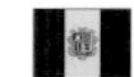

American Samoa
United States Unincorporated Territory

Area Sq Km	197	Religions	Protestant, Roman Catholic
Area Sq Miles	76		
Population	67 000	Currency	United States dollar
Capital	Fagatogo	Map page	49
Languages	Samoan, English		

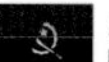

ANDORRA
Principality of Andorra

Area Sq Km	465	Religions	Roman Catholic
Area Sq Miles	180	Currency	Euro
Population	71 000	Organizations	UN
Capital	Andorra la Vella	Map page	104
Languages	Spanish, Catalan, French		

ANGOLA
Republic of Angola

Area Sq Km	1 246 700	Religions	Roman Catholic, Protestant, traditional beliefs
Area Sq Miles	481 354		
Population	13 625 000		
Capital	Luanda	Currency	Kwanza
Languages	Portuguese, Bantu, local languages	Organizations	SADC, UN
		Map page	120

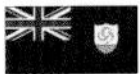

Anguilla
United Kingdom Overseas Territory

Area Sq Km	155	Religions	Protestant, Roman
Area Sq Miles	60		Catholic
Population	12 000	Currency	East Caribbean dollar
Capital	The Valley	Map page	147
Languages	English		

ANTIGUA AND BARBUDA

Area Sq Km	442	Religions	Protestant, Roman
Area Sq Miles	171		Catholic
Population	73 000	Currency	East Caribbean dollar
Capital	St John's	Organizations	CARICOM,
Languages	English, creole		Comm., UN
		Map page	147

ARGENTINA
Argentine Republic

Area Sq Km	2 766 889	Religions	Roman Catholic,
Area Sq Miles	1 068 302		Protestant
Population	38 428 000	Currency	Argentinian peso
Capital	Buenos Aires	Organizations	UN
Languages	Spanish, Italian,	Map page	152–153
	Amerindian		
	languages		

ARMENIA
Republic of Armenia

Area Sq Km	29 800	Religions	Armenian Orthodox
Area Sq Miles	11 506	Currency	Dram
Population	3 061 000	Organizations	CIS, UN
Capital	Yerevan (Erevan)	Map page	81
Languages	Armenian, Azeri		

Aruba
Self-governing Netherlands Territory

Area Sq Km	193	Religions	Roman Catholic,
Area Sq Miles	75		Protestant
Population	100 000	Currency	Aruban florin
Capital	Oranjestad	Map page	147
Languages	Papiamento, Dutch,		
	English		

Ascension
Dependency of St Helena

Area Sq Km	88	Religions	Protestant, Roman
Area Sq Miles	34		Catholic
Population	1 122	Currency	Pound sterling
Capital	Georgetown	Map page	113
Languages	English		

AUSTRALIA
Commonwealth of Australia

Area Sq Km	7 692 024	Religions	Protestant, Roman
Area Sq Miles	2 969 907		Catholic, Orthodox
Population	19 731 000	Currency	Australian dollar
Capital	Canberra	Organizations	APEC, Comm.,
Languages	English, Italian,		OECD, UN
	Greek	Map page	50–51

Australian Capital Territory (Federal Territory)

Area Sq Km	2 358	Population	321 680
Area Sq Miles	910	Capital	Canberra

Jervis Bay Territory (Territory)

Area Sq Km	73	Population	611
Area Sq Miles	28		

New South Wales (State)

Area Sq Km	800 642	Population	6 609 304
Area Sq Miles	309 130	Capital	Sydney

Northern Territory (Territory)

Area Sq Km	1 349 129	Population	200 019
Area Sq Miles	520 902	Capital	Darwin

Queensland (State)

Area Sq Km	1 730 648	Population	3 635 121
Area Sq Miles	668 207	Capital	Brisbane

South Australia (State)

Area Sq Km	983 482	Population	1 514 854
Area Sq Miles	379 725	Capital	Adelaide

Tasmania (State)

Area Sq Km	68 401	Population	472 931
Area Sq Miles	26 410	Capital	Hobart

Victoria (State)

Area Sq Km	227 416	Population	4 822 663
Area Sq Miles	87 806	Capital	Melbourne

Western Australia (State)

Area Sq Km	2 529 875	Population	1 906 114
Area Sq Miles	976 790	Capital	Perth

AUSTRIA
Republic of Austria

Area Sq Km	83 855	Religions	Roman Catholic,
Area Sq Miles	32 377		Protestant
Population	8 116 000	Currency	Euro
Capital	Vienna (Wien)	Organizations	EU, OECD, UN
Languages	German, Croatian,	Map page	102–103
	Turkish		

AZERBAIJAN
Azerbaijani Republic

Area Sq Km	86 600	Religions	Shi'a Muslim, Sunni
Area Sq Miles	33 436		Muslim, Russian and
Population	8 370 000		Armenian Orthodox
Capital	Baku (Bakı)	Currency	Azerbaijani manat
Languages	Azeri, Armenian,	Organizations	CIS, UN
	Russian, Lezgian	Map page	81

Azores (Arquipélago dos Açores)
Autonomous Region of Portugal

Area Sq Km	2 300	Religions	Roman Catholic,
Area Sq Miles	888		Protestant
Population	242 073	Currency	Euro
Capital	Ponta Delgada	Map page	112
Languages	Portuguese		

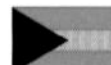

THE BAHAMAS
Commonwealth of The Bahamas

Area Sq Km	13 939	Religions	Protestant, Roman
Area Sq Miles	5 382		Catholic
Population	314 000	Currency	Bahamian dollar
Capital	Nassau	Organizations	CARICOM, Comm.,
Languages	English, creole		UN
		Map page	146–147

BAHRAIN
Kingdom of Bahrain

Area Sq Km	691	Religions	Shi'a Muslim, Sunni
Area Sq Miles	267		Muslim, Christian
Population	724 000	Currency	Bahraini dinar
Capital	Manama	Organizations	UN
	(Al Manāmah)	Map page	79
Languages	Arabic, English		

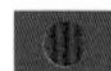

BANGLADESH
People's Republic of Bangladesh

Area Sq Km	143 998	Religions	Sunni Muslim, Hindu
Area Sq Miles	55 598	Currency	Taka
Population	146 736 000	Organizations	Comm., UN
Capital	Dhaka (Dacca)	Map page	75
Languages	Bengali, English		

BARBADOS

Area Sq Km	430	Religions	Protestant, Roman
Area Sq Miles	166		Catholic
Population	270 000	Currency	Barbados dollar
Capital	Bridgetown	Organizations	CARICOM,
Languages	English, creole		Comm., UN
		Map page	147

BELARUS
Republic of Belarus

Area Sq Km	207 600	Religions	Belorussian Orthodox,
Area Sq Miles	80 155		Roman Catholic
Population	9 895 000	Currency	Belarus rouble
Capital	Minsk	Organizations	CIS, UN
Languages	Belorussian, Russian	Map page	88–89

BELGIUM
Kingdom of Belgium

Area Sq Km	30 520	Religions	Roman Catholic,
Area Sq Miles	11 784		Protestant
Population	10 318 000	Currency	Euro
Capital	Brussels (Bruxelles)	Organizations	EU, OECD, UN
Languages	Dutch (Flemish),	Map page	100
	French (Walloon),		
	German		

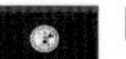

BELIZE

Area Sq Km	22 965	Religions	Roman Catholic,
Area Sq Miles	8 867		Protestant
Population	256 000	Currency	Belize dollar
Capital	Belmopan	Organizations	CARICOM, Comm.,
Languages	English, Spanish,		UN
	Mayan, creole	Map page	147

BENIN
Republic of Benin

Area Sq Km	112 620	Religions	Traditional beliefs,
Area Sq Miles	43 483		Roman Catholic,
Population	6 736 000		Sunni Muslim
Capital	Porto-Novo	Currency	CFA franc
Languages	French, Fon,	Organization	UN
	Yoruba, Adja,	Map page	114
	local languages		

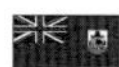

Bermuda
United Kingdom Overseas Territory

Area Sq Km	54	Religions	Protestant, Roman
Area Sq Miles	21		Catholic
Population	82 000	Currency	Bermuda dollar
Capital	Hamilton	Map page	125
Languages	English		

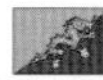

BHUTAN
Kingdom of Bhutan

Area Sq Km	46 620	Religions	Buddhist, Hindu
Area Sq Miles	18 000	Currency	Ngultrum,
Population	2 257 000		Indian rupee
Capital	Thimphu	Organizations	UN
Languages	Dzongkha,	Map page	75
	Nepali, Assamese		

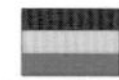

BOLIVIA
Republic of Bolivia

Area Sq Km	1 098 581	Religions	Roman Catholic,
Area Sq Miles	424 164		Protestant, Baha'i
Population	8 808 000	Currency	Boliviano
Capital	La Paz/Sucre	Organizations	UN
Languages	Spanish, Quechua,	Map page	152
	Aymara		

Bonaire
part of Netherlands Antilles

Area Sq Km	288	Religions	Roman Catholic,
Area Sq Miles	111		Protestant
Population	10 114	Currency	Netherlands Antilles
Capital	Kralendijk		guilder
Languages	Dutch, Papiamento	Map page	147

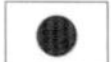

Bonin Islands (Ogasawara-shotō)
part of Japan

Area Sq Km	104	Religions	Shintoist, Buddhist,
Area Sq Miles	40		Christian
Population	2 300	Currency	Yen
Capital	Omura	Map page	69
Languages	Japanese		

BOSNIA-HERZEGOVINA
Republic of Bosnia and Herzegovina

Area Sq Km	51 130	Religions	Sunni Muslim, Serbian
Area Sq Miles	19 741		Orthodox, Roman
Population	4 161 000		Catholic, Protestant
Capital	Sarajevo	Currency	Marka
Languages	Bosnian, Serbian,	Organizations	UN
	Croatian	Map page	109

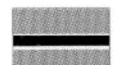

BOTSWANA
Republic of Botswana

Area Sq Km	581 370	Religions	Traditional beliefs,
Area Sq Miles	224 468		Protestant, Roman
Population	1 785 000		Catholic
Capital	Gaborone	Currency	Pula
Languages	English, Setswana,	Organizations	Comm., SADC, UN
	Shona, local	Map page	120
	languages		

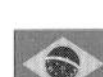

BRAZIL
Federative Republic of Brazil

Area Sq Km	8 514 879	Religions	Roman Catholic,
Area Sq Miles	3 287 613		Protestant
Population	178 470 000	Currency	Real
Capital	Brasília	Organizations	UN
Languages	Portuguese	Map page	150–151

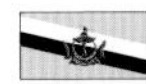

BRUNEI
State of Brunei Darussalam

Area Sq Km	5 765	Religions	Sunni Muslim, Buddhist,
Area Sq Miles	2 226		Christian
Population	358 000	Currency	Brunei dollar
Capital	Bandar Seri Begawan	Organizations	APEC, ASEAN,
Languages	Malay, English,		Comm., UN
	Chinese	Map page	61

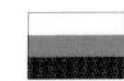

BULGARIA
Republic of Bulgaria

Area Sq Km	110 994	Religions	Bulgarian Orthodox,
Area Sq Miles	42 855		Sunni Muslim
Population	7 897 000	Currency	Lev
Capital	Sofia (Sofiya)	Organizations	UN
Languages	Bulgarian, Turkish,	Map page	110
	Romany,		
	Macedonian		

BURKINA
Democratic Republic of Burkina Faso

Area Sq Km	274 200	Religions	Sunni Muslim,
Area Sq Miles	105 869		traditional beliefs,
Population	13 002 000		Roman Catholic
Capital	Ouagadougou	Currency	CFA franc
Languages	French, Moore	Organizations	UN
	(Mossi), Fulani, local	Map page	114
	languages		

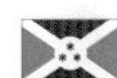

BURUNDI
Republic of Burundi

Area Sq Km	27 835	Religions	Roman Catholic,
Area Sq Miles	10 747		traditional beliefs,
Population	6 825 000		Protestant
Capital	Bujumbura	Currency	Burundian franc
Languages	Kirundi (Hutu,	Organizations	UN
	Tutsi), French	Map page	119

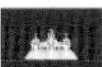

CAMBODIA
Kingdom of Cambodia

Area Sq Km	181 000	Religions	Buddhist, Roman
Area Sq Miles	69 884		Catholic, Sunni
Population	14 144 000		Muslim
Capital	Phnom Pénh	Currency	Riel
	(Phnom Penh)	Organizations	ASEAN, UN
Languages	Khmer, Vietnamese	Map page	63

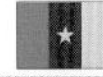

CAMEROON
Republic of Cameroon

Area Sq Km	475 442	Religions	Roman Catholic,
Area Sq Miles	183 569		traditional beliefs,
Population	16 018 000		Sunni Muslim,
Capital	Yaoundé		Protestant
Languages	French, English,	Currency	CFA franc
	Fang, Bamileke,	Organizations	Comm., UN
	local languages	Map page	118

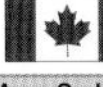

CANADA

Area Sq Km	9 984 670	Religions	Roman Catholic,
Area Sq Miles	3 855 103		Protestant, Eastern
Population	31 510 000		Orthodox, Jewish
Capital	Ottawa	Currency	Canadian dollar
Languages	English, French,	Organizations	APEC, Comm.,
	Inuktitut		OECD, UN
		Map page	126–127

Alberta (Province)

Area Sq Km	661 848	Population	3 113 600
Area Sq Miles	255 541	Capital	Edmonton

British Columbia (Province)

Area Sq Km	944 735	Population	4 141 300
Area Sq Miles	364 764	Capital	Victoria

Manitoba (Province)

Area Sq Km	647 797	Population	1 150 800
Area Sq Miles	250 116	Capital	Winnipeg

New Brunswick (Province)

Area Sq Km	72 908	Population	756 700
Area Sq Miles	28 150	Capital	Fredericton

Newfoundland and Labrador (Province)

Area Sq Km	405 212	Population	531 600
Area Sq Miles	156 453	Capital	St John's

Northwest Territories (Territory)

Area Sq Km	1 346 106	Population	41 400
Area Sq Miles	519 734	Capital	Yellowknife

CANADA

Nova Scotia (Province)

Area Sq Km	55 284	Population	944 800
Area Sq Miles	21 345	Capital	Halifax

Nunavut (Territory)

Area Sq Km	2 093 190	Population	28 700
Area Sq Miles	808 185	Capital	Iqaluit (Frobisher Bay)

Ontario (Province)

Area Sq Km	1 076 395	Population	12 068 300
Area Sq Miles	415 598	Capital	Toronto

Prince Edward Island (Province)

Area Sq Km	5 660	Population	139 900
Area Sq Miles	2 185	Capital	Charlottetown

Québec (Province)

Area Sq Km	1 542 056	Population	7 455 200
Area Sq Miles	595 391	Capital	Québec

Saskatchewan (Province)

Area Sq Km	651 036	Population	1 011 800
Area Sq Miles	251 366	Capital	Regina

Yukon Territory (Territory)

Area Sq Km	482 443	Population	29 900
Area Sq Miles	186 272	Capital	Whitehorse

Canary Islands (Islas Canarias)
Autonomous Community of Spain

Area Sq Km	7 447	Languages	Spanish
Area Sq Miles	2 875	Religions	Roman Catholic
Population	1 694 477	Currency	Euro
Capital	Santa Cruz de Tenerife/Las Palmas	Map page	114

CAPE VERDE
Republic of Cape Verde

Area Sq Km	4 033	Religions	Roman Catholic, Protestant
Area Sq Miles	1 557		
Population	463 000	Currency	Cape Verde escudo
Capital	Praia	Organizations	UN
Languages	Portuguese, creole	Map page	46

Cayman Islands
United Kingdom Overseas Territory

Area Sq Km	259	Religions	Protestant, Roman Catholic
Area Sq Miles	100		
Population	40 000	Currency	Cayman Islands dollar
Capital	George Town	Map page	146
Languages	English		

CENTRAL AFRICAN REPUBLIC

Area Sq Km	622 436	Religions	Protestant, Roman Catholic, traditional beliefs, Sunni Muslim
Area Sq Miles	240 324		
Population	3 865 000		
Capital	Bangui	Currency	CFA franc
Languages	French, Sango, Banda, Baya, local languages	Organizations	UN
		Map page	118

Ceuta
Autonomous Community of Spain

Area Sq Km	19	Religions	Roman Catholic, Muslim
Area Sq Miles	7		
Population	71 505	Currency	Euro
Capital	Ceuta	Map page	106
Languages	Spanish, Arabic		

CHAD
Republic of Chad

Area Sq Km	1 284 000	Religions	Sunni Muslim, Roman Catholic, Protestant, traditional beliefs
Area Sq Miles	495 755		
Population	8 598 000		
Capital	Ndjamena	Currency	CFA franc
Languages	Arabic, French,Sara, local languages	Organizations	UN
		Map page	115

Chatham Islands
part of New Zealand

Area Sq Km	963	Religions	Protestant
Area Sq Miles	372	Currency	New Zealand dollar
Population	717	Map page	49
Capital	Waitangi		
Languages	English		

CHILE
Republic of Chile

Area Sq Km	756 945	Religions	Roman Catholic, Protestant
Area Sq Miles	292 258		
Population	15 805 000	Currency	Chilean peso
Capital	Santiago	Organizations	APEC, UN
Languages	Spanish, Amerindian languages	Map page	152–153

CHINA
People's Republic of China

Area Sq Km	9 584 492	Religions	Confucian, Taoist, Buddhist, Christian, Sunni Muslim
Area Sq Miles	3 700 593		
Population	1 289 161 000		
Capital	Beijing (Peking)	Currency	Yuan, Hong Kong dollar, Macau pataca
Languages	Mandarin, Wu, Cantonese, Hsiang, regional languages	Organizations	APEC, UN
		Map page	68–69

Anhui (Province)

Area Sq Km	139 000	Population	59 860 000
Area Sq Miles	53 668	Capital	Hefei

Bejing (Municipality)

Area Sq Km	16 800	Population	13 820 000
Area Sq Miles	6 487	Capital	Beijing (Peking)

Chongqing (Municipality)

Area Sq Km	23 000	Population	30 900 000
Area Sq Miles	8 880	Capital	Chongqing

Fujian (Province)

Area Sq Km	121 400	Population	34 710 000
Area Sq Miles	46 873	Capital	Fuzhou

Gansu (Province)

Area Sq Km	453 700	Population	25 620 000
Area Sq Miles	175 175	Capital	Lanzhou

Macau (Special Administrative Region)

Area Sq Km	17	Population	440 000
Area Sq Mile	7		

Guangdong (Province)

Area Sq Km	178 000	Population	86 420 000
Area Sq Miles	68 726	Capital	Guangzhou (Canton)

Nei Mongol Zizhiqu (Inner Mongolia) (Autonomous Region)

Area Sq Km	1 183 000	Population	23 760 000
Area Sq Miles	456 759	Capital	Hohhot

Guangxi Zhuangzu Zizhiqu (Autonomous Region)

Area Sq Km	236 000	Population	44 890 000
Area Sq Miles	91 120	Capital	Nanning

Ningxia Huizu Zizhiqu (Autonomous Region)

Area Sq Km	66 400	Population	5 620 000
Area Sq Miles	25 637	Capital	Yinchuan

Guizhou (Province)

Area Sq Km	176 000	Population	35 250 000
Area Sq Miles	67 954	Capital	Guiyang

Qinghai (Province)

Area Sq Km	721 000	Population	5 180 000
Area Sq Miles	278 380	Capital	Xining

Hainan (Province)

Area Sq Km	34 000	Population	7 870 000
Area Sq Miles	13 127	Capital	Haikou

Shaanxi (Province)

Area Sq Km	205 600	Population	36 050 000
Area Sq Miles	79 383	Capital	Xi'an

Hebei (Province)

Area Sq Km	187 700	Population	67 440 000
Area Sq Miles	72 471	Capital	Shijiazhuang

Shandong (Province)

Area Sq Km	153 300	Population	90 790 000
Area Sq Miles	59 189	Capital	Jinan

Heilongjiang (Province)

Area Sq Km	454 600	Population	36 890 000
Area Sq Miles	175 522	Capital	Harbin

Shanghai (Municipality)

Area Sq Km	6 300	Population	16 740 000
Area Sq Miles	2 432	Capital	Shanghai

Henan (Province)

Area Sq Km	167 000	Population	92 560 000
Area Sq Miles	64 479	Capital	Zhengzhou

Shanxi (Province)

Area Sq Km	156 300	Population	32 970 000
Area Sq Miles	60 348	Capital	Taiyuan

Hong Kong (Special Administrative Region)

Area Sq Km	1 075	Population	6 780 000
Area Sq Miles	415	Capital	Hong Kong

Sichuan (Province)

Area Sq Km	569 000	Population	83 290 000
Area Sq Miles	219 692	Capital	Chengdu

Hubei (Province)

Area Sq Km	185 900	Population	60 280 000
Area Sq Miles	71 776	Capital	Wuhan

Tianjin (Municipality)

Area Sq Km	11 300	Population	10 010 000
Area Sq Miles	4 363	Capital	Tianjin

Hunan (Province)

Area Sq Km	210 000	Population	64 400 000
Area Sq Miles	81 081	Capital	Changsha

Xinjiang Uygur Zizhiqu (Sinkiang) (Autonomous Region)

Area Sq Km	1 600 000	Population	19 250 000
Area Sq Miles	617 763	Capital	Ürümqi

Jiangsu (Province)

Area Sq Km	102 600	Population	74 380 000
Area Sq Miles	39 614	Capital	Nanjing

Xizang Zizhiqu (Tibet) (Autonomous Region)

Area Sq Km	1 228 400	Population	2 620 000
Area Sq Miles	474 288	Capital	Lhasa

Jiangxi (Province)

Area Sq Km	166 900	Population	41 400 000
Area Sq Miles	64 440	Capital	Nanchang

Yunnan (Province)

Area Sq Km	394 000	Population	42 880 000
Area Sq Miles	152 124	Capital	Kunming

Jilin (Province)

Area Sq Km	187 000	Population	27 280 000
Area Sq Miles	72 201	Capital	Changchun

Zhejiang (Province)

Area Sq Km	101 800	Population	46 770 000
Area Sq Miles	39 305	Capital	Hangzhou

Liaoning (Province)

Area Sq Km	147 400	Population	42 380 000
Area Sq Miles	56 911	Capital	Shenyang

Christmas Island
Australian External Territory

Area Sq Km	135	Religions	Buddhist, Sunni
Area Sq Miles	52		Muslim, Protestant,
Population	1 560		Roman Catholic
Capital	The Settlement	Currency	Australian dollar
Languages	English	Map page	58

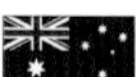

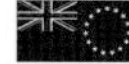

Cook Islands
Self-governing New Zealand Territory

Area Sq Km	293	Religions	Protestant, Roman
Area Sq Miles	113		Catholic
Population	18 000	Currency	New Zealand dollar
Capital	Avarua	Map page	49
Languages	English, Maori		

Cocos Islands (Keeling Islands)
Australian External Territory

Area Sq Km	14	Religions	Sunni Muslim,
Area Sq Miles	5		Christian
Population	632	Currency	Australian dollar
Capital	West Island	Map page	58
Languages	English		

COSTA RICA
Republic of Costa Rica

Area Sq Km	51 100	Religions	Roman Catholic,
Area Sq Miles	19 730		Protestant
Population	4 173 000	Currency	Costa Rican colón
Capital	San José	Organizations	UN
Languages	Spanish	Map page	146

COLOMBIA
Republic of Colombia

Area Sq Km	1 141 748	Religions	Roman Catholic,
Area Sq Miles	440 831		Protestant
Population	44 222 000	Currency	Colombian peso
Capital	Bogotá	Organizations	APEC, UN
Languages	Spanish, Amerindian	Map page	150
	languages		

CÔTE D'IVOIRE
Republic of Côte d'Ivoire

Area Sq Km	322 463	Religions	Sunni Muslim, Roman
Area Sq Miles	124 504		Catholic, traditonal
Population	16 631 000		beliefs, Protestant
Capital	Yamoussoukro	Currency	CFA franc
Languages	French, creole, Akan,	Organizations	UN
	local languages	Map page	114

COMOROS
Union of the Comoros

Area Sq Km	1 862	Religions	Sunni Muslim, Roman
Area Sq Miles	719		Catholic
Population	768 000	Currency	Comoros franc
Capital	Moroni	Organizations	UN
Languages	Comorian, French,	Map page	121
	Arabic		

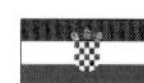

CROATIA
Republic of Croatia

Area Sq Km	56 538	Religions	Roman Catholic,
Area Sq Miles	21 829		Serbian Orthodox,
Population	4 428 000		Sunni Muslim
Capital	Zagreb	Currency	Kuna
Languages	Croatian, Serbian	Organizations	UN
		Map page	109

CONGO
Republic of the Congo

Area Sq Km	342 000	Religions	Roman Catholic,
Area Sq Miles	132 047		Protestant, traditional
Population	3 724 000		beliefs, Sunni Muslim
Capital	Brazzaville	Currency	CFA franc
Languages	French, Kongo,	Organizations	UN
	Monokutuba, local	Map page	118
	languages		

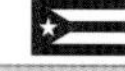

CUBA
Republic of Cuba

Area Sq Km	110 860	Religions	Roman Catholic,
Area Sq Miles	42 803		Protestant
Population	11 300 000	Currency	Cuban peso
Capital	Havana (La Habana)	Organizations	UN
Languages	Spanish	Map page	146

Curaçao
part of Netherlands Antilles

Area Sq Km	444	Religions	Roman Catholic,
Area Sq Miles	171		Protestant
Population	126 816	Currency	Netherlands Antilles
Capital	Willemstad		guilder
Languages	Dutch, Papiamento	Map page	147

CONGO, DEMOCRATIC REPUBLIC OF

Area Sq Km	2 345 410	Religions	Christian, Sunni
Area Sq Miles	905 568		Muslim
Population	52 771 000	Currency	Congolese franc
Capital	Kinshasa	Organizations	SADC, UN
Languages	French, Lingala,	Map page	118–119
	Swahili, Kongo,		
	local languages		

CYPRUS
Republic of Cyprus

Area Sq Km	9 251	Religions	Greek Orthodox, Sunni
Area Sq Miles	3 572		Muslim
Population	802 000	Currency	Cyprus pound
Capital	Nicosia (Lefkosia)	Organizations	Comm., UN
Languages	Greek, Turkish,	Map page	80
	English		

14

CZECH REPUBLIC

Area Sq Km	78 864	Religions	Roman Catholic,
Area Sq Miles	30 450		Protestant
Population	10 236 000	Currency	Czech koruna
Capital	Prague (Praha)	Organizations	UN
Languages	Czech, Moravian ,	Map page	102–103
	Slovakian		

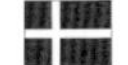

DENMARK
Kingdom of Denmark

Area Sq Km	43 075	Religions	Protestant
Area Sq Miles	16 631	Currency	Danish krone
Population	5 364 000	Organizations	EU, OECD, UN
Capital	Copenhagen	Map page	93
	(København)		
Languages	Danish		

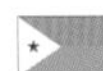

DJIBOUTI
Republic of Djibouti

Area Sq Km	23 200	Religions	Sunni Muslim,
Area Sq Miles	8 958		Christian
Population	703 000	Currency	Djibouti franc
Capital	Djibouti	Organizations	UN
Languages	Somali, Afar, French,	Map page	117
	Arabic		

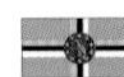

DOMINICA
Commonwealth of Dominica

Area Sq Km	750	Religions	Roman Catholic,
Area Sq Miles	290		Protestant
Population	79 000	Currency	East Caribbean dollar
Capital	Roseau	Organizations	CARICOM, Comm.,
Languages	English, creole		UN
		Map page	147

DOMINICAN REPUBLIC

Area Sq Km	48 442	Religions	Roman Catholic,
Area Sq Miles	18 704		Protestant
Population	8 745 000	Currency	Dominican peso
Capital	Santo Domingo	Organizations	UN
Languages	Spanish, creole	Map page	147

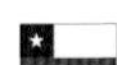

Easter Island (Isla de Pascua)
part of Chile

Area Sq Km	171	Religions	Roman Catholic
Area Sq Miles	66	Currency	Chilean peso
Population	3 791	Map page	157
Capital	Hanga Roa		
Languages	Spanish		

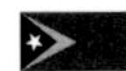

EAST TIMOR
Democratic Republic of East Timor

Area Sq Km	14 874	Religions	Roman Catholic
Area Sq Miles	5 743	Currency	United States dollar
Population	778 000	Organisations	UN
Capital	Dili	Map page	59
Languages	Portuguese, Tetun,		
	English		

ECUADOR
Republic of Ecuador

Area Sq Km	272 045	Religions	Roman Catholic
Area Sq Miles	105 037	Currency	United States dollar
Population	13 003 000	Organizations	APEC, UN
Capital	Quito	Map page	150
Languages	Spanish, Quechua,		
	Amerindian		
	languages		

EGYPT
Arab Republic of Egypt

Area Sq Km	1 000 250	Religions	Sunni Muslim, Coptic
Area Sq Miles	386 199		Christian
Population	71 931 000	Currency	Egyptian pound
Capital	Cairo (Al Qāhira)	Organizations	UN
Languages	Arabic	Map page	116

EL SALVADOR
Republic of El Salvador

Area Sq Km	21 041	Religions	Roman Catholic,
Area Sq Miles	8 124		Protestant
Population	6 515 000	Currency	El Salvador colón,
Capital	San Salvador		United States dollar
Languages	Spanish	Organizations	UN
		Map page	146

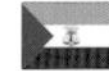

EQUATORIAL GUINEA
Republic of Equatorial Guinea

Area Sq Km	28 051	Religions	Roman Catholic,
Area Sq Miles	10 831		traditional beliefs
Population	494 000	Currency	CFA franc
Capital	Malabo	Organizations	UN
Languages	Spanish, French,	Map page	118
	Fang		

ERITREA
State of Eritrea

Area Sq Km	117 400	Religions	Sunni Muslim, Coptic
Area Sq Miles	45 328		Christian
Population	4 141 000	Currency	Nakfa
Capital	Asmara	Organizations	UN
Languages	Tigrinya, Tigre	Map page	116

ESTONIA
Republic of Estonia

Area Sq Km	45 200	Religions	Protestant, Estonian
Area Sq Miles	17 452		and Russian Orthodox
Population	1 323 000	Currency	Kroon
Capital	Tallinn	Organizations	UN
Languages	Estonian, Russian	Map page	88

ETHIOPIA
Federal Democratic Republic of Ethiopia

Area Sq Km	1 133 880	Religions	Ethiopian Orthodox,
Area Sq Miles	437 794		Sunni Muslim,
Population	70 678 000		traditional beliefs
Capital	Addis Ababa	Currency	Birr
	(Ādīs Ābeba)	Organizations	UN
Languages	Oromo, Amharic,	Map page	117
	Tigrinya, local		
	languages		

Falkland Islands
United Kingdom Overseas Territory

Area Sq Km	12 170	Religions	Protestant, Roman
Area Sq Miles	4 699		Catholic
Population	3 000	Currency	Falkland Islands
Capital	Stanley		pound
Languages	English	Map page	153

GABON
Gabonese Republic

Area Sq Km	267 667	Religions	Roman Catholic,
Area Sq Miles	103 347		Protestant, traditonal
Population	1 329 000		beliefs
Capital	Libreville	Currency	CFA franc
Languages	French, Fang, local	Organizations	UN
	languages	Map page	118

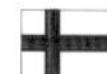

Faroe Islands
Self-governing Danish Territory

Area Sq Km	1 399	Religions	Protestant
Area Sq Miles	540	Currency	Danish krone
Population	47 000	Map page	94
Capital	Tórshavn		
	(Thorshavn)		
Languages	Faroese, Danish		

Galapagos Islands (Islas Galápagos)
part of Ecuador

Area Sq Km	8 010	Religions	Roman Catholic
Area Sq Miles	3 093	Currency	United States dollar
Population	18 640	Map page	125
Capital	Puerto Baquerizo		
	Moreno		
Languages	Spanish		

FIJI
Sovereign Democratic Republic of Fiji

Area Sq Km	18 330	Religions	Christian, Hindu, Sunni
Area Sq Miles	7 077		Muslim
Population	839 000	Currency	Fiji dollar
Capital	Suva	Organizations	UN, Comm.
Languages	English, Fijian,	Map page	49
	Hindi		

THE GAMBIA
Republic of The Gambia

Area Sq Km	11 295	Religions	Sunni Muslim,
Area Sq Miles	4 361		Protestant
Population	1 426 000	Currency	Dalasi
Capital	Banjul	Organizations	Comm., UN
Languages	English, Malinke,	Map page	114
	Fulani, Wolof		

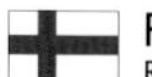

FINLAND
Republic of Finland

Area Sq Km	338 145	Religions	Protestant, Greek
Area Sq Miles	130 559		Orthodox
Population	5 207 000	Currency	Euro
Capital	Helsinki (Helsingfors)	Organizations	EU, OECD, UN
Languages	Finnish, Swedish	Map page	92–93

Gaza
semi-autonomous region

Area Sq Km	363	Religions	Sunni Muslim, Shi'a
Area Sq Miles	140		Muslim
Population	1 203 591	Currency	Israeli shekel
Capital	Gaza	Map page	80
Languages	Arabic		

FRANCE
French Republic

Area Sq Km	543 965	Religions	Roman Catholic,
Area Sq Miles	210 026		Protestant, Sunni
Population	60 144 000		Muslim
Capital	Paris	Currency	Euro
Languages	French, Arabic	Organizations	EU, OECD, UN
		Map page	104–105

GEORGIA
Republic of Georgia

Area Sq Km	69 700	Religions	Georgian Orthodox,
Area Sq Miles	26 911		Russian Orthodox,
Population	5 126 000		Sunni Muslim
Capital	T'bilisi	Currency	Lari
Languages	Georgian, Russian,	Organizations	CIS, UN
	Armenian, Azeri,	Map page	81
	Ossetian, Abkhaz		

French Guiana
French Overseas Department

Area Sq Km	90 000	Religions	Roman Catholic
Area Sq Miles	34 749	Currency	Euro
Population	178 000	Map page	151
Capital	Cayenne		
Languages	French, creole		

GERMANY
Federal Republic of Germany

Area Sq Km	357 022	Religions	Protestant, Roman
Area Sq Miles	137 847		Catholic
Population	82 476 000	Currency	Euro
Capital	Berlin	Organizations	EU, OECD, UN
Languages	German, Turkish	Map page	102

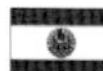

French Polynesia
French Overseas Territory

Area Sq Km	3 265	Religions	Protestant, Roman
Area Sq Miles	1 261		Catholic
Population	244 000	Currency	CFP franc
Capital	Papeete	Map page	49
Languages	French, Tahitian,		
	Polynesian		
	languages		

GHANA
Republic of Ghana

Area Sq Km	238 537	Religions	Christian, Sunni
Area Sq Miles	92 100		Muslim, traditional
Population	20 922 000		beliefs
Capital	Accra	Currency	Cedi
Languages	English, Hausa,	Organizations	Comm., UN
	Akan, local	Map page	114
	languages		

Gibraltar
United Kingdom Overseas Territory

Area Sq Km	7	Religions	Roman Catholic,
Area Sq Miles	3		Protestant, Sunni
Population	27 000		Muslim
Capital	Gibraltar	Currency	Gibraltar pound
Languages	English, Spanish	Map page	106

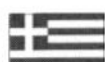

GREECE
Hellenic Republic

Area Sq Km	131 957	Religions	Greek Orthodox, Sunni
Area Sq Miles	50 949		Muslim
Population	10 976 000	Currency	Euro
Capital	Athens (Athina)	Organizations	EU, OECD, UN
Languages	Greek	Map page	111

Greenland
Self-governing Danish Territory

Area Sq Km	2 175 600	Religions	Protestant
Area Sq Miles	840 004	Currency	Danish krone
Population	57 000	Map page	127
Capital	Nuuk (Godthåb)		
Languages	Greenlandic, Danish		

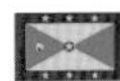

GRENADA

Area Sq Km	378	Religions	Roman Catholic,
Area Sq Miles	146		Protestant
Population	80 000	Currency	East Caribbean dollar
Capital	St George's	Organizations	CARICOM, Comm.,
Languages	English, creole		UN
		Map page	147

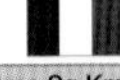

Guadeloupe
French Overseas Department

Area Sq Km	1 780	Religions	Roman Catholic
Area Sq Miles	687	Currency	Euro
Population	440 000	Map page	147
Capital	Basse-Terre		
Languages	French, creole		

Guam
United States Unincorporated Territory

Area Sq Km	541	Religions	Roman Catholic
Area Sq Miles	209	Currency	United States dollar
Population	163 000	Map page	59
Capital	Hagåtña		
Languages	Chamorro, English, Tagalog		

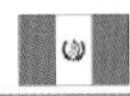

GUATEMALA
Republic of Guatemala

Area Sq Km	108 890	Religion	Roman Catholic,
Area Sq Miles	42 043		Protestant
Population	12 347 000	Currency	Quetzal, United States
Capital	Guatemala City		dollar
Languages	Spanish, Mayan languages	Organizations	UN
		Map page	146

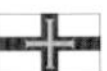

Guernsey
United Kingdom Crown Dependency

Area Sq Km	78	Religions	Protestant, Roman
Area Sq Miles	30		Catholic
Population	62 701	Currency	Pound sterling
Capital	St Peter Port	Map page	95
Languages	English, French		

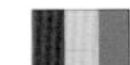

GUINEA
Republic of Guinea

Area Sq Km	245 857	Religions	Sunni Muslim,
Area Sq Miles	94 926		traditional beliefs,
Population	8 480 000		Christian
Capital	Conakry	Currency	Guinea franc
Languages	French, Fulani, Malinke, local languages	Organizations	UN
		Map page	114

GUINEA-BISSAU
Republic of Guinea-Bissau

Area Sq Km	36 125	Religions	Traditional beliefs,
Area Sq Miles	13 948		Sunni Muslim,
Population	1 493 000		Christian
Capital	Bissau	Currency	CFA franc
Languages	Portuguese, crioulo, local languages	Organizations	UN
		Map page	114

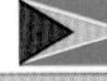

GUYANA
Co-operative Republic of Guyana

Area Sq Km	214 969	Religions	Protestant, Hindu,
Area Sq Miles	83 000		Roman Catholic,
Population	765 000		Sunni Muslim
Capital	Georgetown	Currency	Guyana dollar
Languages	English, creole, Amerindian languages	Organizations	CARICOM, Comm., UN
		Map page	150

HAITI
Republic of Haiti

Area Sq Km	27 750	Religions	Roman Catholic,
Area Sq Miles	10 714		Protestant, Voodoo
Population	8 326 000	Currency	Gourde
Capital	Port-au-Prince	Organizations	CARICOM, UN
Languages	French, creole	Map page	147

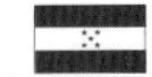

HONDURAS
Republic of Honduras

Area Sq Km	112 088	Religions	Roman Catholic,
Area Sq Miles	43 277		Protestant
Population	6 941 000	Currency	Lempira
Capital	Tegucigalpa	Organizations	UN
Languages	Spanish, Amerindian languages	Map page	147

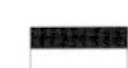

HUNGARY
Republic of Hungary

Area Sq Km	93 030	Religions	Roman Catholic,
Area Sq Miles	35 919		Protestant
Population	9 877 000	Currency	Forint
Capital	Budapest	Organizations	OECD, UN
Languages	Hungarian	Map page	103

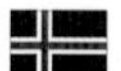

ICELAND
Republic of Iceland

Area Sq Km	102 820	Religions	Protestant
Area Sq Miles	39 699	Currency	Icelandic króna
Population	290 000	Organizations	OECD, UN
Capital	Reykjavík	Map page	92
Languages	Icelandic		

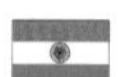

INDIA
Republic of India

Area Sq Km	3 064 898	Religions	Hindu, Sunni Muslim,
Area Sq Miles	1 183 364		Shi'a Muslim, Sikh,
Population	1 065 462 000		Christian
Capital	New Delhi	Currency	Indian rupee
Languages	Hindi, English, many	Organizations	Comm., UN
	regional languages	Map page	72–73

INDONESIA
Republic of Indonesia

Area Sq Km	1 919 445	Religions	Sunni Muslim,
Area Sq Miles	741 102		Protestant, Roman
Population	219 883 000		Catholic, Hindu,
Capital	Jakarta		Buddhist
Languages	Indonesian, local	Currency	Rupiah
	languages	Organizations	APEC, ASEAN,
			OPEC, UN
		Map page	58–59

IRAN
Islamic Republic of Iran

Area Sq Km	1 648 000	Religions	Shi'a Muslim, Sunni
Area Sq Miles	636 296		Muslim
Population	68 920 000	Currency	Iranian rial
Capital	Tehrän	Organizations	OPEC, UN
Languages	Farsi, Azeri, Kurdish,	Map page	81
	regional languages		

IRAQ
Republic of Iraq

Area Sq Km	438 317	Religions	Shi'a Muslim, Sunni
Area Sq Miles	169 235		Muslim, Christian
Population	25 175 000	Currency	Iraqi dinar
Capital	Baghdād	Organizations	OPEC, UN
Languages	Arabic, Kurdish,	Map page	81
	Turkmen		

IRELAND, REPUBLIC OF

Area Sq Km	70 282	Religions	Roman Catholic,
Area Sq Miles	27 136		Protestant,
Population	3 956 000	Currency	Euro
Capital	Dublin	Organizations	EU, OECD, UN
	(Baile Átha Cliath)	Map page	97
Languages	English, Irish		

Isle of Man
United Kingdom Crown Dependency

Area Sq Km	572	Religions	Protestant, Roman
Area Sq Miles	221		Catholic
Population	75 000	Currency	Pound sterling
Capital	Douglas	Map page	98
Languages	English		

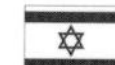

ISRAEL
State of Israel

Area Sq Km	20 770	Religions	Jewish, Sunni Muslim,
Area Sq Miles	8 019		Christian, Druze
Population	6 433 000	Currency	Shekel
Capital	Jerusalem*	Organizations	UN
	(Yerushalayim)	Map page	80
	(El Quds)		
Languages	Hebrew, Arabic		

*De facto capital. Disputed.

ITALY
Italian Republic

Area Sq Km	301 245	Religions	Roman Catholic
Area Sq Miles	116 311	Currency	Euro
Population	57 423 000	Organizations	EU, OECD, UN
Capital	Rome (Roma)	Map page	108–109
Languages	Italian		

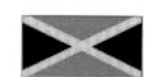

JAMAICA

Area Sq Km	10 991	Religions	Protestant, Roman
Area Sq Miles	4 244		Catholic
Population	2 651 000	Currency	Jamaican dollar
Capital	Kingston	Organizations	CARICOM, Comm.,
Languages	English, creole		UN
		Map page	146

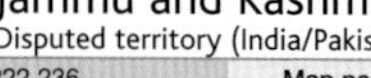

Jammu and Kashmir
Disputed territory (India/Pakistan)

Area Sq Km	222 236	Map page	74–75
Area Sq Miles	85 806		
Population	13 000 000		
Capital	Srinagar		

JAPAN

Area Sq Km	377 727	Religions	Shintoist, Buddhist,
Area Sq Miles	145 841		Christian
Population	127 654 000	Currency	Yen
Capital	Tōkyō	Organizations	APEC, OECD, UN
Languages	Japanese	Map page	66–67

Jersey
United Kingdom Crown Dependency

Area Sq Km	116	Religions	Protestant, Roman
Area Sq Miles	45		Catholic
Population	87 186	Currency	Pound sterling
Capital	St Helier	Map page	95
Languages	English, French		

JORDAN
Hashemite Kingdom of Jordan

Area Sq Km	89 206	Religions	Sunni Muslim,
Area Sq Miles	34 443		Christian
Population	5 473 000	Currency	Jordanian dinar
Capital	'Ammān	Organizations	UN
Languages	Arabic	Map page	80

Juan Fernández Islands
part of Chile

Area Sq Km	179	Religions	Roman Catholic, Protestant
Area Sq Miles	69		
Population	633	Currency	Chilean peso
Capital	San Juan Bautista	Map page	157
Languages	Spanish, Amerindian languages		

KAZAKHSTAN
Republic of Kazakhstan

Area Sq Km	2 717 300	Religions	Sunni Muslim, Russian Orthodox, Protestant
Area Sq Miles	1 049 155		
Population	15 433 000	Currency	Tenge
Capital	Astana (Akmola)	Organizations	CIS, UN
Languages	Kazakh, Russian, Ukrainian, German, Uzbek, Tatar	Map page	76–77

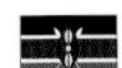

KENYA
Republic of Kenya

Area Sq Km	582 646	Religions	Christian, traditional beliefs
Area Sq Miles	224 961		
Population	31 987 000	Currency	Kenyan shilling
Capital	Nairobi	Organizations	Comm., UN
Languages	Swahili, English, local languages	Map page	119

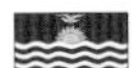

KIRIBATI
Republic of Kiribati

Area Sq Km	717	Religions	Roman Catholic, Protestant
Area Sq Miles	277		
Population	88 000	Currency	Australian dollar
Capital	Bairiki	Organizations	Comm., UN
Languages	Gilbertese, English	Map page	49

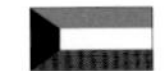

KUWAIT
State of Kuwait

Area Sq Km	17 818	Religions	Sunni Muslim, Shi'a Muslim, Christian, Hindu
Area Sq Miles	6 880		
Population	2 521 000	Currency	Kuwaiti dinar
Capital	Kuwait (Al Kuwayt)	Organizations	OPEC, UN
Languages	Arabic	Map page	78

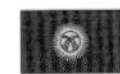

KYRGYZSTAN
Kyrgyz Republic

Area Sq Km	198 500	Religions	Sunni Muslim, Russian Orthodox
Area Sq Miles	76 641		
Population	5 138 000	Currency	Kyrgyz som
Capital	Bishkek (Frunze)	Organizations	CIS, UN
Languages	Kyrgyz, Russian, Uzbek	Map page	77

LAOS
Lao People's Democratic Republic

Area Sq Km	236 800	Religions	Buddhist, traditional beliefs
Area Sq Miles	91 429		
Population	5 657 000	Currency	Kip
Capital	Vientiane (Viangchan)	Organizations	ASEAN, UN
		Map page	62–63
Languages	Lao, local languages		

LATVIA
Republic of Latvia

Area Sq Km	63 700	Religions	Protestant, Roman Catholic, Russian Orthodox
Area Sq Miles	24 595		
Population	2 307 000	Currency	Lats
Capital	Riga	Organizations	UN
Languages	Latvian, Russian	Map page	88

LEBANON
Republic of Lebanon

Area Sq Km	10 452	Religions	Shi'a Muslim, Sunni Muslim, Christian
Area Sq Miles	4 036		
Population	3 653 000	Currency	Lebanese pound
Capital	Beirut (Beyrouth)	Organizations	UN
Languages	Arabic, Armenian, French	Map page	80

LESOTHO
Kingdom of Lesotho

Area Sq Km	30 355	Religions	Christian, traditional beliefs
Area Sq Miles	11 720		
Population	1 802 000	Currency	Loti, South African rand
Capital	Maseru	Organizations	Comm., SADC, UN
Languages	Sesotho, English, Zulu	Map page	123

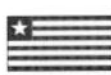

LIBERIA
Republic of Liberia

Area Sq Km	111 369	Religions	Traditional beliefs, Christian, Sunni Muslim
Area Sq Miles	43 000		
Population	3 367 000	Currency	Liberian dollar
Capital	Monrovia	Organizations	UN
Languages	English, creole, local languages	Map page	114

LIBYA
Socialist People's Libyan Arab Jamahiriya

Area Sq Km	1 759 540	Religions	Sunni Muslim
Area Sq Miles	679 362	Currency	Libyan dinar
Population	5 551 000	Organizations	OPEC, UN
Capital	Tripoli (Tarābulus)	Map page	115
Languages	Arabic, Berber		

LIECHTENSTEIN
Principality of Liechtenstein

Area Sq Km	160	Religions	Roman Catholic, Protestant
Area Sq Miles	62		
Population	34 000	Currency	Swiss franc
Capital	Vaduz	Organizations	UN
Languages	German	Map page	105

LITHUANIA
Republic of Lithuania

Area Sq Km	65 200	Religions	Roman Catholic, Protestant, Russian Orthodox
Area Sq Miles	25 174		
Population	3 444 000	Currency	Litas
Capital	Vilnius	Organizations	UN
Languages	Lithuanian, Russian, Polish	Map page	88

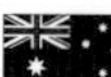

Lord Howe Island
part of Australia

Area Sq Km	17	Religions	Protestant,
Area Sq Miles	6		Roman Catholic
Population	397	Currency	Australian dollar
Languages	English	Map page	51

LUXEMBOURG
Grand Duchy of Luxembourg

Area Sq Km	2 586	Religions	Roman Catholic
Area Sq Miles	998	Currency	Euro
Population	453 000	Organizations	EU, OECD, UN
Capital	Luxembourg	Map page	100
Languages	Letzeburgish, German, French		

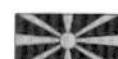

MACEDONIA (F.Y.R.O.M.)
Republic of Macedonia

Area Sq Km	25 713	Religions	Macedonian Orthodox,
Area Sq Miles	9 928		Sunni Muslim
Population	2 056 000	Currency	Macedonian denar
Capital	Skopje	Organizations	UN
Languages	Macedonian, Albanian, Turkish	Map page	111

MADAGASCAR
Republic of Madagascar

Area Sq Km	587 041	Religions	Traditional beliefs,
Area Sq Miles	226 658		Christian, Sunni
Population	17 404 000		Muslim
Capital	Antananarivo	Currency	Malagasy franc
Languages	Malagasy, French	Organizations	UN
		Map page	121

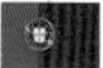

Madeira
Autonomous Region of Portugal

Area Sq Km	779	Religions	Roman Catholic,
Area Sq Miles	301		Protestant
Population	242 603	Currency	Euro
Capital	Funchal	Map page	114
Languages	Portuguese		

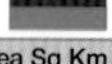

MALAWI
Republic of Malawi

Area Sq Km	118 484	Religions	Christian, traditional
Area Sq Miles	45 747		beliefs, Sunni Muslim
Population	12 105 000	Currency	Malawian kwacha
Capital	Lilongwe	Organizations	Comm.,SADC, UN
Languages	Chichewa, English, local languages	Map page	121

MALAYSIA
Federation of Malaysia

Area Sq Km	332 965	Religions	Sunni Muslim,
Area Sq Miles	128 559		Buddhist,
Population	24 425 000		Hindu, Christian,
Capital	Kuala Lumpur/ Putrajaya		traditional beliefs
		Currency	Ringgit
Languages	Malay, English, Chinese, Tamil, local languages	Organizations	APEC, ASEAN, Comm., UN
		Map page	60–61

MALDIVES
Republic of the Maldives

Area Sq Km	298	Religions	Sunni Muslim
Area Sq Miles	115	Currency	Rufiyaa
Population	318 000	Organizations	Comm., UN
Capital	Male	Map page	56
Languages	Divehi (Maldivian)		

MALI
Republic of Mali

Area Sq Km	1 240 140	Religions	Sunni Muslim,
Area Sq Miles	478 821		traditional beliefs,
Population	13 007 000		Christian
Capital	Bamako	Currency	CFA franc
Languages	French, Bambara, local languages	Organizations	UN
		Map page	114

MALTA
Republic of Malta

Area Sq Km	316	Religions	Roman Catholic
Area Sq Miles	122	Currency	Maltese lira
Population	394 000	Organizations	Comm., UN
Capital	Valletta	Map page	84
Languages	Maltese, English		

MARSHALL ISLANDS
Republic of the Marshall Islands

Area Sq Km	181	Religions	Protestant, Roman
Area Sq Miles	70		Catholic
Population	53 000	Currency	United States dollar
Capital	Delap-Uliga-Djarrit	Organizations	UN
Languages	English, Marshallese	Map page	48

Martinique
French Overseas Department

Area Sq Km	1 079	Religions	Roman Catholic,
Area Sq Miles	417		traditional beliefs
Population	393 000	Currency	Euro
Capital	Fort-de-France	Map page	147
Languages	French, creole		

MAURITANIA
Islamic Arab and African Republic of Mauritania

Area Sq Km	1 030 700	Religions	Sunni Muslim
Area Sq Miles	397 955	Currency	Ouguiya
Population	2 893 000	Organizations	UN
Capital	Nouakchott	Map page	114
Languages	Arabic, French, local languages		

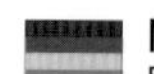

MAURITIUS
Republic of Mauritius

Area Sq Km	2 040	Religions	Hindu, Roman
Area Sq Miles	788		Catholic, Sunni
Population	1 221 000		Muslim
Capital	Port Louis	Currency	Mauritius rupee
Languages	English, creole, Hindi, Bhojpuri, French	Organizations	Comm., SADC, UN
		Map page	113

Mayotte
French Territorial Collectivity

Area Sq Km	373	Religions	Sunni Muslim,
Area Sq Miles	144		Christian
Population	170 879	Currency	Euro
Capital	Dzaoudzi	Map page	121
Languages	French, Mahorian		

Melilla
Autonomous Community of Spain

Area Sq Km	13	Religions	Roman Catholic,
Area Sq Miles	5		Muslim
Population	66 411	Currency	Euro
Capital	Melilla	Map page	114
Languages	Spanish, Arabic		

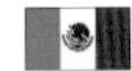

MEXICO
United Mexican States

Area Sq Km	1 972 545	Religions	Roman Catholic,
Area Sq Miles	761 604		Protestant
Population	103 457 000	Currency	Mexican peso
Capital	Mexico City	Organizations	APEC, OECD, UN
Languages	Spanish, Amerindian	Map page	144–145
	languages		

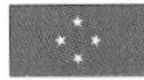

MICRONESIA, FEDERATED STATES OF

Area Sq Km	701	Religions	Roman Catholic,
Area Sq Miles	271		Protestant
Population	109 000	Currency	United States dollar
Capital	Palikir	Organizations	UN
Languages	English, Chuukese,	Map page	48
	Pohnpeian, local		
	languages		

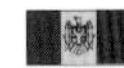

MOLDOVA
Republic of Moldova

Area Sq Km	33 700	Religions	Romanian Orthodox,
Area Sq Miles	13 012		Russian Orthodox
Population	4 267 000	Currency	Moldovan leu
Capital	Chişinău (Kishinev)	Organizations	CIS, UN
Languages	Romanian,	Map page	90
	Ukrainian, Gagauz,		
	Russian		

MONACO
Principality of Monaco

Area Sq Km	2	Religions	Roman Catholic
Area Sq Miles	1	Currency	Euro
Population	34 000	Organizations	UN
Capital	Monaco-Ville	Map page	105
Languages	French, Monégasque,		
	Italian		

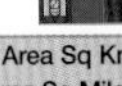

MONGOLIA

Area Sq Km	1 565 000	Religions	Buddhist, Sunni Muslim
Area Sq Miles	604 250	Currency	Tugrik (tögrög)
Population	2 594 000	Organizations	UN
Capital	Ulan Bator	Map page	68–69
	(Ulaanbaatar)		
Languages	Khalka (Mongolian),		
	Kazakh, local		
	languages		

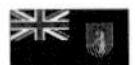

Montserrat
United Kingdom Overseas Territory

Area Sq Km	100	Religions	Protestant, Roman
Area Sq Miles	39		Catholic
Population	4 000	Currency	East Caribbean dollar
Capital	Plymouth	Organizations	CARICOM
Languages	English	Map page	147

MOROCCO
Kingdom of Morocco

Area Sq Km	446 550	Religions	Sunni Muslim
Area Sq Miles	172 414	Currency	Moroccan dirham
Population	30 566 000	Organizations	UN
Capital	Rabat	Map page	114
Languages	Arabic, Berber,		
	French		

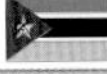

MOZAMBIQUE
Republic of Mozambique

Area Sq Km	799 380	Religions	Traditional beliefs,
Area Sq Miles	308 642		Roman Catholic,
Population	18 863 000		Sunni Muslim
Capital	Maputo	Currency	Metical
Languages	Portuguese, Makua,	Organizations	Comm., SADC, UN
	Tsonga, local	Map page	121
	languages		

MYANMAR
Union of Myanmar

Area Sq Km	676 577	Religions	Buddhist, Christian,
Area Sq Miles	261 228		Sunni Muslim
Population	49 485 000	Currency	Kyat
Capital	Rangoon (Yangôn)	Organizations	ASEAN, UN
Languages	Burmese, Shan,	Map page	62–63
	Karen, local		
	languages		

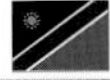

NAMIBIA
Republic of Namibia

Area Sq Km	824 292	Religions	Protestant, Roman
Area Sq Miles	318 261		Catholic
Population	1 987 000	Currency	Namibian dollar
Capital	Windhoek	Organizations	Comm., SADC, UN
Languages	English, Afrikaans,	Map page	121
	German, Ovambo,		
	local languages		

NAURU
Republic of Nauru

Area Sq Km	21	Religions	Protestant, Roman
Area Sq Miles	8		Catholic
Population	13 000	Currency	Australian dollar
Capital	Yaren	Organizations	Comm., UN
Languages	Nauruan, English	Map page	48

NEPAL
Kingdom of Nepal

Area Sq Km	147 181	Religions	Hindu, Buddhist,
Area Sq Miles	56 827		Sunni Muslim
Population	25 164 000	Currency	Nepalese rupee
Capital	Kathmandu	Organizations	UN
Languages	Nepali, Maithili,	Map page	75
	Bhojpuri, English,		
	local languages		

NETHERLANDS
Kingdom of the Netherlands

Area Sq Km	41 526	Religions	Roman Catholic,
Area Sq Miles	16 033		Protestant, Sunni
Population	16 149 000		Muslim
Capital	Amsterdam/	Currency	Euro
	The Hague	Organizations	EU, OECD, UN
	('s-Gravenhage)	Map page	100
Languages	Dutch, Frisian		

Netherlands Antilles
Self-governing Netherlands Territory

Area Sq Km	800	Religions	Roman Catholic,
Area Sq Miles	309		Protestant
Population	221 000	Currency	Netherlands Antilles
Capital	Willemstad		guilder
Languages	Dutch, Papiamento,	Map page	147
	English		

New Caledonia
French Overseas Territory

Area Sq Km	19 058	Religions	Roman Catholic,
Area Sq Miles	7 358		Protestant, Sunni
Population	228 000		Muslim
Capital	Nouméa	Currency	CFP franc
Languages	French, local	Map page	48
	languages		

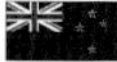

NEW ZEALAND

Area Sq Km	270 534	Religions	Protestant, Roman
Area Sq Miles	104 454		Catholic
Population	3 875 000	Currency	New Zealand dollar
Capital	Wellington	Organizations	APEC, Comm.,
Languages	English, Maori		OECD, UN
		Map page	54

NICARAGUA
Republic of Nicaragua

Area Sq Km	130 000	Religions	Roman Catholic,
Area Sq Miles	50 193		Protestant
Population	5 466 000	Currency	Córdoba
Capital	Managua	Organizations	UN
Languages	Spanish, Amerindian	Map page	146
	languages		

NIGER
Republic of Niger

Area Sq Km	1 267 000	Religions	Sunni Muslim,
Area Sq Miles	489 191		traditional beliefs
Population	11 972 000	Currency	CFA franc
Capital	Niamey	Organizations	UN
Languages	French, Hausa,	Map page	115
	Fulani, local		
	languages		

NIGERIA
Federal Republic of Nigeria

Area Sq Km	923 768	Religions	Sunni Muslim,
Area Sq Miles	356 669		Christian, traditional
Population	124 009 000		beliefs
Capital	Abuja	Currency	Naira
Languages	English, Hausa,	Organizations	Comm., OPEC, UN
	Yoruba, Ibo, Fulani,	Map page	115
	local languages		

Niue
Self-governing New Zealand Overseas Territory

Area Sq Km	258	Religions	Christian
Area Sq Miles	100	Currency	New Zealand dollar
Population	2 000	Map page	48
Capital	Alofi		
Languages	English, Polynesian		

Norfolk Island
Australian External Territory

Area Sq Km	35	Religions	Protestant, Roman
Area Sq Miles	14		Catholic
Population	2 037	Currency	Australian dollar
Capital	Kingston	Map page	48
Languages	English		

Northern Mariana Islands
United States Commonwealth

Area Sq Km	477	Religions	Roman Catholic
Area Sq Miles	184	Currency	United States dollar
Population	79 000	Map page	59
Capital	Capitol Hill		
Languages	English, Chamorro,		
	local languages		

NORTH KOREA
People's Democratic Republic of North Korea

Area Sq Km	120 538	Religions	Traditional beliefs,
Area Sq Miles	46 540		Chondoist, Buddhist
Population	22 664 000	Currency	North Korean won
Capital	P'yŏngyang	Organizations	UN
Languages	Korean	Map page	65

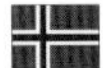

NORWAY
Kingdom of Norway

Area Sq Km	323 878	Religions	Protestant, Roman
Area Sq Miles	125 050		Catholic
Population	4 533 000	Currency	Norwegian krone
Capital	Oslo	Organizations	OECD, UN
Languages	Norwegian	Map page	92–93

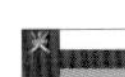

OMAN
Sultanate of Oman

Area Sq Km	309 500	Religions	Ibadhi Muslim, Sunni
Area Sq Miles	119 499		Muslim
Population	2 851 000	Currency	Omani riyal
Capital	Muscat (Masqat)	Organizations	UN
Languages	Arabic, Baluchi,	Map page	79
	Indian languages		

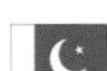

PAKISTAN
Islamic Republic of Pakistan

Area Sq Km	803 940	Religions	Sunni Muslim, Shi'a
Area Sq Miles	310 403		Muslim, Christian,
Population	153 578 000		Hindu
Capital	Islamabad	Currency	Pakistani rupee
Languages	Urdu, Punjabi,	Organizations	Comm., UN
	Sindhi, Pushtu,	Map page	74
	English		

PALAU
Republic of Palau

Area Sq Km	497	Religions	Roman Catholic,
Area Sq Miles	192		Protestant, traditional
Population	20 000		beliefs
Capital	Koror	Currency	United States dollar
Languages	Palauan, English	Organizations	UN
		Map page	59

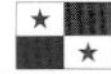

PANAMA
Republic of Panama

Area Sq Km	77 082	Religions	Roman Catholic,
Area Sq Miles	29 762		Protestant, Sunni
Population	3 120 000		Muslim
Capital	Panama City	Currency	Balboa
Languages	Spanish, English,	Organizations	UN
	Amerindian	Map page	146
	languages		

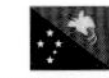

PAPUA NEW GUINEA
Independent State of Papua New Guinea

Area Sq Km	462 840	Religions	Protestant, Roman
Area Sq Miles	178 704		Catholic, traditional
Population	5 711 000		beliefs
Capital	Port Moresby	Currency	Kina
Languages	English, Tok Pisin	Organizations	Comm., UN
	(creole), local	Map page	59
	languages		

PARAGUAY
Republic of Paraguay

Area Sq Km	406 752	Religions	Roman Catholic,
Area Sq Miles	157 048		Protestant
Population	5 878 000	Currency	Guaraní
Capital	Asunción	Organizations	UN
Languages	Spanish, Guaraní	Map page	152

PERU
Republic of Peru

Area Sq Km	1 285 216	Religions	Roman Catholic,
Area Sq Miles	496 225		Protestant
Population	27 167 000	Currency	Sol
Capital	Lima	Organizations	APEC, UN
Languages	Spanish, Quechua,	Map page	150
	Aymara		

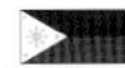

PHILIPPINES
Republic of the Philippines

Area Sq Km	300 000	Religions	Roman Catholic,
Area Sq Miles	115 831		Protestant, Sunni
Population	79 999 000		Muslim, Aglipayan
Capital	Manila	Currency	Philippine peso
Languages	English, Pilipino,	Organizations	APEC, ASEAN, UN
	Tagalog, Cebuano,	Map page	64
	local languages		

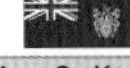

Pitcairn Islands
United Kingdom Overseas Territory

Area Sq Km	45	Religions	Protestant
Area Sq Miles	17	Currency	New Zealand dollar
Population	51	Map page	49
Capital	Adamstown		
Languages	English		

POLAND
Polish Republic

Area Sq Km	312 683	Religions	Roman Catholic,
Area Sq Miles	120 728		Polish Orthodox
Population	38 587 000	Currency	Zloty
Capital	Warsaw (Warszawa)	Organizations	OECD, UN
Languages	Polish, German	Map page	103

PORTUGAL
Portuguese Republic

Area Sq Km	88 940	Religions	Roman Catholic,
Area Sq Miles	34 340		Protestant
Population	10 062 000	Currency	Euro
Capital	Lisbon (Lisboa)	Organizations	EU, OECD, UN
Languages	Portuguese	Map page	106

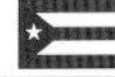

Puerto Rico
United States Commonwealth

Area Sq Km	9 104	Religions	Roman Catholic,
Area Sq Miles	3 515		Protestant
Population	3 879 000	Currency	United States dollar
Capital	San Juan	Map page	147
Languages	Spanish, English		

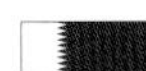

QATAR
State of Qatar

Area Sq Km	11 437	Religions	Sunni Muslim
Area Sq Miles	4 416	Currency	Qatari riyal
Population	610 000	Organizations	OPEC, UN
Capital	Doha (Ad Dawḩah)	Map page	79
Languages	Arabic		

Réunion
French Overseas Department

Area Sq Km	2 551	Religions	Roman Catholic
Area Sq Miles	985	Currency	Euro
Population	756 000	Map page	113
Capital	St-Denis		
Languages	French, creole		

 ## Rodrigues Island
part of Mauritius

Area Sq Km	104	Religions	Christian
Area Sq Miles	40	Currency	Rupee
Population	36 306	Map page	159
Capital	Port Mathurin		
Languages	English, creole		

 ## ROMANIA

Area Sq Km	237 500	Religions	Romanian Orthodox,
Area Sq Miles	91 699		Protestant, Roman
Population	22 334 000		Catholic
Capital	Bucharest (Bucureşti)	Currency	Romanian leu
Languages	Romanian,	Organizations	UN
	Hungarian	Map page	110

 ## RUSSIAN FEDERATION

Area Sq Km	17 075 400	Religions	Russian Orthodox,
Area Sq Miles	6 592 849		Sunni Muslim,
Population	143 246 000		Protestant
Capital	Moscow (Moskva)	Currency	Russian rouble
Languages	Russian, Tatar,	Organizations	APEC, CIS, UN
	Ukrainian, local	Map page	82–83
	languages		

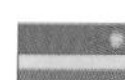

 ## RWANDA
Republic of Rwanda

Area Sq Km	26 338	Religions	Roman Catholic,
Area Sq Miles	10 169		traditional beliefs,
Population	8 387 000		Protestant
Capital	Kigali	Currency	Rwandan franc
Languages	Kinyarwanda,	Organizations	UN
	French, English	Map page	119

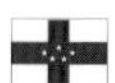

 ## Saba
part of Netherlands Antilles

Area Sq Km	13	Religions	Roman Catholic,
Area Sq Miles	5		Protestant
Population	1 387	Currency	Netherlands Antilles
Capital	Bottom		guilder
Languages	Dutch, English	Map page	147

 ## St Barthélémy
Dependency of Guadeloupe

Area Sq Km	21	Religions	Roman Catholic
Area Sq Miles	8	Currency	Euro
Population	6 852	Map page	147
Capital	Gustavia		
Languages	French, creole		

 ## St Helena
United Kingdom Overseas Territory

Area Sq Km	121	Religions	Protestant, Roman
Area Sq Miles	47		Catholic,
Population	5 644	Currency	St Helena pound
Capital	Jamestown	Map page	113
Languages	English		

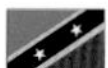

 ## ST KITTS AND NEVIS
Federation of St Kitts and Nevis

Area Sq Km	261	Religions	Protestant, Roman
Area Sq Miles	101		Catholic
Population	42 000	Currency	East Caribbean dollar
Capital	Basseterre	Organizations	CARICOM, Comm.,
Languages	English, creole		UN
		Map page	147

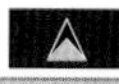

 ## ST LUCIA

Area Sq Km	616	Religions	Roman Catholic,
Area Sq Miles	238		Protestant
Population	149 000	Currency	East Caribbean dollar
Capital	Castries	Organizations	CARICOM, Comm.,
Languages	English, creole		UN
		Map page	147

 ## St Martin
Dependency of Guadeloupe

Area Sq Km	54	Religions	Roman Catholic
Area Sq Miles	21	Currency	Euro
Population	29 078	Map page	147
Capital	Marigot		
Languages	French, creole		

 ## St Pierre and Miquelon
French Territorial Collectivity

Area Sq Km	242	Religions	Roman Catholic
Area Sq Miles	93	Currency	Euro
Population	6 000	Map page	131
Capital	St-Pierre		
Languages	French		

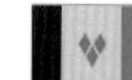

ST VINCENT AND THE GRENADINES

Area Sq Km	389	Religions	Protestant, Roman
Area Sq Miles	150		Catholic
Population	120 000	Currency	East Caribbean dollar
Capital	Kingstown	Organizations	CARICOM, Comm.,
Languages	English, creole		UN
		Map page	147

 ## SAMOA
Independent State of Samoa

Area Sq Km	2 831	Religions	Protestant, Roman
Area Sq Miles	1 093		Catholic
Population	178 000	Currency	Tala
Capital	Apia	Organizations	Comm., UN
Languages	Samoan, English	Map page	49

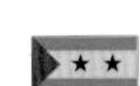

SAN MARINO
Republic of San Marino

Area Sq Km	61	Religions	Roman Catholic
Area Sq Miles	24	Currency	Euro
Population	28 000	Organizations	UN
Capital	San Marino	Map page	108
Languages	Italian		

SÃO TOMÉ AND PRÍNCIPE
Democratic Republic of São Tomé and Príncipe

Area Sq Km	964	Religions	Roman Catholic,
Area Sq Miles	372		Protestant
Population	161 000	Currency	Dobra
Capital	São Tomé	Organizations	UN
Languages	Portuguese, creole	Map page	113

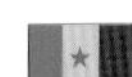

SAUDI ARABIA
Kingdom of Saudi Arabia

Area Sq Km	2 200 000	Religions	Sunni Muslim, Shi'a
Area Sq Miles	849 425		Muslim
Population	24 217 000	Currency	Saudi Arabian riyal
Capital	Riyadh (Ar Riyāḍ)	Organizations	OPEC, UN
Languages	Arabic	Map page	78–79

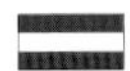

SENEGAL
Republic of Senegal

Area Sq Km	196 720	Religions	Sunni Muslim, Roman
Area Sq Miles	75 954		Catholic, traditional
Population	10 095 000		beliefs
Capital	Dakar	Currency	CFA franc
Languages	French, Wolof, Fulani,	Organizations	UN
	local languages	Map page	114

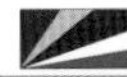

SERBIA AND MONTENEGRO
Federal Republic of Yugoslavia

Area Sq Km	102 173	Religions	Serbian Orthodox,
Area Sq Miles	39 449		Montenegrin Orthodox,
Population	10 527 000		Sunni Muslim
Capital	Belgrade (Beograd)	Currency	Dinar, Euro
Languages	Serbian, Albanian,	Organizations	UN
	Hungarian	Map page	109

SEYCHELLES
Republic of the Seychelles

Area Sq Km	455	Religions	Roman Catholic,
Area Sq Miles	176		Protestant
Population	81 000	Currency	Seychelles rupee
Capital	Victoria	Organizations	Comm., SADC, UN
Languages	English, French,	Map page	113
	creole		

SIERRA LEONE
Republic of Sierra Leone

Area Sq Km	71 740	Religions	Sunni Muslim,
Area Sq Miles	27 699		traditional beliefs
Population	4 971 000	Currency	Leone
Capital	Freetown	Organizations	Comm., UN
Languages	English, creole,	Map page	114
	Mende, Temne,		
	local languages		

SINGAPORE
Republic of Singapore

Area Sq Km	639	Religions	Buddhist, Taoist, Sunni
Area Sq Miles	247		Muslim, Christian,
Population	4 253 000		Hindu
Capital	Singapore	Currency	Singapore dollar
Languages	Chinese, English,	Organizations	APEC, ASEAN,
	Malay, Tamil		Comm., UN
		Map page	60

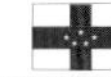

Sint Eustatius
part of Netherlands Antilles

Area Sq Km	21	Religions	Protestant, Roman
Area Sq Miles	8		Catholic
Population	2 829	Currency	Netherlands Antilles
Capital	Oranjestad		guilder
Languages	Dutch, English	Map page	147

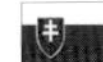

Sint Maarten
part of Netherlands Antilles

Area Sq Km	34	Religions	Protestant, Roman
Area Sq Miles	13		Catholic
Population	31 882	Currency	Netherlands Antilles
Capital	Philipsburg		guilder
Languages	Dutch, English	Map page	147

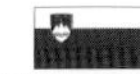

SLOVAKIA
Slovak Republic

Area Sq Km	49 035	Religions	Roman Catholic,
Area Sq Miles	18 933		Protestant, Orthodox
Population	5 402 000	Currency	Slovakian koruna
Capital	Bratislava	Organizations	UN
Languages	Slovakian,	Map page	103
	Hungarian, Czech		

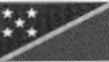

SLOVENIA
Republic of Slovenia

Area Sq Km	20 251	Religions	Roman Catholic,
Area Sq Miles	7 819		Protestant
Population	1 984 000	Currency	Tólar
Capital	Ljubljana	Organizations	UN
Languages	Slovenian, Croatian,	Map page	108–109
	Serbian		

SOLOMON ISLANDS

Area Sq Km	28 370	Religions	Protestant, Roman
Area Sq Miles	10 954		Catholic
Population	477 000	Currency	Solomon Islands dollar
Capital	Honiara	Organizations	Comm., UN
Languages	English, creole, local	Map page	48
	languages		

SOMALIA

Somali Democratic Republic

Area Sq Km	637 657	Religions	Sunni Muslim
Area Sq Miles	246 201	Currency	Somali shilling
Population	9 890 000	Organizations	UN
Capital	Mogadishu	Map page	117
	(Muqdisho)		
Languages	Somali, Arabic		

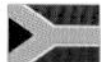

SOUTH AFRICA, REPUBLIC OF

Area Sq Km	1 219 080	Religions	Protestant, Roman
Area Sq Miles	470 689		Catholic, Sunni
Population	45 026 000		Muslim, Hindu
Capital	Pretoria/Cape Town	Currency	Rand
Languages	Afrikaans, English,	Organizations	Comm., SADC, UN
	nine official local	Map page	122–123
	languages		

SOUTH KOREA

Republic of Korea

Area Sq Km	99 274	Religions	Buddhist, Protestant,
Area Sq Miles	38 330		Roman Catholic
Population	47 700 000	Currency	South Korean won
Capital	Seoul (Sŏul)	Organizations	APEC, UN
Languages	Korean	Map page	65

SPAIN
Kingdom of Spain

Area Sq Km	504 782	Religions	Roman Catholic
Area Sq Miles	194 897	Currency	Euro
Population	41 060 000	Organizations	EU, OECD, UN
Capital	Madrid	Map page	106–107
Languages	Castilian, Catalan,		
	Galician, Basque		

SRI LANKA

Democratic Socialist Republic of Sri Lanka

Area Sq Km	65 610	Religions	Buddhist, Hindu,
Area Sq Miles	25 332		Sunni Muslim, Roman
Population	19 065 000		Catholic
Capital	Sri Jayewardenepura	Currency	Sri Lankan rupee
	Kotte	Organizations	Comm., UN
Languages	Sinhalese, Tamil,	Map page	73
	English		

SUDAN

Republic of the Sudan

Area Sq Km	2 505 813	Religions	Sunni Muslim,
Area Sq Miles	967 500		traditional beliefs,
Population	33 610 000		Christian
Capital	Khartoum	Currency	Sudanese dinar
Languages	Arabic, Dinka,	Organizations	UN
	Nubian, Beja, Nuer,	Map page	116–117
	local languages		

SURINAME
Republic of Suriname

Area Sq Km	163 820	Religions	Hindu, Roman
Area Sq Miles	63 251		Catholic, Protestant,
Population	436 000		Sunni Muslim
Capital	Paramaribo	Currency	Suriname guilder
Languages	Dutch,	Organizations	CARICOM, UN
	Surinamese,	Map page	151
	English, Hindi		

Svalbard

part of Norway

Area Sq Km	61 229	Religions	Protestant
Area Sq Miles	23 641	Currency	Norwegian krone
Population	2 515	Map page	82
Capital	Longyearbyen		
Languages	Norwegian		

SWAZILAND

Kingdom of Swaziland

Area Sq Km	17 364	Currency	Emalangeni,
Area Sq Miles	6 704		South African rand
Population	1 077 000	Organizations	Comm., SADC, UN
Capital	Mbabane	Map page	123
Languages	Swazi, English		
Religions	Christian,		
	traditional beliefs		

SWEDEN

Kingdom of Sweden

Area Sq Km	449 964	Religions	Protestant,
Area Sq Miles	173 732		Roman Catholic
Population	8 876 000	Currency	Swedish krona
Capital	Stockholm	Organizations	EU, OECD, UN
Languages	Swedish	Map page	92–93

SWITZERLAND

Swiss Confederation

Area Sq Km	41 293	Religions	Roman Catholic,
Area Sq Miles	15 943		Protestant,
Population	7 169 000	Currency	Swiss franc
Capital	Bern (Berne)	Organizations	OECD, UN
Languages	German, French,	Map page	105
	Italian, Romansch		

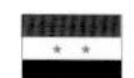

SYRIA
Syrian Arab Republic

Area Sq Km	185 180	Religions	Sunni Muslim, Shi'a
Area Sq Miles	71 498		Muslim, Christian
Population	17 800 000	Currency	Syrian pound
Capital	Damascus (Dimashq)	Organizations	UN
Languages	Arabic, Kurdish,	Map page	80
	Armenian		

TAIWAN

Republic of China

Area Sq Km	36 179	Religions	Buddhist, Taoist,
Area Sq Miles	13 969		Confucian, Christian
Population	22 548 009	Currency	Taiwan dollar
Capital	T'aipei	Organizations	APEC
Languages	Mandarin, Min,	Map page	71
	Hakka, local		
	languages		

TAJIKISTAN
Republic of Tajikistan

Area Sq Km	143 100	Religions	Sunni Muslim
Area Sq Miles	55 251	Currency	Somoni
Population	6 245 000	Organizations	CIS, UN
Capital	Dushanbe	Map page	77
Languages	Tajik, Uzbek, Russian		

TANZANIA
United Republic of Tanzania

Area Sq Km	945 087	Religions	Shi'a Muslim, Sunni
Area Sq Miles	364 900		Muslim, traditional
Population	36 977 000		beliefs, Christian
Capital	Dodoma	Currency	Tanzanian shilling
Languages	Swahili, English,	Organizations	Comm., SADC, UN
	Nyamwezi, local	Map page	119
	languages		

THAILAND
Kingdom of Thailand

Area Sq Km	513 115	Religions	Buddhist, Sunni
Area Sq Miles	198 115		Muslim
Population	62 833 000	Currency	Baht
Capital	Bangkok	Organizations	APEC, ASEAN, UN
	(Krung Thep)	Map page	62–63
Languages	Thai, Lao, Chinese,		
	Malay, Mon-Khmer		
	languages		

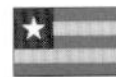

TOGO
Republic of Togo

Area Sq Km	56 785	Religions	Traditional beliefs,
Area Sq Miles	21 925		Christian, Sunni
Population	4 909 000		Muslim
Capital	Lomé	Currency	CFA franc
Languages	French, Ewe, Kabre,	Organizations	UN
	local languages	Map page	114

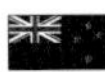

Tokelau
New Zealand Overseas Territory

Area Sq Km	10	Religions	Christian
Area Sq Miles	4	Currency	New Zealand dollar
Population	2 000	Map page	49
Capital	none		
Languages	English, Tokelauan		

TONGA
Kingdom of Tonga

Area Sq Km	748	Religions	Protestant, Roman
Area Sq Miles	289		Catholic
Population	104 000	Currency	Pa'anga
Capital	Nuku'alofa	Organizations	Comm., UN
Languages	Tongan, English	Map page	49

TRINIDAD AND TOBAGO
Republic of Trinidad and Tobago

Area Sq Km	5 130	Religions	Roman Catholic,
Area Sq Miles	1 981		Hindu, Protestant,
Population	1 303 000		Sunni Muslim
Capital	Port of Spain	Currency	Trinidad and Tobago
Languages	English, creole,		dollar
	Hindi	Organizations	CARICOM, Comm.,
			UN
		Map page	147

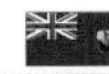

Tristan da Cunha
Dependency of St Helena

Area Sq Km	98	Religions	Protestant, Roman
Area Sq Miles	38		Catholic
Population	284	Currency	Pound sterling
Capital	Settlement of	Map page	113
	Edinburgh		
Languages	English		

TUNISIA
Republic of Tunisia

Area Sq Km	164 150	Religions	Sunni Muslim
Area Sq Miles	63 379	Currency	Tunisian dinar
Population	9 832 000	Organizations	UN
Capital	Tunis	Map page	115
Languages	Arabic, French		

TURKEY
Republic of Turkey

Area Sq Km	779 452	Religions	Sunni Muslim, Shi'a
Area Sq Miles	300 948		Muslim
Population	71 325 000	Currency	Turkish lira
Capital	Ankara	Organizations	OECD, UN
Languages	Turkish, Kurdish	Map page	80

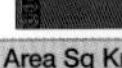

TURKMENISTAN
Republic of Turkmenistan

Area Sq Km	488 100	Religions	Sunni Muslim, Russian
Area Sq Miles	188 456		Orthodox
Population	4 867 000	Currency	Turkmen manat
Capital	Ashgabat (Ashkhabad)	Organizations	CIS, UN
Languages	Turkmen, Uzbek,	Map page	76
	Russian		

Turks and Caicos Islands
United Kingdom Overseas Territory

Area Sq Km	430	Religions	Protestant
Area Sq Miles	166	Currency	United States dollar
Population	21 000	Map page	147
Capital	Grand Turk		
Languages	English		

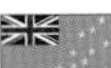

TUVALU

Area Sq Km	25	Religions	Protestant
Area Sq Miles	10	Currency	Australian dollar
Population	11 000	Organizations	Comm.
Capital	Vaiaku	Map page	49
Languages	Tuvaluan, English		

UGANDA
Republic of Uganda

Area Sq Km	241 038	Religions	Roman Catholic, Protestant, Sunni Muslim, traditional beliefs
Area Sq Miles	93 065		
Population	25 827 000		
Capital	Kampala	Currency	Ugandan shilling
Languages	English, Swahili, Luganda, local languages	Organizations	Comm., UN
		Map page	119

UKRAINE
Republic of Ukraine

Area Sq Km	603 700	Religions	Ukrainian Orthodox, Ukrainian Catholic, Roman Catholic
Area Sq Miles	233 090		
Population	48 523 000		
Capital	Kiev (Kyiv)	Currency	Hryvnia
Languages	Ukrainian, Russian	Organizations	CIS, UN
		Map page	90–91

UNITED ARAB EMIRATES
Federation of Emirates

Area Sq Km	77 700	Religions	Sunni Muslim, Shi'a Muslim
Area Sq Miles	30 000		
Population	2 995 000	Currency	United Arab Emirates dirham
Capital	Abu Dhabi (Abū Ẓabī)		
		Organizations	OPEC, UN
Languages	Arabic, English	Map page	79

Abu Dhabi (Abū Ẓabī) (Emirate)

Area Sq Km	67 340	Population	1 248 000
Area Sq Miles	26 000	Capital	Abu Dhabi (Abū Ẓabī)

Ajman (Emirate)

Area Sq Km	259	Population	189 000
Area Sq Miles	100	Capital	Ajman

Dubai (Emirate)

Area Sq Km	3 885	Population	971 000
Area Sq Miles	1 500	Capital	Dubai

Fujairah (Emirate)

Area Sq Km	1 165	Population	103 000
Area Sq Miles	450	Capital	Fujairah

Ras al Khaimah (Emirate)

Area Sq Km	1 684	Population	179 000
Area Sq Miles	650	Capital	Ras al Khaimah

Sharjah (Emirate)

Area Sq Km	2 590	Population	551 000
Area Sq Miles	1 000	Capital	Sharjah

Umm al Qaiwain (Emirate)

Area Sq Km	777	Population	49 000
Area Sq Miles	300	Capital	Umm al Qaiwain

UNITED KINGDOM
of Great Britain and Northern Ireland

Area Sq Km	243 609	Religions	Protestant, Roman Catholic, Muslim
Area Sq Miles	94 058		
Population	58 789 194	Currency	Pound sterling
Capital	London	Organizations	Comm., EU, OECD, UN
Languages	English, Welsh, Gaelic		
		Map page	94–95

England (Constituent country)

Area Sq Km	130 433	Population	49 138 831
Area Sq Miles	50 360	Capital	London

Northern Ireland (Province)

Area Sq Km	13 576	Population	1 685 267
Area Sq Miles	5 242	Capital	Belfast

Scotland (Constituent country)

Area Sq Km	78 822	Population	5 062 011
Area Sq Miles	30 433	Capital	Edinburgh

Wales (Principality)

Area Sq Km	20 778	Population	2 903 085
Area Sq Miles	8 022	Capital	Cardiff

UNITED STATES OF AMERICA
Federal Republic

Area Sq Km	9 826 635	Religions	Protestant, Roman Catholic, Sunni Muslim, Jewish
Area Sq Miles	3 794 085		
Population	294 043 000		
Capital	Washington D.C.	Currency	United States dollar
Languages	English, Spanish	Organizations	APEC, OECD, UN
		Map page	132–133

Alabama (State)

Area Sq Km	135 765	Population	4 486 508
Area Sq Miles	52 419	Capital	Montgomery

Alaska (State)

Area Sq Km	1 717 854	Population	643 786
Area Sq Miles	663 267	Capital	Juneau

Arizona (State)

Area Sq Km	295 253	Population	5 456 453
Area Sq Miles	113 998	Capital	Phoenix

Arkansas (State)

Area Sq Km	137 733	Population	2 710 079
Area Sq Miles	53 179	Capital	Little Rock

California (State)

Area Sq Km	423 971	Population	35 116 033
Area Sq Miles	163 696	Capital	Sacramento

Colorado (State)

Area Sq Km 269 602	Population 4 506 542
Area Sq Miles 104 094	Capital Denver

Connecticut (State)

Area Sq Km 14 356	Population 3 460 503
Area Sq Miles 5 543	Capital Hartford

Delaware (State)

Area Sq Km 6 446	Population 807 385
Area Sq Miles 2 489	Capital Dover

District of Columbia (District)

Area Sq Km 176	Population 570 898
Area Sq Miles 68	Capital Washington

Florida (State)

Area Sq Km 170 305	Population 16 713 149
Area Sq Miles 65 755	Capital Tallahassee

Georgia (State)

Area Sq Km 69 700	Population 5 126 000
Area Sq Miles 26 911	Capital Atlanta

Hawaii (State)

Area Sq Km 28 311	Population 1 244 898
Area Sq Miles 10 931	Capital Honolulu

Idaho (State)

Area Sq Km 216 445	Population 1 341 131
Area Sq Miles 83 570	Capital Boise

Illinois (State)

Area Sq Km 149 997	Population 12 600 620
Area Sq Miles 57 914	Capital Springfield

Indiana (State)

Area Sq Km 94 322	Population 6 159 068
Area Sq Miles 36 418	Capital Indianapolis

Iowa (State)

Area Sq Km 145 744	Population 2 936 760
Area Sq Miles 56 272	Capital Des Moines

Kansas (State)

Area Sq Km 213 096	Population 2 715 884
Area Sq Miles 82 277	Capital Topeka

Kentucky (State)

Area Sq Km 104 659	Population 4 092 891
Area Sq Miles 40 409	Capital Frankfort

Louisiana (State)

Area Sq Km 134 265	Population 4 482 646
Area Sq Miles 51 840	Capital Baton Rouge

Maine (State)

Area Sq Km 91 647	Population 1 294 464
Area Sq Miles 35 385	Capital Augusta

Maryland (State)

Area Sq Km 32 134	Population 5 458 137
Area Sq Miles 12 407	Capital Annapolis

Massachusetts (State)

Area Sq Km 27 337	Population 6 427 801
Area Sq Miles 10 555	Capital Boston

Michigan (State)

Area Sq Km 250 493	Population 10 050 446
Area Sq Miles 96 716	Capital Lansing

Minnesota (State)

Area Sq Km 225 171	Population 5 019 720
Area Sq Miles 86 939	Capital St Paul

Mississippi (State)

Area Sq Km 125 433	Population 2 871 782
Area Sq Miles 48 430	Capital Jackson

Missouri (State)

Area Sq Km 180 533	Population 5 672 579
Area Sq Miles 69 704	Capital Jefferson City

Montana (State)

Area Sq Km 380 837	Population 909 453
Area Sq Miles 147 042	Capital Helena

Nebraska (State)

Area Sq Km 200 346	Population 1 729 180
Area Sq Miles 77 354	Capital Lincoln

Nevada (State)

Area Sq Km 286 352	Population 2 173 491
Area Sq Miles 110 561	Capital Carson City

New Hampshire (State)

Area Sq Km 24 216	Population 1 275 056
Area Sq Miles 9 350	Capital Concord

New Jersey (State)

Area Sq Km 22 587	Population 8 590 300
Area Sq Miles 8 721	Capital Trenton

UNITED STATES OF AMERICA
Federal Republic

New Mexico (State)

Area Sq Km 314 914	Population 1 855 059
Area Sq Miles 121 589	Capital Santa Fe

New York (State)

Area Sq Km 141 299	Population 19 157 532
Area Sq Miles 54 556	Capital Albany

North Carolina (State)

Area Sq Km 139 391	Population 8 320 146
Area Sq Miles 53 819	Capital Raleigh

North Dakota (State)

Area Sq Km 183 112	Population 634 110
Area Sq Miles 70 700	Capital Bismarck

Ohio (State)

Area Sq Km 116 096	Population 11 421 267
Area Sq Miles 44 825	Capital Columbus

Oklahoma (State)

Area Sq Km 181 035	Population 3 493 714
Area Sq Miles 69 898	Capital Oklahoma City

Oregon (State)

Area Sq Km 254 806	Population 3 521 515
Area Sq Miles 98 381	Capital Salem

Pennsylvania (State)

Area Sq Km 119 282	Population 12 335 091
Area Sq Miles 46 055	Capital Harrisburg

Rhode Island (State)

Area Sq Km 4 002	Population 1 069 725
Area Sq Miles 1 545	Capital Providence

South Carolina (State)

Area Sq Km 82 931	Population 4 107 183
Area Sq Miles 32 020	Capital Columbia

South Dakota (State)

Area Sq Km 199 730	Population 761 063
Area Sq Miles 77 116	Capital Pierre

Tennessee (State)

Area Sq Km 109 150	Population 5 797 289
Area Sq Miles 42 143	Capital Nashville

Texas (State)

Area Sq Km 695 622	Population 21 779 893
Area Sq Miles 268 581	Capital Austin

Utah (State)

Area Sq Km 219 887	Population 2 316 256
Area Sq Miles 84 899	Capital Salt Lake City

Vermont (State)

Area Sq Km 24 900	Population 616 592
Area Sq Miles 9 614	Capital Montpelier

Virginia (State)

Area Sq Km 110 784	Population 7 293 542
Area Sq Miles 42 774	Capital Richmond

Washington (State)

Area Sq Km 184 666	Population 6 068 996
Area Sq Miles 71 300	Capital Olympia

West Virginia (State)

Area Sq Km 62 755	Population 1 801 873
Area Sq Miles 24 230	Capital Charleston

Wisconsin (State)

Area Sq Km 169 639	Population 5 441 196
Area Sq Miles 65 498	Capital Madison

Wyoming (State)

Area Sq Km 253 337	Population 498 703
Area Sq Miles 97 814	Capital Cheyenne

URUGUAY
Oriental Republic of Uruguay

Area Sq Km 176 215	Religions Roman Catholic,
Area Sq Miles 68 037	Protestant, Jewish
Population 3 415 000	Currency Uruguayan peso
Capital Montevideo	Organizations UN
Languages Spanish	Map page 153

UZBEKISTAN
Republic of Uzbekistan

Area Sq Km	447 400	Religions	Sunni Muslim, Russian
Area Sq Miles	172 742		Orthodox
Population	26 093 000	Currency	Uzbek som
Capital	Tashkent	Organizations	CIS, UN
Languages	Uzbek, Russian,	Map page	76–77
	Tajik, Kazakh		

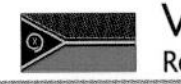

VANUATU
Republic of Vanuatu

Area Sq Km	12 190	Religions	Protestant, Roman
Area Sq Miles	4 707		Catholic, traditional
Population	212 000		beliefs
Capital	Port Vila	Currency	Vatu
Languages	English, Bislama	Organizations	Comm., UN
	(creole), French	Map page	48

VATICAN CITY
Vatican City State

Area Sq Km	0.5	Religions	Roman Catholic
Area Sq Miles	0.2	Currency	Euro
Population	472	Map page	108
Capital	Vatican City		
Languages	Italian		

VENEZUELA
Republic of Venezuela

Area Sq Km	912 050	Religions	Roman Catholic,
Area Sq Miles	352 144		Protestant
Population	25 699 000	Currency	Bolívar
Capital	Caracas	Organizations	OPEC, UN
Languages	Spanish, Amerindian	Map page	150
	languages		

VIETNAM
Socialist Republic of Vietnam

Area Sq Km	329 565	Religions	Buddhist, Taoist,
Area Sq Miles	127 246		Roman Catholic,
Population	81 377 000		Cao Dai, Hoa Hao
Capital	Ha Nôi (Hanoi)	Currency	Dong
Languages	Vietnamese, Thai,	Organizations	APEC, ASEAN, UN
	Khmer, Chinese,	Map page	62–63
	local languages		

Virgin Islands (U.K.)
United Kingdom Overseas Territory

Area Sq Km	153	Religions	Protestant, Roman
Area Sq Miles	59		Catholic
Population	21 000	Currency	United States dollar
Capital	Road Town	Map page	147
Languages	English		

Virgin Islands (U.S.)
United States Unincorporated Territory

Area Sq Km	352	Religions	Protestant,
Area Sq Miles	136		Roman Catholic
Population	111 000	Currency	United States dollar
Capital	Charlotte Amalie	Map page	147
Languages	English, Spanish		

Wallis and Futuna Islands
French Overseas Territory

Area Sq Km	274	Religions	Roman Catholic
Area Sq Miles	106	Currency	CFP franc
Population	15 000	Map page	49
Capital	Matä'utu		
Languages	French, Wallisian,		
	Futunian		

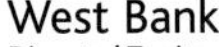

West Bank
Disputed Territory

Area Sq Km	5 860	Religions	Sunni Muslim, Jewish,
Area Sq Miles	2 263		Shi'a Muslim, Christian
Population	2 303 660	Currency	Jordanian dinar,
Capital	none		Isreali shekel
Languages	Arabic, Hebrew	Map page	80

Western Sahara
Disputed territory (Morocco)

Area Sq Km	266 000	Religions	Sunni Muslim
Area Sq Miles	102 703	Currency	Moroccan dirham
Population	308 000	Map page	114
Capital	Laâyoune		
Languages	Arabic		

YEMEN
Republic of Yemen

Area Sq Km	527 968	Religions	Sunni Muslim, Shi'a
Area Sq Miles	203 850		Muslim
Population	20 010 000	Currency	Yemeni riyal
Capital	Şan'a'	Organizations	UN
Languages	Arabic	Map page	78–79

ZAMBIA
Republic of Zambia

Area Sq Km	752 614	Religions	Christian, traditional
Area Sq Miles	290 586		beliefs
Population	10 812 000	Currency	Zambian kwacha
Capital	Lusaka	Organizations	Comm., SADC, UN
Languages	English, Bemba,	Map page	120–121
	Nyanja, Tonga, local		
	languages		

ZIMBABWE
Republic of Zimbabwe

Area Sq Km	390 759	Religions	Christian, traditional
Area Sq Miles	150 873		beliefs
Population	12 891 000	Currency	Zimbabwean dollar
Capital	Harare	Organizations	SADC, UN
Languages	English, Shona,	Map page	121
	Ndebele		

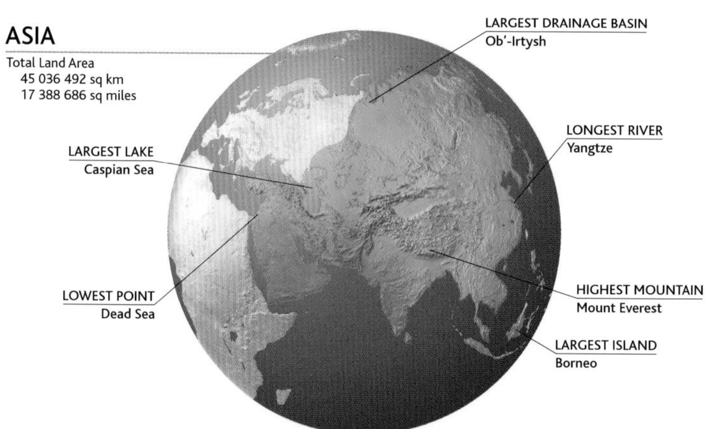

ANTARCTICA
Total Land Area
12 093 000 sq km
4 669 292 sq miles
(excluding ice shelves)

OCEANIA
Total land area
8 844 516 sq km
3 414 887 sq miles
(includes New Guinea and
Pacific Island nations)

HIGHEST MOUNTAIN
Puncak Jaya

LARGEST ISLAND
New Guinea

HIGHEST MOUNTAIN
Vinson Massif
4 897 m / 16 066 ft

LARGEST LAKE AND
LOWEST POINT
Lake Eyre

LONGEST RIVER AND
LARGEST DRAINAGE BASIN
Murray-Darling

HIGHEST MOUNTAINS	HEIGHT metres	feet	LARGEST ISLANDS	AREA sq km	sq miles	LARGEST LAKES	AREA sq km	sq miles	LONGEST RIVERS	LENGTH km	miles
Puncak Jaya	5 030	16 502	New Guinea	808 510	312 167	Lake Eyre	0–8 900	0–3 436	Murray-Darling	3 750	2 330
Puncak Trikora	4 730	15 518	South Island	151 215	58 384	Lake Torrens	0–5 780	0–2 232	Darling	2 739	1 702
Puncak Mandala	4 700	15 420	North Island	115 777	44 702				Murray	2 589	1 608
Puncak Yamin	4 595	15 075	Tasmania	67 800	26 178				Murrumbidgee	1 690	1 050
Mt Wilhelm	4 509	14 793							Lachlan	1 480	919

ASIA
Total Land Area
45 036 492 sq km
17 388 686 sq miles

LARGEST DRAINAGE BASIN
Ob'-Irtysh

LARGEST LAKE
Caspian Sea

LONGEST RIVER
Yangtze

LOWEST POINT
Dead Sea

HIGHEST MOUNTAIN
Mount Everest

LARGEST ISLAND
Borneo

HIGHEST MOUNTAINS	HEIGHT metres	feet	LARGEST ISLANDS	AREA sq km	sq miles	LARGEST LAKES	AREA sq km	sq miles	LONGEST RIVERS	LENGTH km	miles
Mt Everest	8 848	29 028	Borneo	745 561	287 863	Caspian Sea	371 000	143 244	Yangtze	6 380	3 964
K2	8 611	28 251	Sumatra	473 606	182 860	Lake Baikal	30 500	11 776	Ob'-Irtysh	5 568	3 460
Kangchenjunga	8 586	28 169	Honshū	227 414	87 805	Aral Sea	28 687	11 076	Yenisey-Angara-Selenga	5 550	3 448
Lhotse	8 516	27 939	Celebes	189 216	73 057	Lake Balkhash	17 400	6 718	Yellow	5 464	3 395
Makalu	8 463	27 765	Java	132 188	51 038	Ysyk-Köl	6 200	2 393	Irtysh	4 440	2 759

EUROPE

Total Land Area
9 908 599 sq km
3 825 731 sq miles

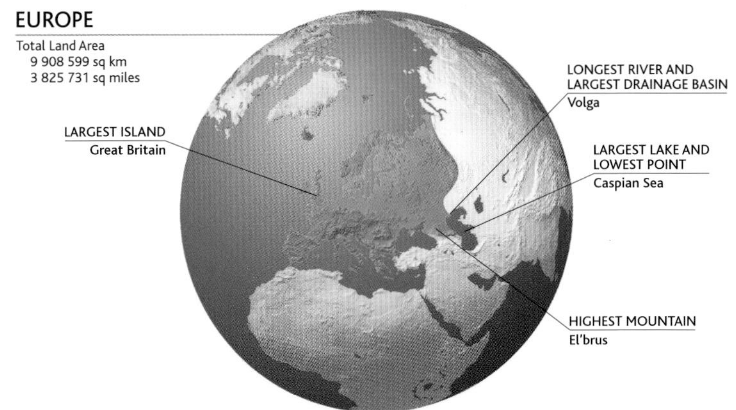

LONGEST RIVER AND
LARGEST DRAINAGE BASIN
Volga

LARGEST ISLAND
Great Britain

LARGEST LAKE AND
LOWEST POINT
Caspian Sea

HIGHEST MOUNTAIN
El'brus

HIGHEST MOUNTAINS	HEIGHT metres	feet	LARGEST ISLANDS	AREA sq km	sq miles	LARGEST LAKES	AREA sq km	sq miles	LONGEST RIVERS	LENGTH km	miles
El'brus	5 642	5 642	Great Britain	218 476	84 354	Caspian Sea	371 000	143 244	Volga	3 688	2 291
Gora Dykh-Tau	5 204	17 073	Iceland	102 820	39 699	Lake Ladoga	18 390	7 100	Danube	2 850	1 770
Shkhara	5 201	17 063	Novaya Zemlya	90 650	35 000	Lake Onega	9 600	3 706	Dnieper	2 285	1 419
Kazbek	5 047	16 558	Ireland	83 045	32 064	Vänern	5 585	2 156	Kama	2 028	1 260
Mont Blanc	4 808	15 774	Spitsbergen	37 814	14 600	Rybinskoye Vdkhr.	5 180	2 000	Don	1 931	1 199

AFRICA

Total Land Area
30 343 578 sq km
11 715 721 sq miles

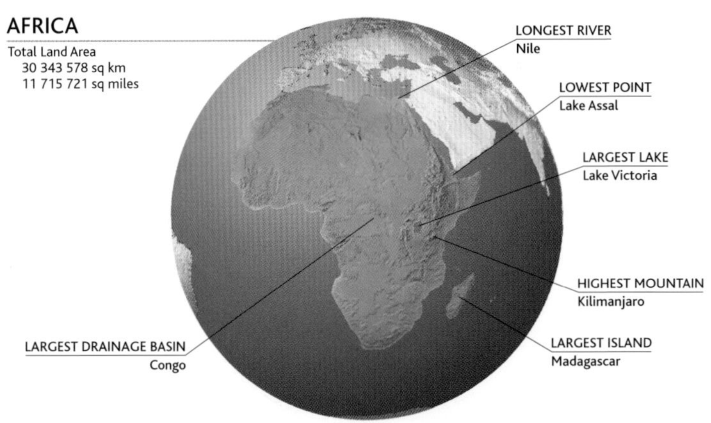

LONGEST RIVER
Nile

LOWEST POINT
Lake Assal

LARGEST LAKE
Lake Victoria

HIGHEST MOUNTAIN
Kilimanjaro

LARGEST DRAINAGE BASIN
Congo

LARGEST ISLAND
Madagascar

HIGHEST MOUNTAINS	HEIGHT metres	feet	LARGEST ISLANDS	AREA sq km	sq miles	LARGEST LAKES	AREA sq km	sq miles	LONGEST RIVERS	LENGTH km	miles
Kilimanjaro	5 892	19 331	Madagascar	587 040	226 657	Lake Victoria	68 800	26 564	Nile	6 695	4 160
Mt Kenya	5 199	17 057				Lake Tanganyika	32 900	12 702	Congo	4 667	2 900
Margherita Peak	5 110	16 765				Lake Nyasa	30 044	11 600	Niger	4 184	2 599
Meru	4 565	14 977				Lake Chad	10 000–26 000	3 861–10 039	Zambezi	2 736	1 700
Ras Dejen	4 533	14 872				Lake Volta	8 485	3 276	Webi Shabeelle	2 490	1 547

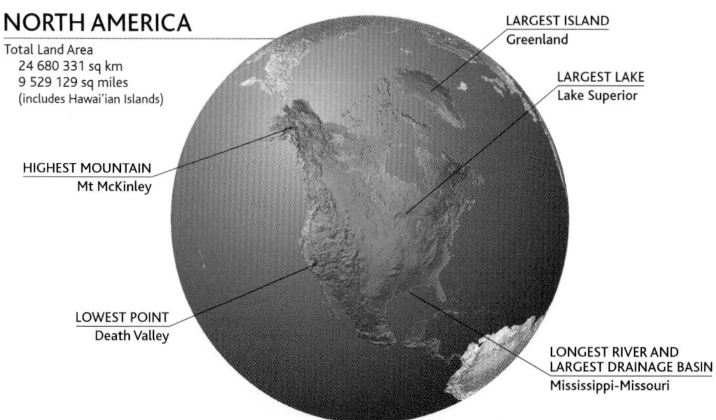

NORTH AMERICA

Total Land Area
24 680 331 sq km
9 529 129 sq miles
(includes Hawai'ian Islands)

HIGHEST MOUNTAIN
Mt McKinley

LOWEST POINT
Death Valley

LARGEST ISLAND
Greenland

LARGEST LAKE
Lake Superior

LONGEST RIVER AND
LARGEST DRAINAGE BASIN
Mississippi-Missouri

HIGHEST MOUNTAINS	HEIGHT metres	feet	LARGEST ISLANDS	AREA sq km	sq miles	LARGEST LAKES	AREA sq km	sq miles	LONGEST RIVERS	LENGTH km	miles
Mt McKinley	6 194	20 321	Greenland	2 175 600	840 004	Lake Superior	82 100	31 699	Mississippi-Missouri	5 969	3 709
Mt Logan	5 959	19 550	Baffin Island	507 451	195 928	Lake Huron	59 600	23 012	Mackenzie-Peace-Finlay	4 241	2 635
Pico de Orizaba	5 747	18 855	Victoria Island	217 291	83 897	Lake Michigan	57 800	22 317	Missouri	4 086	2 539
Mt St Elias	5 489	18 008	Ellesmere Island	196 236	75 767	Great Bear Lake	31 328	12 095	Mississippi	3 765	2 339
Volcán Popocatépetl	5 452	17 887	Cuba	110 860	42 803	Great Slave Lake	28 568	11 030	Yukon	3 185	1 979

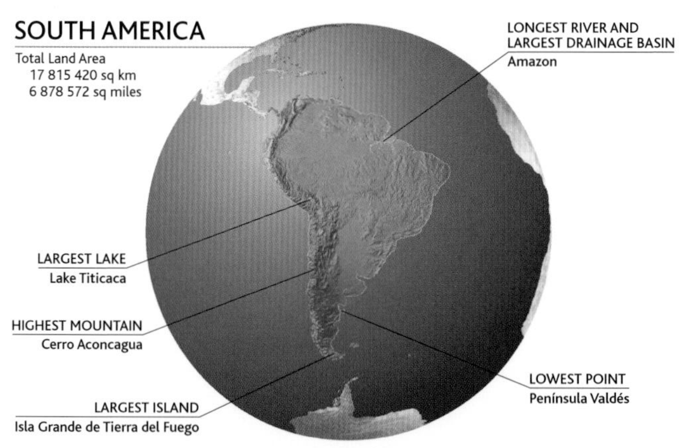

SOUTH AMERICA

Total Land Area
17 815 420 sq km
6 878 572 sq miles

LARGEST LAKE
Lake Titicaca

HIGHEST MOUNTAIN
Cerro Aconcagua

LARGEST ISLAND
Isla Grande de Tierra del Fuego

LONGEST RIVER AND
LARGEST DRAINAGE BASIN
Amazon

LOWEST POINT
Península Valdés

HIGHEST MOUNTAINS	HEIGHT metres	feet	LARGEST ISLANDS	AREA sq km	sq miles	LARGEST LAKES	AREA sq km	sq miles	LONGEST RIVERS	LENGTH km	miles
Cerro Aconcagua	6 959	22 831	Isla Grande de Tierra del Fuego	47 000	18 147	Lake Titicaca	8 340	3 220	Amazon	6 516	4 049
Nevado Ojos del Salado	6 908	22 664	Isla de Chiloé	8 394	3 240				Río de la Plata-Paraná	4 500	2 796
Cerro Bonete	6 872	22 546	East Falkland	6 760	2 610				Purus	3 218	1 999
Cerro Pissis	6 858	22 500	West Falkland	5 413	2 090				Madeira	3 200	1 988
Cerro Tupungato	6 800	22 211							Sao Francisco	2 900	1 802

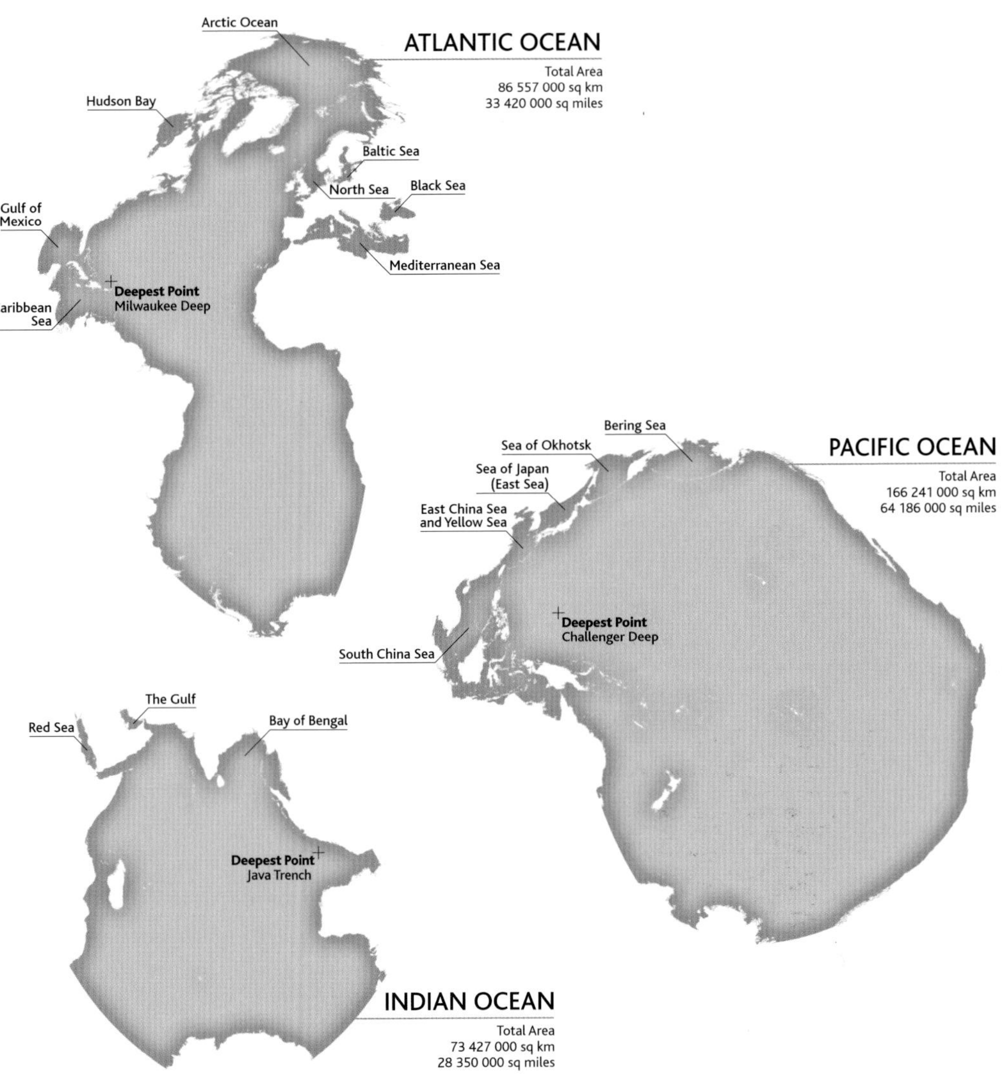

Arctic Ocean

ATLANTIC OCEAN
Total Area
86 557 000 sq km
33 420 000 sq miles

Hudson Bay

Baltic Sea

North Sea   Black Sea

Gulf of
Mexico

Mediterranean Sea

Deepest Point
Milwaukee Deep

Caribbean
Sea

Bering Sea

Sea of Okhotsk

PACIFIC OCEAN
Total Area
166 241 000 sq km
64 186 000 sq miles

Sea of Japan
(East Sea)

East China Sea
and Yellow Sea

Deepest Point
Challenger Deep

South China Sea

The Gulf

Bay of Bengal

Red Sea

Deepest Point
Java Trench

INDIAN OCEAN
Total Area
73 427 000 sq km
28 350 000 sq miles

ATLANTIC OCEAN	AREA		DEEPEST POINT	
	sq km	sq miles	metres	feet
Extent	86 557 000	33 420 000	8 605	28 231
Arctic Ocean	9 485 000	3 662 000	5 450	17 880
Caribbean Sea	2 512 000	970 000	7 680	25 196
Mediterranean Sea	2 510 000	969 000	5 121	16 800
Gulf of Mexico	1 544 000	596 000	3 504	11 495
Hudson Bay	1 233 000	476 000	259	849
North Sea	575 000	222 000	661	2 168
Black Sea	508 000	196 000	2 245	7 365
Baltic Sea	382 000	147 000	460	1 509

INDIAN OCEAN	AREA		DEEPEST POINT	
	sq km	sq miles	metres	feet
Extent	73 427 000	28 350 000	7 125	23 376
Bay of Bengal	2 172 000	839 000	4 500	14 763
Red Sea	453 000	175 000	3 040	9 973
The Gulf	238 000	92 000	73	239

PACIFIC OCEAN	AREA		DEEPEST POINT	
	sq km	sq miles	metres	feet
Extent	166 241 000	64 186 000	10 920	35 826
South China Sea	2 590 000	1 000 000	5 514	18 090
Bering Sea	2 261 000	873 000	4 150	13 615
Sea of Okhotsk	1 392 000	537 000	3 363	11 033
Sea of Japan (East Sea)	1 013 000	391 000	3 743	12 280
East China Sea and Yellow Sea	1 202 000	464 000	2 717	8 913

MAJOR CLIMATIC REGIONS AND SUB-TYPES

Winkel Tripel Projection
1:145 000 000

Köppen classification system

A	Rainy climate with no winter: coolest month above 18°C (64.4°F).
B	Dry climates; limits are defined by formulae based on rainfall effectiveness. **BS** Steppe or semi-arid climate. **BW** Desert or arid climate.
*C	Rainy climates with mild winters: coolest month above 0°C (32°F), but below 18°C (64.4°F); warmest month above 10°C (50°F).
*D	Rainy climates with severe winters: coolest month below 0°C (32°F); warmest month above 10°C (50°F).
E	Polar climates with no warm season: warmest month below 10°C (50°F). **ET** Tundra climate: warmest month below 10°C (50°F) but above 0°C (32°F). **EF** Perpetual frost: all months below 0°C (32°F).
a	Warmest month above 22°C (71.6°F).
b	Warmest month below 22°C (71.6°F).
c	Less than four months over 10°C (50°F).
d	As 'c', but with severe cold: coldest month below -38°C (-36.4°F).
f	Constantly moist rainfall throughout the year.
*h	Warmer dry: all months above 0°C (32°F).
*k	Cooler dry: at least one month below 0°C (32°F).
m	Monsoon rain: short dry season, but is compensated by heavy rains during rest of the year.
n	Frequent fog.
s	Dry season in summer.

* Modification of Köppen definition

- ● World weather extremes– see table

Polar

| EF | Ice cap |
| ET | Tundra |

Cooler humid

Dc Dd	Subarctic
Db	Continental cool summer
Da	Continental warm

Warmer humid

Cb Cc	Temperate
Ca	Humid subtropical
Cs	Mediterranean

Dry

| BS | Steppe |
| BW | Desert |

Tropical humid

| Aw As | Savanna |
| Af Am | Rain forest |

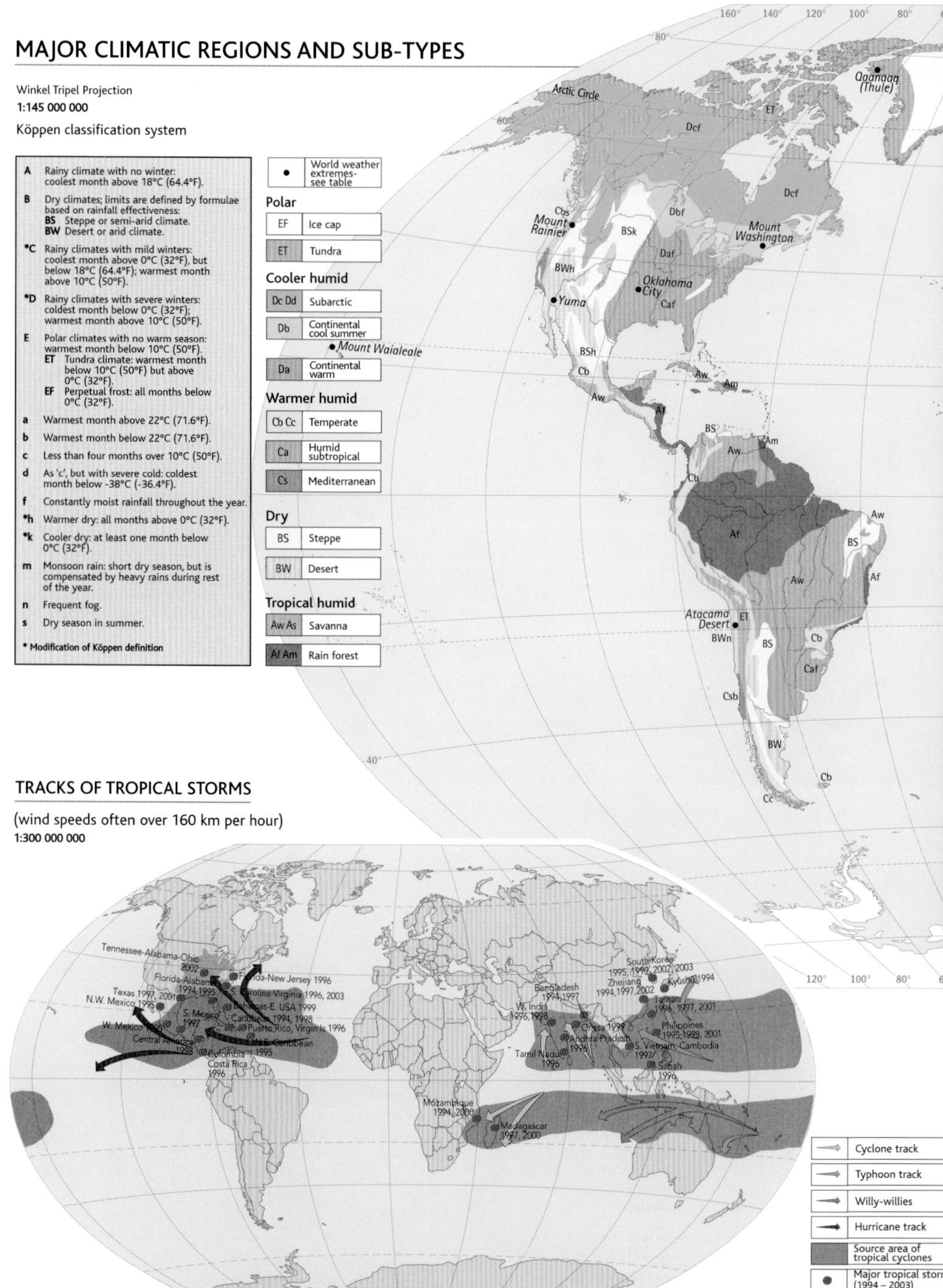

TRACKS OF TROPICAL STORMS

(wind speeds often over 160 km per hour)
1:300 000 000

→	Cyclone track
→	Typhoon track
→	Willy-willies
→	Hurricane track
	Source area of tropical cyclones
●	Major tropical storm (1994 – 2003)
	Tornado high risk areas

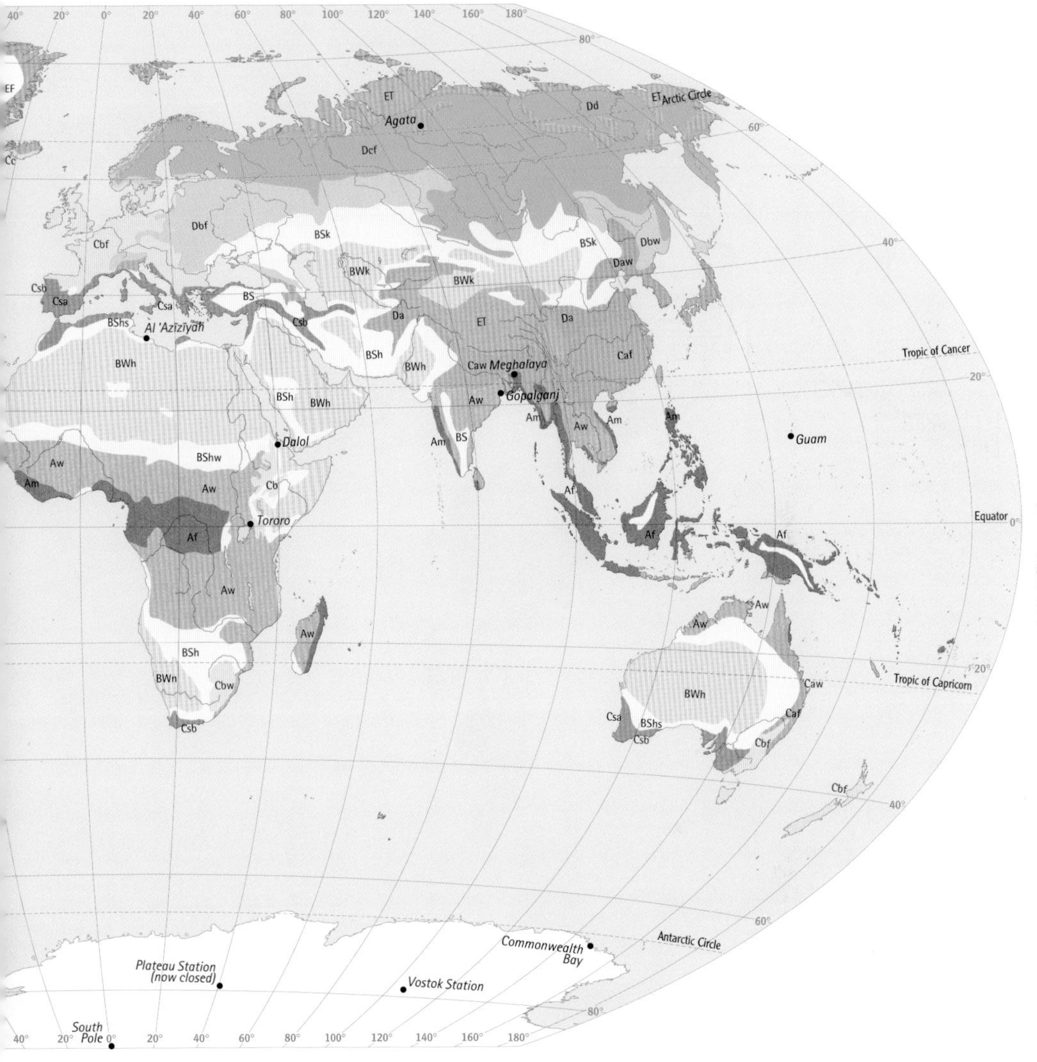

WORLD WEATHER EXTREMES

Highest shade temperature	57.8°C/136°F **Al 'Azīzīyah**, Libya (13th September 1922)	Highest surface wind speed	
Hottest place – Annual mean	34.4°C/93.9°F **Dalol**, Ethiopia	High altitude	372 km per hour/231 miles per hour **Mount Washington**, New Hampshire, USA (12th April 1934)
Driest place – Annual mean	0.1 mm/0.004 inches **Atacama Desert**, Chile	Low altitude	333 km per hour/207 miles per hour **Qaanaaq (Thule)**, Greenland (8th March 1972)
Most sunshine – Annual mean	90% **Yuma**, Arizona, USA (over 4 000 hours)	Tornado	512 km per hour/318 miles per hour **Oklahoma City**, Oklahoma, USA (3rd May 1999)
Least sunshine	Nil for 182 days each year, **South Pole**	Greatest snowfall	31 102 mm/1 224.5 inches **Mount Rainier**, Washington, USA (19th February 1971–18th February 1972)
Lowest screen temperature	-89.2°C/-128.6°F **Vostok Station**, Antarctica (21st July 1983)	Heaviest hailstones	1 kg/2.21 lb **Gopalganj**, Bangladesh (14th April 1986)
Coldest place – Annual mean	-56.6°C/-69.9°F **Plateau Station**, Antarctica	Thunder-days Average	251 days per year **Tororo**, Uganda
Wettest place – Annual mean	11 873 mm/467.4 inches **Meghalaya**, India	Highest barometric pressure	1 083.8 mb **Agata**, Siberia, Rus. Fed. (31st December 1968)
Most rainy days	Up to 350 per year **Mount Waialeale**, Hawaii, USA	Lowest barometric pressure	870 mb 483 km/300 miles west of **Guam**, Pacific Ocean (12th October 1979)
Windiest place	322 km per hour/200 miles per hour in gales, **Commonwealth Bay**, Antarctica		

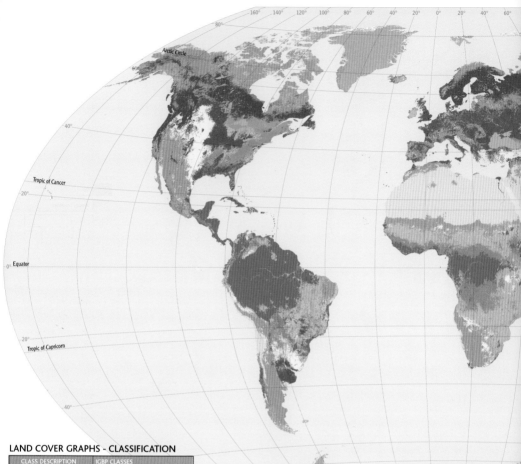

LAND COVER GRAPHS - CLASSIFICATION

CLASS DESCRIPTION	IGBP CLASSES
Forest/Woodland	Evergreen needleleaf forest
	Evergreen broadleaf forest
	Deciduous needleleaf forest
	Deciduous broadleaf forest
	Mixed forest
Shrubland	Closed shrublands
	Open shrublands
Grass/Savanna	Woody savannas
	Savannas
	Grasslands
Wetland	Permanent wetlands
Crops/Mosaic	Croplands
	Cropland/Natural vegetation mosaic
Urban	Urban and built-up
Snow/Ice	Snow and Ice
Barren	Barren or sparsely vegetated

GLOBAL LAND COVER COMPOSITION

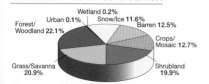

Wetland 0.2%
Urban 0.1%   Snow/Ice 11.6%
Forest/   Barren 12.5%
Woodland 22.1%
                               Crops/
                               Mosaic 12.7%

Grass/Savanna
20.9%   Shrubland
                       19.9%

CONTINENTAL LAND COVER COMPOSITION

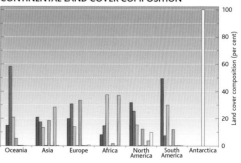

Land cover composition (per cent)

Oceania Asia Europe Africa North   South   Antarctica
                                America America

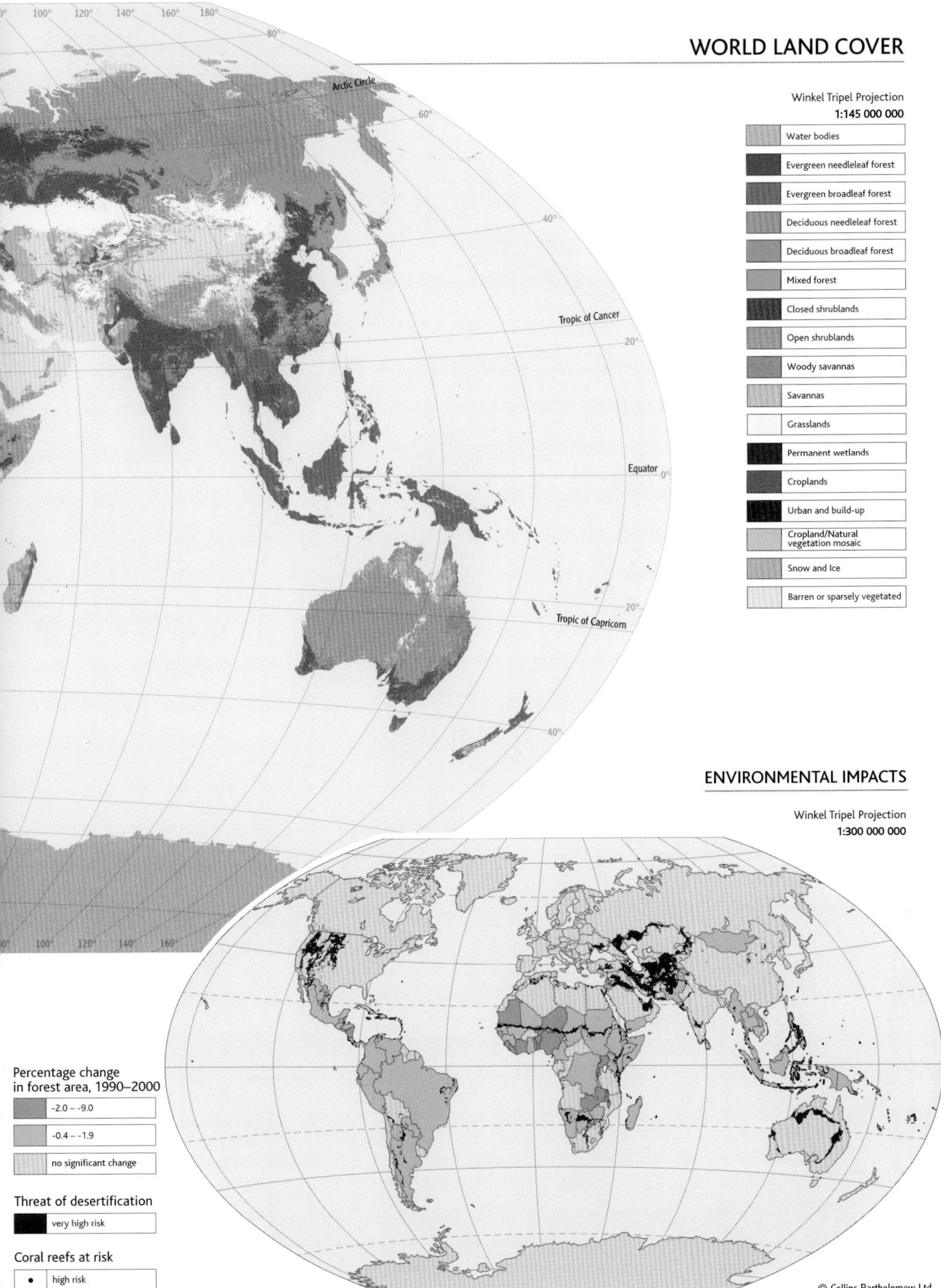

WORLD LAND COVER

Winkel Tripel Projection
1:145 000 000

	Water bodies
	Evergreen needleleaf forest
	Evergreen broadleaf forest
	Deciduous needleleaf forest
	Deciduous broadleaf forest
	Mixed forest
	Closed shrublands
	Open shrublands
	Woody savannas
	Savannas
	Grasslands
	Permanent wetlands
	Croplands
	Urban and build-up
	Cropland/Natural vegetation mosaic
	Snow and Ice
	Barren or sparsely vegetated

ENVIRONMENTAL IMPACTS

Winkel Tripel Projection
1:300 000 000

Percentage change in forest area, 1990–2000

	-2.0 – -9.0
	-0.4 – -1.9
	no significant change

Threat of desertification

	very high risk

Coral reefs at risk

•	high risk

© Collins Bartholomew Ltd

WORLD POPULATION DISTRIBUTION AND THE WORLD'S MAJOR CITIES

Winkel Tripel Projection
1:145 000 000

Population Density

per sq mile
1 250   250   62.5   2.5   0

Inhabitants   Uninhabited

500   100   25   1   0
per sq km

Major Urban Agglomerations

- 5 million–10 million
- 10 million–20 million
- over 20 million

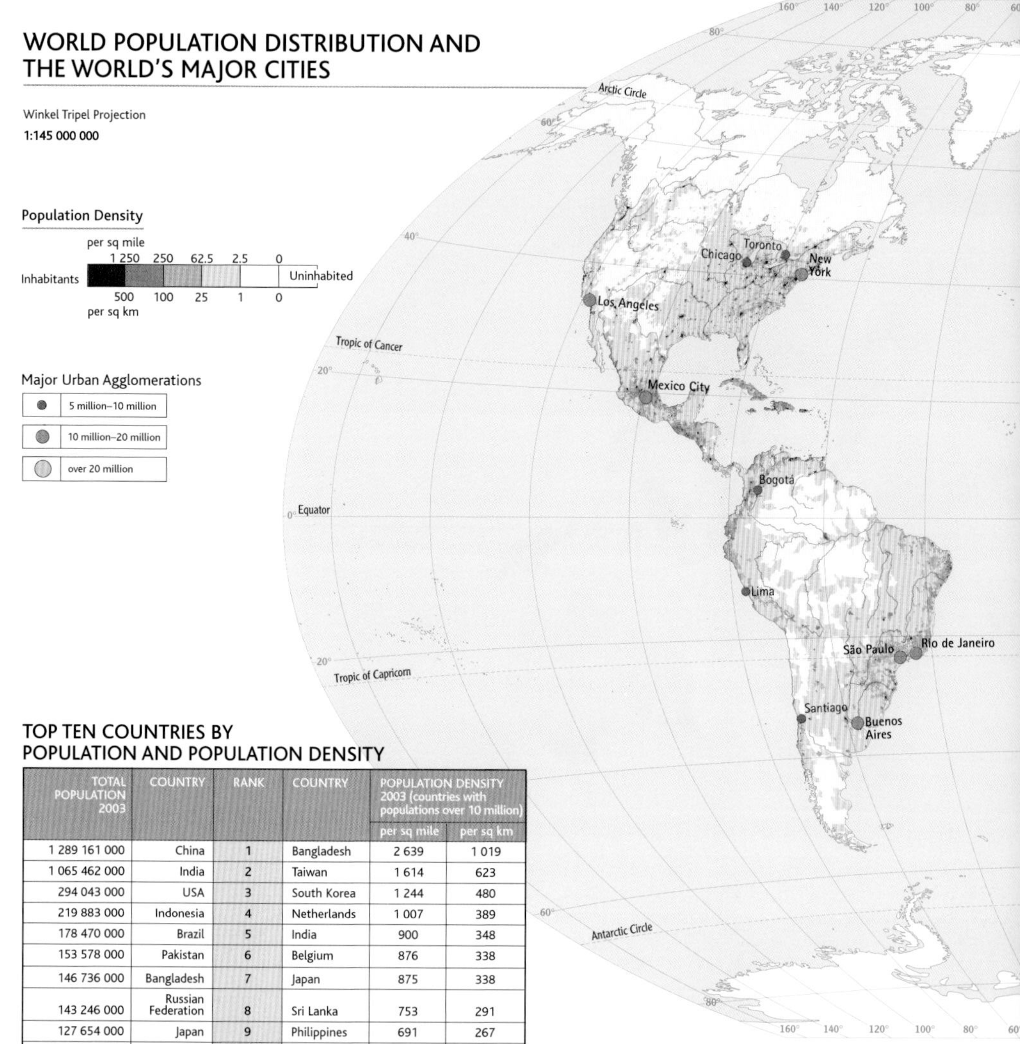

TOP TEN COUNTRIES BY POPULATION AND POPULATION DENSITY

TOTAL POPULATION 2003	COUNTRY	RANK	COUNTRY	POPULATION DENSITY 2003 (countries with populations over 10 million) per sq mile	per sq km
1 289 161 000	China	1	Bangladesh	2 639	1 019
1 065 462 000	India	2	Taiwan	1 614	623
294 043 000	USA	3	South Korea	1 244	480
219 883 000	Indonesia	4	Netherlands	1 007	389
178 470 000	Brazil	5	India	900	348
153 578 000	Pakistan	6	Belgium	876	338
146 736 000	Bangladesh	7	Japan	875	338
143 246 000	Russian Federation	8	Sri Lanka	753	291
127 654 000	Japan	9	Philippines	691	267
124 009 000	Nigeria	10	Vietnam	640	247

KEY POPULATION STATISTICS FOR MAJOR REGIONS

	POPULATION 2003 (millions)	GROWTH (per cent)	INFANT MORTALITY RATE	TOTAL FERTILITY RATE	LIFE EXPECTANCY (years)	% AGED 60 OR OVER 2000	2050
World	6 301	1.2	56	2.7	65	10	21
More developed regions	1 203	0.3	8	1.6	76	19	32
Less developed regions	5 098	1.5	61	2.9	63	8	20
Africa	851	2.2	89	4.9	49	5	10
Asia	3 823	1.3	53	2.6	67	9	23
Europe	726	-0.1	9	1.4	74	20	35
Latin America and the Caribbean	543	1.4	32	2.5	70	8	24
North America	326	1.0	7	2.1	77	16	26
Oceania	32	1.2	26	2.3	74	13	25

Except for population (2003) and % aged 60 and over figures, the data are annual averages projected for the period 2000–2005.

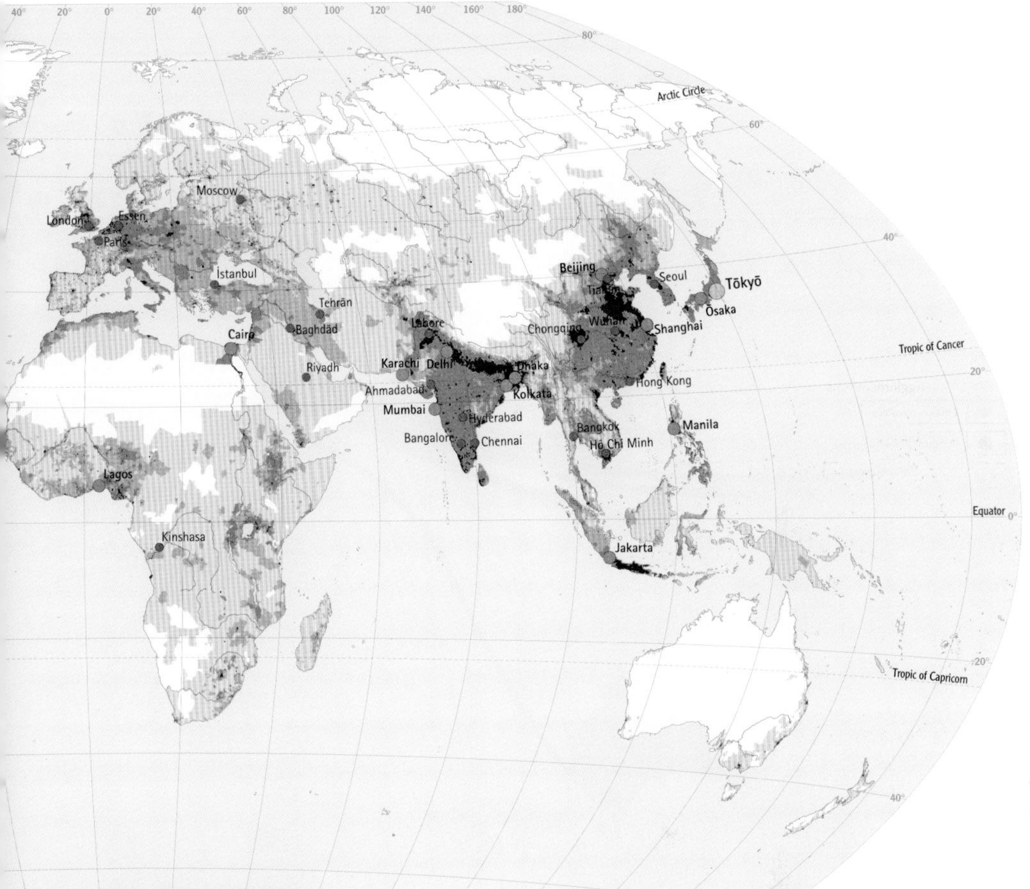

WORLD POPULATION GROWTH BY CONTINENT 1750–2050

THE WORLD'S LARGEST CITIES

CITY	COUNTRY	POPULATION
Tōkyō	Japan	26 849 000
São Paulo	Brazil	19 591 000
Mexico City	Mexico	18 934 000
Mumbai	India	18 337 000
New York	USA	17 147 000
Dhaka	Bangladesh	15 921 000
Delhi	India	15 335 000
Kolkata	India	14 299 000
Los Angeles	USA	13 766 000
Jakarta	Indonesia	13 156 000
Shanghai	China	12 665 000
Buenos Aires	Argentina	12 439 000
Karachi	Pakistan	11 830 000
Rio de Janeiro	Brazil	11 170 000
Lagos	Nigeria	11 134 000
Ōsaka	Japan	11 013 000
Beijing	China	10 849 000
Manila	Philippines	10 684 000
Cairo	Egypt	10 094 000
İstanbul	Turkey	9 946 000

INTERNATIONAL TELECOMMUNICATIONS TRAFFIC 2002

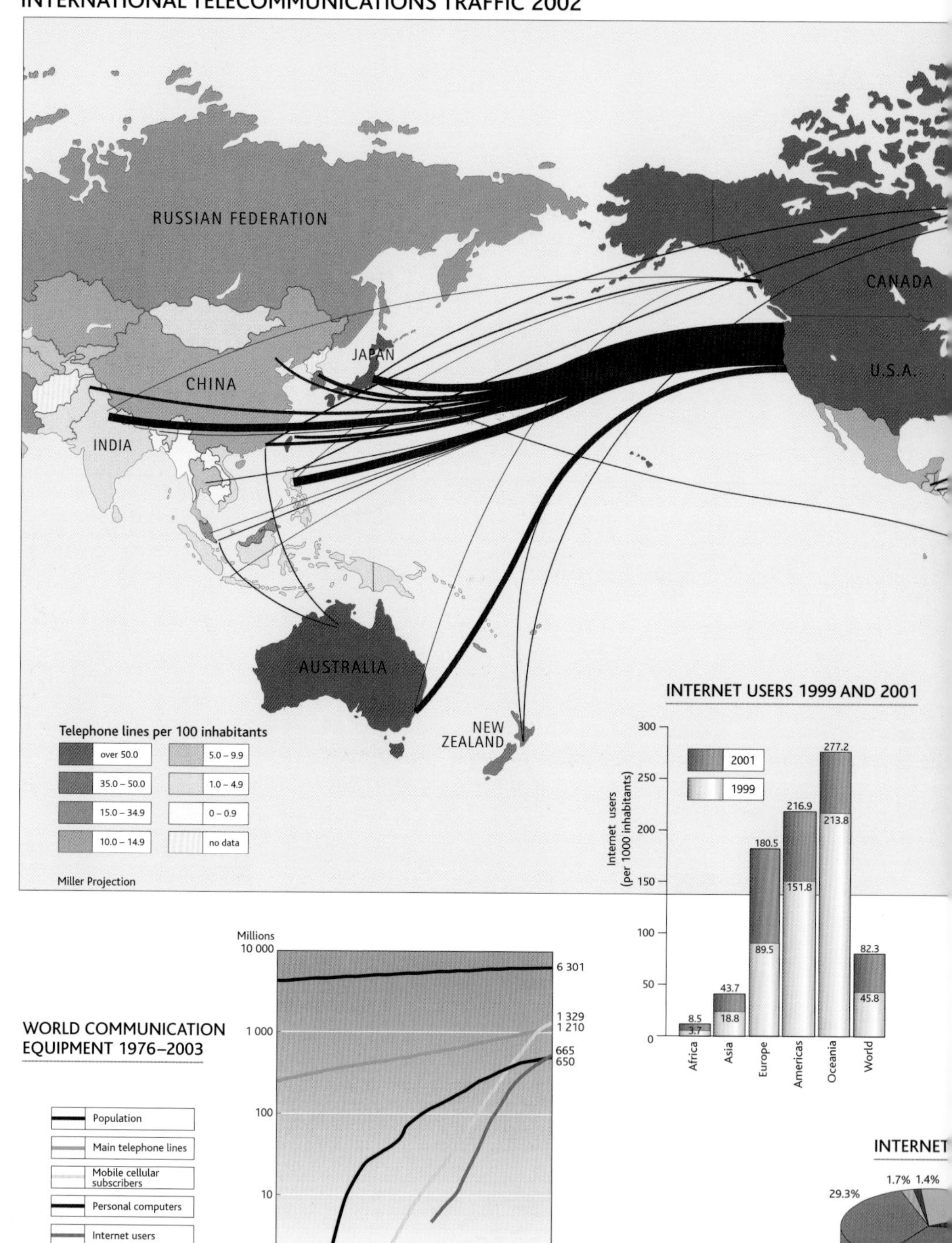

Telephone lines per 100 inhabitants

over 50.0	5.0 – 9.9
35.0 – 50.0	1.0 – 4.9
15.0 – 34.9	0 – 0.9
10.0 – 14.9	no data

Miller Projection

INTERNET USERS 1999 AND 2001

Internet users (per 1000 inhabitants)

- 2001
- 1999

	Africa	Asia	Europe	Americas	Oceania	World
2001	8.5	43.7	180.5	216.9	277.2	82.3
1999	3.7	18.8	89.5	151.8	213.8	45.8

WORLD COMMUNICATION EQUIPMENT 1976–2003

Millions

- Population
- Main telephone lines
- Mobile cellular subscribers
- Personal computers
- Internet users

6 301
1 329
1 210
665
650

1976 1979 1982 1985 1988 1991 1994 1997 2000 2003

INTERNET

1.7% 1.4%
29.3%

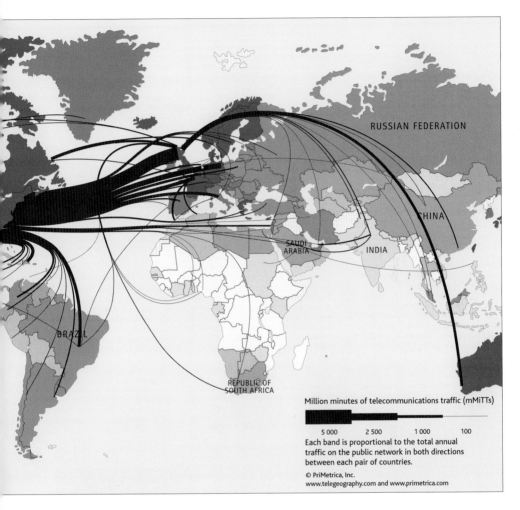

RUSSIAN FEDERATION

CHINA

SAUDI
ARABIA

INDIA

BRAZIL

REPUBLIC OF
SOUTH AFRICA

Million minutes of telecommunications traffic (mMiTTs)

5 000   2 500   1 000   100

Each band is proportional to the total annual
traffic on the public network in both directions
between each pair of countries.

© PriMetrica, Inc.
www.telegeography.com and www.primetrica.com

TELEPHONE MAIN LINES

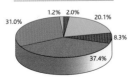

1.2% 2.0%   20.1%
31.0%
8.3%
37.4%

TOP 10 INTERNET SERVICE PROVIDERS (ISPs)

INTERNET SERVICE PROVIDER	WEB ADDRESS	SUBSCRIBERS
AOL (USA)	www.aol.com	20 500 000
T-Online (Germany)	www.t-online.de	4 151 000
Nifty-Serve (Japan)	www.nifty.com	3 500 000
EarthLink (USA)	www.earthlink.com	3 122 000
Biglobe (Japan)	www.biglobe.ne.jp	2 720 000
MSN (USA)	www.msn.com	2 700 000
Chollian (South Korea)	www.chollian.net	2 000 000
Tin.it (Italy)	www.tin.it	1 990 000
Freeserve (UK)	www.freeserve.com	1 575 000
AT&T WorldNet (USA)	www.att.net	1 500 000

USERS

31.1%
5.3%
31.2%

Africa

USA and Canada

Latin America
and the Caribbean

Asia

Europe

Oceania

CELLULAR SUBSCRIBERS

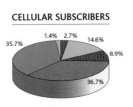

1.4% 2.7%   14.6%
35.7%
8.9%
36.7%

© Collins Bartholomew Ltd

MAP POLICIES AND ABBREVIATIONS

Place Names

The spelling of place names on maps has always been a matter of great complexity, because of the variety of the world's languages and the systems used to write them down. There is no standard way of spelling names or of converting them from one alphabet, or symbol set, to another. Instead, conventional ways of spelling have evolved in each of the world's major languages, and the results often differ significantly from the name as it is spelled in the original language. Familiar examples of English conventional names include Munich (München), Florence (Firenze) and Moscow (from the transliterated form, Moskva).

In this atlas, local name forms are used where these are in the Roman alphabet, though for major cities, and main physical features, conventional English names are given first. The local forms are those which are officially recognized by the government of the country concerned, usually as represented by its official mapping agency. This is a basic principle laid down by the United Kingdom government's Permanent Committee on Geographical Names (PCGN) and the equivalent United States Board on Geographic Names, (BGN). Prominent English-language and historic names are not neglected, however. These, and significant superseded names and alternate spellings, are included in brackets on the maps where space permits, and are cross-referenced in the index.

Country names are shown in conventional English form and include any recent changes promulgated by national governments and adopted by the United Nations. The names of continents, oceans, seas and under-water features in international waters also appear in English throughout the atlas, as do those of other international features where such an English form exists and is in common use. International features are defined as features crossing one or more international boundary.

Boundaries

The status of nations, their names and their boundaries, are shown in this atlas as they are at the time of going to press, as far as can be ascertained. Where an international boundary symbol appears in the sea or ocean it does not necessarily infer a legal maritime boundary, but shows which offshore islands belong to which country. The extent of island nations is shown by a short boundary symbol at the extreme limits of the area of sea or ocean within which all land is part of that nation.

Where international boundaries are the subject of dispute it may be that no portrayal of them will meet with the approval of any of the countries involved, but it is not seen as the function of this atlas to try to adjudicate between the rights and wrongs of political issues. Although reference mapping at atlas scales is not the ideal medium for indicating the claims of many separatist and irredentist movements, every reasonable attempt is made to show where an active territorial dispute exists, and where there is an important difference between 'de facto' (existing in fact, on the ground) and 'de jure' (according to law) boundaries. This is done by the use of a different symbol where international boundaries are disputed, or where the alignment is unconfirmed, to that used for settled international boundaries. Ceasefire lines are also shown by a separate symbol. For clarity, disputed boundaries and areas are annotated where this is considered necessary. The atlas aims to take a strictly neutral viewpoint of all such cases, based on advice from expert consultants.

Map Projections

Map projections have been selected specifically for the area and scale of each map, or suite of maps. As the only way to show the Earth with absolute accuracy is on a globe, all map projections are compromises. Some projections seek to maintain correct area relationships (equal area projections), true distances and bearings from a point (equidistant projections) or correct angles and shapes (conformal projections); others attempt to achieve a balance between these properties. The choice of projections used in this atlas has been made on an individual continental and regional basis. Projections used, and their individual parameters, have been defined to minimize distortion and to reduce scale errors as much as possible. The projection used is indicated at the bottom left of each map page.

Scale

In order to directly compare like with like throughout the world it would be necessary to maintain a single scale throughout the atlas. However, the desirability of mapping the more densely populated areas of the world at larger scales, and other geographical considerations, such as the need to fit a homogeneous physical region within a uniform rectangular page format, mean that a range of scales have been used. Scales for continental maps range between 1:25 000 000 and 1:55 000 000, depending on the size of the continental land mass being covered. Scales for regional maps are typically in the range 1:15 000 000 to 1:25 000 000. Mapping for most countries is at scales between 1:6 000 000 and 1:12 000 000, although for the more densely populated areas of Europe the scale increases to 1:3 000 000.

ABBREVIATIONS

Arch.	Archipelago			L.	Lake			Ra.	Range		mountain range
B.	Bay				Loch	(Scotland)	lake	S.	South, Southern		
	Bahia, Baía	Portuguese	bay		Lough	(Ireland)	lake		Salar, Salina,		
	Bahía	Spanish	bay		Lac	French	lake		Salinas	Spanish	salt pan, salt pans
	Baie	French	bay		Lago	Portuguese, Spanish	lake	Sa	Serra	Portuguese	mountain range
C.	Cape			M.	Mys	Russian	cape, point		Sierra	Spanish	mountain range
	Cabo	Portuguese,		Mt	Mount			Sd	Sound		
		Spanish	cape, headland		Mont	French	hill, mountain	S.E.	Southeast,		
	Cap	French	cape, headland	Mt.	Mountain				Southeastern		
Co	Cerro	Spanish	hill, peak, summit	Mte	Monte	Portuguese, Spanish	hill, mountain	St	Saint		
E.	East, Eastern			Mts	Mountains				Sankt	German	
Est.	Estrecho	Spanish	strait		Monts	French	hills, mountains		Sint	Dutch	saint
G.	Gebel	Arabic	hill, mountain	N.	North, Northern			Sta	Santa	Italian, Portuguese,	
Gt	Great			O.	Ostrov	Russian	island			Spanish	saint
I.	Island, Isle			Pk	Puncak	Indonesian, Malay	hill, mountain	Ste	Sainte	French	saint
	Ilha	Portuguese	island	Pt	Point			Str.	Strait		
	Islas	Spanish	island	Pta	Punta	Italian, Spanish	cape, point	Tk	Teluk	Indonesian, Malay	bay, gulf
Is	Islands, Isles			R.	River			Tg	Tanjong, Tanjung	Indonesian, Malay	cape, point
	Islas	Spanish	islands		Rio	Portuguese	river	Vdkhr.	Vodokhranilishche	Russian	reservoir
Kep.	Kepulauan	Indonesian	islands		Río	Spanish	river	W.	West, Western		
Khr.	Khrebet	Russian	mountain range		Rivière	French	river		Wadi, Wâdi, Wādī	Arabic	watercourse

MAP SYMBOLS

Land and Water Features

- Lake
- Impermanent lake
- Salt lake or lagoon
- Impermanent salt lake
- Dry salt lake or salt pan

- River
- Impermanent river
- Ice cap / Glacier
- 123 Pass
  Height in metres
- ∴ Site of special interest
- ◡ Oasis
- ᴧᴧᴧᴧ Wall

Transport

- Motorway
- Main road
- Track
- Main railway
- Canal
- Main airport

Boundaries

- International boundary
- Disputed international boundary or alignment unconfirmed
- Undefined international boundary in the sea.
  All land within this boundary is part of state or territory named.
- Administrative boundary
  Shown for selected countries only.
- Ceasefire line or other boundary described on the map

Relief

Contour intervals used in layer-colouring, for land height and sea depth

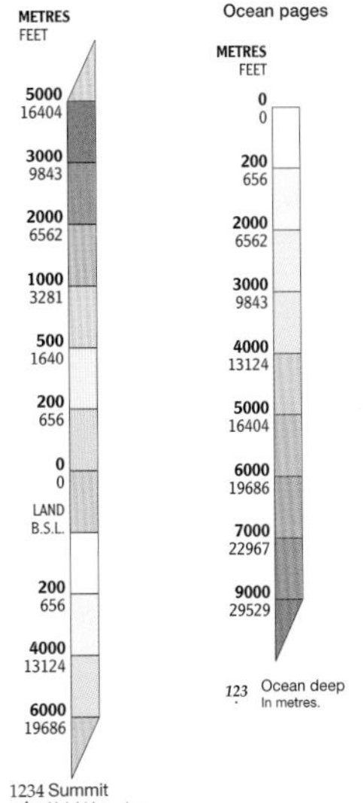

METRES FEET	
5000	16404
3000	9843
2000	6562
1000	3281
500	1640
200	656
0	0
LAND B.S.L.	
200	656
4000	13124
6000	19686

1234 Summit
△ Height in metres

Ocean pages

METRES FEET	
0	0
200	656
2000	6562
3000	9843
4000	13124
5000	16404
6000	19686
7000	22967
9000	29529

123 Ocean deep
In metres.

Styles of Lettering

Cities and towns are explained separately

		Physical features	
Country	**FRANCE**	Island	*Gran Canaria*
Overseas Territory/Dependency	**Guadeloupe**	Lake	*Lake Erie*
Disputed Territory	AKSAI CHIN	Mountain	*Mt Blanc*
Administrative name	**SCOTLAND**	River	*Thames*
Shown for selected countries only.			
Area name	PATAGONIA	Region	*LAPPLAND*

Cities and Towns

Population	National Capital	Administrative Capital	Other City or Town
		Shown for selected countries only	
over 5 million	**BEIJING** ⊡	**Atlanta** ⊙	**New York** ◎
1 million to 5 million	**KĀBUL** ☐	**Sydney** ○	**Koahsiung** ○
500 000 to 1 million	**BANGUI** ☐	**Winnipeg** ○	**Jeddah** ○
100 000 to 500 000	WELLINGTON ☐	Edinburgh ○	Apucarana ○
50 000 to 100 000	PORT OF SPAIN ☐	Bismarck ○	Invercargill ○
under 50 000	MALABO ▫	Charlottetown ○	Ceres ○

CONTINENTAL MAPS

Boundaries

—— International boundary   - - - - - - Disputed international boundary   ·········· Ceasefire line

Cities and Towns

National Capital   **Beijing** ☐   Other City or Town   **New York** ○

METRES
FEET

6000	19686
4000	13124
2000	6562
1000	3281
500	1640
200	656
0 LAND B.S.L.	
200	656
3000	9843
5000	16404
7000	22967

EARTH'S DIMENSIONS

Mass	5.974 X 10^{21} tonnes
Total area	509 450 000 sq km / 196 699 746 sq miles
Land area	148 721 936 sq km / 57 421 861 sq miles
Water area	360 728 064 sq km / 139 277 885 sq miles
Volume	1 083 207 X 10^6 cu km / 259 911 X 10^6 cu miles

Winkel Tripel Projection

HIGHEST MOUNTAINS

	LOCATION	HEIGHT	
		metres	feet
Mt Everest	China/Nepal	8 848	29 028
K2	China/Jammu and Kashmir	8 611	28 251
Kangchenjunga	India/Nepal	8 586	28 169
Lhotse	China/Nepal	8 516	27 939
Makalu	China/Nepal	8 463	27 765

LARGEST ISLANDS

	LOCATION	AREA	
		sq km	sq miles
Greenland	North America	2 175 600	840 004
New Guinea	Oceania	808 510	312 167
Borneo	Asia	745 561	287 863
Madagascar	Africa	587 040	266 657
Baffin Island	North America	507 451	195 928

Equatorial diameter	12 756 km / 7 927 miles
Polar diameter	12 714 km / 7 901 miles
Equatorial circumference	40 075 km / 24 903 miles
Meridional circumference	40 008 km / 24 861 miles

1: 126 000 000

LARGEST LAKES

	LOCATION	AREA	
		sq km	sq miles
Caspian Sea	Asia/Europe	371 000	143 244
Lake Superior	North America	82 100	31 699
Lake Victoria	Africa	68 800	26 564
Lake Huron	North America	59 600	23 012
Lake Michigan	North America	57 800	22 317

LONGEST RIVERS

	LOCATION	LENGTH	
		km	miles
Nile	Africa	6 695	4 160
Amazon	South America	6 516	4 049
Yangtze	Asia	6 380	3 965
Mississippi-Missouri	North America	5 969	3 709
Ob'-Irtysh	Asia	5 568	3 460

TIME COMPARISONS

Time varies around the world due to the
earth's rotation causing different parts of the
world to be in light or darkness at any one time.
To account for this, the world is divided into twenty-
four Standard Time Zones based on 15° intervals of longitude.
The table below gives examples of times observed at different parts
of the world when it is 12 noon in the zone at the Greenwich Meridian
(0° longitude). Daylight Saving Time, normally one hour ahead of local
Standard Time, observed by certain countries for parts of the year, is not considered.

Winkel Tripel Projection

01:00	02:00	03:00	04:00	05:00	06:00	07:00	08:00	09:00	10:00	11:00	12:00
Am. Samoa Samoa	Cook Is Hawaiian Is Tahiti	Anchorage	Vancouver San Francisco Los Angeles Pitcairn Is	Edmonton Denver	Chicago Houston Monterrey Mexico City Easter Island	Ottawa Washington Havana Bogotá Lima	Puerto Rico Caracas La Paz Asunción	Nuuk Brasília Rio de Janeiro Buenos Aires	South Georgia S. Sandwich Is	Azores Cape Verde	Reykjavík London Rabat Nouakchott Accra

Abbreviations

A.	ANDORRA	CZ.R.	CZECH REPUBLIC	M.	MACEDONIA
AL.	ALBANIA	DEN.	DENMARK	MO.	MOLDOVA
ARM.	ARMENIA	EQ.G.	EQUATORIAL GUINEA	NETH.	NETHERLANDS
AUS.	AUSTRIA	FR.G.	FRENCH GUIANA	NI.	NIGERIA
AZ.	AZERBAIJAN	GEOR.	GEORGIA	Q.	QATAR
B.	BURUNDI	GER.	GERMANY	R.	RWANDA
BE.	BENIN	GH.	GHANA	S.	SERBIA AND MONTENEGRO
BEL.	BELGIUM	GUY.	GUYANA	SLA.	SLOVAKIA
B.H.	BOSNIA-HERZEGOVINA	HUN.	HUNGARY	SL.	SLOVENIA
BN.	BAHRAIN	ISR.	ISRAEL	SUR.	SURINAME
BUR.	BURKINA	JOR.	JORDAN	SW.	SWITZERLAND
CAM.	CAMEROON	K.	KUWAIT	T.	TOGO
C.A.R.	CENTRAL AFRICAN REPUBLIC	KYR.	KYRGYZSTAN	TAJIK.	TAJIKISTAN
C.D'I.	CÔTE D'IVOIRE	LEB.	LEBANON	TURKM.	TURKMENISTAN
CR.	CROATIA	LITH.	LITHUANIA	U.A.E.	UNITED ARAB EMIRATES
CYP.	CYPRUS	LUX.	LUXEMBOURG	UZBEK.	UZBEKISTAN

1: 126 000 000

13:00	14:00	15:00	16:00	17:00	18:00	19:00	20:00	21:00	22:00	23:00	24:00
Oslo	Kiev	Moscow	T'bilisi	Yekaterinburg	Omsk	Ha Nôi	Ulaanbaatar	P'yŏngyang	Port Moresby	Magadan	Marshall Is
Paris	Ankara	Baghdad	Muscat	Islamabad	Dhaka	Bangkok	Beijing	Tōkyō	Brisbane	Solomon Is	Tuvalu
Algiers	Cairo	Riyadh	Seychelles	Karachi		Jakarta	Manila	Palau	Canberra	New Caledonia	Fiji
Abuja	Harare	Addis Ababa	Mauritius				Singapore				Wellington
Kinshasa	Cape Town	Dodoma					Perth				

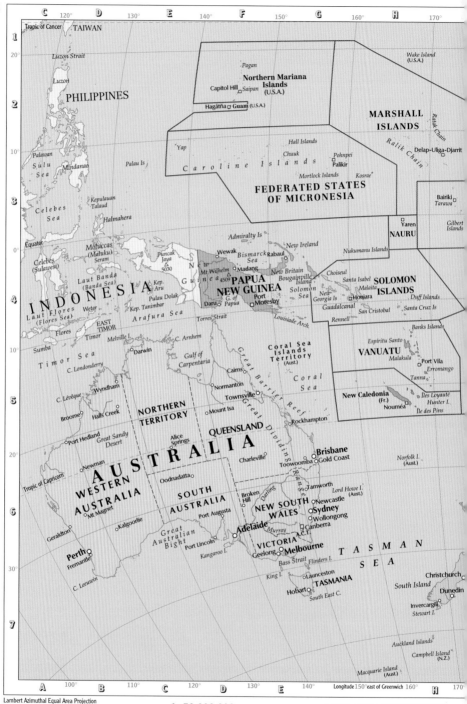

Tropic of Cancer   TAIWAN

20°   Luzon Strait

Luzon

PHILIPPINES

Wake Island
(U.S.A.)

Pagan

Northern Mariana
Islands
(U.S.A.)

Capitol Hill *Saipan*

Hagåtña □ Guam (U.S.A.)

MARSHALL
ISLANDS

Ratak Chain

10°   Palawan

Sulu
Sea

Mindanao

Palau Is

Yap

Hall Islands

Chuuk

C a r o l i n e   I s l a n d s

Ralik Chain

Delap-Uliga-Djarrit

Pohnpei
Palikir

Kepulauan
Talaud

Celebes
Sea

Halmahera

Mortlock Islands   Kosrae

FEDERATED STATES
OF MICRONESIA

Bairiki
Tarawa

Equator

Celebes
(Sulawesi)

Moluccas
(Maluku)
Seram

Puncak
Jaya
5030

Wewak

Bismarck
Sea

Rabaul

Admiralty Is   New Ireland

Nukumanu Islands

Yaren

NAURU

Gilbert
Islands

Laut Banda
(Banda Sea)

Kep.
Aru

Pulau Dolak

N e w

Mt Wilhelm
4500

Madang

G u i n e a

PAPUA
NEW
GUINEA

New Britain
Bougainville
Island

Solomon
Sea

Choiseul

New
Georgia Is

Santa Isabel

Guadalcanal

Honiara

Malaita

SOLOMON
ISLANDS

Duff Islands

San Cristobal   Santa Cruz Is

INDONESIA

Laut Flores
(Flores Sea)

Wetar

Kep. Tanimbar

Arafura Sea

G. of
Papua

Daru

Port
Moresby

Torres Strait   Louisiade Arch.   Rennell

Banks Islands

Flores

EAST
TIMOR

Timor

Melville I.

C. Arnhem

Espíritu Santo

VANUATU

Sumba

Timor

Timor Sea

Darwin

Gulf of
Carpentaria

Malakula

Port Vila
Erromango

C. Londonderry

Coral Sea
Islands
Territory
(Aust.)

Tanna

C. Léveque

Wyndham

Cairns

C o r a l
S e a

New Caledonia
(Fr.)

Nouméa

Îles Loyauté
Hunter I.
Île des Pins

Broome

Halls Creek

Normanton

Townsville

Mount Isa

NORTHERN
TERRITORY

Great Barrier Reef

Rockhampton

Port Hedland

Newman

Great Sandy
Desert

Alice
Springs

QUEENSLAND

Charleville

Toowoomba

Brisbane
Gold Coast

Norfolk I.
(Aust.)

Tropic of Capricorn

WESTERN
AUSTRALIA

A U S T R A L I A

Oodnadatta

SOUTH
AUSTRALIA

Broken
Hill

Darling

Tamworth

NEW SOUTH
WALES

Lord Howe I.
(Aust.)

Mt Magnet

Kalgoorlie

Port Augusta

Newcastle
Sydney
Wollongong

Canberra

Geraldton

Great
Australian
Bight

Port Lincoln

Adelaide

Murray

A.C.T.

VICTORIA

Perth
Fremantle

C. Lecuwin

Kangaroo I.

Geelong

Melbourne

Bass Strait

King I.

Flinders I.

Launceston

T A S M A N
S E A

Christchurch

South Island

Dunedin

30°

Hobart

TASMANIA

South East C.

Invercargill
Stewart I.

Auckland Islands

Campbell Island
(N.Z.)

Macquarie Island
(Aust.)

Longitude 150° east of Greenwich 160°

1 : 50 000 000

MILES 0   500   1000

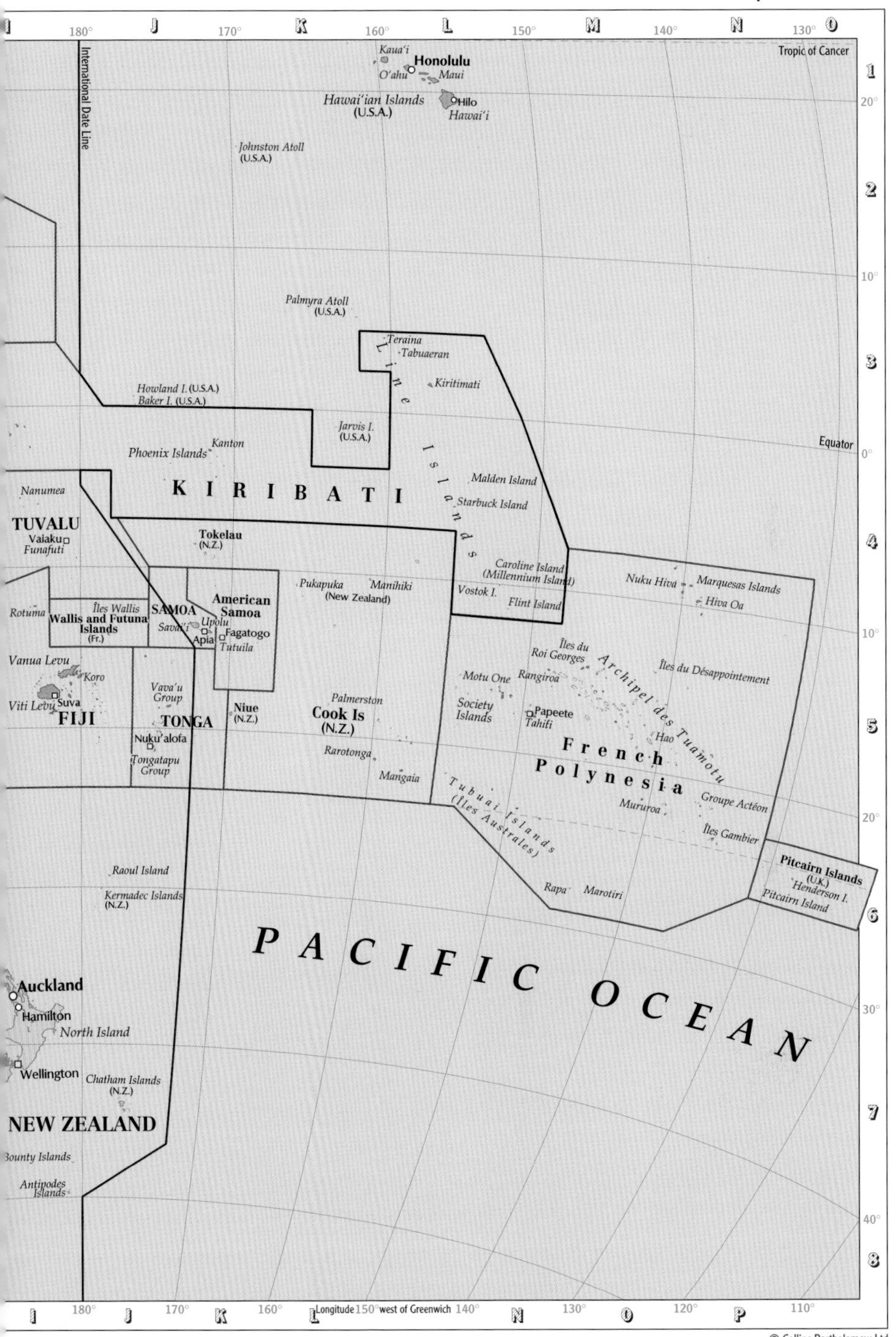

180° 170° 160° 150° 140° 130°

Tropic of Cancer

Kaua'i **Honolulu**
O'ahu Maui

Hawai'ian Islands Hilo
(U.S.A.) *Hawai'i*

20°

Johnston Atoll
(U.S.A.)

International Date Line

10°

Palmyra Atoll
(U.S.A.)

Teraina
·Tabuaeran

Kiritimati

Howland I. (U.S.A.)
Baker I. (U.S.A.)

Jarvis I.
(U.S.A.)

Equator 0°

Nanumea

Kanton

Phoenix Islands·

Malden Island

K I R I B A T I

Starbuck Island

TUVALU
Vaiaku
Funafuti

Tokelau
(N.Z.)

Caroline Island
(Millennium Island)

Nuku Hiva · Marquesas Islands

Rotuma

Îles Wallis

Pukapuka ·Manihiki
(New Zealand)

Vostok I.

· Hiva Oa

Vanua Levu

SAMOA
Savai'i

**American
Samoa**
Upolu
Fagatogo
Apia Tutuila

Flint Island

Îles du
Roi Georges

Îles du Désappointement

**Wallis and Futuna
Islands**
(Fr.)

Motu One · Rangiroa

·Koro

Vava'u
Group

Society
Islands

Papeete
Tahiti

Hao

Viti Levu·Suva
FIJI

TONGA

Niue
(N.Z.)

Palmerston

Cook Is
(N.Z.)

**French
Polynesia**

Groupe Actéon

Nuku'alofa

Rarotonga·

Mururoa

·Tongatapu
Group

Mangaia

Tubuai Islands
(Îles Australes)

Îles Gambier

Raoul Island

Rapa· Marotiri

Pitcairn Islands
(U.K.)
Henderson I.
Pitcairn Island

Kermadec Islands
(N.Z.)

P A C I F I C   O C E A N

Auckland
Hamilton

· North Island

30°

Wellington

Chatham Islands
(N.Z.)

NEW ZEALAND

Bounty Islands

Antipodes
Islands·

40°

180° 170° 160° 150° 140° 130° 120° 110°
Longitude west of Greenwich

0   500   1000   1500 KILOMETRES

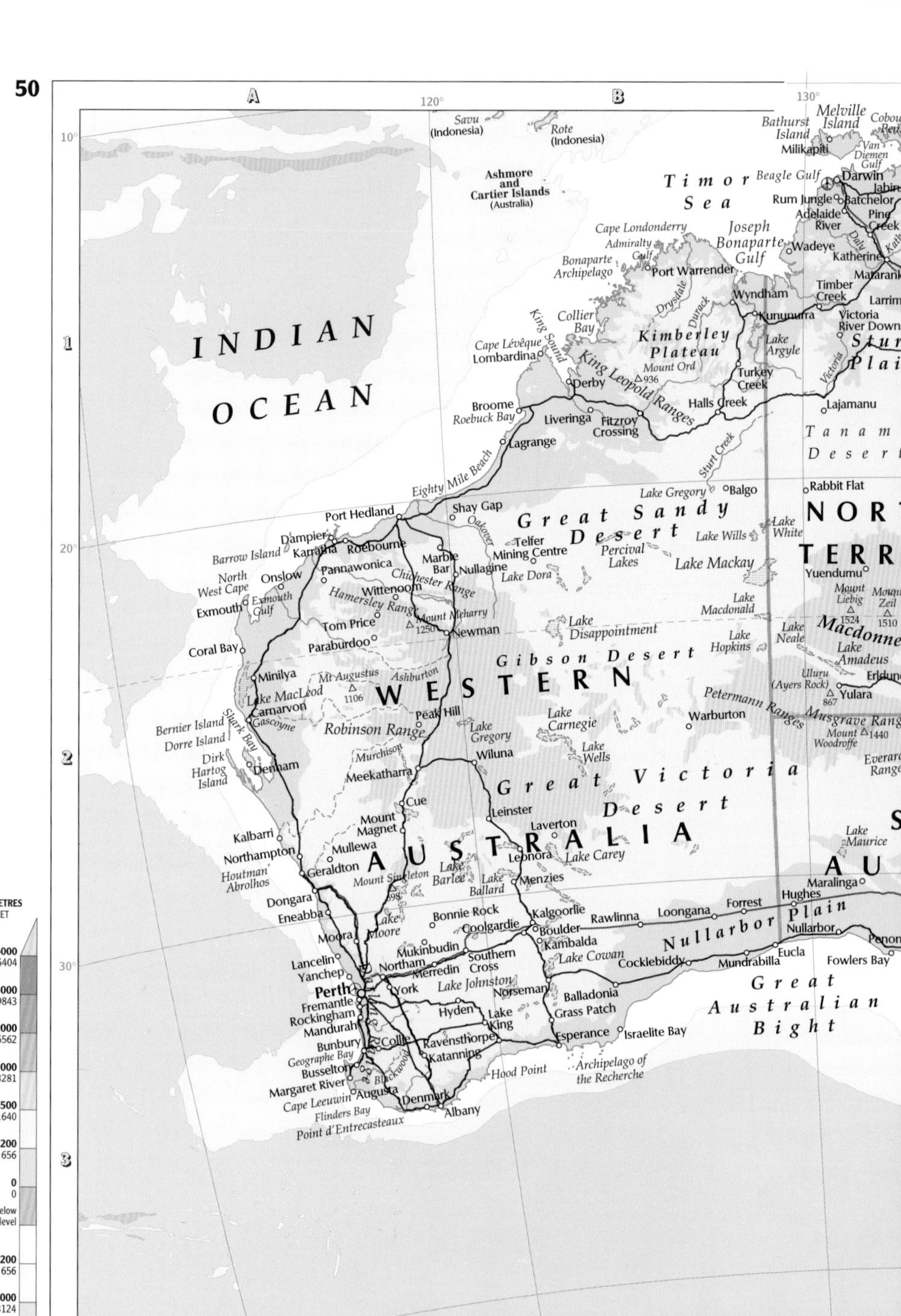

INDIAN

OCEAN

Savu (Indonesia)
Rote (Indonesia)

Ashmore and Cartier Islands (Australia)

Melville Island
Bathurst Island
Cobourg Pen.
Milikapiti
Van Diemen Gulf

T i m o r Beagle Gulf Darwin
S e a Rum Jungle Jabiru
Adelaide Batchelor
River Pine Creek

Cape Londonderry
Admiralty Gulf
Joseph Wyndham Katherine
Bonaparte Matarania
Gulf Kununurra Larrimah

Bonaparte Archipelago
Port Warrender
Cape Lévêque
Lombardina
Collier Bay

Timber Creek
Victoria River Downs
S t u r t
P l a i n

K i m b e r l e y
P l a t e a u
Mount Ord △936
Lake Argyle
Turkey Creek
Lajamanu

Derby
Halls Creek

King Sound
King Leopold Ranges

T a n a m i
D e s e r t

Broome
Roebuck Bay
Liveringa
Fitzroy Crossing
Lagrange

Eighty Mile Beach

Sturt Creek

Lake Gregory
Balgo
Rabbit Flat

Port Hedland
Shay Gap

G r e a t S a n d y
D e s e r t

Lake White
N O R T

Dampier
Karratha
Roebourne

Telfer
Mining Centre
Percival Lakes
Lake Wills
Lake Mackay

T E R R I

North West Cape
Onslow
Pannawonica

Marble Bar
Nullagine
Oakover

Yuendumu

Exmouth
Exmouth Gulf
Wittenoom
Chichester Range
Hamersley Range
Mount Meharry △1250
Lake Dora

Lake Disappointment

Mount Liebig
Mount Zeil △1524 △1510

Coral Bay
Tom Price
Paraburdoo
Newman

G i b s o n D e s e r t

Lake Macdonald
Lake Hopkins

Lake Neale
M a c d o n n e l l
Lake Amadeus
Erldunda

Minilya
Lake MacLeod
Carnarvon
Gascoyne
Mt Augustus △1106
Ashburton

W E S T E R N

Lake Carnegie

Warburton
Uluru (Ayers Rock) △867
Yulara
Petermann Ranges
Musgrave Range
Mount Woodroffe △1440

Bernier Island
Dorre Island
Dirk Hartog Island
Denham
Shark Bay
Robinson Range
Peak Hill
Murchison
Meekatharra
Lake Gregory
Wiluna
Lake Wells

E v e r a r d
R a n g e

Cue
Leinster
G r e a t V i c t o r i a
D e s e r t
Lake Maurice

Mount Magnet
Laverton
A U S

Kalbarri
Northampton
Houtman Abrolhos
Geraldton
Mount Singleton △
Leonora
Lake Carey
Menzies
Lake Barlee
Lake Ballard

Maralinga

Dongara
Eneabba
Lake Moore
Bonnie Rock
Kalgoorlie
Coolgardie
Boulder
Kambalda
Rawlinna
Loongana
Forrest
Hughes
Nullarbor
N u l l a r b o r P l a i n

Lancelin
Yanchep
Moora
Mukinbudin
Southern Cross
Lake Cowan
Cocklebiddy
Mundrabilla
Eucla
Fowlers Bay
Penong

Perth
Fremantle
Rockingham
Mandurah
Northam
York
Merredin
Lake Johnston
Norseman

G r e a t
A u s t r a l i a n
B i g h t

Bunbury
Collie
Hyden
Lake King
Balladonia
Grass Patch

Geographe Bay
Busselton
Blackwood
Ravensthorpe
Katanning
Esperance
Israelite Bay
Archipelago of the Recherche

Margaret River
Cape Leeuwin
Augusta
Denmark
Albany
Hood Point
Flinders Bay
Point d'Entrecasteaux

METRES
FEET

5000	16404
3000	9843
2000	6562
1000	3281
500	1640
200	656
0	0

Land below sea level

200	656
4000	13124
6000	19686

Lambert Azimuthal Equal Area Projection

1 : 20 000 000

Longitude 120° east of Greenwich

MILES 0   100   200   300   400

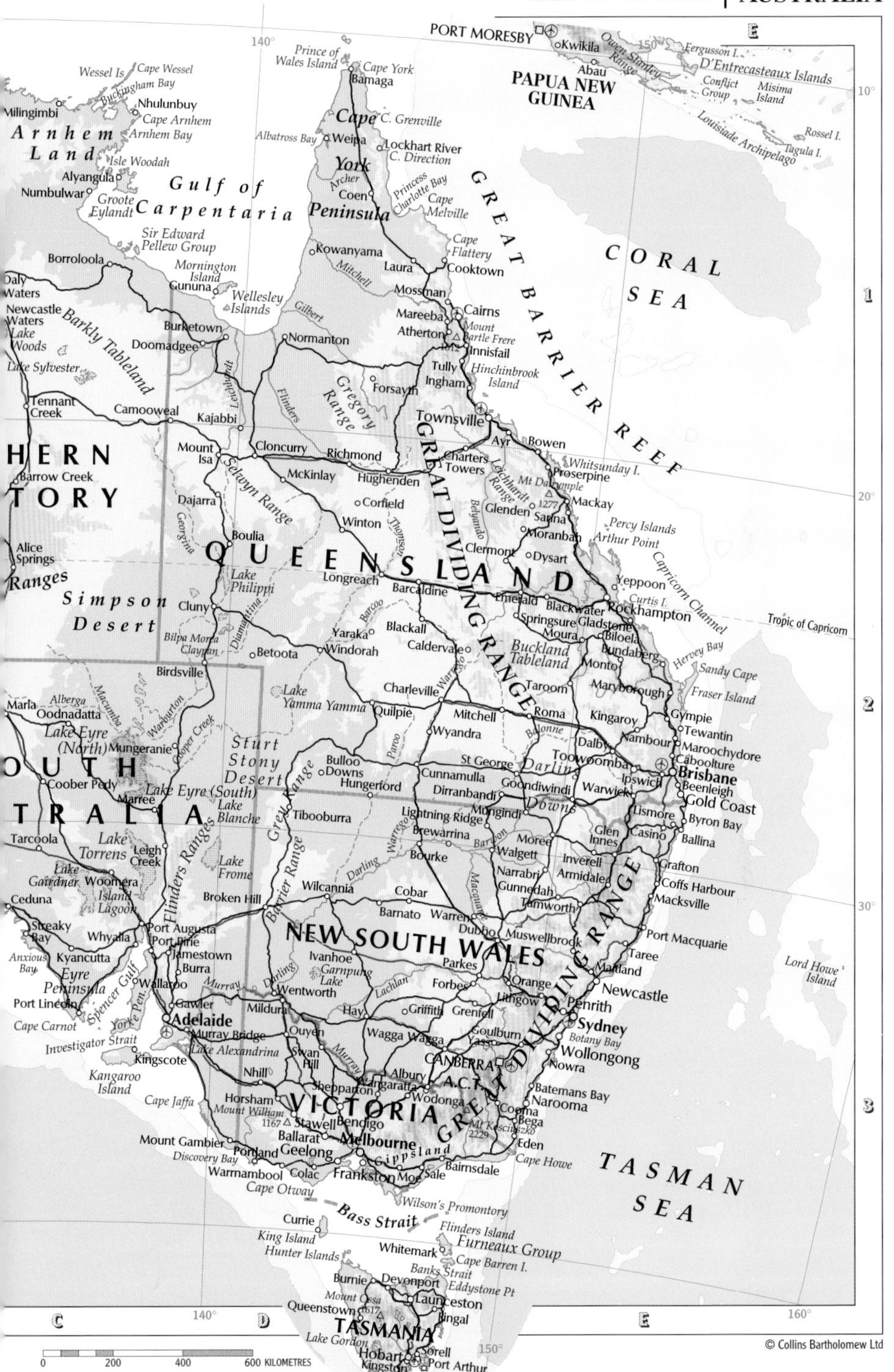

Wessel Is *Cape Wessel*
Buckingham Bay
Milingimbi
Nhulunbuy
Arnhem Land Isle Woodah *Arnhem Bay*
Alyangula *Groote Eylandt*
Numbulwar

Gulf of Carpentaria

Borroloola
Daly Waters
Newcastle Waters
Lake Woods
Lake Sylvester
Tennant Creek
Camooweal

Sir Edward Pellew Group
Mornington Island Gununa
Wellesley Islands

Burketown
Doomadgee
Normanton

Gilbert

Gregory Range

PORT MORESBY Kwikila
PAPUA NEW GUINEA Abau
Owen Stanley Range
Fergusson I.
D'Entrecasteaux Islands
Conflict Group Misima Island
Rossel I.
Tagula I.
Louisiade Archipelago

Prince of Wales Island
Cape York
Bamaga
Cape York
C. Grenville
Albatross Bay Weipa
Lockhart River
C. Direction

Cape York Peninsula
Archer
Coen
Princess Charlotte Bay
Cape Melville

Kowanyama
Cape Flattery
Laura
Cooktown

Mitchell

Mossman
Mareeba
Cairns
Atherton
Innisfail
Mount Bartle Frere
Tully
Ingham
Hinchinbrook Island

Forsayth
Flinders

Cloncurry
Richmond
McKinlay
Hughenden
Corfield
Winton

GREAT DIVIDING RANGE

GREAT BARRIER REEF

CORAL SEA

Townsville
Ayr
Bowen
Charters Towers
Proserpine
Whitsunday I.
Mt Dalrymple
Mackay

Selwyn Range
Mount Isa
Dajarra

Boulia

Thomson

Clermont
Moranbah
Dysart
Glenden Sarina

Percy Islands
Arthur Point

Longreach
Barcaldine
Emerald
Blackwater

Yeppoon
Curtis I.
Rockhampton

Tropic of Capricorn

Capricorn Channel

Simpson Desert

Ranges
Alice Springs

HERN TORY
Barrow Creek

Cluny
Lake Philippi
Yaraka
Blackall
Calderva

Springsure
Moura
Biloela
Gladstone
Monto
Bundaberg
Maryborough
Buckland Tableland
Taroom
Kingaroy
Hervey Bay
Sandy Cape
Fraser Island
Gympie
Tewantin
Nambour
Maroochydore
Caboolture

Birdsville
Lake Yamma Yamma

Betoota
Windorah
Charleville
Mitchell
Roma

Quilpie

Sturt Stony Desert

Marla
Alberga
Oodnadatta
Mungeranie

Coober Pedy
Lake Eyre (North)
Marree
Lake Eyre (South)
Lake Blanche
Tibooburra

Bulloo Downs
Hungerford
Wyandra
Cunnamulla
Dirranbandi

St George
Goondiwindi
Warwick

Toowoomba
Ipswich
Brisbane
Beenleigh
Gold Coast
Byron Bay

Lightning Ridge
Brewarrina
Mungindi
Moree
Glen Innes
Casino
Lismore
Ballina

Tarcoola
Lake Torrens
Leigh Creek
Lake Gairdner
Lake Frome

Bourke
Walgett
Narrabri
Gunnedah
Inverell
Armidale
Grafton
Coffs Harbour
Macksville

SOUTH TRALIA

Ceduna
Woomera
Island Lagoon

Wilcannia
Cobar
Barnato
Warren
Dubbo
Muswellbrook
Tamworth
Port Macquarie

Streaky Bay
Anxious Bay
Whyalla
Kyancutta
Eyre Peninsula
Port Lincoln

Broken Hill
Barrier Range
Ivanhoe
Garnpung
Parkes
Orange
Lithgow
Maitland
Newcastle

Port Augusta
Port Pirie
Jamestown
Burra
Gawler
Adelaide

Mildura
Wentworth
Hay
Griffith
Forbes
Grenfell

Penrith
Sydney
Botany Bay
Wollongong
Nowra

Kangaroo Island
Kingscote
Cape Jaffa

Ouyen
Swan Hill
Nhill
Horsham
Mount William
1167

Ballarat

Shepparton
Wangaratta
Albury
Wodonga
Benalla
Bendigo

Wagga Wagga
CANBERRA
A.C.T.
Cooma
Mt Kosciuszko
2229

Batemans Bay
Narooma
Bega
Eden
Cape Howe

NEW SOUTH WALES

Taree

Lord Howe Island

Stawell
Melbourne
Geelong
Colac
Warrnambool
Cape Otway
Discovery Bay
Portland
Mount Gambier

VICTORIA
Frankston
Sale
Bairnsdale
Gippsland
Wilson's Promontory

TASMAN SEA

Currie
King Island
Hunter Islands
Bass Strait

Whitemark
Flinders Island
Cape Barren I.
Banks Strait
Eddystone Pt
Bingal

Furneaux Group

Burnie
Devonport
Launceston

Mount Ossa

Queenstown
TASMANIA
Lake Gordon
Hobart
Kingston
Sorell
Port Arthur

© Collins Bartholomew Ltd

0   200   400   600 KILOMETRES

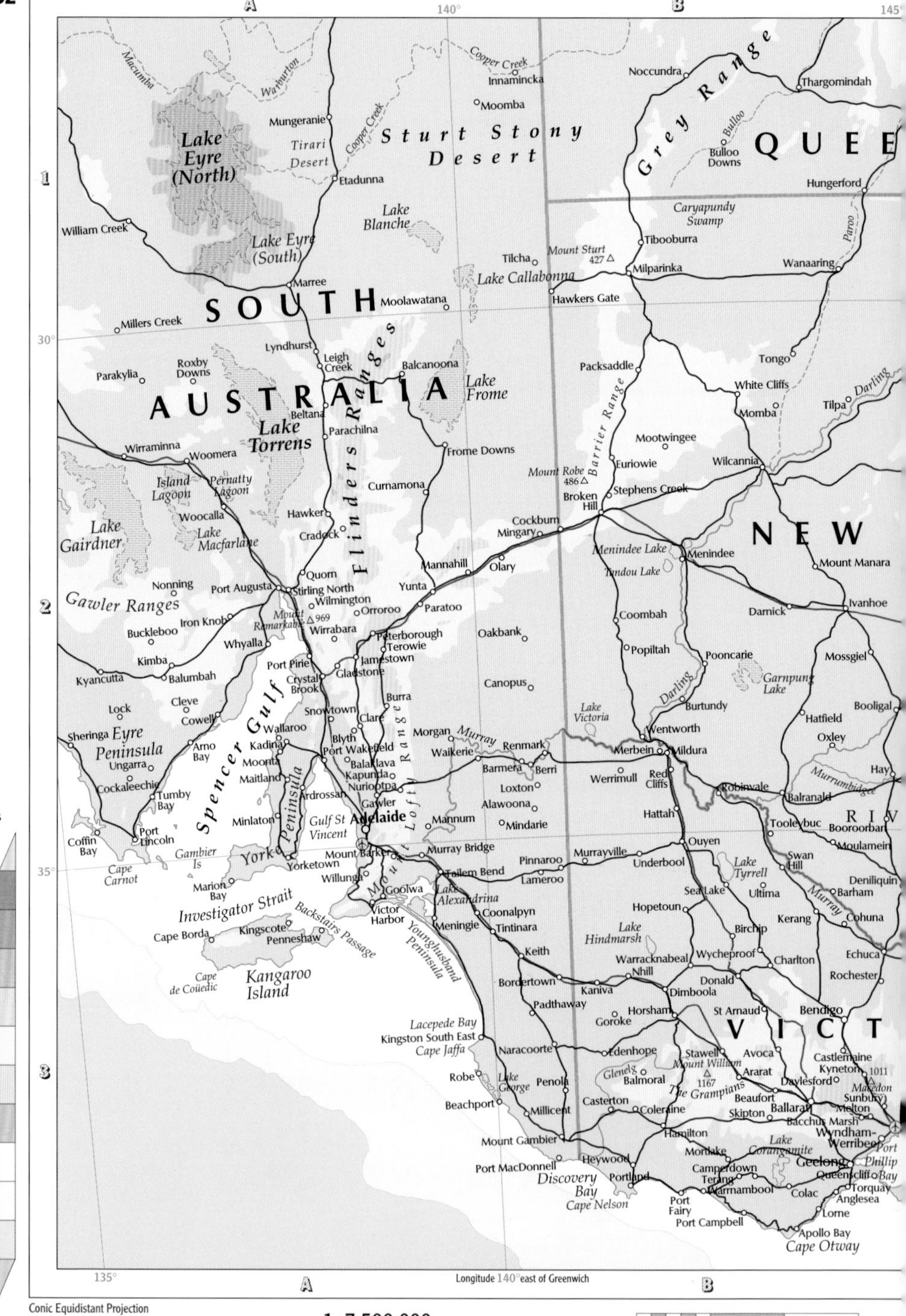

A   140°   B   145°

Macumba

Warburton

Cooper Creek
Inamincka

Noccundra   Thargomindah

Mungeranie

Lake
Eyre
(North)

*Tirari
Desert*

Cooper Creek

S t u r t   S t o n y
D e s e r t

Moomba

Bulloo

G r e y   R a n g e

Q U E E

Etadunna

Bulloo
Downs

1

Lake
Eyre
(South)

Lake
Blanche

Caryapundy
Swamp

Tibooburra

Hungerford

William Creek

Tilcha

Mount Sturt
427 △

Milparinka

Wanaaring

Paroo

Marree

Lake Callabonna

Moolawatana

Hawkers Gate

Millers Creek

S O U T H

30°

Lyndhurst

Leigh
Creek

Balcanoona

Packsaddle

Tongo

Parakylia

Roxby
Downs

White Cliffs

A U S T R A L I A

Beltana

Parachilna

Lake
Frome

Barrier Range

Momba

Tilpa

Darling

Wirraminna

Woomera

Lake
Torrens

Flinders Range

Mootwingee

Island
Lagoon

Pernatty
Lagoon

Curnamona

Frome Downs

Mount Robe
486 △

Euriowie

Wilcannia

N E W

Woocalla

Hawker

Broken
Hill

Stephens Creek

Lake
Gairdner

Lake
Macfarlane

Cradock

Cockburn
Mingary

Meninder Lake

Menindee

Nonning

Quorn

Mannahill

Olary

Tandou Lake

Mount Manara

Gawler Ranges

Port Augusta

Stirling North
Wilmington

Yunta

Darnick

Ivanhoe

2

Buckleboo

Iron Knob

Mount
Remarkable △ 969

Orroroo

Coombah

Kimba

Whyalla

Wirrabara

Peterborough

Oakbank

Popiltah

Pooncarie

Mossgiel

Kyancutta

Balumbah

Port Pirie

Jamestown
Terowie

Canopus

Burtundy

Darling

Garnpung
Lake

Booligal

Lock

Cleve

Crystal
Brook

Gladstone

Burra

Lake
Victoria

Oxley

Sheringa

Cowell

Snowtown

Clare

Morgan

Murray

Wentworth

Hatfield

Hay

Eyre
Peninsula

Amo
Bay

Kadina

Wallaroo

Blyth

Renmark

Merbein

Mildura

Murrumbidgee

Ungarra

Moonta

Balaklava

Waikerie

Red
Cliffs

Robinvale

Balranald

R I V

Cockaleechie

Tumby
Bay

Maitland

Kapunda
Nuriootpa

Barmera
Loxton

Berri

Werrimull

Hattah

Tooleybuc

Booroorbar

Minlaton

Ardrossan

Gawler

Alawoona

Ouyen

Moulamein

Coffin
Bay

Port
Lincoln

Gambier
Is

Gulf St
Vincent

Adelaide

Mannum

Mindarie

York Peninsula

Murray Bridge

Pinnaroo

Murrayville

Underbool

Lake
Tyrrell

Swan
Hill

Deniliquin

35°

Cape
Carnot

Yorketown

Mount Barker

Tailem Bend

Lameroo

Hopetoun

Sea Lake

Ultima

Barham

Marion
Bay

Willunga

Goolwa

Coonalpyn

Birchip

Kerang

Cohuna

Investigator Strait

Kingscote

Penneshaw

Victor
Harbor

Meningie

Lake
Alexandrina

Tintinara

Keith

Lake
Hindmarsh

Warracknabeal
Nhill

Wycheproof

Charlton

Echuca

Cape Borda

Backstairs Passage

Younghusband Peninsula

Bordertown

Kaniva
Padthaway

Donald
Dimboola

Rochester

Cape
de Couedic

Kangaroo
Island

Lacepede Bay

Kingston South East
Cape Jaffa

Naracoorte

Goroke

Horsham

St Arnaud

Bendigo

Edenhope

Stawell
Mount William
△
1167

Avoca

Castlemaine
Kyneton

3

Robe

Lake
George

Penola

Glenelg

Balmoral

Ararat

Beaufort

Daylesford

Macedon
1011
Sunbury

Beachport

Millicent

Casterton

The Grampians

Skipton

Ballarat

Bacchus Marsh

Melton

Coleraine

Hamilton

Mortlake

Lake
Corangamite

Wyndham-
Werribee

Port
Phillip

Mount Gambier

Port MacDonnell

Heywood

Camperdown
Terang

Geelong

Queenscliff

Torquay
Anglesea

Discovery
Bay
Cape Nelson

Portland

Port
Fairy

Warrnambool

Colac

Lorne

Port Campbell

Apollo Bay
Cape Otway

135°

A

Longitude 140° east of Greenwich

B

Conic Equidistant Projection

1 : 7 500 000

MILES 0   50   100   150

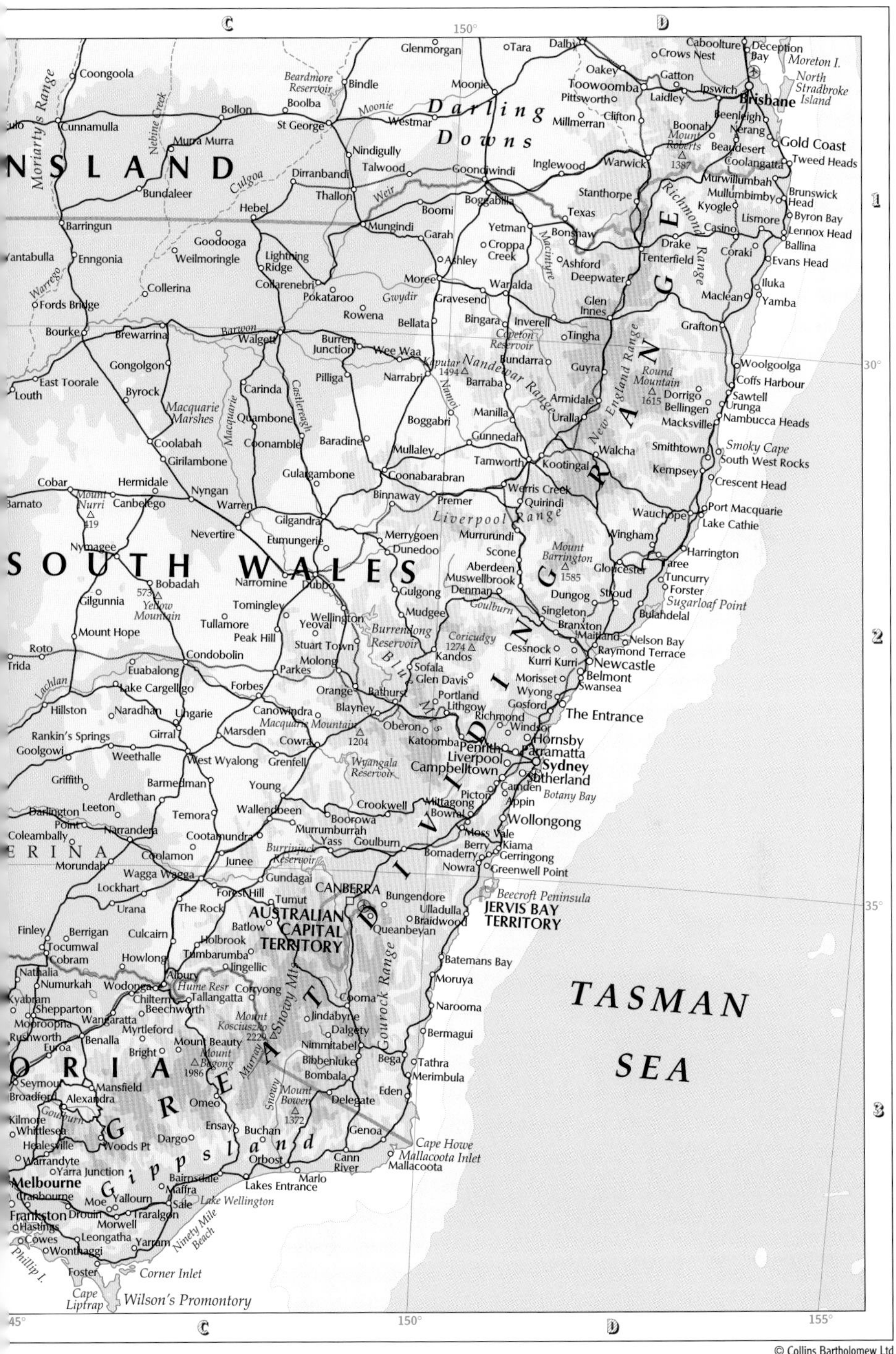
TASMAN SEA
SOUTH WALES
GREAT DIVIDING RANGE
NEW ENGLAND RANGE
Darling Downs
Gippsland
AUSTRALIAN CAPITAL TERRITORY
JERVIS BAY TERRITORY
CANBERRA
Sydney
Newcastle
Wollongong
Brisbane
Melbourne
Gold Coast
0 100 200 KILOMETRES

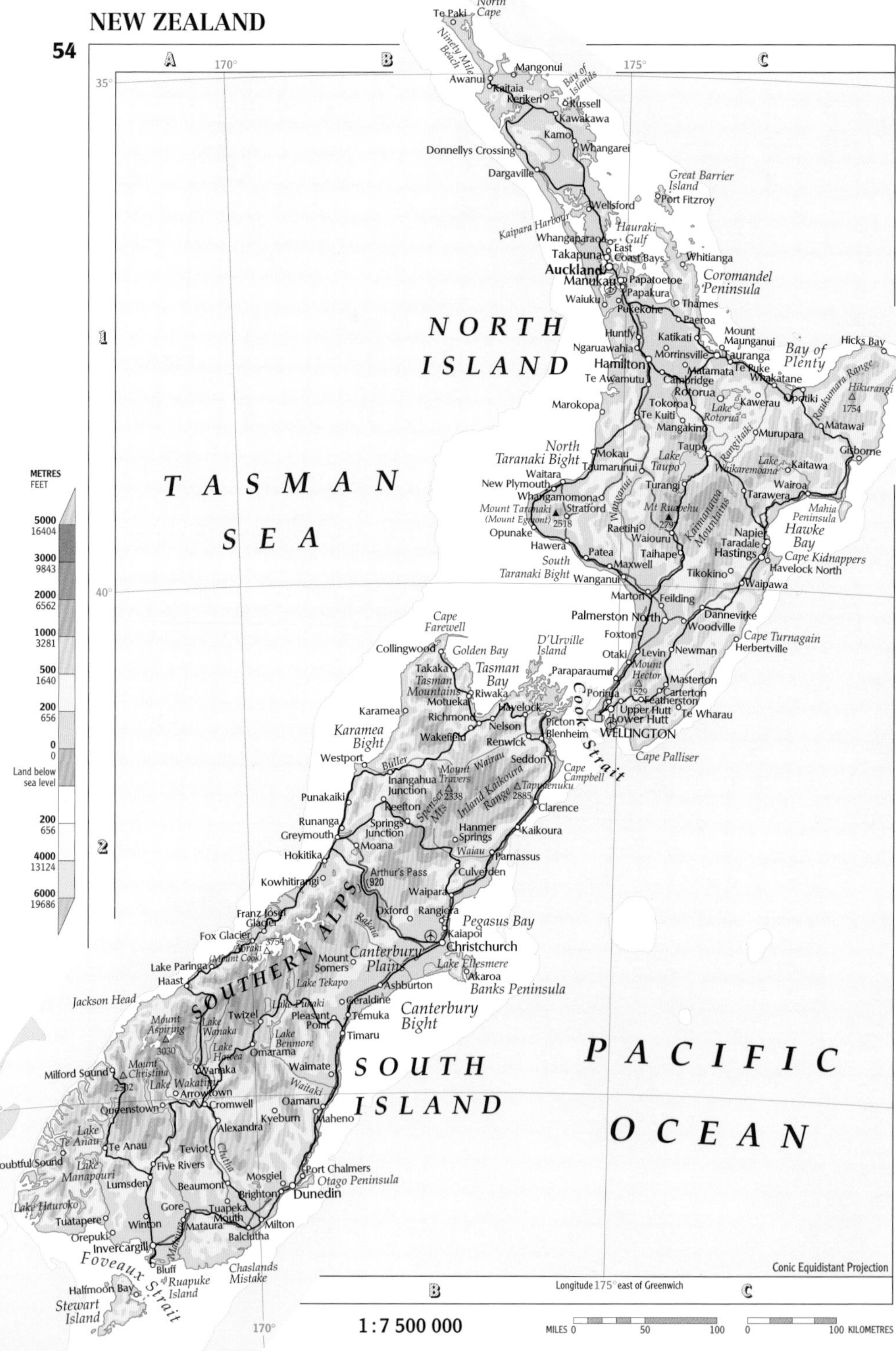

A
B
C
170°
175°
35°
40°
45°
1
2
North Cape
Te Paki
Ninety Mile Beach
Mangonui
Awanui
Kaitaia
Kerikeri
Bay of Islands
Russell
Kawakawa
Kamo
Whangarei
Donnellys Crossing
Dargaville
Great Barrier Island
Port Fitzroy
Wellsford
Kaipara Harbour
Hauraki Gulf
Whangaparaoa
East Coast Bays
Takapuna
Whitianga
Auckland
Coromandel Peninsula
Manukau
Papatoetoe
Papakura
Waiuku
Thames
Pukekohe
Paeroa
NORTH ISLAND
Huntly
Katikati
Mount Maunganui
Ngaruawahia
Morrinsville
Tauranga
Hicks Bay
Bay of Plenty
Hamilton
Matamata
Te Puke
Te Awamutu
Cambridge
Whakatane
Raukumara Range
Hikurangi
1754
Rotorua
Opotiki
Marokopa
Tokoroa
Lake Rotorua
Kawerau
Te Kuiti
Mangakino
Matawai
Murupara
North Taranaki Bight
Mokau
Taupo
Rangitaiki
Lake Taupo
Gisborne
Taumarunui
Lake Waikaremoana
Kaitawa
TASMAN SEA
Waitara
New Plymouth
Turangi
Whangamomona
Wairoa
Tarawera
Mount Taranaki (Mount Egmont)
2518
Stratford
Wanganui
Mt Ruapehu
2797
Kaimanawa Mountains
Mahia Peninsula
Opunake
Raetihi
Waiouru
Napier
Hawke Bay
Taradale
Hawera
Taihape
Hastings
Cape Kidnappers
Patea
South Taranaki Bight
Maxwell
Havelock North
Tikokino
Wanganui
Waipawa
Marton
Feilding
Dannevirke
Palmerston North
Woodville
Cape Farewell
Foxton
Cape Turnagain
Herbertville
Collingwood
Golden Bay
D'Urville Island
Otaki
Levin
Newman
Mount Hector
1529
Takaka
Tasman Bay
Paraparaumu
Tasman Mountains
Masterton
Riwaka
Porirua
Carterton
Motueka
Featherston
Karamea
Havelock
Upper Hutt
Te Wharau
Richmond
Lower Hutt
Nelson
Picton
Cook Strait
Karamea Bight
Wakefield
Blenheim
WELLINGTON
Renwick
Cape Palliser
Westport
Seddon
Buller
Mount Travers
Wairau
Cape Campbell
Inangahua Junction
2338
Inland Kaikoura Range
Tapuaenuku
2885
Punakaiki
Spenser Mts
Reefton
Clarence
Runanga
Springs Junction
Greymouth
Hanmer Springs
Kaikoura
Moana
Waiau
Hokitika
Parnassus
Arthur's Pass
920
Culverden
Kowhitirangi
Waipara
Franz Josef Glacier
Oxford
Rangiora
Pegasus Bay
Rakaia
Fox Glacier
Kaiapoi
3754
Christchurch
Aoraki (Mount Cook)
Canterbury Plains
Mount Somers
Lake Paringa
Lake Ellesmere
SOUTHERN ALPS
Akaroa
Haast
Lake Tekapo
Ashburton
Banks Peninsula
Jackson Head
Lake Pukaki
Geraldine
Canterbury Bight
Twizel
Mount Aspiring
Pleasant Point
Temuka
Lake Wanaka
Timaru
3030
Lake Benmore
Lake Hawea
Omarama
PACIFIC OCEAN
Milford Sound
Mount Christina
2502
Waimate
SOUTH ISLAND
Wanaka
Lake Wakatipu
Waitaki
Arrowtown
Queenstown
Cromwell
Oamaru
Kyeburn
Maheno
Lake Te Anau
Alexandra
Te Anau
Teviot
Clutha
Doubtful Sound
Five Rivers
Lake Manapouri
Port Chalmers
Otago Peninsula
Lumsden
Mosgiel
Beaumont
Brighton
Dunedin
Lake Hauroko
Gore
Tuapeka Mouth
Tuatapere
Winton
Mataura
Milton
Orepuki
Balclutha
Invercargill
Foveaux Strait
Bluff
Ruapuke Island
Chaslands Mistake
Halfmoon Bay
Stewart Island
METRES
FEET
5000
16404
3000
9843
2000
6562
1000
3281
500
1640
200
656
0
0
Land below sea level
200
656
4000
13124
6000
19686
Conic Equidistant Projection
Longitude 175° east of Greenwich
1:7 500 000
MILES 0
50
100
0
100 KILOMETRES

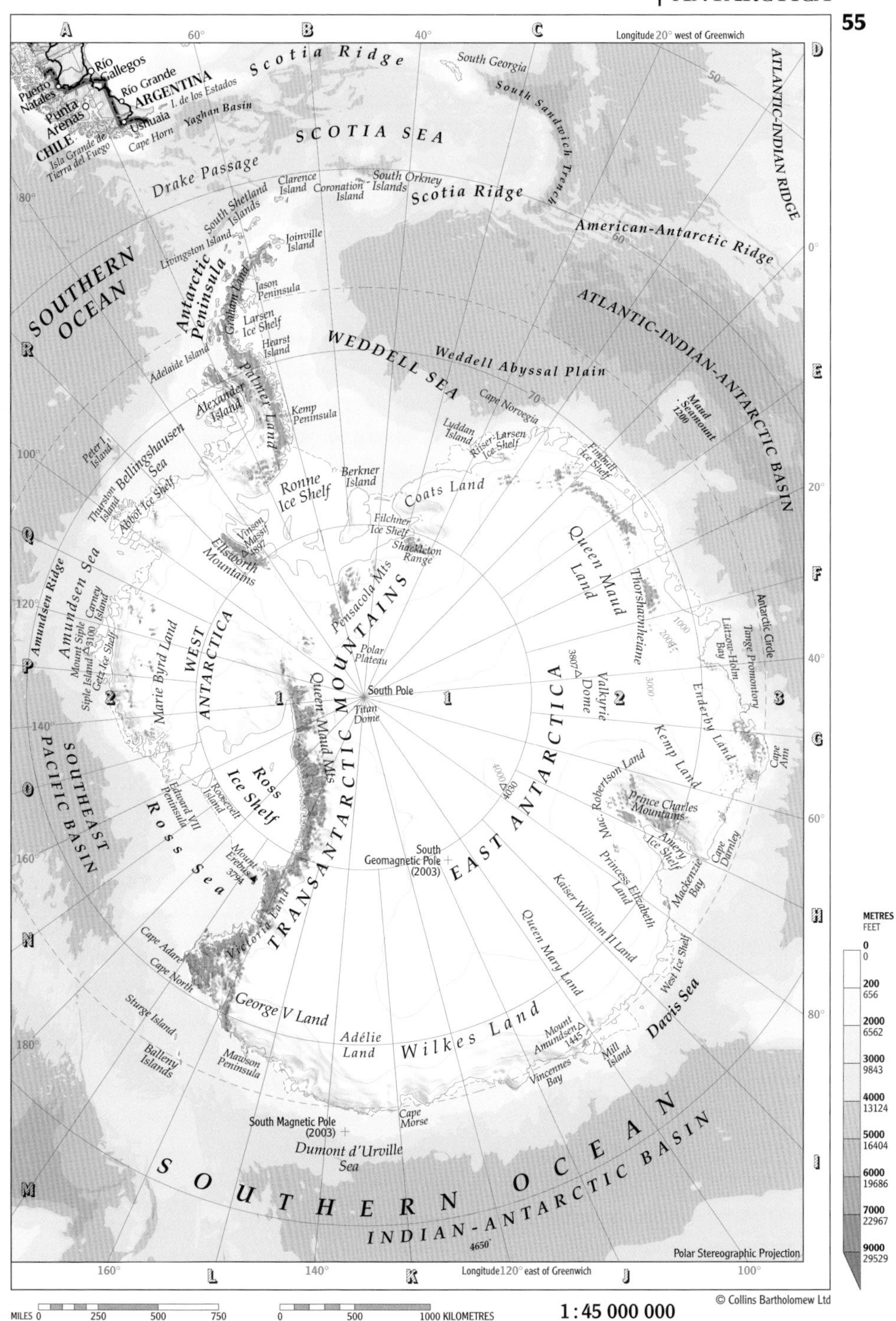

ATLANTIC-INDIAN RIDGE

Longitude 20° west of Greenwich

Scotia Ridge

South Georgia

South Sandwich Trench

SCOTIA SEA

Rio Gallegos
Rio Grande
ARGENTINA
Puerto
Natales
Punta
Arenas
CHILE
Ushuaia
Cape Horn
Yaghan Basin
Isla Grande de
Tierra del Fuego
I. de los Estados

Drake Passage

South Shetland
Islands
Clarence
Island
Coronation
Island
South Orkney
Islands
Scotia Ridge

American-Antarctic Ridge

Livingston Island
Joinville
Island

**SOUTHERN
OCEAN**

Jason
Peninsula

Graham Land

Larsen
Ice Shelf

Hearst
Island

WEDDELL SEA

Weddell Abyssal Plain

ATLANTIC-INDIAN-ANTARCTIC BASIN

Adelaide Island

Antarctic Peninsula

Palmer Land

Kemp
Peninsula

Cape Norvegia

Maud
Seamount
2200

Alexander
Island

Lyddan
Island

Riiser-Larsen
Ice Shelf

Finimbul
Ice Shelf

Peter I
Island

Thurston
Land

Bellingshausen
Sea

Ronne
Ice Shelf

Berkner
Island

Coats Land

**Queen Maud
Land**

Thorshavnheiane

Antarctic Circle

Abbot Ice Shelf

Filchner
Ice Shelf

Shackleton
Range

Tange Promontory

Lützow-Holm
Bay

Amundsen Sea

Vinson
Massif
4897

Ellsworth
Mountains

Pensacola Mts

Valkyrie
Dome
3807

Enderby Land

Cape
Ann

Mount Sidley
3300
Carney
Island

Siple Island

Getz Ice Shelf

**WEST
ANTARCTICA**

Amundsen Ridge

Marie Byrd Land

Queen Maud Mts

Polar
Plateau

South Pole

Titan
Dome

Kemp Land

Mac. Robertson Land

Prince Charles
Mountains

Amery
Ice Shelf

TRANS-ANTARCTIC MOUNTAINS

**SOUTHEAST
PACIFIC BASIN**

Ross
Ice Shelf

EAST ANTARCTICA

Kaiser Wilhelm II Land

Princess Elizabeth
Land

Mackenzie
Bay

Cape
Darnley

Edward VII
Peninsula

Roosevelt
Island

South
Geomagnetic Pole
(2003)

West Ice Shelf

Davis Sea

**R o s s
S e a**

Mount
Erebus
3794

Queen Mary Land

Mill
Island

Cape Adare

Victoria Land

Cape North

Mount
Aurdmundsen TA
1445

Vincennes
Bay

Sturge Island

George V Land

W i l k e s   L a n d

Balleny
Islands

Adélie
Land

Mawson
Peninsula

South Magnetic Pole
(2003)

Cape
Morse

S O U T H E R N   O C E A N

Dumont d'Urville
Sea

INDIAN-ANTARCTIC BASIN

4650

Polar Stereographic Projection

© Collins Bartholomew Ltd

METRES	
FEET	
0	0
200	656
2000	6562
3000	9843
4000	13124
5000	16404
6000	19686
7000	22967
9000	29529

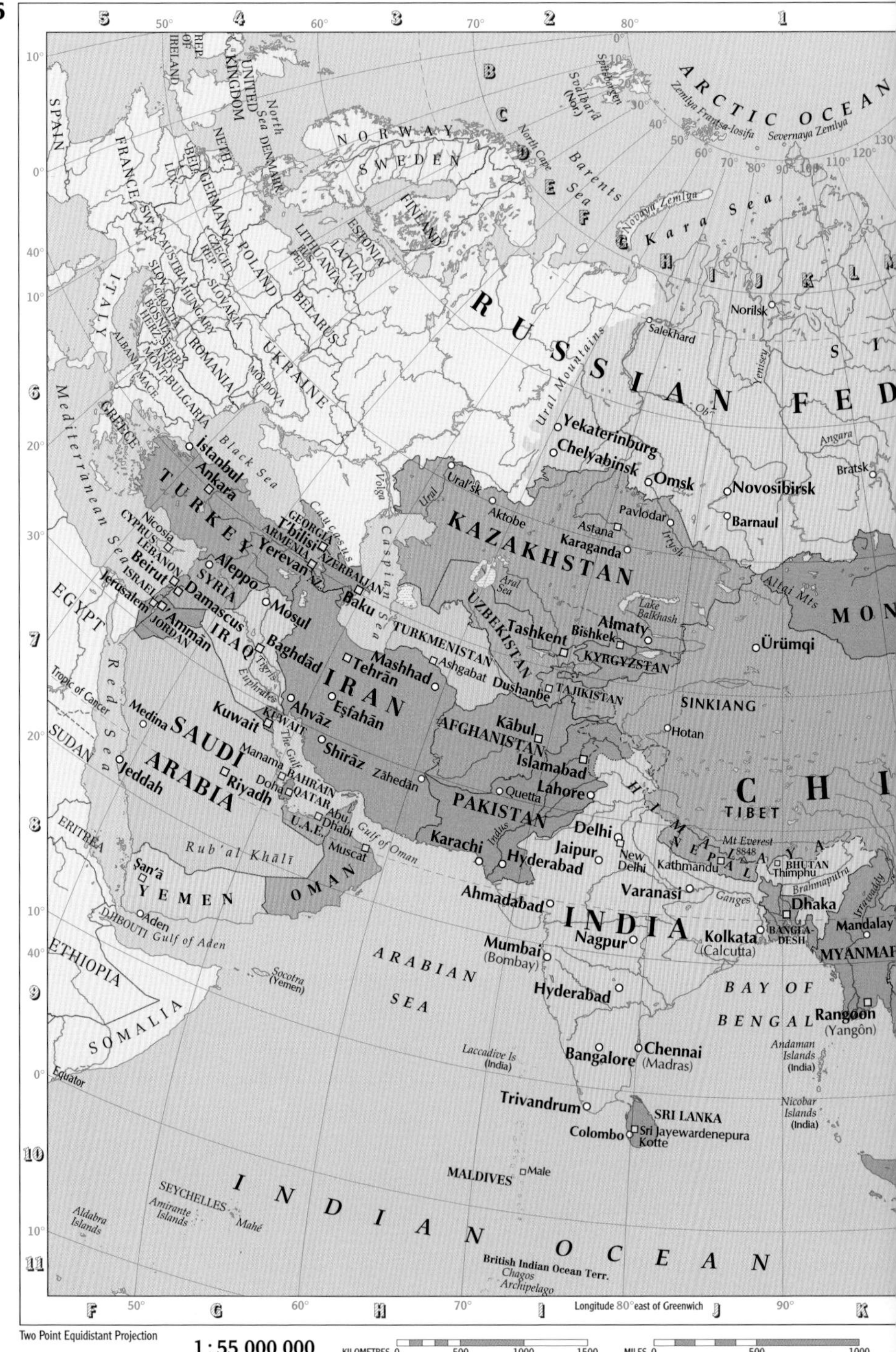

56

Map grid references (top)

5   50°   4   60°   3   70°   2   80°   1

0°

ARCTIC OCEAN

Zemlya Frantsa-Iosifa   Severnaya Zemlya

Spitsbergen
(Nor.)

B
C
D
E
F

G   Kara Sea

H   I   J   K   L

Novaya Zemlya

S I

SPAIN

IRELAND

UNITED KINGDOM

NETH.
BELG.
LUX.
FRANCE
SWITZ.
AUSTRIA
SLO.
CRO.
B&H
SERBIA
MON.
MAC.
ALBANIA
ITALY
GREECE

North Sea

NORWAY

SWEDEN

DENMARK

FINLAND

ESTONIA
LATVIA
LITHUANIA

GERMANY
CZECH REP.
POLAND
SLOVAKIA
HUNGARY
SLOVENIA
ROMANIA
BULGARIA
MOLDOVA

BELARUS

UKRAINE

North Cape (Nor.)

Barents Sea

R U S S I A N   F E D

Norilsk

Salekhard

Ural Mountains

Yekaterinburg
Chelyabinsk
Omsk
Novosibirsk
Bratsk

Mediterranean Sea

Black Sea

Istanbul
Ankara
TURKEY

GEORGIA
T'bilisi
ARMENIA
Yerevan
AZERBAIJAN
Baku

Caspian Sea

Volga
Ural
Ural'sk
Aktobe
Karaganda
Astana
Pavlodar
Irtysh

K A Z A K H S T A N

Lake Balkhash

Altai Mts

MON

Ürümqi

NICOSIA
CYPRUS
LEBANON
Beirut
ISRAEL
Jerusalem
Damascus
SYRIA
Aleppo
Mosul

IRAQ
Baghdad
Euphrates
Tigris

Kuwait
KUWAIT

Tehrān
Mashhad
Eşfahān
I R A N
Ahvāz
Shīrāz
Zāhedān

Aral Sea

TURKMENISTAN
Ashgabat
UZBEKISTAN
Tashkent
Dushanbe
TAJIKISTAN

Bishkek
KYRGYZSTAN
Almaty

SINKIANG
Hotan

C H I
TIBET

EGYPT

Tropic of Cancer

Red Sea

SUDAN

Medina
SAUDI
ARABIA
Jeddah

Riyadh

Manama
BAHRAIN
QATAR
Doha
U.A.E.
Abu Dhabi
The Gulf
Muscat
Gulf of Oman

OMAN

Rub' al Khālī

San'ā
YEMEN

ERITREA

Aden
DJIBOUTI
Gulf of Aden

ETHIOPIA

SOMALIA

Equator

Socotra
(Yemen)

A R A B I A N

S E A

Laccadive Is.
(India)

JORDAN
Amman

Kābul
AFGHANISTAN
Islamabad
Lahore
Quetta
PAKISTAN
Karachi

Delhi
New Delhi
Jaipur
Hyderabad
Ahmadabad

Indus

HIMALAYA
Mt Everest 8848
Kathmandu
NEPAL
BHUTAN
Thimphu
Brahmaputra

Varanasi
Ganges

I N D I A

Nagpur

Mumbai
(Bombay)

Hyderabad

Bangalore

Chennai
(Madras)

Trivandrum

Colombo
SRI LANKA
Sri Jayewardenepura
Kotte

MALDIVES
Male

Dhaka
BANGLA-DESH
Mandalay
MYANMAR
Rangoon
(Yangôn)

Irrawaddy

B A Y   O F

B E N G A L

Andaman Islands (India)

Nicobar Islands (India)

SEYCHELLES
Aldabra Islands
Amirante Islands
Mahé

I N D I A N   O C E A N

British Indian Ocean Terr.
Chagos Archipelago

F   50°   G   60°   H   70°   I   Longitude 80° east of Greenwich   J   90°   K

Two Point Equidistant Projection

1 : 55 000 000

KILOMETRES 0   500   1000   1500   MILES 0   500   1000

East Siberian Sea
Wrangel Island
New Siberia Islands
Arctic Circle
BERING SEA
Aleutian Islands (U.S.A.)
Midway Islands (U.S.A.)
Kure Atoll
Kamchatka Peninsula
Petropavlovsk-Kamchatskiy
Magadan
Sea of Okhotsk
Yakutsk
Lena
Sakhalin
Amur
Kuril Islands
Khabarovsk
Sapporo
Hokkaidō
PACIFIC OCEAN
Tropic of Cancer
Wake Atoll (U.S.A.)
Lake Baikal
Heilong Jiang
Qiqihar
Harbin
Vladivostok
Ulan Bator
Changchun
Sea of Japan (East Sea)
NORTH KOREA
P'yŏngyang
Tōkyō
Honshū
JAPAN
Shenyang
INNER MONGOLIA
Gobi
Beijing
Dalian
Seoul
SOUTH KOREA
Ōsaka
Baotou
Tianjin
Fukuoka
Kyūshū
Bonin Islands (Japan)
Volcano Islands (Japan)
Taiyuan
Huang He
Yellow Sea
Shanghai
East China Sea
Ryukyu Islands
Lanzhou
Xi'an
Nanjing
Wuhan
Chengdu
Yangtze
Changsha
Chongqing
Fuzhou
T'aipei
TAIWAN
Northern Mariana Is (U.S.A.)
Guam (U.S.A.)
Kunming
Guangzhou
Hong Kong
Nanning
Luzon
Caroline Islands
Equator
Ha Nôi
Hainan
Quezon City
Manila
PHILIPPINES
Vientiane
LAOS
VIETNAM
South China Sea
Mekong
PALAU
Koror
Mindanao
THAILAND
Bangkok
CAMBODIA
Admiralty Is
New Britain
Phnom Penh
Hô Chi Minh City
Palawan
Sulu Sea
Davao
Gulf of Thailand
Jayapura
PAPUA NEW GUINEA
Bandar Seri Begawan
BRUNEI
Celebes Sea
Halmahera
Puncak Jaya 5030
New Guinea
MALAYSIA
Manado
Medan
Kuala Lumpur
Putrajaya
Kuching
Moluccas (Maluku)
Seram
Kepulauan Aru
SINGAPORE
Borneo
Balikpapan
Celebes (Sulawesi)
Pulau Dolak
Sumatra (Sumatera)
Banjarmasin
Makassar
INDONESIA
Laut Banda
Kepulauan Tanimbar
Arafura Sea
Palembang
Laut Java
Dili
EAST TIMOR
C. Arnhem
AUSTRALIA
Jakarta
Surabaya
Sumbawa
Laut Sawu
Timor
Bandung
Java
Sumba
80° 50° 40° 30° 170° 180° 20° 10° 160° 0° 140° 150°

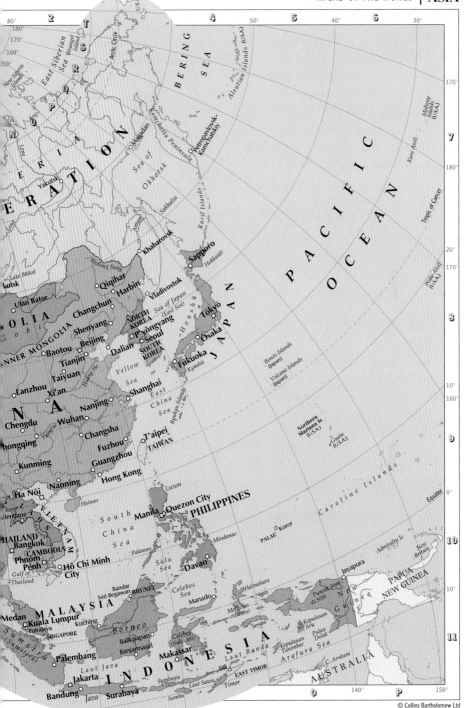

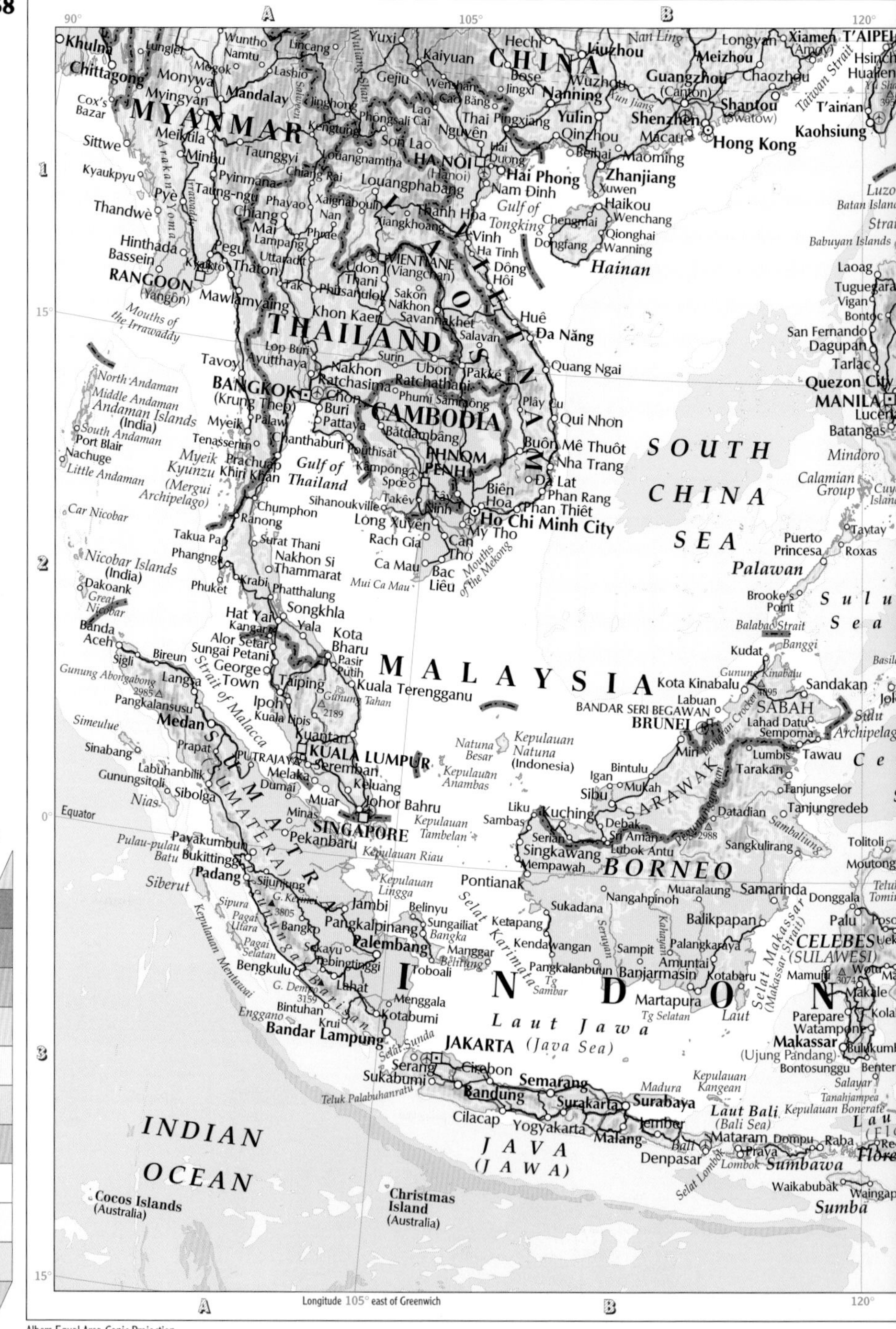

1 : 25 000 000

Albers Equal Area Conic Projection

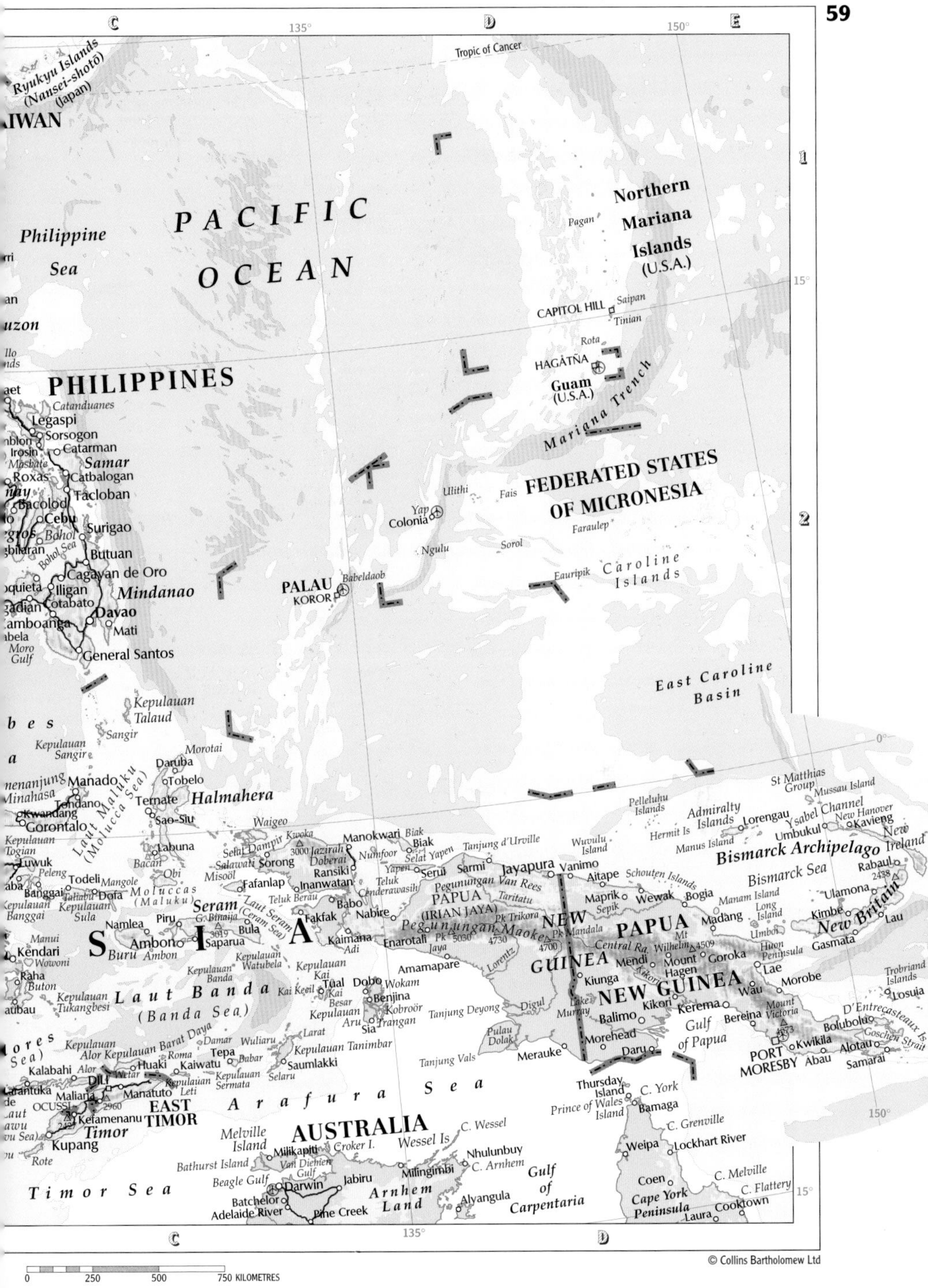

C   135°   D   150°   E

*Ryukyu Islands
(Nansei-shotō)
(Japan)*

Tropic of Cancer

IWAN

1

*Philippine
Sea*

PACIFIC

OCEAN

Pagan

**Northern
Mariana
Islands
(U.S.A.)**

an

uzon

llo
nds

15°

Saipan
CAPITOL HILL
Tinian

PHILIPPINES

Catanduanes

Legaspi
Sorsogon
Irosin   Catarman
Roxas   *Samar*
Catbalogan
may   Bacolod   Tacloban
Cebu
os   Bohol
Bohol Sea   Surigao
Butuan
Cagayan de Oro
quieta   Iligan
  Cotabato
dian   Zamboanga   **Davao**
bela   Mati
*Moro
Gulf*   General Santos

Mindanao

Rota

HAGÅTÑA

**Guam
(U.S.A.)**

Mariana Trench

2

Ulithi   Fais

**FEDERATED STATES
OF MICRONESIA**

Yap
Colonia

Faraulep

Ngulu   Sorol

PALAU   Babeldaob
KOROR

Eauripik

*Caroline
Islands*

*East Caroline
Basin*

0°

bes

a

*Kepulauan
Talaud*

Sangir

*Kepulauan
Sangir*

Morotai

Daruba

Pelleluhu
Islands

St Matthias
Group

Mussau Island

Admiralty

Islands Lorengau

Manus Island

Hermit
Islands

Ysabel Channel   New Hanover

Umbukul   Kavieng

Wuvulu
Island

Bismarck Archipelago Ireland

nenanjung   Manado
Minahasa   oTobelo
kwandang
Gorontalo   Ternate
Togian   Sao-Sio   Tidore
(Molucca Sea)

Laut Maluku

Halmahera

Waigeo

Kwoka

Manokwari   Biak

Selat Dampir   Nunfoor

Salawati   Sorong

Doberai   Selat Yapen

Tanjung d'Urville

Serui

Sarmi

Jayapura

Vanimo

Aitape

Schouten Islands

Maprik   Wewak

Sepik

Bogia

Manam Island

Lorong
Island

New Hanover

Ulamona

Rabaul

Bismarck Sea

*Kepulauan
Togian*

Luwuk

Todeli   Mangole

Banggai   Peleng

Dofa   Bacan

Inanwatan

Fafanlap   Misool

*Moluccas
(Maluku)*

**New
Guinea**

Madang

Hagen

Goroka

Mount

Lae

Huon
Peninsula

Kimbe

Lau

New Britain

Gasmata

*Trobriand
Islands*

Losuia

aba   *Kepulauan
Sula*

Namlea   Piru

Buru   Ambon

Waigeo

Kaimana

Enarotali

Nabire

**PAPUA
(IRIAN JAYA)**

Pegunungan Van Rees

Pegunungan Maoke

Pk Trikora
4700

Pk Mandala
4509

Central Ra Wilhelm
5050   4730

PAPUA

Mendi

Wau

Mt
Victoria

D'Entrecasteaux Is

Boluboluo

Goschen Strait

Samarai

S I A

ASIA

*Laut Banda
(Banda Sea)*

Kendari
Wowoni

Raha

Buton

Manui

Ambon
Seram
(Ceram)

Fakfak

Laut Seram

Bula

Geser

Teluk Berau

Bonasi

Amamapare

Agats

Timika

Lorentz

Jaya

*Kepulauan
Watubela*

Kepulauan

Dobo

Wokam

Aru

Benjina

Kepulauan

Besar

Kobroor

*Kepulauan
Aru*

Sia

Trangan

Tanjung Deyong

Murray

Digul

Balimo

Kikori

Kerema

*Gulf
of Papua*

Bereina   Abau

**PORT
MORESBY**

Alotau

Kwikila

NEW GUINEA

Merauke

Morehead

Daru

150°

ores
Sea)

Kepulauan Barat Daya

Kalabahi   Alor

Damar   Wuliaru

Tepa

Kepulauan Tanimbar

Saumlakki

Tanjung Vals

*Pulau
Dolak*

Larat

Arafura Sea

Thursday
Island

Prince of Wales
Island

C. York

Bamaga

C. Grenville

Dili

Maliana

OCUSSI

Kefamenanu

**EAST
TIMOR**

Larantuka

Timor

Kupang

Rote

Manatuto

Leti

*Kepulauan
Sermata*   Selaru

*Melville
Island*

Milikapiti

Croker I.

Van Diemen
Gulf

Bathurst Island

Beagle Gulf

Batchelor

Adelaide River   Darwin

Pine Creek

Wessel Is

C. Wessel

Nhulunbuy

C. Arnhem

Milingimbi

AUSTRALIA

*Arnhem
Land*

Alyangula

*Gulf
of
Carpentaria*

Weipa

C. Grenville

Lockhart River

Coen

**Cape York
Peninsula**

C. Melville

C. Flattery

Cooktown

Laura

15°

Timor Sea

C   135°   D

© Collins Bartholomew Ltd

0   250   500   750 KILOMETRES

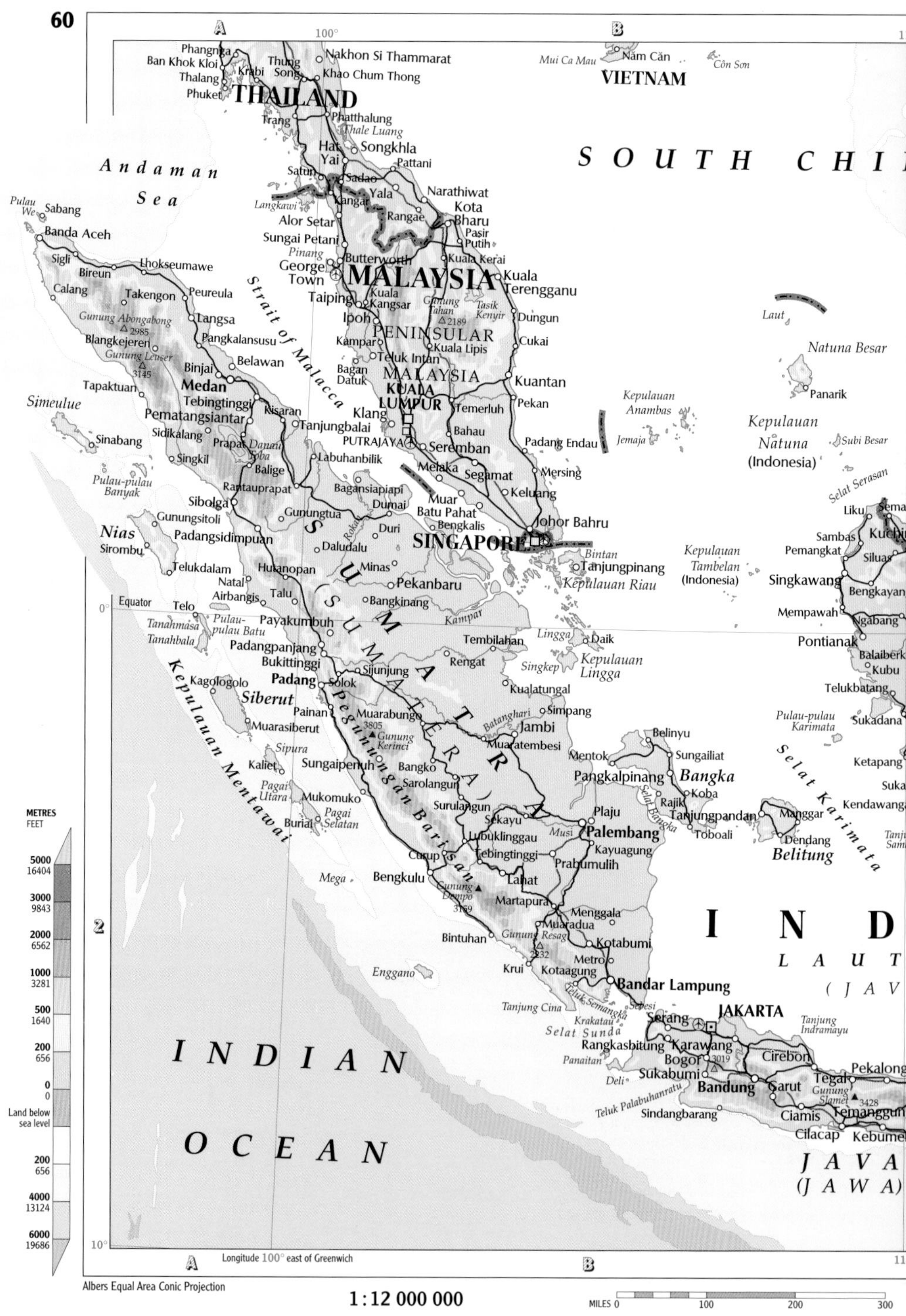

100°

11

Phangnga
Ban Khok Kloi
Thalang
Phuket
Thung Song
Krabi
Nakhon Si Thammarat
Khao Chum Thong
THAILAND
Trang
Phatthalung
Thale Luang
Songkhla
Hat Yai
Satun
Pattani
Sadao
Langkawi
Yala
Narathiwat
Alor Setar
Rangae
Kota Bharu
Sungai Petani
Pasir Putih
Butterworth
Kuala Kerai
George Town
MALAYSIA
Kuala Terengganu
Taiping
Kuala Kangsar
Gunung Tahan △2189
Tasik Kenyir
Dungun
Ipoh
PENINSULAR
Kuala Lipis
Cukai
Kampar
Teluk Intan
Kuantan
Bagan Datuk
MALAYSIA
Binjai
Belawan
KUALA LUMPUR
Klang
Temerluh
Pekan
Tebingtinggi
Risaran
Tanjungbalai
Bahau
Pematangsiantar
Sidikalang
PUTRAJAYA
Seremban
Padang Endau
Prapat
Danau Toba
Labuhanbilik
Melaka
Segamat
Mersing
Baligé
Rantauprapat
Bagansiapiapi
Muar
Batu Pahat
Keluang
Sibolga
Gunungtua
Dumai
Bengkalis
Gunungsitoli
Padangsidimpuan
Duri
Daludalu
SINGAPORE
Sirombu
Hulunopan
Minas
Pekanbaru
Bangkinang
Natal
Airbangis
Talu
Equator
Telo
Payakumbuh
Kampar
Tembilahan

Andaman Sea

Pulau We
Sabang
Banda Aceh
Sigli
Lhokseumawe
Bireun
Calang
Takengon
Peureula
Gunung Abongabong △2985
Langsa
Blangkejeren
Pangkalansusu
Gunung Leuser 3145
Binjai
Tapaktuan
Medan

Simeulue
Sinabang
Pulau-pulau Banyak

Nias

Siberut
Painan
Muarabungo
3805 Gunung Kerinci
Muarasiberut
Sungaipenuh
Bangko
Sipura
Sarolangun
Pagai Utara
Mukomuko
Surulangun
Pagai Selatan
Buriat
Sekayu
Mega
Lubuklinggau
Curup
Bengkulu
Gunung Dempo 3159
Lahat
Martapura
Muaradua
Bintuhan
Gunung Resag
Kotabumi
Enggano
Metro
Krui
Kotaagung
Bandar Lampung
Tanjung Cina
Krakatau
Serang
JAKARTA
Selat Sunda
Rangkasbitung
Karawang
Panaitan
Bogor
Cirebon
Deli
Sukabumi
Bandung
Garut
Sindangbarang
Ciamis
Teluk Palabuhanratu
Cilacap

VIETNAM
Mui Ca Mau
Nam Căn
Côn Son

SOUTH CHIN

Strait of Malacca

Sibolga
Kampar
Bangkinang

Laut

Natuna Besar

Panarik

Kepulauan Anambas

Jemaja

Kepulauan Natuna (Indonesia)

Subi Besar

Selat Serasan
Liku
Lemat
Sambas
Kuch
Pemangkat
Siluas
Singkawang
Bengkayang
Mempawah
Ngabang
Pontianak
Balaiberku
Kubu
Telukbatang
Pulau-pulau Karimata
Sukadana
Ketapang
Sukar
Kendawangan

Tanjungpinang
Bintan
Kepulauan Riau
Kepulauan Tambelan (Indonesia)

Rengat
Lingga
Daik
Singkep
Kepulauan Lingga

SUMATRA

Padangpanjang
Bukittinggi
Sijunjung
Padang
Solok
Muaratembesi
Batanghari
Simpang
Jambi
Belinyu
Mentok
Sungailiat
Pangkalpinang
Bangka
Plaju
Rajik
Tanjungpandan
Palembang
Koba
Kayuagung
Toboali
Prabumulih
Manggar
Dendang
Belitung
Menggala
Metro

I N D

L A U T

(J A V A

Tanjung Indramayu

Tegal
Pekalonga
Gunung Slamet 3428
Temanggung
Kebumen

J A V A (J A W A)

Sulesi

INDIAN

OCEAN

Ⓐ
Longitude 100° east of Greenwich
Ⓑ
110

Albers Equal Area Conic Projection

1 : 12 000 000

MILES 0   100   200   300

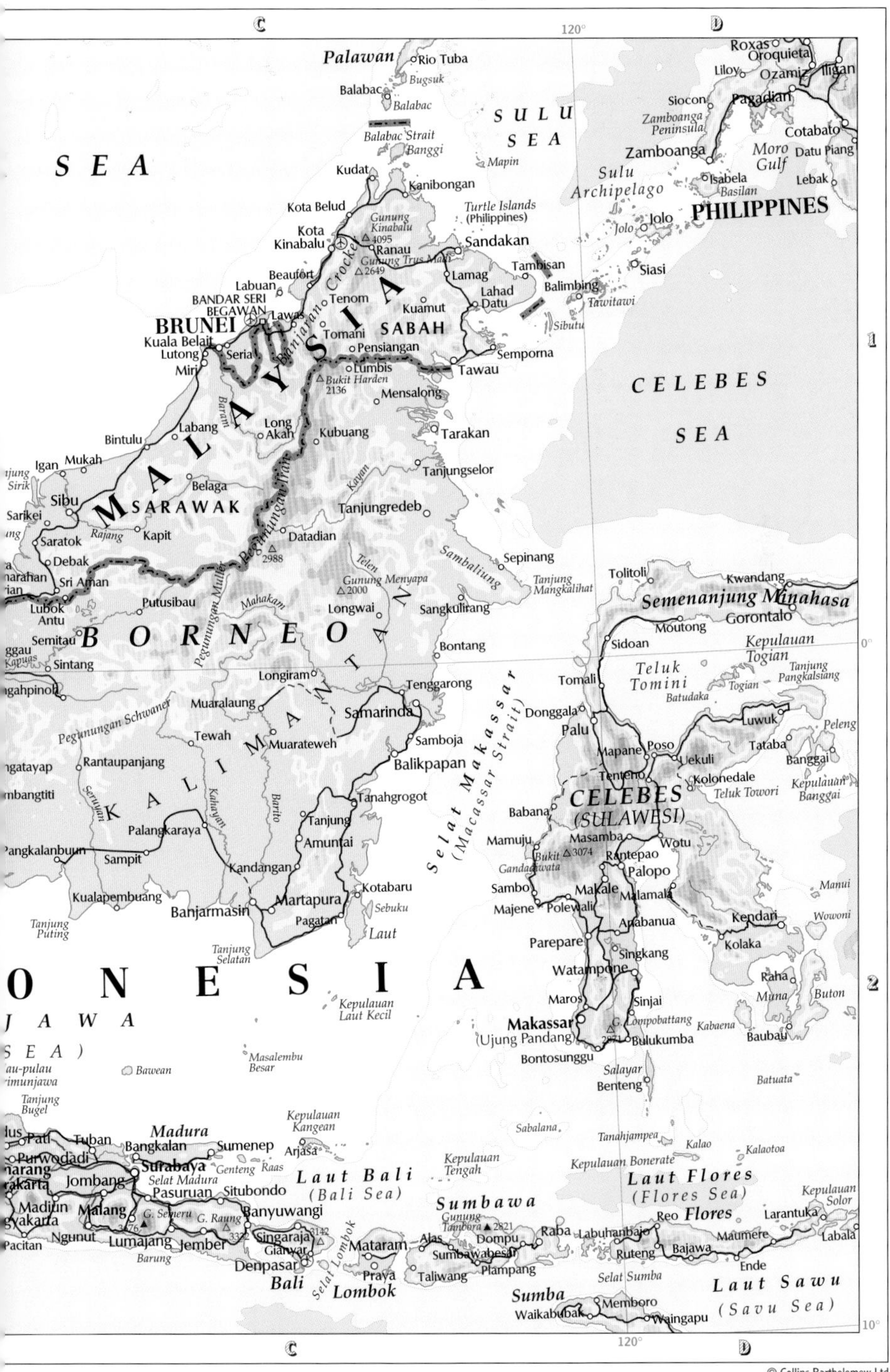
C
D
120°
1
2
0°
10°
SEA
SULU SEA
CELEBES SEA
Palawan
Rio Tuba
Bugsuk
Balabac
Balabac Strait
Banggi
Mapin
Roxas
Oroquieta
Liloy
Ozamiz
Iligan
Siocon
Pagadian
Zamboanga Peninsula
Cotabato
Zamboanga
Moro Gulf
Datu Piang
Sulu Archipelago
Isabela
Basilan
Lebak
PHILIPPINES
Jolo
Siasi
Tawitawi
Sibutu
Balimbing
Kudat
Kanibongan
Kota Belud
Kota Kinabalu
Gunung Kinabalu
4095
Ranau
Turtle Islands (Philippines)
Sandakan
Gunung Trus Madi
2649
Tambisan
Beaufort
Labuan
BANDAR SERI BEGAWAN
BRUNEI
Tenom
Lamag
Lahad Datu
Kuamut
Lawas
Crocker
Banjaran
Tomani
SABAH
Kuala Belait
Lutong
Seria
Miri
Pensiangan
Semporna
Lumbis
Tawau
Bukit Harden
2136
Mensalong
MALAYSIA
Baram
Long Akah
Kubuang
Tarakan
Bintulu
Labang
Igan
Mukah
Tanjungselor
Belaga
Sibu
SARAWAK
Tanjungredeb
Sarikei
Saratok
Rajang
Kapit
Datadian
Debak
2988
Sri Aman
Pegunungan Iran
Kayan
Telen
Sambaliung
Sepinang
Tanjung Mangkalihat
Gunung Menyapa
2000
Lubok Antu
Putusibau
Mahakam
Longwai
Sangkulirang
Semitau
BORNEO
Kapuas
Sintang
Bontang
Pegunungan Muller
Longiram
Tenggarong
Muaralaung
Samarinda
Pegunungan Schwaner
Tewah
Muarateweh
Samboja
Balikpapan
Rantaupanjang
KALIMANTAN
Tanahgrogot
Seruyan
Kahayan
Barito
Tanjung
Palangkaraya
Amuntai
Pangkalanbuun
Sampit
Kandangan
Kotabaru
Kualapembuang
Banjarmasin
Martapura
Sebuku
Pagatan
Laut
Tanjung Puting
Tanjung Selatan
INDONESIA
JAWA
SEA)
Kepulauan Laut Kecil
Masalembu Besar
Bawean
Tanjung Bugel
Kepulauan Kangean
Madura
Pati
Tuban
Bangkalan
Sumenep
Arjasa
Purwodadi
Surabaya
Genteng
Raas
Selat Madura
Jombang
Pasuruan
Situbondo
Madiun
Malang
G. Semeru
G. Raung
Banyuwangi
Ngunut
Lumajang
Jember
Singaraja
Pacitan
Barung
Gianyar
Denpasar
Bali
Selat Lombok
Mataram
Praya
Lombok
Laut Bali
(Bali Sea)
Kepulauan Tengah
Sumbawa
Gunung Tambora
2821
Alas
Dompu
Raba
Sumbawabesar
Taliwang
Plampang
Sumba
Waikabubak
Memboro
Waingapu
Selat Sumba
Laut Sawu
(Savu Sea)
Labuhanbajo
Reo
Flores
Ruteng
Bajawa
Maumere
Ende
Larantuka
Labala
Kepulauan Solor
Laut Flores
(Flores Sea)
Kalao
Kalaotoa
Kepulauan Bonerate
Tanahjampea
Sabalana
Selat Makassar (Macassar Strait)
Tolitoli
Kwandang
Semenanjung Minahasa
Gorontalo
Moutong
Sidoan
Kepulauan Togian
Togian
Tanjung Pangkalsiang
Teluk Tomini
Batudaka
Tomali
Donggala
Palu
Luwuk
Peleng
Tataba
Banggai
Kepulauan Banggai
Mapane
Poso
Uekuli
Tentena
Kolonedale
Teluk Towori
CELEBES (SULAWESI)
Babana
Mamuju
Masamba
Bukit Gandadiwata
3074
Rantepao
Wotu
Palopo
Sambo
Makale
Malamala
Majene
Polewali
Manui
Wowoni
Kendari
Anabanua
Kolaka
Parepare
Singkang
Watampone
Raha
Muna
Buton
Maros
Sinjai
Makassar
(Ujung Pandang)
G. Lompobattang
2871
Bulukumba
Kabaena
Baubau
Bontosunggu
Salayar
Benteng
Batuata
0
200
400 KILOMETRES

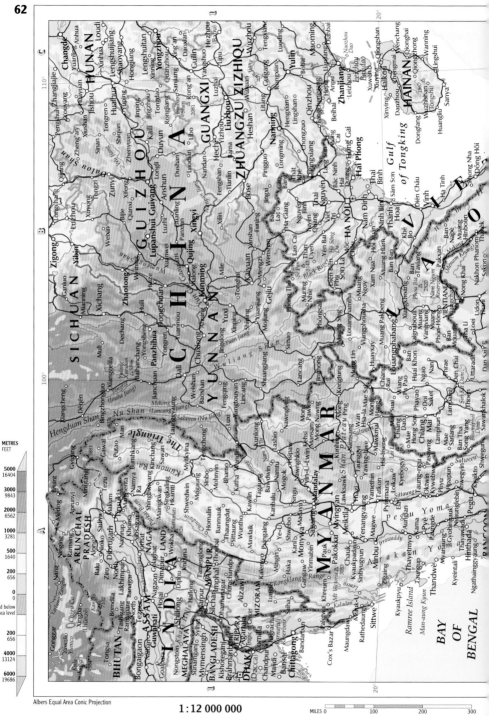

METRES
FEET

5000 16404
3000 9843
2000 6562
1000 3281
500 1640
200 656
0 0
Land below sea level
200 656
4000 13124
6000 19686

Albers Equal Area Conic Projection

1:12 000 000

MILES 0   100   200   300

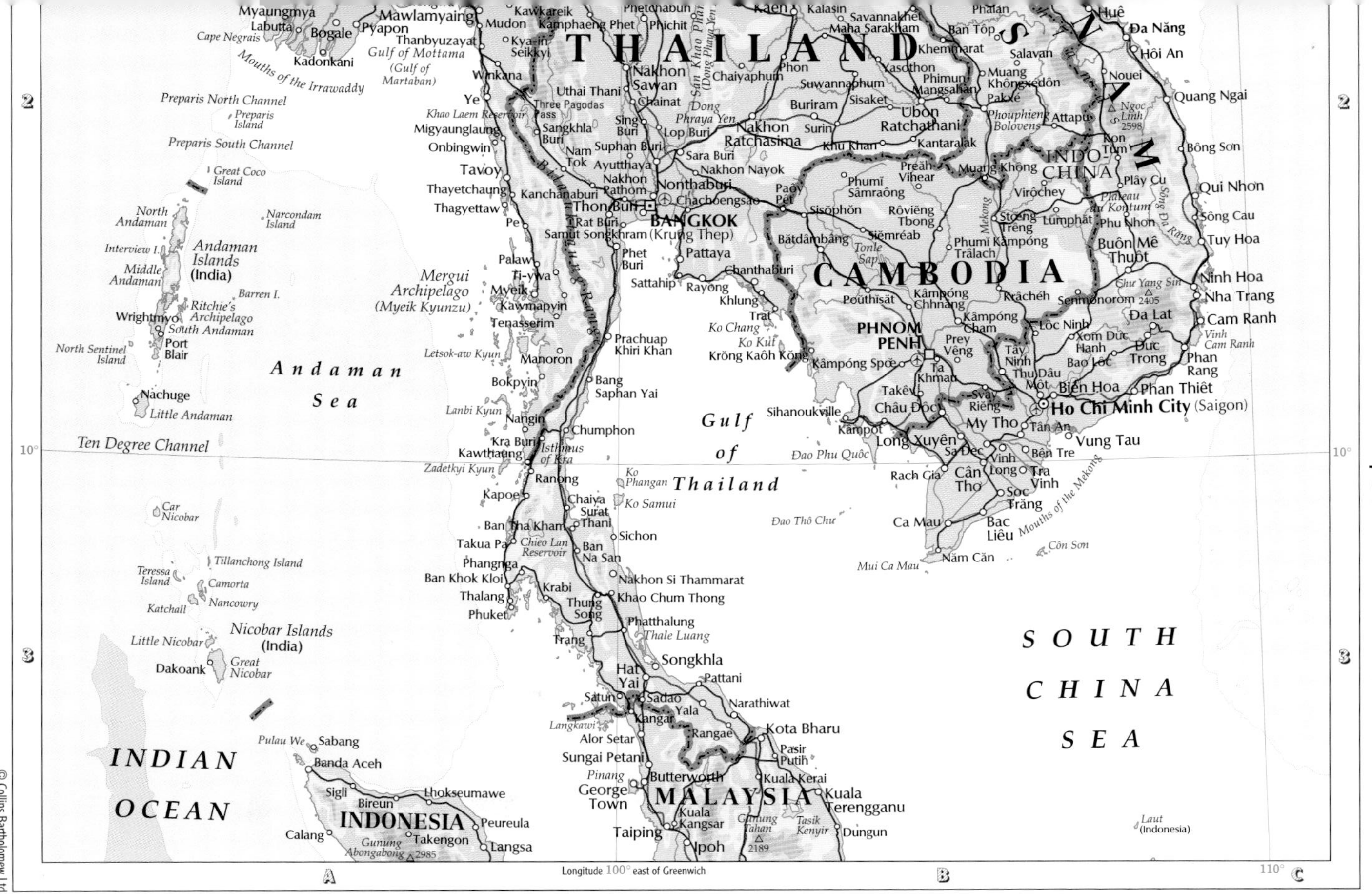

SOUTH

CHINA

SEA

Laut
(Indonesia)

VIETNAM

INDO CHINA

CAMBODIA

PHNOM
PENH

THAILAND

BANGKOK

Gulf

of

Thailand

MALAYSIA

Kuala
Terengganu

George
Town

Andaman

Sea

Meryui
Archipelago
(Myeik Kyunzu)

Nicobar Islands
(India)

INDONESIA

Banda Aceh

Andaman
Islands
(India)

Port
Blair

North
Andaman

Little Andaman

Ten Degree Channel

INDIAN

OCEAN

Myaungmya

Mouths of the Irrawaddy

0   200   400 KILOMETRES

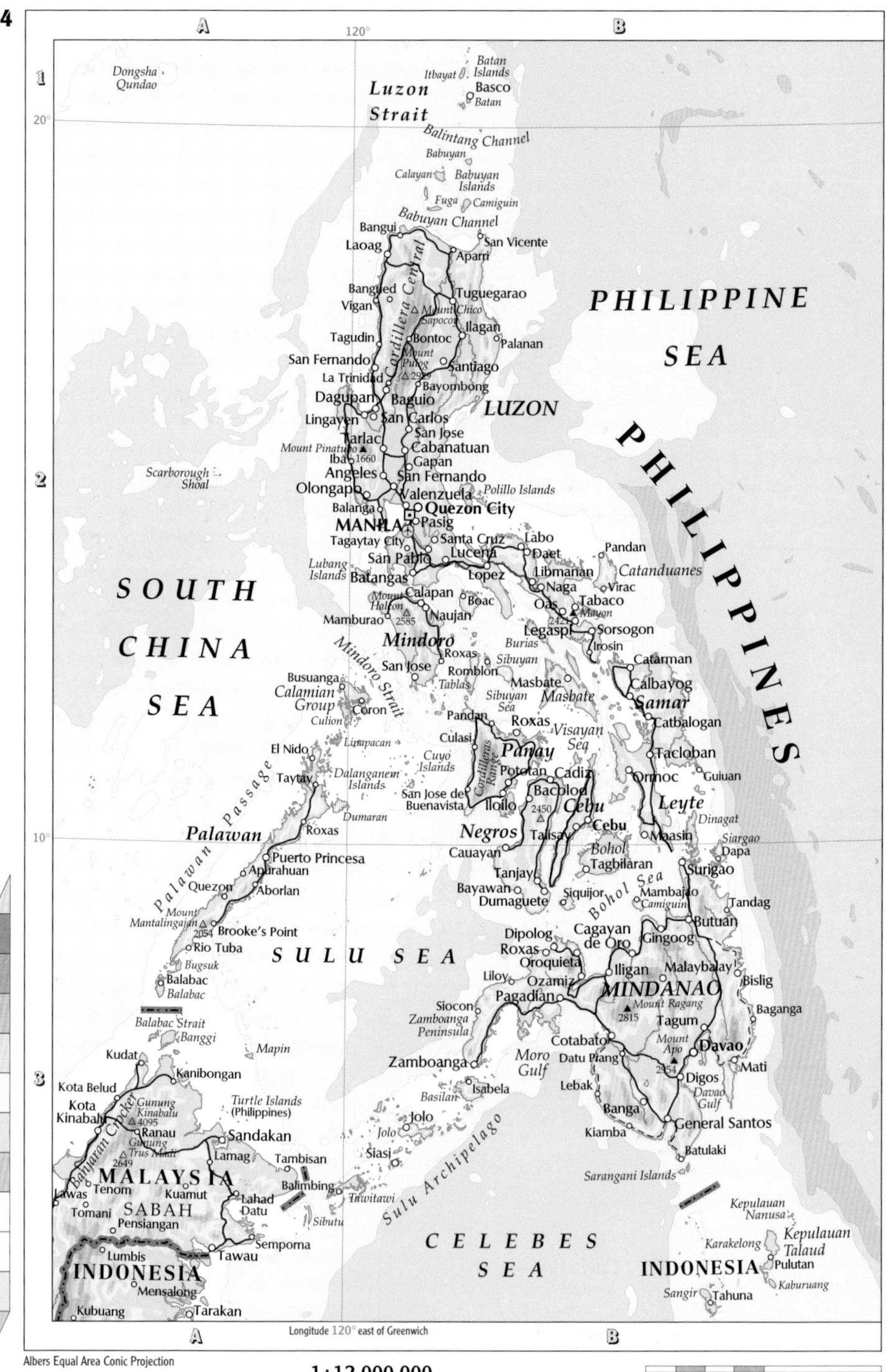

PHILIPPINE

SEA

PHILIPPINES

SOUTH

CHINA

SEA

Dongsha
Qundao

Luzon Strait

Batan Islands
Basco
Batan

Itbayat

Balintang Channel
Babuyan

Calayan *Babuyan Islands*
Fuga *Camiguin*

Babuyan Channel

Bangui
Laoag
San Vicente
Aparri

Bangued
Vigan
Tuguegarao
Ilagan

Tagudin
San Fernando
Bontoc
Palanan

La Trinidad
Bayombong
Santiago

Dagupan
Baguio

Lingayen
San Carlos
San Jose
Cabanatuan

Tarlac
Gapan

Iba
Angeles
San Fernando

Olongapo
Valenzuela
Polillo Islands

Balanga
Quezon City

MANILA
Pasig

Tagaytay City
Santa Cruz
Labo

San Pablo
Lucena
Daet
Pandan

Batangas
Lopez
Libmanan
Naga
Virac
Catanduanes

Calapan
Boac
Oas
Tabaco

Mamburao
Naujan
Legaspi
Sorsogon

Mindoro
Burias
Irosin

Roxas
Sibuyan
Catarman

San Jose
Romblon
Masbate
Calbayog

Busuanga
Tablas
Masbate
Samar
Catbalogan

Calamian Group
Coron
Pandan
Sibuyan Sea
Roxas
Visayan Sea
Tacloban

Culasi
Panay
Ormoc
Guiuan

El Nido
Cuyo Islands
Pototan
Cadiz

Taytay
Dalanganem Islands
San Jose de Buenavista
Iloilo
Bacolod
Cebu
Leyte
Dinagat

Roxas
Dumaran
Negros
Cebu
Dapa

Palawan
Cauayan
Talisay
Bohol
Maasin
Siargao

Puerto Princesa
Tanjay
Tagbilaran
Surigao

Aburahan
Bayawan
Siquijor
Tandag

Quezon
Aborlan
Dumaguete
Camiguin

Rio Tuba
Dipolog
Cagayan de Oro
Gingoog
Butuan

SULU SEA
Roxas
Oroquieta
Iligan
Malaybalay
Bislig

Balabac
Liloy
Ozami
Baganga

Balabac
Siocon
Pagadian
MINDANAO
Tagum

Banggi
Mapin
Zamboanga Peninsula
Cotabato
Davao

Kudat
Zamboanga
Datu Piang
Mati

Kanibongan
Kota Belud
Turtle Islands (Philippines)
Isabela
Lebak
Digos

Kota Kinabalu
Ranau
Sandakan
Jolo
Banga
General Santos

Lamag
Tambisan
Jolo
Kiamba
Batulaki

Tenom
Balimbing
Siasi
Sarangani Islands

MALAYSIA
Lahad Datu
Tawitawi
Sulu Archipelago

Lawas
Kuamut
Semporna
Sibutu

Tomani
SABAH
Pensiangan
CELEBES SEA
INDONESIA

Lumbis
Tawau
Karakelong
Kepulauan Talaud

INDONESIA
Mensalong
Sangir
Tahuna
Pulutan
Kaburuang

Tarakan
Nanusa

Kubuang

METRES
FEET

5000 / 16404
3000 / 9843
2000 / 6562
1000 / 3281
500 / 1640
200 / 656
0 / 0
Land below sea level
200 / 656
4000 / 13124
6000 / 19686

KILOMETRES 0 ... 200 ... 400
MILES 0 ... 100 ... 200 ... 300

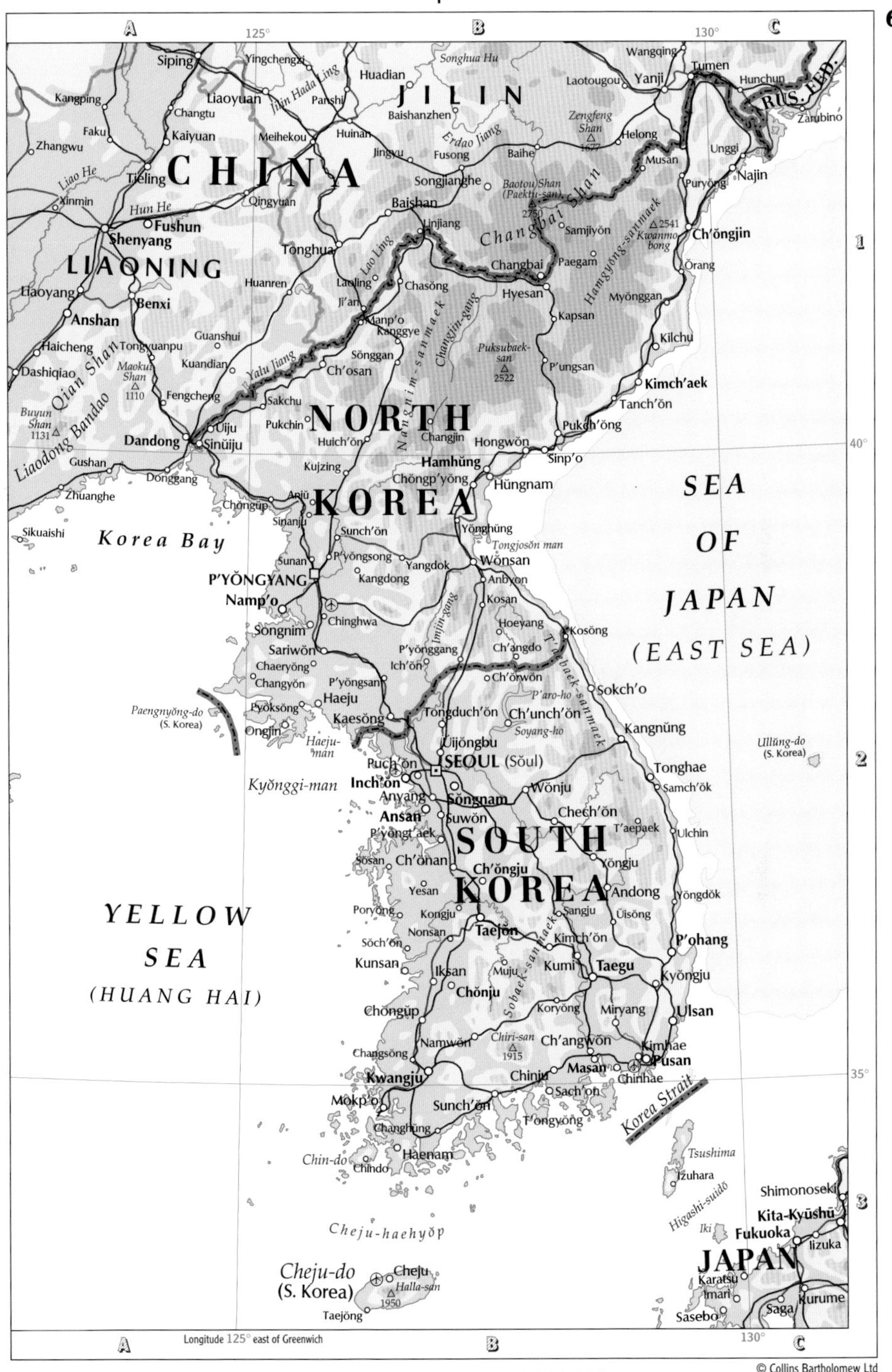

Longitude 125° east of Greenwich

1 : 6 500 000

0   100   200 KILOMETRES
0   50   100   150 MILES

© Collins Bartholomew Ltd

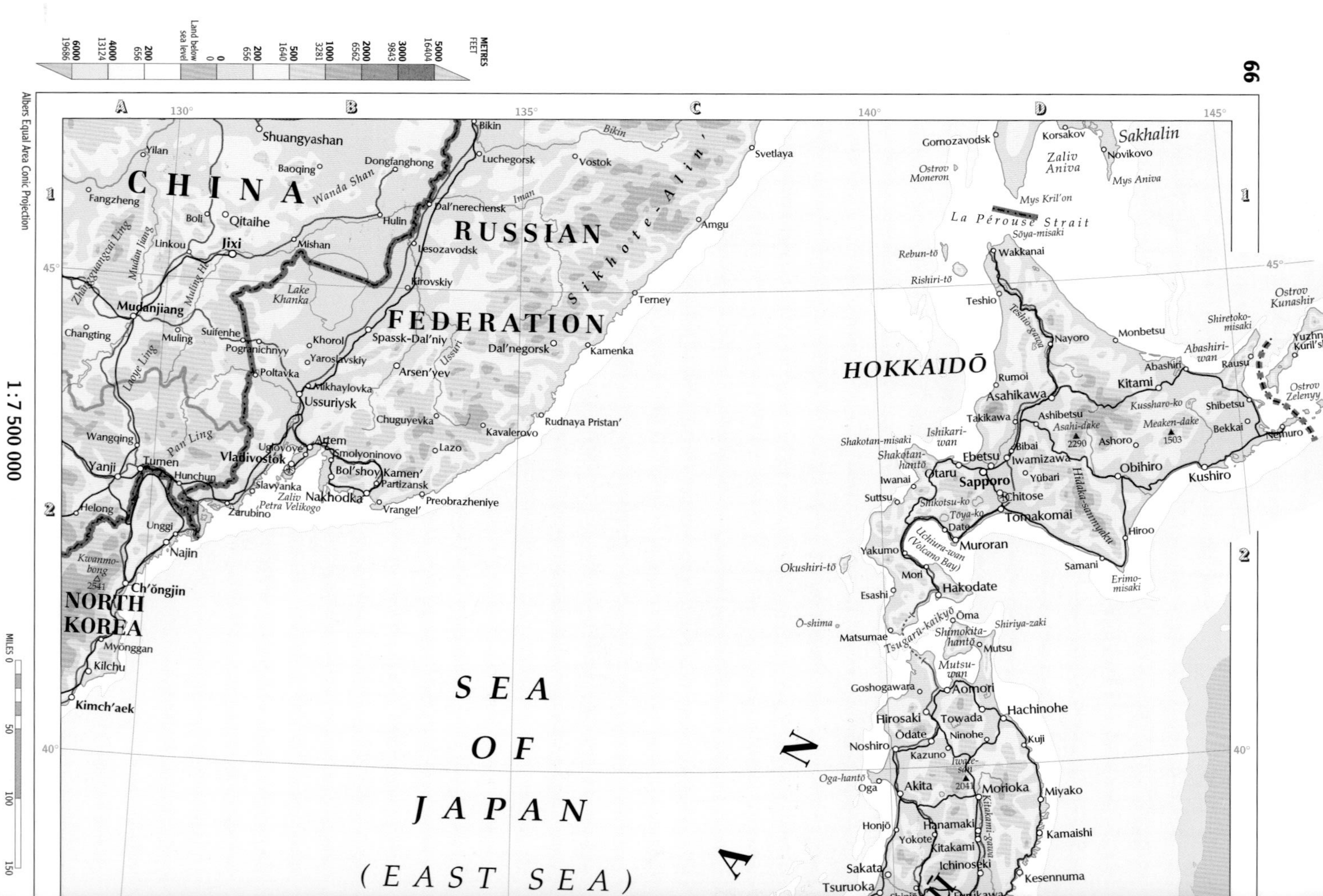

Sakhalin

Kosakov
Novikovo
Mys Aniva

Gornozavodsk

Zaliv
Aniva

Ostrov
Moneron

Rebun-tō

Rishiri-tō

La Pérouse Strait

Mys Krilon

Ostrov
Kunashir

Yuzhno-
Kuril'sk

Ostrov
Zelenyy

45°

145°

1

D

40°

2

Shiretoko-
misaki

Abashiri-
wan

Rausu

Shibetsu

Bekkai

Kushiro

Nemuro

Abashiri

Kitami

Monbetsu

Kussharo-ko
Meakan-dake
1503
Ashoro

Obihiro

Hiroo

Erimo-
misaki

Samani

Hidaka-sammyaku

Nayoro

Asahi-dake
2290

Iwamizawa

Yūbari

Teshio

Wakkanai

Ashibetsu

Ebetsu

Sapporo

Asahikawa

Ishikari-
wan

Shakotan-misaki

Rumoi

Takikawa

Otaru

Iwanai

Suttsu

Chitose

Tomakomai

Abuta-ko

Date

Noboribetsu

Muroran

Yakumo

Mori

Esashi

Okushiri-tō

O-shima

Toya-ko
Uchiura-wan
(Volcano Bay)

Hakodate

Matsumae

Tsu

HOKKAIDŌ

Teshio-gawa

140°

Shimokita-
hantō
Mutsu-
wan

Ōma

Ōminato

Shimokita-
hantō

Shiriya-zaki

Goshogawara

Mutsu

Aomori

Towada

Odate

Noshiro

Hirosaki

Oga-hantō

Oga

Honjō

Noheji

Kuji

Hachinohe

Ninohe

Hachimantai
2041

Towada

Akita

Kazuno

Morioka

Ichinoseki

Yokote

Yokote

Itakami

Kitakami-gawa

Miyako

Kamaishi

Kesennuma

Sakata

Tsuruoka

Shinjō

Fukushima

Ningamaki

N

A

V

Svetlaya

Amgu

Terney

Bikin

Vostok

Kamenka

Rudnaya Pristan'

Kavalerovo

Dal'negorsk

RUSSIAN

FEDERATION

Sikhote-Alin'

Bikin

Luchegorsk

Dal'nerechensk

Ussuriysk

Ostrovskiy

Lesozavodsk

Arsen'yev

Spassk-Dal'niy

Yaroslavskiy

Khorol

Chuguyevka

Lazo

SEA

OF

JAPAN

(EAST SEA)

Mikhaylovka

Kamen'-
Rybolov

Molodyozhnoye

Partizansk

Vrangel'

Preobrazheniye

CHINA

Shuangyashan

Dongfangh ong

Baoqing

Jixi

Hulin

Mishan

Wanda Shan

Lake
Khanka

Kamen-
Rybolov

Bol'shoy
Kamen'

Nakhodka

Zaliv
Petra Velikogo

Ilan

Qitaihe

Boli

Linkou

Pogranichnyy

Poltavka

Razdol'noye

Ussuriysk

Vladivostok

Ussuri

Slavyanka

Zarubino

Mudan Jiang

Muling

Suifenhe

Muling He

Zhang Guangcai Ling

Fangzheng

Changting

Mudanjiang

Wangqing

Helong

Yanji

Tumen

Hunchun

Krasnino

Unggi

Najin

Kraskino

Chongjin

Myŏnggan

Kilchu

Kimch'aek

NORTH
KOREA

Kumgang-
bong
2541

Changbai Shan

Mudan Ling

Laoye Ling

Kanmu-ri

130°

135°

C

B

A

1

2

45°

40°

METRES
FEET

5000	16404
3000	9843
2000	6562
1000	3281
500	1640
200	656
0	0

Land below
sea level

200	656
4000	13124
6000	19686

1:7 500 000

MILES 0   50   100   150

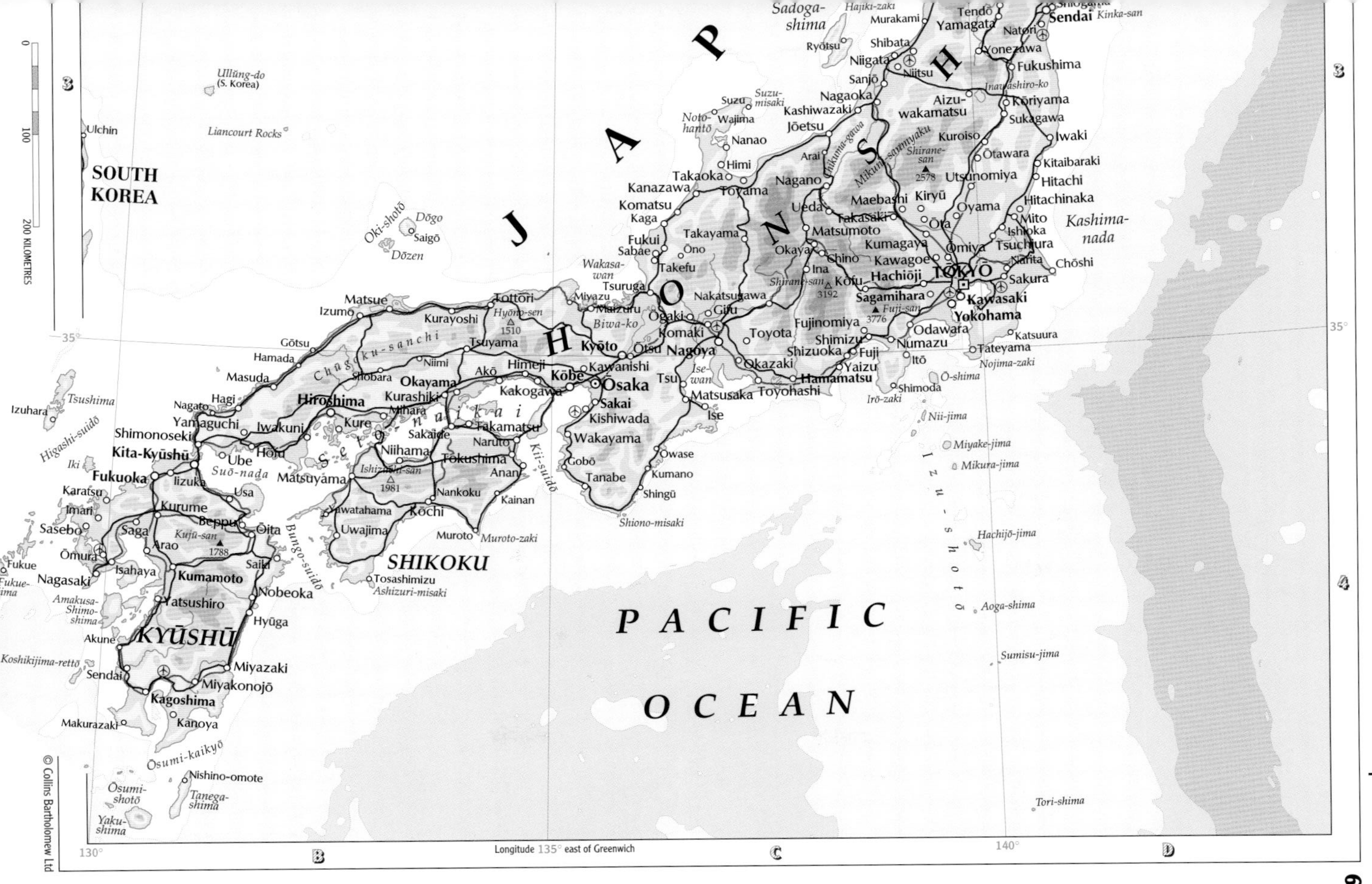

35°

140°

PACIFIC

OCEAN

SOUTH
KOREA

Ulleung-do
(S. Korea)

Liancourt Rocks°

Oki-shotō

Dōgo
Saigo
Dōzen

Tsushima

Iki

Hisashi-suidō

Izuhara

Fukue
Fukue-shima

Koshikijima-rettō

Makurazaki

**SOUTH
KOREA**

Ulchin

Gōtsu
Hamada
Masuda
Hagi

Matsue
Izumo

Tottori
Kurayoshi

Chū-sanchi

Yonago

Niimi
Shōbara
Kurashiki
Okayama

*Hiruzen-san
1510*

Tsuyama

Akō
Himeji

Fukuyama

Onomichi

Hiroshima
Kure
Iwakuni
Hōfu
Shimonoseki
Yamaguchi
Ube
Kita-Kyūshū
Iizuka
Fukuoka
Karatsu
Imari
Saga
Kurume
Sasebo
Ōmura
Nagasaki
Isahaya
Shimabara

Matsuyama
Niihama
Saijō
Sakaide
Marugame
Takamatsu
Naruto
Tokushima

SHIKOKU

Kōchi

*Ishizuchi-san
1981*

Uwajima
Sukumo
Watanabe

Bungo-suidō
Suō-nada
Ōita
Usa
Beppu
Kumamoto
Yatsushiro
Hitoyoshi

*Aso-san
1788*
Kujū-san

KYŪSHŪ

Nobeoka
Hyūga

Miyazaki
Miyakonojō
Satō

Akune
Sendai
Kagoshima
Kanoya

Ōsumi-shotō

Ōsumi-kaikyō
Nishino-omote
Tanega-shima

Yaku-shima

© Collins Bartholomew Ltd

0   100   200 KILOMETRES

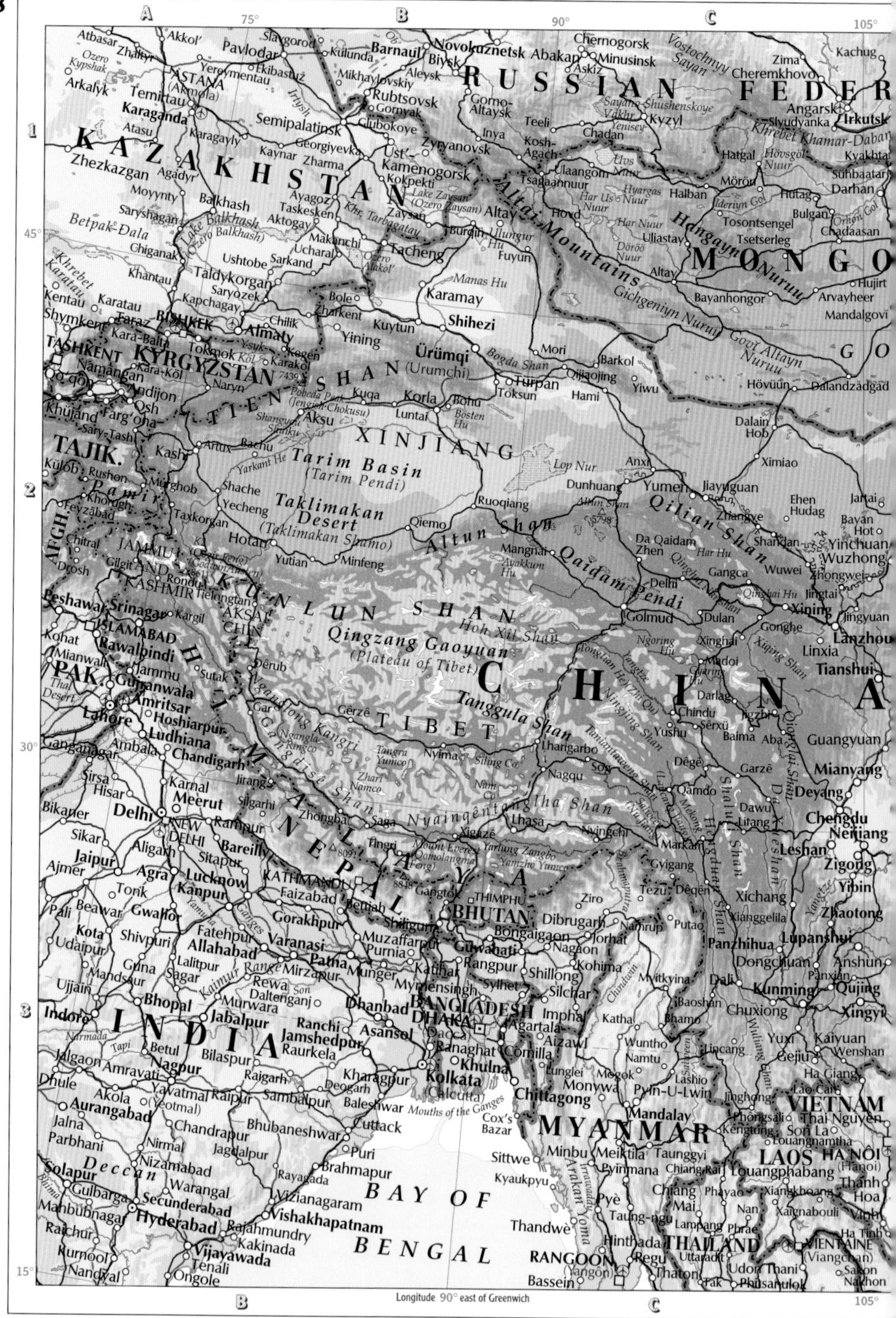

METRES
FEET

5000
16404

3000
9843

2000
6562

1000
3281

500
1640

200
656

0
0

Land below
sea level

200
656

4000
13124

6000
19686

Albers Equal Area Conic Projection

1 : 25 000 000

MILES 0   250   500

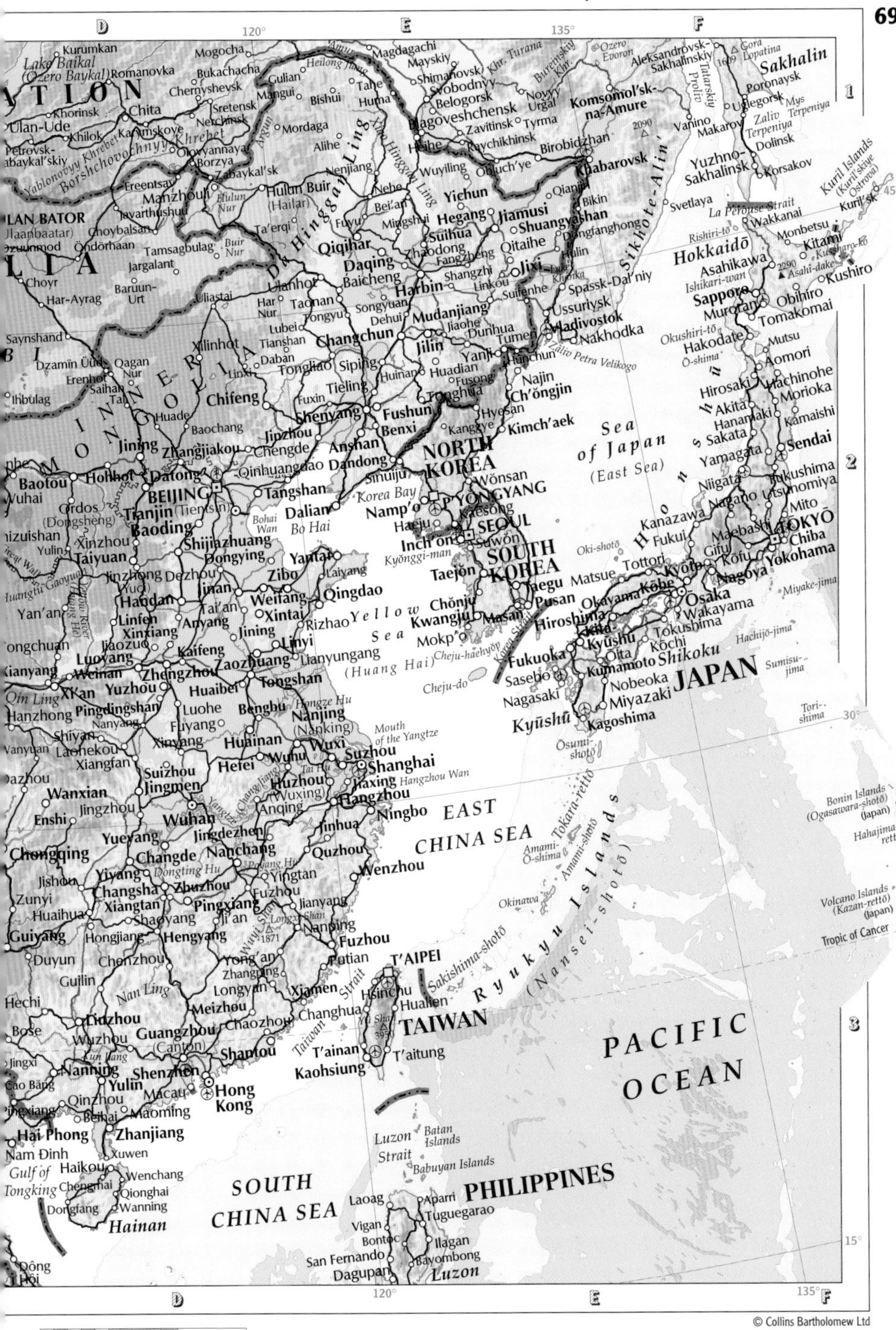

0   250   500   750 KILOMETRES

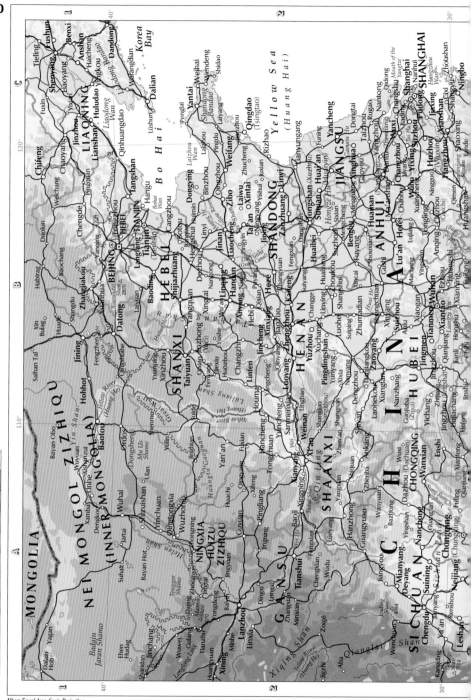

MONGOLIA

NEI MONGOL ZIZHIQU (INNER MONGOLIA)

LIAONING

Korea Bay

Bo Hai

Yellow Sea (Huang Hai)

HEBEI

BEIJING

TIANJIN

SHANDONG

SHANXI

NINGXIA HUIZU ZIZHIQU

GANSU

SHAANXI

HENAN

JIANGSU

ANHUI

SHANGHAI

HUBEI

CHONGQING

SICHUAN

C H I N A

Albers Equal Area Conic Projection

1 : 12 000 000

MILES 0   100   200   300

METRES
FEET

5000 / 16404
3000 / 9843
2000 / 6562
1000 / 3281
500 / 1640
200 / 656
0 / 0
Land below sea level
200 / 656
4000 / 13124
6000 / 19686

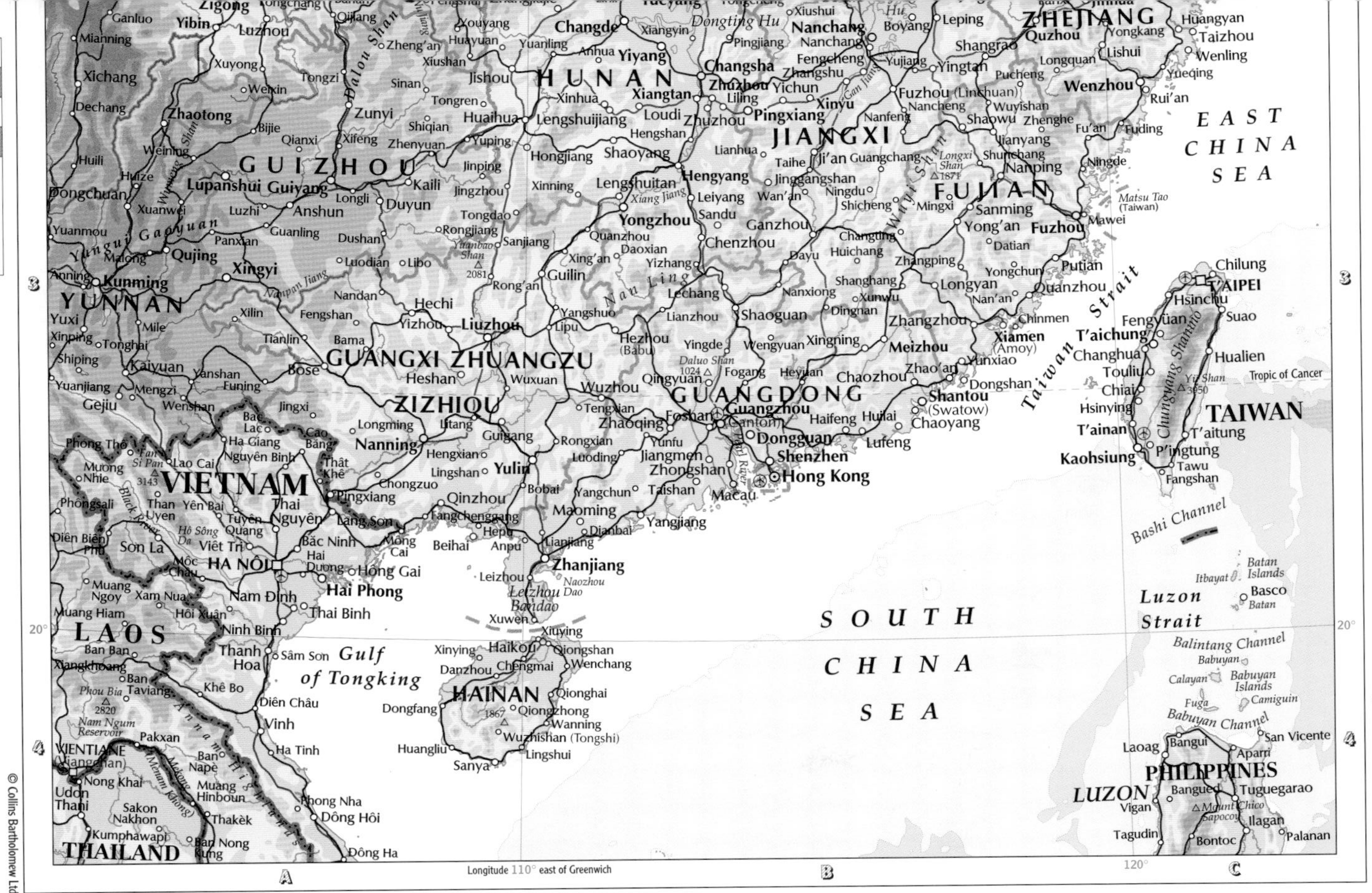

EAST CHINA SEA

SOUTH CHINA SEA

Gulf of Tongking

ZHEJIANG

FUJIAN

JIANGXI

HUNAN

GUIZHOU

GUANGDONG

GUANGXI ZHUANGZU

YUNNAN

HAINAN

TAIWAN

PHILIPPINES

LUZON

VIETNAM

LAOS

THAILAND

Luzon Strait

Balintang Channel

Bashi Channel

Taiwan Strait

Tropic of Cancer

Hong Kong

HANOI

VIENTIANE

Kunming

Changsha

Nanchang

Fuzhou

Guiyang

Nanning

Guangzhou

Shenzhen

Macau

Haikou

Longitude 110° east of Greenwich

0   200   400 KILOMETRES

METRES
FEET

5000
16404
3000
9843
2000
6562
1000
3281
500
1640
200
656
0
0
Land below
sea level
200
656
4000
13124
6000
19686

Albers Equal Area Conic Projection

1 : 15 000 000

MILES 0   100   200   300

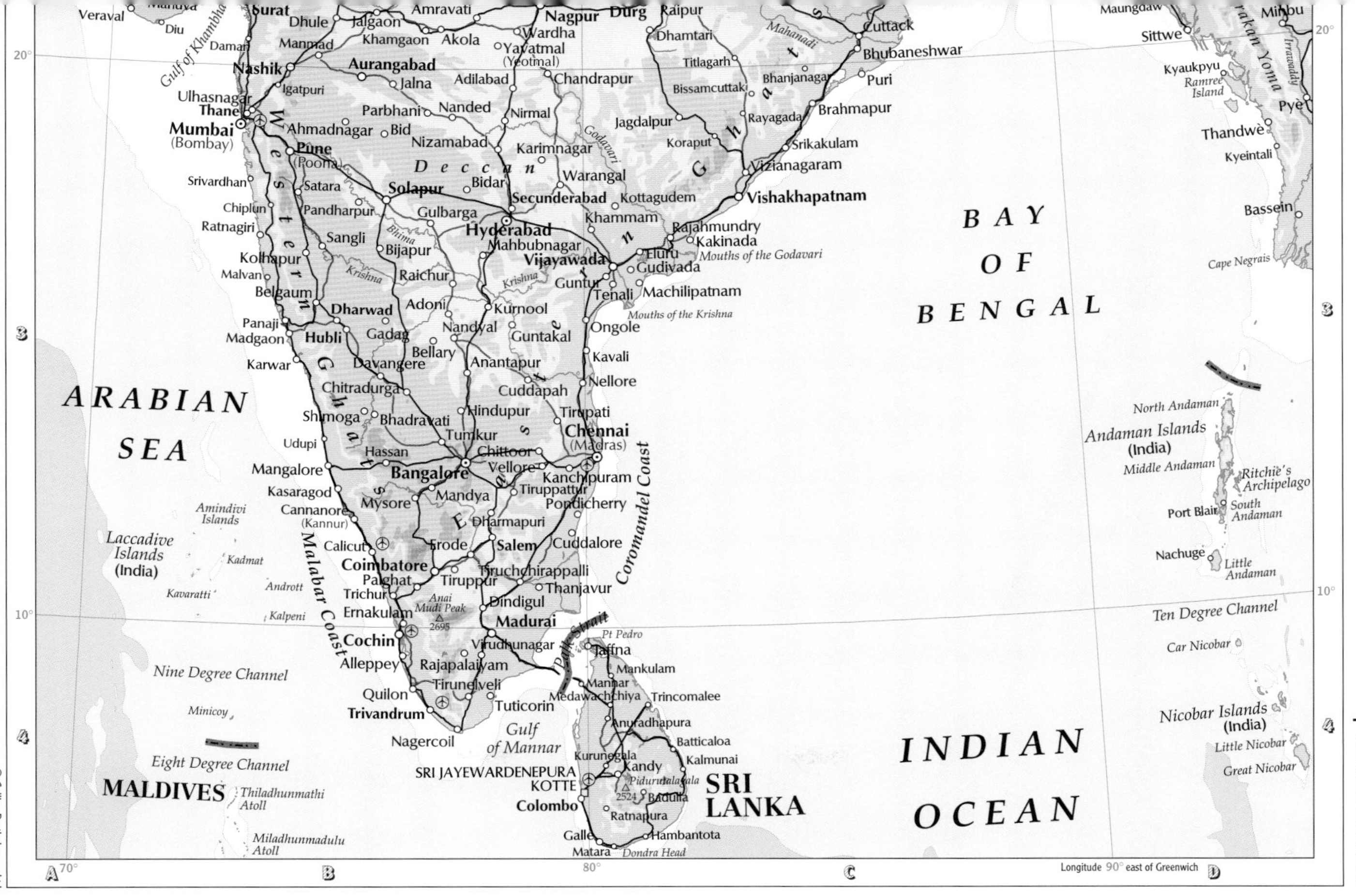
BAY OF BENGAL
ARABIAN SEA
INDIAN OCEAN
SRI LANKA
MALDIVES
Andaman Islands (India)
Nicobar Islands (India)
Laccadive Islands (India)
North Andaman
Middle Andaman
South Andaman
Little Andaman
Ritchie's Archipelago
Car Nicobar
Little Nicobar
Great Nicobar
Ten Degree Channel
Nine Degree Channel
Eight Degree Channel
Gulf of Mannar
Gulf of Khambhat
Palk Strait
Coromandel Coast
Malabar Coast
Deccan
Western Ghats
Eastern Ghats
Mouths of the Godavari
Mouths of the Krishna
Cape Negrais
Arakan Yoma
Irrawaddy
Mahanadi
Godavari
Krishna
Bhima
Amindivi Islands
Kadmat
Kavaratti
Andrott
Kalpeni
Minicoy
Thiladhunmathi Atoll
Miladhunmadulu Atoll
Pt Pedro
Dondra Head
Anai Mudi Peak 2695
Pidurutalagala 2524
Veraval
Diu
Surat
Daman
Dhule
Jalgaon
Amravati
Manmad
Khamgaon
Akola
Nagpur
Durg
Raipur
Wardha
Yavatmal (Yeotmal)
Dhamtari
Cuttack
Bhubaneshwar
Puri
Nashik
Aurangabad
Jalna
Adilabad
Chandrapur
Titlagarh
Bissamcuttak
Bhanjanagar
Brahmapur
Igatpuri
Ulhasnagar
Thane
Mumbai (Bombay)
Parbhani
Nanded
Nirmal
Jagdalpur
Rayagada
Ahmadnagar
Bid
Nizamabad
Karimnagar
Koraput
Srikakulam
Pune (Poona)
Vizianagaram
Vishakhapatnam
Srivardhan
Satara
Solapur
Bidar
Warangal
Secunderabad
Kottagudem
Chiplun
Pandharpur
Gulbarga
Khammam
Hyderabad
Mahbubnagar
Rajahmundry
Kakinada
Ratnagiri
Sangli
Bijapur
Vijayawada
Eluru
Gudivada
Kolhapur
Malvan
Raichur
Guntur
Tenali
Machilipatnam
Belgaum
Dharwad
Adoni
Kurnool
Ongole
Panaji
Madgaon
Hubli
Gadag
Nandyal
Guntakal
Bellary
Kavali
Karwar
Davangere
Anantapur
Nellore
Chitradurga
Cuddapah
Shimoga
Bhadravati
Hindupur
Tirupati
Udupi
Tumkur
Chennai (Madras)
Hassan
Chittoor
Mangalore
Bangalore
Vellore
Kanchipuram
Kasaragod
Tiruppattur
Cannanore (Kannur)
Mysore
Mandya
Pondicherry
Dharmapuri
Calicut
Erode
Salem
Cuddalore
Coimbatore
Palghat
Tiruppur
Tiruchchirappalli
Thanjavur
Trichur
Dindigul
Ernakulam
Madurai
Cochin
Virudhunagar
Alleppey
Rajapalaiyam
Tirunelveli
Quilon
Tuticorin
Trivandrum
Nagercoil
Jaffna
Mankulam
Mannar
Medawachchiya
Trincomalee
Anuradhapura
Batticaloa
Kurunegala
Kalmunai
Kandy
Badulla
SRI JAYEWARDENEPURA KOTTE
Colombo
Ratnapura
Galle
Matara
Hambantota
Maungdaw
Sittwe
Minbu
Kyaukpyu
Ramree Island
Pye
Thandwe
Kyeintali
Bassein
Port Blair
Nachuge
Longitude 90° east of Greenwich
20°
10°
70°
80°
A
B
C
D
E
0
250
500 KILOMETRES

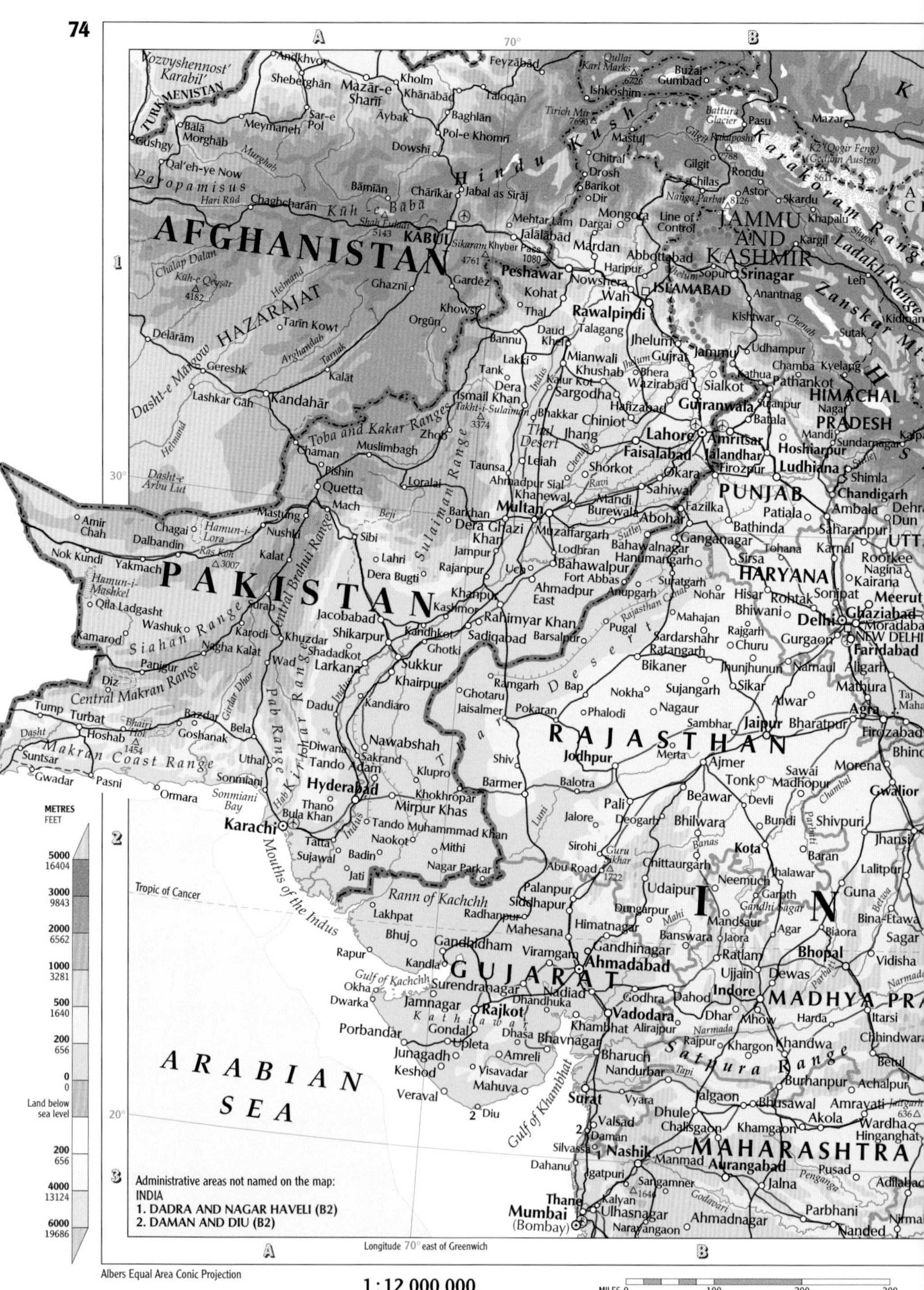

A · 70° · B · K

TURKMENISTAN
Rozvyshennost'
Karabil' Andkhvoy
Gushgy Sheberghan Kholm Feyzabad Qullai Buzai
Bala Meymaneh Mazar-e Khanabad Taloqan Karl Marks Gumbad
Morghab Sar-e Sharif Aybak Ishkoshim 6426
Qal'eh-ye Now Pol Baghlan Tirich Mir Battura Pasu
Murghab Dowshi 7690 Glacier Gilgit Rakaposhi Mazar
Paropamisus Bamian Charikar Pol-e Khomri Drosh Gilgit 7788 (Qogir Feng)
Hari Rud Chaghcharan Kuh-e Jabal as Siraj Barikot Dir Mongora Rondu 8611 (Gordwin Austen)
Chalap Dalan Kabe Babe Mehtar Lam Dargai Line of Nanga Parbat 8126 Skardu A.C.
AFGHANISTAN 5143 Shah Fuladi KABUL Sikaram Khyber Pass Mardan Abbottabad Control **JAMMU** Khapalu Ladakh Range
Kahe Ceysar 4761 Gardez 1080 Peshawar Haripur Chitral **AND** Kargil
4182 Ghazni Khost Kohat Nowshera Wah **KASHMIR** Leh
Delaram **HAZARAJAT** Tarin Kowt Orgun Bannu Daud Khel Rawalpindi Jhelum Srinagar Anantnag Zanskar Mts H
30° Gereshk Arghandab Tarnak Lakki Mianwali Khushab Talagang Gujrat Jammu Udhampur Kishtwar Chenab Sutak Kidman
Lashkar Gah Kandahar Kalat Tank Khushab Bhera Wazirabad Sialkot Chamba Kyelang **HIMACHAL**
Helmand Dera Sargodha Hafizabad Gujranwala Batala Nagar Pathankot Sundarnagar **PRADESH**
Dasht-e Toba and Kakar Ranges Ismail Khan Bhakkar Chiniot Lahore Amritsar Hoshiarpur
Arbu Lut Chaman Muslimbagh Zhob Takht-i-Sulaiman Jhang Faisalabad Jalandhar Ludhiana Shimla
Pishin 3374 Shorkot Okara Firozpur Chandigarh
PAKISTAN Quetta Loralai Barkhan Khanewal Mandi Sahiwal Fazilka Bathinda Patiala Ambala Dun
Amir Dalbandin Mastung Mach Sibi Dera Ghazi Burewala Abohar Ganganagar Tohana Sirsa Karnal Rookee UTT
Chah Hamun-i- Lora Nushki Khan Lodhran Bahawalnagar Hanumangarh Nohar **HARYANA** Nagina
Nok Kundi Yakmach 3007 Kalat Lahri Muzaffargarh Bahawalpur Suratgarh Mahajan Hisar Rohtak Sonipat Kairana Meerut
Hamun-i- Dera Bugti Jampur Fort Abbas Anupgarh Pugal Bhiwani Delhi Ghaziabad
Mashkel Rakhshan Range Rajanpur Ahmadpur Sadiqabad Nohar Bikaner Churu Jhunjhunun Gurgaon NEW DELHI Moradabad
Qila Ladgasht Washuk Khuzdar Kashmor East Rahimyar Khan Sardarshahr Ratangarh Sikar Namaul Alwar Faridabad
Central Brahui Range Jacobabad Shikarpur Ghotki Barsalpur Sujangarh Nagaur Sambhar Mathura
Kamarod Nagha Kalat Shadadkot Larkana Wad Pugal **RAJASTHAN** Phalodi Nokha Sambhar Jaipur Bharatpur Agra
Diz Siahan Range Paniigur Dadu Kandiaro Khairpur Jaisalmer Pokaran Nagaur Merta Ajmer Tonk Sawai Madhopur Firozabad Taj
Tump Turbat Central Makran Range Karodi Bela Nawabshah Sakrand Shiv Barmer Jodhpur Tonk Devli Bundi Morena Bhind
Hoshab Bzdar Goshanu Uthal Diwana Klupro Balotra Pali Beawar Devli Shivpuri Gwalior
Dasht Bhairi Hyderabad Tando Adam Barmer Jalore Deogarh Bhilwara Bundi Baran Jhansi
Suntsar Makran Coast Range Sonmiani Thano Bula Khan Mirpur Khas Sirohi Guru Chittaurgarh Kota Lalitpur
Gwadar Pasni Ormara Sonmiani Bay Karachi Tatta Khokhropar Nagar Parkar Abu Road Sikhar Udaipur Neemuch Jhalawar Guna
Mouths of the Indus Badin Mithi Palanpur 1722 Dungarpur Mandsaur I N Bina-
Jati Naokot Sidhpur Himatnagar Banswara Jaora Ratlam Bhopal Biaora Sagar
Tropic of Cancer Lakhpat Radhanpur Mahesana Gandhinagar **I N D I A** Mhow Ujjain Dewas Indore Vidisha
Rapur Bhuj Gandhidham Viramgam **Ahmadabad** Godhra Dahod Mhow Harda **MADHYA PRADESH**
Kandla Surendranagar Nadiad Gandhinagar Khargon Khandwa Itarsi Chhindwara
Okha **GUJARAT** Dhanduka Kheda Vadodara Alirajpur Narmada Nandurbar Burhanpur Achalpur
Gulf of Kachchh Jamnagar Gondal Dhasa Bhavnagar Bharuch Nandurbar Sathpura Range Betul
Dwarka Rajkot Upleta Amreli Nandurbar Tapi Dhule Bhusawal Amravati Jalgaon Wardha
Porbandar Junagadh Keshod Visavadar Mahuva Surat Vyara Talgaon Akola Hinganghat
ARABIAN Veraval Diu Valsad Daman Nandurbar Chalisgaon Khamgaon
SEA 20° Silvassa Dahanu Nashik Manmad **MAHARASHTRA** Jalna Adilabac
gatpuri 1646 Aurangabad Parbhani
Administrative areas not named on the map: Thane Kalyan Sangamner Pusad Nanded
INDIA Mumbai Ulhasnagar Ahmadnagar
1. DADRA AND NAGAR HAVELI (B2) (Bombay) Narayangaon
2. DAMAN AND DIU (B2) A Longitude 70° east of Greenwich B

METRES / FEET
5000 / 16404
3000 / 9843
2000 / 6562
1000 / 3281
500 / 1640
200 / 656
0 / 0
Land below sea level
200 / 656
4000 / 13124
6000 / 19686

Albers Equal Area Conic Projection

1 : 12 000 000

MILES 0 · 100 · 200 · 300

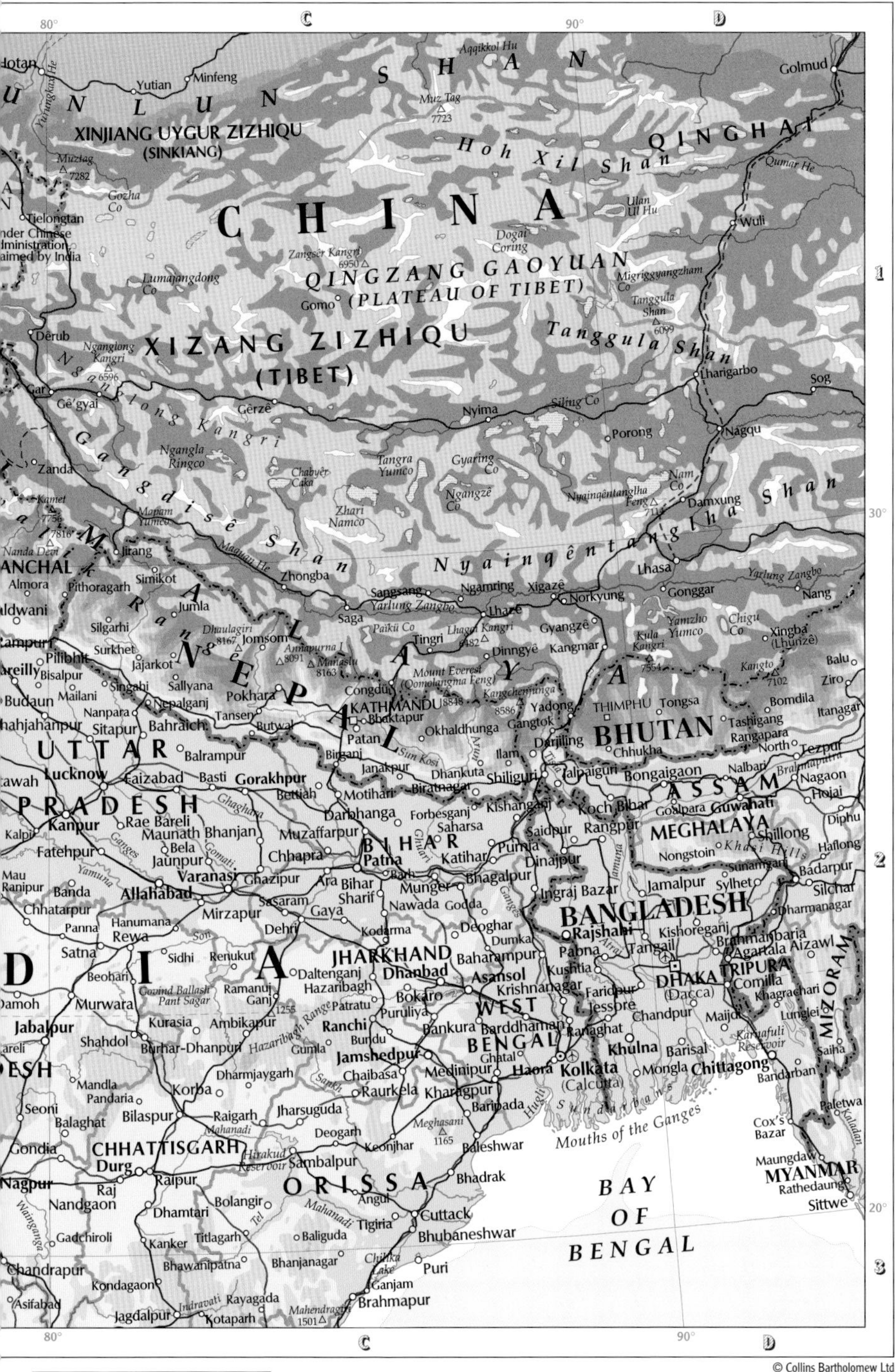
80°
C
90°
D
1
2
3
30°
20°
CHINA
XINJIANG UYGUR ZIZHIQU
(SINKIANG)
QINGHAI
QINGZANG GAOYUAN
(PLATEAU OF TIBET)
XIZANG ZIZHIQU
(TIBET)
Hoh Xil Shan
Tanggula Shan
Nyainqêntanglha Shan
Gangdisê Shan
Nganglong Kangri
HIMALAYA
NEPAL
BHUTAN
BANGLADESH
UTTAR PRADESH
BIHAR
JHARKHAND
WEST BENGAL
ASSAM
MEGHALAYA
TRIPURA
MIZORAM
CHHATTISGARH
ORISSA
MYANMAR
BAY OF BENGAL
Mouths of the Ganges
Golmud
Yutian
Minfeng
Aqqikkol Hu
Muz Tag 7723
Muztag 7282
Gozha Co
Tielongtan
Under Chinese administration claimed by India
Zangser Kangri 6950
Ulan Ul Hu
Dogai Coring
Migriggyangzham Co
Tanggula Shan 6099
Lumajangdong Co
Gomo
Wuli
Qumar He
Dêrub
Nganglong Kangri 6596
Gar
Gê'gyai
Gêrzê
Nyima
Siling Co
Lharigarbo
Sog
Nagqu
Porong
Zanda
Ngangla Ringco
Chabyêr Caka
Tangra Yumco
Gyaring Co
Ngangzê Co
Nam Co
Nyainqêntanglha Feng 7111
Damxung
Kamet 7756
Nanda Devi 7816
Mapam Yumco
Zhari Namco
Jirang
Maquan He
Zhongba
Lhasa
Yarlung Zangbo
Gonggar
Nang
Sangsang
Ngamring
Xigazê
Norkyung
Saga
Lhazê
Paikü Co
Tingri
Lhagoi Kangri 7482
Gyangzê
Yamzho Yumco
Chigu Co
Kula Kangri 7554
Xingba (Lhünzê)
Kangto 7102
Balu
Ziro
Bomdila
Itanagar
Dinngyê
Kangmar
Mount Everest (Qomolangma Feng) 8848
Kangchenjunga 8586
Yadong
THIMPHU
Tongsa
Tashigang
Rangapara North
Tezpur
Gangtok
Darjiling
Chhukha
Dhaulagiri 8167
Annapurna I 8091
Manaslu 8163
Jomsom
Simikot
Jumla
Almora
Pithoragarh
Haldwani
Silgarhi
Surkhet
Jajarkot
Rampur
Pilibhit
Bareilly
Bisalpur
Singahi
Sallyana
Pokhara
Mailani
Budaun
Nanpara
Nepalganj
Tansen
Butwal
Shahjahanpur
Sitapur
Bahraich
Balrampur
Congdü
KATHMANDU
Bhaktapur
Patan
Okhaldhunga
Sun Kosi
Arun
Ilam
Birganj
Janakpur
Dhankuta
Shiliguri
Jalpaiguri
Bongaigaon
Nalbari
Nagaon
Hojai
Etawah
Lucknow
Faizabad
Basti
Gorakhpur
Bettiah
Motihari
Biratnagar
Kishanganj
Koch Bihar
Goalpara
Guwahati
Diphu
Kalpi
Kanpur
Rae Bareli
Maunath Bhanjan
Darbhanga
Forbesganj
Saharsa
Saidpur
Rangpur
Shillong
Fatehpur
Ganges
Bela
Jaunpur
Gomati
Ghaghara
Muzaffarpur
Chhapra
Patna
Katihar
Purnia
Dinajpur
Nongstoin
Khasi Hills
Haflong
Mau Ranipur
Yamuna
Banda
Allahabad
Varanasi
Ghazipur
Ara
Barh
Bihar Sharif
Munger
Bhagalpur
Ingraj Bazar
Jamuna
Jamalpur
Sunamganj
Sylhet
Badarpur
Silchar
Dharmanagar
Chhatarpur
Mirzapur
Sasaram
Gaya
Nawada
Godda
Rajshahi
Kishoreganj
Brahmanbaria
Agartala
Aizawl
Panna
Hanumana
Rewa
Son
Dehri
Kodarma
Deoghar
Dumka
Pabna
Tangail
Atrai
Satna
Sidhi
Renukut
Daltenganj
Hazaribagh
Dhanbad
Baharampur
Kushtia
DHAKA (Dacca)
Comilla
Beohari
Govind Ballash Pant Sagar
Ramanuj Ganj
Asansol
Krishnanagar
Faridpur
Damoh
Murwara
Patratu
Bokaro
Jessore
Chandpur
Maijdi
Khagrachari
Lunglei
Jabalpur
Kurasia
Ambikapur
Hazaribagh Range 1255
Ranchi
Purulia
Bankura
Barddhaman
Ranaghat
Karnafuli Reservoir
Shahdol
Burhar-Dhanpuri
Gumla
Bundu
Khulna
Barisal
Saiha
Jamshedpur
Chaibasa
Ghatal
Haora
Kolkata (Calcutta)
Mongla
Chittagong
Bandarban
Mandla
Pandaria
Dharmjaygarh
Medinipur
Sankh
Korba
Raurkela
Kharagpur
Sundarbans
Seoni
Bilaspur
Raigarh
Jharsuguda
Baripada
Hugli
Paletwa
Kaladan
Balaghat
Mahanadi
Deogarh
Meghasani 1165
Cox's Bazar
Gondia
Hirakud Reservoir
Keonjhar
Baleshwar
Maungdaw
Durg
Sambalpur
Bhadrak
Rathedaung
Nagpur
Raipur
Angul
Sittwe
Raj Nandgaon
Bolangir
Dhamtari
Tel
Tigiria
Cuttack
Wainganga
Gadchiroli
Kanker
Titlagarh
Baliguda
Bhubaneshwar
Bhawanipatna
Bhanjanagar
Chilika Lake
Puri
Chandrapur
Kondagaon
Ganjam
Asifabad
Indravati
Rayagada
Brahmapur
Jagdalpur
Kotaparh
Mahendragiri 1501
0
200
400 KILOMETRES

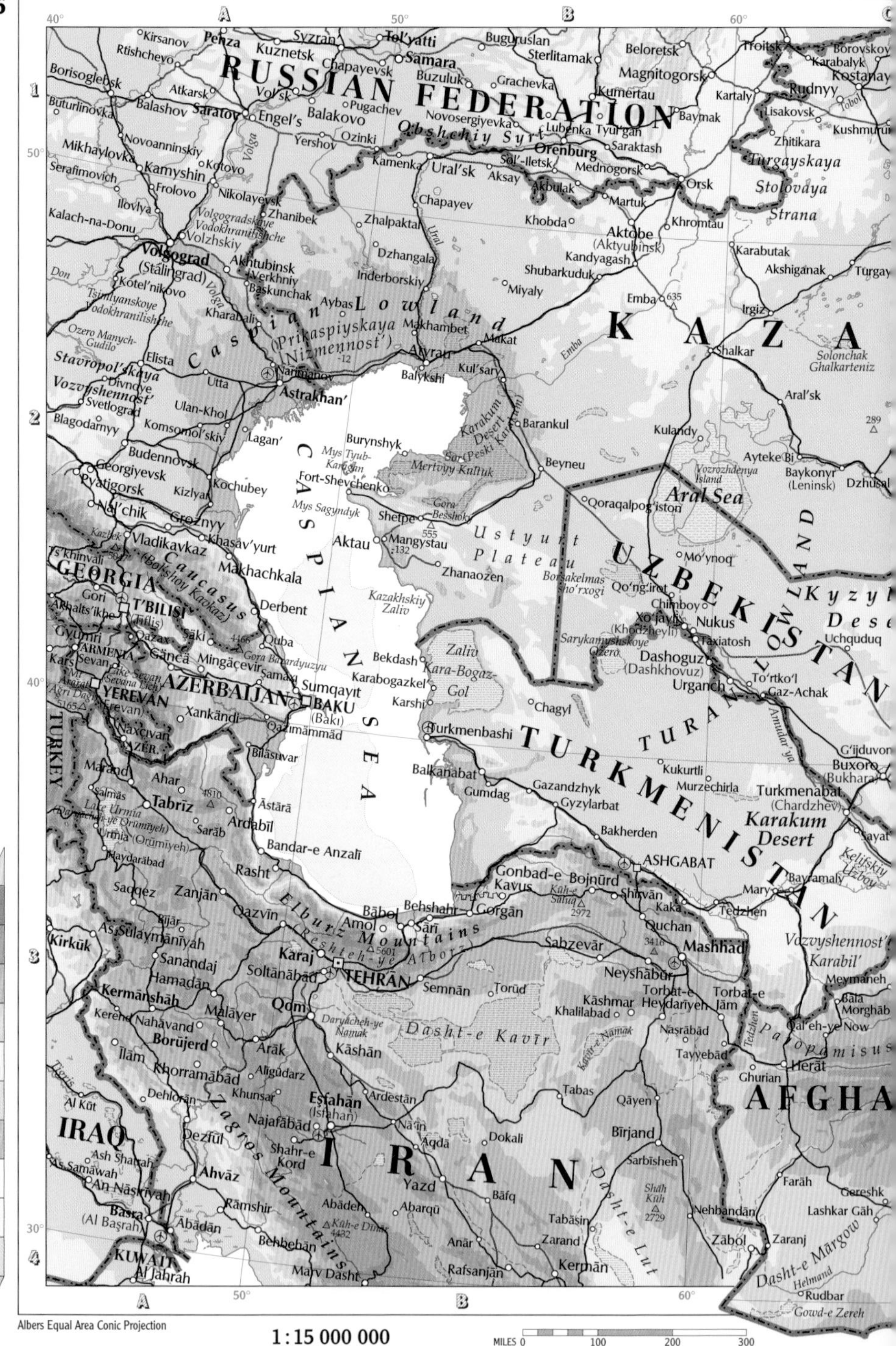

METRES
FEET

5000   16404

3000   9843

2000   6562

1000   3281

500   1640

200   656

0   0

Land below
sea level

200   656

4000   13124

6000   19686

Albers Equal Area Conic Projection

1:15 000 000

MILES 0   100   200   300

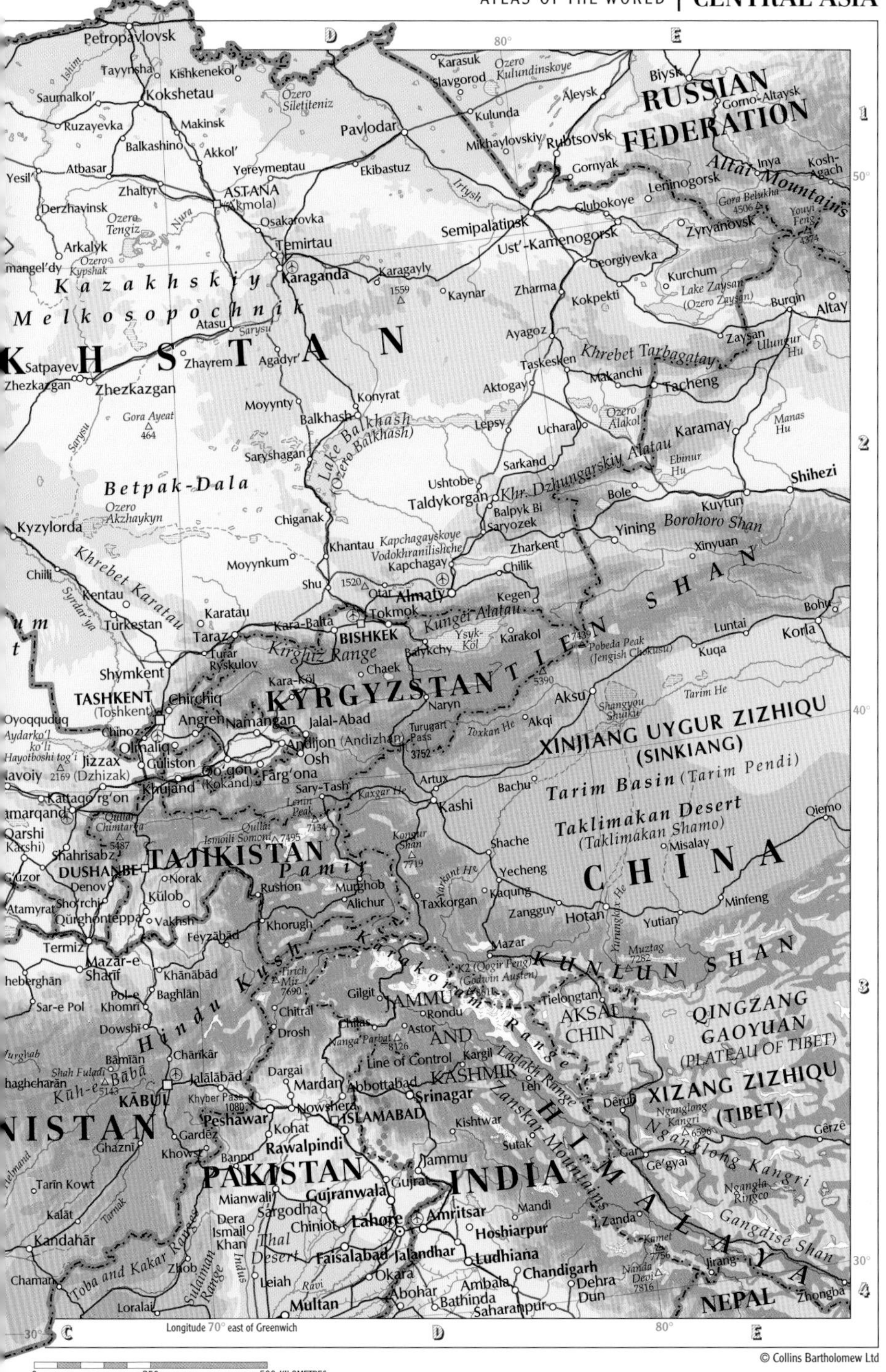

Petropavlovsk
Karasuk
80°
Biysk
RUSSIAN
Tayynsha Kishkenekol' Slavgorod Ozero Kulundinskoye
Aleysk Gorno-Altaysk
FEDERATION
Saumalkol' Kokshetau Kulunda
Ruzayevka Makinsk Ozero Pavlodar Mikhaylovskiy Rubtsovsk
Inya Kosh-
Siletiteniz Gornyak Leninogorsk Altai Mountains Agach
Atbasar Akkol' Ekibastuz Irtysh Gora Belukha 50°
Yesil' Balkashino Yereymentau Gornyak 4506 Youyi
Derzhavinsk Zhaltyr ASTANA Osakarovka Semipalatinsk Glubokoye Zyryanovsk Feng
(Akmola) Ust'-Kamenogorsk Georgiyevka Kurchum Lake Zaysan
mangel'dy Arkalyk Ozero Temirtau Karagayly Kokpekti (Ozero Zaysan) Burqin
Tengiz Karaganda Kaynar Zharma Zaysan Ulungu Altay
Ozero 1559 Ayagoz Khrebet Tarbagatay Hu
Kazakhskiy Kypshak Atasu Taskesken Makanchi Tacheng
K Satpayev Zhayrem Agadyr Aktogay Karamay Manas
Zhezkazgan Melkosopochnik Aktogay Ozero Karamay Hu
Zhezkargan Konyrat Lepsy Alakol Karamay Shihezi
Gora Ayeat Balkhash Ushtobe Ucharal Karamay
464 Lake Balkhash Sarkand Ebinur Hu
Betpak-Dala Saryshagan (Ozero Balkhash) Taldykorgan Balpyq Bi Bole Kuytun Yining Borohoro Shan
Kyzylorda Ozero Khantau Kapchagayskoye Zharkent Xinyuan
Akzhaykyn Vodokhranilishche Kapchagay Chilik Kegen
Chili Moyynkum Shu Kapchagay Karakol SHAN
Kentau Shu 1520 Otar Almaty Pobeda Peak Kuqa Luntai Korla
um Turkestan Kara-Balta Tokmok Kunge Alatau (Jengish Chokusu) Bohu
t Karatau Taraz BISHKEK Ysyk-Kol Aksu Tarim He
Shymkent Turar Ryskulov Kirghiz Range Balykchy Karakol TIEN 7439 Shayou Shuide
TASHKENT Chirchiq Kara-Kol Chaek 5390 Kashi Tarim Basin (Tarim Pendi)
(Toshkent) Namangan Naryn Akqi XINJIANG UYGUR ZIZHIQU
Oyoqquduq Angren Jalal-Abad Toxkan He (SINKIANG)
Aydarko'l Chinoz Olmaliq Andijon (Andizhan) Artux Bachu Shache Taklimakan Desert
ko'li Guliston Osh 3752 Kashi (Taklimakan Shamo)
Hayotboshi tog'i Jizzax Fargʻona Sary-Tash Kaxgar He Yecheng Misalay CHINA
avoiy 2169 (Dzhizak) Khujand (Kokand) Lenin Kongur Qiemo
amarqand Kattaqoʻrgʻon (Kokand) Peak 7135 Shan Shache Minfeng
Qarshi Ismoili Somoni Pamir Yecheng Hotan Yutian
Kashi Shahrisabz 7495 Qullai Zangguy Minfeng
izor DUSHANBE TAJIKISTAN Norak Rushon Murghob Kaqung KUNLUN SHAN Muztag
Atamyrat Shoʻrchi Kulob Rushon Alichur Taxkorgan Mazar 7282 Tielongtan
Termiz Qurghonteppa Vakhsh Feyzabad Khorugh K2 (Qogir Feng) AKSAI QINGZANG
Mazar-e Khanabad Khorugh (Godwin Austen) JAMMU CHIN GAOYUAN
heberghan Sharif Pol-e Baghlan Gilgit Rondu Ladakh Range (PLATEAU OF TIBET)
Sar-e Pol Khomri Chitral Astor AND Kargil Deruh XIZANG ZIZHIQU
Dowshi Bamian Charikar Drosh Nanga Parbat Line of Control KASHMIR Leh Zanskar Mountains (TIBET)
furghab Shah Fuladi Charikar Dargai 8126 Srinagar Kishtwar N Gangdise Shan
haghcharan Kuh-e Baba 5143 Jalalabad Mardan Abbottabad Srinagar HIMALAYA Gerze
NISTAN KABUL Khyber Pass Peshawar Kohat ISLAMABAD Jammu Sutak Ge'gyai
Ghazni Gardez Khowst Bannu Rawalpindi Kishtwar Gangdise Shan
Tarin Kowt Pol-e Khomri Mianwali Jhelum Mandi Zanda Neangang Kangri
Kalat Dera Chiniot Lahore Amritsar Hoshiarpur Jirang Zhongba
Kandahar Ismail Khan Faisalabad Jalandhar Ludhiana Chandigarh Dehra
Chaman PAKISTAN Leiah INDIA Ambala Saharanpur Dun NEPAL Zhongba
Toba and Kakar Range Multan Okara Abohar Bathinda
Loralai Sulaiman Range Dera Ghazi Khan Ravi

0   250   500 KILOMETRES

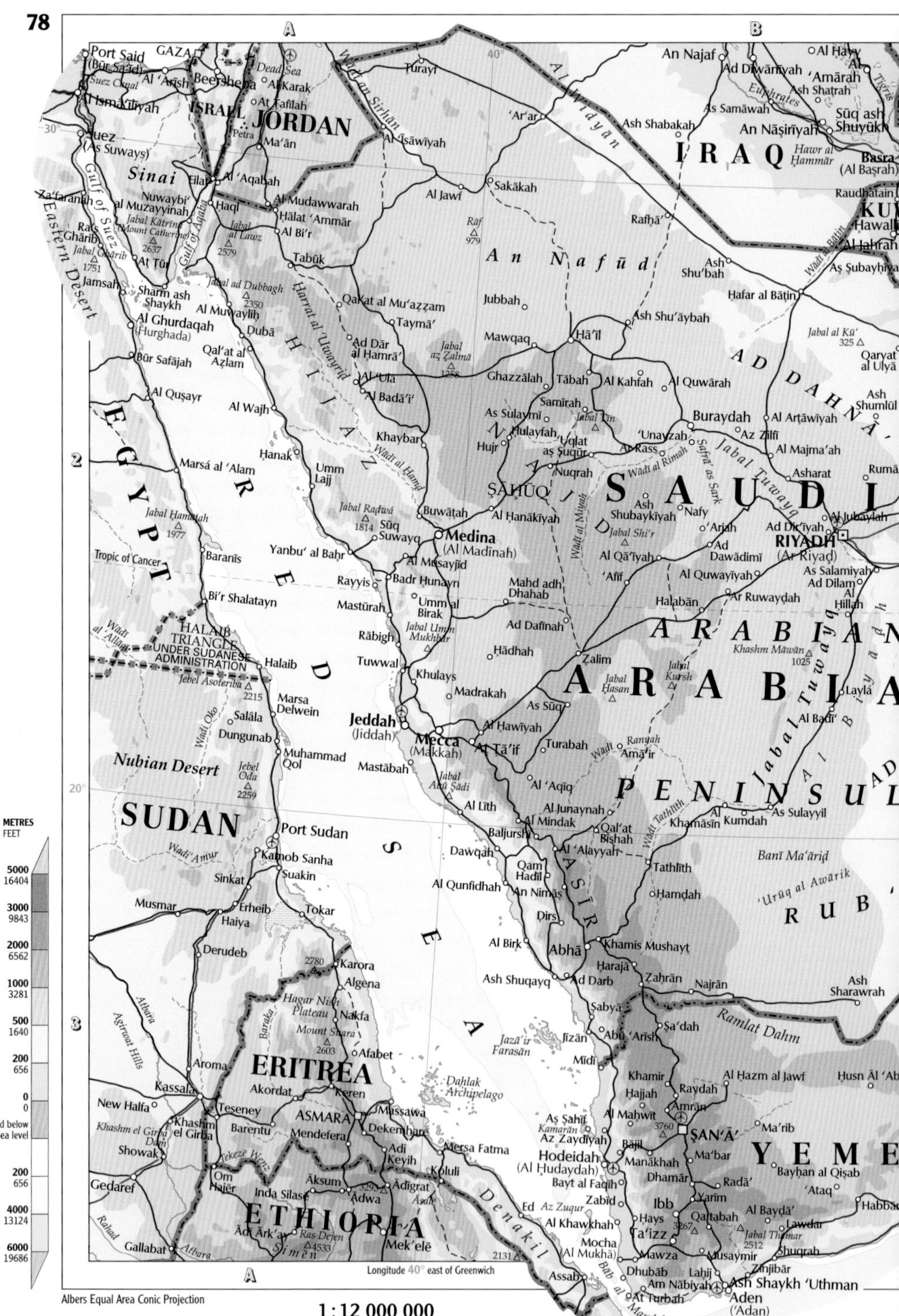

Port Said
(Būr Saʿīd) GAZA
Dead Sea
Suez Canal Al ʿArīsh Beersheba Al Karak
Ismāʿīlīyah ISRAEL Aṭ Ṭafīlah JORDAN
(As Suways) Petra Maʿān
Suez Jabal Katrīna Al ʿIsāwīyah ʿArʿar
Ras Nuwaybiʿ Al ʿAqabah Al Mudawwarah
Gharib al Muzayyinah Ḥaql Ḥālat ʿAmmār
Jamsah Jabal Katrīn Al Biʾr
Sharm ash Mount Catherine At Ṭūr Tabūk
Shaykh 2637 Jabal ad Dubbāgh
Al Muwaylih 2350
Al Ghurdaqah Dubā
(Hurghada) Qalʿat al
Būr Safājah Azlam
Al Quṣayr Ad Dār
Marsá al ʿAlam al Ḥamrāʾ
Jabal Ḥamāṭah Baranīs Khaybar
1977 Yanbuʿ al Baḥr
Tropic of Cancer
Biʾr Shalatayn
Buwāṭah
HALAIB Sūq
TRIANGLE Suwayq
UNDER SUDANESE
ADMINISTRATION Medina
Jebel Asoteriba (Al Madīnah)
2215 Badr Ḥunayn
Halaib Umm al
Marsa Birak
Dungunab Delwein Rābigh
Muhammad Khulays
Salāla Qol Madrakah
Jeddah
Nubian Desert (Jiddah)
Jebel Mastābah Mecca
Oda (Makkah)
2259 Taʾif

SUDAN Port Sudan
Kamob Sanha
Sinkat
Musmar Suakin
Haiya
Derudeb

ETHIOPIA

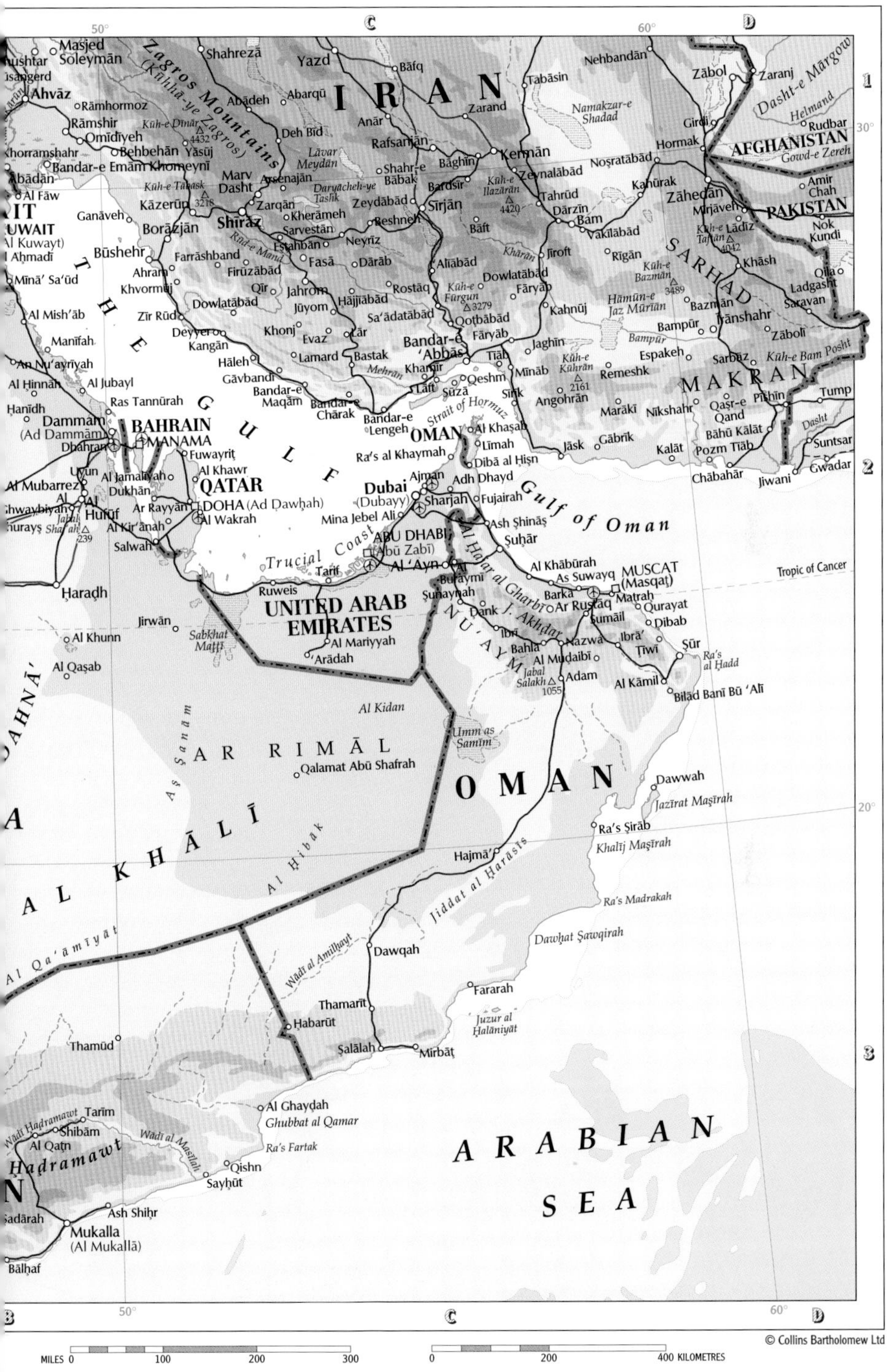

MILES 0   100   200   300   0   200   400 KILOMETRES

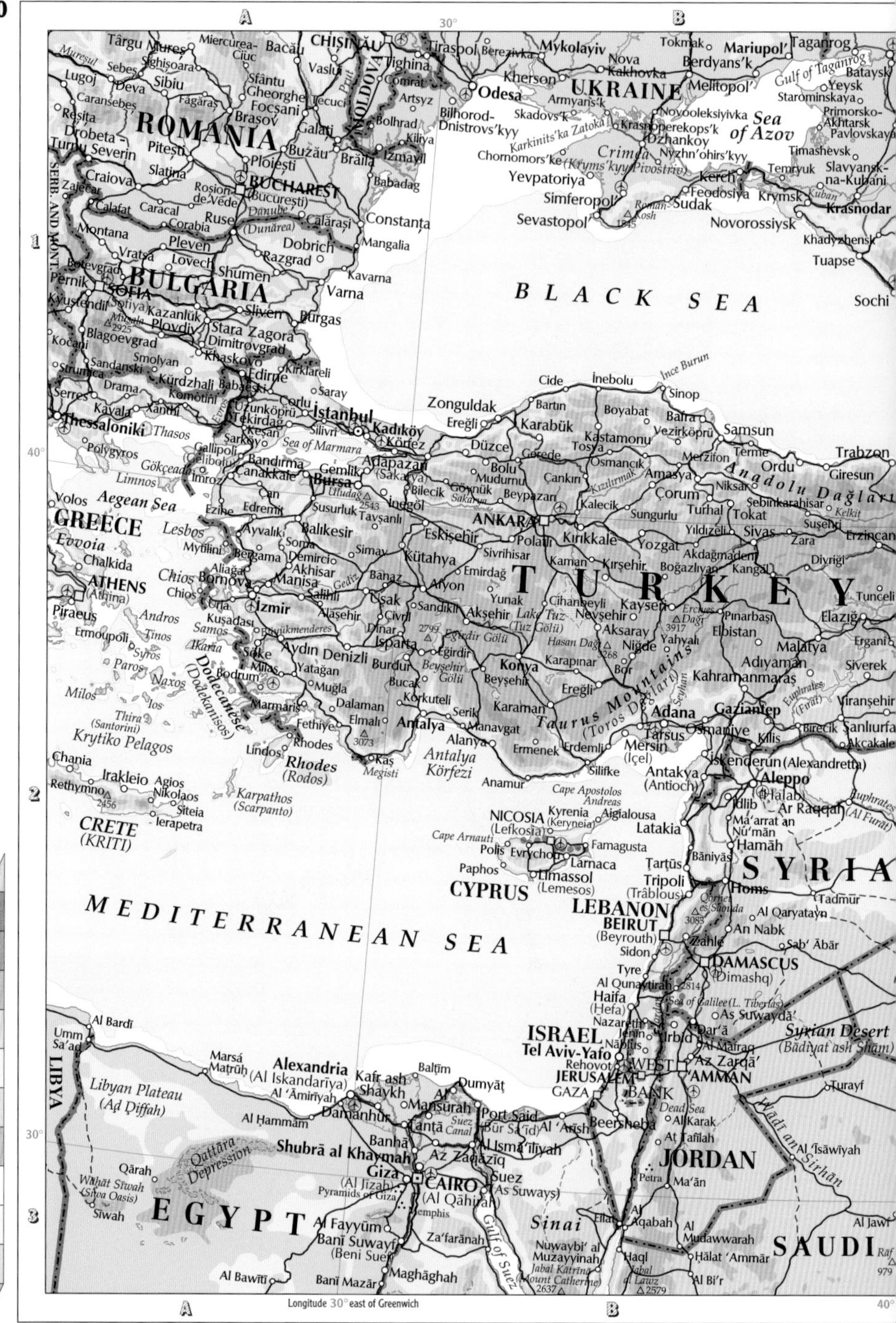

Târgu Mureş, Miercurea-Ciuc, Bacău, **CHIŞINĂU**, Tiraspol, Berezivka, Mykolayiv, Tokmak, Berdyans'k, **Mariupol'**, Taganrog
Sighişoara, Sebeş, Vaslui, Tighina, Comrat, Kherson, Nova Kakhovka, Melitopol', Gulf of Taganrog, Yeysk, Bataysk
Lugoj, Deva, Sibiu, Sfântu Gheorghe, Iecuci, Artsyz, Odesa, Skadovs'k, Novooleksiyivka, Primorsko-Akhtarsk, Staromins'ka
Caransebeş, Făgăraş, Focşani, Bilhorod-Dnistrovs'kyy, Karkinits'ka Zatoka, Krasnoperekops'k, Pavlovskaya
Reşita, Braşov, Galaţi, Izmayil, Kiliya, Chornomors'ke (Krym), Nyzhn'ohirs'kyy, Timashevsk
Drobeta, Piteşti, Buzău, Brăila, Izmayil, Chornomors'ke, Krymskyy, Kerch, Slavyans'k-na-Kubani
Turnu Severin, **ROMANIA**, **BUCHAREST** (Bucureşti), Babadag, Yevpatoriya, Simferopol', Feodosiya, Krymsk, Krasnodar
Craiova, Slatina, Roşiori de Vede, Ruse (Dunărea), Constanţa, Sevastopol', Sudak, Novorossiysk
Calafat, Caracal, Corabia, Pleven, Dobrich, Razgrad, Khadyzhensk
Montana, Vratsa, Lovech, Shumen, Kavarna, **BLACK SEA**, Tuapse
Botevgrad, **BULGARIA**, Varna, Sochi
Pernik, **SOFIA**, Kazanlŭk, Sliven, Burgas
Kyustendil, Plovdiv, Stara Zagora, Dimitrovgrad
Blagoevgrad, Smolyan, Khaskovo, Kŭrdzhali, Edirne, Kırklareli
Sandanski, Drama, Komotini, Lüleburgaz, Saray, Çorlu, **İstanbul**, Zonguldak, Bartın, Cide, İnebolu, Ince Burun, Sinop
Serres, Kavala, Xanthi, Tekirdağ, Çerkezköy, Silivri, Kadıköy, Ereğli, Karabük, Kastamonu, Boyabat, Vezirköprü, Samsun
Thessaloniki, Thasos, Gallipoli, Sea of Marmara, Adapazarı, Düzce, Bolu, Gerede, Tosya, Merzifon, Terme, Ordu, Trabzon
Polygyros, Gökçeada, İmroz, Çanakkale, Bandırma, Gemlik, **Bursa**, Bilecik, Mudurnu, Çankırı, Amasya, Çorum, Niksar, Giresun
Volos, Limnos, Edremit, Uludağ, İnegöl, Eskişehir, **ANKARA**, Kalecik, Sungurlu, Turhal, Tokat, Erzincan
GREECE, Lesbos, Ayvalık, Balıkesir, Simav, Kütahya, Sivrihisar, Polatlı, Kırıkkale, Yozgat, Yıldızeli, Sivas, Suşehri
Evvoia, Chalkida, Mytilini, Bergama, Demirci, Afyon, Emirdağ, Kaman, Kırşehir, Akdağmadeni, Boğazlıyan, Diyriği, Diyarbakır
ATHENS (Athina), Chios, Manisa, İzmir, Alaşehir, Banaz, Uşak, Cihanbeyli, Kayseri, Nevşehir, Pınarbaşı, Tunceli
Piraeus, Andros, Kuşadası, Ödemiş, Sarayköy, Sandıklı, Akşehir, Lake Tuz (Tuz Gölü), Niğde, Elbistan, Elazığ
Ermoupoli, Tinos, Ikaria, Söke, Aydın, Nazilli, Dinar, Isparta, Eğirdir Gölü, Hasan Dağı, Yahyalı, Ergani
Naxos, Paros, Milos, Ios, Bodrum, Milas, Muğla, Burdur, Beyşehir, Karapınar, **Konya**, Kahramanmaraş, Siverek, Şanlıurfa
Thira (Santorini), Krytiko Pelagos, Dalaman, Elmalı, Beyşehir, Karaman, Ereğli, Adana, Osmaniye, Kilis, Gaziantep, Birecik
Chania, Fethiye, Kaş, **Antalya**, Manavgat, Serik, Ermenek, Erdemli, Tarsus, Mersin (İçel), İskenderun (Alexandretta)
Rethymno, Irakleio, Agios Nikolaos, Rhodes, Megisti, **Rhodes** (Rodos), Antalya Körfezi, Anamur, Silifke, Antakya (Antioch), **Aleppo** (Halab)
CRETE (KRITI), Ierapetra, Siteia, Karpathos (Scarpanto), Lindos, Cape Apostolos Andreas, Latakia, İdlib, Ar Raqqah (Al Furāt)
Kyrenia (Keryneia), Aigialousa, Ma'arrat an Nu'mān, Hamāh, **SYRIA**
Cape Arnauti, **NICOSIA** (Lefkosia), Famagusta, Bāniyās
Polis, Evrychou, Larnaca, Tartūs, Homs, Tadmur
Paphos, Lemesos (Limassol), Tripoli (Trâblous), Al Qaryatayn
MEDITERRANEAN SEA, **CYPRUS**, **LEBANON**, An Nabk, Sab' Ābār
BEIRUT (Beyrouth), Zahlé
Sidon, **DAMASCUS** (Dimashq)
Tyre, Al Qunayţirah, As Suwaydā', Syrian Desert (Bādiyat ash Shām)
Haifa (Hefa), Sea of Galilee (L. Tiberias), Dar'ā
ISRAEL, Nazareth, Irbid, Al Mafraq, Turayf
Marsá Matrûh, Kafr ash Shaykh, Baltīm, Dumyāţ, Tel Aviv-Yafo, Rehovot, Nablus, **WEST** Az Zarqā'
Al Bardī, Al 'Amirīyah, **JERUSALEM**, GAZA, **BANK**, **AMMAN**
LIBYA, Umm Sa'ad, Libyan Plateau (Aḍ Diffah), Alexandria (Al Iskandariya), Al Manşūrah, Port Said (Bûr Sa'îd), Al 'Arîsh, Beersheba, Al Karak, Ma'ān
Al Hammām, Damanhūr, Ţanţā, Suez Canal, Al Ismā'īlīyah, Dead Sea, **JORDAN**, Petra
Qattara Depression, Shubrā al Khaymah, Banhā, Az Zaqāzīq, Suez (As Suways), Gulf of Suez, Sinai, Al 'Aqabah, At Tafîlah, Wadi an Sirhan
Qārah, Siwah, Wāhat Siwah (Siwa Oasis), **CAIRO** (Al Qāhirah), Nuwaybi' al Muzayyinah, Ḥaql, Ḥālat 'Ammār, Al 'Aţrūn
Al Fayyūm, Giza (Al Jīzah), Pyramids of Giza, Memphis, Za'farānah, **SAUDI**
EGYPT, Banī Suwayf, Bani Mazār, Maghāghah, Mount Catherine, Jabal Lawz, Al Bi'r, Raf, Al Jawf

METRES FEET
5000 16404
3000 9843
2000 6562
1000 3281
500 1640
200 656
0 0
Land below sea level
200 656
4000 13124
6000 19686

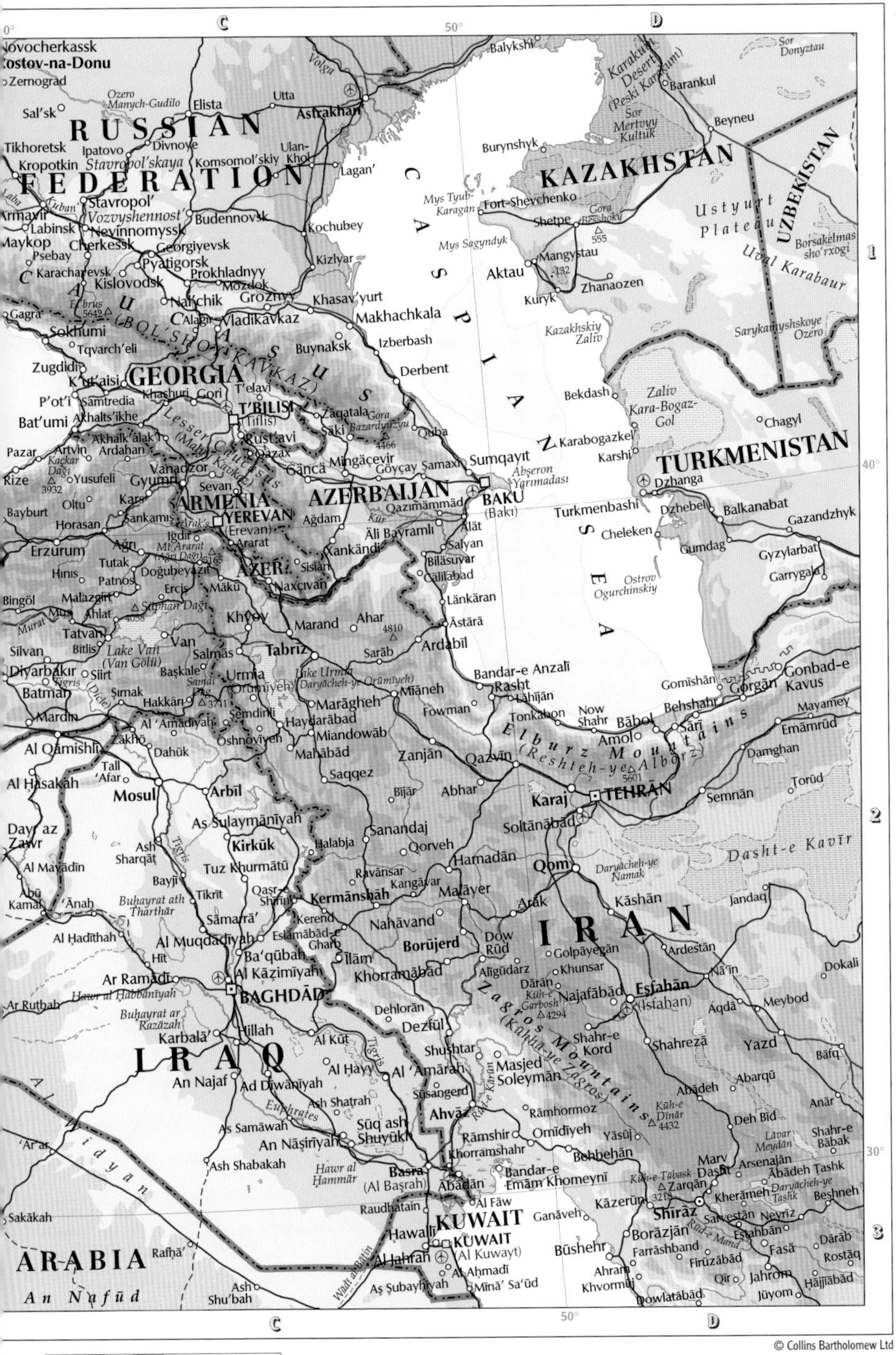

0   200   400 KILOMETRES

② 75° ① 0° 15° 90°

Arctic Circle

TÓRSHAVN
Faroe Islands (Denmark)
Shetland Islands

Norwegian Sea

Jan Mayen (Norway)

Greenland Sea

Svalbard (Norway)
Spitsbergen
LONGYEARBYEN

A R C T I C

Zemlya Aleksandry
Nagurskoye
Ostrov Rudol'fa
Ostrov Greem-Bell
Zemlya Frantsa-Iosifa
Ostrov Vil'cheka

Ostrov Ushakova

60°
0°

Trondheim
Kristiansund
Ålesund
Bergen
OSLO

N O R W A Y

S W E D E N

Lofoten
Tromsø
Hammerfest
North Cape (Nordkapp)
Narvik
Kirkenes
Murmansk
Kola Peninsula (Poluostrov Kola)

B A R E N T S   S E A

Bjørnøya (Norway)

Edgeøya
Nordaustlandet

Stolbovoy
Mezhdusharskiy
Ostrov Kolguyev
Kanin Nos

Novaya Zemlya

Mys Zhelaniya

Ostrova Arkticheskogo Instituta

(Kara Sea) (Karskoye More)

Ostrov Belyy
Yamal Peninsula (Poluostrov Yamal)
Krasino

Dikson

Gulf of Bothnia

F I N L A N D

Baltic Sea

STOCKHOLM
Göteborg

ESTONIA
TALLINN
LATVIA
RIGA
LITHUANIA
VILNIUS

Gulf of Finland
St Petersburg
White Sea (Beloye More)
Arkhangel'sk (Archangel)
Kandalaksha
Onega
Plesetsk
Kotlas
Syktyvkar
Ukhta
Pechora
Vorkuta
Nar'yan-Mar

Usinsk
Usa

Salekhard

U r a l   M o u n t a i n s   (Ural'skiy Khrebet)

Gydan Peninsula (Gydanskiy Poluostrov)

Dudinka
Noril'sk

Igarka

MINSK
BELARUS

MOSCOW
Smolensk
Kaluga
Tula
Orël
Bryansk
Yaroslavl'
Vladimir
Ryazan'
Kostroma
Vologda
Cherepovets
Rybinsk
Ivanovo
Nizhniy Novgorod
Kirov (Vyatka)
Perm'
Berezniki
Solikamsk
Syktyvkar

Berezovo

R U S S I A N

Novyy Urengoy
Nadym
Urengoy
Turukhansk

West Siberian Plain

Khanty-Mansiysk
Surgut
Nefteyugansk
Noyabr'sk
Langepas
Nizhnevartovsk
Strezhevoy

Ob'
Taz

KIEV
UKRAINE
Kharkiv
Kursk
Voronezh
Lipetsk
Tambov
Penza
Saransk
Ul'yanovsk
Tol'yatti
Samara
Kazan'
Cheboksary
Naberezhnyye Chelny
Izhevsk
Glazov
Sarapul
Ufa
Yekaterinburg (Sverdlovsk)
Tyumen'
Tobol'sk
Serov
Ivdel'
Nyagan'

Ishim

Omsk

Tara
Kolpashevo

Tomsk
Asino

Dnipropetrovs'k
Zaporizhzhya
Donets'k
Rostov-na-Donu
Volgograd (Volgograd)
Saratov
Balakovo
Magnitogorsk
Orenburg
Chelyabinsk
Kurgan
Petropavlovsk
Kokshetau
Kostanay
Rudnyy

Novosibirsk
Kemerovo
Iskitim
Kiselevsk
Barnaul
Biysk
Gorno-Altaysk

Sea of Azov
Sevastopol'
Black Sea
Sochi

GEORGIA
Bat'umi
TBILISI
ARMENIA
YEREVAN
AZERBAIJAN
BAKU (Baki)
Nagorno-Karabakh

Groznyy
Makhachkala
Astrakhan'

Caspian Lowland (Prikaspiyskaya Nizmennost')

Caspian Sea (Kaspiyskoye More)

Aktau

ASTANA (Akmola)
Karaganda
Temirtau
Pavlodar
Semipalatinsk
Ust'-
Kamenogorsk
Zyryanovsk
Ayagoz

Lake Zaysan

A l t a i   M o u n t a i n s

K A Z A K H S T A N

Aral Sea
Aral'sk

UZBEKISTAN
TURKMENISTAN
Türkmenbashi

Kyzylkum Desert

Kyzylorda
Betpak-Dala
Balkhash
Lake Balkhash (Ozero Balkhash)

Taldykorgan

C H I N A

Qazvin
Rasht
Ardabil
Tabriz
I R A N

60°

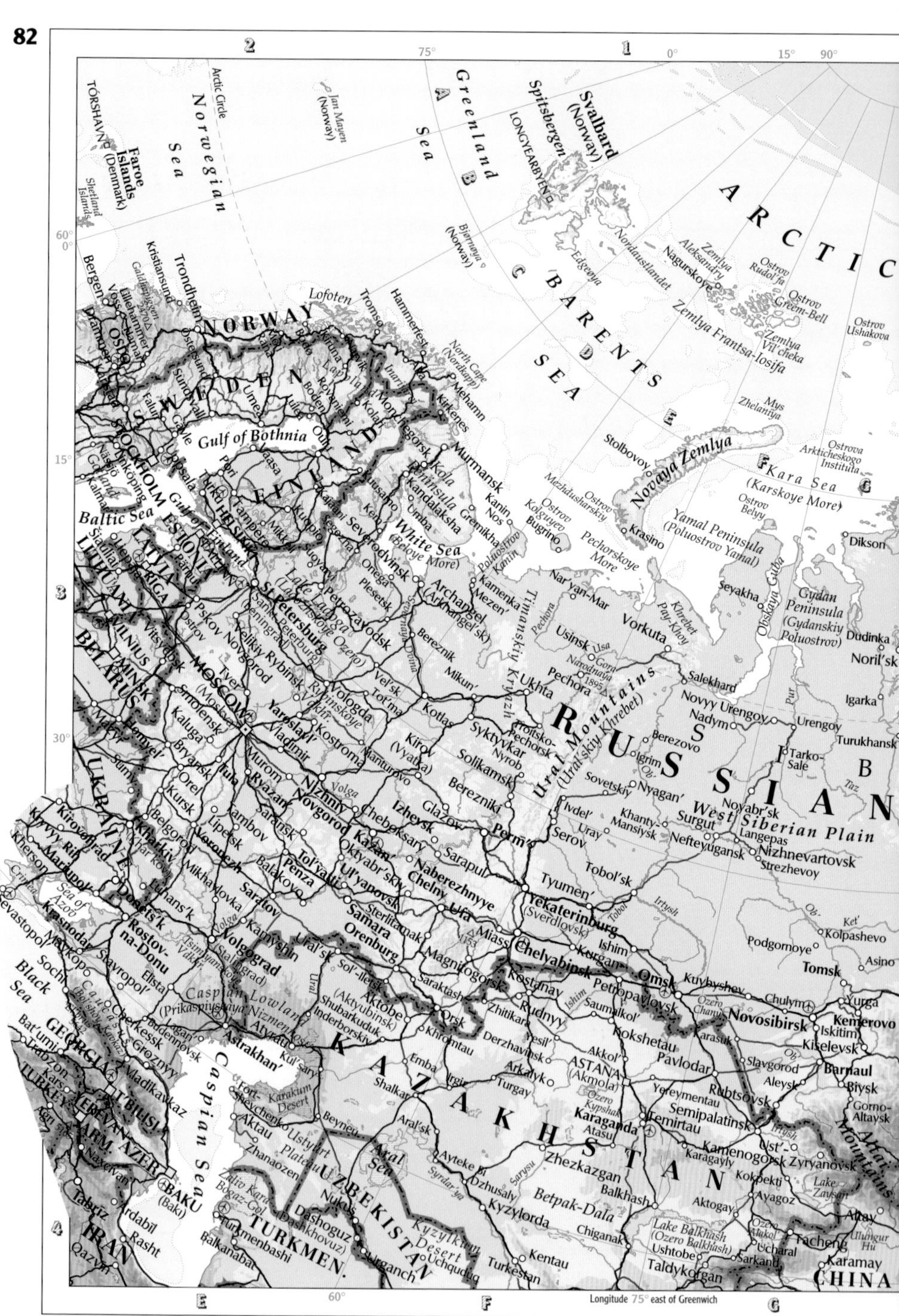

Conic Equidistant Projection

Longitude 75° east of Greenwich

1 : 30 000 000

MILES 0   200   400   600

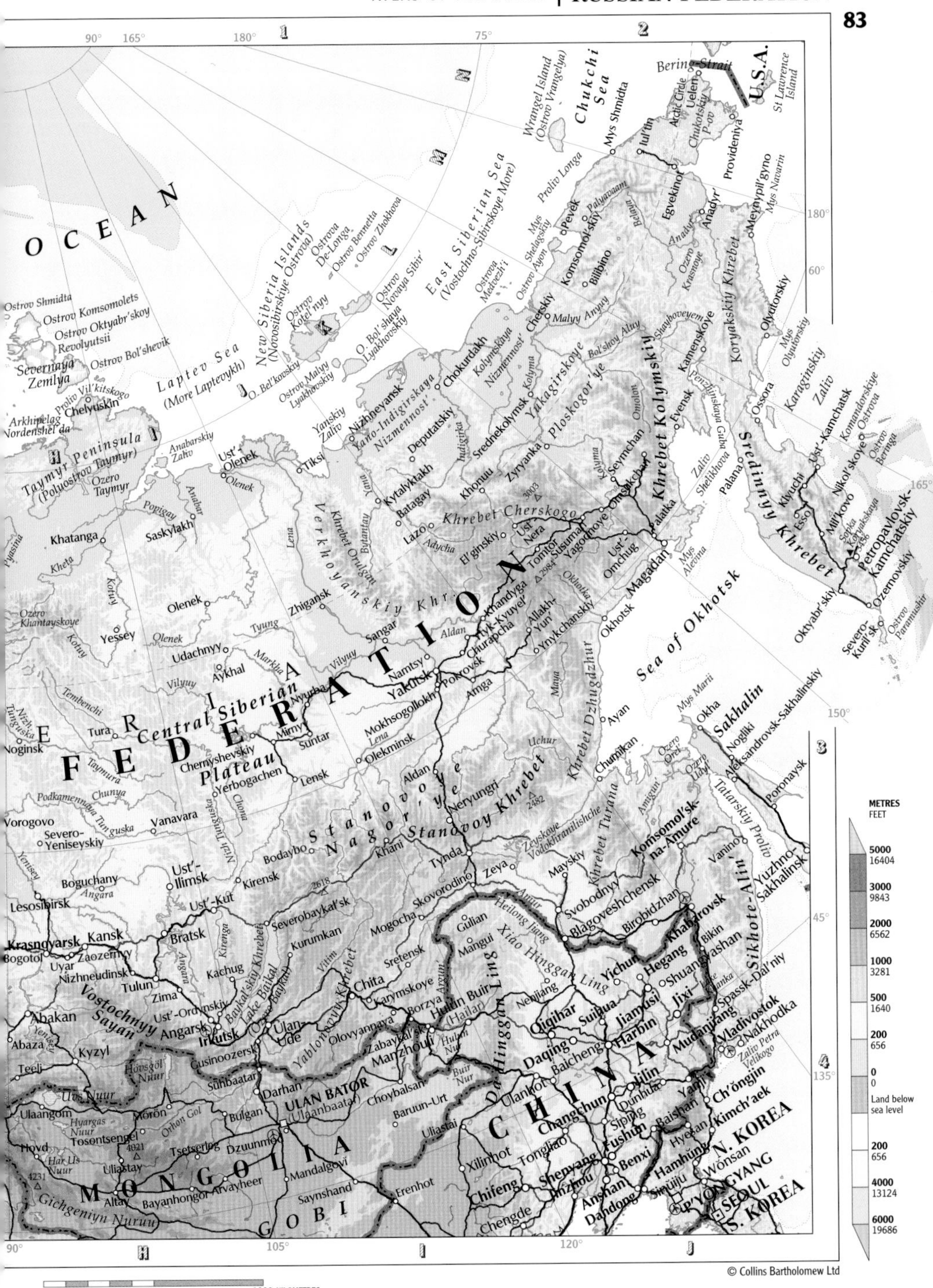

© Collins Bartholomew Ltd

90°
165°
180°
75°
1
2
3
4
OCEAN
Ostrov Shmidta
Ostrov Komsomolets
Ostrov Oktyabr'skoy
Revolyutsii
Ostrov Bol'shevik
Severnaya Zemlya
Proliv Vil'kitskogo
Chelyuskin
Arkhipelag Nordenshel'da
Taymyr Peninsula (Poluostrov Taymyr)
Ozero Taymyr
Anabarskiy Zaliv
Laptev Sea (More Laptevykh)
New Siberia Islands (Novosibirskiye Ostrova)
O. Bel'kovskiy
Ostrov Kotel'nyy
Ostrova De-Longa
Ostrov Bennetta
Ostrov Zhokhova
Ostrov Novaya Sibir'
O. Bol'shoy Lyakhovskiy
Ostrov Malyy Lyakhovskiy
East Siberian Sea (Vostochno-Sibirskoye More)
Ostrova Medvezh'i
Ostrov Ayon
Mys Shelagskiy
Proliv Longa
Wrangel Island (Ostrov Vrangelya)
Chukchi Sea
Mys Shmidta
Bering Strait
U.S.A.
St Lawrence Island
Arctic Circle
Uelen
Chukotskiy P-ov
Iul'tin
Provideniya
Egvekinot
Anadyr'
Meynypil'gyno
Mys Navarin
Pevek
Palyavaam
Komsomol'skiy
Bilibino
Ozero Krasnoye
Koryakskiy Khrebet
Olyutorskiy
Mys Olyutorskiy
Karaginskiy Zaliv
Ossora
Ust'-Kamchatsk
Komandorskiye Ostrova
Ostrov Beringa
Nikol'skoye
Klyuchi
Esso
Mil'kovo
Sopka Koryakskaya 3456
Petropavlovsk-Kamchatskiy
Sredinnyy Khrebet
Ust'-Khayryuzovo
Palana
Zaliv Shelikhova
Penzhinskaya Guba
Evensk
Kamenskoye
Cherskiy
Malyy Anyuy
Bol'shoy Anyuy
Kolymskaya Nizmennost'
Chokurdakh
Yukagirskoye Ploskogor'ye
Srednekolymsk
Zyryanka
Seymchan
Omsukchan
Khrebet Kolymskiy
Omolon
Kolyma
Palatka
Magadan
Mys Alevina
Ust'-Omchug
Yagodnoye
Susuman
Tomtor
Ust'-Nera
El'ginskiy
Khrebet Cherskogo
3003
2984
Khonuu
Indigirka
Deputatskiy
Yano-Indigirskaya Nizmennost'
Nizhneyansk
Yanskiy Zaliv
Tiksi
Ust'-Olenek
Olenek
Kytalyktakh
Batagay
Lazo
Adycha
Yana
Khrebet Orulgan
Verkhoyanskiy Khr.
Zhigansk
Lena
Sangar
Aldan
Khandyga
Tyk-Kyuyel'
Churapcha
Allakh-Yun'
Ynykchanskiy
Okhotsk
Sea of Okhotsk
Oktyabr'skiy
Ozernovskiy
Ostrov Paramushir
Severo-Kuril'sk
Popigay
Anabar
Saskylakh
Khatanga
Kheta
Kotuy
Pyasina
Ozero Khantayskoye
Yessey
Olenek
Udachnyy
Aykhal
Markha
Tyung
Vilyuy
Namtsy
Yakutsk
Pokrovsk
Amga
Nyurba
Mirnyy
Suntar
Mokhsogollokh
Olekminsk
Central Siberian Plateau
Tembenchi
Nizh. Tunguska
Tura
Noginsk
Taymura
Chernyshevskiy
Yerbogachen
Lensk
Chunya
Podkamennaya Tunguska
Vanavara
Chona
Vorogovo
Severo-Yeniseyskiy
Yenisey
RUSSIAN FEDERATION
Aldan
Neryungri
Stanovoye Nagor'ye
Stanovoy Khrebet
2482
Uchur
Maya
Khrebet Dzhugdzhur
Ayan
Chumikan
Ozero Orel'
Ozero Udyl'
Mys Marii
Okha
Sakhalin
Nogliki
Aleksandrovsk-Sakhalinskiy
Poronaysk
Tatarskiy Proliv
Yuzhno-Sakhalinsk
Vanino
Amguni
Khrebet Turana
Zeyskoye Vodokhranilishche
Komsomol'sk-na-Amure
Sikhote-Alin'
Tynda
Khani
Bodaybo
2618
Zeya
Mayskiy
Svobodnyy
Blagoveshchensk
Birobidzhan
Khabarovsk
Bikin
Skovorodino
Ust'-Ilimsk
Kirensk
Ust'-Kut
Boguchany
Angara
Lesosibirsk
Krasnoyarsk
Kansk
Zaozernyy
Bogotol
Uyar
Nizhneudinsk
Tulun
Bratsk
Zima
Kachug
Kirenga
Severobaykal'sk
Baykal'skiy Khrebet
Lake Baikal (Ozero Baykal)
Kurumkan
Vitim
Mogocha
Sretensk
Chita
Karymskoye
Yablonovyy Khrebet
Argun'
Amur
Heilong Jiang
Gulian
Mangui
Xiao Hinggan Ling
Da Hinggan Ling
Vostochnyy Sayan
Abakan
Abaza
Angarsk
Irkutsk
Ust'-Ordynskiy
Ulan-Ude
Olovyannaya
Borzya
Zabaykal'sk
Manzhouli
Hulun Buir (Hailar)
Hulun Nur
Buir Nur
Nenjiang
Qiqihar
Suihua
Yichun
Hegang
Jiamusi
Shuangyashan
Jixi
Spassk-Dal'niy
Ozero Khanka
Harbin
Mudanjiang
Vladivostok
Nakhodka
Zaliv Petra Velikogo
Daqing
Baicheng
Jilin
Dunhua
Yanji
Ch'ŏngjin
Kimch'aek
Changchun
Siping
Baishan
Hyesan
N. KOREA
Hamhŭng
Wŏnsan
P'YŎNGYANG
SEOUL
S. KOREA
Sinŭiju
Dandong
Anshan
Benxi
Fushun
Shenyang
Jinzhou
Tongliao
Chifeng
Chengde
Ulanhot
Xilinhot
CHINA
Uliastai
Erenhot
Kyzyl
Teeli
Hövsgöl Nuur
Gusinoozersk
Sühbaatar
Darhan
ULAN BATOR (Ulaanbaatar)
Choybalsan
Baruun-Urt
Uvs Nuur
Ulaangom
Mörön
Orhon Gol
Bulgan
Hyargas Nuur
Tosontsengel
4021
Hovd
Har Us Nuur
Uliastay
Tsetserleg
Dzuunmod
Mandalgovĭ
4231
Altay
Bayanhongor
Arvayheer
Saynshand
MONGOLIA
Gichgeniyn Nuruu
GOBI
90°
105°
120°
135°
150°
165°
180°
60°
45°
J
K
METRES
FEET
5000
16404
3000
9843
2000
6562
1000
3281
500
1640
200
656
0
0
Land below sea level
200
656
4000
13124
6000
19686
0
500
1000 KILOMETRES

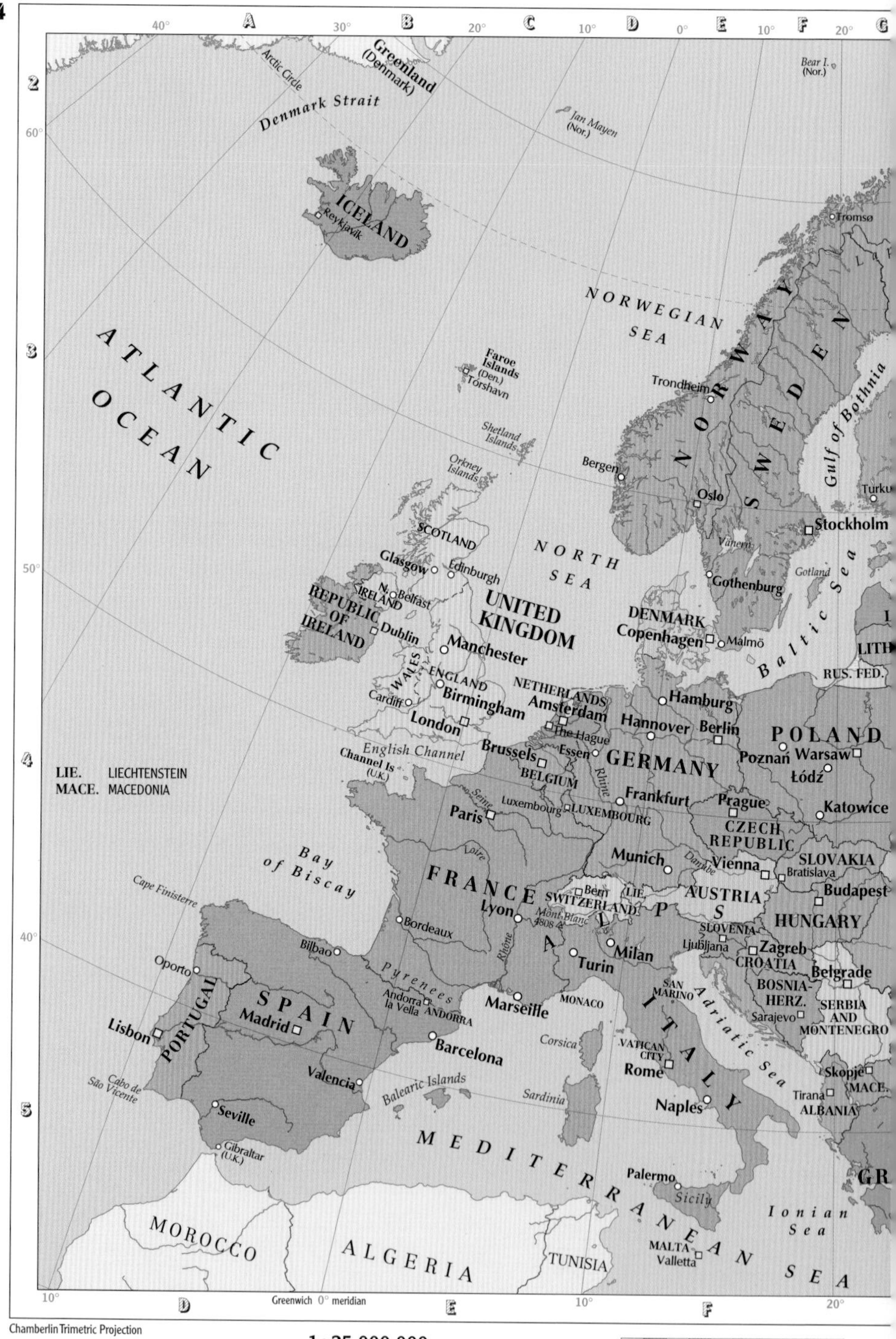

LIE. LIECHTENSTEIN
MACE. MACEDONIA

Chamberlin Trimetric Projection

1 : 25 000 000

MILES 0   250   500

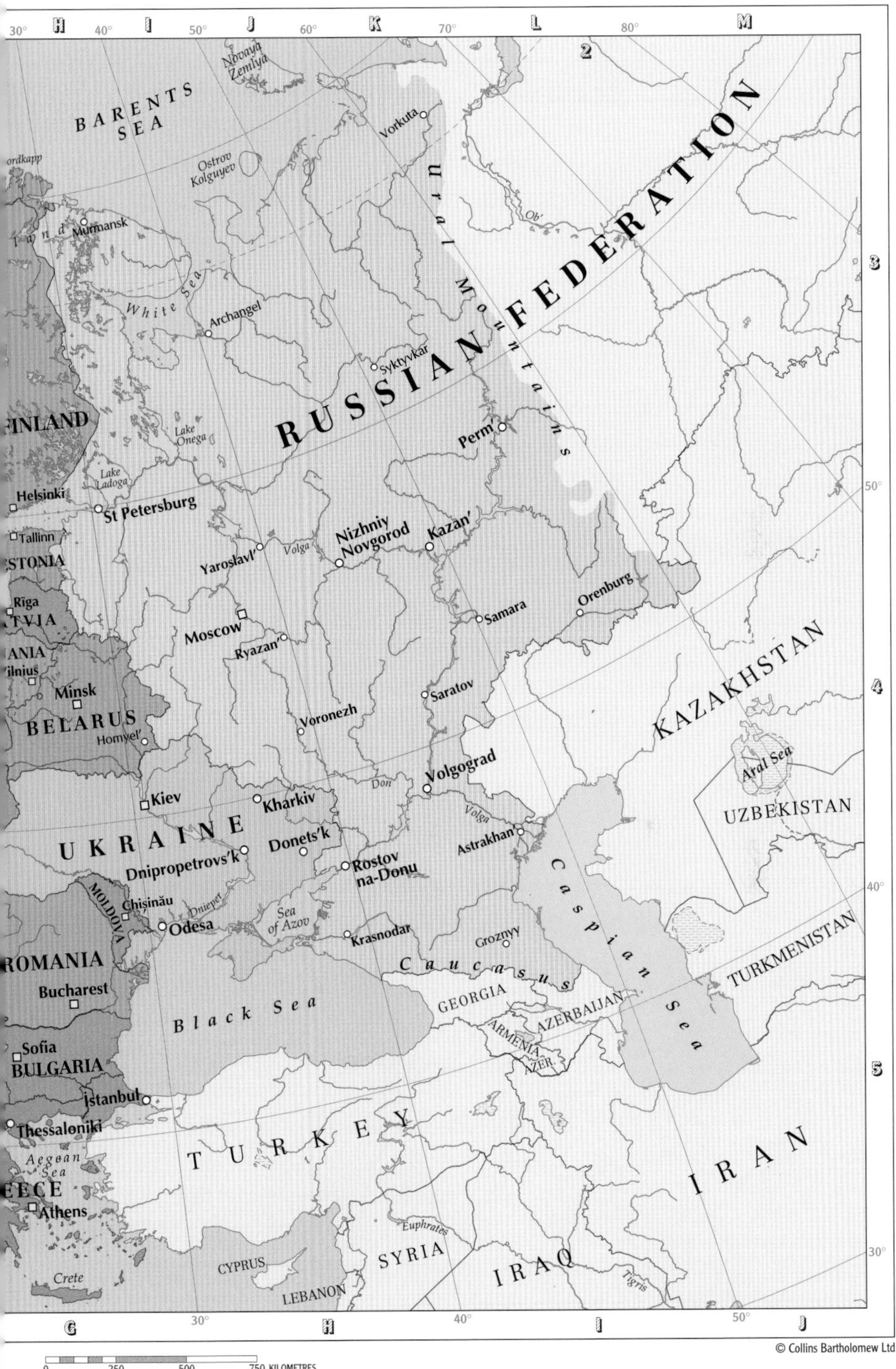

BARENTS SEA

Novaya Zemlya

RUSSIAN FEDERATION

Vorkuta

Ostrov Kolguyev

Nordkapp

Murmansk

l a n d

White Sea

Archangel

Ob'

U r a l   M o u n t a i n s

Syktyvkar

FINLAND

Lake Onega

Lake Ladoga

Perm'

Helsinki

St Petersburg

Tallinn

Nizhniy Novgorod

Kazan'

ESTONIA

Yaroslavl'

Volga

Riga

LATVIA

Samara

Orenburg

Moscow

Ryazan'

Vilnius

LITHUANIA

Saratov

Minsk

KAZAKHSTAN

BELARUS

Homyel'

Voronezh

Aral Sea

Kiev

Kharkiv

Volgograd

Don

UZBEKISTAN

UKRAINE

Dnipropetrovs'k

Donets'k

Volga

Astrakhan'

Chişinău

Rostov na-Donu

Odesa

Dnieper

Sea of Azov

Krasnodar

Grozny

MOLDOVA

Caspian Sea

TURKMENISTAN

ROMANIA

Black Sea

C a u c a s u s

Bucharest

GEORGIA

AZERBAIJAN

ARMENIA

Sofia

BULGARIA

AZER.

İstanbul

Thessaloniki

IRAN

Aegean Sea

GREECE

T U R K E Y

Athens

Crete

CYPRUS

SYRIA

Euphrates

IRAQ

LEBANON

Tigris

30° 40° 50° 60° 70° 80°

H I J K L M

2

3

50°

4

40°

5

30°

G H I J

30° 40° 50°

0 250 500 750 KILOMETRES

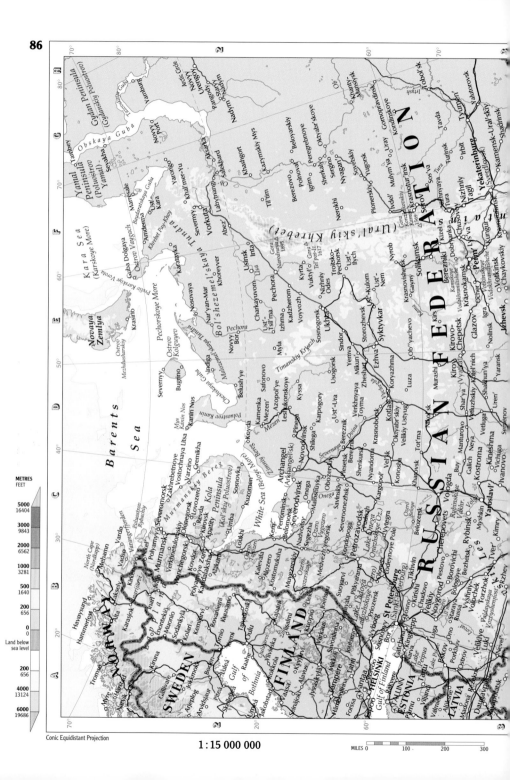

METRES
FEET

5000
16404

3000
9843

2000
6562

1000
3281

500
1640

200
656

0
0

Land below
sea level

200
656

4000
13124

6000
19686

Conic Equidistant Projection

1 : 15 000 000

MILES 0   100   200   300

RUSSIAN FEDERATION

NORWAY

SWEDEN

FINLAND

ESTONIA

LATVIA

Barents Sea

Kara Sea
(Karskoye More)

Novaya Zemlya

Pechorskoye More

White Sea
(Beloye More)

Gulf of Bothnia

Gulf of Finland

St Petersburg
(Sankt-Peterburg)

HELSINKI

TALLINN

Murmansk

Arctic Circle

Ural'skiy Khrebet)

Kola Peninsula
(Kol'skiy Poluostrov)

Yamal Peninsula
(Poluostrov Yamal)

Gydan Peninsula
(Gydanskiy Poluostrov)

Obskaya Guba

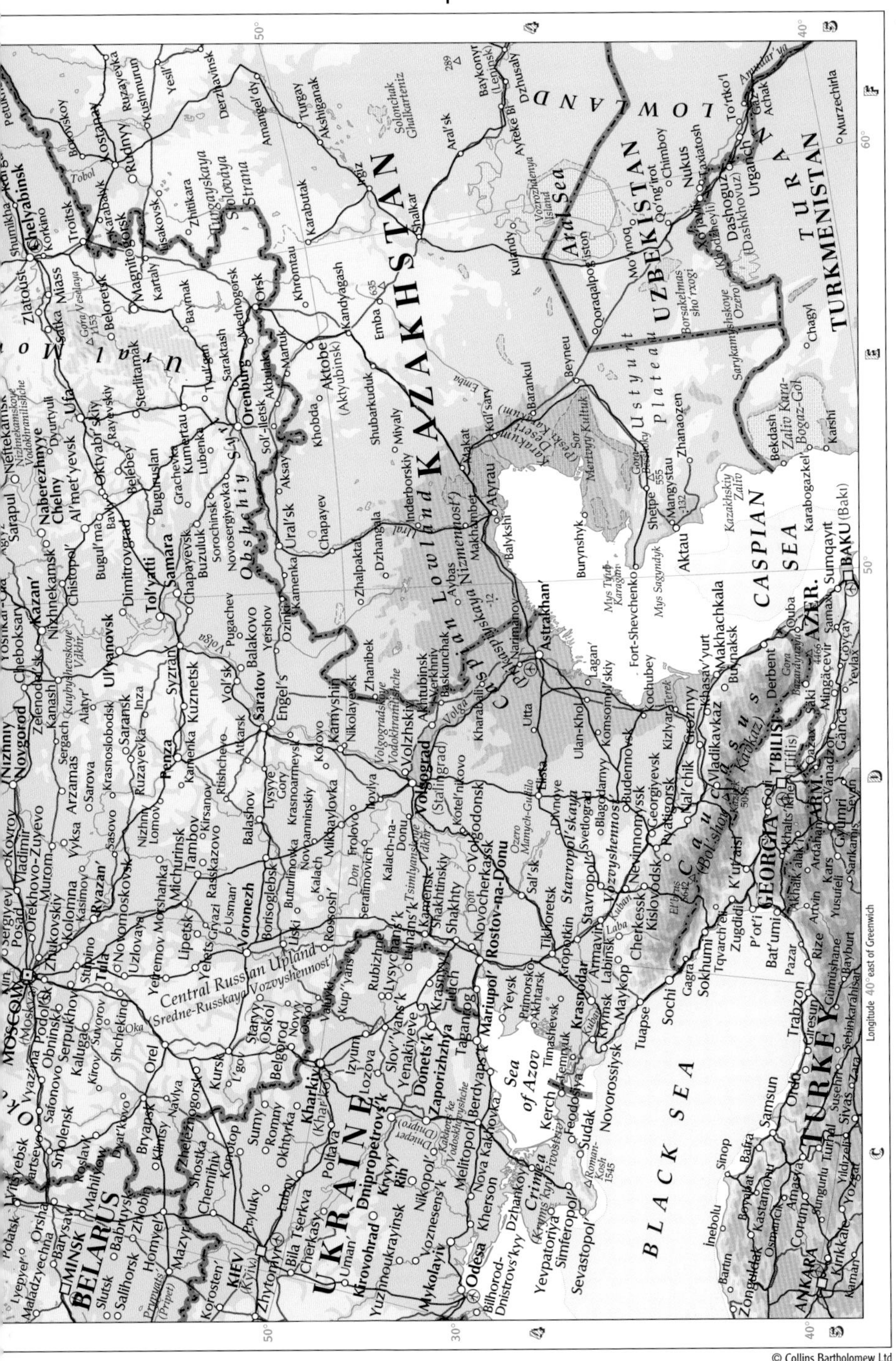
KAZAKHSTAN
UKRAINE
BELARUS
UZBEKISTAN
TURKMENISTAN
GEORGIA
ARM.
AZER.
TURKEY
BLACK SEA
CASPIAN SEA
Sea of Azov
Aral Sea
Caspian Lowland
Central Russian Upland
Obshchiy Syrt
Ustyurt plateau
Ural Mountains
Caucasus
TURAN LOWLAND
Longitude 40° east of Greenwich
0
250
500 KILOMETRES

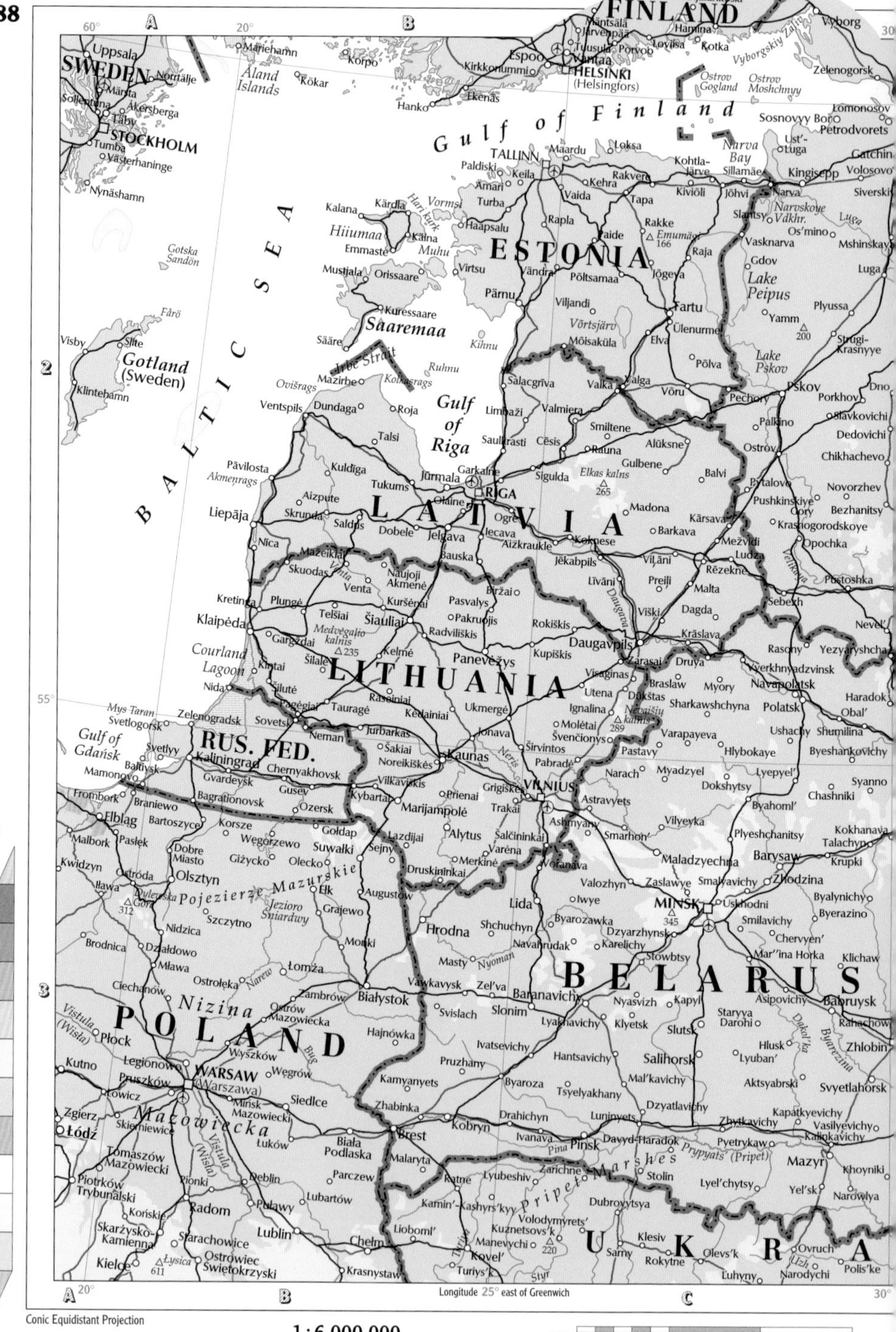

FINLAND

SWEDEN

Uppsala
Norrtälje
Märsta
Åkersberga
Sollentuna
Täby
STOCKHOLM
Tumba
Västerhaninge
Nynäshamn

Mariehamn
Korpo
Åland Islands
Rökär

Kirkkonummi
Ekenäs
Hanko

Kouvola
Anjalankoski
Hamina
Mäntsälä
Järvenpää
Tuusula Porvoo Loviisa Kotka
Espoo Vantaa
HELSINKI
(Helsingfors)

Vyborgskiy Zaliv
Vyborg
Zelenogorsk

Gulf of Finland

Sosnovyy Bor
Lomonosov
Petrodvorets
Gatchin
Ostrov Gogland
Ostrov Moshchnyy

TALLINN
Paldiski
Keila
Kehra
Maardu
Loksa
Amari
Vaida
Rakvere
Kohtla-Järve
Sillamäe
Kingisepp Volosovo
Narva
Siverski

ESTONIA

Kärdla
Hiiumaa
Emmaste
Mustjala
Orissaare
Kuressaare
Saaremaa
Sääre

Kalana
Vormsi
Haapsalu
Virtsu
Kihnu
Ruhnu

Turba
Rapla
Türi
Paide
Põltsamaa
Viljandi
Pärnu
Võrtsjärv
Jändra

Kehra
Tapa
Rakke
Emumägi 166
Raja
Jõgeva
Elva
Põltsamaa
Tartu
Ülenurme
Mõisaküla
Põlva

Vaskanarva
Os'mino
Gdov
Plyussa
Yamm
Strugi-Krasnyye
Lake Peipus
Pskov
Pechory
Palkino
Ostrov

Luga
Mshinskaya
Luga
200

BALTIC SEA

Gotska Sandön

Visby
Slite
Klintehamn
Gotland (Sweden)
Fårö

Salacgrīva
Limbaži
Valmiera
Cēsis
Smiltene
Rauna
Gulbene
Balvi

Valka
Valga
Alūksne

Porkhov
Slavkovichi
Dedovichi
Chikhachevo

Ovīšrags
Kolkasrags
Mazirbe
Roja
Dundaga
Ventspils
Talsi

Gulf of Riga

Saulkrasti

Bytalov
Pushkinskiye Gory
Krasnogorodskoye
Ostrov
Novorzhev
Bezhanitsy
Opochka

Pāvilosta
Akmeņrags
Kuldīga
Aizpute
Tukums
Jūrmala
Olaine
RIGA
Sigulda
Madona
Kārsava
Rēzekne

Pustoshka
Sebezh
Nevel'

LATVIA

Liepāja
Skrunda
Saldus
Dobele
Jelgava
Iecava
Bauska
Aizkraukle
Jēkabpils
Viļāni
Preiļi
Malta
Krāslava
Dagda

Rasony
Verkhnyadzvinsk
Yezyaryshcha
Haradok

Nīca
Mažeikiai
Naujoji Akmenė
Venta
Pasvalys
Biržai
Rokiškis
Līvāni
Viški
Daugavpils
Druya
Braslaw
Myory
Navapolatsk
Polatsk
Obal'
Ushachy
Shumilina

Kretinga
Plungė
Telšiai
Šiauliai
Pakruojis
Radviliškis
Kupiškis
Visaginas
Zarasai
Dūkštas
Sharkawshchyna

Klaipėda
Gargždai
Medvėgalio kalnis △235
Šilalė
Kelmė
Panevėžys
Utena
Ignalina
Nevaišių kalnas 289
Pastavy
Varapayeva
Hlybokaye
Byesharkovichy
Sharkawshchyna
Sharkawshchyna
Syanno
Chashniki

Courland Lagoon
Nida
Šilutė
Rusnė
Taurage
Kėdainiai
Ukmergė
Molėtai
Švenčionys
Narach
Myadzyel
Lyepyel'
Byahoml'
Kokhanava
Talachyn
Krupki

LITHUANIA

Mys Taran
Svetlogorsk
Zelenogradsk

Gulf of Gdansk

Svetlyy
Baltiysk
Mamonovo
Frombork
Braniewo

Sovetsk
Neman
Jurbarkas
Šakiai
Vilkaviškis
Kaunas
Jonava
Širvintos
Grigiškės
Trakai
VILNIUS
Ašmyany
Astravyets
Vilyeyka
Plyeshchanitsy
Maladzyechna
Smalyavichy
Barysaw
Zhodzina
Byalynichy
Byerazino

RUS. FED.
Kaliningrad
Gvardeysk
Chernyakhovsk
Gusev
Ozersk

Bagrationovsk
Bartoszyce
Korsze
Gołdap
Wegorzewo
Węgorzewo
Suwałki
Sejny
Marijampolė
Prienai
Lazdijai
Alytus
Varėna
Salčininkai
Smarhon'
Valozhyn
Ivyė
Dzyarzhynsk
MINSK
Ushodni
Smilavichy
Chervyen'

Elbląg
Malbork
Pasłęk
Dobre Miasto
Olsztyn

Ełk
Olecko
Druskininkai
Merkinė
Lida
Byarozawka
Navahrudak
Karelichy

345
Klichaw
Mar''ina Horka

Kwidzyn
Iława
Ostróda
Dylewska Góra 312
Pojezierze Mazurskie
Nidzica
Jezioro Śniardwy
Grajewo
Mońki
Hrodna
Shchuchyn
Masty
Navahrudak
Stowbtsy
Vawkavysk
Zel'va
Baranavichy
Nyasvizh
Kapyl
Asipovichy
Babruysk

Brodnica
Działdowo
Mława
Ciechanów
Łomża
Nareew
Ostrołęka
Zambrów
Wyszków
Białystok
Hajnówka
Svisloch
Slonim
Lyakhavichy
Klyetsk
Slutsk
Staryya Darohi
Hlusk
Svyetlahorsk

POLAND

Nizina Mazowiecka

Kutno
Legionowo
Płock
WARSAW (Warszawa)
Żyrardów
Skierniewice
Łowicz
Żgierz
Łódź

Wyszków
Pruszków
Węgrów
Siedlce
Mińsk Mazowiecki
Łuków
Parczew
Lubartów

Kamyanyets
Pruzhany
Byaroza
Tsyelyakhany
Mal'kavichy
Hantsavichy
Salihorsk
Lyuban'
Aktsyabrski
Zhytkavichy

BELARUS

Ivatsevichy
Kobryn
Drahichyn
Ivanava
Pinsk
Dayd-Harodak
Luninyets
Zhabinka
Brest
Biała Podlaska
Malaryta
Pinsk
Stolin
Lyel'chytsy
Dubrovytsya

Tomaszów Mazowiecki
Piotrków Trybunalski
Koriskiai
Skarżysko-Kamienna
Starachowice
Kielce
Łysica 611
Ostrowiec Świętokrzyski
Radom
Puławy
Lublin
Chełm
Krasnystaw

Zharichne
Lyubeshiv
Kamin'-Kashyrs'kyy
Kuznetsov'k 220
Manevychi
Kovel'
Turiys'k

Pripyats' (Pripet)
Pripet Marshes
Pripyat'
Volodymyrets'
Sarny
Rokytne
Luhyny
Narodychi

Mazyr
Khoyniki
Yel'sk
Narowlya
Ovruch
Polis'ke

UKRA

METRES FEET

5000 16404
3000 9843
2000 6562
1000 3281
500 1640
200 656
0 0
Land below sea level
200 656
4000 13124
6000 19686

Conic Equidistant Projection

1:6 000 000

Longitude 25° east of Greenwich

MILES 0   50   100   150

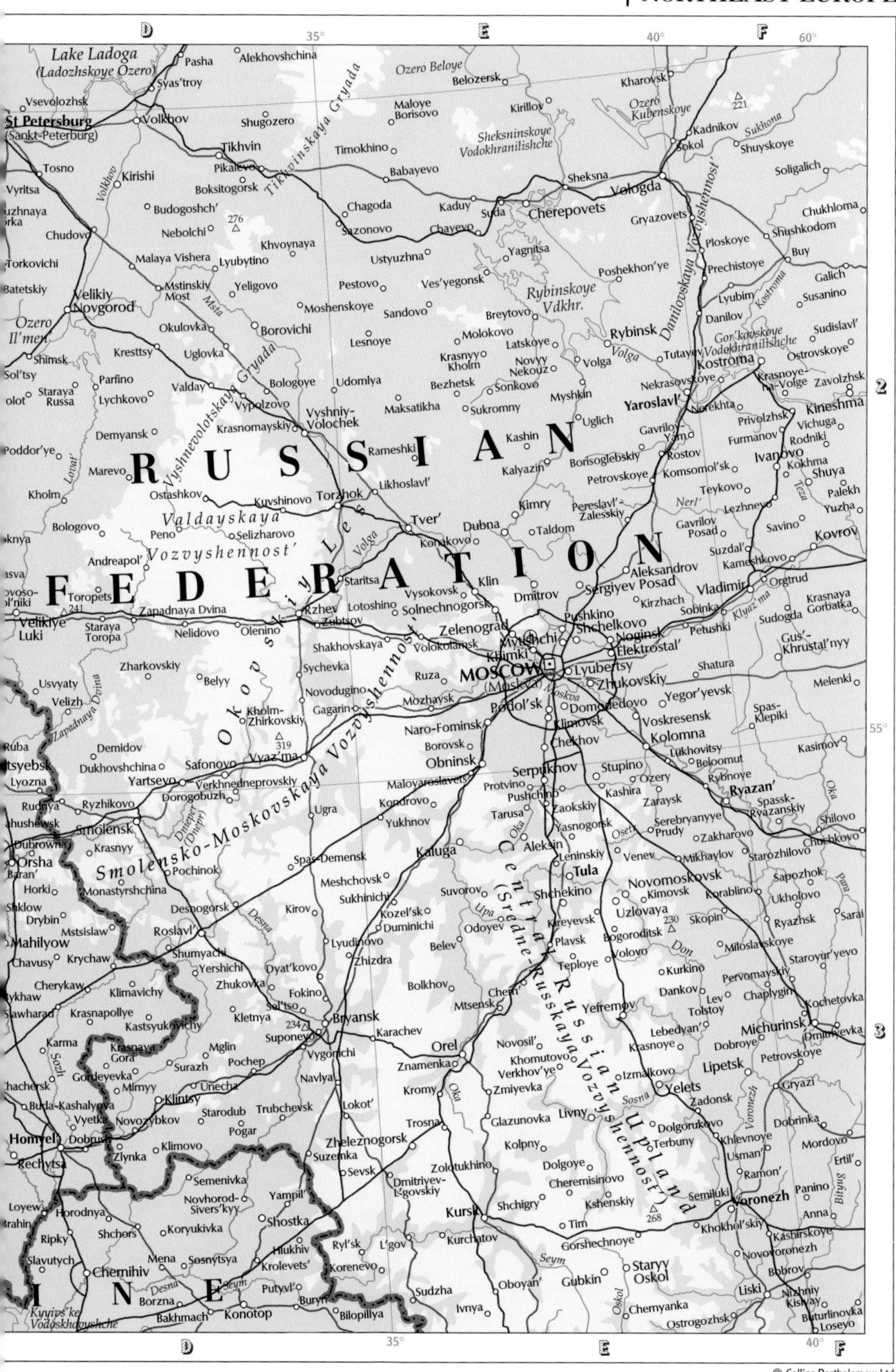
D
35°
E
40°
F
60°
Lake Ladoga
(Ladozhskoye Ozero)
Pasha
Alekhovshchina
Syas'troy
Ozero Beloye
Belozersk
Kharovsk
Vsevolozhsk
Maloye Borisovo
Kirillov
221
St Petersburg
(Sankt-Peterburg)
Volkhov
Shugozero
Ozero Kubenskoye
Kadnikov
Sukhona
Sheksninskoye Vodokhranilishche
Sokol
Shuyskoye
Tikhvin
Timokhino
Tikhvinskaya Gryada
Tosno
Pikalevo
Babayevo
Soligalich
Kirishi
Volkhov
Boksitogorsk
Sheksna
Vologda
Vyritsa
Budogoshch'
Chagoda
Kaduy
Suda
Cherepovets
Gryazovets
Chukhloma
276
Sazonovo
Chayevo
Shushkodom
Chudovo
Nebolchi
Khvoynaya
Ploskoye
Yagnitsa
Buy
Malaya Vishera
Lyubytino
Ustyuzhna
Torkovichi
Poshekhon'ye
Prechistoye
Danilovskaya Vozvyshennost'
Galich
Batetskiy
Mstinskiy Most
Yeligovo
Pestovo
Ves'yegonsk
Rybinskoye Vdkhr.
Susanino
Velikiy Novgorod
Moshenskoye
Sandovo
Breytovo
Lyubim
Kostroma
Msta
Danilov
Ozero Il'men'
Okulovka
Borovichi
Molokovo
Rybinsk
Sudislavl'
Lesnoye
Gor'kovskoye Vodokhranilishche
Kresttsy
Uglovka
Krasnyy Kholm
Latskoye
Volga
Tutayev
Ostrovskoye
Shimsk
Novyy Nekouz
Volga
Kostroma
Sol'tsy
Parfino
Bologoye
Udomlya
Bezhetsk
Sonkovo
Nekrasovskoye
Krasnoye-na-Volge
Zavolzhsk
Staraya Russa
Valday
Lychkovo
Vypolzovo
Maksatikha
Myshkin
Yaroslavl'
Nerekhta
Kineshma
Vyshniy-Volochek
Sukromny
Privolzhsk
Vichuga
Uglich
Krasnomayskiy
Gavrilov-Yam
Furmanov
Rodniki
Demyansk
Kashin
Rameshki
Rostov
Ivanovo
Poddor'ye
Borisoglebskiy
Kokhma
Marevo
RUSSIAN FEDERATION
Kalyazin
Komsomol'sk
Shuya
Lovat'
Likhoslavl'
Petrovskoye
Teykovo
Palekh
Kholm
Ostashkov
Kuvshinovo
Torzhok
Kimry
Pereslavl'-Zalesskiy
Nerl'
Lezhnevo
Teza
Yuzha
Valdayskaya Vozvyshennost'
Tver'
Dubna
Taldom
Gavrilov Posad
Savino
Bologovo
Peno
Selizharovo
Konakovo
Suzdal'
Kovrov
Volga
Andreapol'
Kameshkovo
Aleksandrov
Staritsa
Vysokovsk
Klin
Dmitrov
Sergiyev Posad
Vladimir
Orgtrud
Toropets
241
Lotoshino
Solnechnogorsk
Kirzhach
Krasnaya Gorbatka
Zapadnaya Dvina
Rzhev
Pushkino
Sobinka
Klyaz'ma
Velikiye Luki
Staraya Toropa
Nelidovo
Olenino
Zubtsov
Zelenograd
Shchelkovo
Sudogda
Petushki
Mytishchi
Noginsk
Gus'-Khrustal'nyy
Shakhovskaya
Volokolamsk
Khimki
Elektrostal'
Zharkovskiy
Sychevka
MOSCOW
(Moskva)
Lyubertsy
Shatura
Ruza
Melenki
Usvyaty
Belyy
Novodugino
Zhukovskiy
Moskva
Yegor'yevsk
Velizh
Zapadnaya Dvina
Gagarin
Mozhaysk
Podol'sk
Domodedovo
Spas-Klepiki
Kholm-Zhirkovskiy
Voskresensk
Okovskiy Les
Naro-Fominsk
Klimovsk
Kolomna
55°
Demidov
319
Borovsk
Chekhov
Lukhovitsy
Kasimov
Vyaz'ma
Obninsk
Beloomut
Dukhovshchina
Safonovo
Serpukhov
Stupino
Rybnoye
Lyozna
Yartsevo
Verkhnedneprovskiy
Maloyaroslavets
Protvino
Ozery
Ryazan'
Oka
Pushchino
Kashira
Zaraysk
Spassk-Ryazanskiy
Rudnya
Ryzhikovo
Dorogobuzh
Kondrovo
Tarusa
Zaokskiy
Smolensk
Ugra
Yukhnov
Dnieper (Dnepr)
Oka
Yasnogorsk
Serebryanyye Prudy
Shilovo
Dubrowna
Krasnyy
Smolensko-Moskovskaya Vozvyshennost'
Aleksin
Osetr
Zakharovo
Chuchkovo
Orsha
Spas-Demensk
Kaluga
Leninskiy
Venev
Mikhaylov
Starozhilovo
Baran'
Pochinok
Meshchovsk
Tula
Novomoskovsk
Sapozhok
Horki
Monastyrshchina
Suvorov
Shchekino
Kimovsk
Korablino
Ukholovo
Para
Sukhinichi
Uzlovaya
Sarai
Shklow
Desnogorsk
Kirov
Kozel'sk
Upa
Kireyevsk
230
Skopin
Drybin
Desna
Duminichi
Odoyev
Central Russian Upland
(Sredne-Russkaya Vozvyshennost')
Bogoroditsk
Ryazhsk
Mstsislaw
Roslavl'
Lyudinovo
Plavsk
Mahilyow
Belev
Volovo
Don
Miloslavskoye
Chavusy
Krychaw
Shumyachi
Zhizdra
Teploye
Staroyur'yevo
Yershichi
Dyat'kovo
Kurkino
Pervomayskiy
Cherykaw
Klimavichy
Zhukovka
Bolkhov
Chern'
Dankov
Lev Tolstoy
Chaplygin
Krasnapollye
Fokino
Mtsensk
Yefremov
Slawharad
Kochetovka
Kletnya
Sel'tso
Kastsyukovichy
Bryansk
Lebedyan'
Michurinsk
Karma
234
Karachev
Dmitriyevka
Krasnaya Gora
Mglin
Suponevo
Orel
Novosil'
Krasnoye
Dobroye
Sozh
Surazh
Pochep
Vygonichi
Znamenka
Khomutovo
Petrovskoye
Gordeyevka
Verkhov'ye
Izmalkovo
Lipetsk
Mirnyy
Unecha
Navlya
Kromy
Oka
Zmiyevka
Yelets
Gryazi
Buda-Kashalyova
Klintsy
Trubchevsk
Sosna
Zadonsk
Vyetka
Novozybkov
Starodub
Lokot'
Glazunovka
Livny
Voronezh
Dobrinka
Homyel'
Dobrush
Pogar
Trosna
Dolgorukovo
Khlevnoye
Zlynka
Klimovo
Zheleznogorsk
Kolpny
Terbuny
Mordovo
Rechytsa
Suzemka
Usman'
Sevsk
Zolotukhino
Dolgoye
Ertil'
Semenivka
Ramon'
Dmitriyev-L'govskiy
Cheremisinovo
Novhorod-Sivers'kyy
Yampil'
Panino
Loyew
Horodnya
Kursk
Shchigry
Kshenskiy
Semiluki
Voronezh
Bityug
Anna
Brahin
Shostka
268
Koryukivka
Tim
Khokhol'skiy
Kashirskoye
Ripky
Shchors
Hlukhiv
Ryl'sk
L'gov
Kurchatov
Gorshechnoye
Slavutych
Mena
Sosnytsya
Krolevets'
Seym
Novovoronezh
Chernihiv
Seym
Korenevo
Staryy Oskol
Desna
Putyvl'
Oboyan'
Gubkin
Bobrov
Borzna
Buryn'
Sudzha
Liski
Nizhniy Kislyay
Kyyivs'ke Vodoskhovyshche
Bakhmach
Konotop
Bilopillya
Ivnya
Oskol
Chernyanka
Ostrogozhsk
Buturlinovka
Loseyevo
35°
40°
2
3
0
100
200 KILOMETRES

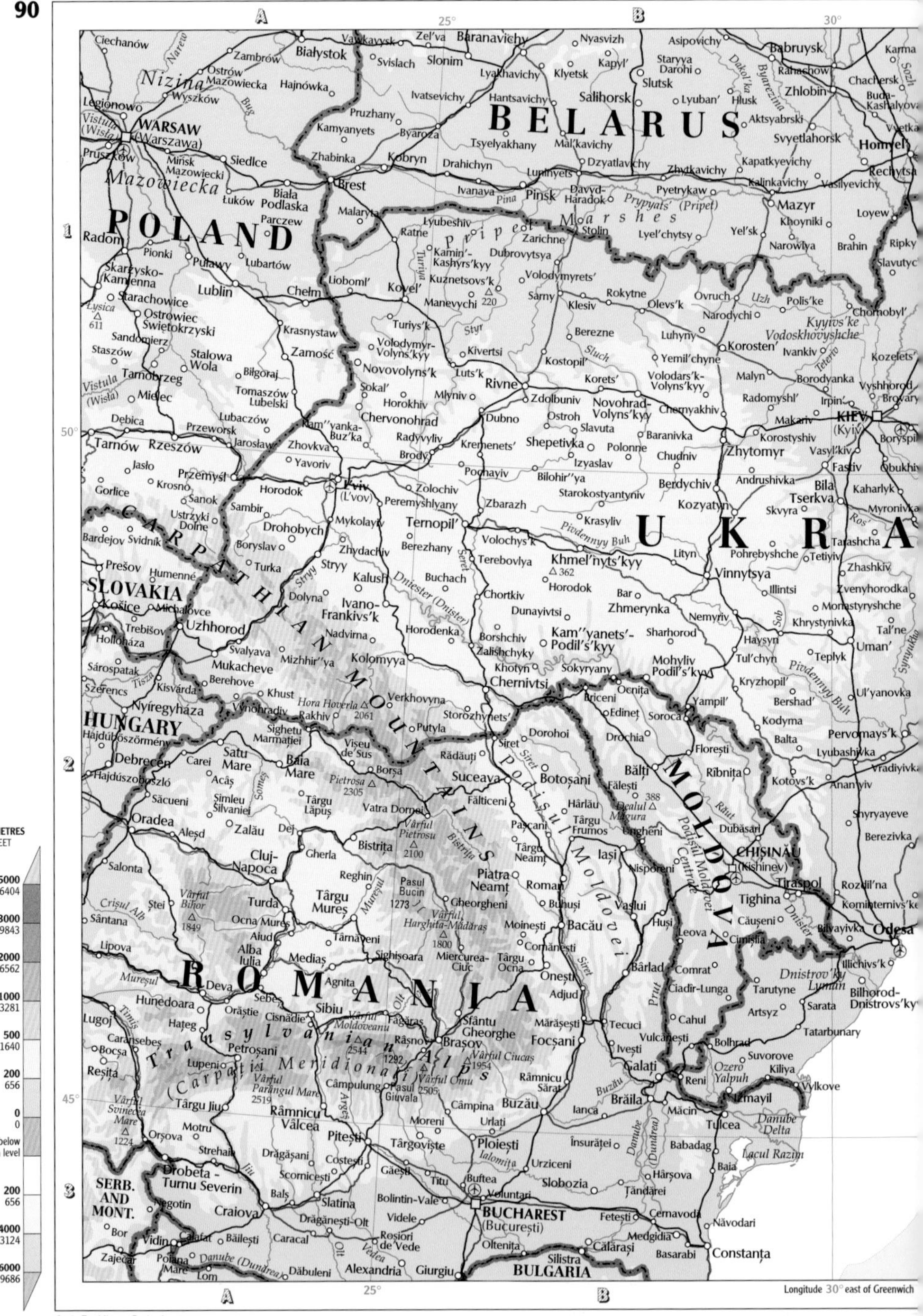

1 : 6 000 000

MILES 0   50   100   150

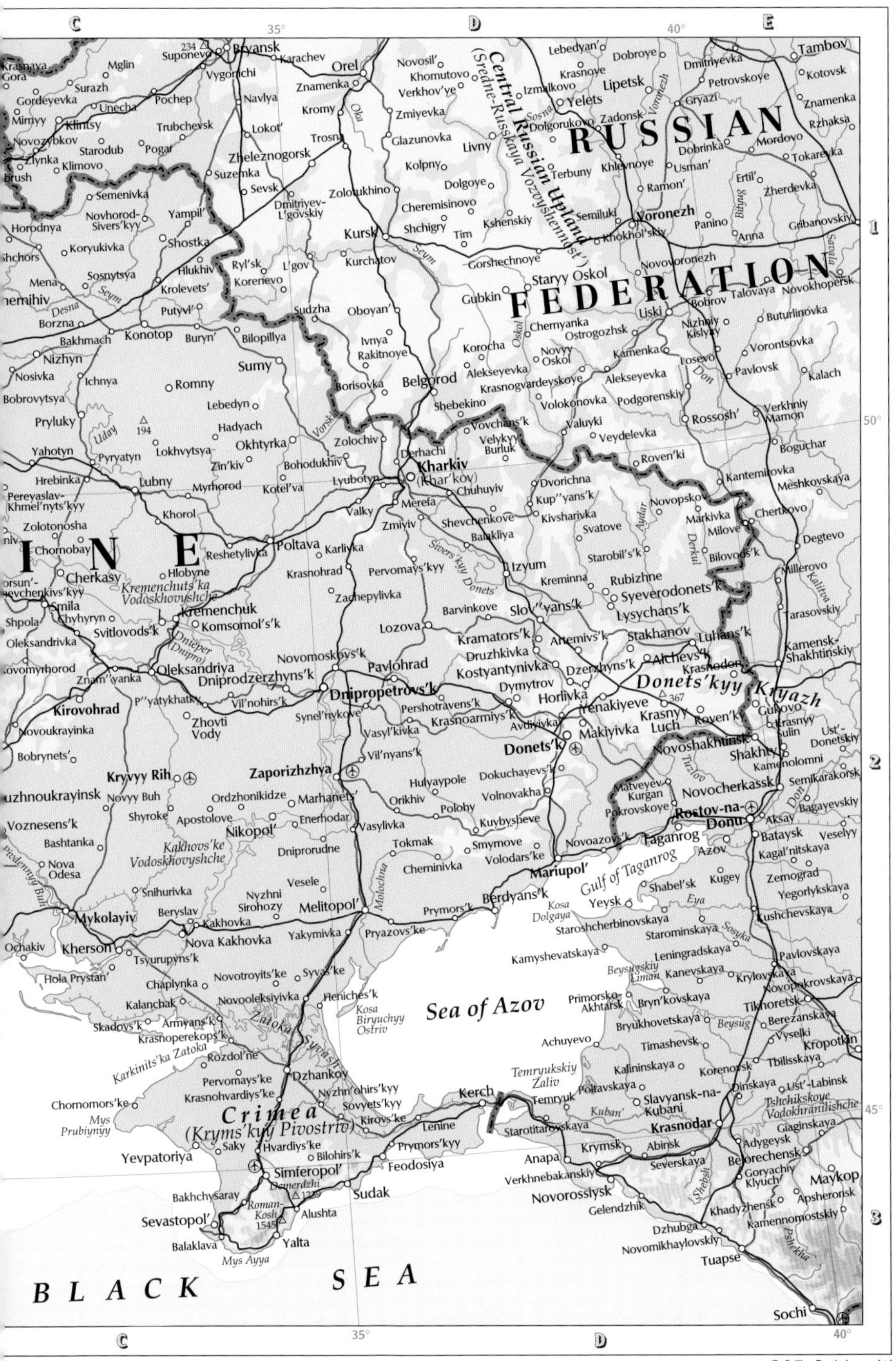
RUSSIAN FEDERATION
Central Russian Upland (Sredne-Russkaya Vozvyshennost')
Sea of Azov
BLACK SEA
Crimea (Kryms'kyy Pivostriv)
Donets'kyy Kryazh
Gulf of Taganrog
Kharkiv (Khar'kov)
Dnipropetrovs'k
Zaporizhzhya
Donets'k
Rostov-na-Donu
Voronezh
Kursk
Belgorod
Sumy
Poltava
Simferopol'
Sevastopol'
Mariupol'
Luhans'k
Krasnodar
Kremenchuk
Mykolayiv
Kherson
Kirovohrad
Kryvyy Rih
Melitopol'
Kerch
Novorossiysk
Taganrog
0 100 200 KILOMETRES

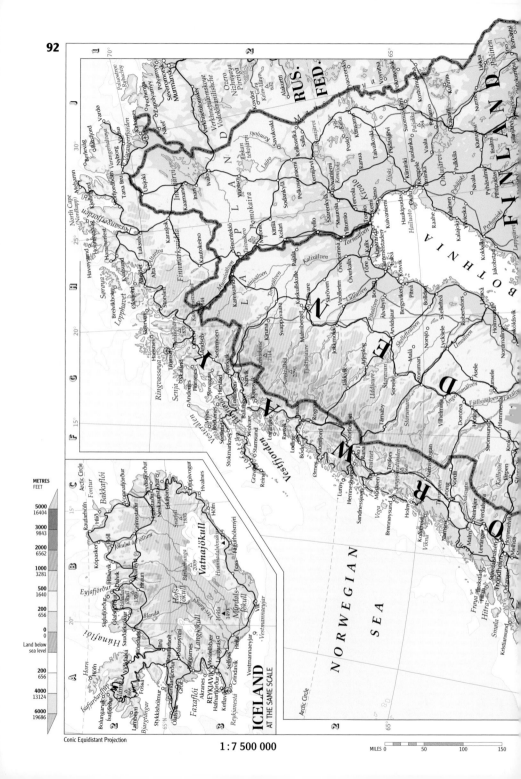

RUS. FED.

FINLAND

GULF OF BOTHNIA

VINHLOU

North Cape
(Nordkapp)

S W E D E N

N O R W A Y

NORWEGIAN SEA

Arctic Circle

METRES
FEET

5000
16404

3000
9843

2000
6562

1000
3281

500
1640

200
656

0
0

Land below
sea level

200
656

4000
13124

6000
19686

ICELAND
AT THE SAME SCALE

Bakkaflói

Vatnajökull

Eyjafjörður

Hofs-
jökull

Langjökull

Mýrdals-
jökull

Hunaflói

Faxaflói

REYKJAVIK

Húnaflói

Conic Equidistant Projection

1 : 7 500 000

MILES 0   50   100   150

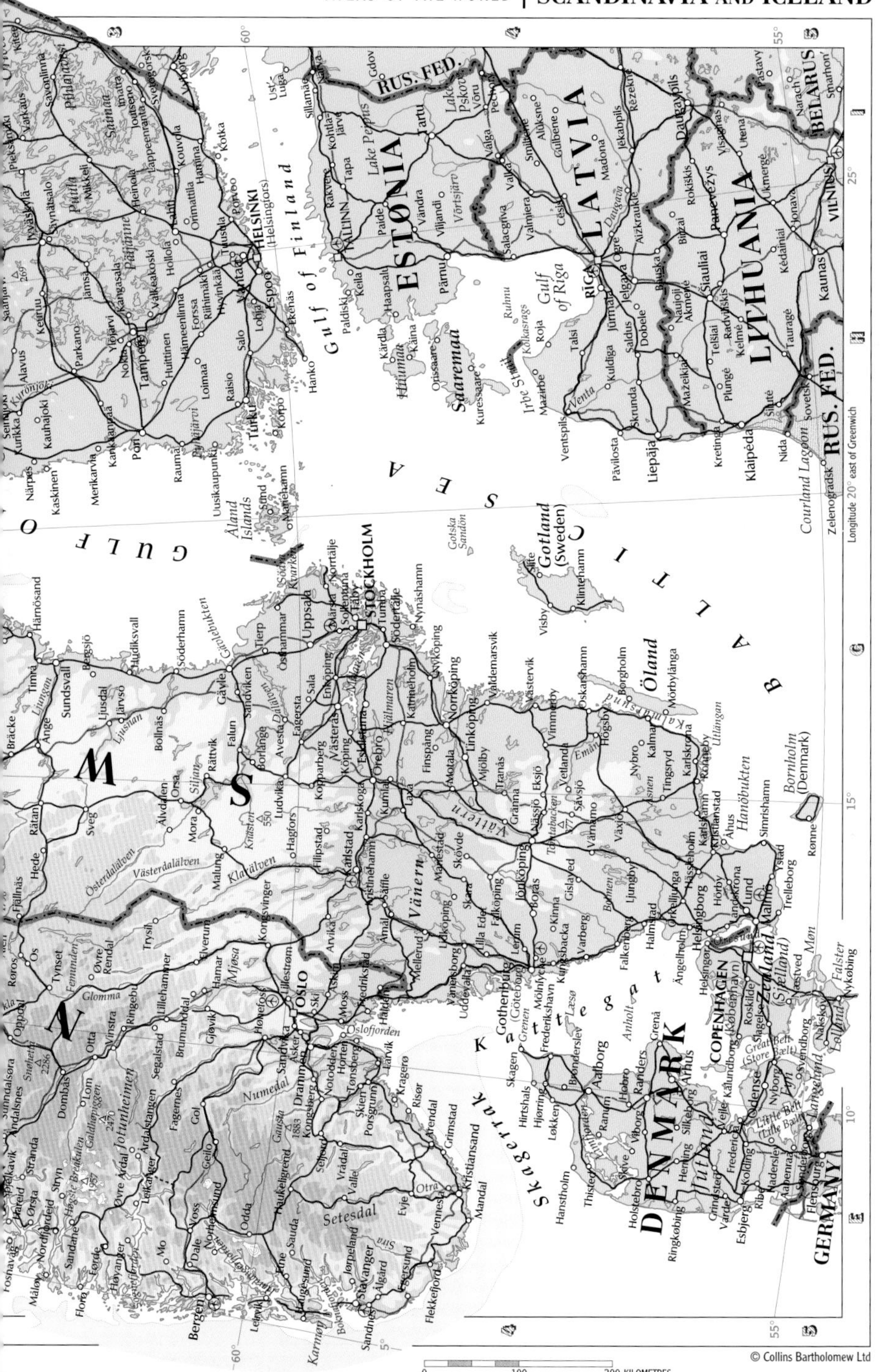

0   100   200 KILOMETRES

© Collins Bartholomew Ltd

NORWAY
SWEDEN
DENMARK
ESTONIA
LATVIA
LITHUANIA
RUS. FED.
BELARUS
GERMANY
GULF OF BOTHNIA
BALTIC SEA
Gulf of Finland
Gulf of Riga
Kattegat
Skagerrak
OSLO
STOCKHOLM
HELSINKI (Helsingfors)
TALLINN
RIGA
VILNIUS
COPENHAGEN (København)
Gotland (Sweden)
Öland
Saaremaa
Hiiumaa
Bornholm (Denmark)
Åland Islands
Vänern
Vättern
Zealand (Sjælland)
Jutland
Longitude 20° east of Greenwich

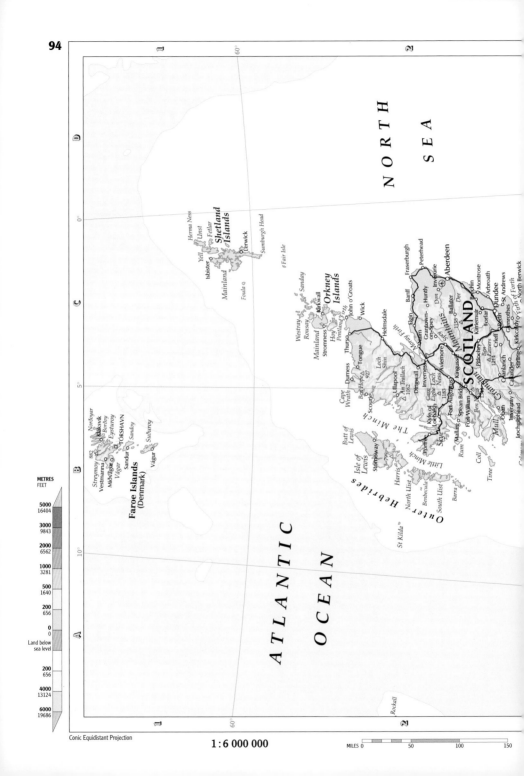

METRES
FEET

5000	16404
3000	9843
2000	6562
1000	3281
500	1640
200	656
0	0

Land below
sea level

200	656
4000	13124
6000	19686

Conic Equidistant Projection

1 : 6 000 000

MILES 0   50   100   150

N O R T H

S E A

Herma Ness

Yell *Unst*
Fetlar
**Shetland
Islands**
○ Lerwick

Isbister ○

Mainland

Sumburgh Head

○ *Fair Isle*

Foula ○

Fraserburgh
Peterhead
○ Aberdeen

Westray
Rousay
Sanday

Kirkwall
**Orkney
Islands**
Mainland
Stromness
Hoy
Pentland Firth
John o'Groats

Banff
Huntly
Elgin
Grantown-
on-Spey

Invurie

Ballater
Dee

Montrose
Arbroath
St Andrews
Dundee
Brechin
Forfar

Thurso
Wick
Helmsdale

Moray Firth
Dornoch

Fettercairn
Kirriemuir
1155
Cairn
Perth
Crieff
Dollar

Durness
Tongue
*Loch
Shin*

Lairg
927

An Teallach
1062

Ullapool

SCOTLAND

Callander

Inverness
Loch Ness

Grampian Mountains

Kingussie
Aviemore

Kirkcaldy
Firth of Forth
Stirling
North Berwick

Cape
Wrath
Scourie

1183

Fort Augustus
Spean Bridge
Ben Nevis
1214

Kyle of
Lochalsh

Ben A'an

*Butt of
Lewis*

Stornoway

Fort William
Skye
Mallaig

Rum

*Isle of
Lewis*

Harris

North Uist

Benbecula

South Uist

Barra

Portree

Inveraray

Oban

Lochgilphead

Mull

Coll

Tiree

Colon...

St Kilda ○

Little Minch

The Minch

O u t e r   H e b r i d e s

Faroe Islands
(Denmark)

Nordoyar
Borðoy
882
Klaksvík
Eysturoy
Streymoy
TÓRSHAVN
Vágar
Vestmanna
Miðvágur
Vágur
Sandur
Sandoy
Suðuroy
Vágur

A T L A N T I C

O C E A N

Rockall

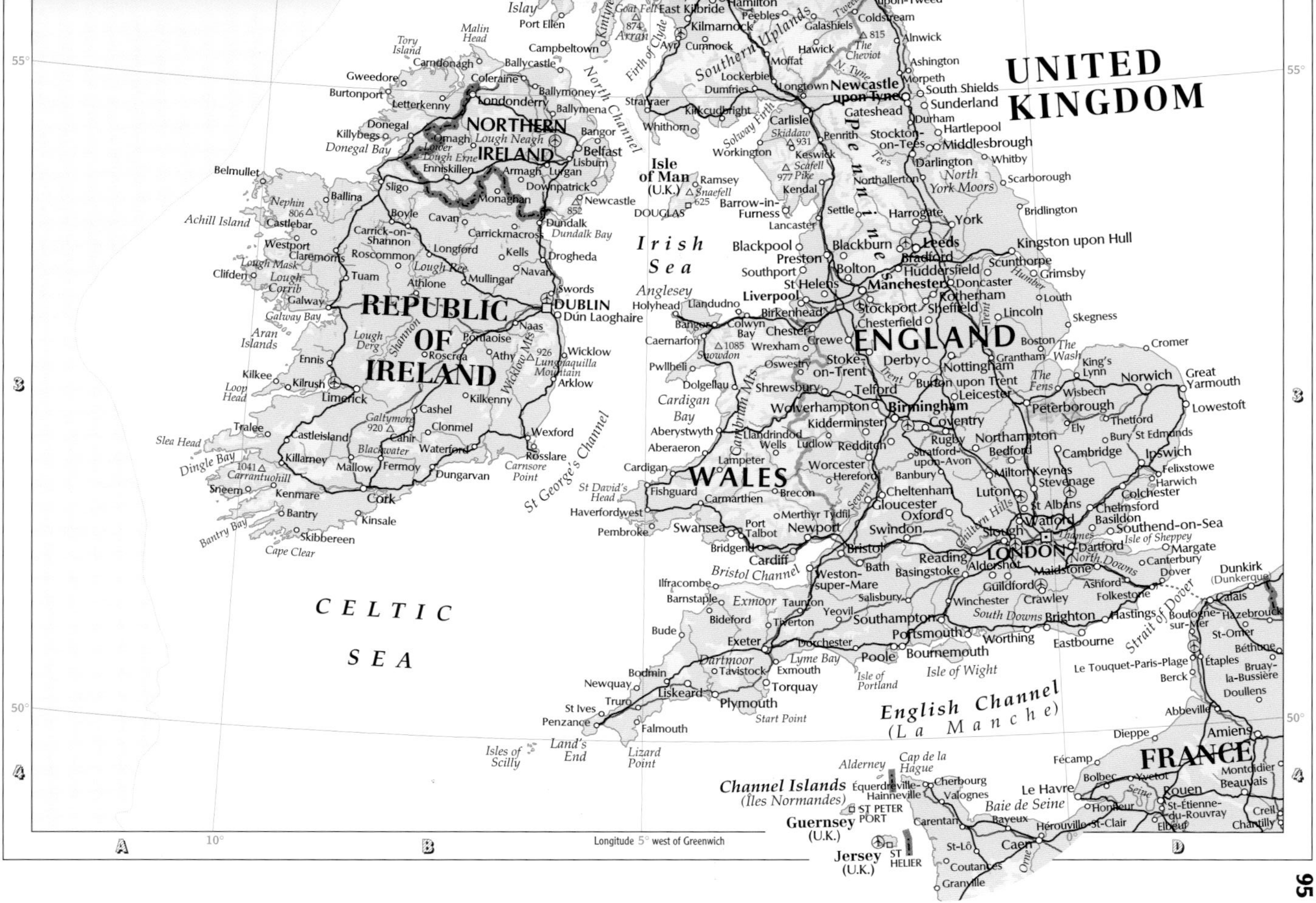
UNITED KINGDOM
REPUBLIC OF IRELAND
NORTHERN IRELAND
ENGLAND
WALES
FRANCE
LONDON
DUBLIN
Belfast
Cardiff
Irish Sea
CELTIC SEA
English Channel
(La Manche)
St George's Channel
Bristol Channel
North Channel
Strait of Dover
Isle of Man (U.K.)
DOUGLAS
Channel Islands (Îles Normandes)
Guernsey (U.K.)
Jersey (U.K.)
ST PETER PORT
ST HELIER
Isle of Wight
Isles of Scilly
Pennines
Cambrian Mts
Wicklow Mts
Southern Uplands
Newcastle upon Tyne
Manchester
Liverpool
Birmingham
Leeds
Sheffield
Bristol
Plymouth
Southampton
Norwich
Kingston upon Hull
Cork
Limerick
Galway
Waterford
Londonderry
Land's End
Lizard Point
Longitude 5° west of Greenwich
0 100 200 KILOMETRES

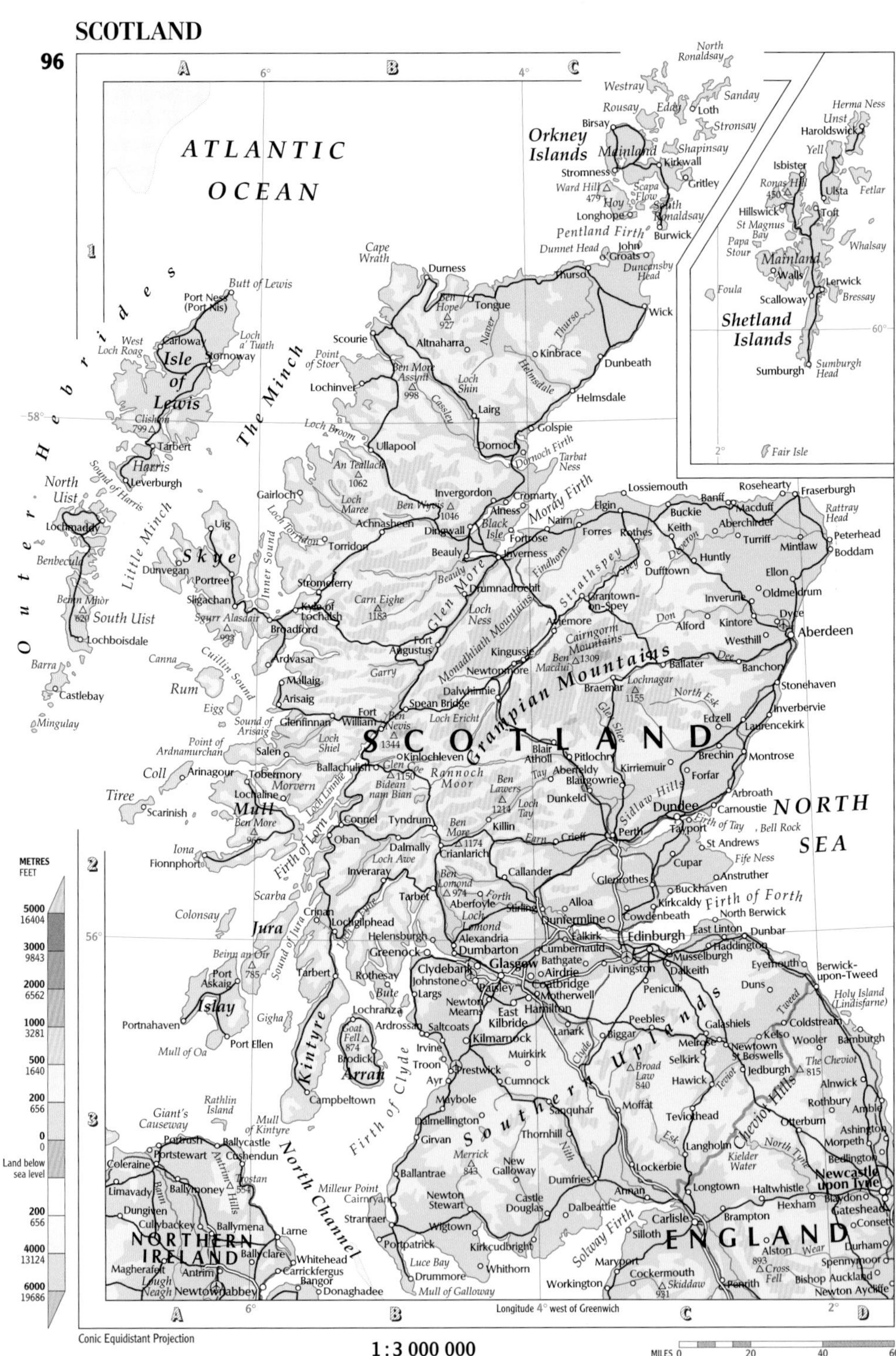

A 10°   B   8°   C   6°   D

SCOTLAND
Port Askaig
Jura
Islay
Gigha
Portnahaven
Port Ellen
Mull of Oa
Campbeltown
Kintyre

ATLANTIC

OCEAN

Malin Head
West Town Tory Island
Tory Sound
Inishowen
Malin
Rathlin Island
Giant's Causeway
Mull of Kintyre
Ballycastle
Bloody Foreland
Falcarragh
Carndonagh
Portstewart
Portrush
Coleraine
Cushendun
Brinlack
Gweedore
Buncrana
Lough Foyle
Limavady
Ballymoney
Bunbeg
Errigal 752
Ramelton
Londonderry
Ballybofey
Dungiven
Cullybackey
Larne
Aran Island
Burtonport
Letterkenny
Ballymena
Gweebarra Bay
Glenties
ULSTER
Strabane
Lifford
Antrim
Ballymena
Carrickfergus
Whitehead
Bangor
Malin More
Blue Stack Mts 676
Newtownstewart
NORTHERN
Magherafelt
Antrim
Rossan Point
Donegal
Castlederg
Cookstown
Newtownabbey
Donaghadee
Killybegs
Ballyshannon
Omagh
IRELAND
Dungannon
Lough Neagh
Belfast
Lisburn
Dunmurry
Newtownards
Strangford Lough
Donegal Bay
Bundoran
Lower Lough Erne
Fintona
Portadown
Dromore
Saintfield
Benwee Head
Erris Head
Ballycastle
Killala Bay
Sligo Bay
Enniskillen
Upper Lough Erne
Monaghan
Armagh
Ballynahinch
Downpatrick
The Mullet
Killala
Ballina
Sligo
Dromahair
Lisnaskea
Clones
Keady
Rathfriland
Ardglass
Blacksod Bay
Lough Conn
Collooney
Swanlinbar
Newtownbutler
Castleblayney
Newry
Newcastle
Dundrum Bay
Nephin 806
Lough Allen
Belturbet
Cootehill
Warrenpoint
Slieve Donard
Kilkeel
Achill Island
Nephin Beg Range
Carrick-on-Shannon
Cavan
Shercock
Dundalk
Greenore
Clare Island
Castlebar
Boyle
Lough Gara
Carrickmacross
Dundalk Bay
Clew Bay
Westport
Ballaghaderreen
Kingscourt
Ardee
Dunany Point
Louisburgh
Coagh Patrick 765
Ballyhaunis
Castlerea
Granard
Kells
Drogheda
Inishbofin
Leenane
CONNAUGHT
Ballinrobe
Claremorris
Longford
Lough Sheelin
Navan
Balbriggan
Clifden
Lough Mask
Roscommon
Castlepollard
Athboy
Deleek
Skerries
Connemara
Oughterard
Tuam
Mount Bellew
Lough Ree
Mullingar
Trim
Boyne
Slyne Head
Lough Corrib
Athlone
Moate
Clara
Enfield
Swords
Gorumna Island
Galway
Ballinasloe
Tullamore
Bog of Allen
Kildare
DUBLIN (Baile Átha Cliath)
Dun Laoghaire
Inishmore
Aran Islands
Galway Bay
Burren
Athenry
Loughrea
Portumna
Birr
Mountmellick
Portlaoise
Naas
Newbridge
Enniskerry
Bray
Greystones
Hag's Head
Liscannor Bay
Lisdoonvarna
Ennistymon
Lough Derg
LEINSTER
Roscrea
Athy
Wicklow Mts 926
Ashford
Wicklow
Spanish Point
Ennis
Killaloe
Nenagh
Templemore
Baltinglass
Lugnaquilla Mountain
Wicklow Head
Kilkee
Kilrush
Newmarket-on-Fergus
Thurles
Carlow
Tullow
Shillelagh
Arklow
Loop Head
Tarbert
Foynes
Limerick
Golden Vale
Kilkenny
Leighlinbridge
Muine Bheag
Mount Leinster 795
Bunclody
Gorey
Mouth of the Shannon
Kerry Head
Listowel
Newcastle
Adare
Tipperary
Cashel
Callan
Graiguenamanagh
Ferns
Cahore Point
Enniscorthy
Brandon Mountain 953
Tralee
Abbeyfeale
Rathluirc
Galtymore 920
Cahir
Clonmel
Thomastown
New Ross
Wexford
Wexford Harbour
Rosslare
Dingle
Castleisland
Newmarket
Mitchelstown
Fethard
Carrick-on-Suir
Waterford
Rosslare Harbour
Slea Head
Killorglin
Kanturk
Fermoy
Blackwater
Lismore
Tramore
Carnsore Point
Dingle Bay
Carrantuohill 1041
Killarney
Mallow
Dungarvan
Helvick Head
Valencia Island
Macgillycuddy's Reeks
Blarney
Midleton
Youghal
Cahersiveen
Kenmare
Macroom
Cork
Knockaboy 707
Lee
Cobh
Waterville
Sneem
Ballineen
Bandon
Kinsale
Cahermore
Dunmanway
Bantry
Dursey Island
Bantry Bay
Skibbereen
Clonakilty
Old Head of Kinsale
Schull
Baltimore
Mizen Head
Cape Clear
Caha Mts

CELTIC SEA

Longitude 8° west of Greenwich

A 10°   B   C   6°   D

North Channel
St George's Channel

	METRES	FEET
	5000	16404
	3000	9843
	2000	6562
	1000	3281
	500	1640
	200	656
	0	0
Land below sea level		
	200	656
	4000	13124
	6000	19686

0   50   100 KILOMETRES

1:3 000 000

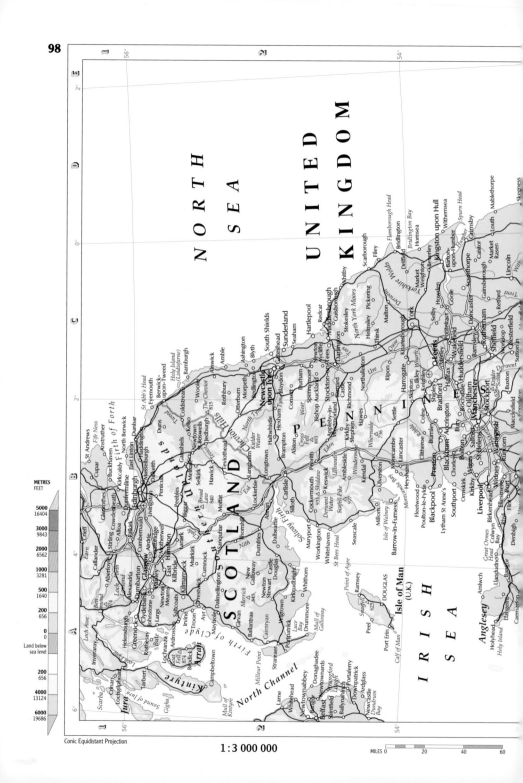

NORTH SEA

UNITED KINGDOM

SCOTLAND

PENNINES

IRISH SEA

Anglesey

Isle of Man (U.K.)

North Channel

Kintyre

1 : 3 000 000

MILES 0   20   40   60

METRES
FEET

5000 16404
3000 9843
2000 6562
1000 3281
500 1640
200 656
0 0
Land below sea level
200 656
4000 13124
6000 19686

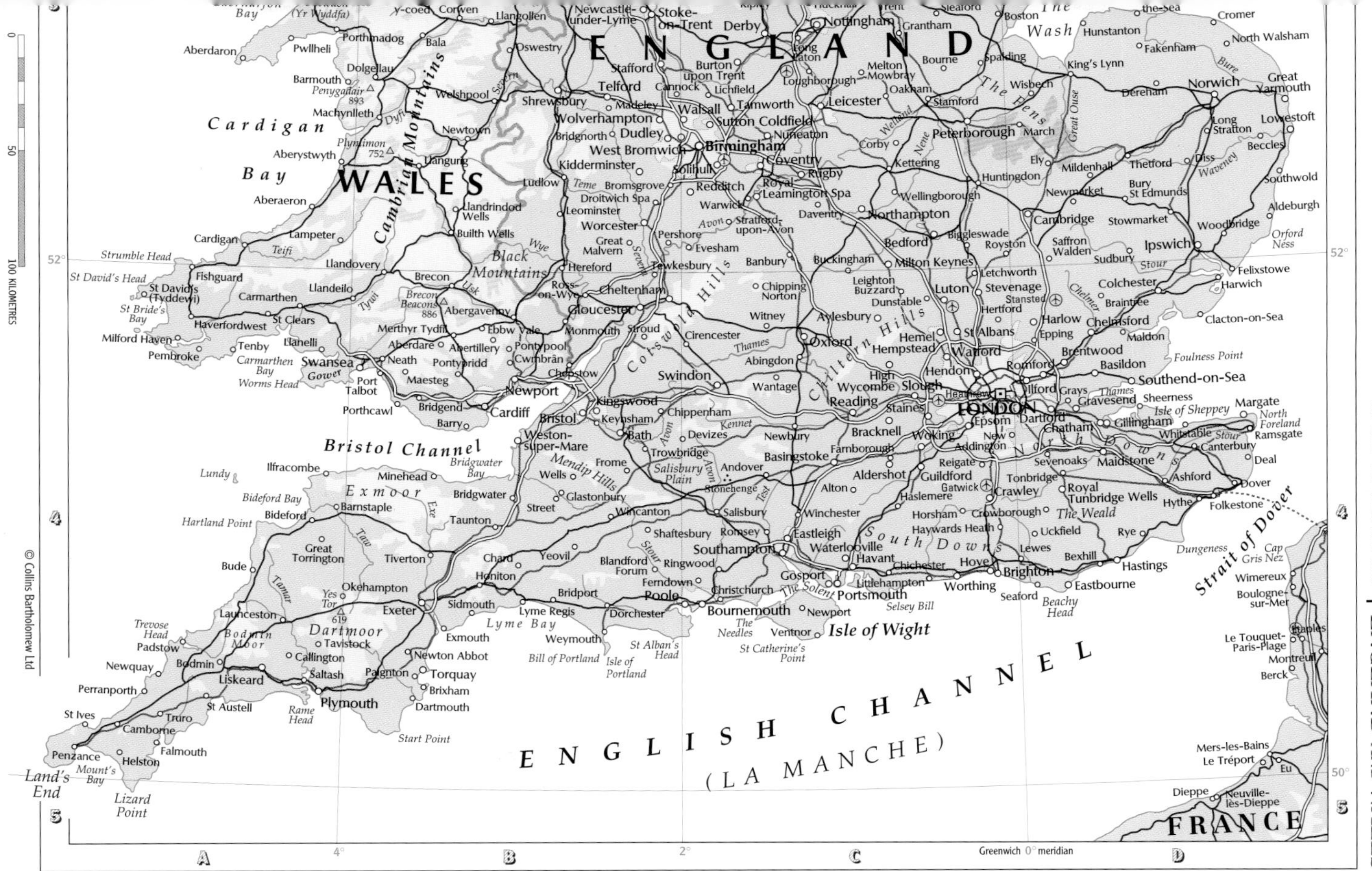

ENGLAND

WALES

Cambrian Mountains

Cardigan Bay

ENGLISH CHANNEL (LA MANCHE)

Strait of Dover

FRANCE

Bristol Channel

Wash

The Fens

Isle of Wight

LONDON

0   50   100 KILOMETRES

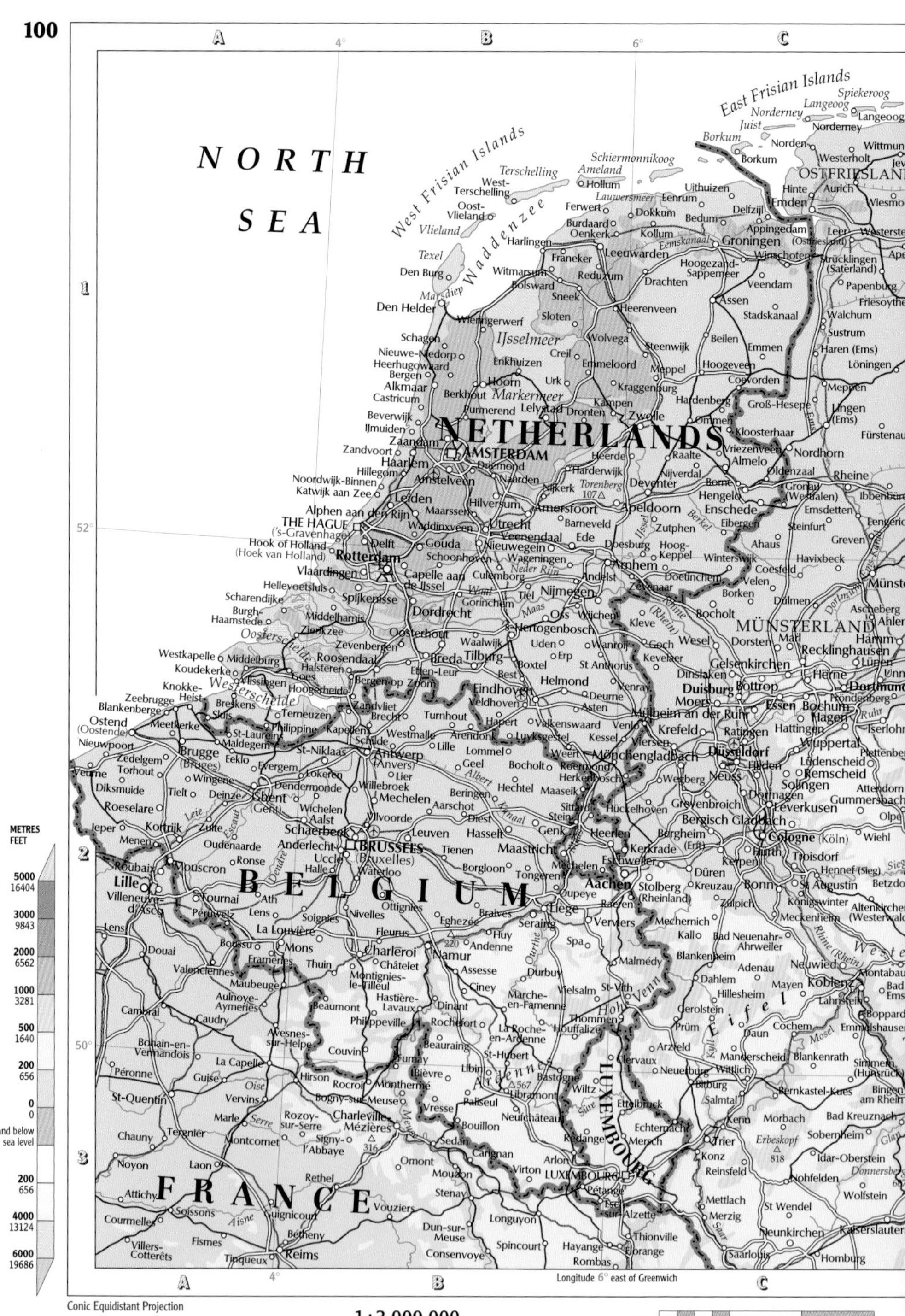

NORTH SEA

West Frisian Islands

East Frisian Islands

Spiekeroog
Langeoog
Norderney Langeoog
Juist Nordemey
Borkum Norden Wittmun
Borkum Westerholt Iev Wiesmo
Norden
OSTFRIESLAND
Aurich

Schiermonnikoog
Terschelling Ameland
West- Hollum
Terschelling Uithuizen Hinte Emden (Ostheim)
Oost- Ferwert Delfzijl Winschoten
Vlieland Dokkum Bedum Appingedam Leer Westerste
Vlieland Burdaard Eenrum Groningen Winschoten Rücklingen
Harlingen Kollum Emskanaal Leer (Saterland)
Texel Franeker Redux Drachten Veendam Papenburg
Den Burg Witmarsum Leeuwarden Sappemeer Friesoythe
Den Helder Bolsward Sneek Heerenveen Assen Stadskanaal Walchum
Wieringwerf Sloten Steenwijk Beilen Emmen Haren (Ems) Sustrum
Schagen Wolvega Löningen
Nieuwe-Nedorp Meppel Hoogeveen Coevorden Meppen
Heerhugoward Enkhuizen Creil Emmeloord Hardenberg Groß-Hesepe Lingen (Ems)
Bergen Hoorn Urk Kraggenburg Kloosterhaar Fürstenau
Alkmaar Berkhout Markermeer Kampen Zwolle Vriezenveen Nordhorn
Castricum Purmerend Lelystad Dronten Raalte Almelo Rheine
Beverwijk Ijmuiden Zaandam Heerde Börg Oldenzaal Gronau (Westfalen)
Zaandvoort AMSTERDAM Harderwijk Nijverdal Hengelo Enschede Ibbenbüren
Haarlem NETHERLANDS Apeldoorn Borne Emsdetten
Hillegom Amstelveen Naarden Torenberg Deventer Eibergen Steinfurt Greven
Noordwijk-Binnen Hilversum Amersfoort 107 Winterswijk Ahaus
Katwijk aan Zee Leiden Barneveld Doesburg Hoog- Coesfeld Havixbeck
Alphen aan den Rijn Maarssen Utrecht Ede Keppel Doetinchem Borken Münste
THE HAGUE Waddinxveen Veenendaal Arnhem Dülmen Ascheberg
('s-Gravenhage) Gouda Neder Rijn Bocholt MÜNSTERLAND Ahlen
Hook of Holland Delft Nieuwegein Wageningen Nijmegen Kleve Dorsten Mall Hamm
(Hoek van Holland) Rotterdam Schoonhoven Tiel Wesel Gelsenkirchen Recklinghausen Herne Lünen
Vlaardingen Capelle aan Culemborg Maas Goch Kevelaer Dortmund
de Ijssel Gorinchem Wichen Dinslaken Bottrop Hagen
Hellevoetsluis Spijkenisse Nijmegen Geldern Mülheim an der Ruhr Essen Bochum
Scharendijke Dordrecht Oss Boxmeer St Antonis Duisburg Iserlohn
Burgh- Middelharnis Oosterhout Waalwijk Uden Viersen Krefeld Ratingen Hattingen Wuppertal Plettenber
Haamstede Zevenbergen Hertogenbosch Erp Kessel Venlo Mönchengladbach Lüdenscheid
Westkapelle Middelburg Roosendaal Tilburg Boxtel Deurne Weert Wegberg Neuss Solingen Remscheid Attendorn
Koudekerke Halsteren Breda Helmond Roermond Hückelhoven Grevenbroich Bergisch Gladbach Leverkusen Olpe
Knokke-Heist Bergen op Zoom Eindhoven Asten Herkenbosch Erft Cologne (Köln) Wiehl
Zeebrugge Vlissingen Hoogerheide Veldhoven Aarschot Geel Sittard Köln Brühl Betzdo
Ostend Breskens Zandvliet Someren Maaseik Heinsberg Düren Hennef (sieg)
(Oostende) Sluis St-Laureins Turnhout Lille Genk Erkelenz Stolberg Bonn St Augustin
Nieuwpoort Maldegem Antwerp Arendonk Lommel Heerlen Kerkrade Aachen (Rheinland) Kreuzau Königswinter Altenkirchen (Westerwald)
Veurne Zedelgem Kapellen Westmalle Hechtel Maasmechelen Mechernich Bad Neuenahr- Neuwied
Diksmuide Torhout Brugge (Anvers) Geel Bocholt Beringen Maastricht Valkenburg Kallo Ahrweiler Westei
Roeselare Wingene (Bruges) Lier Lommel Hasselt Borgloon Tongeren Verviers Malmedy Blankenheim Adenau Mayen Koblenz
Deinze Tielt Ghent Mechelen Diest Spa Dahlem Cochem Bad
Ieper Eeklo Willebroek Aarschot Leuven Tienen Liège Dinant St-Vith Gerolstein Lahnstein Ems
Kortrijk (Gent) Aalst Vilvoorde Herve Verviers Prüm Emmelshausen Montaba
Menen Oudenaarde Anderlecht BRUSSELS Borgloon Seraing Wiesalm Wittlich Boppard
Roubaix Ronse Uccle (Bruxelles) Tongeren Houffalize Neuerburg Simmern Bad Kreuznach
Mouscron Schaerbeek Halle Waterloo Andenne Durbuy St-Hubert Bitburg Bernkastel-Kues Bingen am Rhein
Tournai Lille La Louvière Nivelles Fleurus Eghezée Marche- Vielsalm Clervaux Arzfeld Morbach
Lens Soignies en-Famenne Mandscheid Blankenrath Idar-Oberstein
Douai BELGIUM Mons Charleroi Namur Assesse Huy Bastogne Wittlich LUXEMBOURG Trier Kern
Valenciennes Maubeuge Thuin Châtelet Ciney Rochefort La Roche- Houffalize Wiltz Wiltz Erbeskopf Sobernheim
Cambrai Beaumont Montignies- Dinant en-Ardenne St-Hubert Diekirch 818 Idar-Oberstein
Aulnoye- le-Tilleul Philippeville Rochefort Libin Libramont Ettelbruck Echternach Saarburg Idar-Oberstein Donnersb
Aymeries Avesnes- Hirson Couvin Beauraing St-Hubert Larochette Merzig Hofelden Wolfstein
St-Quentin sur-Helpe Rocroi Monthermé Vresse Bouillon Neufchâteau LUXEMBOURG Mettlach St Wendel Neunkirchen Kaiserslautern
Péronne La Capelle Charleville- Sedan Carignan Arlon Pétange Merzig Saarlouis Homburg
Guise Mézières Montcornet Virton Mondorf Thionville Saarbrücken
FRANCE Rethel Omont Mouzon Stenay Longwy Alzette Saaralbe Neunkirchen
Chauny Laon Signy- Longuyon Hayange Orange
Vervins l'Abbaye Rozoy- Dun-sur- Longuyon Rombas
Noyon sur-Serre Meuse Spincourt Hagondange
Attichy Serre Marle Verdun Consenvoye Thionville
Soissons Montcornet Aisne Étain
Courmelles Fismes Tinqueux Béthény Reims

Longitude 6° east of Greenwich

1 : 3 000 000

METRES FEET

5000 16404
3000 9843
2000 6562
1000 3281
500 1640
200 656
0 0
Land below sea level
200 656
4000 13124
6000 19686

MILES 0   20   40   60

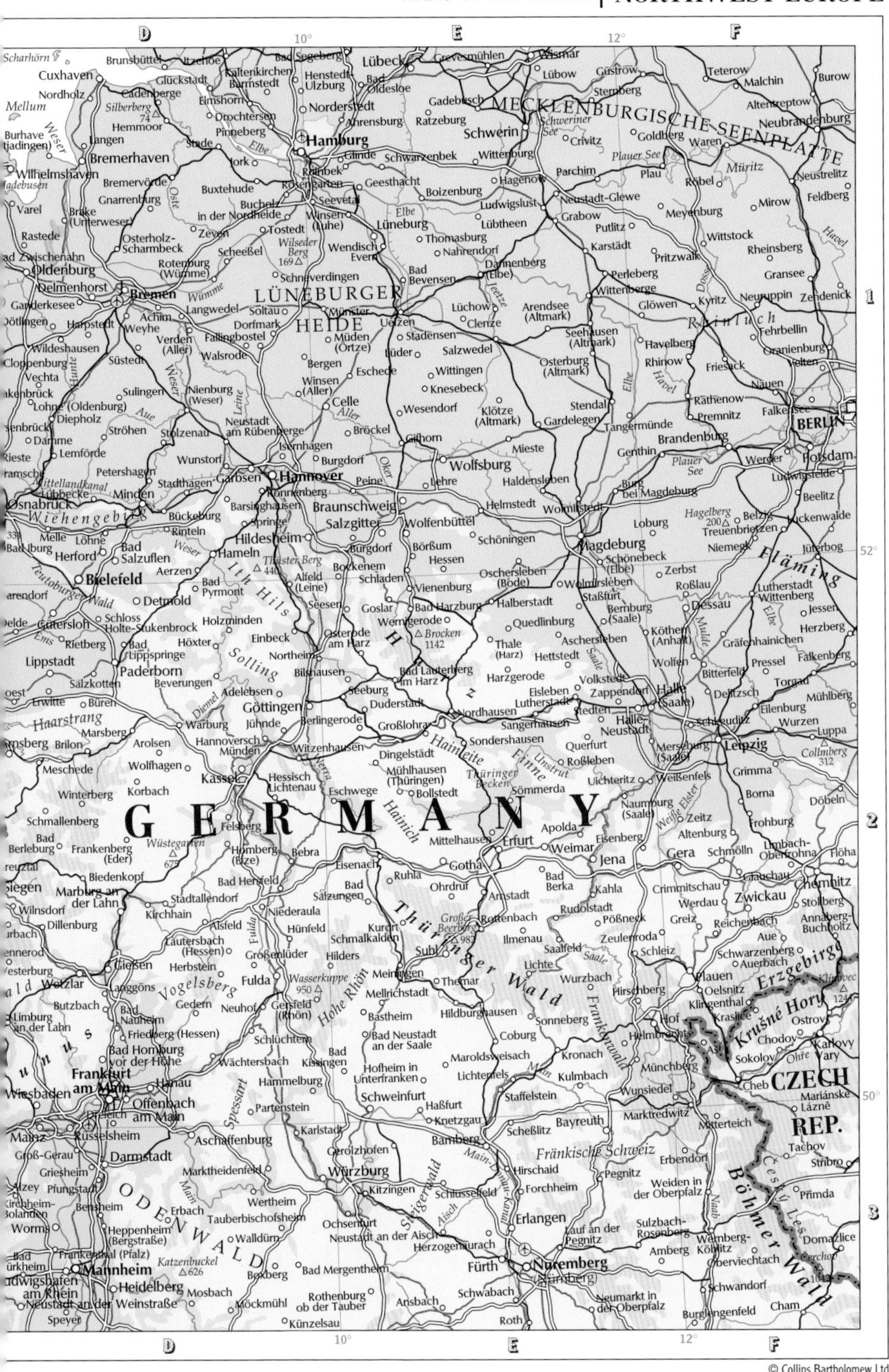

0   50   100 KILOMETRES

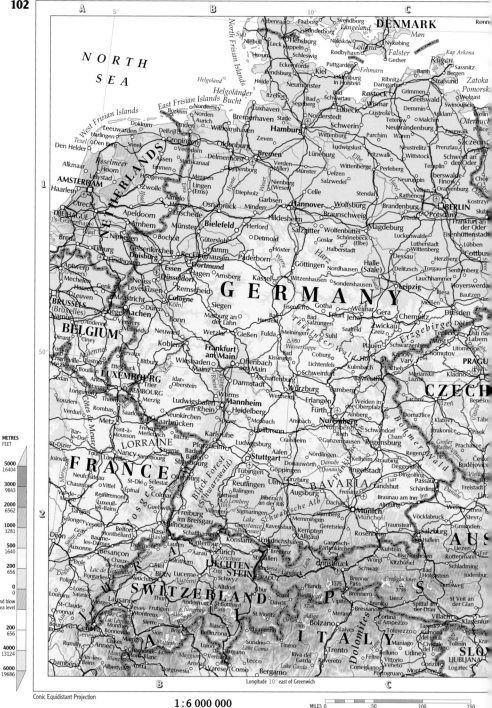

NORTH
SEA

DENMARK

NETHERLANDS

AMSTERDAM

THE HAGUE
('s-Gravenhage)

BELGIUM

BRUSSELS
(Bruxelles)

GERMANY

Hamburg

Bremen

Hannover

BERLIN

Dortmund
Essen
Düsseldorf
Cologne
(Köln)

Frankfurt
am Main

LUXEMBOURG

LUXEMBOURG

Mannheim

Nuremberg
(Nürnberg)

CZECH

PRAGUE
(Praha)

FRANCE

LORRAINE

Black Forest
(Schwarzwald)

Stuttgart

BAVARIA

Munich
(München)

AUS

SWITZERLAND

LIECHTEN-
STEIN

VADUZ

ALPS

BERN

ITALY

SLO

LJUBLJANA

METRES
FEET

5000
16404

3000
9843

2000
6562

1000
3281

500
1640

200
656

0
0

Land below
sea level

200
656

4000
13124

6000
19686

Conic Equidistant Projection

1 : 6 000 000

Longitude 10° east of Greenwich

MILES 0   50   100   150

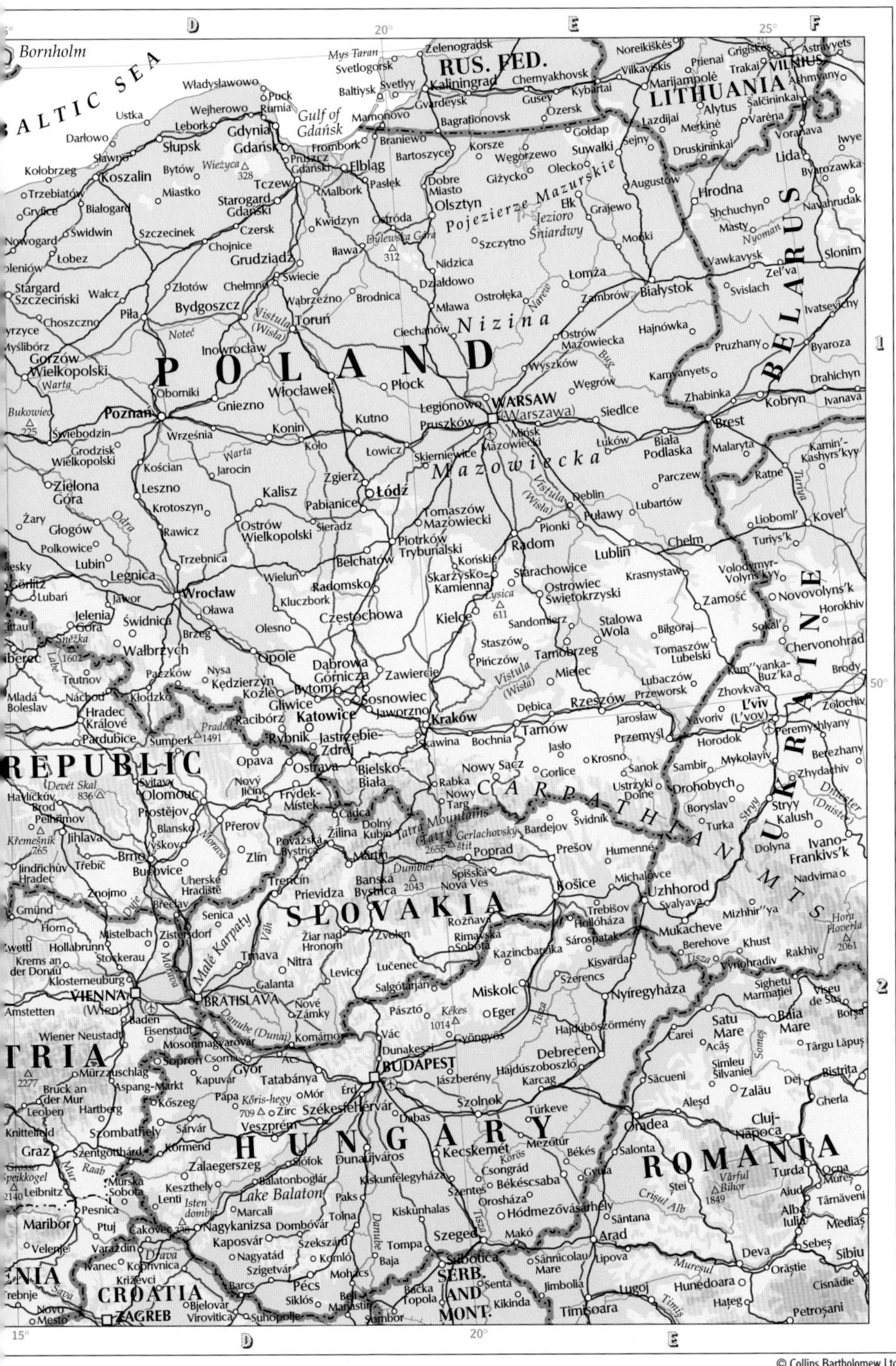

© Collins Bartholomew Ltd

0   100   200 KILOMETRES

BALTIC SEA
Bornholm
RUS. FED.
LITHUANIA
BELARUS
POLAND
REPUBLIC
SLOVAKIA
UKRAINE
HUNGARY
ROMANIA
CROATIA
SERB. AND MONT.
TRIA
ENIA
Gulf of Gdańsk
Mys Taran
Zelenogradsk
Svetlogorsk
Baltiysk
Svetlyy
Kaliningrad
Chernyakhovsk
Gvardeysk
Gusev
Kybartai
Bagrationovsk
Ozersk
Mamonovo
Noreikiškės
Vilkaviškis
Marijampolė
Prienai
Grigiškės
Trakai
VILNIUS
Astravyets
Ashmyany
Alytus
Šalčininkai
Lazdijai
Merkinė
Varėna
Druskininkai
Voranava
Lida
Iwye
Byarozawka
Hrodna
Shchuchyn
Navahrudak
Masty
Nyoman
Vawkavysk
Slonim
Zel'va
Svislach
Ivatsevichy
Pruzhany
Byaroza
Kamyanyets
Drahichyn
Zhabinka
Kobryn
Ivanava
Brest
Malaryta
Kamin'-Kashyrs'kyy
Ratne
Turiya
Liuboml'
Kovel'
Turiys'k
Volodymyr-Volyns'kyy
Novovolyns'k
Horokhiv
Sokal'
Chervonohrad
Kam''yanka-Buz'ka
Brody
Zhovkva
L'viv (L'vov)
Zolochiv
Peremyshlyany
Yavoriv
Horodok
Berezhany
Sambir
Mykolayiv
Zhydachiv
Drohobych
Boryslav
Stryy
Stryy
Dnister (Dniester)
Kalush
Turka
Dolyna
Ivano-Frankivs'k
Nadvirna
Uzhhorod
Svalyava
Mizhhir''ya
Hora Hoverla 2061
Mukacheve
Berehove
Khust
Rakhiv
Tisza
Vynohradiv
CARPATHIAN MTS
Władysławowo
Puck
Rumia
Wejherowo
Gdynia
Gdańsk
Ustka
Lębork
Słupsk
Darłowo
Sławno
Kołobrzeg
Koszalin
Bytów
Wieżyca 328
Pruszcz Gdański
Frombork
Braniewo
Elbląg
Bartoszyce
Korsze
Węgorzewo
Gołdap
Suwałki
Sejny
Trzebiatów
Miastko
Tczew
Malbork
Pasłęk
Dobre Miasto
Giżycko
Olecko
Augustów
Gryfice
Białogard
Starogard Gdański
Kwidzyn
Ostróda
Olsztyn
Pojezierze Mazurskie
Ełk
Jezioro Śniardwy
Grajewo
Nowogard
Świdwin
Szczecinek
Czersk
Chojnice
Iława
Dylewska Góra 312
Szczytno
Mońki
Łobez
Grudziądz
Nidzica
Goleniów
Świecie
Działdowo
Łomża
Stargard Szczeciński
Wałcz
Złotów
Chełmno
Wąbrzeźno
Brodnica
Mława
Ostrołęka
Narew
Zambrów
Białystok
Piła
Bydgoszcz
Vistula (Wisła)
Toruń
Pyrzyce
Choszczno
Noteć
Ciechanów
Nizina
Ostrów Mazowiecka
Hajnówka
Myślibórz
Inowrocław
Gorzów Wielkopolski
Warta
Wyszków
Bug
Płock
Węgrów
Oborniki
Gniezno
Włocławek
Legionowo
WARSAW (Warszawa)
Siedlce
Bukowiec 225
Poznań
Kutno
Pruszków
Mińsk Mazowiecki
Świebodzin
Września
Konin
Koło
Łowicz
Skierniewice
Łuków
Biała Podlaska
Grodzisk Wielkopolski
Mazowiecka
Kościan
Jarocin
Zgierz
Łódź
Parczew
Zielona Góra
Leszno
Kalisz
Pabianice
Tomaszów Mazowiecki
Dęblin
Puławy
Lubartów
Żary
Krotoszyn
Odra
Głogów
Rawicz
Ostrów Wielkopolski
Sieradz
Pionki
Polkowice
Piotrków Trybunalski
Radom
Chełm
Lubin
Trzebnica
Bełchatów
Końskie
Starachowice
Lublin
Krasnystaw
Legnica
Wieluń
Radomsko
Skarżysko-Kamienna
Ostrowiec Świętokrzyski
Görlitz
Lubań
Jawor
Wrocław
Kluczbork
Łysica 611
Zamość
Jelenia Góra
Świdnica
Oława
Częstochowa
Kielce
Sandomierz
Stalowa Wola
Biłgoraj
Śnieżka 1602
Brzeg
Olesno
Staszów
Wałbrzych
Opole
Pińczów
Tarnobrzeg
Tomaszów Lubelski
Labe
Trutnov
Paczków
Nysa
Dąbrowa Górnicza
Zawiercie
Mielec
Lubaczów
Náchod
Kłodzko
Kędzierzyn-Koźle
Bytom
Sosnowiec
Przeworsk
Mladá Boleslav
Hradec Králové
Gliwice
Katowice
Jaworzno
Kraków
Dębica
Rzeszów
Jarosław
Pradĕd 1491
Racibórz
Šumperk
Rybnik
Jastrzębie-Zdrój
Tarnów
Przemyśl
Pardubice
Skawina
Bochnia
Jasło
Krosno
Opava
Ostrava
Bielsko-Biała
Nowy Sącz
Gorlice
Sanok
Devět Skal 836
Svitavy
Nový Jičín
Frýdek-Místek
Rabka
Ustrzyki Dolne
Havlíčkův Brod
Olomouc
Nowy Targ
Čadca
Pelhřimov
Prostějov
Přerov
Dolný Kubín
Tatra Mountains
Svidník
Křemešník 765
Jihlava
Blansko
Vyškov
Žilina
Tatry
Gerlachovský štít 2655
Bardejov
Považská Bystrica
Brno
Zlín
Martin
Poprad
Prešov
Humenné
Jindřichův Hradec
Třebíč
Břeclav
Uherské Hradiště
Dumbier 2043
Spišská Nová Ves
Michalovce
Znojmo
Trenčín
Banská Bystrica
Košice
Gmünd
Prievidza
Morava
Trebišov
Horn
Senica
Rožňava
Hollóháza
Mistelbach
Zistersdorf
Váh
Žiar nad Hronom
Zvolen
Rimavská Sobota
Sárospatak
Zwettl
Hollabrunn
Malé Karpaty
Kazincbarcika
Krems an der Donau
Stockerau
Trnava
Nitra
Lučenec
Kisvárda
Klosterneuburg
Levice
Szerencs
Galanta
Salgótarján
Miskolc
Nyíregyháza
VIENNA (Wien)
BRATISLAVA
Nové Zámky
Sighetu Marmației
Vișeu de Sus
Amstetten
Baden
Pásztó
Kékes 1014
Eger
Tisza
Satu Mare
Baia Mare
Borșa
Eisenstadt
Danube (Dunaj)
Hajdúböszörmény
Wiener Neustadt
Mosonmagyaróvár
Komárno
Vác
Gyöngyös
Carei
Someș
Târgu Lăpuș
Dunakeszi
Acâș
Sopron
Csorna
Győr
Ács
Debrecen
Şimleu Silvaniei
2277
Mürzzuschlag
Tatabánya
BUDAPEST
Hajdúszoboszló
Săcueni
Bistrița
Kapuvár
Jászberény
Karcag
Zalău
Dej
Bruck an der Mur
Spang-Markt
Pápa
Kőris-hegy 709
Mór
Érd
Szolnok
Aleșd
Gherla
Leoben
Hartberg
Kőszeg
Zirc
Székesfehérvár
Dabas
Túrkeve
Cluj-Napoca
Knittelfeld
Szombathely
Sárvár
Veszprém
Oradea
Graz
Szentgotthárd
Körmend
Kecskemét
Mezőtúr
Salonta
Dunaújváros
Körös
Békés
Groesser Speikkogel 2140
Raab
Zalaegerszeg
Siófok
Csongrád
Turda
Ocna Mureș
Mur
Balatonboglár
Kiskunfélegyháza
Gyula
Vârful Bihor 1849
Murska Sobota
Keszthely
Lake Balaton
Szentes
Békéscsaba
Ştei
Aiud
Leibnitz
Lenti
Isten dombja
Paks
Orosháza
Crișul Alb
Târnăveni
Pesnica
Marcali
Kiskunhalas
Hódmezővásárhely
Alba Iulia
Maribor
Ptuj
Čakovec 338
Nagykanizsa
Dombóvár
Tolna
Danube
Sântana
Mediaș
Velenje
Varaždin
Kaposvár
Szekszárd
Tompa
Szeged
Tisza
Makó
Arad
Sebeș
Sibiu
Drava
Nagyatád
Komló
Baja
Subotica
Sânnicolau Mare
Lipova
Mureșul
Deva
Orăștie
Vanec
Koprivnica
Szigetvár
Mohács
Senta
Jimbolia
Hunedoara
Cisnădie
Križevci
Sava
Barcs
Pécs
Bačka Topola
Kikinda
Lugoj
Timiș
Hațeg
Trebnje
Bjelovar
Siklós
Beli Manastir
Sombor
Timișoara
Petroșani
Novo Mesto
ZAGREB
Virovitica
Suhopolje
15°
25°
50°
F

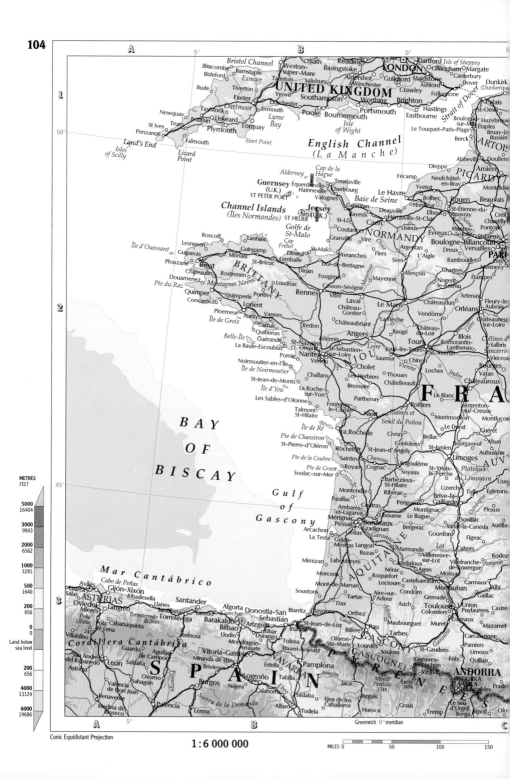

A · 5° · **B** · 0° · **C**

UNITED KINGDOM

Bristol Channel
Ilfracombe Barnstaple Weston- Bath Reading Dartford Isle of Sheppey
Bideford Super-Mare Basingstoke Aldershot Guildford Maidstone Gillingham Margate
Exmoor Taunton Salisbury Winchester Crawley Folkestone Dover Dunkirk
Bude Tiverton Yeovil Southampton Worthing Brighton Hastings (Dunkerque)
Newquay Tavistock Dorchester Exmouth Portsmouth Eastbourne Calais
St Ives Liskeard Bodmin Dartmoor Lyme Poole Bournemouth Isle Boulogne- Hazebrouck
Truro Plymouth Torquay Bay of Wight St-Omer sur-Mer Étaples
Penzance Land's End Falmouth Start Point English Channel Le Touquet-Paris-Plage Bruay-la-
Isles Lizard (La Manche) Berck Bussière
of Scilly Point ARTOIS

Alderney Cap de la Dieppe Abbeville Doullens Amiens
Hague Tréport PICARD
Guernsey Équerdreville- Cherbourg Fécamp Neufchâtel- Montdidier
(U.K.) Hainneville Tourlaville Le Havre Yvetot Bolbec en-Bray Beauvais
ST PETER PORT Valognes Baie de Seine Honfleur Rouen St-Étienne-du- Creil
Channel Islands Carentan Deauville Étretat Rouvray Chantilly
(Îles Normandes) Jersey St-Lô Bayeux Hérouville-St-Clair Lisieux Évreux Mantes- Pontoise St-Denis
Golfe de ST HELIER (U.K.) Coutances Caen NORMANDY la-Jolie Versailles Boulogne-Billancourt
St-Malo Granville Avranches Orne Flers Argentan Sées L'Aigle Dreux Rambouillet PARIS
Roscoff Cap Fréhel Dinard St-Malo Bol-de-Bretagne Mayenne Alençon Chartres Nogent- Étampes Mennecy
Île d'Ouessant Lannion Dinan Fougères le-Rotrou Artenay Fleury-les-
Lesneven Guingamp Lamballe Dol-de-Bretagne Châteaudun Aubrais
Guipavas St-Brieuc BRITTANY Vitré Laval Mayenne Le Mans Vendôme Orléans
Plouzane Brest Morlaix Rostrenen Loudéac Cesson-Sévigné Château- La Flèche Baugé Blois Châteauneu Collines d
Châteaulin Douarnenez Montagnes Noires Pontivy Rennes Gontier Baugé-du-Loir Romorantin- sur-Loire Sancerro
Pte du Raz Quimper Quimperlé Loire Angers Saumur Tours Joué-lès-Tours Lanthenay St-Aver Vierzor
Concarneau Lorient Auray Vannes Redon Châteaubriant ANJOU Vendôme Chinon Loches Bourges
Ploemeur Guérande Nantes St-Sébastien- Vertou Cholet Loire Saumur Vienne Indre Vatan Châteauroux
Belle-Île Île de Groix La Baule-Escoublac St-Nazaire Orvault sur-Loire Thouars Châtellerault FRA
Île d'Yeu Noirmoutier-en-l'Île Challans Les Herbiers Bressuire Poitiers Argenton-
St-Jean-de-Monts Île de Noirmoutier La Roche- Fontenay- Parthenay Montmorillon sur-Creuse Montluçon
sur-Yon le-Comte Vallans et Seuil du Poitou Le Dorat Guéret
Les Sables-d'Olonne Talmont- Niort Civray Bellac Bourganeuf Ahun
St-Hilaire La Rochelle Confolens St-Junien
Île de Ré La Rochelle Aubusson
Pte de Chassiron Rochefort St-Jean-d'Angély Angoulême St-Yrieix- Limoges AUV
Pte de la Coubre St-Pierre-d'Oléron Saintes Charente la-Perche Plateau
BAY Royan Cognac Soyaux Uzerche Tulle au Limousin Égletons
Pte de Grave Soulac-sur-Mer Barbézieux- Brive-la- Ussel
OF Montendre St-Hilaire Périgueux Gaillarde
Pauillac Ribérac Dordogne Souillac
BISCAY Ambarès- Coutras Brantôme Sarlat-la-Canéda Aurillac
et-Lagrave Libourne Le Bugue Gourdon Figeac
Gulf Mérignac Bordeaux Bergerac
of Arcachon Pessac Gradignan Marmande Lot Cahors Rodez
Gascony La Teste Gujan- Villeneuve- Villefranche-
Mestras Langon sur-Lot Agen de-Rouergue
Mimizan Labouheyre Morcenx Nérac Moissac Carmaux Albi
Mar Cantábrico Roquefort Castelsarrasin Montauban
Cabo de Peñas Mont-de-Marsan Lectoure Grenade Gaillac
Avilés Gijón-Xixón Soustons Aire-sur- Auch Colomiers Union Castre
Luarca Salas Ribadesella l'Adour Tartas Toulouse Puylaurens
ASTURIAS Mieres Dax Grenade Cugnaux Mazamet
Oviedo Llanes Algorta Donostia-San Bayonne Muret
Peña Langreo Santander Barakaldo Sebastián Biarritz Orthez Mont-de-Marsan Maubourguet Carcassonne
Ubiña Torrecerredo Torrelavega Algorta (Guecho) St-Jean-de-Luz Peyrehorade Pau Tarbes Pamiers
Pola Arizgoiti Hendaye Irun Billère Limoux
de Lena Bilbao Elibar Lourdes St-Gaudens Foix Quillan
Reinosa Llodio Mondragón Arrasate Oloron- Bagnères-de- ANDORRA
Cordillera Cantábrica Durango Tolosa Ste-Marie Soulom Luchon
Guardo Vitoria-Gasteiz Vielha ANDORRA
San Andrés Aguilar Estella Pamplona Monte Anéto LA VELLA
del Rabanedo León de Campoo Miranda de Ebro NAVARRA Perdido 3404 La Seu Prade
Astorga Saldaña Briviesca Aragón Jaca 3348 d'Urgell Caldes
Villablino Osorno Burgos Tafalla PYRENEES Berga Ripoll
Valencia Sahagún Logroño Ejea de los d'Urgell Olo
de Don Juan Nájera Caballeros Huesca
SPAIN Estella Sádaba Tremp
Benavente Palencia Lerma Arguis
Medina de Sierra de la Demanda Alfaro Tudela
Rioseco Villalpando

METRES / FEET

5000	16404
3000	9843
2000	6562
1000	3281
500	1640
200	656
0	0
Land below sea level	
200	656
4000	13124
6000	19686

Conic Equidistant Projection

1 : 6 000 000

Greenwich 0° meridian

MILES 0 · 50 · 100 · 150

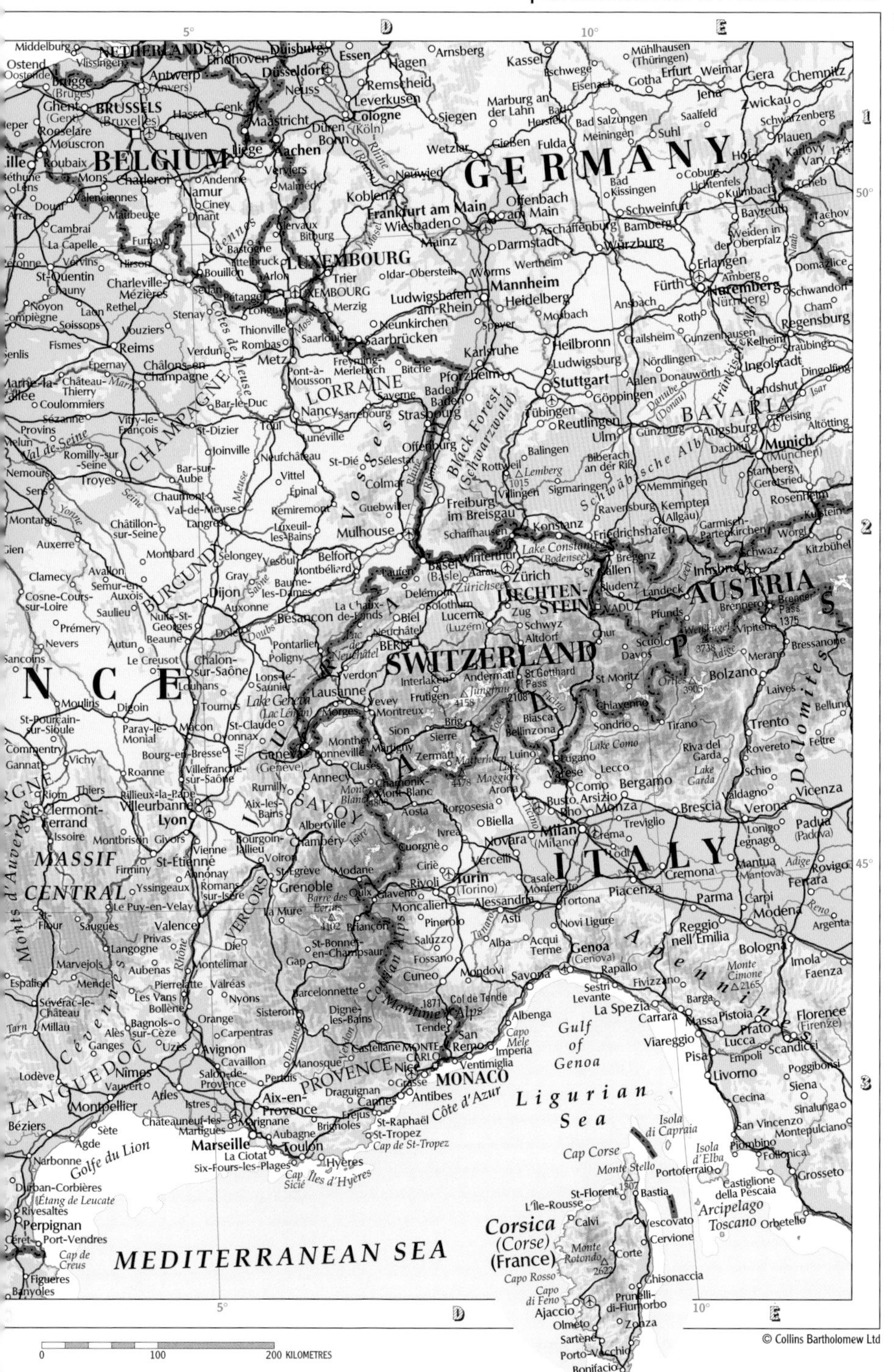
NETHERLANDS
BELGIUM
LUXEMBOURG
GERMANY
SWITZERLAND
LIECHTENSTEIN
AUSTRIA
ITALY
MONACO
N C E
MEDITERRANEAN SEA
Ligurian Sea
Gulf of Genoa
Golfe du Lion
Corsica (Corse) (France)
Arcipelago Toscano
BRUSSELS (Bruxelles)
Antwerp (Anvers)
Brugge (Bruges)
Ghent (Gent)
Ostend
Middelburg
Vlissingen
Eindhoven
Duisburg
Düsseldorf
Essen
Arnsberg
Hagen
Remscheid
Neuss
Leverkusen
Cologne (Köln)
Maastricht
Liège
Aachen
Bonn
Düren
Siegen
Kassel
Eschwege
Eisenach
Mühlhausen (Thüringen)
Gotha
Erfurt
Weimar
Jena
Gera
Chemnitz
Zwickau
Plauen
Schwarzenberg
Saalfeld
Suhl
Meiningen
Bad Salzungen
Marburg an der Lahn
Gießen
Fulda
Wetzlar
Koblenz
Neuwied
Frankfurt am Main
Wiesbaden
Mainz
Offenbach am Main
Aschaffenburg
Darmstadt
Bamberg
Coburg
Lichtenfels
Kulmbach
Bayreuth
Hof
Karlovy Vary
Cheb
Tachov
Weiden in der Oberpfalz
Bad Kissingen
Schweinfurt
Würzburg
Erlangen
Fürth
Nuremberg (Nürnberg)
Amberg
Regensburg
Ingolstadt
Kelheim
Straubing
Dingolfing
Landshut
Munich (München)
Freising
Augsburg
Altötting
Rosenheim
Kufstein
Mannheim
Heidelberg
Ludwigshafen am Rhein
Worms
Wertheim
Mosbach
Heilbronn
Karlsruhe
Pforzheim
Baden-Baden
Stuttgart
Ludwigsburg
Göppingen
Tübingen
Reutlingen
Ulm
Aalen
Nördlingen
Donauwörth
Ansbach
Crailsheim
Roth
Gunzenhausen
BAVARIA
Schwäbische Alb
Black Forest (Schwarzwald)
Freiburg im Breisgau
Konstanz
Friedrichshafen
Lake Constance (Bodensee)
Kempten (Allgäu)
Memmingen
Ravensburg
Garmisch-Partenkirchen
Innsbruck
Bregenz
Kitzbühel
Wörgl
Schwaz
Landeck
Brennero
Brenner Pass 1375
Vipiteno
Bressanone
Merano
Bolzano
Dolomites
Trento
Rovereto
Feltre
Vicenza
Padua (Padova)
Verona
Brescia
Bergamo
Lecco
Como
Monza
Milan (Milano)
Busto Arsizio
Novara
Vercelli
Biella
Turin (Torino)
Alessandria
Asti
Piacenza
Cremona
Parma
Reggio nell'Emilia
Modena
Bologna
Ferrara
Mantua (Mantova)
Rovigo
Imola
Faenza
Florence (Firenze)
Prato
Pistoia
Lucca
Pisa
Livorno
Viareggio
Massa
Carrara
La Spezia
Genoa (Genova)
Savona
Imperia
San Remo
Ventimiglia
Siena
Grosseto
Piombino
Isola d'Elba
Isola di Capraia
Bastia
Ajaccio
Corte
Calvi
Porto-Vecchio
Bonifacio
Apennines
Lake Como
Lake Garda
Lake Maggiore
Alps
Cottian Alps
Maritime Alps
Lake Geneva (Lac Léman)
Geneva (Genève)
Lausanne
Bern
Basel (Basle)
Zürich
Lucerne (Luzern)
Interlaken
Jungfrau 4158
Matterhorn 4478
Mont Blanc
Sion
Zermatt
Brig
Chamonix-Mont-Blanc
Annecy
Chambéry
Grenoble
Lyon
Villeurbanne
Saint-Étienne
Valence
Avignon
Nîmes
Montpellier
Marseille
Toulon
Aix-en-Provence
Nice
Cannes
Antibes
Hyères
Perpignan
Narbonne
Béziers
Sète
MASSIF CENTRAL
Clermont-Ferrand
LANGUEDOC
PROVENCE
SAVOY
BURGUNDY
CHAMPAGNE
LORRAINE
Vosges
Dijon
Besançon
Mulhouse
Colmar
Strasbourg
Nancy
Metz
Reims
Troyes
Lille
Roubaix
Mons
Charleroi
Namur
Ardennes
Côte d'Azur
0 100 200 KILOMETRES

A   10°   B   5°   C

ATLANTIC

OCEAN

Mar Cantábrico

Cabo
Ortegal
Punta da
Estaca de Bares
Ortigueira   Cervo
Cabo de Peñas
Viveiro   Luarca   Avilés   Gijón-Xixón
Ferrol   Gándara   Ribadeo   Salas   Santander
A Coruña   Villalba   Cangas   Oviedo   Pola de   Ribadesella   Laredo   Algorta
Betanzos   Lugo   del Narcea   Mieres   Siero   Llanes   (Guecho)
Santiago   Ordes   Langreo   Torrecerredo   Torrelavega   Santillana   Barakaldo   Bilbao   Fibar
de Compostela   Melide   Villablino   Cabañaquinta 2648   Reinosa   Mondragon-   Llodio
Cape Finisterre   Estrada   Sarria   Peña Ubiña   Guardo   Vitoria-Gasteiz   Arrasate
(Cabo Fisterra)   Muros   Chantada   2417   San Andrés   Aguilar   Miranda de Ebro
Vilagarcía de Arousa   Lalín   del Rabanedo   León   de Campóo   Briviesca   Logroño
Santa Uxía de Ribeira   Pontevedra   Ponferrada   Astorga   Saldaña   Osorno   Burgos   Nájera
Marín   Redondela   Monforte   Sahagún   Lerma   Soria
Cangas   O Barco   Benavente   Medina   Palencia   Sierra de la Demanda
Vigo   Xinzo   Valencia   de Rioseco   Aranda
Tui   de Limia   Truchas   de Don Juan   Olmedo   de Duero   Almazán
Miño   Verín   Sierra de la Cabrera   Zamora   Valladolid   Ayllón
Tondevila   Bragança   Toro   Tordesillas   Cuéllar   Cerezo   Medinaceli
Viana do Castelo   Chaves   CASTILLA Y LEÓN   Duero   de Abajo   Sigüenza
Braga   Macedo   Embalse   Medina   Arévalo   Segovia   Guadalajara
Póvoa de Varzim   Guimarães   de Cavaleiros   de Almendra   del Campo   Peñaranda   Alcalá de
Maia   Vila Real   Mirandela   Ledesma   de Bracamonte   Ávila   Henares   Embalse
Matosinhos   Torre de   Fermoselle   Salamanca   Peñalara   MADRID   de
Vila Nova de Gaia   Oporto   Moncorvo   Vilar   Ciudad   2430   Móstoles   Getafe   Buendia
Porto   Pedroso   Formoso   Rodrigo   Nuñomoral   Béjar   Sierra de Gredos   Fuenlabrada   Parla
Ovar   São João   Lamego   Guarda   Sierra de Guadarrama   Ocaña   Tarancón
Aveiro   da Madeira   Meda   Plasencia   Navalmoral   Torrijos   Aranjuez
Ílhavo   Águeda   Visau   Coria   de la Mata   Valle de Tiétar   Toledo
Mangualde   Covilhã   Sierra de San Pedro   Talavera   CASTILLA-LA MANCHA   Alcázar de
Mealhada   Mondego   Torre   Fundão   de la Reina   Montes de Toledo   San Juan
Figueira   Coimbra   1993   Sabugal   Alcántara   Embalse   Madridejos   Socuéllamos
da Foz   Lousã   Serra da Estrela   Cáceres   de Valdecañas   Sierra   Villarrobledo
Marinha   Pombal   Castelo   Trujillo   de Guadalupe   Embalse   Tomelloso
Grande   Tomar   Branco   Herrera   de Cijara   Ciudad   Daimiel   Manzanares
Batalha   Leiria   Abrantes   Ponte   del Duque   Miajadas   Real   Valdepeñas
Caldas da Rainha   Torres   Entroncamento   de Sôr   Portalegre   Navalvillar   Almadén   Villanueva   Alcaraz
Peniche   Novas   Santarém   Campo Maior   Mérida   de Pela   Jabalón   de los Infantes
Torres Vedras   Coruche   Elvas   Montijo   Don   Villanueva   Puertollano
Vila Franca de Xira   Amadora   Estremoz   Badajoz   Benito   de la Serena   Los Pedroches
LISBON   Cacem   Recondo   Olivenza   Cabeza del Buey   Pozoblanco
Cascais   Almada   (Lisboa)   Évora   Almendralejo   Hinojosa   Peñarroya-Pueblonuevo   Sierra
Cabo Espichel   Montijo   Zafra   del Duque   Andújar
Setúbal   Alcácer do Sal   Fregenal   Azuaga   Sierra Morena   Linares
Baía de Setúbal   de la Sierra   Córdoba   Baeza   Úbeda
Grândola   Torrão   Moura   Rosal de la   Constantina   Palma del Río   Martos   Jaén   Huéscar
Sines   Beja   Frontera   Guadalquivir   Montilla   Alcaudete
Cabo de   Aljustrel   Serpa   Cortegana   Lora   Écija   Cabra   Alcalá la Real   Baza
Sines   Castro   Constantina   del Río   Priego de
Odemira   Verde   Mértola   Valverde   Carmona   Marchena   Loja   Córdoba   Guadix
del Camino   Seville   Utrera   Osuna   Granada   Sierra Nevada
Almodôvar   (Sevilla)   Mulhacén
Aljezur   ALGARVE   Huelva   Las Marismas   Lebrija   Morón de   Antequera   Vélez-   3482
Cabo de   Lagos   Portimão   Loulé   Almonte   Coria   la Frontera   Málaga   Motril   Almería
São Vicente   Albufeira   Olhão   Tavira   del Río   Sanlúcar   Arcos de   Ronda   Málaga   El Ejido
Sagres   Cabo de Faro   Playa de   de Barrameda   la Frontera   Costa del Sol   Adra   Golfo de
Santa Maria   Castilla   El Puerto de   Jerez de la   Torremolinos   Almuñécar   Almería
Golfo de la Luz   Santa María   Frontera   Marbella   Estepona
Cádiz   San   Chiclana de   La Línea de
de Cádiz   Fernando   la Frontera   la Concepción
Vejer de la Frontera   Algeciras   Gibraltar (U.K.)
Barbate de Franco   Pta Almina
Cabo Trafalgar   Strait of Gibraltar   Ceuta (Spain)
Tangier   Cabo Negro
(Tanger)   Tétouan   Cap des
Asilah   MOROCCO   Trois Fourches

ASTURIAS

Cordillera Cantábrica

Sierra de Guadarrama

GALICIA

PORTUGAL

SPAIN

EXTREMADURA

ANDALUCÍA

Duero   Tâmega   Támega   Douro   Côa   Tagus (Tejo)   Guadiana   Zújar   Guadalquivir   Genil   Guadalete

1

40°

2

A   10°   B   5°   C

METRES
FEET

5000   16404
3000   9843
2000   6562
1000   3281
500   1640
200   656
0   0
Land below
sea level
200   656
4000   13124
6000   19686

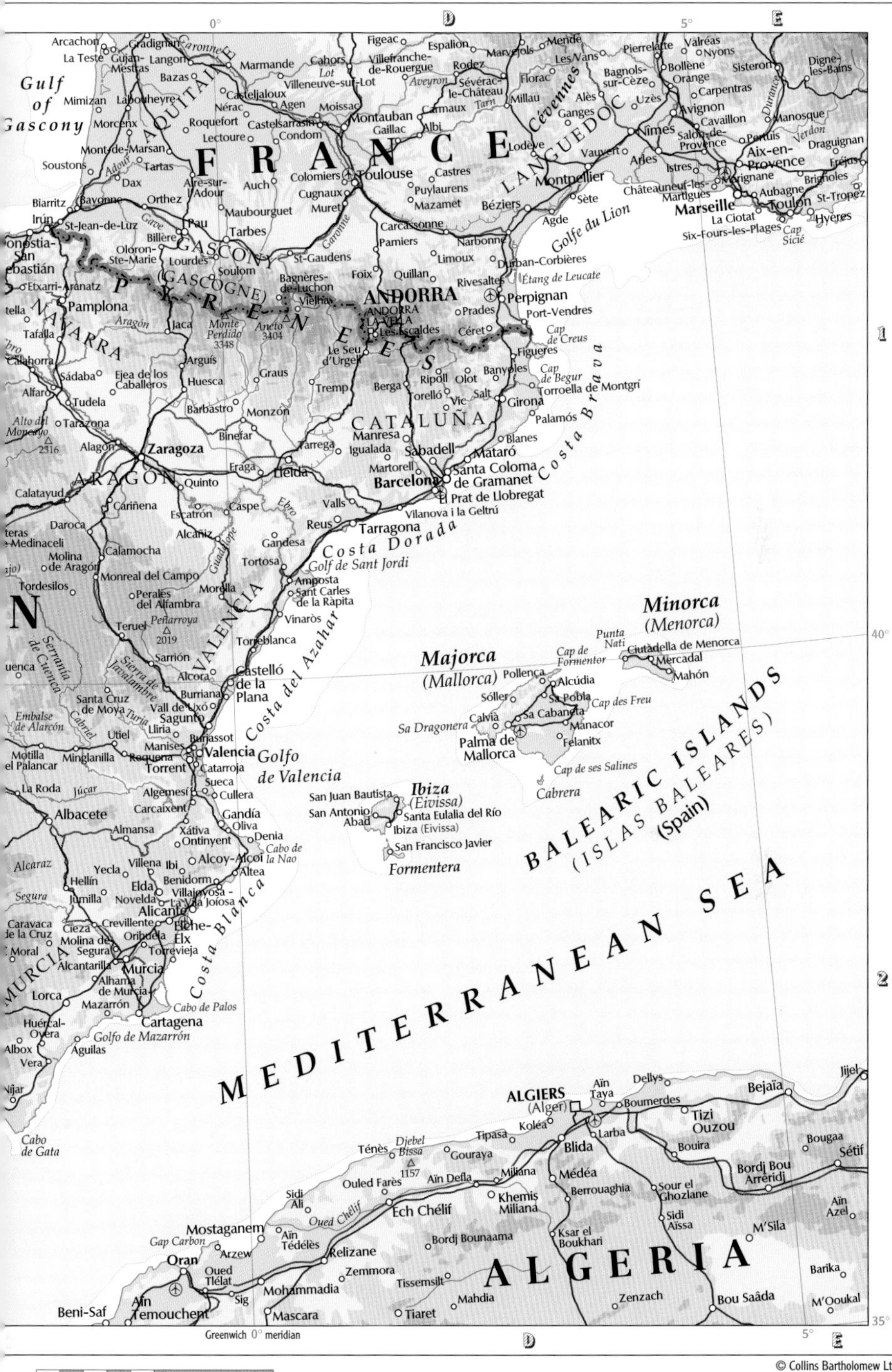

Gulf of Gascony

FRANCE

GASCON

(GASCOGNE)

P Y R E N E E S

NAVARRA

ARAGON

CATALUÑA

VALENCIA

MURCIA

Costa Brava

Costa Dorada

Costa del Azahar

Costa Blanca

Golfo de Valencia

ANDORRA
ANDORRA LA VELLA
Les Escaldes

LANGUEDOC

Marseille

Majorca
(Mallorca)

Minorca
(Menorca)

Ibiza
(Eivissa)

Formentera

BALEARIC ISLANDS
(ISLAS BALEARES)
(Spain)

M E D I T E R R A N E A N   S E A

ALGIERS
(Alger)

A L G E R I A

0   100   200 KILOMETRES

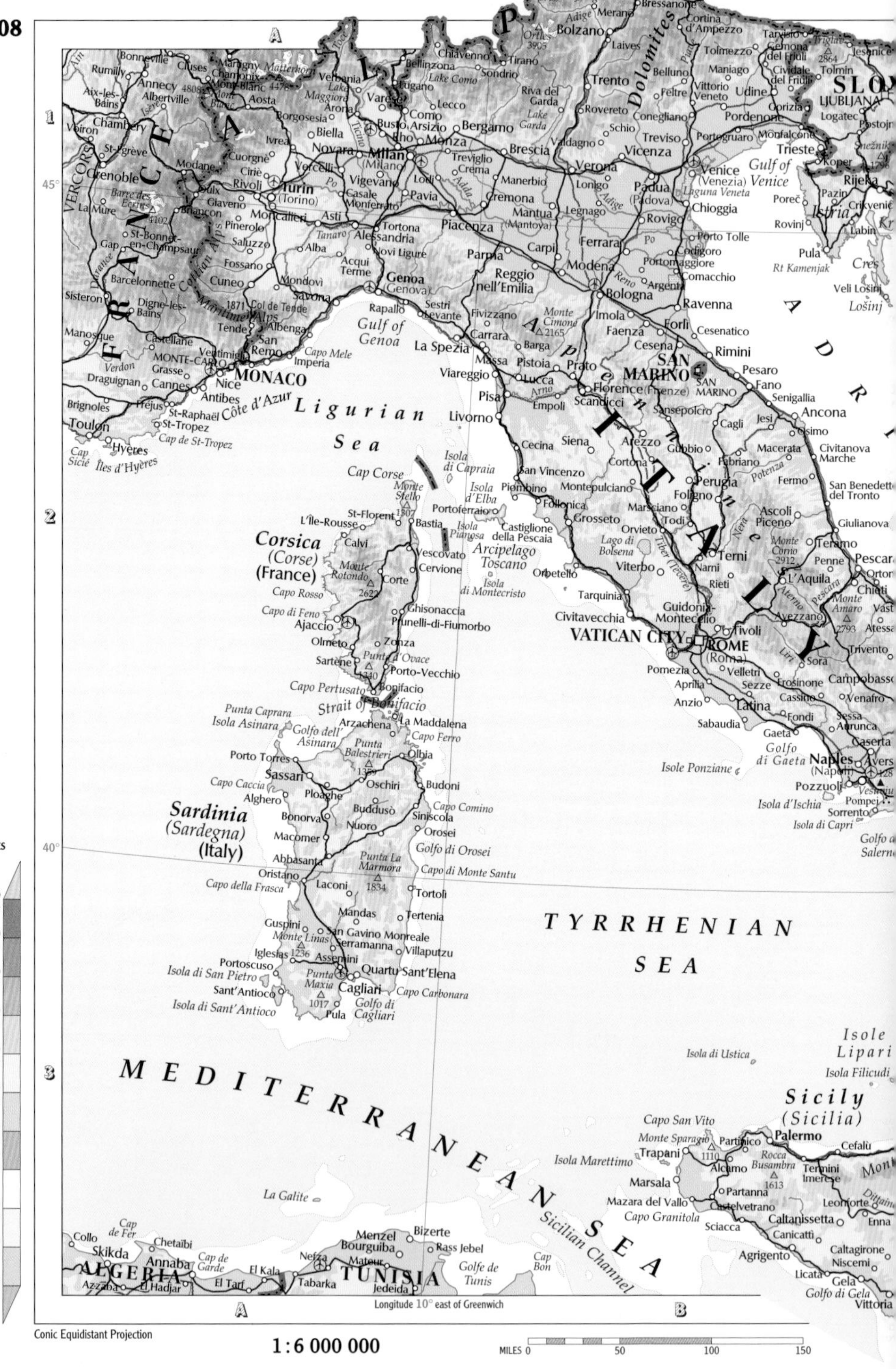

METRES
FEET

METRES	FEET
5000	16404
3000	9843
2000	6562
1000	3281
500	1640
200	656
0	0
Land below sea level	
200	656
4000	13124
6000	19686

Conic Equidistant Projection

1:6 000 000

MILES 0 50 100 150

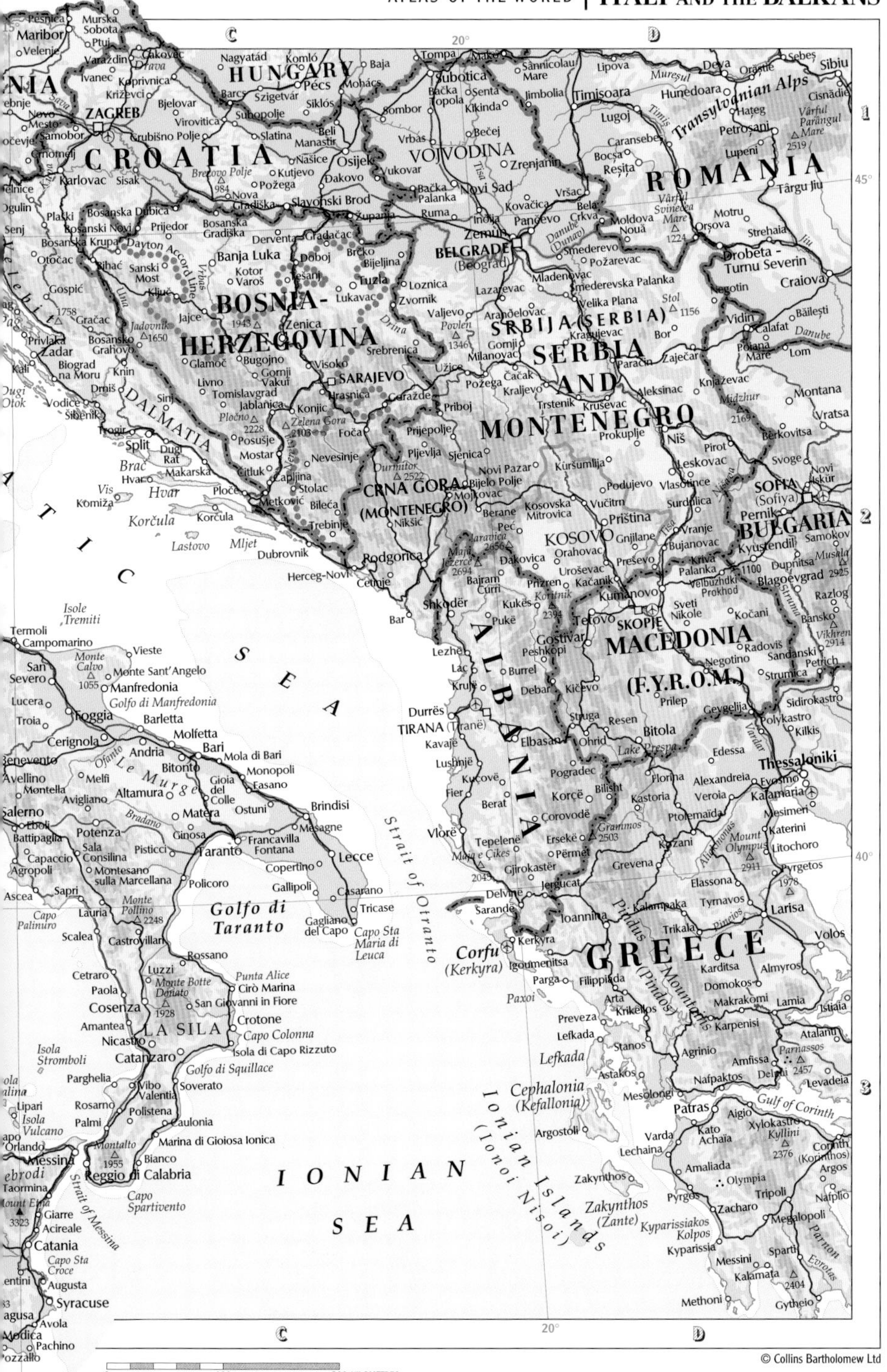

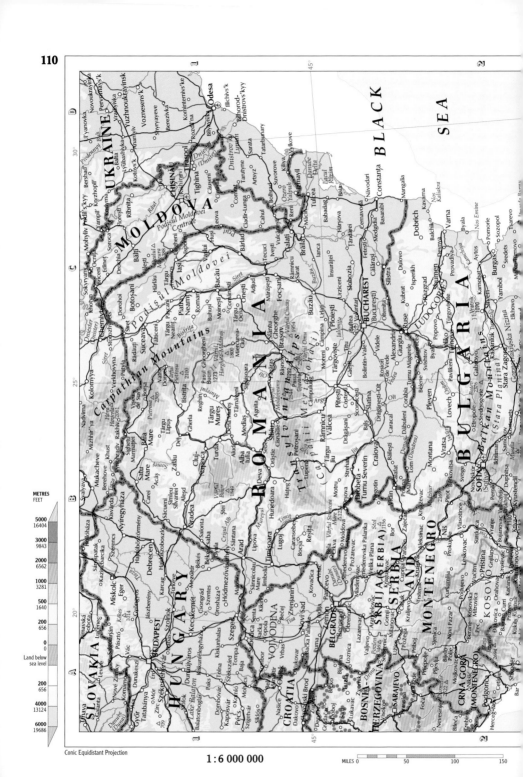

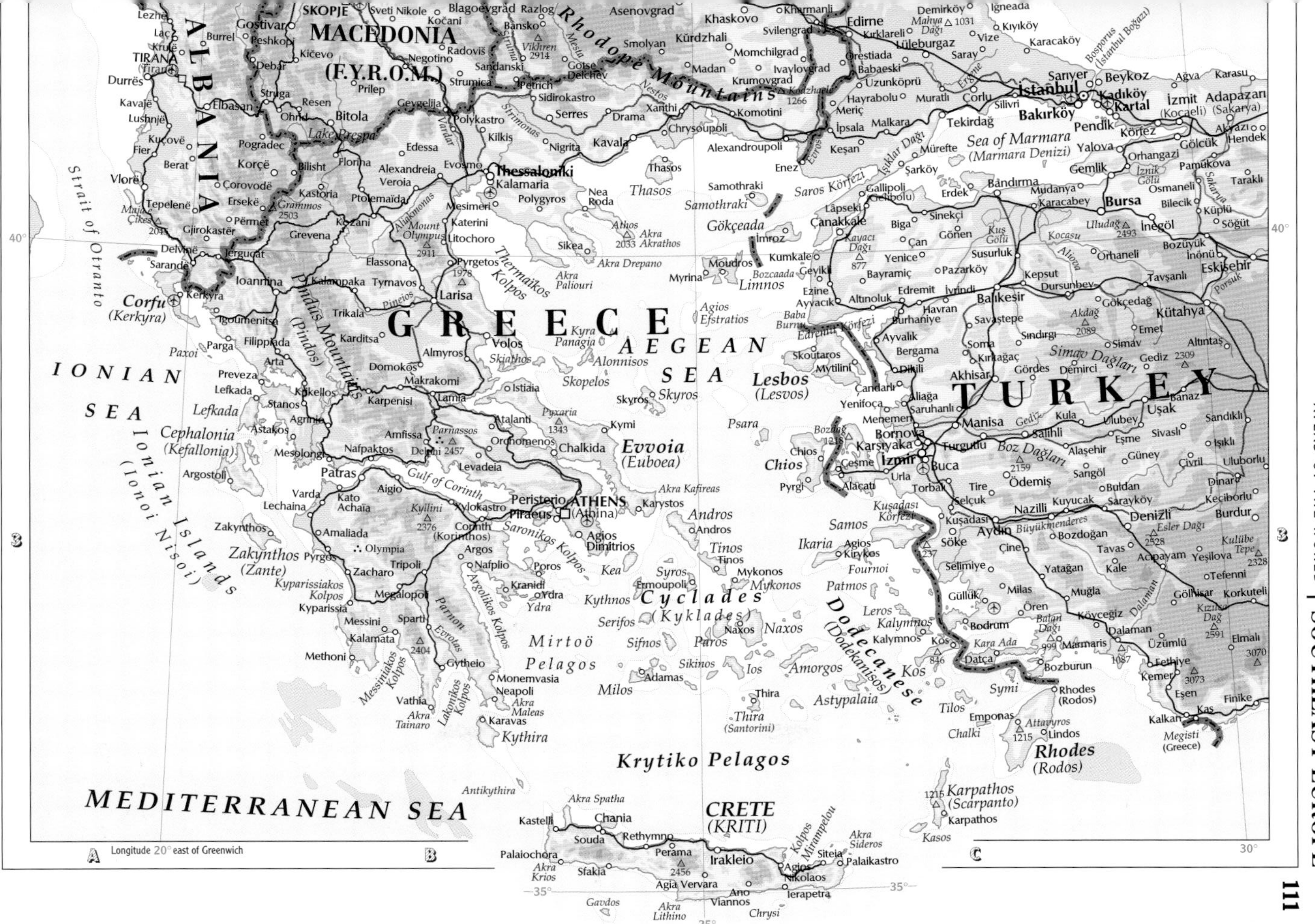
ALBANIA
MACEDONIA
(F.Y.R.O.M.)
GREECE
TURKEY
AEGEAN SEA
IONIAN SEA
MEDITERRANEAN SEA
Krytiko Pelagos
Mirtoö Pelagos
Sea of Marmara
(Marmara Denizi)
Strait of Otranto
Rhodope Mountains
Pindus Mountains
(Pindos)
Ionian Islands
(Ionoi Nisoi)
Corfu
(Kerkyra)
Lefkada
Cephalonia
(Kefallonia)
Zakynthos
(Zante)
Evvoia
(Euboea)
Lesbos
(Lesvos)
Chios
Samos
Cyclades
(Kyklades)
Dodecanese
(Dodekanisos)
Rhodes
(Rodos)
Karpathos
(Scarpanto)
CRETE
(KRITI)
Thira
(Santorini)
Naxos
Milos
Kythira
Thasos
Limnos
Gökçeada
Skyros
ATHENS
(Athina)
Thessaloniki
TIRANA
(Tiranë)
SKOPJE
İstanbul
İzmir
Bursa
Longitude 20° east of Greenwich
0 100 200 KILOMETRES

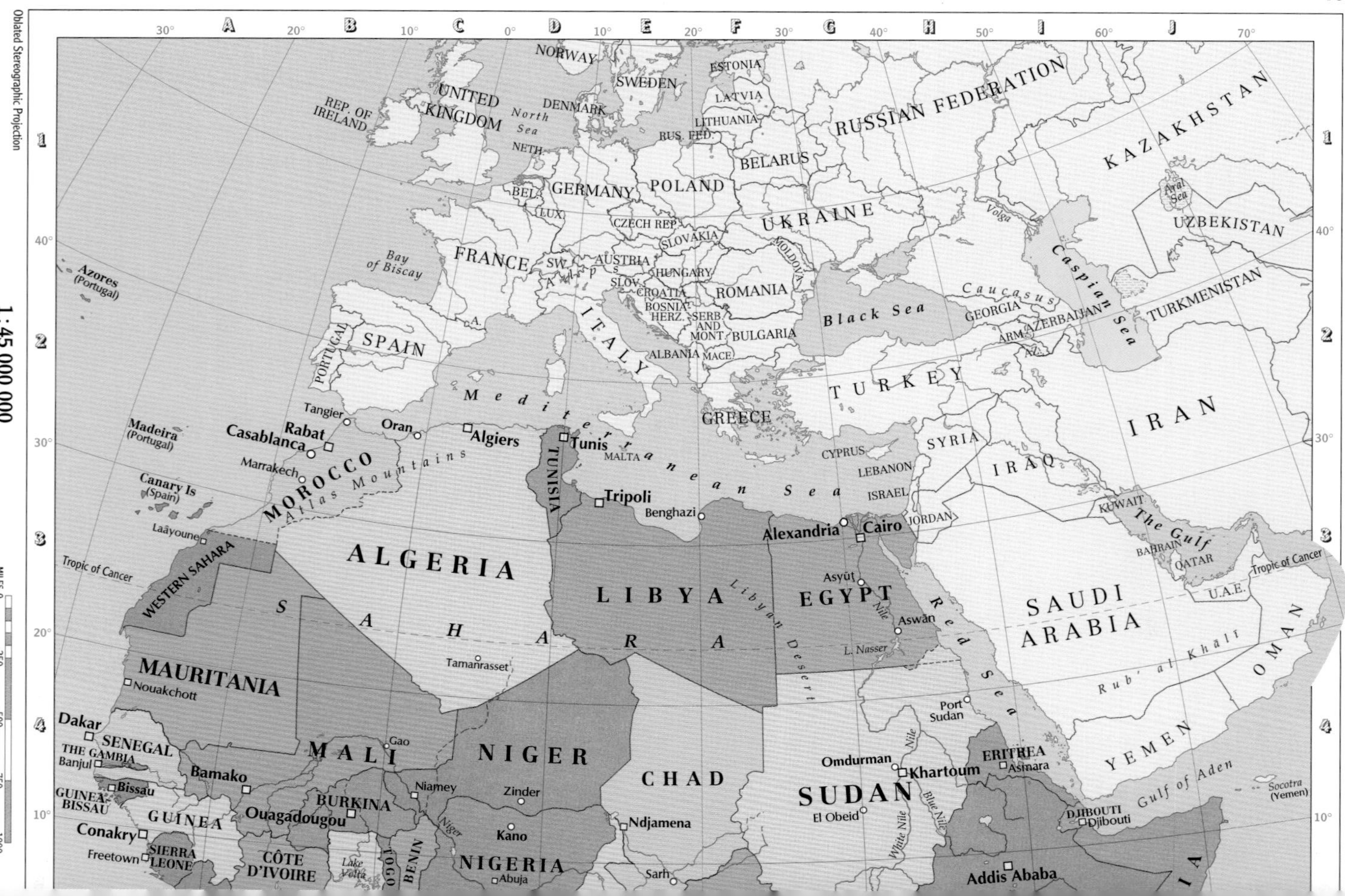

Oblated Stereographic Projection

1 : 45 000 000

MILES 0   250   500   750   1000

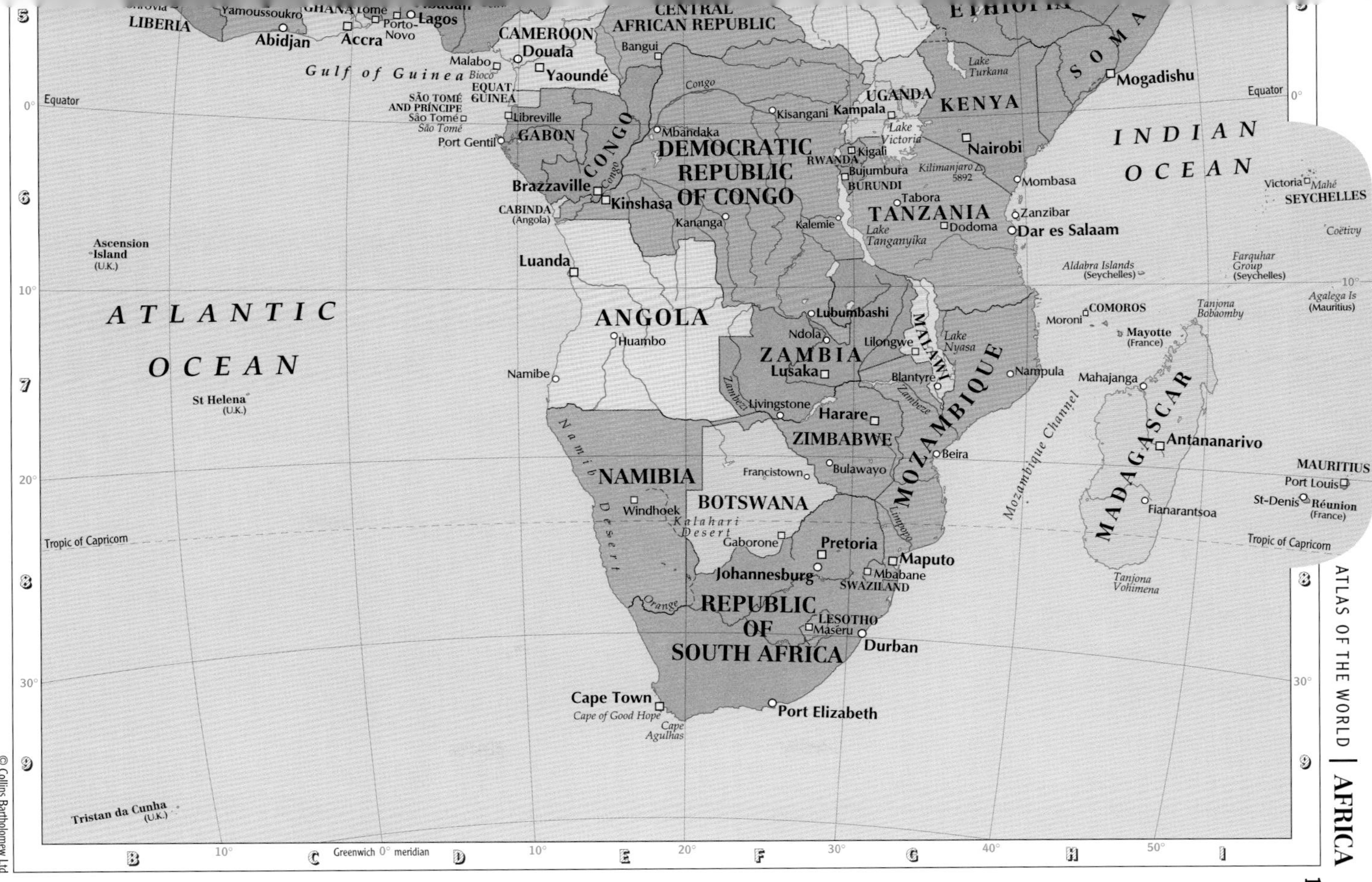

0   500   1000   1500 KILOMETRES

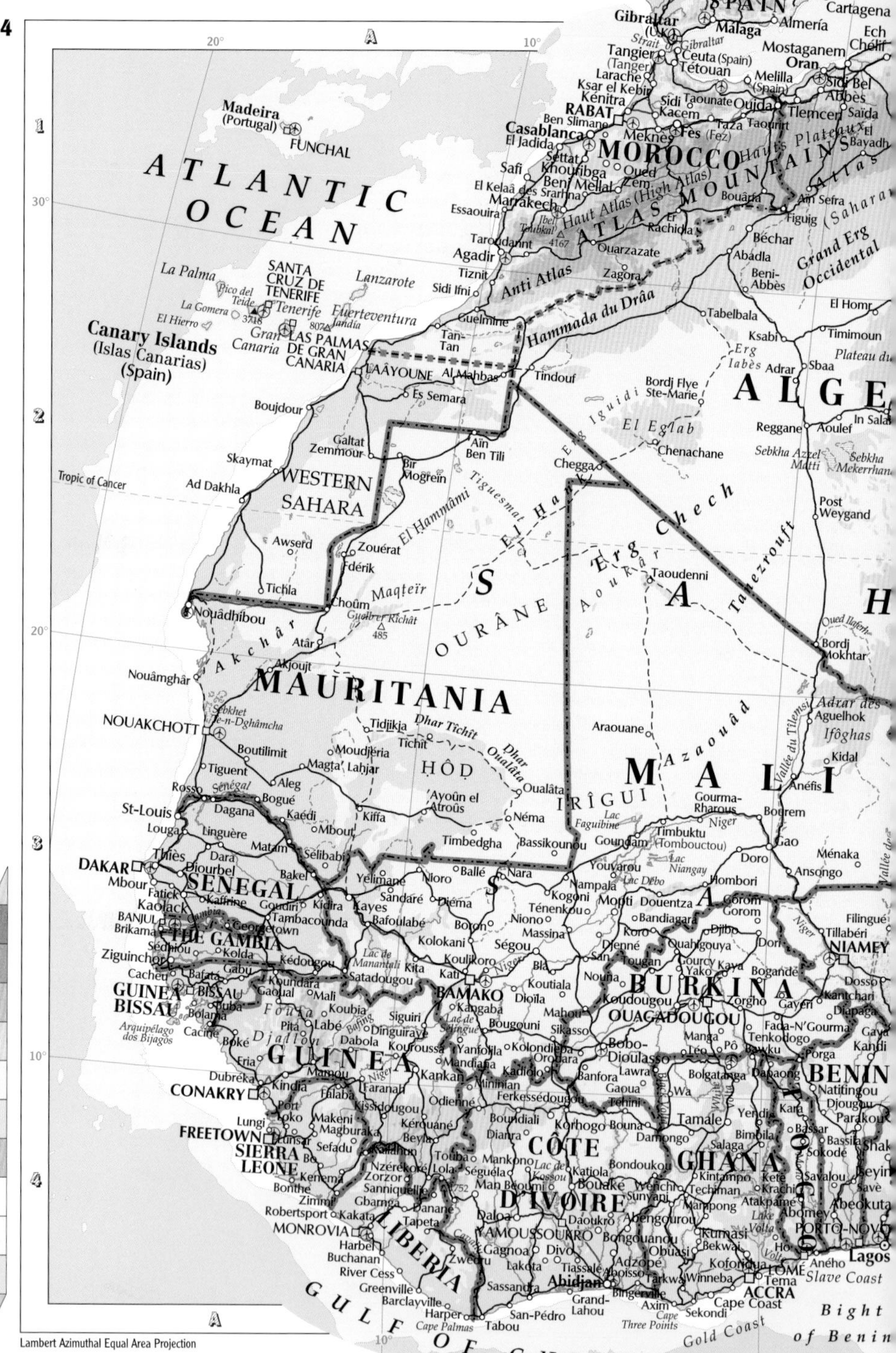

ATLANTIC OCEAN

Madeira (Portugal) ✈ FUNCHAL

Canary Islands (Islas Canarias) (Spain)

La Palma
SANTA CRUZ DE TENERIFE
Pico del Teide 3718
La Gomera
El Hierro
Tenerife
Gran Canaria
LAS PALMAS DE GRAN CANARIA
Lanzarote
Fuerteventura
Jandía 802

Tropic of Cancer

Ad Dakhla

Skaymat
Galtat Zemmour
Bir Mogreïn

Boujdour

WESTERN SAHARA

Es Semara
LAAYOUNE
Al Mahbas
Ain Ben Tili

Awserd
Zouérat
El Hammâmi
Choûm
Güelta Richât 485

Nouâdhibou

Akchâr

Tichla
Fdérik
Maqteïr

Atâr

Nouâmghâr
Akjoujt

MAURITANIA

NOUAKCHOTT
Sebkhet Te-n-Dghâmcha
Tidjikja
Moudjéria
Magta'Lahjar
Tichit
Dhar Tichît
Boutilimit
Tiguent
Aleg
Bogué

St-Louis
Rosso
Dagana
Sénégal
Kaédi
Kiffa
Néma
Ayoûn el Atroûs
Oualâta
HÔD
Dhar Oualâta

Louga
Linguère
Matam
Sélibabi
Nioro
Ballé
Nara

Thiès
DAKAR
Diourbel
Bakel
Yélimané
Diéma
Nampala

Mbour
Fatick
Kaffrine
Goudiry
Kidira
Hayes
Sandaré
Kogoni
Ténénkou
Massina

SENEGAL
Kaolack
Gossas
Tambacounda
Bafoulabé
Boron
Niono
Ségou
Djenné

BANJUL
Brikama
THE GAMBIA
Kolda
Kédougou
Kita
Kali
Koutiala

Ziguinchor
Cacheu
Bignona
Kouniara
Mali
Koubia
Siguiri
Kolokani
Koulikoro
Dioila
Sikasso

Cacine
GUINEA BISSAU
Gabú
Bafatá
Bissorã
Koundara
Pita
Labé
Dinguiraye
BAMAKO
Mahou
Bougouni
Bobo-Dioulasso
Banfora

Bolama
Arquipélago dos Bijagós
Boké
Fria
Dubréka
Télimélé
Dalaba
Mamou
Faranah
Kankan
Kérouané
Odienné
Korhogo
Gaoua
Wa

GUINEA
CONAKRY
Kindia
Kissidougou
Mankono
Bondoukou

Lungi
Makeni
Magburaka
Kabala
Beyla
Séguéla
Bouaké

FREETOWN
Lunsar
Sefadu
Nzérékoré
Lola
Man
Bouaflé

SIERRA LEONE
Kenema
Zorzor
Sanniquellie
Daloa

Bonthe
Zimmi
Robertsport
Kakata
Tapeta
Tabou
YAMOUSSOUKRO

MONROVIA
Harbel
LIBERIA
Gagnoa
Divo
CÔTE D'IVOIRE

Buchanan
River Cess
Lakota
Tiassalé
ABIDJAN

Greenville
Sassandra
Grand-Lahou

Barclayville
Harper
San-Pédro
Cape Palmas

GULF OF GUINEA

MOROCCO

RABAT
Gibraltar (UK)
Tangier (Tanger)
Ceuta (Spain)
Tetouan
Larache
Ksar el Kebir
Kénitra
Casablanca
El Jadida
Settat
Khouribga
Safi
Essaouira
Marrakech
Agadir
Taroudannt
Sidi Ifni
Tan-Tan
Guelmime
Tiznit
Anti Atlas
Haut Atlas (High Atlas)
Jbel Toubkal 4167

SPAIN
Gibraltar
Strait of Gibraltar
Málaga
Almería
Cartagena
Melilla (Spain)
Oran
Mostaganem
Sidi Bel Abbès
Tlemcen
Saïda
Bayadh
Béchar
Abadla
Beni-Abbès
Figuig
Aïn Sefra
Haut Plateaux

Meknès
Fès (Fez)
Faza
Taourirt
Oujda
Sidi Slimane
Oued Zem
Beni Mellal
El Kelaâ des Srarhna
Ksabi
Rachidia
Ouarzazate
Zagora
Hammada du Drâa

ALGE...
Grand Erg Occidental
Sahara
El Homr
Tabelbala
Timimoun
Ksabi
Reggane
Aoulef
In Salah
Plateau du Tademaït

LAAYOUNE
Tindouf
Iguidi
El Eglab
Chenachane
Sebkha Azzel Matti
Sebkha Mekerrhane
Post Weygand

Tiguesmat
El Hammâmi
Chegga
Erg Chech
Taoudenni
El Erg
Aouk
Erg
Aguelhok
Erg Tarezrouft

El Mzereb
Bordj Mokhtar
Oued Ifetessene

SAHARA

Adrar des Ifôghas
Aguelhok
Araouane
Kidal
Anéfis

MALI
Timbuktu (Tombouctou)
Goundam
Niafunké
Gao
Ménaka
Ansongo
Gourma-Rharous
Bourem
Doro
Hombori

OURÂNE
Aoukâr
Azaouad
Vallée du Tilemsi

IRÎGUI
Lac Faguibine
Niger
Lac Débo
Lac Niangay

Timbedgha
Bassikounou
Douentza
Gorom-Gorom
Dori
Djibo
Filingué
Tillabéri
NIAMEY

Mopti
Bandiagara
Ouahigouya
Kaya
Zorgho
Fada-N'Gourma
Kantchari
Diapaga
Dosso
Birnin

BURKINA
Koudougou
OUAGADOUGOU
Manga
Pô
Bawku
Tenkodogo
Bolgatanga
Gaya
Kandi

Orodara
Léo
Dapaong
Malanville
BENIN

Tamale
Yendi
Natitingou
Djougou
Parakou

Ferkessédougou
Bouna
Kara
Bassila
Bassari
Sokodé

Katiola
Bondoukou
Bole
Salaga
Atakpamé
Kpalimé
Savé
Abeokuta

CÔTE D'IVOIRE
Bouaké
Yamoussoukro
Dimbokro
Bongouanou
Obuasi
Kumasi
Koforidua
TOGO
Aného
PORTO-NOVO
LOMÉ
Lagos

Agboville
Aboisso
Tarkwa
Winneba
ACCRA
Tema

Grand-Bassam
Axim
Sekondi
Cape Coast
Gold Coast
Slave Coast

GHANA
Techiman
Sunyani
Lake Volta
Ho

BIGHT of BENIN

Lambert Azimuthal Equal Area Projection

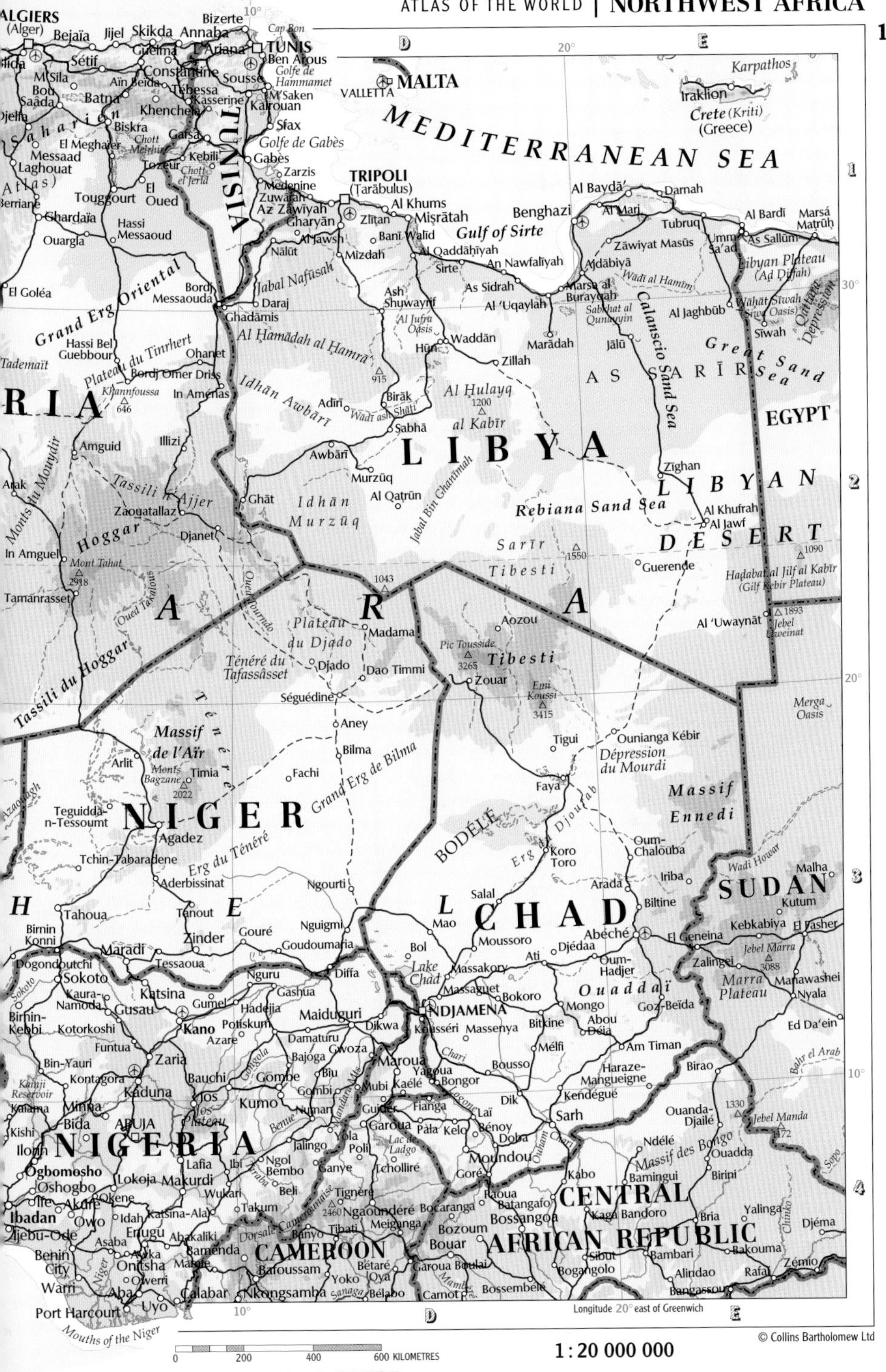

ALGIERS (Alger)
Bejaïa
Jijel
Skikda
Annaba
Bizerte
Cap Bon
TUNIS
VALLETTA **MALTA**
MEDITERRANEAN SEA
Iraklion
Crete (Kriti) (Greece)
Karpathos

Béjaïa
Sétif
Aïn Beïda
Constantine
Souss
Ben Arous
Golfe de Hammamet
Karpathos

M'Sila
Bou Saâda
Batna
Khenchela
Kasserine
Kairouan
Sfax
Golfe de Gabès

Djelfa
Biskra
El Meghaïer
Gafsa
Chott Melrhir
Kebili
Gabès
Zarzis

Messaad
Laghouat
Touggourt
El Oued
Chott el Jerid
Medenine
Zuwārah
Al Khums
Mişrātah
Al Baydā'
Darnah

Atlas
Berriane
Ghardaïa
Hassi Messaoud
Bordj Messaouda
Daraj
Ghadāmis
Az Zāwiyah
Gharyān
Al Jawsh
Nālūt
Banī Walīd
Zlitan
TRIPOLI (Ţarābulus)
Al Qaddāḩīyah
Sirte
Mizdah
An Nawfalīyah
Benghazi
Al Marj
Zāwiyat Masūs
Tubruq
Marsá Maţrūḩ
As Sallūm

El Goléa
Ouargla
Hassi Bel Guebbour
Jabal Nafūsah
Al Ḩamādah al Ḩamrā'
Waddān
Ash Shuwayrif
As Sidrah
Al 'Uqaylah
Marsá al Burayqah
Sabḩat al Qunayyin
Al Jaghbūb
Siwah
Siwah Oasis
Libyan Plateau (Ad Diffah)
Wāḩāt Siwah

Plateau du Tinrhert
Bordj Omer Driss
Ohanet
Al Ḩulayq al Kabīr
Marādah
Zillah
Al Jaghbūb
Jālū
AS SARĪR Sand Sea
Great Sand Sea
EGYPT

Tademaït
Khanfoussa
646
In Amenas
Adiri
Wādi ash Shāṭi'
Sabhā
Bi'r al 'Abd
Ţighan
LIBYAN DESERT

Amguid
Illizi
Awbārī
Murzūq
Al Qaţrūn
Rebiana Sand Sea
Al Khufrah
Al Jawf
1090

Hoggar
Tassili N'Ajjer
Ghāt
Idhān Murzūq
Jabal Bin Ghanīmah
Sarīr
Guerende
1550
Ḩaḑabat al Jilf al Kabīr (Gilf Kebir Plateau)
1893
Jebel 'Uwaynāt

In Amguel
Mont Tahat 2918
Oued Tafassasset
Djanet
Plateau du Djado
Madama
Pic Toussidé 3265
Zouar
Tibesti
Emi Koussi 3415
Al 'Uwaynāt

Tamanrasset
Tassili du Hoggar
Ténéré du Tafassâsset
Dao Timmi
Séguédine
Aozou
Tigui
Ounianga Kébir
Dépression du Mourdi
Merga Oasis

Azaougah
Massif de l'Aïr
Monts Bagzane 2022
Timia
Aney
Bilma
Grand Erg de Bilma
Faya
Koro Toro
Massif Ennedi

Arlit
Teguidda-n-Tessoumt
Agadez
Fachi
Ngourti
BODÉLÉ
Erg du Djourab
Oum-Chalouba
Iriba
Wadi Howar
Malha
Kutum

NIGER
Tchin-Tabaradene
Aderbissinat
Erg du Ténéré
Arada
Biltine
SUDAN
Kebkabiya
El Fasher

Tahoua
Tanout
Zinder
Gouré
Goudoumaria
Salal
Mao
CHAD
Ati
Djédaa
El Geneina
Zalingei
Jebel Marra 3088
Manawashei
Nyala

Birnin Konni
Maradi
Tessaoua
Nguigmi
Bol
Lake Chad
Massakory
Bokoro
Mongo
Goz-Beïda
Ed Da'ein

Dogondoutchi
Sokoto
Katsina
Gusau
Gumel
Hadejia
Diffa
Gashua
Maïduguri
Dikwa
NDJAMENA
Massenya
Bitkine
Abou Déia
Am Timan
Haraze-Mangueigne
Birao

Birnin-Kebbi
Funtua
Kano
Potiskum
Damaturu
Gwoza
Maroua
Mubi
Kaélé
Bongor
Melfi
Bousso
Kendégué
Ouanda-Djallé 1330
Jebel Manda 1372

Kaura-Namoda
Kotorkoshi
Zaria
Azare
Gombe
Biu
Garoua
Guider
Figuil
Laï
Sarh
Ndélé
Ouadda
Birini

NIGERIA
Kaduna
Bauchi
Jos
Kumo
Numan
Yola
Pala
Kelo
Dik
Bénoy
Doba
Kyabé
Massif des Bongo

Minna
Lafia
Makurdi
Wukari
Jalingo
Ngol
Bembo
Poli
Tcholliré
Moundou
Batangafo
Bozoum
Bozoum
Bangassou

ABUJA
Lokoja
Ibi
Takum
Tignère
Ngaoundéré 2460
Bocaranga
Bossangoa
Kaga Bandoro
Bambari
Alindao
Zémio

Ogbomosho
Oshogbo
Okene
Idah
Katsina-Ala
Banyo
Tibati
Meiganga
Bouar
CENTRAL AFRICAN REPUBLIC
Sibut
Bria
Yalinga
Djéma

Ibadan
Akure
Owo
Enugu
Abakaliki
Bamenda
Foumban
Yoko
Bétaré Oya
Bogangolo
Bambari

Benin City
Asaba
Onitsha
Calabar
Krangsamba
Bafoussam
Garoua Boulaï
Bélabo
Carnot
Bossembélé
Banassou

Warri
Aba
Uyo
Port Harcourt
Mouths of the Niger

METRES
FEET

METRES	FEET
5000	16404
3000	9843
2000	6562
1000	3281
500	1640
200	656
0	0
Land below sea level	
200	656
4000	13124
6000	19686

Lambert Azimuthal Equal Area Projection

1:20 000 000

MILES 0 100 200 300 400

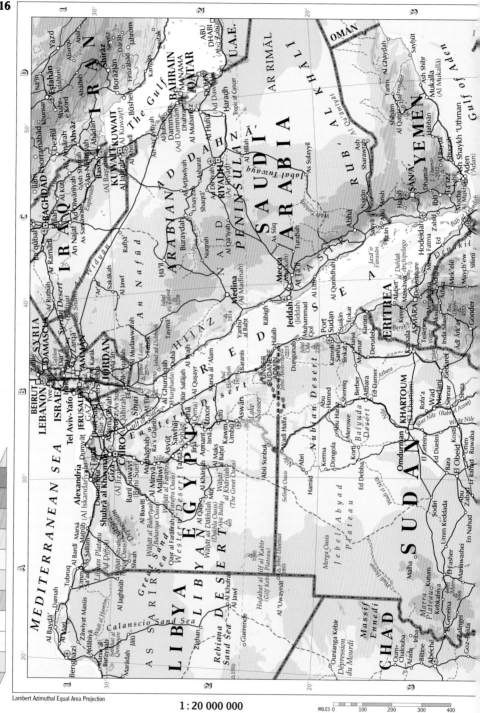

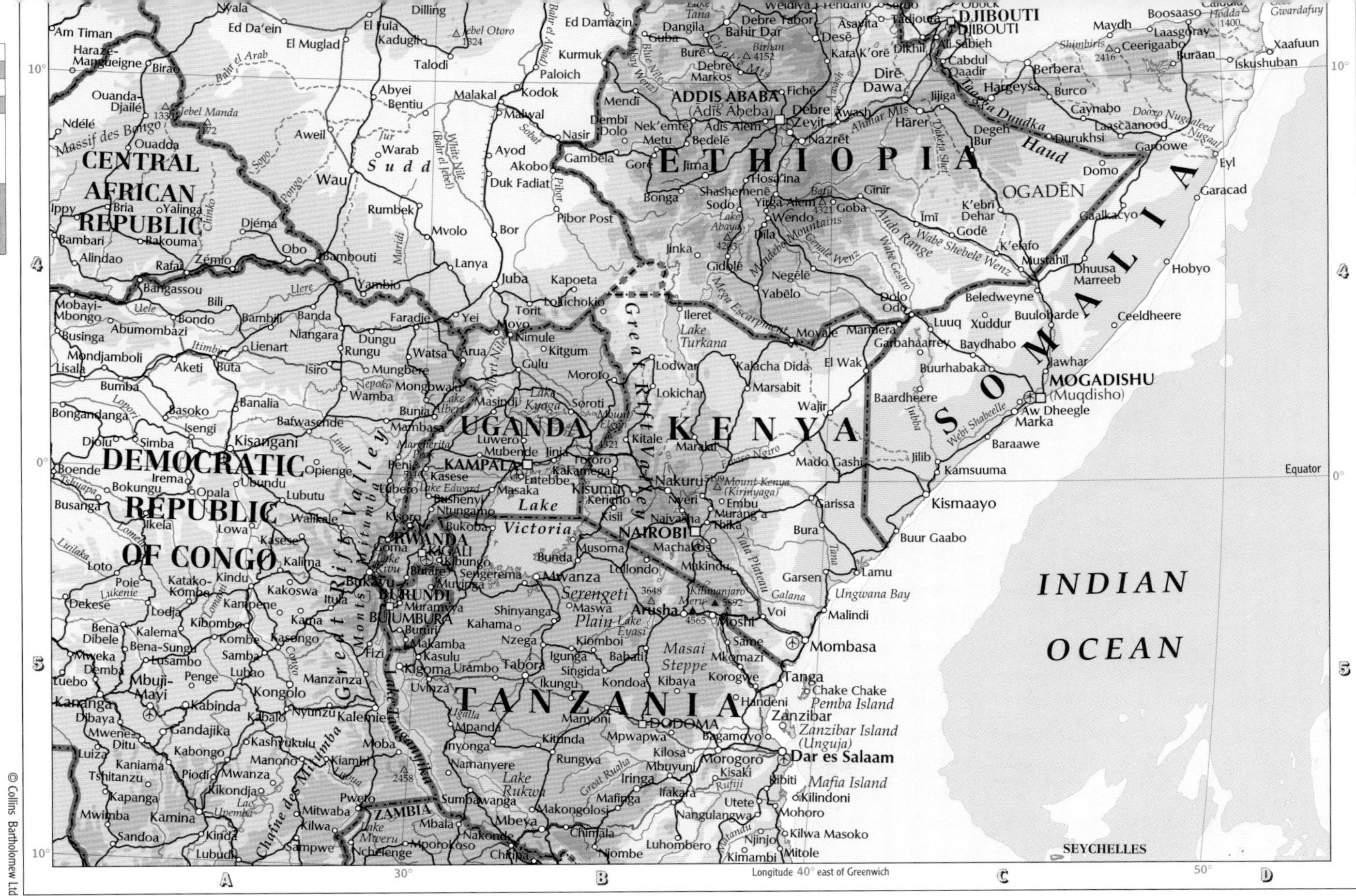

INDIAN

OCEAN

SOMALIA

ETHIOPIA

KENYA

TANZANIA

UGANDA

DEMOCRATIC
REPUBLIC
OF CONGO

CENTRAL
AFRICAN
REPUBLIC

DJIBOUTI

SEYCHELLES

ZAMBIA

Great Rift Valley

MOGADISHU
(Muqdisho)

NAIROBI

ADDIS ABABA
(Adis Abeba)

KAMPALA

BUJUMBURA

Equator

Longitude 40° east of Greenwich

White Nile
(Bahr el Jebel)

Lake
Victoria

Lake
Tanganyika

Dar es Salaam

Mombasa

Zanzibar

0   200   400   600 KILOMETRES

© Collins Bartholomew Ltd

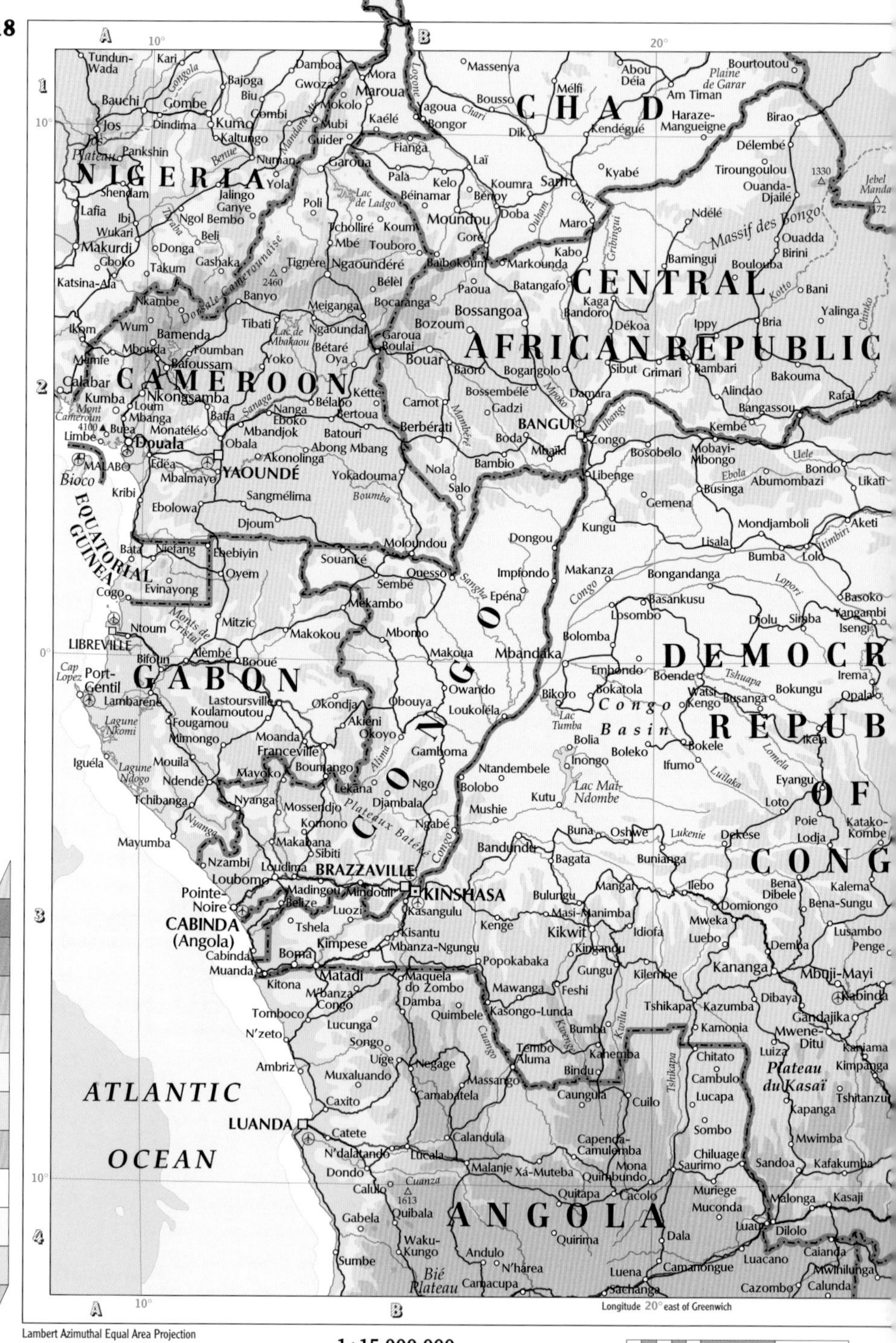

A   10°   B   20°

1

10°

C H A D

Tundun-
Wada   Kari   Damboa
Bauchi Gombe   Bajoga Gwoza Mora   Massenya   Abou   Bourtoutou
        Biu   Combi Mokolo Maroua   Boussa Mélfi Déïa   Plaine
Jos Dindima Kumo Kaltungo Kaélé Yagoua Bongor Dik   Am Timan de Garar
        Mubi   Guider   Fianga   Kendégué Haraze- Birao
NIGERIA Shendam Numan Garoua Pala Kelo Laï   Kyabé Mangueigne Délembé
Lafia Ibi Yola Poli Béïnamar Koumra Sarh   Tiroungoulou Ouanda- 1330
Wukari Ngol Ganye Lac Mbé Touboro Moundou Doba Maro Ndélé   Djallé Jebel
Makurdi Bembo Beli de Ladgo Koum   Gore Oham Kabo Bamingui Ouadda Marra 1472
Gboko Takum Gashaka Tchollíré Ngaoundéré Baïbokoum Markounda Batangafo Boulouba Birini Massif des Bongo
Katsina-Ala Ikom Banyo Tibati Méïganga Bélel Paoua Bozoum Dékoa Ippy Bria Yalinga
Ikom Wum Bamenda Ngaoundal Bétaré Bocaranga   Bossangoa Kaga Bandoro Bambari Bakouma
Calabar Mbouda Foumban Yoko Oya Bouar **CENTRAL**   Sibut Grimari Alindao Rafaï
Kumba Nkongsamba Bafoussam Kétté Carnot Bogangolo Damara **AFRICAN REPUBLIC** Bangassou
Loum Mbanga Nanga Bélabo Bertoua Berbérati Gadzi Mbaïki **BANGUI** Zongo Bosobolo Mobayi- Bondo Likati
Douala Monatélé Eboko Batouri Boda   Libenge Mbongo Abumombazi
MALABO Edéa Obala Akonolinga Abong Mbang Bambio Salo Dongou Businga Akéti
Bioco Mbalmayo YAOUNDÉ Yokadouma Nola   Kungu Gemena Mondjamboli
Kribi Ebolowa Sangmélima   Boumba Impfondo Basankusu Bumba Lolo
EQUATORIAL Djoum Souanké Moloundou Ouesso Épéna Bongandanga Basoko
GUINEA Bata Niefang Ebebiyin Sembé Mékambo Bolomba Djolu Yangambi
Cogo Evinayong Oyem Makokou Mbomo Makua Mbandaka Boende **DEMOCR**
LIBREVILLE Mitzic Booué Owando Bikoro Embondo Watsi Bokungu Opala
Ntoum Alembé Okondja Bolia Kengo Busanga Eyangu Kataka-
Port- Bifoun **GABON** Akéni Gamboma Bokatola Ifumo Loto Kombe
Gentil Lambaréné Lastoursville Okoyo Ntandembele Inongo Boleko **REPUB** Lodja
Koulamoutou Moanda Lac Bokele Lusambo
Fougamou Franceville Ngo Tumba Poie **OF** Demba
Iguéla Mouila Mimongo Boumango Bolobo Lac Maï- Dekese
Mayoko Lekana Mushie Ndombe Buniang **CONG** Penge
Tchibanga Ndendé Nyanga Mossendjo Komono Buna Oshwe Lukenie Bena Mbuji-Mayi
Mayumba Nzambi Makabana Djambala Ngabé Bandundu Bagata Dibele Bena-Sungu
Loubomo Sibiti Bulungu Mangai Mweka Dibaya Nebinda
BRAZZAVILLE Madingou Mindouli **KINSHASA** Kasangulu Masi-Manimba Idiofa Luebo Kananga Dibaya
Pointe- Belize Luozi Kisantu Kenge Kikwit Kipushi Luiza Kamonia Kanyama
Noire Tshela Mbanza-Ngungu Popokabaka Gungu Kilembe Tshikapa Kazumba Mwene- Kimpanga
CABINDA Kimpese Boma Feshi Mawanga Kasongo-Lunda Bumba Kamonia Ditu Gandajika
(Angola) Cabinda Muanda Kitona Matadi M'banza Lucunga Songo Quimbele Kahemba Chitato Luiza
Tomboco Congo do Zombo Damba Tembo Bindu Tshikapa Mwinilunga
N'zeto Uíge Quimbele Aluma Caungula Cuilo Cambulo Plateau
Ambriz Negage Massango Lucapa du Kasaï
Muxaluando Camabatela Mona Kapanga
Caxito **ANGOLA**

0°

10°

ATLANTIC

OCEAN

LUANDA Catete
N'dalatando Lucala Malanje Xá-Muteba Quitapa Cacolo Saurimo Muriege Malonga Kasaji
Dondo Calulo Cuanza Cacolo Chiluage Muconda Sandoa Kafakumba
Gabela Quibala 1613 Quirima Quimbundo Dala Cazombo Luau Caianda Mwihulunga
Waku- Quibala Quirima Cuilo Chitato Luena Camanongue Luacano Calunda
Kungo Andulo N'harea Camacupa Luena Sachanga

4

Sumbe Bié Plateau

METRES FEET
5000 16404
3000 9843
2000 6562
1000 3281
500 1640
200 656
0 0
Land below
sea level
200 656
4000 13124
6000 19686

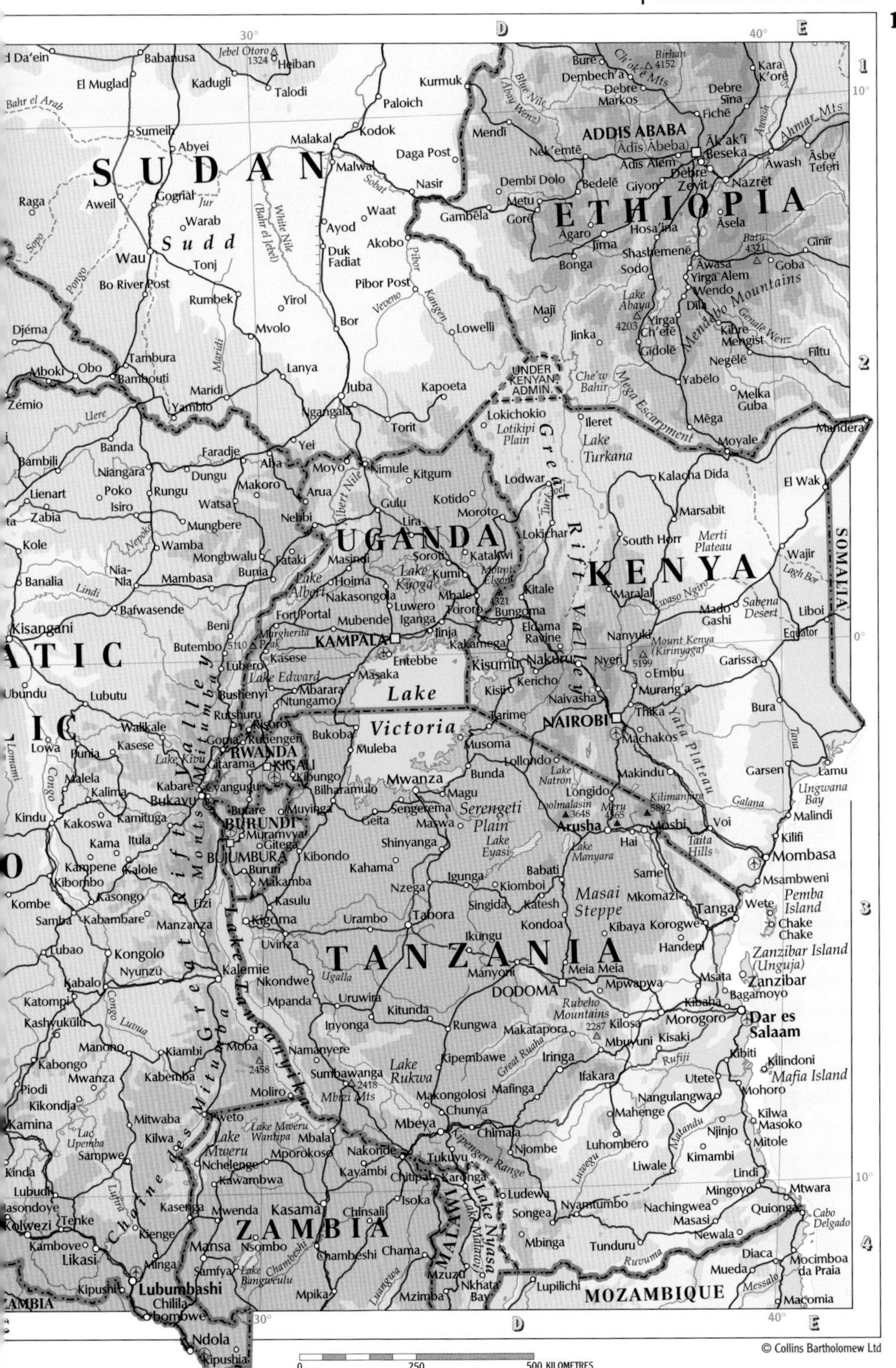
SUDAN
ETHIOPIA
UGANDA
KENYA
TANZANIA
RWANDA
BURUNDI
ZAMBIA
MALAWI
MOZAMBIQUE
SOMALIA
ADDIS ABABA
KAMPALA
NAIROBI
DODOMA
KIGALI
BUJUMBURA
Dar es Salaam
Lake Victoria
Lake Turkana
Lake Tanganyika
Lake Nyasa
Great Rift Valley
0 250 500 KILOMETRES

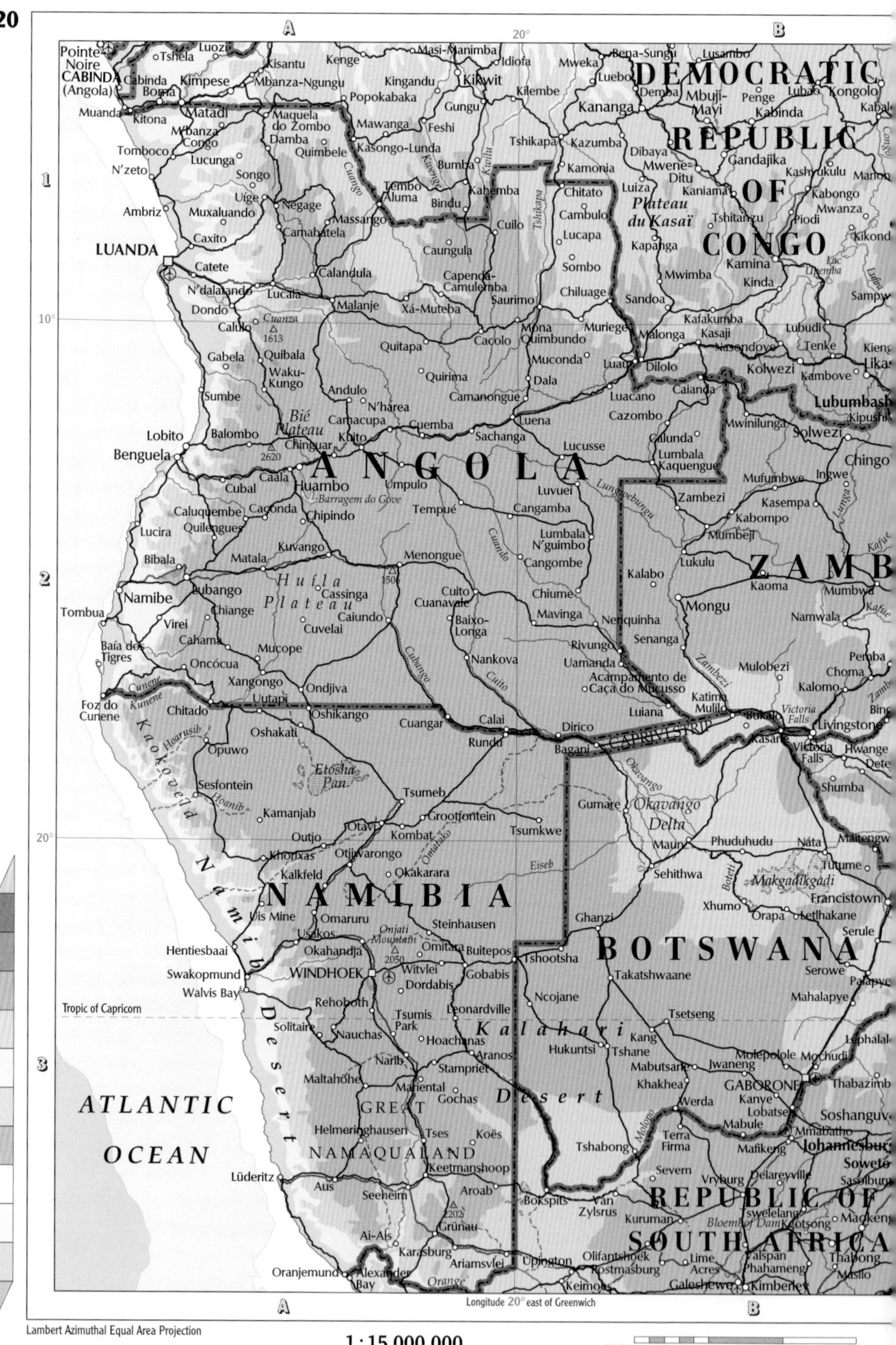

Pointe-Noire
Luozi
Tshela
Kisantu
Kenge
Masi-Manimba
Idiofa
Mweka
Bena-Sungu
Lusambo
CABINDA (Angola)
Cabinda
Kimpese
Mbanza-Ngungu
Kingandu
Kikwit
Kilembe
Luebo
Demba
Mbuji-Mayi
Penge
Lubao
Kongolo
Kabal
DEMOCRATIC
Boma
Popokabaka
Gungu
Kananga
REPUBLIC
Muanda
Kitona
Matadi
Maquela do Zombo
Mawanga
Feshi
Tshikapa
Kazumba
Dibaya
Mwene-Ditu
Gandajika
Kashyukulu
Manon
Mbanza Congo
Damba
Kasongo-Lunda
Bumba
Kamonia
Kaniama
Tshibangu
Kabongo
Mwanza
OF
Tomboco
Lucunga
Songo
Quimbele
Chitato
Plateau du Kasaï
Kamina
Kabinda
Piodi
Kikond
N'zeto
Uige
Negage
Tembo Aluma
Bindu
Kahemba
Cuilo
Cambulo
Lucapa
Kapanga
Kamina
Kinda
CONGO
Ambriz
Muxaluando
Massango
Camabatela
Caungula
Sombo
Mwimba
Sampy
Caxito
LUANDA
Catete
Calandula
Capenda-Camulemba
Saurimo
Chiluage
Sandoa
Kafakumba
Lubudi
Kieng
N'dalatando
Dondo
Malanje
Xá-Muteba
Cacolo
Mona Quimbundo
Muriege
Malonga
Kasaji
Nasondoya
Tenke
Likas
Calulo
Cuanza
1613
Quibala
Quitapa
Muconda
Luau
Dilolo
Kolwezi
Kambove
Lubumbash
Gabela
Waku-Kungo
Andulo
Quirima
Dala
Luacano
Caianda
Mwinilunga
Solwezi
Kipushi
Sumbe
Balombo
N'harea
Camacupa
Cuemba
Camanongue
Luena
Cazombo
Calunda
Chingo
Lobito
Bié Plateau
Chinguar
Koito
Sachanga
Lucusse
Lumbala Kaquengue
Ingwe
Benguela
Caála
Huambo
Umpulo
Cangamba
Zambezi
Kasempa
ANGOLA
Mufumbwe
Kabompo
Cubal
ZAMB
Caluquembe
Cagonda
Chipindo
Tempué
Luvuei
Mumbeji
Lucira
Quilengues
Kuvango
Menongue
Lumbala N'guimbo
Cangombe
Lukulu
Kaoma
Mumbwa
Bibala
Matala
Cassinga
Cuito Cuanavale
Chiume
Kalabo
Mongu
Namwala
Tombua
Namibe
Lubango
Huila Plateau
Caiundo
Baixo-Longa
Mavinga
Neriquinha
Senanga
Peroba
Virei
Chiange
Cuvelai
Nankova
Uamanda
Mulobezi
Choma
Kalomo
Baía dos Tigres
Cahama
Mucope
Oncócua
Acampamento de Caça do Mucusso
Katima Mulilo
Zamb
Foz do Cunene
Chitado
Xangongo
Ondjiva
Luiana
Kasan
Victoria Falls
Livingstone
Uutapi
Oshikango
Cuangar
Calai
Dirico
Bagani
Victoria Falls
Kazung
Hwange
Dete
Oshakati
Rundu
Shumba
Opuwo
Etosha Pan
Tsumeb
Gumare
Okavango Delta
Nata
Maitengw
Sesfontein
Kamanjab
Otavi
Grootfontein
Tsumkwe
Maun
Phuduhudu
Tutume
Outjo
Kombat
Otjiwarongo
Eiseb
Sehithwa
Makgadikgadi
Francistown
Khorixas
Kalkfeld
Okakarara
Orapa
Xetlhakane
NAMIBIA
Ghanzi
Xhumo
Serule
Uis Mine
Omaruru
Onjati
Steinhausen
BOTSWANA
Serowe
Palapye
Hentiesbaai
Usakos
Okahandja
Omitara
Buitepos
Tshootsha
Takatshwaane
Mahalapye
Swakopmund
WINDHOEK
Witvlei
Dordabis
Gobabis
Ncojane
Tsetseng
Iphalal
Walvis Bay
Rehoboth
Leonardville
Kalahari
Kang
Hukuntsi
Molepolole
Mochudi
Tropic of Capricorn
Solitaire
Tsumis Park
Nauchas
Hoachanas
Tshane
Mabutsane
Jwaneng
Thabazim
Thabazimb
Narib
Aranos
Stampriet
Khakhea
Werda
GABORONE
Kanye
Soshanguv
Maltahöhe
Mariental
Gochas
Desert
Terra Firma
Mabule
Mmabatho
Johannesbur
Helmeringhausen
Tses
Koës
Tshabong
Mafikeng
Soweto
GREAT
NAMAQUALAND
Keetmanshoop
Severn
Vryburg
Delareyville
Sasolbur
Lüderitz
Aus
Seeheim
Aroab
Bokspits
Van Zylsrus
Kuruman
Taung
REPUBLIC OF
Bloemhof Dam
Klerksdorp
Macken
Ai-Ais
Karasburg
Ariamsvlei
Upington
Olifantshoek
Lime Acres
Warrenton
Vaalspan
Phahameng
Thabong
SOUTH AFRICA
Oranjemund
Alexander Bay
Orange
Keimoes
Galeshewe
Kimberle

ATLANTIC OCEAN

Lambert Azimuthal Equal Area Projection

Longitude 20° east of Greenwich

1 : 15 000 000

MILES 0   100   200   300

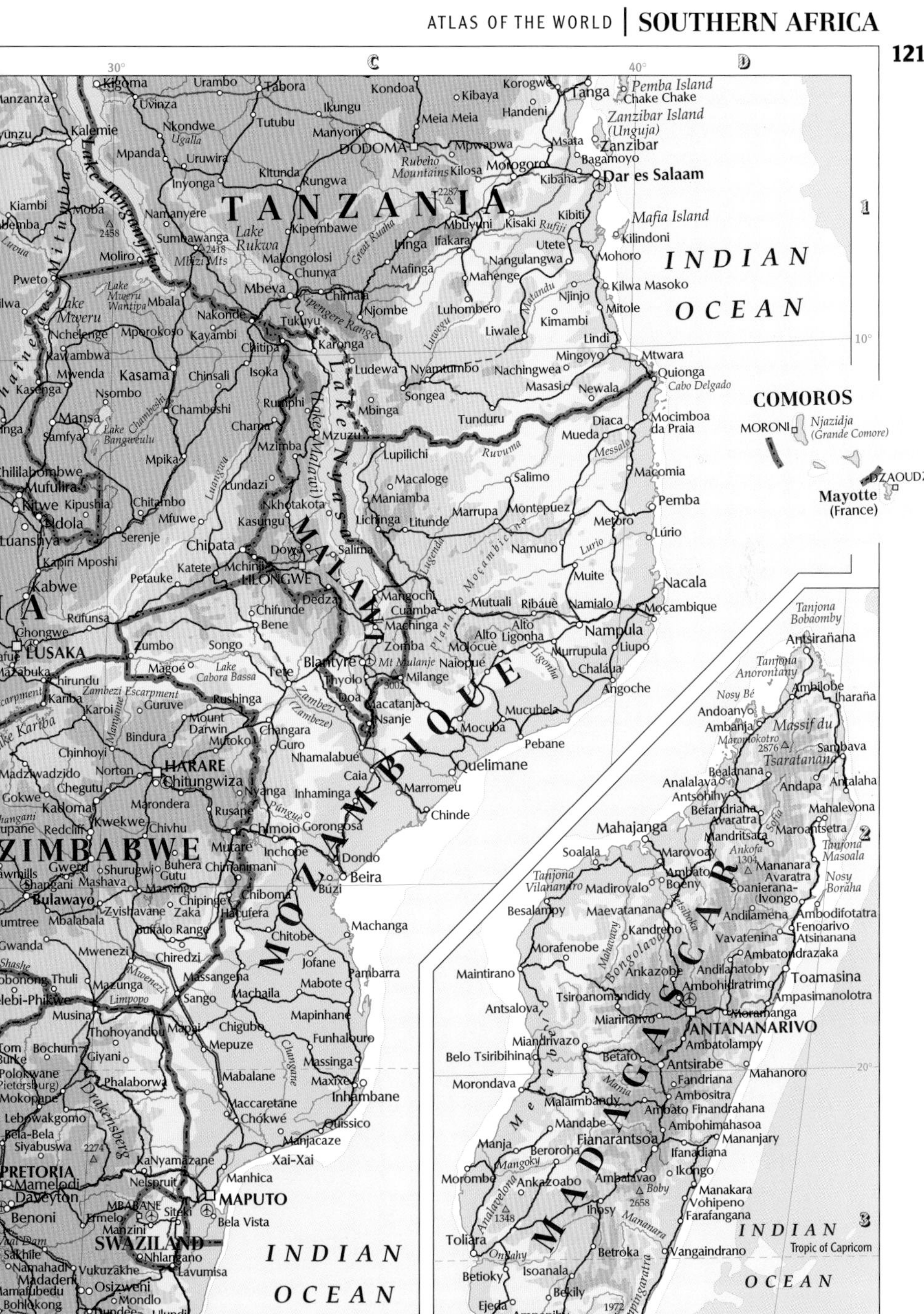

0   250   500 KILOMETRES

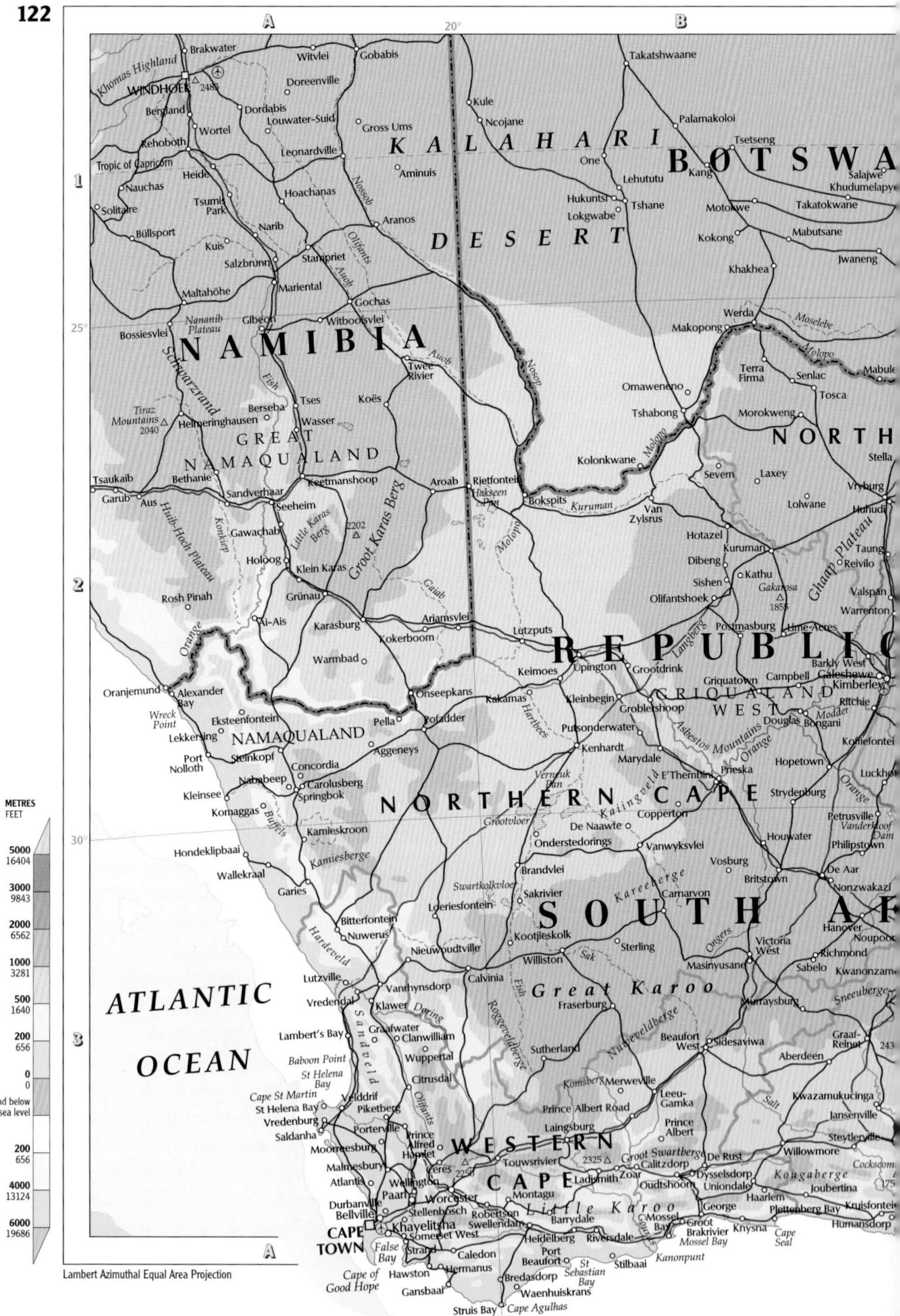

A · B

20°

WINDHOEK 2488
Khomas Highland
Brakwater
Witvlei
Gobabis
Kule
Takatshwaane
Bergland
Doreenville
Ncojane
Palamakoloi
Tsetseng
Dordabis
Louwater-Suid
Gross Ums
One
Lehututu
Kang
Khudumelapye
Salajwe
Wortel
Rehoboth
Leonardville
Aminuis
Hukuntsi
Tshane
Motokwe
Takatokwane
Tropic of Capricorn
Heide
Hoachanas
Lokgwabe
Mabutsane
Nauchas
Tsumis
Park
Narib
Aranos
Kokong
Khakhea
Jwaneng

1

K A L A H A R I
B O T S W A

Solitaire
Bullsport
Kuis
Salzbrunn
Stampriet
Marienthal
Gochas
D E S E R T
Werda
Makopong
Moselebe
Molopo

Maltahöhe
Gibeon
Witbooisvlei
Mabule

25°
Nananib
Plateau
Bossievlei
N A M I B I A
Twee
Rivier
Omaweneno
Terra
Firma
Senlac
Tosca
Schwarzrand
Fish
Auob
Tshabong
Morokweng
Tiraz
Mountains
2040
Helmeringhausen
Berseba
Tses
Wasser
Koës
Kolonkwane
Molopo
Severn
Laxey
Stella
N O R T H
G R E A T
N A M A Q U A L A N D
Tsaukaib
Bethanie
Sandverhaar
Keetmanshoop
Aroab
Rietfontein
Bokspits
Kuruman
Vryburg
Hotazel
Dibeng
Kuruman
Reivilo
Taung
Garub
Aus
Gawachab
Seeheim
Groot Karas Berg
Inkseen
Pan
Van
Zylsrus
Lolwane
Huhudi
Konkiep
Little Karas
Berg
2202
Moloye
Kathu
Sishen
Olifantshoek
Gakarosa
1851
Valspan
Warrenton
Holoog
Klein Karas
Postmasburg
Lime Acres

2
Rosh Pinah
Grünau
Caub
Ariamsvlei
Kokerboom
Lutzputs
Upington
Grootdrink
Griquatown
Campbell
Barkly West
Kimberley
Ai-Ais
Karasburg
R E P U B L I C
Warmbad
Keimoes
Kleinbegin
Groblershoop
G R I Q U A L A N D
Douglas
Ritchie
Orange
Oranjemund
Alexander
Bay
Eksteenfontein
Onseepkans
Kakamas
Putsonderwater
W E S T
Modder
Kotjiesfontein
Wreck
Point
Lekkersing
Pella
Pofadder
Kenhardt
Marydale
Prieska
Hopetown
Luckhoff
Port
Nolloth
Steinkopf
Aggeneys
Vermuk
Pan
E'Thembini
Strydenburg
Petrusville
Vanderkloof
Dam
Nababeep
Concordia
Carolusberg
Springbok
N O R T H E R N C A P E
Copperton
Houwater
Philipstown
Kleinsee
Komaggas
Kamieskroon
Grootvloer
De Naawte
Vanwyksvlei
Vosburg
Britstown
De Aar
Hanover
30°
Hondeklipbaai
Onderstedorings
Brandvlei
Kareeberge
Carnarvon
Victoria
West
Richmond
Noupoort
Garies
Sakrivier
Sterling
Masinyusane
Sabelo
Kwanonzame
Wallekraal
Loeriesfontein
Swartkolkvloer
Kootjieskolk
S O U T H A F
Bitterfontein
Nuwerus
Williston
G r e a t   K a r o o
Fraserburg
Murraysburg
Graaf-
Reinet
243
Lutzville
Vanrhynsdorp
Calvinia
Beaufort
West
Sidesaviwa
Aberdeen
Vredendal
Klawer
Nieuwoudtville
Sutherland
Kwazamukucinga
Cockscom
175
W E S T E R N
Clanwilliam
Wuppertal
Citrusdal
Komsber
Merweville
Prince Albert Road
Prince
Albert
Leeu-
Gamka
Willowmore
Uitenhage
Steytlerville
C A P E
Ladismith
Zoar
Oudtshoorn
De Rust
Dysselsdorp
Kougaberge
Lambert's Bay
Baboon Point
St Helena
Bay
Cape St Martin
St Helena Bay
Velddrif
Piketberg
Porterville
Laingsburg
Touwsrivier
2325
Calitzdorp
Uniondale
Haarlem
Knysna
Vredenburg
Moorreesburg
Prince
Alfred
Hamlet
Ceres
Montagu
Barrydale
Little Karoo
George
Plettenberg Bay
Knysfontein
Saldanha
Malmesbury
Atlantis
Wellington
Worcester
Robertson
Swellendam
Heidelberg
Riversdale
Brakrivier
Mossel
Bay
Cape
Seal
Durbanville
Bellville
Paarl
Stellenbosch
Somerset West
Barrydale
Humansdorp
CAPE
TOWN
Khayelitsha
Strand
Caledon
Port
Beaufort
St
Sebastian
Bay
Stilbaai
Kanonpunt
False
Bay
Hawston
Hermanus
Bredasdorp
Cape of
Good Hope
Gansbaai
Waenhuiskrans
Struis Bay
Cape Agulhas
20°

A T L A N T I C

O C E A N

3

Buffels
Kamiesberge
N A M A Q U A L A N D
Hardeveld
Sandveld
Olifants
Doring
Fish
Roggeveldberge
Nuweveldberge
Sak
Ongers
Sak
Sneeuberge
Great Karoo
Kareeberge

METRES
FEET

5000 16404
3000 9843
2000 6562
1000 3281
500 1640
200 656
0 0
Land below
sea level
200 656
4000 13124
6000 19686

Lambert Azimuthal Equal Area Projection

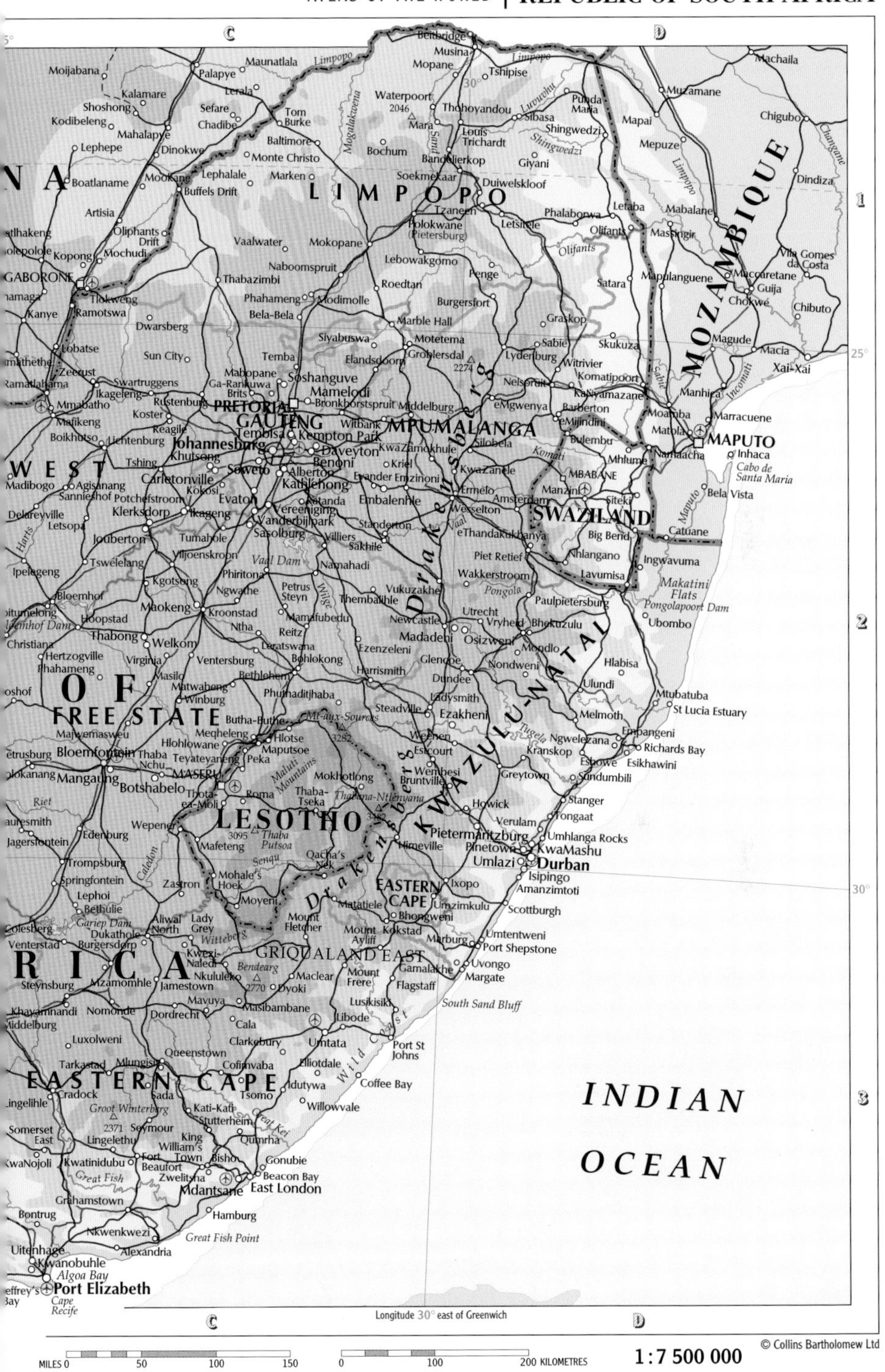

INDIAN

OCEAN

Longitude 30° east of Greenwich

© Collins Bartholomew Ltd

MILES 0   50   100   150

0   100   200 KILOMETRES

1 : 7 500 000

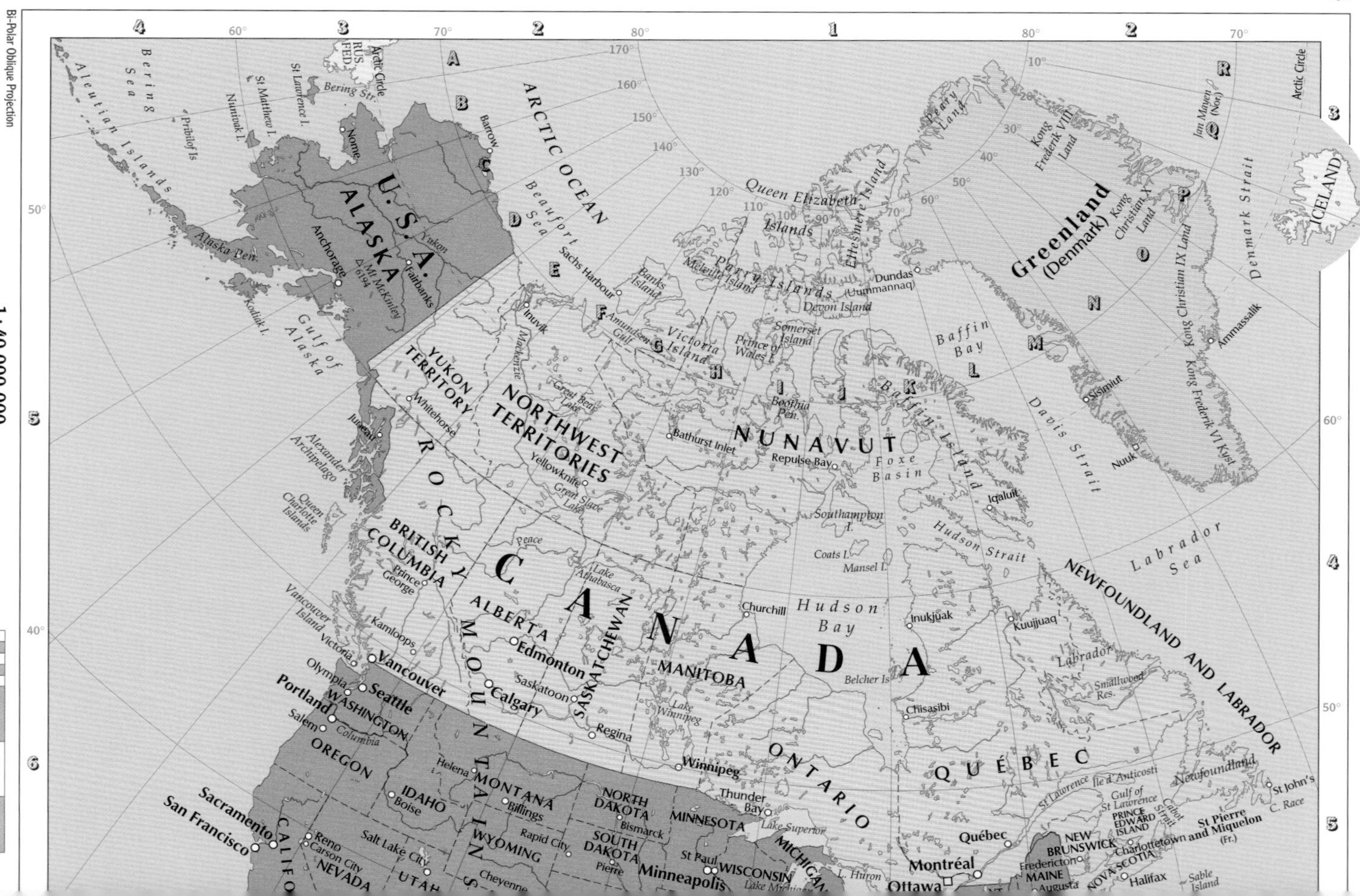

ICELAND

Arctic Circle

70°

Jan Mayen (Nor.)

Denmark Strait

Ammassalik

Kong Frederik VI Kyst

Kong Christian IX Land

Kong Christian X Land

Kong Frederik VIII Land

Greenland
(Denmark)

Nuuk

Davis Strait

Baffin
Bay

NEWFOUNDLAND AND LABRADOR

Labrador
Sea

St John's
Race

Newfoundland

St Pierre and Miquelon (Fr.)

NOVA
SCOTIA

Halifax

Sable I.

NEW
BRUNSWICK

Fredericton

MAINE

Augusta

Nain

Labrador

Smallwood
Res.

Gulf of St Lawrence

Gaspé Pén.

St Lawrence

Anticosti I.

PRINCE EDWARD
ISLAND

Ellesmere Island

Queen Elizabeth
Islands

Devon Island

Axel Heiberg
Island

Grinnell Pen.

Dundas

Somerset
Island

Prince of
Wales I.

Prince
Leopold I.

Baffin Island

Foxe
Basin

Southampton I.

Repulse Bay

Coats I.

Mansel I.

Hudson Strait

Iqaluit

Kingston

Chisasibi

Ungava Bay

Belcher Is.

Kuujjuaq

QUÉBEC

Québec

Montréal

Ottawa

ONTARIO

Lake Superior

MICHIGAN

WISCONSIN

Thunder Bay

Lake Huron

Hudson

Bay

NUNAVUT

Churchill

Banks
Island

Victoria
Island

Prince of
Wales Island

King
William I.

Boothia
Pen.

Bathurst Inlet

MANITOBA

Winnipeg

Lake
Winnipeg

SASKATCHEWAN

Regina

Saskatoon

Lake
Athabasca

MINNESOTA

St Paul

Minneapolis

NORTH
DAKOTA

Bismarck

SOUTH
DAKOTA

Pierre

Rapid City

ARCTIC OCEAN

Beaufort
Sea

Sachs Harbour

Amundsen
Gulf

Ulukhaktok

Great Bear
Lake

Great Slave
Lake

Yellowknife

NORTHWEST
TERRITORIES

Mackenzie

Inuvik

C A N A D A

ALBERTA

Edmonton

Calgary

Peace

BRITISH
COLUMBIA

R O C K Y   M O U N T A I N

MONTANA

Helena

Billings

WYOMING

Cheyenne

Barrow

U.S.A.

ALASKA

Fairbanks

△ Mt McKinley
6194

Yukon

YUKON
TERRITORY

Whitehorse

Prince
George

Kamloops

Vancouver

Seattle

WASHINGTON

Olympia

Portland

OREGON

Salem

IDAHO

Boise

NEVADA

Reno

Carson City

UTAH

Salt Lake City

Juneau

Vancouver
Island

Victoria

Columbia

Queen
Charlotte
Islands

Alexander
Archipelago

Gulf of
Alaska

Nome

Anchorage

RUS.
FED.

Arctic Circle

St Lawrence I.

Bering Str.

St Matthew I.

Nunivak I.

Pribilof Is

Kodiak I.

Alaska Pen.

B e r i n g
S e a

Aleutian Islands

CALIFO

Sacramento

San Francisco

70°

60°

80°

50°

10°

40°

130°

140°

150°

160°

170°

50°

60°

70°

80°

60°

50°

40°

2

1

2

3

4

5

6

7

8

9

10

11

12

13

14

15

1 : 40 000 000

MILES 0   200   400   600   800

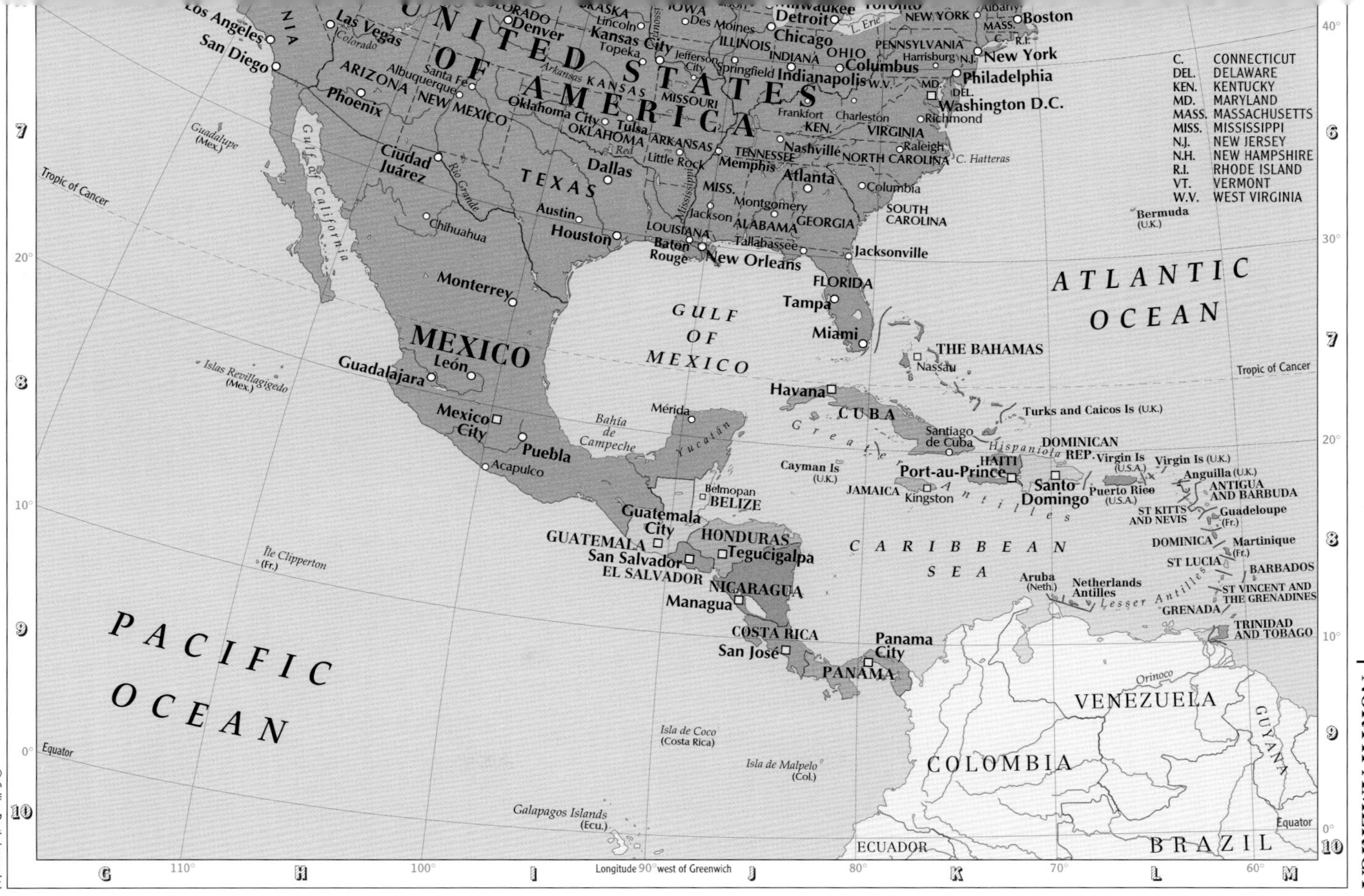
ATLANTIC OCEAN
PACIFIC OCEAN
GULF OF MEXICO
CARIBBEAN SEA
UNITED STATES OF AMERICA
MEXICO
CUBA
THE BAHAMAS
HAITI
DOMINICAN REP.
JAMAICA
BELIZE
GUATEMALA
HONDURAS
EL SALVADOR
NICARAGUA
COSTA RICA
PANAMA
VENEZUELA
COLOMBIA
GUYANA
BRAZIL
ECUADOR
C. CONNECTICUT
DEL. DELAWARE
KEN. KENTUCKY
MD. MARYLAND
MASS. MASSACHUSETTS
MISS. MISSISSIPPI
N.J. NEW JERSEY
N.H. NEW HAMPSHIRE
R.I. RHODE ISLAND
VT. VERMONT
W.V. WEST VIRGINIA
Bermuda (U.K.)
Turks and Caicos Is (U.K.)
Virgin Is (U.K.)
Virgin Is (U.S.A.)
Anguilla (U.K.)
ANTIGUA AND BARBUDA
ST KITTS AND NEVIS
Guadeloupe (Fr.)
DOMINICA
Martinique (Fr.)
ST LUCIA
BARBADOS
ST VINCENT AND THE GRENADINES
GRENADA
TRINIDAD AND TOBAGO
Puerto Rico (U.S.A.)
Netherlands Antilles
Aruba (Neth.)
Cayman Is (U.K.)
Isla de Malpelo (Col.)
Isla de Coco (Costa Rica)
Galapagos Islands (Ecu.)
Île Clipperton (Fr.)
Islas Revillagigedo (Mex.)
Guadalupe (Mex.)
Gulf of California
Bahía de Campeche
Tropic of Cancer
Equator
Longitude 90° west of Greenwich
Boston
New York
Philadelphia
Washington D.C.
Richmond
Raleigh
C. Hatteras
Columbia
Jacksonville
Miami
Tampa
Atlanta
Nashville
Memphis
New Orleans
Baton Rouge
Houston
Dallas
Austin
Chicago
Detroit
Columbus
Indianapolis
Kansas City
Denver
Oklahoma City
Tulsa
Little Rock
Phoenix
Las Vegas
Los Angeles
San Diego
Albuquerque
Santa Fe
Ciudad Juárez
Chihuahua
Monterrey
Guadalajara
León
Mexico City
Puebla
Acapulco
Mérida
Havana
Santiago de Cuba
Nassau
Port-au-Prince
Santo Domingo
Kingston
Belmopan
Guatemala City
San Salvador
Tegucigalpa
Managua
San José
Panama City
0 400 800 1200 KILOMETRES

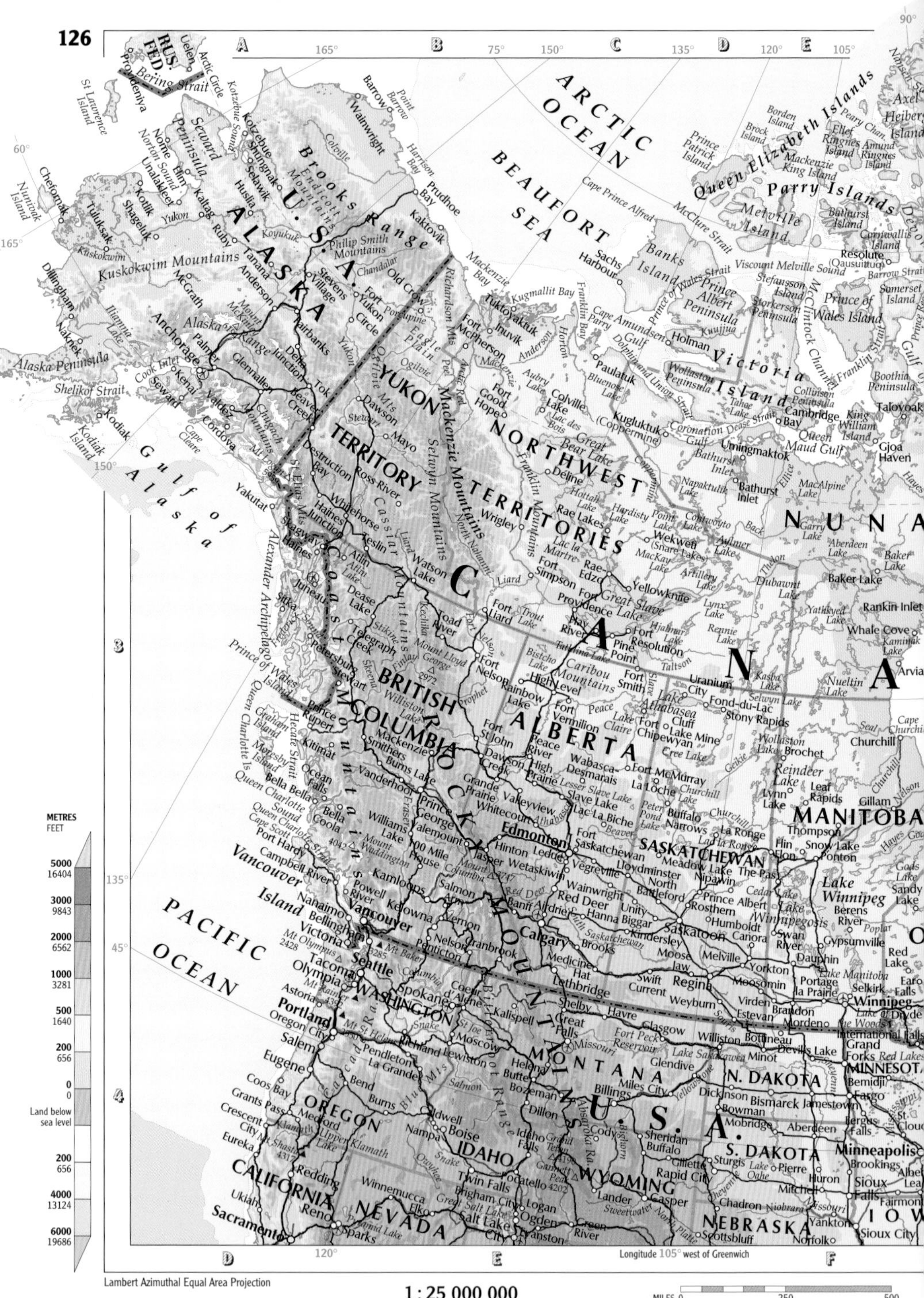
ARCTIC OCEAN
BEAUFORT SEA
PACIFIC OCEAN
Gulf of Alaska
ALASKA
U.S.A.
CANADA
YUKON TERRITORY
NORTHWEST TERRITORIES
NUNA
BRITISH COLUMBIA
ALBERTA
SASKATCHEWAN
MANITOBA
WASHINGTON
OREGON
IDAHO
MONTANA
WYOMING
N. DAKOTA
S. DAKOTA
NEBRASKA
CALIFORNIA
NEVADA
RUS. FED.
Bering Strait
Brooks Range
Kuskokwim Mountains
Alaska Range
Mackenzie Mountains
Selwyn Mountains
Cassiar Mountains
Coast Mountains
ROCKY MOUNTAINS
Queen Elizabeth Islands
Parry Islands
Banks Island
Victoria Island
Melville Island
Great Bear Lake
Great Slave Lake
Lake Athabasca
Lake Winnipeg
Vancouver Island
Anchorage
Fairbanks
Juneau
Whitehorse
Dawson
Yellowknife
Edmonton
Calgary
Vancouver
Victoria
Seattle
Portland
Saskatoon
Regina
Winnipeg
Boise
Salt Lake City
Sacramento
METRES
FEET
5000
16404
3000
9843
2000
6562
1000
3281
500
1640
200
656
0
0
Land below sea level
200
656
4000
13124
6000
19686
Longitude 105° west of Greenwich
Lambert Azimuthal Equal Area Projection
1:25 000 000
MILES 0
250
500

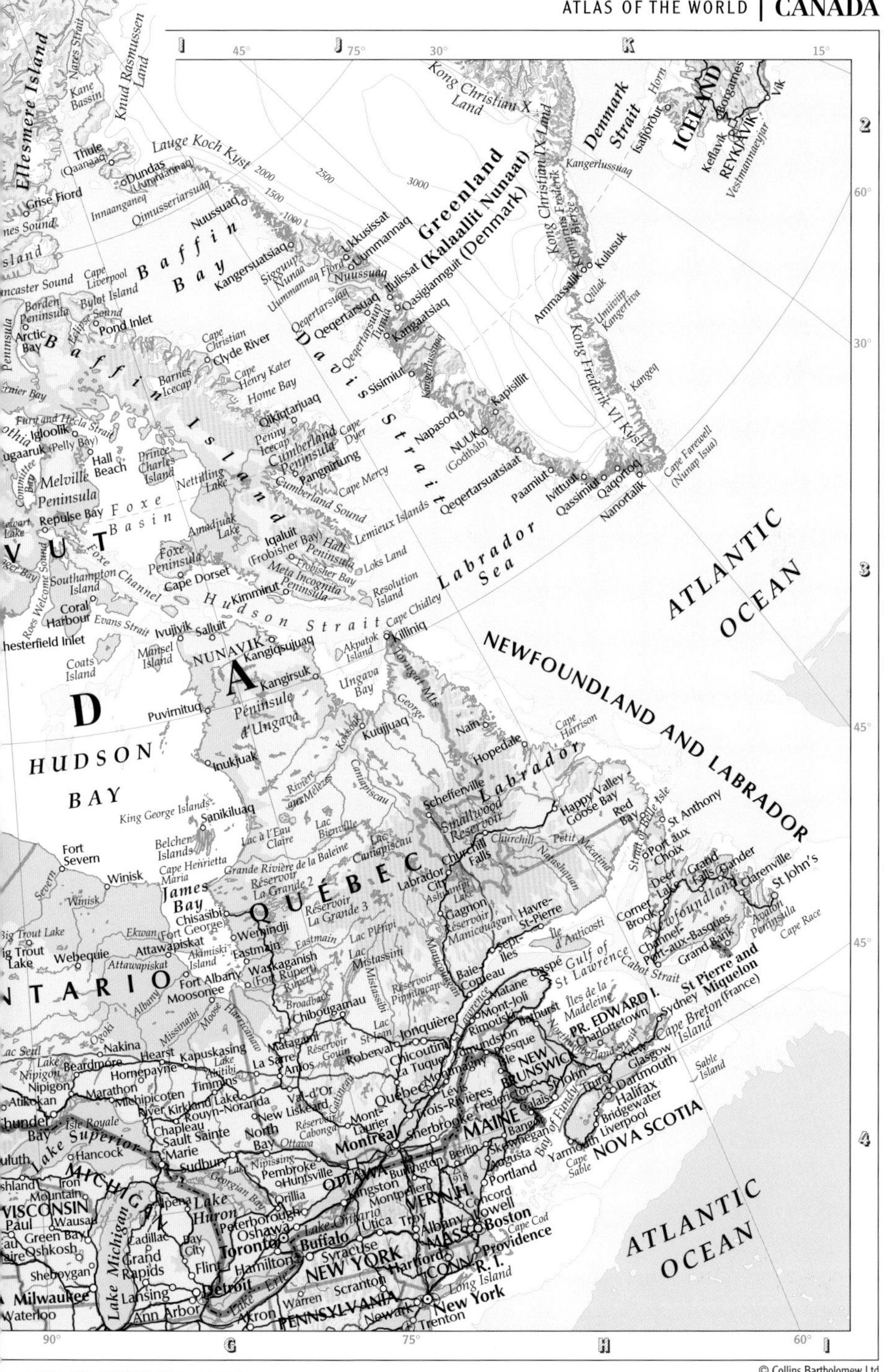

Ellesmere Island
Naves Strait
Kane Basin
Knud Rasmussen Land
Thule (Qaanaaq)
Dundas (Uummannaq)
Innaanganeq
Grise Fiord
nes Sound

Lauge Koch Kyst 2000
Qimusseriarsuaq
1500
Nuussuaq
Kangersuatsiaq
Siggup Nunaa
Upernavik
Uummannaq
Uummannaq Fjord
Nuussuaq
Qeqertarsuaq
Ilulissat

Kong Christian X Land

**Greenland
(Kalaallit Nunaat) (Denmark)**

Kong Christian IX Land
Kong Frederik VIII Land
Kangerlussuaq

Denmark Strait
Horn
Isafjorður
ICELAND

Keflavik
REYKJAVIK
Vestmannaeyjar
Vik

Dengarnes

lancaster Sound
Cape Liverpool
Borden Peninsula
Bylot Island
Arctic Bay
Pond Inlet

**Baffin
Bay**

Cape Christian
Clyde River

Kangerdlugssuaq
Qeqertarsuaq
Aasiaat
Qasigiannguit
Qeqertarsuaq
Kangaatsiaq
Sisimiut

Kangerlussuaq
Maniitsoq

Ammassalik
Qillak
Umiivik
Kangertittivaq
Kangeq

land
Cape Barnes Icecap
Cape Henry Kater
Home Bay

Napasoq
NUUK (Godthåb)
Qeqertarsuatsiaat
Paamiut

Kong Frederik VI Kyst

Davis Strait

Fury and Hecla Strait
othia
Igloolik
ugaruk (Pelly Bay)
Hall Beach

Oikiqtarjuaq
Penny Icecap
Cumberland Peninsula
Cape Dyer
Kangiqtugaapik
Pangnirtung
Cumberland Sound
Cape Mercy

Kapisillit

Ivittuut
Qassimiut
Nanortalik
Qaqortoq

Cape Farewell (Nunap Isua)

Prince Charles Island
Nettilling Lake
Melville Peninsula
Repulse Bay

Foxe Basin
Amadjuak Lake

Foxe Peninsula
Cape Dorset

Iqaluit
Frobisher Bay Hall
Lemieux Islands
Meta Incognita Peninsula
Frobisher Bay
Loks Land
Resolution Island

Labrador
Sea

Kimmirut

**ATLANTIC
OCEAN**

VUT

Southampton Island
Roes Welcome Sound
Coral Harbour

Evans Strait
Ivujivik
Salluit

Cape Chidley
Akpatok Island
Killiniq

Hudson Strait

hesterfield Inlet
Coats Island
Mansel Island

Kangiqsujuaq

NUNAVIK
Kangirsuk

NEWFOUNDLAND AND LABRADOR

D A

King George Islands

Puvirnituq

Péninsule
d'Ungava

Ungava
Bay
George
Rivière

Kuujjuaq

Nain

Hopedale

Cape
Harrison

**HUDSON
BAY**

Belcher
Islands
Sanikiluaq

Inukjuak

Cape Henrietta Maria

Rivière Caniapiscau

Kuujjuarapik

Labrador

Schefferville
Smallwood
Reservoir
Churchill

Happy Valley-
Goose Bay
Red
Bay

St Anthony

Fort
Severn
Winisk

James
Bay

Grande Rivière de la Baleine
Réservoir
La Grande 2
Chisasibi
Fort George

Réservoir
La Grande 3

Labrador City
Churchill
Falls

Gagnon

Petit Mécatina

Strait of Belle Isle
Port aux
Choix

Deer
Lake
Gander

St John's

ig Trout Lake
ig Trout
Lake
Webeque

Ekwan
Attawapiskat
Attawapiskat

Akimiski
Island

Wemindji
Eastmain
Eastmain
Waskaganish
(Fort Rupert)

Lac
Bienville

Réservoir
Manicouagan

Lac
St-Pierre

Manitou

Cabonga

d'Anticosti

Corner
Brook

Newfoundland

Grand
Falls-Windsor

Clarenville

Grand Bank

Avalon
Peninsula
Cape Race

N T A R I O
Albany
Fort Albany
Moosonee

Lac
Mistassini

Sept-
Îles

Baie-
Comeau

Gaspé

Gulf of
St Lawrence

Îles de la
Madeleine

Cape Breton
Island

Sable
Island

ac Seul
Lac
Seul
Nakina

Oba

Nipigon
Beardmore
Hornepayne
Hearst
Kapuskasing
Timmins

Broadback
Chibougamau
Lac

Matagami
Amos
Val-d'Or

Roberval
La Tuque
Chicoutimi

Jonquière

Rimouski
Matane

Rivière-du-Loup

Mont-Joli

PR. EDWARD I.
Charlottetown
Summerside

Sydney

NOVA SCOTIA

ac Seil
Atikokan
hunder
Bay
Isle Royale

Nipigon
Marathon

Michipicoten
River
Chapleau

Kirkland Lake
Rouyn-Noranda

New Liskeard

North
Bay

Québec

Trois-Rivières
Montréal

Drummondville

Sherbrooke

Lévis
MAINE

Bangor
Bay of Fundy
Saint John
**NEW
BRUNSWICK**
Moncton
Fredericton

Truro
Glasgow
Dartmouth
HALIFAX
Bridgewater
Liverpool
Yarmouth
Cape
Sable

WISCONSIN
Paul

shland
uluth
Iron
Mountain

MICHIGAN

Lake Michigan
Cadillac
Saginaw

Sault
Sainte
Marie
Sudbury

Huntsville
Pembroke

OTTAWA

Georgian
Bay
Orillia

Nipissing
Huntsville

VERMONT
Montpelier
N.H.
Concord

Augusta
Portland

Portsmouth

**ATLANTIC
OCEAN**

au Green Bay
aire
Oshkosh
Sheboygan

Lansing
Flint

Grand
Rapids

Hamilton
Buffalo
Syracuse
Utica
Albany
Lowell
Hartford
MASS.
Boston
Providence
R.I.
Cape Cod

Milwaukee
Waterloo

Ann Arbor
Detroit

Akron

Toronto
Oshawa
Lake Ontario
Peterborough
Kingston

Rochester
NEW YORK
Binghamton

CONN.
Long Island

Warren
Scranton

Trenton
Newark
New York

PENNSYLVANIA

0   250   500   750 KILOMETRES

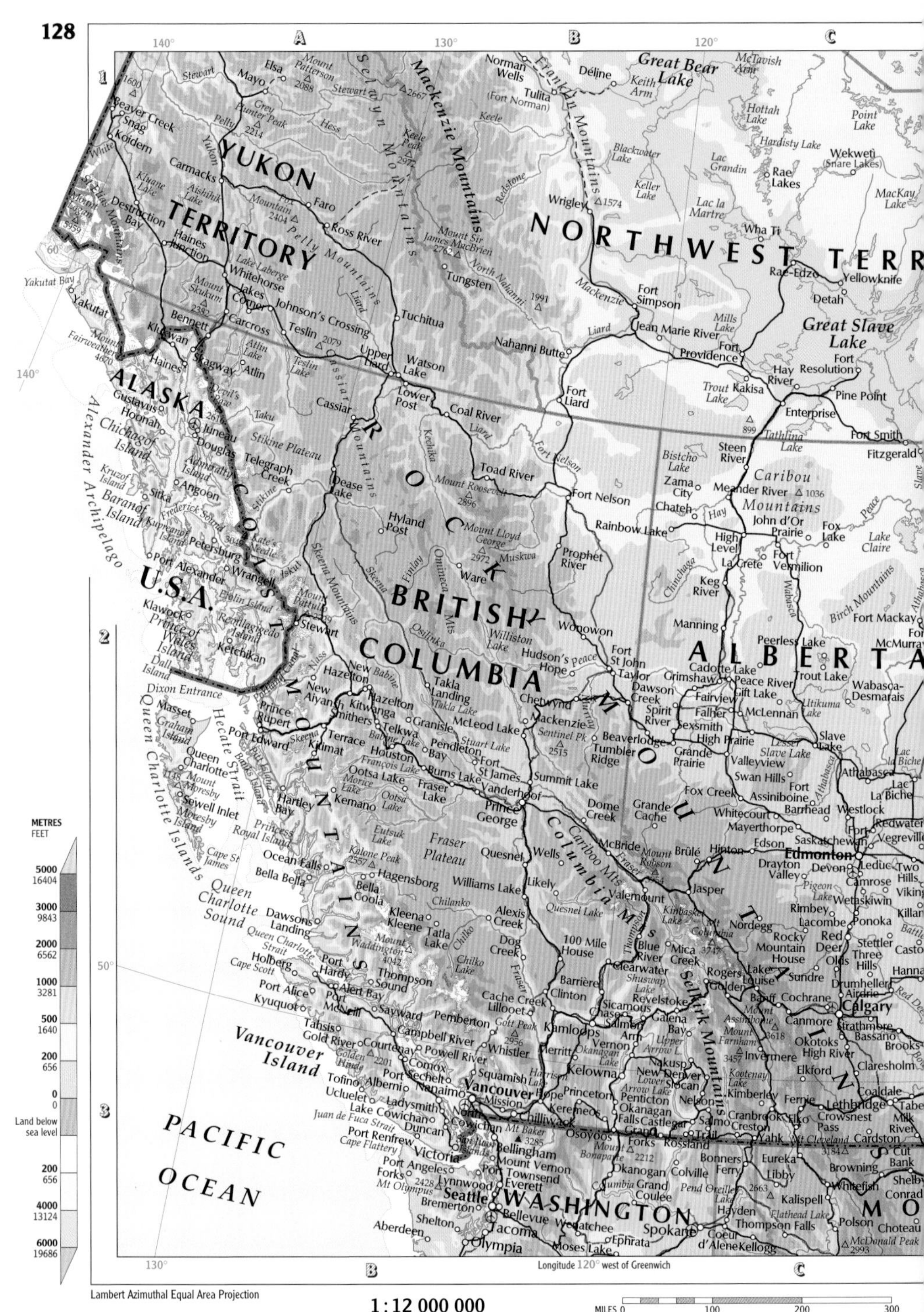

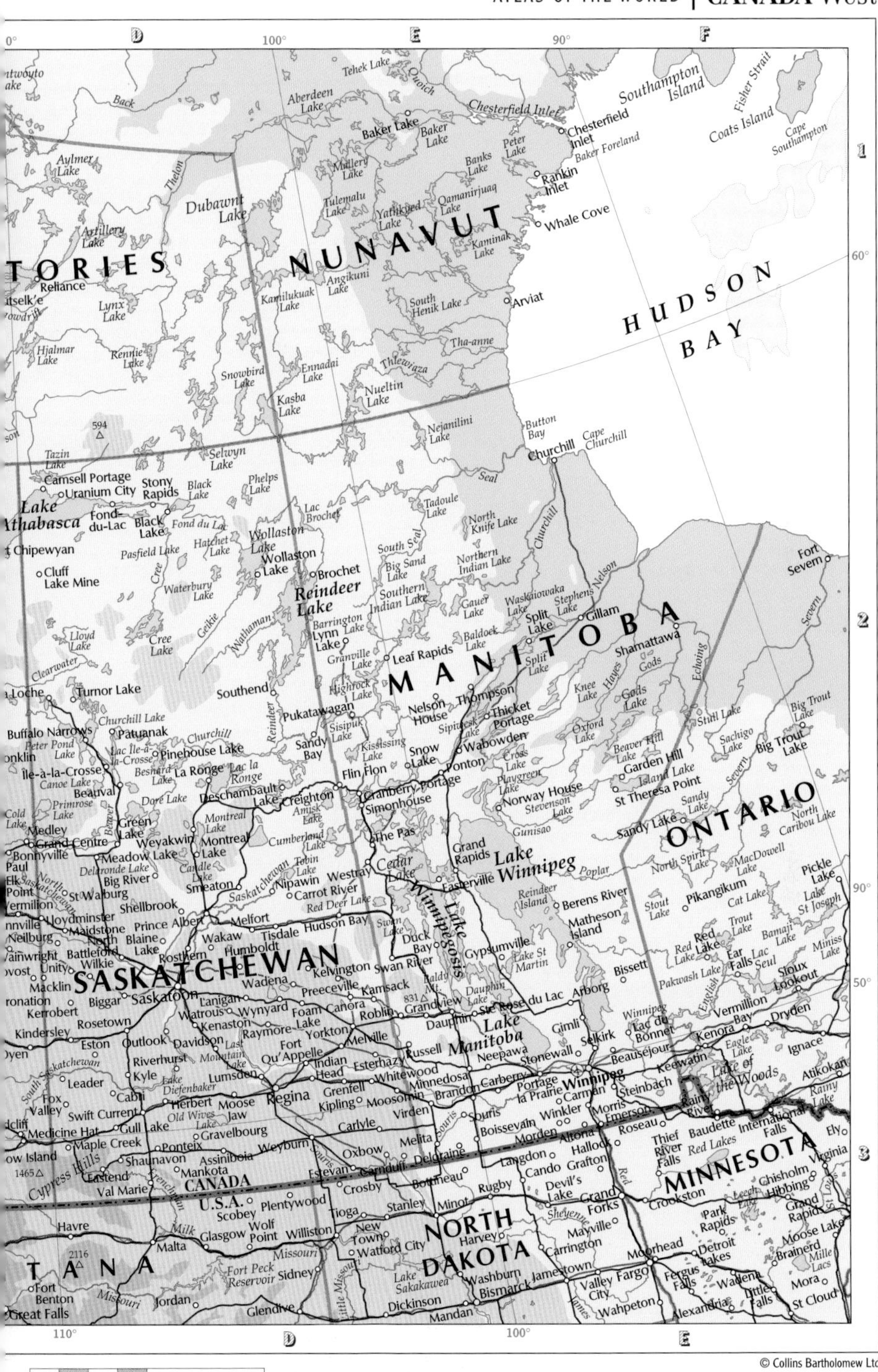

0　　　　200　　　　400 KILOMETRES

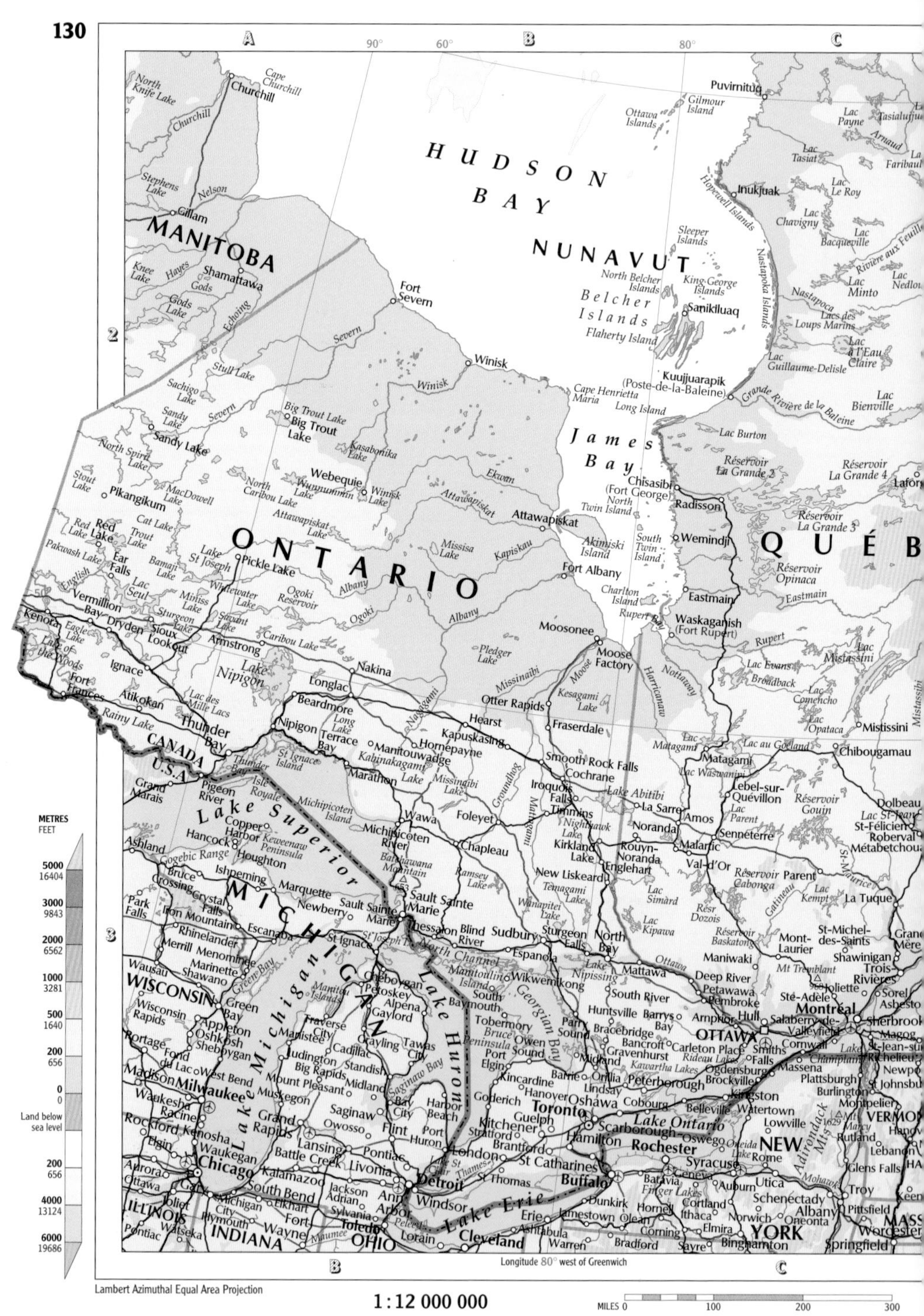

A 90° 60° B 80° C

North Knife Lake
Cape Churchill
Churchill

MANITOBA

Stephens Lake
Nelson
Gillam

Knee Lake
Gods
Hayes
Shamattawa

Sachigo Lake
Fort Severn

Stull Lake
Severn

Winisk

Stout Lake
North Spirit Lake
Sandy Lake
MacDowell
Winisk

Red Lake
Cat Lake
Big Trout Lake
Kasabonika Lake
Webequie
Winisk Lake
Ekwan

Pakwash Lake
Trout Falls
Bamaji Lake
Pickle Lake
St Joseph Lake
Attawapiskat

Vermilion Bay
Lac Seul
Sturgeon Lake
Whitewater Lake
Ogoki Reservoir
Missisa Lake
Kapiskau
Fort Albany

Kenora
Eagle Lake
Dryden
Sioux Lookout
Caribou Lake
Ogoki
Nakina
Albany

Lake of the Woods
Fort Frances
Ignace
Armstrong
Lake Nipigon
Longlac

HUDSON BAY

NUNAVUT

Puvirnitug
Gilmour Island
Ottawa Islands

Hopewell Islands
Inukjuak

Sleeper Islands

North Belcher Islands
King George Islands
Saniklluaq

Belcher Islands
Flaherty Island

Cape Henrietta Maria
Kuujjuarapik (Poste-de-la-Baleine)
Long Island

James Bay
Chisasibi (Fort George)
North Twin Island
Radisson

Akimiski Island
South Twin Island
Wemindji

Charlton Island
Eastmain
Waskaganish (Fort Rupert)

Moosonee
Moose Factory

Lac Payne
Lac Tasiat
Tasiujaq

Lac Le Roy
Lac Chavigny
Lac Minto
Lac Faribault

Lacs des Loups Marins
Lac Bacquevile
Rivière aux Feuilles
Lac Nedlou

Lac Guillaume-Delisle
Lac à l'Eau Claire

Grande Rivière de la Baleine
Lac Bienville

Lac Burton
Réservoir La Grande 2
Réservoir La Grande 4

QUÉB

Réservoir La Grande 3
Lafor

Réservoir Opinaca

Rupert
Lac Evans
Broadback

Lac Mistassini
Lac Conchcho

Lac Opataca
Mistissini

ONTARIO

Pikangikum
North Caribou Lake
Wunnummin Lake
Attawapiskat Lake

Ear Falls
Miniss Lake

Thunder Bay
Beardmore
Nipigon
Terrace Bay
Manitouwadge
Hornepayne
Kapuskasing

Hearst
Fraserdale

Otter Rapids
Kesagami Lake

Missinaibi
Moose River
Harricana

CANADA
U.S.A.

Grand Marais
Pigeon River
Isle Royale

Copper Harbor
Keweenaw Peninsula

Ashland
Gogebic Range
Hancock
Houghton

Crystal Falls
Iron Mountain
Marquette
Newberry

Ishpeming
Michipicoten Island

Bruce Crossing

Michipicoten River
Wawa
Chapleau
Foleyet
Timmins
Iroquois Falls
Cochrane
Smooth Rock Falls

Matheson
New Liskeard
Kirkland Lake
Englehart

Rouyn-Noranda
Norranda
Matalic
Val-d'Or

MICHIGAN

Merrill
Rhinelander
Menominee

Wausau
Shawano
Marinette

WISCONSIN

Wisconsin Rapids
Green Bay
Appleton
Oshkosh
Sheboygan

Portage
Fond du Lac

Madison
Milwaukee
Waukesha
Racine
Kenosha

Rockford
Waukegan

Elgin
Aurora
Chicago

Joliet
Kankakee
Pontiac

ILLINOIS
Watseka

INDIANA

Sault Sainte Marie
Sault Sainte Marie
Blind River
Espanola
Sudbury
Sturgeon Falls
North Bay

Lake Superior

Lake Michigan

Lake Huron

Georgian Bay

Toronto
Hamilton
Scarborough
Oshawa

Lake Ontario
Rochester

NEW YORK

Buffalo

Lake Erie

Cleveland

OHIO

Detroit
Windsor
London

NUNAVUT

Lambert Azimuthal Equal Area Projection

1:12 000 000

MILES 0   100   200   300

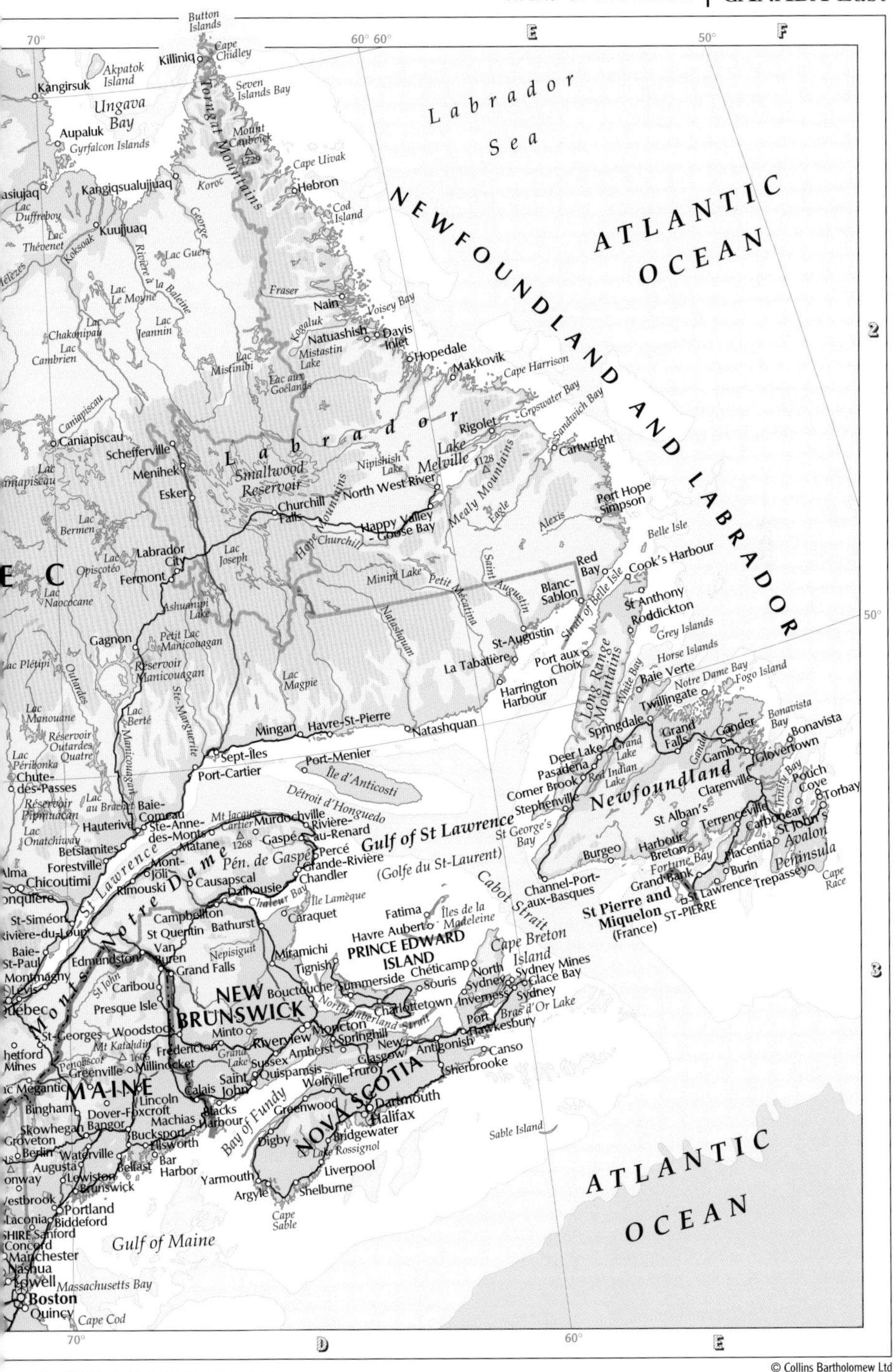

Button
Islands
70°   Cape
Killiniq   Chidley   60° 60°   E   50°   F
Akpatok   Seven
Kangirsuk   Island   Islands Bay
Aupaluk   Mount
Gyrfalcon Islands   Caubvick
·asiujaq   Kangiqsualujjuaq   Koroc   Cape Uivak
Lac   Kuujjuaq
Duffreboy   Lac   Hebron
Thévenet   Kaksouk   Rivière a la Baleine   Cod
Island
·telraz   Lac Guers
Lac   Fraser
Le Moyne   Nain
Lac   Voisey Bay
Lac   Jeannin   Koroluk   Natuashish Davis
Cambrien   Mistastin   Inlet
Mistinibi   Lake   Hopedale
Lac aux   Makkovik
Lac   Goélands   Cape Harrison
Caniapiscau   Groswater Bay
Caniapiscau   Labrador   Rigolet   Cartwright
Lac   Scheff
Bermen   Scheffefferville   Lake
Menihek   Smallwood   Nipishish   Melville
Esker   Reservoir   Lake   1128
Churchill   North West River   Mealy Mountains   Port Hope
Falls   Happy Valley-   Simpson
·apiscau   Labrador   Goose Bay   Alexis
City   Lac   Eagle
Fermont   Joseph   Haut Churchill   Belle Isle
Gagnon   Minipi Lake   Petit Mécatina   Red   Cook's Harbour
Petit Lac   Bay   St Anthony
Lac   Manicouagan   Blanc-   Roddickton
Nascaune   Manicouagan   Sablon   Grey Islands
Lac Plétipi   Réservoir   St-Augustin   Horse Islands
Manicouagan   La Tabatière   Port aux   Baie Verte
Lac   Choix   Twillingate   Fogo Island
Manouane   Lac   Harrington   Springdale   Notre Dame Bay
Réservoir   Berté   Harbour   Bonavista
Outardes   Deer Lake   Grand   Gander   Bonavista
Chute-   Quatre   Mingan   Havre-St-Pierre   Pasadena   Falls   Gambo   Glovertown
des-Passes   Natashquan   Corner Brook   Torbay
Réservoir   Sept-Îles   Port-Menier   Stephenville   Clarenville   Pouch
Pipmuacan   Île d'Anticosti   St Alban's   Cove
Lac   Port-Cartier   Détroit d'Honguedo   Newfoundland   Carbonear   St John's
Onatchiway   Baie-   Mt Jacques   Murdochville   St George's   Burin   Placentia   Avalon
Alma   Hauterive   Comeau   Cartier   Rivière-   Bay   Terrenceville   Peninsula
Chicoutimi   Ste-Anne-   au-Renard   Burgeo   Grand Bank   Trepassey
·onguiere   Matane   1268   des-Monts   Gaspé   Fortune Bay
St-Siméon   Mont-   Pén. de Gaspé   Channel-Port-   St Pierre and   Cape
Rimouski   Joli   Grande-Rivière   aux-Basques   Miquelon   Race
Baie-   Causapscal   Chandler   Cabot Strait   (France) ST-PIERRE
riviere-du-Loup   Dalhousie   Île Lamèque
Baie-   Campbellton   Chaleur Bay   Caraquet
St-Paul   St Quentin   Bathurst   Fatima   Îles de la
Montmagny   Van   Nepisiguit   Miramichi   Havre Aubert   Madeleine
·évis   Buren   Grand Falls   Tignish   PRINCE EDWARD   Cape Breton
·uebec   St   Caribou   ISLAND   Island
hetford   Presque Isle   Bouctouche   Summerside   North   Sydney Mines
Mines   MAINE   NEW   Minto   Chéticamp   Sydney   Glace Bay
Mt Katahdin   BRUNSWICK   Moncton   Charlottetown   Inverness   Sydney
ac Mégantic   Bingham   1606   Springhill   New   Bras d'Or Lake
Penobscot   Fredericton   Riverview   Port   Hawkesbury
Skowhegan   Dover-Foxcroft   Greenville   Amherst   Glasgow   Antigonish   Canso
Groveton   Millinocket   Sussex   Springhill   Truro
·Berlin   Waterville   Lincoln   Saint   Quispamsis   Sherbrooke
onway   Bangor   Machias   John   NOVA
·estbrook   Belfast   Bucksport   Greenwood   Wolfville   SCOTIA   Sable Island
·aconia   Augusta   Bar   Bay of Fundy   Halifax
HIRE Sanford   Lewiston   Harbour   Digby   Dartmouth
Concord   onway   Brunswick   Yarmouth   Bridgewater
·ashua   Portland   Lac Rossignol
·owell   Biddeford   Cape   Liverpool
·Manchester   Sable   Shelburne
Boston   Massachusetts Bay   Argyle
Quincy   Cape Cod

Torngat Mountains
Ungava Bay
Labrador Sea
ATLANTIC OCEAN
NEWFOUNDLAND AND LABRADOR
Labrador
Gulf of St Lawrence
(Golfe du St-Laurent)
Northumberland Strait
Long Range Mountains
Mont Notre Dam
Gulf of Maine
ATLANTIC OCEAN

70°   60°
0   200   400 KILOMETRES

© Collins Bartholomew Ltd

50° 130°   **A**   120°   **B**   110°   **C**   100°

C A N A D A

BRITISH COLUMBIA   **ALBERTA**   **SASKATCHEWAN**   **MAN**

Port Hardy · Gold River · Campbell River · Powell River · Jasper · Leduc · Edmonton · Lloydminster · Meadow Lake · The Pas · Cedar Lake · Vancouver Island · Nanaimo · Kamloops · 100 Mile House · Mount Washington 2093 · Wetaskiwin · Wainwright · Prince Albert · Nipawin · Swan River

Cape Flattery · Victoria · Vancouver · Kelowna · Vernon · Red Deer · Airdrie · Hanna · Unity · Saskatoon · Biggar · Humboldt · Canora · Yorkton · Winnipegosis · Swan Lake

Bellingham · Penticton · Nelson · Cranbrook · Okotoks · Calgary · Brooks · Kindersley · Rosthern · Davidson · Melville · Dauphin Lake

Tacoma · Seattle · Spokane · Coeur d'Alene · Lethbridge · Medicine Hat · Moose Jaw · Regina · Moosomin · Virden · Brandon · Morden · Portage la Prairie

Olympia · Mt Olympus · Columbia · Kalispell · Shelby · Swift Current · Weyburn · Estevan · Bottineau · Morden

WASHINGTON · Yakima · Snake · Havre · Glasgow · Williston · Minot · Devil's Lake · Jamestown

Astoria · Portland · Mt St Helens · Richland · Moscow · Lewiston · St Joe · Missoula · Helena · Great Falls · Fort Peck Reservoir · Glendive · Dickinson · Bismarck

Salem · Oregon City · Pendleton · La Grande · **MONTANA** · Butte · Bozeman · Billings · Miles City · Bowman · Mobridge · **N. DAKOTA**

Eugene · Albany · Bend · Burns · Blue Mountains · Salmon · Dillon · Cody · Sheridan · Gillette · Aberdeen

Coos Bay · Crater Lake · Caldwell · Nampa · Boise · Idaho Falls · Big Horn Mts · Buffalo · Rapid City · Black Hills · **S. DAKOTA** · Pierre · Huron

OREGON · Grants Pass · Klamath Falls · Upper Klamath Lake · Lakeview · Jerome · Twin Falls · Brigham City · Pinedale · Lander · Gillette · Chadron · Scottsbluff · Niobrara

Crescent City · Eureka · Redding · Mt Shasta · Alturas · Winnemucca · Elko · Great Salt Lake · Wendover · Ogden · Logan · Casper · **NEBRASKA** · Ogallala · Grand Island

Point Arena · Ukiah · Red Bluff · Pyramid Lake · Lovelock · Humboldt · Salt Lake City · Evanston · Green River · Laramie · Cheyenne · Sidney · North Platte · Kearney

Santa Rosa · Sacramento · Reno · Sparks · Carson City · **NEVADA** · Provo · Craig · Boulder · Greeley · **COLORADO** · McCook

San Francisco · Oakland · Stockton · Modesto · Great Basin · Ely · Wheeler Peak · **UTAH** · Grand Junction · Denver · Aurora · Burlington · **KAN**

San Jose · Monterey Bay · Salinas · Fresno · Visalia · Tonopah · Caliente · Richfield · Moab · Mount Elbert 4398 · Colorado Springs · Pueblo · Great Bend · Dodge City · Pratt

Santa Maria · Bakersfield · Beatty · St George · **UNITED STATES** · Cedar City · Lake Powell · Page · Durango · Alamosa · Trinidad · Ulysses · Liberal · **OKL**

Santa Barbara · Pt Conception · Charleston · Las Vegas · Henderson · Kanab · Kayenta · Farmington · Taos · Clayton · Stratford · Dumas · Elk City · Amarillo

Oxnard · Los Angeles · Pasadena · Riverside · Barstow · Kingman · Grand Canyon · Tuba City · Gallup · Los Alamos · Santa Fe · Canadian · Lawton

Long Beach · Oceanside · Santa Ana · Lake Havasu City · Flagstaff · Winslow · Albuquerque · Las Vegas · Tucumcari · Clovis · Portales · Vernon · Wichita Falls

San Diego · Tijuana · Channel Islands · Salton Sea · Glendale · **ARIZONA** · Phoenix · Mesa · St Johns · Socorro · **NEW MEXICO** · Llano Estacado · Lubbock · Post · Snyder

Ensenada · Mexicali · Yuma · Casa Grande · Tucson · Silver City · Alamogordo · Roswell · Artesia · Covington · Hobbs · Midland · Abilene

Lázaro Cárdenas · C. San Quintín · Picacho del Diablo 3096 · San Felipe · Puerto Peñasco · Nogales · Douglas · Deming · Las Cruces · El Paso · Ciudad Juárez · Pecos · Odessa · San Angelo · Brady

PACIFIC OCEAN

Guadalupe (Mexico) · Bahía Sebastián Vizcaíno · Isla Cedros · Punta Eugenia · Bahía Tortugas · Santa Rosalía · Cabora · Benjamin Hill · Magdalena · Nuevo Casas Grandes · Moctezuma · Van Horn · Fort Stockton · Sonora · **TEXAS** · San Antonio

Rosarito · Isla Ángel de la Guarda · Isla Tiburón · Hermosillo · Madera · Chihuahua · Ciudad Delicias · Ciudad Camargo · Sabinas · Laredo

Villa Insurgentes · Isla Carmen · Guaymas · Yécora · Cuauhtémoc · Hidalgo del Parral · Bolsón de Mapimí · Monclova · Hidalgo · McAllen · Reynosa

Santa Margarita · Isla San José · Isla Cerralvo · Ciudad Obregón · Navojoa · Los Mochis · Guasave · Guamúchil · Culiacán · Gómez Palacio · Torreón · Saltillo · Monclova · Monterrey · Monemorelos

La Paz · San José del Cabo · Costa Rica · Durango · Río Grande · Mazatlán · Matehuala · Linares · Ciudad Victoria

Tropic of Cancer · **M E X I C O** · Gulf of California · Sierra Madre Occidental

20° · 120° · **B** · Longitude 110° west of Greenwich · **C** · 100°

Lambert Azimuthal Equal Area Projection

1 : 20 000 000

MILES 0   100   200   300   400

METRES FEET	
5000	16404
3000	9843
2000	6562
1000	3281
500	1640
200	656
0	0
Land below sea level	
200	656
4000	13124
6000	19686

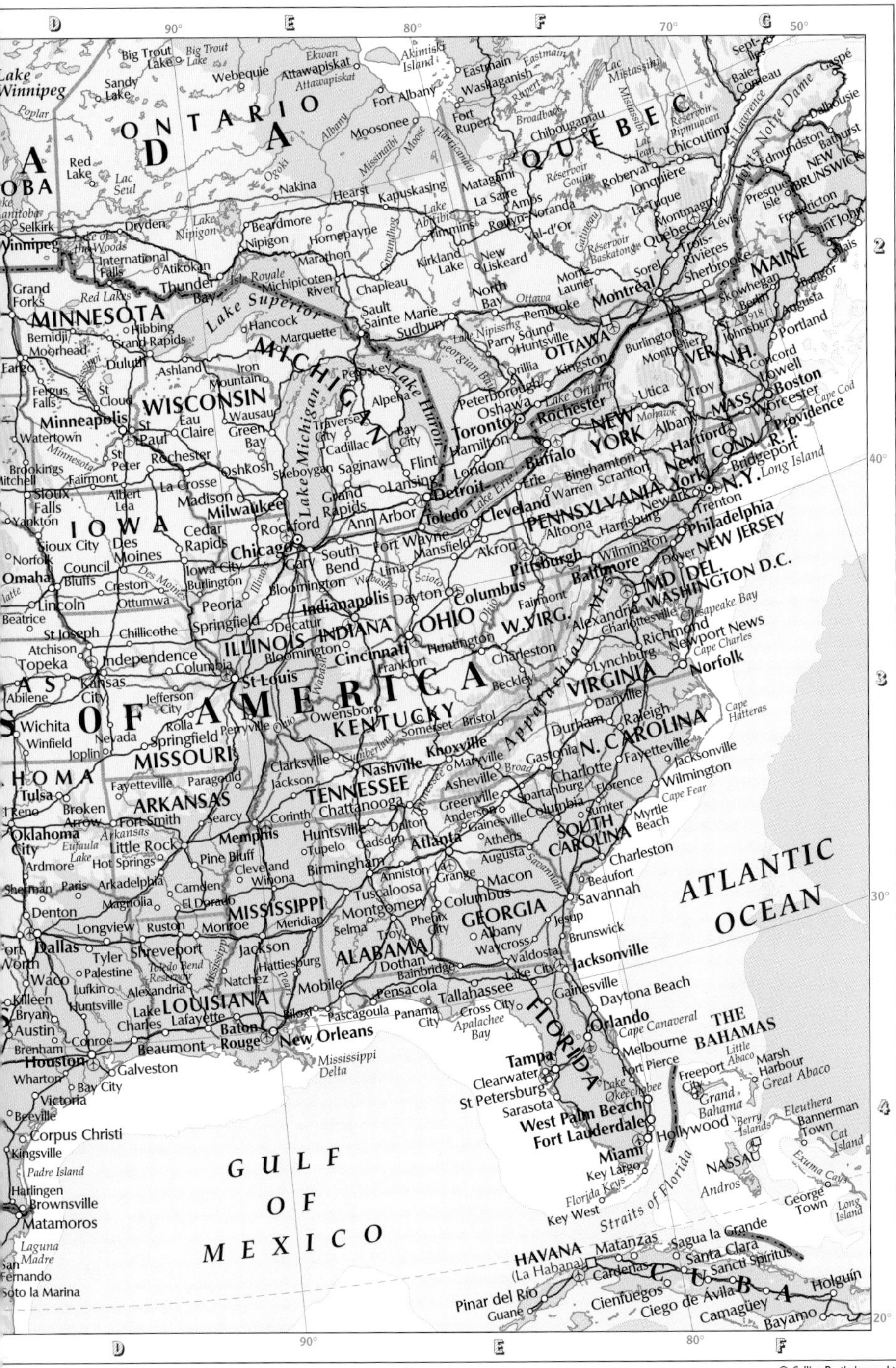

CANADA

ONTARIO

QUEBEC

NEW BRUNSWICK

Lake Winnipeg

MANITOBA

MINNESOTA

WISCONSIN

MICHIGAN

MAINE

Winnipeg

Grand Forks

Fargo

Bemidji
Moorhead

Duluth

Hibbing
Grand Rapids

VERMONT

N.H.

Minneapolis
St Paul

Eau Claire
Green Bay

Traverse City
Cadillac

MASS.

Boston
Worcester
Providence

Watertown

Rochester

Oshkosh

Saginaw

Bay City

Flint

Albany

CONN.

R.I.

Bridgeport

Sioux Falls
Yankton

Albert Lea

Madison
Milwaukee
Rockford

Grand Rapids

Lansing

Detroit

Toledo

Cleveland

NEW YORK

Buffalo

Scranton

Hartford

New Haven

N.Y.

Long Island

IOWA

Cedar Rapids

Chicago

Fort Wayne

Akron

PENNSYLVANIA

Newark
New York
Trenton

NEW JERSEY

Sioux City
Omaha
Council Bluffs
Lincoln

Des Moines

Iowa City

South Bend

Gary

Peoria

Bloomington

Lima

Mansfield

Pittsburgh

Philadelphia

MD.

DEL.

Topeka
Kansas City

Springfield

Decatur

INDIANA

Indianapolis

Dayton

OHIO

Columbus

Harrisburg
Baltimore

WASHINGTON D.C.

Chesapeake Bay

ILLINOIS

Bloomington

Cincinnati

Frankfort

W.VIRG.

Fairmont

Alexandria

Charlottesville

Richmond

Wichita

St Louis

Owensboro

Beckley

Lynchburg

Newport News

Cape Charles

Norfolk

MISSOURI

Springfield
Joplin

Rolla

KENTUCKY

Somerset

Bristol

VIRGINIA

Danville

Raleigh

Cape Hatteras

OKLAHOMA

Tulsa

Fort Smith

Fayetteville

Clarksville

Nashville

TENNESSEE

Knoxville
Maryville

Asheville

Durham

N. CAROLINA

Oklahoma City

Little Rock

ARKANSAS

Searcy

Memphis

Chattanooga

Dalton

Greenville
Spartanburg

Charlotte
Gastonia

Wilmington

Jacksonville

Cape Fear

Ardmore

Pine Bluff

Tupelo

Huntsville

Gadsden

Athens

Anderson

Columbia

SOUTH CAROLINA

Myrtle Beach

Denton
Dallas

Fort Worth

Paris

Longview
Tyler

Arkadelphia
Magnolia

El Dorado

Camden

Winona

Birmingham

Tuscaloosa

Anniston

La Grange

Augusta

Sumter

Charleston

MISSISSIPPI

Montgomery

Columbus

Macon

Savannah

Beaufort

Waco

Shreveport

Ruston
Monroe

Meridian

Selma

Troy

Phenix City

GEORGIA

Albany

Jesup

Brunswick

ATLANTIC OCEAN

Killeen
Bryan
Austin

Palestine
Lufkin
Alexandria

Jackson

Hattiesburg

ALABAMA

Dothan

Bainbridge

Valdosta

Lake City

Jacksonville

Houston

Beaumont

LOUISIANA

Lake Charles
Lafayette

Baton Rouge

Biloxi

Pascagoula
Mobile

Pensacola

Panama City

Tallahassee

Cross City

Gainesville

Daytona Beach

Galveston

New Orleans

Mississippi Delta

Apalachee Bay

Orlando

Cape Canaveral

Melbourne

THE BAHAMAS

Victoria
Bay City

Wharton

Tampa

Clearwater
St Petersburg
Sarasota

FLORIDA

Fort Pierce

West Palm Beach

Fort Lauderdale

Freeport

Little Abaco
Great Abaco

Corpus Christi

Hollywood

Miami

NASSAU

Eleuthera

Bannerman Town

Kingsville

Padre Island

Harlingen
Brownsville
Matamoros

GULF
OF
MEXICO

Key Largo

Florida Keys

Key West

Straits of Florida

Andros

Cat Island

Exuma

Long Island

HAVANA
(La Habana)

Pinar del Río

Matanzas

Cárdenas

CUBA

Santa Clara

Sancti Spíritus

Holguín

Cienfuegos

Ciego de Ávila

Camagüey

Bayamo

© Collins Bartholomew Ltd

0   200   400   600 KILOMETRES

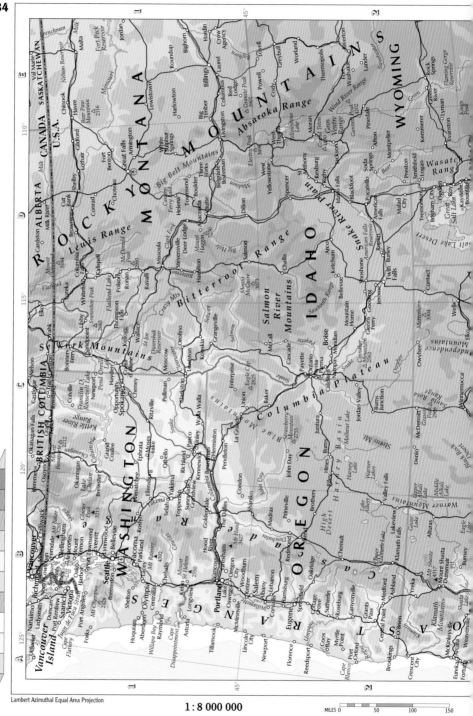

METRES
FEET

5000 | 16404
3000 | 9843
2000 | 6562
1000 | 3281
500 | 1640
200 | 656
0 | 0
Land below
sea level
200 | 656
4000 | 13124
6000 | 19686

Lambert Azimuthal Equal Area Projection

1 : 8 000 000

MILES 0   50   100   150

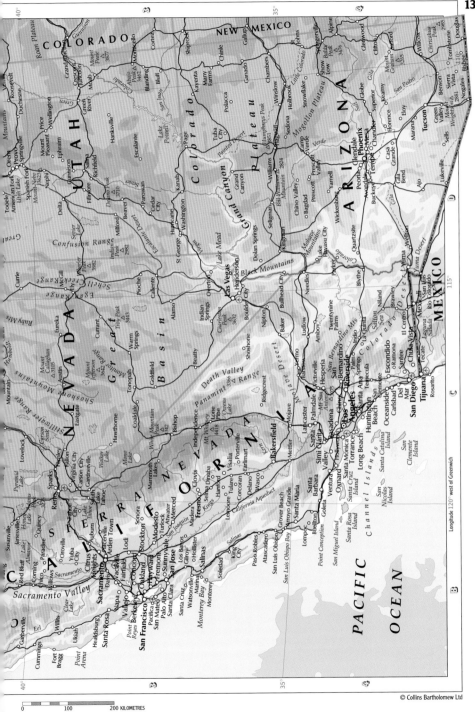

40°

COLORADO

Roan Plateau

Yampa
Roosevelt
Duchesne
Mount
Roosevelt
Green

Gunnison

Grand Junction
Green River
Moab
Crescent Junction

NEW MEXICO

Cortez
Gallup

Alpine
Clearwood

Douglas

Chiricahua
Peak
△2985

Willcox

Price
Wellington

Mount
Peale
△3877

Monticello

Blanding
Bluff

Shiprock

Johns

Tombstone

Clifton

Safford
Sierra
Vista

Bisbee

Nogales

Benson

San Pedro

UTAH

Orem
Provo
Springville
Spanish Fork
American Fork
Tooele
Utah Lake

Salt
Lake

Nephi
Mount Nebo
△3623
Levan

Fillmore

Delta

Hanksville

Escalante

Capitol Reef

Lake Powell

Kayenta

Many
Farms

Chinle

Chambers

Ganado

Winslow

Holbrook
Snowflake

Show
Low

Superior

Globe

Kearny

Eloy

Florence
Casa
Grande

Marana

Tucson

Sells

Green
Valley
Sahuarita
△Mount
Wrightson
2881

ARIZONA

MEXICO

115°

Ephraim
Gunnison
Salina
Richfield

Sevier Desert

Sevier

Dolores Peak
△3710

Abajo
Peak
△3462

Colorado

Page

Tuba
City

Sedona

Flagstaff
△
Humphreys Peak
3851

Mogollon Plateau

Verde

Payson

Prescott
Valley
Prescott

Camp
Verde

Yarnell

Wickenburg

Peoria
Glendale
Phoenix
Tempe
Mesa
Chandler

Buckeye

Gila Bend

Ajo

Lukeville

Yuma Desert

Great

Sevier Lake

Beaver

Cedar
City

St George

Hurricane

Washington
Kanab

Grand
Canyon

Grand Canyon

Plateau

Williams

Bill Williams
Mountain
△2824

Chino Valley

Seligman

Kingman

Mohave
Mountains

Lake
Havasu City

Quartzsite

Blythe

Colorado

Yuma

Gila

Confusion Range

Escalante Desert

Indian
Peak
△2982

Pioche

Calliente

Lake Mead

Dolan Springs

Black Mountains

Boulder City
Henderson
Las Vegas

Overton

Needles

Topock

Lake Havasu
City

Parker

San Luis Rio Colorado

El Centro

Calexico
Mexicali

Tecate

Rosarito

Tijuana

Currie

Wendover

Schell Creek Range

Egan Range

Ely

McGill

Clarkston
Peak
△3632

Indian
Springs

Alamo

Nipton

Baker

Ludlow

Amboy

Twentynine
Palms

Indio

Coachella

Salton
Sea

Brawley

Westmorland

Holtville

Laguna Mexicali

Del
Mar

Santee
Chula
Vista

San Diego

Oceanside
Carlsbad
Encinitas

Escondido
Ramona

Ruby Mts

Eureka

Austin

Warm
Springs

Tonopah

Goldfield

Beatty

Shoshone

Death Valley

Panamint Range

Ridgecrest

Trona

Mojave

Barstow

Victorville
Hesperia

Yermo

San Bernardino
Mts

Big Bear

Redlands

Banning

Palm
Springs

Temecula

NEVADA

Mount
Callaghan
△3105

Monitor Range

Mount
Jefferson
△3642

Diamond Peak
△3743

Troy Peak
△3443

Clarkston
Peak

Death Valley
△3366

Panamint
Range

Owens
Lake

Mt Whitney
△4418

Mt San
Antonio
△3068

Palmdale

Lancaster

Santa
Clarita

Simi
Valley

Pasadena

Glendale

Los
Angeles

Santa Ana

Anaheim

Riverside

Corona

Long Beach

Huntington
Beach

Shoshone Mountains

Stillwater Range

Lovelock

Fallon

Walker
Lake

Hawthorne

Coaldale

Bishop

Independence

Lone
Pine

Mammoth

Inyokern

Tehachapi

Mojave

Tehachapi

Oxnard
Ventura

Santa
Barbara

Goleta

Oxnard

Santa Monica
Torrance

Santa Catalina
Island

San
Clemente
Island

PACIFIC

OCEAN

Pyramid
Lake

Sparks
Reno

Carson City
Gardnerville

Virginia City

Minden

South
Lake
Tahoe

Lake
Tahoe

Carson
Sink

Honey
Lake

Mono
Lake

Mammoth

Sonora

Coalinga

Clovis

Fresno

Visalia

Tulare

Delano

Wasco

Porterville

Earlimart

Bakersfield

Shafter

Maricopa

Santa
Maria

Lompoc

Point
Conception

San Miguel Island

Santa Rosa
Island

Santa Cruz
Island

San
Nicolas
Island

Channel Islands

CALIFORNIA

Mount
Callaghan

SIERRA

NEVADA

Yuba
City

Oroville

Paradise

Chico

Willows

Corning

Red Bluff

Susanville

Janesville

Quincy

Eagle
Lake

Lake
Almanor

Orland

Cummings

Fort
Bragg

Garberville

Willits

Ukiah

Healdsburg

Clear
Lake

Eel

Point
Arena

Santa Rosa

Napa
Vallejo

Fairfield

Vacaville

Citrus
Heights

Sacramento

Arden Town

Davis

Stockton

Lodi

Manteca

Modesto

Turlock

Merced

Los Banos

Madera

San Joaquin

Sacramento Valley

Sacramento

Berkeley
Oakland
San Francisco
Daly City
Pacifica
San Mateo
Palo Alto
Sunnyvale
Santa Clara
San Jose

Fremont
Hayward

Gilroy

Hollister

Watsonville

Santa Cruz

Monterey

Marina

Salinas

Soledad

King
City

Paso Robles

Atascadero

San Luis Obispo

Grover Beach
Arroyo Grande

Monterey Bay

Point
Reyes

San Joaquin

California Aqueduct

Kings

Lemoore

Hanford

Corcoran

Selma

Point Sur

40°

35°

35°

0   100   200 KILOMETRES

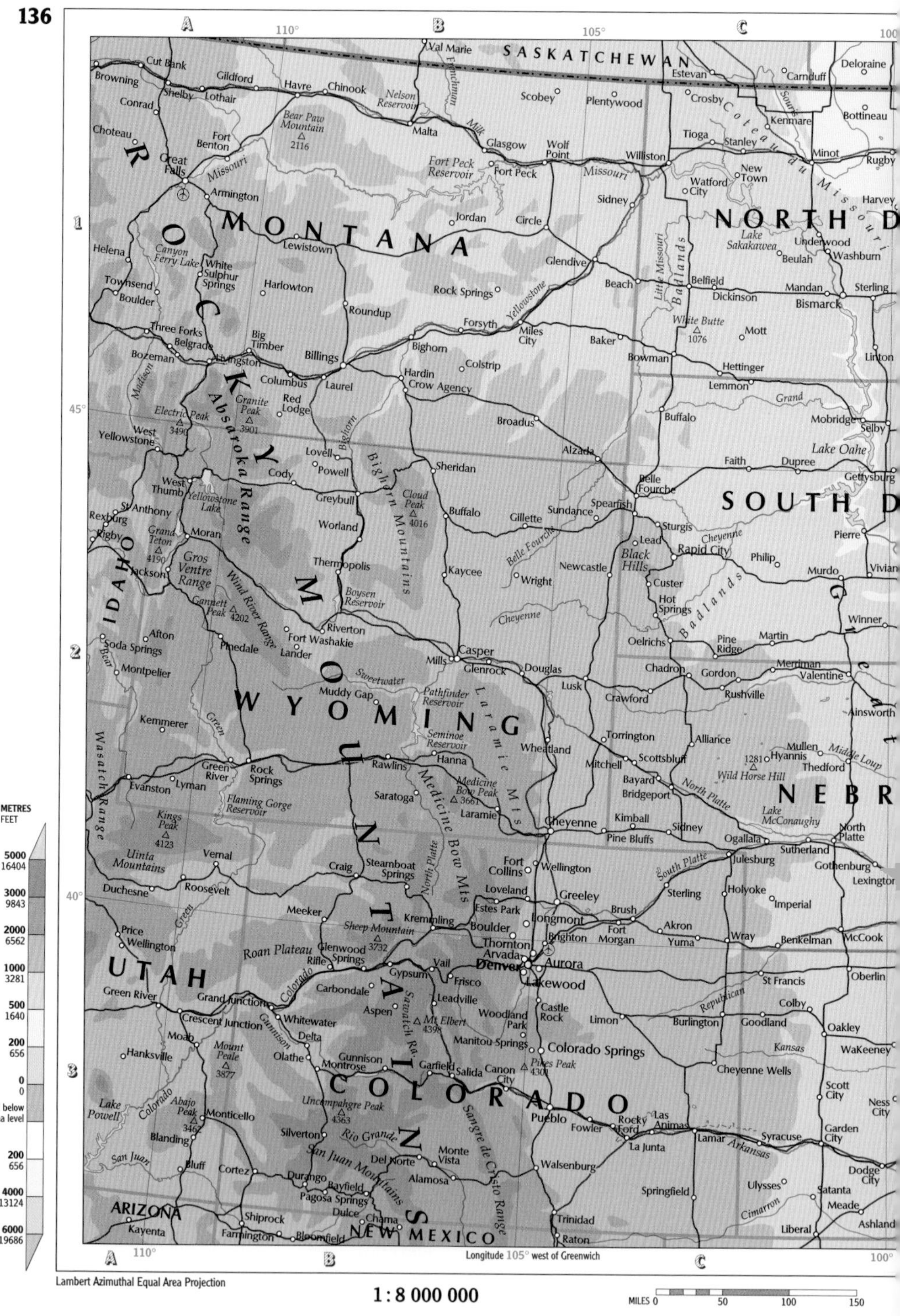

SASKATCHEWAN

Val Marie · Estevan · Carnduff · Deloraine

Browning · Cut Bank · Gildford · Havre · Chinook · Scobey · Plentywood · Crosby · Kenmare · Bottineau
Conrad · Shelby · Lothair · Nelson Reservoir · Glasgow · Wolf Point · Williston · Tioga · Stanley · New Town · Minot · Rugby
Choteau · Fort Benton · Bear Paw Mountain 2116 · Malta · Fort Peck Reservoir · Fort Peck · Watford City · Underwood · Beulah · Washburn
Great Falls · Armington · Missouri · Jordan · Circle · Sidney · Glendive · NORTH D

MONTANA

Helena · Lewistown · Lake Sakakawea · Belfield · Dickinson · Mandan · Bismarck · Sterling
Townsend · White Sulphur Springs · Harlowton · Rock Springs · Beach · White Butte 1076 · Mott · Linton
Boulder · Canyon Ferry Lake · Roundup · Forsyth · Miles City · Baker · Hettinger · Lemmon · Grand · Mobridge · Selby
Three Forks · Belgrade · Big Timber · Billings · Bighorn · Colstrip · Bowman · Buffalo · Faith · Lake Oahe · Gettysburg
Bozeman · Livingston · Columbus · Laurel · Hardin · Crow Agency · Broadus · Alzada · Dupree · SOUTH D
Red Lodge · Granite Peak 3901 · Sheridan · Belle Fourche · Sturgis · Rapid City · Philip · Pierre
West Yellowstone · Electric Peak 3349 · Cody · Lovell · Powell · Buffalo · Gillette · Sundance · Spearfish · Lead · Black Hills · Custer · Murdo · Vivian
South Thumb · West Thumb · Greybull · Cloud Peak 4016 · Newcastle · Hot Springs · Pine Ridge · Martin · Winner
Rexburg · Yellowstone Lake · Worland · Wright · Oelrichs · Merriman · Valentine · Ainsworth

WYOMING

Casper · Glenrock · Douglas · Chadron · Gordon · Rushville
Muddy Gap · Lusk · Crawford · Alliance · Mullen · Hyannis · Thedford
Torrington · Scottsbluff · Mitchell · Bayard · Bridgeport · Wild Horse Hill 1281 · NEBR

COLORADO

NEW MEXICO

ARIZONA

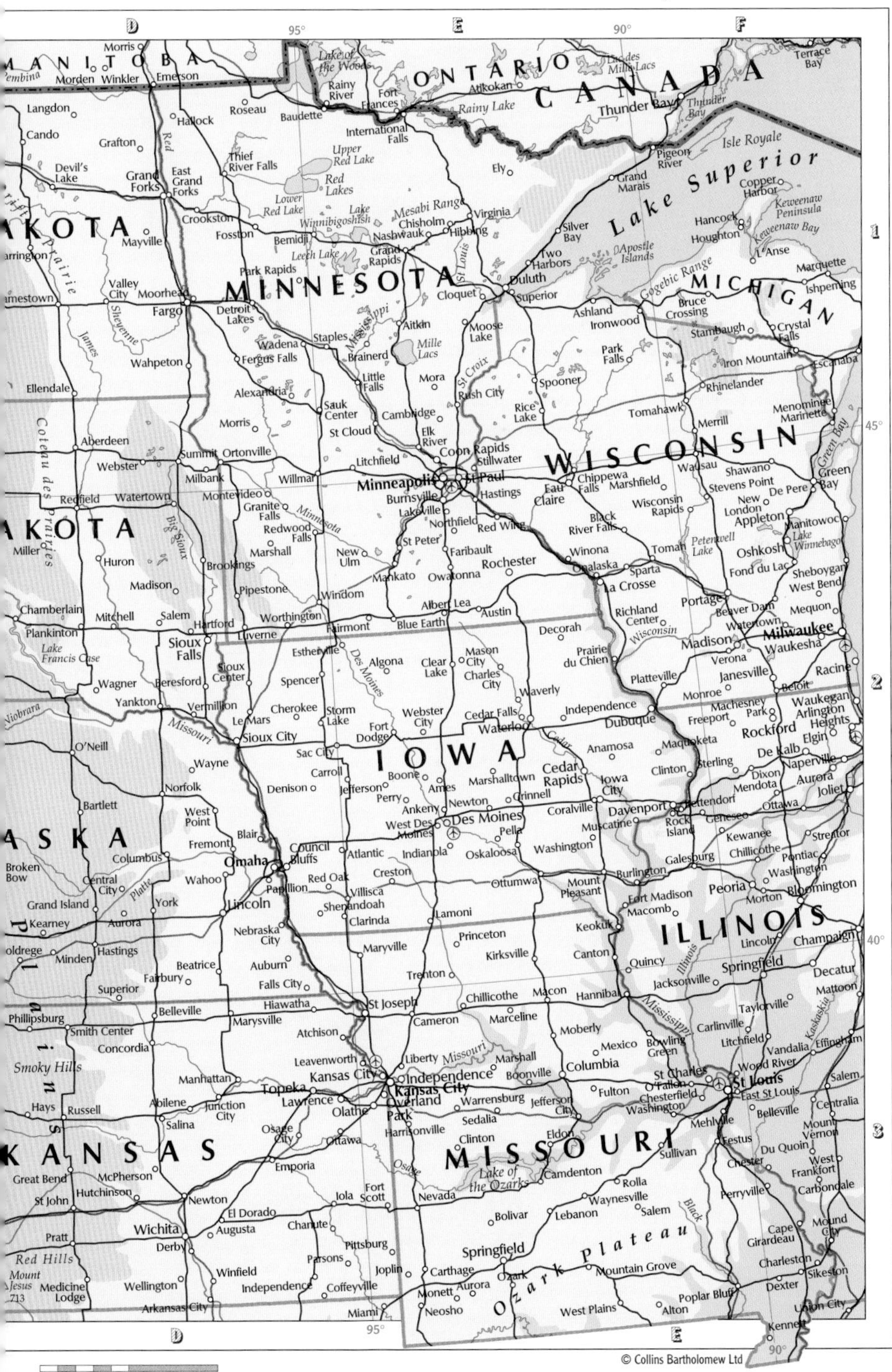
D
95°
E
90°
F
1
2
3
45°
40°
MANITOBA
ONTARIO
CANADA
MINNESOTA
WISCONSIN
MICHIGAN
IOWA
ILLINOIS
MISSOURI
KANSAS
AKOTA
AKOTA
ASKA
Morris
Pembina
Morden
Winkler
Emerson
Lake of the Woods
Rainy River
Fort Frances
Atikokan
Lac des Mille Lacs
Thunder Bay
Terrace Bay
Rainy Lake
International Falls
Langdon
Hallock
Roseau
Baudette
Cando
Grafton
Red
Thief River Falls
Upper Red Lake
Red Lakes
Lower Red Lake
Devil's Lake
Grand Forks
East Grand Forks
Crookston
Fosston
Lake Winnibigoshish
Mesabi Range
Chisholm
Nashwauk
Hibbing
Virginia
Ely
Pigeon River
Isle Royale
Grand Marais
Lake Superior
Copper Harbor
Keweenaw Peninsula
Keweenaw Bay
Hancock
Houghton
L'Anse
Mayville
Bemidji
Leech Lake
Grand Rapids
Silver Bay
Two Harbors
Apostle Islands
Park Rapids
St Louis
Duluth
Superior
Gogebic Range
Marquette
Ishpeming
Valley City
Moorhead
Fargo
Detroit Lakes
Cloquet
Ashland
Ironwood
Bruce Crossing
Stambaugh
Crystal Falls
Sheyenne
James
Wadena
Staples
Mississippi
Aitkin
Mille Lacs
Moose Lake
Park Falls
Iron Mountain
Escanaba
Wahpeton
Fergus Falls
Brainerd
Little Falls
Mora
St Croix
Spooner
Rhinelander
Ellendale
Alexandria
Rush City
Sauk Centre
Cambridge
Rice Lake
Tomahawk
Menominee
Marinette
Morris
St Cloud
Elk River
Merrill
Green Bay
Aberdeen
Ortonville
Litchfield
Coon Rapids
Stillwater
Webster
Summit
Milbank
Willmar
Minneapolis
St Paul
Chippewa Falls
Eau Claire
Marshfield
Wausau
Shawano
Stevens Point
De Pere
Redfield
Watertown
Montevideo
Granite Falls
Burnsville
Lakeville
Hastings
Wisconsin Rapids
New London
Appleton
Manitowoc
Minnesota
Big Sioux
Northfield
Red Wing
Black River Falls
Miller
Huron
Redwood Falls
Marshall
St Peter
New Ulm
Faribault
Rochester
Winona
Tomah
Petenwell Lake
Oshkosh
Lake Winnebago
Fond du Lac
Sheboygan
West Bend
Brookings
Madison
Mankato
Owatonna
Onalaska
Sparta
La Crosse
Pipestone
Windom
Portage
Chamberlain
Mitchell
Salem
Worthington
Albert Lea
Austin
Richland Center
Beaver Dam
Mequon
Plankinton
Hartford
Luverne
Fairmont
Blue Earth
Decorah
Watertown
Milwaukee
Waukesha
Lake Francis Case
Sioux Falls
Estherville
Des Moines
Algona
Clear Lake
Mason City
Charles City
Prairie du Chien
Verona
Racine
Janesville
Sioux Center
Spencer
Wagner
Beresford
Platteville
Monroe
Beloit
Yankton
Vermillion
Cherokee
Storm Lake
Webster City
Cedar Falls
Waverly
Independence
Machesney Park
Freeport
Waukegan
Arlington Heights
Niobrara
Missouri
Le Mars
Sioux City
Fort Dodge
Waterloo
Dubuque
Rockford
Elgin
O'Neill
Sac City
Anamosa
Maquoketa
De Kalb
Wayne
Carroll
Boone
Cedar
Cedar Rapids
Clinton
Sterling
Naperville
Aurora
Norfolk
Denison
Jefferson
Ames
Marshalltown
Iowa City
Dixon
Mendota
Joliet
Bartlett
Perry
Ankeny
Grinnell
Newton
Coralville
Davenport
Bettendorf
Ottawa
West Point
West Des Moines
Des Moines
Pella
Muscatine
Rock Island
Geneseo
Kewanee
Streator
Blair
Fremont
Council Bluffs
Atlantic
Indianola
Oskaloosa
Washington
Chillicothe
Pontiac
Columbus
Omaha
Broken Bow
Wahoo
Red Oak
Creston
Galesburg
Washington
Central City
Papillion
Villisca
Ottumwa
Mount Pleasant
Burlington
Peoria
Bloomington
Grand Island
York
Lincoln
Shenandoah
Clarinda
Fort Madison
Macomb
Morton
Kearney
Aurora
Lamoni
Keokuk
Holdrege
Minden
Hastings
Nebraska City
Princeton
Kirksville
Canton
Lincoln
Champaign
Beatrice
Auburn
Quincy
Illinois
Springfield
Decatur
Fairbury
Falls City
Trenton
Jacksonville
Superior
Mattoon
Hiawatha
St Joseph
Chillicothe
Macon
Hannibal
Taylorville
Phillipsburg
Belleville
Marysville
Cameron
Marceline
Kaskaskia
Smith Center
Atchison
Moberly
Carlinville
Concordia
Litchfield
Effingham
Leavenworth
Liberty
Marshall
Mexico
Bowling Green
Vandalia
Smoky Hills
Manhattan
Kansas City
Independence
Boonville
Columbia
Wood River
Topeka
Kansas City
St Charles
O'Fallon
St Louis
Salem
Hays
Russell
Abilene
Junction City
Lawrence
Olathe
Overland Park
Warrensburg
Jefferson City
Fulton
Chesterfield
Washington
East St Louis
Belleville
Centralia
Salina
Osage City
Harrisonville
Sedalia
Mehlville
Mount Vernon
Ottawa
Clinton
Eldon
Festus
Du Quoin
Sullivan
Great Bend
McPherson
Emporia
Lake of the Ozarks
Camdenton
Chester
West Frankfort
Hutchinson
Fort Scott
Iola
Nevada
Rolla
Perryville
Carbondale
St John
Newton
El Dorado
Waynesville
Salem
Black
Bolivar
Lebanon
Wichita
Augusta
Chanute
Pratt
Derby
Pittsburg
Springfield
Cape Girardeau
Mound City
Red Hills
Parsons
Ozark Plateau
Joplin
Carthage
Mountain Grove
Charleston
Sikeston
Mount Jesus
713
Medicine Lodge
Winfield
Wellington
Independence
Coffeyville
Ozark
Aurora
Monett
Dexter
Poplar Bluff
West Plains
Alton
Arkansas City
Miami
Neosho
Union City
Kennett
Plains
0
100
200 KILOMETRES

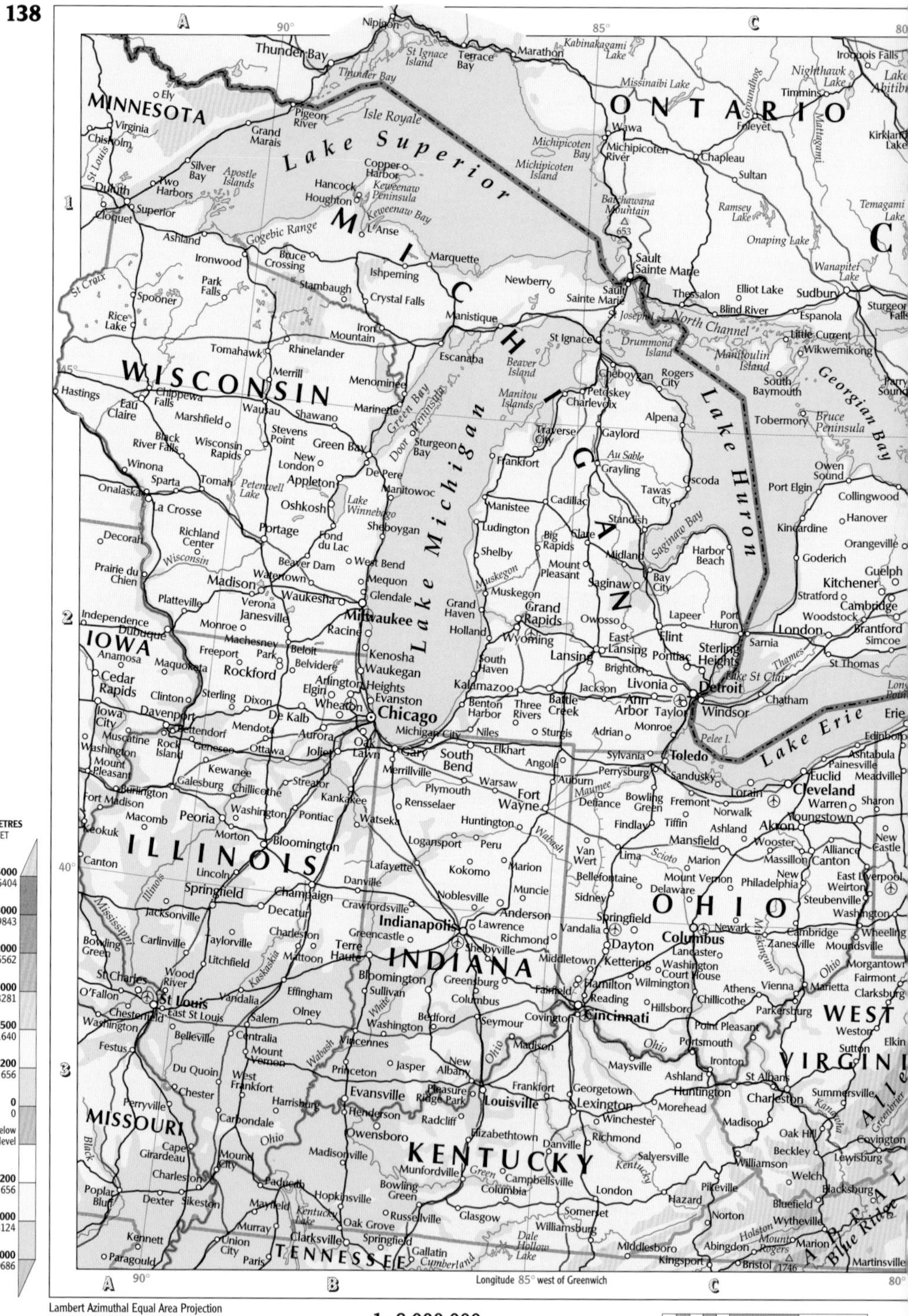

MINNESOTA

Ely
Virginia
Chisholm

St Louis R.
Duluth
Superior
Cloquet

Silver
Bay
Two
Harbors

Ashland

Spooner

Park
Falls

Ironwood

Hancock
Houghton

Copper
Harbor

Keweenaw
Peninsula

Keweenaw Bay

L'Anse

Ishpeming

Marquette

Bruce
Crossing

Stambaugh
Crystal Falls

Iron
Mountain

Menominee

Marinette

Escanaba

Newberry

ONTARIO

Thunder Bay

Nipigon

St Ignace
Island

Terrace
Bay

Marathon

Kabinakagami
Lake

Missinaibi Lake

Iroquois Falls

Nighthawk
Lake

Timmins

Kirkland
Lake

Lake Abitibi

Temagami
Lake

Onaping Lake

Wanapitei
Lake

Sudbury

Espanola

Little Current

Sturgeon

Manitoulin
Island

Wikwemikong

South
Baymouth

Tobermory

Bruce
Peninsula

Georgian Bay

Owen
Sound

Collingwood

Kincardine

Hanover

Goderich

Orangeville

Guelph

Kitchener

Stratford

Woodstock

Cambridge

Brantford

London

St Thomas

Simcoe

Chatham

Windsor

Detroit

Lake Erie

Erie

Edinboro

Painesville

Euclid

Cleveland

Meadville

Sharon

Warren

Youngstown

Akron

Wooster

Canton

Alliance

New
Castle

East Liverpool

Steubenville

Washington

Wheeling

Moundsville

Morgantown

Fairmont

Clarksburg

WEST
VIRGINIA

MICHIGAN

Lake Superior

Isle Royale

Pigeon
River

Grand
Marais

Gogebic Range

Apostle
Islands

Rice
Lake

St Croix R.

Hastings

WISCONSIN

Eau
Claire

Chippewa
Falls

Black
River Falls

Wisconsin
Rapids

Marshfield

Wausau

Merrill

Rhinelander

Tomahawk

Manistique

Manitou
Islands

Beaver
Island

St Ignace

Cheboygan

Petoskey

Charlevoix

Traverse
City

Frankfort

Manistee

Ludington

Big
Rapids

Cadillac

Grayling

Au Sable R.

Gaylord

Alpena

Rogers
City

Tawas
City

Oscoda

Standish

Midland

Saginaw Bay

Bay
City

Harbor
Beach

Port Elgin

Saugeen

North Channel

Drummond
Island

Manitoulin

Blind River

Elliot Lake

Thessalon

Sault
Sainte Marie

St Joseph I.

Lake Huron

Ramsey
Lake

Sultan

Chapleau

Batchawana
Mountain
653

Michipicoten
Island

Michipicoten
Bay

Michipicoten
River

Wawa

Onaping Lake

METRES
FEET

5000 16404
3000 9843
2000 6562
1000 3281
500   1640
200   656
0   0
Land below
sea level
200   656
4000 13124
6000 19686

Lambert Azimuthal Equal Area Projection

Longitude 85° west of Greenwich

1 : 8 000 000

MILES 0   50   100   150

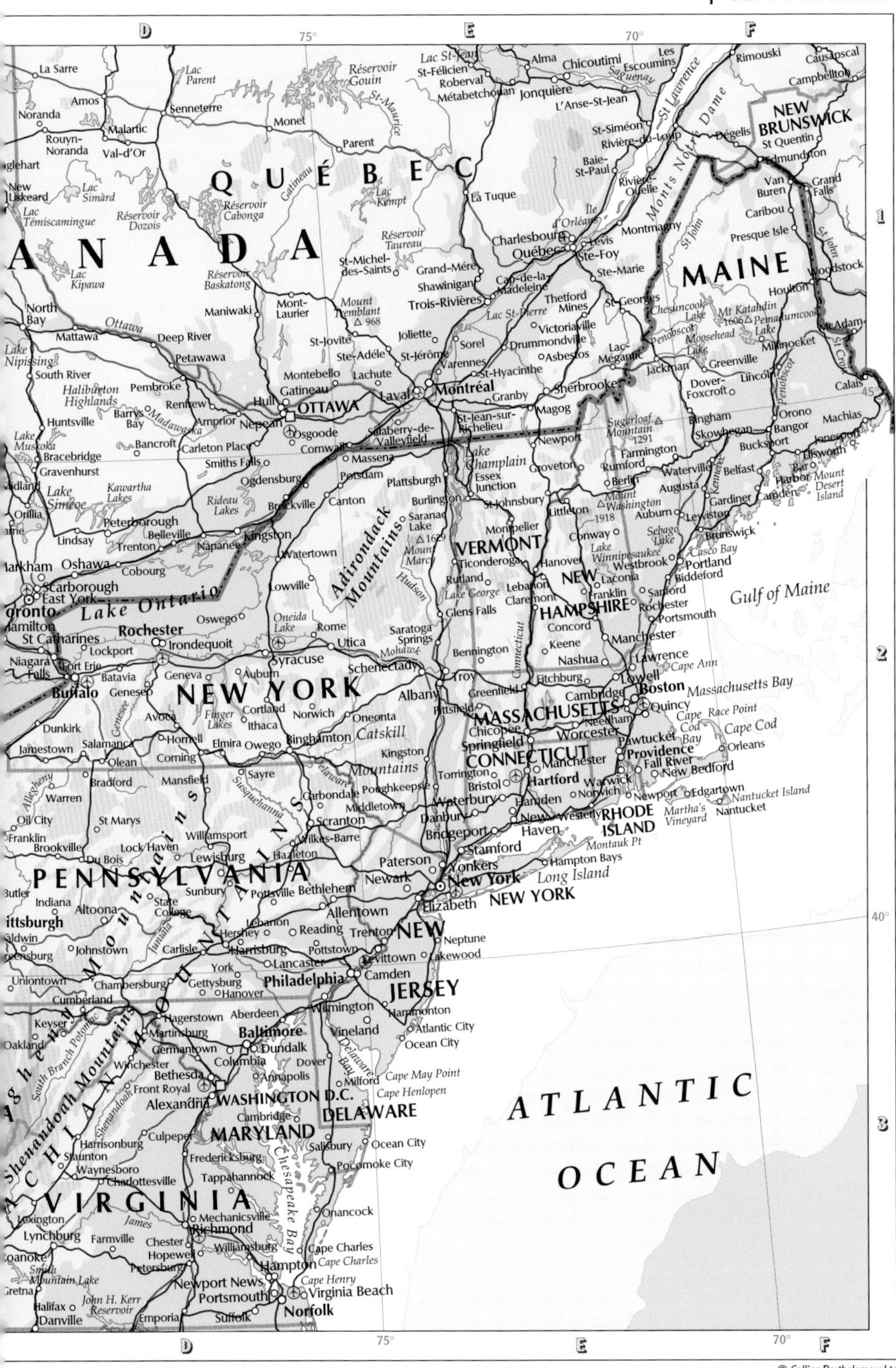
D
E
F
75°
70°
1
2
3
40°
45°
QUÉBEC
CANADA
MAINE
NEW BRUNSWICK
VERMONT
NEW HAMPSHIRE
MASSACHUSETTS
CONNECTICUT
RHODE ISLAND
NEW YORK
PENNSYLVANIA
NEW JERSEY
DELAWARE
MARYLAND
VIRGINIA
WASHINGTON D.C.
ATLANTIC OCEAN
Gulf of Maine
Massachusetts Bay
Cape Cod Bay
Cape Cod
Cape Ann
Race Point
Long Island
Montauk Pt
Martha's Vineyard
Nantucket Island
Cape May Point
Cape Henlopen
Cape Charles
Cape Henry
Chesapeake Bay
Delaware Bay
Lake Ontario
Lake Champlain
Lake George
Oneida Lake
Finger Lakes
Lake Simcoe
Lake Nipissing
Lake Muskoka
Kawartha Lakes
Rideau Lakes
Lac Témiscamingue
Lac Kipawa
Lac Simard
Lac Parent
Lac St-Jean
Lac Kempt
Lac St-Pierre
Réservoir Gouin
Réservoir Cabonga
Réservoir Dozois
Réservoir Taureau
Réservoir Baskatong
Moosehead Lake
Chesuncook Lake
Pemadumcook Lake
Sebago Lake
Lake Winnipesaukee
Smith Mountain Lake
John H. Kerr Reservoir
St Lawrence
Saguenay
St-Maurice
Gatineau
Ottawa
Madawaska
Hudson
Mohawk
Connecticut
Delaware
Susquehanna
Genesee
Allegheny
Juniata
South Branch Potomac
Shenandoah
James
St John
Penobscot
Kennebec
St Croix
Adirondack Mountains
Catskill Mountains
Appalachian Mountains
Allegheny Mountains
Shenandoah Mountains
Monts Notre Dame
Haliburton Highlands
Mount Tremblant △ 968
Mt Katahdin 1606 △
Sugarloaf Mountain △ 1291
Mount Washington △ 1918
Mount Marcy △ 1629
Mount Desert Island
Île d'Orléans
OTTAWA
Montréal
Québec
Toronto
Boston
New York
Philadelphia
Baltimore
Pittsburgh
Buffalo
Rochester
Syracuse
Albany
Hartford
Providence
Portland
Richmond
Norfolk
La Sarre
Amos
Noranda
Rouyn-Noranda
Malartic
Val-d'Or
Senneterre
Monet
Parent
New Liskeard
St-Félicien
Roberval
Métabetchouan
Alma
Chicoutimi
Jonquière
Les Escoumins
L'Anse-St-Jean
Rimouski
Causapscal
Campbellton
St-Siméon
Rivière-du-Loup
Dégelis
St Quentin
Edmundston
Baie-St-Paul
Rivière-Ouelle
Montmagny
Van Buren
Grand Falls
Caribou
Presque Isle
Woodstock
Houlton
McAdam
Millinocket
Calais
La Tuque
Charlesbourg
Lévis
Ste-Foy
Ste-Marie
St-Georges
St-Michel-des-Saints
Grand-Mère
Shawinigan
Trois-Rivières
Cap-de-la-Madeleine
Thetford Mines
Victoriaville
Drummondville
Asbestos
Lac-Mégantic
Jackman
Greenville
Dover-Foxcroft
Lincoln
Maniwaki
Mont-Laurier
St-Jovite
Ste-Adèle
Joliette
Sorel
St-Jérôme
Varennes
St-Hyacinthe
Sherbrooke
Montebello
Lachute
Gatineau
Hull
Laval
Granby
Magog
St-Jean-sur-Richelieu
Salaberry-de-Valleyfield
North Bay
Mattawa
Deep River
Petawawa
South River
Pembroke
Renfrew
Arnprior
Nepean
Osgoode
Cornwall
Huntsville
Barrys Bay
Bancroft
Carleton Place
Smiths Falls
Bracebridge
Gravenhurst
Midland
Orillia
Ogdensburg
Brockville
Peterborough
Belleville
Trenton
Napanee
Kingston
Lindsay
Oshawa
Cobourg
Markham
Scarborough
East York
Hamilton
St Catharines
Niagara Falls
Fort Erie
Lockport
Irondequoit
Oswego
Watertown
Lowville
Massena
Potsdam
Plattsburgh
Canton
Burlington
Saranac Lake
Ticonderoga
Rutland
Glens Falls
Saratoga Springs
Rome
Utica
Schenectady
Troy
Bennington
Newport
Coaticook
St Johnsbury
Montpelier
Littleton
Groveton
Conway
Hanover
Lebanon
Claremont
Laconia
Franklin
Concord
Keene
Nashua
Manchester
Fitchburg
Lowell
Lawrence
Cambridge
Quincy
Needham
Worcester
Greenfield
Pittsfield
Chicopee
Springfield
Manchester
Torrington
Bristol
Waterbury
Hamden
New Haven
Danbury
Bridgeport
Stamford
Yonkers
Norwich
Westerly
Warwick
Newport
Pawtucket
Fall River
New Bedford
Edgartown
Nantucket
Orleans
Hampton Bays
Rumford
Farmington
Berlin
Waterville
Augusta
Belfast
Gardiner
Camden
Lewiston
Auburn
Brunswick
Westbrook
Biddeford
Sanford
Rochester
Portsmouth
Bingham
Skowhegan
Orono
Bangor
Bucksport
Machias
Jonesport
Ellsworth
Bar Harbor
Batavia
Geneseo
Geneva
Auburn
Cortland
Ithaca
Norwich
Oneonta
Dunkirk
Jamestown
Salamanca
Olean
Hornell
Corning
Elmira
Owego
Binghamton
Kingston
Poughkeepsie
Middletown
Avoca
Bradford
Warren
Oil City
Franklin
St Marys
Mansfield
Sayre
Carbondale
Scranton
Wilkes-Barre
Hazleton
Williamsport
Lock Haven
Lewisburg
Brookville
Du Bois
Butler
Indiana
Altoona
State College
Sunbury
Pottsville
Bethlehem
Allentown
Paterson
Newark
Elizabeth
Trenton
Neptune
Lakewood
Levittown
Camden
Pottstown
Reading
Lebanon
Hershey
Harrisburg
Carlisle
Lancaster
York
Gettysburg
Hanover
Chambersburg
Johnstown
Baldwin
Greensburg
Uniontown
Cumberland
Hagerstown
Aberdeen
Martinsburg
Keyser
Oakland
Germantown
Columbia
Dundalk
Wilmington
Hammonton
Vineland
Atlantic City
Ocean City
Dover
Milford
Annapolis
Winchester
Bethesda
Front Royal
Alexandria
Cambridge
Salisbury
Ocean City
Pocomoke City
Culpeper
Harrisonburg
Staunton
Waynesboro
Charlottesville
Fredericksburg
Tappahannock
Lexington
Lynchburg
Farmville
Mechanicsville
Chester
Hopewell
Petersburg
Williamsburg
Hampton
Newport News
Portsmouth
Suffolk
Virginia Beach
Onancock
Roanoke
Gretna
Halifax
Danville
Emporia
0
100
200 KILOMETRES

MISSOURI
TENNESSEE
KENTUCKY
ARKANSAS
OKLAHOMA
MISSISSIPPI
ALABAMA
TEXAS
LOUISIANA

GULF OF MEXICO

Vinita, Owasso, Tulsa, Pryor, Siloam Springs, Bentonville, Rogers, Springdale, Fayetteville, West Plains, Poplar Bluff, Alton, Charleston, Sikeston, Paducah, Glasgow, Hopkinsville, Oak Grove, Russellville, Clarksville, Gallatin

Sapulpa, Broken Arrow, Muskogee, Okmulgee, Henryetta, Tahlequah, Boston Mts, Mountain Home, Pocahontas, Kennett, Dexter, Mayfield, Murray, Kentucky Lake, Springfield, Nashville, Lebanon, Cumberland

Chicotah, Sallisaw, Van Buren, Clarksville, Heber Springs, Batesville, Newport, Trumann, Hoxie, Jonesboro, Blytheville, Humboldt, Jackson, Dyersburg, McKenzie, Dickson, Franklin, Murfreesboro

Fort Smith, Magazine Mountain, Russellville, Searcy, Conway, Jacksonville, Wynne, Forrest City, West Memphis, Bartlett, Brownsville, Linden, Columbia, Shelbyville, Manchester, McMinnville, Lewisburg, Tullahoma, Fayetteville

Eufaula Lake, McAlester, Poteau, Ouachita Mts, LITTLE ROCK, Stuttgart, Marianna, Memphis, Southaven, Corinth, Bolivar, Lawrenceburg

Atoka, Mena, Lake Ouachita, Hot Springs, Arkadelphia, Malvern, Pine Bluff, Helena, Holly Springs, Oxford, Booneville, Athens, Huntsville, Florence, Russellville, Wheeler Lake, Decatur, Fort Payne

Hugo, Idabel, De Queen, Hope, Fordyce, Monticello, Clarksdale, Batesville, Tupelo, Hamilton, Cullman, Gadsden

Paris, New Boston, Ashdown, Camden, Warren, Dumas, Cleveland, Grenada, Amory, Jasper, Center Point, Anniston

Commerce, Texarkana, Magnolia, El Dorado, Hamburg, Crossett, Greenville, Leland, Greenwood, Winona, Starkville, Columbus, Birmingham, Vestavia Hills, Bessemer, Cheaha Mountain, Sylacauga

Sulphur Springs, Mount Pleasant, Homer, Minden, Bastrop, Yazoo City, Louisville, Macon, Tuscaloosa, Alabaster, Alexander City

Tyler, Gladewater, Longview, Shreveport, Ruston, Monroe, Canton, Vicksburg, Ridgeland, Eutaw, Demopolis, Clanton, Auburn, Tuskegee

Athens, Henderson, Marshall, Carthage, Bossier City, Jonesboro, Driskill Mountain, Tallulah, JACKSON, Meridian, York, Selma, Prattville, Montgomery

Jacksonville, Tenaha, Natchitoches, Mansfield, Winnsboro, Olla, Crystal Springs, Forest, Thomasville, Greenville, Troy

Palestine, Nacogdoches, Toledo Bend Reservoir, Many, Winfield, Natchez, Brookhaven, Laurel, Jackson, Monroeville, Ozark, Enterprise

Crockett, Lufkin, Jasper, Alexandria, Pineville, Leesville, Marksville, Lecompte, Hattiesburg, Petal, Evergreen, Andalusia, Atmore

Huntsville, Corrigan, De Ridder, Oakdale, McComb, Lumberton, Century, Crestview, De Funiak Springs

Lake Livingston, Livingston, Conroe, Ville Platte, Opelousas, Jennings, Kentwood, Bogalusa, Picayune, Mobile, Prichard, Pensacola, Fort Walton Beach, Panama City

The Woodlands, Humble, Beaumont, Orange, Nederland, Vidor, Lake Charles, Crowley, Lafayette, Baker, Port Allen, BATON ROUGE, Hammond, Gulfport, Biloxi, Pascagoula, Santa Rosa Island, Mobile Bay, Mobile Point

Houston, Baytown, Pasadena, Groves, Port Arthur, White Lake, Abbeville, New Iberia, Plaquemine, Kenner, Metairie, NEW ORLEANS, Gretna, Mississippi Sound, Chandeleur Islands

Sugar Land, Texas City, Lake Jackson, Galveston Bay, Galveston, Galveston Island, Freeport, Marsh Island, Morgan City, Thibodaux, Raceland, Cut Off, Port Sulphur, Houma, Breton Sound, Mississippi Delta

Atchafalaya Bay, Terrebonne Bay, Grand Isle

METRES	FEET
5000	16404
3000	9843
2000	6562
1000	3281
500	1640
200	656
0	0
Land below sea level	
200	656
4000	13124
6000	19686

Lambert Azimuthal Equal Area Projection

Longitude 90° west of Greenwich

1 : 8 000 000

MILES 0 50 100 150

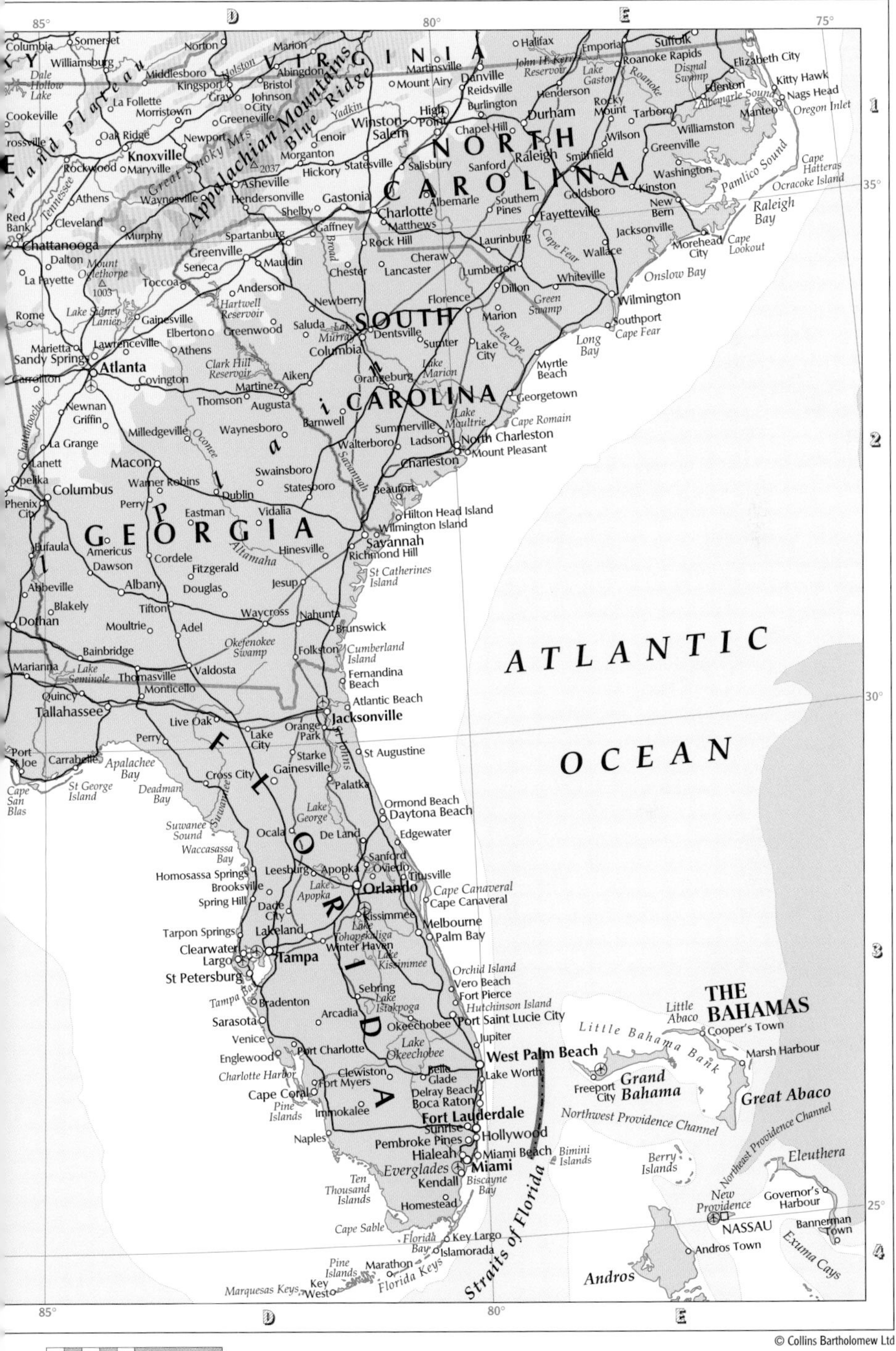
NORTH CAROLINA
SOUTH CAROLINA
GEORGIA
FLORIDA
VIRGINIA
ATLANTIC OCEAN
THE BAHAMAS
Appalachian Mountains
Blue Ridge
Great Smoky Mts
Atlanta
Charlotte
Raleigh
Columbia
Savannah
Jacksonville
Orlando
Tampa
Miami
Fort Lauderdale
West Palm Beach
Tallahassee
Charleston
Wilmington
Knoxville
Chattanooga
Asheville
Augusta
Macon
Columbus
Gainesville
St Petersburg
Daytona Beach
Hollywood
Key West
Florida Keys
Straits of Florida
Grand Bahama
Great Abaco
Andros
NASSAU
Eleuthera
Cape Hatteras
Pamlico Sound
Okefenokee Swamp
Lake Okeechobee
Everglades
Cape Canaveral
Onslow Bay
Long Bay
Raleigh Bay
Apalachee Bay
Northwest Providence Channel
Little Bahama Bank
200 KILOMETRES

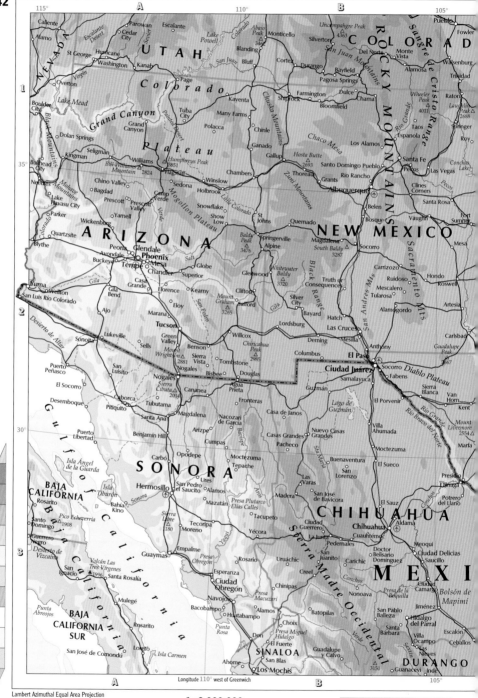

Lambert Azimuthal Equal Area Projection

1 : 8 000 000

MILES 0   50   100   150

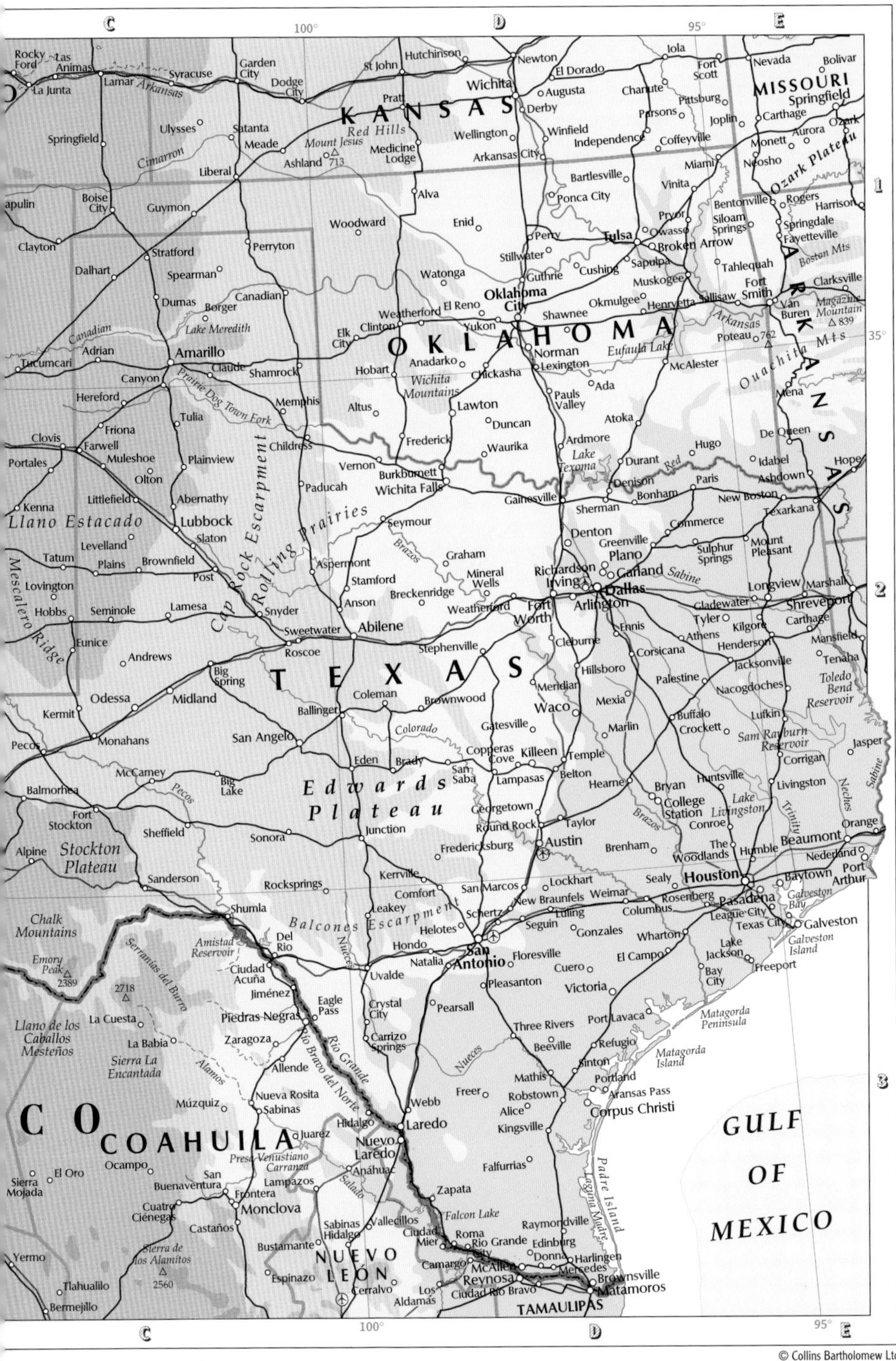
C
100°
D
95°
E
1
2
3
35°
KANSAS
MISSOURI
OKLAHOMA
ARKANSAS
TEXAS
COAHUILA
NUEVO LEÓN
TAMAULIPAS
GULF OF MEXICO
Rocky Ford
Las Animas
La Junta
Lamar
Arkansas
Syracuse
Garden City
Dodge City
St John
Hutchinson
Newton
Iola
El Dorado
Fort Scott
Nevada
Bolivar
Wichita
Augusta
Chanute
Pittsburg
Springfield
Pratt
Derby
Parsons
Joplin
Carthage
Ozark
Red Hills
Mount Jesus
713
Wellington
Winfield
Independence
Coffeyville
Monett
Aurora
Ozark Plateau
Springfield
Ulysses
Satanta
Meade
Ashland
Medicine Lodge
Arkansas City
Cimarron
Liberal
Bartlesville
Miami
Neosho
Vinita
Alva
Ponca City
Bentonville
Rogers
Harrison
Siloam Springs
Springdale
Fayetteville
Boise City
Guymon
Woodward
Enid
Perry
Pryor
Owasso
Tulsa
Broken Arrow
Clayton
Stratford
Perryton
Stillwater
Cushing
Sapulpa
Tahlequah
Boston Mts
Dalhart
Spearman
Watonga
Guthrie
Muskogee
Fort Smith
Clarksville
Canadian
Oklahoma City
Okmulgee
Henryetta
Sallisaw
Van Buren
Magazine Mountain
839
Dumas
Borger
Weatherford
El Reno
Yukon
Shawnee
Lake Meredith
Clinton
Elk City
Arkansas
Poteau
762
Adrian
Amarillo
Norman
Eufaula Lake
Ouachita Mts
Tucumcari
Claude
Anadarko
Lexington
McAlester
Canyon
Shamrock
Hobart
Chickasha
Ada
Wichita Mountains
Mena
Hereford
Prairie Dog Town Fork
Memphis
Altus
Lawton
Pauls Valley
Tulia
Duncan
Atoka
Friona
Clovis
Farwell
Childress
Frederick
Waurika
Ardmore
De Queen
Hugo
Portales
Muleshoe
Plainview
Vernon
Lake Texoma
Durant
Idabel
Hope
Olton
Burkburnett
Red
Denison
Paris
Ashdown
Paducah
Wichita Falls
Kenna
Littlefield
Abernathy
Gainesville
Bonham
New Boston
Llano Estacado
Lubbock
Sherman
Texarkana
Rolling Prairies
Seymour
Denton
Commerce
Slaton
Brazos
Greenville
Mount Pleasant
Levelland
Graham
Sulphur Springs
Tatum
Plains
Brownfield
Aspermont
Plano
Garland
Sabine
Post
Mineral Wells
Richardson
Lovington
Stamford
Breckenridge
Irving
Dallas
Longview
Marshall
Caprock Escarpment
Anson
Weatherford
Fort Worth
Arlington
Gladewater
Shreveport
Mescalero Ridge
Hobbs
Seminole
Lamesa
Snyder
Tyler
Kilgore
Carthage
Sweetwater
Abilene
Ennis
Mansfield
Athens
Henderson
Eunice
Roscoe
Stephenville
Cleburne
Corsicana
Tenaha
Andrews
Big Spring
Hillsboro
Jacksonville
Toledo Bend Reservoir
Palestine
Odessa
Midland
Coleman
Brownwood
Meridian
Nacogdoches
Kermit
Ballinger
Waco
Mexia
Buffalo
Lufkin
Gatesville
Marlin
Crockett
Colorado
Pecos
Monahans
San Angelo
Sam Rayburn Reservoir
Jasper
Copperas Cove
Killeen
Temple
Corrigan
McCamey
Eden
Brady
San Saba
Lampasas
Belton
Huntsville
Big Lake
Edwards Plateau
Hearne
Bryan
Livingston
Balmorhea
Lake Livingston
College Station
Neches
Sabine
Pecos
Georgetown
Trinity
Fort Stockton
Round Rock
Taylor
Conroe
Sheffield
Junction
Orange
Sonora
Austin
Beaumont
Alpine
Stockton Plateau
Brenham
The Woodlands
Humble
Fredericksburg
Nederland
Port Arthur
Sanderson
Lockhart
Sealy
Houston
Baytown
Kerrville
Rockprings
San Marcos
Comfort
New Braunfels
Weimar
Rosenberg
Pasadena
Galveston Bay
Chalk Mountains
Shumla
Leakey
Balcones Escarpment
Schertz
Luling
Seguin
Columbus
League City
Texas City
Galveston
Gonzales
Amistad Reservoir
Del Rio
Helotes
Hondo
Wharton
Lake Jackson
Galveston Island
Emory Peak
2389
Serranías del Burro
Ciudad Acuña
Nueces
Natalia
San Antonio
Floresville
El Campo
Freeport
Uvalde
Cuero
Bay City
2718
Jiménez
Pleasanton
Victoria
Eagle Pass
Crystal City
Pearsall
Port Lavaca
Matagorda Peninsula
La Cuesta
Piedras Negras
Three Rivers
Llano de los Caballos Mesteños
Zaragoza
Carrizo Springs
Beeville
Refugio
La Babia
Matagorda Island
Sierra La Encantada
Allende
Río Bravo del Norte
Rio Grande
Álamos
Nueces
Sinton
Mathis
Portland
Aransas Pass
Freer
Nueva Rosita
Robstown
Múzquiz
Sabinas
Webb
Alice
Corpus Christi
Hidalgo
Laredo
Kingsville
Juárez
Nuevo Laredo
Presa Venustiano Carranza
Ocampo
Anáhuac
Falfurrias
Padre Island
Sierra Mojada
El Oro
San Buenaventura
Lampazos
Salado
Zapata
Laguna Madre
Frontera
Cuatro Ciénegas
Monclova
Falcon Lake
Raymondville
Castaños
Sabinas Hidalgo
Vallecillos
Ciudad Mier
Roma
Rio Grande City
Edinburg
Bustamante
Yermo
Sierra de los Alamitos
2560
Donna
Harlingen
Camargo
McAllen
Mercedes
Brownsville
Espinazo
Tlahualilo
Reynosa
Cerralvo
Los Aldamas
Ciudad Río Bravo
Matamoros
Bermejillo
0
100
200 KILOMETRES

ARIZONA

NEW MEXICO

UNITED

U N I T E D

El Paso

Ciudad Juárez

Tijuana

Mexicali

Ensenada

Gulf of California

Baja California

M E X I C O

Chihuahua

Hermosillo

Guaymas

Ciudad Obregón

Los Mochis

Culiacán

La Paz

Durango

Torreón

Gómez Palacio

Mazatlán

Tepic

Guadalajara

León

Irapuato

Colima

Tropic of Cancer

20°

P A C I F I C

O C E A N

Islas Revillagigedo
(Mexico)

Isla Clarión

Isla Socorro

Isla San Benedicto

METRES
FEET

5000	16404
3000	9843
2000	6562
1000	3281
500	1640
200	656
0	0

Land below
sea level

200	656
4000	13124
6000	19686

Lambert Azimuthal Equal Area Projection

Longitude 110° west of Greenwich

1 : 12 000 000

MILES 0   100   200   300

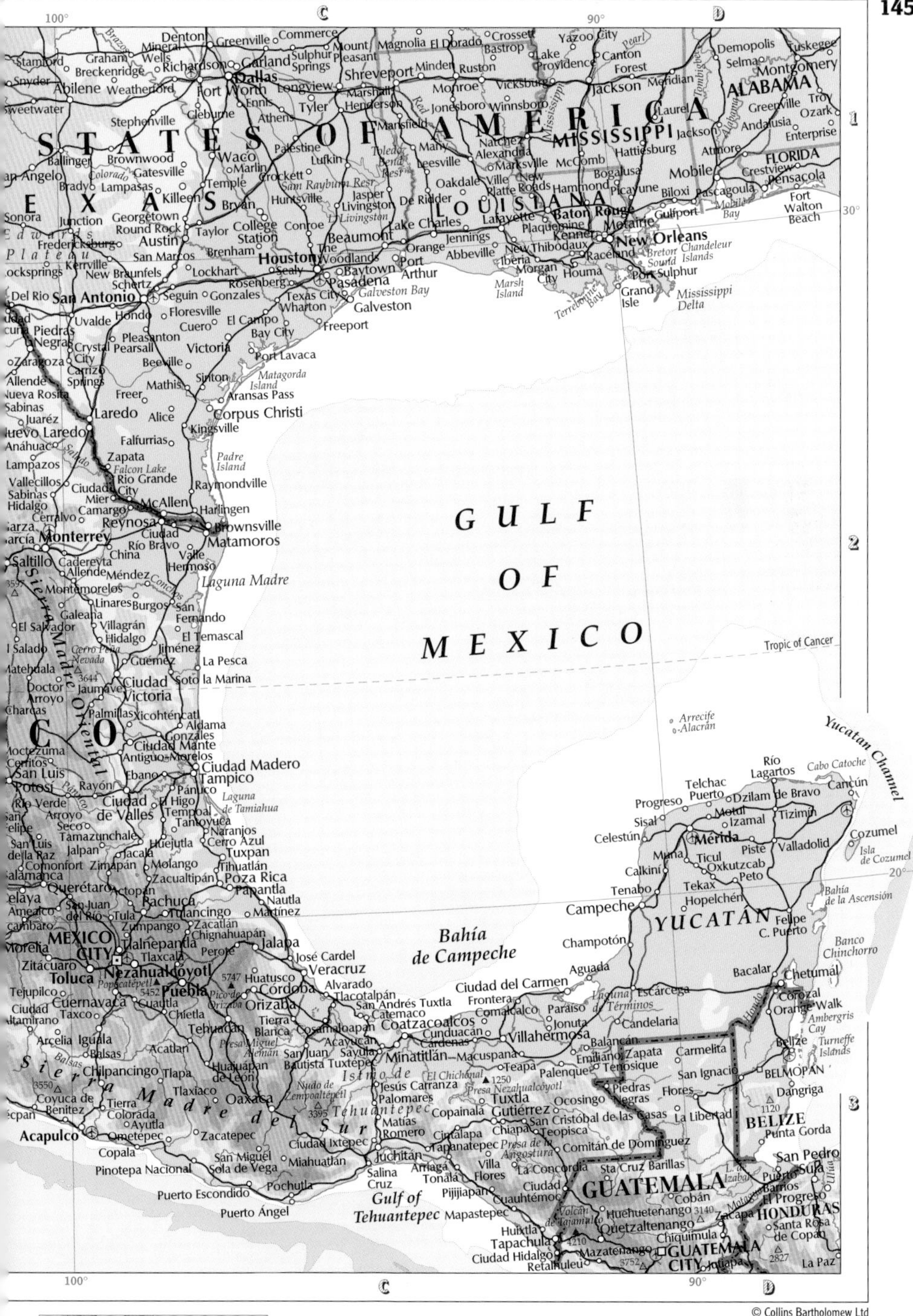

GULF

OF

MEXICO

Tropic of Cancer

GULF OF MEXICO

Bahía
de Campeche

YUCATÁN

BELIZE

GUATEMALA

HONDURAS

Gulf of
Tehuantepec

STATES OF AMERICA

TEXAS

MISSISSIPPI

ALABAMA

FLORIDA

LOUISIANA

100°

90°

0   200   400 KILOMETRES

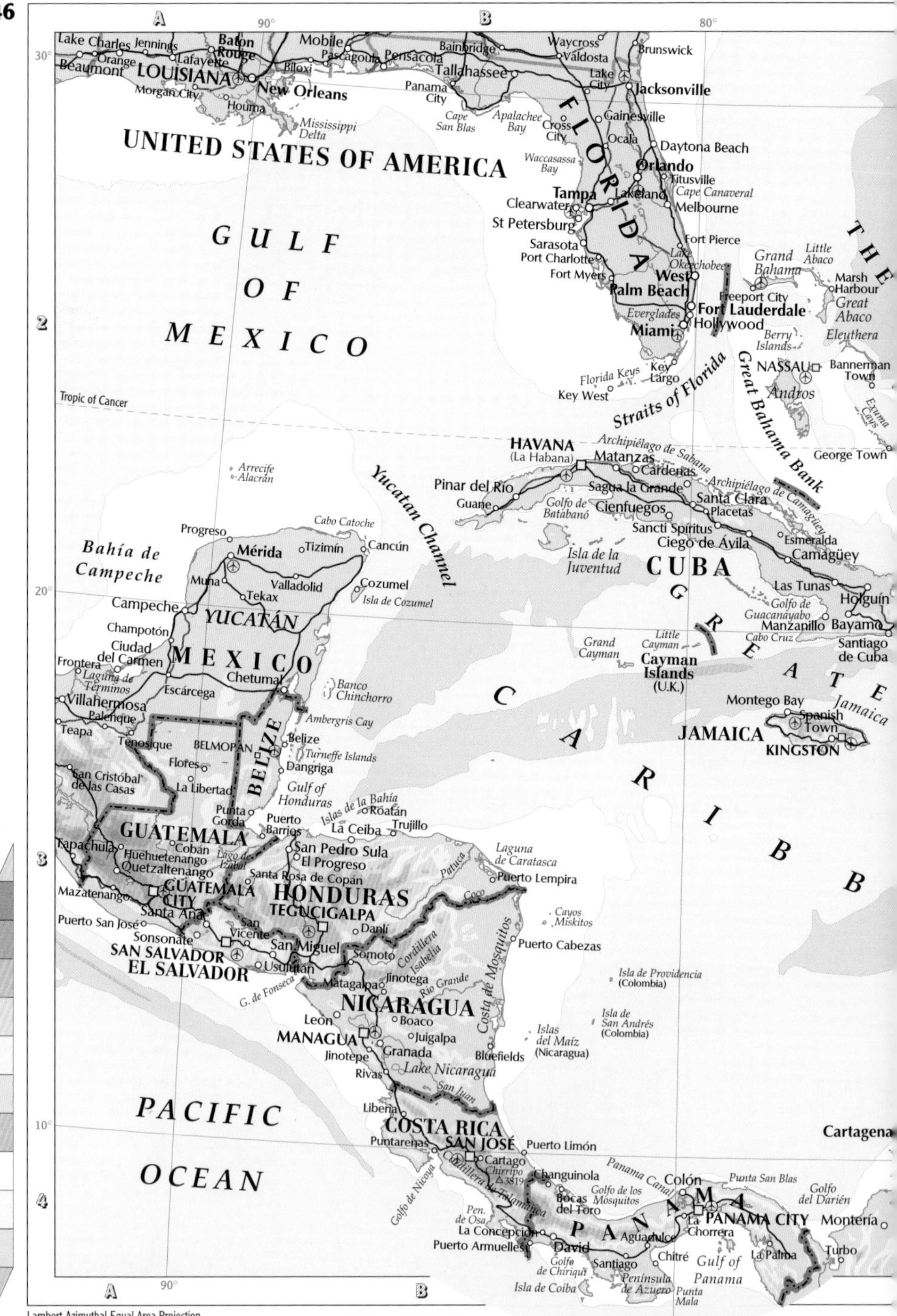

A   90°   B   80°

30°

UNITED STATES OF AMERICA

Lake Charles Jennings Mobile Waycross Brunswick
Orange Lafayette Baton Pascagoula Pensacola Valdosta
Beaumont Rouge Biloxi Bainbridge Jacksonville
LOUISIANA New Orleans Panama Tallahassee Lake Gainesville
Morgan City Houma City Cape Apalachee Cross Ocala Daytona Beach
Mississippi San Blas Bay City Orlando Titusville
Delta Waccasassa FLORIDA Cape Canaveral
Bay Tampa Lakeland Melbourne
Clearwater St Petersburg Fort Pierce
Sarasota Lake West Grand Little
Port Charlotte Okeechobee Palm Beach Bahama Abaco
Fort Myers Palm Beach Freeport City Great

GULF

OF

MEXICO

Tropic of Cancer

Arrecife
Alacrán

Bahía de
Campeche

Progreso Cabo Catoche
Mérida Tizimín Cancún
Muna Valladolid Cozumel
Campeche YUCATÁN Tekax Isla de Cozumel
Champotón
Ciudad
del Carmen MEXICO Chetumal
Frontera Escárcega
Villahermosa Palenque
Teapa Tenosique BELMOPAN Belize
San Cristóbal Flores Dangriga
de las Casas La Libertad Gulf of
Punta Honduras
GUATEMALA Gorda Puerto
Tapachula Cobán Barrios
Huehuetenango Santa Rosa de Copán
Quetzaltenango San Pedro Sula
Mazatenango El Progreso
Puerto San José GUATEMALA HONDURAS
Santa Ana CITY TEGUCIGALPA
Sonsonate San Danlí
SAN SALVADOR Vicente San Miguel Somoto
EL SALVADOR Usulután Jinotega
Matagalpa
León NICARAGUA
MANAGUA Boaco
Jinotepe Granada Bluefields
Rivas Lake Nicaragua
Liberia
COSTA RICA SAN JOSÉ Puerto Limón
Puntarenas Cartago Colón
Changuinola PANAMA
Bocas PANAMA CITY
del Toro Chorrera
La Concepción Aguadulce Chitré
Puerto Armuelles David Santiago

PACIFIC

OCEAN

HAVANA Matanzas
(La Habana) Cárdenas
Pinar del Río Sagua la Grande
Guane Golfo de Santa Clara
Batabanó Cienfuegos Placetas
Sancti Spíritus
Ciego de Ávila Esmeralda
Isla de la Camagüey
Juventud CUBA
Las Tunas
Grand Little Holguín
Cayman Cayman Manzanillo Bayamo
Cayman Santiago
Islands de Cuba
(U.K.)
Montego Bay JAMAICA
KINGSTON

CARIBBEAN

NASSAU Bannerman
Andros Town

George Town

Cartagena

1 : 15 000 000

Lambert Azimuthal Equal Area Projection

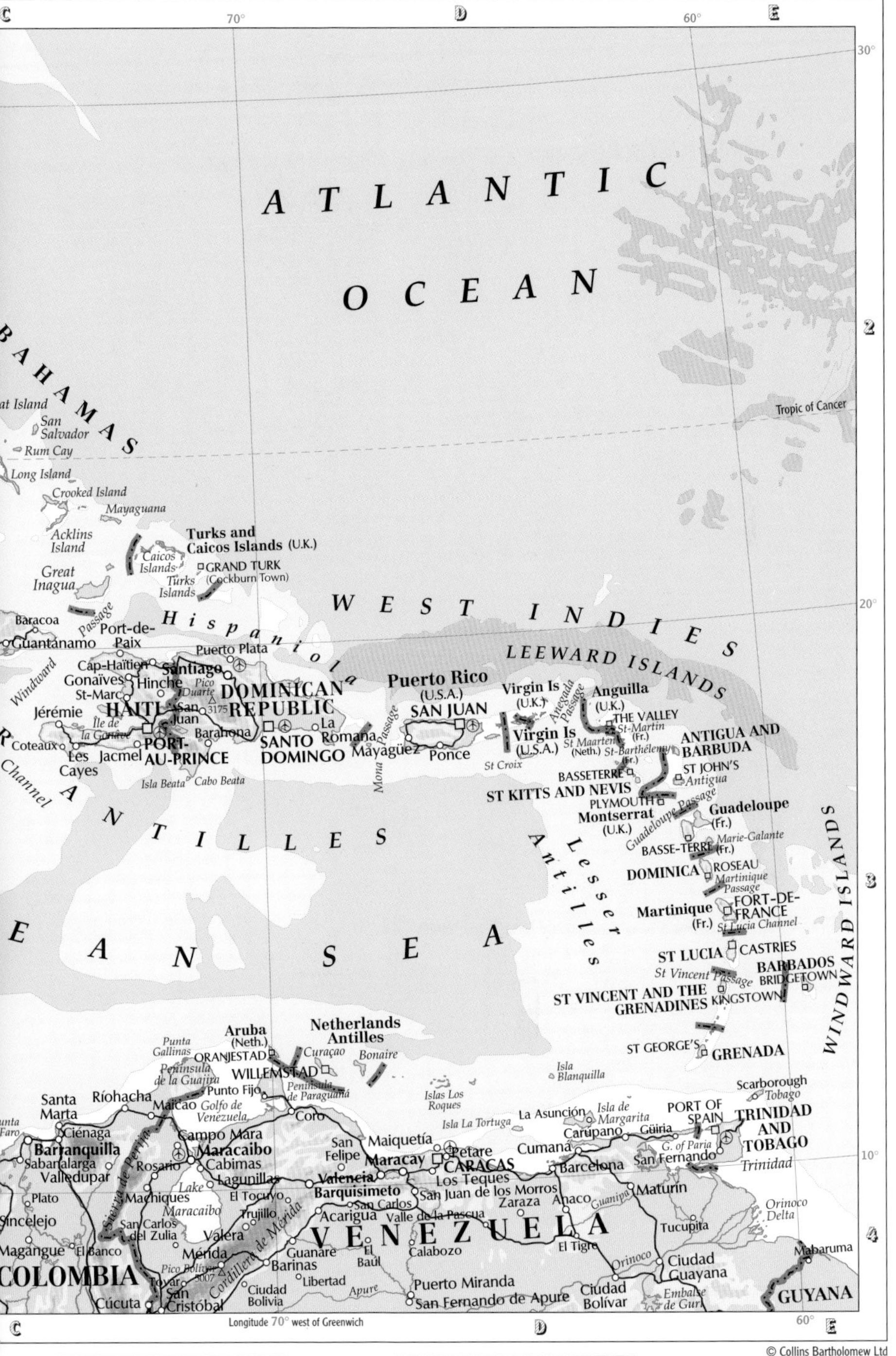

ATLANTIC OCEAN

CARIBBEAN SEA

BRAZIL
COLOMBIA
VENEZUELA
GUYANA
SURINAME
French Guiana
ECUADOR
PERU
BOLIVIA
PARAGUAY
PANAMA
COSTA RICA
NICARAGUA

Barranquilla
Maracaibo
Barquisimeto
Caracas
Aruba (Neth.)
Netherlands Antilles
ST VINCENT AND THE GRENADINES
ST LUCIA
GRENADA
BARBADOS
TRINIDAD AND TOBAGO
Ciudad Bolívar
Orinoco
Georgetown
Paramaribo
Cayenne
Medellín
Bogotá
Cali
Quito
Guayaquil
Isla de Malpelo (Colombia)
Lake Nicaragua
Boa Vista
Branco
Negro
Manaus
Japurá
Amazon
Iquitos
Marañón
Trujillo
Callao
Lima
Pucallpa
Ayacucho
Arequipa
Arica
Antofagasta
Lake Titicaca
La Paz
Sucre
Santa Cruz
Asunción
Rio Branco
Porto Velho
Madeira
Purus
Juruá
SELVAS
ANDES
Desert
Macapá
Santarém
Tapajós
Xingu
Iriri
Mouths of the Amazon
Ilha de Marajó
Belém
Marabá
Tocantins
Araguaia
São Luís
Teresina
Parnaíba
Fortaleza
Natal
João Pessoa
Recife
Maceió
Aracaju
Salvador
Barragem de Sobradinho
São Francisco
Brasília
Goiânia
Cuiabá
Belo Horizonte
Vitória
Rio de Janeiro
Campinas
São Paulo
Santos
Curitiba
Campo Grande
Paraná
Paraguay
Ilha da Trindade (Brazil)
Tropic of Capricorn
Equator

Bi-Polar Oblique Projection

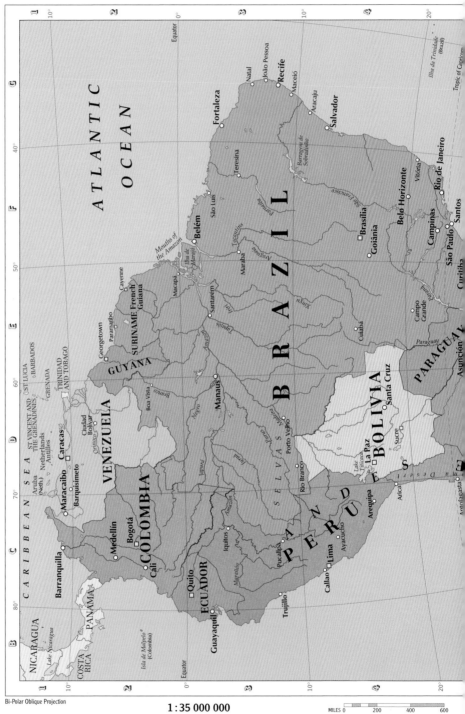

1 : 35 000 000

MILES 0 200 400 600

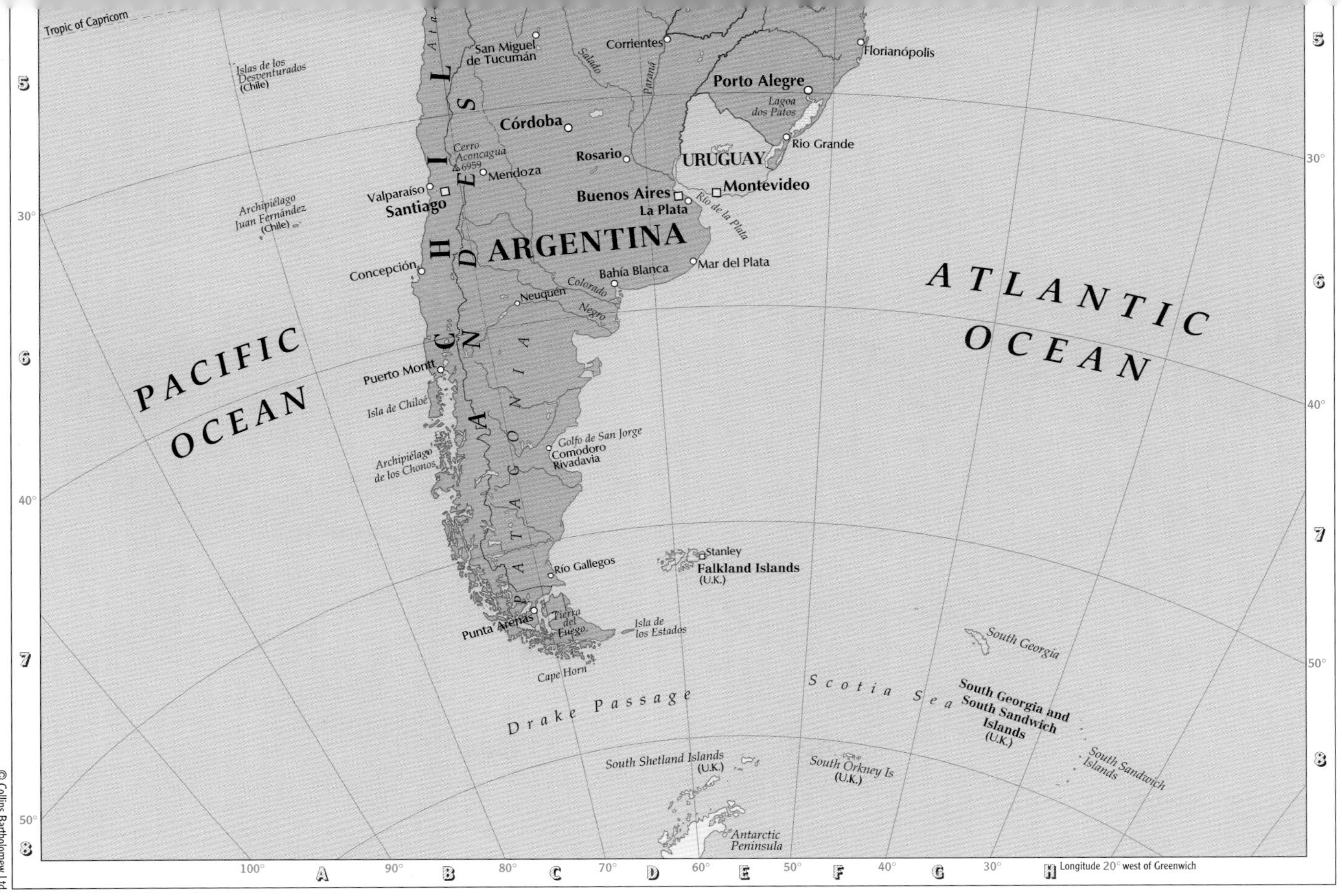

ATLANTIC OCEAN

PACIFIC OCEAN

Scotia Sea

Drake Passage

South Georgia

South Georgia and South Sandwich Islands (U.K.)

South Sandwich Islands

South Orkney Is (U.K.)

South Shetland Islands (U.K.)

Antarctic Peninsula

Stanley
Falkland Islands (U.K.)

Isla de los Estados
Tierra del Fuego
Cape Horn
Punta Arenas
Río Gallegos

Comodoro Rivadavia
Golfo de San Jorge

P A T A G O N I A

Puerto Montt
Isla de Chiloé
Archipiélago de los Chonos

Concepción

Valparaíso
Santiago
Mendoza
Cerro Aconcagua

Córdoba
San Miguel de Tucumán

A N D E S

C H I L E

B O L I V I A

ARGENTINA

Rosario
Buenos Aires
La Plata
Bahía Blanca
Neuquén
Colorado
Negro

Río de la Plata
Mar del Plata
Montevideo
URUGUAY

Paraná
Corrientes
Salado

Porto Alegre
Río Grande
Lagoa dos Patos

Florianópolis

Archipiélago Juan Fernández (Chile)

Islas de los Desventurados (Chile)

Tropic of Capricorn

Longitude 20 west of Greenwich

© Collins Bartholomew Ltd

0   500   1000 KILOMETRES

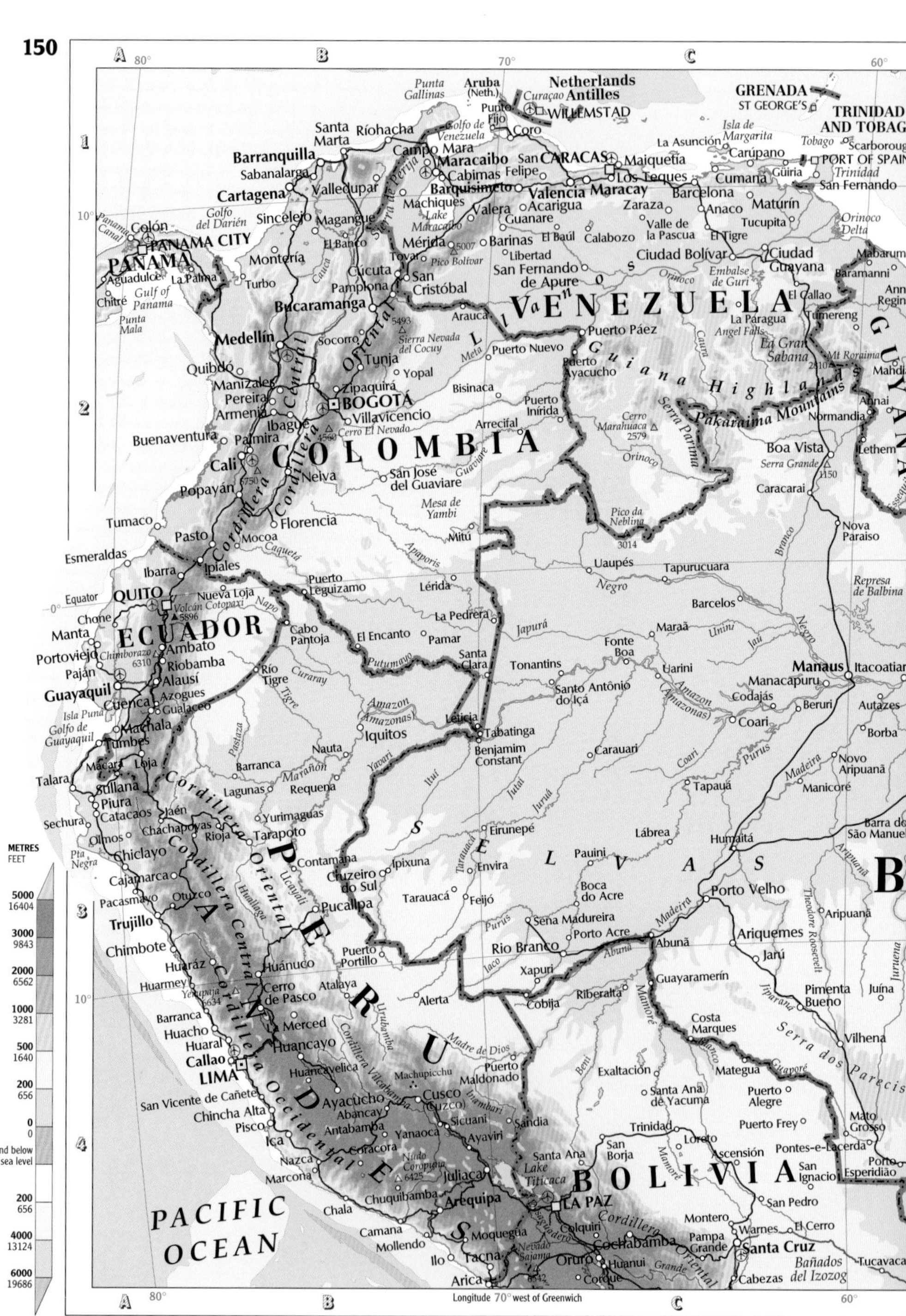

PANAMA

COLOMBIA

VENEZUELA

GUYANA

ECUADOR

PERU

BOLIVIA

PACIFIC
OCEAN

METRES
FEET

5000	16404
3000	9843
2000	6562
1000	3281
500	1640
200	656
0	0
Land below sea level	
200	656
4000	13124
6000	19686

Lambert Azimuthal Equal Area Projection

Longitude 70° west of Greenwich

1 : 20 000 000

MILES 0   100   200   300   400

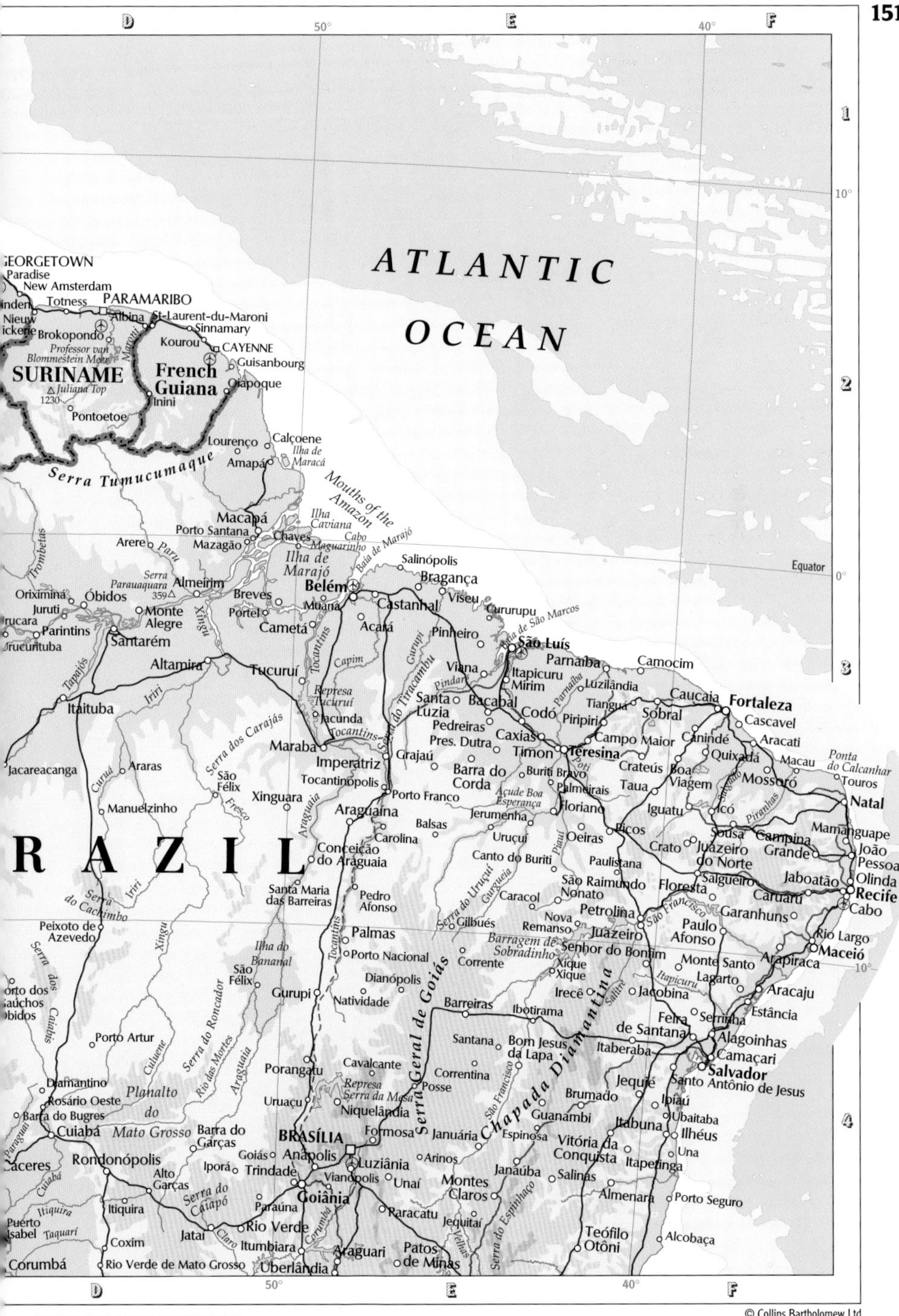

ATLANTIC

OCEAN

GEORGETOWN
Paradise
New Amsterdam
Totness PARAMARIBO
inden Albina St-Laurent-du-Maroni
Nieuw Brokopondo Sinnamary
ickerie Kourou
Professor van CAYENNE
Blommestein Meer Guisanbourg
SURINAME French
△ Juliana Top Guiana Oiapoque
1230 Inini
Pontoetoe
Lourenço Calçoene
Serra Tumucumaque Amapá Ilha de
Maracá
Mouths of the
Amazon
Macapá Ilha
Porto Santana Caviana
Arere Mazagão Chaves Cabo
Serra Maguarinho Salinópolis
Oriximiná Parauaquara Almeirim Baía de Marajó Bragança
Óbidos 359△ Ilha de Belém Viseu
rucara Juruti Monte Breves Marajó Castanhal Cururupu
ucurituba Parintins Alegre Portel Muaná Acará Pinheiro
Santarém Cametá Baía de São Marcos
Altamira Tucuruí Capim São Luís
Itaituba Irriri Represa Viana Parnaíba Camocim
Tucuruí Itapicuru Luzilândia
Jacunda Santa Mirim Tianguá Caucaia Fortaleza
Maraba Tocantins Luzia Codó Piripiri Sobral Cascavel
Imperatriz Pedreiras Timon Campo Maior Caninde Quixadá Aracati
Xinguara Pres. Dutra Caxias Teresina Crateús Boa Macau do Calcanhar
Jacareacanga Araras São Tocantinópolis Grajaú Barra do Buriti Bravo Taua Viagem Mossoró Touros
Félix Porto Franco Corda Açude Boa Palmeirais Iguatu Icó Natal
Manuelzinho Araguaína Esperança Floriano Picos Crato Juazeiro Campina
Carolina Balsas Jerumenha Oeiras do Norte Grande João
B R A Z I L Conceição Uruçuí Nova Salgueiro Jaboatão Pessoa
do Araguaia Canto do Buriti São Raimundo Floresta Caruaru Olinda
Santa Maria Nonato Petrolina Recife
Peixoto de das Barreiras Pedro Gilbués Remanso Paulo Garanhuns Cabo
Azevedo Afonso Juazeiro Afonso Rio Largo
Palmas Corrente Barragem de Monte Santo Arapiraca Maceió
orto dos Ilha do Porto Nacional Sobradinho Senhor do Bonfim Lagarto
auchos Bananal Dianópolis Xique- Irecé Jacobina Aracaju
bidos Porto Artur São Natividade Xique Serrinha Estância
Félix Gurupi Barreiras Ibotirama Feira Alagoinhas
Diamantino Santana Bom Jesus de Santana Camaçari
Rosário Oeste Porangatu Cavalcante da Lapa Itaberaba Salvador
Barra do Bugres Uruaçu Correntina Posse Jequié Santo Antônio de Jesus
Cuiabá Planalto do Niquelândia Brumado Ibiaú Ilhéus
áceres Mato Grosso Barra do Formosa Guanambi Itabuna Ubaitaba
Garças Januária Vitória da Una
Rondonópolis Alto BRASÍLIA Anápolis Arinos Espinosa Conquista Itapetinga
Garças Goiás Luziânia Janaúba Salinas
Iporá Trindade Unaí Montes Porto Seguro
Iquira Coxim Paraúna Goiânia Vianópolis Claros Almenara
Puerto Itiquira Jataí Itumbiara Araraquara Teófilo Alcobaça
sabel Rio Verde de Mato Grosso Uberlândia Araguari Patos Otôni
Corumbá de Minas

© Collins Bartholomew Ltd

0   200   400   600 KILOMETRES

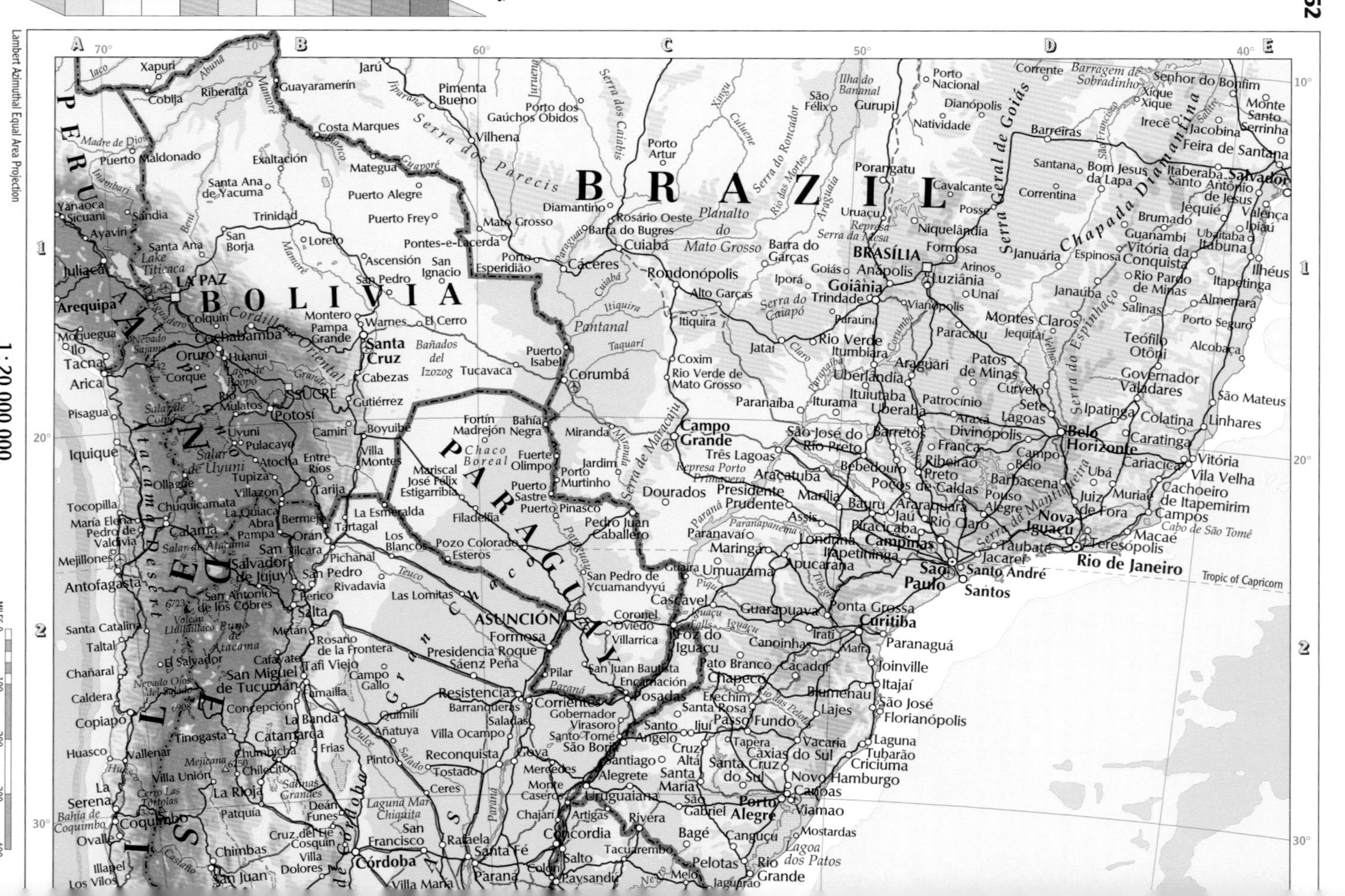

METRES
FEET

5000	16404
3000	9843
2000	6562
1000	3281
500	1640
200	656
0	0
Land below sea level	
200	656
4000	13124
6000	19686

Lambert Azimuthal Equal Area Projection

1 : 20 000 000

MILES 0   100   200   300   400

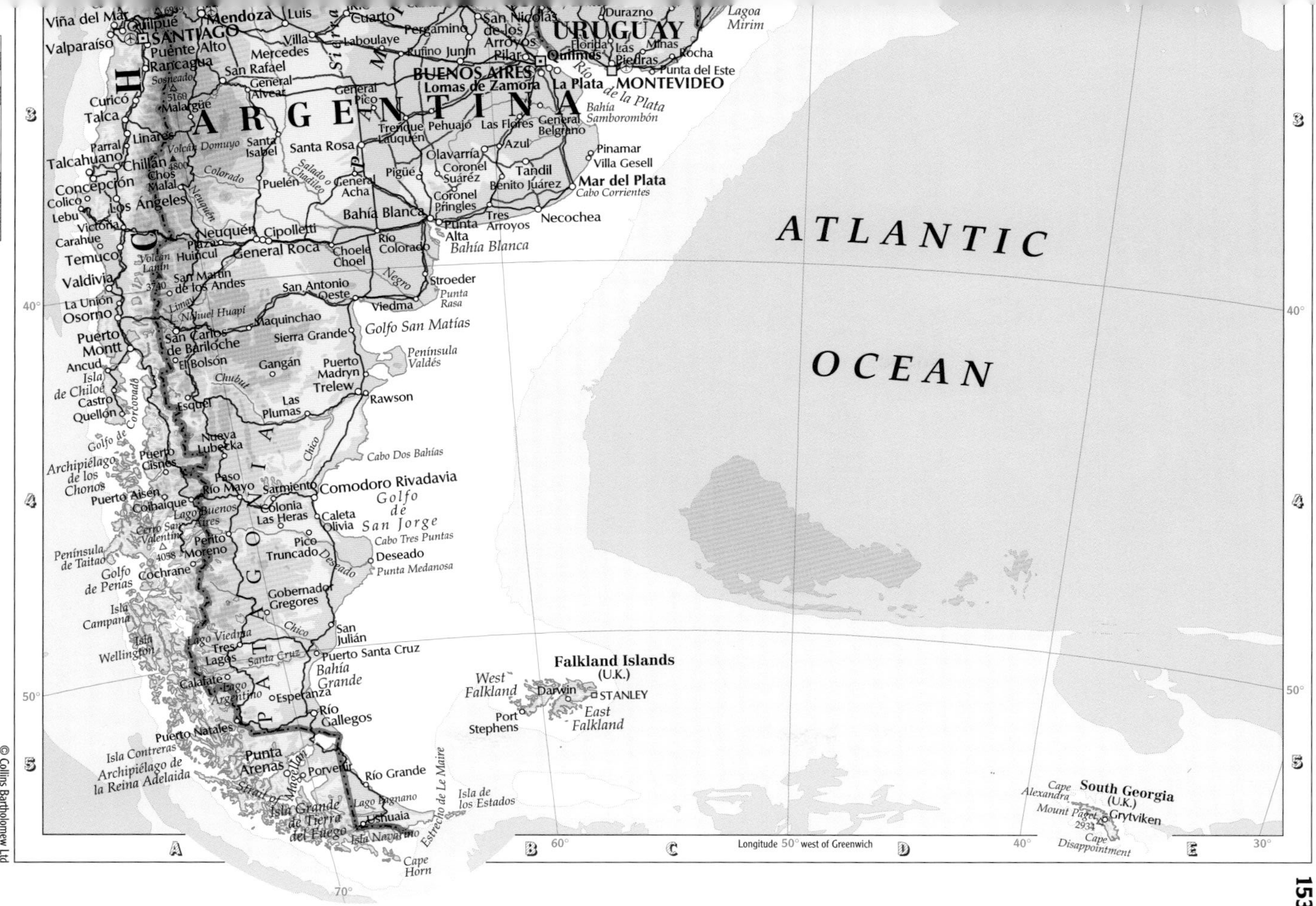
ATLANTIC
OCEAN
ARGENTINA
CHILE
PATAGONIA
URUGUAY
BUENOS AIRES
Lomas de Zamora
La Plata
MONTEVIDEO
SANTIAGO
Mendoza
Mar del Plata
Bahía Blanca
Comodoro Rivadavia
Golfo San Matías
Golfo de San Jorge
Río Gallegos
Punta Arenas
Ushuaia
Cape Horn
Isla Grande de Tierra del Fuego
Falkland Islands
(U.K.)
STANLEY
West Falkland
East Falkland
South Georgia
(U.K.)
Grytviken
Valparaíso
Concepción
Puerto Montt
Valdivia
Temuco
Neuquén
Longitude 50° west of Greenwich
0
200
400
600 KILOMETRES

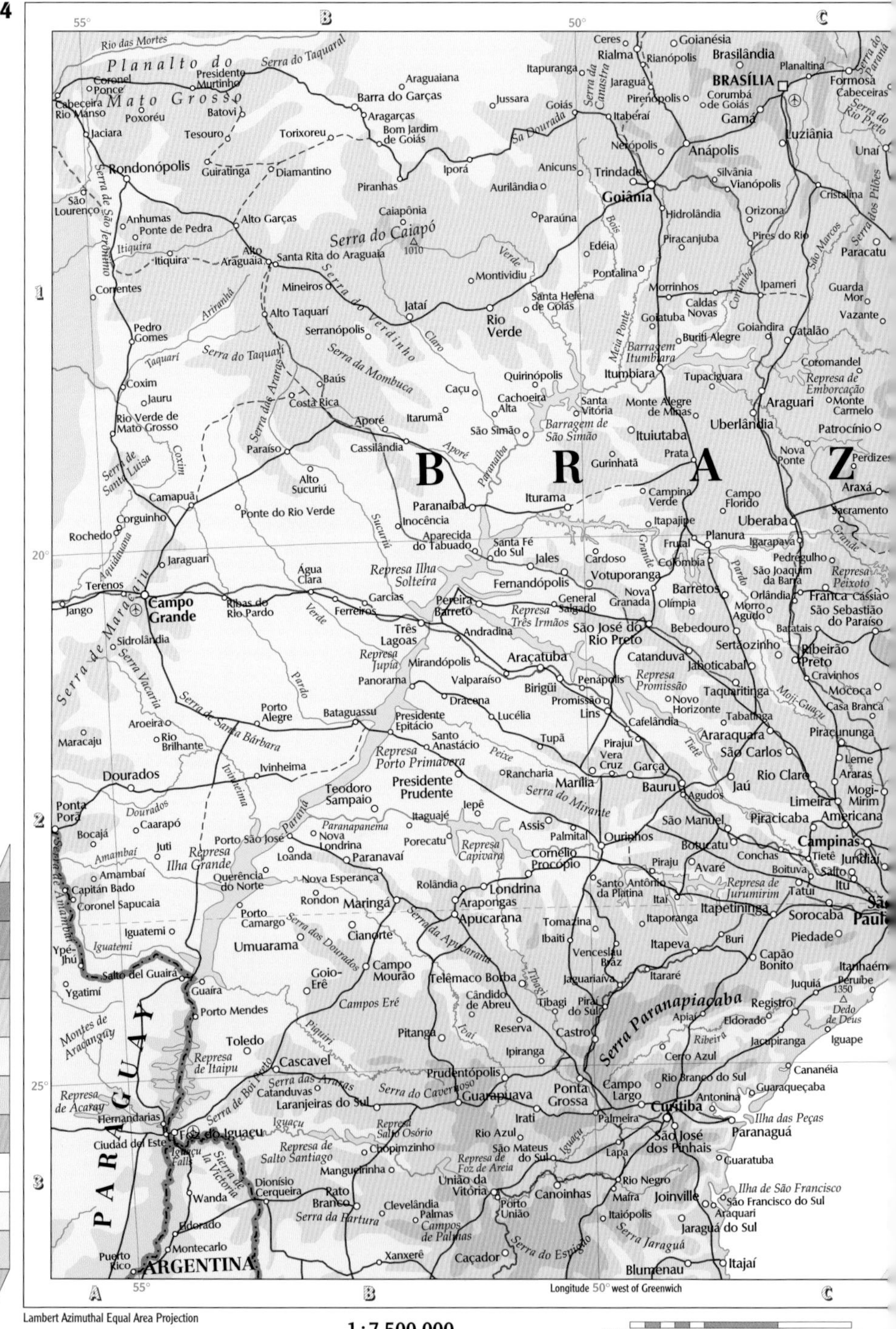

55°   B   50°   C

Rio das Mortes
Planalto do
Coronel
Ponce
Cabeceira
Rio Manso
Jaciara
Presidente
Murtinho
Mato Grosso
Poxoréu
Batovi
Tesouro
Diamantino
Barra do Garças
Aragarças
Bom Jardim
de Goiás
Torixoreu
Piranhas
Serra do Taquaral
Araguaiana
Jussara
Goiás
Ceres
Rianápolis
Itapuranga
Jaraguá
Pirenópolis
Goianésia
Goianápolis
Brasilândia
BRASÍLIA
Planaltina
Formosa
Cabeceiras

Rondonópolis
São
Lourenço
Anhumas
Ponte de Pedra
Guiratinga
Itiquira
Alto Garças
Alto
Araguaia
Santa Rita do Araguaia
Mineiros
Serra do Caiapó
1010
Iporá
Anicuns
Trindade
Nerópolis
Itaberaí
Corumbá
de Goiás
Gama
Anápolis
Luziânia
Unaí

1

Correntes
Pedro
Gomes
Alto Taquari
Jataí
Serra do Perdinho
Rio
Verde
Santa Helena
de Goiás
Aurilândia
Paraúna
Edéia
Goiânia
Silvânia
Vianópolis
Hidrolândia
Piracanjuba
Orizona
Cristalina
Paracatu

Serranópolis
Coxim
Jauru
Rio Verde de
Mato Grosso
Baús
Costa Rica
Serra do Taquari
Aporé
Itarumã
Caçu
Quirinópolis
Cachoeira
Alta
Santa
Vitória
São Simão
Monte Alegre
de Minas
Ituiutaba
Prata
Morrinhos
Goiatuba
Pontalina
Gurinhatã
Buriti Alegre
Goiandira
Catalão
Coromandel
Goiás
Guarda
Mor
Vazante
Represa de Emborcação
Monte
Carmelo
Patrocínio
Araguari
Uberlândia

Camapuã
Corguinho
Rochedo
Paraíso
Cassilândia
Alto
Sucuriú
Ponte do Rio Verde
Paranaíba
Inocência
Iturama
Campina
Verde
Itapagipe
Frutal
Planura
Igarapava
Prata
Campo
Florido
Nova
Ponte
Sacramento
Perdizes
Araxá
Uberaba
Represa de
Peixoto
Franca
Cássia

B   R   A   Z

20°

Terenos
Jango
Jaraguari
Água
Clara
Garças
Represa Ilha Solteira
Fernandópolis
Jales
Santa Fé
do Sul
Cardoso
Votuporanga
Colômbia
Nova
Granada
Olímpia
Barretos
Orlândia
Morro
Agudo
São Joaquim
da Barra
Batatais
São Sebastião
do Paraíso

**Campo
Grande**
Sidrolândia
Ribas do
Rio Pardo
Ferreiros
Pereira
Barreto
General
Salgado
*Represa
Três Irmãos*
São José do
Rio Preto
Catanduva
Bebedouro
Sertãozinho
Jaboticabal
Cravinhos
Mococa
Casa Branca
Ribeirão
Preto

Maracaju
Aroeira
Rio
Brilhante
Três
Lagoas
*Represa
Jupiá*
Mirandópolis
Nova
Panorama
Valparaíso
Andradina
Araçatuba
Birigui
Dracena
Lucélia
Penápolis
*Represa
Promissão*
Novo
Horizonte
Tabatinga
Taquaritinga
Araraquara
São Carlos
Piracununga
Leme
Araras
Rio Claro

Dourados
Ponta
Porã
Bocajá
Porto
Alegre
Bataguassu
Presidente
Epitácio
Santo
Anastácio
Ivinheima
*Represa
Porto Primavera*
Teodoro
Sampaio
Presidente
Prudente
Iepê
Rancharia
Pirajuí
Promissão
Lins
Cafelândia
Garça
Marília
Bauru
Agudos
Jaú
Limeira
Americana
Piracicaba
Mogi-
Mirim

2

Caarapó
Juti
Amambaí
Capitán Bado
Coronel Sapucaia
Iguatemi
Dourados
*Represa
Ilha Grande*
Porto São José
Loanda
Paranavaí
Paranapanema
Nova
Londrina
Querência
do Norte
Porto
Camargo
Rondon
Porecatu
Rolândia
*Represa
Capivara*
Assis
Palmital
Cornélio
Procópio
Ourinhos
Santo Antônio
da Platina
Piraju
Avaré
Conchas
Tietê
Botucatu
São Manuel
Salto
Itu
Boituva
Tatuí
Campinas
Jundiaí
Sorocaba
São
Paulo

Ypé-
Jhú
Amambaí
Ygatimí
Salto del Guairá
Guaíra
Porto Mendes
Umuarama
Goio-
Erê
Campos Eré
Cianorte
Campo
Mourão
Maringá
Apucarana
Araponga
Ibaiti
Londrina
Tomazina
Venceslau
Braz
Ibaiti
Jaguariaíva
Itararé
Itapeva
Buri
Piedade
Capão
Bonito
Itapetininga
Itapeva
Itanhaém

1000

Ciudad del Este
Iguatemi
Toledo
*Represa
de Itaipu*
Cascavel
Catanduvas
Laranjeiras do Sul
Pitanga
Pitanga
Reserva
Prudentópolis
Castro
Tibagi
Telêmaco Borba
Cândido
de Abreu
Ipiranga
Ponta
Grossa
Campo
Largo
Apiaí
Cerro Azul
Eldorado
Registro
Iguape
Cananéia

25°

Hernandárias
Foz do Iguaçu
Wanda
Dionísio
Cerqueira
Mato
Branco
Clevelândia
Serra da Fartura
Reprêsa
Salto Osório
Chopinzinho
Mangueirinha
Palmas
*Campos
de Palmas*
União da
Vitória
Porto
União
Canoinhas
Rio Azul
São Mateus
do Sul
Lapa
Palmeira
Irati
São José
dos Pinhais
Curitiba
Guaratuba
Paranaguá
Ilha das Peças
Antonina
Rio Branco do Sul

3

Puerto
Rico
Montecarlo
Eldorado
ARGENTINA
Xanxerê
Caçador
Xanxerê
União da
Vitória
Rio Negro
Mafra
Itaiópolis
Joinville
Jaguá do Sul
Itajaí
Blumenau
Ilha de São Francisco
São Francisco do Sul

P A R A G U A Y

A   55°   B   Longitude 50° west of Greenwich   C

Lambert Azimuthal Equal Area Projection

1 : 7 500 000

MILES 0   50   100   150

METRES
FEET

5000	16404
3000	9843
2000	6562
1000	3281
500	1640
200	656
0	0

Land below
sea level

200	656
4000	13124
6000	19686

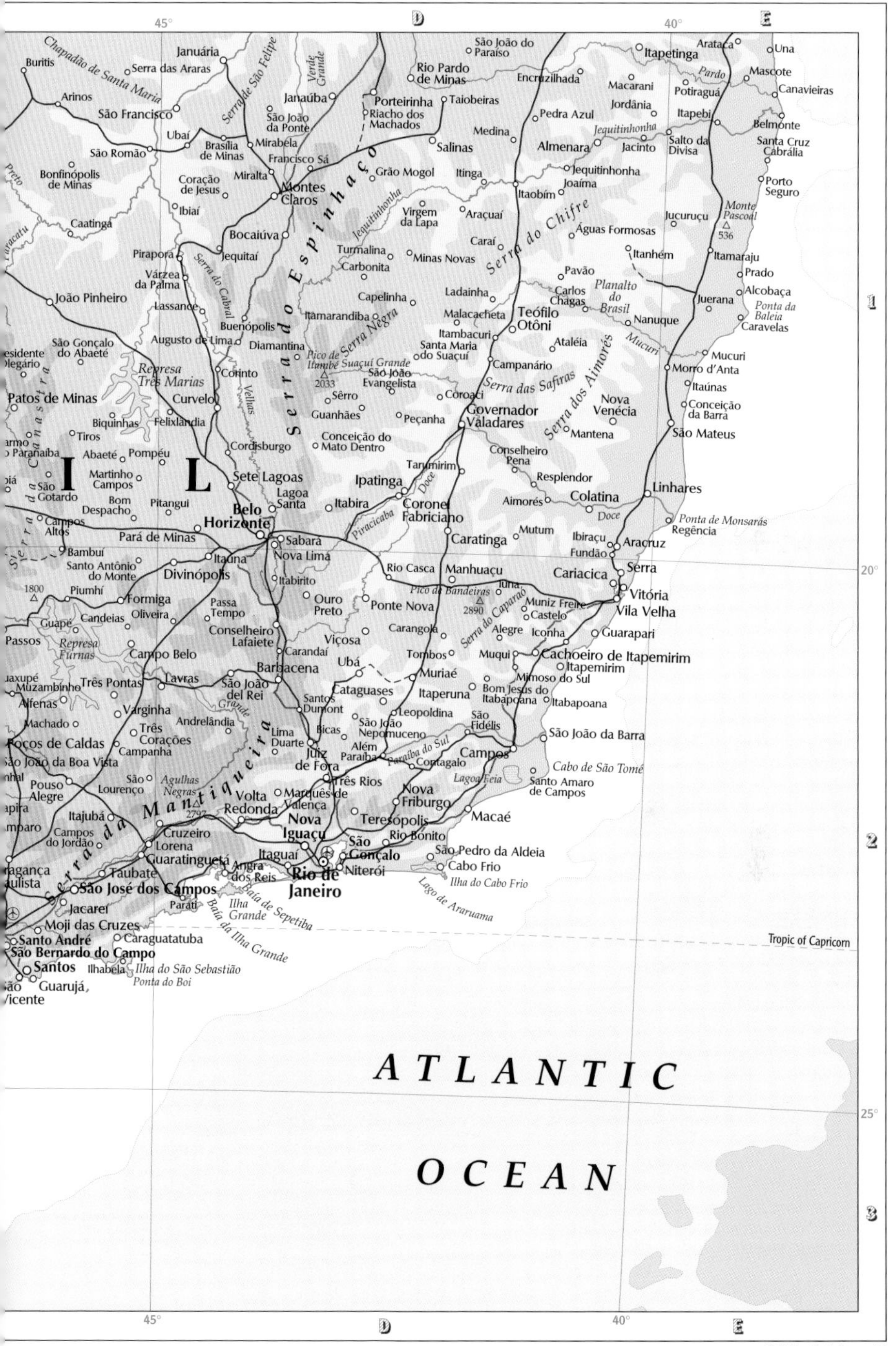

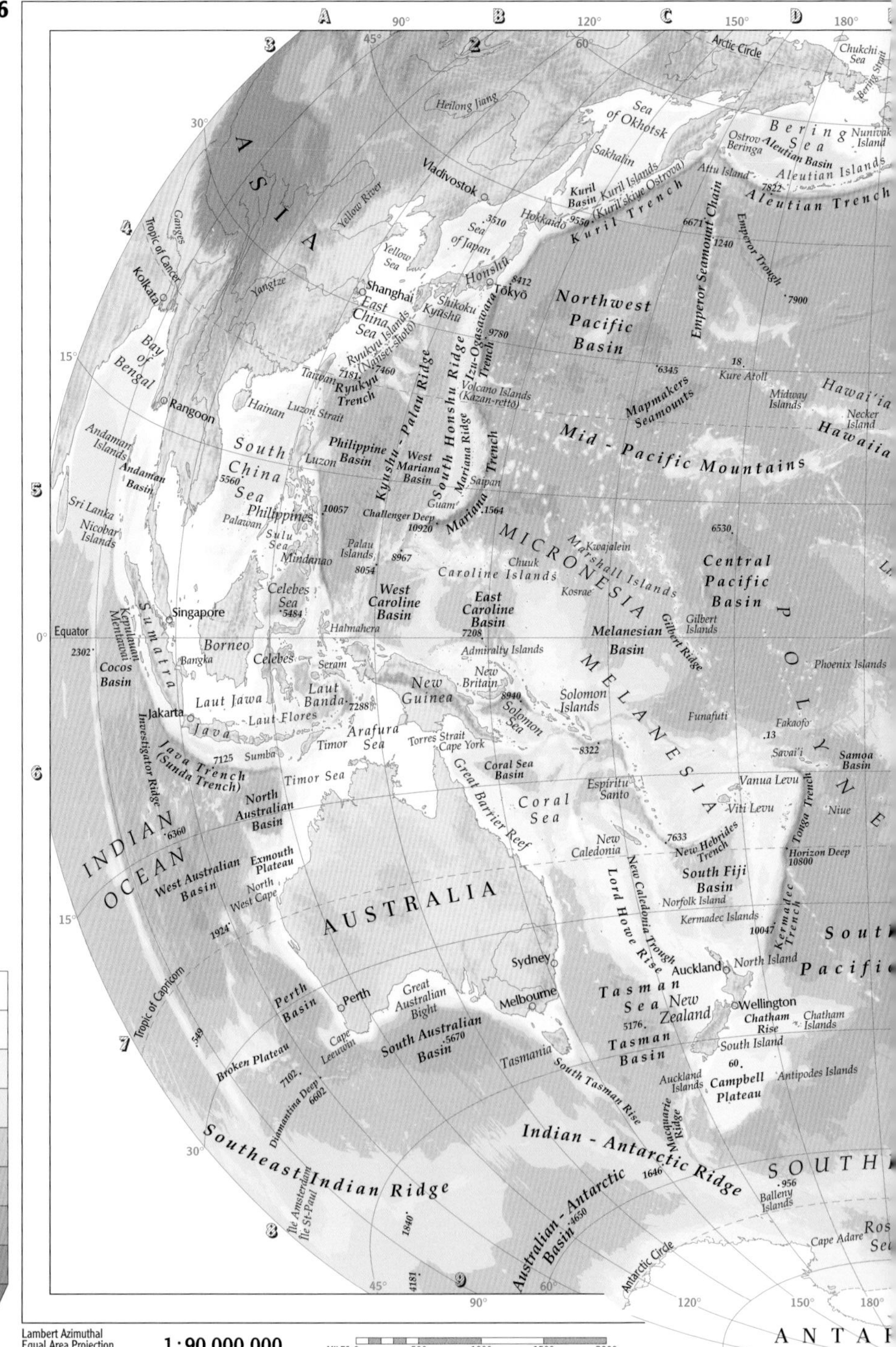

ASIA

Arctic Circle

Chukchi Sea

Heilong Jiang

Sea of Okhotsk

Vladivostok

Sakhalin

Bering Sea

Ostrov Beringa

Nunivak Island

Aleutian Basin

Attu Island

Aleutian Islands

Aleutian Trench

Yellow River

Kuril Basin

Hokkaido

Kuril Islands
Kuril'skiye Ostrova

.3510

9550

Kuril Trench

6671

7822

Emperor Seamount Chain

Emperor Trough

Sea of Japan

Honshu

.812

Tōkyō

Northwest Pacific Basin

1240

.7900

Ganges

Tropic of Cancer

Yellow Sea

Shanghai

Shikoku
Kyushu

Kolkata

Yangtze

East China Sea

Ryukyu Islands
(Nansei-shoto)

9780

Izu-Ogasawara Trench

Volcano Islands
(Kazan-retto)

18

.6345

Kure Atoll

Midway Islands

Hawai'ia

Bay of Bengal

Rangoon

Hainan

Tanpan

7181

.7460

Ryukyu Trench

Mid - Pacific Mountains

Mapmakers Seamounts

Necker Island

Hawaiia

Andaman Islands

South China Sea

Luzon Strait

Kyushu - Palau Ridge

Philippine Basin

Luzon

West Mariana Basin

South Honshu Ridge

Mariana Ridge

Saipan

Mariana Trench

MICRONESIA

6530

Central Pacific Basin

Andaman Basin

5560

10057

Challenger Deep
10920

Guam

.1564

Sri Lanka

Philippines

Palawan

Palau Islands

8967

8054

Mindanao

West Caroline Basin

Caroline Islands

Chuuk

Kwajalein

Marshall Islands

Kosrae

POLYNE

Nicobar Islands

Sulu Sea

Celebes Sea

.5484

Halmahera

East Caroline Basin

7208

Gilbert Ridge

Melanesian Basin

Gilbert Islands

Equator

2302

Cocos Basin

Bangka

Borneo

Celebes

Seram

Admiralty Islands

New Britain

MELANESIA

Phoenix Islands

Sumatra

Kepulauan Mentawai

Singapore

Laut Jawa

Laut Banda

7288

8940

Solomon Sea

Solomon Islands

Funafuti

Fakaofo

.13

Savai'i

Samoa Basin

Jakarta

Java

Laut Flores

Timor

New Guinea

Sumba

.8322

Espiritu Santo

Vanua Levu

Niue

7125

Arafura Sea

Torres Strait

Cape York

Viti Levu

Investigator Ridge
(Sunda Trench)

Java Trench
(Sunda Trench)

.6360

Timor Sea

Coral Sea Basin

Tonga Trench

INDIAN

North Australian Basin

Great Barrier Reef

Coral Sea

New Caledonia

.7633

New Hebrides Trench

Horizon Deep
10800

OCEAN

West Australian Basin

Exmouth Plateau

North West Cape

New Caledonia Trough

South Fiji Basin

Norfolk Island

Lord Howe Rise

Kermadec Islands

10047

Sout

Pacific

1924'

AUSTRALIA

Sydney

Auckland

North Island

Perth Basin

Perth

Great Australian Bight

Melbourne

Tasman Sea

New Zealand

Wellington

Chatham Rise

Chatham Islands

Broken Plateau

549

Cape Leeuwin

South Australian Basin

.5670

Tropic of Capricorn

Tasmania

Tasman Basin

5176.

South Island

Diamantina Deep
6002

7102.

South Tasman Rise

Auckland Islands

Campbell Plateau

60.

Antipodes Islands

Ile Amsterdam
Ile St-Paul

1540'

Indian - Antarctic Ridge

1646.

Southeast Indian Ridge

4181'

Australian - Antarctic Basin

.3650

956.

SOUTH

Ballery Islands

Antarctic Circle

Cape Adare

Ros
Se

ANTAR

METRES / FEET

METRES	FEET
0	0
200	656
2000	6562
3000	9843
4000	13124
5000	16404
6000	19686
7000	22967
9000	29529

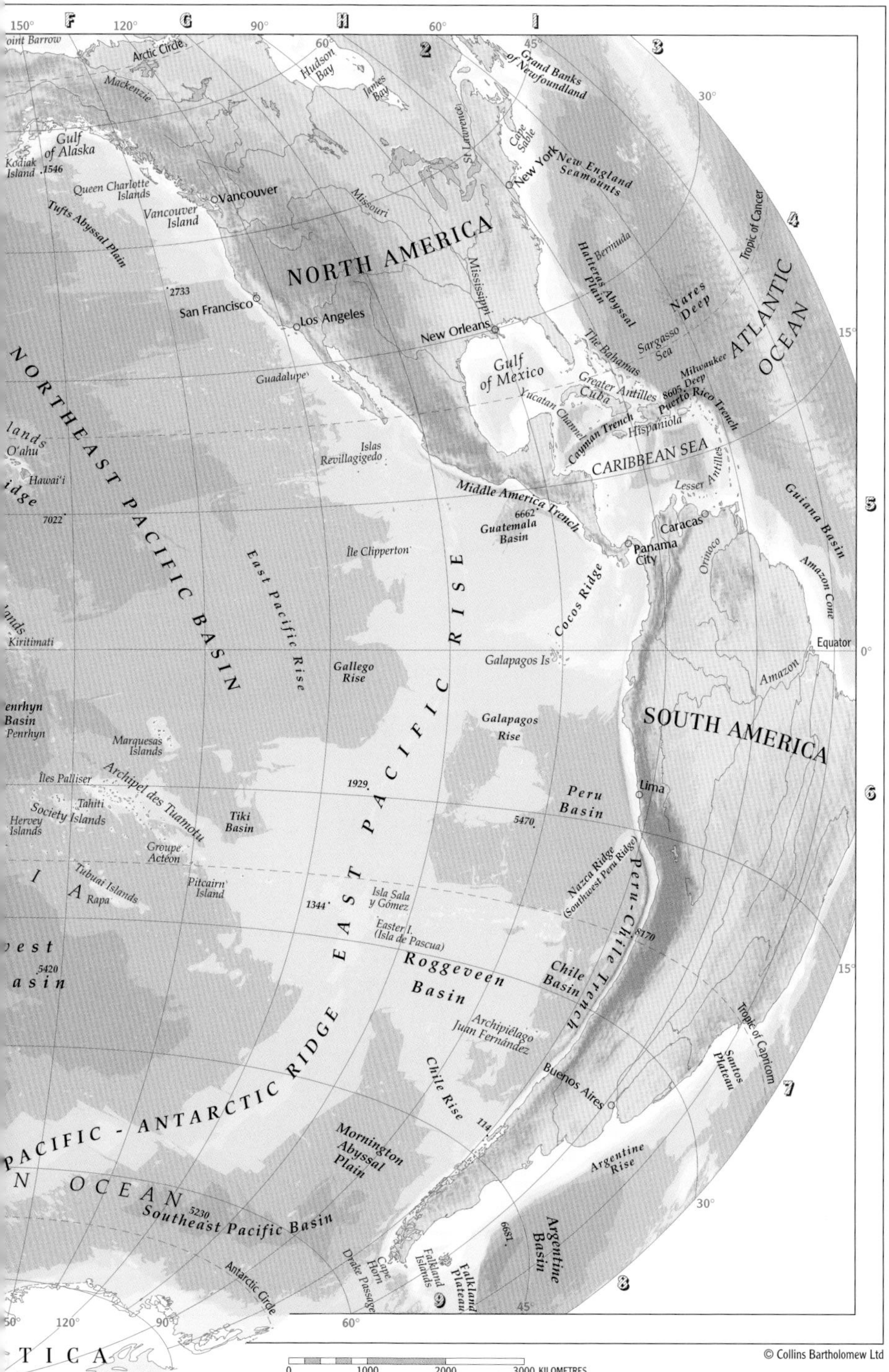

0   1000   2000   3000 KILOMETRES

© Collins Bartholomew Ltd

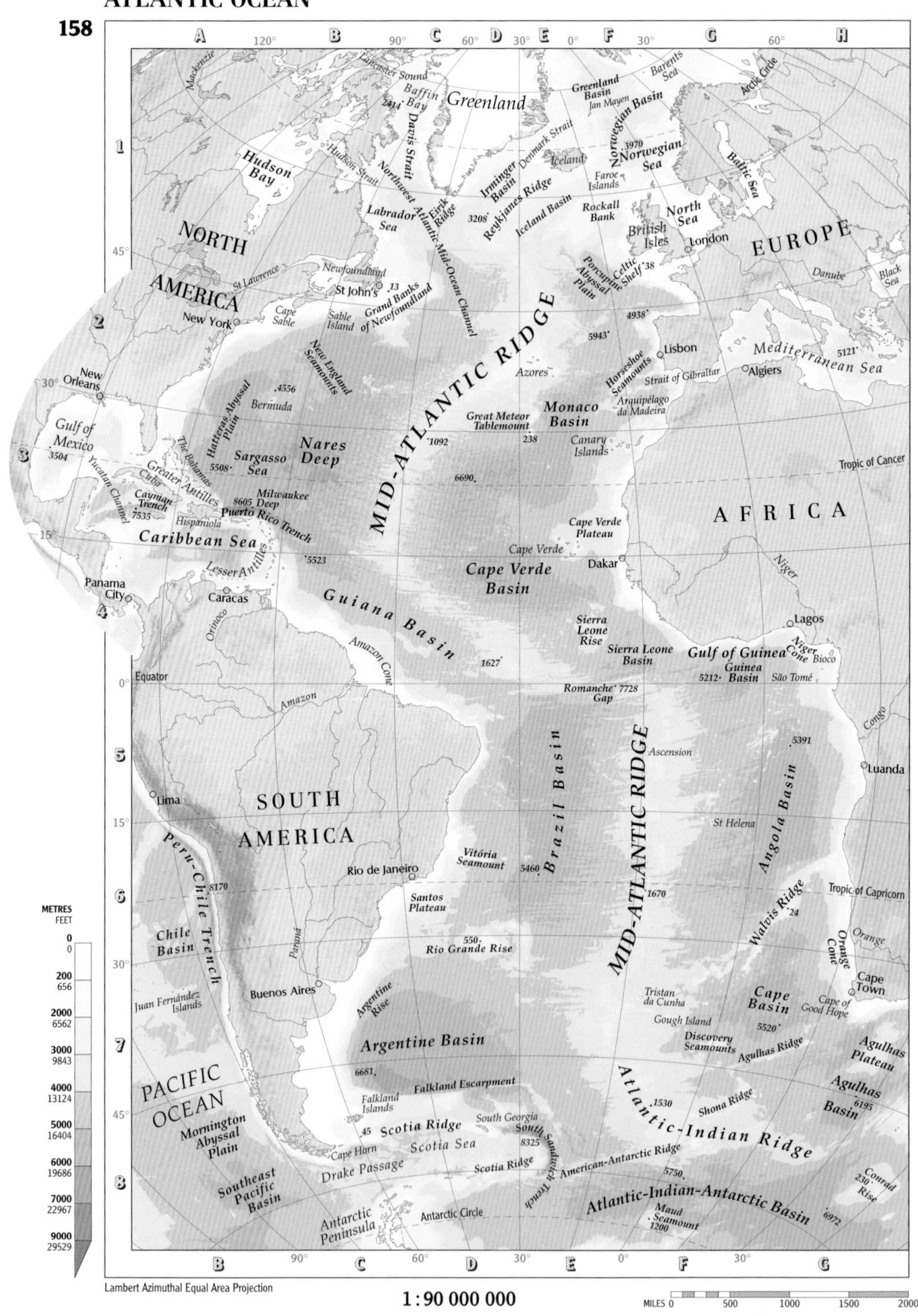

ATLANTIC OCEAN

NORTH AMERICA

Mackenzie

Hudson Bay

Baffin Bay

Lancaster Sound

2411

Greenland

Greenland Basin

Jan Mayen

Barents Sea

Arctic Circle

Davis Strait

Northwest Atlantic Mid-Ocean Channel

Hudson Strait

Labrador Sea

Imminger Basin

Eirik Ridge

3208

Reykjanes Ridge

Denmark Strait

Iceland

Iceland Basin

Norwegian Basin

3970

Norwegian Sea

Faroe Islands

Rockall Bank

Baltic Sea

British Isles

North Sea

London

EUROPE

Danube

Black Sea

St Lawrence

Newfoundland

St John's

13

Grand Banks of Newfoundland

New York

Cape Sable

Sable Island

Mid-Atlantic Ridge

Porcupine Abyssal Plain

Celtic Shelf

38

Lisbon

Algiers

Mediterranean Sea

5121

New Orleans

Bermuda

4556

New England Seamounts

Azores

4938

5943

Horseshoe Seamounts

Strait of Gibraltar

Gulf of Mexico

3504

The Bahamas

Hatteras Abyssal Plain

Sargasso Sea

Nares Deep

Great Meteor Tablemount

1092

238

Monaco Basin

Arquipélago da Madeira

Canary Islands

Tropic of Cancer

Greater Antilles

Cuba

5508

Milwaukee Deep

8605

6690

AFRICA

Yucatan Channel

Cayman Trench

7535

Puerto Rico Trench

Hispaniola

Caribbean Sea

5523

Cape Verde Plateau

Panama City

Lesser Antilles

Caracas

Guiana Basin

Cape Verde

Cape Verde Basin

Dakar

Niger

Lagos

Orinoco

Amazon Cont.

1627

Sierra Leone Rise

Sierra Leone Basin

Gulf of Guinea

5212

Guinea Basin

Niger Cone

Bioco

São Tomé

Equator

Amazon

Romanche 7728 Gap

Congo

SOUTH AMERICA

Lima

Brazil Basin

Ascension

5391

Angola Basin

Luanda

Rio de Janeiro

Vitória Seamount

5460

St Helena

Peru-Chile Trench

8170

Santos Plateau

1670

Mid-Atlantic Ridge

Walvis Ridge

24

Tropic of Capricorn

Orange Cone

Chile Basin

Rio Grande Rise

550

Orange

Juan Fernández Islands

Cape Town

Buenos Aires

Paraná

Argentine Rise

Tristan da Cunha

Gough Island

Cape Basin

5520

Cape of Good Hope

Agulhas Plateau

PACIFIC OCEAN

Argentine Basin

6681

Falkland Islands

Falkland Escarpment

Discovery Seamounts

Agulhas Ridge

Agulhas Basin

6195

Mornington Abyssal Plain

45

Scotia Ridge

South Georgia

1530

Shona Ridge

Atlantic-Indian Ridge

Conrad Rise

230

6972

Cape Horn

Drake Passage

Scotia Sea

Scotia Ridge

South Sandwich Trench

8325

American-Antarctic Ridge

5750

Southeast Pacific Basin

Antarctic Peninsula

Antarctic Circle

Atlantic-Indian-Antarctic Basin

Maud Seamount

1200

Lambert Azimuthal Equal Area Projection

1 : 90 000 000

MILES 0   500   1000   1500   2000

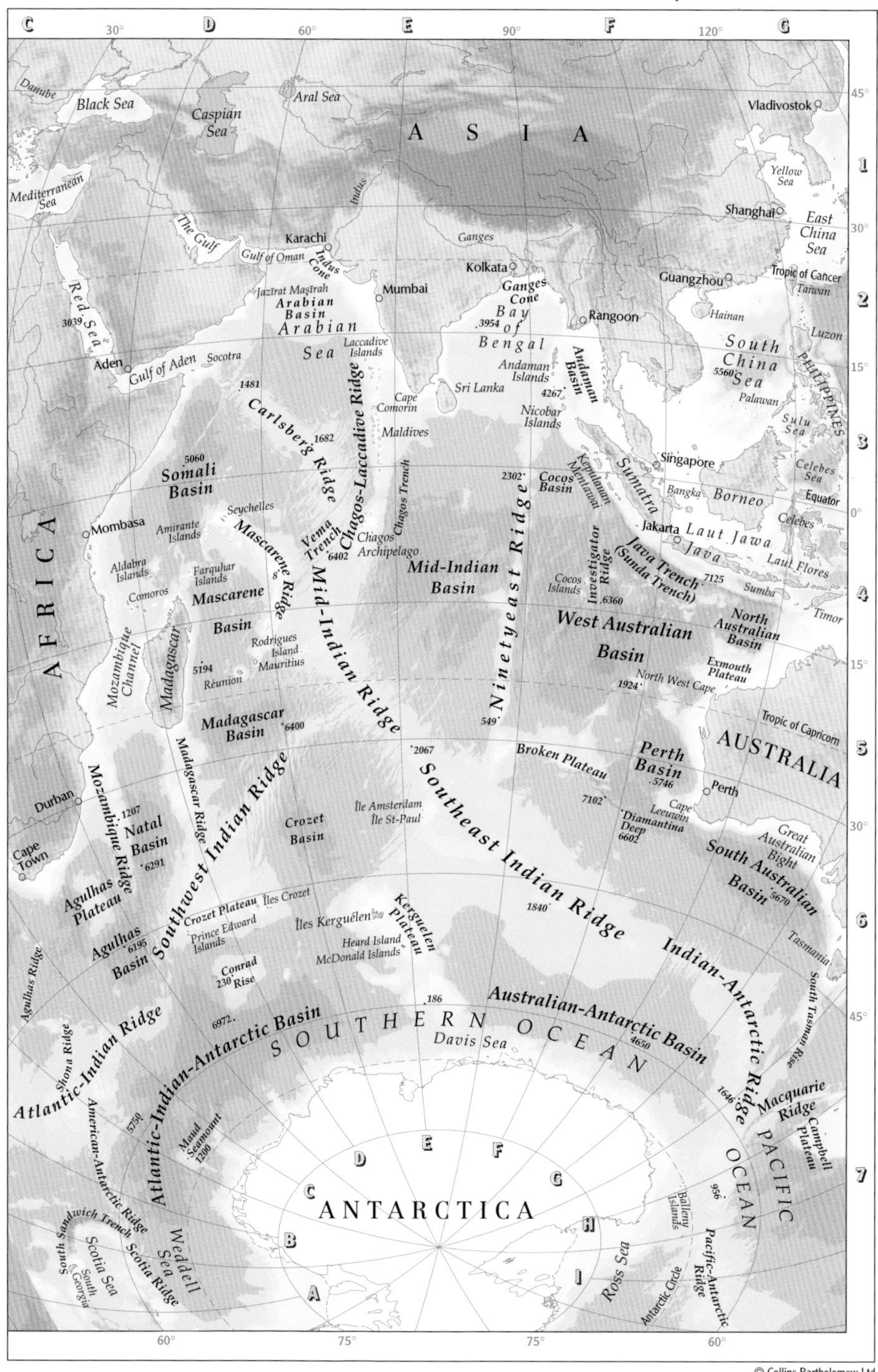

1 : 90 000 000

© Collins Bartholomew Ltd

0   1000   2000   3000 KILOMETRES

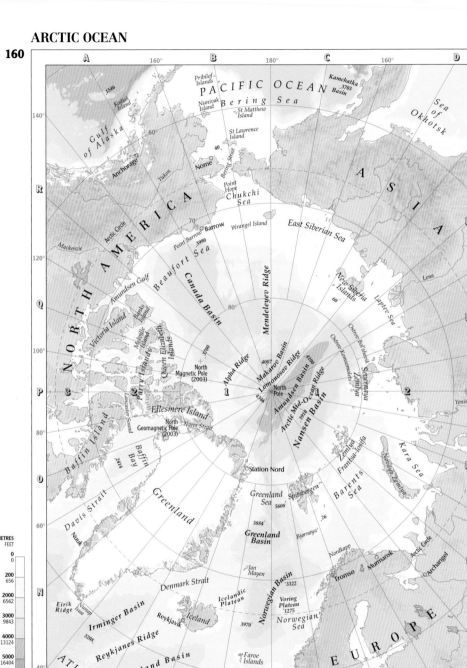

ARCTIC OCEAN

160

A   160°   B   180°   C   160°   D

PACIFIC OCEAN

Pribilof
Islands

Bering   Sea

Nunivak
Island   St Matthew
Island

1546

Kodiak
Island

Gulf
of
Alaska

St Lawrence
Island

Anchorage

40

Nome   Bering Strait

Point
Hope

Yukon

Chukchi
Sea

Arctic Circle

Point Barrow   Barrow   Wrangel Island

Beaufort
Sea   3990

Kamchatka
Basin   3703

Sea
of
Okhotsk

A   S   I   A

East Siberian Sea

Mackenzie

NORTH   AMERICA

Amundsen Gulf

Banks
Island

Victoria Island

Melville
Island

Parry Islands

Canada Basin

80°

Mendeleyev Ridge

New Siberia
Islands   60

Laptev Sea

Lena

5700

North
Magnetic Pole
(2003)

Queen Elizabeth
Islands

Alpha Ridge

4007

Makarov Basin

Lomonosov Ridge

North
Pole   4100

Amundsen Basin

Ostrov Komsomolets

Ostrov Bol'shevik

Severnaya
Zemlya

Yenisey

Lancaster Sound

Ellesmere Island

North
Geomagnetic Pole
(2003)

Baffin Island

Nares Strait   4346

Arctic Mid-Ocean Ridge   3910

Nansen Basin

Zemlya
Franstsa-Iosifa

Novaya Zemlya

Kara
Sea

Baffin
Bay   2414

Station Nord

Spitsbergen

Barents
Sea

Davis Strait

Greenland

Greenland
Sea   5608

26

Bjørnøya

Nordkapp

Arctic Circle

Archangel

Nuuk

3884

Greenland
Basin

Murmansk

Tromsø

Jan
Mayen

Eirik
Ridge   Nunap
Isua

Denmark Strait

Irminger Basin

3208

Reykjanes Ridge

Reykjavik

Iceland

Icelandic
Plateau   3970

Norwegian Basin   3322

Voring
Plateau   1275

Norwegian
Sea

Bergen

EUROPE

Baltic Sea

ATLANTIC OCEAN

Iceland Basin

Rockall
Bank

Faroe
Islands

British
Isles

North
Sea

M   20°   L   Greenwich 0°meridian   K   20°   J

Polar Stereographic Projection

1 : 45 000 000

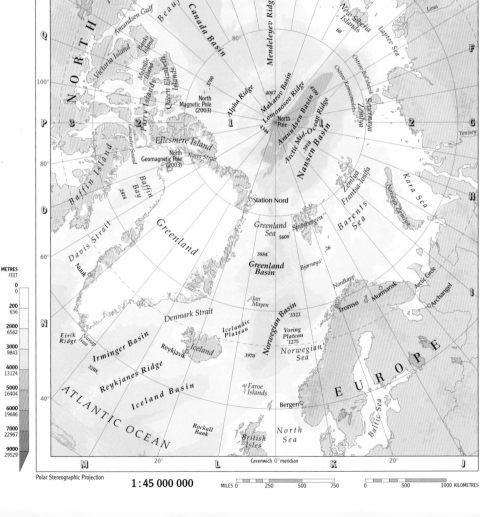

METRES	FEET
0	0
200	656
2000	6562
3000	9843
4000	13124
5000	16404
6000	19686
7000	22967
9000	29529

MILES 0   250   500   750

0   500   1000 KILOMETRES

INTRODUCTION TO THE INDEX

The index includes all names shown on the maps in the Atlas of the World. Names are referenced by page number and by a grid reference. The grid reference correlates to the alphanumeric values which appear within each map frame. Each entry also includes the country or geographical area in which the feature is located. Entries relating to names appearing on insets are indicated by a small box symbol: □, followed by a grid reference if the inset has its own alphanumeric values.

Name forms are as they appear on the maps, with additional alternative names or name forms included as cross-references which refer the user to the entry for the map form of the name. Names beginning with Mc or Mac are alphabetized exactly as they appear. The terms Saint, Sainte, Sankt, etc, are abbreviated to St, Ste, St, etc, but alphabetized as if in the full form.

Names of physical features beginning with generic geographical terms are permuted – the descriptive term is placed after the main part of the name. For example, Lake Superior is indexed as Superior, Lake; Mount Everest as Everest, Mount. This policy is applied to all languages.

Entries, other than those for towns and cities, include a descriptor indicating the type of geographical feature. Descriptors are not included where the type of feature is implicit in the name itself.

Administrative divisions are included to differentiate entries of the same name and feature type within the one country. In such cases, duplicate names are alphabetized in order of administrative division. Additional qualifiers are also included for names within selected geographical areas.

INDEX ABBREVIATIONS

admin. div.	administrative division	g.	gulf	Port.	Portugal
Afgh.	Afghanistan	Ger.	Germany	prov.	province
Alg.	Algeria	Guat.	Guatemala	pt	point
Arg.	Argentina	hd	headland	r.	river
Austr.	Australia	Hond.	Honduras	r. mouth	river mouth
aut. comm.	autonomous community	i.	island	reg.	region
aut. reg.	autonomous region	imp. l.	impermanent lake	resr	reservoir
aut. rep.	autonomous republic	Indon.	Indonesia	rf	reef
Azer.	Azerbaijan	is.	islands	Rus. Fed.	Russian Federation
b.	bay	isth.	isthmus	S.	South
B.I.O.T.	British Indian Ocean Territory	Kazakh.	Kazakhstan	salt l.	salt lake
		Kyrg.	Kyrgyzstan	sea chan.	sea channel
Bangl.	Bangladesh	l.	lake	Serb. and Mont.	Serbia and Montenegro
Bol.	Bolivia	lag.	lagoon	special admin. reg.	special administrative region
Bos.-Herz.	Bosnia Herzegovina	Lith.	Lithuania		
Bulg.	Bulgaria	Lux.	Luxembourg	str.	strait
c.	cape	Madag.	Madagascar	Switz.	Switzerland
Can.	Canada	Maur.	Mauritania	Tajik.	Tajikistan
C.A.R.	Central African Republic	Mex.	Mexico	Tanz.	Tanzania
Col.	Colombia	Moz.	Mozambique	terr.	territory
Czech Rep.	Czech Republic	mt.	mountain	Thai.	Thailand
Dem. Rep. Congo	Democratic Republic of Congo	mts	mountains	Trin. and Tob.	Trinidad and Tobago
		mun.	municipality	Turkm.	Turkmenistan
depr.	depression	N.	North	U.A.E.	United Arab Emirates
des.	desert	Neth.	Netherlands	U.K.	United Kingdom
Dom. Rep.	Dominican Republic	Neth. Antilles	Netherland Antilles	Ukr.	Ukraine
Equat. Guinea	Equatorial Guinea	Nic.	Nicaragua	union terr.	union territory
		N.Z.	New Zealand	Uru.	Uruguay
esc.	escarpment	Pak.	Pakistan	U.S.A.	United States of America
est.	estuary	Para.	Paraguay	Uzbek.	Uzbekistan
Eth.	Ethiopia	pen.	peninsula	val.	valley
Fin.	Finland	Phil.	Philippines	Venez.	Venezuela
for.	forest	plat.	plateau	vol.	volcano
Fr. Guiana	French Guiana	P.N.G.	Papua New Guinea	vol. crater	volcanic crater
Fr. Polynesia	French Polynesia	Pol.	Poland		

A

93 E4 **Aabenraa** Denmark
100 C2 **Aachen** Ger.
93 E4 **Aalborg** Denmark
102 C2 **Aalen** Ger.
100 B2 **Aalst** Belgium
93 I3 **Äänekoski** Fin.
105 D2 **Aarau** Switz.
100 B2 **Aarschot** Belgium
70 A2 **Aba** China
119 D2 **Aba** Dem. Rep. Congo
115 C4 **Aba** Nigeria
81 C2 **Ābādān** Iran
81 D2 **Ābādeh** Iran
81 D3 **Ābādeh Ṭashk** Iran
114 B1 **Abadla** Alg.
155 C1 **Abaeté** Brazil
Abagnar Qi China *see* **Xilinhot**
135 E3 **Abajo Peak** U.S.A.
115 C4 **Abakaliki** Nigeria
83 H3 **Abakan** Rus. Fed.
150 B4 **Abancay** Peru
81 D2 **Abarqū** Iran
66 D2 **Abashiri** Japan
66 D2 **Abashiri-wan** *b.* Japan
59 D3 **Abau** P.N.G.
Abaya, Lake Eth. *see* **Lake Abaya**
Ābay Wenz *r.* Eth. *see* **Blue Nile**
83 H3 **Abaza** Rus. Fed.
108 A2 **Abbasanta** *Sardinia* Italy
104 C1 **Abbeville** France
141 C2 **Abbeville** *AL* U.S.A.
140 B3 **Abbeville** *LA* U.S.A.
97 B2 **Abbeyfeale** Rep. of Ireland
55 R2 **Abbot Ice Shelf** Antarctica
74 B1 **Abbottabad** Pak.
115 E3 **Abéché** Chad
114 B4 **Abengourou** Côte d'Ivoire
114 C4 **Abeokuta** Nigeria
99 A3 **Aberaeron** U.K.
96 C2 **Aberchirder** U.K.
Abercorn Zambia *see* **Mbala**
99 B4 **Aberdare** U.K.
99 A3 **Aberdaron** U.K.
53 D2 **Aberdeen** Austr.
122 B3 **Aberdeen** S. Africa
96 C2 **Aberdeen** U.K.
139 D3 **Aberdeen** *MD* U.S.A.
137 D1 **Aberdeen** *SD* U.S.A.
134 B1 **Aberdeen** *WA* U.S.A.
129 E1 **Aberdeen Lake** Can.
96 C2 **Aberfeldy** U.K.
96 B2 **Aberfoyle** U.K.
99 B4 **Abergavenny** U.K.
Abergwaun U.K. *see* **Fishguard**
Aberhonddu U.K. *see* **Brecon**
143 C2 **Abernathy** U.S.A.
134 B2 **Abert, Lake** U.S.A.
Abertawe U.K. *see* **Swansea**
Aberteifi U.K. *see* **Cardigan**
99 B4 **Abertillery** U.K.
99 A3 **Aberystwyth** U.K.
86 F2 **Abez'** Rus. Fed.
78 B3 **Abhā** Saudi Arabia
81 C2 **Abhar** Iran
Abiad, Bahr el *r.* Sudan/Uganda *see* **White Nile**
114 B4 **Abidjan** Côte d'Ivoire
137 D3 **Abilene** *KS* U.S.A.
143 D2 **Abilene** *TX* U.S.A.
99 C4 **Abingdon** U.K.
138 C3 **Abingdon** U.S.A.
91 D3 **Abinsk** Rus. Fed.
130 B3 **Abitibi, Lake** Can.
Åbo Fin. *see* **Turku**
74 B1 **Abohar** India
114 B4 **Aboisso** Côte d'Ivoire
114 C4 **Abomey** Benin
60 A1 **Abongabong, Gunung** *mt.* Indon.
118 B2 **Abong Mbang** Cameroon
64 A3 **Aborlan** Phil.
115 D3 **Abou Déia** Chad
106 B2 **Abrantes** Port.
152 B2 **Abra Pampa** Arg.
142 A3 **Abreojos, Punta** *pt* Mex.
116 B2 **'Abri** Sudan
136 A2 **Absaroka Range** *mts* U.S.A.
81 C1 **Abşeron Yarımadası** *pen.* Azer.
78 B3 **Abū 'Arīsh** Saudi Arabia
116 A2 **Abū Ballāş** *hill* Egypt
79 C2 **Abu Dhabi** U.A.E.
116 B3 **Abu Hamed** Sudan
116 B3 **Abu Haraz** Sudan
115 C4 **Abuja** Nigeria
81 C2 **Abū Kamāl** Syria
118 C2 **Abumombazi** Dem. Rep. Congo
152 B1 **Abunã** *r.* Bol.
150 C3 **Abunã** Brazil
74 B2 **Abu Road** India
78 B2 **Abū Şādi, Jabal** *hill* Saudi Arabia
116 B2 **Abū Sunbul** Egypt
116 A3 **Abu Zabad** Sudan
Abū Ẓabī U.A.E. *see* **Abu Dhabi**
117 A4 **Abyei** Sudan
145 B2 **Acambaro** Mex.
120 B2 **Acampamento de Caça do Mucusso** Angola
106 B1 **A Cañiza** Spain
144 B2 **Acaponeta** Mex.
145 C3 **Acapulco** Mex.
151 E3 **Acará** Brazil
154 A3 **Acaray, Represa de** *resr* Para.
150 C2 **Acarigua** Venez.
110 B1 **Acâş** Romania
145 C3 **Acatlan** Mex.
145 C3 **Acayucán** Mex.
114 B4 **Accra** Ghana
98 B3 **Accrington** U.K.
74 B2 **Achalpur** India
97 A2 **Achill Island** Rep. of Ireland
101 D1 **Achim** Ger.
96 B2 **Achnasheen** U.K.
91 D2 **Achuyevo** Rus. Fed.
111 C3 **Acıpayam** Turkey
109 C3 **Acireale** *Sicily* Italy
147 C2 **Acklins Island** Bahamas
153 A3 **Aconcagua, Cerro** *mt.* Arg.
106 B1 **A Coruña** Spain
108 A2 **Acqui Terme** Italy
103 D2 **Ács** Hungary
49 N6 **Actéon, Groupe** *is* Fr. Polynesia
145 C2 **Actopán** Mex.
143 D2 **Ada** U.S.A.
Adabazar Turkey *see* **Adapazarı**
79 C2 **Adam** Oman
111 B3 **Adamas** Greece
135 B3 **Adams Peak** U.S.A.
'Adan Yemen *see* **Aden**
80 B2 **Adana** Turkey
111 D2 **Adapazarı** Turkey
97 B2 **Adare** Rep. of Ireland
55 M2 **Adare, Cape** Antarctica
108 A1 **Adda** *r.* Italy
78 B2 **Ad Dafinah** Saudi Arabia
78 B2 **Ad Dahnā'** *des.* Saudi Arabia
79 B2 **Ad Dahnā'** *des.* Saudi Arabia
114 A2 **Ad Dakhla** Western Sahara
Ad Dammām Saudi Arabia *see* **Dammam**
78 A2 **Ad Dār al Ḥamrā'** Saudi Arabia
78 B3 **Ad Darb** Saudi Arabia
78 B2 **Ad Dawādimī** Saudi Arabia
Ad Dawḥah Qatar *see* **Doha**
Ad Ḍiffah Egypt *see* **Libyan Plateau**
78 B2 **Ad Dilam** Saudi Arabia
78 B2 **Ad Dir'īyah** Saudi Arabia
117 B4 **Addis Ababa** Eth.
81 C2 **Ad Dīwānīyah** Iraq
141 D2 **Adel** U.S.A.
52 A2 **Adelaide** Austr.
55 A3 **Adelaide Island** Antarctica
50 C1 **Adelaide River** Austr.
101 D2 **Adelebsen** Ger.
55 K2 **Adélie Land** Antarctica
78 B3 **Aden** Yemen
116 C3 **Aden, Gulf of** Somalia/Yemen
100 C2 **Adenau** Ger.
115 C3 **Aderbissinat** Niger
79 C2 **Adh Dhayd** U.A.E.
59 C3 **Adi** *i.* Indon.
116 B3 **Ādī Ārk'ay** Eth.
108 B1 **Adige** *r.* Italy
116 B3 **Ādīgrat** Eth.
78 A3 **Adi Keyih** Eritrea
74 B3 **Adilabad** India
115 D2 **Adīrī** Libya
139 E2 **Adirondack Mountains** U.S.A.
Ādīs Ābeba Eth. *see* **Addis Ababa**
117 B4 **Ādīs Alem** Eth.
80 B2 **Adıyaman** Turkey
110 C1 **Adjud** Romania
50 B1 **Admiralty Gulf** Austr.
128 A2 **Admiralty Island** U.S.A.
59 D3 **Admiralty Islands** P.N.G.
73 B3 **Adoni** India
104 B3 **Adour** *r.* France
106 C2 **Adra** Spain
114 B2 **Adrar** Alg.
138 C2 **Adrian** *MI* U.S.A.
143 C1 **Adrian** *TX* U.S.A.
108 B2 **Adriatic Sea** Europe
Adua Eth. *see* **Ādwa**
116 B3 **Ādwa** Eth.
83 K2 **Adycha** *r.* Rus. Fed.
91 D3 **Adygeysk** Rus. Fed.
114 B4 **Adzopé** Côte d'Ivoire
111 B3 **Aegean Sea** Greece/Turkey
101 D1 **Aerzen** Ger.
106 B1 **A Estrada** Spain
116 B3 **Afabet** Eritrea
Affreville Alg. *see* **Khemis Miliana**
76 C3 **Afghanistan** *country* Asia
78 B2 **'Afīf** Saudi Arabia
136 A2 **Afton** U.S.A.
80 B2 **Afyon** Turkey
115 C3 **Agadez** Niger
114 B1 **Agadir** Morocco
77 D2 **Agadyr'** Kazakh.
113 I7 **Agalega Islands** Mauritius
Agana Guam *see* **Hagåtña**
74 B2 **Agar** India
119 D2 **Āgaro** Eth.
75 D2 **Agartala** India
81 C2 **Ağdam** Azer.
105 C3 **Agde** France
Agedabia Libya *see* **Ajdābiyā**
104 C3 **Agen** France
122 A2 **Aggeneys** S. Africa
111 C3 **Agia Vervara** Greece
111 B3 **Agios Dimitrios** Greece
111 C3 **Agios Efstratios** *i.* Greece
111 C3 **Agios Kirykos** Greece
111 C3 **Agios Nikolaos** Greece
78 A3 **Agirwat Hills** Sudan
123 C2 **Agisanang** S. Africa
110 B1 **Agnita** Romania
74 B2 **Agra** India
81 C2 **Ağrı** Turkey
Ağrı Dağı *mt.* Turkey *see* **Ararat, Mount**
108 B3 **Agrigento** *Sicily* Italy
111 B3 **Agrinio** Greece
109 B2 **Agropoli** Italy
87 E3 **Agryz** Rus. Fed.
144 B2 **Agua Brava, Laguna** *lag.* Mex.
154 B2 **Água Clara** Brazil
145 C3 **Aguada** Mex.
146 B4 **Aguadulce** Panama
144 B2 **Aguanaval** *r.* Mex.
144 B1 **Agua Prieta** Mex.
144 B2 **Aguascalientes** Mex.
155 D1 **Águas Formosas** Brazil
154 C2 **Agudos** Brazil
106 B1 **Águeda** Port.
114 C3 **Aguelhok** Mali
106 C1 **Aguilar de Campóo** Spain
107 C2 **Águilas** Spain
144 B3 **Aguililla** Mex.
122 B3 **Agulhas, Cape** S. Africa
158 F7 **Agulhas Basin** *sea feature* Southern Ocean
155 D2 **Agulhas Negras** *mt.* Brazil
158 F7 **Agulhas Plateau** *sea feature* Southern Ocean
158 F7 **Agulhas Ridge** *sea feature* S. Atlantic Ocean
111 C2 **Ağva** Turkey
81 C2 **Ahar** Iran
100 C1 **Ahaus** Ger.
81 C2 **Ahlat** Turkey
100 C2 **Ahlen** Ger.
74 B2 **Ahmadabad** India
74 B3 **Ahmadnagar** India
74 B2 **Ahmadpur East** Pak.
74 B1 **Ahmadpur Sial** Pak.
117 C4 **Ahmar Mountains** Eth.
Ahmedabad India *see* **Ahmadabad**
Ahmednagar India *see* **Ahmadnagar**
144 B2 **Ahome** Mex.
81 D3 **Ahram** Iran
101 E1 **Ahrensburg** Ger.
104 C2 **Ahun** France
93 F4 **Åhus** Sweden
81 C2 **Ahvāz** Iran
Ahvenanmaa *is* Fin. *see* **Åland Islands**
122 A2 **Ai-Ais** Namibia
80 B2 **Aigialousa** Cyprus
111 B3 **Aigio** Greece
Aihui China *see* **Heihe**
Aijal India *see* **Aizawl**
141 D2 **Aiken** U.S.A.
155 D1 **Aimorés** Brazil
155 D1 **Aimorés, Serra dos** *hills* Brazil
105 D2 **Ain** *r.* France
107 E2 **Aïn Azel** Alg.
115 C1 **Aïn Beïda** Alg.
114 B2 **'Aïn Ben Tili** Maur.
107 D2 **Aïn Defla** Alg.
114 B1 **Aïn Sefra** Alg.
136 D2 **Ainsworth** U.S.A.
Aintab Turkey *see* **Gaziantep**
107 D2 **Aïn Taya** Alg.
107 D2 **Aïn Tédélès** Alg.
107 C2 **Aïn Temouchent** Alg.
115 C3 **Aïr, Massif de l'** *mts* Niger
60 A1 **Airbangis** Indon.
128 C2 **Airdrie** Can.
96 C3 **Airdrie** U.K.
104 B3 **Aire-sur-l'Adour** France
101 E3 **Aisch** *r.* Ger.
128 A1 **Aishihik Lake** Can.
100 A3 **Aisne** *r.* France
59 D3 **Aitape** P.N.G.
137 E1 **Aitkin** U.S.A.
110 B1 **Aiud** Romania
105 D3 **Aix-en-Provence** France
Aix-la-Chapelle Ger. *see* **Aachen**
105 D2 **Aix-les-Bains** France
75 D2 **Aizawl** India
88 C2 **Aizkraukle** Latvia
88 B2 **Aizpute** Latvia
67 C3 **Aizu-wakamatsu** Japan
105 D3 **Ajaccio** *Corsica* France
Ajayameru India *see* **Ajmer**
115 E1 **Ajdābiyā** Libya
79 C2 **'Ajman** U.A.E.
74 B2 **Ajmer** India
Ajmer-Merwara India *see* **Ajmer**
142 A2 **Ajo** U.S.A.
119 D2 **Āk'ak'ī Beseka** Eth.
Akamagaseki Japan *see* **Shimonoseki**
54 B2 **Akaroa** N.Z.
87 E3 **Akbulak** Rus. Fed.
80 B2 **Akçakale** Turkey
114 A3 **Akchâr** *reg.* Maur.
111 C3 **Akdağ** *mt.* Turkey
80 B2 **Akdağmadeni** Turkey
88 A2 **Åkersberga** Sweden
118 C2 **Aketi** Dem. Rep. Congo
81 C1 **Akhalk'alak'i** Georgia
81 C1 **Akhalts'ikhe** Georgia
79 C2 **Akhḍar, Jabal** *mts* Oman
111 C3 **Akhisar** Turkey
87 D4 **Akhtubinsk** Rus. Fed.
118 B3 **Akiéni** Gabon
130 B2 **Akimiski Island** Can.
66 D3 **Akita** Japan
114 A3 **Akjoujt** Maur.
Akkerman Ukr. *see* **Bilhorod-Dnistrovs'kyy**
77 D1 **Akkol'** Kazakh.
Ak-Mechet Kazakh. *see* **Kyzylorda**
88 B2 **Akmeņrags** *pt* Latvia
Akmola Kazakh. *see* **Astana**
Akmolinsk Kazakh. *see* **Astana**
67 B4 **Akō** Japan
117 B4 **Akobo** Sudan
74 B2 **Akola** India
118 B2 **Akonolinga** Cameroon
78 A3 **Akordat** Eritrea
131 D1 **Akpatok Island** Can.
77 D2 **Akqi** China
92 □A3 **Akranes** Iceland
111 B2 **Akrathos, Akra** *pt* Greece
136 C2 **Akron** *CO* U.S.A.
138 C2 **Akron** *OH* U.S.A.

75 B1 Aksai Chin *terr.* Asia
80 B2 Aksaray Turkey
86 F2 Aksarka Rus. Fed.
76 B1 Aksay Kazakh.
91 D2 Aksay Rus. Fed.
80 B2 Akşehir Turkey
76 C2 Akshiganak Kazakh.
77 E2 Aksu China
116 B3 Āksum Eth.
76 B2 Aktau Kazakh.
76 B1 Aktobe Kazakh.
77 D2 Aktogay Kazakh.
88 C3 Aktsyabrski Belarus
        Aktyubinsk Kazakh. *see*
        Aktobe
67 B4 Akune Japan
115 C4 Akure Nigeria
92 □B2 Akureyri Iceland
        Akyab Myanmar *see* Sittwe
111 D2 Akyazı Turkey
77 C2 Akzhaykyn, Ozero *salt l.*
        Kazakh.
140 C2 Alabama *r.* U.S.A.
140 C2 Alabama *state* U.S.A.
140 C2 Alabaster U.S.A.
111 C3 Alaçatı Turkey
145 D2 Alacrán, Arrecife *rf* Mex.
81 C1 Alagir Rus. Fed.
151 F4 Alagoinhas Brazil
107 C1 Alagón Spain
78 B2 Al Aḥmadī Kuwait
77 E2 Alakol', Ozero *salt l.*
        Kazakh.
92 J2 Alakurtti Rus. Fed.
78 B3 Al 'Alayyah Saudi Arabia
81 C2 Al 'Amādīyah Iraq
81 C2 Al 'Amārah Iraq
80 A2 Al 'Āmirīyah Egypt
143 C3 Alamitos, Sierra de los
        mt. Mex.
135 C3 Alamo U.S.A.
142 B2 Alamogordo U.S.A.
144 A2 Alamos Mex.
144 B2 Alamos Mex.
144 B2 Alamos *r.* Mex.
136 B3 Alamosa U.S.A.
        Åland Fin. *see*
93 G3 Åland Islands *is* Fin.
80 B2 Alanya Turkey
        Alappuzha India *see*
        Alleppey
80 B3 Al 'Aqabah Jordan
78 B2 Al 'Aqīq Saudi Arabia
107 C2 Alarcón, Embalse de *resr*
        Spain
80 B2 Al 'Arīsh Egypt
78 B2 Al Arţāwīyah Saudi Arabia
61 C2 Alas Indon.
111 C3 Alaşehir Turkey
128 A2 Alaska *state* U.S.A.
124 D4 Alaska, Gulf of U.S.A.
126 B3 Alaska Peninsula U.S.A.
126 C2 Alaska Range *mts* U.S.A.
81 C2 Älät Azer.
87 D3 Alatyr' Rus. Fed.
150 B3 Alausí Ecuador
93 H3 Alavus Fin.
52 B2 Alawoona Austr.
79 C2 Al 'Ayn U.A.E.
108 A2 Alba Italy
107 C2 Albacete Spain
78 A2 Al Badā'i' Saudi Arabia
78 B2 Al Badī' Saudi Arabia
110 B1 Alba Iulia Romania
109 C2 Albania *country* Europe
50 A3 Albany Austr.
130 B2 Albany *r.* Can.
141 D2 Albany *GA* U.S.A.
139 E2 Albany *NY* U.S.A.
134 B2 Albany *OR* U.S.A.
115 E1 Al Bardī Libya
        Al Başrah Iraq *see* Basra
51 D1 Albatross Bay Austr.
116 A2 Al Bawītī Egypt
115 E1 Al Baydā' Libya
78 B3 Al Baydā' Yemen
141 D1 Albemarle U.S.A.
141 E1 Albemarle Sound
        sea chan. U.S.A.
108 A2 Albenga Italy
51 C2 Alberga *watercourse* Austr.
119 D2 Albert, Lake
        Dem. Rep. Congo/Uganda
128 C2 Alberta *prov.* Can.
100 B2 Albert Kanaal *canal*
        Belgium
137 E2 Albert Lea U.S.A.
117 B4 Albert Nile *r.*
        Sudan/Uganda
123 C2 Alberton S. Africa

        Albertville
        Dem. Rep. Congo *see*
        Kalemie
105 D2 Albertville France
104 C3 Albi France
151 D2 Albina Suriname
78 A2 Al Bi'r Saudi Arabia
78 B3 Al Birk Saudi Arabia
78 B2 Al Biyāḍh *reg.*
        Saudi Arabia
        Alborz, Reshteh-ye Iran
        see Elburz Mountains
107 C2 Albox Spain
106 B2 Albufeira Port.
142 B1 Albuquerque U.S.A.
79 C2 Al Buraymī Oman
53 C3 Albury Austr.
106 B2 Alcácer do Sal Port.
106 C1 Alcalá de Henares Spain
106 C2 Alcalá la Real Spain
108 B3 Alcamo *Sicily* Italy
107 C1 Alcañiz Spain
106 B2 Alcántara Spain
107 C2 Alcantarilla Spain
106 C2 Alcaraz Spain
106 C2 Alcaraz, Sierra de *mts*
        Spain
106 C2 Alcaudete Spain
106 C2 Alcázar de San Juan
        Spain
        Alcazarquivir Morocco *see*
        Ksar el Kebir
91 D2 Alchevs'k Ukr.
155 E1 Alcobaça Brazil
107 C1 Alcora Spain
107 C2 Alcoy-Alcoi Spain
107 D2 Alcúdia Spain
113 H6 Aldabra Islands
        Seychelles
142 B2 Aldama Mex.
145 C2 Aldama Mex.
83 J3 Aldan Rus. Fed.
83 J2 Aldan *r.* Rus. Fed.
99 D3 Aldeburgh U.K.
95 C4 Alderney *i.* Channel Is
99 C4 Aldershot U.K.
114 A3 Aleg Maur.
155 D2 Alegre Brazil
152 C2 Alegrete Brazil
89 D1 Aleksandrov Rus. Fed.
89 E2 Aleksandrovsk Ukr. *see*
        Zaporizhzhya
83 K3 Aleksandrovsk-
        Sakhalinskiy Rus. Fed.
82 E1 Aleksandry, Zemlya *i.*
        Rus. Fed.
        Alekseyevka Kazakh. *see*
        Akkol'
91 D1 Alekseyevka Rus. Fed.
91 D1 Alekseyevka Rus. Fed.
89 E3 Aleksin Rus. Fed.
109 D2 Aleksinac Serb. and Mont.
118 B3 Alèmbé Gabon
155 D2 Além Paraíba Brazil
93 F3 Ålen Norway
104 C2 Alençon France
80 B2 Aleppo Syria
150 B4 Alerta Peru
128 B2 Alert Bay Can.
105 C3 Alès France
110 B1 Aleşd Romania
        Aleshki Ukr. *see*
        Tsyurupyns'k
108 A2 Alessandria Italy
        Alessio Albania *see* Lezhë
93 E3 Ålesund Norway
156 D2 Aleutian Basin *sea feature*
        Bering Sea
124 A4 Aleutian Islands U.S.A.
83 L3 Alevina, Mys *c.* Rus. Fed.
128 A2 Alexander Archipelago *is*
        U.S.A.
122 A2 Alexander Bay S. Africa
140 C2 Alexander City U.S.A.
55 A2 Alexander Island
        Antarctica
53 C3 Alexandra Austr.
54 A3 Alexandra N.Z.
153 E5 Alexandra, Cape
        S. Georgia
        Alexandra Land *i.*
        Rus. Fed. *see*
        Aleksandry, Zemlya
111 B2 Alexandreia Greece
116 A1 Alexandria Egypt
110 C2 Alexandria Romania
123 C3 Alexandria S. Africa
96 B3 Alexandria U.K.
140 B2 Alexandria *LA* U.S.A.
137 D1 Alexandria *MN* U.S.A.

139 D3 Alexandria *VA* U.S.A.
52 A3 Alexandrina, Lake Austr.
111 C2 Alexandroupoli Greece
131 E2 Alexis *r.* Can.
128 B2 Alexis Creek Can.
77 E1 Aleysk Rus. Fed.
107 C1 Alfaro Spain
81 C3 Al Fāw Iraq
80 B3 Al Fayyūm Egypt
101 D2 Alfeld (Leine) Ger.
155 C2 Alfenas Brazil
96 C2 Alford U.K.
        Al Fujayrah U.A.E. *see*
        Fujairah
        Al Furāt *r.* Iraq/Syria *see*
        Euphrates
93 E4 Ålgård Norway
106 B2 Algarve *reg.* Port.
106 B2 Algeciras Spain
107 C2 Algemesí Spain
78 A3 Algena Eritrea
        Alger Alg. *see* Algiers
114 C2 Algeria *country* Africa
79 C3 Al Ghaydah Yemen
108 A2 Alghero *Sardinia* Italy
116 B2 Al Ghurdaqah Egypt
79 B2 Al Ghwaybiyah
        Saudi Arabia
115 C1 Algiers Alg.
123 C3 Algoa Bay S. Africa
137 E2 Algona U.S.A.
106 C1 Algorta Spain
        Algueirao Moz. *see*
        Hacufera
81 C2 Al Ḥadīthah Iraq
79 C2 Al Ḥajar al Gharbī *mts*
        Oman
115 D2 Al Ḥamādah al Ḥamrā'
        plat. Libya
107 C2 Alhama de Murcia Spain
80 A2 Al Ḥammām Egypt
78 B2 Al Ḥanākīyah Saudi Arabia
81 C2 Al Ḥasakah Syria
78 B2 Al Ḥawīyah Saudi Arabia
81 C2 Al Ḥayy Iraq
78 B3 Al Ḥazm al Jawf Yemen
79 C3 Al Ḥibāk *des.* Saudi Arabia
        Al Ḥillah Iraq *see* Hillah
78 B2 Al Ḥillah Saudi Arabia
79 B2 Al Ḥinnāh Saudi Arabia
        Al Ḥudaydah Yemen *see*
        Hodeidah
79 B2 Al Hufūf Saudi Arabia
115 D2 Al Ḥulayq al Kabir *hills*
        Libya
79 C2 'Alīābād Iran
111 C3 Aliağa Turkey
111 B2 Aliakmonas *r.* Greece
81 C2 Äli Bayramlı Azer.
107 C2 Alicante Spain
143 D3 Alice U.S.A.
109 C3 Alice, Punta *pt* Italy
51 C2 Alice Springs Austr.
77 D3 Alichur Tajik.
74 B2 Aligarh India
81 C2 Alīgūdarz Iran
69 E1 Alihe China
118 B3 Alima *r.* Congo
118 C2 Alindao C.A.R.
111 C3 Aliova *r.* Turkey
74 B2 Alirajpur India
117 C3 Ali Sabieh Djibouti
78 A1 Al 'Isāwīyah Saudi Arabia
        Al Iskandarīyah Egypt *see*
        Alexandria
78 B2 Al Ismā'īlīyah Egypt
123 C3 Aliwal North S. Africa
115 E2 Al Jaghbūb Libya
78 B2 Al Jahrah Kuwait
78 B2 Al Jamalīyah Qatar
115 E2 Al Jawf Libya
78 A2 Al Jawf Saudi Arabia
115 D1 Al Jawsh Libya
106 B2 Aljezur Port.
        Al Jīzah Egypt *see* Giza
79 B2 Al Jubayl Saudi Arabia
78 B2 Al Jubaylah Saudi Arabia
115 D2 Al Jufra Oasis Libya
78 B2 Al Junaynah Saudi Arabia
106 B2 Aljustrel Port.
78 B2 Al Kahfah Saudi Arabia
79 C2 Al Kāmil Oman
80 B2 Al Karak Jordan
81 C2 Al Kāẓimīyah Iraq
79 C2 Al Khābūrah Oman
78 B2 Al Khamāsīn Saudi Arabia
78 B2 Al Khārijah Egypt
79 C2 Al Khaşab Oman
78 B3 Al Khawkhah Yemen
79 C2 Al Khawr Qatar
115 E2 Al Khufrah Libya

115 D1 Al Khums Libya
79 B2 Al Khunn Saudi Arabia
78 B2 Al Kidan *well* Saudi Arabia
79 C2 Al Kir'ānah Qatar
100 B1 Alkmaar Neth.
81 C2 Al Küt Iraq
        Al Kuwayt Kuwait *see*
        Kuwait
        Al Lādhiqīyah Syria *see*
        Latakia
75 C2 Allahabad India
83 K2 Allakh-Yun' Rus. Fed.
78 A2 'Allāqī, Wādī al
        watercourse Egypt
139 D2 Allegheny *r.* U.S.A.
139 C3 Allegheny Mountains
        U.S.A.
97 B1 Allen, Lough *l.*
        Rep. of Ireland
145 B2 Allende Mex.
145 B2 Allende Mex.
139 D2 Allentown U.S.A.
73 B4 Alleppey India
101 D1 Aller *r.* Ger.
136 C2 Alliance *NE* U.S.A.
138 C2 Alliance *OH* U.S.A.
78 B2 Al Lith Saudi Arabia
96 C2 Alloa U.K.
131 C3 Alma Can.
        Alma-Ata Kazakh. *see*
        Almaty
106 B2 Almada Port.
106 C2 Almadén Spain
        Al Madīnah Saudi Arabia
        see Medina
80 B2 Al Mafraq Jordan
114 B2 Al Mahbas
        Western Sahara
78 B3 Al Maḥwīt Yemen
78 B2 Al Majma'ah Saudi
        Arabia
116 B2 Al Maks al Baḥrī Egypt
        Al Manāmah Bahrain *see*
        Manama
135 B2 Almanor, Lake U.S.A.
107 C2 Almansa Spain
80 B2 Al Manşūrah Egypt
78 B2 Al Mariyyah U.A.E.
115 E1 Al Marj Libya
77 D2 Almaty Kazakh.
        Al Mawşil Iraq *see* Mosul
81 C2 Al Mayādīn Syria
106 C1 Almazán Spain
151 D3 Almeirim Brazil
100 C1 Almelo Neth.
155 D1 Almenara Brazil
106 B1 Almendra, Embalse de
        resr Spain
106 B2 Almendralejo Spain
106 C2 Almería Spain
106 C2 Almería, Golfo de *b.*
        Spain
87 E3 Al'met'yevsk Rus. Fed.
78 B2 Al Mindak Saudi Arabia
116 B2 Al Minyā Egypt
79 B2 Al Mish'āb Saudi Arabia
106 B2 Almodôvar Port.
106 B2 Almonte Spain
75 B2 Almora India
79 B2 Al Mubarrez Saudi Arabia
79 C2 Al Muḍaibī Oman
80 B3 Al Mudawwarah Jordan
        Al Mukallā Yemen *see*
        Mukalla
        Al Mukhā Yemen *see*
        Mocha
106 C2 Almuñécar Spain
81 C2 Al Muqdādīyah Iraq
78 A2 Al Musayjid Saudi Arabia
78 A2 Al Muwaylih Saudi Arabia
111 B3 Almyros Greece
96 B2 Alness U.K.
98 C2 Alnwick U.K.
62 A1 Along India
111 B3 Alonnisos *i.* Greece
59 C3 Alor *i.* Indon.
59 C3 Alor, Kepulauan *is* Indon.
60 B1 Alor Setar Malaysia
        Alor Star Malaysia *see*
        Alor Setar
        Alost Belgium *see* Aalst
153 E6 Alotau P.N.G.
86 C2 Alozero Rus. Fed.
138 C1 Alpena U.S.A.
160 Q1 Alpha Ridge *sea feature*
        Arctic Ocean
100 B1 Alphen aan den Rijn
        Neth.
142 B2 Alpine *AZ* U.S.A.
143 C2 Alpine *TX* U.S.A.
84 E4 Alps *mts* Europe

79 B3 **Al Qaʻāmīyāt** *reg.* Saudi Arabia
115 D1 **Al Qaddāḥīyah** Libya
Al Qāhirah Egypt *see* **Cairo**
78 B2 **Al Qāʻīyah** Saudi Arabia
81 C2 **Al Qāmishlī** Syria
80 B2 **Al Qaryatayn** Syria
79 B2 **Al Qaṣab** Saudi Arabia
116 A2 **Al Qaṣr** Egypt
79 B3 **Al Qaṭn** Yemen
115 D2 **Al Qaṭrūn** Libya
80 B2 **Al Qunayṭirah** Syria
78 B3 **Al Qunfidhah** Saudi Arabia
116 B2 **Al Quṣayr** Egypt
78 B2 **Al Quwārah** Saudi Arabia
78 B2 **Al Quwayīyah** Saudi Arabia
101 D2 **Alsfeld** Ger.
98 B2 **Alston** U.K.
92 H2 **Alta** Norway
92 H2 **Altaelva** *r.* Norway
68 B1 **Altai Mountains** Asia
141 D2 **Altamaha** *r.* U.S.A.
151 D3 **Altamira** Brazil
109 C2 **Altamura** Italy
144 A1 **Altar, Desierto de** *des.* Mex.
77 E2 **Altay** China
68 C1 **Altay** Mongolia
105 D2 **Altdorf** Switz.
107 C2 **Altea** Spain
92 H1 **Alteidet** Norway
101 F2 **Altenburg** Ger.
100 C2 **Altenkirchen (Westerwald)** Ger.
101 F1 **Altentreptow** Ger.
111 C3 **Altınoluk** Turkey
111 D3 **Altıntaş** Turkey
152 B1 **Altiplano** *plain* Bol.
96 B1 **Altnaharra** U.K.
154 B1 **Alto Araguaia** Brazil
107 C1 **Alto del Moncayo** *mt.* Spain
154 B1 **Alto Garças** Brazil
121 C2 **Alto Ligonha** Moz.
121 C2 **Alto Molócuè** Moz.
99 C4 **Alton** U.K.
137 E3 **Alton** U.S.A.
129 E3 **Altona** Can.
139 D2 **Altoona** U.S.A.
154 B1 **Alto Sucuriú** Brazil
154 B1 **Alto Taquarí** Brazil
102 C2 **Altötting** Ger.
68 C2 **Altun Shan** *mt.* China
68 B2 **Altun Shan** *mts* China
134 B2 **Alturas** U.S.A.
143 D2 **Altus** U.S.A.
88 C2 **Alūksne** Latvia
78 A2 **Al ʻUlā** Saudi Arabia
115 D1 **Al ʻUqaylah** Libya
Al Uqṣur Egypt *see* **Luxor**
91 C3 **Alushta** Ukr.
115 E2 **Al ʻUwaynāt** Libya
143 D1 **Alva** U.S.A.
145 C3 **Alvarado** Mex.
93 F3 **Älvdalen** Sweden
93 F3 **Älvdalen** *val.* Sweden
92 H2 **Älvsbyn** Sweden
78 A2 **Al Wajh** Saudi Arabia
79 C2 **Al Wakrah** Qatar
74 B2 **Alwar** India
81 C2 **Al Widyān** *plat.* Iraq/Saudi Arabia
Alxa Youqi China *see* **Ehen Hudag**
Alxa Zuoqi China *see* **Bayan Hot**
51 C1 **Alyangula** Austr.
88 B3 **Alytus** Lith.
136 C1 **Alzada** U.S.A.
101 D3 **Alzey** Ger.
50 C2 **Amadeus, Lake** *salt flat* Austr.
127 H2 **Amadjuak Lake** Can.
106 B2 **Amadora** Port.
78 B2 **Amāʻir** Saudi Arabia
67 B4 **Amakusa-Shimo-shima** *i.* Japan
93 F4 **Åmål** Sweden
111 B3 **Amaliada** Greece
59 D3 **Amamapare** Indon.
154 A2 **Amambaí** Brazil
154 B2 **Amambaí** *r.* Brazil
154 A2 **Amambaí, Serra de** *hills* Brazil/Para.
69 E3 **Amami-Ō-shima** *i.* Japan
69 E3 **Amami-shotō** *is* Japan
77 C1 **Amangel'dy** Kazakh.
109 C3 **Amantea** Italy
123 D3 **Amanzimtoti** S. Africa
151 D2 **Amapá** Brazil
106 B2 **Amareleja** Port.
88 B2 **Ämari** Estonia
143 C1 **Amarillo** U.S.A.
108 B2 **Amaro, Monte** *mt.* Italy
80 B1 **Amasya** Turkey
150 D2 **Amazon** *r.* S. America
151 E2 **Amazon, Mouths of the** Brazil
Amazonas *r.* S. America *see* **Amazon**
157 I5 **Amazon Cone** *sea feature* S. Atlantic Ocean
74 B1 **Ambala** India
121 □D3 **Ambalavao** Madag.
121 □D2 **Ambanja** Madag.
104 B3 **Ambarès-et-Lagarve** France
150 B3 **Ambato** Ecuador
121 □D2 **Ambato Boeny** Madag.
121 □D3 **Ambato Finandrahana** Madag.
121 □D2 **Ambatolampy** Madag.
121 □D2 **Ambatondrazaka** Madag.
101 E3 **Amberg** Ger.
146 B3 **Ambergris Cay** *i.* Belize
75 C2 **Ambikapur** India
121 □D2 **Ambilobe** Madag.
98 C2 **Amble** U.K.
98 B2 **Ambleside** U.K.
121 □D3 **Amboasary** Madag.
121 □D2 **Ambodifotatra** Madag.
121 □D2 **Ambohidratrimo** Madag.
121 □D3 **Ambohimahasoa** Madag.
Amboina Indon. *see* **Ambon**
59 C3 **Ambon** Indon.
59 C3 **Ambon** *i.* Indon.
121 □D3 **Ambositra** Madag.
121 □D3 **Ambovombe** Madag.
135 C4 **Amboy** U.S.A.
Ambre, Cap d' *c.* Madag. *see* **Bobaomby, Tanjona**
120 A1 **Ambriz** Angola
Ambrizete Angola *see* **N'zeto**
86 F2 **Amderma** Rus. Fed.
Amdo China *see* **Lharigarbo**
145 B2 **Amealco** Mex.
144 B2 **Ameca** Mex.
100 B1 **Ameland** *i.* Neth.
154 C2 **Americana** Brazil
55 D4 **American-Antarctic Ridge** *sea feature* S. Atlantic Ocean
134 D2 **American Falls** U.S.A.
134 D2 **American Falls Reservoir** U.S.A.
135 D2 **American Fork** U.S.A.
49 J5 **American Samoa** *terr.* S. Pacific Ocean
141 D2 **Americus** U.S.A.
100 B1 **Amersfoort** Neth.
55 H2 **Amery Ice Shelf** Antarctica
137 E2 **Ames** U.S.A.
111 B3 **Amfissa** Greece
83 J2 **Amga** Rus. Fed.
66 C1 **Amgu** Rus. Fed.
115 C2 **Amguid** Alg.
83 K3 **Amgun'** *r.* Rus. Fed.
131 D3 **Amherst** Can.
104 C2 **Amiens** France
79 C3 **Amilḥayt, Wādī al** *r.* Oman
73 B3 **Amindivi Islands** India
122 A1 **Aminuis** Namibia
74 A2 **Amir Chah** Pak.
129 D2 **Amisk Lake** Can.
143 C3 **Amistad Reservoir** Mex./U.S.A.
98 A3 **Amlwch** U.K.
80 B2 **ʻAmmān** Jordan
127 J2 **Ammassalik** Greenland
78 B3 **Am Nābiyah** Yemen
81 D2 **Amol** Iran
111 C3 **Amorgos** *i.* Greece
140 C2 **Amory** U.S.A.
130 C3 **Amos** Can.
Amoy China *see* **Xiamen**
121 □D3 **Ampanihy** Madag.
155 C2 **Amparo** Brazil
121 □D2 **Ampasimanolotra** Madag.
107 D1 **Amposta** Spain
78 B3 **Amrān** Yemen
Amraoti India *see* **Amravati**
74 B2 **Amravati** India
74 B2 **Amreli** India
74 B1 **Amritsar** India
100 B1 **Amstelveen** Neth.
100 B1 **Amsterdam** Neth.
123 D2 **Amsterdam** S. Africa
156 A8 **Amsterdam, Île** *i.* Indian Ocean
103 C2 **Amstetten** Austria
115 E3 **Am Timan** Chad
76 B2 **Amudar'ya** *r.* Asia
126 F1 **Amund Ringnes Island** Can.
55 J3 **Amundsen, Mount** Antarctica
160 H1 **Amundsen Basin** *sea feature* Arctic Ocean
126 D2 **Amundsen Gulf** Can.
55 P2 **Amundsen Ridge** *sea feature* Southern Ocean
55 P2 **Amundsen Sea** Antarctica
61 C2 **Amuntai** Indon.
Amur *r.* China/Rus. Fed. *see* **Heilong Jiang**
78 A3 **ʻAmur, Wadi** *watercourse* Sudan
61 D2 **Anabanua** Indon.
83 I2 **Anabar** *r.* Rus. Fed.
83 I2 **Anabarskiy Zaliv** *b.* Rus. Fed.
150 C2 **Anaco** Venez.
134 D1 **Anaconda** U.S.A.
134 B1 **Anacortes** U.S.A.
143 D1 **Anadarko** U.S.A.
80 B1 **Anadolu Dağları** *mts* Turkey
83 M2 **Anadyr'** Rus. Fed.
83 M2 **Anadyr'** *r.* Rus. Fed.
81 C2 **ʻĀnah** Iraq
145 B2 **Anáhuac** Mex.
73 B3 **Anai Mudi Peak** India
121 □D2 **Analalava** Madag.
121 □D3 **Analavelona** *mts* Madag.
60 B1 **Anambas, Kepulauan** *is* Indon.
137 E2 **Anamosa** U.S.A.
80 B2 **Anamur** Turkey
67 B4 **Anan** Japan
73 B3 **Anantapur** India
74 B1 **Anantnag** Jammu and Kashmir
90 B2 **Anan'yiv** Ukr.
91 D3 **Anapa** Rus. Fed.
154 C1 **Anápolis** Brazil
81 D2 **Anār** Iran
152 B2 **Añatuya** Arg.
65 B2 **Anbyon** N. Korea
104 B2 **Ancenis** France
126 C2 **Anchorage** U.S.A.
108 B2 **Ancona** Italy
153 A4 **Ancud** Chile
Anda China *see* **Daqing**
93 E3 **Åndalsnes** Norway
106 C2 **Andalucía** *reg.* Spain
Andalusia *reg.* Spain *see* **Andalucía**
140 C2 **Andalusia** U.S.A.
159 F3 **Andaman Basin** *sea feature* Indian Ocean
73 D3 **Andaman Islands** India
63 A2 **Andaman Sea** Indian Ocean
121 □D2 **Andapa** Madag.
100 B2 **Andelst** Neth.
92 G2 **Andenes** Norway
100 B2 **Andenne** Belgium
100 B2 **Anderlecht** Belgium
105 D2 **Andermatt** Switz.
126 D2 **Anderson** *r.* Can.
126 C2 **Anderson** *AK* U.S.A.
138 B2 **Anderson** *IN* U.S.A.
141 D2 **Anderson** *SC* U.S.A.
148 C3 **Andes** *mts* S. America
77 D2 **Andijon** Uzbek.
121 □D2 **Andilamena** Madag.
121 □D2 **Andilanatoby** Madag.
Andizhan Uzbek. *see* **Andijon**
74 A1 **Andkhvoy** Afgh.
121 □D2 **Andoany** Madag.
Andong China *see* **Dandong**
65 B2 **Andong** S. Korea
104 C3 **Andorra** *country* Europe
104 C3 **Andorra la Vella** Andorra
99 C4 **Andover** U.K.
154 B2 **Andradina** Brazil
89 D2 **Andreapol'** Rus. Fed.
155 D2 **Andrelândia** Brazil
143 C2 **Andrews** U.S.A.
109 C2 **Andria** Italy
121 □D3 **Androka** Madag.
Andropov Rus. Fed. *see* **Rybinsk**
146 C2 **Andros** *i.* Bahamas
111 B3 **Andros** Greece
111 B3 **Andros** *i.* Greece
141 E4 **Andros Town** Bahamas
73 B3 **Andrott** *i.* India
90 B1 **Andrushivka** Ukr.
92 G2 **Andselv** Norway
106 C2 **Andújar** Spain
120 A2 **Andulo** Angola
114 C3 **Anéfis** Mali
147 D3 **Anegada Passage** Virgin Is (U.K.)
114 C4 **Aného** Togo
107 D1 **Aneto** *mt.* Spain
115 D3 **Aney** Niger
83 H3 **Angara** *r.* Rus. Fed.
68 C1 **Angarsk** Rus. Fed.
93 G3 **Ånge** Sweden
Angel, Salto del *waterfall* Venez. *see* **Angel Falls**
144 A2 **Ángel de la Guarda, Isla** *i.* Mex.
64 B2 **Angeles** Phil.
150 C2 **Angel Falls** Venez.
93 F4 **Ängelholm** Sweden
92 G3 **Ångermanälven** *r.* Sweden
104 B2 **Angers** France
129 E1 **Angikuni Lake** Can.
52 B3 **Anglesea** Austr.
98 A3 **Anglesey** *i.* U.K.
121 C2 **Angoche** Moz.
79 C2 **Angohrān** Iran
120 A2 **Angola** *country* Africa
138 C2 **Angola** U.S.A.
158 F6 **Angola Basin** *sea feature* S. Atlantic Ocean
128 A2 **Angoon** U.S.A.
104 C2 **Angoulême** France
155 D2 **Angra dos Reis** Brazil
77 D2 **Angren** Uzbek.
147 D3 **Anguilla** *terr.* West Indies
75 C2 **Angul** India
93 F4 **Anholt** *i.* Denmark
71 B3 **Anhua** China
70 B2 **Anhui** *prov.* China
154 B1 **Anhumas** Brazil
Anhwei *prov.* China *see* **Anhui**
154 C1 **Anicuns** Brazil
66 D1 **Aniva, Mys** *c.* Rus. Fed.
66 D1 **Aniva, Zaliv** *b.* Rus. Fed.
88 C1 **Anjalankoski** Fin.
104 B2 **Anjou** *reg.* France
65 B2 **Anjŭ** N. Korea
70 A2 **Ankang** China
80 B2 **Ankara** Turkey
121 □D3 **Ankazoabo** Madag.
121 □D2 **Ankazobe** Madag.
137 E2 **Ankeny** U.S.A.
102 C1 **Anklam** Ger.
121 □D2 **Ankofa** *mt.* Madag.
70 B2 **Anlu** China
55 G3 **Ann, Cape** Antarctica
139 E2 **Ann, Cape** U.S.A.
89 F3 **Anna** Rus. Fed.
115 C1 **Annaba** Alg.
101 F2 **Annaberg-Buchholtz** Ger.
80 B2 **An Nabk** Syria
78 B2 **An Nafūd** *des.* Saudi Arabia
150 D2 **Annai** Guyana
81 C2 **An Najaf** Iraq
63 B2 **Annam Highlands** *mts* Laos/Vietnam
96 C3 **Annan** U.K.
139 D3 **Annapolis** U.S.A.
75 C2 **Annapurna I** *mt.* Jammu and Kashmir/Nepal
138 C2 **Ann Arbor** U.S.A.
150 D2 **Anna Regina** Guyana
An Nás Rep. of Ireland *see* **Naas**
81 C2 **An Nāṣirīyah** Iraq
115 D1 **An Nawfalīyah** Libya
105 D2 **Annecy** France
78 B3 **An Nimāṣ** Saudi Arabia
71 A3 **Anning** China
140 C2 **Anniston** U.S.A.
105 C2 **Annonay** France
79 B2 **An Nuʻayrīyah** Saudi Arabia
121 □D2 **Anorontany, Tanjona** *hd* Madag.
111 C3 **Ano Viannos** Greece
71 B3 **Anpu** China
70 B2 **Anqing** China
65 B2 **Ansan** S. Korea
101 E3 **Ansbach** Ger.
70 C1 **Anshan** China
71 A3 **Anshun** China

78 A1 **An Sirhān, Wādī** *watercourse* Saudi Arabia
143 D2 **Anson** U.S.A.
114 C3 **Ansongo** Mali
96 C2 **Anstruther** U.K.
150 B4 **Antabamba** Peru
80 B2 **Antakya** Turkey
121 □E2 **Antalaha** Madag.
80 B2 **Antalya** Turkey
80 B2 **Antalya Körfezi** *g.* Turkey
121 □D2 **Antananarivo** Madag.
55 A2 **Antarctic Peninsula** Antarctica
96 B2 **An Teallach** *mt.* U.K.
106 C2 **Antequera** Spain
142 B2 **Anthony** U.S.A.
114 B2 **Anti Atlas** *mts* Morocco
105 D3 **Antibes** France
131 D3 **Anticosti, Île d'** *i.* Can.
131 D3 **Antigonish** Can.
147 D3 **Antigua** *i.* Antigua
147 D3 **Antigua and Barbuda** *country* West Indies
145 C2 **Antiguo-Morelos** Mex.
111 B3 **Antikythira** *i.* Greece
Antioch Turkey *see* **Antakya**
49 I8 **Antipodes Islands** N.Z.
An t-Ob U.K. *see* **Leverburgh**
152 A2 **Antofagasta** Chile
154 C3 **Antonina** Brazil
António Enes Moz. *see* **Angoche**
97 C1 **Antrim** U.K.
97 C1 **Antrim Hills** U.K.
121 □D2 **Antsalova** Madag.
Antseranana Madag. *see* **Antsirañana**
121 □D2 **Antsirabe** Madag.
121 □D2 **Antsirañana** Madag.
121 □D2 **Antsohihy** Madag.
100 B2 **Antwerp** Belgium
Antwerpen Belgium *see* **Antwerp**
An Uaimh Rep. of Ireland *see* **Navan**
74 B2 **Anupgarh** India
73 C4 **Anuradhapura** Sri Lanka
Anvers Belgium *see* **Antwerp**
68 C2 **Anxi** China
51 C3 **Anxious Bay** Austr.
70 B2 **Anyang** China
65 B2 **Anyang** S. Korea
108 B2 **Anzio** Italy
67 C4 **Aoga-shima** *i.* Japan
66 D2 **Aomori** Japan
54 B2 **Aoraki** N.Z.
108 A1 **Aosta** Italy
114 B2 **Aoukâr** *reg.* Mali/Maur.
114 C2 **Aoulef** Alg.
115 D2 **Aozou** Chad
141 D3 **Apalachee Bay** U.S.A.
150 C3 **Apaporis** *r.* Col.
154 B2 **Aparecida do Tabuado** Brazil
64 B2 **Aparri** Phil.
86 C2 **Apatity** Rus. Fed.
144 B3 **Apatzingán** Mex.
100 B1 **Apeldoorn** Neth.
100 C1 **Apen** Ger.
108 A2 **Apennines** *mts* Italy
49 J5 **Apia** Samoa
154 C2 **Apiaí** Brazil
64 B3 **Apo, Mount** *vol.* Phil.
101 E2 **Apolda** Ger.
52 B3 **Apollo Bay** Austr.
141 D3 **Apopka** U.S.A.
141 D3 **Apopka, Lake** U.S.A.
154 B1 **Aporé** Brazil
154 B1 **Aporé** *r.* Brazil
138 A1 **Apostle Islands** U.S.A.
80 B2 **Apostolos Andreas, Cape** Cyprus
91 C2 **Apostolove** Ukr.
133 F3 **Appalachian Mountains** U.S.A.
Appennino *mts* Italy *see* **Apennines**
53 D2 **Appin** Austr.
100 C1 **Appingedam** Neth.
98 B2 **Appleby-in-Westmorland** U.K.
138 B2 **Appleton** U.S.A.
108 B2 **Aprilia** Italy
62 A1 **Aprunyi** India
91 D3 **Apsheronsk** Rus. Fed.
Apsheronskaya Rus. Fed. *see* **Apsheronsk**
154 B2 **Apucarana** Brazil
154 B2 **Apucarana, Serra da** *hills* Brazil
64 A3 **Apurahuan** Phil.
147 D4 **Apure** *r.* Venez.
78 A2 **Aqaba, Gulf of** Asia
81 D2 **'Aqdā** Iran
75 C1 **Aqqikkol Hu** *salt l.* China
154 A1 **Aquidauana** *r.* Brazil
104 B3 **Aquitaine** *reg.* France
75 C2 **Ara** India
117 A4 **Arab, Bahr el** *watercourse* Sudan
78 B2 **Arabian Peninsula** Saudi Arabia
56 B4 **Arabian Sea** Indian Ocean
151 F4 **Aracaju** Brazil
154 A2 **Aracanguy, Montes de** *hills* Para.
151 F3 **Aracati** Brazil
154 B2 **Araçatuba** Brazil
155 D1 **Aracruz** Brazil
155 D1 **Araçuaí** Brazil
110 B1 **Arad** Romania
115 E3 **Arada** Chad
79 C2 **'Arādah** U.A.E.
59 C3 **Arafura Sea** Austr./Indon.
154 B1 **Aragarças** Brazil
107 C1 **Aragón** *r.* Spain
107 C1 **Aragón** *reg.* Spain
151 E3 **Araguaia** *r.* Brazil
154 B1 **Araguaiana** Brazil
151 E3 **Araguaína** Brazil
154 C1 **Araguari** Brazil
67 C3 **Arai** Japan
115 C2 **Arak** Alg.
81 C2 **Arāk** Iran
62 A1 **Arakan Yoma** *mts* Myanmar
81 C1 **Arak's** *r.* Armenia/Turkey
76 C2 **Aral Sea** *salt l.* Kazakh./Uzbek.
76 C2 **Aral'sk** Kazakh.
Aral'skoye More *salt l.* Kazakh./Uzbek. *see* **Aral Sea**
106 C1 **Aranda de Duero** Spain
109 D2 **Aranđelovac** Serb. and Mont.
97 B1 **Aran Island** Rep. of Ireland
97 B2 **Aran Islands** Rep. of Ireland
106 C1 **Aranjuez** Spain
122 A1 **Aranos** Namibia
143 D3 **Aransas Pass** U.S.A.
67 B4 **Arao** Japan
114 B3 **Araouane** Mali
151 F3 **Arapiraca** Brazil
154 B2 **Arapongas** Brazil
154 C3 **Araquari** Brazil
78 B1 **'Ar'ar** Saudi Arabia
154 C2 **Araraquara** Brazil
151 D3 **Araras** Brazil
154 C2 **Araras** Brazil
154 B1 **Araras, Serra das** *hills* Brazil
154 B3 **Araras, Serra das** *mts* Brazil
81 C2 **Ararat** Armenia
52 B3 **Ararat** Austr.
81 C2 **Ararat, Mount** Turkey
155 D2 **Araruama, Lago de** *lag.* Brazil
155 E1 **Arataca** Brazil
Aratürük China *see* **Yiwu**
150 B2 **Arauca** Col.
154 C1 **Araxá** Brazil
81 C2 **Arbīl** Iraq
129 E2 **Arborg** Can.
96 C2 **Arbroath** U.K.
74 A2 **Arbu Lut, Dasht-e** *des.* Afgh.
104 B3 **Arcachon** France
141 D3 **Arcadia** U.S.A.
134 B2 **Arcata** U.S.A.
145 B3 **Arcelia** Mex.
86 D2 **Archangel** Rus. Fed.
51 D1 **Archer** *r.* Austr.
49 M5 **Archipel des Tuamotu** *is* Fr. Polynesia
149 B6 **Archipiélago Juan Fernández** S. Pacific Ocean
134 D2 **Arco** U.S.A.
106 B2 **Arcos de la Frontera** Spain
127 G2 **Arctic Bay** Can.
Arctic Institute Islands Rus. Fed. *see* **Arkticheskogo Instituta, Ostrova**
160 J1 **Arctic Mid-Ocean Ridge** *sea feature* Arctic Ocean
160 **Arctic Ocean**
126 D2 **Arctic Red** *r.* Can.
81 C2 **Ardabīl** Iran
81 C1 **Ardahan** Turkey
93 E3 **Årdalstangen** Norway
97 C2 **Ardee** Rep. of Ireland
100 B3 **Ardennes** *plat.* Belgium
135 B3 **Arden Town** U.S.A.
81 D2 **Ardestān** Iran
97 D1 **Ardglass** U.K.
53 C2 **Ardlethan** Austr.
143 D2 **Ardmore** U.S.A.
96 A2 **Ardnamurchan, Point of** U.K.
52 A2 **Ardrossan** Austr.
96 B3 **Ardrossan** U.K.
96 B2 **Ardvasar** U.K.
135 B3 **Arena, Point** U.S.A.
93 E4 **Arendal** Norway
100 B2 **Arendonk** Belgium
101 E1 **Arendsee (Altmark)** Ger.
150 B4 **Arequipa** Peru
151 D3 **Arere** Brazil
106 C1 **Arévalo** Spain
108 B2 **Arezzo** Italy
108 B2 **Argenta** Italy
104 B2 **Argentan** France
153 B4 **Argentina** *country* S. America
158 D7 **Argentine Basin** *sea feature* S. Atlantic Ocean
157 I8 **Argentine Rise** *sea feature* S. Atlantic Ocean
153 A5 **Argentino, Lago** *l.* Arg.
104 C2 **Argenton-sur-Creuse** France
110 C2 **Argeș** *r.* Romania
74 A1 **Arghandab** *r.* Afgh.
111 B3 **Argolikos Kolpos** *b.* Greece
111 B3 **Argos** Greece
111 B3 **Argostoli** Greece
107 C1 **Arguís** Spain
69 E1 **Argun'** *r.* China/Rus. Fed.
131 D3 **Argyle** Can.
50 B1 **Argyle, Lake** Austr.
Argyrokastron Albania *see* **Gjirokastër**
Ar Horqin Qi China *see* **Tianshan**
93 F4 **Århus** Denmark
122 A2 **Ariamsvlei** Namibia
152 A1 **Arica** Chile
96 A2 **Arinagour** U.K.
155 C1 **Arinos** Brazil
150 D4 **Aripuanã** Brazil
150 C3 **Aripuanã** *r.* Brazil
150 C3 **Ariquemes** Brazil
154 B1 **Ariranhá** *r.* Brazil
96 B2 **Arisaig** U.K.
96 B2 **Arisaig, Sound of** *sea chan.* U.K.
104 B3 **Arizgoiti** Spain
142 A2 **Arizona** *state* U.S.A.
144 A1 **Arizpe** Mex.
78 B2 **'Arjah** Saudi Arabia
61 C2 **Arjasa** Indon.
92 G2 **Arjeplog** Sweden
140 B2 **Arkadelphia** U.S.A.
77 C1 **Arkalyk** Kazakh.
140 B2 **Arkansas** *r.* U.S.A.
140 B1 **Arkansas** *state* U.S.A.
137 D3 **Arkansas City** U.S.A.
Arkhangel'sk Rus. Fed. *see* **Archangel**
97 C2 **Arklow** Rep. of Ireland
102 C1 **Arkona, Kap** *c.* Ger.
82 G1 **Arkticheskogo Instituta, Ostrova** *is* Rus. Fed.
105 C3 **Arles** France
143 D2 **Arlington** U.S.A.
138 B2 **Arlington Heights** U.S.A.
115 C3 **Arlit** Niger
100 B3 **Arlon** Belgium
97 C1 **Armagh** U.K.
116 B2 **Armant** Egypt
87 D4 **Armavir** Rus. Fed.
81 C1 **Armenia** *country* Asia
150 B2 **Armenia** Col.
Armenopolis Romania *see* **Gherla**
144 B3 **Armeria** Mex.
53 D2 **Armidale** Austr.
134 D1 **Armington** U.S.A.
130 B2 **Armstrong** Can.
91 C2 **Armyans'k** Ukr.
Armyanskaya S.S.R. *admin. reg.* Asia *see* **Armenia**
Arnaoutis, Cape Cyprus *see* **Arnauti, Cape**
130 D2 **Arnaud** *r.* Can.
80 B2 **Arnauti, Cape** Cyprus
100 B2 **Arnhem** Neth.
51 C1 **Arnhem, Cape** Austr.
51 C1 **Arnhem Bay** Austr.
51 C1 **Arnhem Land** *reg.* Austr.
108 B2 **Arno** *r.* Italy
52 A2 **Arno Bay** Austr.
130 C3 **Arnprior** Can.
101 D2 **Arnsberg** Ger.
101 E2 **Arnstadt** Ger.
122 A2 **Aroab** Namibia
154 B2 **Aroeira** Brazil
101 D2 **Arolsen** Ger.
78 A3 **Aroma** Sudan
108 A1 **Arona** Italy
144 B2 **Aros** *r.* Mex.
Arquipélago dos Açores *aut. reg.* N. Atlantic Ocean *see* **Azores**
Arrah India *see* **Ara**
81 C2 **Ar Ramādī** Iraq
96 B3 **Arran** *i.* U.K.
80 B2 **Ar Raqqah** Syria
105 C1 **Arras** France
78 B2 **Ar Rass** Saudi Arabia
79 C2 **Ar Rayyān** Qatar
150 C2 **Arrecifal** Col.
145 C3 **Arriagá** Mex.
79 C2 **Ar Rimāl** *reg.* Saudi Arabia
Ar Riyāḍ Saudi Arabia *see* **Riyadh**
54 A2 **Arrowtown** N.Z.
135 B3 **Arroyo Grande** U.S.A.
145 C2 **Arroyo Seco** Mex.
79 C2 **Ar Rustāq** Oman
81 C2 **Ar Ruṭbah** Iraq
78 B2 **Ar Ruwayḍah** Saudi Arabia
81 D3 **Arsenajān** Iran
66 B2 **Arsen'yev** Rus. Fed.
111 B3 **Arta** Greece
144 B3 **Arteaga** Mex.
66 B2 **Artem** Rus. Fed.
91 D2 **Artemivs'k** Ukr.
104 C2 **Artenay** France
142 C2 **Artesia** U.S.A.
51 E2 **Arthur Point** Austr.
54 B2 **Arthur's Pass** N.Z.
152 C3 **Artigas** Uru.
129 D1 **Artillery Lake** Can.
123 C1 **Artisia** Botswana
104 C1 **Artois** *reg.* France
90 B2 **Artsyz** Ukr.
Artur de Paiva Angola *see* **Kuvango**
77 D3 **Artux** China
81 C1 **Artvin** Turkey
59 C3 **Aru, Kepulauan** *is* Indon.
119 D2 **Arua** Uganda
147 D3 **Aruba** *terr.* West Indies
75 C2 **Arun** *r.* Nepal
119 D3 **Arusha** Tanz.
136 B3 **Arvada** U.S.A.
68 C1 **Arvayheer** Mongolia
129 E1 **Arviat** Can.
92 G2 **Arvidsjaur** Sweden
93 F4 **Arvika** Sweden
108 A2 **Arzachena** *Sardinia* Italy
87 D3 **Arzamas** Rus. Fed.
107 C2 **Arzew** Alg.
100 C2 **Arzfeld** Ger.
Arzila Morocco *see* **Asilah**
101 F2 **Aš** Czech Rep.
115 C4 **Asaba** Nigeria
66 D2 **Asahi-dake** *vol.* Japan
66 D2 **Asahikawa** Japan
78 B3 **Āsalē** *l.* Eth.
75 C2 **Asansol** India
117 C3 **Āsayita** Eth.
130 C3 **Asbestos** Can.
122 B2 **Asbestos Mountains** S. Africa
119 E2 **Āsbe Teferi** Eth.
109 C2 **Ascea** Italy
152 B1 **Ascensión** Bol.
113 B6 **Ascension** *i.* S. Atlantic Ocean
145 D3 **Ascensión, Bahía de la** *b.* Mex.
101 D3 **Aschaffenburg** Ger.
100 C2 **Ascheberg** Ger.
101 E2 **Aschersleben** Ger.
108 B2 **Ascoli Piceno** Italy
119 D2 **Āsela** Eth.
92 G3 **Åsele** Sweden

111 B2 Asenovgrad Bulg.
78 B2 Asharat Saudi Arabia
50 A2 Ashburton watercourse Austr.
54 B2 Ashburton N.Z.
140 B2 Ashdown U.S.A.
141 D1 Asheville U.S.A.
53 D1 Ashford Austr.
97 C2 Ashford Rep. of Ireland
99 D4 Ashford U.K.
76 B3 Ashgabat Turkm.
66 D2 Ashibetsu Japan
98 C2 Ashington U.K.
67 B4 Ashizuri-misaki pt Japan
Ashkhabad Turkm. see Ashgabat
136 D3 Ashland KS U.S.A.
138 C3 Ashland KY U.S.A.
138 C2 Ashland OH U.S.A.
134 B2 Ashland OR U.S.A.
138 A1 Ashland WI U.S.A.
53 C1 Ashley Austr.
88 C3 Ashmyany Belarus
66 D2 Ashoro Japan
81 C2 Ash Shabakah Iraq
78 B3 Ash Sharawrah Saudi Arabia
Ash Shāriqah U.A.E. see Sharjah
81 C2 Ash Sharqāt Iraq
81 C2 Ash Shaṭrah Iraq
78 B3 Ash Shaykh 'Uthman Yemen
79 B3 Ash Shiḥr Yemen
79 C2 Ash Shināş Oman
78 B2 Ash Shu'aybah Saudi Arabia
78 B2 Ash Shu'bah Saudi Arabia
78 B2 Ash Shubaykīyah Saudi Arabia
78 B2 Ash Shumlūl Saudi Arabia
78 B3 Ash Shuqayq Saudi Arabia
115 D2 Ash Shuwayrif Libya
138 C2 Ashtabula U.S.A.
131 D2 Ashuanipi Lake Can.
75 B3 Asifabad India
106 B2 Asilah Morocco
108 A2 Asinara, Golfo dell' b. Sardinia Italy
108 A2 Asinara, Isola i. Sardinia Italy
82 G3 Asino Rus. Fed.
88 C3 Asipovichy Belarus
78 B2 'Asir reg. Saudi Arabia
93 F4 Asker Norway
93 F4 Askim Norway
68 C1 Askiz Rus. Fed.
116 B3 Asmara Eritrea
93 F4 Åsnen l. Sweden
116 B2 Asoteriba, Jebel mt. Sudan
103 D2 Aspang-Markt Austria
136 B3 Aspen U.S.A.
143 C2 Aspermont U.S.A.
54 A2 Aspiring, Mount N.Z.
116 C3 Assab Eritrea
78 B3 Aş Şahif Saudi Arabia
Aş Şahrā' al Gharbīyah des. Egypt see Western Desert
Aş Şahrā' ash Sharqīyah des. Egypt see Eastern Desert
78 B2 As Salamīyah Saudi Arabia
116 A1 As Sallūm Egypt
75 D2 Assam state India
81 C2 As Samāwah Iraq
79 C2 Aş Şanām reg. Saudi Arabia
115 E2 As Sarīr reg. Libya
108 A3 Assemini Sardinia Italy
100 C1 Assen Neth.
100 B2 Assesse Belgium
115 D1 As Sidrah Libya
129 D3 Assiniboia Can.
128 C2 Assiniboine, Mount Can.
154 B2 Assis Brazil
78 B2 Aş Şubayḥīyah Kuwait
81 C2 As Sulaymānīyah Iraq
78 B2 As Sulaymī Saudi Arabia
78 B2 As Sulayyil Saudi Arabia
78 B2 As Sūq Saudi Arabia
80 B2 As Suwaydā' Syria
79 C2 As Suwayq Oman
As Suways Egypt see Suez
111 B3 Astakos Greece
77 D1 Astana Kazakh.
81 C2 Āstārā Iran
100 B2 Asten Neth.

Asterabad Iran see Gorgān
108 A2 Asti Italy
74 B1 Astor Jammu and Kashmir
72 B1 Astor Jammu and Kashmir
106 B1 Astorga Spain
134 B1 Astoria U.S.A.
Astrabad Iran see Gorgān
87 D4 Astrakhan' Rus. Fed.
Astrakhan' Bazar Azer. see Cälilabad
88 C3 Astravyets Belarus
Astrida Rwanda see Butare
106 B1 Asturias reg. Spain
111 C3 Astypalaia i. Greece
152 C2 Asunción Para.
116 B2 Aswân Egypt
116 B2 Asyūṭ Egypt
Atacama, Desierto de des. Chile see Atacama Desert
152 B2 Atacama, Puna de plat. Arg.
152 B2 Atacama, Salar de salt flat Chile
152 B2 Atacama Desert des. Chile
114 C4 Atakpamé Togo
111 B3 Atalanti Greece
150 B4 Atalaya Peru
155 D1 Ataléia Brazil
77 C3 Atamyrat Turkm.
78 B3 'Ataq Yemen
114 A2 Atâr Maur.
135 B3 Atascadero U.S.A.
77 D2 Atasu Kazakh.
116 B3 Atbara Sudan
116 B3 Atbara r. Sudan
77 C1 Atbasar Kazakh.
140 B3 Atchafalaya Bay U.S.A.
137 D3 Atchison U.S.A.
Aterno r. Italy
108 B2 Atessa Italy
100 A2 Ath Belgium
128 C2 Athabasca Can.
129 C2 Athabasca r. Can.
129 D2 Athabasca, Lake Can.
97 C2 Athboy Rep. of Ireland
97 B2 Athenry Rep. of Ireland
111 B3 Athens Greece
140 C2 Athens AL U.S.A.
141 D2 Athens GA U.S.A.
138 C3 Athens OH U.S.A.
141 D1 Athens TN U.S.A.
143 D2 Athens TX U.S.A.
51 D1 Atherton Austr.
Athina Greece see Athens
97 C2 Athlone Rep. of Ireland
111 B3 Athos mt. Greece
97 C2 Athy Rep. of Ireland
115 D3 Ati Chad
130 A3 Atikokan Can.
87 D4 Atkarsk Rus. Fed.
141 D2 Atlanta U.S.A.
137 D2 Atlantic U.S.A.
141 D2 Atlantic Beach U.S.A.
139 E3 Atlantic City U.S.A.
55 D3 Atlantic-Indian-Antarctic Basin sea feature S. Atlantic Ocean
158 E8 Atlantic-Indian Ridge sea feature Southern Ocean
158 Atlantic Ocean
122 A3 Atlantis S. Africa
114 B1 Atlas Mountains Africa
114 C1 Atlas Saharien mts Alg.
128 A2 Atlin Can.
128 A2 Atlin Lake Can.
140 B2 Atmore U.S.A.
152 B2 Atocha Bol.
143 D2 Atoka U.S.A.
75 C2 Atrai r. India
80 B2 Aṭ Ṭafilah Jordan
78 B2 Aṭ Ṭā'if Saudi Arabia
63 B2 Attapu Laos
111 C3 Attavyros mt. Greece
130 B2 Attawapiskat Can.
130 B2 Attawapiskat r. Can.
130 B2 Attawapiskat Lake Can.
100 C2 Attendorn Ger.
100 A3 Attichy France
116 B2 Aṭ Ṭūr Egypt
78 B3 Aṭ Ṭurbah Yemen
135 B3 Atwater U.S.A.
76 B2 Atyrau Kazakh.
105 D3 Aubagne France
105 C3 Aubenas France

126 D2 Aubry Lake Can.
140 C2 Auburn AL U.S.A.
135 B3 Auburn CA U.S.A.
138 B2 Auburn IN U.S.A.
139 E2 Auburn ME U.S.A.
137 D2 Auburn NE U.S.A.
139 D2 Auburn NY U.S.A.
104 C2 Aubusson France
104 C3 Auch France
54 B1 Auckland N.Z.
48 H9 Auckland Islands N.Z.
117 C4 Audo Range mts Eth.
101 F2 Aue Ger.
101 F2 Auerbach Ger.
102 C2 Augsburg Ger.
50 A3 Augusta Austr.
109 C3 Augusta Sicily Italy
141 D2 Augusta GA U.S.A.
137 D3 Augusta KS U.S.A.
139 F2 Augusta ME U.S.A.
155 D1 Augusto de Lima Brazil
103 E1 Augustów Pol.
50 A2 Augustus, Mount Austr.
100 A2 Aulnoye-Aymeries France
Aumale Alg. see Sour el Ghozlane
62 A2 Aunglan Myanmar
122 B2 Auob watercourse Namibia/S. Africa
131 D2 Aupaluk Can.
74 B3 Aurangabad India
104 B2 Auray France
100 C1 Aurich Ger.
154 B1 Aurilândia Brazil
104 C3 Aurillac France
136 C3 Aurora CO U.S.A.
138 B2 Aurora IL U.S.A.
137 E3 Aurora MO U.S.A.
137 D2 Aurora NE U.S.A.
122 A2 Aus Namibia
138 C2 Au Sable r. U.S.A.
137 E2 Austin MN U.S.A.
135 C3 Austin NV U.S.A.
143 D2 Austin TX U.S.A.
Australes, Îles is Fr. Polynesia see Tubuai Islands
50 B2 Australia country Oceania
55 K4 Australian-Antarctic Basin sea feature Southern Ocean
53 C3 Australian Capital Territory admin. div. Austr.
102 C2 Austria country Europe
150 D3 Autazes Brazil
144 B3 Autlán Mex.
105 C2 Autun France
104 C3 Auvergne reg. France
105 C2 Auvergne, Monts d' mts France
105 C2 Auxerre France
105 C2 Auxonne France
105 C2 Avallon France
131 E3 Avalon Peninsula Can.
154 C2 Avaré Brazil
91 D2 Avdiyivka Ukr.
106 B1 Aveiro Port.
109 B2 Avellino Italy
108 B2 Aversa Italy
100 A2 Avesnes-sur-Helpe France
93 G3 Avesta Sweden
104 C3 Aveyron r. France
108 B2 Avezzano Italy
96 C2 Aviemore U.K.
109 C2 Avigliano Italy
105 C3 Avignon France
106 C1 Avila Spain
106 B1 Avilés Spain
52 B3 Avoca Austr.
139 D2 Avoca U.S.A.
109 C3 Avola Sicily Italy
99 C4 Avon r. England U.K.
99 B4 Avon r. England U.K.
99 B3 Avon r. England U.K.
142 A2 Avondale U.S.A.
104 B2 Avranches France
54 B1 Awanui N.Z.
117 C4 Āwash Eth.
117 C4 Āwash r. Eth.
115 D2 Awbārī Libya
117 C4 Aw Dheegle Somalia
96 B2 Awe, Loch l. U.K.
117 A4 Aweil Sudan
115 C4 Awka Nigeria
114 A2 Awserd Western Sahara
126 F1 Axel Heiberg Island Can.
114 B4 Axim Ghana
150 B4 Ayacucho Peru
77 E2 Ayagoz Kazakh.

Ayaguz Kazakh. see Ayagoz
68 B2 Ayakkum Hu salt l. China
106 B2 Ayamonte Spain
83 K3 Ayan Rus. Fed.
150 B4 Ayaviri Peru
74 A1 Āybak Afgh.
76 A2 Aybas Kazakh.
91 D2 Aydar r. Ukr.
77 C2 Aydarko'l ko'li l. Uzbek.
111 C3 Aydın Turkey
77 C2 Ayeat, Gora hill Kazakh.
Ayers Rock hill Austr. see Uluṟu
83 I2 Aykhal Rus. Fed.
99 C4 Aylesbury U.K.
106 C1 Ayllón Spain
129 D1 Aylmer Lake Can.
117 B4 Ayod Sudan
83 M2 Ayon, Ostrov i. Rus. Fed.
114 B3 'Ayoûn el 'Atroûs Maur.
51 D1 Ayr Austr.
96 B3 Ayr U.K.
98 A2 Ayre, Point of Isle of Man
76 C2 Ayteke Bi Kazakh.
110 C2 Aytos Bulg.
145 C3 Ayutla Mex.
63 B2 Ayutthaya Thai.
111 C3 Ayvacık Turkey
111 C3 Ayvalık Turkey
91 C3 Ayya, Mys pt Ukr.
114 B3 Azaouâd reg. Mali
114 C3 Azaouagh, Vallée de watercourse Mali/Niger
115 D3 Azare Nigeria
Azbine mts Niger see Aïr, Massif de l'
81 C1 Azerbaijan country Asia
Azerbaydzhanskaya S.S.R. admin. reg. Asia see Azerbaijan
150 B3 Azogues Ecuador
86 D2 Azopol'ye Rus. Fed.
112 A2 Azores aut. reg. N. Atlantic Ocean
91 D2 Azov Rus. Fed.
91 D2 Azov, Sea of Rus. Fed./Ukr.
Azraq, Bahr el r. Sudan see Blue Nile
106 B2 Azuaga Spain
146 B4 Azuero, Península de pen. Panama
153 C3 Azul Arg.
108 A3 Azzaba Alg.
78 B2 Az Zahrān Saudi Arabia see Dhahran
80 B2 Az Zaqāzīq Egypt
80 B2 Az Zarqā' Jordan
115 D1 Az Zāwiyah Libya
78 B3 Az Zaydīyah Yemen
114 C2 Azzel Matti, Sebkha salt pan Alg.
78 B2 Az Zilfī Saudi Arabia
78 B3 Az Zuqur i. Yemen

B

117 C4 Baardheere Somalia
77 C3 Bābā, Kūh-e mts Afgh.
111 C3 Baba Burnu pt Turkey
110 C2 Babadag Romania
111 C2 Babaeski Turkey
116 C3 Bāb al Mandab str. Africa/Asia
61 C2 Babana Indon.
119 C1 Babanusa Sudan
59 C3 Babar i. Indon.
119 D3 Babati Tanz.
89 E2 Babayevo Rus. Fed.
59 C2 Babeldaob i. Palau
128 B2 Babine r. Can.
128 B2 Babine Lake Can.
59 C3 Babo Indon.
81 D2 Bābol Iran
122 A3 Baboon Point S. Africa
88 C3 Babruysk Belarus
Babu China see Hezhou
64 B2 Babuyan i. Phil.
64 B2 Babuyan Channel Phil.
64 B2 Babuyan Islands Phil.
151 E3 Bacabal Brazil
145 D3 Bacalar Mex.
59 C3 Bacan i. Indon.
110 C1 Bacău Romania
52 B3 Bacchus Marsh Austr.
77 D3 Bachu China
129 E1 Back r. Can.

109 C1 **Bačka Palanka** Serb. and Mont.
109 C1 **Bačka Topola** Serb. and Mont.
52 A3 **Backstairs Passage** Austr.
62 B1 **Bac Lac** Vietnam
63 B3 **Bac Liêu** Vietnam
62 B1 **Băc Ninh** Vietnam
142 B3 **Bacobampo** Mex.
64 B2 **Bacolod** Phil.
130 C2 **Bacqueville, Lac** *l.* Can.
Bada China *see* **Xilin**
70 A1 **Badain Jaran Shamo** *des.* China
106 B2 **Badajoz** Spain
Badaojiang China *see* Baishan
75 D2 **Badarpur** India
101 E2 **Bad Berka** Ger.
101 D2 **Bad Berleburg** Ger.
101 E1 **Bad Bevensen** Ger.
101 D3 **Bad Dürkheim** Ger.
100 C2 **Bad Ems** Ger.
103 D2 **Baden** Austria
102 B2 **Baden-Baden** Ger.
101 E2 **Bad Harzburg** Ger.
101 D2 **Bad Hersfeld** Ger.
102 C2 **Bad Hofgastein** Austria
101 D2 **Bad Homburg vor der Höhe** Ger.
101 D1 **Bad Iburg** Ger.
74 A2 **Badin** Pak.
Bādiyat ash Shām *des.* Asia *see* **Syrian Desert**
101 E2 **Bad Kissingen** Ger.
100 C3 **Bad Kreuznach** Ger.
136 C1 **Badlands** *reg. ND* U.S.A.
136 C2 **Badlands** *reg. SD* U.S.A.
101 E2 **Bad Lauterberg im Harz** Ger.
101 D2 **Bad Lippspringe** Ger.
101 D3 **Bad Mergentheim** Ger.
101 D2 **Bad Nauheim** Ger.
100 C2 **Bad Neuenahr-Ahrweiler** Ger.
101 E2 **Bad Neustadt an der Saale** Ger.
101 E1 **Bad Oldesloe** Ger.
101 D2 **Bad Pyrmont** Ger.
78 A2 **Badr Ḩunayn** Saudi Arabia
101 D1 **Bad Salzuflen** Ger.
101 E2 **Bad Salzungen** Ger.
102 C1 **Bad Schwartau** Ger.
101 E1 **Bad Segeberg** Ger.
73 C4 **Badulla** Sri Lanka
101 D1 **Bad Zwischenahn** Ger.
106 C2 **Baeza** Spain
114 A3 **Bafatá** Guinea-Bissau
127 H2 **Baffin Bay** *sea* Can./Greenland
127 H2 **Baffin Island** Can.
118 B2 **Bafia** Cameroon
114 A3 **Bafing** *r.* Guinea/Mali
114 A3 **Bafoulabé** Mali
118 B2 **Bafoussam** Cameroon
81 D2 **Bāfq** Iran
80 B1 **Bafra** Turkey
79 C2 **Bāft** Iran
119 C2 **Bafwasende** Dem. Rep. Congo
119 D3 **Bagamoyo** Tanz.
Bagan Datoh Malaysia *see* **Bagan Datuk**
60 B1 **Bagan Datuk** Malaysia
64 B3 **Baganga** Phil.
120 B2 **Bagani** Namibia
60 B1 **Bagansiapiapi** Indon.
118 B3 **Bagata** Dem. Rep. Congo
91 E2 **Bagayevskiy** Rus. Fed.
142 A2 **Bagdad** U.S.A.
152 C3 **Bagé** Brazil
81 C2 **Baghdād** Iraq
79 C1 **Bāghīn** Iran
77 C3 **Baghlān** Afgh.
104 C3 **Bagnères-de-Luchon** France
105 C3 **Bagnols-sur-Cèze** France
Bago Myanmar *see* **Pegu**
88 B3 **Bagrationovsk** Rus. Fed.
Bagrax China *see* **Bohu**
64 B2 **Baguio** Phil.
115 C3 **Bagzane, Monts** *mts* Niger
146 C2 **Bahamas, The** *country* West Indies
75 C2 **Baharampur** India
Bahariya Oasis Egypt *see* Bahrīyah, Wāḩāt al
60 B1 **Bahau** Malaysia
74 B2 **Bahawalnagar** Pak.
74 B2 **Bahawalpur** Pak.
Bahia Brazil *see* **Salvador**
146 B3 **Bahía, Islas de la** *is* Hond.
153 B3 **Bahía Blanca** Arg.
144 A2 **Bahía Kino** Mex.
152 C2 **Bahía Negra** Para.
144 A2 **Bahía Tortugas** Mex.
117 B3 **Bahir Dar** Eth.
79 C2 **Bahlā** Oman
75 C2 **Bahraich** India
79 C2 **Bahrain** *country* Asia
116 A2 **Bahrīyah, Wāḩāt al** Egypt
79 D2 **Bāhū Kālāt** Iran
89 D3 **Bahushewsk** Belarus
110 C2 **Baia** Romania
120 A2 **Baía dos Tigres** Angola
110 B1 **Baia Mare** Romania
118 B2 **Baïbokoum** Chad
69 E1 **Baicheng** China
Baidoa Somalia *see* Baydhabo
Baie-aux-Feuilles Can. *see* **Tasiujaq**
131 D3 **Baie-Comeau** Can.
Baie-du-Poste Can. *see* **Mistissini**
131 C3 **Baie-St-Paul** Can.
131 E3 **Baie Verte** Can.
62 A1 **Baihanchang** China
65 B1 **Baihe** China
69 D1 **Baikal, Lake** Rus. Fed.
Baile Átha Cliath Rep. of Ireland *see* **Dublin**
110 B2 **Băilești** Romania
68 C2 **Baima** China
141 D2 **Bainbridge** U.S.A.
Baingoin China *see* Porong
48 I3 **Bairiki** Kiribati
Bairin Youqi China *see* Daban
53 C3 **Bairnsdale** Austr.
65 B1 **Baishan** *Jilin* China
65 B1 **Baishanzhen** *Jilin* China
120 A2 **Baixo-Longa** Angola
70 A2 **Baiyin** China
116 B3 **Baiyuda Desert** Sudan
103 D2 **Baja** Hungary
144 A1 **Baja California** *pen.* Mex.
61 D2 **Bajawa** Indon.
78 B3 **Bājil** Yemen
115 D3 **Bajoga** Nigeria
109 D2 **Bajram Curri** Albania
114 A3 **Bakel** Senegal
135 C3 **Baker** *CA* U.S.A.
140 B2 **Baker** *LA* U.S.A.
136 C1 **Baker** *MT* U.S.A.
134 C2 **Baker** *OR* U.S.A.
134 B1 **Baker, Mount** *vol.* U.S.A.
129 E1 **Baker Foreland** *hd* Can.
49 J3 **Baker Island** *terr.* N. Pacific Ocean
129 E1 **Baker Lake** Can.
129 E1 **Baker Lake** *l.* Can.
135 C3 **Bakersfield** U.S.A.
Bakharden Turkm. *see* Bakherden
91 C3 **Bakhchysaray** Ukr.
76 B3 **Bakherden** Turkm.
91 C1 **Bakhmach** Ukr.
Bakhmut Ukr. *see* **Artemivs'k**
Bākhtarān Iran *see* **Kermānshāh**
Bakı Azer. *see* **Baku**
111 C2 **Bakırköy** Turkey
92 □C2 **Bakkaflói** *b.* Iceland
118 C2 **Bakouma** C.A.R.
81 C1 **Baku** Azer.
99 B3 **Bala** U.K.
64 A3 **Balabac** Phil.
64 A3 **Balabac** *i.* Phil.
61 C1 **Balabac Strait** Malaysia/Phil.
75 C2 **Balaghat** India
60 C2 **Balaiberkuak** Indon.
52 A2 **Balaklava** Austr.
91 C3 **Balaklava** Ukr.
91 D2 **Balakliya** Ukr.
87 D3 **Balakovo** Rus. Fed.
76 C3 **Bālā Morghāb** Afgh.
145 C3 **Balancán** Mex.
111 C3 **Balan Dağı** *hill* Turkey
64 B2 **Balanga** Phil.
87 D3 **Balashov** Rus. Fed.
Balaton, Lake Hungary *see* **Lake Balaton**
103 D2 **Balatonboglár** Hungary
150 D3 **Balbina, Represa de** *resr* Brazil
97 C2 **Balbriggan** Rep. of Ireland
52 A2 **Balcanoona** Austr.
110 C2 **Balchik** Bulg.
54 A3 **Balclutha** N.Z.
143 C3 **Balcones Escarpment** U.S.A.
129 E2 **Baldock Lake** Can.
138 D2 **Baldwin** U.S.A.
129 D2 **Baldy Mountain** *hill* Can.
142 B2 **Baldy Peak** U.S.A.
Baleares, Islas *is* Spain *see* **Balearic Islands**
107 D2 **Balearic Islands** *is* Spain
155 E1 **Baleia, Ponta da** *pt* Brazil
130 C2 **Baleine, Grande Rivière de la** *r.* Can.
131 D2 **Baleine, Rivière à la** *r.* Can.
75 C2 **Baleshwar** India
50 B2 **Balgo** Austr.
79 B3 **Bālḩaf** Yemen
61 C2 **Bali** *i.* Indon.
60 A1 **Balige** Indon.
75 C2 **Baliguda** India
111 C3 **Balıkesir** Turkey
61 C2 **Balikpapan** Indon.
64 A3 **Balimbing** Phil.
59 D3 **Balimo** P.N.G.
102 B2 **Balingen** Ger.
64 B2 **Balintang Channel** Phil.
Bali Sea Indon. *see* **Laut Bali**
78 B3 **Baljurshī** Saudi Arabia
76 B3 **Balkanabat** Turkm.
110 B2 **Balkan Mountains** Bulg./Serb. and Mont.
77 C1 **Balkashino** Kazakh.
77 D2 **Balkhash** Kazakh.
77 D2 **Balkhash, Lake** Kazakh.
Balkhash, Ozero *l.* Kazakh. *see* **Balkhash, Lake**
Balla Balla Zimbabwe *see* **Mbalabala**
96 B2 **Ballachulish** U.K.
50 B3 **Balladonia** Austr.
97 B2 **Ballaghaderreen** Rep. of Ireland
92 G2 **Ballangen** Norway
96 B3 **Ballantrae** U.K.
52 B3 **Ballarat** Austr.
50 B2 **Ballard, Lake** *salt flat* Austr.
96 C2 **Ballater** U.K.
114 B3 **Ballé** Mali
55 M3 **Balleny Islands** Antarctica
53 D1 **Ballina** Austr.
97 B1 **Ballina** Rep. of Ireland
97 B2 **Ballinasloe** Rep. of Ireland
97 B3 **Ballineen** Rep. of Ireland
143 D2 **Ballinger** U.S.A.
97 B2 **Ballinrobe** Rep. of Ireland
97 B1 **Ballycastle** Rep. of Ireland
97 C1 **Ballycastle** U.K.
97 D1 **Ballyclare** U.K.
97 B2 **Ballyhaunis** Rep. of Ireland
97 C1 **Ballymena** U.K.
97 C1 **Ballymoney** U.K.
97 D1 **Ballynahinch** U.K.
97 B1 **Ballyshannon** Rep. of Ireland
95 B2 **Ballyvoy** U.K.
52 B3 **Balmoral** Austr.
143 C2 **Balmorhea** U.S.A.
120 A2 **Balombo** Angola
51 D2 **Balonne** *r.* Austr.
74 B2 **Balotra** India
77 D2 **Balpyk Bi** Kazakh.
75 C2 **Balrampur** India
52 B2 **Balranald** Austr.
110 B2 **Balș** Romania
151 E3 **Balsas** Brazil
145 C3 **Balsas** Mex.
145 B3 **Balsas** *r.* Mex.
90 B2 **Balta** Ukr.
90 B2 **Bălți** Moldova
93 G4 **Baltic Sea** *g.* Europe
80 B2 **Balṭīm** Egypt
97 B3 **Baltimore** Rep. of Ireland
123 C1 **Baltimore** S. Africa
139 D3 **Baltimore** U.S.A.
97 C2 **Baltinglass** Rep. of Ireland
88 A3 **Baltiysk** Rus. Fed.
75 D2 **Balu** India
52 A2 **Balumbah** Austr.
88 C2 **Balvi** Latvia
77 D2 **Balykchy** Kyrg.
87 E4 **Balykshi** Kazakh.
79 C2 **Bam** Iran
71 A3 **Bama** China
51 D1 **Bamaga** Austr.
130 A2 **Bamaji Lake** Can.
114 B3 **Bamako** Mali
118 C2 **Bambari** C.A.R.
101 E3 **Bamberg** Ger.
119 C2 **Bambili** Dem. Rep. Congo
118 B2 **Bambio** C.A.R.
119 C2 **Bambouti** C.A.R.
155 C2 **Bambuí** Brazil
98 C2 **Bamburgh** U.K.
118 B2 **Bamenda** Cameroon
77 C3 **Bāmīān** Afgh.
118 C2 **Bamingui** C.A.R.
79 D2 **Bampūr** Iran
79 C2 **Bampūr** *watercourse* Iran
152 B1 **Bañados del Izozog** *swamp* Bol.
119 C2 **Banalia** Dem. Rep. Congo
71 A3 **Banan** China
151 D4 **Bananal, Ilha do** *i.* Brazil
74 B2 **Banas** *r.* India
111 C3 **Banaz** Turkey
62 B2 **Ban Ban** Laos
97 C1 **Banbridge** U.K.
99 C3 **Banbury** U.K.
96 C2 **Banchory** U.K.
130 C3 **Bancroft** Can.
Bancroft Zambia *see* **Chililabombwe**
119 C2 **Banda** Dem. Rep. Congo
75 C2 **Banda** India
59 C3 **Banda, Kepulauan** *is* Indon.
59 C3 **Banda, Laut** Indon.
60 A1 **Banda Aceh** Indon.
Bandar India *see* **Machilipatnam**
Bandar Abbas Iran *see* Bandar-e 'Abbās
75 D2 **Bandarban** Bangl.
79 C2 **Bandar-e 'Abbās** Iran
81 C2 **Bandar-e Anzalī** Iran
79 C2 **Bandar-e Chārak** Iran
81 C2 **Bandar-e Emām Khomeynī** Iran
79 C2 **Bandar-e Lengeh** Iran
79 C2 **Bandar-e Maqām** Iran
Bandar-e Pahlavī Iran *see* Bandar-e Anzalī
Bandar-e Shāhpūr Iran *see* **Bandar-e Emām Khomeynī**
60 B2 **Bandar Lampung** Indon.
61 C1 **Bandar Seri Begawan** Brunei
Banda Sea Indon. *see* Banda, Laut
155 D2 **Bandeiras, Pico de** *mt.* Brazil
123 C1 **Bandelierkop** S. Africa
144 B2 **Banderas, Bahía de** *b.* Mex.
114 B3 **Bandiagara** Mali
111 C2 **Bandırma** Turkey
Bandjarmasin Indon. *see* Banjarmasin
97 B3 **Bandon** Rep. of Ireland
97 B3 **Bandon** *r.* Rep. of Ireland
118 B3 **Bandundu** Dem. Rep. Congo
60 B2 **Bandung** Indon.
128 C2 **Banff** Can.
96 C2 **Banff** U.K.
114 B3 **Banfora** Burkina
64 B3 **Banga** Phil.
73 B3 **Bangalore** India
118 C2 **Bangassou** C.A.R.
61 D2 **Banggai** Indon.
59 C3 **Banggai, Kepulauan** *is* Indon.
61 D2 **Banggai, Kepulauan** *is* Indon.
61 C1 **Banggi** *i. Sabah* Malaysia
Banghāzī Libya *see* Benghazi
60 B2 **Bangka** *i.* Indon.
60 B2 **Bangka, Selat** *sea chan.* Indon.
61 C2 **Bangkalan** Indon.
60 B1 **Bangkinang** Indon.
60 B2 **Bangko** Indon.
63 B2 **Bangkok** Thai.
75 C2 **Bangladesh** *country* Asia
97 D1 **Bangor** *Northern Ireland* U.K.
98 A3 **Bangor** *Wales* U.K.
139 F2 **Bangor** U.S.A.
63 A2 **Bang Saphan Yai** Thai.
64 B2 **Bangued** Phil.
118 B2 **Bangui** C.A.R.
64 B2 **Bangui** Phil.
121 B2 **Bangweulu, Lake** Zambia
80 B2 **Banhā** Egypt
62 B2 **Ban Huai Khon** Thai.

Bani

118 C2	Bani C.A.R.
80 B3	Bani Mazār Egypt
116 B2	Bani Suwayf Egypt
115 D1	Bani Walid Libya
80 B2	Bāniyās Syria
109 C2	Banja Luka Bos.-Herz.
61 C2	Banjarmasin Indon.
114 A3	Banjul Gambia
63 A3	Ban Khok Kloi Thai.
128 A2	Banks Island B.C. Can.
126 D2	Banks Island N.W.T. Can.
48 H5	Banks Islands Vanuatu
129 E1	Banks Lake Can.
54 B2	Banks Peninsula N.Z.
51 D4	Banks Strait Austr.
75 C2	Bankura India
62 A1	Banmauk Myanmar
62 B2	Ban Mouang Laos
97 C1	Bann r. U.K.
62 B2	Ban Napè Laos
63 A3	Ban Na San Thai.
146 C2	Bannerman Town Bahamas
	Banningville Dem. Rep. Congo see Bandundu
71 A4	Ban Nong Kung Thai.
74 B1	Bannu Pak.
103 D2	Banská Bystrica Slovakia
111 B2	Bansko Bulg.
74 B2	Banswara India
62 B2	Ban Taviang Laos
63 A3	Ban Tha Kham Thai.
62 A2	Ban Tha Song Yang Thai.
63 B2	Ban Tôp Laos
97 B3	Bantry Rep. of Ireland
97 B3	Bantry Bay Rep. of Ireland
60 A1	Banyak, Pulau-pulau is Indon.
118 B2	Banyo Cameroon
107 D1	Banyoles Spain
61 C2	Banyuwangi Indon.
	Banzyville Dem. Rep. Congo see Mobayi-Mbongo
	Bao'an China see Shenzhen
70 B1	Baochang China
70 B2	Baoding China
70 A2	Baoji China
63 B2	Bao Lôc Vietnam
66 B1	Baoqing China
118 B2	Baoro C.A.R.
62 A1	Baoshan China
70 B1	Baotou China
65 B1	Baotou Shan mt. China/N. Korea
74 B2	Bap India
81 C2	Ba'qūbah Iraq
109 C2	Bar Serb. and Mont.
90 B2	Bar Ukr.
116 B3	Bara Sudan
117 C4	Baraawe Somalia
147 C2	Baracoa Cuba
53 C2	Baradine Austr.
147 C3	Barahona Dom. Rep.
116 B3	Baraka watercourse Eritrea/Sudan
106 C1	Barakaldo Spain
61 C1	Baram r. Sarawak Malaysia
150 D2	Baramanni Guyana
89 D3	Baran' Belarus
74 B2	Baran India
88 C3	Baranavichy Belarus
116 B2	Baranis Egypt
90 B1	Baranivka Ukr.
76 B2	Barankul Kazakh.
128 A2	Baranof Island U.S.A.
	Baranowicze Belarus see Baranavichy
59 C3	Barat Daya, Kepulauan is Indon.
155 D2	Barbacena Brazil
147 E3	Barbados country West Indies
107 D1	Barbastro Spain
106 B2	Barbate de Franco Spain
123 D2	Barberton S. Africa
104 B2	Barbezieux-St-Hilaire France
51 D2	Barcaldine Austr.
107 D1	Barcelona Spain
150 C1	Barcelona Venez.
105 D3	Barcelonnette France
150 C3	Barcelos Brazil
114 B4	Barclayville Liberia
51 D2	Barcoo watercourse Austr.
	Barcoo Creek watercourse Austr. see Cooper Creek
103 D2	Barcs Hungary

92 □B3	Bárðarbunga mt. Iceland
75 C2	Barddhaman India
103 E2	Bardejov Slovakia
	Bardera Somalia see Baardheere
79 C2	Bardsīr Iran
75 B2	Bareilly India
82 D1	Barents Sea Arctic Ocean
78 A3	Barentu Eritrea
72 C1	Barga China
108 B2	Barga Italy
75 C2	Barh India
52 B3	Barham Austr.
139 F2	Bar Harbor U.S.A.
109 C2	Bari Italy
107 E2	Barika Alg.
74 B1	Barikot Afgh.
150 B2	Barinas Venez.
75 C2	Baripada India
75 D2	Barisal Bangl.
60 B2	Barisan, Pegunungan mts Indon.
61 C2	Barito r. Indon.
79 C2	Barkā Oman
88 C2	Barkava Latvia
74 A2	Barkhan Pak.
51 C1	Barkly Tableland reg. Austr.
122 B2	Barkly West S. Africa
68 C2	Barkol China
110 C1	Bârlad Romania
105 D2	Bar-le-Duc France
50 A2	Barlee, Lake salt flat Austr.
109 C2	Barletta Italy
53 C2	Barmedman Austr.
	Barmen-Elberfeld Ger. see Wuppertal
74 B2	Barmer India
52 B2	Barmera Austr.
99 A3	Barmouth U.K.
101 D1	Barmstedt Ger.
98 C2	Barnard Castle U.K.
53 B2	Barnato Austr.
82 G3	Barnaul Rus. Fed.
127 H2	Barnes Icecap Can.
100 B1	Barneveld Neth.
98 C3	Barnsley U.K.
99 A4	Barnstaple U.K.
	Barnstaple Bay U.K. see Bideford Bay
141 D2	Barnwell U.S.A.
	Baroda India see Vadodara
150 C1	Barquisimeto Venez.
96 A2	Barra i. U.K.
53 D2	Barraba Austr.
151 D4	Barra do Bugres Brazil
151 E3	Barra do Corda Brazil
154 B1	Barra do Garças Brazil
150 D3	Barra do São Manuel Brazil
	Barraigh i. U.K. see Barra
150 B4	Barranca Peru
150 B3	Barranca Peru
152 C2	Barranqueras Arg.
150 B1	Barranquilla Col.
105 D3	Barre des Ecrins mt. France
151 E4	Barreiras Brazil
63 A2	Barren Island India
154 C2	Barretos Brazil
128 C2	Barrhead Can.
130 C3	Barrie Can.
128 B2	Barrière Can.
52 B2	Barrier Range hills Austr.
53 D2	Barrington, Mount Austr.
129 D2	Barrington Lake Can.
53 C1	Barringun Austr.
97 C2	Barrow r. Rep. of Ireland
126 B2	Barrow U.S.A.
126 B2	Barrow, Point U.S.A.
51 C2	Barrow Creek Austr.
98 B2	Barrow-in-Furness U.K.
50 A2	Barrow Island Austr.
126 F2	Barrow Strait Can.
99 B4	Barry U.K.
122 B3	Barrydale S. Africa
130 C3	Barrys Bay Can.
74 B2	Barsalpur India
101 D1	Barsinghausen Ger.
135 C4	Barstow U.S.A.
105 C2	Bar-sur-Aube France
102 C1	Barth Ger.
80 B1	Bartın Turkey
51 D1	Bartle Frere, Mount Austr.
143 D1	Bartlesville U.S.A.
129 D2	Bartlett NE U.S.A.
140 C1	Bartlett TN U.S.A.
98 C3	Barton-upon-Humber U.K.

103 E1	Bartoszyce Pol.
61 C2	Barung i. Indon.
69 D1	Baruun-Urt Mongolia
91 D2	Barvinkove Ukr.
53 C2	Barwon r. Austr.
88 C3	Barysaw Belarus
118 B2	Basankusu Dem. Rep. Congo
110 C2	Basarabi Romania
64 B1	Basco Phil.
105 D2	Basel Switz.
71 C3	Bashi Channel Taiwan
91 C2	Bashtanka Ukr.
64 B3	Basilan i. Phil.
99 D4	Basildon U.K.
99 C4	Basingstoke U.K.
81 C2	Başkale Turkey
130 C3	Baskatong, Réservoir resr Can.
	Basle Switz. see Basel
118 C2	Basoko Dem. Rep. Congo
81 C2	Basra Iraq
128 C2	Bassano Can.
114 C4	Bassar Togo
63 A2	Bassein Myanmar
147 D3	Basse-Terre Guadeloupe
147 D3	Basseterre St Kitts and Nevis
114 B3	Bassikounou Maur.
114 C4	Bassila Benin
51 D3	Bass Strait Austr.
79 C2	Bastak Iran
101 E2	Bastheim Ger.
75 C2	Basti India
105 D3	Bastia Corsica France
100 B2	Bastogne Belgium
140 B2	Bastrop U.S.A.
	Basuo China see Dongfang
	Basutoland country Africa see Lesotho
118 A2	Bata Equat. Guinea
146 B2	Batabanó, Golfo de b. Cuba
83 J2	Batagay Rus. Fed.
154 B2	Bataguassu Brazil
74 B1	Batala India
106 B2	Batalha Port.
64 B1	Batan i. Phil.
118 B2	Batangafo C.A.R.
64 B2	Batangas Phil.
60 B2	Batanghari r. Indon.
64 B1	Batan Islands Phil.
154 C2	Batatais Brazil
139 D2	Batavia U.S.A.
91 D2	Bataysk Rus. Fed.
130 B3	Batchawana Mountain hill Can.
50 C1	Batchelor Austr.
63 B2	Bătdâmbâng Cambodia
118 B3	Batéké, Plateaux Congo
53 D3	Batemans Bay Austr.
140 B1	Batesville AR U.S.A.
140 C2	Batesville MS U.S.A.
89 D2	Batetskiy Rus. Fed.
99 B4	Bath U.K.
96 C3	Bathgate U.K.
74 B1	Bathinda India
53 C2	Bathurst Austr.
131 D3	Bathurst Can.
	Bathurst Gambia see Banjul
126 E2	Bathurst Inlet Can.
126 E2	Bathurst Inlet inlet Can.
50 C1	Bathurst Island Austr.
126 F1	Bathurst Island Can.
78 B1	Bāṭin, Wādī al watercourse Asia
53 C3	Batlow Austr.
81 C2	Batman Turkey
115 C1	Batna Alg.
140 B2	Baton Rouge U.S.A.
144 B2	Batopilas Mex.
118 B2	Batouri Cameroon
154 B1	Batovi Brazil
	Batrā' tourist site Jordan see Petra
92 I1	Bátsfjord Norway
73 C4	Batticaloa Sri Lanka
109 B2	Battipaglia Italy
128 D2	Battle r. Can.
138 B2	Battle Creek U.S.A.
135 C2	Battle Mountain U.S.A.
74 B1	Battura Glacier Jammu and Kashmir
117 B4	Batu mt. Eth.
60 A2	Batu, Pulau-pulau is Indon.
61 D2	Batuata i. Indon.
61 D2	Batudaka i. Indon.
64 B3	Batulaki Phil.

	Batum Georgia see Bat'umi
81 C1	Bat'umi Georgia
60 B1	Batu Pahat Malaysia
61 D2	Baubau Indon.
115 C3	Bauchi Nigeria
137 E1	Baudette U.S.A.
	Baudouinville Dem. Rep. Congo see Moba
104 B2	Baugé France
105 D2	Baume-les-Dames France
154 C2	Bauru Brazil
154 B1	Baús Brazil
88 B2	Bauska Latvia
102 C1	Bautzen Ger.
102 C2	Bavaria reg. Ger.
144 B2	Bavispe r. Mex.
87 E3	Bavly Rus. Fed.
62 A1	Bawdwin Myanmar
61 C2	Bawean i. Indon.
114 B3	Bawku Ghana
	Baxian China see Banan
146 C2	Bayamo Cuba
	Bayan Gol China see Dengkou
68 C1	Bayanhongor Mongolia
70 A2	Bayan Hot China
70 A1	Bayan Obo China
136 C2	Bayard NE U.S.A.
142 B2	Bayard NM U.S.A.
64 B3	Bayawan Phil.
81 C1	Bayburt Turkey
138 C2	Bay City MI U.S.A.
143 D3	Bay City TX U.S.A.
86 F2	Baydaratskaya Guba Rus. Fed.
117 C4	Baydhabo Somalia
104 B2	Bayeux France
136 B3	Bayfield U.S.A.
78 B3	Bayhan al Qişab Yemen
	Bay Islands is Hond. see Bahía, Islas de la
81 C2	Bayjī Iraq
	Baykal, Ozero l. Rus. Fed. see Baikal, Lake
	Baykal Range mts Rus. Fed. see Baykal'skiy Khrebet
83 I3	Baykal'skiy Khrebet mts Rus. Fed.
76 C2	Baykonyr Kazakh.
87 E3	Baymak Rus. Fed.
64 B2	Bayombong Phil.
104 B3	Bayonne France
76 C3	Bayramaly Turkm.
111 C3	Bayramiç Turkey
101 E3	Bayreuth Ger.
78 B3	Bayt al Faqīh Yemen
143 D3	Baytown U.S.A.
106 C2	Baza Spain
106 C2	Baza, Sierra de mts Spain
76 A2	Bazardyuzyu, Gora mt. Azer./Rus. Fed.
104 B3	Bazas France
74 A2	Bazdar Pak.
70 A2	Bazhong China
79 D2	Bazmān Iran
79 D2	Bazmān, Kūh-e mt. Iran
	Bé, Nossi i. Madag. see Nosy Bé
136 C1	Beach U.S.A.
52 B3	Beachport Austr.
99 D4	Beachy Head hd U.K.
123 C3	Beacon Bay S. Africa
50 B1	Beagle Gulf Austr.
121 □D2	Bealanana Madag.
121 □D3	Beampingaratra mts Madag.
134 D2	Bear r. U.S.A.
130 B3	Beardmore Can.
53 C1	Beardmore Reservoir Austr.
	Bear Island i. Arctic Ocean see Bjørnøya
134 E1	Bear Paw Mountain U.S.A.
147 C3	Beata, Cabo c. Dom. Rep.
147 C3	Beata, Isla i. Dom. Rep.
137 D2	Beatrice U.S.A.
135 C3	Beatty U.S.A.
53 D1	Beaudesert Austr.
52 B3	Beaufort Austr.
61 C1	Beaufort Sabah Malaysia
141 D2	Beaufort U.S.A.
126 C2	Beaufort Sea Can./U.S.A.
122 B3	Beaufort West S. Africa
96 B2	Beauly r. U.K.
96 B2	Beauly U.K.
100 B2	Beaumont Belgium
54 A3	Beaumont N.Z.

143 E2 Beaumont U.S.A.
105 C2 Beaune France
100 B2 Beauraing Belgium
129 E2 Beauséjour Can.
104 C2 Beauvais France
129 D2 Beauval Can.
129 D2 Beaver *r.* Can.
135 D3 Beaver U.S.A.
128 A1 Beaver Creek Can.
138 B2 Beaver Dam U.S.A.
129 E2 Beaver Hill Lake Can.
138 B1 Beaver Island U.S.A.
128 C2 Beaverlodge Can.
74 B2 Beawar India
154 C2 Bebedouro Brazil
101 D2 Bebra Ger.
99 D3 Beccles U.K.
109 D1 Bečej Serb. and Mont.
106 B1 Becerreá Spain
114 B1 Béchar Alg.
Bechuanaland *country* Africa *see* Botswana
138 C3 Beckley U.S.A.
117 B4 Bedelē Eth.
99 C3 Bedford U.K.
138 B3 Bedford U.S.A.
98 C2 Bedlington U.K.
100 C1 Bedum Neth.
53 C3 Beechworth Austr.
53 D2 Beecroft Peninsula Austr.
101 F1 Beelitz Ger.
53 D1 Beenleigh Austr.
80 B2 Beersheba Israel
Be'ér Sheva' Israel *see* Beersheba
143 D3 Beeville U.S.A.
121 □D2 Befandriana Avaratra Madag.
53 C3 Bega Austr.
107 D1 Begur, Cap de *c.* Spain
81 D2 Behbehān Iran
81 D2 Behshahr Iran
69 E1 Bei'an China
71 A3 Beihai China
70 B2 Beijing China
100 C1 Beilen Neth.
118 B2 Béinamar Chad
96 B3 Beinn an Oir *hill* U.K.
96 A2 Beinn Mhòr *hill* U.K.
Beinn na Faoghlia *i.* U.K. *see* Benbecula
121 C2 Beira Moz.
80 B2 Beirut Lebanon
123 C1 Beitbridge Zimbabwe
106 B2 Beja Port.
115 C1 Bejaïa Alg.
106 B1 Béjar Spain
74 A2 Beji *r.* Pak.
76 B2 Bekdash Turkm.
103 E2 Békés Hungary
103 E2 Békéscsaba Hungary
121 □D3 Bekily Madag.
66 D2 Bekkai Japan
114 B4 Bekwai Ghana
75 C2 Bela India
74 A2 Bela Pak.
123 C1 Bela-Bela S. Africa
118 B2 Bélabo Cameroon
109 D2 Bela Crkva Serb. and Mont.
61 C1 Belaga *Sarawak* Malaysia
88 C3 Belarus *country* Europe
121 C3 Bela Vista Moz.
60 A1 Belawan Indon.
83 M2 Belaya *r.* Rus. Fed.
103 D1 Bełchatów Pol.
Belchatow Pol. *see* Bełchatów
130 C2 Belcher Islands Can.
87 E3 Belebey Rus. Fed.
117 C4 Beledweyne Somalia
118 B2 Bélèl Cameroon
151 E3 Belém Brazil
142 B2 Belen U.S.A.
110 C2 Belene Bulg.
89 E3 Belev Rus. Fed.
97 D1 Belfast U.K.
139 F2 Belfast U.S.A.
136 C1 Belfield U.S.A.
105 D2 Belfort France
73 B3 Belgaum India
Belgian Congo *country* Africa *see* Congo, Democratic Republic of
100 B2 Belgium *country* Europe
91 D1 Belgorod Rus. Fed.
109 D2 Belgrade Serb. and Mont.
134 D1 Belgrade U.S.A.
115 D4 Beli Nigeria
109 C1 Beli Manastir Croatia
60 B2 Belinyu Indon.
60 B2 Belitung *i.* Indon.
118 B3 Belize Angola
146 B3 Belize Belize
146 B3 Belize *country* Central America
83 K1 Bel'kovskiy, Ostrov *i.* Rus. Fed.
128 B2 Bella Bella Can.
104 C2 Bellac France
128 B2 Bella Coola Can.
73 B3 Bellary India
53 C1 Bellata Austr.
138 C2 Bellefontaine U.S.A.
136 C2 Belle Fourche U.S.A.
136 C2 Belle Fourche *r.* U.S.A.
141 D3 Belle Glade U.S.A.
104 B2 Belle-Île *i.* France
131 E2 Belle Isle *i.* Can.
131 E2 Belle Isle, Strait of Can.
130 C3 Belleville Can.
138 B3 Belleville *IL* U.S.A.
137 D3 Belleville *KS* U.S.A.
134 D2 Bellevue *ID* U.S.A.
134 B1 Bellevue *WA* U.S.A.
Bellin Can. *see* Kangirsuk
53 D2 Bellingen Austr.
134 B1 Bellingham U.S.A.
55 R2 Bellingshausen Sea Antarctica
105 D2 Bellinzona Switz.
96 C2 Bell Rock *i.* U.K.
108 B1 Belluno Italy
122 A3 Bellville S. Africa
53 D2 Belmont Austr.
155 E1 Belmonte Brazil
146 B3 Belmopan Belize
97 B1 Belmullet Rep. of Ireland
69 E1 Belogorsk Rus. Fed.
121 □D3 Beloha Madag.
155 D1 Belo Horizonte Brazil
138 B2 Beloit U.S.A.
86 C2 Belomorsk Rus. Fed.
89 E3 Beloomut Rus. Fed.
91 D3 Belorechensk Rus. Fed.
Belorechenskaya Rus. Fed. *see* Belorechensk
87 E3 Beloretsk Rus. Fed.
Belorussia *country* Europe *see* Belarus
Belorusskaya S.S.R. *admin. reg.* Europe *see* Belarus
Belostok Pol. *see* Białystok
121 □D2 Belo Tsiribihina Madag.
86 F2 Beloyarskiy Rus. Fed.
89 E1 Beloye, Ozero *l.* Rus. Fed.
Beloye More *sea* Rus. Fed. *see* White Sea
89 E1 Belozersk Rus. Fed.
52 A2 Beltana Austr.
143 D2 Belton U.S.A.
Bel'ts' Moldova *see* Bălţi
Bel'tsy Moldova *see* Bălţi
97 C1 Belturbet Rep. of Ireland
77 E2 Belukha, Gora *mt.* Kazakh./Rus. Fed.
86 D2 Belush'ye Rus. Fed.
138 B2 Belvidere U.S.A.
51 D2 Belyando *r.* Austr.
89 D2 Belyy Rus. Fed.
82 F2 Belyy, Ostrov *i.* Rus. Fed.
101 F1 Belzig Ger.
137 E1 Bemidji U.S.A.
118 C3 Bena Dibele Dem. Rep. Congo
53 C3 Benalla Austr.
Benares India *see* Varanasi
115 D1 Ben Arous Tunisia
118 C3 Bena-Sungu Dem. Rep. Congo
106 B1 Benavente Spain
96 A2 Benbecula *i.* U.K.
134 B2 Bend U.S.A.
123 C3 Bendearg *mt.* S. Africa
Bender Moldova *see* Tighina
Bendery Moldova *see* Tighina
52 B3 Bendigo Austr.
121 C2 Bene Moz.
102 C2 Benešov Czech Rep.
109 B2 Benevento Italy
73 C3 Bengal, Bay of *sea* Indian Ocean
70 B2 Bengbu China
115 E1 Benghazi Libya
60 B1 Bengkalis Indon.
60 B1 Bengkayang Indon.
60 B2 Bengkulu Indon.
120 A2 Benguela Angola
Benha Egypt *see* Banhā
96 B1 Ben Hope *hill* U.K.
152 B1 Beni *r.* Bol.
119 C2 Beni Dem. Rep. Congo
114 B1 Beni-Abbès Alg.
107 C2 Benidorm Spain
114 B1 Beni Mellal Morocco
114 C3 Benin *country* Africa
114 C4 Benin, Bight of *g.* Africa
115 C4 Benin City Nigeria
107 C2 Beni-Saf Alg.
Beni Suef Egypt *see* Banī Suwayf
153 C3 Benito Juárez Arg.
150 C3 Benjamim Constant Brazil
144 A1 Benjamín Hill Mex.
59 C3 Benjina Indon.
136 C2 Benkelman U.S.A.
96 B2 Ben Lawers *mt.* U.K.
96 B2 Ben Lomond *hill* U.K.
96 C2 Ben Macdui *mt.* U.K.
96 A2 Ben More *hill* U.K.
96 B2 Ben More *mt.* U.K.
54 B2 Benmore, Lake N.Z.
96 B1 Ben More Assynt *hill* U.K.
128 A2 Bennett Can.
83 K1 Bennetta, Ostrov *i.* Rus. Fed.
Bennett Island Rus. Fed. *see* Bennetta, Ostrov
96 B2 Ben Nevis *mt.* U.K.
139 E2 Bennington U.S.A.
123 C2 Benoni S. Africa
115 D4 Bénoy Chad
101 D3 Bensheim Ger.
114 B1 Ben Slimane Morocco
142 A2 Benson U.S.A.
61 D2 Benteng Indon.
117 A4 Bentiu Sudan
138 B2 Benton Harbor U.S.A.
140 B1 Bentonville U.S.A.
63 B2 Bên Tre Vietnam
115 C4 Benue *r.* Nigeria
97 B1 Benwee Head *hd* Rep. of Ireland
96 B2 Ben Wyvis *mt.* U.K.
70 C1 Benxi China
Beograd Serb. and Mont. *see* Belgrade
75 C2 Beohari India
114 B4 Béoumi Côte d'Ivoire
67 B4 Beppu Japan
109 C2 Berane Serb. and Mont.
109 C2 Berat Albania
59 C3 Berau, Teluk *b.* Indon.
116 B3 Berber Sudan
117 C3 Berbera Somalia
118 B2 Berbérati C.A.R.
104 C1 Berck France
91 D2 Berdyans'k Ukr.
90 B2 Berdychiv Ukr.
90 A2 Berehove Ukr.
59 D3 Bereina P.N.G.
129 E2 Berens River Can.
137 D2 Beresford U.S.A.
91 D2 Berezanskaya Rus. Fed.
90 A2 Berezhany Ukr.
90 C2 Berezivka Ukr.
90 B1 Berezne Ukr.
86 D2 Bereznik Rus. Fed.
86 E3 Berezniki Rus. Fed.
Berezov Rus. Fed. *see* Berezovo
86 F2 Berezovo Rus. Fed.
107 D1 Berga Spain
111 C3 Bergama Turkey
108 A1 Bergamo Italy
102 C1 Bergen Ger.
101 D1 Bergen Ger.
100 B1 Bergen Neth.
93 E3 Bergen Norway
100 B2 Bergen op Zoom Neth.
104 C3 Bergerac France
100 C2 Bergheim (Erft) Ger.
100 C2 Bergisch Gladbach Ger.
122 A1 Bergland Namibia
93 G3 Bergsjö Sweden
92 H2 Bergsviken Sweden
Berhampur India *see* Baharampur
83 M3 Beringa, Ostrov *i.* Rus. Fed.
100 B2 Beringen Belgium
124 A4 Bering Sea N. Pacific Ocean
124 B3 Bering Strait Rus. Fed./U.S.A.
100 C1 Berkel *r.* Neth.
135 B3 Berkeley U.S.A.
100 B1 Berkhout Neth.
55 B2 Berkner Island Antarctica
110 B2 Berkovitsa Bulg.
92 I1 Berlevåg Norway
101 F1 Berlin Ger.
139 E2 Berlin U.S.A.
101 E2 Berlingerode Ger.
53 D3 Bermagui Austr.
144 B2 Bermejíllo Mex.
152 B2 Bermejo Bol.
131 D2 Bermen, Lac *l.* Can.
125 L6 Bermuda *terr.* N. Atlantic Ocean
105 D2 Bern Switz.
101 E2 Bernburg (Saale) Ger.
127 G2 Bernier Bay Can.
50 A2 Bernier Island Austr.
100 C3 Bernkastel-Kues Ger.
121 □D3 Beroroha Madag.
52 B2 Berri Austr.
115 C1 Berriane Alg.
53 C3 Berrigan Austr.
107 D2 Berrouaghia Alg.
53 D2 Berry Austr.
146 C2 Berry Islands Bahamas
122 A2 Berseba Namibia
101 C1 Bersenbrück Ger.
90 B2 Bershad' Ukr.
131 D2 Berté, Lac *l.* Can.
118 B2 Bertoua Cameroon
150 C3 Beruri Brazil
98 B2 Berwick-upon-Tweed U.K.
91 C2 Beryslav Ukr.
121 □D2 Besalampy Madag.
105 D2 Besançon France
81 D3 Beshneh Iran
129 D2 Besnard Lake Can.
140 C2 Bessemer U.S.A.
76 B2 Besshoky, Gora *hill* Kazakh.
100 B2 Best Neth.
121 □D2 Betafo Madag.
106 B1 Betanzos Spain
118 B2 Bétaré Oya Cameroon
122 A2 Bethanie Namibia
100 B3 Bétheny France
139 D3 Bethesda U.S.A.
123 C2 Bethlehem S. Africa
139 D2 Bethlehem U.S.A.
123 C3 Bethulie S. Africa
105 C1 Béthune France
121 □D3 Betioky Madag.
51 D2 Betoota Austr.
77 D2 Betpak-Dala *plain* Kazakh.
121 □D3 Betroka Madag.
131 D3 Betsiamites Can.
121 □D2 Betsiboka *r.* Madag.
137 E2 Bettendorf U.S.A.
75 C2 Bettiah India
74 B2 Betul India
74 B2 Betwa *r.* India
99 B3 Betws-y-coed U.K.
100 C2 Betzdorf Ger.
136 C1 Beulah U.S.A.
98 C3 Beverley U.K.
101 D2 Beverungen Ger.
100 B1 Beverwijk Neth.
99 D4 Bexhill U.K.
111 C2 Beykoz Turkey
114 B4 Beyla Guinea
76 B2 Beyneu Kazakh.
80 B1 Beypazarı Turkey
Beyrouth Lebanon *see* Beirut
80 B2 Beyşehir Turkey
80 B2 Beyşehir Gölü *l.* Turkey
91 D2 Beysug *r.* Rus. Fed.
91 D2 Beysugskiy Liman *lag.* Rus. Fed.
88 C2 Bezhanitsy Rus. Fed.
89 E2 Bezhetsk Rus. Fed.
105 C3 Béziers France
Bhadgaon Nepal *see* Bhaktapur
75 C2 Bhadrak India
73 B3 Bhadravati India
75 C2 Bhagalpur India
74 A2 Bhairi Hol *mt.* Pak.
74 B1 Bhakkar Pak.
75 C2 Bhaktapur Nepal
62 A1 Bhamo Myanmar
75 C3 Bhanjanagar India
74 B2 Bharatpur India
74 B2 Bharuch India
74 B2 Bhavnagar India
75 C3 Bhawanipatna India
123 D2 Bhekuzulu S. Africa
74 B1 Bhera Pak.
74 B2 Bhilwara India

73 B3 **Bhima** r. India
74 B2 **Bhind** India
74 B2 **Bhiwani** India
123 C3 **Bhongweni** S. Africa
74 B2 **Bhopal** India
75 C2 **Bhubaneshwar** India
Bhubaneswar India see
Bhubaneshwar
74 A2 **Bhuj** India
62 A2 **Bhumiphol Dam** Thai.
74 B2 **Bhusawal** India
75 D2 **Bhutan** country Asia
62 B2 **Bia, Phou** mt. Laos
Biafra, Bight of g. Africa
see Benin, Bight of
59 D3 **Biak** Indon.
59 D3 **Biak** i. Indon.
103 E1 **Biała Podlaska** Pol.
103 D1 **Białogard** Pol.
103 E1 **Białystok** Pol.
109 C3 **Bianco** Italy
74 B2 **Biaora** India
104 B3 **Biarritz** France
105 D2 **Biasca** Switz.
66 D2 **Bibai** Japan
120 A2 **Bibala** Angola
53 C3 **Bibbenluke** Austr.
102 B2 **Biberach an der Riß** Ger.
155 D2 **Bicas** Brazil
73 B3 **Bid** India
115 C4 **Bida** Nigeria
73 B3 **Bidar** India
139 E2 **Biddeford** U.S.A.
96 B2 **Bidean nam Bian** mt. U.K.
99 A4 **Bideford** U.K.
99 A4 **Bideford Bay** U.K.
Bié Angola see Kuito
101 D2 **Biedenkopf** Ger.
105 D2 **Biel** Switz.
101 D1 **Bielefeld** Ger.
108 A1 **Biella** Italy
103 D2 **Bielsko-Biała** Pol.
63 B2 **Biên Hoa** Vietnam
130 C2 **Bienville, Lac** l. Can.
120 A2 **Bié Plateau** Angola
100 B3 **Bièvre** Belgium
118 B3 **Bifoun** Gabon
111 C2 **Biga** Turkey
134 D1 **Big Belt Mountains** U.S.A.
123 D2 **Big Bend** Swaziland
129 D2 **Biggar** Can.
96 C3 **Biggar** U.K.
99 C3 **Biggleswade** U.K.
134 D1 **Big Hole** r. U.S.A.
134 E1 **Bighorn** U.S.A.
136 B1 **Bighorn** r. U.S.A.
136 B2 **Bighorn Mountains** U.S.A.
143 C2 **Big Lake** U.S.A.
138 B2 **Big Rapids** U.S.A.
129 D2 **Big River** Can.
129 E2 **Big Sand Lake** Can.
137 D2 **Big Sioux** r. U.S.A.
143 C2 **Big Spring** U.S.A.
134 E1 **Big Timber** U.S.A.
130 B2 **Big Trout Lake** Can.
130 A2 **Big Trout Lake** l. Can.
109 C2 **Bihać** Bos.-Herz.
75 C2 **Bihar** state India
75 C2 **Bihar Sharif** India
110 B1 **Bihor, Vârful** mt. Romania
114 A3 **Bijagós, Arquipélago dos**
is Guinea-Bissau
73 B3 **Bijapur** India
81 C2 **Bijär** Iran
109 C2 **Bijeljina** Bos.-Herz.
109 C2 **Bijelo Polje**
Serb. and Mont.
71 A3 **Bijie** China
74 B2 **Bikaner** India
66 B1 **Bikin** Rus. Fed.
66 B1 **Bikin** r. Rus. Fed.
118 B3 **Bikoro** Dem. Rep. Congo
79 C2 **Bilād Banī Bū 'Alī** Oman
75 C2 **Bilaspur** India
81 C2 **Biläsuvar** Azer.
90 C2 **Bila Tserkva** Ukr.
63 A2 **Bilauktaung Range** mts
Myanmar/Thai.
106 C1 **Bilbao** Spain
109 C2 **Bileća** Bos.-Herz.
111 C2 **Bilecik** Turkey
103 E1 **Biłgoraj** Pol.
119 D3 **Bilharamulo** Tanz.
90 C2 **Bilhorod-Dnistrovs'kyy**
Ukr.
119 C2 **Bili** Dem. Rep. Congo
83 M2 **Bilibino** Rus. Fed.
109 D2 **Bilisht** Albania
104 B3 **Billère** France
134 E1 **Billings** U.S.A.
99 B4 **Bill of Portland** hd U.K.

142 A1 **Bill Williams Mountain**
U.S.A.
115 D3 **Bilma** Niger
51 E2 **Biloela** Austr.
91 C2 **Bilohirs'k** Ukr.
90 B1 **Bilohir"ya** Ukr.
91 C1 **Bilopillya** Ukr.
91 D2 **Bilovods'k** Ukr.
140 C2 **Biloxi** U.S.A.
51 C2 **Bilpa Morea Claypan**
salt flat Austr.
101 E2 **Bilshausen** Ger.
115 E3 **Biltine** Chad
90 C2 **Bilyayivka** Ukr.
114 C4 **Bimbila** Ghana
141 E3 **Bimini Islands** Bahamas
74 B2 **Bina-Etawa** India
59 C3 **Binaija, Gunung** mt.
Indon.
53 C1 **Bindle** Austr.
118 B3 **Bindu** Dem. Rep. Congo
121 C2 **Bindura** Zimbabwe
107 D1 **Binefar** Spain
120 B2 **Binga** Zimbabwe
53 D1 **Bingara** Austr.
100 C3 **Bingen am Rhein** Ger.
114 B4 **Bingerville** Côte d'Ivoire
139 F1 **Bingham** U.S.A.
139 D2 **Binghamton** U.S.A.
115 D2 **Bin Ghanīmah, Jabal** hills
Libya
81 C2 **Bingöl** Turkey
62 A1 **Bingzhongluo** China
60 A1 **Binjai** Indon.
53 C2 **Binnaway** Austr.
61 C1 **Bintan** i. Indon.
60 B2 **Bintuhan** Indon.
61 C1 **Bintulu** Sarawak Malaysia
115 C3 **Bin-Yauri** Nigeria
70 B2 **Binzhou** China
118 A2 **Bioco** i. Equat. Guinea
109 C2 **Biograd na Moru** Croatia
155 C1 **Biquinhas** Brazil
115 D2 **Birāk** Libya
118 C1 **Birao** C.A.R.
75 C2 **Biratnagar** Nepal
52 B3 **Birchip** Austr.
128 C2 **Birch Mountains** Can.
51 C2 **Birdsville** Austr.
80 B2 **Birecik** Turkey
Birendranagar Nepal see
Surkhet
60 A1 **Bireun** Indon.
75 C2 **Birganj** Nepal
117 B3 **Birhan** mt. Eth.
154 B2 **Birigüi** Brazil
118 C2 **Birini** C.A.R.
76 B3 **Birjand** Iran
98 B3 **Birkenhead** U.K.
99 C3 **Birmingham** U.K.
140 C2 **Birmingham** U.S.A.
114 A2 **Bîr Mogreïn** Maur.
115 C3 **Birnin-Kebbi** Nigeria
115 C3 **Birnin Konni** Niger
69 E1 **Birobidzhan** Rus. Fed.
97 C2 **Birr** Rep. of Ireland
96 C1 **Birsay** U.K.
78 A2 **Bi'r Shalatayn** Egypt
88 B2 **Biržai** Lith.
75 B2 **Bisalpur** India
115 E3 **Bisbee** U.S.A.
104 A2 **Biscay, Bay of** sea
France/Spain
141 D3 **Biscayne Bay** U.S.A.
102 C2 **Bischofshofen** Austria
77 D2 **Bishkek** Kyrg.
123 C3 **Bisho** S. Africa
135 C3 **Bishop** U.S.A.
98 C2 **Bishop Auckland** U.K.
69 E1 **Bishui** China
115 C1 **Bisinaca** Col.
115 C1 **Biskra** Alg.
64 B3 **Bislig** Phil.
136 C1 **Bismarck** U.S.A.
59 D3 **Bismarck Archipelago** is
P.N.G.
59 D3 **Bismarck Sea** P.N.G.
107 D2 **Bissa, Djebel** mt. Alg.
114 A3 **Bissau** Guinea-Bissau
129 E2 **Bissett** Can.
128 C2 **Bistcho Lake** Can.
110 B1 **Bistriţa** Romania
110 C1 **Bistriţa** r. Romania
100 C3 **Bitburg** Ger.
105 D2 **Bitche** France
115 D3 **Bitkine** Chad
81 C2 **Bitlis** Turkey
111 B2 **Bitola** Macedonia
Bitolj Macedonia see
Bitola
109 C2 **Bitonto** Italy

101 F2 **Bitterfeld** Ger.
122 A3 **Bitterfontein** S. Africa
134 D1 **Bitterroot** r. U.S.A.
134 C1 **Bitterroot Range** mts
U.S.A.
89 E3 **Bityug** r. Rus. Fed.
115 D3 **Biu** Nigeria
67 C3 **Biwa-ko** l. Japan
77 E1 **Biysk** Rus. Fed.
Bizerta Tunisia see Bizerte
115 C1 **Bizerte** Tunisia
92 □A2 **Bjargtangar** hd Iceland
92 G3 **Bjästa** Sweden
109 C1 **Bjelovar** Croatia
92 G2 **Bjerkvik** Norway
Björneborg Fin. see Pori
82 C2 **Bjørnøya** Arctic Ocean
114 B3 **Bla** Mali
137 E3 **Black** r. U.S.A.
51 D2 **Blackall** Austr.
98 B3 **Blackburn** U.K.
134 D2 **Blackfoot** U.S.A.
102 B2 **Black Forest** mts Ger.
136 C2 **Black Hills** U.S.A.
96 B2 **Black Isle** pen. U.K.
129 D2 **Black Lake** Can.
129 D2 **Black Lake** l. Can.
99 B4 **Black Mountains** hills U.K.
142 A1 **Black Mountains** U.S.A.
98 B3 **Blackpool** U.K.
142 B2 **Black Range** mts U.S.A.
62 B1 **Black River** r. Vietnam
138 A2 **Black River Falls** U.S.A.
134 C2 **Black Rock Desert** U.S.A.
138 C3 **Blacksburg** U.S.A.
80 B1 **Black Sea** Asia/Europe
131 D3 **Blacks Harbour** Can.
97 A1 **Blacksod Bay**
Rep. of Ireland
97 C2 **Blackstairs Mountains**
hills Rep. of Ireland
114 B4 **Black Volta** r. Africa
51 D2 **Blackwater** r. Austr.
97 C2 **Blackwater** r.
Rep. of Ireland
128 B1 **Blackwater Lake** Can.
50 A1 **Blackwood** r. Austr.
87 D4 **Blagodarnyy** Rus. Fed.
111 B2 **Blagoevgrad** Bulg.
69 E1 **Blagoveshchensk**
Rus. Fed.
129 D2 **Blaine Lake** Can.
137 D2 **Blair** U.S.A.
96 C2 **Blair Atholl** U.K.
96 C2 **Blairgowrie** U.K.
141 D2 **Blakely** U.S.A.
105 D2 **Blanc, Mont** mt.
France/Italy
153 B3 **Blanca, Bahía** b. Arg.
52 A1 **Blanche, Lake** salt flat
Austr.
152 B1 **Blanco** r. Bol.
134 B2 **Blanco, Cape** U.S.A.
131 E2 **Blanc-Sablon** Can.
92 □A2 **Blanda** r. Iceland
99 B4 **Blandford Forum** U.K.
135 E3 **Blanding** U.S.A.
107 D1 **Blanes** Spain
60 A1 **Blangkejeren** Indon.
100 A2 **Blankenberge** Belgium
100 C2 **Blankenheim** Ger.
100 C2 **Blankenrath** Ger.
147 D3 **Blanquilla, Isla** i. Venez.
103 D2 **Blansko** Czech Rep.
121 C2 **Blantyre** Malawi
97 B3 **Blarney** Rep. of Ireland
98 C2 **Blaydon** U.K.
53 C2 **Blayney** Austr.
54 B2 **Blenheim** N.Z.
115 C1 **Blida** Alg.
130 B3 **Blind River** Can.
123 C2 **Bloemfontein** S. Africa
123 C2 **Bloemhof** S. Africa
123 C2 **Bloemhof Dam** S. Africa
92 □A2 **Blönduós** Iceland
97 B1 **Bloody Foreland** pt
Rep. of Ireland
142 B1 **Bloomfield** U.S.A.
138 B2 **Bloomington** IL U.S.A.
138 B3 **Bloomington** IN U.S.A.
102 B2 **Bludenz** Austria
138 B2 **Blue Earth** U.S.A.
138 C3 **Bluefield** U.S.A.
146 B3 **Bluefields** Nic.
53 C2 **Blue Mountains** Austr.
134 C1 **Blue Mountains** U.S.A.
116 B3 **Blue Nile** r. Eth./Sudan
128 C1 **Bluenose Lake** Can.
138 C3 **Blue Ridge** mts U.S.A.
128 C2 **Blue River** Can.

97 B1 **Blue Stack Mountains**
hills Rep. of Ireland
54 A3 **Bluff** N.Z.
135 E3 **Bluff** U.S.A.
154 C3 **Blumenau** Brazil
52 A2 **Blyth** Austr.
98 C2 **Blyth** U.K.
135 D4 **Blythe** U.S.A.
140 C1 **Blytheville** U.S.A.
114 A4 **Bo** Sierra Leone
64 B2 **Boac** Phil.
146 B3 **Boaco** Nic.
151 E3 **Boa Esperança, Açude**
resr Brazil
134 C1 **Boardman** U.S.A.
123 C1 **Boatlaname** Botswana
151 F3 **Boa Viagem** Brazil
150 C2 **Boa Vista** Brazil
53 C2 **Bobadah** Austr.
71 B3 **Bobai** China
121 □D2 **Bobaomby, Tanjona** c.
Madag.
114 B3 **Bobo-Dioulasso** Burkina
121 B3 **Bobonong** Botswana
Bobriki Rus. Fed. see
Novomoskovsk
89 F3 **Bobrov** Rus. Fed.
91 C1 **Bobrovytsya** Ukr.
91 C2 **Bobrynets'** Ukr.
121 □D3 **Boby** mt. Madag.
150 C3 **Boca do Acre** Brazil
155 D1 **Bocaiúva** Brazil
154 A2 **Bocajá** Brazil
118 B2 **Bocaranga** C.A.R.
141 D3 **Boca Raton** U.S.A.
146 B4 **Bocas del Toro** Panama
103 E2 **Bochnia** Pol.
100 B2 **Bocholt** Belgium
100 C2 **Bocholt** Ger.
100 C2 **Bochum** Ger.
123 C1 **Bochum** S. Africa
101 E1 **Bockenem** Ger.
110 B1 **Bocşa** Romania
118 B2 **Boda** C.A.R.
83 I3 **Bodaybo** Rus. Fed.
96 D2 **Boddam** U.K.
115 D3 **Bodélé** reg. Chad
92 H2 **Boden** Sweden
Bodensee l. Ger./Switz.
see Constance, Lake
99 A4 **Bodmin** U.K.
99 A4 **Bodmin Moor** moorland
U.K.
92 F2 **Bodø** Norway
111 C3 **Bodrum** Turkey
118 C3 **Boende** Dem. Rep. Congo
63 A2 **Bogale** Myanmar
140 C2 **Bogalusa** U.S.A.
114 B3 **Bogandé** Burkina
118 B2 **Bogangolo** C.A.R.
80 B2 **Boğazlıyan** Turkey
68 B2 **Bogda Shan** mts China
53 D1 **Boggabilla** Austr.
53 D2 **Boggabri** Austr.
97 B2 **Boggeragh Mountains**
hills Rep. of Ireland
Boghari Alg. see
Ksar el Boukhari
59 D3 **Bogia** P.N.G.
100 B3 **Bogny-sur-Meuse** France
97 C2 **Bog of Allen** reg.
Rep. of Ireland
53 C3 **Bogong, Mount** Austr.
60 B2 **Bogor** Indon.
89 E3 **Bogorodítsk** Rus. Fed.
150 B2 **Bogotá** Col.
83 G3 **Bogotol** Rus. Fed.
Bogoyavlenskoye
Rus. Fed. see
Pervomayskiy
83 H3 **Boguchany** Rus. Fed.
89 F3 **Boguchar** Rus. Fed.
114 A3 **Bogué** Maur.
70 B2 **Bo Hai** g. China
100 A3 **Bohain-en-Vermandois**
France
70 B2 **Bohai Wan** b. China
Bohemian Forest mts Ger.
see Böhmer Wald
123 C2 **Bohlokong** S. Africa
101 F3 **Böhmer Wald** mts Ger.
91 D1 **Bohodukhiv** Ukr.
64 B3 **Bohol** i. Phil.
64 B3 **Bohol Sea** Phil.
77 E2 **Bohu** China
155 C1 **Boi, Ponta do** pt Brazil
123 C2 **Boikhutso** S. Africa
154 B3 **Boi Preto, Serra de** hills
Brazil
154 B1 **Bois** r. Brazil
126 D2 **Bois, Lac des** l. Can.

134 C2 **Boise** U.S.A.
143 C1 **Boise City** U.S.A.
129 D3 **Boissevain** Can.
123 C2 **Boitumelong** S. Africa
154 C2 **Boituva** Brazil
101 E1 **Boizenburg** Ger.
76 B3 **Bojnūrd** Iran
75 C2 **Bokaro** India
118 B3 **Bokatola** Dem. Rep. Congo
114 A3 **Boké** Guinea
118 C3 **Bokele** Dem. Rep. Congo
93 E4 **Boknafjorden** *sea chan.* Norway
115 D3 **Bokoro** Chad
63 A2 **Bokpyin** Myanmar
89 D2 **Boksitogorsk** Rus. Fed.
122 B2 **Bokspits** S. Africa
118 C3 **Bokungu** Dem. Rep. Congo
115 D3 **Bol** Chad
114 A3 **Bolama** Guinea-Bissau
75 C2 **Bolangir** India
104 C2 **Bolbec** France
77 E2 **Bole** China
118 B3 **Boleko** Dem. Rep. Congo
114 B3 **Bolgatanga** Ghana
90 B2 **Bolhrad** Ukr.
66 B1 **Boli** China
118 B3 **Bolia** Dem. Rep. Congo
92 H3 **Boliden** Sweden
110 C2 **Bolintin-Vale** Romania
137 E3 **Bolivar** *MO* U.S.A.
140 C1 **Bolivar** *TN* U.S.A.
150 B2 **Bolívar, Pico** *mt.* Venez.
152 B1 **Bolivia** *country* S. America
89 E3 **Bolkhov** Rus. Fed.
105 C3 **Bollène** France
93 G3 **Bollnäs** Sweden
53 C1 **Bollon** Austr.
101 E2 **Bollstedt** Ger.
93 F4 **Bolmen** *l.* Sweden
118 B3 **Bolobo** Dem. Rep. Congo
108 B2 **Bologna** Italy
89 D2 **Bologovo** Rus. Fed.
89 D2 **Bologoye** Rus. Fed.
123 C2 **Bolokanang** S. Africa
118 B2 **Bolomba** Dem. Rep. Congo
63 B2 **Bolovens, Phouphieng** *plat.* Laos
108 B2 **Bolsena, Lago di** *l.* Italy
83 H1 **Bol'shevik, Ostrov** *i.* Rus. Fed.
86 E2 **Bol'shezemel'skaya Tundra** *lowland* Rus. Fed.
83 L2 **Bol'shoy Aluy** *r.* Rus. Fed.
66 B2 **Bol'shoy Kamen'** Rus. Fed.
Bol'shoy Kavkaz *mts* Asia/Europe *see* **Caucasus**
83 K2 **Bol'shoy Lyakhovskiy, Ostrov** *i.* Rus. Fed.
Bol'shoy Tokmak Kyrg. *see* **Tokmok**
Bol'shoy Tokmak Ukr. *see* **Tokmak**
100 B1 **Bolsward** Neth.
98 B3 **Bolton** U.K.
80 B1 **Bolu** Turkey
59 E3 **Bolubolu** P.N.G.
92 □A2 **Bolungarvík** Iceland
108 B1 **Bolzano** Italy
118 B3 **Boma** Dem. Rep. Congo
53 D2 **Bomaderry** Austr.
53 C3 **Bombala** Austr.
Bombay India *see* **Mumbai**
155 C1 **Bom Despacho** Brazil
75 D2 **Bomdila** India
154 B1 **Bom Jardim de Goiás** Brazil
151 E4 **Bom Jesus da Lapa** Brazil
155 D2 **Bom Jesus do Itabapoana** Brazil
115 D1 **Bon, Cap** *c.* Tunisia
147 D3 **Bonaire** *i.* Neth. Antilles
134 C1 **Bonaparte, Mount** U.S.A.
50 B1 **Bonaparte Archipelago** *is* Austr.
131 E3 **Bonavista** Can.
131 E3 **Bonavista Bay** Can.
118 C2 **Bondo** Dem. Rep. Congo
114 B4 **Bondoukou** Côte d'Ivoire
Bône Alg. *see* **Annaba**
61 D2 **Bonerate, Kepulauan** *is* Indon.
155 C1 **Bonfinópolis de Minas** Brazil
117 B4 **Bonga** Eth.
75 D2 **Bongaigaon** India
118 C2 **Bongandanga** Dem. Rep. Congo
122 B2 **Bongani** S. Africa
118 C2 **Bongo, Massif des** *mts* C.A.R.
121 □D2 **Bongolava** *mts* Madag.
115 D3 **Bongor** Chad
114 B4 **Bongouanou** Côte d'Ivoire
63 B2 **Bông Sơn** Vietnam
143 D2 **Bonham** U.S.A.
105 D3 **Bonifacio** *Corsica* France
108 A2 **Bonifacio, Strait of** France/Italy
69 F3 **Bonin Islands** *is* Japan
100 C2 **Bonn** Ger.
134 C1 **Bonners Ferry** U.S.A.
105 D2 **Bonneville** France
50 A3 **Bonnie Rock** Austr.
129 C2 **Bonnyville** Can.
108 A2 **Bonorva** *Sardinia* Italy
53 D1 **Bonshaw** Austr.
61 C1 **Bontang** Indon.
114 A4 **Bonthe** Sierra Leone
64 B2 **Bontoc** Phil.
61 C2 **Bontosunggu** Indon.
123 C3 **Bontrug** S. Africa
53 C1 **Boolba** Austr.
52 B2 **Booligal** Austr.
53 C1 **Boomi** Austr.
53 D1 **Boonah** Austr.
137 E2 **Boone** U.S.A.
140 C2 **Booneville** U.S.A.
137 E3 **Boonville** U.S.A.
52 B2 **Booroorban** Austr.
53 C2 **Boorowa** Austr.
117 C3 **Boosaaso** Somalia
126 G2 **Boothia, Gulf of** Can.
126 F2 **Boothia Peninsula** Can.
118 B3 **Booué** Gabon
100 C2 **Boppard** Ger.
144 B2 **Boquilla, Presa de la** *resr* Mex.
109 D2 **Bor** Serb. and Mont.
117 B4 **Bor** Sudan
80 B2 **Bor** Turkey
93 F4 **Borås** Sweden
81 D3 **Borāzjān** Iran
150 D3 **Borba** Brazil
104 B3 **Bordeaux** France
126 E1 **Borden Island** Can.
127 G2 **Borden Peninsula** Can.
52 B3 **Bordertown** Austr.
107 D2 **Bordj Bou Arréridj** Alg.
107 D2 **Bordj Bounaama** Alg.
114 B2 **Bordj Flye Ste-Marie** Alg.
115 C1 **Bordj Messaouda** Alg.
114 C2 **Bordj Mokhtar** Alg.
Bordj Omar Driss Alg. *see* **Bordj Omer Driss**
115 C2 **Bordj Omer Driss** Alg.
94 B1 **Borðoy** *i.* Faroe Is
Borgå Fin. *see* **Porvoo**
92 □A3 **Borgarnes** Iceland
143 C1 **Borger** U.S.A.
93 G4 **Borgholm** Sweden
100 B2 **Borgloon** Belgium
108 A1 **Borgosesia** Italy
87 D3 **Borisoglebsk** Rus. Fed.
89 E2 **Borisoglebskiy** Rus. Fed.
91 D1 **Borisovka** Rus. Fed.
119 C2 **Bo River Post** Sudan
100 C2 **Borken** Ger.
92 G2 **Borkenes** Norway
100 C1 **Borkum** Ger.
100 C1 **Borkum** *i.* Ger.
93 G3 **Borlänge** Sweden
101 F2 **Borna** Ger.
100 C1 **Borne** Neth.
61 C1 **Borneo** *i.* Asia
93 F4 **Bornholm** *i.* Denmark
111 C3 **Bornova** Turkey
90 B1 **Borodyanka** Ukr.
77 E2 **Borohoro Shan** *mts* China
114 B3 **Boron** Mali
89 D2 **Borovichi** Rus. Fed.
89 E2 **Borovsk** Rus. Fed.
76 C1 **Borovskoy** Kazakh.
51 C1 **Borroloola** Austr.
110 B1 **Borşa** Romania
76 B2 **Borsakelmas sho'rxogi** *salt marsh* Uzbek.
90 B2 **Borshchiv** Ukr.
69 D1 **Borshchovochnyy Khrebet** *mts* Rus. Fed.
101 E1 **Börßum** Ger.
Bortala China *see* **Bole**
81 C2 **Borūjerd** Iran
90 A2 **Boryslav** Ukr.
90 C1 **Boryspil'** Ukr.
91 C1 **Borzna** Ukr.
69 D1 **Borzya** Rus. Fed.
109 C1 **Bosanska Dubica** Bos.-Herz.
109 C1 **Bosanska Gradiška** Bos.-Herz.
109 C2 **Bosanska Krupa** Bos.-Herz.
109 C1 **Bosanski Novi** Bos.-Herz.
109 C2 **Bosansko Grahovo** Bos.-Herz.
71 A3 **Bose** China
123 C2 **Boshof** S. Africa
109 C2 **Bosnia-Herzegovina** *country* Europe
118 B2 **Bosobolo** Dem. Rep. Congo
111 C2 **Bosporus** *str.* Turkey
142 B2 **Bosque** U.S.A.
118 B2 **Bossangoa** C.A.R.
118 B2 **Bossembélé** C.A.R.
140 B2 **Bossier City** U.S.A.
122 A2 **Bossiesvlei** Namibia
68 B2 **Bosten Hu** *l.* China
99 C3 **Boston** U.K.
139 E2 **Boston** U.S.A.
140 B1 **Boston Mountains** U.S.A.
53 D2 **Botany Bay** Austr.
120 B3 **Boteti** *r.* Botswana
110 B2 **Botev** *mt.* Bulg.
80 A1 **Botevgrad** Bulg.
92 G3 **Bothnia, Gulf of** Fin./Sweden
110 C1 **Botoşani** Romania
70 B2 **Botou** China
123 C2 **Botshabelo** S. Africa
120 B3 **Botswana** *country* Africa
109 C3 **Botte Donato, Monte** *mt.* Italy
136 C1 **Bottineau** U.S.A.
100 C2 **Bottrop** Ger.
154 C2 **Botucatu** Brazil
114 B4 **Bouaké** Côte d'Ivoire
118 B2 **Bouar** C.A.R.
114 B1 **Bouârfa** Morocco
131 D3 **Bouctouche** Can.
107 E2 **Bougaa** Alg.
48 G4 **Bougainville Island** P.N.G.
Bougie Alg. *see* **Bejaïa**
114 B3 **Bougouni** Mali
100 B3 **Bouillon** Belgium
107 D2 **Bouira** Alg.
114 A2 **Boujdour** Western Sahara
50 B3 **Boulder** Austr.
136 B2 **Boulder** *CO* U.S.A.
134 D1 **Boulder** *MT* U.S.A.
135 D3 **Boulder City** U.S.A.
Boulhaut Morocco *see* Ben Slimane
51 C2 **Boulia** Austr.
104 C2 **Boulogne-Billancourt** France
104 C1 **Boulogne-sur-Mer** France
118 C2 **Boulouba** C.A.R.
118 B3 **Boumango** Gabon
118 B2 **Boumba** *r.* Cameroon
107 D2 **Boumerdes** Alg.
114 B4 **Bouna** Côte d'Ivoire
114 B4 **Boundiali** Côte d'Ivoire
134 D2 **Bountiful** U.S.A.
49 I8 **Bounty Islands** N.Z.
114 B3 **Bourem** Mali
104 C2 **Bourganeuf** France
105 D2 **Bourg-en-Bresse** France
104 C2 **Bourges** France
Bourgogne *reg.* France *see* **Burgundy**
105 D2 **Bourgoin-Jallieu** France
53 C2 **Bourke** Austr.
99 C3 **Bourne** U.K.
99 C4 **Bournemouth** U.K.
118 C1 **Bourtoutou** Chad
115 C1 **Bou Saâda** Alg.
115 D3 **Bousso** Chad
100 A2 **Boussu** Belgium
114 A3 **Boutilimit** Maur.
128 C3 **Bow** *r.* Can.
Bowa China *see* **Muli**
51 D2 **Bowen** Austr.
53 C3 **Bowen, Mount** Austr.
129 C3 **Bow Island** Can.
138 B3 **Bowling Green** *KY* U.S.A.
137 E3 **Bowling Green** *MO* U.S.A.
138 C2 **Bowling Green** *OH* U.S.A.
136 C1 **Bowman** U.S.A.
53 D2 **Bowral** Austr.
101 D3 **Boxberg** Ger.
100 B2 **Boxtel** Neth.
80 B1 **Boyabat** Turkey
71 B3 **Boyang** China
97 B2 **Boyle** Rep. of Ireland
97 C2 **Boyne** *r.* Rep. of Ireland
136 B2 **Boysen Reservoir** U.S.A.
152 B2 **Boyuibe** Bol.
111 C3 **Bozburun** Turkey
111 C3 **Bozcaada** *i.* Turkey
111 C3 **Bozdağ** *mt.* Turkey
111 C3 **Boz Dağları** *mts* Turkey
111 C3 **Bozdoğan** Turkey
134 D1 **Bozeman** U.S.A.
118 B2 **Bozoum** C.A.R.
111 D3 **Bozüyük** Turkey
109 C2 **Brač** *i.* Croatia
130 C3 **Bracebridge** Can.
131 D3 **Brachet, Lac au** *l.* Can.
93 G3 **Bräcke** Sweden
99 C4 **Bracknell** U.K.
109 C2 **Bradano** *r.* Italy
141 D3 **Bradenton** U.S.A.
98 C3 **Bradford** U.K.
139 D2 **Bradford** U.S.A.
143 D2 **Brady** U.S.A.
96 C2 **Braemar** U.K.
106 B1 **Braga** Port.
151 E3 **Bragança** Brazil
106 B1 **Bragança** Port.
155 C2 **Bragança Paulista** Brazil
89 D3 **Brahin** Belarus
75 D2 **Brahmanbaria** Bangl.
75 C3 **Brahmapur** India
62 A1 **Brahmaputra** *r.* China/India
53 C3 **Braidwood** Austr.
110 C1 **Brăila** Romania
137 E1 **Brainerd** U.S.A.
99 D4 **Braintree** U.K.
100 B2 **Braives** Belgium
101 D1 **Brake (Unterweser)** Ger.
122 A1 **Brakwater** Namibia
98 B2 **Brampton** U.K.
101 D1 **Bramsche** Ger.
150 C3 **Branco** *r.* Brazil
101 F1 **Brandenburg** Ger.
129 E3 **Brandon** Can.
140 C2 **Brandon** U.S.A.
97 A2 **Brandon Mountain** *hill* Rep. of Ireland
122 B3 **Brandvlei** S. Africa
103 D1 **Braniewo** Pol.
130 B3 **Brantford** Can.
53 D2 **Branxton** Austr.
131 D3 **Bras d'Or Lake** Can.
155 D1 **Brasil, Planalto do** *plat.* Brazil
154 C1 **Brasilândia** Brazil
154 C1 **Brasília** Brazil
155 D1 **Brasília de Minas** Brazil
88 C2 **Braslaw** Belarus
110 C1 **Braşov** Romania
103 D2 **Bratislava** Slovakia
83 H3 **Bratsk** Rus. Fed.
102 C2 **Braunau am Inn** Austria
101 E1 **Braunschweig** Ger.
92 □A2 **Brautarholt** Iceland
Bravo del Norte, Río *r.* Mex./U.S.A. *see* Rio Grande
135 C4 **Brawley** U.S.A.
97 C2 **Bray** Rep. of Ireland
150 D2 **Brazil** *country* S. America
158 E6 **Brazil Basin** *sea feature* S. Atlantic Ocean
143 D3 **Brazos** *r.* U.S.A.
118 B3 **Brazzaville** Congo
109 C2 **Brčko** Bos.-Herz.
96 C2 **Brechin** U.K.
100 B2 **Brecht** Belgium
143 D2 **Breckenridge** U.S.A.
103 D2 **Břeclav** Czech Rep.
99 B4 **Brecon** U.K.
99 B4 **Brecon Beacons** *reg.* U.K.
100 B2 **Breda** Neth.
122 B3 **Bredasdorp** S. Africa
102 B2 **Bregenz** Austria
92 H1 **Breivikbotn** Norway
92 E3 **Brekstad** Norway
101 D1 **Bremen** Ger.
101 D1 **Bremerhaven** Ger.
Bremersdorp Swaziland *see* **Manzini**
134 B1 **Bremerton** U.S.A.
101 D1 **Bremervörde** Ger.
143 D2 **Brenham** U.S.A.
108 B1 **Brennero** Italy
102 C2 **Brenner Pass** Austria/Italy
99 D4 **Brentwood** U.K.
108 B1 **Brescia** Italy
100 A2 **Breskens** Neth.
108 B1 **Bressanone** Italy
96 □ **Bressay** *i.* U.K.
104 B2 **Bressuire** France
88 B3 **Brest** Belarus
104 B2 **Brest** France

Brest-Litovsk Belarus *see* Brest
Bretagne *reg.* France *see* Brittany
140 C3 **Breton Sound** *b.* U.S.A.
151 D3 **Breves** Brazil
53 C1 **Brewarrina** Austr.
134 C1 **Brewster** U.S.A.
89 E2 **Breytovo** Rus. Fed.
Brezhnev Rus. Fed. *see* Naberezhnyye Chelny
109 C1 **Brezovo Polje** *hill* Croatia
118 C2 **Bria** C.A.R.
105 D3 **Briançon** France
90 B2 **Briceni** Moldova
Brichany Moldova *see* Briceni
99 B4 **Bridgend** U.K.
139 E2 **Bridgeport** *CT* U.S.A.
136 C2 **Bridgeport** *NE* U.S.A.
147 E3 **Bridgetown** Barbados
131 D3 **Bridgewater** Can.
99 B3 **Bridgnorth** U.K.
99 B4 **Bridgwater** U.K.
99 B4 **Bridgwater Bay** U.K.
98 C2 **Bridlington** U.K.
98 C2 **Bridlington Bay** U.K.
99 B4 **Bridport** U.K.
105 D2 **Brig** Switz.
134 D2 **Brigham City** U.S.A.
53 C3 **Bright** Austr.
54 B3 **Brighton** N.Z.
99 C4 **Brighton** U.K.
136 C3 **Brighton** *CO* U.S.A.
138 C2 **Brighton** *MI* U.S.A.
105 D3 **Brignoles** France
114 A3 **Brikama** Gambia
101 D2 **Brilon** Ger.
109 C2 **Brindisi** Italy
97 B1 **Brinlack** Rep. of Ireland
53 D1 **Brisbane** Austr.
99 B4 **Bristol** U.K.
139 E2 **Bristol** *CT* U.S.A.
141 D1 **Bristol** *TN* U.S.A.
99 A4 **Bristol Channel** *est.* U.K.
128 B2 **British Columbia** *prov.* Can.
British Guiana *country* S. America *see* **Guyana**
British Honduras *country* Central America *see* **Belize**
56 C6 **British Indian Ocean Territory** *terr.* Indian Ocean
British Solomon Islands *country* S. Pacific Ocean *see* **Solomon Islands**
123 C2 **Brits** S. Africa
122 B3 **Britstown** S. Africa
104 B2 **Brittany** *reg.* France
104 C2 **Brive-la-Gaillarde** France
106 C1 **Briviesca** Spain
99 B4 **Brixham** U.K.
103 D2 **Brno** Czech Rep.
Broach India *see* **Bharuch**
141 D2 **Broad** *r.* U.S.A.
130 C2 **Broadback** *r.* Can.
53 C3 **Broadford** Austr.
96 B2 **Broadford** U.K.
96 C3 **Broad Law** *hill* U.K.
136 B1 **Broadus** U.S.A.
129 D2 **Brochet** Can.
129 D2 **Brochet, Lac** *l.* Can.
101 E1 **Bröckel** Ger.
101 E2 **Brocken** *mt.* Ger.
126 E1 **Brock Island** Can.
130 C3 **Brockville** Can.
127 G2 **Brodeur Peninsula** Can.
96 B3 **Brodick** U.K.
103 D1 **Brodnica** Pol.
90 B1 **Brody** Ukr.
143 D1 **Broken Arrow** U.S.A.
137 D2 **Broken Bow** U.S.A.
52 B2 **Broken Hill** Austr.
Broken Hill Zambia *see* Kabwe
159 F6 **Broken Plateau** *sea feature* Indian Ocean
151 D2 **Brokopondo** Suriname
99 B3 **Bromsgrove** U.K.
93 E4 **Brønderslev** Denmark
123 C2 **Bronkhorstspruit** S. Africa
92 F2 **Brønnøysund** Norway
64 A3 **Brooke's Point** Phil.
140 B2 **Brookhaven** U.S.A.
134 B2 **Brookings** *OR* U.S.A.
137 D2 **Brookings** *SD* U.S.A.
128 C2 **Brooks** Can.
126 C2 **Brooks Range** *mts* U.S.A.
141 D3 **Brooksville** U.S.A.
139 D2 **Brookville** U.S.A.
96 B2 **Broom, Loch** *inlet* U.K.
50 B1 **Broome** Austr.
134 B2 **Brothers** U.S.A.
Broughton Island Can. *see* **Qikiqtarjuaq**
90 C1 **Brovary** Ukr.
143 C2 **Brownfield** U.S.A.
128 C3 **Browning** U.S.A.
140 C1 **Brownsville** *TN* U.S.A.
143 D3 **Brownsville** *TX* U.S.A.
143 D2 **Brownwood** U.S.A.
92 □A2 **Brú** Iceland
104 C1 **Bruay-la-Bussière** France
138 B1 **Bruce Crossing** U.S.A.
130 B3 **Bruce Peninsula** Can.
103 D2 **Bruck an der Mur** Austria
Bruges Belgium *see* Brugge
100 A2 **Brugge** Belgium
62 A1 **Bruint** India
128 C2 **Brûlé** Can.
151 E4 **Brumado** Brazil
93 F3 **Brumunddal** Norway
61 C1 **Brunei** *country* Asia
Brunei Brunei *see* **Bandar Seri Begawan**
102 C2 **Brunico** Italy
Brünn Czech Rep. *see* Brno
101 D1 **Brunsbüttel** Ger.
141 D2 **Brunswick** *GA* U.S.A.
139 F2 **Brunswick** *ME* U.S.A.
53 D1 **Brunswick Head** Austr.
123 D2 **Bruntville** S. Africa
136 C2 **Brush** U.S.A.
100 B2 **Brussels** Belgium
Bruxelles Belgium *see* Brussels
143 D2 **Bryan** U.S.A.
89 D3 **Bryansk** Rus. Fed.
91 D2 **Bryn'kovskaya** Rus. Fed.
91 D2 **Bryukhovetskaya** Rus. Fed.
103 D1 **Brzeg** Pol.
Brześć nad Bugiem Belarus *see* **Brest**
114 A3 **Buba** Guinea-Bissau
111 C3 **Buca** Turkey
80 B2 **Bucak** Turkey
150 B2 **Bucaramanga** Col.
90 B2 **Buchach** Ukr.
53 C3 **Buchan** Austr.
114 A4 **Buchanan** Liberia
110 C2 **Bucharest** Romania
101 D1 **Bucholz in der Nordheide** Ger.
110 C1 **Bucin, Pasul** *pass* Romania
101 D1 **Bückeburg** Ger.
142 A2 **Buckeye** U.S.A.
96 C2 **Buckhaven** U.K.
96 C2 **Buckie** U.K.
99 C3 **Buckingham** U.K.
51 C1 **Buckingham Bay** Austr.
51 D2 **Buckland Tableland** *reg.* Austr.
52 A2 **Buckleboo** Austr.
139 F2 **Bucksport** U.S.A.
103 D2 **Bučovice** Czech Rep.
Bucureşti Romania *see* Bucharest
89 D3 **Buda-Kashalyova** Belarus
103 D2 **Budapest** Hungary
75 B2 **Budaun** India
108 A2 **Buddusò** *Sardinia* Italy
99 A4 **Bude** U.K.
87 D4 **Budennovsk** Rus. Fed.
Budennoye Rus. Fed. *see* Krasnogvardeyskoye
89 D2 **Budogoshch'** Rus. Fed.
108 A2 **Budoni** *Sardinia* Italy
Budweis Czech Rep. *see* České Budějovice
118 A2 **Buea** Cameroon
135 B4 **Buellton** U.S.A.
150 B2 **Buenaventura** Col.
144 B2 **Buenaventura** Mex.
Buena Vista *i.* N. Mariana Is *see* **Tinian**
106 C1 **Buendia, Embalse de** *resr* Spain
155 D1 **Buenópolis** Brazil
153 C3 **Buenos Aires** Arg.
153 A4 **Buenos Aires, Lago** *l.* Arg./Chile
139 D2 **Buffalo** *NY* U.S.A.
136 C1 **Buffalo** *SD* U.S.A.
143 D2 **Buffalo** *TX* U.S.A.
136 B2 **Buffalo** *WY* U.S.A.
129 D2 **Buffalo Narrows** Can.
121 C3 **Buffalo Range** Zimbabwe
122 A2 **Buffels** *watercourse* S. Africa
123 C1 **Buffels Drift** S. Africa
110 C2 **Buftea** Romania
103 E1 **Bug** *r.* Pol.
61 C2 **Bugel, Tanjung** *pt* Indon.
109 C2 **Bugojno** Bos.-Herz.
86 D2 **Bugrino** Rus. Fed.
64 A3 **Bugsuk** *i.* Phil.
87 E3 **Bugul'ma** Rus. Fed.
87 E3 **Buguruslan** Rus. Fed.
121 C2 **Buhera** Zimbabwe
110 C1 **Buhuşi** Romania
99 B3 **Builth Wells** U.K.
69 D1 **Buir Nur** *l.* Mongolia
120 A3 **Buitepos** Namibia
109 D2 **Bujanovac** Serb. and Mont.
119 C3 **Bujumbura** Burundi
69 D1 **Bukachacha** Rus. Fed.
120 B2 **Bukalo** Namibia
119 C3 **Bukavu** Dem. Rep. Congo
Bukhara Uzbek. *see* Buxoro
60 B2 **Bukittinggi** Indon.
119 D3 **Bukoba** Tanz.
103 D1 **Bukowiec** *hill* Pol.
59 C3 **Bula** Indon.
53 D2 **Bulahdelah** Austr.
121 B3 **Bulawayo** Zimbabwe
111 C3 **Buldan** Turkey
123 D2 **Bulembu** Swaziland
68 C1 **Bulgan** Mongolia
110 C2 **Bulgaria** *country* Europe
54 B2 **Buller** *r.* N.Z.
142 A1 **Bullhead City** U.S.A.
52 B1 **Bulloo** *watercourse* Austr.
52 B1 **Bulloo Downs** Austr.
122 A1 **Büllsport** Namibia
61 D2 **Bulukumba** Indon.
118 B3 **Bulungu** Dem. Rep. Congo
118 B3 **Bumba** Dem. Rep. Congo
118 C2 **Bumba** Dem. Rep. Congo
62 A1 **Bumhkang** Myanmar
118 B3 **Buna** Dem. Rep. Congo
97 B1 **Bunbeg** Rep. of Ireland
50 A3 **Bunbury** Austr.
97 C2 **Bunclody** Rep. of Ireland
97 C1 **Buncrana** Rep. of Ireland
119 D3 **Bunda** Tanz.
51 E2 **Bundaberg** Austr.
53 C1 **Bundaleer** Austr.
53 D2 **Bundarra** Austr.
74 B2 **Bundi** India
97 B1 **Bundoran** Rep. of Ireland
75 C2 **Bundu** India
53 C3 **Bungendore** Austr.
119 D2 **Bungoma** Kenya
67 B4 **Bungo-suidō** *sea chan.* Japan
119 D2 **Bunia** Dem. Rep. Congo
118 C3 **Bunianga** Dem. Rep. Congo
63 B2 **Buôn Mê Thuôt** Vietnam
119 D3 **Bura** Kenya
117 C3 **Buraan** Somalia
Burang China *see* **Jirang**
78 B2 **Buraydah** Saudi Arabia
101 D2 **Burbach** Ger.
117 C4 **Burco** Somalia
100 B1 **Burdaard** Neth.
111 D3 **Burdur** Turkey
Burdwan India *see* Barddhaman
117 B3 **Burē** Eth.
99 D3 **Bure** *r.* U.K.
69 E1 **Bureinskiy Khrebet** *mts* Rus. Fed.
101 D2 **Büren** Ger.
Bureya Range *mts* Rus. Fed. *see* Bureinskiy Khrebet
110 C2 **Burgas** Bulg.
101 E1 **Burg bei Magdeburg** Ger.
101 E1 **Burgdorf** Ger.
101 E1 **Burgdorf** Ger.
131 E3 **Burgeo** Can.
123 C3 **Burgersdorp** S. Africa
123 D1 **Burgersfort** S. Africa
100 A2 **Burgh-Haamstede** Neth.
101 F3 **Burglengenfeld** Ger.
145 C2 **Burgos** Mex.
106 C1 **Burgos** Spain
105 C2 **Burgundy** *reg.* France
111 C3 **Burhaniye** Turkey
74 B2 **Burhanpur** India
75 C2 **Burhar-Dhanpuri** India
101 D1 **Burhave (Butjadingen)** Ger.
154 C2 **Buri** Brazil
60 B2 **Buriai** Indon.
64 B2 **Burias** *i.* Phil.
131 E3 **Burin** Can.
63 B2 **Buriram** Thai.
154 C1 **Buriti Alegre** Brazil
151 E3 **Buriti Bravo** Brazil
155 C1 **Buritis** Brazil
107 C2 **Burjassot** Spain
143 D2 **Burkburnett** U.S.A.
51 C1 **Burketown** Austr.
114 B3 **Burkina** *country* Africa
134 D2 **Burley** U.S.A.
136 C3 **Burlington** *CO* U.S.A.
137 E2 **Burlington** *IA* U.S.A.
141 E1 **Burlington** *NC* U.S.A.
139 E2 **Burlington** *VT* U.S.A.
134 B2 **Burney** U.S.A.
51 D4 **Burnie** Austr.
98 B3 **Burnley** U.K.
134 C2 **Burns** U.S.A.
134 C2 **Burns Junction** U.S.A.
128 B2 **Burns Lake** Can.
137 E2 **Burnsville** U.S.A.
101 F1 **Burow** Ger.
77 E2 **Burqin** China
52 A2 **Burra** Austr.
109 D2 **Burrel** Albania
97 B2 **Burren** *reg.* Rep. of Ireland
53 C2 **Burrendong Reservoir** Austr.
53 C2 **Burren Junction** Austr.
107 C2 **Burriana** Spain
53 C2 **Burrinjuck Reservoir** Austr.
144 B2 **Burro, Serranías del** *mts* Mex.
111 C2 **Bursa** Turkey
116 B2 **Būr Safājah** Egypt
Būr Sa'īd Egypt *see* Port Said
Būr Sa'īd Egypt *see* Port Said
Būr Sudan Sudan *see* Port Sudan
130 C2 **Burton, Lac** *l.* Can.
97 B1 **Burtonport** Rep. of Ireland
99 C3 **Burton upon Trent** U.K.
52 B2 **Burtundy** Austr.
59 C3 **Buru** *i.* Indon.
119 C3 **Burundi** *country* Africa
119 C3 **Bururi** Burundi
96 C1 **Burwick** U.K.
98 B3 **Bury** U.K.
91 C1 **Buryn'** Ukr.
76 B2 **Burynshyk** Kazakh.
99 D3 **Bury St Edmunds** U.K.
118 C3 **Busanga** Dem. Rep. Congo
81 D3 **Būshehr** Iran
119 D3 **Bushenyi** Uganda
Bushire Iran *see* **Būshehr**
118 C2 **Businga** Dem. Rep. Congo
50 A3 **Busselton** Austr.
143 C3 **Bustamante** Mex.
108 A1 **Busto Arsizio** Italy
64 A2 **Busuanga** Phil.
118 C2 **Buta** Dem. Rep. Congo
119 C3 **Butare** Rwanda
96 B3 **Bute** *i.* U.K.
119 C2 **Butembo** Dem. Rep. Congo
123 C2 **Butha-Buthe** Lesotho
139 D2 **Butler** U.S.A.
61 D2 **Buton** *i.* Indon.
134 D1 **Butte** U.S.A.
60 B1 **Butterworth** Malaysia
96 A1 **Butt of Lewis** *hd* U.K.
129 E2 **Button Bay** Can.
131 D1 **Button Islands** Can.
64 B3 **Butuan** Phil.
89 F3 **Buturlinovka** Rus. Fed.
75 C2 **Butwal** Nepal
101 D2 **Butzbach** Ger.
117 C4 **Buulobarde** Somalia
117 C5 **Buur Gaabo** Somalia
117 C4 **Buurhabaka** Somalia
78 A2 **Buwāṭah** Saudi Arabia
76 C3 **Buxoro** Uzbek.
101 D1 **Buxtehude** Ger.
98 C3 **Buxton** U.K.
89 F2 **Buy** Rus. Fed.
87 D4 **Buynaksk** Rus. Fed.
111 C3 **Büyükmenderes** *r.* Turkey
65 A1 **Buyun Shan** *mt.* China
74 B1 **Buzai Gumbad** Afgh.
110 C1 **Buzău** Romania
110 C1 **Buzău** *r.* Romania
121 C2 **Búzi** Moz.
87 E3 **Buzuluk** Rus. Fed.
88 C3 **Byahoml'** Belarus
110 C2 **Byala** Bulg.
110 C2 **Byala** Bulg.

88 C3 **Byalynichy** Belarus
88 D3 **Byarezina** *r.* Belarus
88 B3 **Byaroza** Belarus
88 C3 **Byarozawka** Belarus
103 D1 **Bydgoszcz** Pol.
Byelorussia *country* Europe *see* **Belarus**
88 C3 **Byerazino** Belarus
88 C2 **Byeshankovichy** Belarus
89 D3 **Bykhaw** Belarus
127 G2 **Bylot Island** Can.
53 C2 **Byrock** Austr.
53 D1 **Byron Bay** Austr.
83 J2 **Bytantay** *r.* Rus. Fed.
103 D1 **Bytom** Pol.
103 D1 **Bytów** Pol.

C

120 A2 **Caála** Angola
154 B2 **Caarapó** Brazil
155 C1 **Caatinga** Brazil
144 B2 **Caballos Mesteños, Llano de los** *plain* Mex.
106 B1 **Cabañaquinta** Spain
64 B2 **Cabanatuan** Phil.
117 C3 **Cabdul Qaadir** Somalia
154 A1 **Cabeceira Rio Manso** Brazil
154 C1 **Cabeceiras** Brazil
106 B2 **Cabeza del Buey** Spain
152 B1 **Cabezas** Bol.
150 B1 **Cabimas** Venez.
120 A1 **Cabinda** Angola
118 B3 **Cabinda** *prov.* Angola
151 F3 **Cabo** Brazil
155 D2 **Cabo Frio** Brazil
155 D2 **Cabo Frio, Ilha do** *i.* Brazil
130 C3 **Cabonga, Réservoir** *resr* Can.
53 D1 **Caboolture** Austr.
150 B3 **Cabo Pantoja** Peru
121 C2 **Cabora Bassa, Lake** *resr* Moz.
144 A1 **Caborca** Mex.
131 D3 **Cabot Strait** Can.
106 C2 **Cabra** Spain
155 D1 **Cabral, Serra do** *mts* Brazil
107 D2 **Cabrera** *i.* Spain
106 B1 **Cabrera, Sierra de la** *mts* Spain
129 D2 **Cabri** Can.
107 C2 **Cabriel** *r.* Spain
154 B3 **Caçador** Brazil
109 D2 **Čačak** Serb. and Mont.
108 A2 **Caccia, Capo** *c.* *Sardinia* Italy
106 B2 **Cacém** Port.
151 D4 **Cáceres** Brazil
106 B2 **Cáceres** Spain
128 B2 **Cache Creek** Can.
114 A3 **Cacheu** Guinea-Bissau
151 D3 **Cachimbo, Serra do** *hills* Brazil
154 B1 **Cachoeira Alta** Brazil
155 D2 **Cachoeiro de Itapemirim** Brazil
114 A3 **Cacine** Guinea-Bissau
120 A2 **Cacolo** Angola
120 A2 **Caconda** Angola
154 B1 **Caçu** Brazil
103 D2 **Čadca** Slovakia
101 D1 **Cadenberge** Ger.
145 B2 **Cadereyta** Mex.
138 B2 **Cadillac** U.S.A.
64 B2 **Cadiz** Phil.
106 B2 **Cádiz** Spain
106 B2 **Cádiz, Golfo de** *g.* Spain
128 C2 **Cadotte Lake** Can.
104 B2 **Caen** France
Caerdydd U.K. *see* **Cardiff**
Caerfyrddin U.K. *see* **Carmarthen**
Caergybi U.K. *see* **Holyhead**
98 A3 **Caernarfon** U.K.
99 A3 **Caernarfon Bay** U.K.
Caernarvon U.K. *see* **Caernarfon**
152 B2 **Cafayate** Arg.
154 C2 **Cafelândia** Brazil
64 B3 **Cagayan de Oro** Phil.
108 B2 **Cagli** Italy
108 A3 **Cagliari** *Sardinia* Italy
108 A3 **Cagliari, Golfo di** *b.* *Sardinia* Italy
120 A2 **Cahama** Angola
97 B3 **Caha Mountains** *hills* Rep. of Ireland
97 A3 **Cahermore** Rep. of Ireland
97 A3 **Cahersiveen** Rep. of Ireland
97 C2 **Cahir** Rep. of Ireland
Cahora Bassa, Lago de *resr* Moz. *see* **Cabora Bassa, Lake**
97 C2 **Cahore Point** Rep. of Ireland
104 C3 **Cahors** France
90 B2 **Cahul** Moldova
121 C2 **Caia** Moz.
151 D4 **Caiabis, Serra dos** *hills* Brazil
120 B2 **Caianda** Angola
154 B1 **Caiapó, Serra do** *mts* Brazil
154 B1 **Caiapônia** Brazil
147 C2 **Caicos Islands** Turks and Caicos Is
96 C2 **Cairngorm Mountains** U.K.
96 B3 **Cairnryan** U.K.
51 D1 **Cairns** Austr.
116 B1 **Cairo** Egypt
Caisleán an Bharraigh Rep. of Ireland *see* **Castlebar**
98 C3 **Caistor** U.K.
120 A2 **Caiundo** Angola
150 B3 **Cajamarca** Peru
109 C1 **Čakovec** Croatia
123 C3 **Cala** S. Africa
115 C4 **Calabar** Nigeria
150 C2 **Calabozo** Venez.
110 B2 **Calafat** Romania
153 A5 **Calafate** Arg.
107 C1 **Calahorra** Spain
120 A2 **Calai** Angola
104 C1 **Calais** France
139 F1 **Calais** U.S.A.
152 B2 **Calama** Chile
64 A2 **Calamian Group** *is* Phil.
107 C1 **Calamocha** Spain
120 A1 **Calandula** Angola
60 A1 **Calang** Indon.
115 E1 **Calanscio Sand Sea** *des.* Libya
64 B2 **Calapan** Phil.
110 C2 **Călărași** Romania
107 C1 **Calatayud** Spain
64 B2 **Calayan** *i.* Phil.
64 B2 **Calbayog** Phil.
151 F3 **Calcanhar, Ponta do** *pt* Brazil
151 D2 **Calçoene** Brazil
Calcutta India *see* **Kolkata**
106 B2 **Caldas da Rainha** Port.
154 C1 **Caldas Novas** Brazil
152 A2 **Caldera** Chile
51 D2 **Caldervale** Austr.
134 C2 **Caldwell** U.S.A.
123 C3 **Caledon** *r.* Lesotho/S. Africa
122 A3 **Caledon** S. Africa
153 B4 **Caleta Olivia** Arg.
98 A2 **Calf of Man** *i.* Isle of Man
128 C2 **Calgary** Can.
150 B2 **Cali** Col.
73 B3 **Calicut** India
135 D3 **Caliente** U.S.A.
135 B2 **California** *state* U.S.A.
144 A1 **California, Gulf of** *g.* Mex.
135 B3 **California Aqueduct** *canal* U.S.A.
81 C2 **Cälilabad** Azer.
122 B3 **Calitzdorp** S. Africa
145 C2 **Calkiní** Mex.
52 B1 **Callabonna, Lake** *salt flat* Austr.
135 C3 **Callaghan, Mount** U.S.A.
97 C2 **Callan** Rep. of Ireland
96 B2 **Callander** U.K.
150 B4 **Callao** Peru
99 A4 **Callington** U.K.
108 B3 **Caltagirone** *Sicily* Italy
108 B3 **Caltanissetta** *Sicily* Italy
120 A1 **Calulo** Angola
120 B2 **Calunda** Angola
120 A2 **Caluquembe** Angola
117 D3 **Caluula** Somalia
105 D3 **Calvi** *Corsica* France
107 D2 **Calvià** Spain
144 B2 **Calvillo** Mex.
122 A3 **Calvinia** S. Africa
109 C2 **Calvo, Monte** *mt.* Italy
120 A1 **Camabatela** Angola
151 F4 **Camaçari** Brazil
144 B2 **Camacho** Mex.
120 A2 **Camacupa** Angola
146 C2 **Camagüey** Cuba
146 C2 **Camagüey, Archipiélago de** *is* Cuba
150 B4 **Camana** Peru
120 B2 **Camanongue** Angola
154 B1 **Camapuã** Brazil
145 C2 **Camargo** Mex.
63 B3 **Ca Mau** Vietnam
Cambay India *see* **Khambhat**
63 B2 **Cambodia** *country* Asia
99 A4 **Camborne** U.K.
105 C1 **Cambrai** France
99 B3 **Cambrian Mountains** *hills* U.K.
138 C2 **Cambridge** Can.
54 C1 **Cambridge** N.Z.
99 D3 **Cambridge** U.K.
139 E2 **Cambridge** *MA* U.S.A.
139 D3 **Cambridge** *MD* U.S.A.
137 E1 **Cambridge** *MN* U.S.A.
138 C2 **Cambridge** *OH* U.S.A.
126 E2 **Cambridge Bay** Can.
131 D2 **Cambrien, Lac** *l.* Can.
120 B1 **Cambulo** Angola
53 D2 **Camden** Austr.
140 B2 **Camden** *AR* U.S.A.
139 F2 **Camden** *ME* U.S.A.
139 D3 **Camden** *NJ* U.S.A.
137 E3 **Camdenton** U.S.A.
137 E3 **Cameron** U.S.A.
118 B2 **Cameroon** *country* Africa
118 A2 **Cameroun, Mont** *vol.* Cameroon
151 E3 **Cametá** Brazil
64 B2 **Camiguin** *i.* Phil.
64 B3 **Camiguin** *i.* Phil.
152 B2 **Camiri** Bol.
151 E3 **Camocim** Brazil
51 C1 **Camooweal** Austr.
63 A3 **Camorta** *i.* India
153 A4 **Campana, Isla** *i.* Chile
155 D1 **Campanário** Brazil
155 C2 **Campanha** Brazil
122 B2 **Campbell** S. Africa
54 B2 **Campbell, Cape** N.Z.
48 H9 **Campbell Island** N.Z.
156 D9 **Campbell Plateau** *sea feature* S. Pacific Ocean
128 B2 **Campbell River** Can.
138 B3 **Campbellsville** U.S.A.
131 D3 **Campbellton** Can.
53 D2 **Campbelltown** Austr.
96 B3 **Campbeltown** U.K.
145 C3 **Campeche** Mex.
145 C3 **Campeche, Bahía de** *g.* Mex.
52 B3 **Camperdown** Austr.
110 C1 **Câmpina** Romania
151 F3 **Campina Grande** Brazil
154 C2 **Campinas** Brazil
154 C1 **Campina Verde** Brazil
108 B2 **Campobasso** Italy
155 C2 **Campo Belo** Brazil
154 C1 **Campo Florido** Brazil
152 B2 **Campo Gallo** Arg.
154 B2 **Campo Grande** Brazil
154 C3 **Campo Largo** Brazil
151 E3 **Campo Maior** Brazil
106 B2 **Campo Maior** Port.
150 B1 **Campo Mara** Venez.
109 C2 **Campomarino** Italy
154 B2 **Campo Mourão** Brazil
155 D2 **Campos** Brazil
155 C1 **Campos Altos** Brazil
155 C2 **Campos do Jordão** Brazil
110 C1 **Câmpulung** Romania
142 A2 **Camp Verde** U.S.A.
63 B2 **Cam Ranh** Vietnam
63 B2 **Cam Ranh, Vinh** *b.* Vietnam
Cam Ranh Bay Vietnam *see* **Cam Ranh, Vinh**
128 C2 **Camrose** Can.
129 D2 **Camsell Portage** Can.
111 C2 **Çan** Turkey
126 F2 **Canada** *country* N. America
160 A2 **Canada Basin** *sea feature* Arctic Ocean
143 C1 **Canadian** U.S.A.
143 D1 **Canadian** *r.* U.S.A.
111 C2 **Çanakkale** Turkey
144 A1 **Cananea** Mex.
154 C2 **Cananéia** Brazil
114 A2 **Canary Islands** *terr.* N. Atlantic Ocean
154 C1 **Canastra, Serra da** *mts* *Goiás* Brazil
155 C1 **Canastra, Serra da** *mts* *Minas Gerais* Brazil
144 B2 **Canatlán** Mex.
141 D3 **Canaveral, Cape** U.S.A.
155 E1 **Canavieiras** Brazil
53 C2 **Canbelego** Austr.
53 C3 **Canberra** Austr.
145 D2 **Cancún** Mex.
111 C3 **Çandarlı** Turkey
155 C2 **Candeias** Brazil
145 C3 **Candelaria** Mex.
154 B2 **Cândido de Abreu** Brazil
129 D2 **Candle Lake** Can.
137 D1 **Cando** U.S.A.
120 A2 **Cangamba** Angola
106 B1 **Cangas** Spain
106 B1 **Cangas del Narcea** Spain
120 B2 **Cangombe** Angola
152 C3 **Canguçu** Brazil
70 B2 **Cangzhou** China
131 D2 **Caniapiscau** Can.
131 D2 **Caniapiscau** *r.* Can.
131 C2 **Caniapiscau, Lac** *l.* Can.
Caniçado Moz. *see* **Guija**
108 B3 **Canicattì** *Sicily* Italy
151 F3 **Canindé** Brazil
144 B2 **Cañitas de Felipe Pescador** Mex.
80 B1 **Çankırı** Turkey
128 C2 **Canmore** Can.
96 A2 **Canna** *i.* U.K.
73 B3 **Cannanore** India
105 D3 **Cannes** France
99 B3 **Cannock** U.K.
53 C3 **Cann River** Austr.
152 C2 **Canoas** Brazil
129 D2 **Canoe Lake** Can.
154 B3 **Canoinhas** Brazil
136 B3 **Canon City** U.S.A.
52 B2 **Canopus** Austr.
129 D2 **Canora** Can.
53 C2 **Canowindra** Austr.
131 D3 **Canso** Can.
Cantabrian Mountains Spain *see* **Cantábrica, Cordillera**
Cantabrian Sea Spain *see* **Cantábrico, Mar**
106 C1 **Cantábrica, Cordillera** *mts* Spain
106 B1 **Cantábrico, Mar** *sea* Spain
99 D4 **Canterbury** U.K.
54 B2 **Canterbury Bight** *b.* N.Z.
54 B2 **Canterbury Plains** N.Z.
63 B2 **Cân Thơ** Vietnam
151 E3 **Canto do Buriti** Brazil
Canton China *see* **Guangzhou**
137 E2 **Canton** *MO* U.S.A.
140 C2 **Canton** *MS* U.S.A.
139 D2 **Canton** *NY* U.S.A.
138 C2 **Canton** *OH* U.S.A.
143 C1 **Canyon** U.S.A.
134 D1 **Canyon Ferry Lake** U.S.A.
134 B2 **Canyonville** U.S.A.
62 B1 **Cao Bằng** Vietnam
109 C2 **Capaccio** Italy
154 C2 **Capão Bonito** Brazil
155 D2 **Caparaó, Serra do** *mts* Brazil
139 E1 **Cap-de-la-Madeleine** Can.
51 D4 **Cape Barren Island** Austr.
158 F7 **Cape Basin** *sea feature* S. Atlantic Ocean
52 A3 **Cape Borda** Austr.
131 D3 **Cape Breton Island** Can.
141 D3 **Cape Canaveral** U.S.A.
139 D3 **Cape Charles** U.S.A.
114 B4 **Cape Coast** Ghana
139 E2 **Cape Cod Bay** U.S.A.
141 D3 **Cape Coral** U.S.A.
127 G2 **Cape Dorset** Can.
141 E2 **Cape Fear** *r.* U.S.A.
137 F3 **Cape Girardeau** U.S.A.
155 D1 **Capelinha** Brazil
100 B2 **Capelle aan de IJssel** Neth.
Capelongo Angola *see* **Kuvango**
139 E3 **Cape May Point** U.S.A.
120 A1 **Capenda-Camulemba** Angola
122 A3 **Cape Town** S. Africa
158 E3 **Cape Verde** *country* N. Atlantic Ocean
158 D4 **Cape Verde Basin** *sea feature* N. Atlantic Ocean

Cape York Peninsula

174

51 D1 Cape York Peninsula Austr.
147 C3 Cap-Haïtien Haiti
151 E3 Capim r. Brazil
154 A2 Capitán Bado Para.
58 D1 Capitol Hill N. Mariana Is
154 B2 Capivara, Represa resr Brazil
109 C2 Čapljina Bos.-Herz.
109 B3 Capo d'Orlando Sicily Italy
108 A2 Capraia, Isola di i. Italy
108 A2 Caprara, Punta pt Sardinia Italy
108 B2 Capri, Isola di i. Italy
51 E2 Capricorn Channel Austr.
120 B2 Caprivi Strip reg. Namibia
143 C2 Cap Rock Escarpment U.S.A.
143 C1 Capulin U.S.A.
150 C3 Caquetá r. Col.
110 B2 Caracal Romania
150 C2 Caracarai Brazil
150 C1 Caracas Venez.
151 E3 Caracol Brazil
155 C2 Caraguatatuba Brazil
153 A3 Carahue Chile
155 D1 Caraí Brazil
151 D3 Carajás, Serra dos hills Brazil
155 D2 Carandaí Brazil
155 D2 Carangola Brazil
110 B1 Caransebeş Romania
131 D3 Caraquet Can.
146 B3 Caratasca, Laguna de lag. Hond.
155 D1 Caratinga Brazil
150 C3 Carauari Brazil
107 C2 Caravaca de la Cruz Spain
155 E1 Caravelas Brazil
129 E3 Carberry Can.
144 A2 Carbó Mex.
108 A3 Carbonara, Capo c. Sardinia Italy
136 B3 Carbondale CO U.S.A.
138 B3 Carbondale IL U.S.A.
139 D2 Carbondale PA U.S.A.
131 E3 Carbonear Can.
155 D1 Carbonita Brazil
107 C2 Carcaixent Spain
104 C3 Carcassonne France
128 A1 Carcross Can.
146 B2 Cárdenas Cuba
145 C3 Cárdenas Mex.
99 B4 Cardiff U.K.
99 A3 Cardigan U.K.
99 A3 Cardigan Bay U.K.
154 C2 Cardoso Brazil
128 C3 Cardston Can.
110 B1 Carei Romania
104 B2 Carentan France
50 B2 Carey, Lake salt flat Austr.
155 D2 Cariacica Brazil
146 B3 Caribbean Sea N. Atlantic Ocean
128 B2 Cariboo Mountains Can.
139 F1 Caribou U.S.A.
130 B2 Caribou Lake Can.
128 C2 Caribou Mountains Can.
144 B2 Carichic Mex.
100 B3 Carignan France
53 C2 Carinda Austr.
107 C1 Cariñena Spain
130 C3 Carleton Place Can.
123 C2 Carletonville S. Africa
135 C2 Carlin U.S.A.
97 C1 Carlingford Lough inlet Rep. of Ireland/U.K.
138 B3 Carlinville U.S.A.
98 B2 Carlisle U.K.
139 D2 Carlisle U.S.A.
155 D1 Carlos Chagas Brazil
97 C2 Carlow Rep. of Ireland
96 A1 Carloway U.K.
135 C4 Carlsbad CA U.S.A.
142 C2 Carlsbad NM U.S.A.
129 D3 Carlyle Can.
128 A1 Carmacks Can.
129 E3 Carman Can.
99 A4 Carmarthen U.K.
99 A4 Carmarthen Bay U.K.
104 C3 Carmaux France
145 C3 Carmelita Guat.
144 A2 Carmen, Isla i. Mex.
155 C1 Carmo do Paranaíba Brazil
Carmona Angola see Uíge
106 B2 Carmona Spain
104 B2 Carnac France
50 A2 Carnarvon Austr.
122 B3 Carnarvon S. Africa
97 C1 Carndonagh Rep. of Ireland
129 D3 Carnduff Can.
50 B2 Carnegie, Lake salt flat Austr.
96 B2 Carn Eighe mt. U.K.
55 P2 Carney Island Antarctica
73 D4 Car Nicobar i. India
118 B2 Carnot C.A.R.
52 A2 Carnot, Cape Austr.
96 C2 Carnoustie U.K.
97 C2 Carnsore Point Rep. of Ireland
151 E3 Carolina Brazil
49 L4 Caroline Island Kiribati
59 D2 Caroline Islands N. Pacific Ocean
122 A2 Carolusberg S. Africa
103 D2 Carpathian Mountains Europe
Carpații Meridionali mts Romania see Transylvanian Alps
51 C1 Carpentaria, Gulf of Austr.
105 D3 Carpentras France
108 B2 Carpi Italy
141 D3 Carrabelle U.S.A.
97 B3 Carrantuohill mt. Rep. of Ireland
108 B2 Carrara Italy
97 D1 Carrickfergus U.K.
97 C2 Carrickmacross Rep. of Ireland
97 B2 Carrick-on-Shannon Rep. of Ireland
97 C2 Carrick-on-Suir Rep. of Ireland
137 D1 Carrington U.S.A.
143 D3 Carrizo Springs U.S.A.
142 B2 Carrizozo U.S.A.
137 E2 Carroll U.S.A.
141 C2 Carrollton U.S.A.
129 D2 Carrot River Can.
135 C3 Carson City U.S.A.
135 C3 Carson Sink l. U.S.A.
Carstensz-top mt. Indon. see Jaya, Puncak
150 B1 Cartagena Col.
107 C2 Cartagena Spain
146 B4 Cartago Costa Rica
54 C2 Carterton N.Z.
137 E3 Carthage MO U.S.A.
143 E2 Carthage TX U.S.A.
131 E2 Cartwright Can.
151 F3 Caruarú Brazil
150 C1 Carúpano Venez.
52 B1 Caryapundy Swamp Austr.
114 B1 Casablanca Morocco
154 C2 Casa Branca Brazil
144 B1 Casa de Janos Mex.
142 A2 Casa Grande U.S.A.
108 A1 Casale Monferrato Italy
109 C2 Casarano Italy
144 B1 Casas Grandes Mex.
134 C2 Cascade U.S.A.
134 B2 Cascade Range mts Can./U.S.A.
106 B2 Cascais Port.
151 F3 Cascavel Brazil
154 B2 Cascavel Brazil
139 F2 Casco Bay U.S.A.
108 B2 Caserta Italy
97 C2 Cashel Rep. of Ireland
153 B3 Casilda Arg.
53 D1 Casino Austr.
Casnewydd U.K. see Newport
107 C1 Caspe Spain
136 B2 Casper U.S.A.
76 A2 Caspian Lowland Kazakh./Rus. Fed.
81 C1 Caspian Sea Asia/Europe
Cassaigne Alg. see Sidi Ali
154 C2 Cássia Brazil
128 B2 Cassiar Can.
128 A2 Cassiar Mountains Can.
154 B1 Cassilândia Brazil
120 A2 Cassinga Angola
108 B2 Cassino Italy
96 B2 Cassley r. U.K.
151 E3 Castanhal Brazil
152 B3 Castaño r. Arg.
144 B2 Castaños Mex.
104 C3 Casteljaloux France
105 D3 Castellane France
107 C2 Castelló de la Plana Spain
155 D2 Castelo Brazil
106 B2 Castelo Branco Port.
104 C3 Castelsarrasin France
108 B3 Castelvetrano Sicily Italy
52 B3 Casterton Austr.
108 B2 Castiglione della Pescaia Italy
106 C2 Castilla - La Mancha reg. Spain
106 C1 Castilla y León reg. Spain
97 B2 Castlebar Rep. of Ireland
96 A2 Castlebay U.K.
97 C1 Castleblayney Rep. of Ireland
97 C1 Castlederg U.K.
96 C3 Castle Douglas U.K.
128 C3 Castlegar Can.
97 B2 Castleisland Rep. of Ireland
52 B3 Castlemaine Austr.
97 C2 Castlepollard Rep. of Ireland
97 B2 Castlerea Rep. of Ireland
53 C2 Castlereagh r. Austr.
136 C3 Castle Rock U.S.A.
128 C2 Castor Can.
104 C3 Castres France
100 B1 Castricum Neth.
147 D3 Castries St Lucia
154 C2 Castro Brazil
153 A4 Castro Chile
106 B2 Castro Verde Port.
109 C3 Castrovillari Italy
150 A3 Catacaos Peru
155 D2 Cataguases Brazil
154 C1 Catalão Brazil
Catalonia reg. Spain see Cataluña
107 D1 Cataluña reg. Spain
152 B2 Catamarca Arg.
64 B2 Catanduanes i. Phil.
154 C2 Catanduva Brazil
154 B3 Catanduvas Brazil
109 C3 Catania Sicily Italy
109 C3 Catanzaro Italy
64 B2 Catarman Phil.
107 C2 Catarroja Spain
64 B2 Catbalogan Phil.
145 C3 Catemaco Mex.
120 A1 Catete Angola
Catherine, Mount mt. Egypt see Kātrīnā, Jabal
147 C2 Cat Island Bahamas
130 A2 Cat Lake Can.
145 D2 Catoche, Cabo c. Mex.
139 E2 Catskill Mountains U.S.A.
123 D2 Catuane Moz.
64 B3 Cauayan Phil.
131 D2 Caubvick, Mount Can.
150 B2 Cauca r. Col.
151 F3 Caucaia Brazil
81 C1 Caucasus mts Asia/Europe
100 A2 Caudry France
109 C3 Caulonia Italy
120 A1 Caungula Angola
150 C2 Caura r. Venez.
131 D3 Causapscal Can.
90 B2 Căuşeni Moldova
105 D3 Cavaillon France
151 E4 Cavalcante Brazil
114 B4 Cavally r. Côte d'Ivoire
97 C2 Cavan Rep. of Ireland
154 B3 Cavernoso, Serra do mts Brazil
151 D2 Caviana, Ilha i. Brazil
Cawnpore India see Kanpur
151 E3 Caxias Brazil
152 C2 Caxias do Sul Brazil
120 A1 Caxito Angola
151 D2 Cayenne Fr. Guiana
146 B3 Cayman Islands terr. West Indies
158 C3 Cayman Trench sea feature Caribbean Sea
117 C4 Caynabo Somalia
120 B2 Cazombo Angola
Ceará Brazil see Fortaleza
Ceatharlach Rep. of Ireland see Carlow
144 B2 Ceballos Mex.
64 B2 Cebu Phil.
64 B2 Cebu i. Phil.
108 B2 Cecina Italy
137 F2 Cedar r. U.S.A.
135 D3 Cedar City U.S.A.
137 E2 Cedar Falls U.S.A.
129 D2 Cedar Lake Can.
137 E2 Cedar Rapids U.S.A.
144 A2 Cedros, Isla i. Mex.
51 C3 Ceduna Austr.
117 C4 Ceeldheere Somalia
117 C3 Ceerigaabo Somalia
108 B3 Cefalù Sicily Italy
145 B2 Celaya Mex.
61 D2 Celebes i. Indon.
156 C5 Celebes Sea Indon./Phil.
145 C2 Celestún Mex.
101 E1 Celle Ger.
95 B3 Celtic Sea Rep. of Ireland/U.K.
59 D3 Cenderawasih, Teluk b. Indon.
140 C2 Center Point U.S.A.
150 B2 Central, Cordillera mts Col.
150 B4 Central, Cordillera mts Peru
64 B2 Central, Cordillera mts Phil.
Central African Empire country Africa see Central African Republic
118 C2 Central African Republic country Africa
74 A2 Central Brahui Range mts Pak.
137 D2 Central City U.S.A.
138 B3 Centralia IL U.S.A.
134 B1 Centralia WA U.S.A.
74 A2 Central Makran Range mts Pak.
156 D5 Central Pacific Basin sea feature Pacific Ocean
134 B2 Central Point U.S.A.
Central Provinces state India see Madhya Pradesh
59 D3 Central Range mts P.N.G.
89 E3 Central Russian Upland hills Rus. Fed.
83 I2 Central Siberian Plateau plat. Rus. Fed.
140 C2 Century U.S.A.
Ceos i. Greece see Kea
111 B3 Cephalonia i. Greece
Ceram i. Indon. see Seram
Ceram Sea Indon. see Laut Seram
101 F3 Čerchov mt. Czech Rep.
152 B2 Ceres Arg.
154 C1 Ceres Brazil
122 A3 Ceres S. Africa
105 C3 Céret France
106 C1 Cerezo de Abajo Spain
109 C2 Cerignola Italy
Cerigo i. Greece see Kythira
110 C2 Cernavodă Romania
145 C2 Cerralvo Mex.
144 B2 Cerralvo, Isla i. Mex.
145 B2 Cerritos Mex.
154 C2 Cerro Azul Brazil
145 C2 Cerro Azul Mex.
150 B4 Cerro de Pasco Peru
105 D3 Cervione Corsica France
106 B1 Cervo Spain
108 B2 Cesena Italy
108 B2 Cesenatico Italy
88 C2 Cēsis Latvia
102 C2 České Budějovice Czech Rep.
101 F3 Český Les mts Czech Rep./Ger.
111 C3 Çeşme Turkey
53 D2 Cessnock Austr.
104 B2 Cesson-Sévigné France
104 B3 Cestas France
109 C2 Cetinje Serb. and Mont.
109 C3 Cetraro Italy
106 B2 Ceuta N. Africa
105 C3 Cévennes mts France
Ceylon country Asia see Sri Lanka
79 D2 Chābahār Iran
75 C1 Chabyêr Caka salt l. China
150 B3 Chachapoyas Peru
89 D3 Chachersk Belarus
63 B2 Chachoengsao Thai.
152 C2 Chaco Boreal reg. Para.
142 B1 Chaco Mesa plat. U.S.A.
115 D3 Chad country Africa
115 D3 Chad, Lake Africa
68 C1 Chadaasan Mongolia
68 C1 Chadan Rus. Fed.
123 C1 Chadibe Botswana
136 C2 Chadron U.S.A.
Chadyr-Lunga Moldova see Ciadîr-Lunga
77 D2 Chaek Kyrg.
65 B2 Chaeryŏng N. Korea
74 A2 Chagai Pak.
77 C3 Chaghcharān Afgh.
89 E2 Chagoda Rus. Fed.

56 I10 **Chagos Archipelago** *is* B.I.O.T.
159 E4 **Chagos-Laccadive Ridge** *sea feature* Indian Ocean
159 E4 **Chagos Trench** *sea feature* Indian Ocean
76 B2 **Chagyl** Turkm.
75 C2 **Chaibasa** India
63 B2 **Chainat** Thai.
63 A3 **Chaiya** Thai.
63 B2 **Chaiyaphum** Thai.
152 C3 **Chajarí** Arg.
119 D3 **Chake Chake** Tanz.
131 D2 **Chakonipau, Lake** Can.
150 B4 **Chala** Peru
74 A1 **Chalap Dalan** *mts* Afgh.
121 C2 **Chaláua** Moz.
131 D3 **Chaleur Bay** *inlet* Can.
74 B2 **Chalisgaon** India
111 C3 **Chalki** *i.* Greece
111 B3 **Chalkida** Greece
143 C3 **Chalk Mountains** U.S.A.
104 B2 **Challans** France
134 D2 **Challis** U.S.A.
105 C2 **Châlons-en-Champagne** France
Châlons-sur-Marne France *see* **Châlons-en-Champagne**
105 C2 **Chalon-sur-Saône** France
101 F3 **Cham** Ger.
142 B1 **Chama** U.S.A.
121 C2 **Chama** Zambia
74 A1 **Chaman** Pak.
74 B1 **Chamba** India
74 B2 **Chambal** *r.* India
137 D2 **Chamberlain** U.S.A.
142 B1 **Chambers** U.S.A.
139 D3 **Chambersburg** U.S.A.
105 D2 **Chambéry** France
121 C2 **Chambeshi** Zambia
121 B2 **Chambeshi** *r.* Zambia
Chamdo China *see* **Qamdo**
105 D2 **Chamonix-Mont-Blanc** France
105 C2 **Champagne** *reg.* France
138 B2 **Champaign** U.S.A.
139 E2 **Champlain, Lake** Can./U.S.A.
145 C3 **Champotón** Mex.
Chanak Turkey *see* **Çanakkale**
152 A2 **Chañaral** Chile
Chanda India *see* **Chandrapur**
126 C2 **Chandalar** *r.* U.S.A.
140 C3 **Chandeleur Islands** U.S.A.
74 B1 **Chandigarh** India
131 D3 **Chandler** Can.
142 A2 **Chandler** U.S.A.
75 D2 **Chandpur** Bangl.
75 B3 **Chandrapur** India
63 B2 **Chang, Ko** *i.* Thai.
Chang'an China *see* **Rong'an**
121 C3 **Changane** *r.* Moz.
121 C2 **Changara** Moz.
65 B1 **Changbai** China
65 B1 **Changbai Shan** *mts* China/N. Korea
Changchow China *see* **Zhangzhou**
Changchow China *see* **Changzhou**
69 E2 **Changchun** China
71 B3 **Changde** China
65 B2 **Ch'angdo** N. Korea
70 B2 **Changge** China
71 C3 **Changhua** Taiwan
65 B3 **Changhŭng** S. Korea
Chang Jiang *r.* China *see* **Yangtze**
Changjiang Kou *r. mouth* China *see* **Yangtze, Mouth of the**
65 B1 **Changjin** N. Korea
65 B1 **Changjin-gang** *r.* N. Korea
Changkiang China *see* **Zhanjiang**
Changning China *see* **Xunwu**
Ch'ang-pai Shan *mts* China/N. Korea *see* **Changbai Shan**
71 B3 **Changsha** China
70 C2 **Changshu** China
65 B2 **Changsŏng** S. Korea
Changteh China *see* **Changde**
71 B3 **Changting** *Fujian* China
66 A2 **Changting** *Heilong.* China
65 A1 **Changtu** China
146 B4 **Changuinola** Panama
65 B2 **Ch'angwŏn** S. Korea
65 B2 **Changyŏn** N. Korea
70 B2 **Changyuan** China
70 B2 **Changzhi** China
70 B2 **Changzhou** China
111 B3 **Chania** Greece
95 C4 **Channel Islands** English Chan.
135 C4 **Channel Islands** U.S.A.
131 E3 **Channel-Port-aux-Basques** Can.
106 B1 **Chantada** Spain
63 B2 **Chanthaburi** Thai.
104 C2 **Chantilly** France
137 D3 **Chanute** U.S.A.
82 G3 **Chany, Ozero** *salt l.* Rus. Fed.
70 B2 **Chaohu** China
71 B3 **Chaoyang** *Guangdong* China
Chaoyang China *see* **Huinan**
70 C1 **Chaoyang** *Liaoning* China
71 B3 **Chaozhou** China
144 B2 **Chapala, Laguna de** *l.* Mex.
76 B1 **Chapayev** Kazakh.
87 D3 **Chapayevsk** Rus. Fed.
152 C2 **Chapecó** Brazil
141 E1 **Chapel Hill** U.S.A.
130 B3 **Chapleau** Can.
89 E3 **Chaplygin** Rus. Fed.
91 C2 **Chaplynka** Ukr.
Chapra India *see* **Chhapra**
145 B2 **Charcas** Mex.
99 B4 **Chard** U.K.
Chardzhev Turkm. *see* **Turkmenabat**
Chardzhou Turkm. *see* **Turkmenabat**
104 B2 **Charente** *r.* France
118 B1 **Chari** *r.* Cameroon/Chad
77 C3 **Chārīkār** Afgh.
86 E2 **Charkayuvom** Rus. Fed.
Charkhlik China *see* **Ruoqiang**
100 B2 **Charleroi** Belgium
139 D3 **Charles, Cape** U.S.A.
139 E1 **Charlesbourg** Can.
137 E2 **Charles City** U.S.A.
138 B3 **Charleston** *IL* U.S.A.
137 F3 **Charleston** *MO* U.S.A.
141 E2 **Charleston** *SC* U.S.A.
138 C3 **Charleston** *WV* U.S.A.
135 C3 **Charleston Peak** U.S.A.
51 D2 **Charleville** Austr.
105 C2 **Charleville-Mézières** France
138 B1 **Charlevoix** U.S.A.
141 D1 **Charlotte** U.S.A.
141 D3 **Charlotte Harbor** *b.* U.S.A.
139 D3 **Charlottesville** U.S.A.
131 D3 **Charlottetown** Can.
52 B3 **Charlton** Austr.
130 C2 **Charlton Island** Can.
51 D2 **Charters Towers** Austr.
104 C2 **Chartres** France
128 C2 **Chase** Can.
88 C3 **Chashniki** Belarus
54 A3 **Chaslands Mistake** *c.* N.Z.
65 B1 **Chasŏng** N. Korea
104 B2 **Chassiron, Pointe de** *pt* France
104 B2 **Châteaubriant** France
104 C2 **Château-du-Loir** France
104 C2 **Châteaudun** France
104 B2 **Château-Gontier** France
104 B2 **Châteaulin** France
105 D3 **Châteauneuf-les-Martigues** France
104 C2 **Châteauneuf-sur-Loire** France
104 C2 **Châteauroux** France
105 C2 **Château-Thierry** France
128 C2 **Chateh** Can.
100 B2 **Châtelet** Belgium
104 C2 **Châtellerault** France
138 C2 **Chatham** Can.
99 D4 **Chatham** U.K.
49 J8 **Chatham Islands** N.Z.
105 C2 **Châtillon-sur-Seine** France
141 D2 **Chattahoochee** *r.* U.S.A.
141 C1 **Chattanooga** U.S.A.
63 B2 **Châu Đôc** Vietnam
62 A1 **Chauk** Myanmar
105 D2 **Chaumont** France
105 C2 **Chauny** France
Chau Phu Vietnam *see* **Châu Đôc**
151 E3 **Chaves** Brazil
106 B1 **Chaves** Port.
130 C2 **Chavigny, Lac** *l.* Can.
89 D3 **Chavusy** Belarus
89 E2 **Chayevo** Rus. Fed.
86 E3 **Chaykovskiy** Rus. Fed.
140 C2 **Cheaha Mountain** *hill* U.S.A.
102 C1 **Cheb** Czech Rep.
87 D3 **Cheboksary** Rus. Fed.
138 C1 **Cheboygan** U.S.A.
65 B2 **Chech'ŏn** S. Korea
140 A1 **Checotah** U.S.A.
Chefoo China *see* **Yantai**
126 B2 **Chefornak** U.S.A.
114 B2 **Chegga** Maur.
121 C2 **Chegutu** Zimbabwe
134 B1 **Chehalis** U.S.A.
65 B3 **Cheju** S. Korea
65 B3 **Cheju-do** *i.* S. Korea
65 B3 **Cheju-haehyŏp** *sea chan.* S. Korea
89 E2 **Chekhov** Rus. Fed.
Chekiang *prov.* China *see* **Zhejiang**
134 B1 **Chelan, Lake** U.S.A.
81 D2 **Cheleken** Turkm.
107 D2 **Chélif, Oued** *r.* Alg.
103 E1 **Chełm** Pol.
99 D4 **Chelmer** *r.* U.K.
103 D1 **Chełmno** Pol.
99 D4 **Chelmsford** U.K.
99 B4 **Cheltenham** U.K.
87 F3 **Chelyabinsk** Rus. Fed.
83 H1 **Chelyuskin** Rus. Fed.
101 F2 **Chemnitz** Ger.
Chemulpo S. Korea *see* **Inch'ŏn**
134 B2 **Chemult** U.S.A.
74 B2 **Chenab** *r.* India/Pak.
114 B2 **Chenachane** Alg.
134 C1 **Cheney** U.S.A.
Chengchow China *see* **Zhengzhou**
70 B1 **Chengde** China
70 A2 **Chengdu** China
Chengjiang China *see* **Taihe**
71 B4 **Chengmai** China
Chengshou China *see* **Yingshan**
Chengtu China *see* **Chengdu**
70 A2 **Chengxian** China
Chengxiang China *see* **Wuxi**
Chengxiang China *see* **Mianning**
Chengyang China *see* **Juxian**
73 C3 **Chennai** India
Chenstokhov Pol. *see* **Częstochowa**
71 B3 **Chenzhou** China
99 B4 **Chepstow** U.K.
141 E2 **Cheraw** U.S.A.
104 B2 **Cherbourg** France
Cherchen China *see* **Qiemo**
89 E3 **Cheremisinovo** Rus. Fed.
68 C1 **Cheremkhovo** Rus. Fed.
89 E2 **Cherepovets** Rus. Fed.
91 C2 **Cherkasy** Ukr.
87 D4 **Cherkessk** Rus. Fed.
89 E3 **Chern'** Rus. Fed.
91 C1 **Chernihiv** Ukr.
91 D2 **Cherninivka** Ukr.
90 B2 **Chernivtsi** Ukr.
68 C1 **Chernogorsk** Rus. Fed.
90 B1 **Chernyakhiv** Ukr.
88 B3 **Chernyakhovsk** Rus. Fed.
89 E3 **Chernyanka** Rus. Fed.
69 D1 **Chernyshevsk** Rus. Fed.
83 I2 **Chernyshevskiy** Rus. Fed.
Chernyy Rynok Rus. Fed. *see* **Kochubey**
137 D2 **Cherokee** U.S.A.
83 L2 **Cherskiy** Rus. Fed.
83 K2 **Cherskogo, Khrebet** *mts* Rus. Fed.
91 E2 **Chertkovo** Rus. Fed.
Chervonoarmeyskoye Ukr. *see* **Vil'nyans'k**
Chervonoarmiys'k Ukr. *see* **Krasnoarmiys'k**
Chervonoarmiys'k Ukr. *see* **Radyvyliv**
90 A1 **Chervonohrad** Ukr.
88 C3 **Chervyen'** Belarus
89 D3 **Cherykaw** Belarus
139 D3 **Chesapeake Bay** U.S.A.
86 D2 **Cheshskaya Guba** *b.* Rus. Fed.
98 B3 **Chester** U.K.
138 B3 **Chester** *IL* U.S.A.
141 D2 **Chester** *SC* U.S.A.
139 D3 **Chester** *VA* U.S.A.
98 C3 **Chesterfield** U.K.
137 E3 **Chesterfield** U.S.A.
129 E1 **Chesterfield Inlet** Can.
129 E1 **Chesterfield Inlet** *inlet* Can.
139 F1 **Chesuncook Lake** U.S.A.
108 A3 **Chetaïbi** Alg.
131 D3 **Chéticamp** Can.
145 D3 **Chetumal** Mex.
128 B2 **Chetwynd** Can.
98 B2 **Cheviot Hills** U.K.
119 D2 **Che'w Bahir** *salt l.* Eth.
136 C2 **Cheyenne** U.S.A.
136 C2 **Cheyenne** *r.* U.S.A.
136 C3 **Cheyenne Wells** U.S.A.
75 C2 **Chhapra** India
75 B2 **Chhatarpur** India
75 C2 **Chhattisgarh** *state* India
74 B2 **Chhindwara** India
75 C2 **Chhukha** Bhutan
71 C3 **Chiai** Taiwan
62 A2 **Chiang Dao** Thai.
120 A2 **Chiange** Angola
62 A2 **Chiang Mai** Thai.
62 A2 **Chiang Rai** Thai.
145 C3 **Chiapa** Mex.
108 A1 **Chiavenno** Italy
69 F2 **Chiba** Japan
70 B3 **Chibi** China
Chibizovka Rus. Fed. *see* **Zherdevka**
121 C3 **Chiboma** Moz.
130 C3 **Chibougamau** Can.
123 D1 **Chibuto** Moz.
138 B2 **Chicago** U.S.A.
128 A2 **Chichagof Island** U.S.A.
99 C4 **Chichester** U.K.
50 A2 **Chichester Range** *mts* Austr.
143 D1 **Chickasha** U.S.A.
106 B2 **Chiclana de la Frontera** Spain
150 B3 **Chiclayo** Peru
153 B4 **Chico** *r.* Arg.
153 B4 **Chico** *r.* Arg.
135 B3 **Chico** U.S.A.
139 E2 **Chicopee** U.S.A.
64 B2 **Chico Sapocoy, Mount** Phil.
131 C3 **Chicoutimi** Can.
131 D1 **Chidley, Cape** Can.
63 A3 **Chieo Lan Reservoir** Thai.
108 B2 **Chieti** Italy
145 C3 **Chietla** Mex.
70 B1 **Chifeng** China
155 D1 **Chifre, Serra do** *mts* Brazil
121 C2 **Chifunde** Moz.
77 D2 **Chiganak** Kazakh.
145 C3 **Chignahuapán** Mex.
121 C3 **Chigubo** Moz.
62 A1 **Chigu Co** *l.* China
144 B2 **Chihuahua** Mex.
77 C2 **Chiili** Kazakh.
88 C2 **Chikhachevo** Rus. Fed.
67 C3 **Chikuma-gawa** *r.* Japan
128 B2 **Chilanko** *r.* Can.
74 B1 **Chilas** Jammu and Kashmir
143 C2 **Childress** U.S.A.
153 A3 **Chile** *country* S. America
158 C6 **Chile Basin** *sea feature* S. Pacific Ocean
152 B2 **Chilecito** Arg.
157 G8 **Chile Rise** *sea feature* S. Pacific Ocean
77 D2 **Chilik** Kazakh.
75 C3 **Chilika Lake** India
121 B2 **Chililabombwe** Zambia
128 B2 **Chilko** *r.* Can.
128 B2 **Chilko Lake** Can.
153 A3 **Chillán** Chile
138 B2 **Chillicothe** *IL* U.S.A.
137 E3 **Chillicothe** *MO* U.S.A.
138 C3 **Chillicothe** *OH* U.S.A.
128 B3 **Chilliwack** Can.
153 A4 **Chiloé, Isla de** *i.* Chile
145 C3 **Chilpancingo** Mex.
53 C3 **Chiltern** Austr.
99 C4 **Chiltern Hills** U.K.
120 B1 **Chiluage** Angola
71 C3 **Chilung** Taiwan

119 D3 Chimala Tanz.
121 C2 Chimanimani Zimbabwe
152 B3 Chimbas Arg.
150 B3 Chimborazo *mt.* Ecuador
150 B3 Chimbote Peru
76 B2 Chimboy Uzbek.
Chimishliya Moldova *see* Cimişlia
Chimkent Kazakh. *see* Shymkent
121 C2 Chimoio Moz.
77 C3 Chimtargha, Qullai *mt.* Tajik.
68 C2 China *country* Asia
145 C2 China Mex.
150 B4 Chincha Alta Peru
128 C2 Chinchaga *r.* Can.
145 D3 Chinchorro, Banco *sea feature* Mex.
121 C2 Chinde Moz.
65 B3 Chindo S. Korea
65 B3 Chin-do *i.* S. Korea
68 C2 Chindu China
62 A1 Chindwin *r.* Myanmar
65 B2 Chinghwa N. Korea
121 B2 Chingola Zambia
120 A2 Chinguar Angola
65 B2 Chinhae S. Korea
121 C2 Chinhoyi Zimbabwe
Chini India *see* Kalpa
Chining China *see* Jining
74 B1 Chiniot Pak.
144 B2 Chinipas Mex.
65 B2 Chinju S. Korea
118 C2 Chinko *r.* C.A.R.
142 B1 Chinle U.S.A.
71 B3 Chinmen Taiwan
Chinnamp'o N. Korea *see* Namp'o
67 C3 Chino Japan
135 C4 Chino U.S.A.
104 C2 Chinon France
134 E1 Chinook U.S.A.
142 A2 Chino Valley U.S.A.
77 C2 Chinoz Uzbek.
121 C2 Chinsali Zambia
108 B1 Chioggia Italy
111 C3 Chios Greece
111 C3 Chios *i.* Greece
121 C2 Chipata Zambia
120 A2 Chipindo Angola
Chipinga Zimbabwe *see* Chipinge
121 C3 Chipinge Zimbabwe
73 B3 Chiplun India
99 B4 Chippenham U.K.
138 A2 Chippewa Falls U.S.A.
99 C4 Chipping Norton U.K.
Chipuriro Zimbabwe *see* Guruve
145 D3 Chiquimula Guat.
77 C2 Chirchiq Uzbek.
121 C3 Chiredzi Zimbabwe
142 B2 Chiricahua Peak U.S.A.
146 B4 Chiriquí, Golfo de *b.* Panama
65 B2 Chiri-san *mt.* S. Korea
146 B4 Chirripo *mt.* Costa Rica
121 B2 Chirundu Zimbabwe
130 C2 Chisasibi Can.
137 E1 Chisholm U.S.A.
Chisimaio Somalia *see* Kismaayo
90 B2 Chişinău Moldova
87 E3 Chistopol' Rus. Fed.
69 D1 Chita Rus. Fed.
120 A2 Chitado Angola
Chitaldrug India *see* Chitradurga
121 C2 Chitambo Zambia
120 B1 Chitato Angola
121 C1 Chitipa Malawi
121 C3 Chitobe Moz.
Chitor India *see* Chittaurgarh
66 D2 Chitose Japan
73 B3 Chitradurga India
74 B1 Chitral Pak.
146 B4 Chitré Panama
75 D2 Chittagong Bangl.
74 B2 Chittaurgarh India
73 B3 Chittoor India
Chittorgarh India *see* Chittaurgarh
121 C2 Chitungwiza Zimbabwe
120 B2 Chiume Angola
121 C2 Chivhu Zimbabwe
70 B2 Chizhou China
Chkalov Rus. Fed. *see* Orenburg
101 F2 Chodov Czech Rep.
153 B3 Choele Choel Arg.
Chogori Feng *mt.* China/Jammu and Kashmir *see* K2
48 G4 Choiseul *i.* Solomon Is
144 B2 Choix Mex.
102 C1 Chojna Pol.
103 D1 Chojnice Pol.
117 B3 Ch'ok'ē Mountains Eth.
Chokue Moz. *see* Chókwé
83 K2 Chokurdakh Rus. Fed.
121 C3 Chókwé Moz.
104 B2 Cholet France
145 C3 Cholula Mex.
120 B2 Choma Zambia
Chomo China *see* Yadong
102 C1 Chomutov Czech Rep.
83 I2 Chona *r.* Rus. Fed.
65 B2 Ch'ŏnan S. Korea
58 A2 Chon Buri Thai.
150 A3 Chone Ecuador
Chong'an China *see* Wuyishan
65 B1 Ch'ŏngjin N. Korea
65 B2 Chŏngju N. Korea
65 B2 Ch'ŏngju S. Korea *see* Chŏngŭp
65 B2 Chŏngp'yŏng N. Korea
70 A3 Chongqing China
70 A2 Chongqing *mun.* China
65 B2 Chŏngŭp S. Korea
121 B2 Chongwe Zambia
71 A3 Chongzuo China
65 B2 Chŏnju S. Korea
153 A4 Chonos, Archipiélago de los *is* Chile
154 B3 Chopimzinho Brazil
98 B3 Chorley U.K.
91 C2 Chornobay Ukr.
90 C1 Chornobyl' Ukr.
91 C2 Chornomors'ke Ukr.
90 B2 Chortkiv Ukr.
65 B2 Ch'ŏrwŏn S. Korea
65 B1 Ch'osan N. Korea
67 D3 Chōshi Japan
153 A3 Chos Malal Arg.
103 D1 Choszczno Pol.
134 D1 Choteau U.S.A.
114 A2 Choûm Maur.
69 D1 Choybalsan Mongolia
69 D1 Choyr Mongolia
54 B2 Christchurch N.Z.
99 C4 Christchurch U.K.
127 H2 Christian, Cape Can.
123 C2 Christiana S. Africa
Christianshåb Greenland *see* Qasigiannguit
54 A2 Christina, Mount N.Z.
58 B3 Christmas Island *terr.* Indian Ocean
111 C3 Chrysi *i.* Greece
111 B2 Chrysoupoli Greece
Chu Kazakh. *see* Shu
Chubarovka Ukr. *see* Polohy
153 B4 Chubut *r.* Arg.
89 F3 Chuchkovo Rus. Fed.
90 B1 Chudniv Ukr.
89 D2 Chudovo Rus. Fed.
126 C2 Chugach Mountains U.S.A.
67 B4 Chūgoku-sanchi *mts* Japan
Chuguchak China *see* Tacheng
66 B2 Chuguyevka Rus. Fed.
91 D2 Chuhuyiv Ukr.
Chukchi Peninsula Rus. Fed. *see* Chukotskiy Poluostrov
160 J3 Chukchi Sea *sea* Rus. Fed./U.S.A.
89 F2 Chukhloma Rus. Fed.
83 N2 Chukotskiy Poluostrov *pen.* Rus. Fed.
Chulaktau Kazakh. *see* Karatau
135 C4 Chula Vista U.S.A.
82 G3 Chulym Rus. Fed.
152 B2 Chumbicha Arg.
83 K3 Chumikan Rus. Fed.
63 A2 Chumphon Thai.
65 B2 Ch'unch'ŏn S. Korea
Chungking China *see* Chongqing
Ch'ungmu S. Korea *see* T'ongyŏng
71 C3 Chungyang Shanmo *mts* Taiwan
83 H2 Chunya *r.* Rus. Fed.
119 D3 Chunya Tanz.
150 B4 Chuquibamba Peru
152 B2 Chuquicamata Chile
105 D2 Chur Switz.
62 A1 Churachandpur India
83 J2 Churapcha Rus. Fed.
129 E2 Churchill Can.
129 E2 Churchill *r. Man.* Can.
131 D2 Churchill *r. Nfld and Lab.* Can.
129 E2 Churchill, Cape Can.
131 D2 Churchill Falls Can.
129 D2 Churchill Lake Can.
74 B2 Churu India
142 B1 Chuska Mountains U.S.A.
86 E3 Chusovoy Rus. Fed.
131 C3 Chute-des-Passes Can.
48 G3 Chuuk *is* Micronesia
62 B1 Chuxiong China
63 B2 Chư Yang Sin *mt.* Vietnam
91 C2 Chyhyryn Ukr.
Chymyshliya Moldova *see* Cimişlia
Ciadâr-Lunga Moldova *see* Ciadîr-Lunga
90 B2 Ciadîr-Lunga Moldova
60 B2 Ciamis Indon.
60 B2 Cianjur Indon.
154 B2 Cianorte Brazil
142 A2 Cibuta, Sierra *mt.* Mex.
80 B1 Cide Turkey
103 E1 Ciechanów Pol.
146 C2 Ciego de Ávila Cuba
147 C3 Ciénaga Col.
146 B2 Cienfuegos Cuba
107 C2 Cieza Spain
106 C2 Cigüela *r.* Spain
80 B2 Cihanbeyli Turkey
144 B3 Cihuatlán Mex.
106 C2 Cijara, Embalse de *resr* Spain
109 C2 Çikes, Maja e *mt.* Albania
60 B2 Cilacap Indon.
Cill Airne Rep. of Ireland *see* Killarney
Cill Chainnigh Rep. of Ireland *see* Kilkenny
143 C1 Cimarron *r.* U.S.A.
90 B2 Cimişlia Moldova
108 B2 Cimone, Monte *mt.* Italy
Cîmpina Romania *see* Câmpina
Cîmpulung Romania *see* Câmpulung
60 B2 Cina, Tanjung *c.* Indon.
138 C3 Cincinnati U.S.A.
Cinco de Outubro Angola *see* Xá-Muteba
111 C3 Çine Turkey
100 B2 Ciney Belgium
134 C2 Cinnabar Mountain U.S.A.
145 C3 Cintalapa Mex.
Ciping China *see* Jinggangshan
153 B3 Cipolletti Arg.
126 C2 Circle *AK* U.S.A.
136 B1 Circle *MT* U.S.A.
60 B2 Cirebon Indon.
99 C4 Cirencester U.K.
108 A1 Ciriè Italy
109 C3 Cirò Marina Italy
110 B1 Cisnădie Romania
109 C2 Čitluk Bos.-Herz.
122 A3 Citrusdal S. Africa
135 B3 Citrus Heights U.S.A.
110 C1 Ciucaş, Vârful *mt.* Romania
145 B2 Ciudad Acuña Mex.
145 B3 Ciudad Altamirano Mex.
150 C2 Ciudad Bolívar Venez.
147 C4 Ciudad Bolivia Venez.
144 B2 Ciudad Camargo Mex.
144 A2 Ciudad Constitución Mex.
145 C3 Ciudad Cuauhtémoc Mex.
145 C3 Ciudad del Carmen Mex.
154 B3 Ciudad del Este Para.
144 B2 Ciudad Delicias Mex.
145 C2 Ciudad de Valles Mex.
150 C2 Ciudad Guayana Venez.
142 B3 Ciudad Guerrero Mex.
144 B3 Ciudad Guzmán Mex.
145 C3 Ciudad Hidalgo Mex.
145 C3 Ciudad Ixtepec Mex.
144 B1 Ciudad Juárez Mex.
145 C2 Ciudad Madero Mex.
145 C2 Ciudad Mante Mex.
145 C2 Ciudad Mier Mex.
144 B2 Ciudad Obregón Mex.
106 C2 Ciudad Real Spain
145 C2 Ciudad Río Bravo Mex.
106 B1 Ciudad Rodrigo Spain
Ciudad Trujillo Dom. Rep. *see* Santo Domingo
145 C2 Ciudad Victoria Mex.
107 D1 Ciutadella de Menorca Spain
108 B1 Cividale del Friuli Italy
108 B2 Civitanova Marche Italy
108 B2 Civitavecchia Italy
104 C2 Civray France
111 C3 Çivril Turkey
70 C2 Cixi China
99 D4 Clacton-on-Sea U.K.
128 C2 Claire, Lake Can.
105 C2 Clamecy France
140 C2 Clanton U.S.A.
122 A3 Clanwilliam S. Africa
97 C2 Clara Rep. of Ireland
52 A2 Clare Austr.
138 C2 Clare U.S.A.
97 A2 Clare Island Rep. of Ireland
139 E2 Claremont U.S.A.
97 B2 Claremorris Rep. of Ireland
54 B2 Clarence N.Z.
55 B3 Clarence Island Antarctica
131 E3 Clarenville Can.
128 C2 Claresholm Can.
137 D2 Clarinda U.S.A.
144 A3 Clarión, Isla *i.* Mex.
123 C3 Clarkebury S. Africa
134 C1 Clark Fork *r.* U.S.A.
141 D2 Clark Hill Reservoir U.S.A.
138 C3 Clarksburg U.S.A.
140 B2 Clarksdale U.S.A.
134 C1 Clarkston U.S.A.
140 B1 Clarksville *AR* U.S.A.
140 C1 Clarksville *TN* U.S.A.
154 B1 Claro *r.* Brazil
143 C1 Claude U.S.A.
143 C1 Clayton U.S.A.
97 B3 Clear, Cape Rep. of Ireland
126 C3 Cleare, Cape U.S.A.
137 E2 Clear Lake U.S.A.
135 B3 Clear Lake *l.* U.S.A.
128 C2 Clearwater Can.
129 C2 Clearwater *r.* Can.
141 D3 Clearwater U.S.A.
134 C1 Clearwater *r.* U.S.A.
143 D2 Cleburne U.S.A.
101 E1 Clenze Ger.
51 D2 Clermont Austr.
105 C2 Clermont-Ferrand France
100 C2 Clervaux Lux.
52 A2 Cleve Austr.
140 B2 Cleveland *MS* U.S.A.
138 C2 Cleveland *OH* U.S.A.
141 D1 Cleveland *TN* U.S.A.
134 D1 Cleveland, Mount U.S.A.
154 B3 Clevelândia Brazil
97 B2 Clew Bay Rep. of Ireland
141 D3 Clewiston U.S.A.
97 A2 Clifden Rep. of Ireland
53 D1 Clifton Austr.
142 B2 Clifton U.S.A.
142 B1 Clines Corners U.S.A.
128 B2 Clinton Can.
137 E2 Clinton *IA* U.S.A.
137 E3 Clinton *MO* U.S.A.
143 D1 Clinton *OK* U.S.A.
125 H8 Clipperton, Île *terr.* N. Pacific Ocean
96 A2 Clisham *hill* U.K.
98 B3 Clitheroe U.K.
97 B3 Clonakilty Rep. of Ireland
51 D2 Cloncurry Austr.
97 C1 Clones Rep. of Ireland
97 C2 Clonmel Rep. of Ireland
101 D1 Cloppenburg Ger.
137 E1 Cloquet U.S.A.
136 B2 Cloud Peak U.S.A.
135 C3 Clovis *CA* U.S.A.
143 C2 Clovis *NM* U.S.A.
Cluain Meala Rep. of Ireland *see* Clonmel
129 D2 Cluff Lake Mine Can.
110 B1 Cluj-Napoca Romania
51 C2 Cluny Austr.
105 D2 Cluses France
54 A3 Clutha *r.* N.Z.
96 B3 Clyde *r.* U.K.
96 B3 Clyde, Firth of *est.* U.K.
96 B3 Clydebank U.K.
127 H2 Clyde River Can.
144 B3 Coalcomán Mex.
128 C3 Coaldale Can.
135 C3 Coaldale U.S.A.

128 B2 **Coal River** Can.
150 C3 **Coari** Brazil
150 C3 **Coari** *r.* Brazil
141 C2 **Coastal Plain** U.S.A.
128 B2 **Coast Mountains** Can.
134 B2 **Coast Ranges** *mts* U.S.A.
96 B3 **Coatbridge** U.K.
129 F1 **Coats Island** Can.
55 C2 **Coats Land** *reg.* Antarctica
145 C3 **Coatzacoalcos** Mex.
146 A3 **Cobán** Guat.
53 C2 **Cobar** Austr.
97 B3 **Cóbh** Rep. of Ireland
152 B1 **Cobija** Bol.
Coblenz Ger. *see* **Koblenz**
130 C3 **Cobourg** Can.
50 C1 **Cobourg Peninsula** Austr.
53 C3 **Cobram** Austr.
101 E2 **Coburg** Ger.
152 B1 **Cochabamba** Bol.
100 C2 **Cochem** Ger.
73 B4 **Cochin** India
128 C2 **Cochrane** *Alta* Can.
130 B3 **Cochrane** *Ont.* Can.
153 A4 **Cochrane** Chile
52 A2 **Cockaleechie** Austr.
52 B2 **Cockburn** Austr.
Cockburn Town Turks and Caicos Is *see* **Grand Turk**
98 B2 **Cockermouth** U.K.
50 B3 **Cocklebiddy** Austr.
122 B3 **Cockscomb** *mt.* S. Africa
146 B3 **Coco** *r.* Hond./Nic.
125 J9 **Coco, Isla de** *i.* N. Pacific Ocean
159 F4 **Cocos Basin** *sea feature* Indian Ocean
58 A3 **Cocos Islands** *terr.* Indian Ocean
144 B2 **Cocula** Mex.
150 B2 **Cocuy, Sierra Nevada del** *mt.* Col.
139 E2 **Cod, Cape** U.S.A.
150 C3 **Codajás** Brazil
108 B2 **Codigoro** Italy
131 D2 **Cod Island** Can.
151 E3 **Codó** Brazil
136 B2 **Cody** U.S.A.
51 D1 **Coen** Austr.
100 C2 **Coesfeld** Ger.
113 I6 **Coëtivy** *i.* Seychelles
134 C1 **Coeur d'Alene** U.S.A.
100 C1 **Coevorden** Neth.
123 C3 **Coffee Bay** S. Africa
137 D3 **Coffeyville** U.S.A.
52 A2 **Coffin Bay** Austr.
53 D2 **Coffs Harbour** Austr.
123 C3 **Cofimvaba** S. Africa
104 B2 **Cognac** France
118 A2 **Cogo** Equat. Guinea
52 B3 **Cohuna** Austr.
146 B4 **Coiba, Isla de** *i.* Panama
153 A4 **Coihaique** Chile
73 B3 **Coimbatore** India
106 B1 **Coimbra** Port.
152 B1 **Coipasa, Salar de** *salt flat* Bol.
52 B3 **Colac** Austr.
155 D1 **Colatina** Brazil
136 C3 **Colby** U.S.A.
99 D4 **Colchester** U.K.
129 C2 **Cold Lake** Can.
96 C3 **Coldstream** U.K.
53 C2 **Coleambally** Austr.
143 D2 **Coleman** U.S.A.
52 B3 **Coleraine** Austr.
97 C1 **Coleraine** U.K.
123 C3 **Colesberg** S. Africa
153 A3 **Colico** Chile
144 B3 **Colima** Mex.
144 B3 **Colima, Nevado de** *vol.* Mex.
96 A2 **Coll** *i.* U.K.
53 C1 **Collarenebri** Austr.
143 D2 **College Station** U.S.A.
53 C1 **Collerina** Austr.
50 A3 **Collie** Austr.
50 B1 **Collier Bay** Austr.
138 C2 **Collingwood** Can.
54 B2 **Collingwood** N.Z.
126 F2 **Collinson Peninsula** Can.
101 F2 **Collmberg** *hill* Ger.
108 A3 **Collo** Alg.
97 B1 **Collooney** Rep. of Ireland
105 D2 **Colmar** France
98 B3 **Colne** U.K.
100 C2 **Cologne** Ger.
Colomb-Béchar Alg. *see* **Béchar**
154 C2 **Colômbia** Brazil
150 B2 **Colombia** *country* S. America
73 B4 **Colombo** Sri Lanka
104 C3 **Colomiers** France
152 C3 **Colón** Arg.
146 C4 **Colón** Panama
59 D2 **Colonia** Micronesia
153 B4 **Colonia Las Heras** Arg.
109 C3 **Colonna, Capo** *c.* Italy
96 A2 **Colonsay** *i.* U.K.
153 B3 **Colorado** *r.* Arg.
142 A2 **Colorado** *r.* Mex./U.S.A.
143 D3 **Colorado** *r.* U.S.A.
136 B3 **Colorado** *state* U.S.A.
135 C4 **Colorado Desert** U.S.A.
135 E3 **Colorado Plateau** U.S.A.
136 C3 **Colorado Springs** U.S.A.
144 B2 **Colotlán** Mex.
152 B1 **Colquiri** Bol.
136 B1 **Colstrip** U.S.A.
138 B3 **Columbia** *KY* U.S.A.
139 D3 **Columbia** *MD* U.S.A.
137 E3 **Columbia** *MO* U.S.A.
141 D2 **Columbia** *SC* U.S.A.
140 C1 **Columbia** *TN* U.S.A.
134 B1 **Columbia** *r.* U.S.A.
128 C2 **Columbia, Mount** Can.
134 D1 **Columbia Falls** U.S.A.
128 B2 **Columbia Mountains** Can.
134 C1 **Columbia Plateau** U.S.A.
141 D2 **Columbus** *GA* U.S.A.
138 B3 **Columbus** *IN* U.S.A.
140 C2 **Columbus** *MS* U.S.A.
134 E1 **Columbus** *MT* U.S.A.
137 D2 **Columbus** *NE* U.S.A.
142 B2 **Columbus** *NM* U.S.A.
138 C3 **Columbus** *OH* U.S.A.
143 D3 **Columbus** *TX* U.S.A.
134 C1 **Colville** U.S.A.
126 B2 **Colville** *r.* U.S.A.
126 D2 **Colville Lake** Can.
98 B3 **Colwyn Bay** U.K.
108 B2 **Comacchio** Italy
145 C3 **Comalcalco** Mex.
110 C1 **Comănești** Romania
130 C2 **Comencho, Lac** *l.* Can.
97 C2 **Comeragh Mountains** *hills* Rep. of Ireland
143 D2 **Comfort** U.S.A.
75 D2 **Comilla** Bangl.
108 A2 **Comino, Capo** *c. Sardinia* Italy
145 C3 **Comitán de Domínguez** Mex.
105 C2 **Commentry** France
143 D2 **Commerce** U.S.A.
127 G2 **Committee Bay** Can.
108 A1 **Como** Italy
Como, Lago di Italy *see* Como, Lake
108 A1 **Como, Lake** *l.* Italy
153 B4 **Comodoro Rivadavia** Arg.
145 B2 **Comonfort** Mex.
121 D2 **Comoros** *country* Africa
128 B3 **Comox** Can.
105 C2 **Compiègne** France
144 B2 **Compostela** Mex.
90 B2 **Comrat** Moldova
114 A4 **Conakry** Guinea
104 B2 **Concarneau** France
155 E1 **Conceição da Barra** Brazil
151 E3 **Conceição do Araguaia** Brazil
155 D1 **Conceição do Mato Dentro** Brazil
152 B2 **Concepción** Arg.
153 A3 **Concepción** Chile
144 B2 **Concepción** Mex.
135 B4 **Conception, Point** U.S.A.
154 C2 **Conchas** Brazil
142 C1 **Conchas Lake** U.S.A.
144 B2 **Conchos** *r.* Mex.
145 C2 **Conchos** *r.* Mex.
135 B3 **Concord** *CA* U.S.A.
139 E2 **Concord** *NH* U.S.A.
152 C3 **Concordia** Arg.
122 A2 **Concordia** S. Africa
137 D3 **Concordia** U.S.A.
53 C2 **Condobolin** Austr.
104 C3 **Condom** France
134 B1 **Condon** U.S.A.
108 B1 **Conegliano** Italy
51 E1 **Conflict Group** *is* P.N.G.
104 C2 **Confolens** France
135 D3 **Confusion Range** *mts* U.S.A.
75 C2 **Congdü** China
98 B3 **Congleton** U.K.
118 B3 **Congo** *country* Africa
118 B3 **Congo** *r.* Congo/Dem. Rep. Congo
118 C3 **Congo, Democratic Republic of** *country* Africa
118 C3 **Congo Basin** Dem. Rep. Congo
Congo (Brazzaville) *country* Africa *see* **Congo**
Congo Free State *country* Africa *see* **Congo, Democratic Republic of**
Congo (Kinshasa) *country* Africa *see* **Congo, Democratic Republic of**
129 C2 **Conklin** Can.
97 B1 **Conn, Lough** *l.* Rep. of Ireland
97 B2 **Connaught** *reg.* Rep. of Ireland
139 E2 **Connecticut** *r.* U.S.A.
139 E2 **Connecticut** *state* U.S.A.
96 B2 **Connel** U.K.
97 B2 **Connemara** *reg.* Rep. of Ireland
134 D1 **Conrad** U.S.A.
159 D7 **Conrad Rise** *sea feature* Southern Ocean
143 D2 **Conroe** U.S.A.
155 D2 **Conselheiro Lafaiete** Brazil
155 D1 **Conselheiro Pena** Brazil
100 B3 **Consenvoye** France
98 C2 **Consett** U.K.
63 B3 **Côn Sơn** *i.* Vietnam
Constance Ger. *see* **Konstanz**
105 D2 **Constance, Lake** Ger./Switz.
110 C2 **Constanța** Romania
106 B2 **Constantina** Spain
115 C1 **Constantine** Alg.
134 D2 **Contact** U.S.A.
155 D2 **Contagalo** Brazil
150 B3 **Contamana** Peru
153 A5 **Contreras, Isla** *i.* Chile
126 E2 **Contwoyto Lake** Can.
140 B1 **Conway** *AR* U.S.A.
139 E2 **Conway** *NH* U.S.A.
51 C2 **Coober Pedy** Austr.
Cooch Behar India *see* **Koch Bihar**
Cook, Mount *mt.* N.Z. *see* **Aoraki**
141 C1 **Cookeville** U.S.A.
126 B2 **Cook Inlet** *sea chan.* U.S.A.
49 K5 **Cook Islands** *terr.* S. Pacific Ocean
131 E2 **Cook's Harbour** Can.
97 C1 **Cookstown** U.K.
54 B2 **Cook Strait** N.Z.
51 D1 **Cooktown** Austr.
53 C2 **Coolabah** Austr.
53 C2 **Coolamon** Austr.
53 D1 **Coolangatta** Austr.
50 B3 **Coolgardie** Austr.
53 C3 **Cooma** Austr.
52 B2 **Coombah** Austr.
53 C2 **Coonabarabran** Austr.
52 A3 **Coonalpyn** Austr.
53 C2 **Coonamble** Austr.
53 C1 **Coongoola** Austr.
137 E1 **Coon Rapids** U.S.A.
52 A1 **Cooper Creek** *watercourse* Austr.
141 E3 **Cooper's Town** Bahamas
134 B2 **Coos Bay** U.S.A.
53 C2 **Cootamundra** Austr.
97 C1 **Cootehill** Rep. of Ireland
145 C3 **Copainalá** Mex.
145 C3 **Copala** Mex.
93 F4 **Copenhagen** Denmark
109 C2 **Copertino** Italy
53 D1 **Copeton Reservoir** Austr.
152 A2 **Copiapó** Chile
143 D2 **Copperas Cove** U.S.A.
138 B1 **Copper Harbor** U.S.A.
Coppermine Can. *see* **Kugluktuk**
126 E2 **Coppermine** *r.* Can.
122 B2 **Copperton** S. Africa
Coquilhatville Dem. Rep. Congo *see* **Mbandaka**
152 A2 **Coquimbo** Chile
152 A2 **Coquimbo, Bahía de** *b.* Chile
110 B2 **Corabia** Romania
155 D1 **Coração de Jesus** Brazil
150 B4 **Coracora** Peru
53 D1 **Coraki** Austr.
50 A2 **Coral Bay** Austr.
127 G2 **Coral Harbour** Can.
51 E1 **Coral Sea** S. Pacific Ocean
48 G5 **Coral Sea Islands Territory** *terr.* Austr.
137 E2 **Coralville** U.S.A.
52 B3 **Corangamite, Lake** Austr.
99 C3 **Corby** U.K.
Corcaigh Rep. of Ireland *see* **Cork**
135 C3 **Corcoran** U.S.A.
153 A4 **Corcovado, Golfo de** *sea chan.* Chile
141 D2 **Cordele** U.S.A.
64 B2 **Cordilleras Range** *mts* Phil.
155 D1 **Cordisburgo** Brazil
152 B3 **Córdoba** Arg.
145 C3 **Córdoba** Mex.
106 C2 **Córdoba** Spain
153 B3 **Córdoba, Sierras de** *mts* Arg.
126 C2 **Cordova** U.S.A.
51 D2 **Corfield** Austr.
111 A3 **Corfu** *i.* Greece
154 B1 **Corguinho** Brazil
106 B2 **Coria** Spain
106 B2 **Coria del Río** Spain
53 D2 **Coricudgy** *mt.* Austr.
111 B3 **Corinth** Greece
140 C2 **Corinth** U.S.A.
Corinth, Gulf of *sea chan.* Greece *see* **Gulf of Corinth**
155 D1 **Corinto** Brazil
97 B3 **Cork** Rep. of Ireland
111 C2 **Çorlu** Turkey
154 B2 **Cornélio Procópio** Brazil
131 E3 **Corner Brook** Can.
53 C3 **Corner Inlet** *b.* Austr.
135 B3 **Corning** *CA* U.S.A.
139 D2 **Corning** *NY* U.S.A.
Corn Islands *is* Nic. *see* **Maíz, Islas del**
108 B2 **Corno, Monte** *mt.* Italy
130 C3 **Cornwall** Can.
126 F1 **Cornwallis Island** Can.
150 C1 **Coro** Venez.
155 D1 **Coroaci** Brazil
154 C1 **Coromandel** Brazil
73 C3 **Coromandel Coast** India
54 C1 **Coromandel Peninsula** N.Z.
64 B2 **Coron** Phil.
129 C2 **Coronation** Can.
126 E2 **Coronation Gulf** Can.
55 B3 **Coronation Island** S. Atlantic Ocean
155 D1 **Coronel Fabriciano** Brazil
152 C2 **Coronel Oviedo** Para.
154 B1 **Coronel Ponce** Brazil
153 B3 **Coronel Pringles** Arg.
154 A2 **Coronel Sapucaia** Brazil
153 B3 **Coronel Suárez** Arg.
109 D2 **Çorovodë** Albania
145 D3 **Corozal** Belize
143 D3 **Corpus Christi** U.S.A.
152 B1 **Corque** Bol.
151 E4 **Corrente** Brazil
154 B1 **Correntes** Brazil
151 E4 **Correntina** Brazil
97 B2 **Corrib, Lough** *l.* Rep. of Ireland
152 C2 **Corrientes** Arg.
153 C3 **Corrientes, Cabo** *c.* Arg.
144 B2 **Corrientes, Cabo** *c.* Mex.
143 E2 **Corrigan** U.S.A.
53 C3 **Corryong** Austr.
Corse *i.* France *see* **Corsica**
105 D3 **Corse, Cap** *c. Corsica* France
105 D3 **Corsica** *i.* France
143 D2 **Corsicana** U.S.A.
105 D3 **Corte** *Corsica* France
106 B2 **Cortegana** Spain
136 B3 **Cortez** U.S.A.
108 B1 **Cortina d'Ampezzo** Italy
139 D2 **Cortland** U.S.A.
108 B2 **Cortona** Italy
106 B2 **Coruche** Port.
Çoruh Turkey *see* **Artvin**
80 B1 **Çorum** Turkey
151 D4 **Corumbá** Brazil
154 C1 **Corumbá** *r.* Brazil
154 C1 **Corumbá de Goiás** Brazil
Corunna Spain *see* **A Coruña**
134 B2 **Corvallis** U.S.A.
99 B3 **Corwen** U.K.

Cos *i.* Greece *see* **Kos**
144 B2 **Cosalá** Mex.
145 C3 **Cosamaloapan** Mex.
109 C3 **Cosenza** Italy
105 C2 **Cosne-Cours-sur-Loire** France
152 B3 **Cosquín** Arg.
107 C2 **Costa Blanca** *coastal area* Spain
107 D1 **Costa Brava** *coastal area* Spain
106 B2 **Costa de la Luz** *coastal area* Spain
107 C2 **Costa del Azahar** *coastal area* Spain
106 B2 **Costa del Sol** *coastal area* Spain
146 B3 **Costa de Mosquitos** *coastal area* Nic.
107 D1 **Costa Dorada** *coastal area* Spain
150 C4 **Costa Marques** Brazil
154 B1 **Costa Rica** Brazil
146 B3 **Costa Rica** *country* Central America
144 B2 **Costa Rica** Mex.
Costermansville Dem. Rep. Congo *see* **Bukavu**
110 B2 **Costeşti** Romania
64 B3 **Cotabato** Phil.
137 D1 **Coteau des Prairies** *slope* U.S.A.
136 C1 **Coteau du Missouri** *slope* U.S.A.
147 C3 **Coteaux** Haiti
105 D3 **Côte d'Azur** *coastal area* France
114 B4 **Côte d'Ivoire** *country* Africa
Côte Française de Somalis *country* Africa *see* **Djibouti**
105 C2 **Côtes de Meuse** *ridge* France
150 B3 **Cotopaxi, Volcán** *vol.* Ecuador
99 B4 **Cotswold Hills** U.K.
134 B2 **Cottage Grove** U.S.A.
102 C1 **Cottbus** Ger.
105 D3 **Cottian Alps** *mts* France/Italy
104 B2 **Coubre, Pointe de la** *pt* France
52 A3 **Coüedic, Cape de** Austr.
105 C2 **Coulommiers** France
137 D2 **Council Bluffs** U.S.A.
88 B2 **Courland Lagoon** *b.* Lith./Rus. Fed.
100 A3 **Courmelles** France
128 B3 **Courtenay** Can.
104 B2 **Coutances** France
104 B2 **Coutras** France
100 B2 **Couvin** Belgium
99 C3 **Coventry** U.K.
106 B1 **Covilhã** Port.
141 D2 **Covington** *GA* U.S.A.
138 C3 **Covington** *KY* U.S.A.
138 C3 **Covington** *VA* U.S.A.
50 B3 **Cowan, Lake** *salt flat* Austr.
96 C2 **Cowdenbeath** U.K.
52 A2 **Cowell** Austr.
53 C3 **Cowes** Austr.
134 B1 **Cowlitz** *r.* U.S.A.
53 C2 **Cowra** Austr.
154 B1 **Coxim** Brazil
154 B1 **Coxim** *r.* Brazil
75 D2 **Cox's Bazar** Bangl.
145 B3 **Coyuca de Benítez** Mex.
145 D2 **Cozumel** Mex.
145 D2 **Cozumel, Isla de** *i.* Mex.
52 A2 **Cradock** Austr.
123 C3 **Cradock** S. Africa
136 B2 **Craig** U.S.A.
102 C2 **Crailsheim** Ger.
110 B2 **Craiova** Romania
129 D2 **Cranberry Portage** Can.
53 C3 **Cranbourne** Austr.
128 C3 **Cranbrook** Can.
151 E3 **Crateús** Brazil
151 F3 **Crato** Brazil
154 C2 **Cravinhos** Brazil
136 C2 **Crawford** U.S.A.
138 B2 **Crawfordsville** U.S.A.
99 C4 **Crawley** U.K.
134 D1 **Crazy Mountains** U.S.A.
129 D2 **Cree** *r.* Can.
144 B2 **Creel** Mex.
129 D2 **Cree Lake** Can.
129 D2 **Creighton** Can.

104 C2 **Creil** France
100 B1 **Creil** Neth.
108 A1 **Crema** Italy
108 B1 **Cremona** Italy
108 B2 **Cres** *i.* Croatia
134 B2 **Crescent City** U.S.A.
53 D2 **Crescent Head** Austr.
135 E3 **Crescent Junction** U.S.A.
128 C3 **Creston** Can.
140 C2 **Creston** U.S.A.
137 E2 **Creston** U.S.A.
140 C2 **Crestview** U.S.A.
111 B3 **Crete** *i.* Greece
107 D1 **Creus, Cap de** *c.* Spain
107 C2 **Crevillente** Spain
98 B3 **Crewe** U.K.
96 B2 **Crianlarich** U.K.
152 D2 **Criciúma** Brazil
96 C2 **Crieff** U.K.
108 B1 **Crikvenica** Croatia
91 C2 **Crimea** *pen.* Ukr.
101 F2 **Crimmitschau** Ger.
96 B2 **Crinan** U.K.
118 B2 **Cristal, Monts de** *mts* Equat. Guinea/Gabon
154 C1 **Cristalina** Brazil
110 B1 **Crişul Alb** *r.* Romania
101 E1 **Crivitz** Ger.
109 C2 **Crna Gora** *aut. rep.* Serb. and Mont.
109 C1 **Črnomelj** Slovenia
97 B2 **Croagh Patrick** *hill* Rep. of Ireland
109 C1 **Croatia** *country* Europe
61 C1 **Crocker, Banjaran** *mts* Malaysia
143 D2 **Crockett** U.S.A.
59 C3 **Croker Island** Austr.
96 B2 **Cromarty** U.K.
99 D3 **Cromer** U.K.
54 A3 **Cromwell** N.Z.
147 C2 **Crooked Island** Bahamas
137 D1 **Crookston** U.S.A.
53 C2 **Crookwell** Austr.
53 D1 **Croppa Creek** Austr.
136 C1 **Crosby** U.S.A.
141 D3 **Cross City** U.S.A.
140 B2 **Crossett** U.S.A.
98 B2 **Cross Fell** *hill* U.K.
129 E2 **Cross Lake** Can.
141 C1 **Crossville** U.S.A.
109 C3 **Crotone** Italy
141 E1 **Crow Agency** U.S.A.
99 C4 **Crowborough** U.K.
99 D4 **Crowley** U.S.A.
53 D1 **Crows Nest** Austr.
128 C3 **Crowsnest Pass** Can.
159 D7 **Crozet, Îles** *is* Indian Ocean
146 C3 **Cruz, Cabo** *c.* Cuba
152 C2 **Cruz Alta** Brazil
152 B3 **Cruz del Eje** Arg.
155 D2 **Cruzeiro** Brazil
150 B3 **Cruzeiro do Sul** Brazil
52 A2 **Crystal Brook** Austr.
143 D3 **Crystal City** U.S.A.
138 B1 **Crystal Falls** U.S.A.
140 B2 **Crystal Springs** U.S.A.
103 E2 **Csongrád** Hungary
103 D2 **Csorna** Hungary
121 C2 **Cuamba** Moz.
120 B2 **Cuando** *r.* Angola/Zambia
120 A2 **Cuangar** Angola
118 B3 **Cuango** *r.* Angola/Dem. Rep. Congo
120 A1 **Cuanza** *r.* Angola
144 B2 **Cuatro Ciénegas** Mex.
144 B2 **Cuauhtémoc** Mex.
145 C3 **Cuautla** Mex.
146 C2 **Cuba** *country* West Indies
120 A2 **Cubal** Angola
120 B2 **Cubango** *r.* Angola/Namibia
150 B2 **Cúcuta** Col.
73 B3 **Cuddalore** India
73 B3 **Cuddapah** India
50 A2 **Cue** Austr.
106 C1 **Cuéllar** Spain
120 A2 **Cuemba** Angola
150 B3 **Cuenca** Ecuador
107 C1 **Cuenca** Spain
107 C1 **Cuenca, Serranía de** *mts* Spain
145 C3 **Cuernavaca** Mex.
143 D3 **Cuero** U.S.A.
104 C3 **Cugnaux** France
151 D4 **Cuiabá** Brazil
151 D4 **Cuiabá** *r.* Brazil
96 A2 **Cuillin Sound** *sea chan.* U.K.
120 A1 **Cuilo** Angola
120 B2 **Cuito** *r.* Angola
120 A2 **Cuito Cuanavale** Angola

60 B1 **Cukai** Malaysia
64 B2 **Culasi** Phil.
53 C3 **Culcairn** Austr.
100 B2 **Culemborg** Neth.
53 C1 **Culgoa** Austr.
144 B2 **Culiacán** Mex.
64 A2 **Culion** *i.* Phil.
107 C2 **Cullera** Spain
140 C2 **Cullman** U.S.A.
97 C1 **Cullybackey** U.K.
139 D3 **Culpeper** U.S.A.
151 D4 **Culuene** *r.* Brazil
54 B2 **Culverden** N.Z.
150 C1 **Cumaná** Venez.
139 D3 **Cumberland** U.S.A.
138 B3 **Cumberland** *r.* U.S.A.
141 D2 **Cumberland Island** U.S.A.
129 D2 **Cumberland Lake** Can.
127 H2 **Cumberland Peninsula** Can.
140 C1 **Cumberland Plateau** U.S.A.
127 H2 **Cumberland Sound** *sea chan.* Can.
96 C3 **Cumbernauld** U.K.
96 B3 **Cummings** U.S.A.
96 B3 **Cumnock** U.K.
144 B1 **Cumpas** Mex.
145 C3 **Cunduacán** Mex.
120 A2 **Cunene** *r.* Angola/Namibia
108 A2 **Cuneo** Italy
53 C1 **Cunnamulla** Austr.
108 A1 **Cuorgnè** Italy
96 C2 **Cupar** U.K.
110 B2 **Ćuprija** Serb. and Mont.
147 D3 **Curaçao** *i.* Neth. Antilles
150 B3 **Curaray** *r.* Ecuador
153 A3 **Curicó** Chile
154 C3 **Curitiba** Brazil
52 A2 **Curnamona** Austr.
51 D3 **Currie** Austr.
135 D2 **Currie** U.S.A.
51 E2 **Curtis Island** Austr.
151 D3 **Curuá** *r.* Brazil
60 B2 **Curup** Indon.
151 E3 **Cururupu** Brazil
155 D1 **Curvelo** Brazil
97 C1 **Cushendun** U.K.
143 D1 **Cushing** U.S.A.
136 C2 **Custer** U.S.A.
134 D1 **Cut Bank** U.S.A.
140 B3 **Cut Off** U.S.A.
75 C2 **Cuttack** India
120 A2 **Cuvelai** Angola
101 D1 **Cuxhaven** Ger.
64 B2 **Cuyo Islands** Phil.
Cuzco Peru *see* **Cusco**
99 B4 **Cwmbrân** U.K.
119 C3 **Cyangugu** Rwanda
111 B3 **Cyclades** *is* Greece
129 C3 **Cypress Hills** Can.
80 B2 **Cyprus** *country* Asia
80 B2 **Cyprus** *i.* Asia
102 C2 **Czech Republic** *country* Europe
103 D1 **Czersk** Pol.
103 D1 **Częstochowa** Pol.

D

Đa, Sông *r.* Vietnam *see* **Black River**
69 D2 **Daban** China
103 D2 **Dabas** Hungary
114 A3 **Dabola** Guinea
103 D1 **Dąbrowa Górnicza** Pol.
110 B2 **Dăbuleni** Romania
Dacca Bangl. *see* **Dhaka**
102 C2 **Dachau** Ger.
Dachuan China *see* **Dazhou**
141 D3 **Dade City** U.S.A.
Dadong China *see* **Donggang**
Dadra India *see* **Achalpur**
74 B2 **Dadra and Nagar Haveli** *union terr.* India
74 A2 **Dadu** Pak.
Daegu S. Korea *see* **Taegu**
64 B2 **Daet** Phil.
114 A3 **Dagana** Senegal
119 D2 **Daga Post** Sudan
88 C2 **Dagda** Latvia
64 B2 **Dagupan** Phil.
Dahalach, Isole *is* Eritrea *see* **Dahlak Archipelago**
74 B3 **Dahanu** India

69 D2 **Da Hinggan Ling** *mts* China
116 C3 **Dahlak Archipelago** *is* Eritrea
100 C2 **Dahlem** Ger.
78 B3 **Dahm, Ramlat** *des.* Saudi Arabia/Yemen
74 B2 **Dahod** India
Dahomey *country* Africa *see* **Benin**
Dahra Senegal *see* **Dara**
81 C2 **Dahūk** Iraq
60 B2 **Daik** Indon.
106 C2 **Daimiel** Spain
Dairen China *see* **Dalian**
51 C2 **Dajarra** Austr.
70 A2 **Dajing** China
114 A3 **Dakar** Senegal
117 C4 **Daketa Shet'** *watercourse* Eth.
116 A2 **Dākhilah, Wāḥāt ad** Egypt
Dakhla Oasis Egypt *see* **Dākhilah, Wāḥāt ad**
63 A3 **Dakoank** India
88 C3 **Dakol'ka** *r.* Belarus
109 D2 **Đakovica** Serb. and Mont.
109 C1 **Đakovo** Croatia
120 B2 **Dala** Angola
70 A1 **Dalain Hob** China
93 G3 **Dalälven** *r.* Sweden
111 C3 **Dalaman** Turkey
111 C3 **Dalaman** *r.* Turkey
68 C2 **Dalandzadgad** Mongolia
64 B2 **Dalanganem Islands** Phil.
63 B2 **Đa Lat** Vietnam
74 A2 **Dalbandin** Pak.
96 C3 **Dalbeattie** U.K.
53 D1 **Dalby** Austr.
93 E3 **Dale** Norway
141 C1 **Dale Hollow Lake** U.S.A.
53 C3 **Dalgety** Austr.
143 C1 **Dalhart** U.S.A.
131 D3 **Dalhousie** Can.
62 B1 **Dali** China
70 C2 **Dalian** China
96 C3 **Dalkeith** U.K.
143 D2 **Dallas** U.S.A.
128 A2 **Dall Island** U.S.A.
Dalmacija *reg.* Croatia *see* **Dalmatia**
96 B2 **Dalmally** U.K.
109 C2 **Dalmatia** *reg.* Croatia
96 B3 **Dalmellington** U.K.
66 C2 **Dal'negorsk** Rus. Fed.
66 B1 **Dal'nerechensk** Rus. Fed.
Dalny China *see* **Dalian**
114 B4 **Daloa** Côte d'Ivoire
71 A3 **Dalou Shan** *mts* China
51 D2 **Dalrymple, Mount** Austr.
92 □A3 **Dalsmynni** Iceland
75 C2 **Daltenganj** India
141 D2 **Dalton** U.S.A.
Daltonganj India *see* **Daltenganj**
60 B1 **Daludalu** Indon.
71 B3 **Daluo Shan** *mt.* China
92 □B2 **Dalvík** Iceland
96 B2 **Dalwhinnie** U.K.
50 C1 **Daly** *r.* Austr.
51 C1 **Daly Waters** Austr.
74 B2 **Daman** India
74 B2 **Daman and Diu** *union terr.* India
116 B1 **Damanhūr** Egypt
59 C3 **Damar** *i.* Indon.
118 B2 **Damara** C.A.R.
80 B2 **Damascus** Syria
115 D3 **Damaturu** Nigeria
76 B3 **Damāvand, Qolleh-ye** *mt.* Iran
120 A1 **Damba** Angola
118 B1 **Damboa** Nigeria
81 D2 **Damghan** Iran
Damietta Egypt *see* **Dumyāţ**
79 C2 **Dammam** Saudi Arabia
101 D1 **Damme** Ger.
75 B2 **Damoh** India
114 B4 **Damongo** Ghana
50 A2 **Dampier** Austr.
59 C3 **Dampir, Selat** *sea chan.* Indon.
75 D1 **Damxung** China
114 B4 **Danané** Côte d'Ivoire
63 B2 **Đa Năng** Vietnam
139 E2 **Danbury** U.S.A.
70 C1 **Dandong** China
117 B3 **Dangila** Eth.
146 B3 **Dangriga** Belize

70 B2 Dangshan China
89 F2 Danilov Rus. Fed.
89 E2 Danilovskaya Vozvyshennost' *hills* Rus. Fed.
70 B2 Danjiangkou China
79 C2 Ḑank Oman
89 E3 Dankov Rus. Fed.
146 B3 Danlí Hond.
101 E1 Dannenberg (Elbe) Ger.
54 C2 Dannevirke N.Z.
62 B2 Dan Sai Thai.
70 B2 Dantu China
110 A1 Danube *r.* Europe
110 C1 Danube Delta Romania
138 B2 Danville *IL* U.S.A.
138 C3 Danville *KY* U.S.A.
139 D3 Danville *VA* U.S.A.
Danxian China *see* Danzhou
71 A4 Danzhou China
Danzig, Gulf of Pol./Rus. Fed. *see* Gdańsk, Gulf of
Daojiang China *see* Daoxian
115 D2 Dao Timmi Niger
Daoud Alg. *see* Aïn Beïda
114 B4 Daoukro Côte d'Ivoire
71 B3 Daoxian China
64 B3 Dapa Phil.
114 C3 Dapaong Togo
68 C2 Da Qaidam Zhen China
69 E1 Daqing China
114 A3 Dara Senegal
80 B2 Dar'ā Syria
81 D3 Dārāb Iran
115 D1 Daraj Libya
81 D2 Dārān Iran
63 B2 Đa Răng, Sông *r.* Vietnam
109 D2 Đaravica *mt.* Serb. and Mont.
75 C2 Darbhanga India
Dardo China *see* Kangding
119 D3 Dar es Salaam Tanz.
74 B1 Dargai Pak.
54 B1 Dargaville N.Z.
53 C3 Dargo Austr.
68 D1 Darhan Mongolia
150 B2 Darién, Golfo del *g.* Col.
Darjeeling India *see* Darjiling
75 C2 Darjiling India
68 C2 Darlag China
52 B2 Darling *r.* Austr.
53 C1 Darling Downs *hills* Austr.
50 A3 Darling Range *hills* Austr.
98 C2 Darlington U.K.
53 C2 Darlington Point Austr.
103 D1 Darłowo Pol.
101 D3 Darmstadt Ger.
115 E1 Darnah Libya
52 B2 Darnick Austr.
55 H3 Darnley, Cape Antarctica
107 C1 Daroca Spain
99 D4 Dartford U.K.
99 A4 Dartmoor *hills* U.K.
131 D3 Dartmouth Can.
99 B4 Dartmouth U.K.
59 D3 Daru P.N.G.
59 C2 Daruba Indon.
50 C1 Darwin Austr.
153 C5 Darwin Falkland Is
79 C2 Dārzīn Iran
65 A1 Dashiqiao China
Dashkhovuz Turkm. *see* Dashoguz
76 B2 Dashoguz Turkm.
74 A2 Dasht *r.* Pak.
61 C1 Datadian Indon.
111 C3 Datça Turkey
66 D2 Date Japan
71 B3 Datian China
70 B1 Datong China
64 B3 Datu Piang Phil.
74 B1 Daud Khel Pak.
88 B2 Daugava *r.* Latvia
88 C2 Daugavpils Latvia
100 C2 Daun Ger.
129 D2 Dauphin Can.
129 E2 Dauphin Lake Can.
73 B3 Davangere India
64 B3 Davao Phil.
64 B3 Davao Gulf Phil.
137 E2 Davenport U.S.A.
99 C3 Daventry U.K.
123 C2 Daveyton S. Africa
146 B4 David Panama
129 D2 Davidson Can.
126 F3 Davidson Lake Can.
135 B3 Davis U.S.A.
131 D2 Davis Inlet Can.
55 I3 Davis Sea *sea* Antarctica
127 I2 Davis Strait *str.* Can./Greenland
105 D2 Davos Switz.
88 C3 Davyd-Haradok Belarus
79 C3 Dawqah Oman
78 B3 Dawqah Saudi Arabia
126 C2 Dawson Can.
141 D2 Dawson U.S.A.
128 B2 Dawson Creek Can.
128 B2 Dawsons Landing Can.
68 C2 Dawu China
Dawukou China *see* Shizuishan
79 C2 Dawwah Oman
104 B3 Dax France
Daxian China *see* Dazhou
68 C2 Da Xueshan *mts* China
52 B3 Daylesford Austr.
Dayong China *see* Zhangjiajie
81 C2 Dayr az Zawr Syria
138 C3 Dayton U.S.A.
141 D3 Daytona Beach U.S.A.
71 B3 Dayu China
70 B2 Da Yunhe *canal* China
70 A2 Dazhou China
122 B3 De Aar S. Africa
141 D3 Deadman Bay U.S.A.
80 B2 Dead Sea *salt l.* Asia
99 D4 Deal U.K.
71 B3 De'an China
152 B3 Deán Funes Arg.
128 B2 Dease Lake Can.
126 E2 Dease Strait Can.
135 C3 Death Valley *depr.* U.S.A.
104 C2 Deauville France
61 C1 Debak *Sarawak* Malaysia
111 B2 Debar Macedonia
103 E1 Dębica Pol.
103 E1 Dęblin Pol.
114 B3 Débo, Lac *l.* Mali
103 E2 Debrecen Hungary
117 B3 Debre Markos Eth.
119 D2 Debre Sīna Eth.
117 B3 Debre Tabor Eth.
117 B4 Debre Zeyit Eth.
140 C2 Decatur *AL* U.S.A.
138 B3 Decatur *IL* U.S.A.
73 B3 Deccan *plat.* India
53 D1 Deception Bay Austr.
71 A3 Dechang China
102 C1 Děčín Czech Rep.
137 E2 Decorah U.S.A.
154 C2 Dedo de Deus *mt.* Brazil
88 C2 Dedovichi Rus. Fed.
121 C2 Dedza Malawi
99 B3 Dee *r. England/Wales* U.K.
96 C2 Dee *r. Scotland* U.K.
130 C3 Deep River Can.
53 D1 Deepwater Austr.
131 E3 Deer Lake Can.
134 D1 Deer Lodge U.S.A.
138 C2 Defiance U.S.A.
140 C2 De Funiak Springs U.S.A.
68 C2 Dêgê China
117 C4 Degeh Bur Eth.
139 F1 Dégelis Can.
102 C2 Deggendorf Ger.
91 E2 Degtevo Rus. Fed.
81 D2 Deh Bīd Iran
81 C2 Dehlorān Iran
74 B1 Dehra Dun India
75 C2 Dehri India
69 E2 Dehui China
100 A2 Deinze Belgium
110 B1 Dej Romania
138 B2 De Kalb U.S.A.
116 B3 Dekemhare Eritrea
118 C3 Dekese Dem. Rep. Congo
118 B2 Dékoa C.A.R.
141 D3 De Land U.S.A.
135 C3 Delano U.S.A.
135 D3 Delano Peak U.S.A.
48 I3 Delap-Uliga-Djarrit Marshall Is
74 A1 Delārām Afgh.
123 C2 Delareyville S. Africa
129 D2 Delaronde Lake Can.
138 C2 Delaware U.S.A.
139 D3 Delaware *r.* U.S.A.
139 D3 Delaware *state* U.S.A.
139 D3 Delaware Bay U.S.A.
53 C3 Delegate Austr.
118 C2 Délembé C.A.R.
105 D2 Delémont Switz.
100 B1 Delft Neth.
100 C1 Delfzijl Neth.
121 D2 Delgado, Cabo *c.* Moz.
68 C2 Delhi China
74 B2 Delhi India
60 B2 Deli *i.* Indon.
128 B1 Déline Can.
Delingha China *see* Delhi
101 F2 Delitzsch Ger.
107 D2 Dellys Alg.
135 C4 Del Mar U.S.A.
101 D1 Delmenhorst Ger.
109 B1 Delnice Croatia
136 B3 Del Norte U.S.A.
83 L1 De-Longa, Ostrova *is* Rus. Fed.
De Long Islands Rus. Fed. *see* De-Longa, Ostrova
De Long Strait Rus. Fed. *see* Longa, Proliv
129 D3 Deloraine Can.
111 B3 Delphi *tourist site* Greece
141 D3 Delray Beach U.S.A.
143 C3 Del Rio U.S.A.
136 B3 Delta *CO* U.S.A.
135 D3 Delta *UT* U.S.A.
126 C2 Delta Junction U.S.A.
109 D3 Delvinë Albania
106 C1 Demanda, Sierra de la *mts* Spain
Demavend *mt.* Iran *see* Damāvand, Qolleh-ye
118 C3 Demba Dem. Rep. Congo
119 D1 Dembech'a Eth.
117 B4 Dembī Dolo Eth.
Demerara Guyana *see* Georgetown
91 C3 Demerdzhi *mt.* Ukr.
89 D2 Demidov Rus. Fed.
142 B2 Deming U.S.A.
111 C3 Demirci Turkey
111 C2 Demirköy Turkey
102 C1 Demmin Ger.
140 C2 Demopolis U.S.A.
60 B2 Dempo, Gunung *vol.* Indon.
89 D2 Demyansk Rus. Fed.
122 B3 De Naawte S. Africa
117 C3 Denakil *reg.* Eritrea/Eth.
98 B3 Denbigh U.K.
100 B1 Den Burg Neth.
62 B2 Den Chai Thai.
60 B2 Dendang Indon.
100 B2 Dendermonde Belgium
100 B2 Dendre *r.* Belgium
Dengjiabu China *see* Yujiang
70 A1 Dengkou China
Dengxian China *see* Dengzhou
70 B2 Dengzhou China
Dengzhou China *see* Penglai
Den Haag Neth. *see* The Hague
50 A2 Denham Austr.
100 B1 Den Helder Neth.
107 D2 Denia Spain
52 B3 Deniliquin Austr.
134 C2 Denio U.S.A.
137 D2 Denison *IA* U.S.A.
143 D2 Denison *TX* U.S.A.
111 C3 Denizli Turkey
53 D2 Denman Austr.
50 A3 Denmark Austr.
93 E4 Denmark *country* Europe
84 B2 Denmark Strait Greenland/Iceland
77 C3 Denov Uzbek.
61 C2 Denpasar Indon.
143 D2 Denton U.S.A.
50 A3 D'Entrecasteaux, Point Austr.
59 E3 D'Entrecasteaux Islands P.N.G.
141 D2 Dentsville U.S.A.
136 B3 Denver U.S.A.
75 C2 Deogarh *Orissa* India
74 B2 Deogarh *Rajasthan* India
75 C2 Deoghar India
138 B2 De Pere U.S.A.
83 K2 Deputatskiy Rus. Fed.
62 A1 Dêqên China
140 B2 De Queen U.S.A.
74 A2 Dera Bugti Pak.
74 B1 Dera Ghazi Khan Pak.
74 B1 Dera Ismail Khan Pak.
87 D4 Derbent Rus. Fed.
50 B1 Derby Austr.
99 C3 Derby U.K.
137 D3 Derby U.S.A.
99 D3 Dereham U.K.
97 B2 Derg, Lough *l.* Rep. of Ireland
91 D1 Derhachi Ukr.
140 B2 De Ridder U.S.A.
91 D2 Derkul *r.* Rus. Fed./Ukr.
75 B1 Dêrub China
116 B3 Derudeb Sudan
122 B3 De Rust S. Africa
109 C2 Derventa Bos.-Herz.
98 C3 Derwent *r. England* U.K.
98 C3 Derwent *r. England* U.K.
98 B2 Derwent Water *l.* U.K.
77 C1 Derzhavinsk Kazakh.
Derzhavinskiy Kazakh. *see* Derzhavinsk
152 B1 Desaguadero *r.* Bol.
49 M5 Désappointement, Îles du *is* Fr. Polynesia
129 D2 Deschambault Lake Can.
134 B1 Deschutes *r.* U.S.A.
117 B3 Desē Eth.
153 B4 Deseado Arg.
153 B4 Deseado *r.* Arg.
142 A2 Desemboque Mex.
137 E2 Des Moines U.S.A.
137 E2 Des Moines *r.* U.S.A.
91 C1 Desna *r.* Rus. Fed./Ukr.
89 D3 Desnogorsk Rus. Fed.
101 F2 Dessau Ger.
Dessye Eth. *see* Desē
128 A1 Destruction Bay Can.
149 C5 Desventurados, Islas de los *is* S. Pacific Ocean
128 C1 Detah Can.
120 B2 Dete Zimbabwe
101 D2 Detmold Ger.
138 C2 Detroit U.S.A.
137 D1 Detroit Lakes U.S.A.
Dett Zimbabwe *see* Dete
100 B2 Deurne Neth.
110 B1 Deva Romania
100 C1 Deventer Neth.
96 C2 Deveron *r.* U.K.
103 D2 Devét Skal *hill* Czech Rep.
137 D1 Devil's Lake U.S.A.
128 A2 Devil's Paw *mt.* U.S.A.
99 C4 Devizes U.K.
74 B2 Devli India
110 C2 Devnya Bulg.
128 C2 Devon Can.
126 F1 Devon Island Can.
51 D4 Devonport Austr.
74 B2 Dewas India
137 F3 Dexter U.S.A.
70 A2 Deyang China
59 D3 Deyong, Tanjung *pt* Indon.
79 C2 Deyyer Iran
81 C2 Dezfūl Iran
70 B2 Dezhou China
79 C2 Dhahran Saudi Arabia
75 D2 Dhaka Bangl.
78 B3 Dhamār Yemen
75 C2 Dhamtari India
75 C2 Dhanbad India
74 B2 Dhandhuka India
75 C2 Dhankuta Nepal
74 B2 Dhar India
75 D2 Dharmanagar India
73 B3 Dharmapuri India
75 C2 Dharmjaygarh India
114 B3 Ḑhar Oualâta *hills* Maur.
114 B3 Ḑhar Tîchît *hills* Maur.
73 B3 Dharwad India
Dharwar India *see* Dharwad
74 B2 Dhasa India
75 C2 Dhaulagiri *mt.* Nepal
78 B3 Dhubāb Yemen
74 B2 Dhule India
Dhulia India *see* Dhule
117 C4 Dhuusa Marreeb Somalia
144 A1 Diablo, Picacho del *mt.* Mex.
142 B2 Diablo Plateau U.S.A.
121 C2 Diaca Moz.
51 C2 Diamantina *watercourse* Austr.
155 D1 Diamantina Brazil
151 E4 Diamantina, Chapada *plat.* Brazil
159 F6 Diamantina Deep *sea feature* Indian Ocean
154 B1 Diamantino Brazil
151 D4 Diamantino Brazil
71 B3 Dianbai China
151 E4 Dianópolis Brazil
114 B4 Dianra Côte d'Ivoire
114 C3 Diapaga Burkina
79 C2 Dibā al Ḩiṣn U.A.E.
79 C2 Ḑibab Oman
118 C3 Dibaya Dem. Rep. Congo
122 B2 Dibeng S. Africa
72 D2 Dibrugarh India
136 C1 Dickinson U.S.A.

140 C1 **Dickson** U.S.A.
Dicle *r.* Turkey *see* **Tigris**
105 D3 **Die** France
Diedenhofen France *see* **Thionville**
129 D2 **Diefenbaker, Lake** Can.
Diégo Suarez Madag. *see* **Antsirañana**
114 B3 **Diéma** Mali
101 D2 **Diemel** *r.* Ger.
62 B1 **Điên Biên Phu** Vietnam
62 B2 **Diên Châu** Vietnam
101 D1 **Diepholz** Ger.
104 C2 **Dieppe** France
100 B2 **Diest** Belgium
115 D3 **Diffa** Niger
131 D3 **Digby** Can.
105 D3 **Digne-les-Bains** France
105 C2 **Digoin** France
64 B3 **Digos** Phil.
59 D3 **Digul** *r.* Indon.
105 D2 **Dijon** France
115 D4 **Dik** Chad
117 C3 **Dikhil** Djibouti
111 C3 **Dikili** Turkey
100 A2 **Diksmuide** Belgium
82 G2 **Dikson** Rus. Fed.
115 D3 **Dikwa** Nigeria
117 B4 **Dīla** Eth.
59 C3 **Dili** East Timor
101 D2 **Dillenburg** Ger.
117 A3 **Dilling** Sudan
126 B3 **Dillingham** U.S.A.
134 D1 **Dillon** *MT* U.S.A.
141 E2 **Dillon** *SC* U.S.A.
118 C4 **Dilolo** Dem. Rep. Congo
72 D2 **Dimapur** India
Dimashq Syria *see* **Damascus**
52 B3 **Dimboola** Austr.
110 C2 **Dimitrovgrad** Bulg.
87 D3 **Dimitrovgrad** Rus. Fed.
Dimitrovo Bulg. *see* **Pernik**
64 B2 **Dinagat** *i.* Phil.
75 C2 **Dinajpur** Bangl.
104 B2 **Dinan** France
100 B2 **Dinant** Belgium
111 D3 **Dinar** Turkey
81 D2 **Dīnār, Kūh-e** *mt.* Iran
104 B2 **Dinard** France
Dinbych U.K. *see* **Denbigh**
73 B3 **Dindigul** India
118 B1 **Dindima** Nigeria
123 D1 **Dindiza** Moz.
101 E2 **Dingelstädt** Ger.
97 A2 **Dingle** Rep. of Ireland
97 A2 **Dingle Bay** Rep. of Ireland
71 B3 **Dingnan** China
102 C2 **Dingolfing** Ger.
114 A3 **Dinguiraye** Guinea
96 B2 **Dingwall** U.K.
70 A2 **Dingxi** China
75 C2 **Dinngyê** China
123 C1 **Dinokwe** Botswana
91 D2 **Dinskaya** Rus. Fed.
100 C2 **Dinslaken** Ger.
135 C3 **Dinuba** U.S.A.
114 B3 **Dioïla** Mali
154 B3 **Dionísio Cerqueira** Brazil
114 A3 **Diourbel** Senegal
75 D2 **Diphu** India
64 B3 **Dipolog** Phil.
74 B1 **Dir** Pak.
51 D1 **Direction, Cape** Austr.
117 C4 **Dirē Dawa** Eth.
120 B2 **Dirico** Angola
50 A2 **Dirk Hartog Island** Austr.
53 C1 **Dirranbandi** Austr.
78 B3 **Ḑirs** Saudi Arabia
153 E5 **Disappointment, Cape** S. Georgia
134 B1 **Disappointment, Cape** U.S.A.
50 B2 **Disappointment, Lake** *salt flat* Austr.
52 B3 **Discovery Bay** Austr.
Disko *i.* Greenland *see* **Qeqertarsuaq**
141 E1 **Dismal Swamp** U.S.A.
99 D3 **Diss** U.K.
108 B3 **Dittaino** *r.* *Sicily* Italy
74 B2 **Diu** India
155 D2 **Divinópolis** Brazil
87 D4 **Divnoye** Rus. Fed.
114 B4 **Divo** Côte d'Ivoire
80 B2 **Divriği** Turkey
74 A2 **Diwana** Pak.
138 B2 **Dixon** U.S.A.
128 A2 **Dixon Entrance** *sea chan.* Can./U.S.A.
81 C2 **Diyarbakır** Turkey
74 A2 **Diz** Pak.
115 D2 **Djado** Niger
115 D2 **Djado, Plateau du** Niger
Djakarta Indon. *see* **Jakarta**
118 B3 **Djambala** Congo
115 C2 **Djanet** Alg.
115 D3 **Djédaa** Chad
115 C1 **Djelfa** Alg.
119 C2 **Djéma** C.A.R.
114 B3 **Djenné** Mali
114 B3 **Djibo** Burkina
117 C3 **Djibouti** *country* Africa
117 C3 **Djibouti** Djibouti
Djidjelli Alg. *see* **Jijel**
118 C2 **Djolu** Dem. Rep. Congo
114 C4 **Djougou** Benin
118 B2 **Djoum** Cameroon
115 D3 **Djourab, Erg du** *des.* Chad
92 □C3 **Djúpivogur** Iceland
89 F3 **Dmitriyevka** Rus. Fed.
89 E3 **Dmitriyev-L'govskiy** Rus. Fed.
Dmitriyevsk Ukr. *see* **Makiyivka**
89 E2 **Dmitrov** Rus. Fed.
Dmytriyevs'k Ukr. *see* **Makiyivka**
Dnepr *r.* Rus. Fed. *see* **Dnieper**
89 D3 **Dnieper** *r.* Rus. Fed.
91 C2 **Dnieper** *r.* Ukr.
90 B2 **Dniester** *r.* Ukr.
Dnipro *r.* Ukr. *see* **Dnieper**
91 C2 **Dniprodzerzhyns'k** Ukr.
91 D2 **Dnipropetrovs'k** Ukr.
91 C2 **Dniprorudne** Ukr.
Dnister *r.* Ukr. *see* **Dniester**
90 C2 **Dnistrov'ky Lyman** *l.* Ukr.
88 C2 **Dno** Rus. Fed.
121 C2 **Doa** Moz.
115 D4 **Doba** Chad
88 B2 **Dobele** Latvia
101 F2 **Döbeln** Ger.
59 C3 **Doberai, Jazirah** *pen.* Indon.
Doberai Peninsula Indon. *see* **Doberai, Jazirah**
59 C3 **Dobo** Indon.
109 C2 **Doboj** Bos.-Herz.
103 E1 **Dobre Miasto** Pol.
110 C2 **Dobrich** Bulg.
89 F3 **Dobrinka** Rus. Fed.
89 E3 **Dobroye** Rus. Fed.
89 D3 **Dobrush** Belarus
86 E3 **Dobryanka** Rus. Fed.
155 E1 **Doce** *r.* Brazil
145 B2 **Doctor Arroyo** Mex.
144 B2 **Doctor Belisario Domínguez** Mex.
Doctor Petru Groza Romania *see* **Ştei**
111 C3 **Dodecanese** *is* Greece
Dodekanisos *is* Greece *see* **Dodecanese**
136 C3 **Dodge City** U.S.A.
119 D3 **Dodoma** Tanz.
100 C1 **Doesburg** Neth.
100 C2 **Doetinchem** Neth.
59 C3 **Dofa** Indon.
75 C1 **Dogai Coring** *salt l.* China
128 B2 **Dog Creek** Can.
67 B3 **Dōgo** *i.* Japan
115 C3 **Dogondoutchi** Niger
81 C2 **Doğubeyazıt** Turkey
79 C2 **Doha** Qatar
62 A2 **Doi Saket** Thai.
81 D2 **Dokali** Iran
100 B1 **Dokkum** Neth.
88 C3 **Dokshytsy** Belarus
91 D2 **Dokuchayevs'k** Ukr.
59 D3 **Dolak, Pulau** *i.* Indon.
142 A1 **Dolan Springs** U.S.A.
130 C3 **Dolbeau** Can.
104 B2 **Dol-de-Bretagne** France
105 D2 **Dole** France
91 D2 **Dolgaya, Kosa** *spit* Rus. Fed.
99 B3 **Dolgellau** U.K.
89 E3 **Dolgorukovo** Rus. Fed.
89 E3 **Dolgoye** Rus. Fed.
69 F1 **Dolinsk** Rus. Fed.
103 D2 **Dolný Kubín** Slovakia
108 B1 **Dolomites** *mts* Italy
Dolomiti *mts* Italy *see* **Dolomites**
Dolonnur China *see* **Duolun**
117 C4 **Dolo Odo** Eth.
144 A2 **Dolores** Mex.
126 E2 **Dolphin and Union Strait** Can.
90 A2 **Dolyna** Ukr.
102 C2 **Domažlice** Czech Rep.
93 E3 **Dombås** Norway
103 D2 **Dombóvár** Hungary
Dombrovitsa Ukr. *see* **Dubrovytsya**
Dombrowa Pol. *see* **Dąbrowa Górnicza**
128 B2 **Dome Creek** Can.
147 D3 **Dominica** *country* West Indies
147 C3 **Dominican Republic** *country* West Indies
118 C3 **Domiongo** Dem. Rep. Congo
117 C4 **Domo** Eth.
89 E2 **Domodedovo** Rus. Fed.
111 B3 **Domokos** Greece
61 C2 **Dompu** Indon.
153 A3 **Domuyo, Volcán** *vol.* Arg.
142 B3 **Don** Mex.
89 E3 **Don** *r.* Rus. Fed.
96 C2 **Don** *r.* U.K.
97 D1 **Donaghadee** U.K.
52 B3 **Donald** Austr.
Donau *r.* Austria/Ger. *see* **Danube**
102 C2 **Donauwörth** Ger.
106 B2 **Don Benito** Spain
98 C3 **Doncaster** U.K.
120 A1 **Dondo** Angola
121 C2 **Dondo** Moz.
73 C4 **Dondra Head** *hd* Sri Lanka
97 B1 **Donegal** Rep. of Ireland
97 B1 **Donegal Bay** Rep. of Ireland
91 D2 **Donets'k** Ukr.
91 D2 **Donets'kyy Kryazh** *hills* Rus. Fed./Ukr.
118 B2 **Donga** Nigeria
50 A2 **Dongara** Austr.
71 A3 **Dongchuan** China
71 A4 **Dongfang** China
66 B1 **Dongfanghong** China
61 C2 **Donggala** Indon.
65 A2 **Donggang** China
Donggou China *see* **Donggang**
71 B3 **Dongguan** China
62 B2 **Đông Ha** Vietnam
Dong Hai *sea* N. Pacific Ocean *see* **East China Sea**
62 B2 **Đông Hôi** Vietnam
116 B3 **Dongola** Sudan
118 B2 **Dongou** Congo
Dong Phaya Yen Range *mts* Thai. *see* **San Khao Phang Hoei**
63 B2 **Dong Phraya Yen** *esc.* Thai.
Dongping China *see* **Anhua**
71 B3 **Dongshan** China
Dongsheng China *see* **Ordos**
70 C2 **Dongtai** China
71 B3 **Dongting Hu** *l.* China
Dong Ujimqin Qi China *see* **Uliastai**
71 C3 **Dongyang** China
70 B2 **Dongying** China
143 D3 **Donna** U.S.A.
54 B1 **Donnellys Crossing** N.Z.
100 C3 **Donnersberg** *hill* Ger.
107 C1 **Donostia - San Sebastián** Spain
81 D1 **Donyztau, Sor** *dry lake* Kazakh.
51 C1 **Doomadgee** Austr.
138 B2 **Door Peninsula** U.S.A.
117 C4 **Dooxo Nugaaleed** *val.* Somalia
50 B2 **Dora, Lake** *salt flat* Austr.
99 B4 **Dorchester** U.K.
122 A1 **Dordabis** Namibia
104 B2 **Dordogne** *r.* France
100 B2 **Dordrecht** Neth.
123 C3 **Dordrecht** S. Africa
122 A1 **Doreenville** Namibia
129 D2 **Doré Lake** Can.
101 D1 **Dorfmark** Ger.
114 B3 **Dori** Burkina
122 A3 **Doring** *r.* S. Africa
100 C2 **Dormagen** Ger.
96 B2 **Dornoch** U.K.
96 B2 **Dornoch Firth** *est.* U.K.
114 B3 **Doro** Mali
89 D3 **Dorogobuzh** Rus. Fed.
110 C1 **Dorohoi** Romania
68 C1 **Döröö Nuur** *salt l.* Mongolia
92 G3 **Dorotea** Sweden
50 A2 **Dorre Island** Austr.
53 D2 **Dorrigo** Austr.
118 B2 **Dorsale Camerounaise** *slope* Cameroon/Nigeria
100 C2 **Dorsten** Ger.
100 C2 **Dortmund** Ger.
100 C2 **Dortmund-Ems-Kanal** *canal* Ger.
153 B4 **Dos Bahías, Cabo** *c.* Arg.
101 F1 **Dosse** *r.* Ger.
114 C3 **Dosso** Niger
141 C2 **Dothan** U.S.A.
101 D1 **Dötlingen** Ger.
105 C1 **Douai** France
118 A2 **Douala** Cameroon
104 B2 **Douarnenez** France
105 D2 **Doubs** *r.* France/Switz.
54 A3 **Doubtful Sound** N.Z.
114 B3 **Douentza** Mali
98 A2 **Douglas** Isle of Man
122 B2 **Douglas** S. Africa
128 A2 **Douglas** *AK* U.S.A.
142 B2 **Douglas** *AZ* U.S.A.
141 D2 **Douglas** *GA* U.S.A.
136 B2 **Douglas** *WY* U.S.A.
104 C1 **Doullens** France
154 B1 **Dourada, Serra** *hills* Brazil
154 B2 **Dourados** Brazil
154 B2 **Dourados** *r.* Brazil
154 B2 **Dourados, Serra dos** *hills* Brazil
106 B1 **Douro** *r.* Port.
99 D4 **Dover** U.K.
139 D3 **Dover** U.S.A.
95 D3 **Dover, Strait of** France/U.K.
139 F1 **Dover-Foxcroft** U.S.A.
121 C2 **Dowa** Malawi
81 D3 **Dowlatābād** Iran
79 C2 **Dowlatābād** Iran
97 D1 **Downpatrick** U.K.
81 C2 **Dow Rūd** Iran
77 C3 **Dowshī** Afgh.
67 B3 **Dōzen** *is* Japan
130 C3 **Dozois, Réservoir** *resr* Can.
154 B2 **Dracena** Brazil
100 C1 **Drachten** Neth.
110 B2 **Drăgănești-Olt** Romania
110 B2 **Drăgășani** Romania
105 D3 **Draguignan** France
88 C3 **Drahichyn** Belarus
53 D1 **Drake** Austr.
123 C2 **Drakensberg** *mts* Lesotho/S. Africa
123 C2 **Drakensberg** *mts* S. Africa
149 C8 **Drake Passage** S. Atlantic Ocean
111 B2 **Drama** Greece
93 F4 **Drammen** Norway
109 C1 **Drava** *r.* Europe
128 C2 **Drayton Valley** Can.
101 D2 **Dreieich** Ger.
111 B3 **Drepano, Akra** *pt* Greece
102 C1 **Dresden** Ger.
104 C2 **Dreux** France
100 B1 **Driemond** Neth.
98 C2 **Driffield** U.K.
137 D1 **Drift Prairie** *reg.* U.S.A.
109 C2 **Drina** *r.* Bos.-Herz./Serb. and Mont.
140 B2 **Driskill Mountain** *hill* U.S.A.
Drissa Belarus *see* **Verkhnyadzvinsk**
109 C2 **Drniš** Croatia
110 B2 **Drobeta-Turnu Severin** Romania
90 B2 **Drochia** Moldova
101 D1 **Drochtersen** Ger.
97 C2 **Drogheda** Rep. of Ireland
90 A2 **Drohobych** Ukr.
99 B3 **Droitwich Spa** U.K.
Drokiya Moldova *see* **Drochia**
97 B1 **Dromahair** Rep. of Ireland
97 C1 **Dromore** U.K.
100 B1 **Dronten** Neth.
74 B1 **Drosh** Pak.
53 C3 **Drouin** Austr.
128 C2 **Drumheller** Can.
138 C1 **Drummond Island** U.S.A.
131 C3 **Drummondville** Can.
96 B3 **Drummore** U.K.
96 B2 **Drumnadrochit** U.K.
Druskieniki Lith. *see* **Druskininkai**

88 B3 **Druskininkai** Lith.
88 C2 **Druya** Belarus
91 D2 **Druzhkivka** Ukr.
88 D2 **Druzhnaya Gorka** Rus. Fed.
89 D3 **Drybin** Belarus
130 A3 **Dryden** Can.
50 B1 **Drysdale** *r.* Austr.
147 C3 **Duarte, Pico** *mt.* Dom. Rep.
78 A2 **Ḍubā** Saudi Arabia
79 C2 **Dubai** U.A.E.
90 B2 **Dubăsari** Moldova
129 D1 **Dubawnt Lake** Can.
Dubayy U.A.E. *see* **Dubai**
78 A2 **Dubbagh, Jabal ad** *mt.* Saudi Arabia
53 C2 **Dubbo** Austr.
Dubesar' Moldova *see* Dubăsari
97 C2 **Dublin** Rep. of Ireland
141 D2 **Dublin** U.S.A.
89 E2 **Dubna** Rus. Fed.
90 B1 **Dubno** Ukr.
139 D2 **Du Bois** U.S.A.
Dubossary Moldova *see* Dubăsari
114 A4 **Dubréka** Guinea
109 C2 **Dubrovnik** Croatia
90 B1 **Dubrovytsya** Ukr.
89 D3 **Dubrowna** Belarus
137 E2 **Dubuque** U.S.A.
135 D2 **Duchesne** U.S.A.
129 D2 **Duck Bay** Can.
63 B2 **Đưc Trong** Vietnam
101 E2 **Duderstadt** Ger.
82 G2 **Dudinka** Rus. Fed.
99 B3 **Dudley** U.K.
106 B1 **Duero** *r.* Spain
48 H4 **Duff Islands** Solomon Is
131 C2 **Duffreboy, Lac** *l.* Can.
96 C2 **Dufftown** U.K.
109 C2 **Dugi Otok** *i.* Croatia
109 C2 **Dugi Rat** Croatia
100 C2 **Duisburg** Ger.
123 D1 **Duiwelskloof** S. Africa
123 C3 **Dukathole** S. Africa
117 B4 **Duk Fadiat** Sudan
79 C2 **Dukhān** Qatar
89 D2 **Dukhovshchina** Rus. Fed.
Dukou China *see* Panzhihua
88 C2 **Dūkštas** Lith.
68 C2 **Dulan** China
152 B3 **Dulce** *r.* Arg.
142 B1 **Dulce** U.S.A.
97 C2 **Duleek** Rep. of Ireland
100 C2 **Dülmen** Ger.
110 C2 **Dulovo** Bulg.
137 E1 **Duluth** U.S.A.
64 B3 **Dumaguete** Phil.
60 B1 **Dumai** Indon.
64 B2 **Dumaran** *i.* Phil.
140 B2 **Dumas** *AR* U.S.A.
143 C1 **Dumas** *TX* U.S.A.
96 B3 **Dumbarton** U.K.
103 D2 **Ďumbier** *mt.* Slovakia
96 C3 **Dumfries** U.K.
89 E3 **Duminichi** Rus. Fed.
75 C2 **Dumka** India
55 L3 **Dumont d'Urville Sea** Antarctica
116 B1 **Dumyāṭ** Egypt
Duna *r.* Hungary *see* Danube
Dünaburg Latvia *see* Daugavpils
103 D2 **Dunakeszi** Hungary
97 C2 **Dunany Point** Rep. of Ireland
Dunărea *r.* Romania *see* Danube
Dunării, Delta Romania *see* **Danube Delta**
103 D2 **Dunaújváros** Hungary
Dunav *r.* Bulg./Croatia/Serb. and Mont. *see* Danube
90 B2 **Dunayivtsi** Ukr.
96 C2 **Dunbar** U.K.
96 C1 **Dunbeath** U.K.
128 B3 **Duncan** Can.
143 D2 **Duncan** U.S.A.
96 C1 **Duncansby Head** *hd* U.K.
88 B2 **Dundaga** Latvia
97 C1 **Dundalk** Rep. of Ireland
139 D3 **Dundalk** U.S.A.
97 C2 **Dundalk Bay** Rep. of Ireland
127 H1 **Dundas** Greenland
Dún Dealgan Rep. of Ireland *see* **Dundalk**
123 D2 **Dundee** S. Africa
96 C2 **Dundee** U.K.
97 D1 **Dundrum Bay** U.K.
54 B3 **Dunedin** N.Z.
53 C2 **Dunedoo** Austr.
96 C2 **Dunfermline** U.K.
97 C1 **Dungannon** U.K.
74 B2 **Dungarpur** India
97 C2 **Dungarvan** Rep. of Ireland
99 D4 **Dungeness** *hd* U.K.
97 C1 **Dungiven** U.K.
53 D2 **Dungog** Austr.
119 C2 **Dungu** Dem. Rep. Congo
60 B1 **Dungun** Malaysia
116 B2 **Dungunab** Sudan
69 E2 **Dunhua** China
68 C2 **Dunhuang** China
96 C2 **Dunkeld** U.K.
Dunkerque France *see* Dunkirk
104 C1 **Dunkirk** France
139 D2 **Dunkirk** U.S.A.
97 C2 **Dún Laoghaire** Rep. of Ireland
97 B3 **Dunmanway** Rep. of Ireland
97 D1 **Dunmurry** U.K.
96 C1 **Dunnet Head** *hd* U.K.
96 C3 **Duns** U.K.
134 B2 **Dunsmuir** U.S.A.
99 C4 **Dunstable** U.K.
100 B3 **Dun-sur-Meuse** France
96 A2 **Dunvegan** U.K.
70 B1 **Duolun** China
Duperré Alg. *see* **Aïn Defla**
110 B2 **Dupnitsa** Bulg.
136 C1 **Dupree** U.S.A.
Duque de Bragança Angola *see* **Calandula**
138 B3 **Du Quoin** U.S.A.
50 B1 **Durack** *r.* Austr.
105 C3 **Durance** *r.* France
144 B2 **Durango** Mex.
106 C1 **Durango** Spain
136 B3 **Durango** U.S.A.
143 D2 **Durant** U.S.A.
153 C3 **Durazno** Uru.
Durazzo Albania *see* Durrës
123 D2 **Durban** S. Africa
105 C3 **Durban-Corbières** France
122 A3 **Durbanville** S. Africa
100 B2 **Durbuy** Belgium
100 C2 **Düren** Ger.
75 C2 **Durg** India
98 C2 **Durham** U.K.
141 E1 **Durham** U.S.A.
60 B1 **Duri** Indon.
109 C2 **Durmitor** *mt.* Serb. and Mont.
96 B1 **Durness** U.K.
109 C2 **Durrës** Albania
97 A3 **Dursey Island** Rep. of Ireland
111 C3 **Dursunbey** Turkey
117 C4 **Durukhsi** Somalia
59 D3 **D'Urville, Tanjung** *pt* Indon.
54 B2 **D'Urville Island** N.Z.
71 A3 **Dushan** China
77 C3 **Dushanbe** Tajik.
100 C2 **Düsseldorf** Ger.
Dutch East Indies *country* Asia *see* **Indonesia**
Dutch Guiana *country* S. America *see* **Suriname**
Dutch West Indies *terr.* West Indies *see* **Netherlands Antilles**
Duvno Bos.-Herz. *see* Tomislavgrad
71 A3 **Duyun** China
80 B1 **Düzce** Turkey
91 D2 **Dvorichna** Ukr.
74 A2 **Dwarka** India
123 C1 **Dwarsberg** S. Africa
134 C1 **Dworshak Reservoir** U.S.A.
89 D3 **Dyat'kovo** Rus. Fed.
96 C2 **Dyce** U.K.
127 H2 **Dyer, Cape** Can.
140 C1 **Dyersburg** U.S.A.
99 B3 **Dyfi** *r.* U.K.
Dyfrdwy *r.* U.K. *see* **Dee**
103 D2 **Dyje** *r.* Austria/Czech Rep.
103 D1 **Dylewska Góra** *hill* Pol.
91 D2 **Dymytrov** Ukr.
123 C3 **Dyoki** S. Africa
51 D2 **Dysart** Austr.
122 B3 **Dysselsdorp** S. Africa
87 E3 **Dyurtyuli** Rus. Fed.
69 D2 **Dzamïn Üüd** Mongolia
121 D2 **Dzaoudzi** Mayotte
91 D2 **Dzerzhyns'k** Ukr.
Dzhaltyr Kazakh. *see* Zhaltyr
Dzhambul Kazakh. *see* Taraz
81 D1 **Dzhanga** Turkm.
76 B2 **Dzhangala** Kazakh.
91 C2 **Dzhankoy** Ukr.
Dzharkent Kazakh. *see* Zharkent
81 D2 **Dzhebel** Turkm.
Dzhetygara Kazakh. *see* Zhitikara
Dzhezkazgan Kazakh. *see* Zhezkazgan
Dzhizak Uzbek. *see* **Jizzax**
91 D3 **Dzhubga** Rus. Fed.
83 K3 **Dzhugdzhur, Khrebet** *mts* Rus. Fed.
77 D2 **Dzhungarskiy Alatau, Khrebet** *mts* China/Kazakh.
76 C2 **Dzhusaly** Kazakh.
103 E1 **Działdowo** Pol.
145 D2 **Dzilam de Bravo** Mex.
69 D1 **Dzuunmod** Mongolia
88 C3 **Dzyarzhynsk** Belarus
88 C3 **Dzyatlavichy** Belarus

E

131 E2 **Eagle** *r.* Can.
134 C1 **Eagle Cap** *mt.* U.S.A.
130 A3 **Eagle Lake** Can.
134 B2 **Eagle Lake** U.S.A.
143 C3 **Eagle Pass** U.S.A.
126 C2 **Eagle Plain** Can.
Eap *i.* Micronesia *see* **Yap**
130 A2 **Ear Falls** Can.
135 C3 **Earlimart** U.S.A.
96 C2 **Earn** *r.* U.K.
55 J2 **East Antarctica** *reg.* Antarctica
East Bengal *country* Asia *see* **Bangladesh**
99 D4 **Eastbourne** U.K.
59 D2 **East Caroline Basin** *sea feature* N. Pacific Ocean
69 E2 **East China Sea** N. Pacific Ocean
54 B1 **East Coast Bays** N.Z.
East Dereham U.K. *see* Dereham
129 D3 **Eastend** Can.
157 G7 **Easter Island** S. Pacific Ocean
123 C3 **Eastern Cape** *prov.* S. Africa
116 B2 **Eastern Desert** Egypt
73 B3 **Eastern Ghats** *mts* India
Eastern Samoa *terr.* S. Pacific Ocean *see* **American Samoa**
Eastern Sayan Mountains Rus. Fed. *see* **Vostochnyy Sayan**
Eastern Transvaal *prov.* S. Africa *see* **Mpumalanga**
129 E2 **Easterville** Can.
153 C5 **East Falkland** *i.* Falkland Is
100 C1 **East Frisian Islands** Ger.
135 C3 **Eastgate** U.S.A.
137 D1 **East Grand Forks** U.S.A.
96 B3 **East Kilbride** U.K.
138 C2 **East Lansing** U.S.A.
99 C4 **Eastleigh** U.K.
96 C3 **East Linton** U.K.
138 C2 **East Liverpool** U.S.A.
123 C3 **East London** S. Africa
130 C2 **Eastmain** Can.
130 C2 **Eastmain** *r.* Can.
141 D2 **Eastman** U.S.A.
157 G8 **East Pacific Rise** *sea feature* N. Pacific Ocean
East Pakistan *country* Asia *see* **Bangladesh**
East Sea N. Pacific Ocean *see* **Japan, Sea of**
83 K2 **East Siberian Sea** Rus. Fed.
138 A3 **East St Louis** U.S.A.
59 C3 **East Timor** *country* Asia
53 C2 **East Toorale** Austr.
139 D2 **East York** Can.
138 A2 **Eau Claire** U.S.A.
130 C2 **Eau Claire, Lac à l'** *l.* Can.
59 D2 **Eauripik** *atoll* Micronesia
145 C2 **Ebano** Mex.
99 B4 **Ebbw Vale** U.K.
118 B2 **Ebebiyin** Equat. Guinea
102 C1 **Eberswalde-Finow** Ger.
66 D2 **Ebetsu** Japan
77 E2 **Ebinur Hu** *salt l.* China
118 C2 **Ebola** *r.* Dem. Rep. Congo
109 C2 **Eboli** Italy
118 B2 **Ebolowa** Cameroon
107 D1 **Ebro** *r.* Spain
114 C1 **Ech Chélif** Alg.
Echeng China *see* **Ezhou**
144 A2 **Echeverria, Pico** *mt.* Mex.
129 E2 **Echoing** *r.* Can.
100 C3 **Echternach** Lux.
52 B3 **Echuca** Austr.
106 B2 **Écija** Spain
102 B1 **Eckernförde** Ger.
127 G2 **Eclipse Sound** *sea chan.* Can.
150 B3 **Ecuador** *country* S. America
116 C3 **Ed** Eritrea
96 C1 **Eday** *i.* U.K.
117 A3 **Ed Da'ein** Sudan
117 B3 **Ed Damazin** Sudan
116 B3 **Ed Damer** Sudan
116 B3 **Ed Debba** Sudan
116 B3 **Ed Dueim** Sudan
51 D4 **Eddystone Point** Austr.
100 B1 **Ede** Neth.
118 B2 **Edéa** Cameroon
154 C1 **Edéia** Brazil
53 C3 **Eden** Austr.
98 B2 **Eden** *r.* U.K.
143 D2 **Eden** U.S.A.
123 C2 **Edenburg** S. Africa
97 C2 **Edenderry** Rep. of Ireland
52 B3 **Edenhope** Austr.
141 E1 **Edenton** U.S.A.
111 B2 **Edessa** Greece
139 E2 **Edgartown** U.S.A.
Edge Island Svalbard *see* Edgeøya
82 C1 **Edgeøya** *i.* Svalbard
141 D3 **Edgewater** U.S.A.
138 C2 **Edinboro** U.S.A.
143 D3 **Edinburg** U.S.A.
96 C3 **Edinburgh** U.K.
90 B2 **Edineț** Moldova
111 C2 **Edirne** Turkey
Edith Ronne Land *ice feature* Antarctica *see* Ronne Ice Shelf
128 C2 **Edmonton** Can.
131 D3 **Edmundston** Can.
111 C3 **Edremit** Turkey
111 C3 **Edremit Körfezi** *b.* Turkey
128 C2 **Edson** Can.
119 C3 **Edward, Lake** Dem. Rep. Congo/Uganda
Edwardesabad Pak. *see* Bannu
143 D2 **Edwards Plateau** U.S.A.
55 O2 **Edward VII Peninsula** Antarctica
96 C2 **Edzell** U.K.
100 A2 **Eeklo** Belgium
135 B2 **Eel** *r.* U.S.A.
100 C1 **Eemskanaal** *canal* Neth.
100 C1 **Eenrum** Neth.
138 B3 **Effingham** U.S.A.
135 C3 **Egan Range** *mts* U.S.A.
103 E2 **Eger** Hungary
93 E4 **Egersund** Norway
100 B2 **Eghezée** Belgium
92 C2 **Egilsstaðir** Iceland
80 B2 **Eğirdir** Turkey
80 B2 **Eğirdir Gölü** *l.* Turkey
104 C2 **Égletons** France
Egmont, Mount *vol.* N.Z. *see* **Taranaki, Mount**
83 M2 **Egvekinot** Rus. Fed.
116 A2 **Egypt** *country* Africa
70 A2 **Ehen Hudag** China
106 C1 **Eibar** Spain
100 C1 **Eibergen** Neth.
100 C2 **Eifel** *hills* Ger.
96 A2 **Eigg** *i.* U.K.
73 B4 **Eight Degree Channel** India/Maldives
50 B1 **Eighty Mile Beach** Austr.
80 B3 **Eilat** Israel
101 F2 **Eilenburg** Ger.
101 D2 **Einbeck** Ger.
100 B2 **Eindhoven** Neth.

160 N4 **Eirik Ridge** *sea feature* N. Atlantic Ocean
150 C3 **Eirunepé** Brazil
120 B2 **Eiseb** *watercourse* Namibia
101 E2 **Eisenach** Ger.
101 E2 **Eisenberg** Ger.
102 C1 **Eisenhüttenstadt** Ger.
103 D2 **Eisenstadt** Austria
101 E2 **Eisleben Lutherstadt** Ger.
Eivissa Spain *see* Ibiza
Eivissa *i.* Spain *see* Ibiza
107 C1 **Ejea de los Caballeros** Spain
121 □D3 **Ejeda** Madag.
Ejin Qi China *see* Dalain Hob
93 H4 **Ekenäs** Fin.
77 D1 **Ekibastuz** Kazakh.
93 F4 **Eksjö** Sweden
122 A2 **Eksteenfontein** S. Africa
130 B2 **Ekwan** *r.* Can.
62 A2 **Ela** Myanmar
El Aaiún Western Sahara *see* Laâyoune
123 C2 **Elandsdoorn** S. Africa
El Araïche Morocco *see* Larache
El Asnam Alg. *see* Ech Chélif
111 B3 **Elassona** Greece
Elat Israel *see* Eilat
80 B2 **Elazığ** Turkey
108 B2 **Elba, Isola d'** *i.* Italy
150 B2 **El Banco** Col.
109 D2 **Elbasan** Albania
150 C2 **El Baúl** Venez.
114 C1 **El Bayadh** Alg.
101 D1 **Elbe** *r.* Ger.
136 B3 **Elbert, Mount** U.S.A.
141 D2 **Elberton** U.S.A.
104 C2 **Elbeuf** France
80 B2 **Elbistan** Turkey
103 D1 **Elbląg** Pol.
153 A4 **El Bolsón** Arg.
87 D4 **El'brus** *mt.* Rus. Fed.
81 C2 **Elburz Mountains** *mts* Iran
150 C2 **El Callao** Venez.
143 D3 **El Campo** U.S.A.
135 C4 **El Centro** U.S.A.
152 B1 **El Cerro** Bol.
107 C2 **Elche-Elx** Spain
145 C3 **El Chichónal** *vol.* Mex.
107 C2 **Elda** Spain
119 D2 **Eldama Ravine** Kenya
137 E3 **Eldon** U.S.A.
153 B3 **Eldorado** Arg.
154 C2 **Eldorado** Brazil
144 B2 **El Dorado** Mex.
140 B2 **El Dorado** AR U.S.A.
137 D3 **El Dorado** KS U.S.A.
134 D1 **Electric Peak** U.S.A.
114 B2 **El Eglab** *plat.* Alg.
106 C2 **El Ejido** Spain
89 E2 **Elektrostal'** Rus. Fed.
150 B3 **El Encanto** Col.
146 C2 **Eleuthera** *i.* Bahamas
116 A3 **El Fasher** Sudan
144 B2 **El Fuerte** Mex.
117 A3 **El Fula** Sudan
116 A3 **El Geneina** Sudan
116 B3 **El Geteina** Sudan
96 C2 **Elgin** U.K.
138 B2 **Elgin** U.S.A.
83 K2 **El'ginskiy** Rus. Fed.
El Gîza Egypt *see* Giza
115 C1 **El Goléa** Alg.
144 A1 **El Golfo de Santa Clara** Mex.
119 D2 **Elgon, Mount** Uganda
108 A3 **El Hadjar** Alg.
114 A2 **El Hammâmi** *reg.* Maur.
114 B2 **El Hank** *esc.* Mali/Maur.
114 A2 **El Hierro** *i.* Canary Is
145 C2 **El Higo** Mex.
114 C2 **El Homr** Alg.
Elichpur India *see* Achalpur
126 B2 **Elim** U.S.A.
Élisabethville Dem. Rep. Congo *see* Lubumbashi
El Iskandarîya Egypt *see* Alexandria
87 D4 **Elista** Rus. Fed.
139 E2 **Elizabeth** U.S.A.
141 E1 **Elizabeth City** U.S.A.
138 B3 **Elizabethton** U.S.A.
114 B1 **El Jadida** Morocco
103 E1 **Ełk** Pol.

108 A3 **El Kala** Alg.
88 C2 **Elkas kalns** *hill* Latvia
143 D1 **Elk City** U.S.A.
114 B1 **El Kelaâ des Srarhna** Morocco
128 C2 **Elkford** Can.
138 B2 **Elkhart** U.S.A.
El Khartûm Sudan *see* Khartoum
110 C2 **Elkhovo** Bulg.
139 D3 **Elkins** U.S.A.
128 C3 **Elko** Can.
134 C2 **Elko** U.S.A.
129 C2 **Elk Point** Can.
137 E1 **Elk River** U.S.A.
126 F1 **Elief Ringnes Island** Can.
137 D1 **Ellendale** U.S.A.
134 B1 **Ellensburg** U.S.A.
54 B2 **Ellesmere, Lake** N.Z.
127 G1 **Ellesmere Island** Can.
98 B3 **Ellesmere Port** U.K.
126 F2 **Ellice** *r.* Can.
Ellice Islands *country* S. Pacific Ocean *see* Tuvalu
123 C3 **Elliotdale** S. Africa
138 C1 **Elliot Lake** Can.
96 C2 **Ellon** U.K.
139 F2 **Ellsworth** U.S.A.
55 R2 **Ellsworth Mountains** Antarctica
111 C3 **Elmalı** Turkey
115 C1 **El Meghaïer** Alg.
139 D2 **Elmira** U.S.A.
107 C2 **El Moral** Spain
101 D1 **Elmshorn** Ger.
117 A3 **El Muglad** Sudan
150 B2 **El Nevado, Cerro** *mt.* Col.
64 A2 **El Nido** Phil.
116 B3 **El Obeid** Sudan
144 B2 **El Oro** Mex.
115 C1 **El Oued** Alg.
142 A2 **Eloy** U.S.A.
El Paso U.S.A. *see* Derby
142 B2 **El Paso** U.S.A.
145 D3 **El Pinalón, Cerro** *mt.* Guat.
144 B1 **El Porvenir** Mex.
107 D1 **El Prat de Llobregat** Spain
146 B3 **El Progreso** Hond.
106 B2 **El Puerto de Santa María** Spain
El Qâhira Egypt *see* Cairo
El Quds Israel/West Bank *see* Jerusalem
143 D1 **El Reno** U.S.A.
128 A1 **Elsa** Can.
145 B2 **El Salado** Mex.
144 B2 **El Salto** Mex.
146 B3 **El Salvador** *country* Central America
152 B2 **El Salvador** Chile
145 B2 **El Salvador** Mex.
142 B3 **El Sauz** Mex.
144 A1 **El Socorro** Mex.
142 B3 **El Sueco** Mex.
El Suweis Egypt *see* Suez
108 A3 **El Tarf** Alg.
106 B1 **El Teleno** *mt.* Spain
145 C2 **El Temascal** Mex.
150 C2 **El Tigre** Venez.
147 D4 **El Tocuyo** Venez.
El Uqşur Egypt *see* Luxor
73 C3 **Eluru** India
88 C2 **Elva** Estonia
106 B2 **Elvas** Port.
93 F3 **Elverum** Norway
119 E2 **El Wak** Kenya
99 D3 **Ely** U.K.
137 E1 **Ely** MN U.S.A.
135 D3 **Ely** NV U.S.A.
81 D2 **Emämrüd** Iran
93 G4 **Emån** *r.* Sweden
76 B2 **Emba** Kazakh.
76 B2 **Emba** *r.* Kazakh.
123 C2 **Embalenhle** S. Africa
118 B2 **Embondo** Dem. Rep. Congo
154 C1 **Emborcação, Represa de** *resr* Brazil
119 D3 **Embu** Kenya
100 C1 **Emden** Ger.
51 D2 **Emerald** Austr.
129 E3 **Emerson** Can.
111 C3 **Emet** Turkey
123 C2 **eMgwenya** S. Africa
123 C2 **eMijindini** S. Africa
115 D3 **Emi Koussi** *mt.* Chad
145 C3 **Emiliano Zapata** Mex.
110 C2 **Emine, Nos** *pt* Bulg.

80 B2 **Emirdağ** Turkey
88 B2 **Emmaste** Estonia
100 B1 **Emmeloord** Neth.
100 C2 **Emmelshausen** Ger.
100 C1 **Emmen** Neth.
143 C2 **Emory Peak** U.S.A.
144 A2 **Empalme** Mex.
123 D2 **Empangeni** S. Africa
156 D2 **Emperor Trough** *sea feature* N. Pacific Ocean
108 B2 **Empoli** Italy
111 C3 **Emponas** Greece
137 D3 **Emporia** KS U.S.A.
139 D3 **Emporia** VA U.S.A.
Empty Quarter *des.* Saudi Arabia *see* Rub' al Khālī
100 C1 **Ems** *r.* Ger.
100 C1 **Emsdetten** Ger.
88 C2 **Emumägi** *hill* Estonia
123 C2 **Emzinoni** S. Africa
59 D3 **Enarotali** Indon.
144 B2 **Encarnación** Mex.
152 C2 **Encarnación** Para.
155 D1 **Encruzilhada** Brazil
61 D2 **Ende** Indon.
55 G2 **Enderby Land** *reg.* Antarctica
126 B2 **Endicott Mountains** U.S.A.
50 A2 **Eneabba** Austr.
91 C2 **Enerhodar** Ukr.
111 C2 **Enez** Turkey
97 C2 **Enfield** Rep. of Ireland
87 D3 **Engel's** Rus. Fed.
60 B2 **Enggano** *i.* Indon.
99 C3 **England** *admin. div.* U.K.
English Bazar India *see* Ingraj Bazar
130 C3 **Englehart** Can.
141 D3 **Englewood** U.S.A.
130 A2 **English** *r.* Can.
95 C4 **English Channel** France/U.K.
143 D1 **Enid** U.S.A.
Enkeldoorn Zimbabwe *see* Chivhu
100 B1 **Enkhuizen** Neth.
93 G4 **Enköping** Sweden
108 B3 **Enna** Sicily Italy
128 C1 **Ennadai Lake** Can.
116 A3 **En Nahud** Sudan
115 E3 **Ennedi, Massif** *mts* Chad
53 C1 **Enngonia** Austr.
97 B2 **Ennis** Rep. of Ireland
143 D2 **Ennis** U.S.A.
97 C2 **Enniscorthy** Rep. of Ireland
97 C1 **Enniskerry** Rep. of Ireland
97 C1 **Enniskillen** U.K.
97 B2 **Ennistymon** Rep. of Ireland
102 C2 **Enns** *r.* Austria
102 C2 **Enns** Austria
92 J3 **Eno** Fin.
92 H2 **Enontekiö** Fin.
53 C3 **Ensay** Austr.
100 C1 **Enschede** Neth.
144 A1 **Ensenada** Mex.
70 A2 **Enshi** China
119 D2 **Entebbe** Uganda
126 C2 **Enterprise** Can.
140 C2 **Enterprise** AL U.S.A.
134 C1 **Enterprise** OR U.S.A.
152 B2 **Entre Ríos** Bol.
106 B2 **Entroncamento** Port.
115 C4 **Enugu** Nigeria
150 B3 **Envira** Brazil
118 B2 **Epéna** Congo
105 C2 **Épernay** France
135 D3 **Ephraim** U.S.A.
134 C1 **Ephrata** U.S.A.
105 D2 **Épinal** France
99 D3 **Epping** U.K.
99 C4 **Epsom** U.K.
118 A2 **Equatorial Guinea** *country* Africa
104 B2 **Équerdreville-Hainneville** France
101 D2 **Erbach** Ger.
101 F3 **Erbendorf** Ger.
100 C3 **Erbeskopf** *hill* Ger.
81 C2 **Erciş** Turkey
80 B2 **Erciyes Dağı** *mt.* Turkey
103 D2 **Érd** Hungary
Erdaobaihe China *see* Baihe
65 B1 **Erdao Jiang** *r.* China
111 C2 **Erdek** Turkey
80 B2 **Erdemli** Turkey

154 B2 **Eré, Campos** *hills* Brazil
55 M2 **Erebus, Mount** *vol.* Antarctica
152 C2 **Erechim** Brazil
69 D1 **Ereentsav** Mongolia
80 B2 **Ereğli** Turkey
80 B1 **Ereğli** Turkey
69 D2 **Erenhot** China
Erevan Armenia *see* Yerevan
101 E2 **Erfurt** Ger.
80 B2 **Ergani** Turkey
114 B2 **'Erg Chech** *des.* Alg./Mali
111 C2 **Ergene** *r.* Turkey
78 A3 **Erheib** Sudan
96 B2 **Ericht, Loch** *l.* U.K.
138 C2 **Erie** U.S.A.
138 C2 **Erie, Lake** Can./U.S.A.
66 D2 **Erimo-misaki** *c.* Japan
116 B3 **Eritrea** *country* Africa
101 E3 **Erlangen** Ger.
50 C2 **Erldunda** Austr.
123 C2 **Ermelo** S. Africa
80 B2 **Ermenek** Turkey
111 B3 **Ermoupoli** Greece
73 B4 **Ernakulam** India
97 B1 **Erne** *r.* Rep. of Ireland/U.K.
73 B3 **Erode** India
100 B2 **Erp** Neth.
114 B1 **Er Rachidia** Morocco
116 B3 **Er Rahad** Sudan
97 B1 **Errigal** *hill* Rep. of Ireland
97 A1 **Erris Head** *hd* Rep. of Ireland
48 H5 **Erromango** *i.* Vanuatu
109 D2 **Ersekë** Albania
89 F3 **Ertil'** Rus. Fed.
101 D2 **Erwitte** Ger.
101 F2 **Erzgebirge** *mts* Czech Rep./Ger.
80 B2 **Erzincan** Turkey
81 C2 **Erzurum** Turkey
66 D2 **Esashi** Japan
93 E4 **Esbjerg** Denmark
135 D3 **Escalante** U.S.A.
135 D3 **Escalante Desert** U.S.A.
144 B2 **Escalón** Mex.
138 B1 **Escanaba** U.S.A.
145 C3 **Escárcega** Mex.
107 C1 **Escatrón** Spain
100 A2 **Escaut** *r.* Belgium
101 E1 **Eschede** Ger.
100 B3 **Esch-sur-Alzette** Lux.
101 E2 **Eschwege** Ger.
100 C2 **Eschweiler** Ger.
135 C4 **Escondido** U.S.A.
144 B2 **Escuinapa** Mex.
111 C3 **Eşen** Turkey
81 D2 **Eşfahān** Iran
123 D2 **Eshowe** S. Africa
123 D2 **Esikhawini** S. Africa
98 B2 **Esk** *r.* U.K.
131 D2 **Esker** Can.
92 □C2 **Eskifjörður** Iceland
93 G4 **Eskilstuna** Sweden
Eskimo Point Can. *see* Arviat
111 D3 **Eskişehir** Turkey
81 C2 **Eslāmābād-e Gharb** Iran
111 C3 **Esler Dağı** *mt.* Turkey
111 C3 **Eşme** Turkey
146 C2 **Esmeralda** Cuba
150 B2 **Esmeraldas** Ecuador
79 D2 **Espakeh** Iran
105 C3 **Espalion** France
130 B3 **Espanola** Can.
142 B1 **Espanola** U.S.A.
50 B3 **Esperance** Austr.
153 A5 **Esperanza** Arg.
144 B2 **Esperanza** Mex.
106 B2 **Espichel, Cabo** *c.* Port.
154 B3 **Espigão, Serra do** *mts* Brazil
143 C3 **Espinazo** Mex.
155 D1 **Espinhaço, Serra do** *mts* Brazil
151 E4 **Espinosa** Brazil
Espírito Santo Brazil *see* Vila Velha
48 H5 **Espíritu Santo** *i.* Vanuatu
144 A2 **Espíritu Santo, Isla** *i.* Mex.
93 H3 **Espoo** Fin.
153 A4 **Esquel** Arg.
114 B1 **Essaouira** Morocco
114 A2 **Es Semara** Western Sahara
100 C2 **Essen** Ger.
150 D2 **Essequibo** *r.* Guyana
139 E2 **Essex Junction** U.S.A.
83 L3 **Esso** Rus. Fed.

106 B1 **Estaca de Bares, Punta da** *pt* Spain
153 B5 **Estados, Isla de los** *i.* Arg.
81 D3 **Eşţahbān** Iran
151 F4 **Estância** Brazil
123 C2 **Estcourt** S. Africa
107 C1 **Estella** Spain
106 D2 **Estepona** Spain
106 C1 **Esteras de Medinaceli** Spain
129 D2 **Esterhazy** Can.
152 B2 **Esteros** Para.
136 B2 **Estes Park** U.S.A.
129 D3 **Estevan** Can.
137 E2 **Estherville** U.S.A.
129 D2 **Eston** Can.
88 C2 **Estonia** *country* Europe
Estonskaya S.S.R. *admin. reg.* Europe *see* Estonia
106 B1 **Estrela, Serra da** *mts* Port.
106 B2 **Estremoz** Port.
52 A1 **Etadunna** Austr.
104 C2 **Étampes** France
104 C1 **Étaples** France
75 B2 **Etawah** India
123 D2 **eThandakukhanya** S. Africa
122 B2 **E'Thembini** S. Africa
117 B4 **Ethiopia** *country* Africa
Etna, Monte *vol.* Italy *see* Etna, Mount
109 C3 **Etna, Mount** *vol. Sicily* Italy
93 E4 **Etne** Norway
128 A2 **Etolin Island** U.S.A.
120 A2 **Etosha Pan** *salt pan* Namibia
110 B2 **Etropole** Bulg.
100 C3 **Ettelbruck** Lux.
100 B2 **Etten-Leur** Neth.
107 C1 **Etxarri-Aranatz** Spain
99 D4 **Eu** France
53 C2 **Euabalong** Austr.
Euboea *i.* Greece *see* Evvoia
50 B3 **Eucla** Austr.
138 C2 **Euclid** U.S.A.
141 C2 **Eufaula** U.S.A.
143 D1 **Eufaula Lake** *resr* U.S.A.
134 B2 **Eugene** U.S.A.
144 A2 **Eugenia, Punta** *pt* Mex.
53 C1 **Eulo** Austr.
53 C2 **Eumungerie** Austr.
143 C2 **Eunice** U.S.A.
81 C2 **Euphrates** *r.* Asia
134 B2 **Eureka** *CA* U.S.A.
134 C1 **Eureka** *MT* U.S.A.
135 C3 **Eureka** *NV* U.S.A.
52 B2 **Euriowie** Austr.
53 C3 **Euroa** Austr.
106 B2 **Europa Point** Gibraltar
140 C2 **Eutaw** U.S.A.
128 B2 **Eutsuk Lake** Can.
123 C2 **Evander** S. Africa
130 C2 **Evans, Lac** *l.* Can.
53 D1 **Evans Head** Austr.
127 G2 **Evans Strait** Can.
138 B2 **Evanston** *IL* U.S.A.
136 A2 **Evanston** *WY* U.S.A.
138 B3 **Evansville** U.S.A.
Eva Perón Arg. *see* La Plata
123 C2 **Evaton** S. Africa
79 C2 **Evaz** Iran
83 L2 **Evensk** Rus. Fed.
50 C2 **Everard Range** *hills* Austr.
75 C2 **Everest, Mount** China/Nepal
134 B1 **Everett** U.S.A.
100 A2 **Evergem** Belgium
141 D3 **Everglades** *swamp* U.S.A.
140 C2 **Evergreen** U.S.A.
99 C3 **Evesham** U.K.
118 B2 **Evinayong** Equat. Guinea
93 E4 **Evje** Norway
106 B2 **Évora** Port.
69 F1 **Evoron, Ozero** *l.* Rus. Fed.
111 B2 **Evosmo** Greece
104 C2 **Évreux** France
111 C2 **Evros** *r.* Greece/Turkey
111 B3 **Evrotas** *r.* Greece
104 C2 **Évry** France
80 B2 **Evrychou** Cyprus
111 B3 **Evvoia** *i.* Greece
119 E2 **Ewaso Ngiro** *r.* Kenya
152 B1 **Exaltación** Bol.
99 B4 **Exe** *r.* U.K.
99 B4 **Exeter** U.K.
99 B4 **Exmoor** *hills* U.K.
50 A2 **Exmouth** Austr.
99 B4 **Exmouth** U.K.
50 A2 **Exmouth Gulf** Austr.
106 B2 **Extremadura** *reg.* Spain
146 C2 **Exuma Cays** *is* Bahamas
91 D2 **Eya** *r.* Rus. Fed.
118 C3 **Eyangu** Dem. Rep. Congo
119 D3 **Eyasi, Lake** *salt l.* Tanz.
96 C3 **Eyemouth** U.K.
92 □B2 **Eyjafjörður** *inlet* Iceland
117 C4 **Eyl** Somalia
52 A1 **Eyre, Lake** *salt flat* Austr.
52 A2 **Eyre Peninsula** Austr.
94 B1 **Eysturoy** *i.* Faroe Is
123 D2 **Ezakheni** S. Africa
123 C2 **Ezenzeleni** S. Africa
70 B2 **Ezhou** China
86 E2 **Ezhva** Rus. Fed.
111 C3 **Ezine** Turkey

F

102 C1 **Faaborg** Denmark
142 B2 **Fabens** U.S.A.
108 B2 **Fabriano** Italy
115 D3 **Fachi** Niger
114 C3 **Fada-N'Gourma** Burkina
108 B2 **Faenza** Italy
Faeroes *terr.* N. Atlantic Ocean *see* **Faroe Islands**
59 C3 **Fafanlap** Indon.
110 B1 **Făgăraş** Romania
49 J5 **Fagatogo** American Samoa
93 E3 **Fagernes** Norway
93 G4 **Fagersta** Sweden
153 B5 **Fagnano, Lago** *l.* Arg./Chile
114 B3 **Faguibine, Lac** *l.* Mali
92 □B3 **Fagurhólsmýri** Iceland
126 C2 **Fairbanks** U.S.A.
137 D2 **Fairbury** U.S.A.
135 B3 **Fairfield** *CA* U.S.A.
138 C3 **Fairfield** *OH* U.S.A.
96 □ **Fair Isle** *i.* U.K.
137 E2 **Fairmont** *MN* U.S.A.
138 C3 **Fairmont** *WV* U.S.A.
128 C2 **Fairview** Can.
128 A2 **Fairweather, Mount** Can./U.S.A.
59 D2 **Fais** *i.* Micronesia
74 B1 **Faisalabad** Pak.
136 C1 **Faith** U.S.A.
75 C2 **Faizabad** India
156 E6 **Fakaofo** *atoll* Tokelau
99 D3 **Fakenham** U.K.
59 C3 **Fakfak** Indon.
65 A1 **Faku** China
114 A4 **Falaba** Sierra Leone
97 B1 **Falcarragh** Rep. of Ireland
143 D3 **Falcon Lake** Mex./U.S.A.
Faleshty Moldova *see* Făleşti
90 B2 **Făleşti** Moldova
143 D3 **Falfurrias** U.S.A.
128 C2 **Falher** Can.
101 F2 **Falkenberg** Ger.
93 F4 **Falkenberg** Sweden
101 F1 **Falkensee** Ger.
96 C3 **Falkirk** U.K.
158 D8 **Falkland Escarpment** *sea feature* S. Atlantic Ocean
153 C5 **Falkland Islands** *terr.* S. Atlantic Ocean
157 I9 **Falkland Plateau** *sea feature* S. Atlantic Ocean
93 F4 **Falköping** Sweden
101 D1 **Fallingbostel** Ger.
135 C3 **Fallon** U.S.A.
139 E2 **Fall River** U.S.A.
137 D2 **Falls City** U.S.A.
99 A4 **Falmouth** U.K.
122 A3 **False Bay** S. Africa
144 B2 **Falso, Cabo** *c.* Mex.
93 F5 **Falster** *i.* Denmark
110 C1 **Fălticeni** Romania
93 G3 **Falun** Sweden
152 B2 **Famailla** Arg.
121 □D3 **Fandriana** Madag.
Fangcheng China *see* Fangchenggang
71 A3 **Fangchenggang** China
71 C3 **Fangshan** Taiwan
66 A1 **Fangzheng** China
108 B2 **Fano** Italy
62 B1 **Fan Si Pan** *mt.* Vietnam
119 C2 **Faradje** Dem. Rep. Congo
121 □D3 **Farafangana** Madag.
116 A2 **Farāfirah, Wāḩāt al** Egypt
Farafra Oasis Egypt *see* **Farāfirah, Wāḩāt al**
76 C3 **Farāh** Afgh.
114 A3 **Faranah** Guinea
79 C3 **Fararah** Oman
78 B3 **Farasān, Jazā'ir** *is* Saudi Arabia
59 D2 **Faraulep** *atoll* Micronesia
127 J2 **Farewell, Cape** *c.* Greenland
54 B2 **Farewell, Cape** N.Z.
137 D1 **Fargo** U.S.A.
77 D2 **Farg'ona** Uzbek.
137 E2 **Faribault** U.S.A.
130 C2 **Faribault, Lac** *l.* Can.
74 B2 **Faridabad** India
75 C2 **Faridpur** Bangl.
139 E2 **Farmington** *ME* U.S.A.
142 B1 **Farmington** *NM* U.S.A.
139 D3 **Farmville** U.S.A.
99 C4 **Farnborough** U.K.
128 C2 **Farnham, Mount** Can.
128 A1 **Faro** Can.
106 B2 **Faro** Port.
88 A2 **Fårö** *i.* Sweden
147 C3 **Faro, Punta** *pt* Col.
106 B1 **Faro, Serra do** *mts* Spain
94 B1 **Faroe Islands** *terr.* N. Atlantic Ocean
113 I6 **Farquhar Group** *atoll* Seychelles
81 D3 **Farrāshband** Iran
Farrukhabad India *see* Fatehgarh
79 C3 **Fartak, Ra's** *c.* Yemen
154 B3 **Fartura, Serra da** *mts* Brazil
143 C2 **Farwell** U.S.A.
79 C2 **Fāryāb** Iran
79 C2 **Fāryāb** Iran
81 D3 **Fasā** Iran
109 C2 **Fasano** Italy
90 B1 **Fastiv** Ukr.
119 D2 **Fataki** Dem. Rep. Congo
75 B2 **Fatehgarh** India
75 C2 **Fatehpur** India
114 A3 **Fatick** Senegal
131 D3 **Fatima** Can.
123 C2 **Fauresmith** S. Africa
92 G2 **Fauske** Norway
92 □A3 **Faxaflói** *b.* Iceland
92 G3 **Faxälven** *r.* Sweden
115 D3 **Faya** Chad
140 B1 **Fayetteville** *AR* U.S.A.
141 E1 **Fayetteville** *NC* U.S.A.
140 C1 **Fayetteville** *TN* U.S.A.
74 B1 **Fazilka** India
114 A2 **Fdérik** Maur.
141 E2 **Fear, Cape** U.S.A.
54 C2 **Featherston** N.Z.
104 C2 **Fécamp** France
Federated Malay States *country* Asia *see* **Malaysia**
48 G3 **Federated States of Micronesia** *country* N. Pacific Ocean
102 C1 **Fehmarn** *i.* Ger.
101 F1 **Fehrbellin** Ger.
155 D2 **Feia, Lagoa** *lag.* Brazil
150 B3 **Feijó** Brazil
54 C2 **Feilding** N.Z.
151 F4 **Feira de Santana** Brazil
107 D2 **Felanitx** Spain
101 F1 **Feldberg** Ger.
145 D3 **Felipe C. Puerto** Mex.
155 D1 **Felixlândia** Brazil
99 D4 **Felixstowe** U.K.
101 D2 **Felsberg** Ger.
108 B1 **Feltre** Italy
93 F3 **Femunden** *l.* Norway
Fénérive Madag. *see* **Fenoarivo Atsinanana**
Fengcheng China *see* **Fengshan**
71 B3 **Fengcheng** *Jiangxi* China
65 A1 **Fengcheng** *Liaoning* China
62 A1 **Fengqing** China
71 A3 **Fengshan** China
Fengshan China *see* **Fengqing**
70 B2 **Fengxian** *Jiangsu* China
70 A2 **Fengxian** *Shaanxi* China
Fengxiang China *see* **Lincang**
Fengyi China *see* **Zheng'an**
71 C3 **Fengyüan** Taiwan
70 B1 **Fengzhen** China
105 D3 **Feno, Capo di** *c. Corsica* France
121 □D2 **Fenoarivo Atsinanana** Madag.
70 B2 **Fenyang** China
91 D2 **Feodosiya** Ukr.
108 A3 **Fer, Cap de** *c.* Alg.
137 D1 **Fergus Falls** U.S.A.
51 E1 **Fergusson Island** P.N.G.
114 B4 **Ferkessédougou** Côte d'Ivoire
108 B2 **Fermo** Italy
131 D2 **Fermont** Can.
106 B1 **Fermoselle** Spain
97 B2 **Fermoy** Rep. of Ireland
141 D2 **Fernandina Beach** U.S.A.
154 B2 **Fernandópolis** Brazil
Fernando Poó *i.* Equat. Guinea *see* **Bioco**
134 B1 **Ferndale** U.S.A.
99 C4 **Ferndown** U.K.
128 C3 **Fernie** Can.
135 C3 **Fernley** U.S.A.
97 C2 **Ferns** Rep. of Ireland
Ferozepore India *see* **Firozpur**
108 B2 **Ferrara** Italy
154 B2 **Ferreiros** Brazil
108 A2 **Ferro, Capo** *c. Sardinia* Italy
106 B1 **Ferrol** Spain
Ferryville Tunisia *see* **Menzel Bourguiba**
100 B1 **Ferwert** Neth.
114 B1 **Fès** Morocco
118 B3 **Feshi** Dem. Rep. Congo
137 E3 **Festus** U.S.A.
110 C2 **Feteşti** Romania
97 C2 **Fethard** Rep. of Ireland
111 C3 **Fethiye** Turkey
96 □ **Fetlar** *i.* U.K.
130 C2 **Feuilles, Rivière aux** *r.* Can.
77 D3 **Feyzābād** Afgh.
Fez Morocco *see* **Fès**
121 □D3 **Fianarantsoa** Madag.
115 D4 **Fianga** Chad
117 B4 **Fichē** Eth.
109 C2 **Fier** Albania
96 C2 **Fife Ness** *pt* U.K.
104 C3 **Figeac** France
106 B1 **Figueira da Foz** Port.
107 D1 **Figueres** Spain
114 B1 **Figuig** Morocco
49 I5 **Fiji** *country* S. Pacific Ocean
152 B2 **Filadelfia** Para.
55 B2 **Filchner Ice Shelf** Antarctica
98 C2 **Filey** U.K.
108 B3 **Filicudi, Isola** *i.* Italy
114 C3 **Filingué** Niger
111 B3 **Filippiada** Greece
93 F4 **Filipstad** Sweden
92 E3 **Fillan** Norway
135 D3 **Fillmore** U.S.A.
119 E2 **Fīltu** Eth.
55 D2 **Fimbull Ice Shelf** Antarctica
96 C2 **Findhorn** *r.* U.K.
138 C2 **Findlay** U.S.A.
51 D4 **Fingal** Austr.
139 D2 **Finger Lakes** U.S.A.
111 D3 **Finike** Turkey
106 B1 **Finisterre, Cape** *c.* Spain
93 I3 **Finland** *country* Europe
93 H4 **Finland, Gulf of** Europe
128 B2 **Finlay** *r.* Can.
53 C3 **Finley** Austr.
134 C1 **Finley** U.S.A.
101 E2 **Finne** *ridge* Ger.
92 H2 **Finnmarksvidda** *reg.* Norway
92 G2 **Finnsnes** Norway
93 G4 **Finspång** Sweden
97 C1 **Fintona** U.K.
96 A2 **Fionnphort** U.K.
Fırat *r.* Turkey *see* **Euphrates**
Firenze Italy *see* **Florence**
105 C2 **Firminy** France
74 B2 **Firozabad** India
74 B1 **Firozpur** India
81 D3 **Fīrūzābād** Iran
122 A2 **Fish** *watercourse* Namibia
122 B3 **Fish** *r.* S. Africa
129 F1 **Fisher Strait** Can.
99 A4 **Fishguard** U.K.
105 C2 **Fismes** France
Fisterra, Cabo Spain *see* **Finisterre, Cape**

139 E2 **Fitchburg** U.S.A.
128 C2 **Fitzgerald** Can.
141 D2 **Fitzgerald** U.S.A.
50 B1 **Fitzroy Crossing** Austr.
Fiume Croatia *see* **Rijeka**
54 A3 **Five Rivers** N.Z.
108 B2 **Fivizzano** Italy
119 C3 **Fizi** Dem. Rep. Congo
93 F3 **Fjällnäs** Sweden
92 G3 **Fjällsjöälven** *r.* Sweden
123 C3 **Flagstaff** S. Africa
142 A1 **Flagstaff** U.S.A.
130 C2 **Flaherty Island** Can.
98 C2 **Flamborough Head** *hd* U.K.
101 F1 **Fläming** *hills* Ger.
136 B2 **Flaming Gorge Reservoir** U.S.A.
134 D1 **Flathead** *r.* U.S.A.
134 D1 **Flathead Lake** U.S.A.
51 D1 **Flattery, Cape** Austr.
134 B1 **Flattery, Cape** U.S.A.
98 B3 **Fleetwood** U.K.
93 E4 **Flekkefjord** Norway
102 B1 **Flensburg** Ger.
104 B2 **Flers** France
100 B2 **Fleurus** Belgium
104 C2 **Fleury-les-Aubrais** France
51 D1 **Flinders** *r.* Austr.
50 A3 **Flinders Bay** Austr.
51 D3 **Flinders Island** Austr.
52 A2 **Flinders Ranges** *mts* Austr.
129 D2 **Flin Flon** Can.
98 B3 **Flint** U.K.
138 C2 **Flint** U.S.A.
49 L5 **Flint Island** Kiribati
101 F2 **Flöha** Ger.
107 D1 **Florac** France
100 C3 **Florange** France
108 B2 **Florence** Italy
140 C2 **Florence** *AL* U.S.A.
142 A2 **Florence** *AZ* U.S.A.
134 B2 **Florence** *OR* U.S.A.
141 E2 **Florence** *SC* U.S.A.
150 B2 **Florencia** Col.
146 B3 **Flores** Guat.
61 D2 **Flores** *i.* Indon.
61 C2 **Flores, Laut** Indon.
Floreshty Moldova *see* **Florești**
Flores Sea Indon. *see* **Flores, Laut**
151 F3 **Floresta** Brazil
90 B2 **Florești** Moldova
143 D3 **Floresville** U.S.A.
151 E3 **Floriano** Brazil
152 D2 **Florianópolis** Brazil
153 C3 **Florida** Uru.
141 D2 **Florida** *state* U.S.A.
141 D4 **Florida, Straits of** Bahamas/U.S.A.
141 D4 **Florida Bay** U.S.A.
141 D4 **Florida Keys** *is* U.S.A.
111 B2 **Florina** Greece
93 E3 **Florø** Norway
129 D2 **Foam Lake** Can.
109 C2 **Foča** Bos.-Herz.
110 C1 **Focșani** Romania
71 B3 **Fogang** China
109 C2 **Foggia** Italy
131 E3 **Fogo Island** Can.
104 C3 **Foix** France
89 D3 **Fokino** Rus. Fed.
130 B3 **Foleyet** Can.
108 B2 **Foligno** Italy
99 D4 **Folkestone** U.K.
141 D2 **Folkston** U.S.A.
108 B2 **Follonica** Italy
129 D2 **Fond-du-Lac** Can.
129 D2 **Fond du Lac** *r.* Can.
138 B2 **Fond du Lac** U.S.A.
106 B1 **Fondevila** Spain
108 B2 **Fondi** Italy
146 B3 **Fonseca, Golfo do** *b.* Central America
150 C3 **Fonte Boa** Brazil
104 B2 **Fontenay-le-Comte** France
92 □C2 **Fontur** *pt* Iceland
Foochow China *see* **Fuzhou**
53 C2 **Forbes** Austr.
75 C2 **Forbesganj** India
101 E3 **Forchheim** Ger.
93 E3 **Førde** Norway
53 C1 **Fords Bridge** Austr.
140 B2 **Fordyce** U.S.A.
140 C2 **Forest** U.S.A.
53 C3 **Forest Hill** Austr.
131 D3 **Forestville** Can.
96 C2 **Forfar** U.K.
134 B1 **Forks** U.S.A.
108 B2 **Forlì** Italy
107 D2 **Formentera** *i.* Spain
107 D2 **Formentor, Cap de** *c.* Spain
155 C2 **Formiga** Brazil
152 C2 **Formosa** Arg.
Formosa Asia *see* **Taiwan**
154 C1 **Formosa** Brazil
Formosa Strait China/Taiwan *see* **Taiwan Strait**
Føroyar *terr.* N. Atlantic Ocean *see* **Faroe Islands**
96 C2 **Forres** U.K.
50 B3 **Forrest** Austr.
140 B1 **Forrest City** U.S.A.
51 D1 **Forsayth** Austr.
93 H3 **Forssa** Fin.
53 D2 **Forster** Austr.
136 B1 **Forsyth** U.S.A.
74 B2 **Fort Abbas** Pak.
130 B2 **Fort Albany** Can.
151 F3 **Fortaleza** Brazil
Fort Archambault Chad *see* **Sarh**
128 C2 **Fort Assiniboine** Can.
96 B2 **Fort Augustus** U.K.
123 C3 **Fort Beaufort** S. Africa
134 D1 **Fort Benton** U.S.A.
Fort Brabant Can. *see* **Tuktoyaktuk**
135 B3 **Fort Bragg** U.S.A.
Fort Carnot Madag. *see* **Ikongo**
Fort Charlet Alg. *see* **Djanet**
Fort Chimo Can. *see* **Kuujjuaq**
129 C2 **Fort Chipewyan** Can.
136 B2 **Fort Collins** U.S.A.
Fort Crampel C.A.R. *see* **Kaga Bandoro**
Fort-Dauphin Madag. *see* **Tôlañaro**
147 D3 **Fort-de-France** Martinique
Fort de Polignac Alg. *see* **Illizi**
137 E2 **Fort Dodge** U.S.A.
139 D2 **Fort Erie** Can.
Fort Flatters Alg. *see* **Bordj Omer Driss**
Fort Foureau Cameroon *see* **Kousséri**
130 A3 **Fort Frances** Can.
Fort Franklin Can. *see* **Déljne**
Fort Gardel Alg. *see* **Zaouatallaz**
Fort George Can. *see* **Chisasibi**
126 D2 **Fort Good Hope** Can.
Fort Gouraud Maur. *see* **Fdérik**
96 C2 **Forth** *r.* U.K.
96 C2 **Forth, Firth of** *est.* U.K.
Fort Hall Kenya *see* **Murang'a**
Fort Hertz Myanmar *see* **Putao**
152 C2 **Fortín Madrejón** Para.
Fort Jameson Zambia *see* **Chipata**
Fort Johnston Malawi *see* **Mangochi**
Fort Lamy Chad *see* **Ndjamena**
Fort Laperrine Alg. *see* **Tamanrasset**
141 D3 **Fort Lauderdale** U.S.A.
128 B1 **Fort Liard** Can.
128 C2 **Fort Mackay** Can.
137 E2 **Fort Madison** U.S.A.
Fort Manning Malawi *see* **Mchinji**
128 C2 **Fort McMurray** Can.
126 D2 **Fort McPherson** Can.
136 C2 **Fort Morgan** U.S.A.
141 D3 **Fort Myers** U.S.A.
128 B2 **Fort Nelson** Can.
128 B2 **Fort Nelson** *r.* Can.
Fort Norman Can. *see* **Tulita**
140 C2 **Fort Payne** U.S.A.
136 B1 **Fort Peck** U.S.A.
136 B1 **Fort Peck Reservoir** U.S.A.
141 D3 **Fort Pierce** U.S.A.
119 D2 **Fort Portal** Uganda
128 C1 **Fort Providence** Can.
129 D2 **Fort Qu'Appelle** Can.
128 C1 **Fort Resolution** Can.
96 B2 **Fortrose** U.K.
Fort Rosebery Zambia *see* **Mansa**
Fort Rousset Congo *see* **Owando**
Fort Rupert Can. *see* **Waskaganish**
Fort Sandeman Pak. *see* **Zhob**
128 C2 **Fort Saskatchewan** Can.
137 E3 **Fort Scott** U.S.A.
130 B2 **Fort Severn** Can.
76 B2 **Fort-Shevchenko** Kazakh.
128 B1 **Fort Simpson** Can.
128 C1 **Fort Smith** Can.
140 B1 **Fort Smith** U.S.A.
128 B2 **Fort St James** Can.
128 B2 **Fort St John** Can.
143 C2 **Fort Stockton** U.S.A.
142 C2 **Fort Sumner** U.S.A.
Fort Trinquet Maur. *see* **Bîr Mogreïn**
134 B2 **Fortuna** U.S.A.
131 E3 **Fortune Bay** Can.
128 C2 **Fort Vermilion** Can.
Fort Victoria Zimbabwe *see* **Masvingo**
Fort Walton U.S.A. *see* **Fort Walton Beach**
140 C2 **Fort Walton Beach** U.S.A.
136 B2 **Fort Washakie** U.S.A.
138 B2 **Fort Wayne** U.S.A.
96 B2 **Fort William** U.K.
143 D2 **Fort Worth** U.S.A.
126 C2 **Fort Yukon** U.S.A.
71 B3 **Foshan** China
92 F3 **Fosna** *pen.* Norway
93 E3 **Fosnavåg** Norway
92 □B3 **Foss** Iceland
92 □A2 **Fossá** Iceland
108 A2 **Fossano** Italy
137 D1 **Fosston** U.S.A.
53 C3 **Foster** Austr.
118 B3 **Fougamou** Gabon
104 B2 **Fougères** France
96 □ **Foula** *i.* U.K.
99 D4 **Foulness Point** U.K.
118 B2 **Foumban** Cameroon
111 C3 **Fournoi** *i.* Greece
114 A3 **Fouta Djallon** *reg.* Guinea
54 A3 **Foveaux Strait** N.Z.
136 C3 **Fowler** U.S.A.
50 C3 **Fowlers Bay** Austr.
81 C2 **Fowman** Iran
128 C2 **Fox Creek** Can.
127 G2 **Foxe Basin** *g.* Can.
127 G2 **Foxe Channel** Can.
127 G2 **Foxe Peninsula** Can.
54 B2 **Fox Glacier** N.Z.
128 C2 **Fox Lake** Can.
128 A1 **Fox Mountain** Can.
54 C2 **Foxton** N.Z.
129 D2 **Fox Valley** Can.
97 C1 **Foyle** *r.* Rep. of Ireland/U.K.
97 C1 **Foyle, Lough** *b.* Rep. of Ireland/U.K.
97 B2 **Foynes** Rep. of Ireland
154 B3 **Foz de Areia, Represa de** *resr* Brazil
120 A2 **Foz do Cunene** Angola
154 B3 **Foz do Iguaçu** Brazil
107 D1 **Fraga** Spain
100 A2 **Frameries** Belgium
154 C2 **Franca** Brazil
109 C2 **Francavilla Fontana** Italy
104 C2 **France** *country* Europe
118 B3 **Franceville** Gabon
137 D2 **Francis Case, Lake** U.S.A.
155 D1 **Francisco Sá** Brazil
120 B3 **Francistown** Botswana
128 B2 **François Lake** Can.
100 B1 **Franeker** Neth.
101 D2 **Frankenberg (Eder)** Ger.
101 D3 **Frankenthal (Pfalz)** Ger.
101 E2 **Frankenwald** *mts* Ger.
138 C3 **Frankfort** *KY* U.S.A.
138 B2 **Frankfort** *MI* U.S.A.
Frankfurt Ger. *see* Frankfurt am Main
101 D2 **Frankfurt am Main** Ger.
102 C1 **Frankfurt an der Oder** Ger.
102 C2 **Fränkische Alb** *hills* Ger.
101 E3 **Fränkische Schweiz** *reg.* Ger.
139 E2 **Franklin** *NH* U.S.A.
139 D2 **Franklin** *PA* U.S.A.
140 C1 **Franklin** *TN* U.S.A.
126 D2 **Franklin Bay** Can.
134 C1 **Franklin D. Roosevelt Lake** U.S.A.
128 B1 **Franklin Mountains** Can.
126 F2 **Franklin Strait** Can.
53 C3 **Frankston** Austr.
82 E1 **Frantsa-Iosifa, Zemlya** *is* Rus. Fed.
54 B2 **Franz Josef Glacier** N.Z.
Franz Josef Land *is* Rus. Fed. *see* **Frantsa-Iosifa, Zemlya**
108 A3 **Frasca, Capo della** *c.* *Sardinia* Italy
128 B3 **Fraser** *r. B.C.* Can.
131 D2 **Fraser** *r. Nfld and Lab.* Can.
122 B3 **Fraserburg** S. Africa
96 C2 **Fraserburgh** U.K.
130 B3 **Fraserdale** Can.
51 E2 **Fraser Island** Austr.
128 B2 **Fraser Lake** Can.
128 B2 **Fraser Plateau** Can.
153 C3 **Fray Bentos** Uru.
93 E4 **Fredericia** Denmark
143 D2 **Frederick** U.S.A.
143 D2 **Fredericksburg** *TX* U.S.A.
139 D3 **Fredericksburg** *VA* U.S.A.
128 A2 **Frederick Sound** *sea chan.* U.S.A.
131 D3 **Fredericton** Can.
Frederikshåb Greenland *see* **Paamiut**
93 F4 **Frederikshavn** Denmark
Fredrikshamn Fin. *see* **Hamina**
93 F4 **Fredrikstad** Norway
138 B2 **Freeport** *IL* U.S.A.
143 D3 **Freeport** *TX* U.S.A.
146 C2 **Freeport City** Bahamas
143 D3 **Freer** U.S.A.
123 C2 **Free State** *prov.* S. Africa
114 A4 **Freetown** Sierra Leone
106 B2 **Fregenal de la Sierra** Spain
104 B2 **Fréhel, Cap** *c.* France
102 B2 **Freiburg im Breisgau** Ger.
102 C2 **Freising** Ger.
102 C2 **Freistadt** Austria
105 D3 **Fréjus** France
50 A3 **Fremantle** Austr.
135 B3 **Fremont** *CA* U.S.A.
137 D2 **Fremont** *NE* U.S.A.
138 C2 **Fremont** *OH* U.S.A.
French Congo *country* Africa *see* **Congo**
151 D2 **French Guiana** *terr.* S. America
French Guinea *country* Africa *see* **Guinea**
134 E1 **Frenchman** *r.* U.S.A.
49 M5 **French Polynesia** *terr.* S. Pacific Ocean
French Somaliland *country* Africa *see* **Djibouti**
French Sudan *country* Africa *see* **Mali**
French Territory of the Afars and Issas *country* Africa *see* **Djibouti**
151 D3 **Fresco** *r.* Brazil
144 B2 **Fresnillo** Mex.
135 C3 **Fresno** U.S.A.
107 D2 **Freu, Cap des** *c.* Spain
105 D2 **Freyming-Merlebach** France
114 A3 **Fria** Guinea
152 B2 **Frias** Arg.
101 D2 **Friedberg (Hessen)** Ger.
102 B2 **Friedrichshafen** Ger.
101 F1 **Friesack** Ger.
100 C1 **Friesoythe** Ger.
143 C2 **Friona** U.S.A.
136 B3 **Frisco** U.S.A.
Frobisher Bay Can. *see* **Iqaluit**
127 H2 **Frobisher Bay** *b.* Can.
101 F2 **Frohburg** Ger.
87 D4 **Frolovo** Rus. Fed.
103 D1 **Frombork** Pol.
99 B4 **Frome** U.K.
52 A2 **Frome, Lake** *salt flat* Austr.
52 A2 **Frome Downs** Austr.
100 C2 **Fröndenberg** Ger.
143 C3 **Frontera** Mex.
145 C3 **Frontera** Mex.
144 B1 **Fronteras** Mex.
139 D3 **Front Royal** U.S.A.
108 B2 **Frosinone** Italy

92 E3 **Frøya** i. Norway
Frunze Kyrg. see **Bishkek**
154 C2 **Frutal** Brazil
105 D2 **Frutigen** Switz.
103 D2 **Frýdek-Místek**
Czech Rep.
71 B3 **Fu'an** China
71 C3 **Fuding** China
106 C1 **Fuenlabrada** Spain
152 C2 **Fuerte Olimpo** Para.
114 A2 **Fuerteventura** i. Canary
Is
64 B2 **Fuga** i. Phil.
79 C2 **Fujairah** U.A.E.
67 C3 **Fuji** Japan
71 B3 **Fujian** prov. China
67 C3 **Fujinomiya** Japan
67 C3 **Fuji-san** vol. Japan
Fukien prov. China see
Fujian
67 A4 **Fukue** Japan
67 A4 **Fukue-jima** i. Japan
67 C3 **Fukui** Japan
67 B4 **Fukuoka** Japan
67 D3 **Fukushima** Japan
101 D2 **Fulda** Ger.
101 D2 **Fulda** r. Ger.
70 A3 **Fuling** China
137 E3 **Fulton** U.S.A.
105 C2 **Fumay** France
49 I4 **Funafuti** atoll Tuvalu
114 A1 **Funchal** Madeira
155 D1 **Fundão** Brazil
106 B1 **Fundão** Port.
131 D3 **Fundy, Bay of** g. Can.
121 C3 **Funhalouro** Moz.
70 B2 **Funing** Jiangsu China
71 A3 **Funing** Yunnan China
115 C3 **Funtua** Nigeria
79 C2 **Fūrgun, Kūh-e** mt. Iran
89 F2 **Furmanov** Rus. Fed.
Furmanovka Kazakh. see
Moyynkum
Furmanovo Kazakh. see
Zhalpaktal
155 C2 **Furnas, Represa** resr
Brazil
51 D4 **Furneaux Group** is Austr.
Furong China see **Wan'an**
100 C1 **Fürstenau** Ger.
101 E3 **Fürth** Ger.
66 D3 **Furukawa** Japan
127 G2 **Fury and Hecla Strait**
Can.
70 C1 **Fushun** China
65 B1 **Fusong** China
79 C2 **Fuwayriţ** Qatar
Fuxian China see
Wafangdian
70 A2 **Fuxian** China
70 C1 **Fuxin** China
70 B2 **Fuyang** China
69 E1 **Fuyu** China
Fuyu China see **Songyuan**
68 B1 **Fuyun** China
71 B3 **Fuzhou** China
71 B3 **Fuzhou** China
93 F4 **Fyn** i. Denmark
96 B3 **Fyne, Loch** inlet U.K.
F.Y.R.O.M. country Europe
see **Macedonia**

G

117 C4 **Gaalkacyo** Somalia
120 A2 **Gabela** Angola
Gaberones Botswana see
Gaborone
115 D1 **Gabès** Tunisia
115 D1 **Gabès, Golfe de** g. Tunisia
118 B3 **Gabon** country Africa
123 C1 **Gaborone** Botswana
79 C2 **Gābrīk** Iran
110 C2 **Gabrovo** Bulg.
114 A3 **Gabú** Guinea-Bissau
73 B3 **Gadag** India
75 C2 **Gadchiroli** India
101 E1 **Gadebusch** Ger.
140 C2 **Gadsden** U.S.A.
118 B2 **Gadzi** C.A.R.
110 C2 **Găeşti** Romania
108 B2 **Gaeta** Italy
108 B2 **Gaeta, Golfo di** g. Italy
141 D1 **Gaffney** U.S.A.
115 C1 **Gafsa** Tunisia
89 E2 **Gagarin** Rus. Fed.
109 C3 **Gagliano del Capo** Italy
114 B4 **Gagnoa** Côte d'Ivoire
131 D2 **Gagnon** Can.

Gago Coutinho Angola
see **Lumbala N'guimbo**
81 C1 **Gagra** Georgia
122 A2 **Gaiab** watercourse
Namibia
104 C3 **Gaillac** France
Gaillimh Rep. of Ireland
see **Galway**
141 D3 **Gainesville** FL U.S.A.
141 D2 **Gainesville** GA U.S.A.
143 D2 **Gainesville** TX U.S.A.
98 C3 **Gainsborough** U.K.
52 A2 **Gairdner, Lake** salt flat
Austr.
96 B2 **Gairloch** U.K.
122 B2 **Gakarosa** mt. S. Africa
119 E3 **Galana** r. Kenya
103 D2 **Galanta** Slovakia
Galápagos, Islas is
Pacific Ocean see
Galapagos Islands
125 I10 **Galapagos Islands** is
Pacific Ocean
157 G6 **Galapagos Rise**
sea feature Pacific Ocean
96 C3 **Galashiels** U.K.
110 C1 **Galaţi** Romania
93 E3 **Galdhøpiggen** mt. Norway
145 B2 **Galeana** Mex.
128 C2 **Galena Bay** Can.
138 A2 **Galesburg** U.S.A.
122 B2 **Galeshewe** S. Africa
89 F2 **Galich** Rus. Fed.
106 B1 **Galicia** reg. Spain
Galilee, Sea of l. Israel
78 A3 **Gallabat** Sudan
140 C1 **Gallatin** U.S.A.
73 C4 **Galle** Sri Lanka
157 G6 **Gallego Rise** sea feature
Pacific Ocean
150 B1 **Gallinas, Punta** pt Col.
109 C2 **Gallipoli** Italy
111 C2 **Gallipoli** Turkey
92 H2 **Gällivare** Sweden
142 B1 **Gallup** U.S.A.
114 A2 **Galtat Zemmour**
Western Sahara
97 B2 **Galtymore** hill
Rep. of Ireland
143 E3 **Galveston** U.S.A.
143 E3 **Galveston Bay** U.S.A.
143 E3 **Galveston Island** U.S.A.
97 B2 **Galway** Rep. of Ireland
97 B2 **Galway Bay**
Rep. of Ireland
154 C1 **Gamá** Brazil
123 D3 **Gamalakhe** S. Africa
117 B4 **Gambēla** Eth.
114 A3 **Gambia** r. Gambia
114 A3 **Gambia, The** country
Africa
49 N6 **Gambier, Îles** is
Fr. Polynesia
52 A3 **Gambier Islands** Austr.
131 E3 **Gambo** Can.
118 B3 **Gamboma** Congo
92 H2 **Gammelstaden** Sweden
142 B1 **Ganado** U.S.A.
81 D3 **Ganāveh** Iran
81 C1 **Gäncä** Azer.
61 C2 **Gandadiwata, Bukit** mt.
Indon.
118 C3 **Gandajika**
Dem. Rep. Congo
106 B1 **Gándara** Spain
131 E3 **Gander** Can.
131 E3 **Gander** r. Can.
101 D1 **Ganderkesee** Ger.
107 D1 **Gandesa** Spain
74 B2 **Gandhidham** India
74 B2 **Gandhinagar** India
74 B2 **Gandhi Sagar** resr India
107 C2 **Gandía** Spain
153 B4 **Gangán** Arg.
74 B2 **Ganganagar** India
62 A1 **Gangaw** Myanmar
68 C2 **Gangca** China
75 C1 **Gangdisê Shan** mts China
75 C2 **Ganges** r. Bangl./India
105 C3 **Ganges** France
75 C2 **Ganges, Mouths of the**
Bangl./India
159 E2 **Ganges Cone** sea feature
Indian Ocean
75 C2 **Gangtok** India
75 C3 **Ganjam** India
71 A3 **Gan Jiang** r. China
71 A3 **Ganluo** China
105 C2 **Gannat** France

136 B2 **Gannett Peak** U.S.A.
122 A3 **Gansbaai** S. Africa
70 A1 **Gansu** prov. China
115 D4 **Ganye** Nigeria
71 B3 **Ganzhou** China
114 B3 **Gao** Mali
Gaoleshan China see
Xianfeng
114 B3 **Gaoua** Burkina
114 A3 **Gaoual** Guinea
70 B2 **Gaoyou** China
70 B2 **Gaoyou Hu** l. China
105 D3 **Gap** France
64 B2 **Gapan** Phil.
107 C2 **Gap Carbon** hd Alg.
75 C1 **Gar** China
72 C1 **Gar** China
97 B2 **Gara, Lough** l.
Rep. of Ireland
117 C4 **Garacad** Somalia
53 C1 **Garah** Austr.
151 F3 **Garanhuns** Brazil
123 C2 **Ga-Rankuwa** S. Africa
118 C1 **Garar, Plaine de** plain
Chad
117 C4 **Garbahaarrey** Somalia
135 B2 **Garberville** U.S.A.
81 D2 **Garbosh, Kūh-e** mt. Iran
101 D1 **Garbsen** Ger.
154 C2 **Garça** Brazil
154 B2 **Garcias** Brazil
108 B1 **Garda, Lago** l. Italy
108 A3 **Garde, Cap de** c. Alg.
101 E1 **Gardelegen** Ger.
136 C3 **Garden City** U.S.A.
129 E2 **Garden Hill** Can.
77 C3 **Gardēz** Afgh.
139 F2 **Gardner** atoll Micronesia
Gardner atoll Micronesia
see **Faraulep**
135 C3 **Gardnerville** U.S.A.
136 B3 **Garfield** U.S.A.
88 B2 **Gargždai** Lith.
123 C3 **Gariep Dam** resr S. Africa
122 A3 **Garies** S. Africa
119 D3 **Garissa** Kenya
88 B2 **Garkalne** Latvia
143 D2 **Garland** U.S.A.
102 C2 **Garmisch-Partenkirchen**
Ger.
52 B2 **Garnpung Lake** imp. l.
Austr.
104 B3 **Garonne** r. France
117 C4 **Garoowe** Somalia
74 B2 **Garoth** India
118 B2 **Garoua** Cameroon
118 B2 **Garoua Boulaï** Cameroon
Garqêntang China see **Sog**
96 B2 **Garry** r. U.K.
81 D2 **Garrygala** Turkm.
126 F2 **Garry Lake** Can.
119 E3 **Garsen** Kenya
122 A2 **Garub** Namibia
60 D2 **Garut** Indon.
138 B2 **Gary** U.S.A.
145 B2 **Garza García** Mex.
68 C2 **Garzê** China
104 B3 **Gascogne** reg. France see
Gascony
Gascogne, Golfe de g.
France/Spain see
Gascony, Gulf of
104 B3 **Gascony** reg. France
104 B3 **Gascony, Gulf of**
France/Spain
50 A2 **Gascoyne** r. Austr.
118 B2 **Gashaka** Nigeria
115 D3 **Gashua** Nigeria
59 E3 **Gasmata** P.N.G.
131 D3 **Gaspé** Can.
131 D3 **Gaspé, Péninsule de** pen.
Can.
141 E1 **Gaston, Lake** U.S.A.
141 D1 **Gastonia** U.S.A.
107 C2 **Gata, Cabo de** c. Spain
88 D2 **Gatchina** Rus. Fed.
98 C2 **Gateshead** U.K.
143 D2 **Gatesville** U.S.A.
141 D1 **Gatineau** Can.
130 C3 **Gatineau** r. Can.
Gatooma Zimbabwe see
Kadoma
53 D1 **Gatton** Austr.
129 E2 **Gauer Lake** Can.
93 E4 **Gausta** mt. Norway
123 C2 **Gauteng** prov. S. Africa
79 C2 **Gāvbandī** Iran
111 B3 **Gavdos** i. Greece
81 D2 **Gave** r. France
93 G3 **Gävle** Sweden
93 G3 **Gävlebukten** b. Sweden

89 F2 **Gavrilov Posad** Rus. Fed.
89 E2 **Gavrilov-Yam** Rus. Fed.
122 A2 **Gawachab** Namibia
62 A1 **Gawai** Myanmar
52 A2 **Gawler** Austr.
52 A2 **Gawler Ranges** hills Austr.
75 C2 **Gaya** India
114 C3 **Gaya** Niger
114 C3 **Gayéri** Burkina
138 C1 **Gaylord** U.S.A.
86 F2 **Gayny** Rus. Fed.
116 B1 **Gaza** terr. Asia
80 B2 **Gaza** Gaza
76 C2 **Gaz-Achak** Turkm.
76 B3 **Gazandzhyk** Turkm.
80 B2 **Gaziantep** Turkey
114 B4 **Gbarnga** Liberia
118 A2 **Gboko** Nigeria
103 D1 **Gdańsk** Pol.
88 A3 **Gdańsk, Gulf of**
Pol./Rus. Fed.
88 C2 **Gdov** Rus. Fed.
103 D1 **Gdynia** Pol.
116 B3 **Gedaref** Sudan
101 D2 **Gedern** Ger.
111 C3 **Gediz** Turkey
111 C3 **Gediz** r. Turkey
102 C1 **Gedser** Denmark
100 B2 **Geel** Belgium
52 B3 **Geelong** Austr.
101 E1 **Geesthacht** Ger.
75 C1 **Gê'gyai** China
129 C2 **Geikie** r. Can.
93 E3 **Geilo** Norway
119 D3 **Geita** Tanz.
71 A3 **Gejiu** China
108 B3 **Gela** Sicily Italy
108 B3 **Gela, Golfo di** g. Sicily
Italy
91 D3 **Gelendzhik** Rus. Fed.
Gelibolu Turkey see
Gallipoli
100 C2 **Gelsenkirchen** Ger.
118 B2 **Gemena** Dem. Rep. Congo
111 C2 **Gemlik** Turkey
108 B1 **Gemona del Friuli** Italy
117 C4 **Genalē Wenz** r. Eth.
153 B3 **General Acha** Arg.
153 B3 **General Alvear** Arg.
153 C3 **General Belgrano** Arg.
144 B2 **General Cepeda** Mex.
General Freire Angola see
Muxaluando
General Machado Angola
see **Camacupa**
153 B3 **General Pico** Arg.
153 B3 **General Roca** Arg.
154 B2 **General Salgado** Brazil
64 B3 **General Santos** Phil.
139 D2 **Genesee** r. U.S.A.
138 A2 **Geneseo** IL U.S.A.
139 D2 **Geneseo** NY U.S.A.
105 D2 **Geneva** Switz.
139 D2 **Geneva** U.S.A.
105 D2 **Geneva, Lake** l.
France/Switz.
Genève Switz. see **Geneva**
106 B2 **Genil** r. Spain
100 B2 **Genk** Belgium
53 C3 **Genoa** Austr.
108 A2 **Genoa** Italy
108 A2 **Genoa, Gulf of** g. Italy
Genova Italy see **Genoa**
Gent Belgium see **Ghent**
61 C2 **Genteng** i. Indon.
101 F1 **Genthin** Ger.
50 A3 **Geographe Bay** Austr.
131 D2 **George** r. Can.
122 B3 **George** S. Africa
52 A3 **George, Lake** Austr.
141 D3 **George, Lake** FL U.S.A.
139 E2 **George, Lake** NY U.S.A.
146 C2 **George Town** Bahamas
114 A3 **Georgetown** Gambia
151 D2 **Georgetown** Guyana
60 B1 **George Town** Malaysia
138 C3 **Georgetown** KY U.S.A.
141 E2 **Georgetown** SC U.S.A.
143 D2 **Georgetown** TX U.S.A.
55 L2 **George V Land** reg.
Antarctica
81 C1 **Georgia** country Asia
141 D2 **Georgia** state U.S.A.
130 B3 **Georgian Bay** Can.
51 C2 **Georgina** watercourse
Austr.
Georgiu-Dezh Rus. Fed.
see **Liski**
77 E2 **Georgiyevka** Kazakh.
87 D4 **Georgiyevsk** Rus. Fed.
101 F2 **Gera** Ger.

151 E4 Geral de Goiás, Serra hills Brazil
54 B2 Geraldine N.Z.
50 A2 Geraldton Austr.
80 B1 Gerede Turkey
76 C3 Gereshk Afgh.
102 C2 Geretsried Ger.
135 C2 Gerlach U.S.A.
103 E2 Gerlachovský štit mt. Slovakia
139 D3 Germantown U.S.A.
102 C1 Germany country Europe
100 C2 Gerolstein Ger.
101 E3 Gerolzhofen Ger.
53 D2 Gerringong Austr.
101 D2 Gersfeld (Rhön) Ger.
Géryville Alg. see El Bayadh
75 C1 Gêrzê China
106 C1 Getafe Spain
139 D3 Gettysburg PA U.S.A.
136 D1 Gettysburg SD U.S.A.
55 P2 Getz Ice Shelf Antarctica
111 B2 Gevgelija Macedonia
111 C3 Geyikli Turkey
122 B2 Ghaap Plateau S. Africa
Ghadamés Libya see Ghadāmis
115 C1 Ghadāmis Libya
75 C2 Ghaghara r. India
76 C2 Ghalkarteniz, Solonchak salt marsh Kazakh.
114 B4 Ghana country Africa
120 B3 Ghanzi Botswana
115 C1 Ghardaïa Alg.
78 A2 Ghārib, Jabal mt. Egypt
115 D1 Gharyān Libya
115 D2 Ghāt Libya
75 C2 Ghatal India
75 B2 Ghaziabad Uttar Prad. India
75 C2 Ghazipur India
77 C3 Ghaznī Afgh.
78 B2 Ghazzālah Saudi Arabia
100 A2 Ghent Belgium
Gheorghe Gheorghiu-Dej Romania see Onești
110 C1 Gheorgheni Romania
110 B1 Gherla Romania
105 D3 Ghisonaccia Corsica France
74 B2 Ghotaru India
74 A2 Ghotki Pak.
75 C2 Ghuari r. India
76 C3 Ghurian Afgh.
91 E3 Giaginskaya Rus. Fed.
97 C1 Giant's Causeway lava field U.K.
61 C2 Gianyar Indon.
109 C3 Giarre Sicily Italy
108 A1 Giaveno Italy
122 A2 Gibeon Namibia
106 B2 Gibraltar terr. Europe
106 B2 Gibraltar, Strait of Morocco/Spain
140 B2 Gibsland U.S.A.
50 B2 Gibson Desert Austr.
68 C1 Gichgeniyn Nuruu mts Mongolia
117 B4 Gīdolē Eth.
105 C2 Gien France
101 D2 Gießen Ger.
101 E1 Gifhorn Ger.
128 C2 Gift Lake Can.
67 C3 Gifu Japan
96 B3 Gigha i. U.K.
76 C2 G'ijduvon Uzbek.
106 B1 Gijón-Xixón Spain
142 A2 Gila r. U.S.A.
142 A2 Gila Bend U.S.A.
51 D1 Gilbert r. Austr.
48 I4 Gilbert Islands country Pacific Ocean
156 D5 Gilbert Ridge sea feature Pacific Ocean
151 E3 Gilbués Brazil
134 D1 Gildford U.S.A.
Gilf Kebir Plateau Egypt see Haḍabat al Jilf al Kabīr
53 C2 Gilgandra Austr.
74 B1 Gilgit Jammu and Kashmir
74 B1 Gilgit r. Jammu and Kashmir
53 C2 Gilgunnia Austr.
129 E2 Gillam Can.
136 B2 Gillette U.S.A.
99 D4 Gillingham U.K.
130 C2 Gilmour Island Can.
135 B3 Gilroy U.S.A.
129 E2 Gimli Can.
64 B3 Gingoog Phil.
117 C4 Gīnīr Eth.
109 C2 Ginosa Italy
109 C2 Gioia del Colle Italy
53 C3 Gippsland reg. Austr.
74 A2 Girdar Dhor r. Pak.
79 D1 Girdi Iran
80 B1 Giresun Turkey
Girgenti Italy see Agrigento
53 C2 Girilambone Austr.
Giron Sweden see Kiruna
107 D1 Girona Spain
104 B2 Gironde est. France
53 C2 Girral Austr.
96 B3 Girvan U.K.
54 C1 Gisborne N.Z.
93 F4 Gislaved Sweden
119 C3 Gitarama Rwanda
119 C3 Gitega Burundi
Giuba r. Somalia see Jubba
108 B2 Giulianova Italy
110 C2 Giurgiu Romania
110 C1 Giuvala, Pasul pass Romania
105 C2 Givors France
123 D1 Giyani S. Africa
119 D2 Giyon Eth.
116 B2 Giza Egypt
103 E1 Giżycko Pol.
109 D2 Gjirokastër Albania
126 F2 Gjoa Haven Can.
93 F3 Gjøvik Norway
131 E3 Glace Bay Can.
134 B1 Glacier Peak vol. U.S.A.
143 E2 Gladewater U.S.A.
51 E2 Gladstone Qld Austr.
52 A2 Gladstone S.A. Austr.
92 □A2 Gláma mts Iceland
109 C2 Glamoč Bos.-Herz.
100 C3 Glan r. Ger.
97 B2 Glanaruddery Mountains hills Rep. of Ireland
96 B3 Glasgow U.K.
138 B3 Glasgow KY U.S.A.
136 B1 Glasgow MT U.S.A.
99 B4 Glastonbury U.K.
101 F2 Glauchau Ger.
86 E3 Glazov Rus. Fed.
89 E3 Glazunovka Rus. Fed.
123 D2 Glencoe S. Africa
96 B2 Glen Coe val. U.K.
142 A2 Glendale AZ U.S.A.
138 B2 Glendale WI U.S.A.
53 D2 Glen Davis Austr.
51 D2 Glenden Austr.
136 C1 Glendive U.S.A.
52 B3 Glenelg r. Austr.
96 B2 Glenfinnan U.K.
53 D1 Glen Innes Austr.
96 B2 Glen More val. U.K.
53 C1 Glenmorgan Austr.
126 C2 Glennallen U.S.A.
134 C2 Glenns Ferry U.S.A.
136 B2 Glenrock U.S.A.
96 C2 Glenrothes U.K.
139 E2 Glens Falls U.S.A.
96 C2 Glen Shee val. U.K.
97 B1 Glenties Rep. of Ireland
142 B2 Glenwood U.S.A.
136 B3 Glenwood Springs U.S.A.
101 E1 Glinde Ger.
103 D1 Gliwice Pol.
142 A2 Globe U.S.A.
103 D1 Głogów Pol.
92 F2 Glomfjord Norway
93 F4 Glomma r. Norway
53 D2 Gloucester Austr.
99 B4 Gloucester U.K.
131 E3 Glovertown Can.
101 F1 Glöwen Ger.
77 E1 Glubokoye Kazakh.
101 D1 Glückstadt Ger.
103 C2 Gmünd Austria
102 C2 Gmunden Austria
101 D1 Gnarrenburg Ger.
103 D1 Gniezno Pol.
109 D2 Gnjilane Serb. and Mont.
75 D2 Goalpara India
96 B3 Goat Fell hill U.K.
117 C4 Goba Eth.
122 A1 Gobabis Namibia
153 A4 Gobernador Gregores Arg.
152 C2 Gobernador Virasoro Arg.
68 D2 Gobi des. China/Mongolia
67 C4 Gobō Japan
100 C2 Goch Ger.
122 A1 Gochas Namibia
74 B3 Godavari r. India
73 C3 Godavari, Mouths of the India
75 C2 Godda India
117 C4 Godē Eth.
130 B3 Goderich Can.
Godhavn Greenland see Qeqertarsuaq
74 B2 Godhra India
129 E2 Gods r. Can.
129 E2 Gods Lake Can.
Godthåb Greenland see Nuuk
Godwin-Austen, Mount China/Jammu and Kashmir see K2
Goedgegun Swaziland see Nhlangano
130 C3 Goéland, Lac au l. Can.
131 D2 Goélands, Lac aux l. Can.
100 A2 Goes Neth.
138 B1 Gogebic Range hills U.S.A.
88 C1 Gogland, Ostrov i. Rus. Fed.
Gogra r. India see Ghaghara
119 C2 Gogrial Sudan
154 C1 Goiandira Brazil
154 C1 Goianésia Brazil
154 C1 Goiânia Brazil
154 B1 Goiás Brazil
154 C1 Goiatuba Brazil
154 B2 Goio-Erê Brazil
111 C2 Gökçeada i. Turkey
111 C3 Gökçedağ Turkey
121 B2 Gokwe Zimbabwe
93 E3 Gol Norway
62 A1 Golaghat India
111 C2 Gölcük Turkey
103 E1 Gołdap Pol.
101 F1 Goldberg Ger.
Gold Coast country Africa see Ghana
53 D1 Gold Coast Austr.
114 B4 Gold Coast coastal area Ghana
128 C2 Golden Can.
54 B2 Golden Bay N.Z.
134 B1 Goldendale U.S.A.
128 B3 Golden Hinde mt. Can.
97 B2 Golden Vale lowland Rep. of Ireland
135 C3 Goldfield U.S.A.
128 B3 Gold River Can.
141 E1 Goldsboro U.S.A.
103 C1 Goleniów Pol.
135 C4 Goleta U.S.A.
Golfe du St-Laurent g. Can. see St Lawrence, Gulf of
111 C3 Gölhisar Turkey
Gollel Swaziland see Lavumisa
75 D1 Golmud China
81 D2 Golpāyegān Iran
96 C2 Golspie U.K.
Golyshi Rus. Fed. see Vetluzhskiy
119 C3 Goma Dem. Rep. Congo
75 C2 Gomati r. India
115 D3 Gombe Nigeria
115 D3 Gombi Nigeria
Gomel' Belarus see Homyel'
144 B2 Gómez Palacio Mex.
81 D2 Gomīshān Iran
75 C1 Gomo China
147 C3 Gonaïves Haiti
147 C3 Gonâve, Île de la i. Haiti
81 D2 Gonbad-e Kavus Iran
74 B2 Gondal India
Gondar Eth. see Gonder
116 B3 Gonder Eth.
75 C2 Gondia India
111 C2 Gönen Turkey
62 A1 Gonggar China
70 A3 Gongga Shan mt. China
68 C2 Gonghe China
115 D4 Gongola r. Nigeria
53 C2 Gongolgon Austr.
Gongtang China see Damxung
123 C3 Gonubie S. Africa
145 C2 Gonzáles Mex.
143 D3 Gonzales U.S.A.
122 A3 Good Hope, Cape of S. Africa
134 D2 Gooding U.S.A.
136 C3 Goodland U.S.A.
53 C1 Goodooga Austr.
98 C3 Goole U.K.
53 C2 Goolgowi Austr.
52 A3 Goolwa Austr.
53 D1 Goondiwindi Austr.
134 B2 Goose Lake U.S.A.
102 B2 Göppingen Ger.
75 C2 Gorakhpur India
109 C2 Goražde Bos.-Herz.
111 C3 Gördes Turkey
89 D3 Gordeyevka Rus. Fed.
136 C2 Gordon U.S.A.
51 D4 Gordon, Lake Austr.
115 D4 Goré Chad
117 B4 Gorē Eth.
54 A3 Gore N.Z.
97 C2 Gorey Rep. of Ireland
81 D2 Gorgān Iran
81 C1 Gori Georgia
100 B2 Gorinchem Neth.
108 B1 Gorizia Italy
Gor'kiy Rus. Fed. see Nizhniy Novgorod
89 F2 Gor'kovskoye Vodokhranilishche resr Rus. Fed.
103 E2 Gorlice Pol.
103 C1 Görlitz Ger.
Gorna Dzhumaya Bulg. see Blagoevgrad
109 D2 Gornji Milanovac Serb. and Mont.
109 C2 Gornji Vakuf Bos.-Herz.
77 E1 Gorno-Altaysk Rus. Fed.
86 F2 Gornopravdinsk Rus. Fed.
110 C2 Gornotrakiyska Nizina lowland Bulg.
66 D1 Gornozavodsk Rus. Fed.
77 E1 Gornyak Rus. Fed.
59 D3 Goroka P.N.G.
52 B3 Goroke Austr.
114 B3 Gorom Gorom Burkina
121 C2 Gorongosa Moz.
61 D1 Gorontalo Indon.
89 E3 Gorshechnoye Rus. Fed.
97 B2 Gorumna Island Rep. of Ireland
91 D3 Goryachiy Klyuch Rus. Fed.
103 D1 Gorzów Wielkopolski Pol.
59 E3 Goschen Strait P.N.G.
53 D2 Gosford Austr.
74 A2 Goshanak Pak.
66 D2 Goshogawara Japan
101 E2 Goslar Ger.
109 C2 Gospić Croatia
99 C4 Gosport U.K.
111 B2 Gostivar Macedonia
Göteborg Sweden see Gothenburg
101 E2 Gotha Ger.
93 F4 Gothenburg Sweden
136 C2 Gothenburg U.S.A.
93 G4 Gotland i. Sweden
111 B2 Gotse Delchev Bulg.
93 G4 Gotska Sandön i. Sweden
67 B4 Gōtsu Japan
101 D2 Göttingen Ger.
128 B2 Gott Peak Can.
Gottwaldow Czech Rep. see Zlín
Gotval'd Ukr. see Zmiyiv
100 B1 Gouda Neth.
114 A3 Goudiri Senegal
115 D3 Goudoumaria Niger
158 E7 Gough Island S. Atlantic Ocean
130 C3 Gouin, Réservoir resr Can.
53 C2 Goulburn Austr.
53 D2 Goulburn r. N.S.W. Austr.
53 C3 Goulburn r. Vic. Austr.
114 B3 Goundam Mali
107 D2 Gouraya Alg.
114 B3 Gourcy Burkina
104 C3 Gourdon France
115 D3 Gouré Niger
122 B3 Gourits r. S. Africa
114 B3 Gourma-Rharous Mali
53 C3 Gourock Range mts Austr.
155 D1 Governador Valadares Brazil
141 E3 Governor's Harbour Bahamas
68 C2 Govĭ Altayn Nuruu mts Mongolia
75 C2 Govind Ballash Pant Sagar resr India
76 C4 Gowd-e Zereh plain Afgh.
99 A3 Gower pen. U.K.
152 C2 Goya Arg.
81 C1 Göyçay Azer.
80 B1 Göynük Turkey

115 E3 Goz-Beïda Chad
75 C1 Gozha Co salt l. China
122 B3 Graaf-Reinet S. Africa
122 A3 Graafwater S. Africa
101 E1 Grabow Ger.
109 C2 Gračac Croatia
87 E3 Grachevka Rus. Fed.
109 C2 Gradačac Bos.-Herz.
104 B3 Gradignan France
101 F2 Gräfenhainichen Ger.
53 D1 Grafton Austr.
137 D1 Grafton U.S.A.
143 D2 Graham U.S.A.
142 B2 Graham, Mount U.S.A.
Graham Bell Island
Rus. Fed. see Greem-
Bell, Ostrov
128 A2 Graham Island Can.
55 A3 Graham Land reg.
Antarctica
123 C3 Grahamstown S. Africa
97 C2 Graiguenamanagh
Rep. of Ireland
151 E3 Grajaú Brazil
103 E1 Grajewo Pol.
111 B2 Grammos mt. Greece
96 B2 Grampian Mountains U.K.
146 B3 Granada Nic.
106 C2 Granada Spain
97 C2 Granard Rep. of Ireland
139 E1 Granby Can.
114 A2 Gran Canaria i. Canary Is
152 B3 Gran Chaco reg.
Arg./Para.
136 F2 Grand r. MO U.S.A.
136 C1 Grand r. SD U.S.A.
146 C2 Grand Bahama i.
Bahamas
131 E3 Grand Bank Can.
158 D2 Grand Banks of
Newfoundland sea feature
N. Atlantic Ocean
Grand Canal canal China
see Da Yunhe
Grand Canary i. Canary Is
see Gran Canaria
142 A1 Grand Canyon U.S.A.
142 A1 Grand Canyon gorge
U.S.A.
146 B3 Grand Cayman i.
Cayman Is
129 C2 Grand Centre Can.
134 C1 Grand Coulee U.S.A.
152 B1 Grande r. Bol.
154 B2 Grande r. Brazil
153 B5 Grande, Bahía b. Arg.
155 D2 Grande, Ilha i. Brazil
150 C2 Grande, Serra mt. Brazil
128 C2 Grande Cache Can.
Grande Comore i.
Comoros see Njazidja
128 C2 Grande Prairie Can.
115 D3 Grand Erg de Bilma des.
Niger
114 B1 Grand Erg Occidental
des. Alg.
115 C2 Grand Erg Oriental des.
Alg.
131 D3 Grande-Rivière Can.
152 B3 Grandes, Salinas
salt marsh Arg.
131 D3 Grand Falls N.B. Can.
131 E3 Grand Falls Nfld and Lab.
Can.
128 C3 Grand Forks Can.
137 D1 Grand Forks U.S.A.
138 B2 Grand Haven U.S.A.
128 C1 Grandin, Lac l. Can.
137 D2 Grand Island Can.
140 B3 Grand Isle U.S.A.
136 B3 Grand Junction U.S.A.
114 B4 Grand-Lahou Côte d'Ivoire
131 D3 Grand Lake N.B. Can.
131 E3 Grand Lake Nfld and Lab.
Can.
137 E1 Grand Marais U.S.A.
130 C3 Grand-Mère Can.
106 B2 Grândola Port.
129 E2 Grand Rapids Can.
138 B2 Grand Rapids MI U.S.A.
137 E1 Grand Rapids MN U.S.A.
136 A2 Grand Teton mt. U.S.A.
147 C2 Grand Turk
Turks and Caicos Is
129 D2 Grandview Can.
134 C1 Grandview U.S.A.
134 C1 Grangeville U.S.A.
138 C2 Granisle Can.
137 D2 Granite Falls U.S.A.
134 E1 Granite Peak MT U.S.A.
134 C2 Granite Peak NV U.S.A.

108 B3 Granitola, Capo c. Sicily
Italy
93 F4 Gränna Sweden
101 F1 Gransee Ger.
99 C3 Grantham U.K.
96 C2 Grantown-on-Spey U.K.
142 B1 Grants U.S.A.
134 B2 Grants Pass U.S.A.
104 B2 Granville France
129 D2 Granville Lake Can.
155 D1 Grão Mogol Brazil
123 D1 Graskop S. Africa
105 D3 Grasse France
50 B3 Grass Patch Austr.
107 D1 Graus Spain
92 F2 Gravdal Norway
104 B2 Grave, Pointe de pt
France
129 D3 Gravelbourg Can.
130 C3 Gravenhurst Can.
53 D1 Gravesend Austr.
99 D4 Gravesend U.K.
105 D2 Gray France
141 D1 Gray U.S.A.
138 C2 Grayling U.S.A.
99 D4 Grays U.K.
103 D2 Graz Austria
146 C2 Great Abaco i. Bahamas
50 B3 Great Australian Bight g.
Austr.
146 C2 Great Bahama Bank
sea feature Bahamas
54 C1 Great Barrier Island N.Z.
51 D1 Great Barrier Reef Austr.
135 C3 Great Basin U.S.A.
128 C1 Great Bear Lake Can.
93 F4 Great Belt sea chan.
Denmark
137 D3 Great Bend U.S.A.
63 A2 Great Coco Island
Cocos Is
53 B3 Great Dividing Range mts
Austr.
Great Eastern Erg des.
Alg. see
Grand Erg Oriental
146 B2 Greater Antilles is
Caribbean Sea
Greater Khingan
Mountains China see
Da Hinggan Ling
134 D1 Great Falls U.S.A.
123 C3 Great Fish r. S. Africa
123 C3 Great Fish Point S. Africa
147 C2 Great Inagua i. Bahamas
122 B3 Great Karoo plat. S. Africa
123 C3 Great Kei r. S. Africa
99 D3 Great Malvern U.K.
122 A2 Great Namaqualand reg.
Namibia
73 D4 Great Nicobar i. India
98 B3 Great Ormes Head hd
U.K.
99 D3 Great Ouse r. U.K.
136 C2 Great Plains U.S.A.
119 D3 Great Rift Valley Africa
119 D3 Great Ruaha r. Tanz.
134 D2 Great Salt Lake U.S.A.
134 D2 Great Salt Lake Desert
U.S.A.
116 A2 Great Sand Sea des.
Egypt/Libya
50 B2 Great Sandy Desert Austr.
128 C1 Great Slave Lake Can.
141 D1 Great Smoky Mountains
U.S.A.
99 A4 Great Torrington U.K.
50 B2 Great Victoria Desert
Austr.
70 B1 Great Wall tourist site
China
Great Western Erg des.
Alg. see
Grand Erg Occidental
99 D3 Great Yarmouth U.K.
Grebenkovskiy Ukr. see
Hrebinka
106 B1 Gredos, Sierra de mts
Spain
111 B3 Greece country Europe
136 C2 Greeley U.S.A.
82 F1 Greem-Bell, Ostrov i.
Rus. Fed.
138 F1 Green r. Can.
138 B3 Green r. KY U.S.A.
138 B3 Green r. WY U.S.A.
138 B1 Green Bay U.S.A.
138 B1 Green Bay b. U.S.A.
138 C3 Greenbrier r. U.S.A.
138 B3 Greencastle U.S.A.
141 D1 Greeneville U.S.A.

139 E2 Greenfield U.S.A.
129 D2 Green Lake Can.
127 J2 Greenland terr. N. America
160 L2 Greenland Basin
sea feature Arctic Ocean
160 R2 Greenland Sea sea
Greenland/Svalbard
96 B3 Greenock U.K.
97 C1 Greenore Rep. of Ireland
135 D3 Green River UT U.S.A.
136 B2 Green River WY U.S.A.
138 B3 Greensburg IN U.S.A.
139 D2 Greensburg PA U.S.A.
141 E2 Green Swamp U.S.A.
142 A2 Green Valley U.S.A.
114 B4 Greenville Liberia
140 C2 Greenville AL U.S.A.
139 F1 Greenville ME U.S.A.
140 B2 Greenville MS U.S.A.
141 E1 Greenville NC U.S.A.
141 D2 Greenville SC U.S.A.
143 D2 Greenville TX U.S.A.
53 D2 Greenwell Point Austr.
131 D3 Greenwood Can.
140 B3 Greenwood MS U.S.A.
141 D2 Greenwood SC U.S.A.
50 B2 Gregory, Lake salt flat
Austr.
102 C1 Greifswald Ger.
101 F2 Greiz Ger.
86 C2 Gremikha Rus. Fed.
93 F4 Grená Denmark
140 C2 Grenada country
West Indies
104 C3 Grenade France
93 F4 Grenen spit Denmark
53 C2 Grenfell Austr.
129 D2 Grenfell Can.
105 D2 Grenoble France
51 D1 Grenville, Cape Austr.
134 B1 Gresham U.S.A.
140 B3 Gretna LA U.S.A.
139 D3 Gretna VA U.S.A.
100 C1 Greven Ger.
111 B2 Grevena Greece
100 C2 Grevenbroich Ger.
101 E1 Grevesmühlen Ger.
136 B2 Greybull U.S.A.
128 A1 Grey Hunter Peak Can.
131 E2 Grey Islands Can.
54 B2 Greymouth N.Z.
52 B1 Grey Range hills Austr.
97 C2 Greystones Rep. of Ireland
123 D2 Greytown S. Africa
91 E1 Gribanovskiy Rus. Fed.
118 B2 Gribingui r. C.A.R.
101 D3 Griesheim Ger.
141 D2 Griffin U.S.A.
53 C2 Griffith Austr.
88 C3 Grigishkés Lith.
118 C2 Grimari C.A.R.
101 F2 Grimma Ger.
102 C1 Grimmen Ger.
98 C3 Grimsby U.K.
128 C2 Grimshaw Can.
92 □B2 Grímsstaðir Iceland
93 E4 Grimstad Norway
92 □A3 Grindavík Iceland
93 E4 Grindsted Denmark
137 E2 Grinnell Can.
123 C3 Griqualand East reg.
S. Africa
122 B2 Griqualand West reg.
S. Africa
123 C2 Griquatown S. Africa
127 G1 Grise Fiord Can.
Grishino Ukr. see
Krasnoarmiys'k
99 D4 Gris Nez, Cap c. France
96 C1 Gritley U.K.
123 C2 Groblersdal S. Africa
122 B2 Groblershoop S. Africa
Grodno Belarus see
Hrodna
103 D1 Grodzisk Wielkopolski
Pol.
92 □A3 Gróf Iceland
104 B2 Groix, Île de i. France
100 C1 Gronau (Westfalen) Ger.
92 F3 Grong Norway
100 C1 Groningen Neth.
122 B3 Groot Brakrivier S. Africa
122 B2 Grootdrink S. Africa
51 C1 Groote Eylandt i. Austr.
120 A2 Grootfontein Namibia
122 A2 Groot Karas Berg plat.
Namibia
122 B3 Groot Swartberge mts

122 B2 Grootvloer salt pan
S. Africa
123 C3 Groot Winterberg mt.
S. Africa
101 D2 Großenlüder Ger.
101 E2 Großer Beerberg hill Ger.
102 C2 Großer Rachel mt. Ger.
103 C2 Grosser Speikkogel mt.
Austria
108 B2 Grosseto Italy
101 D3 Groß-Gerau Ger.
102 C2 Großglockner mt. Austria
100 C1 Groß-Hesepe Ger.
101 E2 Großlohra Ger.
122 A1 Gross Ums Namibia
136 A2 Gros Ventre Range mts
U.S.A.
131 E2 Groswater Bay Can.
130 B3 Groundhog r. Can.
135 B3 Grover Beach U.S.A.
140 B3 Groves U.S.A.
139 E2 Groveton U.S.A.
87 D4 Groznyy Rus. Fed.
109 C1 Grubišno Polje Croatia
Grudovo Bulg. see
Sredets
103 D1 Grudziądz Pol.
122 A2 Grünau Namibia
92 □A3 Grundarfjörður Iceland
Gruzinskaya S.S.R.
admin. reg. Asia see
Georgia
89 E3 Gryazi Rus. Fed.
89 F2 Gryazovets Rus. Fed.
103 D1 Gryfice Pol.
102 C1 Gryfino Pol.
153 E5 Grytviken S. Georgia
146 C2 Guacanayabo, Golfo de
b. Cuba
144 B2 Guadalajara Mex.
106 C1 Guadalajara Spain
48 H4 Guadalcanal i. Solomon Is
107 C1 Guadalope r. Spain
106 B2 Guadalquivir r. Spain
132 B4 Guadalupe i. Mex.
106 B2 Guadalupe, Sierra de mts
Spain
142 C2 Guadalupe Peak U.S.A.
144 B2 Guadalupe Victoria Mex.
144 B2 Guadalupe y Calvo Mex.
106 C1 Guadarrama, Sierra de
mts Spain
147 D3 Guadeloupe terr.
West Indies
147 D3 Guadeloupe Passage
Caribbean Sea
106 B2 Guadiana r. Port./Spain
106 C2 Guadix Spain
154 B2 Guaíra Brazil
147 C3 Guajira, Península de la
pen. Col.
150 B3 Gualaceo Ecuador
59 D2 Guam terr.
N. Pacific Ocean
144 B2 Guamúchil Mex.
144 B2 Guanacevi Mex.
151 E4 Guanambi Brazil
150 C2 Guanare Venez.
146 B2 Guane Cuba
70 A2 Guang'an China
71 B3 Guangchang China
71 B3 Guangdong prov. China
Guanghua China see
Laohekou
71 A3 Guangxi Zhuangzu
Zizhiqu aut. reg. China
70 A2 Guangyuan China
71 B3 Guangzhou China
155 D1 Guanhães Brazil
147 D4 Guanipa r. Venez.
71 A3 Guanling China
65 A1 Guanshui China
71 B3 Guansuo China see
Guanling
147 C2 Guantánamo Cuba
155 C2 Guapé Brazil
150 C4 Guaporé r. Bol./Brazil
155 D2 Guaporé Brazil
154 B3 Guarapuava Brazil
155 C2 Guaraqueçaba Brazil
155 C2 Guaratinguetá Brazil
154 C3 Guaratuba Brazil
106 B1 Guarda Port.
Guardafui, Cape Somalia
see Gwardafuy, Gees
154 C1 Guarda Mor Brazil
106 C1 Guardo Spain
155 C2 Guarujá Brazil
144 B2 Guasave Mex.
146 A3 Guatemala country
Central America

Guatemala Guat. see Guatemala City
157 G5 Guatemala Basin sea feature N. Pacific Ocean
146 A3 Guatemala City Guat.
150 C2 Guaviare r. Col.
155 C2 Guaxupé Brazil
150 B3 Guayaquil Ecuador
150 A3 Guayaquil, Golfo de g. Ecuador
152 B1 Guayaramerín Bol.
144 A2 Guaymas Mex.
117 B3 Guba Eth.
86 E1 Guba Dolgaya Rus. Fed.
108 B2 Gubbio Italy
89 E3 Gubkin Rus. Fed.
73 C3 Gudivada India
105 D2 Guebwiller France
Guecho Spain see Algorta
114 A2 Guelb er Rîchât hill Maur.
115 C1 Guelma Alg.
114 A2 Guelmine Morocco
130 B3 Guelph Can.
145 C2 Guémez Mex.
104 B2 Guérande France
115 E2 Guerende Libya
104 C2 Guéret France
95 C4 Guernsey i. Channel Is
95 C4 Guernsey terr. Channel Is
144 A2 Guerrero Negro Mex.
131 D2 Guers, Lac l. Can.
158 D4 Guiana Basin sea feature N. Atlantic Ocean
150 C2 Guiana Highlands mts Guyana/Venez.
Guichi China see Chizhou
118 B2 Guider Cameroon
108 B2 Guidonia-Montecelio Italy
71 A3 Guigang China
100 A3 Guignicourt France
123 D1 Guija Moz.
99 C4 Guildford U.K.
71 B3 Guilin China
130 C2 Guillaume-Delisle, Lac l. Can.
106 B1 Guimarães Port.
114 A3 Guinea country Africa
113 D5 Guinea, Gulf of Africa
114 A3 Guinea-Bissau country Africa
104 B2 Guingamp France
104 B2 Guipavas France
154 B1 Guiratinga Brazil
150 C1 Güiria Venez.
151 D2 Guisanbourg Fr. Guiana
98 C2 Guisborough U.K.
100 A3 Guise France
64 B2 Guiuan Phil.
71 A3 Guiyang China
71 A3 Guizhou prov. China
104 B3 Gujan-Mestras France
74 B2 Gujarat state India
Gujerat state India see Gujarat
74 B1 Gujranwala Pak.
74 B1 Gujrat Pak.
91 D2 Gukovo Rus. Fed.
70 A2 Gulang China
53 C2 Gulargambone Austr.
73 B3 Gulbarga India
88 C2 Gulbene Latvia
79 C2 Gulf, The Asia
Gulf of California Mex. see California, Gulf of
Gulf of Chihli China see Bo Hai
111 B3 Gulf of Corinth sea chan. Greece
140 C2 Gulfport U.S.A.
53 C2 Gulgong Austr.
69 E1 Gulian China
77 C2 Guliston Uzbek.
Gulja China see Yining
129 D2 Gull Lake Can.
111 C3 Güllük Turkey
Gulü China see Xincai
119 D2 Gulu Uganda
120 B2 Gumare Botswana
76 B3 Gumdag Turkm.
115 C3 Gumel Nigeria
75 C2 Gumla India
100 C2 Gummersbach Ger.
87 C4 Gümüşhane Turkey
74 B2 Guna India
Gunan China see Qijiang
53 C3 Gundagai Austr.
111 C3 Güney Turkey
118 B3 Gungu Dem. Rep. Congo
129 E2 Gunisao r. Can.
53 D2 Gunnedah Austr.
136 B3 Gunnison CO U.S.A.
135 D3 Gunnison UT U.S.A.
136 B3 Gunnison r. U.S.A.
73 B3 Guntakal India
73 C3 Guntur India
51 C1 Gununa Austr.
60 A1 Gunungsitoli Indon.
60 A1 Gunungtua Indon.
102 C2 Günzburg Ger.
102 C2 Gunzenhausen Ger.
70 B2 Guojiaba China
Guoluezhen China see Lingbao
74 B2 Gurgaon India
151 E3 Gurgueia r. Brazil
150 C2 Guri, Embalse de resr Venez.
154 C1 Gurinhatã Brazil
121 C2 Guro Moz.
151 E4 Gurupi Brazil
151 E3 Gurupi r. Brazil
74 B2 Guru Sikhar mt. India
121 C2 Guruve Zimbabwe
Gur'yev Kazakh. see Atyrau
115 C3 Gusau Nigeria
88 B3 Gusev Rus. Fed.
65 A2 Gushan China
74 A1 Gushgy Turkm.
70 B2 Gushi China
83 I3 Gusinoozersk Rus. Fed.
89 F2 Gus'-Khrustal'nyy Rus. Fed.
108 A3 Guspini Sardinia Italy
128 A2 Gustavus U.S.A.
101 F1 Güstrow Ger.
101 D2 Gütersloh Ger.
143 D1 Guthrie U.S.A.
152 B1 Gutiérrez Bol.
121 C2 Gutu Zimbabwe
75 D2 Guwahati India
150 D2 Guyana country S. America
Guyi China see Sanjiang
143 C1 Guymon U.S.A.
53 D2 Guyra Austr.
70 A2 Guyuan China
Guzhou China see Rongjiang
144 B1 Guzmán Mex.
144 B1 Guzmán, Lago de l. Mex.
77 C3 G'uzor Uzbek.
88 B3 Gvardeysk Rus. Fed.
74 A2 Gwadar Pak.
Gwador Pak. see Gwadar
74 B2 Gwalior India
121 B3 Gwanda Zimbabwe
117 D3 Gwardafuy, Gees c. Somalia
97 B1 Gweebarra Bay Rep. of Ireland
97 B1 Gweedore Rep. of Ireland
Gwelo Zimbabwe see Gweru
121 B2 Gweru Zimbabwe
115 D3 Gwoza Nigeria
53 D2 Gwydir r. Austr.
Gya'gya China see Saga
Gyandzha Azer. see Gäncä
Gyangkar China see Dinngyê
Gyangtse China see Gyangzê
75 C2 Gyangzê China
75 C1 Gyaring Co l. China
68 C2 Gyaring Hu l. China
86 G1 Gydan Peninsula pen. Rus. Fed.
Gydanskiy Poluostrov pen. Rus. Fed. see Gydan Peninsula
Gyêgu China see Yushu
62 A1 Gyigang China
Gyixong China see Gonggar
51 E2 Gympie Austr.
62 A2 Gyobingauk Myanmar
103 D2 Gyöngyös Hungary
103 D2 Győr Hungary
136 B3 Gypsum U.S.A.
129 E2 Gypsumville Can.
131 D2 Gyrfalcon Islands Can.
111 B3 Gytheio Greece
103 E2 Gyula Hungary
81 C1 Gyumri Armenia
76 B3 Gyzylarbat Turkm.
Gzhatsk Rus. Fed. see Gagarin

H

88 B2 Haapsalu Estonia
100 B1 Haarlem Neth.
122 B3 Haarlem S. Africa
101 C2 Haarstrang ridge Ger.
54 A2 Haast N.Z.
74 A2 Hab r. Pak.
79 C3 Ḩabarūt Oman
78 B3 Habbān Yemen
81 C2 Ḩabbānīyah, Hawr al l. Iraq
70 B1 Habirag China
67 C4 Hachijō-jima i. Japan
66 D2 Hachinohe Japan
67 C3 Hachiōji Japan
121 C3 Hacufera Moz.
116 A2 Ḩaḑabat al Jilf al Kabīr Egypt
79 C2 Ḩadd, Ra's al pt Oman
96 C3 Haddington U.K.
115 D3 Hadejia Nigeria
93 E4 Haderslev Denmark
78 B2 Ḩādhah Saudi Arabia
79 B3 Ḩaḑramawt reg. Yemen
79 B3 Ḩaḑramawt, Wādī watercourse Yemen
91 C1 Hadyach Ukr.
65 B2 Haeju N. Korea
65 B2 Haeju-man b. N. Korea
65 B3 Haenam S. Korea
78 B2 Ḩafar al Bāṭin Saudi Arabia
74 B1 Hafizabad Pak.
75 D2 Haflong India
92 □A3 Hafnarfjörður Iceland
78 A3 Hagar Nish Plateau Eritrea
59 D2 Hagåtña Guam
101 F1 Hagelberg hill Ger.
100 C2 Hagen Ger.
101 E1 Hagenow Ger.
128 B2 Hagensborg Can.
139 D3 Hagerstown U.S.A.
93 F3 Hagfors Sweden
134 D1 Haggin, Mount U.S.A.
67 B4 Hagi Japan
62 B1 Ha Giang Vietnam
97 B2 Hag's Head hd Rep. of Ireland
104 B2 Hague, Cap de la c. France
69 F3 Hahajima-rettō is Japan
119 D3 Hai Tanz.
Haicheng China see Haifeng
70 C1 Haicheng China
62 B1 Hai Dương Vietnam
80 B2 Haifa Israel
71 B3 Haifeng China
Haikang China see Leizhou
71 B3 Haikou China
78 B2 Ḩā'il Saudi Arabia
Hailar China see Hulun Buir
Hailong China see Meihekou
92 H2 Hailuoto i. Fin.
69 D3 Hainan i. China
71 A4 Hainan prov. China
128 A2 Haines U.S.A.
128 A1 Haines Junction Can.
101 E2 Hainich ridge Ger.
101 E2 Hainleite ridge Ger.
62 B1 Hai Phong Vietnam
Haiphong Vietnam see Hai Phong
147 C3 Haiti country West Indies
116 B3 Haiya Sudan
103 E2 Hajdúböszörmény Hungary
103 E2 Hajdúszoboszló Hungary
67 C3 Hajiki-zaki pt Japan
78 B3 Ḩajjah Yemen
81 D3 Ḩājjīābād Iran
103 E1 Hajnówka Pol.
62 A1 Haka Myanmar
81 C2 Hakkâri Turkey
66 D2 Hakodate Japan
122 B2 Hakseen Pan salt pan S. Africa
Ḩalab Syria see Aleppo
78 B2 Ḩalabān Saudi Arabia
81 C2 Ḩalabja Iraq
116 B2 Halaib Sudan
78 A2 Halaib Triangle terr. Egypt/Sudan
79 C3 Ḩalāniyāt, Juzur al is Oman
78 A2 Ḩālat 'Ammār Saudi Arabia
68 C1 Halban Mongolia
101 E2 Halberstadt Ger.
64 B2 Halcon, Mount Phil.
93 F4 Halden Norway
101 E1 Haldensleben Ger.
75 B2 Haldwani India
79 C2 Ḩāleh Iran
54 A3 Halfmoon Bay N.Z.
139 D1 Haliburton Highlands hills Can.
131 D3 Halifax Can.
98 C3 Halifax U.K.
139 D3 Halifax U.S.A.
65 B3 Halla-san mt. S. Korea
127 G2 Hall Beach Can.
100 B2 Halle Belgium
102 C2 Hallein Austria
101 E2 Halle-Neustadt Ger.
101 E2 Halle (Saale) Ger.
48 G3 Hall Islands Micronesia
137 D1 Hallock U.S.A.
127 H2 Hall Peninsula Can.
50 B1 Halls Creek Austr.
59 C2 Halmahera i. Indon.
93 F4 Halmstad Sweden
Hälsingborg Sweden see Helsingborg
100 B2 Halsteren Neth.
98 B2 Haltwhistle U.K.
67 B4 Hamada Japan
81 C2 Hamadān Iran
80 B2 Ḩamāh Syria
67 C4 Hamamatsu Japan
93 F3 Hamar Norway
116 B2 Ḩamāṭah, Jabal mt. Egypt
73 C4 Hambantota Sri Lanka
101 D1 Hamburg Ger.
123 C3 Hamburg S. Africa
140 B2 Hamburg U.S.A.
78 A2 Ḩamḑ, Wādī al watercourse Saudi Arabia
78 B3 Ḩamḑah Saudi Arabia
139 E2 Hamden U.S.A.
93 H3 Hämeenlinna Fin.
101 D1 Hameln Ger.
50 A2 Hamersley Range mts Austr.
65 B1 Hamgyŏng-sanmaek mts N. Korea
65 B2 Hamhŭng N. Korea
68 C2 Hami China
116 B2 Hamid Sudan
52 B3 Hamilton Austr.
130 C3 Hamilton Can.
Hamilton r. Can. see Churchill
54 C1 Hamilton N.Z.
96 B3 Hamilton U.K.
140 C2 Hamilton AL U.S.A.
134 D1 Hamilton MT U.S.A.
138 C3 Hamilton OH U.S.A.
115 E1 Hamīm, Wādī al watercourse Libya
93 I3 Hamina Fin.
100 C2 Hamm Ger.
114 B2 Hammada du Drâa plat. Alg.
115 D1 Hammamet, Golfe de g. Tunisia
81 C2 Ḩammār, Hawr al imp. l. Iraq
101 D2 Hammelburg Ger.
92 G3 Hammerdal Sweden
92 H1 Hammerfest Norway
140 B2 Hammond U.S.A.
139 E3 Hammonton U.S.A.
139 D3 Hampton U.S.A.
139 E2 Hampton Bays U.S.A.
79 C2 Hāmūn-e Jaz Mūrīān salt marsh Iran
74 A2 Hamun-i-Lora dry lake Pak.
74 A2 Hamun-i-Mashkel salt flat Pak.
78 A2 Ḩanak Saudi Arabia
66 D3 Hanamaki Japan
101 D2 Hanau Ger.
70 B2 Hancheng China
138 B1 Hancock U.S.A.
70 B2 Handan China
119 D3 Handeni Tanz.
135 C3 Hanford U.S.A.
68 C1 Hangayn Nuruu mts Mongolia
Hangchow China see Hangzhou
Hanggin Houqi China see Xamba
Hangö Fin. see Hanko

70 B2 **Hangu** China
70 C2 **Hangzhou** China
70 C2 **Hangzhou Wan** *b.* China
79 B2 **Ḩanīdh** Saudi Arabia
Hanjia China *see* **Pengshui**
Hanjiang China *see* **Yangzhou**
93 H4 **Hanko** Fin.
135 D3 **Hanksville** U.S.A.
54 B2 **Hanmer Springs** N.Z.
128 C2 **Hanna** Can.
136 B2 **Hanna** U.S.A.
137 E3 **Hannibal** U.S.A.
101 D1 **Hannover** Ger.
101 D2 **Hannoversch Münden** Ger.
93 F4 **Hanöbukten** *b.* Sweden
62 B1 **Ha Nôi** Vietnam
Hanoi Vietnam *see* **Ha Nôi**
130 B3 **Hanover** Can.
Hanover Ger. *see* **Hannover**
122 B3 **Hanover** S. Africa
139 E2 **Hanover** *NH* U.S.A.
139 D3 **Hanover** *PA* U.S.A.
92 G2 **Hansnes** Norway
93 E4 **Hanstholm** Denmark
88 C3 **Hantsavichy** Belarus
75 C2 **Hanumana** India
74 B2 **Hanumangarh** India
70 A2 **Hanzhong** China
49 M5 **Hao** *atoll* Fr. Polynesia
75 C2 **Haora** India
92 H2 **Haparanda** Sweden
100 B2 **Hapert** Neth.
131 D2 **Happy Valley-Goose Bay** Can.
78 A2 **Ḩaql** Saudi Arabia
79 B2 **Ḩaradh** Saudi Arabia
88 C2 **Haradok** Belarus
78 B3 **Ḩarajā** Saudi Arabia
121 C2 **Harare** Zimbabwe
79 C3 **Ḩarāsīs, Jiddat al** *des.* Oman
69 D1 **Har-Ayrag** Mongolia
115 E3 **Haraze-Mangueigne** Chad
114 A4 **Harbel** Liberia
69 E1 **Harbin** China
138 C2 **Harbor Beach** U.S.A.
131 E3 **Harbour Breton** Can.
74 B2 **Harda** India
92 E4 **Hardangerfjorden** *sea chan.* Norway
61 C1 **Harden, Bukit** *mt.* Indon.
100 C1 **Hardenberg** Neth.
100 B1 **Harderwijk** Neth.
122 A3 **Hardeveld** *mts* S. Africa
134 E1 **Hardin** U.S.A.
128 C1 **Hardisty Lake** Can.
93 E3 **Hareid** Norway
100 C1 **Haren (Ems)** Ger.
117 C4 **Hārer** Eth.
117 C4 **Hargeysa** Somalia
110 C1 **Harghita-Mădăraş, Vârful** *mt.* Romania
68 C2 **Har Hu** *l.* China
88 B2 **Hari kurk** *sea chan.* Estonia
74 B1 **Haripur** Pak.
74 A1 **Hari Rūd** *r.* Afgh./Iran
110 C1 **Hârlău** Romania
100 B1 **Harlingen** Neth.
143 D3 **Harlingen** U.S.A.
99 D4 **Harlow** U.K.
134 E1 **Harlowton** U.S.A.
134 C2 **Harney Basin** U.S.A.
134 C2 **Harney Lake** U.S.A.
93 G3 **Härnösand** Sweden
69 E1 **Har Nur** China
68 C1 **Har Nuur** *l.* Mongolia
96 □ **Haroldswick** U.K.
114 B4 **Harper** Liberia
101 D1 **Harpstedt** Ger.
130 C2 **Harricanaw** *r.* Can.
53 D2 **Harrington** Austr.
131 E2 **Harrington Harbour** Can.
96 A2 **Harris** *pen.* U.K.
96 A2 **Harris, Sound of** *sea chan.* U.K.
138 B3 **Harrisburg** *IL* U.S.A.
134 B2 **Harrisburg** *OR* U.S.A.
139 D2 **Harrisburg** *PA* U.S.A.
123 C2 **Harrismith** S. Africa
140 B1 **Harrison** U.S.A.
131 E2 **Harrison, Cape** Can.
126 B2 **Harrison Bay** U.S.A.
139 D3 **Harrisonburg** U.S.A.
128 B3 **Harrison Lake** Can.
137 E3 **Harrisonville** U.S.A.
98 C3 **Harrogate** U.K.
110 C2 **Hârşova** Romania
92 G2 **Harstad** Norway
122 B2 **Hartbees** *watercourse* S. Africa
103 D2 **Hartberg** Austria
139 E2 **Hartford** *CT* U.S.A.
137 D2 **Hartford** *SD* U.S.A.
99 A4 **Hartland Point** U.K.
98 C2 **Hartlepool** U.K.
Hartley Zimbabwe *see* **Chegutu**
128 B2 **Hartley Bay** Can.
123 B2 **Harts** *r.* S. Africa
141 D2 **Hartwell Reservoir** U.S.A.
68 C1 **Har Us Nuur** *l.* Mongolia
136 C1 **Harvey** U.S.A.
99 D4 **Harwich** U.K.
74 B2 **Haryana** *state* India
101 E2 **Harz** *hills* Ger.
101 E2 **Harzgerode** Ger.
78 B2 **Ḩasan, Jabal** *hill* Saudi Arabia
80 B2 **Hasan Dağı** *mts* Turkey
99 C4 **Haslemere** U.K.
73 B3 **Hassan** India
100 B2 **Hasselt** Belgium
101 E2 **Haßfurt** Ger.
115 C2 **Hassi Bel Guebbour** Alg.
115 C1 **Hassi Messaoud** Alg.
93 F4 **Hässleholm** Sweden
100 B2 **Hastière-Lavaux** Belgium
53 C3 **Hastings** *Vic.* Austr.
54 C1 **Hastings** N.Z.
99 D4 **Hastings** U.K.
137 E2 **Hastings** *MN* U.S.A.
137 D2 **Hastings** *NE* U.S.A.
Hatay Turkey *see* **Antakya**
142 B2 **Hatch** U.S.A.
129 D2 **Hatchet Lake** Can.
110 B1 **Haţeg** Romania
52 B2 **Hatfield** Austr.
68 C1 **Hatgal** Mongolia
62 B2 **Ha Tinh** Vietnam
52 B2 **Hattah** Austr.
141 E1 **Hatteras, Cape** U.S.A.
157 H3 **Hatteras Abyssal Plain** *sea feature* S. Atlantic Ocean
140 C2 **Hattiesburg** U.S.A.
100 C2 **Hattingen** Ger.
63 B3 **Hat Yai** Thai.
117 C4 **Haud** *reg.* Eth.
93 E4 **Haugesund** Norway
93 E4 **Haukeligrend** Norway
92 I2 **Haukipudas** Fin.
54 C1 **Hauraki Gulf** N.Z.
54 A3 **Hauroko, Lake** N.Z.
114 B1 **Haut Atlas** *mts* Morocco
131 D3 **Hauterive** Can.
Haute-Volta *country* Africa *see* **Burkina**
114 B1 **Hauts Plateaux** Alg.
146 B2 **Havana** Cuba
99 C4 **Havant** U.K.
101 E1 **Havel** *r.* Ger.
101 F1 **Havelberg** Ger.
54 B2 **Havelock** N.Z.
Havelock Swaziland *see* **Bulembu**
54 C1 **Havelock North** N.Z.
99 A4 **Haverfordwest** U.K.
100 C2 **Havixbeck** Ger.
103 D2 **Havlíčkův Brod** Czech Rep.
92 H1 **Havøysund** Norway
111 C3 **Havran** Turkey
134 E1 **Havre** U.S.A.
131 D3 **Havre Aubert** Can.
131 D2 **Havre-St-Pierre** Can.
49 L2 **Hawai'i** *i.* U.S.A.
156 E4 **Hawai'ian Islands** *is* N. Pacific Ocean
78 B2 **Ḩawallī** Kuwait
98 B3 **Hawarden** U.K.
54 A2 **Hawea, Lake** N.Z.
54 B1 **Hawera** N.Z.
98 B2 **Hawes** U.K.
96 C3 **Hawick** U.K.
54 C1 **Hawke Bay** N.Z.
52 A2 **Hawker** Austr.
52 B1 **Hawkers Gate** Austr.
122 A3 **Hawston** S. Africa
135 C3 **Hawthorne** U.S.A.
52 B2 **Hay** Austr.
128 C1 **Hay** *r.* Can.
100 C3 **Hayange** France
81 C2 **Haydarābad** Iran
134 C1 **Hayden** U.S.A.
129 E2 **Hayes** *r. Man.* Can.
126 F2 **Hayes** *r. Nunavut* Can.
79 C3 **Haymā'** Oman
77 C2 **Hayotboshi tog'i** *mt.* Uzbek.
111 C2 **Hayrabolu** Turkey
128 C1 **Hay River** Can.
137 D3 **Hays** U.S.A.
78 B3 **Ḩays** Yemen
90 B2 **Haysyn** Ukr.
135 B3 **Hayward** U.S.A.
99 C4 **Haywards Heath** U.K.
74 A1 **Hazarajat** *reg.* Afgh.
138 C3 **Hazard** U.S.A.
75 C2 **Hazaribagh** India
75 C2 **Hazaribagh Range** *mts* India
104 C1 **Hazebrouck** France
128 B2 **Hazelton** Can.
139 D2 **Hazleton** U.S.A.
135 B3 **Healdsburg** U.S.A.
53 C3 **Healesville** Austr.
159 E7 **Heard Island** Indian Ocean
143 D2 **Hearne** U.S.A.
130 B3 **Hearst** Can.
55 A3 **Hearst Island** Antarctica
70 B2 **Hebei** *prov.* China
53 C1 **Hebel** Austr.
140 B1 **Heber Springs** U.S.A.
70 B2 **Hebi** China
131 D2 **Hebron** Can.
128 A2 **Hecate Strait** Can.
71 A3 **Hechi** China
100 B2 **Hechtel** Belgium
54 C2 **Hector, Mount** N.Z.
93 F3 **Hede** Sweden
100 C1 **Heerde** Neth.
100 B1 **Heerenveen** Neth.
100 B1 **Heerhugowaard** Neth.
100 B2 **Heerlen** Neth.
Ḩefa Israel *see* **Haifa**
70 B2 **Hefei** China
70 B3 **Hefeng** China
69 E1 **Hegang** China
119 D1 **Heiban** Sudan
102 B1 **Heide** Ger.
122 A1 **Heide** Namibia
101 D3 **Heidelberg** Ger.
122 B3 **Heidelberg** S. Africa
69 E1 **Heihe** China
102 B2 **Heilbronn** Ger.
69 E1 **Heilong Jiang** *r.* China/Rus. Fed.
93 I3 **Heinola** Fin.
Hejaz *reg.* Saudi Arabia *see* **Hijaz**
92 A3 **Hekla** *vol.* Iceland
92 F3 **Helagsfjället** *mt.* Sweden
70 A2 **Helan Shan** *mts* China
140 B2 **Helena** *AR* U.S.A.
134 D1 **Helena** *MT* U.S.A.
96 B2 **Helensburgh** U.K.
102 B1 **Helgoland** *i.* Ger.
102 B1 **Helgoländer Bucht** *b.* Ger.
Heligoland *i.* Ger. *see* **Helgoland**
Heligoland Bight *b.* Ger. *see* **Helgoländer Bucht**
Helixi China *see* **Ningguo**
92 □A3 **Hella** Iceland
100 B2 **Hellevoetsluis** Neth.
107 C2 **Hellín** Spain
Hell-Ville Madag. *see* **Andoany**
76 C3 **Helmand** *r.* Afgh.
101 E2 **Helmbrechts** Ger.
122 A2 **Helmeringhausen** Namibia
100 B2 **Helmond** Neth.
96 C1 **Helmsdale** U.K.
96 C1 **Helmsdale** *r.* U.K.
98 C2 **Helmsley** U.K.
101 E1 **Helmstedt** Ger.
65 B1 **Helong** China
143 D3 **Helotes** U.S.A.
93 F4 **Helsingborg** Sweden
Helsingfors Fin. *see* **Helsinki**
93 F4 **Helsingør** Denmark
93 H3 **Helsinki** Fin.
99 A4 **Helston** U.K.
97 C2 **Helvick Head** *hd* Rep. of Ireland
99 C4 **Hemel Hempstead** U.K.
101 D1 **Hemmoor** Ger.
92 F2 **Hemnesberget** Norway
70 B2 **Henan** *prov.* China
111 D2 **Hendek** Turkey
138 B3 **Henderson** *KY* U.S.A.
141 E1 **Henderson** *NC* U.S.A.
135 D3 **Henderson** *NV* U.S.A.
143 E2 **Henderson** *TX* U.S.A.
49 O6 **Henderson Island** Pitcairn Is
141 D1 **Hendersonville** U.S.A.
99 C4 **Hendon** U.K.
62 A1 **Hengduan Shan** *mts* China
100 C1 **Hengelo** Neth.
Hengnan China *see* **Hengyang**
71 B3 **Hengshan** China
70 B2 **Hengshui** China
71 A3 **Hengxian** China
71 B3 **Hengyang** China
Hengzhou China *see* **Hengxian**
91 C2 **Heniches'k** Ukr.
139 D3 **Henlopen, Cape** U.S.A.
100 C2 **Hennef (Sieg)** Ger.
130 B2 **Henrietta Maria, Cape** Can.
Henrique de Carvalho Angola *see* **Saurimo**
139 D3 **Henry, Cape** U.S.A.
143 D1 **Henryetta** U.S.A.
127 H2 **Henry Kater, Cape** Can.
101 D1 **Henstedt-Ulzburg** Ger.
120 A3 **Hentiesbaai** Namibia
101 D3 **Heppenheim (Bergstraße)** Ger.
71 A3 **Hepu** China
76 C3 **Herāt** Afgh.
129 D2 **Herbert** Can.
54 C2 **Herbertville** N.Z.
101 D2 **Herbstein** Ger.
109 C2 **Herceg-Novi** Serb. and Mont.
99 B3 **Hereford** U.K.
143 C2 **Hereford** U.S.A.
101 D1 **Herford** Ger.
100 C2 **Herkenbosch** Neth.
96 □ **Herma Ness** *hd* U.K.
122 A3 **Hermanus** S. Africa
53 C2 **Hermidale** Austr.
134 C1 **Hermiston** U.S.A.
59 D3 **Hermit Islands** P.N.G.
144 A2 **Hermosillo** Mex.
154 B3 **Hernandarias** Para.
100 C2 **Herne** Ger.
93 E4 **Herning** Denmark
104 B2 **Hérouville-St-Clair** France
106 B2 **Herrera del Duque** Spain
139 D2 **Hershey** U.S.A.
99 C4 **Hertford** U.K.
123 C2 **Hertzogville** S. Africa
51 E2 **Hervey Bay** Austr.
101 F2 **Herzberg** Ger.
101 E3 **Herzogenaurach** Ger.
71 A3 **Heshan** China
135 C4 **Hesperia** U.S.A.
128 A1 **Hess** *r.* Can.
101 E1 **Hessen** Ger.
101 D2 **Hessisch Lichtenau** Ger.
136 C1 **Hettinger** U.S.A.
101 E2 **Hettstedt** Ger.
98 B2 **Hexham** U.K.
98 B2 **Heysham** U.K.
71 B3 **Heyuan** China
52 B3 **Heywood** Austr.
70 B2 **Heze** China
71 B3 **Hezhou** China
141 D3 **Hialeah** U.S.A.
137 D3 **Hiawatha** U.S.A.
137 E1 **Hibbing** U.S.A.
141 D1 **Hickory** U.S.A.
54 C1 **Hicks Bay** N.Z.
66 D2 **Hidaka-sanmyaku** *mts* Japan
143 D3 **Hidalgo** Mex.
145 C2 **Hidalgo** Mex.
144 B2 **Hidalgo del Parral** Mex.
154 C1 **Hidrolândia** Brazil
67 A4 **Higashi-suidō** *sea chan.* Japan
High Atlas *mts* Morocco *see* **Haut Atlas**
134 B2 **High Desert** U.S.A.
128 C2 **High Level** Can.
141 E1 **High Point** U.S.A.
128 C2 **High Prairie** Can.
128 C2 **High River** Can.
129 D2 **Highrock Lake** Can.
High Tatras *mts* Pol./Slovakia *see* **Tatry**
99 C4 **High Wycombe** U.K.
88 B2 **Hiiumaa** *i.* Estonia
78 A2 **Hijaz** *reg.* Saudi Arabia
54 C1 **Hikurangi** *mt.* N.Z.
101 E2 **Hildburghausen** Ger.
100 C2 **Hilden** Ger.
101 E2 **Hilders** Ger.
101 D1 **Hildesheim** Ger.
81 C2 **Hillah** Iraq
100 B1 **Hillegom** Neth.

100 C2 **Hillesheim** Ger.
138 C3 **Hillsboro** *OH* U.S.A.
143 D2 **Hillsboro** *TX* U.S.A.
53 C2 **Hillston** Austr.
96 □ **Hillswick** U.K.
49 L2 **Hilo** U.S.A.
141 D2 **Hilton Head Island** U.S.A.
100 B1 **Hilversum** Neth.
74 B1 **Himachal Pradesh** *state* India
68 B2 **Himalaya** *mts* Asia
74 B2 **Himatnagar** India
67 B4 **Himeji** Japan
123 C2 **Himeville** S. Africa
67 C3 **Himi** Japan
Ḥimṣ Syria *see* **Homs**
147 C3 **Hinche** Haiti
51 D1 **Hinchinbrook Island** Austr.
52 B3 **Hindmarsh, Lake** *dry lake* Austr.
74 A1 **Hindu Kush** *mts* Afgh./Pak.
73 B3 **Hindupur** India
134 C2 **Hines** U.S.A.
141 D2 **Hinesville** U.S.A.
74 B2 **Hinganghat** India
81 C2 **Hınıs** Turkey
92 G2 **Hinnøya** *i.* Norway
106 B2 **Hinojosa del Duque** Spain
100 C1 **Hinte** Ger.
62 A2 **Hinthada** Myanmar
128 C2 **Hinton** Can.
75 C2 **Hirakud Reservoir** India
Hîrlău Romania *see* **Hârlău**
66 D2 **Hiroo** Japan
66 D2 **Hirosaki** Japan
67 B4 **Hiroshima** Japan
101 E3 **Hirschaid** Ger.
101 E2 **Hirschberg** Ger.
105 C2 **Hirson** France
Hîrşova Romania *see* **Hârşova**
93 E4 **Hirtshals** Denmark
74 B2 **Hisar** India
147 C2 **Hispaniola** *i.* Caribbean Sea
81 C2 **Hīt** Iraq
67 D3 **Hitachi** Japan
67 D3 **Hitachinaka** Japan
92 E3 **Hitra** *i.* Norway
49 N4 **Hiva Oa** *i.* Fr. Polynesia
93 G4 **Hjälmaren** *l.* Sweden
129 D1 **Hjalmar Lake** Can.
93 F4 **Hjørring** Denmark
123 D2 **Hlabisa** S. Africa
92 □B2 **Hlíð** Iceland
91 C2 **Hlobyne** Ukr.
123 C2 **Hlohlowane** S. Africa
123 C2 **Hlotse** Lesotho
91 C1 **Hlukhiv** Ukr.
88 C3 **Hlusk** Belarus
88 C2 **Hlybokaye** Belarus
114 C4 **Ho** Ghana
122 A1 **Hoachanas** Namibia
120 A2 **Hoanib** *watercourse* Namibia
120 A2 **Hoarusib** *watercourse* Namibia
51 D4 **Hobart** Austr.
143 D1 **Hobart** U.S.A.
143 C2 **Hobbs** U.S.A.
93 E4 **Hobro** Denmark
117 C4 **Hobyo** Somalia
Hô Chi Minh Vietnam *see* **Ho Chi Minh City**
63 B2 **Ho Chi Minh City** Vietnam
114 B3 **Ḥôḍ** *reg.* Maur.
117 D3 **Hodda** *mt.* Somalia
78 B3 **Hodeidah** Yemen
103 E2 **Hódmezővásárhely** Hungary
Hoek van Holland Neth. *see* **Hook of Holland**
65 B2 **Hoeyang** N. Korea
101 E2 **Hof** Ger.
101 E2 **Hofheim in Unterfranken** Ger.
92 □B3 **Höfn** Iceland
92 □A2 **Höfn** Iceland
92 □B3 **Hofsjökull** *ice cap* Iceland
67 B4 **Hōfu** Japan
115 C2 **Hoggar** *plat.* Alg.
93 G4 **Högsby** Sweden
93 E3 **Høgste Breakulen** *mt.* Norway
101 D2 **Hohe Rhön** *mts* Ger.
100 C2 **Hohe Venn** *moorland* Belgium
70 B1 **Hohhot** China
75 C1 **Hoh Xil Shan** *mts* China
63 B2 **Hôi An** Vietnam
119 D2 **Hoima** Uganda
62 B1 **Hôi Xuân** Vietnam
75 D2 **Hojai** India
54 B2 **Hokitika** N.Z.
66 D2 **Hokkaidō** *i.* Japan
91 C2 **Hola Prystan'** Ukr.
128 B2 **Holberg** Can.
53 C3 **Holbrook** Austr.
142 A2 **Holbrook** U.S.A.
137 D2 **Holdrege** U.S.A.
146 C2 **Holguín** Cuba
92 □B2 **Hóll** Iceland
103 D2 **Hollabrunn** Austria
138 B2 **Holland** U.S.A.
Hollandia Indon. *see* **Jayapura**
135 B3 **Hollister** U.S.A.
103 E2 **Hollóháza** Hungary
93 I3 **Hollola** Fin.
100 B1 **Hollum** Neth.
140 C2 **Holly Springs** U.S.A.
134 C4 **Hollywood** U.S.A.
141 D3 **Hollywood** U.S.A.
92 F2 **Holm** Norway
126 E2 **Holman** Can.
92 H3 **Holmsund** Sweden
122 A2 **Holoog** Namibia
93 E4 **Holstebro** Denmark
141 D1 **Holston** *r.* U.S.A.
98 A3 **Holyhead** U.K.
98 C2 **Holy Island** *England* U.K.
98 A3 **Holy Island** *Wales* U.K.
136 C2 **Holyoke** U.S.A.
Holy See Europe *see* **Vatican City**
101 D2 **Holzminden** Ger.
62 A1 **Homalin** Myanmar
101 D2 **Homberg (Efze)** Ger.
114 B3 **Hombori** Mali
100 C3 **Homburg** Ger.
127 H2 **Home Bay** Can.
140 B2 **Homer** U.S.A.
141 D3 **Homestead** U.S.A.
92 F3 **Hommelvik** Norway
141 D3 **Homosassa Springs** U.S.A.
80 B2 **Homs** Syria
89 D3 **Homyel'** Belarus
Honan *prov.* China *see* **Henan**
122 A3 **Hondeklipbaai** S. Africa
145 D3 **Hondo** *r.* Belize/Mex.
142 B2 **Hondo** *NM* U.S.A.
143 D3 **Hondo** *TX* U.S.A.
146 B3 **Honduras** *country* Central America
146 B3 **Honduras, Gulf of** Belize/Hond.
93 F3 **Hønefoss** Norway
135 B2 **Honey Lake** U.S.A.
104 C2 **Honfleur** France
62 B1 **Hông Gai** Vietnam
70 B3 **Honghu** China
71 A3 **Hongjiang** China
71 B3 **Hong Kong** China
71 B3 **Hong Kong** *special admin. reg.* China
Hongqizhen China *see* **Wuzhishan**
131 D3 **Honguedo, Détroit d'** *sea chan.* Can.
65 B1 **Hongwŏn** N. Korea
70 B2 **Hongze Hu** *l.* China
48 H4 **Honiara** Solomon Is
99 B4 **Honiton** U.K.
66 D3 **Honjō** Japan
92 I1 **Honningsvåg** Norway
49 L1 **Honolulu** U.S.A.
67 B3 **Honshū** *i.* Japan
134 B1 **Hood, Mount** *vol.* U.S.A.
50 A3 **Hood Point** Austr.
134 B1 **Hood River** U.S.A.
100 B2 **Hoogerheide** Neth.
100 C1 **Hoogeveen** Neth.
100 C1 **Hoogezand-Sappemeer** Neth.
100 C2 **Hoog-Keppel** Neth.
100 B2 **Hook of Holland** Neth.
128 A2 **Hoonah** U.S.A.
123 C2 **Hoopstad** S. Africa
100 B1 **Hoorn** Neth.
49 J5 **Hoorn, Îles de** *is* Wallis and Futuna Is
128 B3 **Hope** Can.
140 B2 **Hope** U.S.A.
83 N2 **Hope, Point** U.S.A.
131 D2 **Hopedale** Can.
Hopei *prov.* China *see* **Hebei**
145 D3 **Hopelchén** Mex.
131 D2 **Hope Mountains** Can.
Hopes Advance Bay Can. *see* **Aupaluk**
52 B3 **Hopetoun** Austr.
122 B2 **Hopetown** S. Africa
139 D3 **Hopewell** U.S.A.
130 C2 **Hopewell Islands** Can.
50 B2 **Hopkins, Lake** *salt flat* Austr.
138 B3 **Hopkinsville** U.S.A.
134 B1 **Hoquiam** U.S.A.
81 C1 **Horasan** Turkey
93 F4 **Hörby** Sweden
89 D3 **Horki** Belarus
91 D2 **Horlivka** Ukr.
79 D2 **Hormak** Iran
79 C2 **Hormuz, Strait of** Iran/Oman
103 D2 **Horn** Austria
92 □A2 **Horn** *c.* Iceland
153 B5 **Horn, Cape** Chile
139 D2 **Hornell** U.S.A.
130 B3 **Hornepayne** Can.
Hornos, Cabo de *c.* Chile *see* **Horn, Cape**
53 D2 **Hornsby** Austr.
98 C3 **Hornsea** U.K.
90 B2 **Horodenka** Ukr.
91 C1 **Horodnya** Ukr.
90 B2 **Horodok** Ukr.
90 A2 **Horodok** Ukr.
90 A1 **Horokhiv** Ukr.
Horqin Youyi Qianqi China *see* **Ulanhot**
131 E2 **Horse Islands** Can.
52 B3 **Horsham** Austr.
99 C4 **Horsham** U.K.
93 F4 **Horten** Norway
126 D2 **Horton** *r.* Can.
117 B4 **Hosa'ina** Eth.
74 A2 **Hoshab** Pak.
74 B1 **Hoshiarpur** India
142 B1 **Hosta Butte** *mt.* U.S.A.
75 C1 **Hotan** China
122 B2 **Hotazel** S. Africa
92 G3 **Hoting** Sweden
140 B2 **Hot Springs** *AR* U.S.A.
Hot Springs U.S.A. *see* **Truth or Consequences**
136 C2 **Hot Springs** *SD* U.S.A.
128 C1 **Hottah Lake** Can.
100 B2 **Houffalize** Belgium
138 B1 **Houghton** U.S.A.
139 F1 **Houlton** U.S.A.
70 B2 **Houma** China
140 B3 **Houma** U.S.A.
128 B2 **Houston** Can.
143 D3 **Houston** U.S.A.
50 A2 **Houtman Abrolhos** *is* Austr.
122 B3 **Houwater** S. Africa
68 C1 **Hovd** Mongolia
99 C4 **Hove** U.K.
90 A2 **Hoverla, Hora** *mt.* Ukr.
68 C1 **Hövsgöl Nuur** *l.* Mongolia
68 C2 **Hövüün** Mongolia
116 A3 **Howar, Wadi** *watercourse* Sudan
98 C3 **Howden** U.K.
53 C3 **Howe, Cape** Austr.
123 D2 **Howick** S. Africa
49 J3 **Howland Island** *terr.* N. Pacific Ocean
53 C3 **Howlong** Austr.
Howrah India *see* **Haora**
140 B1 **Hoxie** U.S.A.
101 D2 **Höxter** Ger.
96 C1 **Hoy** *i.* U.K.
93 E3 **Høyanger** Norway
102 C1 **Hoyerswerda** Ger.
62 A2 **Hpapun** Myanmar
103 D1 **Hradec Králové** Czech Rep.
109 C2 **Hrasnica** Bos.-Herz.
92 □B2 **Hraun** Iceland
91 C1 **Hrebinka** Ukr.
88 B3 **Hrodna** Belarus
62 A1 **Hsi-hseng** Myanmar
71 C3 **Hsinchu** Taiwan
71 C3 **Hsinying** Taiwan
62 A1 **Hsipaw** Myanmar
70 A2 **Huachi** China
150 B4 **Huacho** Peru
70 B1 **Huade** China
65 B1 **Huadian** China
70 B2 **Huai'an** China
70 B2 **Huaibei** China
70 B2 **Huai He** *r.* China
71 A3 **Huaihua** China
70 B2 **Huainan** China
70 B2 **Huaiyang** China
145 C3 **Huajuápan de León** Mex.
59 C3 **Huaki** Indon.
71 C3 **Hualien** Taiwan
150 B3 **Huallaga** *r.* Peru
120 A2 **Huambo** Angola
150 B4 **Huancavelica** Peru
150 B4 **Huancayo** Peru
Huangcaoba China *see* **Xingyi**
70 B2 **Huangchuan** China
Huang Hai *sea* N. Pacific Ocean *see* **Yellow Sea**
Huang He *r.* China *see* **Yellow River**
71 A4 **Huangliu** China
70 B3 **Huangshan** China
70 B2 **Huangshi** China
70 A2 **Huangtu Gaoyuan** *plat.* China
71 C3 **Huangyan** China
70 A2 **Huangyuan** China
65 B1 **Huanren** China
150 B3 **Huánuco** Peru
152 B1 **Huanuni** Bol.
150 B4 **Huaral** Peru
150 B3 **Huaráz** Peru
150 B4 **Huarmey** Peru
152 A2 **Huasco** Chile
152 A2 **Huasco** *r.* Chile
144 B2 **Huatabampo** Mex.
145 C3 **Huatusco** Mex.
71 A3 **Huayuan** China
62 B1 **Huayxay** Laos
70 B2 **Hubei** *prov.* China
73 B3 **Hubli** India
100 C2 **Hückelhoven** Ger.
99 C3 **Hucknall** U.K.
98 C3 **Huddersfield** U.K.
93 G3 **Hudiksvall** Sweden
139 E2 **Hudson** *r.* U.S.A.
129 D2 **Hudson Bay** Can.
127 G3 **Hudson Bay** *sea* Can.
128 B2 **Hudson's Hope** Can.
127 H2 **Hudson Strait** Can.
63 B2 **Huê** Vietnam
146 A3 **Huehuetenango** Guat.
144 B2 **Huehueto, Cerro** *mt.* Mex.
145 C2 **Huejutla** Mex.
106 B2 **Huelva** Spain
107 C2 **Huércal-Overa** Spain
107 C1 **Huesca** Spain
106 C2 **Huéscar** Spain
51 D2 **Hughenden** Austr.
50 B3 **Hughes** Austr.
75 C2 **Hugli** *r. mouth* India
143 D2 **Hugo** U.S.A.
Huhehot China *see* **Hohhot**
122 B2 **Huhudi** S. Africa
122 A2 **Huib-Hoch Plateau** Namibia
71 B3 **Huichang** China
Huicheng China *see* **Huilai**
65 B1 **Huich'ŏn** N. Korea
71 B3 **Huilai** China
120 A2 **Huíla Plateau** Angola
71 A3 **Huili** China
70 B2 **Huimin** China
69 E2 **Huinan** China
Huinan China *see* **Nanhui**
93 H3 **Huittinen** Fin.
145 C3 **Huixtla** Mex.
71 A3 **Huize** China
68 C1 **Hujirt** Mongolia
78 B2 **Hujr** Saudi Arabia
122 B1 **Hukuntsi** Botswana
78 B2 **Ḥulayfah** Saudi Arabia
66 B1 **Hulin** China
130 C3 **Hull** Can.
70 C1 **Huludao** China
69 D1 **Hulun Buir** China
69 D1 **Hulun Nur** *l.* China
91 D2 **Hulyaypole** Ukr.
69 E1 **Huma** China
150 C3 **Humaitá** Brazil
122 B3 **Humansdorp** S. Africa
98 C2 **Humber** *est.* U.K.
143 D3 **Humble** U.S.A.
129 D2 **Humboldt** Can.
135 C2 **Humboldt** *NV* U.S.A.
140 C1 **Humboldt** *TN* U.S.A.
135 C2 **Humboldt** *r.* U.S.A.
103 E2 **Humenné** Slovakia
53 C3 **Hume Reservoir** Austr.
142 A1 **Humphreys Peak** U.S.A.
115 D2 **Hūn** Libya
92 □A2 **Húnaflói** *b.* Iceland
71 B3 **Hunan** *prov.* China
65 C1 **Hunchun** China
110 B1 **Hunedoara** Romania
101 D2 **Hünfeld** Ger.

103 D2 **Hungary** *country* Europe
52 B1 **Hungerford** Austr.
65 B2 **Hŭngnam** N. Korea
65 A1 **Hun He** *r.* China
Hunjiang China *see* **Baishan**
99 D3 **Hunstanton** U.K.
101 D1 **Hunte** *r.* Ger.
48 I6 **Hunter Island** S. Pacific Ocean
51 D4 **Hunter Islands** Austr.
99 C3 **Huntingdon** U.K.
138 B2 **Huntington** *IN* U.S.A.
138 C3 **Huntington** *WV* U.S.A.
135 C4 **Huntington Beach** U.S.A.
54 C1 **Huntly** N.Z.
96 C2 **Huntly** U.K.
130 C3 **Huntsville** Can.
140 C2 **Huntsville** *AL* U.S.A.
143 D2 **Huntsville** *TX* U.S.A.
Hunyani *r.* Moz./Zimbabwe *see* **Manyame**
59 D3 **Huon Peninsula** P.N.G.
Huoxian China *see* **Huozhou**
70 B2 **Huozhou** China
Hupeh *prov.* China *see* **Hubei**
Hurghada Egypt *see* **Al Ghurdaqah**
137 D2 **Huron** U.S.A.
138 C2 **Huron, Lake** Can./U.S.A.
135 D3 **Hurricane** U.S.A.
100 C2 **Hürth** Ger.
92 □B2 **Húsavík** Iceland
110 C1 **Huşi** Romania
126 B2 **Huslia** U.S.A.
78 B3 **Ḩuşn Āl 'Abr** Yemen
102 B1 **Husum** Ger.
68 C1 **Hutag** Mongolia
60 A1 **Hutanopan** Indon.
137 D3 **Hutchinson** U.S.A.
141 D3 **Hutchinson Island** U.S.A.
70 B2 **Hutuo He** *r.* China
100 B2 **Huy** Belgium
70 C2 **Huzhou** China
92 □C3 **Hvalnes** Iceland
92 □B3 **Hvannadalshnúkur** *vol.* Iceland
109 C2 **Hvar** Croatia
109 C2 **Hvar** *i.* Croatia
91 C2 **Hvardiys'ke** Ukr.
120 B2 **Hwange** Zimbabwe
Hwang Ho *r.* China *see* **Yellow River**
136 C2 **Hyannis** U.S.A.
68 C1 **Hyargas Nuur** *salt l.* Mongolia
50 A3 **Hyden** Austr.
73 B3 **Hyderabad** India
74 A2 **Hyderabad** Pak.
Hydra *i.* Greece *see* **Ydra**
105 D3 **Hyères** France
105 D3 **Hyères, Îles d'** *is* France
65 B1 **Hyesan** N. Korea
128 B2 **Hyland Post** Can.
67 B3 **Hyōno-sen** *mt.* Japan
99 D4 **Hythe** U.K.
67 B4 **Hyūga** Japan
93 H3 **Hyvinkää** Fin.

I

114 B2 **Iabès, Erg** *des.* Alg.
150 C3 **Iaco** *r.* Brazil
110 C2 **Ialomiţa** *r.* Romania
110 C1 **Ianca** Romania
110 C1 **Iaşi** Romania
64 A2 **Iba** Phil.
115 C4 **Ibadan** Nigeria
150 B2 **Ibagué** Col.
154 B2 **Ibaiti** Brazil
150 B2 **Ibarra** Ecuador
78 B3 **Ibb** Yemen
100 C1 **Ibbenbüren** Ger.
115 C4 **Ibi** Nigeria
107 C2 **Ibi** Spain
155 C1 **Ibiá** Brazil
155 D1 **Ibiaí** Brazil
155 D1 **Ibiraçu** Brazil
107 D2 **Ibiza** Spain
107 D2 **Ibiza** *i.* Spain
151 E4 **Ibotirama** Brazil
79 C2 **Ibrā'** Oman
79 C2 **Ibrī** Oman
150 B4 **Ica** Peru
Icaria *i.* Greece *see* **Ikaria**
İçel Turkey *see* **Mersin**
92 □B2 **Iceland** *country* Europe
160 M4 **Iceland Basin** *sea feature* N. Atlantic Ocean
160 L3 **Icelandic Plateau** *sea feature* N. Atlantic Ocean
66 D3 **Ichinoseki** Japan
91 C1 **Ichnya** Ukr.
65 B2 **Ich'ŏn** N. Korea
151 F3 **Icó** Brazil
155 D2 **Iconha** Brazil
143 E2 **Idabel** U.S.A.
115 C4 **Idah** Nigeria
134 D2 **Idaho** *state* U.S.A.
134 D2 **Idaho Falls** U.S.A.
100 C3 **Idar-Oberstein** Ger.
68 C1 **Ideriyn Gol** *r.* Mongolia
116 B2 **Idfū** Egypt
115 D2 **Idhān Awbārī** *des.* Libya
115 D2 **Idhān Murzūq** *des.* Libya
Idi Amin Dada, Lake Dem. Rep. Congo/Uganda *see* **Edward, Lake**
118 B3 **Idiofa** Dem. Rep. Congo
80 B2 **Idlib** Syria
123 C3 **Idutywa** S. Africa
88 B2 **Iecava** Latvia
154 B2 **Iepê** Brazil
100 A2 **Ieper** Belgium
111 C3 **Ierapetra** Greece
119 D3 **Ifakara** Tanz.
121 □D3 **Ifanadiana** Madag.
115 C4 **Ife** Nigeria
114 C3 **Ifôghas, Adrar des** *hills* Mali
118 C3 **Ifumo** Dem. Rep. Congo
61 C1 **Igan** *Sarawak* Malaysia
119 D2 **Iganga** Uganda
154 C2 **Igarapava** Brazil
82 G2 **Igarka** Rus. Fed.
74 B3 **Igatpuri** India
81 C2 **Iğdır** Turkey
108 A3 **Iglesias** *Sardinia* Italy
127 G2 **Igloolik** Can.
Igluligaarjuk Can. *see* **Chesterfield Inlet**
130 A3 **Ignace** Can.
88 C2 **Ignalina** Lith.
111 C2 **İğneada** Turkey
110 C2 **İğneada Burnu** *pt* Turkey
111 B3 **Igoumenitsa** Greece
86 E3 **Igra** Rus. Fed.
86 F2 **Igrim** Rus. Fed.
154 B3 **Iguaçu** *r.* Brazil
154 B3 **Iguaçu Falls** Arg./Brazil
145 C3 **Iguala** Mex.
107 D1 **Igualada** Spain
154 C2 **Iguape** Brazil
154 B2 **Iguatemi** Brazil
154 B2 **Iguatemi** *r.* Brazil
151 F3 **Iguatu** Brazil
118 A3 **Iguéla** Gabon
114 B2 **Iguidi, Erg** *des.* Alg./Maur.
119 D3 **Igunga** Tanz.
121 □D2 **Iharaña** Madag.
69 D2 **Ihbulag** Mongolia
121 □D3 **Ihosy** Madag.
92 I2 **Iijoki** *r.* Fin.
92 I3 **Iisalmi** Fin.
67 B4 **Iizuka** Japan
115 C4 **Ijebu-Ode** Nigeria
100 B1 **IJmuiden** Neth.
100 B1 **IJssel** *r.* Neth.
100 B1 **IJsselmeer** *l.* Neth.
152 C2 **Ijuí** Brazil
Ikaahuk Can. *see* **Sachs Harbour**
123 C2 **Ikageleng** S. Africa
123 C2 **Ikageng** S. Africa
111 C3 **Ikaria** *i.* Greece
118 C3 **Ikela** Dem. Rep. Congo
110 B2 **Ikhtiman** Bulg.
67 A4 **Iki** *i.* Japan
118 A2 **Ikom** Nigeria
121 □D3 **Ikongo** Madag.
65 B2 **Iksan** S. Korea
119 D3 **Ikungu** Tanz.
114 C2 **Ilaferh, Oued** *watercourse* Alg.
64 B2 **Ilagan** Phil.
81 C2 **Īlām** Iran
75 C2 **Ilam** Nepal
103 D1 **Iława** Pol.
79 C2 **Ilazārān, Kūh-e** *mt.* Iran
129 D2 **Île-à-la-Crosse** Can.
129 D2 **Île-à-la-Crosse, Lac** *l.* Can.
118 C3 **Ilebo** Dem. Rep. Congo
119 D2 **Ileret** Kenya
99 D4 **Ilford** U.K.
99 A4 **Ilfracombe** U.K.
155 C2 **Ilhabela** Brazil
155 D2 **Ilha Grande, Baía da** *b.* Brazil
154 B2 **Ilha Grande, Represa** *resr* Brazil
154 B2 **Ilha Solteíra, Represa** *resr* Brazil
106 B1 **Ílhavo** Port.
151 F4 **Ilhéus** Brazil
Ili Kazakh. *see* **Kapchagay**
126 B3 **Iliamna Lake** U.S.A.
64 B3 **Iligan** Phil.
Iliysk Kazakh. *see* **Kapchagay**
98 C3 **Ilkley** U.K.
152 A3 **Illapel** Chile
90 C2 **Illichivs'k** Ukr.
138 A3 **Illinois** *r.* U.S.A.
138 B3 **Illinois** *state* U.S.A.
90 B2 **Illintsi** Ukr.
115 C2 **Illizi** Alg.
89 D2 **Il'men', Ozero** *l.* Rus. Fed.
101 E2 **Ilmenau** Ger.
150 B4 **Ilo** Peru
64 B2 **Iloilo** Phil.
92 J3 **Ilomantsi** Fin.
115 C4 **Ilorin** Nigeria
87 D4 **Ilovlya** Rus. Fed.
53 D1 **Iluka** Austr.
127 I2 **Ilulissat** Greenland
Iman Rus. Fed. *see* **Dal'nerechensk**
66 B1 **Iman** *r.* Rus. Fed.
67 A4 **Imari** Japan
93 I3 **Imatra** Fin.
imeni Petra Stuchki Latvia *see* **Aizkraukle**
117 C4 **Īmī** Eth.
65 B2 **Imjin-gang** *r.* N. Korea/S. Korea
141 D3 **Immokalee** U.S.A.
108 B2 **Imola** Italy
151 E3 **Imperatriz** Brazil
108 A2 **Imperia** Italy
136 C2 **Imperial** U.S.A.
118 B2 **Impfondo** Congo
72 D2 **Imphal** India
111 C2 **İmroz** Turkey
67 C3 **Ina** Japan
150 C4 **Inambari** *r.* Peru
115 C2 **In Aménas** Alg.
115 C2 **In Amguel** Alg.
54 B2 **Inangahua Junction** N.Z.
59 C3 **Inanwatan** Indon.
92 I2 **Inari** Fin.
92 I2 **Inarijärvi** *l.* Fin.
67 D3 **Inawashiro-ko** *l.* Japan
80 B1 **İnce Burun** *pt* Turkey
65 B2 **Inch'ŏn** S. Korea
121 C2 **Inchope** Moz.
123 D2 **Incomati** *r.* Moz.
116 B3 **Inda Silasē** Eth.
144 B2 **Indé** Mex.
135 C3 **Independence** *CA* U.S.A.
137 E2 **Independence** *IA* U.S.A.
137 D3 **Independence** *KS* U.S.A.
137 E3 **Independence** *MO* U.S.A.
134 C2 **Independence Mountains** U.S.A.
76 B2 **Inderborskiy** Kazakh.
72 B2 **India** *country* Asia
139 D2 **Indiana** U.S.A.
138 B2 **Indiana** *state* U.S.A.
138 B3 **Indianapolis** U.S.A.
129 D2 **Indian Head** Can.
159 **Indian Ocean**
137 E2 **Indianola** *IA* U.S.A.
140 B2 **Indianola** *MS* U.S.A.
135 D3 **Indian Peak** U.S.A.
135 C3 **Indian Springs** U.S.A.
86 D2 **Indiga** Rus. Fed.
83 K2 **Indigirka** *r.* Rus. Fed.
109 D1 **Inđija** Serb. and Mont.
135 C4 **Indio** U.S.A.
58 B3 **Indonesia** *country* Asia
74 B2 **Indore** India
60 B2 **Indramayu, Tanjung** *pt* Indon.
Indrapura, Gunung *vol.* Indon. *see* **Kerinci, Gunung**
75 C3 **Indravati** *r.* India
104 C2 **Indre** *r.* France
74 A2 **Indus** *r.* China/Pak.
74 A2 **Indus, Mouths of the** Pak.
159 E2 **Indus Cone** *sea feature* Indian Ocean
80 B1 **İnebolu** Turkey
111 C2 **İnegöl** Turkey
Infantes Spain *see* **Villanueva de los Infantes**
144 B3 **Infiernillo, Presa** *resr* Mex.
51 D1 **Ingham** Austr.
53 D1 **Inglewood** Austr.
102 C2 **Ingolstadt** Ger.
75 C2 **Ingraj Bazar** India
123 D2 **Ingwavuma** S. Africa
120 B2 **Ingwe** Zambia
123 D2 **Inhaca** Moz.
121 C3 **Inhambane** Moz.
121 C2 **Inhaminga** Moz.
151 D2 **Inini** Fr. Guiana
Inis Rep. of Ireland *see* **Ennis**
97 A2 **Inishbofin** *i.* Rep. of Ireland
97 B2 **Inishmore** *i.* Rep. of Ireland
97 C1 **Inishowen** *pen.* Rep. of Ireland
54 B2 **Inland Kaikoura Range** *mts* N.Z.
Inland Sea Japan *see* **Seto-naikai**
102 C2 **Inn** *r.* Europe
127 H1 **Innaanganeq** *c.* Greenland
52 B1 **Innamincka** Austr.
70 A1 **Inner Mongolia** *aut. reg.* China
96 B2 **Inner Sound** *sea chan.* U.K.
51 D1 **Innisfail** Austr.
102 C2 **Innsbruck** Austria
97 C2 **Inny** *r.* Rep. of Ireland
154 B1 **Inocência** Brazil
118 B3 **Inongo** Dem. Rep. Congo
111 D3 **İnönü** Turkey
Inoucdjouac Can. *see* **Inukjuak**
103 D1 **Inowrocław** Pol.
114 C2 **In Salah** Alg.
62 A2 **Insein** Myanmar
110 C2 **Însurăţei** Romania
86 F2 **Inta** Rus. Fed.
105 D2 **Interlaken** Switz.
137 E1 **International Falls** U.S.A.
63 A2 **Interview Island** India
130 C2 **Inukjuak** Can.
126 D2 **Inuvik** Can.
96 B2 **Inveraray** U.K.
96 C2 **Inverbervie** U.K.
54 A3 **Invercargill** N.Z.
53 D1 **Inverell** Austr.
96 B2 **Invergordon** U.K.
128 C2 **Invermere** Can.
131 D3 **Inverness** Can.
96 B2 **Inverness** U.K.
96 C2 **Inverurie** U.K.
159 F4 **Investigator Ridge** *sea feature* Indian Ocean
52 A3 **Investigator Strait** Austr.
77 E1 **Inya** Rus. Fed.
Inyanga Zimbabwe *see* **Nyanga**
119 D3 **Inyonga** Tanz.
87 D3 **Inza** Rus. Fed.
111 B3 **Ioannina** Greece
137 D3 **Iola** U.S.A.
96 A2 **Iona** *i.* U.K.
111 B3 **Ionian Islands** Greece
109 C3 **Ionian Sea** Greece/Italy
Ionioi Nisoi *is* Greece *see* **Ionian Islands**
111 C3 **Ios** *i.* Greece
137 E2 **Iowa** *state* U.S.A.
137 E2 **Iowa City** U.S.A.
154 C1 **Ipameri** Brazil
155 D1 **Ipatinga** Brazil
81 C1 **Ipatovo** Rus. Fed.
123 C2 **Ipelegeng** S. Africa
150 B2 **Ipiales** Col.
151 F4 **Ipiaú** Brazil
154 B3 **Ipiranga** Brazil
150 B3 **Ipixuna** Brazil
60 B1 **Ipoh** Malaysia
154 B1 **Iporá** Brazil
118 C2 **Ippy** C.A.R.
111 C2 **İpsala** Turkey
53 D1 **Ipswich** Austr.
99 D3 **Ipswich** U.K.
127 H2 **Iqaluit** Can.
152 A2 **Iquique** Chile
150 B3 **Iquitos** Peru
Irakleio Greece *see* **Iraklion**
111 C3 **Iraklion** Greece
81 D2 **Iran** *country* Asia
61 C1 **Iran, Pegunungan** *mts* Indon.
79 D2 **Īrānshahr** Iran
144 B2 **Irapuato** Mex.
81 C2 **Iraq** *country* Asia
154 B3 **Irati** Brazil

88 B2 **Irbe Strait** Estonia/Latvia
80 B2 **Irbid** Jordan
86 F3 **Irbit** Rus. Fed.
151 E4 **Irecê** Brazil
97 C2 **Ireland, Republic of** *country* Europe
118 C3 **Irema** Dem. Rep. Congo
76 C2 **Irgiz** Kazakh.
Iri S. Korea see **Iksan**
Irian Jaya *reg.* Indon. see **Papua**
115 E3 **Iriba** Chad
114 B3 **Irîgui** *reg.* Mali/Maur.
119 D3 **Iringa** Tanz.
151 D3 **Iriri** *r.* Brazil
Irish Free State *country* Europe see **Ireland, Republic of**
95 B3 **Irish Sea** Rep. of Ireland/U.K.
68 C1 **Irkutsk** Rus. Fed.
160 M4 **Irminger Basin** *sea feature* N. Atlantic Ocean
139 D2 **Irondequoit** U.S.A.
52 A2 **Iron Knob** Austr.
138 B1 **Iron Mountain** U.S.A.
138 C3 **Ironton** U.S.A.
138 A1 **Ironwood** U.S.A.
130 B3 **Iroquois Falls** Can.
64 B2 **Irosin** Phil.
67 C4 **Irō-zaki** *pt* Japan
90 C1 **Irpin'** Ukr.
62 A2 **Irrawaddy** *r.* Myanmar
63 A2 **Irrawaddy, Mouths of the** Myanmar
86 F2 **Irtysh** *r.* Kazakh./Rus. Fed.
107 C1 **Irún** Spain
96 B3 **Irvine** U.K.
143 D2 **Irving** U.S.A.
64 B3 **Isabela** Phil.
146 B3 **Isabelia, Cordillera** *mts* Nic.
92 □A2 **Ísafjarðardjúp** *est.* Iceland
92 □A2 **Ísafjörður** Iceland
67 B4 **Isahaya** Japan
102 C2 **Isar** *r.* Ger.
96 □ **Isbister** U.K.
108 B2 **Ischia, Isola d'** *i.* Italy
67 C4 **Ise** Japan
118 C2 **Isengi** Dem. Rep. Congo
105 C3 **Isère** *r.* France
100 C2 **Iserlohn** Ger.
101 D1 **Isernhagen** Ger.
67 C4 **Ise-wan** *b.* Japan
114 C4 **Iseyin** Nigeria
Isfahan Iran see **Eşfahān**
66 D2 **Ishikari-wan** *b.* Japan
77 D1 **Ishim** *r.* Kazakh./Rus. Fed.
82 F3 **Ishim** Rus. Fed.
67 D3 **Ishinomaki** Japan
67 D3 **Ishioka** Japan
67 B4 **Ishizuchi-san** *mt.* Japan
74 B1 **Ishkoshim** Tajik.
138 B1 **Ishpeming** U.S.A.
111 C2 **Işıklar Dağı** *mts* Turkey
111 C3 **Işıklı** Turkey
123 D2 **Isipingo** S. Africa
119 C2 **Isiro** Dem. Rep. Congo
80 B2 **İskenderun** Turkey
82 G3 **Iskitim** Rus. Fed.
110 B2 **Iskŭr** *r.* Bulg.
117 D3 **Iskushuban** Somalia
128 A2 **Iskut** *r.* Can.
74 B1 **Islamabad** Pak.
141 D4 **Islamorada** U.S.A.
52 A2 **Island Lagoon** *salt flat* Austr.
129 E2 **Island Lake** Can.
54 B1 **Islands, Bay of** N.Z.
Islas Canarias *is* N. Atlantic Ocean see **Canary Islands**
96 A3 **Islay** *i.* U.K.
98 A2 **Isle of Man** *i.* Irish Sea
Ismail Ukr. see **Izmayil**
77 D3 **Ismoili Somoní, Qullai** *mt.* Tajik.
116 B2 **Isnā** Egypt
121 □D3 **Isoanala** Madag.
121 C2 **Isoka** Zambia
93 H3 **Isokyrö** Fin.
109 C3 **Isola di Capo Rizzuto** Italy
Ispahan Iran see **Eşfahān**
80 B2 **Isparta** Turkey
110 C2 **Isperikh** Bulg.
Ispisar Tajik. see **Khŭjand**
80 B2 **Israel** *country* Asia
50 B3 **Israelite Bay** Austr.
105 C2 **Issoire** France
Issyk-Kul' Kyrg. see **Balykchy**
111 C2 **İstanbul** Turkey
İstanbul Boğazı *str.* Turkey see **Bosporus**
103 D2 **Isten dombja** *hill* Hungary
111 B3 **Istiaia** Greece
141 D3 **Istokpoga, Lake** U.S.A.
Istra *pen.* Croatia see **Istria**
105 C3 **Istres** France
108 B1 **Istria** *pen.* Croatia
155 D2 **Itabapoana** Brazil
151 E4 **Itaberaba** Brazil
154 C1 **Itaberaí** Brazil
155 D1 **Itabira** Brazil
155 D2 **Itabirito** Brazil
151 F4 **Itabuna** Brazil
150 D3 **Itacoatiara** Brazil
155 D2 **Itaguaí** Brazil
154 B2 **Itaguajé** Brazil
154 C2 **Itaí** Brazil
154 C3 **Itaiópolis** Brazil
154 B3 **Itaipu, Represa de** *resr* Brazil
151 D3 **Itaituba** Brazil
154 C3 **Itajaí** Brazil
155 C2 **Itajubá** Brazil
108 B2 **Italy** *country* Europe
155 E1 **Itamaraju** Brazil
155 D1 **Itamarandiba** Brazil
155 D1 **Itambacuri** Brazil
155 D1 **Itambé, Pico de** *mt.* Brazil
75 D2 **Itanagar** India
154 C2 **Itanhaém** Brazil
155 D1 **Itanhém** Brazil
155 D1 **Itaobím** Brazil
154 C1 **Itapajipe** Brazil
155 E1 **Itapebi** Brazil
155 D2 **Itapemirim** Brazil
155 D2 **Itaperuna** Brazil
155 D1 **Itapetinga** Brazil
154 C2 **Itapetininga** Brazil
154 C2 **Itapeva** Brazil
151 F4 **Itapicuru** *r.* Brazil
151 E3 **Itapicuru Mirim** Brazil
155 C2 **Itapira** Brazil
154 C2 **Itaporanga** Brazil
154 C1 **Itapuranga** Brazil
154 C2 **Itararé** Brazil
74 B2 **Itarsi** India
154 B1 **Itarumã** Brazil
155 D2 **Itaúna** Brazil
155 E1 **Itaúnas** Brazil
64 B1 **Itbayat** *i.* Phil.
139 D2 **Ithaca** U.S.A.
101 D1 **Ith Hils** *ridge* Ger.
118 C2 **Itimbiri** *r.* Dem. Rep. Congo
155 D1 **Itinga** Brazil
154 B1 **Itiquira** Brazil
154 A1 **Itiquira** *r.* Brazil
67 C4 **Itō** Japan
154 C2 **Itu** Brazil
150 B3 **Ituí** *r.* Brazil
154 C1 **Ituiutaba** Brazil
119 C3 **Itula** Dem. Rep. Congo
154 C1 **Itumbiara** Brazil
154 C1 **Itumbiara, Barragem** *resr* Brazil
154 B1 **Iturama** Brazil
101 D1 **Itzehoe** Ger.
83 N2 **Iul'tin** Rus. Fed.
155 D2 **Iúna** Brazil
154 B2 **Ivaí** *r.* Brazil
92 I2 **Ivalo** Fin.
88 C3 **Ivanava** Belarus
109 C1 **Ivanec** Croatia
Ivangrad Serb. and Mont. see **Berane**
52 B2 **Ivanhoe** Austr.
90 B1 **Ivankiv** Ukr.
90 A2 **Ivano-Frankivs'k** Ukr.
89 F2 **Ivanovo** Rus. Fed.
88 C3 **Ivatsevichy** Belarus
111 C2 **Ivaylovgrad** Bulg.
86 F2 **Ivdel'** Rus. Fed.
110 C1 **Iveşti** Romania
154 B2 **Ivinheima** Brazil
154 B2 **Ivinheima** *r.* Brazil
127 I2 **Ivittuut** Greenland
Iviza *i.* Spain see **Ibiza**
89 E3 **Ivnya** Rus. Fed.
Ivory Coast *country* Africa see **Côte d'Ivoire**
108 A1 **Ivrea** Italy
111 C3 **İvrindi** Turkey
Ivugivik Can. see **Ivujivik**
127 G2 **Ivujivik** Can.
67 D3 **Iwaki** Japan
67 B4 **Iwakuni** Japan
66 D2 **Iwamizawa** Japan
66 D2 **Iwanai** Japan
66 D3 **Iwate-san** *vol.* Japan
88 C3 **Iwye** Belarus
123 D3 **Ixopo** S. Africa
144 B2 **Ixtlán** Mex.
146 B3 **Izabal, Lago de** *l.* Guat.
145 D2 **Izamal** Mex.
81 C1 **Izberbash** Rus. Fed.
86 E3 **Izhevsk** Rus. Fed.
86 E2 **Izhma** Rus. Fed.
Izhma Rus. Fed. see **Sosnogorsk**
89 E3 **Izmalkovo** Rus. Fed.
90 B2 **Izmayil** Ukr.
111 C3 **İzmir** Turkey
111 C2 **İzmit** Turkey
111 C2 **İznik Gölü** *l.* Turkey
67 A4 **Izuhara** Japan
67 B3 **Izumo** Japan
156 C4 **Izu-Ogasawara Trench** *sea feature* N. Pacific Ocean
67 C4 **Izu-shotō** *is* Japan
90 B1 **Izyaslav** Ukr.
91 D2 **Izyum** Ukr.

J

74 A1 **Jabal as Sirāj** Afgh.
106 C2 **Jabalón** *r.* Spain
75 B2 **Jabalpur** India
50 C1 **Jabiru** Austr.
109 C2 **Jablanica** Bos.-Herz.
151 E2 **Jaboatão** Brazil
154 C2 **Jaboticabal** Brazil
107 C1 **Jaca** Spain
145 C2 **Jacala** Mex.
151 D3 **Jacareacanga** Brazil
155 C2 **Jacareí** Brazil
154 B1 **Jaciara** Brazil
155 D1 **Jacinto** Brazil
139 E1 **Jackman** U.S.A.
140 C2 **Jackson** *AL* U.S.A.
138 C2 **Jackson** *MI* U.S.A.
140 B2 **Jackson** *MS* U.S.A.
140 C1 **Jackson** *TN* U.S.A.
136 A2 **Jackson** *WY* U.S.A.
54 A2 **Jackson Head** *hd* N.Z.
140 B2 **Jacksonville** *AR* U.S.A.
141 D2 **Jacksonville** *FL* U.S.A.
138 A3 **Jacksonville** *IL* U.S.A.
141 E2 **Jacksonville** *NC* U.S.A.
143 D2 **Jacksonville** *TX* U.S.A.
147 C3 **Jacmel** Haiti
74 A2 **Jacobabad** Pak.
151 E4 **Jacobina** Brazil
131 D3 **Jacques Cartier, Mont** *mt.* Can.
151 E3 **Jacunda** Brazil
154 C2 **Jacupiranga** Brazil
101 D1 **Jadebusen** *b.* Ger.
Jadotville Dem. Rep. Congo see **Likasi**
109 C2 **Jadovnik** *mt.* Bos.-Herz.
150 B3 **Jaén** Peru
106 C2 **Jaén** Spain
Jaffa Israel see **Tel Aviv-Yafo**
52 A3 **Jaffa, Cape** Austr.
73 B4 **Jaffna** Sri Lanka
75 C3 **Jagdalpur** India
123 C2 **Jagersfontein** S. Africa
79 C2 **Jaghīn** Iran
152 C3 **Jaguarão** Uru.
154 C2 **Jaguariaíva** Brazil
81 D3 **Jahrom** Iran
74 B2 **Jaipur** India
74 B2 **Jaisalmer** India
74 B2 **Jaitgarh** *hill* India
75 C2 **Jajarkot** Nepal
109 C2 **Jajce** Bos.-Herz.
Jajnagar *state* India see **Orissa**
60 B2 **Jakarta** Indon.
128 A1 **Jakes Corner** Can.
92 G2 **Jäkkvik** Sweden
Jakobshavn Greenland see **Ilulissat**
92 H3 **Jakobstad** Fin.
77 D3 **Jalālābād** Afgh.
77 D2 **Jalal-Abad** Kyrg.
74 B1 **Jalandhar** India
145 C3 **Jalapa** Mex.
154 B2 **Jales** Brazil
74 B2 **Jalgaon** India
115 D4 **Jalingo** Nigeria
74 B3 **Jalna** India
74 B2 **Jalore** India
144 B2 **Jalostotitlán** Mex.
144 B2 **Jalpa** Mex.
75 C2 **Jalpaiguri** India
145 C2 **Jalpan** Mex.
115 E2 **Jālū** Libya
146 C3 **Jamaica** *country* West Indies
146 C3 **Jamaica Channel** Haiti/Jamaica
75 C2 **Jamalpur** Bangl.
60 B2 **Jambi** Indon.
137 D2 **James** *r. ND/SD* U.S.A.
139 D3 **James** *r. VA* U.S.A.
130 B2 **James Bay** Can.
52 A2 **Jamestown** Austr.
Jamestown Can. see **Wawa**
123 C3 **Jamestown** S. Africa
137 D1 **Jamestown** *ND* U.S.A.
139 D2 **Jamestown** *NY* U.S.A.
74 B1 **Jammu** Jammu and Kashmir
74 B1 **Jammu and Kashmir** *terr.* Asia
74 B2 **Jamnagar** India
74 B2 **Jampur** Pak.
93 I3 **Jämsä** Fin.
78 A2 **Jamsah** Egypt
75 C2 **Jamshedpur** India
75 C2 **Jamuna** *r.* Bangl.
75 C2 **Janakpur** Nepal
155 D1 **Janaúba** Brazil
81 D2 **Jandaq** Iran
114 A2 **Jandía** *hill* Canary Islands
135 B2 **Janesville** *CA* U.S.A.
138 B2 **Janesville** *WI* U.S.A.
154 A2 **Jango** Brazil
82 A2 **Jan Mayen** *i.* Arctic Ocean
122 B3 **Jansenville** S. Africa
155 D1 **Januária** Brazil
74 B2 **Jaora** India
67 C3 **Japan** *country* Asia
66 B3 **Japan, Sea of** N. Pacific Ocean
150 C3 **Japurá** *r.* Brazil
154 C1 **Jaraguá** Brazil
154 C3 **Jaraguá, Serra** *mts* Brazil
154 C3 **Jaraguá do Sul** Brazil
154 B2 **Jaraguari** Brazil
152 C2 **Jardim** Brazil
69 D1 **Jargalant** Mongolia
103 D1 **Jarocin** Pol.
103 E1 **Jarosław** Pol.
92 F3 **Järpen** Sweden
70 A2 **Jartai** China
150 C4 **Jarú** Brazil
Jarud China see **Lubei**
88 C1 **Järvenpää** Fin.
49 K4 **Jarvis Island** *terr.* S. Pacific Ocean
93 G3 **Järvsö** Sweden
79 C2 **Jāsk** Iran
103 E2 **Jasło** Pol.
55 A3 **Jason Peninsula** Antarctica
128 C2 **Jasper** Can.
140 C2 **Jasper** *AL* U.S.A.
138 B3 **Jasper** *IN* U.S.A.
143 E2 **Jasper** *TX* U.S.A.
Jassy Romania see **Iaşi**
103 D2 **Jastrzębie-Zdrój** Pol.
103 D2 **Jászberény** Hungary
154 B1 **Jataí** Brazil
74 A2 **Jati** Pak.
154 C2 **Jaú** Brazil
150 C3 **Jaú** *r.* Brazil
145 C2 **Jaumave** Mex.
75 C2 **Jaunpur** India
154 B1 **Jauru** Brazil
61 B2 **Java** *i.* Indon.
107 C1 **Javalambre, Sierra de** *mts* Spain
69 D1 **Javarthushuu** Mongolia
Java Sea Indon. see **Laut Jawa**
156 B6 **Java Trench** *sea feature* Indian Ocean
Jawa *i.* Indon. see **Java**
117 C4 **Jawhar** Somalia
103 D1 **Jawor** Pol.
103 D1 **Jaworzno** Pol.
59 D3 **Jaya, Puncak** *mt.* Indon.
59 D3 **Jayapura** Indon.
79 C2 **Jazīrat Maşīrah** *i.* Oman
128 B1 **Jean Marie River** Can.
131 D2 **Jeannin, Lac** *l.* Can.
Jebel, Bahr el *r.* Sudan/Uganda see **White Nile**
116 A3 **Jebel Abyad Plateau** Sudan

96 C3 Jedburgh U.K.
78 A2 Jeddah Saudi Arabia
108 A3 Jedeida Tunisia
101 E1 Jeetze r. Ger.
137 E2 Jefferson U.S.A.
135 C3 Jefferson, Mount U.S.A.
137 E3 Jefferson City U.S.A.
122 B3 Jeffrey's Bay S. Africa
88 C2 Jēkabpils Latvia
103 D1 Jelenia Góra Pol.
88 B2 Jelgava Latvia
60 B1 Jemaja i. Indon.
61 C2 Jember Indon.
101 E2 Jena Ger.
Jengish Chokusu mt.
China/Kyrg. see
Pobeda Peak
80 B2 Jenin West Bank
140 B2 Jennings U.S.A.
151 E4 Jequié Brazil
155 D1 Jequitaí Brazil
155 D1 Jequitinhonha Brazil
155 E1 Jequitinhonha r. Brazil
147 C3 Jérémie Haiti
144 B2 Jerez Mex.
106 B2 Jerez de la Frontera
Spain
109 D3 Jergucat Albania
115 C1 Jerid, Chott el salt l.
Tunisia
134 D2 Jerome U.S.A.
95 C4 Jersey i. Channel Is
95 C4 Jersey terr. Channel Is
151 E3 Jerumenha Brazil
80 B2 Jerusalem
Israel/West Bank
53 D3 Jervis Bay Territory
admin. div. Austr.
108 B1 Jesenice Slovenia
108 B2 Jesi Italy
Jesselton Malaysia see
Kota Kinabalu
101 F2 Jessen Ger.
75 C2 Jessore Bangl.
141 D2 Jesup U.S.A.
137 D3 Jesus, Mount hill U.S.A.
145 C3 Jesús Carranza Mex.
100 C1 Jever Ger.
74 B2 Jhalawar India
74 B1 Jhang Pak.
74 B2 Jhansi India
75 C2 Jharkhand state India
75 C2 Jharsuguda India
74 B1 Jhelum r. India/Pak.
74 B1 Jhelum Pak.
74 B2 Jhunjhunun India
70 C2 Jiading China
69 E1 Jiamusi China
71 B3 Ji'an Jiangxi China
65 B1 Ji'an Jilin China
Jianchang China see
Nancheng
62 A1 Jianchuan China
70 B3 Jiande China
Jiangling China see
Jingzhou
71 B3 Jiangmen China
70 B2 Jiangsu prov. China
71 B3 Jiangxi prov. China
70 A2 Jiangyou China
70 B3 Jianli China
70 B2 Jianqiao Hebei China
71 B3 Jianyang Fujian China
70 A2 Jianyang Sichuan China
69 E2 Jiaohe Jilin China
Jiaojiang China see
Taizhou
70 C2 Jiaozhou China
70 B2 Jiaozuo China
Jiashan China see
Mingguang
70 C2 Jiaxing China
68 C2 Jiayuguan China
Jiddah Saudi Arabia see
Jeddah
92 G2 Jiehkkevárri mt. Norway
70 B2 Jiexiu China
70 A2 Jigzhi China
103 D2 Jihlava Czech Rep.
115 C1 Jijel Alg.
117 C4 Jijiga Eth.
117 C4 Jilib Somalia
69 E2 Jilin China
65 B1 Jilin prov. China
65 A1 Jilin Hada Ling mts China
117 B4 Jima Eth.
110 B1 Jimbolia Romania
144 B2 Jiménez Mex.
145 C3 Jiménez Mex.
145 C2 Jiménez Mex.
70 B2 Jinan China

70 A2 Jinchang China
70 B2 Jincheng China
Jinchuan China see
Jinchang
53 C3 Jindabyne Austr.
103 D2 Jindřichův Hradec
Czech Rep.
Jin'e China see
Longchang
70 A2 Jingbian China
71 B3 Jingdezhen China
62 B1 Jingdong China
53 C3 Jingellic Austr.
71 B3 Jinggangshan China
62 B1 Jinghong China
70 B2 Jingmen China
70 A2 Jingning China
Jingsha China see
Jingzhou
70 A2 Jingtai China
71 A3 Jingxi China
Jingxian China see
Jingzhou
65 B1 Jingyu China
70 A2 Jingyuan China
70 B2 Jingzhou China
70 B2 Jingzhou Hubei China
70 B2 Jingzhou Hunan China
71 B3 Jinhua China
70 B1 Jining Nei Mongol China
70 B2 Jining Shandong China
119 D2 Jinja Uganda
117 B4 Jinka Eth.
146 B3 Jinotega Nic.
146 B3 Jinotepe Nic.
71 A3 Jinping China
Jinsha Jiang r. China see
Yangtze
Jinshi China see Xinning
70 B3 Jinshi China
Jinxi China see Lianshan
70 B2 Jinzhong China
70 C1 Jinzhou China
150 C3 Jiparaná r. Brazil
75 C1 Jirang China
116 B2 Jirjā Egypt
79 C2 Jīroft Iran
79 C2 Jirwan Saudi Arabia
71 A3 Jishou China
110 B2 Jiu r. Romania
70 A2 Jiuding Shan mt. China
70 B3 Jiujiang China
Jiulian China see Mojiang
79 D2 Jiwani Pak.
66 B1 Jixi China
78 B3 Jīzān Saudi Arabia
77 C2 Jizzax Uzbek.
155 D1 Joaima Brazil
João Belo Moz. see Xai-
Xai
151 F3 João Pessoa Brazil
155 C1 João Pinheiro Brazil
74 B2 Jodhpur India
92 I3 Joensuu Fin.
67 C3 Jōetsu Japan
121 C3 Jofane Moz.
88 C2 Jõgeva Estonia
Jogjakarta Indon. see
Yogyakarta
123 C2 Johannesburg S. Africa
134 C2 John Day U.S.A.
134 B1 John Day r. U.S.A.
128 C2 John d'Or Prairie Can.
141 E1 John H. Kerr Reservoir
U.S.A.
96 C1 John o'Groats U.K.
141 D1 Johnson City U.S.A.
128 A1 Johnson's Crossing Can.
50 B3 Johnston, Lake salt flat
Austr.
49 J2 Johnston Atoll
N. Pacific Ocean
96 B3 Johnstone U.K.
Johnstone Lake Can. see
Old Wives Lake
139 D2 Johnstown U.S.A.
60 B1 Johor Bahru Malaysia
88 C2 Jõhvi Estonia
154 C3 Joinville Brazil
105 D2 Joinville France
55 B3 Joinville Island Antarctica
92 G2 Jokkmokk Sweden
92 □B2 Jökulsá á Fjöllum r.
Iceland
138 B2 Joliet U.S.A.
130 C3 Joliette Can.
64 B3 Jolo Phil.
64 B3 Jolo i. Phil.
61 C2 Jombang Indon.
75 C2 Jomsom Nepal
88 B2 Jonava Lith.

140 B1 Jonesboro AR U.S.A.
140 B2 Jonesboro LA U.S.A.
139 F2 Jonesport U.S.A.
127 G1 Jones Sound sea chan.
Can.
93 F4 Jönköping Sweden
131 C3 Jonquière Can.
145 C3 Jonuta Mex.
137 E3 Joplin U.S.A.
80 B2 Jordan country Asia
80 B2 Jordan r. Asia
134 E1 Jordan U.S.A.
155 D1 Jordânia Brazil
134 C2 Jordan Valley U.S.A.
72 D2 Jorhat India
101 D1 Jork Ger.
93 E4 Jørpeland Norway
115 C4 Jos Nigeria
145 C3 José Cardel Mex.
131 D2 Joseph, Lac l. Can.
50 B1 Joseph Bonaparte Gulf
Austr.
115 C4 Jos Plateau Nigeria
93 E3 Jotunheimen mts Norway
122 B3 Joubertina S. Africa
123 C2 Jouberton S. Africa
104 C2 Joué-lès-Tours France
93 I3 Joutseno Fin.
134 B1 Juan de Fuca Strait
Can./U.S.A.
149 B6 Juan Fernández Islands
S. Pacific Ocean
Juanshui China see
Tongcheng
145 B2 Juárez Mex.
144 A1 Juárez, Sierra de mts
Mex.
151 E3 Juàzeiro Brazil
151 F3 Juàzeiro do Norte Brazil
117 B4 Juba r. Somalia
117 C5 Jubba r. Somalia
78 B2 Jubbah Saudi Arabia
Jubbulpore India see
Jabalpur
107 C2 Júcar r. Spain
145 C3 Juchitán Mex.
155 E1 Jucuruçu Brazil
102 C2 Judenburg Austria
155 E1 Juerana Brazil
101 D2 Jühnde Ger.
146 B3 Juigalpa Nic.
100 C1 Juist i. Ger.
155 D2 Juiz de Fora Brazil
136 C2 Julesburg U.S.A.
150 B4 Juliaca Peru
Julianatop mt. Indon. see
Mandala, Puncak
151 D2 Juliana Top mt. Suriname
Jullundur India see
Jalandhar
107 C2 Jumilla Spain
75 C2 Jumla Nepal
Jumna r. India see Yamuna
74 B2 Junagadh India
143 D2 Junction U.S.A.
137 D3 Junction City U.S.A.
154 C2 Jundiaí Brazil
128 A2 Juneau U.S.A.
53 C2 Junee Austr.
105 D2 Jungfrau mt. Switz.
139 D2 Juniata r. U.S.A.
153 B3 Junín Arg.
92 G3 Junsele Sweden
134 C2 Juntura U.S.A.
Junxi China see Datian
Junxian China see
Danjiangkou
154 B2 Jupiá, Represa resr Brazil
141 D3 Jupiter U.S.A.
154 C2 Juquiá Brazil
117 A4 Jur r. Sudan
105 D2 Jura mts France/Switz.
96 B2 Jura i. U.K.
96 B3 Jura, Sound of sea chan.
U.K.
88 B2 Jurbarkas Lith.
88 B2 Jūrmala Latvia
150 C3 Juruá r. Brazil
154 C2 Jurumirim, Represa de
resr Brazil
151 D3 Juruti Brazil
154 B1 Jussara Brazil
150 C3 Jutaí r. Brazil
101 F2 Jüterbog Ger.
154 B2 Juti Brazil
145 D3 Jutiapa Guat.
93 E4 Jutland pen. Denmark
146 B2 Juventud, Isla de la i.
Cuba

70 B2 Juxian China
81 D3 Jūyom Iran
122 B1 Jwaneng Botswana
Jylland pen. Denmark see
Jutland
93 I3 Jyväskylä Fin.

K

74 B1 K2 mt.
China/Jammu and Kashmir
Kaakhka Turkm. see Kaka
92 I2 Kaamanen Fin.
61 D2 Kabaena i. Indon.
119 C3 Kabalo Dem. Rep. Congo
119 C3 Kabambare
Dem. Rep. Congo
119 C3 Kabare Dem. Rep. Congo
119 C3 Kabemba
Dem. Rep. Congo
130 B3 Kabinakagami Lake Can.
118 C3 Kabinda Dem. Rep. Congo
118 B2 Kabo C.A.R.
120 B2 Kabompo Zambia
119 C3 Kabongo
Dem. Rep. Congo
77 C3 Kābul Afgh.
64 B3 Kaburuang i. Indon.
121 B2 Kabwe Zambia
109 D2 Kačanik Serb. and Mont.
74 A2 Kachchh, Gulf of India
83 I3 Kachug Rus. Fed.
81 C1 Kaçkar Dağı mt. Turkey
111 C2 Kadıköy Turkey
52 A2 Kadina Austr.
114 B3 Kadiolo Mali
Kadiyevka Ukr. see
Stakhanov
73 B3 Kadmat i. India
89 F2 Kadnikov Rus. Fed.
121 B2 Kadoma Zimbabwe
63 A2 Kadonkani Myanmar
117 A3 Kadugli Sudan
115 C3 Kaduna Nigeria
89 E2 Kaduy Rus. Fed.
86 E2 Kadzherom Rus. Fed.
114 A3 Kaédi Maur.
118 B1 Kaélé Cameroon
65 B2 Kaesŏng N. Korea
118 C3 Kafakumba
Dem. Rep. Congo
114 A3 Kaffrine Senegal
111 B3 Kafireas, Akra pt Greece
80 B2 Kafr ash Shaykh Egypt
121 B2 Kafue Zambia
120 B2 Kafue r. Zambia
67 C3 Kaga Japan
118 B2 Kaga Bandoro C.A.R.
91 E2 Kagal'nitskaya Rus. Fed.
Kaganovichi Pervyye Ukr.
see Polis'ke
60 A2 Kagologolo Indon.
67 B4 Kagoshima Japan
Kagul Moldova see Cahul
119 D3 Kahama Tanz.
90 C2 Kaharlyk Ukr.
61 C2 Kahayan r. Indon.
118 B3 Kahemba
Dem. Rep. Congo
101 E2 Kahla Ger.
79 C2 Kahnūj Iran
92 H2 Kahperusvaarat mts Fin.
80 B2 Kahramanmaraş Turkey
79 C2 Kahūrak Iran
59 C3 Kai, Kepulauan is Indon.
115 C4 Kaiama Nigeria
54 B2 Kaiapoi N.Z.
59 C3 Kai Besar i. Indon.
70 B2 Kaifeng China
Kaihua China see
Wenshan
122 B2 Kaiingveld reg. S. Africa
59 C3 Kai Kecil i. Indon.
54 B2 Kaikoura N.Z.
114 A4 Kailahun Sierra Leone
Kailas Range mts China
see Gangdisê Shan
71 A3 Kaili China
59 C3 Kaimana Indon.
54 C1 Kaimanawa Mountains
N.Z.
72 C2 Kaimur Range hills India
88 B2 Käina Estonia
67 C4 Kainan Japan
115 C3 Kainji Reservoir Nigeria
54 B1 Kaipara Harbour N.Z.
74 B2 Kairana India
115 D1 Kairouan Tunisia
100 C3 Kaiserslautern Ger.

55 I2 **Kaiser Wilhelm II Land** reg. Antarctica
54 B1 **Kaitaia** N.Z.
54 C1 **Kaitawa** N.Z.
Kaitong China see Tongyu
59 C3 **Kaiwatu** Indon.
65 A1 **Kaiyuan** Liaoning China
71 A3 **Kaiyuan** Yunnan China
92 I3 **Kajaani** Fin.
51 D2 **Kajabbi** Austr.
76 B3 **Kaka** Turkm.
122 B2 **Kakamas** S. Africa
119 D2 **Kakamega** Kenya
114 A4 **Kakata** Liberia
91 C2 **Kakhovka** Ukr.
91 C2 **Kakhovs'ke Vodoskhovyshche** resr Ukr.
Kakhul Moldova see Cahul
73 C3 **Kakinada** India
128 C1 **Kakisa** Can.
67 B4 **Kakogawa** Japan
119 C3 **Kakoswa** Dem. Rep. Congo
126 C2 **Kaktovik** U.S.A.
Kalaallit Nunaat terr. N. America see Greenland
59 C3 **Kalabahi** Indon.
120 B2 **Kalabo** Zambia
91 E1 **Kalach** Rus. Fed.
119 D2 **Kalacha Dida** Kenya
87 D4 **Kalach-na-Donu** Rus. Fed.
62 A1 **Kaladan** r. India/Myanmar
120 B3 **Kalahari Desert** Africa
92 H3 **Kalajoki** Fin.
123 C1 **Kalamare** Botswana
111 B2 **Kalamaria** Greece
111 B3 **Kalamata** Greece
138 B2 **Kalamazoo** U.S.A.
111 B3 **Kalampaka** Greece
88 B2 **Kalana** Estonia
91 C2 **Kalanchak** Ukr.
61 D2 **Kalao** i. Indon.
61 D2 **Kalaotoa** i. Indon.
63 B2 **Kalasin** Thai.
77 C3 **Kalāt** Afgh.
79 C2 **Kalāt** Iran
74 A2 **Kalat** Pak.
50 A2 **Kalbarri** Austr.
111 C3 **Kale** Turkey
80 B1 **Kalecik** Turkey
118 C3 **Kalema** Dem. Rep. Congo
119 C3 **Kalemie** Dem. Rep. Congo
62 A1 **Kalemyo** Myanmar
86 C2 **Kalevala** Rus. Fed.
Kalgan China see Zhangjiakou
50 B3 **Kalgoorlie** Austr.
109 C2 **Kali** Croatia
110 C2 **Kaliakra, Nos** pt Bulg.
60 A2 **Kaliet** Indon.
119 C3 **Kalima** Dem. Rep. Congo
61 C2 **Kalimantan** reg. Indon.
88 B3 **Kaliningrad** Rus. Fed. see Tver'
91 D2 **Kalininskaya** Rus. Fed.
88 C3 **Kalinkavichy** Belarus
134 D1 **Kalispell** U.S.A.
103 D1 **Kalisz** Pol.
91 E2 **Kalitva** r. Rus. Fed.
92 H2 **Kalix** Sweden
92 H2 **Kalixälven** r. Sweden
111 C3 **Kalkan** Turkey
120 A3 **Kalkfeld** Namibia
100 C2 **Kall** Ger.
92 I3 **Kallavesi** l. Fin.
92 F3 **Kallsjön** l. Sweden
93 G4 **Kalmar** Sweden
93 G4 **Kalmarsund** sea chan. Sweden
73 C4 **Kalmunai** Sri Lanka
119 C3 **Kalole** Dem. Rep. Congo
120 B2 **Kalomo** Zambia
128 B2 **Kalone Peak** Can.
74 B1 **Kalpa** India
73 B3 **Kalpeni** i. India
75 B2 **Kalpi** India
126 B2 **Kaltag** U.S.A.
101 D1 **Kaltenkirchen** Ger.
118 B2 **Kaltungo** Nigeria
89 E3 **Kaluga** Rus. Fed.
93 F4 **Kalundborg** Denmark
74 B1 **Kalur Kot** Pak.
90 A2 **Kalush** Ukr.
74 B3 **Kalyan** India
89 E2 **Kalyazin** Rus. Fed.
111 C3 **Kalymnos** Greece
111 C3 **Kalymnos** i. Greece
119 C3 **Kama** Dem. Rep. Congo
62 A2 **Kama** Myanmar
86 E3 **Kama** r. Rus. Fed.

66 D3 **Kamaishi** Japan
80 B2 **Kaman** Turkey
120 A2 **Kamanjab** Namibia
78 B3 **Kamarān** i. Yemen
Kamaran Island Yemen see Kamarān
74 A2 **Kamarod** Pak.
50 B3 **Kambalda** Austr.
119 C4 **Kambove** Dem. Rep. Congo
160 C4 **Kamchatka Basin** sea feature Bering Sea
57 Q4 **Kamchatka Peninsula** Rus. Fed.
110 C2 **Kamchiya** r. Bulg.
108 B2 **Kamenjak, Rt** pt Croatia
76 B1 **Kamenka** Kazakh.
86 D2 **Kamenka** Rus. Fed.
87 D3 **Kamenka** Rus. Fed.
66 C2 **Kamenka** Rus. Fed.
91 D1 **Kamenka** Rus. Fed.
Kamenka-Strumilovskaya Ukr. see Kam"yanka-Buz'ka
91 E3 **Kamennomostskiy** Rus. Fed.
91 E2 **Kamenolomni** Rus. Fed.
Kamenongue Angola see Camanongue
83 M2 **Kamenskoye** Rus. Fed.
Kamenskoye Ukr. see Dniprodzerzhyns'k
91 E2 **Kamensk-Shakhtinskiy** Rus. Fed.
86 F3 **Kamensk-Ural'skiy** Rus. Fed.
89 F2 **Kameshkovo** Rus. Fed.
75 B1 **Kamet** mt. China
72 C1 **Kamet** mt. China
122 A3 **Kamiesberge** mts S. Africa
122 A3 **Kamieskroon** S. Africa
129 D1 **Kamilukuak Lake** Can.
119 C3 **Kamina** Dem. Rep. Congo
129 E1 **Kaminak Lake** Can.
90 A1 **Kamin'-Kashyrs'kyy** Ukr.
119 C3 **Kamituga** Dem. Rep. Congo
128 B2 **Kamloops** Can.
54 B1 **Kamo** N.Z.
118 C3 **Kamob Sanha** Sudan
118 C3 **Kamonia** Dem. Rep. Congo
119 D2 **Kampala** Uganda
60 B1 **Kampar** r. Indon.
60 B1 **Kampar** Malaysia
100 B1 **Kampen** Neth.
119 C3 **Kampene** Dem. Rep. Congo
63 A2 **Kamphaeng Phet** Thai.
63 B2 **Kâmpóng Cham** Cambodia
63 B2 **Kâmpóng Chhnǎng** Cambodia
Kâmpóng Saôm Cambodia see Sihanoukville
63 B2 **Kâmpóng Spœ** Cambodia
63 B2 **Kâmpôt** Cambodia
Kampuchea country Asia see Cambodia
129 D2 **Kamsack** Can.
86 E3 **Kamskoye Vodokhranilishche** resr Rus. Fed.
117 C4 **Kamsuuma** Somalia
90 B2 **Kam"yanets'-Podil's'kyy** Ukr.
90 A1 **Kam"yanka-Buz'ka** Ukr.
88 B3 **Kamyanyets** Belarus
91 D2 **Kamyshevatskaya** Rus. Fed.
87 D3 **Kamyshin** Rus. Fed.
135 D3 **Kanab** U.S.A.
118 C3 **Kananga** Dem. Rep. Congo
87 D3 **Kanash** Rus. Fed.
138 C3 **Kanawha** r. U.S.A.
67 C3 **Kanazawa** Japan
62 A1 **Kanbalu** Myanmar
63 A2 **Kanchanaburi** Thai.
73 B3 **Kanchipuram** India
77 C3 **Kandahār** Afgh.
86 C2 **Kandalaksha** Rus. Fed.
61 C2 **Kandangan** Indon.
74 A2 **Kandhkot** Pak.
114 C3 **Kandi** Benin
74 A2 **Kandiaro** Pak.
74 B2 **Kandla** India
53 C2 **Kandos** Austr.
121 □D2 **Kandreho** Madag.
73 C4 **Kandy** Sri Lanka

76 B2 **Kandyagash** Kazakh.
127 H1 **Kane Bassin** b. Greenland
91 D2 **Kanevskaya** Rus. Fed.
122 B1 **Kang** Botswana
127 I2 **Kangaatsiaq** Greenland
114 B3 **Kangaba** Mali
80 B2 **Kangal** Turkey
79 C2 **Kangān** Iran
60 B1 **Kangar** Malaysia
52 A3 **Kangaroo Island** Austr.
93 H3 **Kangasala** Fin.
81 C2 **Kangāvar** Iran
75 C2 **Kangchenjunga** mt. India/Nepal
70 A2 **Kangding** China
65 B2 **Kangdong** N. Korea
61 C2 **Kangean, Kepulauan** is Indon.
119 D2 **Kangen** r. Sudan
127 J2 **Kangeq** c. Greenland
127 J2 **Kangerlussuaq** inlet Greenland
127 I2 **Kangerlussuaq** inlet Greenland
127 I2 **Kangersuatsiaq** Greenland
65 B1 **Kanggye** N. Korea
131 D2 **Kangiqsualujjuaq** Can.
127 H2 **Kangiqsujuaq** Can.
131 C1 **Kangirsuk** Can.
75 C2 **Kangmar** China
65 B2 **Kangnŭng** S. Korea
65 A1 **Kangping** China
72 D2 **Kangto** mt. China/India
62 A1 **Kani** Myanmar
118 C3 **Kaniama** Dem. Rep. Congo
61 C1 **Kanibongan** Sabah Malaysia
76 B2 **Kanin, Poluostrov** pen. Rus. Fed.
86 D2 **Kanin Nos** Rus. Fed.
86 D2 **Kanin Nos, Mys** c. Rus. Fed.
91 C2 **Kaniv** Ukr.
52 B3 **Kaniva** Austr.
93 H3 **Kankaanpää** Fin.
138 B2 **Kankakee** U.S.A.
114 B3 **Kankan** Guinea
75 C2 **Kanker** India
Kannur India see Cannanore
115 C3 **Kano** Nigeria
122 B3 **Kanonpunt** pt S. Africa
67 B4 **Kanoya** Japan
75 C2 **Kanpur** India
136 C3 **Kansas** r. U.S.A.
137 D3 **Kansas** state U.S.A.
137 E3 **Kansas City** KS U.S.A.
137 E3 **Kansas City** MO U.S.A.
83 H3 **Kansk** Rus. Fed.
Kansu prov. China see Gansu
63 B2 **Kantaralak** Thai.
114 C3 **Kantchari** Burkina
91 D2 **Kantemirovka** Rus. Fed.
49 J1 **Kanton** i. Kiribati
97 B2 **Kanturk** Rep. of Ireland
123 D2 **KaNyamazane** S. Africa
123 C1 **Kanye** Botswana
71 C3 **Kaohsiung** Taiwan
120 A2 **Kaokoveld** plat. Namibia
114 A3 **Kaolack** Senegal
120 B2 **Kaoma** Zambia
118 C3 **Kapanga** Dem. Rep. Congo
88 C3 **Kapatkyevichy** Belarus
77 D2 **Kapchagay** Kazakh.
77 D2 **Kapchagayskoye Vodokhranilishche** resr Kazakh.
100 B2 **Kapellen** Belgium
121 B2 **Kapiri Mposhi** Zambia
127 I2 **Kapisillit** Greenland
130 B2 **Kapiskau** r. Can.
61 C1 **Kapit** Sarawak Malaysia
63 A3 **Kapoe** Thai.
117 B4 **Kapoeta** Sudan
103 D2 **Kaposvár** Hungary
102 B1 **Kappeln** Ger.
65 B1 **Kapsan** N. Korea
Kapsukas Lith. see Marijampolé
61 B2 **Kapuas** r. Indon.
52 A2 **Kapunda** Austr.
130 A2 **Kapuskasing** Can.
53 C2 **Kaputar** mt. Austr.
103 D2 **Kapuvár** Hungary
88 C3 **Kapyl'** Belarus
77 D3 **Kaqung** China
114 C4 **Kara** Togo

111 C3 **Kara Ada** i. Turkey
77 D2 **Kara-Balta** Kyrg.
76 C1 **Karabalyk** Kazakh.
76 C3 **Karabil', Vozvyshennost'** hills Turkm.
Kara-Bogaz-Gol Turkm. see Karabogazkel'
76 B2 **Kara-Bogaz-Gol, Zaliv** b. Turkm.
76 B2 **Karabogazkel'** Turkm.
80 B1 **Karabük** Turkey
76 C2 **Karabutak** Kazakh.
111 C2 **Karacabey** Turkey
111 C2 **Karacaköy** Turkey
81 C1 **Karachayevsk** Rus. Fed.
89 D3 **Karachev** Rus. Fed.
74 A2 **Karachi** Pak.
77 D2 **Karaganda** Kazakh.
77 D2 **Karagayly** Kazakh.
83 L3 **Karaginskiy Zaliv** b. Rus. Fed.
81 D2 **Karaj** Iran
Kara-Kala Turkm. see Garrygala
64 B3 **Karakelong** i. Indon.
Karaklis Armenia see Vanadzor
77 D2 **Kara-Köl** Kyrg.
77 D2 **Karakol** Kyrg.
74 B1 **Karakoram Range** mts Asia
72 B1 **Karakoram Range** mts Asia
117 B3 **Kara K'orē** Eth.
Karakum, Peski des. Kazakh. see
76 B2 **Karakum Desert** des. Kazakh.
76 C3 **Karakum Desert** Turkm.
Karakumy, Peski des. Turkm. see Karakum Desert
80 B2 **Karaman** Turkey
77 E2 **Karamay** China
54 B2 **Karamea** N.Z.
54 B2 **Karamea Bight** b. N.Z.
80 B2 **Karapınar** Turkey
122 A2 **Karasburg** Namibia
86 F1 **Kara Sea** Rus. Fed.
92 I2 **Karasjok** Norway
Kara Strait Rus. Fed. see Karskiye Vorota, Proliv
111 D2 **Karasu** Turkey
Karasubazar Ukr. see Bilohirs'k
77 D1 **Karasuk** Rus. Fed.
77 D2 **Karatau** Kazakh.
77 C2 **Karatau, Khrebet** mts Kazakh.
86 F2 **Karatayka** Rus. Fed.
67 A4 **Karatsu** Japan
111 B3 **Karavas** Greece
60 B2 **Karawang** Indon.
81 C2 **Karbalā'** Iraq
103 E2 **Karcag** Hungary
Kardeljevo Croatia see Ploče
111 B3 **Karditsa** Greece
88 B2 **Kärdla** Estonia
122 B3 **Kareeberge** mts S. Africa
75 B2 **Kareli** India
88 C3 **Karelichy** Belarus
92 H2 **Karesuando** Sweden
Karghalik China see Yecheng
74 B1 **Kargil** Jammu and Kashmir
Kargilik China see Yecheng
89 E2 **Kargopol'** Rus. Fed.
118 B1 **Kari** Nigeria
121 B2 **Kariba** Zimbabwe
121 B2 **Kariba, Lake** resr Zambia/Zimbabwe
60 B2 **Karimata, Pulau-pulau** is Indon.
60 B2 **Karimata, Selat** str. Indon.
73 B3 **Karimnagar** India
61 C2 **Karimunjawa, Pulau-pulau** is Indon.
91 C2 **Karkinits'ka Zatoka** g. Ukr.
91 D2 **Karlivka** Ukr.
Karl-Marx-Stadt Ger. see Chemnitz
109 C1 **Karlovac** Croatia
102 C1 **Karlovy Vary** Czech Rep.
Karlsburg Romania see Alba Iulia
93 F4 **Karlshamn** Sweden
93 F4 **Karlskoga** Sweden

93 G4 Karlskrona Sweden
102 B2 Karlsruhe Ger.
93 F4 Karlstad Sweden
101 D3 Karlstadt Ger.
89 D3 Karma Belarus
93 E4 Karmøy i. Norway
75 D2 Karnafuli Reservoir Bangl.
74 B2 Karnal India
110 C2 Karnobat Bulg.
74 A2 Karodi Pak.
121 B2 Karoi Zimbabwe
121 C1 Karonga Malawi
116 B3 Karora Eritrea
111 C3 Karpathos Greece
111 C3 Karpathos i. Greece
111 B3 Karpenisi Greece
Karpilovka Belarus see Aktsyabrski
86 D2 Karpogory Rus. Fed.
50 A2 Karratha Austr.
81 C1 Kars Turkey
88 C2 Kārsava Latvia
76 B2 Karshi Turkm.
Karshi Uzbek. see Qarshi
111 C3 Karşıyaka Turkey
86 E2 Karskiye Vorota, Proliv str. Rus. Fed.
Karskoye More sea Rus. Fed. see Kara Sea
101 E1 Karstädt Ger.
111 C2 Kartal Turkey
87 F3 Kartaly Rus. Fed.
81 C2 Kārūn, Rūd-e r. Iran
73 B3 Karwar India
83 I3 Karymskoye Rus. Fed.
111 B3 Karystos Greece
111 C3 Kaş Turkey
130 B2 Kasabonika Lake Can.
118 C3 Kasaï, Plateau du Dem. Rep. Congo
118 C4 Kasaji Dem. Rep. Congo
121 C2 Kasama Zambia
120 B2 Kasane Botswana
118 B3 Kasangulu Dem. Rep. Congo
73 B3 Kasaragod India
129 D1 Kasba Lake Can.
120 B2 Kasempa Zambia
119 C4 Kasenga Dem. Rep. Congo
119 C3 Kasese Dem. Rep. Congo
119 D2 Kasese Uganda
Kasevo Rus. Fed. see Neftekamsk
81 D2 Kāshān Iran
Kashgar China see Kashi
77 D3 Kashi China
67 D3 Kashima-nada b. Japan
89 E2 Kashin Rus. Fed.
89 E3 Kashira Rus. Fed.
89 E3 Kashirskoye Rus. Fed.
67 C3 Kashiwazaki Japan
76 B3 Kāshmar Iran
Kashmir terr. Asia see Jammu and Kashmir
74 A2 Kashmor Pak.
119 C3 Kashyukulu Dem. Rep. Congo
89 F3 Kasimov Rus. Fed.
138 B3 Kaskaskia r. U.S.A.
93 H3 Kaskinen Fin.
119 C3 Kasongo Dem. Rep. Congo
118 B3 Kasongo-Lunda Dem. Rep. Congo
111 C3 Kasos i. Greece
Kaspiyskiy Rus. Fed. see Lagan'
116 B3 Kassala Sudan
101 D2 Kassel Ger.
115 C1 Kasserine Tunisia
80 B1 Kastamonu Turkey
111 B3 Kastelli Greece
Kastellorizon i. Greece see Megisti
111 B2 Kastoria Greece
89 D3 Kastsyukovichy Belarus
119 D3 Kasulu Tanz.
121 C2 Kasungu Malawi
139 F1 Katahdin, Mount U.S.A.
118 C3 Katako-Kombe Dem. Rep. Congo
119 D2 Katakwi Uganda
50 A3 Katanning Austr.
63 A3 Katchall i. India
111 B2 Katerini Greece
119 D3 Katesh Tanz.
128 A2 Kate's Needle mt. Can./U.S.A.
121 C2 Katete Zambia
62 A1 Katha Myanmar
50 C1 Katherine Austr.
50 C1 Katherine r. Austr.
74 B2 Kathiawar pen. India
123 C2 Kathlehong S. Africa
75 C2 Kathmandu Nepal
122 B2 Kathu S. Africa
74 B1 Kathua Jammu and Kashmir
114 B3 Kati Mali
75 C2 Katihar India
54 C1 Katikati N.Z.
123 C3 Kati-Kati S. Africa
120 B2 Katima Mulilo Namibia
114 B4 Katiola Côte d'Ivoire
Katmandu Nepal see Kathmandu
111 B3 Kato Achaïa Greece
119 C3 Katompi Dem. Rep. Congo
53 D2 Katoomba Austr.
103 D1 Katowice Pol.
80 B3 Kātrīnā, Jabal mt. Egypt
93 G4 Katrineholm Sweden
115 C3 Katsina Nigeria
115 C4 Katsina-Ala Nigeria
67 D3 Katsuura Japan
77 C3 Kattaqo'rg'on Uzbek.
93 F4 Kattegat str. Denmark/Sweden
100 B1 Katwijk aan Zee Neth.
101 D3 Katzenbuckel hill Ger.
49 L1 Kaua'i i. U.S.A.
93 H3 Kauhajoki Fin.
88 B3 Kaunas Lith.
115 C3 Kaura-Namoda Nigeria
Kaushany Moldova see Căuşeni
92 H2 Kautokeino Norway
109 D2 Kavadarci Macedonia
109 C2 Kavajë Albania
111 B2 Kavala Greece
66 C2 Kavalerovo Rus. Fed.
73 C3 Kavali India
73 B3 Kavaratti i. India
110 C2 Kavarna Bulg.
59 E3 Kavieng P.N.G.
81 D2 Kavīr, Dasht-e des. Iran
67 C3 Kawagoe Japan
54 B1 Kawakawa N.Z.
121 B1 Kawambwa Zambia
67 C3 Kawanishi Japan
130 C3 Kawartha Lakes Can.
67 C3 Kawasaki Japan
54 C1 Kawerau N.Z.
63 A2 Kawkareik Myanmar
62 A1 Kawlin Myanmar
63 A2 Kawmapyin Myanmar
116 B2 Kawm Umbū Egypt
63 A2 Kawthaung Myanmar
Kaxgar China see Kashi
77 D3 Kaxgar He r. China
114 B3 Kaya Burkina
111 C3 Kayacı Dağı hill Turkey
121 C1 Kayambi Zambia
61 C1 Kayan r. Indon.
136 B2 Kaycee U.S.A.
Kaydanovo Belarus see Dzyarzhynsk
142 A1 Kayenta U.S.A.
114 A3 Kayes Mali
77 D2 Kaynar Kazakh.
80 B2 Kayseri Turkey
134 D2 Kaysville U.S.A.
60 B2 Kayuagung Indon.
Kazakhskaya S.S.R. admin. reg. Asia see Kazakhstan
77 D1 Kazakhskiy Melkosopochnik plain Kazakh.
76 B2 Kazakhskiy Zaliv b. Kazakh.
76 C2 Kazakhstan country Asia
Kazakhstan Kazakh. see Aksay
87 D3 Kazan' Rus. Fed.
Kazandzhik Turkm. see Gazandzhyk
110 C2 Kazanlŭk Bulg.
Kazan-rettō Japan see Volcano Islands
76 A2 Kazbek mt. Georgia/Rus. Fed.
81 D3 Kāzerūn Iran
103 E2 Kazincbarcika Hungary
118 C3 Kazumba Dem. Rep. Congo
66 D2 Kazuno Japan
86 F2 Kazymskiy Mys Rus. Fed.
111 B3 Kea i. Greece
97 C1 Keady U.K.
137 D2 Kearney U.S.A.
142 A2 Kearny U.S.A.
115 C1 Kebili Tunisia
116 A3 Kebkabiya Sudan
92 G2 Kebnekaise mt. Sweden
117 C4 K'ebrī Dehar Eth.
60 B2 Kebumen Indon.
128 B2 Kechika r. Can.
111 D3 Keçiborlu Turkey
103 D2 Kecskemét Hungary
88 B2 Kėdainiai Lith.
114 A3 Kédougou Senegal
103 D1 Kędzierzyn-Koźle Pol.
128 B1 Keele r. Can.
128 A1 Keele Peak Can.
Keelung Taiwan see Chilung
139 E2 Keene U.S.A.
122 A2 Keetmanshoop Namibia
129 E3 Keewatin Can.
Kefallonia i. Greece see Cephalonia
59 C3 Kefamenanu Indon.
92 □A3 Keflavík Iceland
77 D2 Kegen Kazakh.
128 C2 Keg River Can.
88 C2 Kehra Estonia
62 A1 Kehsi Mansam Myanmar
98 C3 Keighley U.K.
88 B2 Keila Estonia
122 B2 Keimoes S. Africa
92 I3 Keitele l. Fin.
52 B3 Keith Austr.
96 C2 Keith U.K.
128 B1 Keith Arm b. Can.
134 B2 Keizer U.S.A.
103 E2 Kékes mt. Hungary
117 C4 K'elafo Eth.
Kelang Malaysia see Klang
92 J2 Keles-Uayv, Gora hill Rus. Fed.
102 C2 Kelheim Ger.
76 C3 Kelifskiy Uzboy marsh Turkm.
80 B1 Kelkit r. Turkey
128 B1 Keller Lake Can.
134 C1 Kellogg U.S.A.
92 I2 Kelloselkä Fin.
97 C2 Kells Rep. of Ireland
88 B2 Kelmė Lith.
115 D4 Kelo Chad
128 C3 Kelowna Can.
96 C3 Kelso U.K.
134 B1 Kelso U.S.A.
60 B1 Keluang Malaysia
129 D2 Kelvington Can.
86 C2 Kem' Rus. Fed.
Ke Macina Mali see Massina
128 B2 Kemano Can.
118 C2 Kembé C.A.R.
111 C3 Kemer Turkey
82 G3 Kemerovo Rus. Fed.
92 H2 Kemi Fin.
92 I2 Kemijärvi Fin.
92 I2 Kemijärvi l. Fin.
92 I2 Kemijoki r. Fin.
136 A2 Kemmerer U.S.A.
92 I3 Kempele Fin.
55 G2 Kemp Land reg. Antarctica
55 A2 Kemp Peninsula Antarctica
53 D2 Kempsey Austr.
130 C3 Kempt, Lac l. Can.
102 C2 Kempten (Allgäu) Ger.
123 C2 Kempton Park S. Africa
61 C2 Kemujan i. Indon.
126 B2 Kenai U.S.A.
129 D2 Kenaston Can.
98 B2 Kendal U.K.
141 D3 Kendall U.S.A.
61 D2 Kendari Indon.
60 C2 Kendawangan Indon.
115 D3 Kendégué Chad
114 A4 Kenema Sierra Leone
118 B3 Kenge Dem. Rep. Congo
62 A1 Kengtung Myanmar
122 B2 Kenhardt S. Africa
114 B1 Kénitra Morocco
97 B3 Kenmare Rep. of Ireland
136 C1 Kenmare U.S.A.
97 A3 Kenmare River inlet Rep. of Ireland
100 C3 Kenn Ger.
143 C2 Kenna U.S.A.
139 F2 Kennebec r. U.S.A.
Kennedy, Cape U.S.A. see Canaveral, Cape
140 B3 Kenner U.S.A.
99 C4 Kennet r. U.K.
137 E3 Kennett U.S.A.
134 C1 Kennewick U.S.A.
130 A3 Kenora Can.
138 B2 Kenosha U.S.A.
142 C2 Kent U.S.A.
77 C2 Kentau Kazakh.
138 B3 Kentucky r. U.S.A.
138 C3 Kentucky state U.S.A.
138 B3 Kentucky Lake U.S.A.
140 B2 Kentwood U.S.A.
119 D2 Kenya country Africa
119 D3 Kenya, Mount mt. Kenya
60 B1 Kenyir, Tasik resr Malaysia
137 E2 Keokuk U.S.A.
75 C2 Keonjhar India
111 C3 Kepsut Turkey
52 B3 Kerang Austr.
91 D2 Kerch Ukr.
59 D3 Kerema P.N.G.
128 C3 Keremeos Can.
116 B3 Keren Eritrea
81 C2 Kerend Iran
159 E7 Kerguélen, Îles is Indian Ocean
159 E7 Kerguelen Plateau sea feature Indian Ocean
119 D3 Kericho Kenya
54 B1 Kerikeri N.Z.
60 B2 Kerinci, Gunung vol. Indon.
Kerintji vol. Indon. see Kerinci, Gunung
100 C2 Kerkrade Neth.
111 A3 Kerkyra Greece
Kerkyra i. Greece see Corfu
116 B3 Kerma Sudan
49 J7 Kermadec Islands S. Pacific Ocean
79 C1 Kermān Iran
81 C2 Kermānshāh Iran
Kermine Uzbek. see Navoiy
143 C2 Kermit U.S.A.
135 C3 Kern r. U.S.A.
114 B4 Kérouané Guinea
100 C2 Kerpen Ger.
129 D2 Kerrobert Can.
143 D2 Kerrville U.S.A.
97 B2 Kerry Head hd Rep. of Ireland
Keryneia Cyprus see Kyrenia
130 B2 Kesagami Lake Can.
111 C2 Keşan Turkey
66 D3 Kesennuma Japan
74 B2 Keshod India
100 C2 Kessel Neth.
98 B2 Keswick U.K.
103 D2 Keszthely Hungary
82 G3 Ket' r. Rus. Fed.
60 C2 Ketapang Indon.
128 A2 Ketchikan U.S.A.
134 D2 Ketchum U.S.A.
114 B4 Kete Krachi Ghana
118 B2 Kétté Cameroon
99 C3 Kettering U.K.
138 C3 Kettering U.S.A.
134 C1 Kettle River Range mts U.S.A.
93 H3 Keuruu Fin.
100 C2 Kevelaer Ger.
138 B2 Kewanee U.S.A.
138 B1 Keweenaw Bay U.S.A.
138 B1 Keweenaw Peninsula U.S.A.
141 D3 Key Largo U.S.A.
99 B4 Keynsham U.K.
139 D3 Keyser U.S.A.
141 D4 Key West U.S.A.
123 C2 Kgotsong S. Africa
69 F1 Khabarovsk Rus. Fed.
91 D3 Khadyzhensk Rus. Fed.
75 D2 Khagrachari Bangl.
74 A2 Khairpur Pak.
122 B1 Khakhea Botswana
76 B3 Khalilabad Iran
86 F2 Khal'mer-Yu Rus. Fed.
68 C1 Khamar-Daban, Khrebet mts Rus. Fed.
74 B2 Khambhat India
74 B3 Khambhat, Gulf of India
74 B2 Khamgaon India
79 C2 Khamīr Iran
78 B3 Khamir Yemen
78 B3 Khamis Mushayṭ Saudi Arabia
77 C3 Khānābād Afgh.
74 B2 Khandwa India
83 K2 Khandyga Rus. Fed.
74 B1 Khanewal Pak.

Khan Hung Vietnam *see* **Soc Trăng**
83 J3 **Khani** Rus. Fed.
66 B2 **Khanka, Lake** China/Rus. Fed.
115 C2 **Khannfoussa** *hill* Alg.
74 B2 **Khanpur** Pak.
77 D2 **Khantau** Kazakh.
83 H2 **Khantayskoye, Ozero** *l.* Rus. Fed.
86 F2 **Khanty-Mansiysk** Rus. Fed.
63 A3 **Khao Chum Thong** Thai.
63 A2 **Khao Laem Reservoir** Thai.
74 B1 **Khapalu** Jammu and Kashmir
87 D4 **Kharabali** Rus. Fed.
75 C2 **Kharagpur** India
79 C2 **Khārān** *r.* Iran
Kharga Oasis Egypt *see* **Khārijah, Wāḩāt al**
74 B2 **Khargon** India
116 B2 **Khārijah, Wāḩāt al** Egypt
91 D2 **Kharkiv** Ukr.
Khar'kov Ukr. *see* **Kharkiv**
111 C2 **Kharmanli** Bulg.
89 F2 **Kharovsk** Rus. Fed.
116 B3 **Khartoum** Sudan
87 D4 **Khasav'yurt** Rus. Fed.
79 D2 **Khāsh** Iran
86 F2 **Khashgort** Rus. Fed.
78 A3 **Khashm el Girba** Sudan
78 A3 **Khashm el Girba Dam** Sudan
81 C1 **Khashuri** Georgia
75 D2 **Khasi Hills** India
111 C2 **Khaskovo** Bulg.
83 H2 **Khatanga** Rus. Fed.
123 C3 **Khayamnandi** S. Africa
78 A2 **Khaybar** Saudi Arabia
122 A3 **Khayelitsha** S. Africa
62 B2 **Khê Bo** Vietnam
107 D2 **Khemis Miliana** Alg.
63 B2 **Khemmarat** Thai.
115 C1 **Khenchela** Alg.
81 D3 **Kherāmeh** Iran
91 C2 **Kherson** Ukr.
83 H2 **Kheta** *r.* Rus. Fed.
69 D1 **Khilok** Rus. Fed.
89 E2 **Khimki** Rus. Fed.
89 E3 **Khlevnoye** Rus. Fed.
63 B2 **Khlung** Thai.
90 B2 **Khmel'nyts'kyy** Ukr.
Khmer Republic *country* Asia *see* **Cambodia**
76 B1 **Khobda** Kazakh.
Khodzheyli Uzbek. *see* **Xo'jayli**
89 E3 **Khokhol'skiy** Rus. Fed.
74 B2 **Khokhropar** Pak.
74 A1 **Kholm** Afgh.
89 D2 **Kholm** Rus. Fed.
89 D2 **Kholm-Zhirkovskiy** Rus. Fed.
122 A1 **Khomas Highland** *hills* Namibia
89 E3 **Khomutovo** Rus. Fed.
79 C2 **Khonj** Iran
63 B2 **Khon Kaen** Thai.
62 A1 **Khonsa** India
83 K2 **Khonuu** Rus. Fed.
86 E2 **Khoreyver** Rus. Fed.
69 D1 **Khorinsk** Rus. Fed.
120 A3 **Khorixas** Namibia
66 B2 **Khorol** Rus. Fed.
91 C2 **Khorol** Ukr.
81 C2 **Khorramābād** Iran
81 C2 **Khorramshahr** Iran
77 D3 **Khorugh** Tajik.
Khotan China *see* **Hotan**
90 B2 **Khotyn** Ukr.
114 B1 **Khouribga** Morocco
77 C3 **Khowst** Afgh.
88 C3 **Khoyniki** Belarus
62 A1 **Khreum** Myanmar
76 B1 **Khromtau** Kazakh.
Khrushchev Ukr. *see* **Svitlovods'k**
90 B2 **Khrystynivka** Ukr.
123 B1 **Khudumelapye** Botswana
77 C2 **Khŭjand** Tajik.
63 B2 **Khu Khan** Thai.
78 A2 **Khulays** Saudi Arabia
75 C2 **Khulna** Bangl.
Khūnīnshahr Iran *see* **Khorramshahr**
81 D2 **Khunsar** Iran
79 B2 **Khurayş** Saudi Arabia
74 B1 **Khushab** Pak.
90 A2 **Khust** Ukr.
123 C2 **Khutsong** S. Africa
74 A2 **Khuzdar** Pak.
81 D3 **Khvormūj** Iran
81 C2 **Khvoy** Iran
89 D2 **Khvoynaya** Rus. Fed.
77 D3 **Khyber Pass** Afgh./Pak.
53 D2 **Kiama** Austr.
64 B3 **Kiamba** Phil.
119 C3 **Kiambi** Dem. Rep. Congo
Kiangsi *prov.* China *see* **Jiangxi**
Kiangsu *prov.* China *see* **Jiangsu**
119 D3 **Kibaha** Tanz.
119 D3 **Kibaya** Tanz.
119 D3 **Kibiti** Tanz.
119 C3 **Kibombo** Dem. Rep. Congo
119 D3 **Kibondo** Tanz.
119 D2 **Kibre Mengist** Eth.
119 D3 **Kibungo** Rwanda
111 B2 **Kičevo** Macedonia
114 C3 **Kidal** Mali
99 B3 **Kidderminster** U.K.
114 A3 **Kidira** Senegal
74 B1 **Kidmang** Jammu and Kashmir
54 C1 **Kidnappers, Cape** N.Z.
102 C1 **Kiel** Ger.
103 E1 **Kielce** Pol.
98 B2 **Kielder Water** *resr* U.K.
119 C4 **Kienge** Dem. Rep. Congo
90 C1 **Kiev** Ukr.
114 A3 **Kiffa** Maur.
119 D3 **Kigali** Rwanda
119 C3 **Kigoma** Tanz.
88 B2 **Kihnu** *i.* Estonia
92 I2 **Kiiminki** Fin.
67 B4 **Kii-suidō** *sea chan.* Japan
109 D1 **Kikinda** Serb. and Mont.
119 C3 **Kikondja** Dem. Rep. Congo
59 D3 **Kikori** P.N.G.
59 D3 **Kikori** *r.* P.N.G.
118 B3 **Kikwit** Dem. Rep. Congo
65 B1 **Kilchu** N. Korea
97 C2 **Kilcock** Rep. of Ireland
97 C2 **Kildare** Rep. of Ireland
118 B3 **Kilembe** Dem. Rep. Congo
143 E2 **Kilgore** U.S.A.
119 D3 **Kilifi** Kenya
119 D3 **Kilimanjaro** *vol.* Tanz.
119 D3 **Kilindoni** Tanz.
80 B2 **Kilis** Turkey
90 B2 **Kiliya** Ukr.
97 B2 **Kilkee** Rep. of Ireland
97 D1 **Kilkeel** U.K.
97 C2 **Kilkenny** Rep. of Ireland
111 B2 **Kilkis** Greece
97 B1 **Killala** Rep. of Ireland
97 B1 **Killala Bay** Rep. of Ireland
97 B2 **Killaloe** Rep. of Ireland
128 C2 **Killam** Can.
97 B2 **Killarney** Rep. of Ireland
143 D2 **Killeen** U.S.A.
96 B2 **Killin** U.K.
131 D1 **Killiniq** Can.
97 B2 **Killorglin** Rep. of Ireland
97 B1 **Killybegs** Rep. of Ireland
96 B3 **Kilmarnock** U.K.
53 B3 **Kilmore** Austr.
119 D3 **Kilosa** Tanz.
97 B2 **Kilrush** Rep. of Ireland
119 C3 **Kilwa** Dem. Rep. Congo
119 D3 **Kilwa Masoko** Tanz.
119 D3 **Kimambi** Tanz.
52 A2 **Kimba** Austr.
136 C2 **Kimball** U.S.A.
59 E3 **Kimbe** P.N.G.
128 C3 **Kimberley** Can.
122 B2 **Kimberley** S. Africa
50 B1 **Kimberley Plateau** Austr.
65 B1 **Kimch'aek** N. Korea
65 B2 **Kimch'ŏn** S. Korea
65 B2 **Kimhae** S. Korea
127 H2 **Kimmirut** Can.
89 E3 **Kimovsk** Rus. Fed.
118 C3 **Kimpanga** Dem. Rep. Congo
118 B3 **Kimpese** Dem. Rep. Congo
89 E2 **Kimry** Rus. Fed.
61 C1 **Kinabalu, Gunung** *mt. Sabah* Malaysia
128 C2 **Kinbasket Lake** Can.
96 C1 **Kinbrace** U.K.
130 B3 **Kincardine** Can.
62 A1 **Kinchang** Myanmar
119 C3 **Kinda** Dem. Rep. Congo
98 C3 **Kinder Scout** *hill* U.K.
129 D2 **Kindersley** Can.
114 A3 **Kindia** Guinea
119 C3 **Kindu** Dem. Rep. Congo
89 F2 **Kineshma** Rus. Fed.
118 B3 **Kingandu** Dem. Rep. Congo
51 E2 **Kingaroy** Austr.
135 B3 **King City** U.S.A.
130 C2 **King George Islands** Can.
88 C2 **Kingisepp** Rus. Fed.
51 D3 **King Island** Austr.
Kingisseppa Estonia *see* **Kuressaare**
50 B1 **King Leopold Ranges** *hills* Austr.
142 A1 **Kingman** U.S.A.
135 B3 **Kings** *r.* U.S.A.
52 A3 **Kingscote** Austr.
97 C2 **Kingscourt** Rep. of Ireland
99 D3 **King's Lynn** U.K.
50 B1 **King Sound** *b.* Austr.
134 D2 **Kings Peak** U.S.A.
141 D1 **Kingsport** U.S.A.
51 D4 **Kingston** Austr.
130 C3 **Kingston** Can.
146 C3 **Kingston** Jamaica
139 E2 **Kingston** U.S.A.
52 A3 **Kingston South East** Austr.
98 C3 **Kingston upon Hull** U.K.
147 D3 **Kingstown** St Vincent
143 D3 **Kingsville** U.S.A.
99 B4 **Kingswood** U.K.
96 B2 **Kingussie** U.K.
126 F2 **King William Island** Can.
123 C3 **King William's Town** S. Africa
67 D3 **Kinka-san** *i.* Japan
96 B2 **Kinlochleven** U.K.
93 F4 **Kinna** Sweden
97 B3 **Kinsale** Rep. of Ireland
118 B3 **Kinshasa** Dem. Rep. Congo
141 E1 **Kinston** U.S.A.
88 B2 **Kintai** Lith.
114 B4 **Kintampo** Ghana
96 C2 **Kintore** U.K.
96 B3 **Kintyre** *pen.* U.K.
119 D3 **Kiomboi** Tanz.
130 C3 **Kipawa, Lac** *l.* Can.
119 D3 **Kipembawe** Tanz.
119 D3 **Kipengere Range** *mts* Tanz.
129 D2 **Kipling** Can.
Kipling Station Can. *see* **Kipling**
119 C4 **Kipushi** Dem. Rep. Congo
119 C4 **Kipushia** Dem. Rep. Congo
101 D2 **Kirchhain** Ger.
101 D3 **Kirchheim-Bolanden** Ger.
83 I3 **Kirenga** *r.* Rus. Fed.
83 I3 **Kirensk** Rus. Fed.
89 E3 **Kireyevsk** Rus. Fed.
Kirghizia *country* Asia *see* **Kyrgyzstan**
77 D2 **Kirghiz Range** *mts* Asia
Kirgizskaya S.S.R. *admin. reg.* Asia *see* **Kyrgyzstan**
49 J4 **Kiribati** *country* Pacific Ocean
80 B2 **Kırıkkale** Turkey
89 E2 **Kirillov** Rus. Fed.
Kirin China *see* **Jilin**
Kirin *prov.* China *see* **Jilin**
Kirinyaga Kenya *see* **Kenya, Mount**
89 D2 **Kirishi** Rus. Fed.
48 L3 **Kiritimati** *i.* Kiribati
111 C3 **Kırkağaç** Turkey
98 B3 **Kirkby** U.K.
98 B2 **Kirkby Stephen** U.K.
96 C2 **Kirkcaldy** U.K.
96 B3 **Kirkcudbright** U.K.
92 J2 **Kirkenes** Norway
88 B1 **Kirkkonummi** Fin.
130 B3 **Kirkland Lake** Can.
111 C2 **Kırklareli** Turkey
137 E2 **Kirksville** U.S.A.
81 C2 **Kirkūk** Iraq
96 C1 **Kirkwall** U.K.
Kīrov Kazakh. *see* **Balpyk Bi**
89 D3 **Kirov** Rus. Fed.
86 D3 **Kirov** Rus. Fed.
Kirovabad Azer. *see* **Gäncä**
Kirovakan Armenia *see* **Vanadzor**
Kirovo Ukr. *see* **Kirovohrad**
86 E3 **Kirovo-Chepetsk** Rus. Fed.
Kirovo-Chepetskiy Rus. Fed. *see* **Kirovo-Chepetsk**
91 C2 **Kirovohrad** Ukr.
86 C2 **Kirovsk** Rus. Fed.
91 D2 **Kirovs'ke** Ukr.
Kirovskiy Kazakh. *see* **Balpyk Bi**
66 B1 **Kirovskiy** Rus. Fed.
96 C2 **Kirriemuir** U.K.
86 E3 **Kirs** Rus. Fed.
87 D3 **Kirsanov** Rus. Fed.
80 B2 **Kırşehir** Turkey
74 A2 **Kirthar Range** *mts* Pak.
92 H2 **Kiruna** Sweden
67 C3 **Kiryū** Japan
89 E2 **Kirzhach** Rus. Fed.
119 D3 **Kisaki** Tanz.
119 C2 **Kisangani** Dem. Rep. Congo
118 B3 **Kisantu** Dem. Rep. Congo
60 A1 **Kisaran** Indon.
82 G3 **Kiselevsk** Rus. Fed.
75 C2 **Kishanganj** India
115 C4 **Kishi** Nigeria
Kishinev Moldova *see* **Chişinău**
67 C4 **Kishiwada** Japan
77 D1 **Kishkenekol'** Kazakh.
75 D2 **Kishoreganj** Bangl.
74 B1 **Kishtwar** Jammu and Kashmir
119 D3 **Kisii** Kenya
103 D2 **Kiskunfélegyháza** Hungary
103 D2 **Kiskunhalas** Hungary
87 D4 **Kislovodsk** Rus. Fed.
117 C5 **Kismaayo** Somalia
Kismayu Somalia *see* **Kismaayo**
119 C3 **Kisoro** Uganda
114 A4 **Kissidougou** Guinea
141 D3 **Kissimmee** U.S.A.
141 D3 **Kissimmee, Lake** U.S.A.
129 D2 **Kississing Lake** Can.
Kistna *r.* India *see* **Krishna**
119 D3 **Kisumu** Kenya
103 E2 **Kisvárda** Hungary
Kisykkamys Kazakh. *see* **Dzhangala**
114 B3 **Kita** Mali
67 D3 **Kitaibaraki** Japan
66 D3 **Kitakami** Japan
66 D3 **Kitakami-gawa** *r.* Japan
67 B4 **Kita-Kyūshū** Japan
119 D2 **Kitale** Kenya
66 D2 **Kitami** Japan
130 B3 **Kitchener** Can.
93 J3 **Kitee** Fin.
119 D2 **Kitgum** Uganda
128 B2 **Kitimat** Can.
118 B3 **Kitona** Dem. Rep. Congo
92 H2 **Kittilä** Fin.
141 E1 **Kitty Hawk** U.S.A.
119 D3 **Kitunda** Tanz.
128 B2 **Kitwanga** Can.
121 B2 **Kitwe** Zambia
102 C2 **Kitzbühel** Austria
101 E3 **Kitzingen** Ger.
59 D3 **Kiunga** P.N.G.
92 I3 **Kiuruvesi** Fin.
92 I2 **Kivalo** *ridge* Fin.
90 B1 **Kivertsi** Ukr.
88 C2 **Kiviõli** Estonia
91 D2 **Kivsharivka** Ukr.
119 C3 **Kivu, Lake** Dem. Rep. Congo/Rwanda
111 C2 **Kıyıköy** Turkey
86 E3 **Kizel** Rus. Fed.
111 C3 **Kızılca Dağ** *mt.* Turkey
80 B1 **Kızılırmak** *r.* Turkey
87 D4 **Kizlyar** Rus. Fed.
Kizyl-Arbat Turkm. *see* **Gyzylarbat**
92 I1 **Kjøllefjord** Norway
92 G2 **Kjøpsvik** Norway
102 C1 **Kladno** Czech Rep.
102 C2 **Klagenfurt** Austria
88 B2 **Klaipėda** Lith.
94 B1 **Klaksvík** Faroe Is
134 B2 **Klamath** *r.* U.S.A.
134 B2 **Klamath Falls** U.S.A.
134 B2 **Klamath Mountains** U.S.A.
60 B1 **Klang** Malaysia
102 C2 **Klatovy** Czech Rep.
122 A3 **Klawer** S. Africa
128 A2 **Klawock** U.S.A.
128 B2 **Kleena Kleene** Can.
122 B2 **Kleinbegin** S. Africa
122 A2 **Klein Karas** Namibia

122 A2 Kleinsee S. Africa
123 C2 Klerksdorp S. Africa
90 B1 Klesiv Ukr.
89 D3 Kletnya Rus. Fed.
100 C2 Kleve Ger.
88 C3 Klichaw Belarus
89 D3 Klimavichy Belarus
89 D3 Klimovo Rus. Fed.
89 E2 Klimovsk Rus. Fed.
89 E2 Klin Rus. Fed.
101 F2 Klingenthal Ger.
101 F2 Klínovec mt. Czech Rep.
93 G4 Klintehamn Sweden
89 D3 Klintsy Rus. Fed.
109 C2 Ključ Bos.-Herz.
103 D1 Kłodzko Pol.
100 C1 Kloosterhaar Neth.
103 D2 Klosterneuburg Austria
101 E1 Klötze (Altmark) Ger.
128 A1 Kluane Lake Can.
Kluang Malaysia see Keluang
103 D1 Kluczbork Pol.
Klukhori Rus. Fed. see Karachayevsk
128 A2 Klukwan U.S.A.
74 A2 Klupro Pak.
89 F2 Klyaz'ma r. Rus. Fed.
88 C3 Klyetsk Belarus
83 L3 Klyuchi Rus. Fed.
98 C2 Knaresborough U.K.
93 F3 Knästen hill Sweden
129 E2 Knee Lake Can.
101 E1 Knebeck Ger.
101 E3 Knetzgau Ger.
109 C2 Knin Croatia
103 C2 Knittelfeld Austria
109 D2 Knjaževac Serb. and Mont.
Knob Lake Can. see Schefferville
97 B3 Knockaboy hill Rep. of Ireland
100 A2 Knokke-Heist Belgium
141 D1 Knoxville U.S.A.
127 H1 Knud Rasmussen Land reg. Greenland
122 B3 Knysna S. Africa
60 B2 Koba Indon.
67 C4 Kôbe Japan
København Denmark see Copenhagen
100 C2 Koblenz Ger.
59 C3 Kobroör i. Indon.
88 B3 Kobryn Belarus
Kocaeli Turkey see İzmit
111 B2 Koçani Macedonia
111 C2 Kocasu r. Turkey
109 B1 Kočevje Slovenia
75 C2 Koch Bihar India
89 F3 Kochetovka Rus. Fed.
Kochi India see Cochin
67 B4 Kôchi Japan
87 D4 Kochubey Rus. Fed.
75 C2 Kodarma India
126 B3 Kodiak U.S.A.
126 B3 Kodiak Island U.S.A.
123 C1 Kodibeleng Botswana
117 B4 Kodok Sudan
90 B2 Kodyma Ukr.
111 C2 Kodzhaele mt. Bulg./Greece
122 A2 Koës Namibia
122 C2 Koffiefontein S. Africa
114 B4 Koforidua Ghana
67 C3 Kôfu Japan
131 D2 Kogaluk r. Can.
114 B3 Kogoni Mali
74 B1 Kohat Pak.
72 D2 Kohima India
88 C2 Kohtla-Järve Estonia
128 A1 Koidern Can.
Kokand Uzbek. see Qo'qon
88 B2 Kökar Fin.
Kokchetav Kazakh. see Kokshetau
122 A2 Kokerboom Namibia
88 C3 Kokhanava Belarus
89 F2 Kokhma Rus. Fed.
92 H3 Kokkola Fin.
88 C2 Koknese Latvia
138 B2 Kokomo U.S.A.
122 B1 Kokong Botswana
123 C2 Kokosi S. Africa
77 E2 Kokpekti Kazakh.
77 C1 Kokshetau Kazakh.
131 D2 Koksoak r. Can.
123 C3 Kokstad S. Africa
Koktokay China see Fuyun
61 D2 Kolaka Indon.

86 C2 Kola Peninsula Rus. Fed.
92 H2 Kolari Fin.
Kolarovgrad Bulg. see Shumen
114 A3 Kolda Senegal
93 E4 Kolding Denmark
119 C2 Kole Dem. Rep. Congo
107 D2 Koléa Alg.
86 D2 Kolguyev, Ostrov i. Rus. Fed.
73 B3 Kolhapur India
88 B2 Kolkasrags pt Latvia
75 C2 Kolkata India
Kollam India see Quilon
100 C1 Kollum Neth.
Köln Ger. see Cologne
103 D1 Koło Pol.
103 D1 Kołobrzeg Pol.
114 B3 Kolokani Mali
89 E2 Kolomna Rus. Fed.
90 B2 Kolomyya Ukr.
114 B3 Kolondiéba Mali
61 D2 Kolonedale Indon.
122 B2 Kolonkwane Botswana
82 G3 Kolpashevo Rus. Fed.
89 E3 Kolpny Rus. Fed.
Kol'skiy Poluostrov pen. Rus. Fed. see Kola Peninsula
78 B3 Koluli Eritrea
92 F3 Kolvereid Norway
119 C4 Kolwezi Dem. Rep. Congo
83 L2 Kolyma r. Rus. Fed.
Kolyma Lowland Rus. Fed. see Kolymskaya Nizmennost'
Kolyma Range mts Rus. Fed. see Kolymskiy, Khrebet
83 L2 Kolymskaya Nizmennost' lowland Rus. Fed.
83 M2 Kolymskiy, Khrebet mts Rus. Fed.
122 A2 Komaggas S. Africa
67 C3 Komaki Japan
83 M3 Komandorskiye Ostrova is Rus. Fed.
103 D2 Komárno Slovakia
123 D2 Komati r. Swaziland
123 D2 Komatipoort S. Africa
67 C3 Komatsu Japan
120 A2 Kombat Namibia
119 C3 Kombe Dem. Rep. Congo
Komintern Ukr. see Marhanets'
Kominternivs'ke Ukr.
90 C2 Komiža Croatia
109 C2 Komló Hungary
103 D2 Kommunarsk Ukr. see Alchevs'k
118 B3 Komono Congo
111 C2 Komotini Greece
Kompong Som Cambodia see Sihanoukville
Komrat Moldova see Comrat
122 B3 Komsberg mts S. Africa
83 H1 Komsomolets, Ostrov i. Rus. Fed.
89 F2 Komsomol'sk Rus. Fed.
91 C2 Komsomol's'k Ukr.
83 M2 Komsomol'skiy Rus. Fed. see Yugorsk
87 D4 Komsomol'skiy Rus. Fed.
83 K3 Komsomol'sk-na-Amure Rus. Fed.
89 E2 Konakovo Rus. Fed.
75 C3 Kondagaon India
86 F2 Kondinskoye Rus. Fed. see Oktyabr'skoye
119 D3 Kondoa Tanz.
86 C2 Kondopoga Rus. Fed.
89 E3 Kondrovo Rus. Fed.
127 J2 Kong Christian IX Land reg. Greenland
127 K2 Kong Christian X Land reg. Greenland
127 J2 Kong Frederik VI Kyst coastal area Greenland
65 B2 Kongju S. Korea
119 C3 Kongolo Dem. Rep. Congo
93 E4 Kongsberg Norway
93 F3 Kongsvinger Norway
77 D3 Kongur Shan mt. China
100 C2 Königswinter Ger.
103 D1 Konin Pol.
109 C2 Konjic Bos.-Herz.
122 A2 Konkiep watercourse Namibia

86 D2 Konosha Rus. Fed.
91 C1 Konotop Ukr.
103 E1 Końskie Pol.
Konstantinograd Ukr. see Krasnohrad
102 B2 Konstanz Ger.
115 C3 Kontagora Nigeria
63 B2 Kon Tum Vietnam
63 B2 Kontum, Plateau du Vietnam
80 B2 Konya Turkey
77 D2 Konyrat Kazakh.
100 C3 Konz Ger.
86 E3 Konzhakovskiy Kamen', Gora mt. Rus. Fed.
134 C1 Kooskia U.S.A.
128 C3 Kootenay Lake Can.
53 D2 Kootingal Austr.
122 B3 Kootjieskolk S. Africa
92 □B2 Kópasker Iceland
108 B1 Koper Slovenia
93 G4 Köping Sweden
123 C1 Kopong Botswana
93 G4 Kopparberg Sweden
109 C1 Koprivnica Croatia
89 F3 Korablino Rus. Fed.
73 B3 Koraput India
75 C2 Korba India
101 D2 Korbach Ger.
109 C2 Korçë Albania
109 C2 Korčula Croatia
109 C2 Korčula i. Croatia
65 B1 Korea, North country Asia
65 B2 Korea, South country Asia
70 C2 Korea Bay g. China/N. Korea
65 B3 Korea Strait Japan/S. Korea
89 D3 Korenevo Rus. Fed.
91 D2 Korenovsk Rus. Fed.
Korenovskaya Rus. Fed. see Korenovsk
90 B1 Korets' Ukr.
111 C2 Körfez Turkey
114 B4 Korhogo Côte d'Ivoire
Korinthos Greece see Corinth
103 D2 Köris-hegy hill Hungary
109 D2 Koritnik mt. Albania
Koritsa Albania see Korçë
67 D3 Kõriyama Japan
87 F3 Korkino Rus. Fed.
111 D3 Korkuteli Turkey
77 E2 Korla China
103 D2 Körmend Hungary
49 I5 Koro i. Fiji
114 B3 Koro Mali
131 D2 Koroc r. Can.
91 D1 Korocha Rus. Fed.
119 D3 Korogwe Tanz.
59 C2 Koror Palau
103 E2 Körös r. Romania
90 B1 Korosten' Ukr.
90 B1 Korostyshiv Ukr.
115 D3 Koro Toro Chad
93 H3 Korpo Fin.
66 D1 Korsakov Rus. Fed.
91 C2 Korsun'-Shevchenkivs'kyy Ukr.
103 E1 Korsze Pol.
116 B3 Korti Sudan
100 A2 Kortrijk Belgium
83 L3 Koryakskaya, Sopka vol. Rus. Fed.
83 M2 Koryakskiy Khrebet mts Rus. Fed.
86 D2 Koryazhma Rus. Fed.
65 B2 Koryŏng S. Korea
91 C1 Koryukivka Ukr.
111 C3 Kos Greece
111 C3 Kos i. Greece
91 D2 Kosa Biryuchyy Ostriv i. Ukr.
65 B2 Kosan N. Korea
103 D1 Kościan Pol.
Kosciusko, Mount Austr. see Kosciuszko, Mount
53 C3 Kosciuszko, Mount Austr.
77 E2 Kosh-Agach Rus. Fed.
67 A4 Koshikijima-rettō is Japan
103 E2 Košice Slovakia
92 H2 Koskullskulle Sweden
65 B2 Kosŏng N. Korea
109 D2 Kosovo prov. Serb. and Mont.
109 D2 Kosovska Mitrovica Serb. and Mont.
48 H3 Kosrae atoll Micronesia
114 B4 Kossou, Lac de l. Côte d'Ivoire
76 C1 Kostanay Kazakh.

110 B2 Kostenets Bulg.
123 C2 Koster S. Africa
116 B3 Kosti Sudan
92 J3 Kostomuksha Rus. Fed.
90 B1 Kostopil' Ukr.
89 F2 Kostroma Rus. Fed.
89 F2 Kostroma r. Rus. Fed.
102 C1 Kostrzyn Pol.
91 D2 Kostyantynivka Ukr.
103 D1 Koszalin Pol.
103 D2 Kőszeg Hungary
74 B2 Kota India
60 B2 Kotaagung Indon.
61 C2 Kotabaru Indon.
61 C1 Kota Belud Sabah Malaysia
60 B1 Kota Bharu Malaysia
60 B2 Kotabumi Indon.
61 C1 Kota Kinabalu Sabah Malaysia
75 C3 Kotaparh India
61 C1 Kota Samarahan Sarawak Malaysia
86 D3 Kotel'nich Rus. Fed.
87 D4 Kotel'nikovo Rus. Fed.
83 K1 Kotel'nyy, Ostrov i. Rus. Fed.
91 C1 Kotel'va Ukr.
101 E2 Köthen (Anhalt) Ger.
119 D2 Kotido Uganda
93 I3 Kotka Fin.
86 D2 Kotlas Rus. Fed.
126 B2 Kotlik U.S.A.
115 C3 Kotorkoshi Nigeria
109 C2 Kotor Varoš Bos.-Herz.
87 D3 Kotovo Rus. Fed.
91 E1 Kotovsk Rus. Fed.
90 B2 Kotovs'k Ukr.
73 C3 Kottagudem India
118 C2 Kotto r. C.A.R.
83 H2 Kotuy r. Rus. Fed.
126 B2 Kotzebue U.S.A.
126 B2 Kotzebue Sound sea chan. U.S.A.
114 A3 Koubia Guinea
100 A2 Koudekerke Neth.
114 B3 Koudougou Burkina
122 B3 Kougaberge mts S. Africa
118 B3 Koulamoutou Gabon
114 B3 Koulikoro Mali
118 B2 Koum Cameroon
114 B3 Koumra Chad
114 A3 Koundâra Guinea
Kounradskiy Kazakh. see Konyrat
151 D2 Kourou Fr. Guiana
114 B3 Kouroussa Guinea
115 D3 Kousséri Cameroon
114 B3 Koutiala Mali
93 I3 Kouvola Fin.
109 D1 Kovačica Serb. and Mont.
92 J2 Kovdor Rus. Fed.
90 A1 Kovel' Ukr.
Kovno Lith. see Kaunas
89 F2 Kovrov Rus. Fed.
51 D1 Kowanyama Austr.
54 B2 Kowhitirangi N.Z.
111 C3 Köyceğiz Turkey
86 D2 Koyda Rus. Fed.
126 B2 Koyukuk r. U.S.A.
111 B2 Kozani Greece
90 C1 Kozelets' Ukr.
89 E3 Kozel'sk Rus. Fed.
Kozhikode India see Calicut
90 B2 Kozyatyn Ukr.
63 A2 Kra, Isthmus of Thai.
63 A3 Krabi Thai.
63 A2 Kra Buri Thai.
63 B2 Krâchéh Cambodia
93 E4 Kragerø Norway
100 B1 Kraggenburg Neth.
109 D2 Kragujevac Serb. and Mont.
60 B2 Krakatau i. Indon.
103 D1 Kraków Pol.
109 D2 Kraljevo Serb. and Mont.
91 D2 Kramators'k Ukr.
93 G3 Kramfors Sweden
111 B3 Kranidi Greece
109 C1 Kranj Slovenia
123 C2 Kranskop S. Africa
86 E1 Krasino Rus. Fed.
88 C2 Krāslava Latvia
101 F2 Kraslice Czech Rep.
89 D3 Krasnapollye Belarus
89 D3 Krasnaya Gora Rus. Fed.
89 F2 Krasnaya Gorbatka Rus. Fed.
Krasnoarmeysk Kazakh. see Tayynsha

87 D3 **Krasnoarmeysk** Rus. Fed.
Krasnoarmeyskaya Rus. Fed. see **Poltavskaya**
91 D2 **Krasnoarmiys'k** Ukr.
86 D2 **Krasnoborsk** Rus. Fed.
91 D2 **Krasnodar** Rus. Fed.
91 D2 **Krasnodon** Ukr.
88 C2 **Krasnogorodskoye** Rus. Fed.
91 D1 **Krasnogvardeyskoye** Rus. Fed.
91 D2 **Krasnohrad** Ukr.
91 C2 **Krasnohvardiys'ke** Ukr.
86 E3 **Krasnokamsk** Rus. Fed.
89 D2 **Krasnomayskiy** Rus. Fed.
91 C2 **Krasnoperekops'k** Ukr.
87 D3 **Krasnoslobodsk** Rus. Fed.
86 F3 **Krasnotur'insk** Rus. Fed.
86 E3 **Krasnoufimsk** Rus. Fed.
86 E2 **Krasnovishersk** Rus. Fed.
Krasnovodsk Turkm. see **Turkmenbashi**
83 H3 **Krasnoyarsk** Rus. Fed.
89 E3 **Krasnoye** Rus. Fed.
83 M2 **Krasnoye, Ozero** *l.* Rus. Fed.
89 F2 **Krasnoye-na-Volge** Rus. Fed.
103 E1 **Krasnystaw** Pol.
89 D3 **Krasnyy** Rus. Fed.
Krasnyy Kamyshanik Rus. Fed. see **Komsomol'skiy**
89 E2 **Krasnyy Kholm** Rus. Fed.
91 D2 **Krasnyy Luch** Ukr.
91 E2 **Krasnyy Sulin** Rus. Fed.
90 B2 **Krasyliv** Ukr.
Kraulshavn Greenland see **Nuussuaq**
100 C2 **Krefeld** Ger.
91 C2 **Kremenchuk** Ukr.
91 C2 **Kremenchuts'ka Vodoskhovyshche** *resr* Ukr.
90 B1 **Kremenets'** Ukr.
103 D2 **Křemešník** *hill* Czech Rep.
Kremges Ukr. see **Svitlovods'k**
91 D2 **Kreminna** Ukr.
136 B2 **Kremmling** U.S.A.
103 D2 **Krems an der Donau** Austria
89 D2 **Kresttsy** Rus. Fed.
88 B2 **Kretinga** Lith.
100 C2 **Kreuzau** Ger.
101 C2 **Kreuztal** Ger.
118 A2 **Kribi** Cameroon
123 C2 **Kriel** S. Africa
111 B3 **Krikellos** Greece
66 D1 **Kril'on, Mys** *c.* Rus. Fed.
111 B3 **Krios, Akra** *pt* Greece
73 C3 **Krishna** *r.* India
73 C3 **Krishna, Mouths of the** India
75 C2 **Krishnanagar** India
93 E4 **Kristiansand** Norway
93 F4 **Kristianstad** Sweden
92 E3 **Kristiansund** Norway
93 F4 **Kristinehamn** Sweden
Kristinopol' Ukr. see **Chervonohrad**
Kriti *i.* Greece see **Crete**
110 B2 **Kriva Palanka** Macedonia
Krivoy Rog Ukr. see **Kryvyy Rih**
109 C1 **Križevci** Croatia
108 B1 **Krk** *i.* Croatia
92 F3 **Krokom** Sweden
91 C1 **Krolevets'** Ukr.
89 E3 **Kromy** Rus. Fed.
101 E2 **Kronach** Ger.
63 B2 **Krŏng Kaôh Kŏng** Cambodia
127 J2 **Kronprins Frederik Bjerge** *nunataks* Greenland
123 C2 **Kroonstad** S. Africa
91 E2 **Kropotkin** Rus. Fed.
103 E2 **Krosno** Pol.
103 D1 **Krotoszyn** Pol.
60 B2 **Krui** Indon.
122 B3 **Kruisfontein** S. Africa
109 C2 **Krujë** Albania
111 C2 **Krumovgrad** Bulg.
Krung Thep Thai. see **Bangkok**
88 C3 **Krupki** Belarus
109 D2 **Kruševac** Serb. and Mont.
101 E2 **Krušné Hory** *mts* Czech Rep.
128 A2 **Kruzof Island** U.S.A.
89 D3 **Krychaw** Belarus
91 D2 **Krylovskaya** Rus. Fed.
91 D3 **Krymsk** Rus. Fed.
Krymskaya Rus. Fed. see **Krymsk**
Kryms'kyy Pivostriv *pen.* Ukr. see **Crimea**
Krystynopol Ukr. see **Chervonohrad**
111 C3 **Krytiko Pelagos** *sea* Greece
91 C2 **Kryvyy Rih** Ukr.
90 B2 **Kryzhopil'** Ukr.
114 B2 **Ksabi** Alg.
107 D2 **Ksar el Boukhari** Alg.
114 B1 **Ksar el Kebir** Morocco
Ksar-es-Souk Morocco see **Er Rachidia**
89 E3 **Kshenskiy** Rus. Fed.
78 B2 **Kū', Jabal al** *hill* Saudi Arabia
61 C1 **Kuala Belait** Brunei
Kuala Dungun Malaysia see **Dungun**
60 B1 **Kuala Kangsar** Malaysia
60 B1 **Kuala Kerai** Malaysia
60 B1 **Kuala Lipis** Malaysia
60 B1 **Kuala Lumpur** Malaysia
61 C2 **Kualapembuang** Indon.
60 B1 **Kuala Terengganu** Malaysia
60 B2 **Kualatungal** Indon.
61 C1 **Kuamut** *Sabah* Malaysia
65 A1 **Kuandian** China
60 B1 **Kuantan** Malaysia
91 D2 **Kuban'** *r.* Rus. Fed.
89 E2 **Kubenskoye, Ozero** *l.* Rus. Fed.
110 C2 **Kubrat** Bulg.
60 B2 **Kubu** Indon.
61 C1 **Kubuang** Indon.
60 C1 **Kuching** *Sarawak* Malaysia
109 C2 **Kuçovë** Albania
61 C1 **Kudat** *Sabah* Malaysia
61 C2 **Kudus** Indon.
102 C2 **Kufstein** Austria
127 G2 **Kugaaruk** Can.
91 D2 **Kugey** Rus. Fed.
126 E2 **Kugluktuk** Can.
126 D2 **Kugmallit Bay** Can.
92 I3 **Kuhmo** Fin.
79 C2 **Kūhrān, Kūh-e** *mt.* Iran
122 A1 **Kuis** Namibia
Kuitin China see **Kuytun**
120 A2 **Kuito** Angola
92 I2 **Kuivaniemi** Fin.
65 B2 **Kujang** N. Korea
66 D2 **Kuji** Japan
67 B4 **Kujū-san** *vol.* Japan
109 D2 **Kukës** Albania
76 B3 **Kukurtli** Turkm.
111 C3 **Kula** Turkey
89 G3 **Kula Kangri** *mt.* Bhutan
76 B2 **Kulandy** Kazakh.
88 B2 **Kuldīga** Latvia
Kuldja China see **Yining**
122 B1 **Kule** Botswana
101 E2 **Kulmbach** Ger.
77 C3 **Kŭlob** Tajik.
76 B2 **Kul'sary** Kazakh.
111 D3 **Kulübe Tepe** *mt.* Turkey
77 D1 **Kulunda** Rus. Fed.
77 D1 **Kulundinskoye, Ozero** *salt l.* Rus. Fed.
127 J2 **Kulusuk** Greenland
67 C3 **Kumagaya** Japan
67 B4 **Kumamoto** Japan
67 C4 **Kumano** Japan
110 B2 **Kumanovo** Macedonia
114 B4 **Kumasi** Ghana
118 A2 **Kumba** Cameroon
Kum-Dag Turkm. see **Gumdag**
78 B2 **Kumdah** Saudi Arabia
87 E3 **Kumertau** Rus. Fed.
65 B2 **Kumi** S. Korea
119 D2 **Kumi** Uganda
111 C3 **Kumkale** Turkey
93 G4 **Kumla** Sweden
115 D3 **Kumo** Nigeria
62 A1 **Kumon Range** *mts* Myanmar
62 B2 **Kumphawapi** Thai.
Kumul China see **Hami**
66 D2 **Kunashir, Ostrov** *i.* Rus. Fed.
120 A2 **Kunene** *r.* Angola/Namibia
77 D2 **Kungei Alatau** *mts* Kazakh./Kyrg.
93 F4 **Kungsbacka** Sweden
118 B2 **Kungu** Dem. Rep. Congo
86 E3 **Kungur** Rus. Fed.
62 A1 **Kunhing** Myanmar
62 A1 **Kunlong** Myanmar
75 B1 **Kunlun Shan** *mts* China
71 A3 **Kunming** China
65 B2 **Kunsan** S. Korea
50 B1 **Kununurra** Austr.
101 D3 **Künzelsau** Ger.
92 I3 **Kuopio** Fin.
109 C1 **Kupa** *r.* Croatia/Slovenia
59 C3 **Kupang** Indon.
88 B2 **Kupiškis** Lith.
111 C2 **Küplü** Turkey
128 A2 **Kupreanof Island** U.S.A.
91 D2 **Kup"yans'k** Ukr.
77 E2 **Kuqa** China
81 C2 **Kür** *r.* Azer.
67 B4 **Kurashiki** Japan
75 C2 **Kurasia** India
67 B3 **Kurayoshi** Japan
89 E3 **Kurchatov** Rus. Fed.
77 E2 **Kurchum** Kazakh.
111 C2 **Kŭrdzhali** Bulg.
67 B4 **Kure** Japan
57 T7 **Kure Atoll** U.S.A.
88 B2 **Kuressaare** Estonia
87 F3 **Kurgan** Rus. Fed.
Kuria Muria Islands Oman see **Ḥalāniyāt, Juzur al**
93 H3 **Kurikka** Fin.
156 C2 **Kuril Basin** *sea feature* Sea of Okhotsk
69 F1 **Kuril Islands** *is* Rus. Fed.
69 F1 **Kuril'sk** Rus. Fed.
Kuril'skiye Ostrova Rus. Fed. see **Kuril Islands**
156 C3 **Kuril Trench** *sea feature* N. Pacific Ocean
89 E3 **Kurkino** Rus. Fed.
Kurmashkino Kazakh. see **Kurchum**
117 B3 **Kurmuk** Sudan
73 B3 **Kurnool** India
67 D3 **Kuroiso** Japan
101 E2 **Kurort Schmalkalden** Ger.
53 D2 **Kurri Kurri** Austr.
88 B2 **Kuršėnai** Lith.
78 B2 **Kursh, Jabal** *hill* Saudi Arabia
89 E3 **Kursk** Rus. Fed.
109 D2 **Kuršumlija** Serb. and Mont.
122 B2 **Kuruman** S. Africa
122 B2 **Kuruman** *watercourse* S. Africa
67 B4 **Kurume** Japan
83 I3 **Kurumkan** Rus. Fed.
73 C4 **Kurunegala** Sri Lanka
81 D1 **Kuryk** Kazakh.
111 C3 **Kuşadası** Turkey
111 C3 **Kuşadası Körfezi** *b.* Turkey
111 C2 **Kuş Gölü** *l.* Turkey
91 D2 **Kushchevskaya** Rus. Fed.
66 D2 **Kushiro** Japan
Kushka Turkm. see **Gushgy**
76 C1 **Kushmurun** Kazakh.
75 C2 **Kushtia** Bangl.
126 B2 **Kuskokwim** *r.* U.S.A.
126 B2 **Kuskokwim Mountains** U.S.A.
66 D2 **Kussharo-ko** *l.* Japan
Kustanay Kazakh. see **Kostanay**
63 B2 **Kut, Ko** *i.* Thai.
111 C3 **Kütahya** Turkey
81 C1 **K'ut'aisi** Georgia
Kutaraja Indon. see **Banda Aceh**
Kutch, Gulf of India see **Kachchh, Gulf of**
109 C1 **Kutjevo** Croatia
103 D1 **Kutno** Pol.
118 B3 **Kutu** Dem. Rep. Congo
116 A3 **Kutum** Sudan
126 E2 **Kuujjua** *r.* Can.
131 D2 **Kuujjuaq** Can.
130 C2 **Kuujjuarapik** Can.
92 I2 **Kuusamo** Fin.
120 A2 **Kuvango** Angola
89 D2 **Kuvshinovo** Rus. Fed.
78 B2 **Kuwait** *country* Asia
78 B2 **Kuwait** Kuwait
82 G3 **Kuybyshev** Rus. Fed.
Kuybyshev Rus. Fed. see **Samara**
91 D2 **Kuybysheve** Ukr.
Kuybyshevka-Vostochnaya Rus. Fed. see **Belogorsk**
87 D3 **Kuybyshevskoye Vodokhranilishche** *resr* Rus. Fed.
77 E2 **Kuytun** China
111 C3 **Kuyucak** Turkey
87 D3 **Kuznetsk** Rus. Fed.
90 B1 **Kuznetsovs'k** Ukr.
86 C2 **Kuzomen'** Rus. Fed.
92 H1 **Kvalsund** Norway
123 D2 **KwaMashu** S. Africa
61 D1 **Kwandang** Indon.
Kwangchow China see **Guangzhou**
65 B2 **Kwangju** S. Korea
Kwangtung *prov.* China see **Guangdong**
65 B1 **Kwanmo-bong** *mt.* N. Korea
123 C3 **Kwanobuhle** S. Africa
123 C3 **KwaNojoli** S. Africa
122 B3 **Kwanonzame** S. Africa
123 C3 **Kwatinidubu** S. Africa
123 C2 **KwaZamokhule** S. Africa
122 B3 **Kwazamukucinga** S. Africa
123 C2 **KwaZanele** S. Africa
123 D2 **Kwazulu-Natal** *prov.* S. Africa
Kweichow *prov.* China see **Guizhou**
Kweiyang China see **Guiyang**
121 B2 **Kwekwe** Zimbabwe
118 B3 **Kwenge** *r.* Dem. Rep. Congo
123 C3 **Kwezi-Naledi** S. Africa
103 D1 **Kwidzyn** Pol.
59 D3 **Kwikila** P.N.G.
118 B3 **Kwilu** *r.* Angola/Dem. Rep. Congo
59 C3 **Kwoka** *mt.* Indon.
118 B2 **Kyabé** Chad
53 C3 **Kyabram** Austr.
62 A2 **Kyaikto** Myanmar
63 A2 **Kya-in Seikkyi** Myanmar
68 D1 **Kyakhta** Rus. Fed.
52 A2 **Kyancutta** Austr.
62 A1 **Kyaukpadaung** Myanmar
62 A2 **Kyaukpyu** Myanmar
88 B3 **Kybartai** Lith.
62 A2 **Kyebogyi** Myanmar
54 B3 **Kyeburn** N.Z.
62 A2 **Kyeintali** Myanmar
74 B1 **Kyelang** India
Kyiv Ukr. see **Kiev**
Kyklades *is* Greece see **Cyclades**
129 D2 **Kyle** Can.
96 B2 **Kyle of Lochalsh** U.K.
100 C3 **Kyll** *r.* Ger.
111 B3 **Kyllini** *mt.* Greece
111 B3 **Kymi** Greece
52 B3 **Kyneton** Austr.
119 D2 **Kyoga, Lake** Uganda
53 D1 **Kyogle** Austr.
65 B2 **Kyŏnggi-man** *b.* S. Korea
65 B2 **Kyŏngju** S. Korea
67 C4 **Kyōto** Japan
111 B3 **Kyparissia** Greece
111 B3 **Kyparissiakos Kolpos** *b.* Greece
111 B3 **Kyra Panagia** *i.* Greece
80 B2 **Kyrenia** Cyprus
77 D2 **Kyrgyzstan** *country* Asia
101 F1 **Kyritz** Ger.
93 H3 **Kyrönjoki** *r.* Fin.
86 E2 **Kyrta** Rus. Fed.
86 D2 **Kyssa** Rus. Fed.
83 J2 **Kytalyktakh** Rus. Fed.
111 B3 **Kythira** *i.* Greece
111 B3 **Kythnos** *i.* Greece
128 B2 **Kyuquot** Can.
67 B4 **Kyūshū** *i.* Japan
110 B2 **Kyustendil** Bulg.
62 A2 **Kywebwe** Myanmar
90 C1 **Kyyivs'ke Vodoskhovyshche** *resr* Ukr.
92 H3 **Kyyjärvi** Fin.
68 C1 **Kyzyl** Rus. Fed.
76 C2 **Kyzylkum Desert** Kazakh./Uzbek.
77 C2 **Kyzylorda** Kazakh.
Kzyl-Orda Kazakh. see **Kyzylorda**
Kzyltu Kazakh. see **Kishkenekol'**

L

145 C3 La Angostura, Presa de resr Mex.
117 C4 Laascaanood Somalia
117 C3 Laasgoray Somalia
150 C1 La Asunción Venez.
114 A2 Laâyoune Western Sahara
87 D4 Laba r. Rus. Fed.
144 B2 La Babia Mex.
61 D2 Labala Indon.
152 B2 La Banda Arg.
61 C1 Labang Sarawak Malaysia
104 B2 La Baule-Escoublac France
102 C1 Labe r. Czech Rep.
114 A3 Labé Guinea
128 A1 Laberge, Lake Can.
128 C2 La Biche, Lac l. Can.
108 B1 Labin Croatia
87 D4 Labinsk Rus. Fed.
64 B2 Labo Phil.
104 B3 Labouheyre France
153 B3 Laboulaye Arg.
131 D2 Labrador reg. Can.
131 D2 Labrador City Can.
127 I2 Labrador Sea Can./Greenland
150 C3 Lábrea Brazil
61 C1 Labuan Malaysia
61 C2 Labuhanbajo Indon.
60 B1 Labuhanbilik Indon.
59 C3 Labuna Indon.
63 A2 Labutta Myanmar
86 F2 Labytnangi Rus. Fed.
109 C2 Laç Albania
La Calle Alg. see El Kala
105 C2 La Capelle France
73 B3 Laccadive Islands India
129 E2 Lac du Bonnet Can.
146 B3 La Ceiba Hond.
52 A3 Lacepede Bay Austr.
134 B1 Lacey U.S.A.
105 D2 La Chaux-de-Fonds Switz.
53 B2 Lachlan r. Austr.
146 C4 La Chorrera Panama
139 E1 Lachute Can.
105 D3 La Ciotat France
128 C2 Lac La Biche Can.
Lac la Martre Can. see Wha Ti
139 E1 Lac-Mégantic Can.
128 C2 Lacombe Can.
146 B4 La Concepción Panama
145 C3 La Concordia Mex.
108 A3 Laconi Sardinia Italy
139 E2 Laconia U.S.A.
128 C2 La Crete Can.
138 A2 La Crosse U.S.A.
144 B2 La Cruz Mex.
144 B2 La Cuesta Mex.
155 D1 Ladainha Brazil
74 B1 Ladakh Range mts India
122 B3 Ladismith S. Africa
79 D2 Lādīz Iran
89 D1 Ladoga, Lake Rus. Fed.
Ladozhskoye Ozero l. Rus. Fed. see Ladoga, Lake
141 D2 Ladson U.S.A.
123 C3 Lady Grey S. Africa
128 B3 Ladysmith Can.
123 C2 Ladysmith S. Africa
59 D3 Lae P.N.G.
143 C3 La Encantada, Sierra mts Mex.
152 B2 La Esmeralda Bol.
93 F4 Læsø i. Denmark
Lafayette Alg. see Bougaa
141 C2 La Fayette U.S.A.
138 B2 Lafayette IN U.S.A.
140 B2 Lafayette LA U.S.A.
115 C4 Lafia Nigeria
104 B2 La Flèche France
141 D1 La Follette U.S.A.
130 C2 Laforge Can.
79 C2 Lāft Iran
108 A3 La Galite i. Tunisia
87 D4 Lagan' Rus. Fed.
151 F4 Lagarto Brazil
118 B2 Lagdo, Lac de l. Cameroon
119 E2 Lagh Bor watercourse Kenya/Somalia
115 C1 Laghouat Alg.
155 D1 Lagoa Santa Brazil
114 A2 La Gomera i. Canary Is
114 C4 Lagos Nigeria
106 B2 Lagos Port.

134 C1 La Grande U.S.A.
130 C2 La Grande 2, Réservoir resr Can.
130 C2 La Grande 3, Réservoir resr Can.
130 C2 La Grande 4, Réservoir resr Can.
50 B1 Lagrange Austr.
141 C2 La Grange U.S.A.
150 C2 La Gran Sabana plat. Venez.
152 D2 Laguna Brazil
144 A2 Laguna, Picacho de la mt. Mex.
150 B3 Lagunas Peru
147 C3 Lagunillas Venez.
La Habana Cuba see Havana
61 C1 Lahad Datu Sabah Malaysia
60 B2 Lahat Indon.
78 B3 Laḥij Yemen
81 C2 Lāhījān Iran
100 C2 Lahnstein Ger.
74 B1 Lahore Pak.
74 A2 Lahri Pak.
93 I3 Lahti Fin.
115 D4 Laï Chad
53 D1 Laidley Austr.
104 C2 L'Aigle France
122 B3 Laingsburg S. Africa
92 H2 Lainioälven r. Sweden
96 B1 Lairg U.K.
108 B1 Laives Italy
70 B2 Laiwu China
70 C2 Laiyang China
70 B2 Laiyuan China
70 B2 Laizhou China
70 B2 Laizhou Wan b. China
50 C1 Lajamanu Austr.
152 C2 Lajes Brazil
144 B2 La Junta Mex.
136 C3 La Junta U.S.A.
117 B4 Lake Abaya l. Eth.
103 D2 Lake Balaton l. Hungary
53 C2 Lake Cargelligo Austr.
53 D2 Lake Cathie Austr.
140 B2 Lake Charles U.S.A.
141 D2 Lake City FL U.S.A.
141 E2 Lake City SC U.S.A.
128 B3 Lake Cowichan Can.
Lake Harbour Can. see Kimmirut
142 A2 Lake Havasu City U.S.A.
143 D3 Lake Jackson U.S.A.
50 A3 Lake King Austr.
141 D3 Lakeland U.S.A.
128 C2 Lake Louise Can.
134 B1 Lake Oswego U.S.A.
54 C1 Lake Paringa N.Z.
140 B2 Lake Providence U.S.A.
53 C3 Lakes Entrance Austr.
117 B3 Lake Tana l. Eth.
134 B2 Lakeview U.S.A.
137 E2 Lakeville U.S.A.
136 B3 Lakewood CO U.S.A.
139 E2 Lakewood NJ U.S.A.
141 D3 Lake Worth U.S.A.
74 A2 Lakhpat India
74 B1 Lakki Pak.
111 B3 Lakonikos Kolpos b. Greece
114 B4 Lakota Côte d'Ivoire
92 H1 Lakselv Norway
146 A3 La Libertad Guat.
106 B1 Lalín Spain
106 B2 La Línea de la Concepción Spain
74 B2 Lalitpur India
Lalitpur Nepal see Patan
129 D2 La Loche Can.
100 B2 La Louvière Belgium
108 A2 La Maddalena Sardinia Italy
61 C1 Lamag Sabah Malaysia
La Manche str. France/U.K. see English Channel
136 C3 Lamar U.S.A.
79 C2 Lamard Iran
108 A3 La Marmora, Punta mt. Sardinia Italy
128 C1 La Martre, Lac l. Can.
104 B2 Lamballe France
118 B3 Lambaréné Gabon
122 A3 Lambert's Bay S. Africa
92 □A2 Lambeyri Iceland
106 B1 Lamego Port.
131 D3 Lamèque, Île l. Can.
150 B4 La Merced Peru
52 B3 Lameroo Austr.

143 C2 Lamesa U.S.A.
111 B3 Lamia Greece
137 E2 Lamoni U.S.A.
62 A2 Lampang Thai.
143 D2 Lampasas U.S.A.
145 B2 Lampazos Mex.
99 A3 Lampeter U.K.
62 A2 Lamphun Thai.
119 E3 Lamu Kenya
105 D3 La Mure France
96 C3 Lanark U.K.
63 A2 Lanbi Kyun i. Myanmar
62 A1 Lancang China
Lancang Jiang r. China see Mekong
98 B2 Lancaster U.K.
135 C4 Lancaster CA U.S.A.
138 C3 Lancaster OH U.S.A.
139 D2 Lancaster PA U.S.A.
141 D2 Lancaster SC U.S.A.
127 G2 Lancaster Sound str. Can.
50 A3 Lancelin Austr.
Lanchow China see Lanzhou
102 C2 Landeck Austria
136 B2 Lander U.S.A.
99 A4 Land's End pt U.K.
102 C2 Landshut Ger.
93 F4 Landskrona Sweden
141 C2 Lanett U.S.A.
122 B2 Langberg mts S. Africa
137 D1 Langdon U.S.A.
93 F4 Langeland i. Denmark
101 D1 Langen Ger.
100 C1 Langeoog Ger.
100 C1 Langeoog i. Ger.
82 G2 Langepas Rus. Fed.
70 B2 Langfang China
101 D2 Langgöns Ger.
96 C3 Langholm U.K.
92 □A3 Langjökull ice cap Iceland
60 A1 Langkawi i. Malaysia
105 C3 Langogne France
104 B3 Langon France
106 B1 Langreo Spain
105 D2 Langres France
60 A1 Langsa Indon.
62 B1 Lang Son Vietnam
105 C3 Languedoc reg. France
101 D1 Langwedel Ger.
129 D2 Lanigan Can.
153 A3 Lanín, Volcán vol. Arg./Chile
81 C2 Länkäran Azer.
104 B2 Lannion France
138 B1 L'Anse U.S.A.
139 E1 L'Anse-St-Jean Can.
138 C2 Lansing U.S.A.
71 B3 Lanxi China
117 B4 Lanya Sudan
114 A2 Lanzarote i. Canary Is
70 A2 Lanzhou China
64 B2 Laoag Phil.
62 B1 Lao Cai Vietnam
70 B2 Laohekou China
Laojunmiao China see Yumen
65 B1 Laoling China
65 B1 Lao ling mts China
105 C2 Laon France
62 B2 Laos country Asia
65 B1 Laotougou China
66 A2 Laoye Ling mts China
154 C3 Lapa Brazil
114 A2 La Palma i. Canary Is
146 C4 La Palma Panama
150 C2 La Paragua Venez.
152 B1 La Paz Bol.
145 D3 La Paz Hond.
144 A2 La Paz Mex.
150 C3 La Pedrera Col.
138 C2 Lapeer U.S.A.
66 D1 La Pérouse Strait Japan/Rus. Fed.
145 C2 La Pesca Mex.
144 B2 La Piedad Mex.
153 C3 La Plata Arg.
153 C3 La Plata, Río de sea chan. Arg./Uru.
92 H3 Lappajärvi l. Fin.
93 I3 Lappeenranta Fin.
92 G2 Lappland reg. Europe
111 C2 Lâpseki Turkey
Laptevo Rus. Fed. see Yasnogorsk
83 J1 Laptev Sea Rus. Fed.
Laptevykh, More sea Rus. Fed. see Laptev Sea
92 H3 Lapua Fin.
152 B3 La Quiaca Arg.
108 B2 L'Aquila Italy

135 C4 La Quinta U.S.A.
79 C2 Lār Iran
114 B1 Larache Morocco
136 B2 Laramie U.S.A.
136 B2 Laramie Mountains U.S.A.
154 B3 Laranjeiras do Sul Brazil
61 D2 Larantuka Indon.
59 C3 Larat i. Indon.
107 D2 Larba Alg.
L'Ardenne, Plateau de Belgium see Ardennes
106 C1 Laredo Spain
143 D3 Laredo U.S.A.
141 D3 Largo U.S.A.
96 B3 Largs U.K.
115 D1 L'Ariana Tunisia
152 B2 La Rioja Arg.
111 B3 Larisa Greece
74 A2 Larkana Pak.
80 B2 Larnaca Cyprus
Larnaka Cyprus see Larnaca
97 D1 Larne U.K.
100 B2 La Roche-en-Ardenne Belgium
104 B2 La Rochelle France
104 B2 La Roche-sur-Yon France
107 C2 La Roda Spain
147 D3 La Romana Dom. Rep.
129 D2 La Ronge Can.
129 D2 La Ronge, Lac l. Can.
50 C1 Larrimah Austr.
55 A3 Larsen Ice Shelf Antarctica
93 F4 Larvik Norway
136 C3 Las Animas U.S.A.
Las Anod Somalia see Laascaanood
130 C3 La Sarre Can.
142 B2 Las Cruces U.S.A.
152 A2 La Serena Chile
153 C3 Las Flores Arg.
153 B3 Las Heras Arg.
62 A1 Lashio Myanmar
76 C3 Lashkar Gāh Afgh.
109 C3 La Sila reg. Italy
152 B2 Las Lomitas Arg.
106 B2 Las Marismas marsh Spain
144 B2 Las Nieves Mex.
114 A2 Las Palmas de Gran Canaria Canary Is
108 A2 La Spezia Italy
153 C3 Las Piedras Uru.
153 B4 Las Plumas Arg.
155 D1 Lassance Brazil
129 D2 Last Mountain Lake Can.
152 B2 Las Tórtolas, Cerro mt. Chile
118 B3 Lastoursville Gabon
109 C2 Lastovo i. Croatia
144 A2 Las Tres Vírgenes, Volcán vol. Mex.
146 C2 Las Tunas Cuba
144 B2 Las Varas Mex.
144 B2 Las Varas Mex.
142 B1 Las Vegas NM U.S.A.
135 C3 Las Vegas NV U.S.A.
131 E2 La Tabatière Can.
80 B2 Latakia Syria
104 B3 La Teste France
108 B2 Latina Italy
147 D3 La Tortuga, Isla i. Venez.
64 B2 La Trinidad Phil.
89 E2 Latskoye Rus. Fed.
130 C3 La Tuque Can.
88 B2 Latvia country Europe
Latviyskaya S.S.R. admin. reg. Europe see Latvia
59 E3 Lau P.N.G.
102 C1 Lauchhammer Ger.
101 E3 Lauf an der Pegnitz Ger.
105 D2 Laufen Switz.
92 □A3 Laugarás Iceland
127 H1 Lauge Koch Kyst reg. Greenland
142 C1 Laughlin Peak U.S.A.
51 D4 Launceston Austr.
99 A4 Launceston U.K.
62 A1 Launggyaung Myanmar
153 A4 La Unión Chile
51 D1 Laura Austr.
141 C2 Laurel MS U.S.A.
134 E1 Laurel MT U.S.A.
96 C2 Laurencekirk U.K.
109 C2 Lauria Italy
141 E2 Laurinburg U.S.A.
105 D2 Lausanne Switz.
60 B1 Laut i. Indon.
61 C2 Laut i. Indon.
61 C2 Laut Bali Indon.

101 D2 **Lautersbach (Hessen)** Ger.
60 C2 **Laut Jawa** Indon.
61 C2 **Laut Kecil, Kepulauan** *is* Indon.
59 C3 **Laut Maluku** Indon.
61 C2 **Laut Sawu** Indon.
59 C3 **Laut Seram** Indon.
100 C1 **Lauwersmeer** *l.* Neth.
139 E1 **Laval** Can.
104 B2 **Laval** France
81 D2 **Lāvar Meydān** *salt marsh* Iran
50 B2 **Laverton** Austr.
155 D2 **Lavras** Brazil
123 D2 **Lavumisa** Swaziland
61 C1 **Lawas** *Sarawak* Malaysia
78 B3 **Lawdar** Yemen
62 A1 **Lawksawk** Myanmar
114 B3 **Lawra** Ghana
138 B3 **Lawrence** *IN* U.S.A.
137 D3 **Lawrence** *KS* U.S.A.
139 E2 **Lawrence** *MA* U.S.A.
140 C1 **Lawrenceburg** U.S.A.
141 D2 **Lawrenceville** U.S.A.
143 D2 **Lawton** U.S.A.
78 A2 **Lawz, Jabal al** *mt.* Saudi Arabia
93 F4 **Laxå** Sweden
122 B2 **Laxey** S. Africa
78 B2 **Laylá** Saudi Arabia
109 D2 **Lazarevac** Serb. and Mont.
144 A1 **Lázaro Cárdenas** Mex.
144 B3 **Lázaro Cárdenas** Mex.
88 B3 **Lazdijai** Lith.
66 B2 **Lazo** Rus. Fed.
83 K2 **Lazo** Rus. Fed.
136 C2 **Lead** U.S.A.
129 D2 **Leader** Can.
136 B3 **Leadville** U.S.A.
Leaf Bay Can. *see* Tasiujaq
129 D2 **Leaf Rapids** Can.
143 D3 **League City** U.S.A.
143 D3 **Leakey** U.S.A.
99 C3 **Leamington Spa, Royal** U.K.
97 B2 **Leane, Lough** *l.* Rep. of Ireland
137 E3 **Leavenworth** U.S.A.
64 B3 **Lebak** Phil.
80 B2 **Lebanon** *country* Asia
137 E3 **Lebanon** *MO* U.S.A.
139 E2 **Lebanon** *NH* U.S.A.
134 B2 **Lebanon** *OR* U.S.A.
139 D2 **Lebanon** *PA* U.S.A.
140 C1 **Lebanon** *TN* U.S.A.
89 E3 **Lebedyan'** Rus. Fed.
91 C1 **Lebedyn** Ukr.
130 C3 **Lebel-sur-Quévillon** Can.
104 C2 **Le Blanc** France
103 D1 **Lębork** Pol.
123 C1 **Lebowakgomo** S. Africa
106 B2 **Lebrija** Spain
153 A3 **Lebu** Chile
104 C3 **Le Bugue** France
109 C2 **Lecce** Italy
108 A1 **Lecco** Italy
102 C2 **Lech** *r.* Austria/Ger.
111 B3 **Lechaina** Greece
71 B3 **Lechang** China
102 B1 **Leck** Ger.
140 B2 **Lecompte** U.S.A.
105 C2 **Le Creusot** France
104 C3 **Lectoure** France
106 B1 **Ledesma** Spain
104 C2 **Le Dorat** France
128 C2 **Leduc** Can.
97 B3 **Lee** *r.* Rep. of Ireland
137 E1 **Leech Lake** U.S.A.
98 C3 **Leeds** U.K.
99 B3 **Leek** U.K.
97 B2 **Leenane** Rep. of Ireland
100 C1 **Leer (Ostfriesland)** Ger.
141 D3 **Leesburg** U.S.A.
140 B2 **Leesville** U.S.A.
53 C2 **Leeton** Austr.
122 B3 **Leeu-Gamka** S. Africa
100 B1 **Leeuwarden** Neth.
50 A3 **Leeuwin, Cape** Austr.
147 D3 **Leeward Islands** Caribbean Sea
111 B3 **Lefkada** Greece
111 B3 **Lefkada** *i.* Greece
Lefkosia Cyprus *see* Nicosia
64 B2 **Legaspi** Phil.
103 E1 **Legionowo** Pol.
108 B1 **Legnago** Italy
103 D1 **Legnica** Pol.
74 B1 **Leh** Jammu and Kashmir

104 C2 **Le Havre** France
101 E1 **Lehre** Ger.
122 B1 **Lehututu** Botswana
74 B1 **Leiah** Pak.
103 D2 **Leibnitz** Austria
99 C3 **Leicester** U.K.
51 C1 **Leichhardt** *r.* Austr.
51 D2 **Leichhardt Range** *mts* Austr.
100 B1 **Leiden** Neth.
100 A2 **Leie** *r.* Belgium
52 A2 **Leigh Creek** Austr.
97 C2 **Leighlinbridge** Rep. of Ireland
99 C4 **Leighton Buzzard** U.K.
93 E3 **Leikanger** Norway
101 D1 **Leine** *r.* Ger.
50 B2 **Leinster** Austr.
97 C2 **Leinster** *reg.* Rep. of Ireland
97 C2 **Leinster, Mount** *hill* Rep. of Ireland
101 F2 **Leipzig** Ger.
92 F2 **Leirangar** Norway
106 B2 **Leiria** Port.
93 E4 **Leirvik** Norway
97 C2 **Leixlip** Rep. of Ireland
71 B3 **Leiyang** China
71 B3 **Leizhou** China
71 A3 **Leizhou Bandao** *pen.* China
118 B3 **Lékana** Congo
122 A2 **Lekkersing** S. Africa
66 B1 **Leland** U.S.A.
Leli China *see* Tianlin
100 B1 **Lelystad** Neth.
153 B5 **Le Maire, Estrecho de** *sea chan.* Arg.
Léman, Lac France/Switz. *see* Geneva, Lake
104 C2 **Le Mans** France
137 D2 **Le Mars** U.S.A.
102 B2 **Lemberg** *mt.* Ger.
154 C2 **Leme** Brazil
Lemesos Cyprus *see* Limassol
101 D1 **Lemförde** Ger.
127 H2 **Lemieux Islands** Can.
136 C1 **Lemmon** U.S.A.
135 C3 **Lemoore** U.S.A.
131 D2 **Le Moyne, Lac** *l.* Can.
62 A1 **Lemro** *r.* Myanmar
109 C2 **Le Murge** *hills* Italy
83 J2 **Lena** *r.* Rus. Fed.
100 C1 **Lengerich** Ger.
70 A2 **Lenglong Ling** *mts* China
71 B3 **Lengshuijiang** China
71 B3 **Lengshuitan** China
Leninabad Tajik. *see* Khŭjand
Leninakan Armenia *see* Gyumri
Lenine Ukr.
Leningrad Rus. Fed. *see* St Petersburg
91 D2 **Leningradskaya** Rus. Fed.
Leninobod Tajik. *see* Khŭjand
77 E1 **Leninogorsk** Kazakh.
77 D3 **Lenin Peak** Kyrg./Tajik.
Leninsk Kazakh. *see* Baykonyr
89 E3 **Leninskiy** Rus. Fed.
53 D1 **Lennox Head** Austr.
141 D1 **Lenoir** U.S.A.
100 A2 **Lens** Belgium
105 C1 **Lens** France
83 I2 **Lensk** Rus. Fed.
103 D2 **Lenti** Hungary
109 C3 **Lentini** *Sicily* Italy
114 B3 **Léo** Burkina
103 D2 **Leoben** Austria
99 D4 **Leodhais, Eilean** *i.* U.K. *see* Lewis, Isle of
99 B3 **Leominster** U.K.
144 B3 **León** Mex.
146 B3 **León** Nic.
106 B1 **León** Spain
122 A1 **Leonardville** Namibia
108 B3 **Leonforte** *Sicily* Italy
53 C3 **Leongatha** Austr.
50 B2 **Leonora** Austr.
Léopold II, Lac *l.* Dem. Rep. Congo *see* Mai-Ndombe, Lac
155 D2 **Leopoldina** Brazil
Léopoldville Dem. Rep. Congo *see* Kinshasa
90 B2 **Leova** Moldova
Leovo Moldova *see* Leova

123 C1 **Lephalale** S. Africa
123 C1 **Lephepe** Botswana
123 C3 **Lephoi** S. Africa
71 B3 **Leping** China
77 D2 **Lepsy** Kazakh.
105 C2 **Le Puy-en-Velay** France
123 C1 **Lerala** Botswana
123 C2 **Leratswana** S. Africa
150 B3 **Lérida** Col.
Lérida Spain *see* Lleida
106 C1 **Lerma** Spain
111 C3 **Leros** *i.* Greece
130 C2 **Le Roy, Lac** *l.* Can.
93 F4 **Lerum** Sweden
96 □ **Lerwick** U.K.
111 C3 **Lesbos** *i.* Greece
147 C3 **Les Cayes** Haiti
104 C3 **Les Escaldes** Andorra
139 F1 **Les Escoumins** Can.
107 D1 **Le Seu d'Urgell** Spain
70 A3 **Leshan** China
104 B2 **Les Herbiers** France
86 D2 **Leshukonskoye** Rus. Fed.
Leskhimstroy Ukr. *see* Syeverodonets'k
109 D2 **Leskovac** Serb. and Mont.
104 B2 **Lesneven** France
89 E2 **Lesnoy** Rus. Fed. *see* Umba
83 H3 **Lesosibirsk** Rus. Fed.
123 C2 **Lesotho** *country* Africa
66 B1 **Lesozavodsk** Rus. Fed.
104 B2 **Les Sables-d'Olonne** France
147 D3 **Lesser Antilles** *is* Caribbean Sea
81 C1 **Lesser Caucasus** *mts* Asia
Lesser Khingan Mountains China *see* Xiao Hinggan Ling
128 C2 **Lesser Slave Lake** Can.
105 C3 **Les Vans** France
Lesvos *i.* Greece *see* Lesbos
103 D1 **Leszno** Pol.
123 D1 **Letaba** S. Africa
99 C4 **Letchworth** U.K.
128 C3 **Lethbridge** Can.
150 D2 **Lethem** Guyana
59 C3 **Leti, Kepulauan** *is* Indon.
150 C3 **Leticia** Col.
123 B3 **Letlhakane** Botswana
123 C1 **Letlhakeng** Botswana
104 C1 **Le Touquet-Paris-Plage** France
99 D4 **Le Tréport** France
123 D1 **Letsitele** S. Africa
63 A2 **Letsok-aw Kyun** *i.* Myanmar
123 C2 **Letsopa** S. Africa
97 C1 **Letterkenny** Rep. of Ireland
105 C3 **Leucate, Étang de** *l.* France
Leukas Greece *see* Lefkada
60 A1 **Leuser, Gunung** *mt.* Indon.
100 B2 **Leuven** Belgium
111 B3 **Levadeia** Greece
92 F3 **Levanger** Norway
143 C2 **Levelland** U.S.A.
50 B1 **Lévêque, Cape** Austr.
96 A2 **Leverburgh** U.K.
100 C2 **Leverkusen** Ger.
103 D2 **Levice** Slovakia
54 C2 **Levin** N.Z.
131 C3 **Lévis** Can.
139 E2 **Levittown** U.S.A.
89 E3 **Lev Tolstoy** Rus. Fed.
99 D4 **Lewes** U.K.
96 A1 **Lewis, Isle of** *i.* U.K.
139 D2 **Lewisburg** *PA* U.S.A.
140 C1 **Lewisburg** *TN* U.S.A.
138 C3 **Lewis Range** *mts* U.S.A.
134 D1 **Lewiston** *ID* U.S.A.
139 E2 **Lewiston** *ME* U.S.A.
134 E1 **Lewistown** U.S.A.
138 C3 **Lexington** *KY* U.S.A.
136 C2 **Lexington** *NE* U.S.A.
143 D1 **Lexington** *OK* U.S.A.
139 D3 **Lexington** *VA* U.S.A.
64 B2 **Leyte** *i.* Phil.
109 C2 **Lezhë** Albania
89 F2 **Lezhnevo** Rus. Fed.
89 E3 **L'gov** Rus. Fed.
75 C2 **Lhagoi Kangri** *mt.* China
75 D1 **Lharigarbo** China

75 D2 **Lhasa** China
75 C2 **Lhazê** China
60 A1 **Lhokseumawe** Indon.
Lhünzê China *see* Xingba
67 B3 **Liancourt Rocks** *i.* N. Pacific Ocean
Liangzhou China *see* Wuwei
70 B2 **Liangzi Hu** *l.* China
Lianhe China *see* Qianjiang
71 B3 **Lianhua** China
71 B3 **Lianjiang** China
Lianran China *see* Anning
70 C1 **Lianshan** China
Liantang China *see* Nanchang
Lianxian China *see* Lianzhou
70 B2 **Lianyungang** China
71 B3 **Lianzhou** China
Lianzhou China *see* Hepu
70 B2 **Liaocheng** China
70 C1 **Liaodong Bandao** *pen.* China
70 C1 **Liaodong Wan** *b.* China
65 A1 **Liao He** *r.* China
70 C1 **Liaoning** *prov.* China
70 C1 **Liaoyang** China
65 B1 **Liaoyuan** China
128 B1 **Liard** *r.* Can.
134 C1 **Libby** U.S.A.
118 B2 **Libenge** Dem. Rep. Congo
136 C3 **Liberal** U.S.A.
103 D1 **Liberec** Czech Rep.
114 B4 **Liberia** *country* Africa
146 B3 **Liberia** Costa Rica
150 C2 **Libertad** Venez.
137 E3 **Liberty** U.S.A.
100 B3 **Libin** Belgium
64 B2 **Libmanan** Phil.
71 A3 **Libo** China
123 C3 **Libode** S. Africa
119 E2 **Liboi** Kenya
104 B3 **Libourne** France
100 B3 **Libramont** Belgium
142 A3 **Libre, Sierra** *mts* Mex.
118 A2 **Libreville** Gabon
115 D2 **Libya** *country* Africa
115 E2 **Libyan Desert** Egypt/Libya
116 A1 **Libyan Plateau** Egypt
108 B3 **Licata** *Sicily* Italy
Licheng China *see* Lipu
99 C3 **Lichfield** U.K.
121 C3 **Lichinga** Moz.
101 E2 **Lichte** Ger.
123 C2 **Lichtenburg** S. Africa
101 E2 **Lichtenfels** Ger.
88 C3 **Lida** Belarus
93 F4 **Lidköping** Sweden
50 C2 **Liebig, Mount** Austr.
105 D2 **Liechtenstein** *country* Europe
100 B2 **Liège** Belgium
92 J3 **Lieksa** Fin.
119 C2 **Lienart** Dem. Rep. Congo
102 C2 **Lienz** Austria
88 B2 **Liepāja** Latvia
100 B2 **Lier** Belgium
102 C2 **Liezen** Austria
97 C2 **Liffey** *r.* Rep. of Ireland
97 C1 **Lifford** Rep. of Ireland
53 C1 **Lightning Ridge** Austr.
121 C2 **Ligonha** *r.* Moz.
105 D3 **Ligurian Sea** France/Italy
119 C4 **Likasi** Dem. Rep. Congo
118 C2 **Likati** Dem. Rep. Congo
128 B2 **Likely** Can.
Likhachevo Ukr. *see* Pervomays'kyy
Likhachyovo Ukr. *see* Pervomays'kyy
89 E2 **Likhoslavl'** Rus. Fed.
60 B1 **Liku** Indon.
105 D3 **L'Île-Rousse** *Corsica* France
71 B3 **Liling** China
93 F4 **Lilla Edet** Sweden
100 B2 **Lille** Belgium
105 C1 **Lille** France
Lille Bælt *sea chan.* Denmark *see* Little Belt
Lillehammer Norway
93 F4 **Lillestrøm** Norway
128 B2 **Lillooet** Can.
121 C2 **Lilongwe** Malawi
64 B3 **Liloy** Phil.
150 B4 **Lima** Peru
134 D2 **Lima** U.S.A.
155 D2 **Lima Duarte** Brazil
79 C2 **Limah** Oman

80 B2 **Limassol** Cyprus
97 C1 **Limavady** U.K.
153 B3 **Limay** *r.* Arg.
101 F2 **Limbach-Oberfrohna** Ger.
88 B2 **Limbaži** Latvia
118 A2 **Limbe** Cameroon
101 D2 **Limburg an der Lahn** Ger.
122 B2 **Lime Acres** S. Africa
154 C2 **Limeira** Brazil
97 B2 **Limerick** Rep. of Ireland
93 E4 **Limfjorden** *sea chan.* Denmark
92 I3 **Liminka** Fin.
111 C3 **Limnos** *i.* Greece
104 C2 **Limoges** France
136 C3 **Limon** U.S.A.
104 C2 **Limousin, Plateaux du** France
104 C3 **Limoux** France
123 C2 **Limpopo** *prov.* S. Africa
121 C3 **Limpopo** *r.* S. Africa/Zimbabwe
64 A2 **Linapacan** *i.* Phil.
153 A3 **Linares** Chile
145 C2 **Linares** Mex.
106 C2 **Linares** Spain
108 A3 **Linas, Monte** *mt. Sardinia* Italy
62 B1 **Lincang** China
Linchuan China *see* **Fuzhou**
98 C3 **Lincoln** U.K.
138 B2 **Lincoln** *IL* U.S.A.
139 F1 **Lincoln** *ME* U.S.A.
137 D2 **Lincoln** *NE* U.S.A.
134 B2 **Lincoln City** U.S.A.
151 D2 **Linden** Guyana
140 C1 **Linden** U.S.A.
119 C2 **Lindi** *r.* Dem. Rep. Congo
119 D3 **Lindi** Tanz.
Lindisfarne *i.* U.K. *see* **Holy Island**
111 C3 **Lindos** Greece
130 C3 **Lindsay** Can.
48 K3 **Line Islands** Kiribati
70 B2 **Linfen** China
64 B2 **Lingayen** Phil.
70 B2 **Lingbao** China
Lingcheng China *see* **Lingshan**
Lingcheng China *see* **Lingshui**
123 C3 **Lingelethu** S. Africa
123 C3 **Lingelihle** S. Africa
100 C1 **Lingen (Ems)** Ger.
60 B2 **Lingga** *i.* Indon.
60 B2 **Lingga, Kepulauan** *is* Indon.
71 A3 **Lingshan** China
71 A4 **Lingshui** China
114 A3 **Linguère** Senegal
155 D1 **Linhares** Brazil
70 A1 **Linhe** China
Linjiang China *see* **Shanghang**
65 B1 **Linjiang** China
93 G4 **Linköping** Sweden
66 B1 **Linkou** China
71 B3 **Linli** China
96 B2 **Linnhe, Loch** *inlet* U.K.
70 B2 **Linqing** China
154 C2 **Lins** Brazil
136 C1 **Linton** U.S.A.
69 D2 **Linxi** China
70 A2 **Linxia** China
70 B2 **Linyi** *Shandong* China
70 B2 **Linyi** *Shandong* China
70 B2 **Linying** China
102 C2 **Linz** Austria
90 A1 **Lioboml'** Ukr.
105 C3 **Lion, Golfe du** *g.* France
Lions, Gulf of France *see* **Lion, Golfe du**
109 B3 **Lipari** Italy
108 B3 **Lipari, Isole** *is* Italy
89 E3 **Lipetsk** Rus. Fed.
110 B1 **Lipova** Romania
101 D2 **Lippstadt** Ger.
53 C3 **Liptrap, Cape** Austr.
71 B3 **Lipu** China
119 D2 **Lira** Uganda
108 B2 **Liri** *r.* Italy
76 C1 **Lisakovsk** Kazakh.
118 C2 **Lisala** Dem. Rep. Congo
Lisboa Port. *see* **Lisbon**
106 B2 **Lisbon** Port.
97 C1 **Lisburn** U.K.
97 B2 **Liscannor Bay** Rep. of Ireland
97 B2 **Lisdoonvarna** Rep. of Ireland
Lishi China *see* **Dingnan**
71 B3 **Lishui** China
104 C2 **Lisieux** France
99 A4 **Liskeard** U.K.
89 E3 **Liski** Rus. Fed.
53 D1 **Lismore** Austr.
97 C2 **Lismore** Rep. of Ireland
97 C1 **Lisnaskea** U.K.
97 B2 **Listowel** Rep. of Ireland
71 A3 **Litang** *Guangxi* China
68 C2 **Litang** *Sichuan* China
138 B3 **Litchfield** *IL* U.S.A.
137 E1 **Litchfield** *MN* U.S.A.
53 D2 **Lithgow** Austr.
111 B3 **Lithino, Akra** *pt* Greece
88 B2 **Lithuania** *country* Europe
111 B2 **Litochoro** Greece
102 C1 **Litoměřice** Czech Rep.
Litovskaya S.S.R. *admin. reg.* Europe *see* **Lithuania**
146 C2 **Little Abaco** *i.* Bahamas
73 D3 **Little Andaman** *i.* India
141 E3 **Little Bahama Bank** *sea feature* Bahamas
93 E4 **Little Belt** *sea chan.* Denmark
146 B3 **Little Cayman** *i.* Cayman Is
142 A1 **Little Colorado** *r.* U.S.A.
138 C1 **Little Current** Can.
137 E1 **Little Falls** U.S.A.
143 C2 **Littlefield** U.S.A.
99 C4 **Littlehampton** U.K.
122 A2 **Little Karas Berg** *plat.* Namibia
122 B3 **Little Karoo** *plat.* S. Africa
96 A2 **Little Minch** *sea chan.* U.K.
136 C1 **Little Missouri** *r.* U.S.A.
73 D4 **Little Nicobar** *i.* India
140 B2 **Little Rock** U.S.A.
139 E2 **Littleton** U.S.A.
121 C2 **Litunde** Moz.
90 B2 **Lityn** Ukr.
Liuchow China *see* **Liuzhou**
70 B2 **Liujiachang** China
Liupanshui China *see* **Lupanshui**
121 C2 **Liupo** Moz.
71 A3 **Liuzhou** China
88 C2 **Līvāni** Latvia
141 D2 **Live Oak** U.S.A.
50 B1 **Liveringa** Austr.
142 C2 **Livermore, Mount** U.S.A.
53 D2 **Liverpool** Austr.
131 D3 **Liverpool** Can.
98 B3 **Liverpool** U.K.
127 G2 **Liverpool, Cape** Can.
53 C2 **Liverpool Range** *mts* Austr.
96 C3 **Livingston** U.K.
134 D1 **Livingston** *MT* U.S.A.
143 E2 **Livingston** *TX* U.S.A.
143 D2 **Livingston, Lake** U.S.A.
120 B2 **Livingstone** Zambia
55 A3 **Livingston Island** Antarctica
109 C2 **Livno** Bos.-Herz.
89 E3 **Livny** Rus. Fed.
138 C2 **Livonia** U.S.A.
108 B2 **Livorno** Italy
119 D3 **Liwale** Tanz.
99 A5 **Lizard Point** U.K.
108 B1 **Ljubljana** Slovenia
93 G3 **Ljungan** *r.* Sweden
93 F4 **Ljungby** Sweden
93 G3 **Ljusdal** Sweden
93 G3 **Ljusnan** *r.* Sweden
99 B4 **Llandeilo** U.K.
99 B4 **Llandovery** U.K.
99 B3 **Llandrindod Wells** U.K.
98 B3 **Llandudno** U.K.
99 A4 **Llanelli** U.K.
106 C1 **Llanes** Spain
98 A3 **Llangefni** U.K.
99 B3 **Llangollen** U.K.
99 B3 **Llangurig** U.K.
143 C2 **Llano Estacado** *plain* U.S.A.
150 C2 **Llanos** *reg.* Col./Venez.
107 D1 **Lleida** Spain
99 A3 **Lleyn Peninsula** U.K.
107 C2 **Llíria** Spain
106 C1 **Llodio** Spain
128 B2 **Lloyd George, Mount** Can.
129 D2 **Lloyd Lake** Can.
129 C2 **Lloydminster** Can.
152 B2 **Llullaillaco, Volcán** *vol.* Chile
154 B2 **Loanda** Brazil
123 C2 **Lobatse** Botswana
103 D1 **Łobez** Pol.
120 A2 **Lobito** Angola
101 F1 **Loburg** Ger.
96 B2 **Lochaber** *mts* U.K.
96 B2 **Lochaline** U.K.
96 A1 **Loch a' Tuath** U.K.
Loch Baghasdail U.K. *see* **Lochboisdale**
96 A2 **Lochboisdale** U.K.
104 C2 **Loches** France
96 B2 **Lochgilphead** U.K.
96 B1 **Lochinver** U.K.
96 A2 **Lochmaddy** U.K.
96 C2 **Lochnagar** *mt.* U.K.
Loch nam Madadh U.K. *see* **Lochmaddy**
96 B3 **Lochranza** U.K.
52 A2 **Lock** Austr.
96 C3 **Lockerbie** U.K.
53 C3 **Lockhart** Austr.
143 D3 **Lockhart** U.S.A.
51 D1 **Lockhart River** Austr.
139 D2 **Lock Haven** U.S.A.
139 D2 **Lockport** U.S.A.
63 B2 **Lôc Ninh** Vietnam
105 C3 **Lodève** France
86 C2 **Lodeynoye Pole** Rus. Fed.
74 B2 **Lodhran** Pak.
108 A1 **Lodi** Italy
135 B3 **Lodi** U.S.A.
92 F2 **Løding** Norway
92 G2 **Lødingen** Norway
118 C3 **Lodja** Dem. Rep. Congo
119 D2 **Lodwar** Kenya
103 D1 **Łódź** Pol.
62 B2 **Loei** Thai.
122 A3 **Loeriesfontein** S. Africa
92 F2 **Lofoten** *is* Norway
134 D2 **Logan** U.S.A.
128 A1 **Logan, Mount** Can.
138 B2 **Logansport** U.S.A.
108 B1 **Logatec** Slovenia
115 D3 **Logone** *r.* Africa
106 C1 **Logroño** Spain
93 H3 **Lohja** Fin.
101 D1 **Löhne** Ger.
101 D1 **Lohne (Oldenburg)** Ger.
62 A2 **Loikaw** Myanmar
62 A2 **Loi Lan** *mt.* Myanmar/Thai.
93 H3 **Loimaa** Fin.
104 B2 **Loire** *r.* France
150 B3 **Loja** Ecuador
106 C2 **Loja** Spain
92 I2 **Lokan tekojärvi** *l.* Fin.
100 B2 **Lokeren** Belgium
122 B1 **Lokgwabe** Botswana
91 C1 **Lokhvytsya** Ukr.
119 D2 **Lokichar** Kenya
119 D2 **Lokichokio** Kenya
93 E4 **Løkken** Denmark
89 D2 **Loknya** Rus. Fed.
115 C4 **Lokoja** Nigeria
89 D3 **Lokot'** Rus. Fed.
88 C2 **Loksa** Estonia
127 H2 **Loks Land** *i.* Can.
114 B4 **Lola** Guinea
93 F5 **Lolland** *i.* Denmark
119 D3 **Lollondo** Tanz.
118 C2 **Lolo** Dem. Rep. Congo
122 B2 **Lolwane** S. Africa
110 B2 **Lom** Bulg.
93 E3 **Lom** Norway
119 C2 **Lomami** *r.* Dem. Rep. Congo
153 C3 **Lomas de Zamora** Arg.
50 B1 **Lombardina** Austr.
61 C2 **Lombok** *i.* Indon.
61 C2 **Lombok, Selat** *sea chan.* Indon.
114 C4 **Lomé** Togo
118 C3 **Lomela** *r.* Dem. Rep. Congo
100 B2 **Lommel** Belgium
96 B2 **Lomond, Loch** *l.* U.K.
88 C2 **Lomonosov** Rus. Fed.
160 A1 **Lomonosov Ridge** *sea feature* Arctic Ocean
61 C2 **Lompobattang, Gunung** *mt.* Indon.
135 B4 **Lompoc** U.S.A.
63 B2 **Lom Sak** Thai.
103 E1 **Łomża** Pol.
130 B3 **London** Can.
99 C4 **London** U.K.
138 C3 **London** U.S.A.
97 C1 **Londonderry** U.K.
50 B1 **Londonderry, Cape** Austr.
154 B2 **Londrina** Brazil
135 C3 **Lone Pine** U.S.A.
83 M2 **Longa, Proliv** *sea chan.* Rus. Fed.
61 C1 **Long Akah** *Sarawak* Malaysia
141 E2 **Long Bay** U.S.A.
135 C4 **Long Beach** U.S.A.
71 A3 **Longchang** China
99 C3 **Long Eaton** U.K.
97 C2 **Longford** Rep. of Ireland
96 C1 **Longhope** U.K.
119 D3 **Longido** Tanz.
61 C2 **Longiram** Indon.
147 C2 **Long Island** Bahamas
130 C2 **Long Island** Can.
59 D3 **Long Island** P.N.G.
139 E2 **Long Island** U.S.A.
130 B3 **Longlac** Can.
130 B3 **Long Lake** Can.
71 A3 **Longli** China
71 A3 **Longming** China
136 B2 **Longmont** U.S.A.
Longping China *see* **Luodian**
138 C2 **Long Point** Can.
71 B3 **Longquan** China
131 E3 **Long Range Mountains** Can.
51 D2 **Longreach** Austr.
Longshan China *see* **Longli**
99 D3 **Long Stratton** U.K.
98 B2 **Longtown** U.K.
105 D2 **Longuyon** France
143 E2 **Longview** *TX* U.S.A.
134 B1 **Longview** *WA* U.S.A.
61 C1 **Longwai** Indon.
70 A2 **Longxi** China
Longxian China *see* **Wengyuan**
71 B3 **Longxi Shan** *mt.* China
63 B2 **Long Xuyên** Vietnam
71 B3 **Longyan** China
82 C1 **Longyearbyen** Svalbard
108 B1 **Lonigo** Italy
100 C1 **Löningen** Ger.
105 D2 **Lons-le-Saunier** France
141 E2 **Lookout, Cape** U.S.A.
119 D3 **Loolmalasin** *vol. crater* Tanz.
50 B3 **Loongana** Austr.
97 B2 **Loop Head** *hd* Rep. of Ireland
Lopasnya Rus. Fed. *see* **Chekhov**
63 B2 **Lop Buri** Thai.
64 B2 **Lopez** Phil.
118 A3 **Lopez, Cap** *c.* Gabon
68 C2 **Lop Nur** *salt l.* China
118 B2 **Lopori** *r.* Dem. Rep. Congo
92 H1 **Lopphavet** *b.* Norway
106 B2 **Lora del Río** Spain
138 C2 **Lorain** U.S.A.
74 A1 **Loralai** Pak.
107 C2 **Lorca** Spain
51 E3 **Lord Howe Island** Austr.
142 B2 **Lordsburg** U.S.A.
155 C2 **Lorena** Brazil
59 D3 **Lorengau** P.N.G.
59 D3 **Lorentz** *r.* Indon.
152 B1 **Loreto** Bol.
144 A2 **Loreto** Mex.
104 B2 **Lorient** France
96 B2 **Lorn, Firth of** *est.* U.K.
52 B3 **Lorne** Austr.
105 D2 **Lorraine** *reg.* France
142 B1 **Los Alamos** U.S.A.
143 D3 **Los Aldamas** Mex.
153 A3 **Los Ángeles** Chile
135 C4 **Los Angeles** U.S.A.
135 B3 **Los Banos** U.S.A.
152 B2 **Los Blancos** Arg.
89 F3 **Losevo** Rus. Fed.
108 B2 **Lošinj** *i.* Croatia
144 B2 **Los Mochis** Mex.
118 B2 **Losombo** Dem. Rep. Congo
106 B2 **Los Pedroches** *plat.* Spain
147 D3 **Los Roques, Islas** *is* Venez.
96 C2 **Lossiemouth** U.K.
150 C1 **Los Teques** Venez.
59 E3 **Losuia** P.N.G.
152 A3 **Los Vilos** Chile
104 C3 **Lot** *r.* France
96 C1 **Loth** U.K.
134 D1 **Lothair** U.S.A.
Lothringen *reg.* France *see* **Lorraine**
119 D2 **Lotikipi Plain** Kenya
118 C3 **Loto** Dem. Rep. Congo
89 E2 **Lotoshino** Rus. Fed.

62 B1 **Louangnamtha** Laos
62 B2 **Louangphabang** Laos
118 B3 **Loubomo** Congo
104 B2 **Loudéac** France
71 B3 **Loudi** China
118 B3 **Loudima** Congo
114 A3 **Louga** Senegal
99 C3 **Loughborough** U.K.
97 B2 **Loughrea** Rep. of Ireland
105 D2 **Louhans** France
97 B2 **Louisburgh** Rep. of Ireland
51 E1 **Louisiade Archipelago** *is* P.N.G.
140 B2 **Louisiana** *state* U.S.A.
123 C1 **Louis Trichardt** S. Africa
138 B3 **Louisville** *KY* U.S.A.
140 C2 **Louisville** *MS* U.S.A.
86 C2 **Loukhi** Rus. Fed.
118 B3 **Loukoléla** Congo
106 B2 **Loulé** Port.
118 A2 **Loum** Cameroon
130 C2 **Loups Marins, Lacs des** *lakes* Can.
104 B3 **Lourdes** France
151 D2 **Lourenço** Brazil
Lourenço Marques Moz. see **Maputo**
106 B1 **Lousã** Port.
53 C2 **Louth** Austr.
98 C3 **Louth** U.K.
Louvain Belgium see Leuven
122 A1 **Louwater-Suid** Namibia
89 D2 **Lovat'** *r.* Rus. Fed.
110 B2 **Lovech** Bulg.
136 B2 **Loveland** U.S.A.
136 B2 **Lovell** U.S.A.
135 C2 **Lovelock** U.S.A.
88 C1 **Loviisa** Fin.
143 C2 **Lovington** U.S.A.
86 C2 **Lovozero** Rus. Fed.
119 C3 **Lowa** Dem. Rep. Congo
139 E2 **Lowell** U.S.A.
119 D2 **Lowelli** Sudan
128 C3 **Lower Arrow Lake** Can.
Lower California *pen.* Mex. see **Baja California**
54 B2 **Lower Hutt** N.Z.
97 C1 **Lower Lough Erne** *l.* U.K.
128 B2 **Lower Post** Can.
137 E1 **Lower Red Lake** U.S.A.
Lower Tunguska *r.* Rus. Fed. see **Nizhnyaya Tunguska**
99 D3 **Lowestoft** U.K.
103 D1 **Łowicz** Pol.
139 D2 **Lowville** U.S.A.
52 B2 **Loxton** Austr.
Loyang China see **Luoyang**
48 H6 **Loyauté, Îles** New Caledonia
89 D3 **Loyew** Belarus
92 F2 **Løypskardtinden** *mt.* Norway
109 C2 **Loznica** Serb. and Mont.
91 D2 **Lozova** Ukr.
120 B2 **Luacano** Angola
70 B2 **Lu'an** China
120 A1 **Luanda** Angola
63 B3 **Luang, Thale** *lag.* Thai.
121 C2 **Luangwa** *r.* Zambia
121 B2 **Luanshya** Zambia
Luao Angola see **Luau**
106 B1 **Luarca** Spain
120 B2 **Luau** Angola
103 E1 **Lubaczów** Pol.
103 D1 **Lubań** Pol.
64 A2 **Lubang Islands** Phil.
120 A2 **Lubango** Angola
119 C3 **Lubao** Dem. Rep. Congo
103 E1 **Lubartów** Pol.
101 D1 **Lübbecke** Ger.
102 C1 **Lübben** Ger.
143 C2 **Lubbock** U.S.A.
101 E1 **Lübeck** Ger.
69 E2 **Lubei** China
76 B1 **Lubenka** Kazakh.
119 C3 **Lubero** Dem. Rep. Congo
103 D1 **Lubin** Pol.
103 E1 **Lublin** Pol.
91 C1 **Lubny** Ukr.
61 C1 **Lubok Antu** *Sarawak* Malaysia
101 E1 **Lübow** Ger.
101 E1 **Lübtheen** Ger.
119 C3 **Lubudi** Dem. Rep. Congo
60 B2 **Lubuklinggau** Indon.
119 C4 **Lubumbashi** Dem. Rep. Congo
120 B2 **Lubungu** Zambia
119 C3 **Lubutu** Dem. Rep. Congo
120 A1 **Lucala** Angola
97 C2 **Lucan** Rep. of Ireland
120 B1 **Lucapa** Angola
108 B2 **Lucca** Italy
96 B3 **Luce Bay** U.K.
154 B2 **Lucélia** Brazil
64 B2 **Lucena** Phil.
106 C2 **Lucena** Spain
103 D2 **Lučenec** Slovakia
109 C2 **Lucera** Italy
105 D2 **Lucerne** Switz.
66 B1 **Luchegorsk** Rus. Fed.
101 E1 **Lüchow** Ger.
120 A2 **Lucira** Angola
Łuck Ukr. see **Luts'k**
101 F1 **Luckenwalde** Ger.
122 B2 **Luckhoff** S. Africa
75 C2 **Lucknow** India
120 A1 **Lucunga** Angola
120 B2 **Lucusse** Angola
Lüda China see **Dalian**
100 C2 **Lüdenscheid** Ger.
101 E1 **Lüder** Ger.
120 A3 **Lüderitz** Namibia
119 D4 **Ludewa** Tanz.
74 B1 **Ludhiana** India
138 B2 **Ludington** U.S.A.
99 B3 **Ludlow** U.K.
135 C4 **Ludlow** U.S.A.
110 C2 **Ludogorie** *reg.* Bulg.
93 G3 **Ludvika** Sweden
102 B2 **Ludwigsburg** Ger.
101 F1 **Ludwigsfelde** Ger.
101 D3 **Ludwigshafen am Rhein** Ger.
101 E1 **Ludwigslust** Ger.
88 C2 **Ludza** Latvia
118 C3 **Luebo** Dem. Rep. Congo
120 A2 **Luena** Angola
70 A2 **Lüeyang** China
71 B3 **Lufeng** China
119 C3 **Lufira** *r.* Dem. Rep. Congo
143 E2 **Lufkin** U.S.A.
88 C2 **Luga** Rus. Fed.
88 C2 **Luga** *r.* Rus. Fed.
105 D2 **Lugano** Switz.
121 C2 **Lugenda** *r.* Moz.
106 B1 **Lugo** Spain
110 B1 **Lugoj** Romania
91 D2 **Luhans'k** Ukr.
119 D3 **Luhombero** Tanz.
90 B1 **Luhyny** Ukr.
120 B2 **Luiana** Angola
Luichow Peninsula China see **Leizhou Bandao**
118 C3 **Luilaka** *r.* Dem. Rep. Congo
Luimneach Rep. of Ireland see **Limerick**
105 D2 **Luino** Italy
92 I2 **Luiro** *r.* Fin.
118 C3 **Luiza** Dem. Rep. Congo
70 B2 **Lujiang** China
Lukapa Angola see **Lucapa**
109 C2 **Lukavac** Bos.-Herz.
118 B3 **Lukenie** *r.* Dem. Rep. Congo
142 A2 **Lukeville** U.S.A.
89 E3 **Lukhovitsy** Rus. Fed.
Lukou China see **Zhuzhou**
103 E1 **Łuków** Pol.
120 B2 **Lukulu** Zambia
92 H2 **Luleå** Sweden
92 H2 **Luleälven** *r.* Sweden
111 C2 **Lüleburgaz** Turkey
70 B2 **Lüliang Shan** *mts* China
143 D3 **Luling** U.S.A.
Luluabourg Dem. Rep. Congo see Kananga
61 C2 **Lumajang** Indon.
75 C1 **Lumajangdong Co** *salt l.* China
Lumbala Angola see Lumbala Kaquengue
Lumbala Angola see Lumbala N'guimbo
120 B2 **Lumbala Kaquengue** Angola
120 B2 **Lumbala N'guimbo** Angola
140 C2 **Lumberton** *MS* U.S.A.
141 E2 **Lumberton** *NC* U.S.A.
61 C1 **Lumbis** Indon.
106 B1 **Lumbrales** Spain
63 B2 **Lumphăt** Cambodia
129 D2 **Lumsden** Can.
54 A3 **Lumsden** N.Z.
93 F4 **Lund** Sweden
121 C2 **Lundazi** Zambia
99 A4 **Lundy** U.K.
101 E1 **Lüneburg** Ger.
101 E1 **Lüneburger Heide** *reg.* Ger.
100 C2 **Lünen** Ger.
105 D2 **Lunéville** France
120 B2 **Lunga** *r.* Zambia
114 A4 **Lungi** Sierra Leone
Lungleh India see **Lunglei**
75 D2 **Lunglei** India
97 C2 **Lungnaquilla Mountain** *hill* Rep. of Ireland
120 B2 **Lungwebungu** *r.* Zambia
74 B2 **Luni** *r.* India
88 C3 **Luninyets** Belarus
104 C3 **L'Union** France
114 A4 **Lunsar** Sierra Leone
77 E2 **Luntai** China
71 A3 **Luodian** China
71 B3 **Luoding** China
70 B2 **Luohe** China
70 B2 **Luoyang** China
118 B3 **Luozi** Dem. Rep. Congo
121 B2 **Lupane** Zimbabwe
71 A3 **Lupanshui** China
110 B1 **Lupeni** Romania
121 C2 **Lupilichi** Moz.
101 F2 **Luppa** Ger.
95 B3 **Lurgan** U.K.
Luring China see **Gêrzê**
121 D2 **Lúrio** Moz.
121 D2 **Lurio** *r.* Moz.
92 F2 **Lurøy** Norway
121 B2 **Lusaka** Zambia
118 C3 **Lusambo** Dem. Rep. Congo
109 C2 **Lushnjë** Albania
70 C2 **Lüshun** China
123 C3 **Lusikisiki** S. Africa
136 C2 **Lusk** U.S.A.
Luso Angola see **Luena**
76 B3 **Lut, Dasht-e** *des.* Iran
101 F2 **Lutherstadt Wittenberg** Ger.
99 C4 **Luton** U.K.
61 C1 **Lutong** *Sarawak* Malaysia
129 C1 **Łutselk'e** Can.
90 B1 **Luts'k** Ukr.
55 F3 **Lützow-Holm Bay** Antarctica
122 B2 **Lutzputs** S. Africa
122 A3 **Lutzville** S. Africa
117 C4 **Luuq** Somalia
137 D2 **Luverne** U.S.A.
119 C3 **Luvua** *r.* Dem. Rep. Congo
120 B2 **Luvuei** Angola
123 D1 **Luvuvhu** *r.* S. Africa
119 D3 **Luwegu** *r.* Tanz.
119 D2 **Luwero** Uganda
61 D2 **Luwuk** Indon.
100 C3 **Luxembourg** *country* Europe
100 C3 **Luxembourg** Lux.
105 D2 **Luxeuil-les-Bains** France
62 A1 **Luxi** China
123 C3 **Luxolweni** S. Africa
116 B2 **Luxor** Egypt
100 B2 **Luyksgestel** Neth.
86 D2 **Luza** Rus. Fed.
Luzern Switz. see **Lucerne**
62 B1 **Luzhai** China
71 A3 **Luzhi** China
71 A3 **Luzhou** China
154 C1 **Luziânia** Brazil
151 E3 **Luzilândia** Brazil
64 B2 **Luzon** *i.* Phil.
64 B1 **Luzon Strait** Phil.
109 C3 **Luzzi** Italy
90 A2 **L'viv** Ukr.
L'vov Ukr. see **L'viv**
Lwów Ukr. see **L'viv**
88 C3 **Lyakhavichy** Belarus
Lyallpur Pak. see Faisalabad
89 D2 **Lychkovo** Rus. Fed.
92 G3 **Lycksele** Sweden
55 C2 **Lyddan Island** Antarctica
123 D2 **Lydenburg** S. Africa
88 C3 **Lyel'chytsy** Belarus
88 C3 **Lyepyel'** Belarus
136 A2 **Lyman** U.S.A.
99 B4 **Lyme Bay** U.K.
99 B4 **Lyme Regis** U.K.
139 D3 **Lynchburg** U.S.A.
52 A2 **Lyndhurst** Austr.
129 D2 **Lynn Lake** Can.
134 B1 **Lynnwood** U.S.A.
129 D1 **Lynx Lake** Can.
105 C2 **Lyon** France
Lyons France see **Lyon**
89 D2 **Lyozna** Belarus
103 E1 **Łysica** *hill* Pol.
86 E3 **Lys'va** Rus. Fed.
91 D2 **Lysychans'k** Ukr.
87 D3 **Lysyye Gory** Rus. Fed.
98 B3 **Lytham St Anne's** U.K.
88 C3 **Lyuban'** Belarus
90 C2 **Lyubashivka** Ukr.
89 E2 **Lyubertsy** Rus. Fed.
90 B1 **Lyubeshiv** Ukr.
89 F2 **Lyubim** Rus. Fed.
91 D2 **Lyubotyn** Ukr.
89 D2 **Lyubytino** Rus. Fed.
89 D3 **Lyudinovo** Rus. Fed.

M

80 B2 **Ma'ān** Jordan
70 B2 **Ma'anshan** China
88 C2 **Maardu** Estonia
78 B3 **Ma'āriḍ, Banī** *des.* Saudi Arabia
80 B2 **Ma'arrat an Nu'mān** Syria
100 B1 **Maarssen** Neth.
100 B2 **Maas** *r.* Neth.
100 B2 **Maaseik** Belgium
64 B2 **Maasin** Phil.
100 B2 **Maastricht** Neth.
121 C3 **Mabalane** Moz.
78 B3 **Ma'bar** Yemen
150 D2 **Mabaruma** Guyana
98 D3 **Mablethorpe** U.K.
123 C2 **Mabopane** S. Africa
121 C3 **Mabote** Moz.
122 B2 **Mabule** Botswana
122 B1 **Mabutsane** Botswana
155 D2 **Macaé** Brazil
121 C2 **Macaloge** Moz.
126 F2 **MacAlpine Lake** Can.
151 D2 **Macapá** Brazil
150 B3 **Macará** Ecuador
155 D1 **Macarani** Brazil
Macassar Indon. see **Makassar**
Macassar Strait Indon. see **Makassar, Selat**
121 C2 **Macatanja** Moz.
151 F3 **Macau** Brazil
71 B3 **Macau** *special admin. reg.* China
121 C3 **Maccaretane** Moz.
98 B3 **Macclesfield** U.K.
50 B2 **Macdonald, Lake** *salt flat* Austr.
50 C2 **Macdonnell Ranges** *mts* Austr.
130 A2 **MacDowell Lake** Can.
96 C2 **Macduff** U.K.
106 B1 **Macedo de Cavaleiros** Port.
52 B3 **Macedon** *mt.* Austr.
111 B2 **Macedonia** *country* Europe
151 F3 **Maceió** Brazil
108 B2 **Macerata** Italy
52 A2 **Macfarlane, Lake** *salt flat* Austr.
97 B3 **Macgillycuddy's Reeks** *mts* Rep. of Ireland
74 A2 **Mach** Pak.
155 C2 **Machado** Brazil
121 C3 **Machaila** Moz.
119 D3 **Machakos** Kenya
150 B3 **Machala** Ecuador
121 C3 **Machanga** Moz.
Machaze Moz. see **Chitobe**
70 B2 **Macheng** China
138 B2 **Machesney Park** U.S.A.
139 F2 **Machias** U.S.A.
73 C3 **Machilipatnam** India
121 C2 **Machinga** Malawi
150 B1 **Machiques** Venez.
150 B4 **Machupicchu** Peru
99 B3 **Machynlleth** U.K.
123 D2 **Macia** Moz.
Macias Nguema *i.* Equat. Guinea see **Bioco**
110 C1 **Măcin** Romania
53 D1 **Macintyre** *r.* Austr.
51 D2 **Mackay** Austr.
50 B2 **Mackay, Lake** *salt flat* Austr.
128 C1 **MacKay Lake** Can.
128 B2 **Mackenzie** Can.
128 A1 **Mackenzie** *r.* Can.
Mackenzie Guyana see **Linden**
Mackenzie *atoll* Micronesia see **Ulithi**
55 H3 **Mackenzie Bay** Antarctica

126 C2 **Mackenzie Bay** Can.
126 E1 **Mackenzie King Island** Can.
128 A1 **Mackenzie Mountains** Can.
Mackillop, Lake *salt flat* Austr. *see* Yamma Yamma, Lake
129 D2 **Macklin** Can.
53 D2 **Macksville** Austr.
53 D1 **Maclean** Austr.
123 C3 **Maclear** S. Africa
50 A2 **MacLeod, Lake** *imp. l.* Austr.
138 A2 **Macomb** U.S.A.
108 A2 **Macomer** *Sardinia* Italy
121 D2 **Macomia** Moz.
105 C2 **Mâcon** France
141 D2 **Macon** *GA* U.S.A.
137 E3 **Macon** *MO* U.S.A.
140 C2 **Macon** *MS* U.S.A.
53 C2 **Macquarie** *r.* Austr.
48 G9 **Macquarie Island** S. Pacific Ocean
53 C2 **Macquarie Marshes** Austr.
53 C2 **Macquarie Mountain** Austr.
156 D9 **Macquarie Ridge** *sea feature* S. Pacific Ocean
55 H2 **Mac. Robertson Land** *reg.* Antarctica
97 B3 **Macroom** Rep. of Ireland
52 A1 **Macumba** *watercourse* Austr.
145 C3 **Macuspana** Mex.
144 B2 **Macuzari, Presa** *resr* Mex.
123 D2 **Madadeni** S. Africa
121 □D3 **Madagascar** *country* Africa
159 D5 **Madagascar Ridge** *sea feature* Indian Ocean
115 D2 **Madama** Niger
111 B2 **Madan** Bulg.
59 D3 **Madang** P.N.G.
139 D1 **Madawaska** *r.* Can.
62 A1 **Madaya** Myanmar
150 D3 **Madeira** *r.* Brazil
114 A1 **Madeira** *terr.* N. Atlantic Ocean
131 D3 **Madeleine, Îles de la** *is* Can.
99 B3 **Madeley** U.K.
144 B2 **Madera** Mex.
135 B3 **Madera** U.S.A.
73 B3 **Madgaon** India
74 B2 **Madhya Pradesh** *state* India
123 C2 **Madibogo** S. Africa
118 B3 **Madingou** Congo
121 □D2 **Madirovalo** Madag.
138 B3 **Madison** *IN* U.S.A.
137 D2 **Madison** *SD* U.S.A.
138 B2 **Madison** *WI* U.S.A.
138 C3 **Madison** *WV* U.S.A.
134 D1 **Madison** *r.* U.S.A.
138 B3 **Madisonville** U.S.A.
61 C2 **Madiun** Indon.
119 D2 **Mado Gashi** Kenya
68 C2 **Madoi** China
88 C2 **Madona** Latvia
78 A2 **Madrakah** Saudi Arabia
79 C3 **Madrakah, Ra's** *c.* Oman
Madras India *see* **Chennai**
134 B2 **Madras** U.S.A.
145 C2 **Madre, Laguna** *lag.* Mex.
143 D3 **Madre, Laguna** *lag.* U.S.A.
150 C4 **Madre de Dios** *r.* Peru
145 B3 **Madre del Sur, Sierra** *mts* Mex.
144 B2 **Madre Occidental, Sierra** *mts* Mex.
145 B2 **Madre Oriental, Sierra** *mts* Mex.
106 C1 **Madrid** Spain
106 C2 **Madridejos** Spain
61 C2 **Madura** *i.* Indon.
61 C2 **Madura, Selat** *sea chan.* Indon.
73 B4 **Madurai** India
121 B2 **Madziwadzido** Zimbabwe
67 C3 **Maebashi** Japan
62 A2 **Mae Hong Son** Thai.
62 A1 **Mae Sai** Thai.
62 A2 **Mae Sariang** Thai.
99 B4 **Maesteg** U.K.
62 A2 **Mae Suai** Thai.
121 □D2 **Maevatanana** Madag.
Mafeking S. Africa *see* **Mafikeng**
123 C2 **Mafeteng** Lesotho
53 C3 **Maffra** Austr.
119 D3 **Mafia Island** Tanz.
123 C2 **Mafikeng** S. Africa
119 D3 **Mafinga** Tanz.
154 C3 **Mafra** Brazil
83 L3 **Magadan** Rus. Fed.
Magallanes Chile *see* Punta Arenas
Magallanes, Estrecho de Chile *see* Magellan, Strait of
150 B2 **Magangue** Col.
140 B1 **Magazine Mountain** *hill* U.S.A.
114 A4 **Magburaka** Sierra Leone
69 E1 **Magdagachi** Rus. Fed.
144 A1 **Magdalena** Mex.
142 B2 **Magdalena** U.S.A.
144 A2 **Magdalena, Bahía** *b.* Mex.
101 E1 **Magdeburg** Ger.
153 A5 **Magellan, Strait of** *sea chan.* Chile
Maggiore, Lago Italy *see* Maggiore, Lake
108 A1 **Maggiore, Lake** *l.* Italy
116 B2 **Maghāghah** Egypt
97 C1 **Magherafelt** U.K.
87 E3 **Magnitogorsk** Rus. Fed.
140 B2 **Magnolia** U.S.A.
121 C2 **Màgoé** Moz.
130 C3 **Magog** Can.
131 D2 **Magpie, Lac** *l.* Can.
114 A3 **Magṭa' Laḥjar** Maur.
119 D3 **Magu** Tanz.
151 E3 **Maguarinho, Cabo** *c.* Brazil
123 D2 **Magude** Moz.
90 B2 **Măgura, Dealul** *hill* Moldova
62 A1 **Magwe** Myanmar
81 C2 **Mahābād** Iran
74 B2 **Mahajan** India
121 □D2 **Mahajanga** Madag.
61 C2 **Mahakam** *r.* Indon.
123 C1 **Mahalapye** Botswana
121 □D2 **Mahalevona** Madag.
75 C2 **Mahanadi** *r.* India
121 □D2 **Mahanoro** Madag.
74 B3 **Maharashtra** *state* India
63 B2 **Maha Sarakham** Thai.
121 □D2 **Mahavavy** *r.* Madag.
68 B3 **Mahbubnagar** India
78 B2 **Mahd adh Dhahab** Saudi Arabia
107 D2 **Mahdia** Alg.
150 D2 **Mahdia** Guyana
113 I6 **Mahé** *i.* Seychelles
75 C3 **Mahendragiri** *mt.* India
119 D3 **Mahenge** Tanz.
54 B3 **Maheno** N.Z.
74 B2 **Mahesana** India
74 B2 **Mahi** *r.* India
54 C1 **Mahia Peninsula** N.Z.
89 D3 **Mahilyow** Belarus
107 D2 **Mahón** Spain
114 B3 **Mahou** Mali
Mahsana India *see* Mahesana
74 B2 **Mahuva** India
111 C2 **Mahya Dağı** *mt.* Turkey
106 B1 **Maia** Port.
Maiaia Moz. *see* **Nacala**
147 C3 **Maicao** Col.
129 D2 **Maidstone** Can.
99 D4 **Maidstone** U.K.
115 D3 **Maiduguri** Nigeria
75 D2 **Maijdi** Bangl.
75 C2 **Mailani** India
101 D2 **Main** *r.* Ger.
118 B3 **Mai-Ndombe, Lac** *l.* Dem. Rep. Congo
101 E3 **Main-Donau-Kanal** *canal* Ger.
139 F1 **Maine** *state* U.S.A.
131 D3 **Maine, Gulf of** Can./U.S.A.
62 A1 **Maingkwan** Myanmar
96 C1 **Mainland** *i. Orkney Is, Scotland* U.K.
96 □ **Mainland** *i. Shetland Is, Scotland* U.K.
121 □D2 **Maintirano** Madag.
101 D2 **Mainz** Ger.
150 C1 **Maiquetía** Venez.
120 B3 **Maitengwe** Botswana
53 D2 **Maitland** *N.S.W.* Austr.
52 A2 **Maitland** *S.A.* Austr.
146 B3 **Maíz, Islas del** *is* Nic.
67 C3 **Maizuru** Japan
109 C2 **Maja Jezercë** *mt.* Albania
61 C2 **Majene** Indon.
119 D2 **Majī** Eth.
107 D2 **Majorca** *i.* Spain
Majunga Madag. *see* Mahajanga
123 C2 **Majwemasweu** S. Africa
118 B3 **Makabana** Congo
61 C2 **Makale** Indon.
119 C3 **Makamba** Burundi
77 E2 **Makanchi** Kazakh.
118 B2 **Makanza** Dem. Rep. Congo
90 B1 **Makariv** Ukr.
69 F1 **Makarov** Rus. Fed.
160 B1 **Makarov Basin** *sea feature* Arctic Ocean
109 C2 **Makarska** Croatia
61 C2 **Makassar** Indon.
61 C2 **Makassar, Selat** Indon.
76 B2 **Makat** Kazakh.
119 D3 **Makatapora** Tanz.
123 D2 **Makatini Flats** *lowland* S. Africa
114 A4 **Makeni** Sierra Leone
120 B3 **Makgadikgadi** *salt pan* Botswana
87 D4 **Makhachkala** Rus. Fed.
76 B2 **Makhambet** Kazakh.
119 D3 **Makindu** Kenya
77 D1 **Makinsk** Kazakh.
91 D2 **Makiyivka** Ukr.
Makkah Saudi Arabia *see* Mecca
131 E2 **Makkovik** Can.
103 E2 **Makó** Hungary
118 B2 **Makokou** Gabon
119 D3 **Makongolosi** Tanz.
122 B2 **Makopong** Botswana
119 C2 **Makoro** Dem. Rep. Congo
118 B3 **Makoua** Congo
111 B3 **Makrakomi** Greece
79 D2 **Makran** *reg.* Iran/Pak.
74 A2 **Makran Coast Range** *mts* Pak.
89 E2 **Maksatikha** Rus. Fed.
81 C2 **Mākū** Iran
62 A1 **Makum** India
67 B4 **Makurazaki** Japan
115 C4 **Makurdi** Nigeria
92 G2 **Malå** Sweden
146 B4 **Mala, Punta** *pt* Panama
73 B3 **Malabar Coast** India
118 A2 **Malabo** Equat. Guinea
155 D1 **Malacacheta** Brazil
Malacca Malaysia *see* Melaka
60 A1 **Malacca, Strait of** Indon./Malaysia
134 D2 **Malad City** U.S.A.
88 C3 **Maladzyechna** Belarus
106 C2 **Málaga** Spain
Malagasy Republic *country* Africa *see* Madagascar
121 □D3 **Malaimbandy** Madag.
48 H4 **Malaita** *i.* Solomon Is
117 B4 **Malakal** Sudan
48 H5 **Malakula** *i.* Vanuatu
61 D2 **Malamala** Indon.
61 C2 **Malang** Indon.
Malange Angola *see* Malanje
120 A1 **Malanje** Angola
93 G4 **Mälaren** *l.* Sweden
153 B3 **Malargüe** Arg.
130 C3 **Malartic** Can.
88 B3 **Malaryta** Belarus
80 B2 **Malatya** Turkey
121 C2 **Malawi** *country* Africa
Malawi, Lake Africa *see* Nyasa, Lake
89 D2 **Malaya Vishera** Rus. Fed.
64 B3 **Malaybalay** Phil.
81 C2 **Malāyer** Iran
60 B1 **Malaysia** *country* Asia
81 C2 **Malazgirt** Turkey
103 D1 **Malbork** Pol.
101 F1 **Malchin** Ger.
100 A2 **Maldegem** Belgium
48 L4 **Malden Island** Kiribati
56 C5 **Maldives** *country* Indian Ocean
99 D4 **Maldon** U.K.
56 I9 **Male** Maldives
111 B3 **Maleas, Akra** *pt* Greece
103 D2 **Malé Karpaty** *hills* Slovakia
119 C3 **Malela** Dem. Rep. Congo
116 A3 **Malha** Sudan
134 C2 **Malheur Lake** U.S.A.
114 B3 **Mali** *country* Africa
114 A3 **Mali** Guinea
59 C3 **Maliana** East Timor
58 C3 **Malili** Indon.
97 C1 **Malin** Rep. of Ireland
119 E3 **Malindi** Kenya
97 C1 **Malin Head** *hd* Rep. of Ireland
97 B1 **Malin More** Rep. of Ireland
111 C2 **Malkara** Turkey
88 C3 **Mal'kavichy** Belarus
110 C2 **Malko Tŭrnovo** Bulg.
53 C3 **Mallacoota** Austr.
53 C3 **Mallacoota Inlet** *b.* Austr.
96 B2 **Mallaig** U.K.
116 B2 **Mallawī** Egypt
129 E1 **Mallery Lake** Can.
Mallorca *i.* Spain *see* Majorca
97 B2 **Mallow** Rep. of Ireland
92 F3 **Malm** Norway
92 H2 **Malmberget** Sweden
100 C2 **Malmédy** Belgium
122 A3 **Malmesbury** S. Africa
93 F4 **Malmö** Sweden
71 A3 **Malong** China
118 C4 **Malonga** Dem. Rep. Congo
86 C2 **Maloshuyka** Rus. Fed.
93 E3 **Måløy** Norway
89 E2 **Maloyaroslavets** Rus. Fed.
89 E2 **Maloye Borisovo** Rus. Fed.
86 D2 **Malozemel'skaya Tundra** *lowland* Rus. Fed.
125 J9 **Malpelo, Isla de** *i.* N. Pacific Ocean
84 F5 **Malta** *country* Europe
88 C2 **Malta** Latvia
134 E1 **Malta** U.S.A.
122 A1 **Maltahöhe** Namibia
98 C2 **Malton** U.K.
Maluku *is* Indon. *see* Moluccas
93 F3 **Malung** Sweden
123 C2 **Maluti Mountains** Lesotho
73 B3 **Malvan** India
140 B2 **Malvern** U.S.A.
117 B4 **Malwal** Sudan
90 B1 **Malyn** Ukr.
83 L2 **Malyy Anyuy** *r.* Rus. Fed.
Malyy Kavkaz *mts* Asia *see* **Lesser Caucasus**
83 K2 **Malyy Lyakhovskiy, Ostrov** *i.* Rus. Fed.
123 C2 **Mamafubedu** S. Africa
151 F3 **Mamanguape** Brazil
64 B3 **Mambajao** Phil.
119 C2 **Mambasa** Dem. Rep. Congo
118 B2 **Mambéré** *r.* C.A.R.
64 B2 **Mamburao** Phil.
123 C2 **Mamelodi** S. Africa
118 A2 **Mamfe** Cameroon
135 C3 **Mammoth Lakes** U.S.A.
88 A3 **Mamonovo** Rus. Fed.
150 C4 **Mamoré** *r.* Bol./Brazil
114 A3 **Mamou** Guinea
114 B4 **Mampong** Ghana
61 C2 **Mamuju** Indon.
114 B4 **Man** Côte d'Ivoire
98 A2 **Man, Isle of** *i.* Irish Sea
150 C3 **Manacapuru** Brazil
107 D2 **Manacor** Spain
59 C2 **Manado** Indon.
146 B3 **Managua** Nic.
121 □D3 **Manakara** Madag.
78 B3 **Manākhah** Yemen
79 C2 **Manama** Bahrain
59 D3 **Manam Island** P.N.G.
121 □D3 **Mananara** *r.* Madag.
121 □D2 **Mananara Avaratra** Madag.
121 □D3 **Mananjary** Madag.
114 A3 **Manantali, Lac de** *l.* Mali
54 A3 **Manapouri, Lake** N.Z.
77 E2 **Manas Hu** *l.* China
75 C2 **Manaslu** *mt.* Nepal
Manastir Macedonia *see* Bitola
59 C3 **Manatuto** East Timor
62 A2 **Man-aung Kyun** Myanmar
150 C3 **Manaus** Brazil
80 B2 **Manavgat** Turkey
116 A3 **Manawashei** Sudan
98 B3 **Manchester** U.K.
139 E2 **Manchester** *CT* U.S.A.
139 E2 **Manchester** *NH* U.S.A.
140 C1 **Manchester** *TN* U.S.A.
81 D3 **Mand, Rūd-e** *r.* Iran
117 A4 **Manda, Jebel** *mt.* Sudan
121 □D3 **Mandabe** Madag.
93 E4 **Mandal** Norway

59 D3 **Mandala, Puncak** *mt.* Indon.
62 A1 **Mandalay** Myanmar
68 D1 **Mandalgovĭ** Mongolia
136 C1 **Mandan** U.S.A.
118 B1 **Mandara Mountains** Cameroon/Nigeria
108 A3 **Mandas** *Sardinia* Italy
119 E2 **Mandera** Kenya
100 C2 **Manderscheid** Ger.
74 B1 **Mandi** India
114 B3 **Mandiana** Guinea
74 B1 **Mandi Burewala** Pak.
   Mandidzuzure Zimbabwe *see* Chimanimani
75 C2 **Mandla** India
121 □D2 **Mandritsara** Madag.
74 B2 **Mandsaur** India
50 A3 **Mandurah** Austr.
73 B3 **Mandya** India
108 B1 **Manerbio** Italy
90 B1 **Manevychi** Ukr.
109 C2 **Manfredonia** Italy
109 C2 **Manfredonia, Golfo di** *g.* Italy
114 B3 **Manga** Burkina
118 B3 **Mangai** Dem. Rep. Congo
49 L6 **Mangaia** *i.* Cook Is
54 C1 **Mangakino** N.Z.
110 C2 **Mangalia** Romania
73 B3 **Mangalore** India
123 C2 **Mangaung** S. Africa
60 B2 **Manggar** Indon.
   Mangghyshlaq Kazakh. *see* Mangystau
61 C1 **Mangkalihat, Tanjung** *pt* Indon.
68 C2 **Mangnai** China
121 C2 **Mangochi** Malawi
121 □D3 **Mangoky** *r.* Madag.
59 C3 **Mangole** *i.* Indon.
54 B1 **Mangonui** N.Z.
   Mangshi China *see* Luxi
106 B1 **Mangualde** Port.
154 B3 **Mangueirinha** Brazil
69 E1 **Mangui** China
   Mangyshlak Kazakh. *see* Mangystau
76 B2 **Mangystau** Kazakh.
137 D3 **Manhattan** U.S.A.
121 C3 **Manhica** Moz.
155 D2 **Manhuaçu** Brazil
121 □D2 **Mania** *r.* Madag.
108 B1 **Maniago** Italy
121 C2 **Maniamba** Moz.
150 C3 **Manicoré** Brazil
131 D3 **Manicouagan** *r.* Can.
131 D2 **Manicouagan, Réservoir** *resr* Can.
79 B2 **Manīfah** Saudi Arabia
49 K5 **Manihiki** *atoll* Cook Is
64 B2 **Manila** Phil.
53 D2 **Manilla** Austr.
   Manipur India *see* Imphal
111 C3 **Manisa** Turkey
107 C2 **Manises** Spain
98 A2 **Man, Isle of** *i.* Irish Sea
138 B2 **Manistee** U.S.A.
138 B1 **Manistique** U.S.A.
129 E2 **Manitoba** *prov.* Can.
129 E2 **Manitoba, Lake** Can.
138 B1 **Manitou Islands** U.S.A.
130 B3 **Manitoulin Island** Can.
136 C3 **Manitou Springs** U.S.A.
130 B3 **Manitouwadge** Can.
138 B2 **Manitowoc** U.S.A.
130 C3 **Maniwaki** Can.
150 B2 **Manizales** Col.
121 □D3 **Manja** Madag.
121 C3 **Manjacaze** Moz.
137 E2 **Mankato** U.S.A.
114 B4 **Mankono** Côte d'Ivoire
129 D3 **Mankota** Can.
73 C4 **Mankulam** Sri Lanka
74 B2 **Manmad** India
52 A2 **Mannahill** Austr.
73 B4 **Mannar** Sri Lanka
73 B4 **Mannar, Gulf of** India/Sri Lanka
101 D3 **Mannheim** Ger.
128 C2 **Manning** Can.
52 A2 **Mannum** Austr.
129 C2 **Mannville** Can.
59 C3 **Manokwari** Indon.
119 C3 **Manono** Dem. Rep. Congo
63 A2 **Manoron** Myanmar
105 D3 **Manosque** France
131 C2 **Manouane, Lac** *l.* Can.
65 B1 **Manp'o** N. Korea
107 D1 **Manresa** Spain
121 B2 **Mansa** Zambia

127 G2 **Mansel Island** Can.
92 I2 **Mansel'kya** *ridge* Fin./Rus. Fed.
53 C3 **Mansfield** Austr.
98 C3 **Mansfield** U.K.
140 B1 **Mansfield** *AR* U.S.A.
140 B2 **Mansfield** *LA* U.S.A.
138 C2 **Mansfield** *OH* U.S.A.
139 D2 **Mansfield** *PA* U.S.A.
150 A3 **Manta** Ecuador
64 A3 **Mantalingajan, Mount** Phil.
155 D1 **Mantena** Brazil
141 E1 **Manteo** U.S.A.
104 C2 **Mantes-la-Jolie** France
155 C2 **Mantiqueira, Serra da** *mts* Brazil
   Mantova Italy *see* Mantua
88 C1 **Mäntsälä** Fin.
108 B1 **Mantua** Italy
86 D3 **Manturovo** Rus. Fed.
151 D3 **Manuelzinho** Brazil
61 D2 **Manui** *i.* Indon.
54 B1 **Manukau** N.Z.
59 D3 **Manus Island** P.N.G.
140 B2 **Many** U.S.A.
121 C2 **Manyame** *r.* Moz./Zimbabwe
119 D3 **Manyara, Lake** *salt l.* Tanz.
   Manyas Gölü *l.* Turkey *see* Kuş Gölü
87 D4 **Manych-Gudilo, Ozero** *l.* Rus. Fed.
142 B1 **Many Farms** U.S.A.
119 D3 **Manyoni** Tanz.
106 C2 **Manzanares** Spain
146 C2 **Manzanillo** Cuba
144 B3 **Manzanillo** Mex.
119 C3 **Manzanza** Dem. Rep. Congo
69 D1 **Manzhouli** China
123 D2 **Manzini** Swaziland
115 D3 **Mao** Chad
   Maó Spain *see* Mahón
59 D3 **Maoke, Pegunungan** *mts* Indon.
123 C2 **Maokeng** S. Africa
65 A1 **Maokui Shan** *mt.* China
70 A2 **Maomao Shan** *mt.* China
71 B3 **Maoming** China
121 C3 **Mapai** Moz.
75 C1 **Mapam Yumco** *l.* China
61 D2 **Mapane** Indon.
145 C3 **Mapastepec** Mex.
144 B2 **Mapimí** Mex.
144 B2 **Mapimí, Bolsón de** *des.* Mex.
64 A3 **Mapin** *i.* Phil.
121 C3 **Mapinhane** Moz.
129 D3 **Maple Creek** Can.
156 D4 **Mapmakers Seamounts** *sea feature* N. Pacific Ocean
59 D3 **Maprik** P.N.G.
123 D1 **Mapulanguene** Moz.
123 D2 **Maputo** Moz.
123 D2 **Maputo** *r.* Moz./S. Africa
123 C2 **Maputsoe** Lesotho
114 A2 **Maqteïr** *reg.* Maur.
75 C2 **Maquan He** *r.* China
120 A1 **Maquela do Zombo** Angola
153 B4 **Maquinchao** Arg.
137 E2 **Maquoketa** U.S.A.
123 C1 **Mara** S. Africa
150 C3 **Maraã** Brazil
151 E3 **Maraba** Brazil
151 D2 **Maracá, Ilha de** *i.* Brazil
150 B1 **Maracaibo** Venez.
150 B1 **Maracaibo, Lago de** Venez. *see* Maracaibo, Lake
   Maracaibo, Lake *l.* Venez.
154 A2 **Maracaju** Brazil
154 A2 **Maracaju, Serra de** *hills* Brazil
150 C1 **Maracay** Venez.
115 D2 **Marādah** Libya
115 C3 **Maradi** Niger
81 C2 **Marāgheh** Iran
150 C2 **Marahuaca, Cerro** *mt.* Venez.
151 E3 **Marajó, Baía de** *est.* Brazil
151 D3 **Marajó, Ilha de** *i.* Brazil
79 C2 **Marākī** Iran
119 D2 **Maralal** Kenya
   Maralbashi China *see* Bachu
50 C3 **Maralinga** Austr.
   Maralwexi China *see* Bachu

142 A2 **Marana** U.S.A.
81 C2 **Marand** Iran
   Marandellas Zimbabwe *see* Marondera
150 B3 **Marañón** *r.* Peru
   Maraş Turkey *see* Kahramanmaraş
110 C1 **Mărăşeşti** Romania
130 B3 **Marathon** Can.
141 D4 **Marathon** U.S.A.
106 C2 **Marbella** Spain
50 A2 **Marble Bar** Austr.
123 C1 **Marble Hall** S. Africa
123 D3 **Marburg** S. Africa
101 D2 **Marburg an der Lahn** Ger.
103 D2 **Marcali** Hungary
137 E3 **Marceline** U.S.A.
99 D3 **March** U.K.
100 B2 **Marche-en-Famenne** Belgium
106 B2 **Marchena** Spain
152 B3 **Mar Chiquita, Laguna** *l.* Arg.
150 B4 **Marcona** Peru
139 E2 **Marcy, Mount** U.S.A.
74 B1 **Mardan** Pak.
153 C3 **Mar del Plata** Arg.
81 C2 **Mardın** Turkey
96 B2 **Maree, Loch** *l.* U.K.
51 D1 **Mareeba** Austr.
108 B3 **Marettimo, Isola** *i.* *Sicily* Italy
89 D2 **Marevo** Rus. Fed.
142 C2 **Marfa** U.S.A.
   Margao India *see* Madgaon
150 A3 **Margaret River** Austr.
150 C1 **Margarita, Isla de** *i.* Venez.
123 D3 **Margate** S. Africa
99 D4 **Margate** U.K.
62 A1 **Margherita** India
   Margherita, Lake Eth. *see* Lake Abaya
119 C2 **Margherita Peak** Dem. Rep. Congo/Uganda
76 C3 **Märgow, Dasht-e** *des.* Afgh.
91 C2 **Marhanets'** Ukr.
62 A1 **Mari** Myanmar
152 B2 **María Elena** Chile
156 C5 **Mariana Trench** *sea feature* N. Pacific Ocean
   Mariánica, Cordillera *mts* Spain *see* Morena, Sierra
140 B2 **Marianna** *AR* U.S.A.
141 C2 **Marianna** *FL* U.S.A.
102 C2 **Mariánské Lázně** Czech Rep.
144 B2 **Marías, Islas** *is* Mex.
78 B3 **Ma'rib** Yemen
109 C1 **Maribor** Slovenia
   Maricourt Can. *see* Kangiqsujuaq
119 C2 **Maridi** Sudan
117 A4 **Maridi** *watercourse* Sudan
55 P2 **Marie Byrd Land** *reg.* Antarctica
147 D3 **Marie-Galante** *i.* Guadeloupe
93 G3 **Mariehamn** Fin.
122 A1 **Mariental** Namibia
93 F4 **Mariestad** Sweden
141 D2 **Marietta** *GA* U.S.A.
138 C3 **Marietta** *OH* U.S.A.
105 D3 **Marignane** France
141 D2 **Mariinsk** Rus. Fed.
88 B3 **Marijampolė** Lith.
154 C2 **Marília** Brazil
106 B1 **Marín** Spain
135 B3 **Marina** U.S.A.
109 C3 **Marina di Gioiosa Ionica** Italy
88 C3 **Mar"ina Horka** Belarus
138 B1 **Marinette** U.S.A.
154 B2 **Maringá** Brazil
106 B2 **Marinha Grande** Port.
138 B2 **Marion** *IN* U.S.A.
141 E2 **Marion** *SC* U.S.A.
138 C3 **Marion** *VA* U.S.A.
141 D2 **Marion, Lake** U.S.A.
52 A3 **Marion Bay** Austr.
152 B2 **Mariscal José Félix Estigarribia** Para.
105 D3 **Maritime Alps** *mts* France/Italy
81 C1 **Maritsa** *r.* Bulg.
91 D2 **Mariupol'** Ukr.
117 C4 **Marka** Somalia

68 C3 **Markam** China
123 C1 **Marken** S. Africa
100 B1 **Markermeer** *l.* Neth.
98 C3 **Market Rasen** U.K.
98 C3 **Market Weighton** U.K.
83 I2 **Markha** *r.* Rus. Fed.
139 D2 **Markham** Can.
91 D2 **Markivka** Ukr.
118 B2 **Markounda** C.A.R.
140 B2 **Marksville** U.S.A.
101 D3 **Marktheidenfeld** Ger.
101 F2 **Marktredwitz** Ger.
100 C2 **Marl** Ger.
51 C2 **Marla** Austr.
100 A3 **Marle** France
143 D2 **Marlin** U.S.A.
53 C3 **Marlo** Austr.
104 C3 **Marmande** France
111 C2 **Marmara, Sea of** *g.* Turkey
   Marmara Denizi *g.* Turkey *see* Marmara, Sea of
111 C3 **Marmaris** Turkey
105 C2 **Marne** *r.* France
105 C2 **Marne-la-Vallée** France
118 B2 **Maro** Chad
121 □D2 **Maroantsetra** Madag.
54 B1 **Marokopa** N.Z.
101 E2 **Maroldsweisach** Ger.
121 □D2 **Maromokotro** *mt.* Madag.
121 C2 **Marondera** Zimbabwe
151 C1 **Maroni** *r.* Fr. Guiana
51 E2 **Maroochydore** Austr.
61 C2 **Maros** Indon.
49 M6 **Marotiri** *is* Fr. Polynesia
118 B1 **Maroua** Cameroon
121 □D2 **Marovoay** Madag.
49 N4 **Marquesas Islands** Fr. Polynesia
141 D4 **Marquesas Keys** *is* U.S.A.
155 D2 **Marquês de Valença** Brazil
138 B1 **Marquette** U.S.A.
116 A3 **Marra, Jebel** *mt.* Sudan
123 D2 **Marracuene** Moz.
114 B1 **Marrakech** Morocco
   Marrakesh Morocco *see* Marrakech
116 A3 **Marra Plateau** Sudan
52 A1 **Marree** Austr.
86 F2 **Marresale** Rus. Fed.
121 C2 **Marromeu** Moz.
121 C2 **Marrupa** Moz.
116 B2 **Marsá al 'Alam** Egypt
115 D1 **Marsa al Burayqah** Libya
119 D2 **Marsabit** Kenya
78 A2 **Marsa Delwein** Sudan
108 B3 **Marsala** *Sicily* Italy
116 A1 **Marsá Maţrūḩ** Egypt
101 D2 **Marsberg** Ger.
108 B2 **Marsciano** Italy
53 C2 **Marsden** Austr.
100 B1 **Marsdiep** *sea chan.* Neth
105 D3 **Marseille** France
   Marseilles France *see* Marseille
140 B1 **Marshall** *AR* U.S.A.
137 D2 **Marshall** *MN* U.S.A.
137 E3 **Marshall** *MO* U.S.A.
143 E2 **Marshall** *TX* U.S.A.
48 H2 **Marshall Islands** *country* N. Pacific Ocean
137 E2 **Marshalltown** U.S.A.
138 A2 **Marshfield** U.S.A.
146 C2 **Marsh Harbour** Bahamas
140 B3 **Marsh Island** U.S.A.
93 G4 **Märsta** Sweden
   Martaban, Gulf of Myanmar *see* Mottama, Gulf of
61 C2 **Martapura** Indon.
60 B2 **Martapura** Indon.
139 E2 **Martha's Vineyard** *i.* U.S.A.
105 D2 **Martigny** Switz.
103 D2 **Martin** Slovakia
136 C2 **Martin** U.S.A.
145 C2 **Martínez** Mex.
141 D2 **Martinez** U.S.A.
155 C1 **Martinho Campos** Brazil
147 D3 **Martinique** *terr.* West Indies
147 D3 **Martinique Passage** Dominica/Martinique
139 D3 **Martinsburg** U.S.A.
138 D3 **Martinsville** U.S.A.
54 C2 **Marton** N.Z.
107 D1 **Martorell** Spain
106 C2 **Martos** Spain
76 B1 **Martuk** Kazakh.
81 D3 **Marv Dasht** Iran

105 C3 **Marvejols** France
76 C3 **Mary** Turkm.
51 E2 **Maryborough** Austr.
122 B2 **Marydale** S. Africa
139 D3 **Maryland** *state* U.S.A.
98 B2 **Maryport** U.K.
137 D3 **Marysville** U.S.A.
137 E2 **Maryville** *MO* U.S.A.
141 D1 **Maryville** *TN* U.S.A.
119 D3 **Masai Steppe** *plain* Tanz.
119 D3 **Masaka** Uganda
61 C2 **Masalembu Besar** *i.* Indon.
61 D2 **Masamba** Indon.
65 B2 **Masan** S. Korea
119 D4 **Masasi** Tanz.
64 B2 **Masbate** Phil.
64 B2 **Masbate** *i.* Phil.
107 D2 **Mascara** Alg.
155 E1 **Mascote** Brazil
123 C2 **Maseru** Lesotho
Mashaba Zimbabwe *see* Mashava
121 C3 **Mashava** Zimbabwe
76 B3 **Mashhad** Iran
123 C3 **Masibambane** S. Africa
79 C3 **Masīlah, Wādī al** *watercourse* Yemen
123 C2 **Masilo** S. Africa
118 B3 **Masi-Manimba** Dem. Rep. Congo
119 D2 **Masindi** Uganda
122 B3 **Masinyusane** S. Africa
Masira, Gulf of Oman *see* **Maşīrah, Khalīj**
79 C3 **Maşīrah, Khalīj** Oman
81 C2 **Masjed Soleymān** Iran
97 B2 **Mask, Lough** *l.* Rep. of Ireland
121 □E2 **Masoala, Tanjona** *c.* Madag.
137 E2 **Mason City** U.S.A.
Masqaţ Oman *see* **Muscat**
108 B2 **Massa** Italy
139 E2 **Massachusetts** *state* U.S.A.
139 E2 **Massachusetts Bay** U.S.A.
115 D3 **Massaguet** Chad
115 D3 **Massakory** Chad
121 C3 **Massangena** Moz.
120 A1 **Massango** Angola
116 B3 **Massawa** Eritrea
139 E2 **Massena** U.S.A.
115 D3 **Massenya** Chad
128 A2 **Masset** Can.
105 C2 **Massif Central** *mts* France
115 C3 **Massif de l'Aïr** *mts* Niger
138 C2 **Massillon** U.S.A.
114 B3 **Massina** Mali
121 C3 **Massinga** Moz.
123 D1 **Massingir** Moz.
78 A2 **Mastābah** Saudi Arabia
54 C2 **Masterton** N.Z.
74 B1 **Mastuj** Pak.
74 A2 **Mastung** Pak.
78 A2 **Mastūrah** Saudi Arabia
88 B3 **Masty** Belarus
67 B4 **Masuda** Japan
Masuku Gabon *see* **Franceville**
121 C3 **Masvingo** Zimbabwe
119 D3 **Maswa** Tanz.
118 B3 **Matadi** Dem. Rep. Congo
146 B3 **Matagalpa** Nic.
130 C3 **Matagami** Can.
130 C3 **Matagami, Lac** *l.* Can.
143 D3 **Matagorda Island** U.S.A.
143 D3 **Matagorda Peninsula** U.S.A.
120 A2 **Matala** Angola
114 A3 **Matam** Senegal
54 C1 **Matamata** N.Z.
144 B2 **Matamoros** Mex.
145 C2 **Matamoros** Mex.
119 D3 **Matandu** *r.* Tanz.
131 D3 **Matane** Can.
146 B2 **Matanzas** Cuba
Matapan, Cape *pt* Greece *see* **Tainaro, Akra**
73 C4 **Matara** Sri Lanka
61 C2 **Mataram** Indon.
50 C1 **Mataranka** Austr.
107 D1 **Mataró** Spain
123 C3 **Matatiele** S. Africa
54 A3 **Mataura** N.Z.
54 A3 **Mataura** *r.* N.Z.
54 C1 **Matawai** N.Z.
152 B1 **Mategua** Bol.
145 B2 **Matehuala** Mex.
109 C2 **Matera** Italy
108 A3 **Mateur** Tunisia
129 E2 **Matheson Island** Can.
143 D3 **Mathis** U.S.A.
74 B2 **Mathura** India
64 B3 **Mati** Phil.
145 C3 **Matías Romero** Mex.
98 C3 **Matlock** U.K.
150 D4 **Mato Grosso** Brazil
154 B1 **Mato Grosso, Planalto do** *plat.* Brazil
123 D2 **Matola** Moz.
106 B1 **Matosinhos** Port.
Matou China *see* **Pingguo**
79 C2 **Maţraḩ** Oman
67 B3 **Matsue** Japan
66 D2 **Matsumae** Japan
67 C3 **Matsumoto** Japan
67 C4 **Matsusaka** Japan
71 C3 **Matsu Tao** *i.* Taiwan
67 B4 **Matsuyama** Japan
130 B2 **Mattagami** *r.* Can.
130 C3 **Mattawa** Can.
105 D2 **Matterhorn** *mt.* Italy/Switz.
134 C2 **Matterhorn** *mt.* U.S.A.
141 D1 **Matthews** U.S.A.
79 C2 **Maţţī, Sabkhat** *salt pan* Saudi Arabia
138 B3 **Mattoon** U.S.A.
150 C2 **Maturín** Venez.
91 D2 **Matveyev Kurgan** Rus. Fed.
123 C2 **Matwabeng** S. Africa
105 C1 **Maubeuge** France
104 C3 **Maubourguet** France
55 E3 **Maud Seamount** *sea feature* S. Atlantic Ocean
49 L1 **Maui** *i.* U.S.A.
141 D2 **Mauldin** U.S.A.
138 C2 **Maumee** *r.* U.S.A.
61 D2 **Maumere** Indon.
120 B2 **Maun** Botswana
75 C2 **Maunath Bhanjan** India
123 C1 **Maunatlala** Botswana
62 A1 **Maungdaw** Myanmar
75 B2 **Mau Ranipur** India
50 C2 **Maurice, Lake** *salt flat* Austr.
114 A3 **Mauritania** *country* Africa
113 I8 **Mauritius** *country* Indian Ocean
120 B2 **Mavinga** Angola
123 C3 **Mavuya** S. Africa
78 B2 **Māwān, Khashm** *hill* Saudi Arabia
118 B3 **Mawanga** Dem. Rep. Congo
71 B3 **Mawei** China
62 A1 **Mawkmai** Myanmar
62 A1 **Mawlaik** Myanmar
63 A2 **Mawlamyaing** Myanmar
78 B2 **Mawqaq** Saudi Arabia
55 L3 **Mawson Peninsula** Antarctica
78 B3 **Mawza** Yemen
108 A3 **Maxia, Punta** *mt. Sardinia* Italy
121 C3 **Maxixe** Moz.
54 B1 **Maxwell** N.Z.
83 J2 **Maya** *r.* Rus. Fed.
147 C2 **Mayaguana** *i.* Bahamas
147 D3 **Mayagüez** Puerto Rico
81 D2 **Mayamey** Iran
96 B3 **Maybole** U.K.
116 B3 **Maych'ew** Eth.
117 C3 **Maydh** Somalia
100 C2 **Mayen** Ger.
104 B2 **Mayenne** France
104 B2 **Mayenne** *r.* France
128 C2 **Mayerthorpe** Can.
138 B3 **Mayfield** U.S.A.
91 E3 **Maykop** Rus. Fed.
128 A1 **Mayo** Can.
118 B3 **Mayoko** Congo
Mayo Landing Can. *see* Mayo
64 B2 **Mayon** *vol.* Phil.
121 D2 **Mayotte** *terr.* Africa
83 J3 **Mayskiy** Rus. Fed.
138 C3 **Maysville** U.S.A.
118 B3 **Mayumba** Gabon
137 D1 **Mayville** U.S.A.
120 B2 **Mazabuka** Zambia
Mazagan Morocco *see* El Jadida
151 D3 **Mazagão** Brazil
104 C3 **Mazamet** France
74 B1 **Mazar** China
108 B3 **Mazara del Vallo** *Sicily* Italy
77 C3 **Mazār-e Sharīf** Afgh.
107 C2 **Mazarrón** Spain
107 C2 **Mazarrón, Golfo de** *b.* Spain
144 A2 **Mazatán** Mex.
146 A3 **Mazatenango** Guat.
144 B2 **Mazatlán** Mex.
88 B2 **Mažeikiai** Lith.
88 B2 **Mazirbe** Latvia
121 B3 **Mazunga** Zimbabwe
103 E1 **Mazurskie, Pojezierze** *reg.* Pol.
88 C3 **Mazyr** Belarus
123 D2 **Mbabane** Swaziland
118 B2 **Mbaïki** C.A.R.
118 B2 **Mbakaou, Lac de** *l.* Cameroon
121 C1 **Mbala** Zambia
121 B3 **Mbalabala** Zimbabwe
119 D2 **Mbale** Uganda
118 B2 **Mbalmayo** Cameroon
118 B3 **Mbandaka** Dem. Rep. Congo
118 B2 **Mbandjok** Cameroon
118 A2 **Mbanga** Cameroon
120 A1 **M'banza Congo** Angola
118 B3 **Mbanza-Ngungu** Dem. Rep. Congo
119 D3 **Mbarara** Uganda
118 B2 **Mbé** Cameroon
119 D3 **Mbeya** Tanz.
119 D4 **Mbinga** Tanz.
119 D3 **Mbizi Mountains** Tanz.
119 C2 **Mboki** C.A.R.
118 B2 **Mbomo** Congo
118 B2 **Mbouda** Cameroon
114 A3 **Mbour** Senegal
114 A3 **Mbout** Maur.
118 C3 **Mbuji-Mayi** Dem. Rep. Congo
119 D3 **Mbuyuni** Tanz.
139 F1 **McAdam** Can.
143 D2 **McAlester** U.S.A.
143 D3 **McAllen** U.S.A.
128 B2 **McBride** Can.
134 C2 **McCall** U.S.A.
143 C2 **McCamey** U.S.A.
126 F2 **McClintock Channel** Can.
126 E2 **McClure Strait** Can.
140 B2 **McComb** U.S.A.
136 C2 **McConaughy, Lake** U.S.A.
136 C2 **McCook** U.S.A.
134 C2 **McDermitt** U.S.A.
159 E7 **McDonald Islands** Indian Ocean
134 D1 **McDonald Peak** U.S.A.
135 D3 **McGill** U.S.A.
126 B2 **McGrath** U.S.A.
134 D1 **McGuire, Mount** U.S.A.
121 C2 **Mchinji** Malawi
140 C1 **McKenzie** U.S.A.
51 D2 **McKinlay** Austr.
134 B2 **McKinleyville** U.S.A.
128 C2 **McLennan** Can.
128 B2 **McLeod Lake** Can.
134 B1 **McMinnville** *OR* U.S.A.
140 C1 **McMinnville** *TN* U.S.A.
137 D3 **McPherson** U.S.A.
128 C1 **McTavish Arm** *b.* Can.
123 C3 **Mdantsane** S. Africa
135 D3 **Mead, Lake** *resr* U.S.A.
136 C3 **Meade** U.S.A.
129 D2 **Meadow Lake** Can.
138 C2 **Meadville** U.S.A.
66 D2 **Meaken-dake** *vol.* Japan
106 B1 **Mealhada** Port.
131 E2 **Mealy Mountains** Can.
128 C2 **Meander River** Can.
78 A2 **Mecca** Saudi Arabia
139 D3 **Mechanicsville** U.S.A.
100 B2 **Mechelen** Belgium
100 B2 **Mechelen** Neth.
100 C2 **Mechernich** Ger.
100 C2 **Meckenheim** Ger.
101 E1 **Mecklenburgische Seenplatte** *reg.* Ger.
106 B1 **Meda** Port.
60 A1 **Medan** Indon.
153 B4 **Medanosa, Punta** *pt* Arg.
73 C4 **Medawachchiya** Sri Lanka
107 D2 **Médéa** Alg.
150 B2 **Medellín** Col.
115 D1 **Medenine** Tunisia
134 B2 **Medford** U.S.A.
110 C2 **Medgidia** Romania
110 B1 **Mediaş** Romania
136 B2 **Medicine Bow Mountains** U.S.A.
136 B2 **Medicine Bow Peak** U.S.A.
129 C2 **Medicine Hat** Can.
137 D3 **Medicine Lodge** U.S.A.
155 D1 **Medina** Brazil
78 A2 **Medina** Saudi Arabia
106 C1 **Medinaceli** Spain
106 C1 **Medina del Campo** Spain
106 B1 **Medina de Rioseco** Spain
75 C2 **Medinipur** India
84 E5 **Mediterranean Sea**
129 C2 **Medley** Can.
87 E3 **Mednogorsk** Rus. Fed.
62 A1 **Mêdog** China
88 B2 **Medvėgalio kalnis** *hill* Lith.
83 L2 **Medvezh'i, Ostrova** *is* Rus. Fed.
86 C2 **Medvezh'yegorsk** Rus. Fed.
50 A2 **Meekatharra** Austr.
136 B2 **Meeker** U.S.A.
74 B2 **Meerut** India
100 A2 **Meetkerke** Belgium
119 D2 **Mēga** Eth.
60 B2 **Mega** *i.* Indon.
119 D2 **Mega Escarpment** Eth./Kenya
111 B3 **Megalopoli** Greece
75 D2 **Meghalaya** *state* India
75 C2 **Meghasani** *mt.* India
111 C3 **Megisti** *i.* Greece
92 I1 **Mehamn** Norway
50 A2 **Meharry, Mount** Austr.
137 E3 **Mehlville** U.S.A.
79 C2 **Mehrān** *watercourse* Iran
74 B1 **Mehtar Lām** Afgh.
119 D3 **Meia Meia** Tanz.
154 C1 **Meia Ponte** *r.* Brazil
118 B2 **Meiganga** Cameroon
65 B1 **Meihekou** China
Meijiang China *see* **Ningdu**
62 A1 **Meiktila** Myanmar
101 E2 **Meiningen** Ger.
102 C1 **Meißen** Ger.
Meixian China *see* Meizhou
71 B3 **Meizhou** China
152 B2 **Mejicana** *mt.* Arg.
152 A2 **Mejillones** Chile
118 B2 **Mékambo** Gabon
116 B3 **Mek'elē** Eth.
114 C2 **Mekerrhane, Sebkha** *salt pan* Alg.
114 B1 **Meknès** Morocco
63 B2 **Mekong** *r.* Asia
63 B3 **Mekong, Mouths of the** Vietnam
60 B1 **Melaka** Malaysia
156 D6 **Melanesia** *is* Pacific Ocean
156 D5 **Melanesian Basin** *sea feature* Pacific Ocean
53 B3 **Melbourne** Austr.
141 D3 **Melbourne** U.S.A.
108 A2 **Mele, Capo** *c.* Italy
Melekess Rus. Fed. *see* **Dimitrovgrad**
89 F2 **Melenki** Rus. Fed.
131 C2 **Mélèzes, Rivière aux** *r.* Can.
115 D3 **Mélfi** Chad
109 C2 **Melfi** Italy
129 D2 **Melfort** Can.
92 F3 **Melhus** Norway
106 B1 **Melide** Spain
114 B1 **Melilla** N. Africa
129 D3 **Melita** Can.
91 D2 **Melitopol'** Ukr.
119 D2 **Melka Guba** Eth.
101 D1 **Melle** Ger.
93 F4 **Mellerud** Sweden
101 E2 **Mellrichstadt** Ger.
101 D1 **Mellum** *i.* Ger.
123 D2 **Melmoth** S. Africa
152 C3 **Melo** Uru.
115 C1 **Melrhir, Chott** *salt l.* Alg.
96 C3 **Melrose** U.K.
Melsetter Zimbabwe *see* **Chimanimani**
52 B3 **Melton** Austr.
99 C3 **Melton Mowbray** U.K.
105 C2 **Melun** France
129 D2 **Melville** Can.
51 D1 **Melville, Cape** Austr.
131 E2 **Melville, Lake** Can.
50 C1 **Melville Island** Austr.
126 E1 **Melville Island** Can.
127 G2 **Melville Peninsula** Can.
61 C2 **Memboro** Indon.
102 C2 **Memmingen** Ger.
60 B1 **Mempawah** Indon.
80 B3 **Memphis** *tourist site* Egypt
140 B1 **Memphis** *TN* U.S.A.

143 C2 Memphis *TX* U.S.A.
91 C1 Mena Ukr.
140 B2 Mena U.S.A.
121 ▢D3 Menabe *mts* Madag.
114 C3 Ménaka Mali
Mènam Khong *r.*
Laos/Thai. *see* Mekong
105 C3 Mende France
117 B4 Mendebo Mountains Eth.
116 B3 Mendefera Eritrea
160 B1 Mendeleyev Ridge
sea feature Arctic Ocean
145 C2 Méndez Mex.
117 B4 Mendī Eth.
59 D3 Mendi P.N.G.
99 B4 Mendip Hills U.K.
138 B2 Mendota U.S.A.
153 B3 Mendoza Arg.
111 C3 Menemen Turkey
100 A2 Menen Belgium
70 B2 Mengcheng China
60 B2 Menggala Indon.
71 A3 Mengzi China
131 D2 Menihek Can.
52 B2 Menindee Austr.
52 B2 Menindee Lake Austr.
52 A3 Meningie Austr.
104 C2 Mennecy France
138 B1 Menominee U.S.A.
120 A2 Menongue Angola
Menorca *i.* Spain *see*
Minorca
61 C1 Mensalong Indon.
60 A2 Mentawai, Kepulauan *is*
Indon.
60 B2 Mentok Indon.
61 C1 Menyapa, Gunung *mt.*
Indon.
108 A3 Menzel Bourguiba Tunisia
50 B2 Menzies Austr.
144 B2 Meoqui Mex.
100 C1 Meppel Neth.
100 C1 Meppen Ger.
121 C3 Mepuze Moz.
123 C2 Meqheleng S. Africa
138 B2 Mequon U.S.A.
108 B1 Merano Italy
59 D3 Merauke Indon.
52 B2 Merbein Austr.
Merca Somalia *see* Marka
107 D2 Mercadal Spain
135 B3 Merced U.S.A.
152 C2 Mercedes Arg.
143 D3 Mercedes U.S.A.
127 H2 Mercy, Cape Can.
143 C1 Meredith, Lake U.S.A.
91 D2 Merefa Ukr.
116 A3 Merga Oasis Sudan
63 A2 Mergui Archipelago *is*
Myanmar
110 C2 Meriç *r.* Greece/Turkey
111 C2 Meriç Turkey
145 D2 Mérida Mex.
106 B2 Mérida Spain
150 B2 Mérida Venez.
147 C4 Mérida, Cordillera de *mts*
Venez.
134 C2 Meridian *ID* U.S.A.
140 C2 Meridian *MS* U.S.A.
143 D2 Meridian *TX* U.S.A.
104 B3 Mérignac France
93 H3 Merikarvia Fin.
53 C3 Merimbula Austr.
88 B3 Merkinė Lith.
116 B3 Merowe Sudan
50 A3 Merredin Austr.
96 B3 Merrick *hill* U.K.
138 B1 Merrill U.S.A.
138 B2 Merrillville U.S.A.
136 C2 Merriman U.S.A.
128 B2 Merritt Can.
53 C2 Merrygoen Austr.
116 C3 Mersa Fatma Eritrea
100 C3 Mersch Lux.
101 E2 Merseburg (Saale) Ger.
98 B2 Mersey *r.* U.K.
80 B2 Mersin Turkey
60 B1 Mersing Malaysia
99 D4 Mers-les-Bains France
74 B2 Merta India
99 B4 Merthyr Tydfil U.K.
119 D2 Merti Plateau Kenya
106 B2 Mértola Port.
76 B2 Mertvyy Kultuk, Sor
dry lake Kazakh.
119 D3 Meru *vol.* Tanz.
122 B3 Merweville S. Africa
80 B1 Merzifon Turkey
100 C3 Merzig Ger.
142 A2 Mesa *AZ* U.S.A.
142 C2 Mesa *NM* U.S.A.

137 E1 Mesabi Range *hills* U.S.A.
109 C2 Mesagne Italy
142 B2 Mescalero U.S.A.
143 C2 Mescalero Ridge U.S.A.
101 D2 Meschede Ger.
89 E3 Meshchovsk Rus. Fed.
Meshed Iran *see* Mashhad
91 E2 Meshkovskaya Rus. Fed.
142 B2 Mesilla U.S.A.
111 B2 Mesimeri Greece
111 B3 Mesolongi Greece
115 C1 Messaad Alg.
121 D2 Messalo *r.* Moz.
109 C3 Messina *Sicily* Italy
109 C3 Messina, Strait of *str.* Italy
Messina, Stretta di Italy
see Messina, Strait of
111 B3 Messini Greece
111 B3 Messiniakos Kolpos *b.*
Greece
111 B2 Mesta *r.* Bulg.
Mesta *r.* Greece *see*
Nestos
150 C2 Meta *r.* Col./Venez.
130 C3 Métabetchouan Can.
127 H2 Meta Incognita Peninsula
Can.
140 B3 Metairie U.S.A.
152 B2 Metán Arg.
111 B3 Methoni Greece
109 C2 Metković Croatia
121 C2 Metoro Moz.
60 B2 Metro Indon.
100 C3 Mettlach Ger.
135 C3 Mettler U.S.A.
117 B4 Metu Eth.
105 D2 Metz France
100 D2 Meuse *r.* Belgium/France
143 D2 Mexia U.S.A.
144 A1 Mexicali Mex.
144 B2 Mexico *country*
Central America
México Mex. *see*
Mexico City
137 E3 Mexico U.S.A.
125 I7 Mexico, Gulf of
Mex./U.S.A.
54 C3 Mexico City Mex.
81 D2 Meybod Iran
101 F1 Meyenburg Ger.
76 C3 Meymaneh Afgh.
83 M2 Meynypil'gyno Rus. Fed.
86 D2 Mezen' Rus. Fed.
86 D2 Mezen' *r.* Rus. Fed.
86 E1 Mezhdusharskiy, Ostrov *i.*
Rus. Fed.
103 E2 Mezőtúr Hungary
132 C4 Mezquital *r.* Mex.
144 B2 Mezquitic Mex.
88 C2 Mežvidi Latvia
121 C2 Mfuwe Zambia
89 D3 Mglin Rus. Fed.
123 D2 Mhlume Swaziland
74 B2 Mhow India
145 C3 Miahuatlán Mex.
106 B2 Miajadas Spain
141 D3 Miami *FL* U.S.A.
143 E1 Miami *OK* U.S.A.
141 D3 Miami Beach U.S.A.
81 C2 Miandowāb Iran
121 ▢D2 Miandrivazo Madag.
81 C2 Mīāneh Iran
71 A3 Mianning China
74 B1 Mianwali Pak.
Mianyang China *see*
Xiantao
70 A2 Mianyang China
121 ▢D2 Miarinarivo Madag.
87 F3 Miass Rus. Fed.
103 D1 Miastko Pol.
128 C2 Mica Creek Can.
103 E2 Michalovce Slovakia
138 B1 Michigan *state* U.S.A.
138 B2 Michigan, Lake U.S.A.
138 B2 Michigan City U.S.A.
138 B1 Michipicoten Bay Can.
130 B3 Michipicoten Island Can.
130 B3 Michipicoten River Can.
Michurin Bulg. *see*
Tsarevo
89 F3 Michurinsk Rus. Fed.
156 D5 Micronesia *is*
Pacific Ocean
48 G3 Micronesia, Federated
States of *country*
N. Pacific Ocean
158 E6 Mid-Atlantic Ridge
sea feature Atlantic Ocean
100 A2 Middelburg Neth.
123 C3 Middelburg *E. Cape*
S. Africa

123 C2 Middelburg *Mpumalanga*
S. Africa
100 B2 Middelharnis Neth.
134 B2 Middle Alkali Lake U.S.A.
73 D3 Middle Andaman *i.* India
Middle Congo *country*
Africa *see* Congo
136 D2 Middle Loup *r.* U.S.A.
138 C3 Middlesboro U.S.A.
98 C2 Middlesbrough U.K.
139 E2 Middletown *NY* U.S.A.
138 C3 Middletown *OH* U.S.A.
78 B3 Midī Yemen
130 C3 Midland Can.
138 C2 Midland *MI* U.S.A.
143 C2 Midland *TX* U.S.A.
97 B3 Midleton Rep. of Ireland
Midnapore India *see*
Medinipur
94 B1 Miðvágur Faroe Is
Midway Oman *see*
Thamarīt
57 T7 Midway Islands *terr.*
N. Pacific Ocean
109 D2 Midzhur *mt.*
Bulg./Serb. and Mont.
103 E1 Mielec Pol.
110 C1 Miercurea-Ciuc Romania
106 B1 Mieres Spain
101 E1 Mieste Ger.
75 D1 Migriggyangzham Co *l.*
China
145 C3 Miguel Alemán, Presa
resr Mex.
144 B2 Miguel Auza Mex.
144 B2 Miguel Hidalgo, Presa
resr Mex.
63 A2 Migyaunglaung Myanmar
67 B4 Mihara Japan
89 E3 Mikhaylov Rus. Fed.
Mikhaylovgrad Bulg. *see*
Montana
66 B2 Mikhaylovka Rus. Fed.
Mikhaylovka Rus. Fed. *see*
Kimovsk
87 D3 Mikhaylovka Rus. Fed.
77 D1 Mikhaylovskiy Rus. Fed.
93 I3 Mikkeli Fin.
86 E2 Mikun' Rus. Fed.
67 C3 Mikuni-sanmyaku *mts*
Japan
67 C4 Mikura-jima *i.* Japan
73 B4 Miladhunmadulu Atoll
Maldives
108 A1 Milan Italy
121 C2 Milange Moz.
Milano Italy *see* Milan
111 C3 Milas Turkey
137 D1 Milbank U.S.A.
99 D3 Mildenhall U.K.
52 B2 Mildura Austr.
71 A3 Mile China
136 B1 Miles City U.S.A.
139 D3 Milford *DE* U.S.A.
135 D3 Milford *UT* U.S.A.
99 A4 Milford Haven U.K.
54 A2 Milford Sound N.Z.
Milḥ, Baḥr al *l.* Iraq *see*
Razāzah, Buḥayrat ar
107 D2 Miliana Alg.
50 C1 Milikapiti Austr.
51 C1 Milingimbi Austr.
116 B3 Milk, Wadi el *watercourse*
Sudan
83 L3 Mil'kovo Rus. Fed.
128 C3 Milk River Can.
105 C3 Millau France
141 D2 Milledgeville U.S.A.
137 E1 Mille Lacs *lakes* U.S.A.
130 A3 Mille Lacs, Lac des *l.*
Can.
Millennium Island Kiribati
see Caroline Island
137 D2 Miller U.S.A.
91 E2 Millerovo Rus. Fed.
52 A2 Millers Creek Austr.
96 B3 Milleur Point U.K.
137 E1 Millicent Austr.
140 C1 Millington U.S.A.
139 F1 Millinocket U.S.A.
55 J3 Mill Island Antarctica
137 E1 Millmerran Austr.
98 B2 Millom U.K.
136 B2 Mills U.S.A.
128 C1 Mills Lake Can.
111 B3 Milos *i.* Greece
89 E3 Miloslavskoye Rus. Fed.
91 E2 Milove Ukr.
52 B1 Milparinka Austr.
54 A3 Milton N.Z.

99 C3 Milton Keynes U.K.
138 B2 Milwaukee U.S.A.
158 C3 Milwaukee Deep
sea feature Caribbean Sea
104 B3 Mimizan France
118 B3 Mimongo Gabon
155 D2 Mimoso do Sul Brazil
79 C2 Mīnāb Iran
61 D1 Minahasa, Semenanjung
pen. Indon.
Minahassa Peninsula
Indon. *see*
Minahasa, Semenanjung
79 C2 Mina Jebel Ali U.A.E.
Minaker Can. *see*
Prophet River
60 B1 Minas Indon.
153 C3 Minas Uru.
79 B2 Mīnāʾ Saʿūd Kuwait
145 D3 Minas, Cerro de las *mt.*
Hond.
155 D1 Minas Novas Brazil
145 C3 Minatitlán Mex.
62 A1 Minbu Myanmar
64 B3 Mindanao *i.* Phil.
62 A1 Mindarie Austr.
101 D1 Minden Ger.
140 B2 Minden *LA* U.S.A.
137 D2 Minden *NE* U.S.A.
64 B2 Mindoro *i.* Phil.
64 A2 Mindoro Strait Phil.
118 B3 Mindouli Congo
99 B4 Minehead U.K.
154 B1 Mineiros Brazil
143 D2 Mineral Wells U.S.A.
75 C1 Minfeng China
119 C4 Minga Dem. Rep. Congo
81 C1 Mingäçevir Azer.
131 D2 Mingan Can.
52 B2 Mingary Austr.
70 B2 Mingguang China
62 A1 Mingin Myanmar
107 C2 Minglanilla Spain
119 D4 Mingoyo Tanz.
69 E1 Mingshui China
96 A2 Mingulay *i.* U.K.
71 B3 Mingxi China
Mingzhou China *see*
Suide
70 A2 Minhe China
73 B4 Minicoy *i.* India
50 A2 Minilya Austr.
114 B3 Mininian Côte d'Ivoire
131 D2 Minipi Lake Can.
130 A2 Miniss Lake Can.
52 A2 Minlaton Austr.
115 C4 Minna Nigeria
137 E2 Minneapolis U.S.A.
129 E2 Minnedosa Can.
137 E2 Minnesota *r.* U.S.A.
137 E1 Minnesota *state* U.S.A.
106 B1 Miño *r.* Port./Spain
107 D1 Minorca *i.* Spain
136 C1 Minot U.S.A.
88 C3 Minsk Belarus
103 E1 Mińsk Mazowiecki Pol.
96 D2 Mintlaw U.K.
131 D3 Minto Can.
130 C2 Minto, Lac *l.* Can.
68 C1 Minusinsk Rus. Fed.
62 A1 Minutang India
89 D2 Minxian China
155 D1 Mirabela Brazil
155 D1 Miralta Brazil
131 D2 Miramichi Can.
111 C3 Mirampelou, Kolpos *b.*
Greece
152 C2 Miranda Brazil
152 C1 Miranda *r.* Brazil
Miranda Moz. *see*
Macal"oge
106 C1 Miranda de Ebro Spain
106 B1 Mirandela Port.
154 B2 Mirandópolis Brazil
154 B2 Mirante, Serra do *hills*
Brazil
79 C3 Mirbāt Oman
61 C1 Miri Sarawak Malaysia
153 C3 Mirim, Lagoa *l.* Brazil
79 D2 Mīrjāveh Iran
83 J2 Mirnyy Rus. Fed.
83 I2 Mirnyy Rus. Fed.
101 F1 Mirow Ger.
74 A2 Mirpur Khas Pak.
Mirtoan Sea Greece *see*
Mirtoö Pelagos
111 B3 Mirtoö Pelagos *sea*
Greece
65 B2 Miryang S. Korea
Mirzachirla Turkm. *see*
Murzechirla

Mirzachul Uzbek. *see* Guliston
75 C2 **Mirzapur** India
77 E3 **Misalay** China
66 B1 **Mishan** China
51 E1 **Misima Island** P.N.G.
146 B3 **Miskitos, Cayos** *is* Nic.
103 E2 **Miskolc** Hungary
59 C3 **Misoöl** *i.* Indon.
115 D1 **Mişrātah** Libya
130 B2 **Missinaibi** *r.* Can.
130 B3 **Missinaibi Lake** Can.
128 B3 **Mission** Can.
130 B2 **Missisa Lake** Can.
140 C3 **Mississippi** *r.* U.S.A.
140 C2 **Mississippi** *state* U.S.A.
140 C3 **Mississippi Delta** U.S.A.
140 C2 **Mississippi Sound** *sea chan.* U.S.A.
Missolonghi Greece *see* Mesolongi
134 D1 **Missoula** U.S.A.
137 E3 **Missouri** *r.* U.S.A.
137 E3 **Missouri** *state* U.S.A.
130 C3 **Mistassibi** *r.* Can.
130 C2 **Mistassini, Lac** *l.* Can.
131 D2 **Mistastin Lake** Can.
103 D2 **Mistelbach** Austria
131 D2 **Mistinibi, Lac** *l.* Can.
130 C2 **Mistissini** Can.
51 D2 **Mitchell** Austr.
51 D1 **Mitchell** *r.* Austr.
136 C2 **Mitchell** *NE* U.S.A.
137 D2 **Mitchell** *SD* U.S.A.
97 B2 **Mitchelstown** Rep. of Ireland
74 A2 **Mithi** Pak.
67 D3 **Mito** Japan
119 D3 **Mitole** Tanz.
53 D2 **Mittagong** Austr.
101 E2 **Mittelhausen** Ger.
101 D1 **Mittellandkanal** *canal* Ger.
101 F3 **Mitterteich** Ger.
Mittimatalik Can. *see* Pond Inlet
150 B2 **Mitú** Col.
119 C4 **Mitumba, Chaîne des** *mts* Dem. Rep. Congo
119 C3 **Mitumba, Monts** *mts* Dem. Rep. Congo
119 C3 **Mitwaba** Dem. Rep. Congo
118 B2 **Mitzic** Gabon
78 B2 **Miyah, Wādī al** *watercourse* Saudi Arabia
67 C4 **Miyake-jima** *i.* Japan
66 D3 **Miyako** Japan
67 B4 **Miyakonojō** Japan
76 B2 **Miyaly** Kazakh.
Miyang China *see* **Mile**
67 B4 **Miyazaki** Japan
67 C3 **Miyazu** Japan
115 D1 **Mizdah** Libya
97 B3 **Mizen Head** *hd* Rep. of Ireland
90 A2 **Mizhhir"ya** Ukr.
Mizo Hills *state* India *see* **Mizoram**
75 D2 **Mizoram** *state* India
93 G4 **Mjölby** Sweden
93 F3 **Mjøsa** *l.* Norway
119 D3 **Mkomazi** Tanz.
103 C1 **Mladá Boleslav** Czech Rep.
109 D2 **Mladenovac** Serb. and Mont.
103 E1 **Mława** Pol.
109 C2 **Mljet** *i.* Croatia
123 C3 **Mlungisi** S. Africa
90 B1 **Mlyniv** Ukr.
123 C2 **Mmabatho** S. Africa
123 C2 **Mmathethe** Botswana
93 E3 **Mo** Norway
135 E3 **Moab** U.S.A.
123 D2 **Moamba** Moz.
54 B2 **Moana** N.Z.
118 B3 **Moanda** Gabon
97 C2 **Moate** Rep. of Ireland
119 C3 **Moba** Dem. Rep. Congo
118 C2 **Mobayi-Mbongo** Dem. Rep. Congo
137 E3 **Moberly** U.S.A.
140 C2 **Mobile** U.S.A.
140 C2 **Mobile Bay** U.S.A.
140 C2 **Mobile Point** U.S.A.
136 C1 **Mobridge** U.S.A.
Mobutu, Lake Dem. Rep. Congo/Uganda *see* **Albert, Lake**
Mobutu Sese Seko, Lake Dem. Rep. Congo/Uganda *see* **Albert, Lake**
121 C2 **Moçambicano, Planalto** *plat.* Moz.
121 D2 **Moçambique** Moz.
Moçâmedes Angola *see* **Namibe**
62 B1 **Môc Châu** Vietnam
78 B3 **Mocha** Yemen
123 C1 **Mochudi** Botswana
121 D2 **Mocimboa da Praia** Moz.
101 D3 **Möckmühl** Ger.
150 B2 **Mocoa** Col.
154 C2 **Mococa** Brazil
144 B2 **Mocorito** Mex.
144 B1 **Moctezuma** Mex.
145 B2 **Moctezuma** Mex.
144 B2 **Moctezuma** Mex.
121 C2 **Mocuba** Moz.
105 D2 **Modane** France
122 B2 **Modder** *r.* S. Africa
108 B2 **Modena** Italy
135 B3 **Modesto** U.S.A.
109 B3 **Modica** *Sicily* Italy
123 C1 **Modimolle** S. Africa
53 C3 **Moe** Austr.
Moero, Lake Dem. Rep. Congo/Zambia *see* **Mweru, Lake**
100 C2 **Moers** Ger.
96 C3 **Moffat** U.K.
117 C4 **Mogadishu** Somalia
Mogador Morocco *see* **Essaouira**
106 B1 **Mogadouro, Serra de** *mts* Port.
123 C1 **Mogalakwena** *r.* S. Africa
62 A1 **Mogaung** Myanmar
Mogilev Belarus *see* **Mahilyow**
154 C2 **Mogi-Mirim** Brazil
83 I3 **Mogocha** Rus. Fed.
123 C1 **Mogoditshane** Botswana
62 A1 **Mogok** Myanmar
142 A2 **Mogollon Plateau** U.S.A.
103 D2 **Mohács** Hungary
123 C3 **Mohale's Hoek** Lesotho
107 D2 **Mohammadia** Alg.
142 A2 **Mohave Mountains** U.S.A.
139 E2 **Mohawk** *r.* U.S.A.
62 A1 **Mohnyin** Myanmar
119 D3 **Mohoro** Tanz.
90 B2 **Mohyliv Podil's'kyy** Ukr.
123 C1 **Moijabana** Botswana
110 C1 **Moinești** Romania
Mointy Kazakh. *see* **Moyynty**
92 F2 **Mo i Rana** Norway
88 C2 **Mõisaküla** Estonia
104 C3 **Moissac** France
135 C3 **Mojave** U.S.A.
135 C3 **Mojave Desert** U.S.A.
62 B1 **Mojiang** China
155 C2 **Moji das Cruzes** Brazil
154 C2 **Moji-Guaçu** *r.* Brazil
109 C2 **Mojkovac** Serb. and Mont.
54 B1 **Mokau** N.Z.
123 C2 **Mokhotlong** Lesotho
83 J2 **Mokhsogollokh** Rus. Fed.
118 B1 **Mokolo** Cameroon
123 C1 **Mokopane** S. Africa
65 B3 **Mokp'o** S. Korea
109 C2 **Mola di Bari** Italy
145 C2 **Molango** Mex.
Moldavia *country* Europe *see* **Moldova**
Moldavskaya S.S.R. *admin. reg.* Europe *see* **Moldova**
93 E3 **Molde** Norway
90 B2 **Moldova** *country* Europe
110 B2 **Moldova Nouă** Romania
110 B1 **Moldoveanu, Vârful** *mt.* Romania
110 B1 **Moldovei, Podişul** *plat.* Romania
90 B2 **Moldovei Centrale, Podişul** *plat.* Moldova
123 C1 **Molepolole** Botswana
88 C2 **Molėtai** Lith.
109 C2 **Molfetta** Italy
Molière Alg. *see* **Bordj Bounaama**
107 C1 **Molina de Aragón** Spain
107 C2 **Molina de Segura** Spain
119 D3 **Moliro** Dem. Rep. Congo
150 B4 **Mollendo** Peru
93 F4 **Mölnlycke** Sweden
91 D2 **Molochna** *r.* Ukr.
89 E2 **Molokovo** Rus. Fed.
53 C2 **Molong** Austr.
122 B2 **Molopo** *watercourse* Botswana/S. Africa
Molotov Rus. Fed. *see* **Perm'**
Molotovsk Rus. Fed. *see* **Severodvinsk**
Molotovsk Rus. Fed. *see* **Nolinsk**
118 B2 **Moloundou** Cameroon
59 C3 **Moluccas** *is* Indon.
Molucca Sea Indon. *see* **Laut Maluku**
52 B2 **Momba** Austr.
119 D3 **Mombasa** Kenya
154 B1 **Mombuca, Serra da** *hills* Brazil
111 C2 **Momchilgrad** Bulg.
93 F4 **Møn** *i.* Denmark
105 D3 **Monaco** *country* Europe
96 B2 **Monadhliath Mountains** U.K.
97 C1 **Monaghan** Rep. of Ireland
143 C2 **Monahans** U.S.A.
147 D3 **Mona Passage** Dom. Rep./Puerto Rico
120 A1 **Mona Quimbundo** Angola
Monastir Macedonia *see* **Bitola**
89 D3 **Monastyrshchina** Rus. Fed.
90 B2 **Monastyryshche** Ukr.
118 B2 **Monatélé** Cameroon
66 D2 **Monbetsu** Japan
108 A1 **Moncalieri** Italy
86 C2 **Monchegorsk** Rus. Fed.
100 C2 **Mönchengladbach** Ger.
144 B2 **Monclova** Mex.
131 D3 **Moncton** Can.
106 B1 **Mondego** *r.* Port.
118 C2 **Mondjamboli** Dem. Rep. Congo
123 D2 **Mondlo** S. Africa
108 A2 **Mondovì** Italy
106 C1 **Mondragón-Arrasate** Spain
111 B3 **Monemvasia** Greece
66 D1 **Moneron, Ostrov** *i.* Rus. Fed.
139 D1 **Monet** Can.
137 E3 **Monett** U.S.A.
108 B1 **Monfalcone** Italy
106 B1 **Monforte** Spain
119 D2 **Mongbwalu** Dem. Rep. Congo
62 B1 **Mông Cai** Vietnam
62 A1 **Mong Hang** Myanmar
Monghyr India *see* **Munger**
75 C2 **Mongla** Bangl.
62 B1 **Mong Lin** Myanmar
62 A1 **Mong Nawng** Myanmar
115 D3 **Mongo** Chad
68 C1 **Mongolia** *country* Asia
74 B1 **Mongora** Pak.
62 A1 **Mong Pawk** Myanmar
62 A1 **Mong Ping** Myanmar
120 B2 **Mongu** Zambia
135 C3 **Monitor Range** *mts* U.S.A.
103 E1 **Mońki** Pol.
99 B4 **Monmouth** U.K.
114 C4 **Mono** *r.* Togo
135 C3 **Mono Lake** U.S.A.
109 C2 **Monopoli** Italy
107 C1 **Monreal del Campo** Spain
140 B2 **Monroe** *LA* U.S.A.
138 C2 **Monroe** *MI* U.S.A.
138 B2 **Monroe** *WI* U.S.A.
140 C2 **Monroeville** U.S.A.
114 A4 **Monrovia** Liberia
100 A2 **Mons** Belgium
155 E1 **Monsarás, Ponta de** *pt* Brazil
100 C2 **Montabaur** Ger.
122 B3 **Montagu** S. Africa
109 C3 **Montalto** *mt.* Italy
110 B2 **Montana** Bulg.
134 E1 **Montana** *state* U.S.A.
105 C2 **Montargis** France
104 C3 **Montauban** France
139 E2 **Montauk Point** U.S.A.
123 C2 **Mont-aux-Sources** *mt.* Lesotho
105 C2 **Montbard** France
105 D2 **Montbéliard** France
105 D2 **Mont Blanc** *mt.* France/Italy
105 C2 **Montbrison** France
100 B3 **Montcornet** France
104 B3 **Mont-de-Marsan** France
104 C2 **Montdidier** France
151 D3 **Monte Alegre** Brazil
154 C1 **Monte Alegre de Minas** Brazil
139 E1 **Montebello** Can.
154 B3 **Montecarlo** Arg.
105 D3 **Monte-Carlo** Monaco
154 C1 **Monte Carmelo** Brazil
152 C3 **Monte Caseros** Arg.
123 C1 **Monte Christo** S. Africa
108 B2 **Montecristo, Isola di** *i.* Italy
146 C3 **Montego Bay** Jamaica
105 C3 **Montélimar** France
109 C2 **Montella** Italy
145 C2 **Montemorelos** Mex.
104 B2 **Montendre** France
Montenegro *aut. rep.* Serb. and Mont. *see* **Crna Gora**
121 C2 **Montepuez** Moz.
108 B2 **Montepulciano** Italy
135 B3 **Monterey** U.S.A.
135 B3 **Monterey Bay** U.S.A.
150 B2 **Montería** Col.
152 B1 **Montero** Bol.
145 B2 **Monterrey** Mex.
109 C2 **Montesano sulla Marcellana** Italy
109 C2 **Monte Sant'Angelo** Italy
151 F4 **Monte Santo** Brazil
108 A2 **Monte Santu, Capo di** *c.* *Sardinia* Italy
155 D1 **Montes Claros** Brazil
153 C3 **Montevideo** Uru.
137 D2 **Montevideo** U.S.A.
136 B3 **Monte Vista** U.S.A.
140 C2 **Montgomery** U.S.A.
100 B3 **Monthermé** France
105 D2 **Monthey** Switz.
140 B2 **Monticello** *AR* U.S.A.
141 D2 **Monticello** *FL* U.S.A.
135 E3 **Monticello** *UT* U.S.A.
104 C2 **Montignac** France
100 B2 **Montignies-le-Tilleul** Belgium
106 B2 **Montijo** Port.
106 B2 **Montijo** Spain
106 C2 **Montilla** Spain
154 B1 **Montividiu** Brazil
131 D3 **Mont-Joli** Can.
130 C3 **Mont-Laurier** Can.
104 C2 **Montluçon** France
131 C3 **Montmagny** Can.
104 C2 **Montmorillon** France
51 E2 **Monto** Austr.
134 D2 **Montpelier** *ID* U.S.A.
139 E2 **Montpelier** *VT* U.S.A.
105 C3 **Montpellier** France
130 C3 **Montréal** Can.
129 D2 **Montreal Lake** Can.
129 D2 **Montreal Lake** *l.* Can.
99 D4 **Montreuil** France
105 D2 **Montreux** Switz.
96 C2 **Montrose** U.K.
136 B3 **Montrose** U.S.A.
147 D3 **Montserrat** *terr.* West Indies
62 A1 **Monywa** Myanmar
108 A1 **Monza** Italy
107 D1 **Monzón** Spain
123 C1 **Mookane** Botswana
52 A1 **Moolawatana** Austr.
52 B1 **Moomba** Austr.
53 D1 **Moonie** Austr.
53 C1 **Moonie** *r.* Austr.
52 A2 **Moonta** Austr.
50 A3 **Moora** Austr.
50 A2 **Moore, Lake** *salt flat* Austr.
137 D1 **Moorhead** U.S.A.
53 C3 **Mooroopna** Austr.
122 A3 **Moorreesburg** S. Africa
130 B2 **Moose** *r.* Can.
130 B2 **Moose Factory** Can.
139 F1 **Moosehead Lake** U.S.A.
129 D2 **Moose Jaw** Can.
137 E1 **Moose Lake** U.S.A.
129 D2 **Moosomin** Can.
130 B2 **Moosonee** Can.
52 B2 **Mootwingee** Austr.
107 E2 **M'Oukal** Alg.
123 C1 **Mopane** S. Africa
114 B3 **Mopti** Mali
150 B4 **Moquegua** Peru
103 D2 **Mór** Hungary
118 B1 **Mora** Cameroon
93 F3 **Mora** Sweden
137 E1 **Mora** U.S.A.
74 B2 **Moradabad** India
121 □D2 **Morafenobe** Madag.
121 □D2 **Moramanga** Madag.
136 A2 **Moran** U.S.A.
51 D2 **Moranbah** Austr.
103 D2 **Morava** *r.* Europe
96 B2 **Moray Firth** *b.* U.K.

100 C3 **Morbach** Ger.
74 B2 **Morbi** India
93 G4 **Mörbylånga** Sweden
104 B3 **Morcenx** France
69 E1 **Mordaga** China
129 E3 **Morden** Can.
89 F3 **Mordovo** Rus. Fed.
98 B2 **Morecambe** U.K.
98 B2 **Morecambe Bay** U.K.
53 C1 **Moree** Austr.
59 D3 **Morehead** P.N.G.
138 C3 **Morehead** U.S.A.
141 E2 **Morehead City** U.S.A.
145 B3 **Morelia** Mex.
107 C1 **Morella** Spain
74 B2 **Morena** India
106 B2 **Morena, Sierra** *mts* Spain
110 C2 **Moreni** Romania
142 A3 **Moreno** Mex.
128 A2 **Moresby, Mount** Can.
128 A2 **Moresby Island** Can.
53 D1 **Moreton Island** Austr.
52 A2 **Morgan** Austr.
140 B3 **Morgan City** U.S.A.
141 D1 **Morganton** U.S.A.
139 D3 **Morgantown** U.S.A.
105 D2 **Morges** Switz.
68 C2 **Mori** China
66 D2 **Mori** Japan
53 C1 **Moriarty's Range** *hills* Austr.
128 B2 **Morice Lake** Can.
66 D3 **Morioka** Japan
53 D2 **Morisset** Austr.
104 B2 **Morlaix** France
98 C3 **Morley** U.K.
157 G9 **Mornington Abyssal Plain** *sea feature* S. Atlantic Ocean
51 C1 **Mornington Island** Austr.
59 D3 **Morobe** P.N.G.
114 B1 **Morocco** *country* Africa
119 D3 **Morogoro** Tanz.
64 B3 **Moro Gulf** Phil.
122 B2 **Morokweng** S. Africa
121 □D3 **Morombe** Madag.
68 C1 **Mörön** Mongolia
121 □D3 **Morondava** Madag.
106 B2 **Morón de la Frontera** Spain
121 D2 **Moroni** Comoros
59 C2 **Morotai** *i.* Indon.
119 D2 **Moroto** Uganda
98 C2 **Morpeth** U.K.
140 B1 **Morrilton** U.S.A.
154 C1 **Morrinhos** Brazil
54 C1 **Morrinsville** N.Z.
129 E3 **Morris** Can.
137 D1 **Morris** U.S.A.
141 D1 **Morristown** U.S.A.
154 C2 **Morro Agudo** Brazil
155 E1 **Morro d'Anta** Brazil
55 K3 **Morse, Cape** Antarctica
87 D3 **Morshanka** Rus. Fed.
Morshansk Rus. Fed. *see* Morshanka
151 C3 **Mortes, Rio das** *r.* Brazil
52 B3 **Mortlake** Austr.
48 G3 **Mortlock Islands** Micronesia
138 B2 **Morton** U.S.A.
53 C2 **Morundah** Austr.
53 D3 **Moruya** Austr.
96 B2 **Morvern** *reg.* U.K.
Morvi India *see* **Morbi**
53 C3 **Morwell** Austr.
101 D3 **Mosbach** Ger.
89 E2 **Moscow** Rus. Fed.
134 C1 **Moscow** U.S.A.
100 C2 **Mosel** *r.* Ger.
122 B2 **Moselebe** *watercourse* Botswana
105 D2 **Moselle** *r.* France
134 C1 **Moses Lake** U.S.A.
92 □A3 **Mosfellsbær** Iceland
54 B3 **Mosgiel** N.Z.
88 C2 **Moshchnyy, Ostrov** *i.* Rus. Fed.
89 D2 **Moshenskoye** Rus. Fed.
119 D3 **Moshi** Tanz.
92 F2 **Mosjøen** Norway
Moskva Rus. Fed. *see* Moscow
89 E2 **Moskva** *r.* Rus. Fed.
103 D2 **Mosonmagyaróvár** Hungary
146 B4 **Mosquitos, Golfo de los** *b.* Panama
93 F4 **Moss** Norway
Mossâmedes Angola *see* Namibe
122 B3 **Mossel Bay** S. Africa
122 B3 **Mossel Bay** *b.* S. Africa
118 B3 **Mossendjo** Congo
52 B2 **Mossgiel** Austr.
51 D1 **Mossman** Austr.
151 F3 **Mossoró** Brazil
53 D2 **Moss Vale** Austr.
102 C1 **Most** Czech Rep.
114 C1 **Mostaganem** Alg.
109 C2 **Mostar** Bos.-Herz.
152 C3 **Mostardas** Brazil
106 C1 **Móstoles** Spain
81 C2 **Mosul** Iraq
145 D3 **Motagua** *r.* Guat.
93 G4 **Motala** Sweden
123 C2 **Motetema** S. Africa
96 C3 **Motherwell** U.K.
75 C2 **Motihari** India
107 C2 **Motilla del Palancar** Spain
122 B1 **Motokwe** Botswana
106 C2 **Motril** Spain
110 B2 **Motru** Romania
136 C1 **Mott** U.S.A.
63 A2 **Mottama** Myanmar
63 A2 **Mottama, Gulf of** Myanmar
54 B2 **Motueka** N.Z.
145 D2 **Motul** Mex.
49 L5 **Motu One** *atoll* Fr. Polynesia
114 A3 **Moudjéria** Maur.
111 C3 **Moudros** Greece
118 B3 **Mouila** Gabon
52 B3 **Moulamein** Austr.
105 C2 **Moulins** France
141 D2 **Moultrie** U.S.A.
141 E2 **Moultrie, Lake** U.S.A.
138 B3 **Mound City** U.S.A.
115 D4 **Moundou** Chad
138 C3 **Moundsville** U.S.A.
137 E3 **Mountain Grove** U.S.A.
140 B1 **Mountain Home** *AR* U.S.A.
134 C2 **Mountain Home** *ID* U.S.A.
141 D1 **Mount Airy** U.S.A.
123 C3 **Mount Ayliff** S. Africa
52 A3 **Mount Barker** Austr.
53 C3 **Mount Beauty** Austr.
97 B2 **Mount Bellew** Rep. of Ireland
121 C2 **Mount Darwin** Zimbabwe
139 F2 **Mount Desert Island** U.S.A.
123 C3 **Mount Fletcher** S. Africa
123 C3 **Mount Frere** S. Africa
52 B3 **Mount Gambier** Austr.
59 D3 **Mount Hagen** P.N.G.
53 C2 **Mount Hope** Austr.
51 C2 **Mount Isa** Austr.
52 A3 **Mount Lofty Range** *mts* Austr.
50 A2 **Mount Magnet** Austr.
52 B2 **Mount Manara** Austr.
54 C1 **Mount Maunganui** N.Z.
97 C2 **Mountmellick** Rep. of Ireland
111 B2 **Mount Olympus** *mt.* Greece
137 E2 **Mount Pleasant** *IA* U.S.A.
138 C2 **Mount Pleasant** *MI* U.S.A.
141 E2 **Mount Pleasant** *SC* U.S.A.
143 E2 **Mount Pleasant** *TX* U.S.A.
135 D3 **Mount Pleasant** *UT* U.S.A.
99 A4 **Mount's Bay** U.K.
134 B2 **Mount Shasta** U.S.A.
54 B2 **Mount Somers** N.Z.
138 B3 **Mount Vernon** *IL* U.S.A.
138 C2 **Mount Vernon** *OH* U.S.A.
134 B1 **Mount Vernon** *WA* U.S.A.
51 D2 **Moura** Austr.
106 B2 **Moura** Port.
115 E3 **Mourdi, Dépression du** *depr.* Chad
97 C1 **Mourne Mountains** *hills* U.K.
100 A2 **Mouscron** Belgium
115 D3 **Moussoro** Chad
61 D1 **Moutong** Indon.
115 C2 **Mouydir, Monts du** *plat.* Alg.
100 B3 **Mouzon** France
97 B1 **Moy** *r.* Rep. of Ireland
117 B4 **Moyale** Eth.
Moyen Congo *country* Africa *see* **Congo**
123 C3 **Moyeni** Lesotho
76 B2 **Mo'ynoq** Uzbek.
119 D2 **Moyo** Uganda
77 D2 **Moyynkum** Kazakh.
77 D2 **Moyynty** Kazakh.
121 C3 **Mozambique** *country* Africa
113 G8 **Mozambique Channel** Africa
81 C1 **Mozdok** Rus. Fed.
89 E2 **Mozhaysk** Rus. Fed.
119 D3 **Mpanda** Tanz.
121 C2 **Mpika** Zambia
118 B2 **Mpoko** *r.* C.A.R.
121 C1 **Mporokoso** Zambia
123 C2 **Mpumalanga** *prov.* S. Africa
119 D3 **Mpwapwa** Tanz.
62 A1 **Mrauk-U** Myanmar
115 D1 **M'Saken** Tunisia
119 D3 **Msambweni** Kenya
119 D3 **Msata** Tanz.
88 C2 **Mshinskaya** Rus. Fed.
115 C1 **M'Sila** Alg.
89 D2 **Msta** *r.* Rus. Fed.
89 D2 **Mstinskiy Most** Rus. Fed.
89 D3 **Mstsislaw** Belarus
Mtoko Zimbabwe *see* Mutoko
89 E3 **Mtsensk** Rus. Fed.
123 D2 **Mtubatuba** S. Africa
119 E4 **Mtwara** Tanz.
151 E3 **Muana** Brazil
118 B3 **Muanda** Dem. Rep. Congo
62 B1 **Muang Hiam** Laos
62 B2 **Muang Hinboun** Laos
63 B2 **Muang Không** Laos
63 B2 **Muang Khôngxédôn** Laos
62 B1 **Muang Ngoy** Laos
62 B2 **Muang Pakbeng** Laos
63 B2 **Muang Phalan** Laos
62 B2 **Muang Phôn-Hông** Laos
62 B1 **Muang Sing** Laos
62 B2 **Muang Vangviang** Laos
60 B1 **Muar** Malaysia
60 B2 **Muarabungo** Indon.
60 B2 **Muaradua** Indon.
61 C2 **Muaralaung** Indon.
60 A2 **Muarasiberut** Indon.
60 B2 **Muaratembesi** Indon.
61 C2 **Muarateweh** Indon.
Muara Tuang Malaysia *see* Kota Samarahan
119 D2 **Mubende** Uganda
115 D3 **Mubi** Nigeria
120 B2 **Muconda** Angola
120 A2 **Mucope** Angola
121 C2 **Mucubela** Moz.
155 E1 **Mucuri** Brazil
155 E1 **Mucuri** *r.* Brazil
66 A2 **Mudanjiang** China
66 A1 **Mudan Jiang** *r.* China
111 C2 **Mudanya** Turkey
136 B2 **Muddy Gap** U.S.A.
101 E1 **Müden (Örtze)** Ger.
53 C2 **Mudgee** Austr.
63 A2 **Mudon** Myanmar
80 B1 **Mudurnu** Turkey
121 C2 **Mueda** Moz.
121 B2 **Mufulira** Zambia
120 B2 **Mufumbwe** Zambia
111 C3 **Muğla** Turkey
116 B2 **Muhammad Qol** Sudan
Muhammarah Iran *see* Khorramshahr
101 F2 **Mühlberg** Ger.
101 E2 **Mühlhausen (Thüringen)** Ger.
88 B2 **Muhu** *i.* Estonia
63 B3 **Mui Ca Mau** *c.* Vietnam
97 C2 **Muine Bheag** Rep. of Ireland
96 B3 **Muirkirk** U.K.
121 C2 **Muite** Moz.
65 B2 **Muju** S. Korea
Mukačevo Ukr. *see* Mukacheve
90 A2 **Mukacheve** Ukr.
61 C1 **Mukah** *Sarawak* Malaysia
79 B3 **Mukalla** Yemen
63 B2 **Mukdahan** Thai.
Mukden China *see* Shenyang
Mukhtuya Rus. Fed. *see* Lensk
50 A3 **Mukinbudin** Austr.
60 B2 **Mukomuko** Indon.
121 C2 **Mulanje, Mount** Malawi
101 F2 **Mulde** *r.* Ger.
119 D3 **Muleba** Tanz.
144 A2 **Mulegé** Mex.
143 C2 **Muleshoe** U.S.A.
106 C2 **Mulhacén** *mt.* Spain
100 C2 **Mülheim an der Ruhr** Ger.
105 D2 **Mulhouse** France
62 B1 **Muli** China
66 B2 **Muling** China
66 B1 **Muling He** *r.* China
96 B2 **Mull** *i.* U.K.
53 C2 **Mullaley** Austr.
136 C2 **Mullen** U.S.A.
61 C1 **Muller, Pegunungan** *mts* Indon.
50 A2 **Mullewa** Austr.
97 C2 **Mullingar** Rep. of Ireland
96 B3 **Mull of Galloway** *c.* U.K.
96 B3 **Mull of Kintyre** *hd* U.K.
96 A3 **Mull of Oa** *hd* U.K.
53 D1 **Mullumbimby** Austr.
120 B2 **Mulobezi** Zambia
74 B1 **Multan** Pak.
86 F2 **Mulym'ya** Rus. Fed.
74 B3 **Mumbai** India
120 B2 **Mumbeji** Zambia
120 B2 **Mumbwa** Zambia
61 D2 **Muna** *i.* Indon.
145 D2 **Muna** Mex.
101 E2 **Münchberg** Ger.
München Ger. *see* Munich
München-Gladbach Ger. *see* Mönchengladbach
138 B2 **Muncie** U.S.A.
50 B3 **Mundrabilla** Austr.
138 B3 **Munfordville** U.S.A.
119 C2 **Mungbere** Dem. Rep. Congo
75 C2 **Munger** India
52 A1 **Mungeranie** Austr.
53 C1 **Mungindi** Austr.
102 C2 **Munich** Ger.
155 D2 **Muniz Freire** Brazil
101 E1 **Münster** Ger.
100 C2 **Münster** Ger.
97 B2 **Munster** *reg.* Rep. of Ireland
100 C2 **Münsterland** *reg.* Ger.
62 B1 **Mường Nhie** Vietnam
92 H2 **Muonio** Fin.
92 H2 **Muonioälven** *r.* Fin./Sweden
Muqdisho Somalia *see* Mogadishu
155 D2 **Muqui** Brazil
103 D2 **Mur** *r.* Austria
67 C3 **Murakami** Japan
119 C3 **Muramvya** Burundi
119 D3 **Murang'a** Kenya
86 D3 **Murashi** Rus. Fed.
81 B2 **Murat** *r.* Turkey
111 C2 **Muratlı** Turkey
67 D3 **Murayama** Japan
50 A2 **Murchison** *watercourse* Austr.
107 C2 **Murcia** Spain
107 C2 **Murcia** *reg.* Spain
136 C2 **Murdo** U.S.A.
131 D3 **Murdochville** Can.
111 C2 **Mürefte** Turkey
110 B1 **Mureşul** *r.* Romania
104 C3 **Muret** France
140 C1 **Murfreesboro** U.S.A.
77 C3 **Murghab** *r.* Afgh.
77 D3 **Murghob** Tajik.
155 D2 **Muriaé** Brazil
120 B1 **Muriege** Angola
101 F1 **Müritz** *l.* Ger.
92 J2 **Murmansk** Rus. Fed.
86 C2 **Murmanskiy Bereg** *coastal area* Rus. Fed.
87 D3 **Murom** Rus. Fed.
66 D2 **Muroran** Japan
106 B1 **Muros** Spain
67 B4 **Muroto** Japan
67 B4 **Muroto-zaki** *pt* Japan
141 D1 **Murphy** U.S.A.
53 C1 **Murra Murra** Austr.
52 A3 **Murray** *r.* Austr.
128 B2 **Murray** *r.* Can.
138 B3 **Murray** U.S.A.
59 D3 **Murray, Lake** P.N.G.
141 D2 **Murray, Lake** U.S.A.
52 A3 **Murray Bridge** Austr.
122 B3 **Murraysburg** S. Africa
52 B3 **Murrayville** Austr.
52 B2 **Murrumbidgee** *r.* Austr.
53 C2 **Murrumburrah** Austr.
121 C2 **Murrupula** Moz.
53 D2 **Murrurundi** Austr.
109 C1 **Murska Sobota** Slovenia
54 C1 **Murupara** N.Z.
49 N6 **Mururoa** *atoll* Fr. Polynesia
75 C2 **Murwara** India
53 D1 **Murwillumbah** Austr.
76 C3 **Murzechirla** Turkm.
115 D2 **Murzūq** Libya

103 D2 Mürzzuschlag Austria
81 C2 Muş Turkey
110 B2 Musala mt. Bulg.
65 B1 Musan N. Korea
78 B3 Musaymir Yemen
79 C2 Muscat Oman
Muscat and Oman
country Asia see Oman
137 E2 Muscatine U.S.A.
50 C2 Musgrave Ranges mts
Austr.
118 B3 Mushie Dem. Rep. Congo
60 B2 Musi r. Indon.
123 D1 Musina S. Africa
138 B2 Muskegon U.S.A.
138 B2 Muskegon r. U.S.A.
138 C3 Muskingum r. U.S.A.
143 D1 Muskogee U.S.A.
139 D1 Muskoka, Lake Can.
128 B2 Muskwa r. Can.
74 A1 Muslimbagh Pak.
116 B3 Musmar Sudan
119 D3 Musoma Tanz.
59 D3 Mussau Island P.N.G.
96 C3 Musselburgh U.K.
117 C4 Mustahil Eth.
88 B2 Mustjala Estonia
53 D2 Muswellbrook Austr.
116 A2 Mūţ Egypt
121 C2 Mutare Zimbabwe
121 C2 Mutoko Zimbabwe
66 D2 Mutsu Japan
66 D2 Mutsu-wan b. Japan
121 C2 Mutuali Moz.
155 D1 Mutum Brazil
92 I2 Muurola Fin.
70 A2 Mu Us Shamo des. China
120 A1 Muxaluando Angola
86 C2 Muyezerskiy Rus. Fed.
119 D3 Muyinga Burundi
74 B1 Muzaffargarh Pak.
75 C2 Muzaffarpur India
123 D1 Muzamane Moz.
155 C2 Muzambinho Brazil
144 B2 Múzquiz Mex.
75 C1 Muz Tag mt. China
117 A4 Mvolo Sudan
119 C3 Mwanza Dem. Rep.
Congo
119 D3 Mwanza Tanz.
118 C3 Mweka Dem. Rep. Congo
121 B2 Mwenda Zambia
118 C3 Mwene-Ditu
Dem. Rep. Congo
121 C3 Mwenezi Zimbabwe
121 C3 Mwenezi r. Zimbabwe
119 C3 Mweru, Lake
Dem. Rep. Congo/Zambia
121 B1 Mweru Wantipa, Lake
Zambia
118 C3 Mwimba Dem. Rep. Congo
120 B2 Mwinilunga Zambia
88 C3 Myadzyel Belarus
62 A2 Myanaung Myanmar
62 A1 Myanmar country Asia
63 A2 Myaungmya Myanmar
63 A2 Myeik Myanmar
Mergui Archipelago is
Myanmar see
Mergui Archipelago
62 A1 Myingyan Myanmar
62 A1 Myitkyina Myanmar
90 A2 Mykolayiv Ukr.
91 C2 Mykolayiv Ukr.
111 C3 Mykonos Greece
111 C3 Mykonos i. Greece
86 E2 Myla Rus. Fed.
75 D2 Mymensingh Bangl.
65 B1 Myŏnggan N. Korea
88 C2 Myory Belarus
92 □B3 Mýrdalsjökull ice cap
Iceland
92 A2 Myre Norway
91 C2 Myrhorod Ukr.
111 C3 Myrina Greece
90 C2 Myronivka Ukr.
141 E2 Myrtle Beach U.S.A.
53 C3 Myrtleford Austr.
134 B2 Myrtle Point U.S.A.
89 E2 Myshkin Rus. Fed.
Myshkino Rus. Fed. see
Myshkin
103 C1 Myślibórz Pol.
73 B3 Mysore India
83 N2 Mys Shmidta Rus. Fed.
63 B2 My Tho Vietnam
111 C3 Mytilini Greece
89 E3 Mytishchi Rus. Fed.
121 C3 Mzamomhle S. Africa
121 C2 Mzimba Malawi
121 C2 Mzuzu Malawi

N

101 F3 Naab r. Ger.
100 B1 Naarden Neth.
97 C2 Naas Rep. of Ireland
122 A2 Nababeep S. Africa
87 E3 Naberezhnyye Chelny
Rus. Fed.
59 D3 Nabire Indon.
80 B2 Nāblus West Bank
123 C1 Naboomspruit S. Africa
121 D2 Nacala Moz.
119 D4 Nachingwea Tanz.
103 D1 Náchod Czech Rep.
73 D3 Nachuge India
143 E2 Nacogdoches U.S.A.
144 B1 Nacozari de García Mex.
Nada China see Danzhou
74 B2 Nadiad India
90 A2 Nadvirna Ukr.
86 C2 Nadvoitsy Rus. Fed.
86 G2 Nadym Rus. Fed.
93 F4 Næstved Denmark
111 B3 Nafpaktos Greece
111 B3 Nafplio Greece
115 D1 Nafūsah, Jabal hills Libya
78 B2 Nafy Saudi Arabia
64 B2 Naga Phil.
130 B2 Nagagami r. Can.
67 C3 Nagano Japan
67 C3 Nagaoka Japan
75 D2 Nagaon India
74 B1 Nagar India
74 B2 Nagar Parkar Pak.
67 A4 Nagasaki Japan
67 B4 Nagato Japan
74 B2 Nagaur India
73 B4 Nagercoil India
74 A2 Nagha Kalat Pak.
74 B2 Nagina India
67 C3 Nagoya Japan
75 B2 Nagpur India
75 D1 Nagqu China
141 E1 Nags Head U.S.A.
82 E1 Nagurskoye Rus. Fed.
103 D2 Nagyatád Hungary
103 D2 Nagykanizsa Hungary
128 B1 Nahanni Butte Can.
81 C2 Nahāvand Iran
101 E1 Nahrendorf Ger.
153 A4 Nahuel Huapí, Lago l. Arg.
141 D2 Nahunta U.S.A.
131 D2 Nain Can.
81 D2 Nā'īn Iran
121 C2 Naiopué Moz.
96 C2 Nairn U.K.
119 D3 Nairobi Kenya
Naissus Serb. and Mont.
see Niš
119 D3 Naivasha Kenya
81 D2 Najafābād Iran
78 B2 Najd reg. Saudi Arabia
106 C1 Nájera Spain
65 C1 Najin N. Korea
78 B3 Najrān Saudi Arabia
119 D2 Nakasongola Uganda
67 C3 Nakatsugawa Japan
78 A3 Nakfa Eritrea
66 B2 Nakhodka Rus. Fed.
63 B2 Nakhon Nayok Thai.
63 B2 Nakhon Pathom Thai.
62 B2 Nakhon Phanom Thai.
63 B2 Nakhon Ratchasima Thai.
63 B2 Nakhon Sawan Thai.
63 A3 Nakhon Si Thammarat
Thai.
Nakhrachi Rus. Fed. see
Kondinskoye
130 B2 Nakina Can.
126 B3 Naknek U.S.A.
121 C1 Nakonde Zambia
93 F5 Nakskov Denmark
119 D3 Nakuru Kenya
128 C2 Nakusp Can.
75 D2 Nalbari India
87 D4 Nal'chik Rus. Fed.
115 D1 Nālūt Libya
123 D2 Namaacha Moz.
123 C2 Namahadi S. Africa
81 D2 Namak, Daryācheh-ye
salt flat Iran
76 B3 Namak, Kavīr-e salt flat
Iran
79 C1 Namakzar-e Shadad
salt flat Iran
77 D2 Namangan Uzbek.
119 D3 Namanyere Tanz.
122 A2 Namaqualand reg.
S. Africa
51 E2 Nambour Austr.

53 D2 Nambucca Heads Austr.
63 B3 Năm Căn Vietnam
75 D1 Nam Co salt l. China
62 B1 Nam Đinh Vietnam
121 C2 Namialo Moz.
120 A3 Namib Desert Namibia
120 A2 Namibe Angola
120 A3 Namibia country Africa
72 D2 Namjagbarwa Feng mt.
China
59 C3 Namlea Indon.
62 B2 Nam Ngum Reservoir
Laos
53 C2 Namoi r. Austr.
134 C2 Nampa U.S.A.
114 B3 Nampala Mali
65 B2 Namp'o N. Korea
121 C2 Nampula Moz.
72 D2 Namrup India
62 A1 Namsang Myanmar
92 F3 Namsos Norway
92 F3 Namsskogan Norway
63 A2 Nam Tok Thai.
75 D1 Namtsy Rus. Fed.
62 A1 Namtu Myanmar
121 C2 Namuno Moz.
100 B2 Namur Belgium
120 B2 Namwala Zambia
65 B2 Namwŏn S. Korea
62 A1 Namya Ra Myanmar
62 B2 Nan Thai.
128 B3 Nanaimo Can.
71 B3 Nan'an China
122 A1 Nananib Plateau Namibia
Nan'ao China see Dayu
67 C3 Nanao Japan
71 B3 Nanchang Jiangxi China
71 B3 Nanchang Jiangxi China
71 B3 Nancheng China
70 A2 Nanchong China
63 A3 Nancowry i. India
105 D2 Nancy France
75 C1 Nanda Devi mt. India
71 A3 Nandan China
74 B3 Nanded India
Nander India see Nanded
53 D2 Nandewar Range mts
Austr.
74 B2 Nandurbar India
73 B3 Nandyal India
71 B3 Nanfeng China
62 A1 Nang China
118 B2 Nanga Eboko Cameroon
61 C2 Nangahpinoh Indon.
77 D3 Nanga Parbat mt.
Jammu and Kashmir
61 C2 Nangatayap Indon.
63 A2 Nangin Myanmar
65 B1 Nangnim-sanmaek mts
N. Korea
70 B2 Nangong China
119 D3 Nangulangwa Tanz.
70 C2 Nanhui China
70 B2 Nanjiang China
Nanking China see Nanjing
67 B4 Nankoku Japan
120 A2 Nankova Angola
70 B2 Nanle China
71 B3 Nan Ling mts China
71 A3 Nanning China
127 I2 Nanortalik Greenland
71 A3 Nanpan Jiang r. China
75 C2 Nanpara India
71 B3 Nanping China
Nanping China see Pucheng
Nansei-shotō Japan see
Ryukyu Islands
160 I1 Nansen Basin sea feature
Arctic Ocean
126 F1 Nansen Sound sea chan.
Can.
104 B2 Nantes France
70 C2 Nantong China
139 E2 Nantucket U.S.A.
139 F2 Nantucket Island U.S.A.
99 B3 Nantwich U.K.
49 I4 Nanumea i. Tuvalu
155 D1 Nanuque Brazil
64 B3 Nanusa, Kepulauan is
Indon.
71 B3 Nanxiong China
70 B2 Nanyang China
119 D3 Nanyuki Kenya
70 B2 Nanzhang China
Nanzhao China see
Zhao'an
107 D2 Nao, Cabo de la c. Spain
131 C2 Naococane, Lac l. Can.
74 A2 Naokot Pak.
71 B3 Naozhou Dao i. China
135 B3 Napa U.S.A.

126 E2 Napaktulik Lake Can.
139 D2 Napanee Can.
127 I2 Napasoq Greenland
137 F2 Naperville U.S.A.
54 C1 Napier N.Z.
108 B2 Naples Italy
141 D3 Naples U.S.A.
150 B3 Napo r. Ecuador
Napoli Italy see Naples
Napug China see Gê'gyai
114 B3 Nara Mali
88 C3 Narach Belarus
52 B3 Naracoorte Austr.
53 C2 Naradhan Austr.
145 C2 Naranjos Mex.
63 B3 Narathiwat Thai.
74 B3 Narayangaon India
105 C3 Narbonne France
63 A2 Narcondam Island India
127 H1 Nares Strait
Can./Greenland
103 E1 Narew r. Pol.
122 A1 Narib Namibia
87 D4 Narimanov Rus. Fed.
67 D3 Narita Japan
74 B2 Narmada r. India
74 B2 Narnaul India
108 B2 Narni Italy
86 F2 Narodnaya, Gora mt.
Rus. Fed.
90 B1 Narodychi Ukr.
89 E2 Naro-Fominsk Rus. Fed.
53 D3 Narooma Austr.
88 C2 Narowlya Belarus
93 H3 Närpes Fin.
53 C2 Narrabri Austr.
53 C2 Narrandera Austr.
53 C2 Narromine Austr.
67 B4 Naruto Japan
88 C2 Narva Estonia
88 C2 Narva Bay
Estonia/Rus. Fed.
92 G2 Narvik Norway
88 C2 Narvskoye
Vodokhranilishche resr
Estonia/Rus. Fed.
86 E2 Nar'yan-Mar Rus. Fed.
77 D2 Naryn Kyrg.
74 B2 Nashik India
139 E2 Nashua U.S.A.
140 C1 Nashville U.S.A.
137 E1 Nashwauk U.S.A.
109 C1 Našice Croatia
117 B4 Nasir Sudan
Nasirabad Bangl. see
Mymensingh
119 C4 Nasondoye
Dem. Rep. Congo
76 B3 Naşrābād Iran
128 B2 Nass r. Can.
146 C2 Nassau Bahamas
116 B2 Nasser, Lake resr Egypt
93 F4 Nässjö Sweden
130 C2 Nastapoca r. Can.
130 C2 Nastapoka Islands Can.
89 D2 Nasva Rus. Fed.
120 B3 Nata Botswana
151 F3 Natal Brazil
60 A1 Natal Indon.
Natal prov. S. Africa see
Kwazulu-Natal
159 D6 Natal Basin sea feature
Indian Ocean
143 D3 Natalia U.S.A.
131 D2 Natashquan Can.
131 D2 Natashquan r. Can.
140 B2 Natchez U.S.A.
140 B2 Natchitoches U.S.A.
53 C3 Nathalia Austr.
107 C1 Nati, Punta pt Spain
114 C3 Natitingou Benin
151 E4 Natividade Brazil
67 D3 Natori Japan
119 D3 Natron, Lake salt l. Tanz.
60 B1 Natuna, Kepulauan is
Indon.
60 B1 Natuna Besar i. Indon.
122 A1 Nauchas Namibia
101 F1 Nauen Ger.
64 B2 Naujan Phil.
88 B2 Naujoji Akmenė Lith.
101 E2 Naumburg (Saale) Ger.
48 H34 Nauru country
S. Pacific Ocean
150 B3 Nauta Peru
145 C2 Nautla Mex.
88 C3 Navahrudak Belarus
106 B2 Navalmoral de la Mata
Spain
106 B2 Navalvillar de Pela Spain
97 C2 Navan Rep. of Ireland

Navangar India *see* **Jamnagar**
88 C2 **Navapolatsk** Belarus
83 M2 **Navarin, Mys** *c.* Rus. Fed.
153 B5 **Navarino, Isla** *i.* Chile
107 C1 **Navarra** *reg.* Spain
Navarre *aut. comm.* Spain *see* **Navarra**
96 B1 **Naver** *r.* U.K.
89 D3 **Navlya** Rus. Fed.
110 C2 **Năvodari** Romania
77 C2 **Navoiy** Uzbek.
144 B2 **Navojoa** Mex.
144 B2 **Navolato** Mex.
74 A2 **Nawabshah** Pak.
75 C2 **Nawada** India
62 A1 **Nawnghkio** Myanmar
62 A1 **Nawngleng** Myanmar
81 C2 **Naxçıvan** Azer.
111 C3 **Naxos** Greece
111 C3 **Naxos** *i.* Greece
144 B2 **Nayar** Mex.
66 D2 **Nayoro** Japan
80 B2 **Nazareth** Israel
144 B2 **Nazas** Mex.
144 B2 **Nazas** *r.* Mex.
150 B4 **Nazca** Peru
157 H7 **Nazca Ridge** *sea feature* S. Pacific Ocean
111 C3 **Nazilli** Turkey
117 B4 **Nazrēt** Eth.
79 C2 **Nazwá** Oman
121 B1 **Nchelenge** Zambia
122 B1 **Ncojane** Botswana
120 A1 **N'dalatando** Angola
118 C2 **Ndélé** C.A.R.
118 B3 **Ndendé** Gabon
115 D3 **Ndjamena** Chad
118 A3 **Ndogo, Lagune** *lag.* Gabon
121 B2 **Ndola** Zambia
97 C1 **Neagh, Lough** *l.* U.K.
50 C2 **Neale, Lake** *salt flat* Austr.
111 B3 **Neapoli** Greece
111 B2 **Nea Roda** Greece
99 B4 **Neath** U.K.
119 D2 **Nebbi** Uganda
53 C1 **Nebine Creek** *r.* Austr.
150 C2 **Neblina, Pico da** *mt.* Brazil
135 D3 **Nebo, Mount** U.S.A.
89 D2 **Nebolchi** Rus. Fed.
136 C2 **Nebraska** *state* U.S.A.
137 D2 **Nebraska City** U.S.A.
108 B3 **Nebrodi, Monti** *mts Sicily* Italy
143 E3 **Neches** *r.* U.S.A.
156 E4 **Necker Island** U.S.A.
153 C3 **Necochea** Arg.
143 E3 **Nederland** U.S.A.
100 B2 **Neder Rijn** *r.* Neth.
130 C2 **Nedlouc, Lac** *l.* Can.
139 E2 **Needham** U.S.A.
135 D4 **Needles** U.S.A.
74 B2 **Neemuch** India
129 E2 **Neepawa** Can.
87 E3 **Neftekamsk** Rus. Fed.
82 F2 **Nefteyugansk** Rus. Fed.
108 A3 **Nefza** Tunisia
120 A1 **Negage** Angola
117 B4 **Negēlē** Eth.
109 D2 **Negotin** Serb. and Mont.
111 B2 **Negotino** Macedonia
150 A3 **Negra, Punta** *pt* Peru
155 D1 **Negra, Serra** *mts* Brazil
63 A2 **Negrais, Cape** Myanmar
153 B4 **Negro** *r.* Arg.
150 D3 **Negro** *r.* S. America
152 C3 **Negro** *r.* Uru.
106 B2 **Negro, Cabo** *c.* Morocco
64 B3 **Negros** *i.* Phil.
79 D1 **Nehbandān** Iran
69 E1 **Nehe** China
70 A3 **Neijiang** China
129 D2 **Neilburg** Can.
150 B2 **Neiva** Col.
129 E2 **Nejanilini Lake** Can.
Nejd *reg.* Saudi Arabia *see* **Najd**
117 B4 **Nek'emtē** Eth.
89 F2 **Nekrasovskoye** Rus. Fed.
89 D2 **Nelidovo** Rus. Fed.
73 B3 **Nellore** India
128 C3 **Nelson** Can.
129 E2 **Nelson** *r.* Can.
54 B2 **Nelson** N.Z.
52 B3 **Nelson, Cape** Austr.
53 D2 **Nelson Bay** Austr.
129 E2 **Nelson House** Can.
134 E1 **Nelson Reservoir** U.S.A.
123 D2 **Nelspruit** S. Africa
114 B3 **Néma** Maur.
88 B2 **Neman** Rus. Fed.
105 C2 **Nemours** France
66 D2 **Nemuro** Japan
90 B2 **Nemyriv** Ukr.
97 B2 **Nenagh** Rep. of Ireland
99 D3 **Nene** *r.* U.K.
69 E1 **Nenjiang** China
137 E3 **Neosho** U.S.A.
75 C2 **Nepal** *country* Asia
75 C2 **Nepalganj** Nepal
139 D1 **Nepean** Can.
135 D3 **Nephi** U.S.A.
97 B1 **Nephin** *hill* Rep. of Ireland
97 B1 **Nephin Beg Range** *hills* Rep. of Ireland
131 D3 **Nepisiguit** *r.* Can.
119 C2 **Nepoko** *r.* Dem. Rep. Congo
139 E2 **Neptune** U.S.A.
108 B2 **Nera** *r.* Italy
104 C3 **Nérac** France
53 D1 **Nerang** Austr.
69 D1 **Nerchinsk** Rus. Fed.
89 F2 **Nerekhta** Rus. Fed.
109 C2 **Neretva** *r.* Bos.-Herz./Croatia
120 B2 **Neriquinha** Angola
88 B3 **Neris** *r.* Lith.
89 E2 **Nerl'** *r.* Rus. Fed.
86 F2 **Nerokhi** Rus. Fed.
154 C1 **Nerópolis** Brazil
83 J3 **Neryungri** Rus. Fed.
92 □C2 **Neskaupstaður** Iceland
96 B2 **Ness, Loch** *l.* U.K.
136 D3 **Ness City** U.S.A.
Nesterov Ukr. *see* **Zhovkva**
111 B2 **Nestos** *r.* Greece
100 B1 **Netherlands** *country* Europe
147 D3 **Netherlands Antilles** *terr.* West Indies
127 H2 **Nettilling Lake** Can.
101 F1 **Neubrandenburg** Ger.
105 D2 **Neuchâtel** Switz.
105 D2 **Neuchâtel, Lac de** *l.* Switz.
100 C2 **Neuerburg** Ger.
100 B3 **Neufchâteau** Belgium
105 D2 **Neufchâteau** France
104 C2 **Neufchâtel-en-Bray** France
101 D2 **Neuhof** Ger.
101 E3 **Neumarkt in der Oberpfalz** Ger.
102 B1 **Neumünster** Ger.
100 C3 **Neunkirchen** Ger.
153 B3 **Neuquén** Arg.
153 B3 **Neuquén** *r.* Arg.
101 F1 **Neuruppin** Ger.
100 C2 **Neuss** Ger.
101 D1 **Neustadt am Rübenberge** Ger.
101 E3 **Neustadt an der Aisch** Ger.
Neustadt an der Hardt Ger. *see* **Neustadt an der Weinstraße**
101 D3 **Neustadt an der Weinstraße** Ger.
101 E1 **Neustadt-Glewe** Ger.
101 F1 **Neustrelitz** Ger.
99 D5 **Neuville-lès-Dieppe** France
100 C2 **Neuwied** Ger.
137 E3 **Nevada** U.S.A.
135 C3 **Nevada** *state* U.S.A.
106 C2 **Nevada, Sierra** *mts* Spain
135 B2 **Nevada, Sierra** *mts* U.S.A.
88 C2 **Nevaišių kalnis** *hill* Lith.
88 C2 **Nevel'** Rus. Fed.
105 C2 **Nevers** France
53 C2 **Nevertire** Austr.
109 C2 **Nevesinje** Bos.-Herz.
87 D4 **Nevinnomyssk** Rus. Fed.
80 B2 **Nevşehir** Turkey
99 C4 **New Addington** U.K.
128 B2 **New Aiyansh** Can.
119 D4 **Newala** Tanz.
138 B3 **New Albany** U.S.A.
151 D2 **New Amsterdam** Guyana
139 E2 **Newark** *NJ* U.S.A.
138 C2 **Newark** *OH* U.S.A.
99 C3 **Newark-on-Trent** U.K.
139 E2 **New Bedford** U.S.A.
141 E1 **New Bern** U.S.A.
138 B1 **Newberry** *MI* U.S.A.
141 D2 **Newberry** *SC* U.S.A.
143 E2 **New Boston** U.S.A.
143 D3 **New Braunfels** U.S.A.
97 C2 **Newbridge** Rep. of Ireland
59 D3 **New Britain** *i.* P.N.G.
131 D3 **New Brunswick** *prov.* Can.
99 C4 **Newbury** U.K.
48 H6 **New Caledonia** *terr.* S. Pacific Ocean
156 D7 **New Caledonia Trough** *sea feature* Tasman Sea
53 D2 **Newcastle** Austr.
123 C2 **Newcastle** S. Africa
97 D1 **Newcastle** U.K.
138 C2 **New Castle** U.S.A.
136 C2 **Newcastle** U.S.A.
99 B3 **Newcastle-under-Lyme** U.K.
98 C2 **Newcastle upon Tyne** U.K.
51 C1 **Newcastle Waters** Austr.
97 B2 **Newcastle West** Rep. of Ireland
74 B2 **New Delhi** India
128 C3 **New Denver** Can.
53 D2 **New England Range** *mts* Austr.
157 H3 **New England Seamounts** *sea feature* N. Atlantic Ocean
131 E3 **Newfoundland** *i.* Can.
131 E2 **Newfoundland and Labrador** *prov.* Can.
96 B3 **New Galloway** U.K.
48 G4 **New Georgia Islands** Solomon Is
131 D3 **New Glasgow** Can.
59 D3 **New Guinea** *i.* Indon./P.N.G.
78 A3 **New Halfa** Sudan
139 E2 **New Hampshire** *state* U.S.A.
59 E3 **New Hanover** *i.* P.N.G.
139 E2 **New Haven** U.S.A.
128 B2 **New Hazelton** Can.
New Hebrides *country* S. Pacific Ocean *see* **Vanuatu**
156 D7 **New Hebrides Trench** *sea feature* S. Pacific Ocean
140 B2 **New Iberia** U.S.A.
59 E3 **New Ireland** *i.* P.N.G.
139 E3 **New Jersey** *state* U.S.A.
130 C3 **New Liskeard** Can.
138 B2 **New London** U.S.A.
50 A2 **Newman** Austr.
54 C2 **Newman** N.Z.
97 B2 **Newmarket** Rep. of Ireland
99 D3 **Newmarket** U.K.
97 B2 **Newmarket-on-Fergus** Rep. of Ireland
142 B2 **New Mexico** *state* U.S.A.
141 D2 **Newnan** U.S.A.
140 B3 **New Orleans** U.S.A.
138 C2 **New Philadelphia** U.S.A.
54 B1 **New Plymouth** N.Z.
99 C4 **Newport** *England* U.K.
99 B4 **Newport** *Wales* U.K.
140 B1 **Newport** *AR* U.S.A.
134 B2 **Newport** *OR* U.S.A.
139 E2 **Newport** *RI* U.S.A.
141 D1 **Newport** *TN* U.S.A.
139 E2 **Newport** *VT* U.S.A.
134 C1 **Newport** *WA* U.S.A.
139 D3 **Newport News** U.S.A.
141 E3 **New Providence** *i.* Bahamas
99 A4 **Newquay** U.K.
140 B2 **New Roads** U.S.A.
97 C2 **New Ross** Rep. of Ireland
97 C1 **Newry** U.K.
83 K1 **New Siberia Islands** Rus. Fed.
52 B2 **New South Wales** *state* Austr.
137 E2 **Newton** *IA* U.S.A.
137 D3 **Newton** *KS* U.S.A.
99 B4 **Newton Abbot** U.K.
98 C2 **Newton Aycliffe** U.K.
96 B3 **Newton Mearns** U.K.
96 B2 **Newtonmore** U.K.
96 B3 **Newton Stewart** U.K.
97 B2 **Newtown** Rep. of Ireland
99 B3 **Newtown** U.K.
136 C1 **New Town** U.S.A.
97 D1 **Newtownabbey** U.K.
97 D1 **Newtownards** U.K.
Newtownbarry Rep. of Ireland *see* **Bunclody**
97 C1 **Newtownbutler** U.K.
96 C3 **Newtown St Boswells** U.K.
97 C1 **Newtownstewart** U.K.
137 E2 **New Ulm** U.S.A.
139 E2 **New York** U.S.A.
139 D2 **New York** *state* U.S.A.
54 B2 **New Zealand** *country* Oceania
86 D3 **Neya** Rus. Fed.
81 D3 **Neyrīz** Iran
76 B3 **Neyshābūr** Iran
145 C3 **Nezahualcóyotl, Presa** *resr* Mex.
60 B1 **Ngabang** Indon.
118 B3 **Ngabé** Congo
75 C2 **Ngamring** China
119 D2 **Ngangala** Sudan
75 C1 **Ngangla Ringco** *salt l.* China
75 C1 **Nganglong Kangri** *mt.* China
75 C1 **Nganglong Kangri** *mts* China
75 C1 **Ngangzê Co** *salt l.* China
62 A2 **Ngao** Thai.
118 B2 **Ngaoundal** Cameroon
118 B2 **Ngaoundéré** Cameroon
54 C1 **Ngaruawahia** N.Z.
62 A2 **Ngathainggyaung** Myanmar
Ngiva Angola *see* **Ondjiva**
118 B3 **Ngo** Congo
63 B2 **Ngoc Linh** *mt.* Vietnam
115 D4 **Ngol Bembo** Nigeria
115 D3 **Ngourti** Niger
115 D3 **Nguigmi** Niger
59 D2 **Ngulu** *atoll* Micronesia
61 C2 **Ngunut** Indon.
Ngunza Angola *see* **Sumbe**
Ngunza-Kabolu Angola *see* **Sumbe**
115 D3 **Nguru** Nigeria
62 B1 **Nguyên Binh** Vietnam
123 C2 **Ngwathe** S. Africa
123 D2 **Ngwelezana** S. Africa
121 C2 **Nhamalabué** Moz.
120 A2 **N'harea** Angola
63 B2 **Nha Trang** Vietnam
52 B3 **Nhill** Austr.
123 D2 **Nhlangano** Swaziland
51 C1 **Nhulunbuy** Austr.
139 D2 **Niagara Falls** Can.
114 C3 **Niamey** Niger
119 C2 **Niangara** Dem. Rep. Congo
114 B3 **Niangay, Lac** *l.* Mali
119 C2 **Nia-Nia** Dem. Rep. Congo
60 A1 **Nias** *i.* Indon.
88 B2 **Nīca** Latvia
146 B3 **Nicaragua** *country* Central America
Nicaragua, Lago de Nic. *see* **Nicaragua, Lake**
146 B3 **Nicaragua, Lake** *l.* Nic.
109 C3 **Nicastro** Italy
105 D3 **Nice** France
73 D4 **Nicobar Islands** India
80 B2 **Nicosia** Cyprus
146 B4 **Nicoya, Golfo de** *b.* Costa Rica
88 B2 **Nida** Lith.
103 E1 **Nidzica** Pol.
102 B1 **Niebüll** Ger.
101 D2 **Niederaula** Ger.
118 B2 **Niefang** Equat. Guinea
101 F1 **Niemegk** Ger.
101 D1 **Nienburg (Weser)** Ger.
103 C1 **Niesky** Ger.
100 B1 **Nieuwegein** Neth.
100 B1 **Nieuwe-Niedorp** Neth.
151 D2 **Nieuw Nickerie** Suriname
122 A3 **Nieuwoudtville** S. Africa
100 A2 **Nieuwpoort** Belgium
80 B2 **Niğde** Turkey
115 C3 **Niger** *country* Africa
115 C4 **Niger** *r.* Africa
115 C4 **Niger, Mouths of the** Nigeria
115 C4 **Nigeria** *country* Africa
130 B3 **Nighthawk Lake** Can.
111 B2 **Nigrita** Greece
67 C3 **Niigata** Japan
67 B4 **Niihama** Japan
67 C4 **Nii-jima** *i.* Japan
67 B4 **Niimi** Japan
67 C3 **Niitsu** Japan
107 C2 **Níjar** Spain
100 B1 **Nijkerk** Neth.
100 B2 **Nijmegen** Neth.
100 C1 **Nijverdal** Neth.
92 J2 **Nikel'** Rus. Fed.
Nikolayev Ukr. *see* **Mykolayiv**

87 D3 **Nikolayevsk** Rus. Fed.
Nikolayevskiy Rus. Fed. see Nikolayevsk
86 D3 **Nikol'sk** Rus. Fed.
Nikol'skiy Kazakh. see **Satpayev**
83 M3 **Nikol'skoye** Rus. Fed.
Nikol'skoye Rus. Fed. see **Sheksna**
91 C2 **Nikopol'** Ukr.
80 B1 **Niksar** Turkey
79 D2 **Nīkshahr** Iran
109 C2 **Nikšić** Serb. and Mont.
Nīl, Bahr el *r.* Africa see **Nile**
135 C4 **Niland** U.S.A.
116 B1 **Nile** *r.* Africa
138 B2 **Niles** U.S.A.
Nimach India see **Neemuch**
105 C3 **Nîmes** France
53 C3 **Nimmitabel** Austr.
117 B4 **Nimule** Sudan
Nimwegen Neth. see **Nijmegen**
53 C1 **Nindigully** Austr.
73 B4 **Nine Degree Channel** India
53 C3 **Ninety Mile Beach** Austr.
54 B1 **Ninety Mile Beach** N.Z.
70 C3 **Ningbo** China
71 B3 **Ningde** China
71 B3 **Ningdu** China
70 B2 **Ningguo** China
71 C3 **Ninghai** China
72 D2 **Ninging** India
Ningjiang China see **Songyuan**
68 C2 **Ningjing Shan** *mts* China
70 A2 **Ningxia Huizu Zizhiqu** *aut. reg.* China
70 B2 **Ningyang** China
62 B1 **Ninh Binh** Vietnam
63 B2 **Ninh Hoa** Vietnam
66 D2 **Ninohe** Japan
137 D2 **Niobrara** *r.* U.S.A.
62 A1 **Nioko** India
114 B3 **Niono** Mali
114 B3 **Nioro** Mali
104 B2 **Niort** France
129 D2 **Nipawin** Can.
130 B3 **Nipigon** Can.
130 B3 **Nipigon, Lake** Can.
131 D2 **Nipishish Lake** Can.
130 C3 **Nipissing, Lake** Can.
135 C3 **Nipton** U.S.A.
151 E4 **Niquelândia** Brazil
74 B3 **Nirmal** India
109 D2 **Niš** Serb. and Mont.
109 D2 **Nišava** *r.* Serb. and Mont.
108 B3 **Niscemi** *Sicily* Italy
67 B4 **Nishino-omote** Japan
90 B2 **Nisporeni** Moldova
155 D2 **Niterói** Brazil
96 C3 **Nith** *r.* U.K.
103 D2 **Nitra** Slovakia
49 K5 **Niue** *terr.* S. Pacific Ocean
92 H3 **Nivala** Fin.
100 B2 **Nivelles** Belgium
73 B3 **Nizamabad** India
87 E3 **Nizhnekamsk** Rus. Fed.
87 E3 **Nizhnekamskoye Vodokhranilishche** *resr* Rus. Fed.
83 H3 **Nizhneudinsk** Rus. Fed.
82 G2 **Nizhnevartovsk** Rus. Fed.
Nizhnevolzhsk Rus. Fed. see **Narimanov**
83 K2 **Nizhneyansk** Rus. Fed.
Nizhniye Kresty Rus. Fed. see **Cherskiy**
Nizhniye Ustriki Pol. see **Ustrzyki Dolne**
89 F3 **Nizhniy Kislyay** Rus. Fed.
87 D3 **Nizhniy Lomov** Rus. Fed.
87 D3 **Nizhniy Novgorod** Rus. Fed.
86 E2 **Nizhniy Odes** Rus. Fed.
86 E3 **Nizhniy Tagil** Rus. Fed.
83 G2 **Nizhnyaya Tunguska** *r.* Rus. Fed.
86 E3 **Nizhnyaya Tura** Rus. Fed.
91 C1 **Nizhyn** Ukr.
103 E1 **Nizina Mazowiecka** *reg.* Pol.
121 D2 **Njazidja** *i.* Comoros
119 D3 **Njinjo** Tanz.
119 D3 **Njombe** Tanz.
118 B2 **Nkambe** Cameroon
119 D4 **Nkhata Bay** Malawi
121 C2 **Nkhotakota** Malawi
118 A3 **Nkomi, Lagune** *lag.* Gabon
119 D3 **Nkondwe** Tanz.
118 A2 **Nkongsamba** Cameroon
123 C3 **Nkululeko** S. Africa
123 C3 **Nkwenkwezi** S. Africa
67 B4 **Nobeoka** Japan
138 B2 **Noblesville** U.S.A.
52 B1 **Noccundra** Austr.
144 A1 **Nogales** Mex.
142 A2 **Nogales** U.S.A.
104 C2 **Nogent-le-Rotrou** France
83 H2 **Noginsk** Rus. Fed.
89 E2 **Noginsk** Rus. Fed.
83 K3 **Nogliki** Rus. Fed.
74 B2 **Nohar** India
100 C3 **Nohfelden** Ger.
104 B2 **Noires, Montagnes** *hills* France
104 B2 **Noirmoutier, Île de** *i.* France
104 B2 **Noirmoutier-en-l'Île** France
67 C4 **Nojima-zaki** *c.* Japan
74 B2 **Nokha** India
93 H3 **Nokia** Fin.
74 A2 **Nok Kundi** Pak.
118 B2 **Nola** C.A.R.
86 D3 **Nolinsk** Rus. Fed.
126 A2 **Nome** U.S.A.
123 C3 **Nomonde** S. Africa
123 D2 **Nondweni** S. Africa
Nonghui China see **Guang'an**
62 B2 **Nong Khai** Thai.
75 D2 **Nongstoin** India
52 A2 **Nonning** Austr.
144 B2 **Nonoava** Mex.
65 B2 **Nonsan** S. Korea
63 B2 **Nonthaburi** Thai.
122 B3 **Nonzwakazi** S. Africa
100 B1 **Noordwijk-Binnen** Neth.
77 C3 **Norak** Tajik.
130 C3 **Noranda** Can.
82 C1 **Nordaustlandet** *i.* Svalbard
128 C2 **Nordegg** Can.
100 C1 **Norden** Ger.
83 H1 **Nordenshel'da, Arkhipelag** *is* Rus. Fed.
Nordenskjold Archipelago *is* Rus. Fed. see **Nordenshel'da, Arkhipelag**
100 C1 **Norderney** Ger.
100 C1 **Norderney** *i.* Ger.
101 E1 **Norderstedt** Ger.
93 E3 **Nordfjordeid** Norway
Nordfriesische Inseln Ger. see **North Frisian Islands**
101 E2 **Nordhausen** Ger.
101 D1 **Nordholz** Ger.
100 C1 **Nordhorn** Ger.
Nordkapp Norway see **North Cape**
92 F3 **Nordli** Norway
102 C2 **Nördlingen** Ger.
92 G3 **Nordmaling** Sweden
94 B1 **Norðoyar** *i.* Faroe Is
97 C2 **Nore** *r.* Rep. of Ireland
88 B3 **Noreikiškės** Lith.
137 D2 **Norfolk** *NE* U.S.A.
139 D3 **Norfolk** *VA* U.S.A.
48 H6 **Norfolk Island** *terr.* S. Pacific Ocean
93 E3 **Norheimsund** Norway
82 G2 **Noril'sk** Rus. Fed.
75 C2 **Norkyung** China
143 D1 **Norman** U.S.A.
Normandes, Îles *is* English Chan. see **Channel Islands**
150 D2 **Normandia** Brazil
Normandie *reg.* France see **Normandy**
104 B2 **Normandy** *reg.* France
51 D1 **Normanton** Austr.
128 B1 **Norman Wells** Can.
93 G4 **Norrköping** Sweden
93 G4 **Norrtälje** Sweden
50 B3 **Norseman** Austr.
92 G3 **Norsjö** Sweden
55 M2 **North, Cape** Antarctica
98 C2 **Northallerton** U.K.
50 A3 **Northam** Austr.
50 A2 **Northampton** Austr.
99 C3 **Northampton** U.K.
73 D3 **North Andaman** *i.* India
159 F4 **North Australian Basin** *sea feature* Indian Ocean
129 D2 **North Battleford** Can.
130 C3 **North Bay** Can.
130 C2 **North Belcher Islands** Can.
96 C2 **North Berwick** U.K.
North Borneo *state* Malaysia see **Sabah**
92 I1 **North Cape** *c.* Norway
54 B1 **North Cape** N.Z.
130 A2 **North Caribou Lake** Can.
141 E1 **North Carolina** *state* U.S.A.
130 B3 **North Channel** *lake channel* Can.
96 A3 **North Channel** U.K.
141 E2 **North Charleston** U.S.A.
128 B3 **North Cowichan** Can.
136 C1 **North Dakota** *state* U.S.A.
99 C4 **North Downs** *hills* U.K.
157 E3 **Northeast Pacific Basin** *sea feature* N. Pacific Ocean
141 E3 **Northeast Providence Channel** Bahamas
101 D2 **Northeim** Ger.
122 A2 **Northern Cape** *prov.* S. Africa
Northern Dvina *r.* Rus. Fed. see **Severnaya Dvina**
129 E2 **Northern Indian Lake** Can.
97 C1 **Northern Ireland** *prov.* U.K.
59 D1 **Northern Mariana Islands** *terr.* N. Pacific Ocean
Northern Rhodesia *country* Africa see **Zambia**
50 C1 **Northern Territory** *admin. div.* Austr.
Northern Transvaal *prov.* S. Africa see **Limpopo**
96 C2 **North Esk** *r.* U.K.
137 E2 **Northfield** U.S.A.
99 D4 **North Foreland** *c.* U.K.
102 B1 **North Frisian Islands** *is* Ger.
54 B1 **North Island** N.Z.
129 E2 **North Knife Lake** Can.
65 B1 **North Korea** *country* Asia
72 D2 **North Lakhimpur** India
North Land *is* Rus. Fed. see **Severnaya Zemlya**
128 B1 **North Nahanni** *r.* Can.
136 C2 **North Platte** U.S.A.
136 C2 **North Platte** *r.* U.S.A.
96 C1 **North Ronaldsay** *i.* U.K.
129 D2 **North Saskatchewan** *r.* Can.
94 D2 **North Sea** Europe
63 A2 **North Sentinel Island** India
130 A2 **North Spirit Lake** Can.
53 D1 **North Stradbroke Island** Austr.
131 D3 **North Sydney** Can.
54 B1 **North Taranaki Bight** *b.* N.Z.
130 C2 **North Twin Island** Can.
98 B2 **North Tyne** *r.* U.K.
96 A2 **North Uist** *i.* U.K.
131 D3 **Northumberland Strait** Can.
99 D3 **North Walsham** U.K.
123 C2 **North West** *prov.* S. Africa
158 D1 **Northwest Atlantic Mid-Ocean Channel** *sea chan.* N. Atlantic Ocean
50 A2 **North West Cape** Austr.
156 D3 **Northwest Pacific Basin** *sea feature* N. Pacific Ocean
141 E3 **Northwest Providence Channel** Bahamas
131 E2 **North West River** Can.
128 B1 **Northwest Territories** *admin. div.* Can.
98 C2 **North York Moors** *moorland* U.K.
138 C3 **Norton** U.S.A.
121 C2 **Norton** Zimbabwe
Norton de Matos Angola see **Balombo**
126 B2 **Norton Sound** *sea chan.* U.S.A.
55 D2 **Norvegia, Cape** Antarctica
138 C2 **Norwalk** U.S.A.
93 F3 **Norway** *country* Europe
129 E2 **Norway House** Can.
160 L3 **Norwegian Basin** *sea feature* N. Atlantic Ocean
92 E2 **Norwegian Sea** N. Atlantic Ocean
99 D3 **Norwich** U.K.
139 E2 **Norwich** *CT* U.S.A.
139 D2 **Norwich** *NY* U.S.A.
66 D2 **Noshiro** Japan
91 C1 **Nosivka** Ukr.
122 B2 **Nosop** *watercourse* Africa
86 E2 **Nosovaya** Rus. Fed.
79 C2 **Noşratābād** Iran
121 □D2 **Nosy Bé** *i.* Madag.
121 □E2 **Nosy Boraha** *i.* Madag.
103 D1 **Noteć** *r.* Pol.
93 E4 **Notodden** Norway
67 C3 **Noto-hantō** *pen.* Japan
131 D3 **Notre Dame, Monts** *mts* Can.
131 E3 **Notre Dame Bay** Can.
130 C2 **Nottaway** *r.* Can.
99 C3 **Nottingham** U.K.
114 A2 **Nouâdhibou** Maur.
114 A3 **Nouakchott** Maur.
114 A3 **Nouâmghâr** Maur.
63 B2 **Nouei** Vietnam
48 H6 **Nouméa** New Caledonia
114 B3 **Nouna** Burkina
122 B3 **Noupoort** S. Africa
Nouveau-Comptoir Can. see **Wemindji**
Nouvelle Anvers Dem. Rep. Congo see **Makanza**
Nouvelles Hébrides *country* S. Pacific Ocean see **Vanuatu**
Nova Chaves Angola see **Muconda**
154 B2 **Nova Esperança** Brazil
Nova Freixa Moz. see **Cuamba**
155 D2 **Nova Friburgo** Brazil
109 C1 **Nova Gradiška** Croatia
154 C2 **Nova Granada** Brazil
155 D2 **Nova Iguaçu** Brazil
91 C2 **Nova Kakhovka** Ukr.
155 D1 **Nova Lima** Brazil
Nova Lisboa Angola see **Huambo**
154 B2 **Nova Londrina** Brazil
91 C2 **Nova Odesa** Ukr.
150 C2 **Nova Paraiso** Brazil
154 C1 **Nova Ponte** Brazil
108 A1 **Novara** Italy
151 E3 **Nova Remanso** Brazil
131 D3 **Nova Scotia** *prov.* Can.
155 D1 **Nova Venécia** Brazil
83 K1 **Novaya Sibir', Ostrov** *i.* Rus. Fed.
86 E1 **Novaya Zemlya** *is* Rus. Fed.
107 C2 **Novelda** Spain
103 D2 **Nové Zámky** Slovakia
Novgorod Rus. Fed. see **Velikiy Novgorod**
91 C1 **Novhorod-Sivers'kyy** Ukr.
110 B2 **Novi Iskŭr** Bulg.
66 D1 **Novikovo** Rus. Fed.
108 A2 **Novi Ligure** Italy
109 D2 **Novi Pazar** Serb. and Mont.
109 C1 **Novi Sad** Serb. and Mont.
Novoalekseyevka Kazakh. see **Khobda**
87 D3 **Novoanninskiy** Rus. Fed.
150 C3 **Novo Aripuanã** Brazil
91 D2 **Novoazovs'k** Ukr.
91 E2 **Novocherkassk** Rus. Fed.
89 D2 **Novodugino** Rus. Fed.
86 D2 **Novodvinsk** Rus. Fed.
Novoekonomicheskoye Ukr. see **Dymytrov**
152 C2 **Novo Hamburgo** Brazil
154 C2 **Novo Horizonte** Brazil
90 B1 **Novohrad-Volyns'kyy** Ukr.
Novokazalinsk Kazakh. see **Ayteke Bi**
91 E1 **Novokhopersk** Rus. Fed.
68 B1 **Novokuznetsk** Rus. Fed.
109 C1 **Novo Mesto** Slovenia
91 D3 **Novomikhaylovskiy** Rus. Fed.
89 E3 **Novomoskovsk** Rus. Fed.
91 D2 **Novomoskovs'k** Ukr.
91 C2 **Novomyrhorod** Ukr.
Novonikolayevsk Rus. Fed. see **Novosibirsk**
91 C2 **Novooleksiyivka** Ukr.

91 E2 **Novopokrovskaya** Rus. Fed.
91 D2 **Novopskov** Ukr.
Novo Redondo Angola *see* **Sumbe**
91 D3 **Novorossiysk** Rus. Fed.
88 C2 **Novorzhev** Rus. Fed.
87 E3 **Novosergiyevka** Rus. Fed.
91 D2 **Novoshakhtinsk** Rus. Fed.
82 G3 **Novosibirsk** Rus. Fed.
Novosibirskiye Ostrova *is* Rus. Fed. *see* **New Siberia Islands**
89 E3 **Novosil'** Rus. Fed.
89 D2 **Novosokol'niki** Rus. Fed.
91 C2 **Novotroyits'ke** Ukr.
91 C2 **Novoukrayinka** Ukr.
90 A1 **Novovolyns'k** Ukr.
89 E3 **Novovoronezh** Rus. Fed.
Novovoronezhskiy Rus. Fed. *see* Novovoronezh
89 D3 **Novozybkov** Rus. Fed.
103 D2 **Nový Jičín** Czech Rep.
86 E2 **Novyy Bor** Rus. Fed.
91 C2 **Novyy Buh** Ukr.
Novyy Donbass Ukr. *see* **Dymytrov**
Novyye Petushki Rus. Fed. *see* **Petushki**
Novyy Margelan Uzbek. *see* **Farg'ona**
89 E2 **Novyy Nekouz** Rus. Fed.
91 D1 **Novyy Oskol** Rus. Fed.
86 G2 **Novyy Port** Rus. Fed.
86 G2 **Novyy Urengoy** Rus. Fed.
69 E1 **Novyy Urgal** Rus. Fed.
Novyy Uzen' Kazakh. *see* **Zhanaozen**
103 D1 **Nowogard** Pol.
Noworadomsk Pol. *see* **Radomsko**
53 D2 **Nowra** Austr.
81 D2 **Now Shahr** Iran
74 B1 **Nowshera** Pak.
103 E2 **Nowy Sącz** Pol.
103 E2 **Nowy Targ** Pol.
82 G2 **Noyabr'sk** Rus. Fed.
105 C2 **Noyon** France
121 C2 **Nsanje** Malawi
121 B2 **Nsombo** Zambia
118 B3 **Ntandembele** Dem. Rep. Congo
123 C2 **Ntha** S. Africa
118 A2 **Ntoum** Gabon
119 D3 **Ntungamo** Uganda
Nuanetsi *r.* Zimbabwe *see* **Mwenezi**
79 C2 **Nu'aym** *reg.* Oman
116 B2 **Nubian Desert** Sudan
150 B4 **Nudo Coropuna** *mt.* Peru
143 D3 **Nueces** *r.* U.S.A.
129 E1 **Nueltin Lake** Can.
150 B2 **Nueva Loja** Ecuador
153 A4 **Nueva Lubecka** Arg.
145 B2 **Nueva Rosita** Mex.
144 B1 **Nuevo Casas Grandes** Mex.
144 B2 **Nuevo Ideal** Mex.
145 C2 **Nuevo Laredo** Mex.
117 C4 **Nugaal** *watercourse* Somalia
105 C2 **Nuits-St-Georges** France
Nu Jiang *r.* China/Myanmar *see* **Salween**
Nukha Azer. *see* **Şäki**
49 J6 **Nuku'alofa** Tonga
49 M4 **Nuku Hiva** *i.* Fr. Polynesia
48 G4 **Nukumanu Islands** P.N.G.
76 B2 **Nukus** Uzbek.
50 B2 **Nullagine** Austr.
50 C3 **Nullarbor** Austr.
50 B3 **Nullarbor Plain** Austr.
115 D4 **Numan** Nigeria
67 C3 **Numazu** Japan
51 C1 **Numbulwar** Austr.
93 E3 **Numedal** *val.* Norway
59 C3 **Numfoor** *i.* Indon.
53 C3 **Numurkah** Austr.
Nunap Isua *c.* Greenland *see* **Farewell, Cape**
127 G2 **Nunavik** *reg.* Can.
129 E1 **Nunavut** *admin. div.* Can.
99 C3 **Nuneaton** U.K.
127 G2 **Nunavik** *reg.* Can.
126 A3 **Nunivak Island** U.S.A.
106 B1 **Nuñomoral** Spain
108 A2 **Nuoro** *Sardinia* Italy
78 B2 **Nuqrah** Saudi Arabia
77 C1 **Nura** *r.* Kazakh.
101 E3 **Nuremberg** Ger.
52 A2 **Nuriootpa** Austr.
92 I3 **Nurmes** Fin.
Nürnberg Ger. *see* **Nuremberg**
53 C2 **Nurri, Mount** *hill* Austr.
62 A1 **Nu Shan** *mts* China
74 A2 **Nushki** Pak.
127 I2 **Nuuk** Greenland
127 I2 **Nuussuaq** Greenland
127 I2 **Nuussuaq** *pen.* Greenland
80 B3 **Nuwaybi' al Muzayyinah** Egypt
122 A3 **Nuwerus** S. Africa
122 B3 **Nuweveldberge** *mts* S. Africa
86 F2 **Nyagan'** Rus. Fed.
75 D1 **Nyainqêntanglha Feng** *mt.* China
75 D2 **Nyainqêntanglha Shan** *mts* China
Nyakh Rus. Fed. *see* **Nyagan'**
117 A3 **Nyala** Sudan
119 D4 **Nyamtumbo** Tanz.
Nyande Zimbabwe *see* **Masvingo**
86 D2 **Nyandoma** Rus. Fed.
118 B3 **Nyanga** Congo
118 B3 **Nyanga** *r.* Gabon
121 C2 **Nyanga** Zimbabwe
121 C1 **Nyasa, Lake** Africa
Nyasaland *country* Africa *see* **Malawi**
88 C3 **Nyasvizh** Belarus
62 A2 **Nyaunglebin** Myanmar
93 F4 **Nyborg** Denmark
92 I1 **Nyborg** Norway
93 G4 **Nybro** Sweden
Nyenchen Tanglha Range *mts* China *see* **Nyainqêntanglha Shan**
119 D3 **Nyeri** Kenya
75 C1 **Nyima** China
68 C3 **Nyingchi** China
103 E2 **Nyíregyháza** Hungary
93 F5 **Nykøbing** Denmark
93 G4 **Nyköping** Sweden
53 C2 **Nymagee** Austr.
93 G4 **Nynäshamn** Sweden
53 C2 **Nyngan** Austr.
88 B3 **Nyoman** *r.* Belarus/Lith.
105 D3 **Nyons** France
86 E2 **Nyrob** Rus. Fed.
103 D1 **Nysa** Pol.
134 C2 **Nyssa** U.S.A.
119 C3 **Nyunzu** Dem. Rep. Congo
83 I2 **Nyurba** Rus. Fed.
91 C2 **Nyzhni Sirohozy** Ukr.
91 C2 **Nyzhn'ohirs'kyy** Ukr.
118 B3 **Nzambi** Congo
119 D3 **Nzega** Tanz.
114 B4 **Nzérékoré** Guinea
120 A1 **N'zeto** Angola

O

136 C2 **Oahe, Lake** U.S.A.
49 L1 **O'ahu** *i.* U.S.A.
52 B2 **Oakbank** Austr.
140 B2 **Oakdale** U.S.A.
53 D1 **Oakey** Austr.
138 B3 **Oak Grove** U.S.A.
99 C3 **Oakham** U.K.
134 B1 **Oak Harbor** U.S.A.
138 C3 **Oak Hill** U.S.A.
135 B3 **Oakland** *CA* U.S.A.
139 D3 **Oakland** *MD* U.S.A.
138 B2 **Oak Lawn** U.S.A.
136 C3 **Oakley** U.S.A.
50 B2 **Oakover** *r.* Austr.
134 B2 **Oakridge** U.S.A.
141 D1 **Oak Ridge** U.S.A.
54 B3 **Oamaru** N.Z.
64 B2 **Oas** Phil.
145 C3 **Oaxaca** Mex.
86 F2 **Ob'** *r.* Rus. Fed.
Ob, Gulf of *sea chan.* Rus. Fed. *see* **Obskaya Guba**
88 C2 **Obal'** Belarus
118 B2 **Obala** Cameroon
96 B2 **Oban** U.K.
106 B1 **O Barco** Spain
Obbia Somalia *see* **Hobyo**
136 C3 **Oberlin** U.S.A.
53 C2 **Oberon** Austr.
101 F3 **Oberviechtach** Ger.
59 C3 **Obi** *i.* Indon.
151 D3 **Óbidos** Brazil
66 D2 **Obihiro** Japan
69 E1 **Obluch'ye** Rus. Fed.
89 E2 **Obninsk** Rus. Fed.
119 C2 **Obo** C.A.R.
117 C3 **Obock** Djibouti
103 D1 **Oborniki** Pol.
118 B3 **Obouya** Congo
89 E3 **Oboyan'** Rus. Fed.
86 D2 **Obozerskiy** Rus. Fed.
144 B2 **Obregón, Presa** *resr* Mex.
109 D2 **Obrenovac** Serb. and Mont.
134 B2 **O'Brien** U.S.A.
87 E3 **Obshchiy Syrt** *hills* Rus. Fed.
86 G2 **Obskaya Guba** *sea chan.* Rus. Fed.
114 B4 **Obuasi** Ghana
90 C1 **Obukhiv** Ukr.
86 D2 **Ob"yachevo** Rus. Fed.
141 D3 **Ocala** U.S.A.
144 B2 **Ocampo** Mex.
106 C2 **Ocaña** Spain
150 B2 **Occidental, Cordillera** *mts* Col.
150 B4 **Occidental, Cordillera** *mts* Peru
139 D3 **Ocean City** *MD* U.S.A.
139 E3 **Ocean City** *NJ* U.S.A.
128 B2 **Ocean Falls** Can.
135 C4 **Oceanside** U.S.A.
91 C2 **Ochakiv** Ukr.
86 E3 **Ocher** Rus. Fed.
101 E3 **Ochsenfurt** Ger.
110 B1 **Ocna Mureş** Romania
90 B2 **Ocniţa** Moldova
141 D2 **Oconee** *r.* U.S.A.
145 C3 **Ocosingo** Mex.
141 E1 **Ocracoke Island** U.S.A.
October Revolution Island Rus. Fed. *see* **Oktyabr'skoy Revolyutsii, Ostrov**
59 C3 **Ocussi** *enclave* East Timor
116 B2 **Oda, Jebel** *mt.* Sudan
66 D2 **Ōdate** Japan
67 C3 **Odawara** Japan
93 E3 **Odda** Norway
106 B2 **Odemira** Port.
111 C3 **Ödemiş** Turkey
93 F4 **Odense** Denmark
101 D3 **Odenwald** *reg.* Ger.
102 C1 **Oder** *r.* Ger.
102 C1 **Oderbucht** *b.* Ger.
90 C2 **Odesa** Ukr.
143 C2 **Odessa** U.S.A.
114 B4 **Odienné** Côte d'Ivoire
89 E3 **Odoyev** Rus. Fed.
103 D1 **Odra** *r.* Pol.
151 E3 **Oeiras** Brazil
101 D2 **Oelde** Ger.
136 C2 **Oelrichs** U.S.A.
101 F2 **Oelsnitz** Ger.
100 B1 **Oenkerk** Neth.
137 E3 **O'Fallon** U.S.A.
109 C2 **Ofanto** *r.* Italy
101 D2 **Offenbach am Main** Ger.
102 B2 **Offenburg** Ger.
66 C3 **Oga** Japan
117 C4 **Ogadēn** *reg.* Eth.
66 C3 **Oga-hantō** *pen.* Japan
67 C3 **Ōgaki** Japan
136 C2 **Ogallala** U.S.A.
Ogasawara-shotō Japan *see* **Bonin Islands**
115 C4 **Ogbomosho** Nigeria
134 D2 **Ogden** U.S.A.
139 D2 **Ogdensburg** U.S.A.
126 C2 **Ogilvie** *r.* Can.
126 C2 **Ogilvie Mountains** Can.
141 D2 **Oglethorpe, Mount** U.S.A.
130 B2 **Ogoki** *r.* Can.
130 B2 **Ogoki Reservoir** Can.
88 B2 **Ogre** Latvia
109 C1 **Ogulin** Croatia
81 D2 **Ogurchinskiy, Ostrov** *i.* Turkm.
115 C2 **Ohanet** Alg.
138 B3 **Ohio** *r.* U.S.A.
138 C2 **Ohio** *state* U.S.A.
101 E2 **Ohrdruf** Ger.
101 F2 **Ohře** *r.* Czech Rep.
111 B2 **Ohrid** Macedonia
151 D2 **Oiapoque** Brazil
139 D2 **Oil City** U.S.A.
100 A3 **Oise** *r.* France
67 B4 **Ōita** Japan
144 B2 **Ojinaga** Mex.
152 B2 **Ojos del Salado, Nevado** *mt.* Arg./Chile
89 F2 **Oka** *r.* Rus. Fed.
120 A3 **Okahandja** Namibia
120 A3 **Okakarara** Namibia
128 C3 **Okanagan Falls** Can.
128 C3 **Okanagan Lake** Can.
134 C1 **Okanogan** U.S.A.
134 C1 **Okanogan** *r.* U.S.A.
74 B1 **Okara** Pak.
120 B2 **Okavango** *r.* Botswana/Namibia
120 B2 **Okavango Delta** *swamp* Botswana
67 C3 **Okaya** Japan
67 B4 **Okayama** Japan
67 C4 **Okazaki** Japan
141 D3 **Okeechobee** U.S.A.
141 D3 **Okeechobee, Lake** U.S.A.
141 D2 **Okefenokee Swamp** U.S.A.
99 A4 **Okehampton** U.K.
115 C4 **Okene** Nigeria
101 E1 **Oker** *r.* Ger.
74 A2 **Okha** India
83 K3 **Okha** Rus. Fed.
75 C2 **Okhaldhunga** Nepal
83 K3 **Okhotka** *r.* Rus. Fed.
83 K3 **Okhotsk** Rus. Fed.
83 K3 **Okhotsk, Sea of** Japan/Rus. Fed.
Okhotskoye More *sea* Japan/Rus. Fed. *see* **Okhotsk, Sea of**
91 C1 **Okhtyrka** Ukr.
69 E3 **Okinawa** *i.* Japan
67 B3 **Oki-shotō** *is* Japan
143 D1 **Oklahoma** *state* U.S.A.
143 D1 **Oklahoma City** U.S.A.
143 D1 **Okmulgee** U.S.A.
Oknitsa Moldova *see* **Ocniţa**
78 A2 **Oko, Wadi** *watercourse* Sudan
118 B3 **Okondja** Gabon
128 C2 **Okotoks** Can.
89 D3 **Okovskiy Les** *for.* Rus. Fed.
118 B3 **Okoyo** Congo
92 H1 **Øksfjord** Norway
62 A2 **Oktwin** Myanmar
Oktyabr' Kazakh. *see* **Kandyagash**
Oktyabr'sk Kazakh. *see* **Kandyagash**
86 D2 **Oktyabr'skiy** Rus. Fed.
83 L3 **Oktyabr'skiy** Rus. Fed.
87 E3 **Oktyabr'skiy** Rus. Fed.
86 F2 **Oktyabr'skoye** Rus. Fed.
83 H1 **Oktyabr'skoy Revolyutsii, Ostrov** *i.* Rus. Fed.
89 D2 **Okulovka** Rus. Fed.
66 C2 **Okushiri-tō** *i.* Japan
92 □B2 **Ólafsfjörður** Iceland
92 □A3 **Ólafsvík** Iceland
88 B2 **Olaine** Latvia
93 G4 **Öland** *i.* Sweden
52 B2 **Olary** Austr.
136 B3 **Olathe** *CO* U.S.A.
137 E3 **Olathe** *KS* U.S.A.
153 B3 **Olavarría** Arg.
103 D1 **Oława** Pol.
108 A2 **Olbia** *Sardinia* Italy
126 C2 **Old Crow** Can.
101 D1 **Oldenburg** Ger.
102 C1 **Oldenburg in Holstein** Ger.
100 C1 **Oldenzaal** Neth.
98 B3 **Oldham** U.K.
97 B3 **Old Head of Kinsale** *hd* Rep. of Ireland
96 C2 **Oldmeldrum** U.K.
128 C2 **Olds** Can.
129 D2 **Old Wives Lake** Can.
139 D2 **Olean** U.S.A.
103 E1 **Olecko** Pol.
83 J2 **Olekminsk** Rus. Fed.
91 C2 **Oleksandrivka** Ukr.
Oleksandrivs'k Ukr. *see* **Zaporizhzhya**
91 C2 **Oleksandriya** Ukr.
86 C2 **Olenegorsk** Rus. Fed.
83 I2 **Olenek** Rus. Fed.
83 I2 **Olenek** *r.* Rus. Fed.
89 D2 **Olenino** Rus. Fed.
Olenivs'ki Kar"yery Ukr. *see* **Dokuchayevs'k**
Olenya Rus. Fed. *see* Olenegorsk
Oleshky Ukr. *see* **Tsyurupyns'k**
103 D1 **Olesno** Pol.
90 B1 **Olevs'k** Ukr.

106 B2 **Olhão** Port.
123 D1 **Olifants** *r.* Moz./S. Africa
122 A2 **Olifants** *watercourse* Namibia
123 D1 **Olifants** S. Africa
122 A3 **Olifants** *r.* S. Africa
122 B2 **Olifantshoek** S. Africa
154 C2 **Olímpia** Brazil
151 F3 **Olinda** Brazil
123 C1 **Oliphants Drift** S. Africa
107 C2 **Oliva** Spain
155 D2 **Oliveira** Brazil
Olivença Moz. *see* **Lupilichi**
106 B2 **Olivenza** Spain
140 B2 **Olla** U.S.A.
152 B2 **Ollagüe** Chile
77 C2 **Olmaliq** Uzbek.
106 C1 **Olmedo** Spain
105 D3 **Olmeto** *Corsica* France
150 B3 **Olmos** Peru
138 B3 **Olney** U.S.A.
103 D2 **Olomouc** Czech Rep.
86 C2 **Olonets** Rus. Fed.
64 B2 **Olongapo** Phil.
104 B3 **Oloron-Ste-Marie** France
107 D1 **Olot** Spain
69 D1 **Olovyannaya** Rus. Fed.
100 C2 **Olpe** Ger.
103 E1 **Olsztyn** Pol.
110 B2 **Olt** *r.* Romania
110 C2 **Oltenița** Romania
143 C2 **Olton** U.S.A.
81 C1 **Oltu** Turkey
Ol'viopol' Ukr. *see* **Pervomays'k**
111 B3 **Olympia** *tourist site* Greece
134 B1 **Olympia** U.S.A.
Olympus, Mount Greece *see* **Mount Olympus**
134 B1 **Olympus, Mount** U.S.A.
83 M2 **Olyutorskiy** Rus. Fed.
83 M3 **Olyutorskiy, Mys** *c.* Rus. Fed.
66 D2 **Ōma** Japan
97 C1 **Omagh** U.K.
137 D2 **Omaha** U.S.A.
79 C2 **Oman** *country* Asia
79 C2 **Oman, Gulf of** Asia
54 A2 **Omarama** N.Z.
120 A3 **Omaruru** Namibia
120 B2 **Omatako** *watercourse* Namibia
122 B2 **Omaweneno** Botswana
116 B3 **Omdurman** Sudan
53 C3 **Omeo** Austr.
145 C3 **Ometepec** Mex.
78 A3 **Om Hajēr** Eritrea
81 C2 **Omīdīyeh** Iran
128 B2 **Omineca Mountains** Can.
120 A3 **Omitara** Namibia
67 C3 **Ōmiya** Japan
100 C1 **Ommen** Neth.
83 L2 **Omolon** *r.* Rus. Fed.
100 B3 **Omont** France
82 F3 **Omsk** Rus. Fed.
83 L2 **Omsukchan** Rus. Fed.
110 C1 **Omu, Vârful** *mt.* Romania
67 A4 **Ōmura** Japan
138 A2 **Onalaska** U.S.A.
139 D3 **Onancock** U.S.A.
138 C1 **Onaping Lake** Can.
131 C3 **Onatchiway, Lac** *l.* Can.
63 A2 **Onbingwin** Myanmar
120 A2 **Oncócua** Angola
122 B3 **Onderstedorings** S. Africa
120 A2 **Ondjiva** Angola
69 D1 **Öndörhaan** Mongolia
122 B1 **One** Botswana
86 C2 **Onega** Rus. Fed.
86 C2 **Onega** *r.* Rus. Fed.
86 C2 **Onega, Lake** Rus. Fed.
128 B2 **100 Mile House** Can.
139 D2 **Oneida Lake** U.S.A.
137 D2 **O'Neill** U.S.A.
139 D2 **Oneonta** U.S.A.
110 C1 **Onești** Romania
Onezhskoye Ozero *l.* Rus. Fed. *see* **Onega, Lake**
122 B2 **Ongers** *watercourse* S. Africa
65 B2 **Ongjin** N. Korea
73 C3 **Ongole** India
121 □D3 **Onilahy** *r.* Madag.
115 C4 **Onitsha** Nigeria
120 A3 **Onjati Mountain** Namibia
67 C3 **Ōno** Japan
122 A2 **Onseepkans** S. Africa
50 A2 **Onslow** Austr.
141 E2 **Onslow Bay** U.S.A.
130 A2 **Ontario** *prov.* Can.
134 C2 **Ontario** U.S.A.
139 D2 **Ontario, Lake** Can./U.S.A.
107 C2 **Ontinyent** Spain
51 C2 **Oodnadatta** Austr.
Oostende Belgium *see* **Ostend**
100 B2 **Oosterhout** Neth.
100 A2 **Oosterschelde** *est.* Neth.
100 B1 **Oost-Vlieland** Neth.
128 B2 **Ootsa Lake** Can.
128 B2 **Ootsa Lake** *l.* Can.
118 C3 **Opala** Dem. Rep. Congo
130 C2 **Opataca, Lac** *l.* Can.
103 D2 **Opava** Czech Rep.
141 C2 **Opelika** U.S.A.
140 B2 **Opelousas** U.S.A.
117 A4 **Opienge** Dem. Rep. Congo
130 C2 **Opinaca, Réservoir** *resr* Can.
131 D2 **Opiscotéo, Lac** *l.* Can.
88 C2 **Opochka** Rus. Fed.
144 A2 **Opodepe** Mex.
103 D1 **Opole** Pol.
106 B1 **Oporto** Port.
54 C1 **Opotiki** N.Z.
93 E3 **Oppdal** Norway
134 C1 **Opportunity** U.S.A.
54 B1 **Opunake** N.Z.
120 A2 **Opuwo** Namibia
110 B1 **Oradea** Romania
109 D2 **Orahovac** Serb. and Mont.
114 B1 **Oran** Alg.
152 B2 **Orán** Arg.
65 B1 **Ŏrang** N. Korea
53 C2 **Orange** Austr.
105 C3 **Orange** France
122 A2 **Orange** *r.* Namibia/S. Africa
143 E2 **Orange** U.S.A.
141 D2 **Orangeburg** U.S.A.
Orange Free State *prov.* S. Africa *see* **Free State**
141 D2 **Orange Park** U.S.A.
138 C2 **Orangeville** Can.
145 D3 **Orange Walk** Belize
101 F1 **Oranienburg** Ger.
122 A2 **Oranjemund** Namibia
147 C3 **Oranjestad** Aruba
120 B3 **Orapa** Botswana
110 B1 **Orăștie** Romania
Orașul Stalin Romania *see* **Brașov**
108 B2 **Orbetello** Italy
53 C3 **Orbost** Austr.
141 D3 **Orchid Island** U.S.A.
111 B3 **Orchomenos** Greece
50 B1 **Ord, Mount** *hill* Austr.
106 B1 **Ordes** Spain
70 B2 **Ordos** China
80 B1 **Ordu** Turkey
Ordzhonikidze Rus. Fed. *see* **Vladikavkaz**
91 C2 **Ordzhonikidze** Ukr.
93 G4 **Örebro** Sweden
134 B2 **Oregon** *state* U.S.A.
134 B1 **Oregon City** U.S.A.
141 E1 **Oregon Inlet** U.S.A.
87 C3 **Orekhovo-Zuyevo** Rus. Fed.
89 E3 **Orel** Rus. Fed.
83 K3 **Orel', Ozero** *l.* Rus. Fed.
135 D2 **Orem** U.S.A.
111 C3 **Ören** Turkey
87 E3 **Orenburg** Rus. Fed.
54 A3 **Orepuki** N.Z.
111 C2 **Orestiada** Greece
93 F4 **Öresund** *str.* Denmark/Sweden
Oretana, Cordillera *mts* Spain *see* **Toledo, Montes de**
99 D3 **Orford Ness** *hd* U.K.
89 F2 **Orgtrud** Rus. Fed.
74 A1 **Orgūn** Afgh.
111 C3 **Orhaneli** Turkey
111 C2 **Orhangazi** Turkey
68 D1 **Orhon Gol** *r.* Mongolia
152 B1 **Oriental, Cordillera** *mts* Bol.
150 B2 **Oriental, Cordillera** *mts* Col.
150 B4 **Oriental, Cordillera** *mts* Peru
107 C2 **Orihuela** Spain
91 D2 **Orikhiv** Ukr.
130 C3 **Orillia** Can.
93 I3 **Orimattila** Fin.
150 C2 **Orinoco** *r.* Col./Venez.
150 C2 **Orinoco Delta** Venez.
75 C2 **Orissa** *state* India
88 B2 **Orissaare** Estonia
108 A3 **Oristano** *Sardinia* Italy
93 I3 **Orivesi** *l.* Fin.
151 D3 **Oriximiná** Brazil
145 C3 **Orizaba** Mex.
145 C3 **Orizaba, Pico de** *vol.* Mex.
154 C1 **Orizona** Brazil
92 E3 **Orkanger** Norway
93 F4 **Örkelljunga** Sweden
93 E3 **Orkla** *r.* Norway
96 C1 **Orkney Islands** U.K.
154 C2 **Orlândia** Brazil
141 D3 **Orlando** U.S.A.
104 C2 **Orléans** France
139 F2 **Orleans** U.S.A.
139 E1 **Orléans, Île d'** *i.* Can.
Orléansville Alg. *see* **Ech Chélif**
74 A2 **Ormara** Pak.
64 B2 **Ormoc** Phil.
141 D3 **Ormond Beach** U.S.A.
98 B3 **Ormskirk** U.K.
104 B2 **Orne** *r.* France
92 F2 **Ørnes** Norway
92 G3 **Örnsköldsvik** Sweden
114 B3 **Orodara** Burkina
134 C1 **Orofino** U.S.A.
139 F2 **Orono** U.S.A.
Oroqen Zizhiqi China *see* **Alihe**
64 B3 **Oroquieta** Phil.
108 A2 **Orosei** *Sardinia* Italy
108 A2 **Orosei, Golfo di** *b.* *Sardinia* Italy
103 E2 **Orosháza** Hungary
135 B3 **Oroville** U.S.A.
52 A2 **Orroroo** Austr.
93 F3 **Orsa** Sweden
89 D3 **Orsha** Belarus
87 E3 **Orsk** Rus. Fed.
110 B2 **Orșova** Romania
93 E3 **Ørsta** Norway
106 B1 **Ortegal, Cabo** *c.* Spain
104 B3 **Orthez** France
106 B1 **Ortigueira** Spain
108 B1 **Ortles** *mt.* Italy
108 B2 **Ortona** Italy
137 D1 **Ortonville** U.S.A.
83 J2 **Orulgan, Khrebet** *mts* Rus. Fed.
Orūmīyeh Iran *see* **Urmia**
Orūmīyeh, Daryācheh-ye *salt l.* Iran *see* **Urmia, Lake**
152 B1 **Oruro** Bol.
104 B2 **Orvault** France
108 B2 **Orvieto** Italy
93 F3 **Os** Norway
146 B4 **Osa, Península de** *pen.* Costa Rica
137 E3 **Osage** *r.* U.S.A.
137 D3 **Osage City** U.S.A.
67 C4 **Ōsaka** Japan
77 D1 **Osakarovka** Kazakh.
101 E1 **Oschersleben (Bode)** Ger.
108 A2 **Oschiri** *Sardinia* Italy
138 C2 **Oscoda** U.S.A.
89 E3 **Osetr** *r.* Rus. Fed.
139 D1 **Osgoode** Can.
77 D2 **Osh** Kyrg.
120 A2 **Oshakati** Namibia
130 C3 **Oshawa** Can.
120 A2 **Oshikango** Namibia
66 C2 **Ō-shima** *i.* Japan
67 C4 **Ō-shima** *i.* Japan
138 B2 **Oshkosh** U.S.A.
81 C2 **Oshnovīyeh** Iran
115 C4 **Oshogbo** Nigeria
118 B3 **Oshwe** Dem. Rep. Congo
109 C1 **Osijek** Croatia
128 B2 **Osilinka** *r.* Can.
108 B2 **Osimo** Italy
Osipenko Ukr. *see* **Berdyans'k**
123 D2 **Osizweni** S. Africa
137 E2 **Oskaloosa** U.S.A.
93 G4 **Oskarshamn** Sweden
89 E3 **Oskol** *r.* Rus. Fed.
93 F4 **Oslo** Norway
93 F4 **Oslofjorden** *sea chan.* Norway
80 B1 **Osmancık** Turkey
111 C2 **Osmaneli** Turkey
80 B2 **Osmaniye** Turkey
88 C2 **Os'mino** Rus. Fed.
101 D1 **Osnabrück** Ger.
153 A4 **Osorno** Chile
106 C1 **Osorno** Spain
128 C3 **Osoyoos** Can.
100 B2 **Oss** Neth.
51 D4 **Ossa, Mount** Austr.
83 L3 **Ossora** Rus. Fed.
89 D2 **Ostashkov** Rus. Fed.
101 D1 **Oste** *r.* Ger.
100 A2 **Ostend** Belgium
101 E1 **Osterburg (Altmark)** Ger.
93 F3 **Österdalälven** *l.* Sweden
101 D1 **Osterholz-Scharmbeck** Ger.
101 E2 **Osterode am Harz** Ger.
92 F3 **Östersund** Sweden
Ostfriesische Inseln *is* Ger. *see* **East Frisian Islands**
100 C1 **Ostfriesland** *reg.* Ger.
93 G3 **Östhammar** Sweden
103 D2 **Ostrava** Czech Rep.
103 D1 **Ostróda** Pol.
89 E3 **Ostrogozhsk** Rus. Fed.
90 B1 **Ostroh** Ukr.
103 E1 **Ostrołęka** Pol.
101 F2 **Ostrov** Czech Rep.
88 C2 **Ostrov** Rus. Fed.
Ostrovets Pol. *see* **Ostrowiec Świętokrzyski**
89 F2 **Ostrovskoye** Rus. Fed.
103 E1 **Ostrowiec Świętokrzyski** Pol.
103 E1 **Ostrów Mazowiecka** Pol.
Ostrowo Pol. *see* **Ostrów Wielkopolski**
103 D1 **Ostrów Wielkopolski** Pol.
109 C2 **Ostuni** Italy
110 B2 **Osŭm** *r.* Bulg.
67 B4 **Ōsumi-kaikyō** *sea chan.* Japan
67 B4 **Ōsumi-shotō** *is* Japan
106 B2 **Osuna** Spain
139 D2 **Oswego** U.S.A.
99 B3 **Oswestry** U.K.
67 C3 **Ōta** Japan
54 B3 **Otago Peninsula** N.Z.
54 C2 **Otaki** N.Z.
77 D2 **Otar** Kazakh.
66 D2 **Otaru** Japan
120 A2 **Otavi** Namibia
67 D3 **Ōtawara** Japan
92 G2 **Oteren** Norway
134 C1 **Othello** U.S.A.
120 A3 **Otjiwarongo** Namibia
109 C2 **Otočac** Croatia
Otog Qi China *see* **Ulan**
117 B3 **Otoro, Jebel** *mt.* Sudan
Otpor Rus. Fed. *see* **Zabaykal'sk**
93 E4 **Otra** *r.* Norway
109 C2 **Otranto, Strait of** Albania/Italy
67 C3 **Ōtsu** Japan
93 E3 **Otta** Norway
130 C3 **Ottawa** Can.
130 C3 **Ottawa** *r.* Can.
138 B2 **Ottawa** *IL* U.S.A.
137 D3 **Ottawa** *KS* U.S.A.
130 B2 **Ottawa Islands** Can.
98 B2 **Otterburn** U.K.
130 B2 **Otter Rapids** Can.
100 B2 **Ottignies** Belgium
137 E2 **Ottumwa** U.S.A.
150 B3 **Otuzco** Peru
52 B3 **Otway, Cape** Austr.
140 B2 **Ouachita** *r.* U.S.A.
140 B2 **Ouachita, Lake** U.S.A.
140 B2 **Ouachita Mountains** U.S.A.
118 C2 **Ouadda** C.A.R.
115 D3 **Ouaddaï** *reg.* Chad
114 B3 **Ouagadougou** Burkina
114 B3 **Ouahigouya** Burkina
114 B3 **Oualâta** Maur.
118 C2 **Ouanda-Djailé** C.A.R.
114 B2 **Ouarâne** *reg.* Maur.
115 C1 **Ouargla** Alg.
114 B1 **Ouarzazate** Morocco
100 A2 **Oudenaarde** Belgium
122 B3 **Oudtshoorn** S. Africa
107 C2 **Oued Tlélat** Alg.
114 B1 **Oued Zem** Morocco
104 A2 **Ouessant, Île d'** *i.* France
118 B2 **Ouesso** Congo
97 B2 **Oughterard** Rep. of Ireland
118 B2 **Ouham** *r.* C.A.R./Chad
114 B1 **Oujda** Morocco
92 H3 **Oulainen** Fin.
107 D2 **Ouled Farès** Alg.
92 I2 **Oulu** Fin.
92 I3 **Oulujärvi** *l.* Fin.
108 A1 **Oulx** Italy
115 E3 **Oum-Chalouba** Chad
115 D3 **Oum-Hadjer** Chad
115 E3 **Ounianga Kébir** Chad
100 B2 **Oupeye** Belgium
100 C3 **Our** *r.* Lux.

106 B1 Ourense Spain
154 C2 Ourinhos Brazil
155 D2 Ouro Preto Brazil
100 B2 Ourthe r. Belgium
98 C3 Ouse r. U.K.
Outaouais, Rivière des r. Can. see Ottawa
131 D3 Outardes r. Can.
131 D2 Outardes Quatre, Réservoir resr Can.
96 A2 Outer Hebrides is U.K.
Outer Mongolia country Asia see Mongolia
120 A3 Outjo Namibia
129 D2 Outlook Can.
92 I3 Outokumpu Fin.
52 B3 Ouyen Austr.
108 A2 Ovace, Punta d' mt. Corsica France
152 A3 Ovalle Chile
106 B1 Ovar Port.
92 H2 Överkalix Sweden
137 E3 Overland Park U.S.A.
135 D3 Overton U.S.A.
92 H2 Övertorneå Sweden
106 B1 Oviedo Spain
141 D3 Oviedo U.S.A.
88 B2 Ovišrags hd Latvia
93 E3 Øvre Årdal Norway
93 F3 Øvre Rendal Norway
90 B1 Ovruch Ukr.
118 B3 Owando Congo
67 C4 Owase Japan
143 D1 Owasso U.S.A.
137 E2 Owatonna U.S.A.
139 D2 Owego U.S.A.
138 B3 Owensboro U.S.A.
135 C3 Owens Lake U.S.A.
130 B3 Owen Sound Can.
51 D1 Owen Stanley Range mts P.N.G.
115 C4 Owerri Nigeria
115 C4 Owo Nigeria
138 C2 Owosso U.S.A.
134 C2 Owyhee U.S.A.
134 C2 Owyhee r. U.S.A.
129 D3 Oxbow Can.
54 B2 Oxford N.Z.
99 C4 Oxford U.K.
140 C2 Oxford U.S.A.
129 E2 Oxford Lake Can.
145 D2 Oxkutzcab Mex.
52 B2 Oxley Austr.
Ox Mountains hills Rep. of Ireland see Slieve Gamph
135 C4 Oxnard U.S.A.
67 C3 Oyama Japan
118 B2 Oyem Gabon
129 C2 Oyen Can.
105 D2 Oyonnax France
77 C2 Oyoqquduq Uzbek.
64 B3 Ozamiz Phil.
140 C2 Ozark AL U.S.A.
137 E3 Ozark MO U.S.A.
137 E3 Ozark Plateau U.S.A.
137 E3 Ozarks, Lake of the U.S.A.
83 L3 Ozernovskiy Rus. Fed.
88 B3 Ozersk Rus. Fed.
89 E3 Ozery Rus. Fed.
87 D3 Ozinki Rus. Fed.

P

127 I2 Paamiut Greenland
122 A3 Paarl S. Africa
103 D1 Pabianice Pol.
75 C2 Pabna Bangl.
88 C3 Pabradė Lith.
74 A2 Pab Range mts Pak.
150 B3 Pacasmayo Peru
142 B2 Pacheco Mex.
109 C3 Pachino Sicily Italy
145 C2 Pachuca Mex.
135 B3 Pacifica U.S.A.
157 E9 Pacific-Antarctic Ridge sea feature S. Pacific Ocean
156 Pacific Ocean
61 C2 Pacitan Indon.
52 B2 Packsaddle Austr.
103 D1 Paczków Pol.
60 B2 Padang Indon.
60 B1 Padang Endau Malaysia
60 B1 Padangpanjang Indon.
60 A1 Padangsidimpuan Indon.
101 D2 Paderborn Ger.
Padova Italy see Padua

143 D3 Padre Island U.S.A.
99 A4 Padstow U.K.
52 B3 Padthaway Austr.
108 B1 Padua Italy
138 B3 Paducah KY U.S.A.
143 C2 Paducah TX U.S.A.
65 B1 Paegam N. Korea
Paektu-san mt. China/N. Korea see Baotou Shan
65 A2 Paengnyŏng-do i. S. Korea
54 C1 Paeroa N.Z.
Pafos Cyprus see Paphos
109 C2 Pag Croatia
109 B2 Pag i. Croatia
64 B3 Pagadian Phil.
60 B2 Pagai Selatan i. Indon.
60 B2 Pagai Utara i. Indon.
59 D1 Pagan i. N. Mariana Is
61 C2 Pagatan Indon.
142 A1 Page U.S.A.
88 B2 Pagėgiai Lith.
153 E5 Paget, Mount S. Georgia
136 B3 Pagosa Springs U.S.A.
88 C2 Paide Estonia
99 B4 Paignton U.K.
93 I3 Päijänne l. Fin.
75 C2 Paikü Co l. China
60 B2 Painan Indon.
138 C2 Painesville U.S.A.
142 A1 Painted Desert U.S.A.
Paint Hills Can. see Wemindji
96 B3 Paisley U.K.
92 H2 Pajala Sweden
150 A3 Paján Ecuador
150 C2 Pakaraima Mountains mts Brazil
150 D2 Pakaraima Mountains mts Guyana
74 A2 Pakistan country Asia
62 A1 Pakokku Myanmar
88 B2 Pakruojis Lith.
103 D2 Paks Hungary
130 A2 Pakwash Lake Can.
62 B2 Pakxan Laos
63 B2 Pakxé Laos
115 D4 Pala Chad
60 B2 Palabuhanratu, Teluk b. Indon.
111 C3 Palaikastro Greece
111 B3 Palaiochora Greece
Palakkat India see Palghat
122 B1 Palamakoloi Botswana
107 D1 Palamós Spain
83 L3 Palana Rus. Fed.
64 B2 Palanan Phil.
61 C2 Palangkaraya Indon.
74 B2 Palanpur India
123 C1 Palapye Botswana
83 L2 Palatka Rus. Fed.
141 D3 Palatka U.S.A.
59 C2 Palau country N. Pacific Ocean
63 A2 Palaw Myanmar
64 A3 Palawan i. Phil.
64 A3 Palawan Passage str. Phil.
88 B2 Paldiski Estonia
89 F2 Palekh Rus. Fed.
60 B2 Palembang Indon.
106 C1 Palencia Spain
145 C3 Palenque Mex.
108 B3 Palermo Sicily Italy
143 D2 Palestine U.S.A.
62 A1 Paletwa Myanmar
73 B3 Palghat India
74 B2 Pali India
48 G4 Palikir Micronesia
109 C2 Palinuro, Capo c. Italy
111 B3 Paliouri, Akra pt Greece
100 B3 Paliseul Belgium
92 I3 Paljakka hill Fin.
88 C2 Palkino Rus. Fed.
73 B4 Palk Strait India/Sri Lanka
Palla Bianca mt. Austria/Italy see Weißkugel
54 C2 Palliser, Cape N.Z.
157 F7 Palliser, Îles is Fr. Polynesia
106 B2 Palma del Río Spain
107 D2 Palma de Mallorca Spain
154 B3 Palmas Brazil
151 E4 Palmas Tocantins Brazil
154 B3 Palmas, Campos de hills Brazil
114 B4 Palmas, Cape Liberia
141 D3 Palm Bay U.S.A.
135 C4 Palmdale U.S.A.
154 C3 Palmeira Brazil
151 E3 Palmeirais Brazil

126 C2 Palmer U.S.A.
55 A2 Palmer Land reg. Antarctica
49 K5 Palmerston atoll Cook Is
54 C2 Palmerston North N.Z.
109 C3 Palmi Italy
145 C2 Palmillas Mex.
150 B2 Palmira Col.
154 B2 Palmital Brazil
135 C4 Palm Springs U.S.A.
Palmyra Syria see Tadmur
49 K3 Palmyra Atoll N. Pacific Ocean
135 B3 Palo Alto U.S.A.
117 B3 Paloich Sudan
145 C3 Palomares Mex.
61 D2 Palopo Indon.
107 C2 Palos, Cabo de c. Spain
92 I3 Paltamo Fin.
61 C2 Palu Indon.
83 M2 Palyavaam r. Rus. Fed.
150 B3 Pamar Col.
121 C3 Pambarra Moz.
104 C3 Pamiers France
77 D3 Pamir mts Asia
141 E1 Pamlico Sound sea chan. U.S.A.
152 B1 Pampa Grande Bol.
153 B3 Pampas reg. Arg.
150 B2 Pamplona Col.
107 C1 Pamplona Spain
111 D2 Pamukova Turkey
60 B2 Panaitan i. Indon.
73 B3 Panaji India
146 B4 Panama country Central America
Panamá Panama see Panama City
Panamá, Golfo de Panama see Panama, Gulf of
146 C4 Panamá, Gulf of g. Panama
146 C4 Panama Canal canal Panama
146 C4 Panama City Panama
140 C2 Panama City U.S.A.
135 C3 Panamint Range mts U.S.A.
60 B1 Panarik Indon.
64 B2 Panay i. Phil.
109 D2 Pančevo Serb. and Mont.
64 B2 Pandan Phil.
64 B2 Pandan Phil.
75 C2 Pandaria India
73 B3 Pandharpur India
88 B2 Panevėžys Lith.
Panfilov Kazakh. see Zharkent
61 C2 Pangkalanbuun Indon.
60 A1 Pangkalansusu Indon.
60 B2 Pangkalpinang Indon.
61 D2 Pangkalsiang, Tanjung pt Indon.
127 H2 Pangnirtung Can.
86 G2 Pangody Rus. Fed.
89 F3 Panino Rus. Fed.
74 B2 Panipat India
74 A2 Panjgur Pak.
Panjim India see Panaji
118 A2 Pankshin Nigeria
65 C1 Pan Ling mts China
75 C2 Panna India
50 A2 Pannawonica Austr.
154 B2 Panorama Brazil
65 B1 Panshi China
152 C1 Pantanal reg. Brazil
145 C2 Pánuco Mex.
145 C2 Pánuco r. Mex.
71 A3 Panxian China
62 B1 Panzhihua China
109 C3 Paola Italy
118 B2 Paoua C.A.R.
63 B2 Paôy Pêt Cambodia
103 D2 Pápa Hungary
54 B1 Papakura N.Z.
145 C2 Papantla Mex.
96 □ Papa Stour i. U.K.
54 B1 Papatoetoe N.Z.
49 M5 Papeete Fr. Polynesia
100 C1 Papenburg Ger.
80 B2 Paphos Cyprus
137 D2 Papillion U.S.A.
59 D3 Papua reg. Indon.
59 D3 Papua, Gulf of P.N.G.
59 D3 Papua New Guinea country Oceania
89 F3 Pará r. Rus. Fed.
50 A2 Paraburdoo Austr.
154 C1 Paracatu Brazil
155 C1 Paracatu r. Brazil

52 A2 Parachilna Austr.
109 D2 Paraćin Serb. and Mont.
155 D1 Pará de Minas Brazil
151 D2 Paradise Guyana
135 B3 Paradise U.S.A.
140 B1 Paragould U.S.A.
151 D3 Paraguai r. Brazil
147 D3 Paraguaná, Península de pen. Venez.
152 C2 Paraguay r. Arg./Para.
152 C2 Paraguay country S. America
155 D2 Paraíba do Sul r. Brazil
154 B1 Paraíso Brazil
145 C3 Paraíso Mex.
114 C4 Parakou Benin
52 A2 Parakylia Austr.
151 D2 Paramaribo Suriname
83 L3 Paramushir, Ostrov i. Rus. Fed.
152 B3 Paraná Arg.
154 A3 Paraná r. S. America
154 C1 Paraná, Serra do hills Brazil
154 C3 Paranaguá Brazil
154 B1 Paranaíba Brazil
154 B2 Paranaíba r. Brazil
154 B2 Paranapanema r. Brazil
154 B2 Paranapiacaba, Serra mts Brazil
154 B2 Paranavaí Brazil
90 A2 Parângul Mare, Vârful mt. Romania
54 B2 Paraparaumu N.Z.
155 D2 Parati Brazil
52 A2 Paratoo Austr.
151 D3 Parauaquara, Serra hill Brazil
154 B1 Pauna Brazil
105 C2 Paray-le-Monial France
74 B2 Parbati r. India
74 B3 Parbhani India
101 E1 Parchim Ger.
103 E1 Parczew Pol.
155 E1 Pardo r. Brazil
154 B2 Pardo r. Brazil
154 C2 Pardo r. Brazil
103 D1 Pardubice Czech Rep.
152 C1 Parecis, Serra dos hills Brazil
130 C3 Parent Can.
130 C3 Parent, Lac l. Can.
61 C2 Parepare Indon.
89 D2 Parfino Rus. Fed.
111 B3 Parga Greece
109 C3 Parghelia Italy
147 D3 Paria, Gulf of Trin. and Tob./Venez.
150 C2 Parima, Serra mts Brazil
151 D3 Parintins Brazil
104 C2 Paris France
140 C1 Paris TN U.S.A.
143 D2 Paris TX U.S.A.
93 H3 Parkano Fin.
142 A2 Parker U.S.A.
138 C3 Parkersburg U.S.A.
53 C2 Parkes Austr.
138 A1 Park Falls U.S.A.
134 B1 Parkland U.S.A.
137 D1 Park Rapids U.S.A.
106 C1 Parla Spain
108 B2 Parma Italy
134 C2 Parma U.S.A.
151 E3 Parnaíba Brazil
151 E3 Parnaíba r. Brazil
111 B3 Parnassos mts Greece
54 B2 Parnassus N.Z.
111 B3 Parnon mts Greece
88 B2 Pärnu Estonia
65 B2 P'aro-ho l. S. Korea
52 B2 Paroo watercourse Austr.
76 C3 Paropamisus mts Afgh.
111 C3 Paros i. Greece
135 D3 Parowan U.S.A.
153 A3 Parral Chile
53 D2 Parramatta Austr.
144 B2 Parras Mex.
126 D2 Parry, Cape Can.
126 E1 Parry Islands Can.
130 B3 Parry Sound Can.
137 D3 Parsons U.S.A.
108 B3 Partanna Sicily Italy
101 D2 Partenstein Ger.
104 B2 Parthenay France
108 B3 Partinico Sicily Italy
66 B2 Partizansk Rus. Fed.
97 B2 Partry Mountains hills Rep. of Ireland
151 D1 Paru r. Brazil
131 E3 Pasadena Can.
135 C4 Pasadena CA U.S.A.

143 D3 **Pasadena** *TX* U.S.A.
62 A2 **Pasawng** Myanmar
140 C2 **Pascagoula** U.S.A.
110 C1 **Paşcani** Romania
134 C1 **Pasco** U.S.A.
155 E1 **Pascoal, Monte** *hill* Brazil
Pascua, Isla de *i.* S. Pacific Ocean *see* **Easter Island**
Pas de Calais *str.* France/U.K. *see* **Dover, Strait of**
102 C1 **Pasewalk** Ger.
129 D2 **Pasfield Lake** Can.
89 D1 **Pasha** Rus. Fed.
64 B2 **Pasig** Phil.
60 B1 **Pasir Putih** Malaysia
103 D1 **Pasłęk** Pol.
74 A2 **Pasni** Pak.
153 A4 **Paso Río Mayo** Arg.
135 B3 **Paso Robles** U.S.A.
97 B3 **Passage West** Rep. of Ireland
155 D2 **Passa Tempo** Brazil
102 C2 **Passau** Ger.
152 C2 **Passo Fundo** Brazil
155 C2 **Passos** Brazil
88 C2 **Pastavy** Belarus
150 B3 **Pastaza** *r.* Peru
150 B2 **Pasto** Col.
74 B1 **Pasu** Jammu and Kashmir
61 C2 **Pasuruan** Indon.
88 B2 **Pasvalys** Lith.
103 D2 **Pásztó** Hungary
153 A5 **Patagonia** *reg.* Arg.
75 C2 **Patan** Nepal
54 B1 **Patea** N.Z.
139 E2 **Paterson** U.S.A.
74 B1 **Pathankot** India
Pathein Myanmar *see* **Bassein**
136 B2 **Pathfinder Reservoir** U.S.A.
61 C2 **Pati** Indon.
74 B1 **Patiala** India
62 A1 **Patkai Bum** *mts* India/Myanmar
111 C3 **Patmos** *i.* Greece
75 C2 **Patna** India
81 C2 **Patnos** Turkey
154 B3 **Pato Branco** Brazil
152 C3 **Patos, Lagoa dos** *l.* Brazil
155 C1 **Patos de Minas** Brazil
152 B3 **Patquía** Arg.
Patra Greece *see* **Patras**
111 B3 **Patras** Greece
75 C2 **Patratu** India
154 C1 **Patrocínio** Brazil
63 B3 **Pattani** Thai.
63 B2 **Pattaya** Thai.
128 B2 **Pattullo, Mount** Can.
129 D2 **Patuanak** Can.
146 B3 **Patuca** *r.* Hond.
144 B3 **Pátzcuaro** Mex.
104 B3 **Pau** France
104 B2 **Pauillac** France
150 C3 **Pauini** Brazil
62 A1 **Pauk** Myanmar
126 D2 **Paulatuk** Can.
Paulis Dem. Rep. Congo *see* **Isiro**
151 E3 **Paulistana** Brazil
151 F3 **Paulo Afonso** Brazil
123 D2 **Paulpietersburg** S. Africa
143 D2 **Pauls Valley** U.S.A.
62 A2 **Paungde** Myanmar
155 D1 **Pavão** Brazil
108 A1 **Pavia** Italy
88 B2 **Pāvilosta** Latvia
110 C2 **Pavlikeni** Bulg.
77 D1 **Pavlodar** Kazakh.
91 D2 **Pavlohrad** Ukr.
91 E1 **Pavlovsk** Rus. Fed.
91 D2 **Pavlovskaya** Rus. Fed.
139 E2 **Pawtucket** U.S.A.
111 B3 **Paxoi** *i.* Greece
60 B2 **Payakumbuh** Indon.
134 C2 **Payette** U.S.A.
134 C2 **Payette** *r.* U.S.A.
86 F2 **Pay-Khoy, Khrebet** *hills* Rus. Fed.
Payne Can. *see* **Kangirsuk**
130 C2 **Payne, Lac** *l.* Can.
152 C3 **Paysandú** Uru.
81 C1 **Pazar** Turkey
110 B2 **Pazardzhik** Bulg.
111 C3 **Pazarköy** Turkey
108 B1 **Pazin** Croatia
63 A2 **Pe** Myanmar
128 C2 **Peace** *r.* Can.
128 C2 **Peace River** Can.
53 C2 **Peak Hill** *N.S.W.* Austr.
50 A2 **Peak Hill** *W.A.* Austr.
135 E3 **Peale, Mount** U.S.A.
140 C2 **Pearl** *r.* U.S.A.
71 B3 **Pearl River** *r.* China
143 D3 **Pearsall** U.S.A.
126 F1 **Peary Channel** Can.
121 C2 **Pebane** Moz.
109 D2 **Peć** Serb. and Mont.
155 D1 **Peçanha** Brazil
154 C3 **Peças, Ilha das** *i.* Brazil
92 J2 **Pechenga** Rus. Fed.
86 E2 **Pechora** Rus. Fed.
86 E2 **Pechora** *r.* Rus. Fed.
Pechora Sea Rus. Fed. *see* **Pechorskoye More**
86 E2 **Pechorskoye More** *sea* Rus. Fed.
88 C2 **Pechory** Rus. Fed.
142 B1 **Pecos** *NM* U.S.A.
143 C2 **Pecos** *TX* U.S.A.
143 C3 **Pecos** *r.* U.S.A.
103 D2 **Pécs** Hungary
142 B3 **Pedernales** Mex.
155 D1 **Pedra Azul** Brazil
154 C2 **Pedregulho** Brazil
151 E3 **Pedreiras** Brazil
73 C4 **Pedro, Point** Sri Lanka
151 E3 **Pedro Afonso** Brazil
152 B2 **Pedro de Valdivia** Chile
154 B1 **Pedro Gomes** Brazil
152 C2 **Pedro Juan Caballero** Para.
106 B1 **Pedroso** Port.
96 C3 **Peebles** U.K.
141 E2 **Pee Dee** *r.* U.S.A.
126 D2 **Peel** *r.* Can.
98 A2 **Peel** Isle of Man
128 C2 **Peerless Lake** Can.
54 B2 **Pegasus Bay** N.Z.
101 E3 **Pegnitz** Ger.
62 A2 **Pegu** Myanmar
62 A2 **Pegu Yoma** *mts* Myanmar
153 B3 **Pehuajó** Arg.
101 E1 **Peine** Ger.
88 C2 **Peipus, Lake** Estonia/Rus. Fed.
Peiraias Greece *see* **Piraeus**
154 B2 **Peixe** *r.* Brazil
155 C2 **Peixoto, Represa** *resr* Brazil
151 D4 **Peixoto de Azevedo** Brazil
123 C2 **Peka** Lesotho
60 B2 **Pekalongan** Indon.
60 B1 **Pekan** Malaysia
60 B1 **Pekanbaru** Indon.
Peking China *see* **Beijing**
130 B3 **Pelee Island** Can.
61 D2 **Peleng** *i.* Indon.
103 D2 **Pelhřimov** Czech Rep.
92 I2 **Pelkosenniemi** Fin.
122 A2 **Pella** S. Africa
137 E2 **Pella** U.S.A.
59 D3 **Pelleluhu Islands** P.N.G.
92 H2 **Pello** Fin.
128 A1 **Pelly** *r.* Can.
Pelly Bay Can. *see* **Kugaaruk**
128 A1 **Pelly Mountains** Can.
152 C3 **Pelotas** Brazil
152 C2 **Pelotas, Rio das** *r.* Brazil
139 F1 **Pemadumcook Lake** U.S.A.
60 B1 **Pemangkat** Indon.
60 A1 **Pematangsiantar** Indon.
121 D2 **Pemba** Moz.
120 B2 **Pemba** Zambia
119 D3 **Pemba Island** Tanz.
128 B2 **Pemberton** Can.
137 D1 **Pembina** *r.* Can.
137 D1 **Pembina** *r.* U.S.A.
130 C3 **Pembroke** Can.
99 A4 **Pembroke** U.K.
141 D3 **Pembroke Pines** U.S.A.
106 C1 **Peñalara** *mt.* Spain
154 B2 **Penápolis** Brazil
106 B1 **Peñaranda de Bracamonte** Spain
107 C1 **Peñarroya** *mt.* Spain
106 B2 **Peñarroya-Pueblonuevo** Spain
106 B1 **Peñas, Cabo de** *c.* Spain
153 A4 **Penas, Golfo de** *g.* Chile
106 B1 **Peña Ubiña** *mt.* Spain
111 C2 **Pendik** Turkey
134 C1 **Pendleton** U.S.A.
128 B2 **Pendleton Bay** Can.
134 C1 **Pend Oreille Lake** U.S.A.
Penfro U.K. *see* **Pembroke**
74 B3 **Penganga** *r.* India
118 C3 **Penge** Dem. Rep. Congo
123 D1 **Penge** S. Africa
70 C2 **Penglai** China
71 A3 **Pengshui** China
106 B2 **Peniche** Port.
96 C3 **Penicuik** U.K.
60 B1 **Peninsular Malaysia** *pen.* Malaysia
108 B2 **Penne** Italy
52 A3 **Penneshaw** Austr.
98 B2 **Pennines** *hills* U.K.
139 D2 **Pennsylvania** *state* U.S.A.
127 H2 **Penny Icecap** Can.
89 D2 **Peno** Rus. Fed.
139 F2 **Penobscot** *r.* U.S.A.
52 B3 **Penola** Austr.
50 C3 **Penong** Austr.
157 E6 **Penrhyn Basin** *sea feature* S. Pacific Ocean
53 D2 **Penrith** Austr.
98 B2 **Penrith** U.K.
140 C2 **Pensacola** U.S.A.
55 B1 **Pensacola Mountains** Antarctica
61 C1 **Pensiangan** *Sabah* Malaysia
128 C3 **Penticton** Can.
96 C1 **Pentland Firth** *sea chan.* U.K.
99 B3 **Penygadair** *hill* U.K.
87 D3 **Penza** Rus. Fed.
99 A4 **Penzance** U.K.
83 L2 **Penzhinskaya Guba** *b.* Rus. Fed.
142 A2 **Peoria** *AZ* U.S.A.
138 B2 **Peoria** *IL* U.S.A.
107 C1 **Perales del Alfambra** Spain
111 B3 **Perama** Greece
131 D3 **Percé** Can.
50 B2 **Percival Lakes** *salt flat* Austr.
51 E2 **Percy Isles** Austr.
107 D1 **Perdido, Monte** *mt.* Spain
154 C1 **Perdizes** Brazil
86 F2 **Peregrebnoye** Rus. Fed.
150 B2 **Pereira** Col.
154 B2 **Pereira Barreto** Brazil
Pereira de Eça Angola *see* **Ondjiva**
90 A2 **Peremyshlyany** Ukr.
89 E2 **Pereslavl'-Zalesskiy** Rus. Fed.
91 C1 **Pereyaslav-Khmel'nyts'kyy** Ukr.
153 B3 **Pergamino** Arg.
92 H3 **Perhonjoki** *r.* Fin.
131 C2 **Péribonka, Lac** *l.* Can.
152 B2 **Perico** Arg.
144 B2 **Pericos** Mex.
104 C2 **Périgueux** France
150 B2 **Perija, Sierra de** *mts* Venez.
111 B3 **Peristerio** Greece
153 A4 **Perito Moreno** Arg.
101 E1 **Perleberg** Ger.
86 E3 **Perm'** Rus. Fed.
109 D2 **Përmet** Albania
Pernambuco Brazil *see* **Recife**
52 A2 **Pernatty Lagoon** *salt flat* Austr.
110 B2 **Pernik** Bulg.
Pernov Estonia *see* **Pärnu**
105 C2 **Péronne** France
145 C3 **Perote** Mex.
105 C3 **Perpignan** France
99 A4 **Perranporth** U.K.
Perrégaux Alg. *see* **Mohammadia**
141 D2 **Perry** *FL* U.S.A.
141 D2 **Perry** *GA* U.S.A.
137 E2 **Perry** *IA* U.S.A.
143 D1 **Perry** *OK* U.S.A.
138 C2 **Perrysburg** U.S.A.
143 C1 **Perryton** U.S.A.
137 F3 **Perryville** U.S.A.
Pershnotravnevoye Ukr. *see* **Pershotravens'k**
99 B3 **Pershore** U.K.
91 D2 **Pershotravens'k** Ukr.
Persia *country* Asia *see* **Iran**
Persian Gulf Asia *see* **The Gulf**
50 A3 **Perth** Austr.
96 C2 **Perth** U.K.
159 F5 **Perth Basin** *sea feature* Indian Ocean
86 C2 **Pertominsk** Rus. Fed.
105 D3 **Pertuis** France
108 A2 **Pertusato, Capo** *c.* *Corsica* France
150 B3 **Peru** *country* S. America
138 B2 **Peru** U.S.A.
157 H6 **Peru Basin** *sea feature* S. Pacific Ocean
157 H7 **Peru-Chile Trench** *sea feature* S. Pacific Ocean
108 B2 **Perugia** Italy
154 C2 **Peruíbe** Brazil
100 A2 **Péruwelz** Belgium
90 C2 **Pervomays'k** Ukr.
91 C2 **Pervomays'ke** Ukr.
Pervomayskiy Rus. Fed. *see* **Novodvinsk**
89 F3 **Pervomayskiy** Rus. Fed.
91 D2 **Pervomays'kyy** Ukr.
108 B2 **Pesaro** Italy
108 B2 **Pescara** Italy
108 B2 **Pescara** *r.* Italy
74 B1 **Peshawar** Pak.
109 D2 **Peshkopi** Albania
109 C1 **Pesnica** Slovenia
104 B3 **Pessac** France
89 E2 **Pestovo** Rus. Fed.
140 C2 **Petal** U.S.A.
100 B3 **Pétange** Lux.
147 D3 **Petare** Venez.
144 B3 **Petatlán** Mex.
121 C2 **Petauke** Zambia
130 C3 **Petawawa** Can.
138 B2 **Petenwell Lake** U.S.A.
52 A2 **Peterborough** Austr.
130 C3 **Peterborough** Can.
99 C3 **Peterborough** U.K.
96 D2 **Peterhead** U.K.
55 R3 **Peter I Island** Antarctica
129 E1 **Peter Lake** Can.
50 B2 **Petermann Ranges** *mts* Austr.
129 D2 **Peter Pond Lake** Can.
128 A2 **Petersburg** *AK* U.S.A.
139 D3 **Petersburg** *VA* U.S.A.
101 D1 **Petershagen** Ger.
Peter the Great Bay Rus. Fed. *see* **Petra Velikogo, Zaliv**
Petitjean Morocco *see* **Sidi Kacem**
131 D2 **Petit Lac Manicouagan** *l.* Can.
131 E2 **Petit Mécatina** *r.* Can.
145 D2 **Peto** Mex.
138 C1 **Petoskey** U.S.A.
80 B2 **Petra** *tourist site* Jordan
66 B2 **Petra Velikogo, Zaliv** *b.* Rus. Fed.
111 B2 **Petrich** Bulg.
Petroaleksandrovsk Uzbek. *see* **To'rtko'l**
88 C2 **Petrodvorets** Rus. Fed.
Petrokov Pol. *see* **Piotrków Trybunalski**
151 E3 **Petrolina** Brazil
77 C1 **Petropavlovsk** Kazakh.
83 L3 **Petropavlovsk-Kamchatskiy** Rus. Fed.
110 B1 **Petroşani** Romania
Petrovskoye Rus. Fed. *see* **Svetlograd**
89 F3 **Petrovskoye** Rus. Fed.
89 E2 **Petrovskoye** Rus. Fed.
69 D1 **Petrovsk-Zabaykal'skiy** Rus. Fed.
86 C2 **Petrozavodsk** Rus. Fed.
123 C2 **Petrusburg** S. Africa
123 C2 **Petrus Steyn** S. Africa
122 B3 **Petrusville** S. Africa
Petsamo Rus. Fed. *see* **Pechenga**
87 F3 **Petukhovo** Rus. Fed.
89 E2 **Petushki** Rus. Fed.
60 A1 **Peureula** Indon.
83 M2 **Pevek** Rus. Fed.
102 B2 **Pforzheim** Ger.
102 C2 **Pfunds** Austria
101 D3 **Pfungstadt** Ger.
123 C2 **Phahameng** *Free State* S. Africa
123 C1 **Phahameng** *Limpopo* S. Africa
123 D1 **Phalaborwa** S. Africa
74 B2 **Phalodi** India
63 A3 **Phangnga** Thai.
63 B2 **Phan Rang** Vietnam
63 B2 **Phan Thiêt** Vietnam
63 B3 **Phatthalung** Thai.
62 A2 **Phayao** Thai.
129 D2 **Phelps Lake** Can.

141 C2 **Phenix City** U.S.A.
63 A2 **Phet Buri** Thai.
63 B2 **Phetchabun** Thai.
63 B2 **Phichit** Thai.
139 D3 **Philadelphia** U.S.A.
136 C2 **Philip** U.S.A.
 Philip Atoll Micronesia see
  Sorol
 Philippeville Alg. see
  Skikda
100 B2 **Philippeville** Belgium
51 C2 **Philippi, Lake** salt flat
  Austr.
100 A2 **Philippine** Neth.
156 C4 **Philippine Basin**
  sea feature
  N. Pacific Ocean
64 B2 **Philippines** country Asia
64 B2 **Philippine Sea**
  N. Pacific Ocean
126 C2 **Philip Smith Mountains**
  U.S.A.
122 B3 **Philipstown** S. Africa
53 C3 **Phillip Island** Austr.
137 D3 **Phillipsburg** U.S.A.
63 B2 **Phimun Mangsahan** Thai.
123 C2 **Phiritona** S. Africa
63 B2 **Phitsanulok** Thai.
63 B2 **Phnom Penh** Cambodia
 Phnum Pénh Cambodia
 see Phnom Penh
142 A2 **Phoenix** U.S.A.
49 J4 **Phoenix Islands** Kiribati
63 B2 **Phon** Thai.
62 B2 **Phong Nha** Vietnam
62 B1 **Phôngsali** Laos
62 B1 **Phong Thô** Vietnam
62 B2 **Phrae** Thai.
 Phu Cuong Vietnam see
  Thu Dâu Môt
120 B3 **Phuduhudu** Botswana
63 A3 **Phuket** Thai.
63 B2 **Phumí Kâmpóng Trâlach**
  Cambodia
63 B2 **Phumí Sâmraông**
  Cambodia
63 B2 **Phu Nhon** Vietnam
63 B2 **Phu Quôc, Dao** i. Vietnam
123 C2 **Phuthaditjhaba** S. Africa
 Phu Vinh Vietnam see
  Tra Vinh
62 A2 **Phyu** Myanmar
108 A1 **Piacenza** Italy
108 B2 **Pianosa, Isola** i. Italy
110 C1 **Piatra Neamt** Romania
151 E3 **Piauí** r. Brazil
108 B1 **Piave** r. Italy
117 B4 **Pibor** r. Sudan
117 B4 **Pibor Post** Sudan
 Picardie reg. France see
  Picardy
104 C2 **Picardy** reg. France
140 C2 **Picayune** U.S.A.
152 B2 **Pichanal** Arg.
144 A2 **Pichilingue** Mex.
98 C2 **Pickering** U.K.
130 A2 **Pickle Lake** Can.
151 E3 **Picos** Brazil
153 B4 **Pico Truncado** Arg.
53 D2 **Picton** Austr.
54 B2 **Picton** N.Z.
73 C4 **Pidurutalagala** mt.
  Sri Lanka
154 C2 **Piedade** Brazil
145 C3 **Piedras Negras** Guat.
145 B2 **Piedras Negras** Mex.
150 C4 **Piedras, Rio de las** r. Peru
93 I3 **Pieksämäki** Fin.
92 I3 **Pielinen** l. Fin.
136 C2 **Pierre** U.S.A.
105 C3 **Pierrelatte** France
123 D2 **Pietermaritzburg** S. Africa
 Pietersaari Fin. see
  Jakobstad
123 D2 **Pietersburg** S. Africa see
  Polokwane
123 D2 **Piet Retief** S. Africa
110 B1 **Pietrosa** mt. Romania
110 C1 **Pietrosu, Vârful** mt.
  Romania
128 C2 **Pigeon Lake** Can.
137 F1 **Pigeon River** U.S.A.
153 B3 **Pigüé** Arg.
93 I3 **Pihlajavesi** l. Fin.
92 I3 **Pihtipudas** Fin.
145 C3 **Pijijiapan** Mex.
89 D2 **Pikalevo** Rus. Fed.
130 A2 **Pikangikum** Can.
136 C3 **Pikes Peak** U.S.A.
122 A3 **Piketberg** S. Africa
138 C3 **Pikeville** U.S.A.

103 D1 **Piła** Pol.
153 C3 **Pilar** Arg.
152 C2 **Pilar** Para.
75 B2 **Pilibhit** India
53 C2 **Pilliga** Austr.
154 C1 **Pilões, Serra dos** mts
  Brazil
150 C4 **Pimenta Bueno** Brazil
88 C3 **Pina** r. Belarus
153 C3 **Pinamar** Arg.
60 B1 **Pinang** i. Malaysia
80 B2 **Pınarbaşı** Turkey
146 B2 **Pinar del Río** Cuba
64 B2 **Pinatubo, Mount** vol.
  Phil.
103 E1 **Pińczów** Pol.
151 E3 **Pindaré** r. Brazil
 Pindos Greece see
  Pindus Mountains
111 B2 **Pindus Mountains** mts
  Greece
140 B2 **Pine Bluff** U.S.A.
136 C2 **Pine Bluffs** U.S.A.
50 C1 **Pine Creek** Austr.
136 B2 **Pinedale** U.S.A.
86 D2 **Pinega** Rus. Fed.
129 D2 **Pinehouse Lake** Can.
111 B3 **Pineios** r. Greece
141 D3 **Pine Islands** FL U.S.A.
141 D4 **Pine Islands** FL U.S.A.
128 C1 **Pine Point** Can.
136 C2 **Pine Ridge** U.S.A.
108 A2 **Pinerolo** Italy
 Pines, Isle of i. Cuba see
  Juventud, Isla de la
123 D2 **Pinetown** S. Africa
140 B2 **Pineville** U.S.A.
70 B2 **Pingdingshan** China
70 B2 **Pingdu** China
62 B1 **Pingguo** China
71 B3 **Pingjiang** China
70 A2 **Pingliang** China
70 B1 **Pingquan** China
71 C3 **P'ingtung** Taiwan
 Pingxi China see Yuping
71 A3 **Pingxiang** Guangxi China
71 B3 **Pingxiang** Jiangxi China
70 B2 **Pingyin** China
155 C2 **Pinhal** Brazil
151 E3 **Pinheiro** Brazil
52 B3 **Pinnaroo** Austr.
101 D1 **Pinneberg** Ger.
 Pinos, Isla de i. Cuba see
  Juventud, Isla de la
145 C3 **Pinotepa Nacional** Mex.
48 H6 **Pins, Île des** i.
  New Caledonia
88 C3 **Pinsk** Belarus
152 B2 **Pinto** Arg.
135 D3 **Pioche** U.S.A.
119 C3 **Piodi** Dem. Rep. Congo
108 B2 **Piombino** Italy
86 F2 **Pionerskiy** Rus. Fed.
103 E1 **Pionki** Pol.
103 D1 **Piotrków Trybunalski** Pol.
137 D2 **Pipestone** U.S.A.
131 C3 **Pipmuacan, Réservoir**
  resr Can.
154 B2 **Piquiri** r. Brazil
154 C1 **Piracanjuba** Brazil
154 C2 **Piracicaba** Brazil
155 D1 **Piracicaba** r. Brazil
154 C2 **Piraçununga** Brazil
111 B3 **Piraeus** Greece
154 B2 **Piraí do Sul** Brazil
154 C2 **Piraju** Brazil
154 C2 **Pirajuí** Brazil
154 B1 **Piranhas** Brazil
151 F3 **Piranhas** r. Brazil
155 D1 **Pirapora** Brazil
154 C1 **Pirenópolis** Brazil
154 C1 **Pires do Rio** Brazil
 Pyrenees mts Europe see
  Pyrenees
151 E3 **Piripiri** Brazil
109 D2 **Pirot** Serb. and Mont.
59 C3 **Piru** Indon.
108 B2 **Pisa** Italy
152 A1 **Pisagua** Chile
150 B4 **Pisco** Peru
102 C2 **Písek** Czech Rep.
79 D2 **Pīshīn** Iran
74 A1 **Pishin** Pak.
145 D2 **Pisté** Mex.
109 C2 **Pisticci** Italy
108 B2 **Pistoia** Italy
106 C1 **Pisuerga** r. Spain
134 B2 **Pit** r. U.S.A.
114 A3 **Pita** Guinea
154 B2 **Pitanga** Brazil
155 D1 **Pitangui** Brazil

49 O6 **Pitcairn Island**
  S. Pacific Ocean
49 O6 **Pitcairn Islands** terr.
  S. Pacific Ocean
92 H2 **Piteå** Sweden
92 H2 **Piteälven** r. Sweden
110 B2 **Pitești** Romania
75 C2 **Pithoragarh** India
142 A2 **Pitiquito** Mex.
86 C2 **Pitkyaranta** Rus. Fed.
96 C2 **Pitlochry** U.K.
128 B2 **Pitt Island** Can.
137 E3 **Pittsburg** U.S.A.
138 D2 **Pittsburgh** U.S.A.
139 E2 **Pittsfield** U.S.A.
53 D1 **Pittsworth** Austr.
155 C2 **Piumhi** Brazil
150 A3 **Piura** Peru
90 C2 **Pivdennyy Buh** r. Ukr.
131 E3 **Placentia** Can.
135 B3 **Placerville** U.S.A.
146 C2 **Placetas** Cuba
143 C2 **Plains** U.S.A.
143 C2 **Plainview** U.S.A.
60 B2 **Plaju** Indon.
61 C2 **Plampang** Indon.
154 C1 **Planaltina** Brazil
137 D2 **Plankinton** U.S.A.
143 D2 **Plano** U.S.A.
154 C2 **Planura** Brazil
140 B2 **Plaquemine** U.S.A.
106 B1 **Plasencia** Spain
109 C1 **Plaški** Croatia
147 C4 **Plato** Col.
137 D2 **Platte** r. U.S.A.
138 A2 **Platteville** U.S.A.
139 E2 **Plattsburgh** U.S.A.
101 F1 **Plau** Ger.
101 F2 **Plauen** Ger.
101 F1 **Plauer See** l. Ger.
89 E3 **Plavsk** Rus. Fed.
106 B2 **Playa de Castilla**
  coastal area Spain
63 B2 **Plây Cu** Vietnam
129 E2 **Playgreen Lake** Can.
153 B3 **Plaza Huincul** Arg.
143 D3 **Pleasanton** U.S.A.
54 B2 **Pleasant Point** N.Z.
138 B3 **Pleasure Ridge Park**
  U.S.A.
104 C2 **Pleaux** France
130 B2 **Pledger Lake** Can.
54 C1 **Plenty, Bay of** g. N.Z.
136 C1 **Plentywood** U.S.A.
86 D2 **Plesetsk** Rus. Fed.
131 C2 **Plétipi, Lac** l. Can.
100 C2 **Plettenberg** Ger.
122 B3 **Plettenberg Bay** S. Africa
110 B2 **Pleven** Bulg.
 Plevna Bulg. see Pleven
109 C2 **Pljevlja** Serb. and Mont.
108 A2 **Ploaghe** Sardinia Italy
109 C2 **Ploče** Croatia
103 D1 **Płock** Pol.
109 C2 **Pločno** mt. Bos.-Herz.
104 B2 **Ploemeur** France
 Ploeşti Romania see
  Ploieşti
110 C2 **Ploieşti** Romania
89 F2 **Ploskoye** Rus. Fed.
104 B2 **Plouzané** France
110 B2 **Plovdiv** Bulg.
 Plozk Pol. see Płock
121 B3 **Plumtree** Zimbabwe
88 B2 **Plungė** Lith.
144 B2 **Plutarco Elías Calles,**
  Presa resr Mex.
88 C3 **Plyeshchanitsy** Belarus
147 D3 **Plymouth** Montserrat
99 A4 **Plymouth** U.K.
138 B2 **Plymouth** U.S.A.
99 B3 **Plynlimon** hill U.K.
88 C2 **Plyussa** Rus. Fed.
102 C2 **Plzeň** Czech Rep.
114 B3 **Pô** Burkina
108 B1 **Po** r. Italy
61 C1 **Po, Tanjung** pt Malaysia
77 E2 **Pobeda Peak** China/Kyrg.
 Pobedy, Pik mt.
  China/Kyrg. see
  Pobeda Peak
140 B1 **Pocahontas** U.S.A.
134 D2 **Pocatello** U.S.A.
90 B1 **Pochayiv** Ukr.
89 D3 **Pochep** Rus. Fed.
89 D3 **Pochinok** Rus. Fed.
145 C3 **Pochutla** Mex.
139 D3 **Pocomoke City** U.S.A.
154 C2 **Poços de Caldas** Brazil
89 D2 **Poddor'ye** Rus. Fed.
91 D1 **Podgorenskiy** Rus. Fed.

109 C2 **Podgorica** Serb. and Mont.
82 G3 **Podgornoye** Rus. Fed.
83 H2 **Podkamennaya Tunguska**
  r. Rus. Fed.
89 E2 **Podol'sk** Rus. Fed.
109 D2 **Podujevo** Serb. and Mont.
122 A2 **Pofadder** S. Africa
89 D3 **Pogar** Rus. Fed.
105 E3 **Poggibonsi** Italy
109 D2 **Pogradec** Albania
66 B2 **Pogranichnyy** Rus. Fed.
 Po Hai g. China see
  Bo Hai
65 B2 **P'ohang** S. Korea
48 G3 **Pohnpei** atoll Micronesia
90 B2 **Pohrebyshche** Ukr.
110 B2 **Poiana Mare** Romania
118 C3 **Poie** Dem. Rep. Congo
118 B3 **Pointe-Noire** Congo
160 B3 **Point Hope** U.S.A.
128 C1 **Point Lake** Can.
138 C3 **Point Pleasant** U.S.A.
104 C2 **Poitiers** France
104 C2 **Poitou, Plaines et Seuil**
  du plain France
74 B2 **Pokaran** India
53 C1 **Pokataroo** Austr.
75 C2 **Pokhara** Nepal
119 C2 **Poko** Dem. Rep. Congo
83 J2 **Pokrovsk** Rus. Fed.
91 D2 **Pokrovskoye** Rus. Fed.
 Pola Croatia see Pula
142 A1 **Polacca** U.S.A.
106 B1 **Pola de Lena** Spain
106 B1 **Pola de Siero** Spain
103 D1 **Poland** country Europe
55 C1 **Polar Plateau** Antarctica
80 B2 **Polatlı** Turkey
88 C2 **Polatsk** Belarus
77 C3 **Pol-e Khomrī** Afgh.
61 C2 **Polewali** Indon.
118 B2 **Poli** Cameroon
102 C1 **Police** Pol.
109 C2 **Policoro** Italy
105 D2 **Poligny** France
64 B2 **Polillo Islands** Phil.
80 B2 **Polis** Cyprus
90 B1 **Polis'ke** Ukr.
109 C3 **Polistena** Italy
103 D1 **Polkowice** Pol.
107 D2 **Pollença** Spain
109 C3 **Pollino, Monte** mt. Italy
86 F2 **Polnovat** Rus. Fed.
91 D2 **Polohy** Ukr.
123 C1 **Polokwane** S. Africa
90 B1 **Polonne** Ukr.
134 D1 **Polson** U.S.A.
91 C2 **Poltava** Ukr.
66 B2 **Poltavka** Rus. Fed.
91 D2 **Poltavskaya** Rus. Fed.
88 C2 **Põltsamaa** Estonia
88 C2 **Põlva** Estonia
 Polyanovgrad Bulg. see
  Karnobat
92 J2 **Polyarnyy** Rus. Fed.
86 C2 **Polyarnyye Zori** Rus. Fed.
111 B2 **Polygyros** Greece
111 B2 **Polykastro** Greece
156 E6 **Polynesia** is Pacific Ocean
106 B2 **Pombal** Port.
108 B2 **Pomezia** Italy
92 I2 **Pomokaira** reg. Fin.
110 C2 **Pomorie** Bulg.
102 C1 **Pomorska, Zatoka** b. Pol.
154 C2 **Pompéu** Brazil
143 D1 **Ponca City** U.S.A.
147 D3 **Ponce** Puerto Rico
73 B3 **Pondicherry** India
127 G2 **Pond Inlet** Can.
 Ponds Bay Can. see
  Pond Inlet
106 B1 **Ponferrada** Spain
117 A4 **Pongo** watercourse Sudan
123 D2 **Pongola** r. S. Africa
123 D2 **Pongolapoort Dam** l.
  S. Africa
128 C2 **Ponoka** U.S.A.
154 B3 **Ponta Grossa** Brazil
154 C1 **Pontalina** Brazil
105 D2 **Pont-à-Mousson** France
154 A2 **Ponta Porã** Brazil
105 D2 **Pontarlier** France
102 B2 **Pontcharra** France
140 B2 **Pontchartrain, Lake**
  U.S.A.
154 B1 **Ponte de Pedra** Brazil
106 B2 **Ponte de Sor** Port.
154 B1 **Ponte do Rio Verde** Brazil
98 C3 **Pontefract** U.K.
129 D2 **Ponteix** Can.
155 D2 **Ponte Nova** Brazil

150 D4 **Pontes-e-Lacerda** Brazil
106 B1 **Pontevedra** Spain
Ponthierville Dem. Rep. Congo see **Ubundu**
138 B2 **Pontiac** *IL* U.S.A.
138 C2 **Pontiac** *MI* U.S.A.
60 B2 **Pontianak** Indon.
Pontine Islands *is* Italy see **Ponziane, Isole**
104 B2 **Pontivy** France
151 D2 **Pontoetoe** Suriname
104 C2 **Pontoise** France
129 E2 **Ponton** Can.
99 B4 **Pontypool** U.K.
99 B4 **Pontypridd** U.K.
108 B2 **Ponziane, Isole** *is* Italy
99 C4 **Poole** U.K.
Poona India see **Pune**
52 B2 **Pooncarie** Austr.
152 B1 **Poopó, Lago de** *l.* Bol.
150 B2 **Popayán** Col.
83 I2 **Popigay** *r.* Rus. Fed.
52 B2 **Popiltah** Austr.
129 E2 **Poplar** *r.* Can.
137 E3 **Poplar Bluff** U.S.A.
145 C3 **Popocatépetl, Volcán** *vol.* Mex.
118 B3 **Popokabaka** Dem. Rep. Congo
Popovichskaya Rus. Fed. see **Kalininskaya**
110 C2 **Popovo** Bulg.
103 E2 **Poprad** Slovakia
151 E4 **Porangatu** Brazil
74 A2 **Porbandar** India
126 C2 **Porcupine** *r.* Can./U.S.A.
108 B1 **Pordenone** Italy
108 B1 **Poreč** Croatia
154 B2 **Porecatu** Brazil
114 C3 **Porga** Benin
93 H3 **Pori** Fin.
54 B2 **Porirua** N.Z.
88 C2 **Porkhov** Rus. Fed.
104 B2 **Pornic** France
83 K3 **Poronaysk** Rus. Fed.
75 D1 **Porong** China
111 B3 **Poros** Greece
92 I1 **Porsangerfjorden** *sea chan.* Norway
93 E4 **Porsgrunn** Norway
111 D3 **Porsuk** *r.* Turkey
97 C1 **Portadown** U.K.
97 D1 **Portaferry** U.K.
138 B2 **Portage** U.S.A.
129 E3 **Portage la Prairie** Can.
128 B3 **Port Alberni** Can.
106 B2 **Portalegre** Port.
143 C2 **Portales** U.S.A.
128 A2 **Port Alexander** U.S.A.
128 B2 **Port Alice** Can.
140 B2 **Port Allen** U.S.A.
134 B1 **Port Angeles** U.S.A.
97 C2 **Portarlington** Rep. of Ireland
51 D4 **Port Arthur** Austr.
Port Arthur China see **Lüshun**
143 E3 **Port Arthur** U.S.A.
96 A3 **Port Askaig** U.K.
52 A2 **Port Augusta** Austr.
147 C3 **Port-au-Prince** Haiti
131 E2 **Port aux Choix** Can.
122 B3 **Port Beaufort** S. Africa
73 D3 **Port Blair** India
52 B3 **Port Campbell** Austr.
131 D2 **Port-Cartier** Can.
54 B3 **Port Chalmers** N.Z.
141 D3 **Port Charlotte** U.S.A.
147 C3 **Port-de-Paix** Haiti
128 A2 **Port Edward** Can.
155 D1 **Porteirinha** Brazil
151 D3 **Portel** Brazil
130 B3 **Port Elgin** Can.
123 C3 **Port Elizabeth** S. Africa
96 A3 **Port Ellen** U.K.
98 A2 **Port Erin** Isle of Man
122 A3 **Porterville** S. Africa
135 C3 **Porterville** U.S.A.
Port Étienne Maur. see **Nouâdhibou**
52 B3 **Port Fairy** Austr.
54 C1 **Port Fitzroy** N.Z.
Port Francqui Dem. Rep. Congo see **Ilebo**
118 A3 **Port-Gentil** Gabon
115 C4 **Port Harcourt** Nigeria
128 B2 **Port Hardy** Can.
Port Harrison Can. see **Inukjuak**
131 D3 **Port Hawkesbury** Can.
99 B4 **Porthcawl** U.K.
50 A2 **Port Hedland** Austr.
Port Herald Malawi see **Nsanje**
99 A3 **Porthmadog** U.K.
131 E2 **Port Hope Simpson** Can.
138 C2 **Port Huron** U.S.A.
106 B2 **Portimão** Port.
Port Keats Austr. see **Wadeye**
Port Láirge Rep. of Ireland see **Waterford**
53 C2 **Portland** *N.S.W.* Austr.
52 B3 **Portland** *Vic.* Austr.
139 E2 **Portland** *ME* U.S.A.
134 B1 **Portland** *OR* U.S.A.
143 D3 **Portland** *TX* U.S.A.
99 B4 **Portland, Isle of** *pen.* U.K.
128 A2 **Portland Canal** *inlet* Can.
97 C2 **Portlaoise** Rep. of Ireland
143 D3 **Port Lavaca** U.S.A.
52 A2 **Port Lincoln** Austr.
114 A4 **Port Loko** Sierra Leone
113 I8 **Port Louis** Mauritius
Port-Lyautrey Morocco see **Kénitra**
52 B3 **Port MacDonnell** Austr.
53 D2 **Port Macquarie** Austr.
Portmadoc U.K. see **Porthmadog**
128 B2 **Port McNeill** Can.
131 D3 **Port-Menier** Can.
59 D3 **Port Moresby** P.N.G.
96 A3 **Portnahaven** U.K.
96 A1 **Port Ness** U.K.
Port Nis U.K. see **Port Ness**
122 A2 **Port Nolloth** S. Africa
Port-Nouveau-Québec Can. see **Kangiqsualujjuaq**
Porto Port. see **Oporto**
150 C3 **Porto Acre** Brazil
154 B2 **Porto Alegre** Brazil
152 C3 **Porto Alegre** Brazil
Porto Alexandre Angola see **Tombua**
Porto Amélia Moz. see **Pemba**
151 D4 **Porto Artur** Brazil
154 B2 **Porto Camargo** Brazil
151 D4 **Porto dos Gaúchos Óbidos** Brazil
150 D4 **Porto Esperidião** Brazil
108 B2 **Portoferraio** Italy
151 E3 **Porto Franco** Brazil
147 D3 **Port of Spain** Trin. and Tob.
108 B1 **Portogruaro** Italy
108 B2 **Portomaggiore** Italy
154 B2 **Porto Mendes** Brazil
152 C2 **Porto Murtinho** Brazil
151 E4 **Porto Nacional** Brazil
114 C4 **Porto-Novo** Benin
154 B2 **Porto Primavera, Represa** *resr* Brazil
134 B2 **Port Orford** U.S.A.
151 D3 **Porto Santana** Brazil
154 B2 **Porto São José** Brazil
108 A3 **Portoscuso** *Sardinia* Italy
155 E1 **Porto Seguro** Brazil
108 B2 **Porto Tolle** Italy
108 A2 **Porto Torres** *Sardinia* Italy
154 B3 **Porto União** Brazil
105 D3 **Porto-Vecchio** *Corsica* France
150 C3 **Porto Velho** Brazil
150 A3 **Portoviejo** Ecuador
96 B3 **Portpatrick** U.K.
52 B3 **Port Phillip Bay** Austr.
52 A2 **Port Pirie** Austr.
96 A2 **Portree** U.K.
128 B3 **Port Renfrew** Can.
97 C1 **Portrush** U.K.
116 B1 **Port Said** Egypt
123 D3 **Port Shepstone** S. Africa
99 C4 **Portsmouth** U.K.
139 E2 **Portsmouth** *NH* U.S.A.
138 C3 **Portsmouth** *OH* U.S.A.
139 D3 **Portsmouth** *VA* U.S.A.
153 B5 **Port Stephens** Falkland Is
97 C1 **Portstewart** U.K.
141 C3 **Port St Joe** U.S.A.
123 C3 **Port St Johns** S. Africa
141 D3 **Port St Lucie City** U.S.A.
116 B3 **Port Sudan** Sudan
140 C3 **Port Sulphur** U.S.A.
99 B4 **Port Talbot** U.K.
134 B1 **Port Townsend** U.S.A.
106 B2 **Portugal** *country* Europe
Portugália Angola see **Chitato**
Portuguese Guinea *country* Africa see **Guinea-Bissau**
Portuguese Timor *country* Asia see **East Timor**
Portuguese West Africa *country* Africa see **Angola**
97 B2 **Portumna** Rep. of Ireland
105 C3 **Port-Vendres** France
48 H5 **Port Vila** Vanuatu
52 A2 **Port Wakefield** Austr.
50 B1 **Port Warrender** Austr.
153 A5 **Porvenir** Chile
93 I3 **Porvoo** Fin.
65 B2 **Poryŏng** S. Korea
152 C2 **Posadas** Arg.
89 E2 **Poshekhon'ye** Rus. Fed.
Poshekon'ye-Volodarsk Rus. Fed. see **Poshekhon'ye**
92 I2 **Posio** Fin.
61 D2 **Poso** Indon.
151 E4 **Posse** Brazil
101 E2 **Pößneck** Ger.
143 C2 **Post** U.S.A.
Poste-de-la-Baleine Can. see **Kuujjuarapik**
122 B2 **Postmasburg** S. Africa
108 B1 **Postojna** Slovenia
114 C2 **Post Weygand** Alg.
Postysheve Ukr. see **Krasnoarmiys'k**
109 C2 **Posušje** Bos.-Herz.
123 C2 **Potchefstroom** S. Africa
143 E1 **Poteau** U.S.A.
109 C2 **Potenza** Italy
108 B2 **Potenza** *r.* Italy
151 E3 **Poti** *r.* Brazil
81 C1 **P'ot'i** Georgia
155 E1 **Potiraguá** Brazil
115 D3 **Potiskum** Nigeria
139 D3 **Potomac, South Branch** *r.* U.S.A.
152 B1 **Potosí** Bol.
64 B2 **Pototan** Phil.
142 C3 **Potrero del Llano** Mex.
101 F1 **Potsdam** Ger.
139 E2 **Potsdam** U.S.A.
139 D2 **Pottstown** U.S.A.
139 D2 **Pottsville** U.S.A.
131 E3 **Pouch Cove** Can.
139 E2 **Poughkeepsie** U.S.A.
98 B3 **Poulton-le-Fylde** U.K.
155 C2 **Pouso Alegre** Brazil
63 B2 **Poŭthĭsăt** Cambodia
103 D2 **Považská Bystrica** Slovakia
109 C2 **Povlen** *mt.* Serb. and Mont.
106 B1 **Póvoa de Varzim** Port.
136 B2 **Powell** U.S.A.
135 D3 **Powell, Lake** *resr* U.S.A.
128 B3 **Powell River** Can.
154 B1 **Poxoréu** Brazil
Poyang China see **Boyang**
71 B3 **Poyang Hu** *l.* China
109 D2 **Požarevac** Serb. and Mont.
145 C2 **Poza Rica** Mex.
109 C1 **Požega** Croatia
109 D2 **Požega** Serb. and Mont.
79 D2 **Pozm Tiāb** Iran
103 D1 **Poznań** Pol.
106 C2 **Pozoblanco** Spain
152 C2 **Pozo Colorado** Para.
109 B3 **Pozzallo** *Sicily* Italy
108 B2 **Pozzuoli** Italy
60 B2 **Prabumulih** Indon.
102 C2 **Prachatice** Czech Rep.
63 A2 **Prachuap Khiri Khan** Thai.
103 D1 **Praděd** *mt.* Czech Rep.
104 C3 **Prades** France
155 E1 **Prado** Brazil
102 C1 **Prague** Czech Rep.
Praha Czech Rep. see **Prague**
143 C2 **Prairie Dog Town Fork** *r.* U.S.A.
138 A2 **Prairie du Chien** U.S.A.
60 A1 **Prapat** Indon.
154 C1 **Prata** Brazil
108 B2 **Prato** Italy
137 D3 **Pratt** U.S.A.
140 C2 **Prattville** U.S.A.
61 C2 **Praya** Indon.
63 B2 **Preăh Vihear** Cambodia
89 F2 **Prechistoye** Rus. Fed.
129 D2 **Preeceville** Can.
88 C2 **Preiļi** Latvia
53 C2 **Premer** Austr.
105 C2 **Prémery** France
101 F1 **Premnitz** Ger.
102 C1 **Prenzlau** Ger.
66 B2 **Preobrazheniye** Rus. Fed.
63 A2 **Preparis Island** Cocos Is
63 A2 **Preparis North Channel** Cocos Is
63 A2 **Preparis South Channel** Cocos Is
103 D2 **Přerov** Czech Rep.
142 A2 **Prescott** U.S.A.
142 A2 **Prescott Valley** U.S.A.
109 D2 **Preševo** Serb. and Mont.
152 B2 **Presidencia Roque Sáenz Peña** Arg.
151 E3 **Presidente Dutra** Brazil
154 B2 **Presidente Epitácio** Brazil
154 B1 **Presidente Murtinho** Brazil
155 C1 **Presidente Olegário** Brazil
154 B2 **Presidente Prudente** Brazil
142 C3 **Presidio** U.S.A.
103 E2 **Prešov** Slovakia
111 B2 **Prespa, Lake** Europe
139 F1 **Presque Isle** U.S.A.
Pressburg Slovakia see **Bratislava**
101 F2 **Pressel** Ger.
98 B3 **Preston** U.K.
134 D2 **Preston** U.S.A.
96 B3 **Prestwick** U.K.
155 C1 **Preto** *r.* Brazil
123 C2 **Pretoria** S. Africa
Pretoria-Witwatersrand-Vereeniging *prov.* S. Africa see **Gauteng**
111 B3 **Preveza** Greece
63 B2 **Prey Vêng** Cambodia
124 A4 **Pribilof Islands** U.S.A.
109 C2 **Priboj** Serb. and Mont.
135 D3 **Price** U.S.A.
140 C2 **Prichard** U.S.A.
106 C2 **Priego de Córdoba** Spain
88 B3 **Prienai** Lith.
122 B2 **Prieska** S. Africa
103 D2 **Prievidza** Slovakia
109 C2 **Prijedor** Bos.-Herz.
109 C2 **Prijepolje** Serb. and Mont.
Prikaspiyskaya Nizmennost' *lowland* Kazakh./Rus. Fed. see **Caspian Lowland**
111 B2 **Prilep** Macedonia
101 F3 **Přimda** Czech Rep.
91 D2 **Primorsko-Akhtarsk** Rus. Fed.
129 D2 **Primrose Lake** Can.
129 D2 **Prince Albert** Can.
122 B3 **Prince Albert** S. Africa
126 E2 **Prince Albert Peninsula** Can.
122 B3 **Prince Albert Road** S. Africa
126 D2 **Prince Alfred, Cape** Can.
122 A3 **Prince Alfred Hamlet** S. Africa
127 G2 **Prince Charles Island** Can.
55 H2 **Prince Charles Mountains** Antarctica
131 D3 **Prince Edward Island** *prov.* Can.
128 B2 **Prince George** Can.
51 D1 **Prince of Wales Island** Austr.
126 F2 **Prince of Wales Island** Can.
128 A2 **Prince of Wales Island** U.S.A.
126 E2 **Prince of Wales Strait** Can.
126 E1 **Prince Patrick Island** Can.
126 F2 **Prince Regent Inlet** *sea chan.* Can.
128 A2 **Prince Rupert** Can.
51 D1 **Princess Charlotte Bay** Austr.
55 H2 **Princess Elizabeth Land** *reg.* Antarctica
128 B2 **Princess Royal Island** Can.
128 B3 **Princeton** Can.
138 B3 **Princeton** *IN* U.S.A.
137 E2 **Princeton** *MO* U.S.A.
134 B2 **Prineville** U.S.A.
86 C2 **Priozersk** Rus. Fed.
Pripet *r.* Belarus see **Prypyats'**

90 A1 **Pripet Marshes** Belarus/Ukr.
109 D2 **Priština** Serb. and Mont.
101 F1 **Pritzwalk** Ger.
105 C3 **Privas** France
109 C2 **Privlaka** Croatia
89 F2 **Privolzhsk** Rus. Fed.
109 D2 **Prizren** Serb. and Mont.
151 D2 **Professor van Blommestein Meer** *resr* Suriname
145 D2 **Progreso** Mex.
81 C1 **Prokhladnyy** Rus. Fed.
109 D2 **Prokuplje** Serb. and Mont.
Prome Myanmar *see* **Pyè**
154 C2 **Promissão** Brazil
154 C2 **Promissão, Represa** *resr* Brazil
126 D3 **Prophet** *r.* Can.
128 B2 **Prophet River** Can.
51 D2 **Proserpine** Austr.
Proskurov Ukr. *see* **Khmel'nyts'kyy**
103 D2 **Prostějov** Czech Rep.
89 E3 **Protvino** Rus. Fed.
110 C2 **Provadiya** Bulg.
105 D3 **Provence** *reg.* France
139 E2 **Providence** U.S.A.
146 B3 **Providencia, Isla de** *i.* Caribbean Sea
83 N2 **Provideniya** Rus. Fed.
105 C2 **Provins** France
135 D2 **Provo** U.S.A.
129 C2 **Provost** Can.
91 C2 **Prubiynyy, Mys** *pt* Ukr.
154 B3 **Prudentópolis** Brazil
126 C2 **Prudhoe Bay** U.S.A.
100 C2 **Prüm** Ger.
105 D3 **Prunelli-di-Fiumorbo** *Corsica* France
103 D1 **Pruszcz Gdański** Pol.
103 E1 **Pruszków** Pol.
110 C1 **Prut** *r.* Europe
88 B3 **Pruzhany** Belarus
91 D2 **Pryazovs'ke** Ukr.
91 C1 **Pryluky** Ukr.
91 D2 **Prymors'k** Ukr.
91 D2 **Prymors'kyy** Ukr.
143 D1 **Pryor** U.S.A.
90 B1 **Prypyats'** *r.* Belarus/Ukr.
103 E2 **Przemyśl** Pol.
103 E1 **Przeworsk** Pol.
Przheval'sk Kyrg. *see* **Karakol**
111 C3 **Psara** *i.* Greece
81 C1 **Psebay** Rus. Fed.
91 D3 **Pshekha** *r.* Rus. Fed.
88 C2 **Pskov** Rus. Fed.
88 C2 **Pskov, Lake** Estonia/Rus. Fed.
111 B2 **Ptolemaïda** Greece
109 C1 **Ptuj** Slovenia
150 B3 **Pucallpa** Peru
71 B3 **Pucheng** China
65 B2 **Puch'ŏn** S. Korea
103 D1 **Puck** Pol.
92 I2 **Pudasjärvi** Fin.
70 C2 **Pudong** China
86 C2 **Pudozh** Rus. Fed.
Puduchcheri India *see* **Pondicherry**
145 C3 **Puebla** Mex.
136 C3 **Pueblo** U.S.A.
153 B3 **Puelén** Arg.
153 A3 **Puente Alto** Chile
106 C2 **Puente-Genil** Spain
153 A4 **Puerto Aisén** Chile
152 B1 **Puerto Alegre** Bol.
145 C3 **Puerto Ángel** Mex.
146 B4 **Puerto Armuelles** Panama
150 C2 **Puerto Ayacucho** Venez.
146 B3 **Puerto Barrios** Guat.
146 B3 **Puerto Cabezas** Nic.
153 A4 **Puerto Cisnes** Chile
144 A2 **Puerto Cortés** Mex.
145 C3 **Puerto Escondido** Mex.
152 B1 **Puerto Frey** Bol.
150 C2 **Puerto Inírida** Col.
152 C1 **Puerto Isabel** Bol.
150 B3 **Puerto Leguizamo** Col.
146 B3 **Puerto Lempira** Hond.
144 A2 **Puerto Libertad** Mex.
146 B3 **Puerto Limón** Costa Rica
106 C2 **Puertollano** Spain
153 B4 **Puerto Madryn** Arg.
150 C4 **Puerto Maldonado** Peru
Puerto México Mex. *see* **Coatzacoalcos**
147 D4 **Puerto Miranda** Venez.
153 A4 **Puerto Montt** Chile
153 A5 **Puerto Natales** Chile
150 C2 **Puerto Nuevo** Col.
150 C2 **Puerto Páez** Venez.
144 A1 **Puerto Peñasco** Mex.
152 C2 **Puerto Pinasco** Para.
147 C3 **Puerto Plata** Dom. Rep.
150 B3 **Puerto Portillo** Peru
Puerto Presidente Stroessner Para. *see* **Ciudad del Este**
64 A3 **Puerto Princesa** Phil.
154 A3 **Puerto Rico** Arg.
147 D3 **Puerto Rico** *terr.* West Indies
158 C3 **Puerto Rico Trench** *sea feature* Caribbean Sea
146 A3 **Puerto San José** Guat.
153 B5 **Puerto Santa Cruz** Arg.
152 C2 **Puerto Sastre** Para.
144 B2 **Puerto Vallarta** Mex.
87 D3 **Pugachev** Rus. Fed.
74 B2 **Pugal** India
54 B2 **Pukaki, Lake** N.Z.
49 K5 **Pukapuka** *atoll* Cook Is
129 D2 **Pukatawagan** Can.
65 B1 **Pukchin** N. Korea
65 B1 **Pukch'ŏng** N. Korea
109 C2 **Pukë** Albania
54 B1 **Pukekohe** N.Z.
65 B1 **Puksubaek-san** *mt.* N. Korea
Pula China *see* **Nyingchi**
108 B2 **Pula** Croatia
108 A3 **Pula** *Sardinia* Italy
152 B2 **Pulacayo** Bol.
103 E1 **Puławy** Pol.
92 I3 **Pulkkila** Fin.
134 C1 **Pullman** U.S.A.
64 B2 **Pulog, Mount** Phil.
64 B3 **Pulutan** Indon.
150 A3 **Puná, Isla** *i.* Ecuador
54 B2 **Punakaiki** N.Z.
123 D1 **Punda Maria** S. Africa
73 B3 **Pune** India
65 B1 **P'ungsan** N. Korea
121 C2 **Púnguè** *r.* Moz.
119 C3 **Punia** Dem. Rep. Congo
74 B1 **Punjab** *state* India
153 B3 **Punta Alta** Arg.
153 A5 **Punta Arenas** Chile
108 A2 **Punta Balestrieri** *mt.* *Sardinia* Italy
153 C3 **Punta del Este** Uru.
146 B3 **Punta Gorda** Belize
146 B3 **Puntarenas** Costa Rica
150 B1 **Punto Fijo** Venez.
92 I3 **Puolanka** Fin.
Puqi China *see* **Chibi**
82 G2 **Pur** *r.* Rus. Fed.
75 C3 **Puri** India
100 B1 **Purmerend** Neth.
Purnea India *see* **Purnia**
75 C2 **Purnia** India
75 C2 **Puruliya** India
150 C3 **Purus** *r.* Peru
61 B2 **Purwakarta** Indon.
61 C2 **Purwodadi** Indon.
65 B1 **Puryŏng** N. Korea
74 B3 **Pusad** India
65 B2 **Pusan** S. Korea
89 E3 **Pushchino** Rus. Fed.
Pushkino Azer. *see* **Biläsuvar**
89 E2 **Pushkino** Rus. Fed.
88 C2 **Pushkinskiye Gory** Rus. Fed.
88 C2 **Pustoshka** Rus. Fed.
62 A1 **Putao** Myanmar
71 B3 **Putian** China
Puting China *see* **De'an**
61 C2 **Puting, Tanjung** *pt* Indon.
101 F1 **Putlitz** Ger.
60 B1 **Putrajaya** Malaysia
122 B2 **Putsonderwater** S. Africa
102 C1 **Puttgarden** Ger.
150 B3 **Putumayo** *r.* Col.
61 C1 **Putusibau** Indon.
90 B2 **Putyla** Ukr.
91 C1 **Putyvl'** Ukr.
93 I3 **Puula** *l.* Fin.
130 C1 **Puvirnituq** Can.
70 B2 **Puyang** China
104 C3 **Puylaurens** France
119 C3 **Pweto** Dem. Rep. Congo
99 A3 **Pwllheli** U.K.
92 J2 **Pyaozerskiy** Rus. Fed.
63 A2 **Pyapon** Myanmar
83 G2 **Pyasina** *r.* Rus. Fed.
87 D4 **Pyatigorsk** Rus. Fed.
91 C2 **P"yatykhatky** Ukr.
62 A2 **Pyè** Myanmar
88 C3 **Pyetrykaw** Belarus
93 H3 **Pyhäjärvi** *l.* Fin.
92 H3 **Pyhäjoki** *r.* Fin.
92 I3 **Pyhäsalmi** Fin.
62 A1 **Pyingaing** Myanmar
62 A2 **Pyinmana** Myanmar
62 A1 **Pyin-U-Lwin** Myanmar
65 B2 **Pyŏksŏng** N. Korea
65 B2 **P'yŏnggang** N. Korea
65 B2 **P'yŏngsan** N. Korea
65 B2 **P'yŏngsong** N. Korea
65 B2 **P'yŏngt'aek** S. Korea
65 B2 **P'yŏngyang** N. Korea
135 C2 **Pyramid Lake** U.S.A.
80 B3 **Pyramids of Giza** *tourist site* Egypt
107 D1 **Pyrenees** *mts* Europe
111 B3 **Pyrgetos** Greece
111 C3 **Pyrgi** Greece
111 B3 **Pyrgos** Greece
91 C1 **Pyryatyn** Ukr.
103 C1 **Pyrzyce** Pol.
88 C2 **Pytalovo** Rus. Fed.
111 B3 **Pyxaria** *mt.* Greece

Q

Qaanaaq Greenland *see* **Thule**
Qabqa China *see* **Gonghe**
123 C3 **Qacha's Nek** Lesotho
69 D2 **Qagan Nur** China
Qahremānshahr Iran *see* **Kermānshāh**
68 C2 **Qaidam Pendi** *basin* China
79 C2 **Qalamat Abū Shafrah** Saudi Arabia
78 A2 **Qal'at al Aẓlam** Saudi Arabia
78 A2 **Qal'at al Mu'aẓẓam** Saudi Arabia
78 B2 **Qal'at Bīshah** Saudi Arabia
76 C3 **Qal'eh-ye Now** Afgh.
129 E1 **Qamanirjuaq Lake** Can.
Qamanittuaq Can. *see* **Baker Lake**
79 C3 **Qamar, Ghubbat al** *b.* Yemen
68 C2 **Qamdo** China
78 B3 **Qam Hadīl** Saudi Arabia
127 I2 **Qaqortoq** Greenland
80 A3 **Qārah** Egypt
Qarkilik China *see* **Ruoqiang**
Qarqan China *see* **Qiemo**
77 C3 **Qarshi** Uzbek.
78 B2 **Qaryat al Ulyā** Saudi Arabia
127 I2 **Qasigiannguit** Greenland
116 A2 **Qaşr al Farāfirah** Egypt
79 D2 **Qaşr-e Qand** Iran
81 C2 **Qaşr-e Shīrīn** Iran
127 I2 **Qassimiut** Greenland
78 B3 **Qa'tabah** Yemen
79 C2 **Qatar** *country* Asia
116 A2 **Qattāra Depression** Egypt
Qausuittuq Can. *see* **Resolute**
76 B3 **Qāyen** Iran
81 C1 **Qazax** Azer.
81 C1 **Qazımämmäd** Azer.
81 C2 **Qazvīn** Iran
Qena Egypt *see* **Qinā**
127 I2 **Qeqertarsuaq** Greenland
127 I2 **Qeqertarsuaq** *i.* Greenland
127 I2 **Qeqertarsuatsiaat** Greenland
127 I2 **Qeqertarsuup Tunua** *b.* Greenland
79 C2 **Qeshm** Iran
74 A1 **Qeyşār, Kūh-e** *mt.* Afgh.
70 A3 **Qianjiang** *Chongqing* China
70 B2 **Qianjiang** *Hubei* China
69 E1 **Qianjin** China
65 A1 **Qian Shan** *mts* China
71 A3 **Qianxi** China
70 C2 **Qidong** China
77 E3 **Qiemo** China
71 A3 **Qijiang** China
68 C2 **Qijiaojing** China
127 H2 **Qikiqtarjuaq** Can.
74 A2 **Qila Ladgasht** Pak.
68 C2 **Qilian Shan** *mts* China
127 J2 **Qillak** *i.* Greenland
70 B3 **Qimen** China
127 H1 **Qimusseriarsuaq** *b.* Greenland
116 B2 **Qinā** Egypt
Qincheng China *see* **Nanfeng**
70 C2 **Qingdao** China
68 C2 **Qinghai Hu** *salt l.* China
68 C2 **Qinghai Nanshan** *mts* China
Qingjiang China *see* **Huai'an**
Qingjiang China *see* **Zhangshu**
70 B2 **Qingshuihe** China
70 A2 **Qingtongxia** China
70 A2 **Qingyang** China
71 B3 **Qingyuan** *Guangdong* China
Qingyuan China *see* **Yizhou**
65 A1 **Qingyuan** *Liaoning* China
68 B2 **Qingzang Gaoyuan** *plat.* China
70 B2 **Qingzhou** China
70 B2 **Qinhuangdao** China
Qinjiang China *see* **Shicheng**
70 A2 **Qin Ling** *mts* China
Qinting China *see* **Lianhua**
70 B2 **Qinyang** China
71 A3 **Qinzhou** China
71 B4 **Qionghai** China
70 A2 **Qionglai Shan** *mts* China
71 B4 **Qiongshan** China
71 A4 **Qiongzhong** China
69 E1 **Qiqihar** China
81 D3 **Qīr** Iran
Qishan China *see* **Qimen**
79 C3 **Qishn** Yemen
66 B1 **Qitaihe** China
70 B2 **Qixian** *Henan* China
70 B2 **Qixian** *Shanxi* China
Qogir Feng *mt.* China/Jammu and Kashmir *see* **K2**
81 D2 **Qom** Iran
Qomishēh Iran *see* **Shahrezā**
Qomolangma Feng *mt.* China/Nepal *see* **Everest, Mount**
76 B2 **Qo'ng'irot** Uzbek.
Qoqek China *see* **Tacheng**
77 D2 **Qo'qon** Uzbek.
76 B2 **Qoraqalpog'iston** Uzbek.
80 B2 **Qornet es Saouda** *mt.* Lebanon
81 C2 **Qorveh** Iran
79 C2 **Qoţbābād** Iran
101 C1 **Quakenbrück** Ger.
53 C2 **Quambone** Austr.
63 B2 **Quang Ngai** Vietnam
63 B2 **Quang Tri** Vietnam
Quan Long Vietnam *see* **Ca Mau**
Quan Phu Quoc *i.* Vietnam *see* **Phu Quôc, Đao**
71 B3 **Quanzhou** *Fujian* China
71 B3 **Quanzhou** *Guangxi* China
108 A3 **Quartu Sant'Elena** *Sardinia* Italy
142 A2 **Quartzsite** U.S.A.
81 C1 **Quba** Azer.
76 B3 **Quchan** Iran
53 C3 **Queanbeyan** Austr.
131 C3 **Québec** Can.
131 C2 **Québec** *prov.* Can.
101 E2 **Quedlinburg** Ger.
Queen Adelaide Islands Chile *see* **Reina Adelaida, Archipiélago de la**
128 A2 **Queen Charlotte** Can.
128 A2 **Queen Charlotte Islands** Can.
128 B2 **Queen Charlotte Sound** *sea chan.* Can.
128 B2 **Queen Charlotte Strait** Can.
126 E1 **Queen Elizabeth Islands** Can.
55 I2 **Queen Mary Land** *reg.* Antarctica
126 F2 **Queen Maud Gulf** Can.
55 E2 **Queen Maud Land** *reg.* Antarctica
55 P1 **Queen Maud Mountains** Antarctica
52 B3 **Queenscliff** Austr.
52 B1 **Queensland** *state* Austr.
51 D4 **Queenstown** Austr.
54 A3 **Queenstown** N.Z.
Queenstown Rep. of Ireland *see* **Cóbh**
123 C3 **Queenstown** S. Africa

121 C2 Quelimane Moz.
153 A4 Quellón Chile
Quelpart Island S. Korea *see* Cheju-do
142 B2 Quemado U.S.A.
Que Que Zimbabwe *see* Kwekwe
154 B2 Queréncia do Norte Brazil
145 B2 Querétaro Mex.
101 E2 Querfurt Ger.
128 B2 Quesnel Can.
128 B2 Quesnel Lake Can.
74 A1 Quetta Pak.
146 A3 Quetzaltenango Guat.
64 A3 Quezon Phil.
64 B2 Quezon City Phil.
120 A2 Quibala Angola
150 B2 Quibdó Col.
104 B2 Quiberon France
120 A2 Quilengues Angola
104 C3 Quillan France
153 C3 Quilmes Arg.
73 B4 Quilon India
51 D2 Quilpie Austr.
153 A3 Quilpué Chile
120 A1 Quimbele Angola
152 B2 Quimili Arg.
104 B2 Quimper France
104 B2 Quimperlé France
135 B3 Quincy *CA* U.S.A.
141 D2 Quincy *FL* U.S.A.
137 E3 Quincy *IL* U.S.A.
139 E2 Quincy *MA* U.S.A.
63 B2 Qui Nhon Vietnam
107 C1 Quinto Spain
121 D2 Quionga Moz.
120 A2 Quirima Angola
53 D2 Quirindi Austr.
154 B1 Quirinópolis Brazil
131 D3 Quispamsis Can.
121 C3 Quissico Moz.
120 A2 Quitapa Angola
150 B3 Quito Ecuador
151 F3 Quixadá Brazil
71 A3 Qujing China
75 D1 Qumar He *r.* China
123 C3 Qumrha S. Africa
115 E1 Qunayyin, Sabkhat al *salt marsh* Libya
129 E1 Quoich *r.* Can.
52 A2 Quorn Austr.
79 C2 Qurayat Oman
77 C3 Qŭrghonteppa Tajik.
Quxar China *see* Lhazê
Quyang China *see* Jingzhou
71 B3 Quzhou China
Qyteti Stalin Albania *see* Kuçovë
Qyzyltū Kazakh. *see* Kishkenekol'

R

103 D2 Raab *r.* Austria
92 H3 Raahe Fin.
100 C1 Raalte Neth.
61 C2 Raas *i.* Indon.
61 C2 Raba Indon.
114 B1 Rabat Morocco
59 E3 Rabaul P.N.G.
50 C2 Rabbit Flat Austr.
78 A2 Rābigh Saudi Arabia
103 D2 Rabka Pol.
Rābniţa Moldova *see* Rîbniţa
Rabyānah, Ramlat *des.* Libya *see* Rebiana Sand Sea
131 E3 Race, Cape Can.
140 B3 Raceland U.S.A.
139 E2 Race Point U.S.A.
63 B3 Rach Gia Vietnam
103 D1 Racibórz Pol.
138 B2 Racine U.S.A.
78 B3 Radā' Yemen
110 C1 Rădăuţi Romania
138 B3 Radcliff U.S.A.
74 B2 Radhanpur India
130 C2 Radisson Can.
103 E1 Radom Pol.
103 D1 Radomsko Pol.
90 B1 Radomyshl' Ukr.
111 B2 Radoviš Macedonia
88 B2 Radviliškis Lith.
78 A2 Raḑwá, Jabal *mt.* Saudi Arabia
90 B1 Radyvyliv Ukr.
75 C2 Rae Bareli India

128 C1 Rae-Edzo Can.
128 C1 Rae Lakes Can.
100 C2 Raeren Belgium
54 C1 Raetihi N.Z.
78 A2 Rāf *hill* Saudi Arabia
152 B3 Rafaela Arg.
118 C2 Rafaï C.A.R.
78 B2 Rafḩā' Saudi Arabia
79 C1 Rafsanjān Iran
119 C2 Raga Sudan
64 B3 Ragang, Mount *vol.* Phil.
109 B3 Ragusa *Sicily* Italy
61 D2 Raha Indon.
88 D3 Rahachow Belarus
78 A3 Rahad *r.* Sudan
74 B2 Rahimyar Khan Pak.
73 B3 Raichur India
75 C2 Raigarh India
128 C2 Rainbow Lake Can.
134 B1 Rainier, Mount *vol.* U.S.A.
130 A3 Rainy Lake Can.
129 E3 Rainy River Can.
75 C2 Raipur India
93 H3 Raisio Fin.
88 C2 Raja Estonia
73 C3 Rajahmundry India
61 C1 Rajang *r. Sarawak* Malaysia
74 B2 Rajanpur Pak.
73 B4 Rajapalaiyam India
74 B2 Rajasthan *state* India
74 B2 Rajasthan Canal *canal* India
74 B2 Rajgarh India
60 B2 Rajik Indon.
74 B2 Rajkot India
75 C2 Raj Nandgaon India
74 B2 Rajpur India
75 C2 Rajshahi Bangl.
54 B2 Rakaia *r.* N.Z.
74 B1 Rakaposhi *mt.* Jammu and Kashmir
90 A2 Rakhiv Ukr.
91 D1 Rakitnoye Rus. Fed.
88 C2 Rakke Estonia
88 C2 Rakvere Estonia
141 E1 Raleigh U.S.A.
141 E2 Raleigh Bay U.S.A.
48 H3 Ralik Chain *is* Marshall Is
75 C2 Ramanuj Ganj India
123 C2 Ramatlabama S. Africa
104 C2 Rambouillet France
99 A4 Rame Head *hd* U.K.
97 C1 Ramelton Rep. of Ireland
89 E2 Rameshki Rus. Fed.
74 B2 Ramgarh India
81 C2 Rāmhormoz Iran
110 C1 Râmnicu Sărat Romania
110 B1 Râmnicu Vâlcea Romania
89 E3 Ramon' Rus. Fed.
135 C4 Ramona U.S.A.
123 C1 Ramotswa Botswana
75 B2 Rampur India
62 A2 Ramree Island Myanmar
98 A2 Ramsey Isle of Man
130 B3 Ramsey Lake Can.
99 D4 Ramsgate U.K.
81 C2 Rāmshīr Iran
62 A1 Ramsing India
75 C2 Ranaghat India
61 C1 Ranau *Sabah* Malaysia
153 A3 Rancagua Chile
154 B2 Rancharia Brazil
75 C2 Ranchi India
93 F4 Randers Denmark
63 B3 Rangae Thai.
75 D2 Rangapara North India
54 B2 Rangiora N.Z.
49 M5 Rangiroa *atoll* Fr. Polynesia
54 C1 Rangitaiki *r.* N.Z.
60 B2 Rangkasbitung Indon.
63 A2 Rangoon Myanmar
75 C2 Rangpur Bangl.
129 E1 Rankin Inlet Can.
53 C2 Rankin's Springs Austr.
Rankovićevo Serb. and Mont. *see* Kraljevo
96 B2 Rannoch Moor *moorland* U.K.
74 B2 Rann of Kachchh *marsh* India
63 A3 Ranong Thai.
59 C3 Ransiki Indon.
60 A1 Rantauprapat Indon.
61 C2 Rantepao Indon.
92 I2 Ranua Fin.
93 E4 Ranum Denmark
78 B2 Ranyah, Wādī *watercourse* Saudi Arabia

49 J6 Raoul Island Kermadec Is
49 M6 Rapa *i.* Fr. Polynesia
108 A2 Rapallo Italy
136 C2 Rapid City U.S.A.
88 B2 Rapla Estonia
74 A2 Rapur India
49 L6 Rarotonga *i.* Cook Is
153 B4 Rasa, Punta *pt* Arg.
Ras al Khaimah U.A.E. *see* Ra's al Khaymah
79 C2 Ra's al Khaymah U.A.E.
116 B3 Ras Dejen *mt.* Eth.
88 B2 Raseiniai Lith.
116 B2 Ra's Ghārib Egypt
81 C2 Rasht Iran
74 A2 Ras Koh *mt.* Pak.
110 C1 Râşnov Romania
88 C2 Rasony Belarus
79 C2 Ra's Şirāb Oman
108 B3 Rass Jebel Tunisia
87 D3 Rasskazovo Rus. Fed.
79 C2 Ras Tannūrah Saudi Arabia
101 D1 Rastede Ger.
48 I2 Ratak Chain *is* Marshall Is
93 F3 Rätan Sweden
123 C2 Ratanda S. Africa
74 B2 Ratangarh India
63 A2 Rat Buri Thai.
62 A1 Rathedaung Myanmar
101 F1 Rathenow Ger.
97 C1 Rathfriland U.K.
97 C1 Rathlin Island U.K.
97 B2 Rathluirc Rep. of Ireland
100 C2 Ratingen Ger.
74 B2 Ratlam India
73 B3 Ratnagiri India
73 C4 Ratnapura Sri Lanka
90 A1 Ratne Ukr.
142 C1 Raton U.S.A.
96 D2 Rattray Head *hd* U.K.
93 G3 Rättvik Sweden
101 E1 Ratzeburg Ger.
78 B2 Raudhatain Kuwait
92 □B2 Raufarhöfn Iceland
54 C1 Raukumara Range *mts* N.Z.
93 H3 Rauma Fin.
88 C2 Rauna Latvia
61 C2 Raung, Gunung *vol.* Indon.
75 C2 Raurkela India
66 D2 Rausu Japan
90 B2 Rāut *r.* Moldova
134 D1 Ravalli U.S.A.
81 C2 Ravānsar Iran
108 B2 Ravenna Italy
102 B2 Ravensburg Ger.
50 B3 Ravensthorpe Austr.
74 B1 Ravi *r.* Pak.
74 B1 Rawalpindi Pak.
103 D1 Rawicz Pol.
50 B3 Rawlinna Austr.
136 B2 Rawlins U.S.A.
153 B4 Rawson Arg.
75 C3 Rayagada India
69 E1 Raychikhinsk Rus. Fed.
78 B3 Raydah Yemen
87 E3 Rayevskiy Rus. Fed.
134 B1 Raymond U.S.A.
53 D2 Raymond Terrace Austr.
143 D3 Raymondville U.S.A.
129 D2 Raymore Can.
145 C2 Rayón Mex.
63 B2 Rayong Thai.
78 A2 Rayyis Saudi Arabia
104 B2 Raz, Pointe du *pt* France
81 C2 Razāzah, Buḩayrat ar *l.* Iraq
110 C2 Razgrad Bulg.
110 C2 Razim, Lacul *lag.* Romania
111 B2 Razlog Bulg.
Raz"yezd 3km Rus. Fed. *see* Novyy Urgal
104 B2 Ré, Île de *i.* France
99 C4 Reading U.K.
138 C3 Reading *OH* U.S.A.
139 D2 Reading *PA* U.S.A.
123 C2 Reagile S. Africa
115 E2 Rebiana Sand Sea *des.* Libya
66 D1 Rebun-tō *i.* Japan
50 B3 Recherche, Archipelago of the *is* Austr.
89 D3 Rechytsa Belarus
151 F3 Recife Brazil
123 C3 Recife, Cape S. Africa
100 C2 Recklinghausen Ger.
152 C2 Reconquista Arg.
137 D1 Red *r.* Can./U.S.A.
140 B2 Red *r.* U.S.A.

100 B3 Redange Lux.
141 C1 Red Bank U.S.A.
Red Basin China *see* Sichuan Pendi
131 E2 Red Bay Can.
135 B2 Red Bluff U.S.A.
98 C2 Redcar U.K.
129 C2 Redcliff Can.
121 B2 Redcliff Zimbabwe
52 B2 Red Cliffs Austr.
128 C2 Red Deer Can.
126 E3 Red Deer *r.* Can.
129 D2 Red Deer Lake Can.
135 B2 Redding U.S.A.
99 C3 Redditch U.K.
137 D2 Redfield U.S.A.
137 D3 Red Hills U.S.A.
130 A2 Red Lake Can.
130 A2 Red Lake *l.* Can.
137 E1 Red Lakes U.S.A.
134 E1 Red Lodge U.S.A.
134 B2 Redmond U.S.A.
137 D2 Red Oak U.S.A.
104 B2 Redon France
106 B1 Redondela Spain
106 B2 Redondo Port.
78 A2 Red Sea Africa/Asia
128 B1 Redstone *r.* Can.
100 B1 Reduzum Neth.
128 C2 Redwater Can.
137 E2 Red Wing U.S.A.
137 D2 Redwood Falls U.S.A.
97 C2 Ree, Lough *l.* Rep. of Ireland
134 B2 Reedsport U.S.A.
54 B2 Reefton N.Z.
143 D3 Refugio U.S.A.
102 C2 Regen Ger.
155 E1 Regência Brazil
102 C2 Regensburg Ger.
114 C2 Reggane Alg.
109 C3 Reggio di Calabria Italy
108 B2 Reggio nell'Emilia Italy
110 B1 Reghin Romania
129 D2 Regina Can.
154 C2 Registro Brazil
122 A1 Rehoboth Namibia
80 B2 Rehovot Israel
101 F2 Reichenbach Ger.
141 E1 Reidsville U.S.A.
99 C4 Reigate U.K.
105 C2 Reims France
153 A5 Reina Adelaida, Archipiélago de la *is* Chile
101 E1 Reinbek Ger.
129 D2 Reindeer *r.* Can.
129 E2 Reindeer Island Can.
129 D2 Reindeer Lake Can.
92 F2 Reine Norway
106 C1 Reinosa Spain
100 C3 Reinsfeld Ger.
123 C2 Reitz S. Africa
122 B2 Reivilo S. Africa
129 D1 Reliance Can.
107 D2 Relizane Alg.
52 A2 Remarkable, Mount *hill* Austr.
79 C2 Remeshk Iran
105 D2 Remiremont France
100 C2 Remscheid Ger.
102 B1 Rendsburg Ger.
139 D1 Renfrew Can.
60 B2 Rengat Indon.
90 B2 Reni Ukr.
52 B2 Renmark Austr.
48 H5 Rennell *i.* Solomon Is
104 B2 Rennerod Ger.
104 B2 Rennes France
129 D1 Rennie Lake Can.
108 B2 Reno *r.* Italy
135 C3 Reno U.S.A.
70 A3 Renshou China
138 B2 Rensselaer U.S.A.
75 C2 Renukut India
54 B2 Renwick N.Z.
61 C2 Reo Indon.
136 C3 Republican *r.* U.S.A.
127 G2 Repulse Bay Can.
150 B3 Requena Peru
107 C2 Requena Spain
60 B2 Resag, Gunung *mt.* Indon.
111 B3 Resen Macedonia
154 B2 Reserva Brazil
91 C2 Reshetylivka Ukr.
152 C2 Resistencia Arg.
110 B1 Reşiţa Romania
126 F2 Resolute Can.
127 H2 Resolution Island Can.
155 D1 Resplendor Brazil
145 D3 Retalhuleu Guat.
98 C3 Retford U.K.

105 C2	Rethel France
111 B3	Rethymno Greece
113 I8	Réunion *terr.* Indian Ocean
107 D1	Reus Spain
	Reut *r.* Moldova *see* Răut
102 B2	Reutlingen Ger.
86 C2	Revda Rus. Fed.
128 C2	Revelstoke Can.
144 A3	Revillagigedo, Islas *is* Mex.
128 A2	Revillagigedo Island U.S.A.
75 C2	Rewa India
134 D2	Rexburg U.S.A.
135 B3	Reyes, Point U.S.A.
160 M4	Reykjanes Ridge *sea feature* N. Atlantic Ocean
92 □A3	Reykjanestá *pt* Iceland
92 □A3	Reykjavík Iceland
145 C2	Reynosa Mex.
	Rezā'īyeh Iran *see* Urmia
	Rezā'īyeh, Daryācheh-ye *salt l.* Iran *see* Urmia, Lake
88 C2	Rēzekne Latvia
	Rheims France *see* Reims
	Rhein *r.* Ger. *see* Rhine
100 C1	Rheine Ger.
101 F1	Rheinsberg Ger.
100 C2	Rhine *r.* Europe
138 B1	Rhinelander U.S.A.
101 F1	Rhinluch *marsh* Ger.
101 F1	Rhinow Ger.
108 A1	Rho Italy
139 E2	Rhode Island *state* U.S.A.
111 C3	Rhodes Greece
111 C3	Rhodes *i.* Greece
	Rhodesia *country* Africa *see* Zimbabwe
111 B2	Rhodope Mountains Bulg./Greece
105 C3	Rhône *r.* France/Switz.
	Rhum *i.* U.K. *see* Rum
	Rhuthun U.K. *see* Ruthin
98 B3	Rhyl U.K.
155 D1	Riacho dos Machados Brazil
154 C1	Rialma Brazil
154 C1	Rianópolis Brazil
60 B1	Riau, Kepulauan *is* Indon.
106 B1	Ribadeo Spain
106 B1	Ribadesella Spain
154 B2	Ribas do Rio Pardo Brazil
121 C2	Ribáuè Moz.
98 B3	Ribble *r.* U.K.
93 E4	Ribe Denmark
154 C2	Ribeira *r.* Brazil
154 C2	Ribeirão Preto Brazil
104 C2	Ribérac France
152 B1	Riberalta Bol.
90 B2	Rîbniţa Moldova
102 C1	Ribnitz-Damgarten Ger.
138 A1	Rice Lake U.S.A.
123 D2	Richards Bay S. Africa
143 D2	Richardson U.S.A.
126 C2	Richardson Mountains Can.
135 D3	Richfield U.S.A.
134 C1	Richland U.S.A.
138 A2	Richland Center U.S.A.
53 D2	Richmond *N.S.W.* Austr.
51 D2	Richmond *Qld* Austr.
134 B1	Richmond Can.
54 B2	Richmond N.Z.
122 B3	Richmond S. Africa
98 C2	Richmond U.K.
138 C3	Richmond *IN* U.S.A.
138 C3	Richmond *KY* U.S.A.
139 D3	Richmond *VA* U.S.A.
141 D2	Richmond Hill U.S.A.
53 D1	Richmond Range *hills* Austr.
130 C3	Rideau Lakes Can.
135 C3	Ridgecrest U.S.A.
140 B2	Ridgeland U.S.A.
102 C1	Riesa Ger.
101 D1	Rieste Ger.
123 B2	Riet *r.* S. Africa
101 D2	Rietberg Ger.
122 B2	Rietfontein S. Africa
108 B2	Rieti Italy
136 B3	Rifle U.S.A.
88 B2	Rīga Latvia
88 B2	Riga, Gulf of Estonia/Latvia
79 C2	Rīgān Iran
134 D2	Rigby U.S.A.
131 E2	Rigolet Can.
93 H3	Riihimäki Fin.
55 D2	Riiser-Larsen Ice Shelf Antarctica
108 B1	Rijeka Croatia
134 C2	Riley U.S.A.
105 C2	Rillieux-la-Pape France
78 B2	Rimah, Wādī al *watercourse* Saudi Arabia
103 E2	Rimavská Sobota Slovakia
128 C2	Rimbey Can.
108 B2	Rimini Italy
	Rîmnicu Sărat Romania *see* Râmnicu Sărat
	Rîmnicu Vîlcea Romania *see* Râmnicu Vâlcea
131 D3	Rimouski Can.
144 B2	Rincón de Romos Mex.
93 F3	Ringebu Norway
93 E4	Ringkøbing Denmark
92 G2	Ringvassøya *i.* Norway
99 C4	Ringwood U.K.
101 D1	Rinteln Ger.
154 B3	Rio Azul Brazil
150 B3	Riobamba Ecuador
155 D2	Rio Bonito Brazil
154 C2	Rio Branco Brazil
154 C3	Rio Branco do Sul Brazil
154 B2	Rio Brilhante Brazil
155 D2	Rio Casca Brazil
153 B3	Río Claro Brazil
153 B3	Río Colorado Arg.
153 B3	Río Cuarto Arg.
155 D2	Rio de Janeiro Brazil
153 B5	Río Gallegos Arg.
153 B5	Río Grande Arg.
152 C3	Rio Grande Brazil
144 B2	Río Grande Mex.
143 D3	Rio Grande *r.* Mex./U.S.A.
143 D3	Rio Grande City U.S.A.
150 B1	Ríohacha Col.
150 B3	Rioja Peru
145 D2	Río Lagartos Mex.
151 F3	Río Largo Brazil
105 C2	Riom France
152 B1	Río Mulatos Bol.
154 B3	Rio Negro Brazil
155 D1	Rio Pardo de Minas Brazil
154 C1	Rio Preto, Serra do *hills* Brazil
142 B1	Rio Rancho U.S.A.
150 B3	Río Tigre Ecuador
64 A3	Rio Tuba Phil.
154 B1	Rio Verde Brazil
145 C2	Río Verde Mex.
154 B1	Rio Verde de Mato Grosso Brazil
90 C1	Ripky Ukr.
99 C3	Ripley U.K.
107 D1	Ripoll Spain
98 C2	Ripon U.K.
66 D1	Rishiri-tō *i.* Japan
	Rîşnov Romania *see* Râşnov
93 E4	Risør Norway
122 B2	Ritchie S. Africa
73 D3	Ritchie's Archipelago *is* India
134 C1	Ritzville U.S.A.
152 B2	Rivadavia Arg.
108 B1	Riva del Garda Italy
146 B3	Rivas Nic.
152 C3	Rivera Uru.
114 B4	River Cess Liberia
129 D2	Riverhurst Can.
52 C2	Riverina *reg.* Austr.
122 B3	Riversdale S. Africa
135 C4	Riverside U.S.A.
136 B2	Riverton U.S.A.
131 D3	Riverview Can.
105 C3	Rivesaltes France
131 D3	Rivière-au-Renard Can.
131 D3	Rivière-du-Loup Can.
139 F1	Rivière-Ouelle Can.
90 B1	Rivne Ukr.
108 A1	Rivoli Italy
120 B2	Rivungo Angola
54 B2	Riwaka N.Z.
78 B2	Riyadh Saudi Arabia
81 C1	Rize Turkey
70 B2	Rizhao China
105 C2	Roanne France
138 D3	Roanoke U.S.A.
141 E1	Roanoke *r.* U.S.A.
141 E1	Roanoke Rapids U.S.A.
135 E3	Roan Plateau U.S.A.
146 B3	Roatán Hond.
52 A3	Robe Austr.
52 B2	Robe, Mount *hill* Austr.
101 F1	Röbel Ger.
53 D1	Roberts, Mount Austr.
92 H3	Robertsfors Sweden
122 A3	Robertson S. Africa
114 A4	Robertsport Liberia
	Robert Williams Angola *see* Caála
130 C3	Roberval Can.
50 A2	Robinson Range *hills* Austr.
52 B2	Robinvale Austr.
129 D2	Roblin Can.
128 C2	Robson, Mount Can.
143 D3	Robstown U.S.A.
	Roçadas Angola *see* Xangongo
108 B3	Rocca Busambra *mt.* Sicily Italy
153 C3	Rocha Uru.
98 B3	Rochdale U.K.
154 B1	Rochedo Brazil
100 B2	Rochefort Belgium
104 B2	Rochefort France
52 B3	Rochester Austr.
137 E2	Rochester *MN* U.S.A.
139 E2	Rochester *NH* U.S.A.
139 D2	Rochester *NY* U.S.A.
94 A2	Rockall *i.* N. Atlantic Ocean
160 L4	Rockall Bank *sea feature* N. Atlantic Ocean
138 B2	Rockford U.S.A.
51 E2	Rockhampton Austr.
141 D2	Rock Hill U.S.A.
50 A3	Rockingham Austr.
138 A2	Rock Island U.S.A.
136 B3	Rock Springs *MT* U.S.A.
136 C3	Rock Springs *WY* U.S.A.
141 D1	Rockwood U.S.A.
136 C3	Rocky Ford U.S.A.
141 E1	Rocky Mount U.S.A.
128 C2	Rocky Mountain House Can.
124 F4	Rocky Mountains U.S.A.
100 B3	Rocroi France
102 C1	Rødbyhavn Denmark
131 E2	Roddickton Can.
104 C3	Rodez France
	Rodi *i.* Greece *see* Rhodes
89 F2	Rodniki Rus. Fed.
	Rodos Greece *see* Rhodes
	Rodos *i.* Greece *see* Rhodes
	Rodosto Turkey *see* Tekirdağ
50 A2	Roebourne Austr.
50 B1	Roebuck Bay Austr.
123 C1	Roedtan S. Africa
100 B2	Roermond Neth.
100 A2	Roeselare Belgium
127 G2	Roes Welcome Sound *sea chan.* Can.
128 C2	Rogers Can.
140 B1	Rogers U.S.A.
138 C3	Rogers, Mount U.S.A.
138 C1	Rogers City U.S.A.
157 G8	Roggeveen Basin *sea feature* S. Pacific Ocean
122 B3	Roggeveldberge *esc.* S. Africa
92 G2	Rognan Norway
134 B2	Rogue *r.* U.S.A.
74 B2	Rohtak India
49 M5	Roi Georges, Îles du *is* Fr. Polynesia
88 B2	Roja Latvia
60 B1	Rokan *r.* Indon.
88 C2	Rokiškis Lith.
90 B1	Rokytne Ukr.
154 B2	Rolândia Brazil
137 E3	Rolla U.S.A.
143 C2	Rolling Prairies *reg.* U.S.A.
51 D2	Roma Austr.
59 C3	Roma *i.* Indon.
	Roma Italy *see* Rome
123 C2	Roma Lesotho
143 D3	Roma U.S.A.
141 E2	Romain, Cape U.S.A.
110 C1	Roman Romania
158 E5	Romanche Gap *sea feature* S. Atlantic Ocean
110 B1	Romania *country* Europe
91 C3	Roman-Kosh *mt.* Ukr.
69 D1	Romanovka Rus. Fed.
105 D2	Romans-sur-Isère France
123 C2	Rombas France
64 B2	Romblon Phil.
108 B2	Rome Italy
141 C2	Rome *GA* U.S.A.
139 D2	Rome *NY* U.S.A.
99 D4	Romford U.K.
105 C2	Romilly-sur-Seine France
91 C1	Romny Ukr.
104 C2	Romorantin-Lanthenay France
99 C4	Romsey U.K.
134 D1	Ronan U.S.A.
96 □	Ronas Hill U.K.
151 D4	Roncador, Serra do *hills* Brazil
106 B2	Ronda Spain
154 B2	Rondon Brazil
154 B1	Rondonópolis Brazil
74 B1	Rondu Jammu and Kashmir
71 A3	Rong'an China
	Rongcheng China *see* Rongxian
	Rongcheng China *see* Jianli
71 A3	Rongjiang China
62 A1	Rongklang Range *mts* Myanmar
	Rongmei China *see* Hefeng
71 B3	Rongxian China
93 F4	Rønne Denmark
93 G4	Ronneby Sweden
55 A2	Ronne Ice Shelf Antarctica
101 D1	Ronnenberg Ger.
100 A2	Ronse Belgium
	Rooke Island P.N.G. *see* Umboi
74 B2	Roorkee India
100 B2	Roosendaal Neth.
135 E2	Roosevelt U.S.A.
128 B2	Roosevelt, Mount Can.
55 N2	Roosevelt Island Antarctica
104 B3	Roquefort France
150 C2	Roraima, Mount Guyana
93 F3	Røros Norway
90 C2	Ros' *r.* Ukr.
142 B3	Rosa, Punta *pt* Mex.
106 B2	Rosal de la Frontera Spain
153 B3	Rosario Arg.
144 A1	Rosario Mex.
144 B2	Rosario Mex.
144 B2	Rosario Mex.
147 C3	Rosario Venez.
152 B2	Rosario de la Frontera Arg.
151 D4	Rosário Oeste Brazil
144 A2	Rosarito Mex.
144 A1	Rosarito Mex.
142 A3	Rosarito Mex.
109 C3	Rosarno Italy
143 C2	Roscoe U.S.A.
104 B2	Roscoff France
97 B2	Roscommon Rep. of Ireland
97 C2	Roscrea Rep. of Ireland
147 D3	Roseau Dominica
137 D1	Roseau U.S.A.
134 B2	Roseburg U.S.A.
96 C2	Rosehearty U.K.
143 D3	Rosenberg U.S.A.
101 D1	Rosengarten Ger.
102 C2	Rosenheim Ger.
129 D2	Rosetown Can.
122 A2	Rosh Pinah Namibia
110 C2	Roşiori de Vede Romania
93 F4	Roskilde Denmark
89 D3	Roslavl' Rus. Fed.
134 B1	Roslyn U.S.A.
109 C3	Rossano Italy
97 B1	Rossan Point Rep. of Ireland
51 E1	Rossel Island P.N.G.
55 N1	Ross Ice Shelf Antarctica
131 D3	Rossignol, Lake Can.
128 C3	Rossland Can.
97 C2	Rosslare Rep. of Ireland
97 C2	Rosslare Harbour Rep. of Ireland
101 F2	Roßlau Ger.
101 E2	Roßleben Ger.
114 A3	Rosso Maur.
105 D3	Rosso, Capo *c.* Corsica France
99 B4	Ross-on-Wye U.K.
91 D1	Rossosh' Rus. Fed.
128 A1	Ross River Can.
55 N2	Ross Sea Antarctica
92 F2	Røssvatnet *l.* Norway
81 D3	Rostāq Iran
129 D2	Rosthern Can.
102 C1	Rostock Ger.
89 E2	Rostov Rus. Fed.

91 D2 **Rostov-na-Donu** Rus. Fed.
Rostov-on-Don Rus. Fed. *see* **Rostov-na-Donu**
104 B2 **Rostrenen** France
92 G2 **Røsvik** Norway
92 H2 **Rosvik** Sweden
142 C2 **Roswell** U.S.A.
59 D2 **Rota** *i.* N. Mariana Is
59 C3 **Rote** *i.* Indon.
101 D1 **Rotenburg (Wümme)** Ger.
101 E3 **Roth** Ger.
98 C2 **Rothbury** U.K.
101 E3 **Rothenburg ob der Tauber** Ger.
98 C3 **Rotherham** U.K.
96 C2 **Rothes** U.K.
96 B3 **Rothesay** U.K.
53 C2 **Roto** Austr.
105 D3 **Rotondo, Monte** *mt. Corsica* France
54 C1 **Rotorua** N.Z.
54 C1 **Rotorua, Lake** N.Z.
101 E2 **Rottenbach** Ger.
102 C2 **Rottenmann** Austria
100 B2 **Rotterdam** Neth.
102 B2 **Rottweil** Ger.
49 I5 **Rotuma** *i.* Fiji
105 C1 **Roubaix** France
104 C2 **Rouen** France
Roulers Belgium *see* **Roeselare**
53 D2 **Round Mountain** Austr.
131 E3 **Round Pond** *l.* Can.
143 D2 **Round Rock** U.S.A.
134 E1 **Roundup** U.S.A.
96 C1 **Rousay** *i.* U.K.
130 C3 **Rouyn-Noranda** Can.
Rouyuanchengzi China *see* **Huachi**
92 I2 **Rovaniemi** Fin.
91 D2 **Roven'ki** Rus. Fed.
91 D2 **Roven'ky** Ukr.
108 B1 **Rovereto** Italy
63 B2 **Rôviĕng Tbong** Cambodia
108 B1 **Rovigo** Italy
108 B1 **Rovinj** Croatia
53 C1 **Rowena** Austr.
Równe Ukr. *see* **Rivne**
64 B3 **Roxas** Phil.
64 B2 **Roxas** Phil.
64 A2 **Roxas** Phil.
64 B2 **Roxas** Phil.
52 A2 **Roxby Downs** Austr.
142 C1 **Roy** *NM* U.S.A.
134 D2 **Roy** *UT* U.S.A.
138 B1 **Royale, Isle** *i.* U.S.A.
104 B2 **Royan** France
99 C3 **Royston** U.K.
90 C2 **Rozdil'na** Ukr.
91 C2 **Rozdol'ne** Ukr.
103 E2 **Rožňava** Slovakia
100 B3 **Rozoy-sur-Serre** France
87 D3 **Rtishchevo** Rus. Fed.
Ruanda *country* Africa *see* **Rwanda**
54 C1 **Ruapehu, Mount** *vol.* N.Z.
54 A3 **Ruapuke Island** N.Z.
89 D2 **Ruba** Belarus
79 B3 **Rub' al Khālī** *des.* Saudi Arabia
119 D3 **Rubeho Mountains** Tanz.
91 D2 **Rubizhne** Ukr.
77 E1 **Rubtsovsk** Rus. Fed.
126 B2 **Ruby** U.S.A.
135 C2 **Ruby Mountains** U.S.A.
76 C3 **Rudbar** Afgh.
66 C2 **Rudnaya Pristan'** Rus. Fed.
89 D3 **Rudnya** Rus. Fed.
76 C1 **Rudnyy** Kazakh.
Rudolf, Lake *salt l.* Eth./Kenya *see* **Turkana, Lake**
82 E1 **Rudol'fa, Ostrov** *i.* Rus. Fed.
Rudolph Island Rus. Fed. *see* **Rudol'fa, Ostrov**
101 E2 **Rudolstadt** Ger.
116 B3 **Rufa'a** Sudan
119 D3 **Rufiji** *r.* Tanz.
153 B3 **Rufino** Arg.
121 B2 **Rufunsa** Zambia
70 C2 **Rugao** China
99 C3 **Rugby** U.K.
136 C1 **Rugby** U.S.A.
102 C1 **Rügen** *i.* Ger.
119 C3 **Ruhengeri** Rwanda
101 E2 **Ruhla** Ger.
88 B2 **Ruhnu** *i.* Estonia
100 C2 **Ruhr** *r.* Ger.
71 C3 **Rui'an** China
142 B2 **Ruidoso** U.S.A.
144 B2 **Ruiz** Mex.
119 D3 **Rukwa, Lake** Tanz.
96 A2 **Rum** *i.* U.K.
109 C1 **Ruma** Serb. and Mont.
78 B2 **Rumāh** Saudi Arabia
117 A4 **Rumbek** Sudan
147 C2 **Rum Cay** *i.* Bahamas
139 E2 **Rumford** U.S.A.
103 D1 **Rumia** Pol.
105 D2 **Rumilly** France
50 C1 **Rum Jungle** Austr.
66 D2 **Rumoi** Japan
121 C2 **Rumphi** Malawi
54 B2 **Runanga** N.Z.
98 B3 **Runcorn** U.K.
120 A2 **Rundu** Namibia
119 C2 **Rungu** Dem. Rep. Congo
119 D3 **Rungwa** Tanz.
68 B2 **Ruoqiang** China
130 C2 **Rupert** *r.* Can.
134 D2 **Rupert** U.S.A.
130 C2 **Rupert Bay** Can.
Rusaddir N. Africa *see* **Melilla**
121 C2 **Rusape** Zimbabwe
110 C2 **Ruse** Bulg.
137 E1 **Rush City** U.S.A.
121 C2 **Rushinga** Zimbabwe
77 D3 **Rushon** Tajik.
136 C2 **Rushville** U.S.A.
53 C3 **Rushworth** Austr.
129 D2 **Russell** Can.
54 B1 **Russell** N.Z.
137 D3 **Russell** U.S.A.
140 C2 **Russellville** *AL* U.S.A.
140 B1 **Russellville** *AR* U.S.A.
138 B3 **Russellville** *KY* U.S.A.
101 D2 **Rüsselsheim** Ger.
82 F2 **Russian Federation** *country* Asia/Europe
81 C1 **Rust'avi** Georgia
123 C2 **Rustenburg** S. Africa
140 B2 **Ruston** U.S.A.
61 D2 **Ruteng** Indon.
98 B3 **Ruthin** U.K.
139 E2 **Rutland** U.S.A.
Rutog China *see* **Dêrub**
119 C3 **Rutshuru** Dem. Rep. Congo
119 E4 **Ruvuma** *r.* Moz./Tanz.
79 C2 **Ruweis** U.A.E.
89 E2 **Ruza** Rus. Fed.
77 C1 **Ruzayevka** Kazakh.
87 D3 **Ruzayevka** Rus. Fed.
119 C3 **Rwanda** *country* Africa
89 E3 **Ryazan'** Rus. Fed.
89 F3 **Ryazhsk** Rus. Fed.
86 C2 **Rybachiy, Poluostrov** *pen.* Rus. Fed.
Rybach'ye Kyrg. *see* **Balykchy**
89 E2 **Rybinsk** Rus. Fed.
89 E2 **Rybinskoye Vodokhranilishche** *resr* Rus. Fed.
103 D1 **Rybnik** Pol.
Rybnitsa Moldova *see* **Rîbniţa**
89 E3 **Rybnoye** Rus. Fed.
99 D4 **Rye** U.K.
Rykovo Ukr. *see* **Yenakiyeve**
89 D3 **Ryl'sk** Rus. Fed.
Ryojun China *see* **Lüshun**
67 C3 **Ryōtsu** Japan
69 E3 **Ryukyu Islands** *is* Japan
89 D3 **Ryzhikovo** Rus. Fed.
103 E1 **Rzeszów** Pol.
91 E1 **Rzhaksa** Rus. Fed.
89 D2 **Rzhev** Rus. Fed.

S

79 C2 **Sa'ādatābād** Iran
101 E2 **Saale** *r.* Ger.
101 E2 **Saalfeld** Ger.
134 B1 **Saanich** Can.
100 C3 **Saar** *r.* Ger.
102 B2 **Saarbrücken** Ger.
88 B2 **Sääre** Estonia
88 B2 **Saaremaa** *i.* Estonia
92 I2 **Saarenkylä** Fin.
93 I3 **Saarijärvi** Fin.
100 C3 **Saarlouis** Ger.
80 B2 **Sab' Ābār** Syria
107 D1 **Sabadell** Spain
67 C3 **Sabae** Japan
61 C1 **Sabah** *state* Malaysia
61 C2 **Sabalana** *i.* Indon.
146 B2 **Sabana, Archipiélago de** *is* Cuba
150 B1 **Sabanalarga** Col.
60 A1 **Sabang** Indon.
155 D1 **Sabará** Brazil
108 B2 **Sabaudia** Italy
122 B3 **Sabelo** S. Africa
119 D2 **Sabena Desert** Kenya
115 D2 **Sabhā** Libya
123 D2 **Sabie** *r.* Moz./S. Africa
123 D2 **Sabie** S. Africa
145 B2 **Sabinas** Mex.
145 B2 **Sabinas Hidalgo** Mex.
143 E3 **Sabine** *r.* U.S.A.
131 D3 **Sable, Cape** Can.
141 D3 **Sable, Cape** U.S.A.
131 E3 **Sable Island** Can.
106 B1 **Sabugal** Port.
78 B3 **Şabyā** Saudi Arabia
76 B3 **Sabzevār** Iran
107 D2 **Sa Cabaneta** Spain
137 D2 **Sac City** U.S.A.
120 A2 **Sachanga** Angola
130 A2 **Sachigo Lake** Can.
65 B3 **Sach'on** S. Korea
126 D2 **Sachs Harbour** Can.
154 C1 **Sacramento** Brazil
135 B3 **Sacramento** U.S.A.
135 B3 **Sacramento** *r.* U.S.A.
142 B2 **Sacramento Mountains** U.S.A.
135 B2 **Sacramento Valley** U.S.A.
110 B1 **Săcueni** Romania
123 C3 **Sada** S. Africa
107 C1 **Sádaba** Spain
Sá da Bandeira Angola *see* **Lubango**
78 B3 **Şa'dah** Yemen
63 B3 **Sadao** Thai.
79 B3 **Şadārah** Yemen
63 B2 **Sa Đec** Vietnam
74 B2 **Sadiqabad** Pak.
72 D2 **Sadiya** India
67 C3 **Sadoga-shima** *i.* Japan
107 D2 **Sa Dragonera** *i.* Spain
93 F4 **Säffle** Sweden
142 B2 **Safford** U.S.A.
99 D3 **Saffron Walden** U.K.
114 B1 **Safi** Morocco
155 D1 **Safiras, Serra das** *mts* Brazil
86 D2 **Safonovo** Rus. Fed.
89 D2 **Safonovo** Rus. Fed.
78 B2 **Safrā' as Sark** *esc.* Saudi Arabia
75 C2 **Saga** China
67 B4 **Saga** Japan
62 A1 **Sagaing** Myanmar
67 C3 **Sagamihara** Japan
74 B2 **Sagar** India
Sagarmatha *mt.* China/Nepal *see* **Everest, Mount**
138 C2 **Saginaw** U.S.A.
138 C2 **Saginaw Bay** U.S.A.
Saglouc Can. *see* **Salluit**
106 B2 **Sagres** Port.
146 B2 **Sagua la Grande** Cuba
139 F1 **Saguenay** *r.* Can.
107 C2 **Sagunto** Spain
76 B2 **Sagyndyk, Mys** *pt* Kazakh.
106 B1 **Sahagún** Spain
114 C3 **Sahara** *des.* Africa
Saharan Atlas *mts* Alg. *see* **Atlas Saharien**
74 B2 **Saharanpur** India
75 C2 **Saharsa** India
114 B3 **Sahel** *reg.* Africa
74 B1 **Sahiwal** Pak.
144 B2 **Sahuayo** Mex.
78 B2 **Şaḩūq** *reg.* Saudi Arabia
114 C1 **Saïda** Alg.
Saïda Lebanon *see* **Sidon**
75 C2 **Saidpur** Bangl.
67 B3 **Saigō** Japan
Saigon Vietnam *see* **Ho Chi Minh City**
75 D2 **Saiha** India
70 B1 **Saihan Tal** China
67 B4 **Saiki** Japan
93 I3 **Saimaa** *l.* Fin.
144 B2 **Sain Alto** Mex.
96 C3 **St Abb's Head** *hd* U.K.
131 E3 **St Alban's** Can.
99 C4 **St Albans** U.K.
138 C3 **St Albans** U.S.A.
99 B4 **St Alban's Head** *hd* U.K.
St Aldhelm's Head *hd* U.K. *see* **St Alban's Head**
St-André, Cap *pt* Madag. *see* **Vilanandro, Tanjona**
96 C2 **St Andrews** U.K.
131 E2 **St Anthony** Can.
134 D2 **St Anthony** U.S.A.
52 B3 **St Arnaud** Austr.
131 E2 **St-Augustin** Can.
131 E2 **St Augustin** *r.* Can.
141 D3 **St Augustine** U.S.A.
99 A4 **St Austell** U.K.
104 C2 **St-Avertin** France
147 D3 **St-Barthélemy** *i.* West Indies
98 B2 **St Bees Head** *hd* U.K.
105 D3 **St-Bonnet-en-Champsaur** France
99 A4 **St Bride's Bay** U.K.
104 B2 **St-Brieuc** France
130 C3 **St Catharines** Can.
141 D2 **St Catherines Island** U.S.A.
99 C4 **St Catherine's Point** U.K.
137 E3 **St Charles** U.S.A.
138 C2 **St Clair, Lake** Can./U.S.A.
105 D2 **St-Claude** France
99 A4 **St Clears** U.K.
137 E1 **St Cloud** U.S.A.
138 A1 **St Croix** *r.* U.S.A.
147 D3 **St Croix** Virgin Is (U.S.A.)
99 A4 **St David's** U.K.
99 A4 **St David's Head** *hd* U.K.
113 I8 **St-Denis** Can.
104 C2 **St-Denis** France
St-Denis-du-Sig Alg. *see* **Sig**
105 D2 **St-Dié** France
105 C2 **St-Dizier** France
130 C3 **Ste-Adèle** Can.
131 D3 **Ste-Anne-des-Monts** Can.
139 E1 **Ste-Foy** Can.
105 D2 **St-Égrève** France
128 A1 **St Elias Mountains** Can.
131 D2 **Ste-Marguerite** *r.* Can.
139 E1 **Ste-Marie** Can.
Ste-Marie, Cap *c.* Madag. *see* **Vohimena, Tanjona**
Sainte-Marie, Île *i.* Madag. *see* **Nosy Boraha**
Ste-Rose-du-Dégelé Can. *see* **Dégelis**
129 E2 **Ste Rose du Lac** Can.
104 B2 **Saintes** France
105 C2 **St-Étienne** France
104 C2 **St-Étienne-du-Rouvray** France
130 C3 **St-Félicien** Can.
97 D1 **Saintfield** U.K.
105 D3 **St-Florent** *Corsica* France
105 C2 **St-Flour** France
136 C3 **St Francis** U.S.A.
104 C3 **St-Gaudens** France
53 C1 **St George** Austr.
135 D3 **St George** U.S.A.
141 D3 **St George Island** U.S.A.
131 C3 **St-Georges** Can.
147 D3 **St George's** Grenada
131 E3 **St George's Bay** Can.
97 C3 **St George's Channel** Rep. of Ireland/U.K.
105 D2 **St Gotthard Pass** *pass* Switz.
113 C7 **St Helena** *terr.* S. Atlantic Ocean
122 A3 **St Helena Bay** S. Africa
122 A3 **St Helena Bay** *b.* S. Africa
98 B3 **St Helens** U.K.
134 B1 **St Helens, Mount** *vol.* U.S.A.
95 C4 **St Helier** Channel Is
100 B2 **St-Hubert** Belgium
139 E1 **St-Hyacinthe** Can.
138 C1 **St Ignace** U.S.A.
130 B3 **St Ignace Island** Can.
99 A4 **St Ives** U.K.
St Jacques, Cap Vietnam *see* **Vung Tau**
128 A2 **St James, Cape** Can.
130 C3 **St-Jean, Lac** *l.* Can.
104 B2 **St-Jean-d'Angély** France
104 B3 **St-Jean-de-Luz** France
104 B2 **St-Jean-de-Monts** France
130 C3 **St-Jean-sur-Richelieu** Can.
139 E1 **St-Jérôme** Can.
134 C1 **St Joe** *r.* U.S.A.
131 D3 **Saint John** Can.
137 D3 **St John** U.S.A.
139 F1 **St John** *r.* U.S.A.
147 D3 **St John's** Antigua
131 E3 **St John's** Can.
142 B2 **St Johns** U.S.A.

141 D2 **St Johns** *r.* U.S.A.
139 E2 **St Johnsbury** U.S.A.
137 E3 **St Joseph** U.S.A.
130 A2 **St Joseph, Lake** Can.
St-Joseph-d'Alma Can. *see* **Alma**
130 B3 **St Joseph Island** Can.
139 E1 **St-Jovité** Can.
104 C2 **St-Junien** France
94 B2 **St Kilda** *i.* U.K.
147 D3 **St Kitts and Nevis** *country* West Indies
151 D2 **St-Laurent-du-Maroni** Fr. Guiana
131 E3 **St Lawrence** Can.
131 D3 **St Lawrence** *inlet* Can.
131 D3 **St Lawrence, Gulf of** Can.
126 A2 **St Lawrence Island** U.S.A.
104 B2 **St-Lô** France
114 A3 **St-Louis** Senegal
137 E3 **St Louis** U.S.A.
137 E1 **St Louis** *r.* U.S.A.
147 D3 **St Lucia** *country* West Indies
147 D3 **St Lucia Channel** Martinique/St Lucia
123 D2 **St Lucia Estuary** S. Africa
147 D3 **St Maarten** *i.* West Indies
96 □ **St Magnus Bay** U.K.
104 B2 **St-Malo** France
104 B2 **St-Malo, Golfe de** *g.* France
147 C3 **St-Marc** Haiti
St Mark's S. Africa *see* **Cofimvaba**
147 D3 **St-Martin** *i.* West Indies
122 A3 **St Martin, Cape** S. Africa
129 E2 **St Martin, Lake** Can.
139 D2 **St Marys** U.S.A.
124 A3 **St Matthew Island** U.S.A.
59 D3 **St Matthias Group** *is* P.N.G.
130 C3 **St-Maurice** *r.* Can.
130 C3 **St-Michel-des-Saints** Can.
104 B2 **St-Nazaire** France
104 C1 **St-Omer** France
129 C2 **St Paul** Can.
137 E2 **St Paul** U.S.A.
156 A8 **St-Paul, Île** *i.* Indian Ocean
137 E2 **St Peter** U.S.A.
95 C4 **St Peter Port** Channel Is
141 D3 **St Petersburg** U.S.A.
131 E3 **St-Pierre** St Pierre and Miquelon
139 E1 **St-Pierre, Lac** *l.* Can.
131 E3 **St Pierre and Miquelon** *terr.* N. America
104 B2 **St-Pierre-d'Oléron** France
105 C2 **St-Pourçain-sur-Sioule** France
131 D3 **St Quentin** Can.
105 C2 **St-Quentin** France
105 D3 **St-Raphaël** France
122 B3 **St Sebastian Bay** S. Africa
104 B2 **St-Sébastien-sur-Loire** France
131 D3 **St-Siméon** Can.
129 E2 **St Theresa Point** Can.
130 B3 **St Thomas** Can.
105 D3 **St-Tropez** France
105 D3 **St-Tropez, Cap de** *c.* France
St Vincent, Cape Port. *see* **São Vicente, Cabo de**
52 A3 **St Vincent, Gulf** Austr.
147 D3 **St Vincent and the Grenadines** *country* West Indies
147 D3 **St Vincent Passage** St Lucia/St Vincent
129 D2 **St Walburg** Can.
104 C2 **St-Yrieix-la-Perche** France
59 D1 **Saipan** *i.* N. Mariana Is
152 B1 **Sajama, Nevado** *mt.* Bol.
122 B2 **Sak** *watercourse* S. Africa
67 C4 **Sakai** Japan
67 B4 **Sakaide** Japan
78 B2 **Sakākah** Saudi Arabia
136 C1 **Sakakawea, Lake** U.S.A.
Sakarya Turkey *see* **Adapazarı**
111 D2 **Sakarya** *r.* Turkey
66 C3 **Sakata** Japan
65 B1 **Sakchu** N. Korea
66 D1 **Sakhalin** *i.* Rus. Fed.
123 C2 **Sakhile** S. Africa
81 C1 **Şäki** Azer.
88 B3 **Šakiai** Lith.
69 E3 **Sakishima-shotō** *is* Japan
62 B2 **Sakon Nakhon** Thai.
74 A2 **Sakrand** Pak.
122 B3 **Sakrivier** S. Africa
67 D3 **Sakura** Japan
91 C2 **Saky** Ukr.
93 G4 **Sala** Sweden
130 C3 **Salaberry-de-Valleyfield** Can.
88 B2 **Salacgrīva** Latvia
109 C2 **Sala Consilina** Italy
135 C4 **Salada, Laguna** *salt l.* Mex.
152 C2 **Saladas** Arg.
152 B3 **Salado** *r.* Arg.
145 C2 **Salado** *r.* Mex.
153 B3 **Salado o Chadileo** *r.* Arg.
114 B4 **Salaga** Ghana
122 B1 **Salajwe** Botswana
79 C2 **Salakh, Jabal** *mt.* Oman
115 D3 **Salal** Chad
78 A2 **Salâla** Sudan
79 C3 **Şalālah** Oman
145 B2 **Salamanca** Mex.
106 B1 **Salamanca** Spain
139 D2 **Salamanca** U.S.A.
106 B1 **Salas** Spain
63 B2 **Salavan** Laos
59 C3 **Salawati** *i.* Indon.
61 D2 **Salayar** *i.* Indon.
157 G7 **Sala y Gómez, Isla** *i.* S. Pacific Ocean
Salazar Angola *see* **N'dalatando**
104 C2 **Salbris** France
88 C3 **Šalčininkai** Lith.
106 C1 **Saldaña** Spain
122 A3 **Saldanha** S. Africa
88 B2 **Saldus** Latvia
53 C3 **Sale** Austr.
86 F2 **Salekhard** Rus. Fed.
73 B3 **Salem** India
138 B3 **Salem** *IL* U.S.A.
137 E3 **Salem** *MO* U.S.A.
134 B2 **Salem** *OR* U.S.A.
137 D2 **Salem** *SD* U.S.A.
96 B2 **Salen** U.K.
109 B2 **Salerno** Italy
108 B2 **Salerno, Golfo di** *g.* Italy
98 B3 **Salford** U.K.
151 E2 **Salgado** *r.* Brazil
103 D2 **Salgótarján** Hungary
151 F3 **Salgueiro** Brazil
136 B3 **Salida** U.S.A.
111 C3 **Salihli** Turkey
88 C3 **Salihorsk** Belarus
121 C2 **Salima** Malawi
121 C2 **Salimo** Moz.
137 D3 **Salina** *KS* U.S.A.
135 D3 **Salina** *UT* U.S.A.
109 B3 **Salina, Isola** *i.* Italy
145 C3 **Salina Cruz** Mex.
155 D1 **Salinas** Brazil
144 B2 **Salinas** Mex.
135 B3 **Salinas** U.S.A.
135 B3 **Salinas** *r.* U.S.A.
107 D2 **Salines, Cap de ses** *c.* Spain
151 E3 **Salinópolis** Brazil
99 C4 **Salisbury** U.K.
139 D3 **Salisbury** *MD* U.S.A.
141 D1 **Salisbury** *NC* U.S.A.
Salisbury Zimbabwe *see* **Harare**
99 B4 **Salisbury Plain** U.K.
151 E3 **Salitre** *r.* Brazil
92 I2 **Salla** Fin.
143 E1 **Sallisaw** U.S.A.
127 G2 **Salluit** Can.
75 C2 **Sallyana** Nepal
81 C2 **Salmās** Iran
128 C3 **Salmo** Can.
134 D1 **Salmon** U.S.A.
134 C1 **Salmon** *r.* U.S.A.
128 C2 **Salmon Arm** Can.
134 C2 **Salmon River Mountains** U.S.A.
100 C3 **Salmtal** Ger.
118 B2 **Salo** C.A.R.
93 H3 **Salo** Fin.
105 D3 **Salon-de-Provence** France
Salonica Greece *see* **Thessaloniki**
110 B1 **Salonta** Romania
87 D4 **Sal'sk** Rus. Fed.
122 B3 **Salt** *watercourse* S. Africa
107 D1 **Salt** Spain
142 A2 **Salt** *r.* U.S.A.
152 B2 **Salta** Arg.
99 A4 **Saltash** U.K.
96 B3 **Saltcoats** U.K.
145 B2 **Saltillo** Mex.
134 D2 **Salt Lake City** U.S.A.
154 C2 **Salto** Brazil
152 C3 **Salto** Uru.
155 E1 **Salto da Divisa** Brazil
154 B2 **Salto del Guairá** Para.
135 C4 **Salton Sea** *salt l.* U.S.A.
154 B3 **Salto Osório, Represa** *resr* Brazil
154 B3 **Salto Santiago, Represa de** *resr* Brazil
141 D2 **Saluda** U.S.A.
76 B3 **Saluq, Kūh-e** *mt.* Iran
108 A2 **Saluzzo** Italy
151 F4 **Salvador** Brazil
79 C2 **Salwah** Saudi Arabia
62 A2 **Salween** *r.* China/Myanmar
81 C2 **Salyan** Azer.
138 C3 **Salyersville** U.S.A.
122 A1 **Salzbrunn** Namibia
102 C2 **Salzburg** Austria
101 E1 **Salzgitter** Ger.
101 D2 **Salzkotten** Ger.
101 E1 **Salzwedel** Ger.
144 B1 **Samalayuca** Mex.
66 D2 **Samani** Japan
64 B2 **Samar** *i.* Phil.
87 E3 **Samara** Rus. Fed.
Samarahan Malaysia *see* **Sri Aman**
59 E3 **Samarai** P.N.G.
61 C2 **Samarinda** Indon.
77 C3 **Samarqand** Uzbek.
81 C2 **Sāmarrā'** Iraq
81 C1 **Şamaxı** Azer.
119 C3 **Samba** Dem. Rep. Congo
61 C1 **Sambaliung** *mts* Indon.
75 C2 **Sambalpur** India
60 C2 **Sambar, Tanjung** *pt* Indon.
60 B1 **Sambas** Indon.
121 □E2 **Sambava** Madag.
74 B2 **Sambhar** India
90 A2 **Sambir** Ukr.
61 C2 **Sambo** Indon.
61 C2 **Samboja** Indon.
153 C3 **Samborombón, Bahía** *b.* Arg.
65 B2 **Samch'ŏk** S. Korea
Samch'ŏnp'o S. Korea *see* **Sach'on**
81 C2 **Samdi Dag** *mt.* Turkey
119 D3 **Same** Tanz.
121 B2 **Samfya** Zambia
78 B2 **Samīrah** Saudi Arabia
65 B1 **Samjiyŏn** N. Korea
Sam Neua Laos *see* **Xam Nua**
48 J5 **Samoa** *country* S. Pacific Ocean
156 E6 **Samoa Basin** *sea feature* S. Pacific Ocean
Samoa i Sisifo *country* S. Pacific Ocean *see* **Samoa**
109 C1 **Samobor** Croatia
110 B2 **Samokov** Bulg.
111 C3 **Samos** *i.* Greece
Samothrace *i.* Greece *see* **Samothraki**
111 C2 **Samothraki** Greece
111 C2 **Samothraki** *i.* Greece
61 C2 **Sampit** Indon.
119 C3 **Sampwe** Dem. Rep. Congo
143 E2 **Sam Rayburn Reservoir** U.S.A.
62 B2 **Sâm Sơn** Vietnam
80 B1 **Samsun** Turkey
81 C1 **Samtredia** Georgia
63 B3 **Samui, Ko** *i.* Thai.
63 B2 **Samut Songkhram** Thai.
114 B3 **San** Mali
78 B3 **Şan'ā'** Yemen
118 A2 **Sanaga** *r.* Cameroon
81 C2 **Sanandaj** Iran
146 B3 **San Andrés, Isla de** *i.* Caribbean Sea
106 B1 **San Andrés del Rabanedo** Spain
142 B2 **San Andres Mountains** U.S.A.
145 C3 **San Andrés Tuxtla** Mex.
143 C2 **San Angelo** U.S.A.
143 D3 **San Antonio** U.S.A.
135 C4 **San Antonio, Mount** U.S.A.
107 D2 **San Antonio Abad** Spain
152 B2 **San Antonio de los Cobres** Arg.
153 B4 **San Antonio Oeste** Arg.
108 B2 **San Benedetto del Tronto** Italy
144 A3 **San Benedicto, Isla** *i.* Mex.
135 C4 **San Bernardino** U.S.A.
135 C4 **San Bernardino Mountains** U.S.A.
142 B3 **San Blas** Mex.
141 C3 **San Blas, Cape** U.S.A.
146 C4 **San Blas, Punta** *pt* Panama
152 B1 **San Borja** Bol.
144 B2 **San Buenaventura** Mex.
64 B2 **San Carlos** Phil.
147 D4 **San Carlos** Venez.
153 A4 **San Carlos de Bariloche** Arg.
147 C4 **San Carlos del Zulia** Venez.
104 C2 **Sancerrois, Collines du** *hills* France
135 C4 **San Clemente** U.S.A.
135 C4 **San Clemente Island** U.S.A.
105 C2 **Sancoins** France
48 H5 **San Cristobal** *i.* Solomon Is
150 B2 **San Cristóbal** Venez.
145 C3 **San Cristóbal de las Casas** Mex.
146 C2 **Sancti Spíritus** Cuba
123 D1 **Sand** *r.* S. Africa
61 C1 **Sandakan** *Sabah* Malaysia
93 E3 **Sandane** Norway
111 B2 **Sandanski** Bulg.
114 A3 **Sandaré** Mali
96 C1 **Sanday** *i.* U.K.
143 C2 **Sanderson** U.S.A.
150 C4 **Sandia** Peru
135 C4 **San Diego** U.S.A.
111 D3 **Sandıklı** Turkey
93 E4 **Sandnes** Norway
92 F2 **Sandnessjøen** Norway
118 C3 **Sandoa** Dem. Rep. Congo
103 E1 **Sandomierz** Pol.
89 E2 **Sandovo** Rus. Fed.
94 B1 **Sandoy** *i.* Faroe Is
134 C1 **Sandpoint** U.S.A.
71 B3 **Sandu** China
94 B1 **Sandur** Faroe Is
138 C2 **Sandusky** U.S.A.
122 A3 **Sandveld** *mts* S. Africa
122 A2 **Sandverhaar** Namibia
93 F4 **Sandvika** Norway
93 G3 **Sandviken** Sweden
131 E2 **Sandwich Bay** Can.
135 D2 **Sandy** U.S.A.
129 D2 **Sandy Bay** Can.
51 E2 **Sandy Cape** Austr.
130 A2 **Sandy Lake** Can.
130 A2 **Sandy Lake** *l.* Can.
141 D2 **Sandy Springs** U.S.A.
144 A1 **San Felipe** Mex.
145 B2 **San Felipe** Mex.
150 C1 **San Felipe** Venez.
144 A2 **San Fernando** Mex.
145 C2 **San Fernando** Mex.
64 B2 **San Fernando** Phil.
64 B2 **San Fernando** Phil.
106 B2 **San Fernando** Spain
147 D3 **San Fernando** Trin. and Tob.
150 C2 **San Fernando de Apure** Venez.
141 D3 **Sanford** *FL* U.S.A.
139 E2 **Sanford** *ME* U.S.A.
141 E1 **Sanford** *NC* U.S.A.
152 B3 **San Francisco** Arg.
135 B3 **San Francisco** U.S.A.
107 D2 **San Francisco Javier** Spain
74 B3 **Sangamner** India
83 J2 **Sangar** Rus. Fed.
108 A3 **San Gavino Monreale** *Sardinia* Italy
101 E2 **Sangerhausen** Ger.
61 C1 **Sanggau** Indon.
118 B3 **Sangha** *r.* Congo
109 C3 **San Giovanni in Fiore** Italy
59 C2 **Sangir** *i.* Indon.
59 C2 **Sangir, Kepulauan** *is* Indon.
65 B2 **Sangju** S. Korea
63 A2 **Sangkhla Buri** Thai.
61 C1 **Sangkulirang** Indon.
73 B3 **Sangli** India
118 B2 **Sangmélima** Cameroon
121 C3 **Sango** Zimbabwe
San Gottardo, Passo del *pass* Switz. *see* **St Gotthard Pass**

136 B3 Sangre de Cristo Range mts U.S.A.
75 C2 Sangsang China
144 A2 San Hipólito, Punta pt Mex.
145 D3 San Ignacio Belize
152 B1 San Ignacio Bol.
144 A2 San Ignacio Mex.
130 C2 Sanikiluaq Can.
71 A3 Sanjiang China
Sanjiang China see Jinping
67 C3 Sanjō Japan
135 B3 San Joaquin r. U.S.A.
153 B4 San Jorge, Golfo de g. Arg.
146 B4 San José Costa Rica
64 B2 San Jose Phil.
64 B2 San Jose Phil.
135 B3 San Jose U.S.A.
144 A2 San José, Isla i. Mex.
144 B2 San José de Bavicora Mex.
64 B2 San Jose de Buenavista Phil.
144 A2 San José de Comondú Mex.
144 B2 San José del Cabo Mex.
150 B2 San José del Guaviare Col.
152 B3 San Juan Arg.
146 B3 San Juan r. Costa Rica/Nic.
147 C3 San Juan Dom. Rep.
147 D3 San Juan Puerto Rico
135 D3 San Juan r. U.S.A.
152 C2 San Juan Bautista Para.
107 D2 San Juan Bautista Spain
145 C3 San Juan Bautista Tuxtepec Mex.
147 D4 San Juan de los Morros Venez.
145 C2 San Juan del Río Mex.
134 B1 San Juan Islands U.S.A.
144 B2 San Juanito Mex.
136 B3 San Juan Mountains U.S.A.
153 B4 San Julián Arg.
75 C2 Sankh r. India
63 B2 San Khao Phang Hoei mts Thai.
100 C2 St Augustin Ger.
105 D2 St Gallen Switz.
105 D2 St Moritz Switz.
Sankt-Peterburg Rus. Fed. see St Petersburg
89 D2 St Petersburg Rus. Fed.
102 C2 Sankt Veit an der Glan Austria
100 C3 St Wendel Ger.
80 B2 Şanlıurfa Turkey
142 B3 San Lorenzo Mex.
106 B2 Sanlúcar de Barrameda Spain
144 B2 San Lucas Mex.
153 B3 San Luis Arg.
145 B2 San Luis de la Paz Mex.
142 A2 San Luisito Mex.
135 B3 San Luis Obispo U.S.A.
135 B3 San Luis Obispo Bay U.S.A.
145 B2 San Luis Potosí Mex.
144 A1 San Luis Río Colorado Mex.
143 D3 San Marcos U.S.A.
108 B2 San Marino country Europe
108 B2 San Marino San Marino
144 B2 San Martín de Bolaños Mex.
153 A4 San Martín de los Andes Arg.
135 B3 San Mateo U.S.A.
153 B4 San Matías, Golfo g. Arg.
70 B2 Sanmenxia China
146 B3 San Miguel El Salvador
152 B2 San Miguel de Tucumán Arg.
135 B4 San Miguel Island U.S.A.
145 C3 San Miguel Sola de Vega Mex.
71 B3 Sanming China
153 B3 San Nicolás de los Arroyos Arg.
135 C4 San Nicolas Island U.S.A.
110 B1 Sânnicolau Mare Romania
123 C2 Sannieshof S. Africa
114 B4 Sanniquellie Liberia
103 E2 Sanok Pol.
64 B2 San Pablo Phil.

144 B2 San Pablo Balleza Mex.
152 B2 San Pedro Arg.
152 B1 San Pedro Bol.
114 B4 San-Pédro Côte d'Ivoire
144 A2 San Pedro Mex.
142 A2 San Pedro watercourse U.S.A.
106 B2 San Pedro, Sierra de mts Spain
144 B2 San Pedro de las Colonias Mex.
152 C2 San Pedro de Ycuamandyyú Para.
142 A3 San Pedro el Saucito Mex.
146 B3 San Pedro Sula Hond.
108 A3 San Pietro, Isola di i. Sardinia Italy
96 C3 Sanquhar U.K.
144 A1 San Quintín, Cabo c. Mex.
153 B3 San Rafael Arg.
108 A2 San Remo Italy
143 D2 San Saba U.S.A.
147 C2 San Salvador i. Bahamas
146 B3 San Salvador El Salvador
152 B2 San Salvador de Jujuy Arg.
108 B2 Sansepolcro Italy
109 C2 San Severo Italy
109 C2 Sanski Most Bos.-Herz.
152 B1 Santa Ana Bol.
146 B3 Santa Ana El Salvador
144 A1 Santa Ana Mex.
135 C4 Santa Ana U.S.A.
152 B1 Santa Ana de Yacuma Bol.
144 B2 Santa Bárbara Mex.
135 C4 Santa Barbara U.S.A.
154 B2 Santa Bárbara, Serra de hills Brazil
152 B2 Santa Catalina Chile
135 C4 Santa Catalina Island U.S.A.
150 C3 Santa Clara Col.
146 C2 Santa Clara Cuba
135 B3 Santa Clara U.S.A.
135 C4 Santa Clarita U.S.A.
107 D1 Santa Coloma de Gramanet Spain
Santa Comba Angola see Waku-Kungo
109 C3 Santa Croce, Capo c. Sicily Italy
153 B5 Santa Cruz r. Arg.
152 B1 Santa Cruz Bol.
64 B2 Santa Cruz Phil.
135 B3 Santa Cruz U.S.A.
145 C3 Santa Cruz Barillas Guat.
155 E1 Santa Cruz Cabrália Brazil
107 C2 Santa Cruz de Moya Spain
114 A2 Santa Cruz de Tenerife Canary Is
152 C2 Santa Cruz do Sul Brazil
135 C4 Santa Cruz Island U.S.A.
48 H5 Santa Cruz Islands Solomon Is
107 D2 Santa Eulalia del Río Spain
152 B3 Santa Fé Arg.
142 B1 Santa Fe U.S.A.
154 B2 Santa Fé do Sul Brazil
154 B1 Santa Helena de Goiás Brazil
153 B3 Santa Isabel Arg.
Santa Isabel Equat. Guinea see Malabo
48 G4 Santa Isabel i. Solomon Is
154 B1 Santa Luisa, Serra de hills Brazil
151 E3 Santa Luzia Brazil
144 A2 Santa Margarita, Isla i. Mex.
152 C2 Santa Maria Brazil
144 B1 Santa María r. Mex.
135 B4 Santa Maria U.S.A.
123 D2 Santa Maria, Cabo de c. Moz.
106 B2 Santa Maria, Cabo de c. Port.
155 C1 Santa Maria, Chapadão de hills Brazil
151 E3 Santa Maria das Barreiras Brazil
109 C3 Santa Maria di Leuca, Capo c. Italy
155 D1 Santa Maria do Suaçuí Brazil
150 B1 Santa Marta Col.
135 C4 Santa Monica U.S.A.

151 E4 Santana Brazil
110 B1 Sântana Romania
106 C1 Santander Spain
108 A3 Sant'Antioco Sardinia Italy
108 A3 Sant'Antioco, Isola di i. Sardinia Italy
151 D3 Santarém Brazil
106 B2 Santarém Port.
154 B1 Santa Rita do Araguaia Brazil
153 B3 Santa Rosa Arg.
152 C2 Santa Rosa Brazil
135 B3 Santa Rosa CA U.S.A.
142 C2 Santa Rosa NM U.S.A.
146 B3 Santa Rosa de Copán Hond.
135 B4 Santa Rosa Island CA U.S.A.
140 C2 Santa Rosa Island FL U.S.A.
144 A2 Santa Rosalía Mex.
134 C2 Santa Rosa Range mts U.S.A.
106 B1 Santa Uxía de Ribeira Spain
154 B1 Santa Vitória Brazil
107 D1 Sant Carles de la Ràpita Spain
135 C4 Santee U.S.A.
152 C2 Santiago Brazil
153 A3 Santiago Chile
147 C3 Santiago Dom. Rep.
144 B2 Santiago Mex.
146 B4 Santiago Panama
64 B2 Santiago Phil.
106 B1 Santiago de Compostela Spain
146 C2 Santiago de Cuba Cuba
144 B2 Santiago Ixcuintla Mex.
144 B2 Santiago Papasquiaro Mex.
106 C1 Santillana Spain
107 D1 Sant Jordi, Golf de g. Spain
155 D2 Santo Amaro de Campos Brazil
154 B2 Santo Anastácio Brazil
155 C2 Santo André Brazil
152 C2 Santo Angelo Brazil
154 B2 Santo Antônio da Platina Brazil
151 F4 Santo Antônio de Jesus Brazil
150 C3 Santo Antônio do Içá Brazil
155 C2 Santo Antônio do Monte Brazil
147 D3 Santo Domingo Dom. Rep.
144 A2 Santo Domingo Mex.
142 B1 Santo Domingo Pueblo U.S.A.
Santorini i. Greece see Thira
155 C2 Santos Brazil
155 D2 Santos Dumont Brazil
157 I7 Santos Plateau sea feature S. Atlantic Ocean
152 C2 Santo Tomé Arg.
153 A4 San Valentín, Cerro mt. Chile
146 B3 San Vicente El Salvador
144 A1 San Vicente Mex.
64 B2 San Vicente Phil.
150 B4 San Vicente de Cañete Peru
108 B2 San Vincenzo Italy
108 B3 San Vito, Capo c. Sicily Italy
71 A4 Sanya China
155 C2 São Bernardo do Campo Brazil
152 C2 São Borja Brazil
154 C2 São Carlos Brazil
155 D1 São Felipe, Serra de hills Brazil
151 D4 São Félix Brazil
151 D3 São Félix Brazil
155 D2 São Fidélis Brazil
155 D1 São Francisco Brazil
151 F4 São Francisco r. Brazil
154 C3 São Francisco, Ilha de i. Brazil
154 C3 São Francisco do Sul Brazil
152 C3 São Gabriel Brazil
155 D2 São Gonçalo Brazil
155 C1 São Gonçalo do Abaeté Brazil
155 C1 São Gotardo Brazil

154 B1 São Jerônimo, Serra de hills Brazil
155 D2 São João da Barra Brazil
155 C2 São João da Boa Vista Brazil
106 B1 São João da Madeira Port.
155 D1 São João da Ponte Brazil
155 D2 São João del Rei Brazil
155 D1 São João do Paraíso Brazil
155 D1 São João Evangelista Brazil
155 D2 São João Nepomuceno Brazil
154 C2 São Joaquim da Barra Brazil
152 D2 São José Brazil
154 C2 São José do Rio Preto Brazil
155 C2 São José dos Campos Brazil
154 C3 São José dos Pinhais Brazil
154 A1 São Lourenço Brazil
155 C2 São Lourenço Brazil
151 E3 São Luís Brazil
154 C2 São Manuel Brazil
154 C1 São Marcos r. Brazil
151 E3 São Marcos, Baía de b. Brazil
154 E1 São Mateus Brazil
154 B1 São Mateus do Sul Brazil
105 C2 Saône r. France
155 C2 São Paulo Brazil
155 D2 São Pedro da Aldeia Brazil
151 E3 São Raimundo Nonato Brazil
155 C1 São Romão Brazil
São Salvador Angola see M'banza Congo
São Salvador do Congo Angola see M'banza Congo
155 C2 São Sebastião, Ilha do i. Brazil
154 C2 São Sebastião do Paraíso Brazil
154 B1 São Simão Brazil
154 B1 São Simão, Barragem de resr Brazil
59 C2 Sao-Siu Indon.
113 D5 São Tomé
São Tomé and Príncipe
113 D5 São Tomé i. São Tomé and Príncipe
155 D2 São Tomé, Cabo de c. Brazil
113 D5 São Tomé and Príncipe country Africa
155 C2 São Vicente Brazil
106 B2 São Vicente, Cabo de c. Port.
59 C3 Saparua Indon.
107 D2 Sa Pobla Spain
89 F3 Sapozhok Rus. Fed.
66 D2 Sapporo Japan
109 C2 Sapri Italy
143 D1 Sapulpa U.S.A.
81 C2 Saqqez Iran
81 C2 Sarāb Iran
63 B2 Sara Buri Thai.
Saragossa Spain see Zaragoza
89 F3 Sarai Rus. Fed.
109 C2 Sarajevo Bos.-Herz.
87 E3 Saraktash Rus. Fed.
62 A1 Saramati mt. India/Myanmar
139 E2 Saranac Lake U.S.A.
109 D3 Sarandë Albania
64 B3 Sarangani Islands Phil.
87 D3 Saransk Rus. Fed.
87 E3 Sarapul Rus. Fed.
141 D3 Sarasota U.S.A.
90 B2 Saratа Ukr.
136 B2 Saratoga U.S.A.
139 E2 Saratoga Springs U.S.A.
61 C1 Saratok Sarawak Malaysia
87 D3 Saratov Rus. Fed.
79 D2 Sarāvan Iran
61 C1 Sarawak state Malaysia
111 C2 Saray Turkey
111 C3 Sarayköy Turkey
79 D2 Sarbāz Iran
76 B3 Sarbīsheh Iran
74 B2 Sardarshahr India
Sardegna i. Italy see Sardinia
108 A2 Sardinia i. Italy

92 G2 Sarektjåkkå mt. Sweden
77 C3 Sar-e Pol Afgh.
158 C3 Sargasso Sea sea Atlantic Ocean
74 B1 Sargodha Pak.
115 D4 Sarh Chad
79 D2 Sarhad reg. Iran
81 D2 Sārī Iran
111 C3 Sarıgöl Turkey
81 C1 Sarıkamış Turkey
61 C1 Sarikei Sarawak Malaysia
51 D2 Sarina Austr.
115 D2 Sarīr Tibesti des. Libya
65 B2 Sariwŏn N. Korea
111 C2 Sarıyer Turkey
77 D2 Sarkand Kazakh.
111 C2 Şarköy Turkey
104 C3 Sarlat-la-Canéda France
59 D3 Sarmi Indon.
153 B4 Sarmiento Arg.
138 C2 Sarnia Can.
90 B1 Sarny Ukr.
60 B2 Sarolangun Indon.
111 B3 Saronikos Kolpos g. Greece
111 C2 Saros Körfezi b. Turkey
103 E2 Sárospatak Hungary
87 D3 Sarova Rus. Fed.
Sarpan i. N. Mariana Is see Rota
105 D2 Sarrebourg France
106 B1 Sarria Spain
107 C1 Sarrión Spain
105 D3 Sartène Corsica France
Sartu China see Daqing
111 C3 Saruhanlı Turkey
103 D2 Sárvár Hungary
81 D3 Sarvestān Iran
76 B2 Sarykamyshskoye Ozero salt l. Turkm./Uzbek.
77 D2 Saryozek Kazakh.
77 D2 Saryshagan Kazakh.
77 C2 Sarysu watercourse Kazakh.
77 D3 Sary-Tash Kyrg.
75 C2 Sasaram India
67 A4 Sasebo Japan
129 D2 Saskatchewan prov. Can.
129 D2 Saskatchewan r. Can.
129 D2 Saskatoon Can.
83 I2 Saskylakh Rus. Fed.
123 C2 Sasolburg S. Africa
87 D3 Sasovo Rus. Fed.
114 B4 Sassandra Côte d'Ivoire
108 A2 Sassari Sardinia Italy
102 C1 Sassnitz Ger.
114 A3 Satadougou Mali
136 C3 Satanta U.S.A.
73 B3 Satara India
123 D1 Satara S. Africa
87 E3 Satka Rus. Fed.
75 C2 Satna India
77 C2 Satpayev Kazakh.
74 B2 Satpura Range mts India
63 B2 Sattahip Thai.
110 B1 Satu Mare Romania
63 B3 Satun Thai.
144 B2 Saucillo Mex.
93 E4 Sauda Norway
92 □B2 Sauðárkrókur Iceland
78 B2 Saudi Arabia country Asia
105 C3 Saugues France
137 E1 Sauk Center U.S.A.
105 C2 Saulieu France
88 B2 Saulkrasti Latvia
130 B3 Sault Sainte Marie Can.
138 C1 Sault Sainte Marie U.S.A.
77 C1 Saumalkol' Kazakh.
59 C3 Saumlakki Indon.
104 B2 Saumur France
120 B1 Saurimo Angola
109 D2 Sava r. Europe
49 J5 Savai'i i. Samoa
91 E1 Savala r. Rus. Fed.
114 C4 Savalou Benin
141 D2 Savannah GA U.S.A.
140 C1 Savannah TN U.S.A.
141 D2 Savannah r. U.S.A.
63 B2 Savannakhét Laos
130 A2 Savant Lake Can.
111 C3 Savaştepe Turkey
114 C4 Savè Benin
105 D2 Saverne France
89 F2 Savino Rus. Fed.
86 D2 Savinskiy Rus. Fed.
Savoie reg. France see Savoy
108 A2 Savona Italy
93 I3 Savonlinna Fin.
105 D2 Savoy reg. France
93 F4 Sävsjö Sweden
59 C3 Savu i. Indon.
92 I2 Savukoski Fin.
Savu Sea Indon. see Laut Sawu
74 B2 Sawai Madhopur India
62 A1 Sawan Myanmar
62 A2 Sawankhalok Thai.
136 B3 Sawatch Range mts U.S.A.
116 B2 Sawhāj Egypt
121 B2 Sawmills Zimbabwe
79 C3 Şawqirah, Dawḩat b. Oman
Şawqirah Bay Oman see Şawqirah, Dawḩat
53 D2 Sawtell Austr.
134 C2 Sawtooth Range mts U.S.A.
68 C1 Sayano-Shushenskoye Vodokhranilishche resr Rus. Fed.
76 C3 Sayat Turkm.
79 C3 Sayḩūt Yemen
93 I3 Säynätsalo Fin.
69 D2 Saynshand Mongolia
139 D2 Sayre U.S.A.
144 B3 Sayula Mex.
145 C3 Sayula Mex.
128 B2 Sayward Can.
Sayyod Turkm. see Sayat
89 E2 Sazonovo Rus. Fed.
114 B2 Sbaa Alg.
98 B2 Scafell Pike hill U.K.
109 C3 Scalea Italy
96 □ Scalloway U.K.
108 B2 Scandicci Italy
96 C1 Scapa Flow inlet U.K.
96 B2 Scarba i. U.K.
130 C3 Scarborough Can.
147 D3 Scarborough Trin. and Tob.
98 C2 Scarborough U.K.
64 A2 Scarborough Shoal sea feature Phil.
96 A2 Scarinish U.K.
Scarpanto i. Greece see Karpathos
100 B2 Schaerbeek Belgium
105 D2 Schaffhausen Switz.
100 B1 Schagen Neth.
102 C2 Schärding Austria
100 A2 Scharendijke Neth.
101 D1 Scharhörn sea feature Ger.
101 D1 Scheeßel Ger.
131 D2 Schefferville Can.
135 D3 Schell Creek Range mts U.S.A.
139 E2 Schenectady U.S.A.
143 D3 Schertz U.S.A.
101 E3 Scheßlitz Ger.
100 C1 Schiermonnikoog i. Neth.
100 B2 Schilde Belgium
108 B1 Schio Italy
101 F2 Schkeuditz Ger.
101 E1 Schladen Ger.
102 C2 Schladming Austria
101 E2 Schleiz Ger.
102 B1 Schleswig Ger.
101 D2 Schloss Holte-Stukenbrock Ger.
101 D2 Schlüchtern Ger.
101 E3 Schlüsselfeld Ger.
101 D2 Schmallenberg Ger.
Schmidt Island Rus. Fed. see Shmidta, Ostrov
101 F2 Schmölln Ger.
101 D1 Schneverdingen Ger.
101 E1 Schönebeck (Elbe) Ger.
101 E1 Schöningen Ger.
100 B2 Schoonhoven Neth.
59 D3 Schouten Islands P.N.G.
97 B3 Schull Rep. of Ireland
101 E3 Schwabach Ger.
102 B2 Schwäbische Alb mts Ger.
101 F3 Schwandorf Ger.
61 C2 Schwaner, Pegunungan mts Indon.
101 E1 Schwarzenbek Ger.
101 F2 Schwarzenberg Ger.
122 A2 Schwarzrand mts Namibia
Schwarzwald mts Ger. see Black Forest
102 C2 Schwaz Austria
102 C1 Schwedt an der Oder Ger.
101 E2 Schweinfurt Ger.
101 E1 Schwerin Ger.
101 E1 Schweriner See l. Ger.
105 D2 Schwyz Switz.
108 B3 Sciacca Sicily Italy
95 B4 Scilly, Isles of U.K.
138 C3 Scioto r. U.S.A.
136 B1 Scobey U.S.A.
53 D2 Scone Austr.
110 B2 Scorniceşti Romania
55 C3 Scotia Ridge sea feature S. Atlantic Ocean
149 F8 Scotia Sea S. Atlantic Ocean
96 C2 Scotland admin. div. U.K.
128 B2 Scott, Cape Can.
123 D3 Scottburgh S. Africa
136 C3 Scott City U.S.A.
136 C2 Scottsbluff U.S.A.
140 C2 Scottsboro U.S.A.
96 B1 Scourie U.K.
139 D2 Scranton U.S.A.
98 C3 Scunthorpe U.K.
105 E2 Scuol Switz.
Scutari Albania see Shkodër
99 D4 Seaford U.K.
98 C2 Seaham U.K.
129 E2 Seal r. Can.
122 B3 Seal, Cape S. Africa
52 B3 Sea Lake Austr.
143 D3 Sealy U.S.A.
140 B1 Searcy U.S.A.
98 B2 Seascale U.K.
134 B1 Seattle U.S.A.
139 E2 Sebago Lake U.S.A.
144 A2 Sebastián Vizcaíno, Bahía b. Mex.
Sebastopol Ukr. see Sevastopol'
Sebenico Croatia see Šibenik
110 B1 Sebeş Romania
60 B2 Sebesi i. Indon.
88 C2 Sebezh Rus. Fed.
80 B1 Şebinkarahisar Turkey
141 D3 Sebring U.S.A.
61 C2 Sebuku i. Indon.
128 B3 Sechelt Can.
150 A3 Sechura Peru
73 B3 Secunderabad India
137 E3 Sedalia U.S.A.
105 C2 Sedan France
54 B2 Seddon N.Z.
114 A3 Sédhiou Senegal
142 A2 Sedona U.S.A.
101 E2 Seeburg Ger.
101 E1 Seehausen (Altmark) Ger.
122 A2 Seeheim Namibia
104 C2 Sées France
101 E2 Seesen Ger.
101 E1 Seevetal Ger.
114 A4 Sefadu Sierra Leone
123 C1 Sefare Botswana
93 F3 Segalstad Norway
60 B1 Segamat Malaysia
86 C2 Segezha Rus. Fed.
114 B3 Ségou Mali
106 C1 Segovia Spain
86 C2 Segozerskoye, Ozero resr Rus. Fed.
115 D2 Séguédine Niger
114 B4 Séguéla Côte d'Ivoire
143 D3 Seguin U.S.A.
107 C2 Segura r. Spain
106 C2 Segura, Sierra de mts Spain
120 B3 Sehithwa Botswana
93 H3 Seinäjoki Fin.
104 C2 Seine r. France
104 B2 Seine, Baie de b. France
105 C2 Seine, Val de val. France
103 E1 Sejny Pol.
60 B2 Sekayu Indon.
114 B4 Sekondi Ghana
134 B1 Selah U.S.A.
59 C3 Selaru i. Indon.
61 C2 Selatan, Tanjung pt Indon.
126 B2 Selawik U.S.A.
98 C3 Selby U.K.
136 C1 Selby U.S.A.
111 C3 Selçuk Turkey
120 B3 Selebi-Phikwe Botswana
Selebi-Pikwe Botswana see Selebi-Phikwe
105 D2 Sélestat France
Seletyteniz, Oz. salt l. Kazakh. see Siletiteniz, Ozero
92 □A3 Selfoss Iceland
114 A3 Sélibabi Maur.
142 A1 Seligman U.S.A.
116 A2 Selîma Oasis Sudan
111 C3 Selimiye Turkey
114 B3 Sélingué, Lac de l. Mali
89 D2 Selizharovo Rus. Fed.
93 E4 Seljord Norway
129 E2 Selkirk Can.
96 C3 Selkirk U.K.
128 C2 Selkirk Mountains Can.
142 A2 Sells U.S.A.
140 C2 Selma AL U.S.A.
135 C3 Selma CA U.S.A.
105 D2 Selongey France
99 C4 Selsey Bill hd U.K.
89 D3 Sel'tso Rus. Fed.
Selukwe Zimbabwe see Shurugwi
150 B3 Selvas reg. Brazil
134 C1 Selway r. U.S.A.
129 D1 Selwyn Lake Can.
128 A1 Selwyn Mountains Can.
51 C2 Selwyn Range hills Austr.
60 B2 Semangka, Teluk b. Indon.
61 C2 Semarang Indon.
60 B1 Sematan Sarawak Malaysia
118 B2 Sembé Congo
81 C2 Şemdinli Turkey
91 C1 Semenivka Ukr.
87 D3 Semenov Rus. Fed.
61 C2 Semeru, Gunung vol. Indon.
91 E2 Semikarakorsk Rus. Fed.
89 E3 Semiluki Rus. Fed.
136 B2 Seminoe Reservoir U.S.A.
143 C2 Seminole U.S.A.
141 D2 Seminole, Lake U.S.A.
77 E1 Semipalatinsk Kazakh.
61 C1 Semitau Indon.
Sem Kolodezey Ukr. see Lenine
81 D2 Semnān Iran
61 C1 Semporna Sabah Malaysia
105 C2 Semur-en-Auxois France
Semyonovskoye Rus. Fed. see Bereznik
Semyonovskoye Rus. Fed. see Ostrovskoye
150 C3 Sena Madureira Brazil
120 B2 Senanga Zambia
67 B4 Sendai Japan
67 D3 Sendai Japan
141 D2 Seneca U.S.A.
114 A3 Senegal country Africa
114 A3 Sénégal r. Maur./Senegal
102 C1 Senftenberg Ger.
119 D3 Sengerema Tanz.
151 E4 Senhor do Bonfim Brazil
103 D2 Senica Slovakia
108 B2 Senigallia Italy
109 B2 Senj Croatia
92 G2 Senja i. Norway
122 B2 Senlac S. Africa
105 C2 Senlis France
63 B2 Senmonorom Cambodia
116 B3 Sennar Sudan
130 C3 Senneterre Can.
123 C3 Senqu r. Lesotho
105 C2 Sens France
109 D1 Senta Serb. and Mont.
128 B2 Sentinel Peak Can.
75 B2 Seoni India
65 B2 Seoul S. Korea
155 D2 Sepetiba, Baía de b. Brazil
59 D3 Sepik r. P.N.G.
61 C1 Sepinang Indon.
131 D2 Sept-Îles Can.
87 D4 Serafimovich Rus. Fed.
100 B2 Seraing Belgium
59 C3 Seram i. Indon.
60 B2 Serang Indon.
60 B1 Serasan, Selat sea chan. Indon.
Serbia aut. rep. Serb. and Mont. see Srbija
109 D2 Serbia and Montenegro country Europe
117 C3 Serdo Eth.
89 E3 Serebryanyye Prudy Rus. Fed.
60 B1 Seremban Malaysia
119 D3 Serengeti Plain Tanz.
121 C2 Serenje Zambia
90 B2 Seret r. Ukr.
87 D3 Sergach Rus. Fed.
86 F2 Sergino Rus. Fed.
89 E2 Sergiyev Posad Rus. Fed.
Sergo Ukr. see Stakhanov
61 C1 Seria Brunei
61 C1 Serian Sarawak Malaysia
111 B3 Serifos i. Greece
80 B2 Serik Turkey
59 C3 Sermata, Kepulauan is Indon.

Sernyy Zavod Turkm. *see* **Kukurtli**
86 F3 **Serov** Rus. Fed.
120 B3 **Serowe** Botswana
106 B2 **Serpa** Port.
Serpa Pinto Angola *see* **Menongue**
89 E3 **Serpukhov** Rus. Fed.
155 D2 **Serra** Brazil
155 C1 **Serra das Araras** Brazil
108 A3 **Serramanna** *Sardinia* Italy
154 B1 **Serranópolis** Brazil
100 A3 **Serre** *r.* France
111 B2 **Serres** Greece
151 F4 **Serrinha** Brazil
155 D1 **Sêrro** Brazil
154 C2 **Sertãozinho** Brazil
59 D3 **Serui** Indon.
120 B3 **Serule** Botswana
61 C2 **Seruyan** *r.* Indon.
68 C2 **Sêrxü** China
120 A2 **Sesfontein** Namibia
108 B2 **Sessa Aurunca** Italy
108 A2 **Sestri Levante** Italy
105 C3 **Sète** France
155 D1 **Sete Lagoas** Brazil
92 G2 **Setermoen** Norway
93 E4 **Setesdal** *val.* Norway
115 C1 **Sétif** Alg.
67 B4 **Seto-naikai** *sea* Japan
114 B1 **Settat** Morocco
98 B2 **Settle** U.K.
106 B2 **Setúbal** Port.
106 B2 **Setúbal, Baía de** *b.* Port.
130 A2 **Seul, Lac** *l.* Can.
81 C1 **Sevan** Armenia
76 A2 **Sevan, Lake** Armenia
Sevana Lich *l.* Armenia *see* **Sevan, Lake**
91 C3 **Sevastopol'** Ukr.
Seven Islands Can. *see* **Sept-Îles**
131 D2 **Seven Islands Bay** Can.
99 D4 **Sevenoaks** U.K.
105 C3 **Sévérac-le-Château** France
130 B2 **Severn** *r.* Can.
122 B2 **Severn** S. Africa
99 B4 **Severn** *r.* U.K.
86 D2 **Severnaya Dvina** *r.* Rus. Fed.
83 H1 **Severnaya Zemlya** *is* Rus. Fed.
86 D2 **Severnyy** Rus. Fed.
86 F2 **Severnyy** Rus. Fed.
83 I3 **Severobaykal'sk** Rus. Fed.
86 C2 **Severodvinsk** Rus. Fed.
83 L3 **Severo-Kuril'sk** Rus. Fed.
92 J2 **Severomorsk** Rus. Fed.
86 C2 **Severoonezhsk** Rus. Fed.
83 H2 **Severo-Yeniseyskiy** Rus. Fed.
91 D3 **Severskaya** Rus. Fed.
135 D3 **Sevier** *r.* U.S.A.
135 D3 **Sevier Lake** U.S.A.
Sevilla Spain *see* **Seville**
106 B2 **Seville** Spain
Sevlyush Ukr. *see* **Vynohradiv**
89 D3 **Sevsk** Rus. Fed.
126 C2 **Seward** U.S.A.
126 B2 **Seward Peninsula** U.S.A.
128 A2 **Sewell Inlet** Can.
128 C2 **Sexsmith** Can.
144 B2 **Sextín** *r.* Mex.
86 G1 **Seyakha** Rus. Fed.
113 I6 **Seychelles** *country* Indian Ocean
92 □C2 **Seyðisfjörður** Iceland
Seyhan Turkey *see* **Adana**
80 B2 **Seyhan** *r.* Turkey
91 C1 **Seym** *r.* Rus. Fed./Ukr.
83 L2 **Seymchan** Rus. Fed.
53 C3 **Seymour** Austr.
123 C3 **Seymour** S. Africa
138 B3 **Seymour** *IN* U.S.A.
143 D2 **Seymour** *TX* U.S.A.
105 C2 **Sézanne** France
108 B2 **Sezze** Italy
111 B3 **Sfakia** Greece
110 C1 **Sfântu Gheorghe** Romania
115 D1 **Sfax** Tunisia
Sfîntu Gheorghe Romania *see* **Sfântu Gheorghe**
's-Gravenhage Neth. *see* **The Hague**
96 A2 **Sgurr Alasdair** *hill* U.K.
70 A2 **Shaanxi** *prov.* China
Shabani Zimbabwe *see* **Zvishavane**
91 D2 **Shabel'sk** Rus. Fed.
77 D3 **Shache** China
55 C1 **Shackleton Range** *mts* Antarctica
74 A2 **Shadadkot** Pak.
86 F3 **Shadrinsk** Rus. Fed.
99 B4 **Shaftesbury** U.K.
126 B2 **Shageluk** U.S.A.
Shāhābād Iran *see* **Eslāmābād-e Gharb**
75 C2 **Shahdol** India
77 C3 **Shah Fuladi** *mt.* Afgh.
75 B2 **Shahjahanpur** India
76 B3 **Shāh Kūh** *mt.* Iran
81 D2 **Shahr-e Bābak** Iran
81 D2 **Shahr-e Kord** Iran
81 D2 **Shahrezā** Iran
77 C3 **Shahrisabz** Uzbek.
Shāhrūd Iran *see* **Emāmrūd**
79 B2 **Shaj'ah, Jabal** *hill* Saudi Arabia
89 E2 **Shakhovskaya** Rus. Fed.
Shakhterskoye Ukr. *see* **Pershotravens'k**
Shakhty Rus. Fed. *see* **Gusinoozersk**
91 E2 **Shakhty** Rus. Fed.
Shakhtyorskoye Ukr. *see* **Pershotravens'k**
86 D3 **Shakhun'ya** Rus. Fed.
114 C4 **Shaki** Nigeria
66 D2 **Shakotan-hantō** *pen.* Japan
66 D2 **Shakotan-misaki** *c.* Japan
76 B2 **Shalkar** Kazakh.
68 C2 **Shaluli Shan** *mts* China
129 E2 **Shamattawa** Can.
143 C1 **Shamrock** U.S.A.
70 A2 **Shandan** China
70 B2 **Shandong** *prov.* China
70 C2 **Shandong Bandao** *pen.* China
121 B2 **Shangani** Zimbabwe
121 B2 **Shangani** *r.* Zimbabwe
70 B1 **Shangdu** China
70 C2 **Shanghai** China
70 C2 **Shanghai** *mun.* China
71 B3 **Shanghang** China
70 A2 **Shangluo** China
70 B2 **Shangnan** China
71 B3 **Shangrao** China
70 B2 **Shangshui** China
77 E2 **Shangyou Shuiku** *resr* China
70 C2 **Shangyu** China
69 E1 **Shangzhi** China
Shangzhou China *see* **Shangluo**
134 B1 **Shaniko** U.S.A.
97 B2 **Shannon** *r.* Rep. of Ireland
97 B2 **Shannon, Mouth of the** Rep. of Ireland
62 A1 **Shan Plateau** Myanmar
Shansi *prov.* China *see* **Shanxi**
71 B3 **Shantou** China
Shantung *prov.* China *see* **Shandong**
70 B2 **Shanxi** *prov.* China
71 B3 **Shaoguan** China
71 B3 **Shaowu** China
70 C2 **Shaoxing** China
71 B3 **Shaoyang** China
96 C1 **Shapinsay** *i.* U.K.
116 C2 **Shaqrā'** Saudi Arabia
90 B2 **Sharhorod** Ukr.
79 C2 **Sharjah** U.A.E.
88 C2 **Sharkawshchyna** Belarus
50 A2 **Shark Bay** Austr.
78 A2 **Sharm ash Shaykh** Egypt
138 C2 **Sharon** U.S.A.
86 D3 **Shar'ya** Rus. Fed.
121 B3 **Shashe** *r.* Botswana/Zimbabwe
117 B4 **Shashemenē** Eth.
Shashi China *see* **Jingzhou**
134 B2 **Shasta, Mount** *vol.* U.S.A.
134 B2 **Shasta Lake** U.S.A.
115 D2 **Shāţi', Wādī ash** *watercourse* Libya
Shatilki Belarus *see* **Svyetlahorsk**
89 E2 **Shatura** Rus. Fed.
129 D3 **Shaunavon** Can.
138 B2 **Shawano** U.S.A.
130 C3 **Shawinigan** Can.
143 D1 **Shawnee** U.S.A.
83 M2 **Shayboveyem** *r.* Rus. Fed.
50 B2 **Shay Gap** Austr.
89 E3 **Shchekino** Rus. Fed.
89 E2 **Shchelkovo** Rus. Fed.
Shcherbakov Rus. Fed. *see* **Rybinsk**
Shcherbinovka Ukr. *see* **Dzerzhyns'k**
89 E3 **Shchigry** Rus. Fed.
91 C1 **Shchors** Ukr.
88 B3 **Shchuchyn** Belarus
91 D1 **Shebekino** Rus. Fed.
77 C3 **Sheberghān** Afgh.
138 B2 **Sheboygan** U.S.A.
91 D3 **Shebsh** *r.* Rus. Fed.
97 C2 **Sheelin, Lough** *l.* Rep. of Ireland
136 B3 **Sheep Mountain** U.S.A.
99 D4 **Sheerness** U.K.
98 C3 **Sheffield** U.K.
143 C2 **Sheffield** U.S.A.
Sheikh Othman Yemen *see* **Ash Shaykh 'Uthman**
Shekhem West Bank *see* **Nāblus**
89 E2 **Sheksna** Rus. Fed.
89 E2 **Sheksninskoye Vodokhranilishche** *resr* Rus. Fed.
83 M2 **Shelagskiy, Mys** *pt* Rus. Fed.
131 D3 **Shelburne** Can.
138 B2 **Shelby** *MI* U.S.A.
134 D1 **Shelby** *MT* U.S.A.
141 D1 **Shelby** *NC* U.S.A.
138 B3 **Shelbyville** *IN* U.S.A.
140 C1 **Shelbyville** *TN* U.S.A.
83 L2 **Shelikhova, Zaliv** *g.* Rus. Fed.
126 B3 **Shelikof Strait** U.S.A.
129 D2 **Shellbrook** Can.
Shelter Bay Can. *see* **Port-Cartier**
134 B1 **Shelton** U.S.A.
137 D2 **Shenandoah** U.S.A.
139 D3 **Shenandoah** *r.* U.S.A.
139 D3 **Shenandoah Mountains** U.S.A.
118 A2 **Shendam** Nigeria
Shengli Feng *mt.* China/Kyrg. *see* **Pobeda Peak**
86 D2 **Shenkursk** Rus. Fed.
70 B2 **Shenmu** China
Shensi *prov.* China *see* **Shaanxi**
70 C1 **Shenyang** China
71 B3 **Shenzhen** China
90 B1 **Shepetivka** Ukr.
53 C3 **Shepparton** Austr.
99 D4 **Sheppey, Isle of** *i.* U.K.
131 D3 **Sherbrooke** *N.S.* Can.
130 C3 **Sherbrooke** *Que.* Can.
97 C2 **Shercock** Rep. of Ireland
116 B3 **Shereiq** Sudan
136 B2 **Sheridan** U.S.A.
52 A2 **Sheringa** Austr.
86 F2 **Sherkaly** Rus. Fed.
143 D2 **Sherman** U.S.A.
100 B2 **'s-Hertogenbosch** Neth.
96 □ **Shetland Islands** U.K.
76 B2 **Shetpe** Kazakh.
Shevchenko Kazakh. *see* **Aktau**
91 D2 **Shevchenkove** Ukr.
137 D1 **Sheyenne** *r.* U.S.A.
79 B3 **Shibām** Yemen
67 C3 **Shibata** Japan
66 D2 **Shibetsu** Japan
Shibotsu-jima *i.* Rus. Fed. *see* **Zelenyy, Ostrov**
71 B3 **Shicheng** China
70 C2 **Shidao** China
96 B2 **Shiel, Loch** *l.* U.K.
Shigatse China *see* **Xigazê**
77 E2 **Shihezi** China
Shihkiachwang China *see* **Shijiazhuang**
Shijiao China *see* **Fogang**
70 B2 **Shijiazhuang** China
Shijiusuo China *see* **Rizhao**
74 A2 **Shikarpur** Pak.
67 B4 **Shikoku** *i.* Japan
66 D2 **Shikotsu-ko** *l.* Japan
86 D2 **Shilega** Rus. Fed.
75 C2 **Shiliguri** India
97 C2 **Shillelagh** Rep. of Ireland
75 D2 **Shillong** India
89 F3 **Shilovo** Rus. Fed.
69 E1 **Shimanovsk** Rus. Fed.
117 C3 **Shimbiris** *mt.* Somalia
67 C3 **Shimizu** Japan
74 B1 **Shimla** India
67 C4 **Shimoda** Japan
73 B3 **Shimoga** India
66 D2 **Shimokita-hantō** *pen.* Japan
67 B4 **Shimonoseki** Japan
89 D2 **Shimsk** Rus. Fed.
96 B1 **Shin, Loch** *l.* U.K.
62 A1 **Shingbwiyang** Myanmar
67 C4 **Shingū** Japan
123 D1 **Shingwedzi** S. Africa
123 D1 **Shingwedzi** *r.* S. Africa
66 D3 **Shinjō** Japan
119 D3 **Shinyanga** Tanz.
67 D3 **Shiogama** Japan
67 C4 **Shiono-misaki** *c.* Japan
71 A3 **Shiping** China
98 C3 **Shipley** U.K.
142 B1 **Shiprock** U.S.A.
71 A3 **Shiqian** China
Shiqizhen China *see* **Zhongshan**
70 A2 **Shiquan** China
78 B2 **Shi'r, Jabal** *hill* Saudi Arabia
67 C3 **Shirane-san** *mt.* Japan
67 C3 **Shirane-san** *vol.* Japan
81 D3 **Shīrāz** Iran
66 D2 **Shiretoko-misaki** *c.* Japan
66 D2 **Shiriya-zaki** *c.* Japan
76 B3 **Shīrvān** Iran
74 B2 **Shiv** India
74 B2 **Shivpuri** India
70 B2 **Shiyan** China
70 A2 **Shizuishan** China
67 C4 **Shizuoka** Japan
89 D3 **Shklow** Belarus
109 C2 **Shkodër** Albania
83 H1 **Shmidta, Ostrov** *i.* Rus. Fed.
67 B4 **Shōbara** Japan
Sholapur India *see* **Solapur**
158 F8 **Shona Ridge** *sea feature* S. Atlantic Ocean
77 C3 **Sho'rchi** Uzbek.
74 B1 **Shorkot** Pak.
135 C3 **Shoshone** *CA* U.S.A.
134 D2 **Shoshone** *ID* U.S.A.
135 C3 **Shoshone Mountains** U.S.A.
123 C1 **Shoshong** Botswana
91 C1 **Shostka** Ukr.
70 B2 **Shouxian** China
78 A3 **Showak** Sudan
142 A2 **Show Low** U.S.A.
91 C2 **Shpola** Ukr.
140 B2 **Shreveport** U.S.A.
99 B3 **Shrewsbury** U.K.
77 D2 **Shu** Kazakh.
Shuangjiang China *see* **Tongdao**
62 A1 **Shuangjiang** China
Shuangxi China *see* **Shunchang**
66 B1 **Shuangyashan** China
87 E4 **Shubarkuduk** Kazakh.
116 B1 **Shubrā al Khaymah** Egypt
89 D2 **Shugozero** Rus. Fed.
Shuidong China *see* **Dianbai**
120 B2 **Shumba** Zimbabwe
110 C2 **Shumen** Bulg.
87 F3 **Shumikha** Rus. Fed.
88 C2 **Shumilina** Belarus
143 C3 **Shumla** U.S.A.
89 D3 **Shumyachi** Rus. Fed.
71 B3 **Shunchang** China
126 B2 **Shungnak** U.S.A.
78 B3 **Shuqrah** Yemen
121 C2 **Shurugwi** Zimbabwe
89 F2 **Shushkodom** Rus. Fed.
81 C2 **Shushtar** Iran
128 C2 **Shuswap Lake** Can.
89 F2 **Shuya** Rus. Fed.
89 F2 **Shuyskoye** Rus. Fed.
62 A1 **Shwebo** Myanmar
62 A1 **Shwedwin** Myanmar
62 A2 **Shwegun** Myanmar
62 A2 **Shwegyin** Myanmar
62 A1 **Shweli** *r.* Myanmar
77 C2 **Shymkent** Kazakh.
74 B1 **Shyok** *r.* India
91 C2 **Shyroke** Ukr.
90 C2 **Shyryayeve** Ukr.
59 C3 **Sia** Indon.
74 A2 **Siahan Range** *mts* Pak.
74 B1 **Sialkot** Pak.
Siam *country* Asia *see* **Thailand**
Sian China *see* **Xi'an**
64 B3 **Siargao** *i.* Phil.

64 B3 **Siasi** Phil.
88 B2 **Šiauliai** Lith.
123 D1 **Sibasa** S. Africa
109 C2 **Šibenik** Croatia
83 G2 **Siberia** *reg.* Rus. Fed.
60 A2 **Siberut** *i.* Indon.
74 A2 **Sibi** Pak.
Sibir' *reg.* Rus. Fed. *see* **Siberia**
118 B3 **Sibiti** Congo
110 B1 **Sibiu** Romania
60 A1 **Sibolga** Indon.
62 A1 **Sibsagar** India
61 C1 **Sibu** *Sarawak* Malaysia
118 B2 **Sibut** C.A.R.
64 A3 **Sibutu** *i.* Phil.
64 B2 **Sibuyan** *i.* Phil.
64 B2 **Sibuyan Sea** Phil.
128 C2 **Sicamous** Can.
63 A3 **Sichon** Thai.
70 A2 **Sichuan** *prov.* China
70 A3 **Sichuan Pendi** *basin* China
105 D3 **Sicié, Cap** *c.* France
Sicilia *i.* Italy *see* **Sicily**
108 B3 **Sicilian Channel** Italy/Tunisia
108 B3 **Sicily** *i.* Italy
150 B4 **Sicuani** Peru
74 B2 **Siddhapur** India
111 C3 **Sideros, Akra** *pt* Greece
122 B3 **Sidesaviwa** S. Africa
75 C2 **Sidhi** India
107 D2 **Sidi Aïssa** Alg.
107 D2 **Sidi Ali** Alg.
114 B1 **Sidi Bel Abbès** Alg.
114 A2 **Sidi Ifni** Morocco
114 B1 **Sidi Kacem** Morocco
60 A1 **Sidikalang** Indon.
111 B2 **Sidirokastro** Greece
96 C2 **Sidlaw Hills** U.K.
99 B4 **Sidmouth** U.K.
134 B1 **Sidney** Can.
136 C1 **Sidney** *MT* U.S.A.
136 C2 **Sidney** *NE* U.S.A.
138 C2 **Sidney** *OH* U.S.A.
141 D2 **Sidney Lanier, Lake** U.S.A.
61 D1 **Sidoan** Indon.
80 B2 **Sidon** Lebanon
154 B2 **Sidrolândia** Brazil
103 E1 **Siedlce** Pol.
100 C2 **Sieg** *r.* Ger.
101 D2 **Siegen** Ger.
63 B2 **Siĕmréab** Cambodia
Siem Reap Cambodia *see* **Siĕmréab**
108 B2 **Siena** Italy
103 D1 **Sieradz** Pol.
142 B2 **Sierra Blanca** U.S.A.
153 B4 **Sierra Grande** Arg.
114 A4 **Sierra Leone** *country* Africa
158 E4 **Sierra Leone Basin** *sea feature* N. Atlantic Ocean
158 E4 **Sierra Leone Rise** *sea feature* N. Atlantic Ocean
144 B2 **Sierra Mojada** Mex.
142 A2 **Sierra Vista** U.S.A.
105 D2 **Sierre** Switz.
116 C3 **Sīfenī** Eth.
111 B3 **Sifnos** *i.* Greece
107 C2 **Sig** Alg.
127 I2 **Sigguup Nunaa** *pen.* Greenland
110 B1 **Sighetu Marmației** Romania
110 B1 **Sighișoara** Romania
60 A1 **Sigli** Indon.
92 □B2 **Siglufjörður** Iceland
102 B2 **Sigmaringen** Ger.
100 B3 **Signy-l'Abbaye** France
106 C1 **Sigüenza** Spain
114 B3 **Siguiri** Guinea
88 B2 **Sigulda** Latvia
63 B2 **Sihanoukville** Cambodia
92 I3 **Siilinjärvi** Fin.
81 C2 **Siirt** Turkey
60 B2 **Sijunjung** Indon.
74 B2 **Sikar** India
74 A1 **Sikaram** *mt.* Afgh.
114 B3 **Sikasso** Mali
111 B2 **Sikea** Greece
137 F3 **Sikeston** U.S.A.
66 B2 **Sikhote-Alin'** *mts* Rus. Fed.
111 C3 **Sikinos** *i.* Greece
103 D2 **Siklós** Hungary
65 A2 **Sikuaishi** China
88 B2 **Šilalė** Lith.
144 B2 **Silao** Mex.
101 D1 **Silberberg** *hill* Ger.
75 D2 **Silchar** India
77 D1 **Siletiteniz, Ozero** *salt l.* Kazakh.
75 C2 **Silgarhi** Nepal
80 B2 **Silifke** Turkey
75 C1 **Siling Co** *salt l.* China
110 C2 **Silistra** Bulg.
111 C2 **Silivri** Turkey
93 F3 **Siljan** *l.* Sweden
93 E4 **Silkeborg** Denmark
88 C2 **Sillamäe** Estonia
98 B2 **Silloth** U.K.
140 B1 **Siloam Springs** U.S.A.
123 D2 **Silobela** S. Africa
60 B1 **Siluas** Indon.
88 B2 **Šilutė** Lith.
81 C2 **Silvan** Turkey
154 C1 **Silvânia** Brazil
74 B2 **Silvassa** India
137 E1 **Silver Bay** U.S.A.
142 B2 **Silver City** U.S.A.
136 B3 **Silverton** U.S.A.
62 B1 **Simao** China
130 C3 **Simàrd, Lac** *l.* Can.
111 C3 **Simav** Turkey
111 C3 **Simav Dağları** *mts* Turkey
118 C2 **Simba** Dem. Rep. Congo
138 C2 **Simcoe** Can.
139 D2 **Simcoe, Lake** Can.
78 A3 **Simēn** Eth.
60 A1 **Simeulue** *i.* Indon.
91 C3 **Simferopol'** Ukr.
75 C2 **Simikot** Nepal
135 C4 **Simi Valley** U.S.A.
Simla India *see* **Shimla**
110 B1 **Şimleu Silvaniei** Romania
100 C3 **Simmern (Hunsrück)** Ger.
92 I2 **Simo** Fin.
129 D2 **Simonhouse** Can.
60 B2 **Simpang** Indon.
51 C2 **Simpson Desert** Austr.
93 F4 **Simrishamn** Sweden
60 A1 **Sinabang** Indon.
116 B2 **Sinai** *pen.* Egypt
105 E3 **Sinalunga** Italy
71 A3 **Sinan** China
65 B2 **Sinanju** N. Korea
62 A1 **Sinbo** Myanmar
62 A1 **Sinbyugyun** Myanmar
150 B2 **Sincelejo** Col.
60 B2 **Sindangbarang** Indon.
111 C3 **Sındırgı** Turkey
86 E2 **Sindor** Rus. Fed.
111 C2 **Sinekçi** Turkey
106 B2 **Sines** Port.
106 B2 **Sines, Cabo de** *c.* Port.
116 B3 **Singa** Sudan
75 C2 **Singahi** India
60 B1 **Singapore** *country* Asia
61 C2 **Singaraja** Indon.
63 B2 **Sing Buri** Thai.
119 D3 **Singida** Tanz.
62 A1 **Singkaling Hkamti** Myanmar
61 D2 **Singkang** Indon.
60 B1 **Singkawang** Indon.
60 B2 **Singkep** *i.* Indon.
60 A1 **Singkil** Indon.
53 D2 **Singleton** Austr.
Sin'gosan N. Korea *see* **Kosan**
62 A1 **Singu** Myanmar
Sining China *see* **Xining**
108 A2 **Siniscola** *Sardinia* Italy
109 C2 **Sinj** Croatia
61 D2 **Sinjai** Indon.
116 B3 **Sinkat** Sudan
151 D2 **Sinnamary** Fr. Guiana
Sînnicolau Mare Romania *see* **Sânnicolau Mare**
Sinoia Zimbabwe *see* **Chinhoyi**
80 B1 **Sinop** Turkey
65 B1 **Sinp'o** N. Korea
61 C1 **Sintang** Indon.
100 B2 **St Anthonis** Neth.
100 A2 **St-Laureins** Belgium
100 B2 **St-Niklaas** Belgium
143 D3 **Sinton** U.S.A.
100 C2 **St-Vith** Belgium
65 A1 **Sinŭiju** N. Korea
64 B3 **Siocon** Phil.
103 D2 **Siófok** Hungary
105 D2 **Sion** Switz.
137 D2 **Sioux Center** U.S.A.
137 D2 **Sioux City** U.S.A.
137 D2 **Sioux Falls** U.S.A.
130 A2 **Sioux Lookout** Can.
65 A1 **Siping** China
129 E2 **Sipiwesk Lake** Can.
55 P2 **Siple, Mount** Antarctica
55 P2 **Siple Island** Antarctica
Sipolilo Zimbabwe *see* **Guruve**
60 A2 **Sipura** *i.* Indon.
64 B3 **Siquijor** Phil.
93 E4 **Sira** *r.* Norway
Siracusa Italy *see* **Syracuse**
51 C1 **Sir Edward Pellew Group** *is* Austr.
110 C1 **Siret** Romania
110 C1 **Siret** *r.* Romania
79 C2 **Sīrīk** Iran
61 C1 **Sirik, Tanjung** *pt* Malaysia
62 B2 **Siri Kit Dam** Thai.
128 B1 **Sir James MacBrien, Mount** Can.
79 C2 **Sīrjān** Iran
81 C2 **Şırnak** Turkey
74 B2 **Sirohi** India
60 A1 **Sirombu** Indon.
74 B2 **Sirsa** India
115 D1 **Sirte** Libya
115 D1 **Sirte, Gulf of** Libya
88 B2 **Širvintos** Lith.
109 C1 **Sisak** Croatia
63 B2 **Sisaket** Thai.
145 C2 **Sisal** Mex.
122 B2 **Sishen** S. Africa
81 C2 **Sisian** Armenia
127 I2 **Sisimiut** Greenland
129 D2 **Sisipuk Lake** Can.
63 B2 **Sisŏphŏn** Cambodia
105 D3 **Sisteron** France
Sitang China *see* **Sinan**
75 C2 **Sitapur** India
111 C3 **Siteia** Greece
123 D2 **Siteki** Swaziland
128 A2 **Sitka** U.S.A.
100 B2 **Sittard** Neth.
62 A1 **Sittaung** Myanmar
62 A2 **Sittaung** *r.* Myanmar
62 A1 **Sittwe** Myanmar
61 C2 **Situbondo** Indon.
80 B2 **Sivas** Turkey
111 C3 **Sivaslı** Turkey
80 B2 **Siverek** Turkey
88 D2 **Siverskiy** Rus. Fed.
91 D2 **Sivers'kyy Donets'** *r.* Ukr.
80 B2 **Sivrihisar** Turkey
116 A2 **Sīwah** Egypt
75 B1 **Siwalik Range** *mts* India/Nepal
116 A2 **Sīwah, Wāḥāt** Egypt
Siwa Oasis Egypt *see* **Sīwah, Wāḥāt**
105 D3 **Six-Fours-les-Plages** France
70 B2 **Sixian** China
123 C2 **Siyabuswa** S. Africa
Sjælland *i.* Denmark *see* **Zealand**
109 D2 **Sjenica** Serb. and Mont.
92 G2 **Sjøvegan** Norway
91 C2 **Skadovs'k** Ukr.
93 F4 **Skagen** Denmark
93 E4 **Skagerrak** *str.* Denmark/Norway
134 B1 **Skagit** *r.* U.S.A.
128 A2 **Skagway** U.S.A.
92 G2 **Skaland** Norway
93 F4 **Skara** Sweden
74 B1 **Skardu** Jammu and Kashmir
103 E1 **Skarżysko-Kamienna** Pol.
103 D2 **Skawina** Pol.
114 A2 **Skaymat** Western Sahara
128 B2 **Skeena** *r.* Can.
128 B2 **Skeena Mountains** Can.
98 D3 **Skegness** U.K.
92 H3 **Skellefteå** Sweden
92 H3 **Skellefteälven** *r.* Sweden
97 C2 **Skerries** Rep. of Ireland
93 F4 **Ski** Norway
111 B3 **Skiathos** *i.* Greece
97 B3 **Skibbereen** Rep. of Ireland
92 □B2 **Skíðadals-jökull** *glacier* Iceland
98 B2 **Skiddaw** *hill* U.K.
93 E4 **Skien** Norway
103 E1 **Skierniewice** Pol.
115 C1 **Skikda** Alg.
52 B3 **Skipton** Austr.
98 B3 **Skipton** U.K.
93 E4 **Skive** Denmark
92 H1 **Skjervøy** Norway
Skobelev Uzbek. *see* **Farg'ona**
111 B3 **Skopelos** *i.* Greece
89 E3 **Skopin** Rus. Fed.
111 B2 **Skopje** Macedonia
111 C3 **Skoutaros** Greece
93 F4 **Skövde** Sweden
83 J3 **Skovorodino** Rus. Fed.
139 F2 **Skowhegan** U.S.A.
92 H2 **Skröven** Sweden
88 B2 **Skrunda** Latvia
128 A1 **Skukum, Mount** Can.
123 D1 **Skukuza** S. Africa
88 B2 **Skuodas** Lith.
90 B2 **Skvyra** Ukr.
96 A2 **Skye** *i.* U.K.
111 B3 **Skyros** Greece
111 B3 **Skyros** *i.* Greece
93 F4 **Slagelse** Denmark
60 B2 **Slamet, Gunung** *vol.* Indon.
97 C2 **Slaney** *r.* Rep. of Ireland
88 C2 **Slantsy** Rus. Fed.
109 C1 **Slatina** Croatia
110 B2 **Slatina** Romania
143 C2 **Slaton** U.S.A.
129 C1 **Slave** *r.* Can.
114 C4 **Slave Coast** Africa
128 C2 **Slave Lake** Can.
77 D1 **Slavgorod** Rus. Fed.
88 C2 **Slavkovichi** Rus. Fed.
Slavonska Požega Croatia *see* **Požega**
109 C1 **Slavonski Brod** Croatia
90 B1 **Slavuta** Ukr.
90 C1 **Slavutych** Ukr.
66 B2 **Slavyanka** Rus. Fed.
Slavyanskaya Rus. Fed. *see* **Slavyansk-na-Kubani**
91 D2 **Slavyansk-na-Kubani** Rus. Fed.
89 D3 **Slawharad** Belarus
103 D1 **Sławno** Pol.
99 C3 **Sleaford** U.K.
97 A2 **Slea Head** *hd* Rep. of Ireland
130 C2 **Sleeper Islands** Can.
97 D1 **Slieve Donard** *hill* U.K.
97 B1 **Slieve Gamph** *hills* Rep. of Ireland
96 A2 **Sligachan** U.K.
Sligeach Rep. of Ireland *see* **Sligo**
97 B1 **Sligo** Rep. of Ireland
97 B1 **Sligo Bay** Rep. of Ireland
93 G4 **Slite** Sweden
110 C2 **Sliven** Bulg.
Sloboda Rus. Fed. *see* **Ezhva**
110 C2 **Slobozia** Romania
128 C3 **Slocan** Can.
88 C3 **Slonim** Belarus
100 B1 **Sloten** Neth.
99 C4 **Slough** U.K.
103 D2 **Slovakia** *country* Europe
108 B1 **Slovenia** *country* Europe
91 D2 **Slov"yans'k** Ukr.
102 C1 **Słubice** Pol.
90 B1 **Sluch** *r.* Ukr.
100 A2 **Sluis** Neth.
103 D1 **Słupsk** Pol.
88 C3 **Slutsk** Belarus
97 A2 **Slyne Head** *hd* Rep. of Ireland
68 C1 **Slyudyanka** Rus. Fed.
131 D2 **Smallwood Reservoir** Can.
88 C3 **Smalyavichy** Belarus
88 C3 **Smarhon'** Belarus
129 D2 **Smeaton** Can.
109 D2 **Smederevo** Serb. and Mont.
109 D2 **Smederevska Palanka** Serb. and Mont.
91 C2 **Smila** Ukr.
88 C3 **Smilavichy** Belarus
88 C2 **Smiltene** Latvia
137 D3 **Smith Center** U.S.A.
128 B2 **Smithers** Can.
141 E1 **Smithfield** *NC* U.S.A.
134 D2 **Smithfield** *UT* U.S.A.
139 D3 **Smith Mountain Lake** U.S.A.
130 C3 **Smiths Falls** Can.
53 D2 **Smithtown** Austr.
53 D2 **Smoky Cape** Austr.
137 D3 **Smoky Hills** U.S.A.
92 E3 **Smøla** *i.* Norway
89 D3 **Smolensk** Rus. Fed.
89 D3 **Smolensko-Moskovskaya Vozvyshennost'** *hills* Rus. Fed.
111 B2 **Smolyan** Bulg.
66 B2 **Smolyoninovo** Rus. Fed.

130 B3 Smooth Rock Falls Can.
Smyrna Turkey see İzmir
91 D2 Smyrnove Ukr.
92 □B3 Snæfell mt. Iceland
98 A2 Snaefell hill Isle of Man
128 A1 Snag Can.
134 C1 Snake r. U.S.A.
134 D2 Snake River Plain U.S.A.
Snare Lakes Can. see Wekweti
92 F3 Snåsvatn l. Norway
100 B1 Sneek Neth.
97 B3 Sneem Rep. of Ireland
122 B3 Sneeuberge mts S. Africa
Snegurovka Ukr. see Tetiyiv
103 D1 Snêžka mt. Czech Rep.
108 B1 Snežnik mt. Slovenia
103 E1 Śniardwy, Jezioro l. Pol.
Sniečkus Lith. see Visaginas
91 C2 Snihurivka Ukr.
93 E3 Snillfjord r. Norway
Snovsk Ukr. see Shchors
129 D1 Snowbird Lake Can.
99 A3 Snowdon mt. U.K.
Snowdrift Can. see Łutselk'e
129 C1 Snowdrift r. Can.
142 A2 Snowflake U.S.A.
129 D2 Snow Lake Can.
134 C1 Snowshoe Peak U.S.A.
52 A2 Snowtown Austr.
53 C3 Snowy r. Austr.
53 C3 Snowy Mountains Austr.
143 C2 Snyder U.S.A.
121 □D2 Soalala Madag.
121 □D2 Soanierana-Ivongo Madag.
90 B2 Sob r. Ukr.
65 B2 Sobaek-sanmaek mts S. Korea
117 B4 Sobat r. Sudan
100 C3 Sobernheim Ger.
89 F2 Sobinka Rus. Fed.
151 E4 Sobradinho, Barragem de resr Brazil
151 E3 Sobral Brazil
91 D3 Sochi Rus. Fed.
65 B2 Söch'ŏn S. Korea
49 L5 Society Islands Fr. Polynesia
150 B2 Socorro Col.
142 B2 Socorro NM U.S.A.
142 B2 Socorro TX U.S.A.
144 A3 Socorro, Isla i. Mex.
56 B4 Socotra i. Yemen
63 B3 Soc Trăng Vietnam
106 C2 Socuéllamos Spain
92 I2 Sodankylä Fin.
134 D2 Soda Springs U.S.A.
93 G3 Söderhamn Sweden
93 G4 Södertälje Sweden
116 A3 Sodiri Sudan
117 B4 Sodo Eth.
93 G3 Södra Kvarken str. Fin./Sweden
123 C1 Soekmekaar S. Africa
Soerabaia Indon. see Surabaya
101 D2 Soest Ger.
53 C2 Sofala Austr.
110 B2 Sofia Bulg.
121 □D2 Sofia r. Madag.
Sofiya Bulg. see Sofia
Sofiyevka Ukr. see Vil'nyans'k
75 D1 Sog China
93 E3 Sognefjorden inlet Norway
111 D2 Söğüt Turkey
Sohâg Egypt see Sawhāj
Sohar Oman see Şuḩār
100 B2 Soignies Belgium
105 C2 Soissons France
90 A1 Sokal' Ukr.
65 B2 Sokch'o S. Korea
111 C3 Söke Turkey
81 C1 Sokhumi Georgia
114 C4 Sokodé Togo
89 F2 Sokol Rus. Fed.
101 F2 Sokolov Czech Rep.
115 C3 Sokoto Nigeria
115 C3 Sokoto r. Nigeria
90 B2 Sokyryany Ukr.
73 B3 Solapur India
135 B3 Soledad U.S.A.
89 F2 Soligalich Rus. Fed.
99 C3 Solihull U.K.
86 E3 Solikamsk Rus. Fed.
87 E3 Sol'-Iletsk Rus. Fed.
100 C2 Solingen Ger.

122 A1 Solitaire Namibia
92 G3 Sollefteå Sweden
93 G4 Sollentuna Sweden
107 D2 Sóller Spain
101 D2 Solling hills Ger.
89 E2 Solnechnogorsk Rus. Fed.
60 B2 Solok Indon.
48 H4 Solomon Islands country S. Pacific Ocean
48 G4 Solomon Sea P.N.G./Solomon Is
61 D2 Solor, Kepulauan is Indon.
105 D2 Solothurn Switz.
81 D2 Soltānābād Iran
101 D1 Soltau Ger.
89 D2 Sol'tsy Rus. Fed.
96 C3 Solway Firth est. U.K.
120 B2 Solwezi Zambia
111 C3 Soma Turkey
117 C4 Somalia country Africa
120 B1 Sombo Angola
109 C1 Sombor Serb. and Mont.
144 B2 Sombrerete Mex.
138 C3 Somerset U.S.A.
123 C3 Somerset East S. Africa
126 F2 Somerset Island Can.
122 A3 Somerset West S. Africa
110 B1 Someş r. Romania
101 E2 Sömmerda Ger.
146 B3 Somoto Nic.
75 C2 Son r. India
93 E5 Sønderborg Denmark
101 E2 Sondershausen Ger.
Søndre Strømfjord inlet Greenland see Kangerlussuaq
108 A1 Sondrio Italy
63 B2 Sông Cau Vietnam
62 B1 Sông Da, Hô resr Vietnam
119 D4 Songea Tanz.
65 B1 Sŏnggan N. Korea
65 B1 Songhua Hu resr China
65 B1 Songjianghe China
Sŏngjin N. Korea see Kimch'aek
63 B3 Songkhla Thai.
65 B2 Sŏngnam S. Korea
65 B2 Songnim N. Korea
120 A1 Songo Angola
121 C2 Songo Moz.
Songololo Dem. Rep. Congo see Mbanza-Ngungu
69 E1 Songyuan China
Sonid Youqi China see Saihan Tal
74 B2 Sonipat India
89 E2 Sonkovo Rus. Fed.
62 B1 Son La Vietnam
74 A2 Sonmiani Pak.
74 A2 Sonmiani Bay Pak.
101 E2 Sonneberg Ger.
142 A2 Sonoita Mex.
144 A2 Sonora r. Mex.
135 B3 Sonora CA U.S.A.
143 C2 Sonora TX U.S.A.
146 B3 Sonsonate El Salvador
Soochow China see Suzhou
117 A4 Sopo watercourse Sudan
103 D2 Sopron Hungary
74 B1 Sopur Jammu and Kashmir
108 B2 Sora Italy
130 C3 Sorel Can.
51 D4 Sorell Austr.
106 C1 Soria Spain
90 B2 Soroca Moldova
154 C2 Sorocaba Brazil
87 E3 Sorochinsk Rus. Fed.
90 B2 Soroki Moldova see Soroca
59 D2 Sorol atoll Micronesia
59 C3 Sorong Indon.
119 D2 Soroti Uganda
92 H1 Sørøya i. Norway
108 B2 Sorrento Italy
92 G2 Sorsele Sweden
64 B2 Sorsogon Phil.
92 G2 Sortavala Rus. Fed.
92 G2 Sortland Norway
65 B2 Sŏsan S. Korea
123 C2 Soshanguve S. Africa
89 E3 Sosna r. Rus. Fed.
153 B3 Sosneado mt. Arg.
86 E2 Sosnogorsk Rus. Fed.
86 D2 Sosnovka Rus. Fed.
88 C2 Sosnovyy Bor Rus. Fed.
103 D1 Sosnowiec Pol.
91 C1 Sosnytsya Ukr.
86 F3 Sos'va Rus. Fed.
91 D2 Sosyka r. Rus. Fed.

145 C2 Soto la Marina Mex.
118 B2 Souanké Congo
111 B3 Souda Greece
104 C3 Souillac France
Soûl S. Korea see Seoul
104 B2 Soulac-sur-Mer France
104 B3 Soulom France
Soûr Lebanon see Tyre
107 D2 Sour el Ghozlane Alg.
129 D3 Souris Man. Can.
131 D3 Souris P.E.I. Can.
129 E3 Souris r. Can.
151 F3 Sousa Brazil
115 D1 Sousse Tunisia
104 B3 Soustons France
122 B3 South Africa, Republic of country Africa
99 C4 Southampton U.K.
129 F1 Southampton, Cape Can.
129 F1 Southampton Island Can.
73 D3 South Andaman i. India
52 A1 South Australia state Austr.
140 B2 Southaven U.S.A.
142 B2 South Baldy mt. U.S.A.
130 B3 South Baymouth Can.
138 B2 South Bend U.S.A.
141 D2 South Carolina state U.S.A.
58 B2 South China Sea N. Pacific Ocean
South Coast Town Austr. see Gold Coast
136 C2 South Dakota state U.S.A.
99 C4 South Downs hills U.K.
159 E6 Southeast Indian Ridge sea feature Indian Ocean
55 O2 Southeast Pacific Basin sea feature S. Pacific Ocean
129 D2 Southend Can.
99 D4 Southend-on-Sea U.K.
54 B2 Southern Alps mts N.Z.
50 A3 Southern Cross Austr.
129 E2 Southern Indian Lake Can.
159 D7 Southern Ocean
141 E1 Southern Pines U.S.A.
Southern Rhodesia country Africa see Zimbabwe
96 B3 Southern Uplands hills U.K.
55 J2 South Geomagnetic Pole Antarctica
149 G8 South Georgia terr. S. Atlantic Ocean
149 G8 South Georgia and South Sandwich Islands terr. S. Atlantic Ocean
138 B2 South Haven U.S.A.
129 E1 South Henik Lake Can.
119 D2 South Horr Kenya
54 B2 South Island N.Z.
65 B2 South Korea country Asia
135 B3 South Lake Tahoe U.S.A.
55 K3 South Magnetic Pole Antarctica
149 F9 South Orkney Islands S. Atlantic Ocean
136 C2 South Platte r. U.S.A.
98 B3 Southport U.K.
141 E2 Southport U.S.A.
130 C3 South River Can.
96 C1 South Ronaldsay i. U.K.
123 D3 South Sand Bluff pt S. Africa
149 H8 South Sandwich Islands S. Atlantic Ocean
55 C4 South Sandwich Trench sea feature S. Atlantic Ocean
129 D2 South Saskatchewan r. Can.
129 E2 South Seal r. Can.
149 E9 South Shetland Islands Antarctica
98 C2 South Shields U.K.
54 B1 South Taranaki Bight b. N.Z.
156 C8 South Tasman Rise sea feature Southern Ocean
130 C2 South Twin Island Can.
96 A2 South Uist i. U.K.
South-West Africa country Africa see Namibia
Southwest Peru Ridge sea feature S. Pacific Ocean see Nazca Ridge

53 D2 South West Rocks Austr.
99 D3 Southwold U.K.
109 C3 Soverato Italy
88 B2 Sovetsk Rus. Fed.
86 F2 Sovetskiy Rus. Fed.
91 C2 Sovyets'kyy Ukr.
123 C2 Soweto S. Africa
66 D1 Sōya-misaki c. Japan
65 B2 Soyang-ho l. S. Korea
104 C2 Soyaux France
90 C1 Sozh r. Europe
110 C2 Sozopol Bulg.
100 B2 Spa Belgium
106 C1 Spain country Europe
Spalato Croatia see Split
99 C3 Spalding U.K.
135 D2 Spanish Fork U.S.A.
Spanish Guinea country Africa see Equatorial Guinea
97 B2 Spanish Point Rep. of Ireland
Spanish Sahara terr. Africa see Western Sahara
146 C3 Spanish Town Jamaica
108 B3 Sparagio, Monte mt. Sicily Italy
135 C3 Sparks U.S.A.
138 A2 Sparta U.S.A.
141 D2 Spartanburg U.S.A.
111 B3 Sparti Greece
109 C3 Spartivento, Capo c. Italy
89 D3 Spas-Demensk Rus. Fed.
89 F2 Spas-Klepiki Rus. Fed.
66 B2 Spassk-Dal'niy Rus. Fed.
89 F3 Spassk-Ryazanskiy Rus. Fed.
111 B3 Spatha, Akra pt Greece
96 B2 Spean Bridge U.K.
136 C2 Spearfish U.S.A.
143 C1 Spearman U.S.A.
Spence Bay Can. see Taloyoak
137 D2 Spencer IA U.S.A.
134 D2 Spencer ID U.S.A.
52 A2 Spencer Gulf est. Austr.
98 C2 Spennymoor U.K.
54 B2 Spenser Mountains N.Z.
101 D3 Spessart reg. Ger.
96 C2 Spey r. U.K.
101 D3 Speyer Ger.
100 C1 Spiekeroog i. Ger.
100 B2 Spijkenisse Neth.
100 B3 Spincourt France
128 C2 Spirit River Can.
103 E2 Spišská Nová Ves Slovakia
82 C1 Spitsbergen i. Svalbard
102 C2 Spittal an der Drau Austria
93 E3 Spjelkavik Norway
109 C2 Split Croatia
129 E2 Split Lake Can.
129 E2 Split Lake l. Can.
134 C1 Spokane U.S.A.
138 A1 Spooner U.S.A.
102 C1 Spree r. Ger.
122 A2 Springbok S. Africa
131 E3 Springdale Can.
140 B1 Springdale U.S.A.
101 D1 Springe Ger.
142 C1 Springer U.S.A.
142 B2 Springerville U.S.A.
136 C3 Springfield CO U.S.A.
138 B3 Springfield IL U.S.A.
139 E2 Springfield MA U.S.A.
137 E3 Springfield MO U.S.A.
138 C3 Springfield OH U.S.A.
134 B2 Springfield OR U.S.A.
140 C1 Springfield TN U.S.A.
123 C3 Springfontein S. Africa
131 D3 Springhill Can.
141 D3 Spring Hill U.S.A.
54 B2 Springs Junction N.Z.
51 D2 Springsure Austr.
135 D2 Springville U.S.A.
98 D3 Spurn Head hd U.K.
128 B3 Squamish Can.
109 C3 Squillace, Golfo di g. Italy
109 D2 Srbija aut. rep. Serb. and Mont.
108 C2 Srebrenica Bos.-Herz.
110 C2 Sredets Bulg.
83 L3 Sredinnyy Khrebet mts Rus. Fed.
83 L2 Srednekolymsk Rus. Fed.
Sredne-Russkaya Vozvyshennost' hills Rus. Fed. see Central Russian Upland

Sredne-Sibirskoye Ploskogor'ye Rus. Fed. *see* **Central Siberian Plateau**
110 B2 **Srednogorie** Bulg.
69 D1 **Sretensk** Rus. Fed.
61 C1 **Sri Aman** *Sarawak* Malaysia
73 B4 **Sri Jayewardenepura Kotte** Sri Lanka
73 C3 **Srikakulam** India
73 C4 **Sri Lanka** *country* Asia
74 B1 **Srinagar** Jammu and Kashmir
73 B3 **Srivardhan** India
101 D1 **Stade** Ger.
101 E1 **Stadensen** Ger.
100 C1 **Stadskanaal** Neth.
101 D2 **Stadtallendorf** Ger.
101 D1 **Stadthagen** Ger.
101 E2 **Staffelstein** Ger.
99 B3 **Stafford** U.K.
99 C4 **Staines** U.K.
91 D2 **Stakhanov** Ukr.
Stakhanovo Rus. Fed. *see* **Zhukovskiy**
Stalin Bulg. *see* **Varna**
Stalinabad Tajik. *see* **Dushanbe**
Stalingrad Rus. Fed. *see* **Volgograd**
Staliniri Georgia *see* **Ts'khinvali**
Stalino Ukr. *see* **Donets'k**
Stalinogorsk Rus. Fed. *see* **Novomoskovsk**
Stalinogród Pol. *see* **Katowice**
Stalinsk Rus. Fed. *see* **Novokuznetsk**
103 E1 **Stalowa Wola** Pol.
138 B1 **Stambaugh** U.S.A.
99 C3 **Stamford** U.K.
139 E2 **Stamford** *CT* U.S.A.
143 D2 **Stamford** *TX* U.S.A.
Stampalia *i.* Greece *see* **Astypalaia**
122 A1 **Stampriet** Namibia
92 F2 **Stamsund** Norway
123 C2 **Standerton** S. Africa
138 C2 **Standish** U.S.A.
123 D2 **Stanger** S. Africa
Stanislav Ukr. *see* **Ivano-Frankivs'k**
Stanke Dimitrov Bulg. *see* **Dupnitsa**
153 C5 **Stanley** Falkland Is
136 C1 **Stanley** U.S.A.
Stanleyville Dem. Rep. Congo *see* **Kisangani**
Stann Creek Belize *see* **Dangriga**
111 B3 **Stanos** Greece
83 I3 **Stanovoye Nagor'ye** *mts* Rus. Fed.
83 J3 **Stanovoy Khrebet** *mts* Rus. Fed.
53 D1 **Stanthorpe** Austr.
137 E1 **Staples** U.S.A.
103 E1 **Starachowice** Pol.
Stara Planina *mts* Bulg./Serb. and Mont. *see* **Balkan Mountains**
89 D2 **Staraya Russa** Rus. Fed.
89 D2 **Staraya Toropa** Rus. Fed.
110 C2 **Stara Zagora** Bulg.
49 L4 **Starbuck Island** Kiribati
103 D1 **Stargard Szczeciński** Pol.
89 D2 **Staritsa** Rus. Fed.
141 D3 **Starke** U.S.A.
140 C2 **Starkville** U.S.A.
102 C2 **Starnberg** Ger.
91 D2 **Starobil's'k** Ukr.
89 D3 **Starodub** Rus. Fed.
103 D1 **Starogard Gdański** Pol.
90 B2 **Starokostyantyniv** Ukr.
91 D2 **Starominskaya** Rus. Fed.
91 D2 **Staroshcherbinovskaya** Rus. Fed.
91 D2 **Starotitarovskaya** Rus. Fed.
89 F3 **Staroyur'yevo** Rus. Fed.
89 E3 **Starozhilovo** Rus. Fed.
99 B4 **Start Point** U.K.
88 C3 **Staryya Darohi** Belarus
86 G2 **Staryy Nadym** Rus. Fed.
89 E3 **Staryy Oskol** Rus. Fed.
101 E2 **Staßfurt** Ger.
103 E1 **Staszów** Pol.
139 D2 **State College** U.S.A.
141 D2 **Statesboro** U.S.A.
141 D1 **Statesville** U.S.A.
160 L1 **Station Nord** Greenland
139 D3 **Staunton** U.S.A.
93 E4 **Stavanger** Norway
87 D4 **Stavropol'** Rus. Fed.
Stavropol'-na-Volge Rus. Fed. *see* **Tol'yatti**
87 D4 **Stavropol'skaya Vozvyshennost'** *hills* Rus. Fed.
52 B3 **Stawell** Austr.
123 C2 **Steadville** S. Africa
136 B2 **Steamboat Springs** U.S.A.
101 E2 **Stedten** Ger.
128 C2 **Steen River** Can.
134 C2 **Steens Mountain** U.S.A.
100 C1 **Steenwijk** Neth.
126 E2 **Stefansson Island** Can.
Stegi Swaziland *see* **Siteki**
110 B1 **Ştei** Romania
101 E3 **Steigerwald** *mts* Ger.
100 B2 **Stein** Neth.
129 E3 **Steinbach** Can.
100 C1 **Steinfurt** Ger.
120 A3 **Steinhausen** Namibia
92 F3 **Steinkjer** Norway
122 A2 **Steinkopf** S. Africa
122 B2 **Stella** S. Africa
122 A3 **Stellenbosch** S. Africa
105 D3 **Stello, Monte** *mt.* *Corsica* France
105 D2 **Stenay** France
101 E1 **Stendal** Ger.
Steornabhagh U.K. *see* **Stornoway**
Stepanakert Azer. *see* **Xankändi**
52 B2 **Stephens Creek** Austr.
129 E2 **Stephens Lake** Can.
131 E3 **Stephenville** Can.
143 D2 **Stephenville** U.S.A.
Stepnoy Rus. Fed. *see* **Elista**
122 B3 **Sterling** S. Africa
136 C2 **Sterling** *CO* U.S.A.
138 B2 **Sterling** *IL* U.S.A.
136 C1 **Sterling** *ND* U.S.A.
138 C2 **Sterling Heights** U.S.A.
87 E3 **Sterlitamak** Rus. Fed.
101 E1 **Sternberg** Ger.
128 C2 **Stettler** Can.
138 C2 **Steubenville** U.S.A.
99 C4 **Stevenage** U.K.
129 E2 **Stevenson Lake** Can.
138 B2 **Stevens Point** U.S.A.
126 C2 **Stevens Village** U.S.A.
134 D1 **Stevensville** U.S.A.
128 B2 **Stewart** Can.
128 A1 **Stewart** *r.* Can.
54 A3 **Stewart Island** N.Z.
127 G2 **Stewart Lake** Can.
123 C3 **Steynsburg** S. Africa
102 C2 **Steyr** Austria
122 B3 **Steytlerville** S. Africa
128 A2 **Stikine** *r.* Can.
128 A2 **Stikine Plateau** Can.
122 B3 **Stilbaai** S. Africa
137 E1 **Stillwater** *MN* U.S.A.
143 D1 **Stillwater** *OK* U.S.A.
135 C3 **Stillwater Range** *mts* U.S.A.
109 D2 **Štip** Macedonia
96 C2 **Stirling** U.K.
52 A2 **Stirling North** Austr.
92 F3 **Stjørdalshalsen** Norway
103 D2 **Stockerau** Austria
93 G4 **Stockholm** Sweden
98 B3 **Stockport** U.K.
135 B3 **Stockton** U.S.A.
98 C2 **Stockton-on-Tees** U.K.
143 C2 **Stockton Plateau** U.S.A.
63 B2 **Stœng Trêng** Cambodia
96 B1 **Stoer, Point of** U.K.
99 B3 **Stoke-on-Trent** U.K.
98 C2 **Stokesley** U.K.
92 F2 **Stokmarknes** Norway
110 B2 **Stol** *mt.* Serb. and Mont.
109 C2 **Stolac** Bos.-Herz.
100 C2 **Stolberg (Rheinland)** Ger.
82 E2 **Stolbovoy** Rus. Fed.
88 C3 **Stolin** Belarus
101 F2 **Stollberg** Ger.
101 D1 **Stolzenau** Ger.
96 C2 **Stonehaven** U.K.
99 C4 **Stonehenge** *tourist site* U.K.
129 E2 **Stonewall** Can.
129 D2 **Stony Rapids** Can.
92 G2 **Storavan** *l.* Sweden
Store Bælt *sea chan.* Denmark *see* **Great Belt**
92 F3 **Støren** Norway
92 I1 **Storfjordbotn** Norway
92 F2 **Storforshei** Norway
126 E2 **Storkerson Peninsula** Can.
137 D2 **Storm Lake** U.S.A.
93 E3 **Stornosa** *mt.* Norway
96 A1 **Stornoway** U.K.
86 E2 **Storozhevsk** Rus. Fed.
90 B2 **Storozhynets'** Ukr.
92 F3 **Storsjön** *l.* Sweden
92 H2 **Storslett** Norway
92 G2 **Storuman** Sweden
92 G2 **Storuman** *l.* Sweden
99 C4 **Stour** *r.* *England* U.K.
99 D4 **Stour** *r.* *England* U.K.
99 C3 **Stour** *r.* *England* U.K.
130 A2 **Stout Lake** Can.
88 C3 **Stowbtsy** Belarus
99 D3 **Stowmarket** U.K.
97 C1 **Strabane** U.K.
102 C2 **Strakonice** Czech Rep.
102 C1 **Stralsund** Ger.
122 A3 **Strand** S. Africa
93 E3 **Stranda** Norway
97 D1 **Strangford Lough** *inlet* U.K.
96 B3 **Stranraer** U.K.
105 D2 **Strasbourg** France
130 B3 **Stratford** Can.
54 B1 **Stratford** N.Z.
143 C1 **Stratford** U.S.A.
99 C3 **Stratford-upon-Avon** U.K.
128 C2 **Strathmore** Can.
96 C2 **Strathspey** *val.* U.K.
102 C2 **Straubing** Ger.
134 C2 **Strawberry Mountain** U.S.A.
51 C3 **Streaky Bay** Austr.
138 B2 **Streator** U.S.A.
99 B4 **Street** U.K.
110 B2 **Strehaia** Romania
94 B1 **Streymoy** *i.* Faroe Is
82 G2 **Strezhevoy** Rus. Fed.
101 F3 **Stříbro** Czech Rep.
111 B2 **Strimonas** *r.* Greece
153 B4 **Stroeder** Arg.
101 D1 **Ströhen** Ger.
109 C3 **Stromboli, Isola** *i.* Italy
96 B2 **Stromeferry** U.K.
96 C1 **Stromness** U.K.
92 G3 **Strömsund** Sweden
96 C1 **Stronsay** *i.* U.K.
53 D2 **Stroud** Austr.
99 B4 **Stroud** U.K.
100 C1 **Strücklingen (Saterland)** Ger.
111 B2 **Struga** Macedonia
88 C2 **Strugi-Krasnyye** Rus. Fed.
122 B3 **Struis Bay** S. Africa
111 B2 **Struma** *r.* Bulg.
99 A3 **Strumble Head** *hd* U.K.
111 B2 **Strumica** Macedonia
122 B2 **Strydenburg** S. Africa
93 E3 **Stryn** Norway
90 A2 **Stryy** Ukr.
90 A2 **Stryy** *r.* Ukr.
128 B2 **Stuart Lake** Can.
53 C2 **Stuart Town** Austr.
Stuchka Latvia *see* **Aizkraukle**
Stučka Latvia *see* **Aizkraukle**
130 A2 **Stull Lake** Can.
89 E3 **Stupino** Rus. Fed.
55 M3 **Sturge Island** Antarctica
138 B2 **Sturgeon Bay** U.S.A.
130 C3 **Sturgeon Falls** Can.
130 A3 **Sturgeon Lake** Can.
138 B2 **Sturgis** *MI* U.S.A.
136 C2 **Sturgis** *SD* U.S.A.
52 B1 **Sturt, Mount** *hill* Austr.
50 B1 **Sturt Creek** *watercourse* Austr.
50 C1 **Sturt Plain** Austr.
52 B1 **Sturt Stony Desert** Austr.
123 C3 **Stutterheim** S. Africa
102 B2 **Stuttgart** Ger.
140 B2 **Stuttgart** U.S.A.
92 □A2 **Stykkishólmur** Iceland
90 B1 **Styr** *r.* Belarus/Ukr.
155 D1 **Suaçuí Grande** *r.* Brazil
116 B3 **Suakin** Sudan
71 C3 **Suao** Taiwan
78 A3 **Suara, Mount** Eritrea
60 B1 **Subi Besar** *i.* Indon.
109 C1 **Subotica** Serb. and Mont.
110 C1 **Suceava** Romania
Suchan Rus. Fed. *see* **Partizansk**
97 B2 **Suck** *r.* Rep. of Ireland
152 B1 **Sucre** Bol.
154 B2 **Sucuriú** *r.* Brazil
Suczawa Romania *see* **Suceava**
89 E2 **Suda** Rus. Fed.
91 C3 **Sudak** Ukr.
116 A3 **Sudan** *country* Africa
130 B3 **Sudbury** Can.
99 D3 **Sudbury** U.K.
117 A4 **Sudd** *swamp* Sudan
89 F2 **Sudislavl'** Rus. Fed.
89 F2 **Sudogda** Rus. Fed.
94 B1 **Suðuroy** *i.* Faroe Is
89 E3 **Sudzha** Rus. Fed.
107 C2 **Sueca** Spain
116 B2 **Suez** Egypt
116 B2 **Suez, Gulf of** Egypt
80 B2 **Suez Canal** *canal* Egypt
139 D3 **Suffolk** U.S.A.
140 A3 **Sugar Land** U.S.A.
139 E1 **Sugarloaf Mountain** U.S.A.
53 D2 **Sugarloaf Point** Austr.
70 A2 **Suhait** China
79 C2 **Şuḩār** Oman
68 D1 **Sühbaatar** Mongolia
101 E2 **Suhl** Ger.
109 C1 **Suhopolje** Croatia
70 B2 **Suide** China
66 B2 **Suifenhe** China
69 E1 **Suihua** China
70 A2 **Suining** China
70 B2 **Suiping** China
97 C2 **Suir** *r.* Rep. of Ireland
Suixian China *see* **Suizhou**
70 B2 **Suiyang** China
70 B2 **Suizhou** China
74 B2 **Sujangarh** India
74 B1 **Sujanpur** India
74 A2 **Sujawal** Pak.
60 B2 **Sukabumi** Indon.
60 B2 **Sukadana** Indon.
67 D3 **Sukagawa** Japan
60 C2 **Sukaraja** Indon.
Sukarnapura Indon. *see* **Jayapura**
Sukarno, Puntjak *mt.* Indon. *see* **Jaya, Puncak**
89 E3 **Sukhinichi** Rus. Fed.
89 F2 **Sukhona** *r.* Rus. Fed.
62 A2 **Sukhothai** Thai.
74 A2 **Sukkur** Pak.
89 E2 **Sukromny** Rus. Fed.
59 C3 **Sula, Kepulauan** *is* Indon.
74 A1 **Sulaiman Range** *mts* Pak.
Sulawesi *i.* Indon. *see* **Celebes**
101 D1 **Sulingen** Ger.
150 A3 **Sullana** Peru
138 B3 **Sullivan** *IN* U.S.A.
137 E3 **Sullivan** *MO* U.S.A.
140 B2 **Sulphur** U.S.A.
143 D2 **Sulphur Springs** U.S.A.
138 C1 **Sultan** Can.
Sultanabad Iran *see* **Arāk**
64 B3 **Sulu Archipelago** *is* Phil.
64 A3 **Sulu Sea** N. Pacific Ocean
101 E3 **Sulzbach-Rosenberg** Ger.
79 C2 **Sumāil** Oman
Sumatera *i.* Indon. *see* **Sumatra**
60 A1 **Sumatra** *i.* Indon.
61 D2 **Sumba** *i.* Indon.
61 C2 **Sumba, Selat** *sea chan.* Indon.
61 C2 **Sumbawa** *i.* Indon.
61 C2 **Sumbawabesar** Indon.
119 D3 **Sumbawanga** Tanz.
120 A2 **Sumbe** Angola
96 □ **Sumburgh** U.K.
96 □ **Sumburgh Head** *hd* U.K.
119 C2 **Sumeih** Sudan
61 C2 **Sumenep** Indon.
67 D4 **Sumisu-jima** *i.* Japan
131 D3 **Summerside** Can.
138 C3 **Summersville** U.S.A.
141 D2 **Summerville** U.S.A.
137 D1 **Summit** U.S.A.
128 B2 **Summit Lake** Can.
103 D2 **Šumperk** Czech Rep.
81 C1 **Sumqayıt** Azer.
141 D2 **Sumter** U.S.A.
91 C1 **Sumy** Ukr.
75 D2 **Sunamganj** Bangl.
65 B2 **Sunan** N. Korea
79 C2 **Şunaynah** Oman
52 B3 **Sunbury** Austr.
139 D2 **Sunbury** U.S.A.

65 B2 **Sunch'ŏn** N. Korea
65 B3 **Sunch'ŏn** S. Korea
123 C2 **Sun City** S. Africa
93 H3 **Sund** Fin.
60 B2 **Sunda, Selat** *str.* Indon.
136 C2 **Sundance** U.S.A.
75 C2 **Sundarbans** *reg.* Bangl./India
74 B1 **Sundarnagar** India
Sunda Strait Indon. *see* Sunda, Selat
Sunda Trench *sea feature* Indian Ocean *see* Java Trench
98 C2 **Sunderland** U.K.
128 C2 **Sundre** Can.
93 G3 **Sundsvall** Sweden
123 D2 **Sundumbili** S. Africa
60 B2 **Sungailiat** Indon.
60 B2 **Sungaipenuh** Indon.
60 B1 **Sungai Petani** Malaysia
80 B1 **Sungurlu** Turkey
75 C2 **Sun Kosi** *r.* Nepal
93 E3 **Sunndalsøra** Norway
134 C1 **Sunnyside** U.S.A.
135 B3 **Sunnyvale** U.S.A.
141 D3 **Sunrise** U.S.A.
83 I2 **Suntar** Rus. Fed.
74 A2 **Suntsar** Pak.
114 B4 **Sunyani** Ghana
92 I3 **Suomussalmi** Fin.
67 B4 **Suō-nada** *b.* Japan
86 C2 **Suoyarvi** Rus. Fed.
142 A2 **Superior** *AZ* U.S.A.
137 D2 **Superior** *NE* U.S.A.
138 A1 **Superior** *WI* U.S.A.
138 B1 **Superior, Lake** Can./U.S.A.
63 B2 **Suphan Buri** Thai.
81 C2 **Süphan Dağı** *mt.* Turkey
89 D3 **Suponevo** Rus. Fed.
81 C2 **Sūq ash Shuyūkh** Iraq
70 B2 **Suqian** China
78 A2 **Sūq Suwayq** Saudi Arabia
Suquṭrā *i.* Yemen *see* Socotra
79 C2 **Şūr** Oman
74 A2 **Surab** Pak.
61 C2 **Surabaya** Indon.
61 C2 **Surakarta** Indon.
74 B2 **Surat** India
74 B2 **Suratgarh** India
63 A3 **Surat Thani** Thai.
89 D3 **Surazh** Rus. Fed.
109 D2 **Surdulica** Serb. and Mont.
100 C3 **Sûre** *r.* Lux.
74 B2 **Surendranagar** India
82 F2 **Surgut** Rus. Fed.
64 B3 **Surigao** Phil.
63 B2 **Surin** Thai.
151 D2 **Suriname** *country* S. America
75 C2 **Surkhet** Nepal
Surt Libya *see* **Sirte**
Surt, Khalīj *g.* Libya *see* Sirte, Gulf of
60 B2 **Surulangun** Indon.
81 C2 **Sūsangerd** Iran
89 F2 **Susanino** Rus. Fed.
135 B2 **Susanville** U.S.A.
80 B1 **Suşehri** Turkey
139 D3 **Susquehanna** *r.* U.S.A.
131 D3 **Sussex** Can.
101 D1 **Süstedt** Ger.
100 C1 **Sustrum** Ger.
83 K2 **Susuman** Rus. Fed.
111 C3 **Susurluk** Turkey
74 B1 **Sutak** Jammu and Kashmir
53 D2 **Sutherland** Austr.
122 B3 **Sutherland** S. Africa
136 C2 **Sutherland** U.S.A.
134 B2 **Sutherlin** U.S.A.
74 B2 **Sutlej** *r.* India/Pak.
138 C3 **Sutton** U.S.A.
99 C3 **Sutton Coldfield** U.K.
98 C3 **Sutton in Ashfield** U.K.
66 D2 **Suttsu** Japan
49 I5 **Suva** Fiji
Suvalki Pol. *see* **Suwałki**
89 E3 **Suvorov** Rus. Fed.
90 B2 **Suvorove** Ukr.
103 E1 **Suwałki** Pol.
141 D3 **Suwanee Sound** *b.* U.S.A.
63 B2 **Suwannaphum** Thai.
141 D3 **Suwannee** *r.* U.S.A.
Suways, Qanāt as *canal* Egypt *see* **Suez Canal**
65 B2 **Suwŏn** S. Korea
79 C2 **Sūzā** Iran
89 F2 **Suzdal'** Rus. Fed.
89 D3 **Suzemka** Rus. Fed.
70 B2 **Suzhou** *Anhui* China
70 C2 **Suzhou** *Jiangsu* China
67 C3 **Suzu** Japan
67 C3 **Suzu-misaki** *pt* Japan
82 B1 **Svalbard** *terr.* Arctic Ocean
90 A2 **Svalyava** Ukr.
92 H2 **Svappavaara** Sweden
91 D2 **Svatove** Ukr.
63 B2 **Svay Riĕng** Cambodia
93 F3 **Sveg** Sweden
88 C2 **Švenčionys** Lith.
93 F4 **Svendborg** Denmark
Sverdlovsk Rus. Fed. *see* Yekaterinburg
111 B2 **Sveti Nikole** Macedonia
66 C1 **Svetlaya** Rus. Fed.
88 B3 **Svetlogorsk** Rus. Fed.
87 D4 **Svetlograd** Rus. Fed.
88 B3 **Svetlyy** Rus. Fed.
93 I3 **Svetogorsk** Rus. Fed.
103 E2 **Svidník** Slovakia
111 C2 **Svilengrad** Bulg.
110 B2 **Svinecea Mare, Vârful** *mt.* Romania
110 C2 **Svishtov** Bulg.
88 B3 **Svislach** Belarus
103 D2 **Svitavy** Czech Rep.
91 C2 **Svitlovods'k** Ukr.
69 E1 **Svobodnyy** Rus. Fed.
110 B2 **Svoge** Bulg.
92 F2 **Svolvær** Norway
88 C3 **Svyetlahorsk** Belarus
141 D2 **Swainsboro** U.S.A.
120 A3 **Swakopmund** Namibia
52 B3 **Swan Hill** Austr.
128 C2 **Swan Hills** Can.
129 D2 **Swan Lake** Can.
97 C1 **Swanlinbar** Rep. of Ireland
129 D2 **Swan River** Can.
53 D2 **Swansea** Austr.
99 B4 **Swansea** U.K.
122 B3 **Swartkolkvloer** *salt pan* S. Africa
123 C2 **Swartruggens** S. Africa
Swatow China *see* Shantou
123 D2 **Swaziland** *country* Africa
93 G3 **Sweden** *country* Europe
143 C2 **Sweetwater** U.S.A.
136 B2 **Sweetwater** *r.* U.S.A.
122 B3 **Swellendam** S. Africa
103 D1 **Świdnica** Pol.
103 D1 **Świdwin** Pol.
103 D1 **Świebodzin** Pol.
103 D1 **Świecie** Pol.
129 D2 **Swift Current** Can.
97 C1 **Swilly, Lough** *inlet* Rep. of Ireland
99 C4 **Swindon** U.K.
102 C1 **Świnoujście** Pol.
105 D2 **Switzerland** *country* Europe
97 C2 **Swords** Rep. of Ireland
88 C3 **Syanno** Belarus
89 D1 **Syas'troy** Rus. Fed.
89 D2 **Sychevka** Rus. Fed.
53 D2 **Sydney** Austr.
131 D3 **Sydney** Can.
131 D3 **Sydney Mines** Can.
91 D2 **Syeverodonets'k** Ukr.
86 E2 **Syktyvkar** Rus. Fed.
140 C2 **Sylacauga** U.S.A.
75 D2 **Sylhet** Bangl.
102 B1 **Sylt** *i.* Ger.
138 C2 **Sylvania** U.S.A.
51 C1 **Sylvester, Lake** *salt flat* Austr.
111 C3 **Symi** *i.* Greece
91 D2 **Synel'nykove** Ukr.
90 C2 **Synyukha** *r.* Ukr.
109 C3 **Syracuse** *Sicily* Italy
136 C3 **Syracuse** *KS* U.S.A.
139 D2 **Syracuse** *NY* U.S.A.
77 C2 **Syrdar'ya** *r.* Asia
80 B2 **Syria** *country* Asia
80 B2 **Syrian Desert** Asia
111 B3 **Syros** *i.* Greece
91 D2 **Syvash, Zatoka** *lag.* Ukr.
91 C2 **Syvas'ke** Ukr.
87 D3 **Syzran'** Rus. Fed.
102 C1 **Szczecin** Pol.
103 D1 **Szczecinek** Pol.
103 E1 **Szczytno** Pol.
Szechwan *prov.* China *see* Sichuan
103 E2 **Szeged** Hungary
103 D2 **Székesfehérvár** Hungary
103 D2 **Szekszárd** Hungary
103 E2 **Szentes** Hungary
103 D2 **Szentgotthárd** Hungary
103 E2 **Szerencs** Hungary
103 D2 **Szigetvár** Hungary
103 E2 **Szolnok** Hungary
103 D2 **Szombathely** Hungary
Sztálinváros Hungary *see* Dunaújváros

T

117 C4 **Taagga Duudka** *reg.* Somalia
64 B2 **Tabaco** Phil.
78 B2 **Tābah** Saudi Arabia
108 A3 **Tabarka** Tunisia
76 B3 **Ţabas** Iran
79 C1 **Tabāsin** Iran
81 D3 **Tābask, Kūh-e** *mt.* Iran
150 C3 **Tabatinga** Brazil
154 C2 **Tabatinga** Brazil
114 B2 **Tabelbala** Alg.
128 C3 **Taber** Can.
64 B2 **Tablas** *i.* Phil.
102 C2 **Tábor** Czech Rep.
119 D3 **Tabora** Tanz.
114 B4 **Tabou** Côte d'Ivoire
81 C2 **Tabrīz** Iran
48 L3 **Tabuaeran** *i.* Kiribati
78 A2 **Tabūk** Saudi Arabia
93 G4 **Täby** Sweden
77 E2 **Tacheng** China
102 C2 **Tachov** Czech Rep.
64 B2 **Tacloban** Phil.
150 B4 **Tacna** Peru
134 B1 **Tacoma** U.S.A.
152 C3 **Tacuarembó** Uru.
142 B3 **Tacupeto** Mex.
114 C2 **Tademaït, Plateau du** Alg.
Tadjikistan *country* Asia *see* **Tajikistan**
117 C3 **Tadjoura** Djibouti
80 B2 **Tadmur** Syria
129 E2 **Tadoule Lake** Can.
Tadzhikskaya S.S.R. *admin. reg.* Asia *see* Tajikistan
65 B2 **T'aebaek-sanmaek** *mts* N. Korea/S. Korea
Taech'ŏn S. Korea *see* Poryŏng
65 B2 **Taegu** S. Korea
65 B2 **Taejŏn** S. Korea
65 B3 **Taejŏng** S. Korea
65 B2 **T'aepaek** S. Korea
69 E1 **Ta'erqi** China
107 C1 **Tafalla** Spain
152 B2 **Tafi Viejo** Arg.
79 D2 **Taftān, Kūh-e** *mt.* Iran
91 D2 **Taganrog** Rus. Fed.
91 D2 **Taganrog, Gulf of** Rus. Fed./Ukr.
62 A1 **Tagaung** Myanmar
64 B2 **Tagaytay City** Phil.
64 B3 **Tagbilaran** Phil.
64 B2 **Tagudin** Phil.
51 E1 **Tagula Island** P.N.G.
64 B3 **Tagum** Phil.
106 B2 **Tagus** *r.* Port./Spain
60 B1 **Tahan, Gunung** *mt.* Malaysia
115 C2 **Tahat, Mont** *mt.* Alg.
69 E1 **Tahe** China
49 M5 **Tahiti** *i.* Fr. Polynesia
143 E1 **Tahlequah** U.S.A.
135 B3 **Tahoe, Lake** U.S.A.
135 B3 **Tahoe City** U.S.A.
126 E2 **Tahoe Lake** Can.
115 C3 **Tahoua** Niger
79 C2 **Tahrūd** Iran
128 B3 **Tahsis** Can.
116 B2 **Ţahţā** Egypt
64 B3 **Tahuna** Indon.
70 B2 **Tai'an** China
70 A2 **Taibai Shan** *mt.* China
Taibus Qi China *see* Baochang
71 C3 **T'aichung** Taiwan
70 B2 **Taihang Shan** *mts* China
54 C1 **Taihape** N.Z.
71 B3 **Taihe** China
70 C2 **Tai Hu** *l.* China
52 A3 **Tailem Bend** Austr.
71 C3 **T'ainan** Taiwan
111 B3 **Tainaro, Akra** *pt* Greece
155 D1 **Taiobeiras** Brazil
71 C3 **T'aipei** Taiwan
Taiping China *see* Chongzuo
60 B1 **Taiping** Malaysia
Tairbeart U.K. *see* **Tarbert**
71 B3 **Taishan** China
70 B2 **Tai Shan** *hills* China
119 D3 **Taita Hills** Kenya
153 A4 **Taitao, Península de** *pen.* Chile
71 C3 **T'aitung** Taiwan
92 I2 **Taivalkoski** Fin.
92 H2 **Taivaskero** *hill* Fin.
71 C3 **Taiwan** Asia
Taiwan Shan *mts* Taiwan *see* **Chungyang Shanmo**
71 B3 **Taiwan Strait** China/Taiwan
70 B2 **Taiyuan** China
70 B2 **Taizhou** *Jiangsu* China
71 C3 **Taizhou** *Zhejiang* China
78 B3 **Ta'izz** Yemen
145 C3 **Tajamulco, Volcán de** *vol.* Guat.
77 D3 **Tajikistan** *country* Asia
74 B2 **Taj Mahal** *tourist site* India
Tajo *r.* Spain *see* **Tagus**
63 A2 **Tak** Thai.
54 B2 **Takaka** N.Z.
115 C2 **Takalous, Oued** *watercourse* Alg.
67 B4 **Takamatsu** Japan
67 C3 **Takaoka** Japan
54 B1 **Takapuna** N.Z.
67 C3 **Takasaki** Japan
122 B1 **Takatokwane** Botswana
122 B1 **Takatshwaane** Botswana
67 C3 **Takayama** Japan
67 C3 **Takefu** Japan
60 A1 **Takengon** Indon.
63 B2 **Takêv** Cambodia
Takhiatash Uzbek. *see* Taxiatosh
63 B2 **Ta Khmau** Cambodia
74 B1 **Takht-i-Sulaiman** *mt.* Pak.
66 D2 **Takikawa** Japan
128 B2 **Takla Lake** Can.
128 B2 **Takla Landing** Can.
Takla Makan *des.* China *see* **Taklimakan Desert**
77 E3 **Taklimakan Desert** *des.* China
Taklimakan Shamo China *see* **Taklimakan Desert**
128 A2 **Taku** *r.* Can./U.S.A.
63 A3 **Takua Pa** Thai.
115 C4 **Takum** Nigeria
88 C3 **Talachyn** Belarus
74 B1 **Talagang** Pak.
146 B4 **Talamanca, Cordillera de** *mts* Costa Rica
150 A3 **Talara** Peru
59 C2 **Talaud, Kepulauan** *is* Indon.
106 C2 **Talavera de la Reina** Spain
153 A3 **Talca** Chile
153 A3 **Talcahuano** Chile
89 E2 **Taldom** Rus. Fed.
77 D2 **Taldykorgan** Kazakh.
Taldy-Kurgan Kazakh. *see* Taldykorgan
59 C3 **Taliabu** *i.* Indon.
64 B2 **Talisay** Phil.
61 C2 **Taliwang** Indon.
81 C2 **Tall 'Afar** Iraq
141 D2 **Tallahassee** U.S.A.
53 C3 **Tallangatta** Austr.
88 B2 **Tallinn** Estonia
140 B2 **Tallulah** U.S.A.
104 B2 **Talmont-St-Hilaire** France
90 C2 **Tal'ne** Ukr.
117 B3 **Talodi** Sudan
74 A1 **Tāloqān** Afgh.
91 E1 **Talovaya** Rus. Fed.
126 F2 **Taloyoak** Can.
88 B2 **Talsi** Latvia
152 A2 **Taltal** Chile
129 C1 **Taltson** *r.* Can.
60 A1 **Talu** Indon.
53 C1 **Talwood** Austr.
114 B4 **Tamale** Ghana
115 C2 **Tamanrasset** Alg.
99 A4 **Tamar** *r.* U.K.
Tamatave Madag. *see* Toamasina
144 B2 **Tamazula** Mex.
145 C2 **Tamazunchale** Mex.
114 A3 **Tambacounda** Senegal
60 B1 **Tambelan, Kepulauan** *is* Indon.
86 G1 **Tambey** Rus. Fed.
61 C1 **Tambisan** *Sabah* Malaysia
61 C2 **Tambora, Gunung** *vol.* Indon.
91 E1 **Tambov** Rus. Fed.
119 C2 **Tambura** Sudan

62 A1 **Tamenglong** India
145 C2 **Tamiahua, Laguna de** *lag.* Mex.
Tammerfors Fin. *see* Tampere
141 D3 **Tampa** U.S.A.
141 D3 **Tampa Bay** U.S.A.
93 H3 **Tampere** Fin.
145 C2 **Tampico** Mex.
69 D1 **Tamsagbulag** Mongolia
102 C2 **Tamsweg** Austria
53 D2 **Tamworth** Austr.
99 C3 **Tamworth** U.K.
119 E3 **Tana** *r.* Kenya
Tana, Lake Eth. *see* Lake Tana
67 C4 **Tanabe** Japan
92 I1 **Tana Bru** Norway
60 A2 **Tanahbala** *i.* Indon.
61 C2 **Tanahgrogot** Indon.
61 D2 **Tanahjampea** *i.* Indon.
60 A2 **Tanahmasa** *i.* Indon.
50 C1 **Tanami Desert** Austr.
63 B2 **Tân An** Vietnam
126 B2 **Tanana** U.S.A.
Tananarive Madag. *see* Antananarivo
108 A1 **Tanaro** *r.* Italy
65 B1 **Tanch'ŏn** N. Korea
64 B3 **Tandag** Phil.
110 C2 **Tăndărei** Romania
153 C3 **Tandil** Arg.
74 A2 **Tando Adam** Pak.
74 A2 **Tando Muhammmad Khan** Pak.
52 B2 **Tandou Lake** *imp. l.* Austr.
67 B4 **Tanega-shima** *i.* Japan
114 B2 **Tanezrouft** *reg.* Alg./Mali
119 D3 **Tanga** Tanz.
75 C2 **Tangail** Bangl.
Tanganyika *country* Africa *see* Tanzania
119 C3 **Tanganyika, Lake** Africa
55 F3 **Tange Promontory** *hd* Antarctica
Tanger *see* Tangier
101 E1 **Tangermünde** Ger.
75 D1 **Tanggulashan** China
75 C1 **Tanggula Shan** *mts* China
114 B1 **Tangier** Morocco
75 C1 **Tangra Yumco** *salt l.* China
70 B2 **Tangshan** China
68 C2 **Taniantaweng Shan** *mts* China
59 C3 **Tanimbar, Kepulauan** *is* Indon.
64 B3 **Tanjay** Phil.
61 C2 **Tanjung** Indon.
60 A1 **Tanjungbalai** Indon.
Tanjungkarang-Telukbetung Indon. *see* Bandar Lampung
60 B2 **Tanjungpandan** Indon.
60 B1 **Tanjungpinang** Indon.
61 C1 **Tanjungredeb** Indon.
61 C1 **Tanjungselor** Indon.
74 B1 **Tank** Pak.
48 H5 **Tanna** *i.* Vanuatu
115 C3 **Tanout** Niger
75 C2 **Tansen** Nepal
116 B1 **Tanţā** Egypt
114 A2 **Tan-Tan** Morocco
145 C2 **Tantoyuca** Mex.
119 D3 **Tanzania** *country* Africa
Tao'an China *see* Taonan
Taocheng China *see* Yongchun
Taolanaro Madag. *see* Tôlañaro
69 E1 **Taonan** China
109 C3 **Taormina** *Sicily* Italy
142 B1 **Taos** U.S.A.
114 B2 **Taoudenni** Mali
114 B1 **Taounate** Morocco
114 B1 **Taourirt** Morocco
88 C2 **Tapa** Estonia
145 C3 **Tapachula** Mex.
151 D3 **Tapajós** *r.* Brazil
60 A1 **Tapaktuan** Indon.
145 C3 **Tapanatepec** Mex.
150 C3 **Tapauá** Brazil
152 C2 **Tapera** Brazil
114 B4 **Tapeta** Liberia
74 B2 **Tapi** *r.* India
139 D3 **Tappahannock** U.S.A.
54 B2 **Tapuaenuku** *mt.* N.Z.
150 C3 **Tapurucuara** Brazil
154 B1 **Taquaral, Serra do** *hills* Brazil
154 A1 **Taquari** *r.* Brazil

154 B1 **Taquari, Serra do** *hills* Brazil
154 C2 **Taquaritinga** Brazil
53 D1 **Tara** Austr.
115 D4 **Taraba** *r.* Nigeria
Ţarābulus Libya *see* Tripoli
54 C1 **Taradale** N.Z.
61 C1 **Tarakan** Indon.
111 D2 **Taraklı** Turkey
88 A3 **Taran, Mys** *pt* Rus. Fed.
54 B1 **Taranaki, Mount** *vol.* N.Z.
106 C1 **Tarancón** Spain
109 C2 **Taranto** Italy
109 C2 **Taranto, Golfo di** *g.* Italy
150 B3 **Tarapoto** Peru
90 C2 **Tarashcha** Ukr.
91 E2 **Tarasovskiy** Rus. Fed.
150 B3 **Tarauacá** Brazil
150 C3 **Tarauacá** *r.* Brazil
48 I3 **Tarawa** *atoll* Kiribati
54 C1 **Tarawera** N.Z.
77 D2 **Taraz** Kazakh.
107 C1 **Tarazona** Spain
77 E2 **Tarbagatay, Khrebet** *mts* Kazakh.
96 C2 **Tarbat Ness** *pt* U.K.
97 B2 **Tarbert** Rep. of Ireland
96 A2 **Tarbert** *Scotland* U.K.
96 B3 **Tarbert** *Scotland* U.K.
104 C3 **Tarbes** France
96 B2 **Tarbet** U.K.
141 E1 **Tarboro** U.S.A.
51 C3 **Tarcoola** Austr.
53 D2 **Taree** Austr.
110 C2 **Tärgovişte** Romania
110 C1 **Târgu Frumos** Romania
110 B1 **Târgu Jiu** Romania
110 B1 **Târgu Lăpuş** Romania
110 B1 **Târgu Mureş** Romania
110 C1 **Târgu Neamţ** Romania
110 C1 **Târgu Ocna** Romania
79 C2 **Tarif** U.A.E.
152 B2 **Tarija** Bol.
79 B3 **Tarim** Yemen
77 E3 **Tarim Basin** *basin* China
119 D3 **Tarime** Tanz.
77 E2 **Tarim He** *r.* China
Tarim Pendi China *see* Tarim Basin
77 C3 **Tarin Kowt** Afgh.
59 D3 **Taritatu** *r.* Indon.
123 C3 **Tarkastad** S. Africa
82 G2 **Tarko-Sale** Rus. Fed.
114 B4 **Tarkwa** Ghana
64 B2 **Tarlac** Phil.
105 C3 **Tarn** *r.* France
92 G2 **Tärnaby** Sweden
77 C3 **Tarnak** *r.* Afgh.
110 B1 **Târnăveni** Romania
103 E1 **Tarnobrzeg** Pol.
Tarnopol Ukr. *see* Ternopil'
103 E1 **Tarnów** Pol.
51 D2 **Taroom** Austr.
114 B1 **Taroudannt** Morocco
141 D3 **Tarpon Springs** U.S.A.
108 B2 **Tarquinia** Italy
107 D1 **Tarragona** Spain
107 D1 **Tàrrega** Spain
80 B2 **Tarsus** Turkey
153 B3 **Tartagal** Arg.
104 B3 **Tartas** France
88 C2 **Tartu** Estonia
80 B2 **Ţarţūs** Syria
155 D1 **Tarumirim** Brazil
89 E3 **Tarusa** Rus. Fed.
90 B2 **Tarutyne** Ukr.
108 B1 **Tarvisio** Italy
Tashauz Turkm. *see* Dashoguz
75 D2 **Tashigang** Bhutan
81 D3 **Tashk, Daryācheh-ye** *l.* Iran
Tashkent Uzbek. *see* Tashkent
77 C2 **Tashkent** Uzbek.
130 C2 **Tasialujjuaq, Lac** *l.* Can.
130 C2 **Tasiat, Lac** *l.* Can.
131 D2 **Tasiujaq** Can.
77 E2 **Taskesken** Kazakh.
54 B2 **Tasman Bay** N.Z.
51 D4 **Tasmania** *state* Austr.
54 B2 **Tasman Mountains** N.Z.
54 A1 **Tasman Sea** S. Pacific Ocean
115 C2 **Tassili du Hoggar** *plat.* Alg.
115 C2 **Tassili n'Ajjer** *plat.* Alg.
115 D2 **Tataba** Indon.
103 D2 **Tatabánya** Hungary
90 B2 **Tatarbunary** Ukr.
83 K3 **Tatarskiy Proliv** *str.* Rus. Fed.

Tatar Strait Rus. Fed. *see* Tatarskiy Proliv
67 C4 **Tateyama** Japan
128 C1 **Tathlina Lake** Can.
78 B3 **Tathlīth** Saudi Arabia
78 B2 **Tathlīth, Wādī** *watercourse* Saudi Arabia
53 C3 **Tathra** Austr.
62 A1 **Tatkon** Myanmar
128 B2 **Tatla Lake** Can.
103 D2 **Tatra Mountains** *mts* Pol./Slovakia
Tatry *mts* Pol./Slovakia *see* Tatra Mountains
74 A2 **Tatta** Pak.
154 A2 **Tatuí** Brazil
143 C2 **Tatum** U.S.A.
81 C2 **Tatvan** Turkey
151 E3 **Taua** Brazil
155 C2 **Taubaté** Brazil
101 D3 **Tauberbischofsheim** Ger.
54 C1 **Taumarunui** N.Z.
122 B2 **Taung** S. Africa
62 A1 **Taunggyi** Myanmar
62 A2 **Taung-ngu** Myanmar
62 A2 **Taungup** Myanmar
74 B1 **Taunsa** Pak.
99 B4 **Taunton** U.K.
101 C2 **Taunus** *hills* Ger.
54 C1 **Taupo** N.Z.
54 C1 **Taupo, Lake** N.Z.
88 B2 **Tauragė** Lith.
54 C1 **Tauranga** N.Z.
139 E1 **Taureau, Réservoir** *resr* Can.
80 B2 **Taurus Mountains** *mts* Turkey
111 C3 **Tavas** Turkey
86 F3 **Tavda** Rus. Fed.
106 B2 **Tavira** Port.
99 A4 **Tavistock** U.K.
63 A2 **Tavoy** Myanmar
111 C3 **Tavşanlı** Turkey
99 A4 **Taw** *r.* U.K.
138 C2 **Tawas City** U.S.A.
61 C1 **Tawau** *Sabah* Malaysia
64 A3 **Tawitawi** *i.* Phil.
71 C3 **Tawu** Taiwan
145 C3 **Taxco** Mex.
76 B2 **Taxiatosh** Uzbek.
77 D3 **Taxkorgan** China
96 C2 **Tay** *r.* U.K.
96 C2 **Tay, Firth of** *est.* U.K.
96 B2 **Tay, Loch** *l.* U.K.
128 B2 **Taylor** Can.
138 C2 **Taylor** *MI* U.S.A.
143 D2 **Taylor** *TX* U.S.A.
138 B3 **Taylorville** U.S.A.
78 A2 **Taymā'** Saudi Arabia
83 H2 **Taymura** *r.* Rus. Fed.
83 H2 **Taymyr, Ozero** *l.* Rus. Fed.
Taymyr, Poluostrov Rus. Fed. *see* Taymyr Peninsula
83 G2 **Taymyr Peninsula** *pen.* Rus. Fed.
63 B2 **Tây Ninh** Vietnam
96 C2 **Tayport** U.K.
64 A2 **Taytay** Phil.
76 C3 **Tayyebād** Iran
77 C1 **Tayynsha** Kazakh.
82 G2 **Taz** *r.* Rus. Fed.
114 B1 **Taza** Morocco
129 D2 **Tazin Lake** Can.
86 G2 **Tazovskaya Guba** *sea chan.* Rus. Fed.
81 C1 **T'bilisi** Georgia
91 E2 **Tbilisskaya** Rus. Fed.
115 C3 **Tchibanga** Gabon
115 D3 **Tchin-Tabaradene** Niger
118 B2 **Tcholliré** Cameroon
103 D1 **Tczew** Pol.
144 B2 **Teacapán** Mex.
54 A3 **Te Anau** N.Z.
54 A3 **Te Anau, Lake** N.Z.
145 C3 **Teapa** Mex.
54 C1 **Te Awamutu** N.Z.
115 C1 **Tébessa** Alg.
60 B2 **Tebingtinggi** Indon.
60 A1 **Tebingtinggi** Indon.
144 A1 **Tecate** Mex.
114 B4 **Techiman** Ghana
144 B3 **Tecomán** Mex.
144 B2 **Tecoripa** Mex.
145 B3 **Técpan** Mex.
144 B2 **Tecuala** Mex.
110 C1 **Tecuci** Romania
76 C3 **Tedzhen** Turkm.
76 C3 **Tedzhen** *r.* Turkm.
68 C1 **Teeli** Rus. Fed.
98 C2 **Tees** *r.* U.K.

111 C3 **Tefenni** Turkey
60 B2 **Tegal** Indon.
146 B3 **Tegucigalpa** Hond.
115 C3 **Teguidda-n-Tessoumt** Niger
129 E1 **Tehek Lake** Can.
Teheran Iran *see* Tehrān
114 B4 **Téhini** Côte d'Ivoire
81 D2 **Tehrān** Iran
145 C3 **Tehuacán** Mex.
Tehuantepec, Golfo de Mex. *see* Tehuantepec, Gulf of
Tehuantepec, Gulf of Mex. *see*
145 C3 **Tehuantepec, Gulf of** *g.* Mex.
145 C3 **Tehuantepec, Istmo de** *isth.* Mex.
114 A2 **Teide, Pico del** *vol.* Canary Islands
99 A3 **Teifi** *r.* U.K.
Teixeira de Sousa Angola *see* Luau
Tejo *r.* Port. *see* Tagus
145 B3 **Tejupilco** Mex.
54 B2 **Tekapo, Lake** N.Z.
145 D2 **Tekax** Mex.
116 B3 **Tekezē** Wenz *r.* Eritrea/Eth.
111 C2 **Tekirdağ** Turkey
54 C1 **Te Kuiti** N.Z.
75 C2 **Tel** *r.* India
81 C1 **T'elavi** Georgia
80 B2 **Tel Aviv-Yafo** Israel
145 D2 **Telchac Puerto** Mex.
128 A2 **Telegraph Creek** Can.
154 B2 **Telêmaco Borba** Brazil
61 C1 **Telen** *r.* Indon.
50 B2 **Telfer Mining Centre** Austr.
99 B3 **Telford** U.K.
128 B2 **Telkwa** Can.
60 A2 **Telo** Indon.
86 E2 **Tel'pos-Iz, Gora** *mt.* Rus. Fed.
88 B2 **Telšiai** Lith.
60 B2 **Telukbatang** Indon.
60 A1 **Telukdalam** Indon.
60 B1 **Teluk Intan** Malaysia
114 C4 **Tema** Ghana
130 C3 **Temagami Lake** Can.
60 C2 **Temanggung** Indon.
123 C2 **Temba** S. Africa
83 H2 **Tembenchi** *r.* Rus. Fed.
60 B2 **Tembilahan** Indon.
123 C2 **Tembisa** S. Africa
120 A1 **Tembo Aluma** Angola
Tembué Moz. *see* Chifunde
99 B3 **Teme** *r.* U.K.
135 C4 **Temecula** U.S.A.
63 B3 **Temengor, Tasik** *resr* Malaysia
60 B1 **Temerluh** Malaysia
77 D1 **Temirtau** Kazakh.
139 D1 **Témiscamingue, Lac** *l.* Can.
53 C2 **Temora** Austr.
142 A2 **Tempe** U.S.A.
143 D2 **Temple** U.S.A.
97 C2 **Templemore** Rep. of Ireland
102 C1 **Templin** Ger.
145 C2 **Tempoal** Mex.
120 A2 **Tempué** Angola
91 D2 **Temryuk** Rus. Fed.
91 D2 **Temryukskiy Zaliv** *b.* Rus. Fed.
153 A3 **Temuco** Chile
54 B2 **Temuka** N.Z.
145 C2 **Tenabo** Mex.
143 E2 **Tenaha** U.S.A.
73 C3 **Tenali** India
63 A2 **Tenasserim** Myanmar
99 A4 **Tenby** U.K.
117 C3 **Tendaho** Eth.
105 D3 **Tende** France
105 D3 **Tende, Col de** *pass* France/Italy
73 D4 **Ten Degree Channel** India
114 A3 **Te-n-Dghâmcha, Sebkhet** *salt marsh* Maur.
67 D3 **Tendō** Japan
114 B3 **Ténenkou** Mali
115 C2 **Ténéré** *reg.* Niger
115 D2 **Ténéré, Erg du** *des.* Niger
115 D2 **Ténéré du Tafassâsset** *des.* Niger
114 A2 **Tenerife** *i.* Canary Is
107 D2 **Ténès** Alg.
61 C2 **Tengah, Kepulauan** *is* Indon.

	Tengcheng China *see* Tengxian	
62 A1	Tengchong China	
61 C2	Tenggarong Indon.	
70 A2	Tengger Shamo *des.* China	
77 C1	Tengiz, Ozero *salt l.* Kazakh.	
71 B3	Tengxian China	
119 C4	Tenke Dem. Rep. Congo	
114 B3	Tenkodogo Burkina	
51 C1	Tennant Creek Austr.	
140 C1	Tennessee *r.* U.S.A.	
140 C1	Tennessee *state* U.S.A.	
61 C1	Tenom *Sabah* Malaysia	
145 C3	Tenosique Mex.	
61 D2	Tenteno Indon.	
53 D1	Tenterfield Austr.	
141 D3	Ten Thousand Islands U.S.A.	
154 B2	Teodoro Sampaio Brazil	
155 D1	Teófilo Otôni Brazil	
145 C3	Teopisca Mex.	
59 C3	Tepa Indon.	
144 B2	Tepache Mex.	
54 B1	Te Paki N.Z.	
144 B3	Tepalcatepec Mex.	
144 B2	Tepatitlán Mex.	
144 B2	Tepehuanes Mex.	
109 D2	Tepelenë Albania	
144 B2	Tepic Mex.	
102 C1	Teplice Czech Rep.	
89 E3	Teploye Rus. Fed.	
90 B2	Teplyk Ukr.	
54 C1	Te Puke N.Z.	
144 B2	Tequila Mex.	
49 K3	Teraina *i.* Kiribati	
108 B2	Teramo Italy	
52 B3	Terang Austr.	
89 E3	Terbuny Rus. Fed.	
90 B2	Terebovlya Ukr.	
87 D4	Terek *r.* Rus. Fed.	
154 B2	Terenos Brazil	
151 E3	Teresina Brazil	
155 D2	Teresópolis Brazil	
63 A3	Teressa Island India	
100 A3	Tergnier France	
80 B1	Terme Turkey	
108 B3	Termini Imerese *Sicily* Italy	
145 C3	Términos, Laguna de *lag.* Mex.	
77 C3	Termiz Uzbek.	
109 B2	Termoli Italy	
59 C2	Ternate Indon.	
100 A2	Terneuzen Neth.	
66 C1	Terney Rus. Fed.	
108 B2	Terni Italy	
90 B2	Ternopil' Ukr.	
52 A2	Terowie Austr.	
69 F1	Terpeniya, Mys *c.* Rus. Fed.	
69 F1	Terpeniya, Zaliv *g.* Rus. Fed.	
128 B2	Terrace Can.	
130 B3	Terrace Bay Can.	
122 B2	Terra Firma S. Africa	
140 B3	Terrebonne Bay U.S.A.	
138 B3	Terre Haute U.S.A.	
131 E3	Terrenceville Can.	
100 B1	Terschelling *i.* Neth.	
108 A3	Tertenia *Sardinia* Italy	
107 C1	Teruel Spain	
92 H2	Tervola Fin.	
109 C2	Tešanj Bos.-Herz.	
116 B3	Teseney Eritrea	
66 D2	Teshio Japan	
66 D2	Teshio-gawa *r.* Japan	
128 A1	Teslin Can.	
128 A1	Teslin Lake Can.	
154 B1	Tesouro Brazil	
115 C3	Tessaoua Niger	
99 C4	Test *r.* U.K.	
121 C2	Tete Moz.	
90 C1	Teteriv *r.* Ukr.	
101 F1	Teterow Ger.	
90 B2	Tetiyiv Ukr.	
114 B1	Tétouan Morocco	
110 B2	Tetovo Macedonia	
	Tetyukhe Rus. Fed. *see* Dal'negorsk	
	Teuchezhsk Rus. Fed. *see* Adygeysk	
152 B2	Teuco *r.* Arg.	
144 B2	Teul de González Ortega Mex.	
101 D1	Teutoburger Wald *hills* Ger.	
	Tevere *r.* Italy *see* Tiber	
54 A3	Teviot N.Z.	
96 C3	Teviot *r.* U.K.	

96 C3	Teviothead U.K.	
61 C2	Tewah Indon.	
51 E2	Tewantin Austr.	
54 C2	Te Wharau N.Z.	
99 B4	Tewkesbury U.K.	
143 E2	Texarkana U.S.A.	
53 D1	Texas Austr.	
143 D2	Texas *state* U.S.A.	
143 E3	Texas City U.S.A.	
145 C3	Texcoco Mex.	
100 B1	Texel *i.* Neth.	
143 D2	Texoma, Lake U.S.A.	
123 C2	Teyateyaneng Lesotho	
89 F2	Teykovo Rus. Fed.	
89 F2	Teza *r.* Rus. Fed.	
75 D2	Tezpur India	
72 D2	Tezu India	
129 E1	Tha-anne *r.* Can.	
	Thabana-Ntlenyana *mt.* Lesotho	
123 C2	Thaba Nchu S. Africa	
123 C2	Thaba Putsoa *mt.* Lesotho	
123 C2	Thaba-Tseka Lesotho	
123 C1	Thabazimbi S. Africa	
123 C2	Thabong S. Africa	
63 A2	Thagyettaw Myanmar	
62 B1	Thai Binh Vietnam	
63 B2	Thailand *country* Asia	
63 B2	Thailand, Gulf of Asia	
62 B1	Thai Nguyên Vietnam	
62 B2	Thakèk Laos	
74 B1	Thal Pak.	
63 A3	Thalang Thai.	
74 B1	Thal Desert Pak.	
101 E2	Thale (Harz) Ger.	
62 B2	Tha Li Thai.	
53 C1	Thallon Austr.	
123 C1	Thamaga Botswana	
78 B3	Thamar, Jabal *mt.* Yemen	
79 C3	Thamarīt Oman	
130 B3	Thames *r.* Can.	
54 C1	Thames N.Z.	
99 D4	Thames *est.* U.K.	
99 D4	Thames *r.* U.K.	
79 B3	Thamūd Yemen	
	Thana India *see* Thane	
63 A2	Thanbyuzayat Myanmar	
62 A2	Thandwè Myanmar	
74 B3	Thane India	
62 B2	Thanh Hoa Vietnam	
73 B3	Thanjavur India	
63 A2	Thanlyin Myanmar	
74 A2	Thano Bula Khan Pak.	
62 B1	Than Uyen Vietnam	
74 A2	Thar Desert India/Pak.	
52 B1	Thargomindah Austr.	
81 C2	Tharthār, Buḩayrat ath *l.* Iraq	
111 B2	Thasos Greece	
111 B2	Thasos *i.* Greece	
62 B1	Thật Khê Vietnam	
62 A2	Thaton Myanmar	
62 A1	Thaungdut Myanmar	
62 A2	Thayawadi Myanmar	
63 A2	Thayetchaung Myanmar	
62 A2	Thayetmyo Myanmar	
62 A1	Thazi Myanmar	
146 C2	The Bahamas *country* West Indies	
98 B2	The Cheviot *hill* U.K.	
134 B1	The Dalles U.S.A.	
136 C2	Thedford U.S.A.	
53 D2	The Entrance Austr.	
99 C3	The Fens *reg.* U.K.	
114 A3	The Gambia *country* Africa	
	The Great Oasis Egypt *see* Wāḩāt al Khārijah	
79 C2	The Gulf Asia	
100 B1	The Hague Neth.	
129 E1	Thelon *r.* Can.	
101 E2	Themar Ger.	
123 C2	Thembalihle S. Africa	
96 A1	The Minch *sea chan.* U.K.	
97 A1	The Mullet *b.* Rep. of Ireland	
99 C4	The Needles *stack* U.K.	
150 C3	Theodore Roosevelt *r.* Brazil	
129 D2	The Pas Can.	
111 B2	Thermaïkos Kolpos *g.* Greece	
136 B2	Thermopolis U.S.A.	
53 C3	The Rock Austr.	
	The Skaw *spit* Denmark *see* Grenen	
99 C4	The Solent *str.* U.K.	
130 B3	Thessalon Can.	
111 B2	Thessaloniki Greece	

99 D3	Thetford U.K.	
131 C3	Thetford Mines Can.	
62 A1	The Triangle *mts* Myanmar	
147 D3	The Valley Anguilla	
131 D2	Thévenet, Lac *l.* Can.	
99 D3	The Wash *b.* U.K.	
99 D4	The Weald *reg.* U.K.	
143 D2	The Woodlands U.S.A.	
140 B3	Thibodaux U.S.A.	
129 E2	Thicket Portage Can.	
137 D1	Thief River Falls U.S.A.	
	Thiel Neth. *see* Tiel	
105 C2	Thiers France	
114 A3	Thiès Senegal	
119 D3	Thika Kenya	
73 B4	Thiladhunmathi Atoll Maldives	
75 C2	Thimphu Bhutan	
105 D2	Thionville France	
111 C3	Thira Greece	
111 C3	Thira *i.* Greece	
98 C2	Thirsk U.K.	
93 G3	Thiruvananthapuram India *see* Trivandrum	
93 E4	Thisted Denmark	
129 E1	Thlewiaza *r.* Can.	
63 B3	Thô Chu, Ðao *i.* Vietnam	
62 A2	Thoen Thai.	
123 D1	Thohoyandou S. Africa	
101 E1	Thomasburg Ger.	
97 C2	Thomastown Rep. of Ireland	
140 C2	Thomasville *AL* U.S.A.	
141 D2	Thomasville *GA* U.S.A.	
100 C2	Thommen Belgium	
129 E2	Thompson Can.	
128 E3	Thompson *r.* U.S.A.	
134 C1	Thompson Falls U.S.A.	
128 B2	Thompson Sound Can.	
51 D2	Thomson *watercourse* Austr.	
141 D2	Thomson U.S.A.	
63 B2	Thon Buri Thai.	
63 A2	Thongwa Myanmar	
142 B1	Thoreau U.S.A.	
96 C3	Thornhill U.K.	
136 C3	Thornton U.S.A.	
55 F2	Thorshavnheiane *reg.* Antarctica	
123 C2	Thota-ea-Moli Lesotho	
104 B2	Thouars France	
62 A1	Thoubal India	
134 D1	Three Forks U.S.A.	
128 C2	Three Hills Can.	
63 A2	Three Pagodas Pass Myanmar/Thai.	
114 B4	Three Points, Cape Ghana	
138 B2	Three Rivers *MI* U.S.A.	
143 D3	Three Rivers *TX* U.S.A.	
	Thrissur India *see* Trichur	
63 B2	Thu Dâu Môt Vietnam	
100 B2	Thuin Belgium	
	Thule *see* Qaanaaq	
121 B3	Thuli Zimbabwe	
102 B2	Thun Switz.	
130 B3	Thunder Bay Can.	
130 B3	Thunder Bay *b.* Can.	
63 A3	Thung Song Thai.	
101 E2	Thüringer Becken *reg.* Ger.	
101 E2	Thüringer Wald *mts* Ger.	
	Thuringian Forest *mts* Ger. *see* Thüringer Wald	
97 C2	Thurles Rep. of Ireland	
59 D3	Thursday Island Austr.	
96 C1	Thurso U.K.	
96 C1	Thurso *r.* U.K.	
55 R2	Thurston Island Antarctica	
101 D1	Thüster Berg *hill* Ger.	
121 C2	Thyolo Malawi	
	Thysville Dem. Rep. Congo *see* Mbanza-Ngungu	
79 C2	Tiāb Iran	
151 E3	Tianguá Brazil	
70 B2	Tianjin China	
70 B2	Tianjin *mun.* China	
71 A3	Tianlin China	
70 B2	Tianmen China	
69 E2	Tianshan China	
70 A2	Tianshui China	
70 A2	Tianzhu China	
107 D2	Tiaret Alg.	
114 B4	Tiassalé Côte d'Ivoire	
154 B1	Tibagi Brazil	
154 B2	Tibagi *r.* Brazil	
118 B2	Tibati Cameroon	
108 B2	Tiber *r.* Italy	

	Tiberias, Lake Israel *see* Galilee, Sea of	
115 D2	Tibesti *mts* Chad	
75 C1	Tibet *aut. reg.* China	
	Tibet, Plateau of China *see* Qingzang Gaoyuan	
52 B1	Tibooburra Austr.	
144 A2	Tiburón, Isla *i.* Mex.	
114 B3	Tichît Maur.	
114 A2	Tichla Western Sahara	
105 D2	Ticino *r.* Italy/Switz.	
139 E2	Ticonderoga U.S.A.	
145 D2	Ticul Mex.	
114 A3	Tidjikja Maur.	
100 B2	Tiel Neth.	
70 C1	Tieling China	
75 B1	Tielongtan Aksai Chin	
100 A2	Tielt Belgium	
100 B2	Tienen Belgium	
68 B2	Tien Shan *mts* China/Kyrg.	
	Tientsin China *see* Tianjin	
	Tientsin *mun.* China *see* Tianjin	
93 G3	Tierp Sweden	
145 C3	Tierra Blanca Mex.	
145 C3	Tierra Colorada Mex.	
153 B5	Tierra del Fuego, Isla Grande de *i.* Arg./Chile	
106 B1	Tiétar, Valle de *val.* Spain	
154 C2	Tietê Brazil	
154 B2	Tietê *r.* Brazil	
138 C2	Tiffin U.S.A.	
	Tiflis Georgia *see* T'bilisi	
141 D2	Tifton U.S.A.	
90 B2	Tighina Moldova	
75 C2	Tigiria India	
118 B2	Tignère Cameroon	
131 D3	Tignish Can.	
150 B3	Tigre *r.* Ecuador/Peru	
81 C2	Tigris *r.* Asia	
114 A3	Tiguent Maur.	
115 D3	Tigui Chad	
145 C2	Tihuatlán Mex.	
144 A1	Tijuana Mex.	
91 E2	Tikhoretsk Rus. Fed.	
89 D2	Tikhvin Rus. Fed.	
89 D2	Tikhvinskaya Gryada *ridge* Rus. Fed.	
157 F7	Tiki Basin *sea feature* S. Pacific Ocean	
54 C1	Tikokino N.Z.	
81 C2	Tikrīt Iraq	
83 J2	Tiksi Rus. Fed.	
100 B2	Tilburg Neth.	
152 B2	Tilcara Arg.	
52 B1	Tilcha Austr.	
114 C3	Tilemsi, Vallée du *watercourse* Mali	
	Tilimsen Alg. *see* Tlemcen	
114 C3	Tillabéri Niger	
134 B1	Tillamook U.S.A.	
63 A3	Tillanchong Island India	
111 C3	Tilos *i.* Greece	
52 B2	Tilpa Austr.	
86 F2	Til'tim Rus. Fed.	
89 E3	Tim Rus. Fed.	
86 D2	Timanskiy Kryazh *ridge* Rus. Fed.	
54 B2	Timaru N.Z.	
91 D2	Timashevsk Rus. Fed.	
	Timashevskaya Rus. Fed. *see* Timashevsk	
114 B3	Timbedgha Maur.	
50 C1	Timber Creek Austr.	
114 B3	Timbuktu Mali	
115 C3	Timia Niger	
114 C2	Timimoun Alg.	
110 B1	Timiş *r.* Romania	
110 B1	Timişoara Romania	
130 B3	Timmins Can.	
89 E2	Timokhino Rus. Fed.	
151 E3	Timon Brazil	
59 C3	Timor *i.* Indon.	
59 C3	Timor Sea Austr./Indon.	
	Timor Timur *country* Asia *see* East Timor	
93 G3	Timrå Sweden	
78 B2	Tin, Jabal *hill* Saudi Arabia	
114 B2	Tindouf Alg.	
53 D1	Tingha Austr.	
75 C2	Tingri China	
93 F4	Tingsryd Sweden	
92 E3	Tingvoll Norway	
	Tingzhou China *see* Changting	
59 D2	Tinian *i.* N. Mariana Is	
	Tinnelvelly India *see* Tirunelveli	
152 B2	Tinogasta Arg.	
111 C3	Tinos Greece	

111 C3 **Tinos** *i.* Greece
100 A3 **Tinqueux** France
115 C2 **Tinrhert, Plateau du** Alg.
62 A1 **Tinsukia** India
52 B3 **Tintinara** Austr.
136 C1 **Tioga** U.S.A.
107 D2 **Tipasa** Alg.
97 B2 **Tipperary** Rep. of Ireland
151 E3 **Tiracambu, Serra do** *hills* Brazil
109 C2 **Tirana** Albania
Tiranë Albania *see* **Tirana**
108 B1 **Tirano** Italy
52 A1 **Tirari Desert** Austr.
90 B2 **Tiraspol** Moldova
122 A2 **Tiraz Mountains** Namibia
111 C3 **Tire** Turkey
96 A2 **Tiree** *i.* U.K.
Tîrgovişte Romania *see* **Târgovişte**
Tîrgu Frumos Romania *see* **Târgu Frumos**
Tîrgu Jiu Romania *see* **Târgu Jiu**
Tîrgu Lăpuş Romania *see* **Târgu Lăpuş**
Tîrgu Mureş Romania *see* **Târgu Mureş**
Tîrgu Neamţ Romania *see* **Târgu Neamţ**
Tîrgu Ocna Romania *see* **Târgu Ocna**
74 B1 **Tirich Mir** *mt.* Pak.
Tîrnăveni Romania *see* **Târnăveni**
155 C1 **Tiros** Brazil
118 C2 **Tiroungoulou** C.A.R.
73 B3 **Tiruchchirappalli** India
73 B4 **Tirunelveli** India
73 B3 **Tirupati** India
73 B3 **Tiruppattur** India
73 B3 **Tiruppur** India
109 D1 **Tisa** *r.* Europe
Tisa *r.* Hungary *see* **Tisza**
129 D2 **Tisdale** Can.
107 D2 **Tissemsilt** Alg.
75 C2 **Tista** *r.* India
103 E2 **Tisza** *r.* Hungary
55 L1 **Titan Dome** *ice feature* Antarctica
Titicaca, Lago Bol./Peru *see* **Titicaca, Lake**
152 B1 **Titicaca, Lake** *l.* Bol./Peru
75 C2 **Titlagarh** India
Titograd Serb. and Mont. *see* **Podgorica**
Titova Mitrovica Serb. and Mont. *see* **Kosovska Mitrovica**
Titovo Užice Serb. and Mont. *see* **Užice**
Titovo Velenje Slovenia *see* **Velenje**
Titov Veles Macedonia *see* **Veles**
Titov Vrbas Serb. and Mont. *see* **Vrbas**
110 C2 **Titu** Romania
141 D3 **Titusville** U.S.A.
99 B4 **Tiverton** U.K.
108 B2 **Tivoli** Italy
79 C2 **Ţīwī** Oman
63 A2 **Ti-ywa** Myanmar
145 D2 **Tizimín** Mex.
107 D2 **Tizi Ouzou** Alg.
114 B2 **Tiznit** Morocco
92 G2 **Tjaktjajaure** *l.* Sweden
Tjirebon Indon. *see* **Cirebon**
145 C3 **Tlacotalpán** Mex.
144 B2 **Tlahualilo** Mex.
145 C3 **Tlalnepantla** Mex.
145 C3 **Tlapa** Mex.
145 C3 **Tlaxcala** Mex.
145 C3 **Tlaxiaco** Mex.
114 B1 **Tlemcen** Alg.
123 C1 **Tlokweng** Botswana
128 B2 **Toad River** Can.
121 □D2 **Toamasina** Madag.
60 A1 **Toba, Danau** *l.* Indon.
Toba, Lake Indon. *see* **Toba, Danau**
74 A1 **Toba and Kakar Ranges** *mts* Pak.
147 D3 **Tobago** *i.* Trin. and Tob.
59 C2 **Tobelo** Indon.
130 B3 **Tobermory** Can.
96 A2 **Tobermory** U.K.
129 D2 **Tobin Lake** Can.
60 B2 **Toboali** Indon.
76 C1 **Tobol** *r.* Kazakh./Rus. Fed.
86 F3 **Tobol'sk** Rus. Fed.
Tobruk Libya *see* **Tubruq**
151 E3 **Tocantinópolis** Brazil
151 E3 **Tocantins** *r.* Brazil
141 D2 **Toccoa** U.S.A.
108 A1 **Toce** *r.* Italy
152 A2 **Tocopilla** Chile
53 C3 **Tocumwal** Austr.
59 C3 **Todeli** Indon.
108 B2 **Todi** Italy
144 A2 **Todos Santos** Mex.
128 B3 **Tofino** Can.
96 □ **Toft** U.K.
61 D2 **Togian** *i.* Indon.
61 D2 **Togian, Kepulauan** *is* Indon.
Togliatti Rus. Fed. *see* **Tol'yatti**
114 C4 **Togo** *country* Africa
74 B2 **Tohana** India
141 D3 **Tohopekaliga, Lake** U.S.A.
126 C2 **Tok** U.S.A.
116 B3 **Tokar** Sudan
69 E3 **Tokara-rettō** *is* Japan
91 E1 **Tokarevka** Rus. Fed.
80 B1 **Tokat** Turkey
49 J4 **Tokelau** *terr.* S. Pacific Ocean
91 D2 **Tokmak** Ukr.
77 D2 **Tokmok** Kyrg.
54 C1 **Tokoroa** N.Z.
68 B2 **Toksun** China
67 B4 **Tokushima** Japan
67 C3 **Tōkyō** Japan
121 □D3 **Tôlañaro** Madag.
Tolbukhin Bulg. *see* **Dobrich**
154 B2 **Toledo** Brazil
106 C2 **Toledo** Spain
138 C2 **Toledo** U.S.A.
106 C2 **Toledo, Montes de** *mts* Spain
140 B2 **Toledo Bend Reservoir** U.S.A.
121 □D3 **Toliara** Madag.
Toling China *see* **Zanda**
61 D1 **Tolitoli** Indon.
108 B1 **Tolmezzo** Italy
108 B1 **Tolmin** Slovenia
103 D2 **Tolna** Hungary
104 B3 **Tolosa** Spain
145 C3 **Toluca** Mex.
87 D3 **Tol'yatti** Rus. Fed.
138 A2 **Tomah** U.S.A.
138 B1 **Tomahawk** U.S.A.
66 D2 **Tomakomai** Japan
61 D2 **Tomali** Indon.
61 C1 **Tomani** *Sabah* Malaysia
106 B2 **Tomar** Port.
103 E1 **Tomaszów Lubelski** Pol.
103 E1 **Tomaszów Mazowiecki** Pol.
144 B3 **Tomatlán** Mex.
154 C2 **Tomazina** Brazil
140 C2 **Tombigbee** *r.* U.S.A.
120 A1 **Tomboco** Angola
155 D2 **Tombos** Brazil
Tombouctou Mali *see* **Timbuktu**
142 A2 **Tombstone** U.S.A.
120 A2 **Tombua** Angola
123 C1 **Tom Burke** S. Africa
106 C2 **Tomelloso** Spain
53 C2 **Tomingley** Austr.
61 D2 **Tomini, Teluk** *g.* Indon.
109 C2 **Tomislavgrad** Bos.-Herz.
103 D2 **Tompa** Hungary
50 A2 **Tom Price** Austr.
82 G3 **Tomsk** Rus. Fed.
93 F4 **Tomtabacken** *hill* Sweden
83 K2 **Tomtor** Rus. Fed.
145 C3 **Tonalá** Mex.
150 C3 **Tonantins** Brazil
99 D4 **Tonbridge** U.K.
59 C2 **Tondano** Indon.
49 J5 **Tonga** *country* S. Pacific Ocean
123 D2 **Tongaat** S. Africa
49 J6 **Tongatapu Group** *is* Tonga
71 B3 **Tongcheng** China
70 A2 **Tongchuan** China
71 A3 **Tongdao** China
65 B2 **Tongduch'ŏn** S. Korea
100 B2 **Tongeren** Belgium
65 B2 **Tonghae** S. Korea
71 A3 **Tonghai** China
65 B1 **Tonghua** China
65 B2 **Tongjosŏn-man** *b.* N. Korea
62 B1 **Tongking, Gulf of** China/Vietnam
69 E2 **Tongliao** China
70 B2 **Tongling** China
52 B2 **Tongo** Austr.
Tongquan China *see* **Malong**
71 A3 **Tongren** China
75 D2 **Tongsa** Bhutan
70 B2 **Tongshan** China
Tongshi China *see* **Wuzhishan**
Tongtian He *r.* China *see* **Yangtze**
96 B1 **Tongue** U.K.
Tongxian China *see* **Tongzhou**
65 B3 **T'ongyŏng** S. Korea
69 E2 **Tongyu** China
65 A1 **Tongyuanpu** China
70 B2 **Tongzhou** China
71 A3 **Tongzi** China
119 C2 **Tonj** Sudan
74 B2 **Tonk** India
81 D2 **Tonkābon** Iran
Tônlé Sab *l.* Cambodia *see* **Tonle Sap**
63 B2 **Tonle Sap** *l.* Cambodia
135 C3 **Tonopah** U.S.A.
93 F4 **Tønsberg** Norway
135 D2 **Tooele** U.S.A.
52 B3 **Tooleybuc** Austr.
53 D1 **Toowoomba** Austr.
137 D3 **Topeka** U.S.A.
144 B2 **Topia** Mex.
144 B2 **Topolobampo** Mex.
86 C2 **Topozero, Ozero** *l.* Rus. Fed.
134 B1 **Toppenish** U.S.A.
111 C3 **Torbalı** Turkey
76 B3 **Torbat-e Heydarīyeh** Iran
76 C3 **Torbat-e Jām** Iran
131 E3 **Torbay** Can.
106 C1 **Tordesillas** Spain
107 C1 **Tordesilos** Spain
92 H2 **Töre** Sweden
107 D1 **Torelló** Spain
100 B1 **Torenberg** *hill* Neth.
Toretam Kazakh. *see* **Baykonyr**
101 F2 **Torgau** Ger.
100 A2 **Torhout** Belgium
Torino Italy *see* **Turin**
67 D4 **Tori-shima** *i.* Japan
117 B4 **Torit** Sudan
154 B1 **Torixoreu** Brazil
89 D2 **Torkovichi** Rus. Fed.
106 B1 **Tormes** *r.* Spain
92 H2 **Torneälven** *r.* Sweden
131 D2 **Torngat Mountains** Can.
92 H2 **Tornio** Fin.
106 B1 **Toro** Spain
130 C3 **Toronto** Can.
89 D2 **Toropets** Rus. Fed.
119 D2 **Tororo** Uganda
Toros Dağları Turkey *see* **Taurus Mountains**
52 B3 **Torquay** Austr.
99 B4 **Torquay** U.K.
135 C4 **Torrance** U.S.A.
106 B2 **Torrão** Port.
106 B1 **Torre** *mt.* Port.
107 D1 **Torreblanca** Spain
106 C1 **Torrecerredo** *mt.* Spain
106 B1 **Torre de Moncorvo** Port.
106 C1 **Torrelavega** Spain
106 C2 **Torremolinos** Spain
52 A2 **Torrens, Lake** *salt flat* Austr.
107 C2 **Torrent** Spain
144 B2 **Torreón** Mex.
106 B2 **Torres Novas** Port.
156 C6 **Torres Strait** Austr.
106 B2 **Torres Vedras** Port.
107 C2 **Torrevieja** Spain
96 B2 **Torridon** U.K.
96 B2 **Torridon, Loch** *b.* U.K.
106 C2 **Torrijos** Spain
139 E2 **Torrington** *CT* U.S.A.
136 C2 **Torrington** *WY* U.S.A.
107 D1 **Torroella de Montgrí** Spain
94 B1 **Tórshavn** Faroe Is
76 C2 **To'rtko'l** Uzbek.
108 A3 **Tortolì** *Sardinia* Italy
108 A2 **Tortona** Italy
107 D1 **Tortosa** Spain
81 D2 **Ţorūd** Iran
103 D1 **Toruń** Pol.
97 B1 **Tory Island** Rep. of Ireland
97 B1 **Tory Sound** *sea chan.* Rep. of Ireland
89 D2 **Torzhok** Rus. Fed.
67 B4 **Tosashimizu** Japan
122 B2 **Tosca** S. Africa
108 A2 **Toscano, Arcipelago** *is* Italy
Toshkent *see* **Tashkent**
89 D2 **Tosno** Rus. Fed.
68 C1 **Tosontsengel** Mongolia
152 B2 **Tostado** Arg.
101 D1 **Tostedt** Ger.
80 B1 **Tosya** Turkey
86 D3 **Tot'ma** Rus. Fed.
151 D2 **Totness** Suriname
67 B3 **Tottori** Japan
114 B4 **Touba** Côte d'Ivoire
114 B1 **Toubkal, Jbel** *mt.* Morocco
118 B2 **Touboro** Cameroon
114 B3 **Tougan** Burkina
115 C1 **Touggourt** Alg.
105 D2 **Toul** France
71 C3 **Touliu** Taiwan
105 D3 **Toulon** France
104 C3 **Toulouse** France
Tourane Vietnam *see* **Đa Nẵng**
104 B2 **Tourlaville** France
100 A2 **Tournai** Belgium
115 D2 **Tourndo, Oued** *watercourse* Alg./Niger
105 C2 **Tournus** France
151 F3 **Touros** Brazil
104 C2 **Tours** France
115 D2 **Tousside, Pic** *mt.* Chad
122 B3 **Touwsrivier** S. Africa
150 B2 **Tovar** Venez.
66 D2 **Towada** Japan
134 D1 **Townsend** U.S.A.
51 D1 **Townsville** Austr.
61 D2 **Towori, Teluk** *b.* Indon.
77 E2 **Toxkan He** *r.* China
66 D2 **Tōya-ko** *l.* Japan
67 C3 **Toyama** Japan
67 C4 **Toyohashi** Japan
67 C3 **Toyota** Japan
115 C1 **Tozeur** Tunisia
81 C1 **Tqvarch'eli** Georgia
Trâblous Lebanon *see* **Tripoli**
80 B1 **Trabzon** Turkey
106 B2 **Trafalgar, Cabo** *c.* Spain
128 C3 **Trail** Can.
88 B3 **Trakai** Lith.
97 B2 **Tralee** Rep. of Ireland
Trá Li Rep. of Ireland *see* **Tralee**
97 C2 **Tramore** Rep. of Ireland
93 F4 **Tranås** Sweden
63 A3 **Trang** Thai.
59 C3 **Trangan** *i.* Indon.
55 L2 **Transantarctic Mountains** Antarctica
110 B1 **Transylvanian Alps** *mts* Romania
108 B3 **Trapani** *Sicily* Italy
53 C3 **Traralgon** Austr.
63 B2 **Trat** Thai.
102 C2 **Traunstein** Ger.
54 B2 **Travers, Mount** N.Z.
138 B2 **Traverse City** U.S.A.
63 B3 **Tra Vinh** Vietnam
103 D2 **Třebíč** Czech Rep.
109 C2 **Trebinje** Bos.-Herz.
103 E2 **Trebišov** Slovakia
Trebizond Turkey *see* **Trabzon**
109 C1 **Trebnje** Slovenia
Trefynwy U.K. *see* **Monmouth**
153 C3 **Treinta y Tres** Uru.
153 B4 **Trelew** Arg.
93 F4 **Trelleborg** Sweden
130 C3 **Tremblant, Mont** *hill* Can.
109 C2 **Tremiti, Isole** *is* Italy
134 D2 **Tremonton** U.S.A.
107 D1 **Tremp** Spain
103 D2 **Trenčín** Slovakia
153 B3 **Trenque Lauquén** Arg.
Trent Italy *see* **Trento**
98 C3 **Trent** *r.* U.K.
108 B1 **Trento** Italy
139 D2 **Trenton** Can.
137 E2 **Trenton** *MO* U.S.A.
139 E2 **Trenton** *NJ* U.S.A.
131 E3 **Trepassey** Can.
153 B3 **Tres Arroyos** Arg.
155 C2 **Três Corações** Brazil
154 B2 **Três Irmãos, Represa** *resr* Brazil

154 B2 **Três Lagoas** Brazil
153 A4 **Tres Lagos** Arg.
155 C1 **Três Marias, Represa** *resr* Brazil
155 C2 **Três Pontas** Brazil
153 B4 **Tres Puntas, Cabo** *c.* Arg.
155 D2 **Três Rios** Brazil
101 F1 **Treuenbrietzen** Ger.
Treves Ger. *see* **Trier**
108 A1 **Treviglio** Italy
108 B1 **Treviso** Italy
99 A4 **Trevose Head** *hd* U.K.
109 C3 **Tricase** Italy
Trichinopoly India *see* **Tiruchchirappalli**
73 B3 **Trichur** India
53 C2 **Trida** Austr.
100 C3 **Trier** Ger.
108 B1 **Trieste** Italy
108 B1 **Triglav** *mt.* Slovenia
111 B3 **Trikala** Greece
59 D3 **Trikora, Puncak** *mt.* Indon.
97 C2 **Trim** Rep. of Ireland
73 C4 **Trincomalee** Sri Lanka
154 C1 **Trindade** Brazil
148 H5 **Trindade, Ilha da** *i.* S. Atlantic Ocean
152 B1 **Trinidad** Bol.
147 D3 **Trinidad** *i.* Trin. and Tob.
136 C3 **Trinidad** U.S.A.
147 D3 **Trinidad and Tobago** *country* West Indies
143 E3 **Trinity** *r.* U.S.A.
131 E3 **Trinity Bay** Can.
111 B3 **Tripoli** Greece
80 B2 **Tripoli** Lebanon
115 D1 **Tripoli** Libya
75 D2 **Tripura** *state* India
113 B9 **Tristan da Cunha** *i.* S. Atlantic Ocean
73 B4 **Trivandrum** India
108 B2 **Trivento** Italy
103 D2 **Trnava** Slovakia
59 E3 **Trobriand Islands** P.N.G.
92 F2 **Trofors** Norway
109 C2 **Trogir** Croatia
109 C2 **Troia** Italy
100 C2 **Troisdorf** Ger.
106 C2 **Trois Fourches, Cap des** *c.* Morocco
130 C3 **Trois-Rivières** Can.
87 F3 **Troitsk** Rus. Fed.
86 E2 **Troitsko-Pechorsk** Rus. Fed.
151 D3 **Trombetas** *r.* Brazil
Tromelin Island Micronesia *see* **Fais**
123 C3 **Trompsburg** S. Africa
92 G2 **Tromsø** Norway
92 F3 **Trondheim** Norway
96 B3 **Troon** U.K.
89 E3 **Trosna** Rus. Fed.
97 C1 **Trostan** *hill* U.K.
128 C2 **Trout Lake** *Alta* Can.
128 B1 **Trout Lake** *l. N.W.T.* Can.
130 A2 **Trout Lake** *l. Ont.* Can.
99 B4 **Trowbridge** U.K.
140 C2 **Troy** *AL* U.S.A.
139 E2 **Troy** *NY* U.S.A.
105 C2 **Troyes** France
135 C3 **Troy Peak** U.S.A.
109 D2 **Trstenik** Serb. and Mont.
89 D3 **Trubchevsk** Rus. Fed.
Truc Giang Vietnam *see* **Bên Tre**
106 B1 **Truchas** Spain
Trucial Coast *country* Asia *see* **United Arab Emirates**
79 C2 **Trucial Coast** U.A.E.
Trucial States *country* Asia *see* **United Arab Emirates**
146 B3 **Trujillo** Hond.
150 B3 **Trujillo** Peru
106 B2 **Trujillo** Spain
147 C4 **Trujillo** Venez.
Trujillo, Monte *mt.* Dom. Rep. *see* **Duarte, Pico**
140 B1 **Trumann** U.S.A.
131 D3 **Truro** Can.
99 A4 **Truro** U.K.
61 C1 **Trus Madi, Gunung** *mt.* Malaysia
142 B2 **Truth or Consequences** U.S.A.
103 D1 **Trutnov** Czech Rep.
93 F3 **Trysil** Norway
103 D1 **Trzebiatów** Pol.
103 D1 **Trzebnica** Pol.
68 B1 **Tsagaannuur** Mongolia
Tsaidam Basin China *see* **Qaidam Pendi**
121 □D2 **Tsaratanana, Massif du** *mts* Madag.
110 C2 **Tsarevo** Bulg.
122 A2 **Tsaukaib** Namibia
Tselinograd Kazakh. *see* **Astana**
Tsementnyy Rus. Fed. *see* **Fokino**
122 A2 **Tses** Namibia
122 B1 **Tsetseng** Botswana
68 C1 **Tsetserleg** Mongolia
Tsetserleg Mongolia *see* **Halban**
122 B2 **Tshabong** Botswana
122 B1 **Tshane** Botswana
91 D2 **Tshchikskoye Vodokhranilishche** *resr* Rus. Fed.
118 B3 **Tshela** Dem. Rep. Congo
118 C3 **Tshikapa** Dem. Rep. Congo
118 C3 **Tshikapa** *r.* Dem. Rep. Congo
123 C2 **Tshing** S. Africa
123 D1 **Tshipise** S. Africa
118 C3 **Tshitanzu** Dem. Rep. Congo
120 B3 **Tshootsha** Botswana
118 C3 **Tshuapa** *r.* Dem. Rep. Congo
Tshwane S. Africa *see* **Pretoria**
87 D4 **Tsimlyanskoye Vodokhranilishche** *resr* Rus. Fed.
Tsinan China *see* **Jinan**
Tsingtao China *see* **Qingdao**
Tsining China *see* **Jining**
121 □D2 **Tsiroanomandidy** Madag.
Tsitsihar China *see* **Qiqihar**
76 A2 **Ts'khinvali** Georgia
123 C3 **Tsomo** S. Africa
67 C4 **Tsu** Japan
67 D3 **Tsuchiura** Japan
66 D2 **Tsugarū-kaikyō** *str.* Japan
Tsugaru Strait Japan *see* **Tsugarū-kaikyō**
120 A2 **Tsumeb** Namibia
122 A1 **Tsumis Park** Namibia
120 B2 **Tsumkwe** Namibia
67 C3 **Tsuruga** Japan
66 C3 **Tsuruoka** Japan
67 A4 **Tsushima** *is* Japan
67 B3 **Tsuyama** Japan
123 C2 **Tswelelang** S. Africa
88 C3 **Tsyelyakhany** Belarus
91 C2 **Tsyurupyns'k** Ukr.
Tthenaagoo Can. *see* **Nahanni Butte**
59 C3 **Tual** Indon.
97 B2 **Tuam** Rep. of Ireland
54 A3 **Tuapeka Mouth** N.Z.
91 D3 **Tuapse** Rus. Fed.
54 A3 **Tuatapere** N.Z.
142 A1 **Tuba City** U.S.A.
61 C2 **Tuban** Indon.
152 D2 **Tubarão** Brazil
102 B2 **Tübingen** Ger.
115 E1 **Tubruq** Libya
49 L6 **Tubuai Islands** *is* Fr. Polynesia
144 A1 **Tubutama** Mex.
152 C1 **Tucavaca** Bol.
128 B1 **Tuchitua** Can.
142 A2 **Tucson** U.S.A.
143 C1 **Tucumcari** U.S.A.
150 C2 **Tucupita** Venez.
151 E3 **Tucuruí** Brazil
151 E3 **Tucuruí, Represa** *resr* Brazil
107 C1 **Tudela** Spain
106 B1 **Tuela** *r.* Port.
157 F2 **Tufts Abyssal Plain** *sea feature* N. Pacific Ocean
123 D2 **Tugela** *r.* S. Africa
64 B2 **Tuguegarao** Phil.
106 B1 **Tui** Spain
59 C3 **Tukangbesi, Kepulauan** *is* Indon.
126 D2 **Tuktoyaktuk** Can.
88 B2 **Tukums** Latvia
119 D3 **Tukuyu** Tanz.
145 C2 **Tula** Mex.
89 E3 **Tula** Rus. Fed.
Tulach Mhór Rep. of Ireland *see* **Tullamore**
145 C2 **Tulancingo** Mex.
135 C3 **Tulare** U.S.A.
142 B2 **Tularosa** U.S.A.
110 C1 **Tulcea** Romania
90 B2 **Tul'chyn** Ukr.
Tuléar Madag. *see* **Toliara**
129 E1 **Tulemalu Lake** Can.
143 C2 **Tulia** U.S.A.
128 B1 **Tulita** Can.
140 C1 **Tullahoma** U.S.A.
53 C2 **Tullamore** Austr.
97 C2 **Tullamore** Rep. of Ireland
104 C2 **Tulle** France
97 C2 **Tullow** Rep. of Ireland
51 D1 **Tully** Austr.
143 D1 **Tulsa** U.S.A.
126 B2 **Tuluksak** U.S.A.
83 H3 **Tulun** Rus. Fed.
150 B2 **Tumaco** Col.
123 C2 **Tumahole** S. Africa
93 G4 **Tumba** Sweden
118 B3 **Tumba, Lac** *l.* Dem. Rep. Congo
61 C2 **Tumbangtiti** Indon.
53 C3 **Tumbarumba** Austr.
150 A3 **Tumbes** Peru
128 B2 **Tumbler Ridge** Can.
52 A2 **Tumby Bay** Austr.
65 B1 **Tumen** China
150 C2 **Tumereng** Guyana
64 A3 **Tumindao** *i.* Phil.
74 A2 **Tump** Pak.
151 D2 **Tumucumaque, Serra** *hills* Brazil
53 C3 **Tumut** Austr.
99 D4 **Tunbridge Wells, Royal** U.K.
80 B2 **Tunceli** Turkey
53 D2 **Tuncurry** Austr.
118 A1 **Tundun-Wada** Nigeria
119 D4 **Tunduru** Tanz.
110 C2 **Tundzha** *r.* Bulg.
128 B1 **Tungsten** Can.
115 D1 **Tunis** Tunisia
108 B3 **Tunis, Golfe de** *g.* Tunisia
115 C1 **Tunisia** *country* Africa
150 B2 **Tunja** Col.
92 F3 **Tunnsjøen** *l.* Norway
Tunxi China *see* **Huangshan**
154 B2 **Tupã** Brazil
154 C1 **Tupaciguara** Brazil
140 C2 **Tupelo** U.S.A.
152 B2 **Tupiza** Bol.
83 H2 **Tura** Rus. Fed.
86 F3 **Tura** *r.* Rus. Fed.
78 B2 **Turabah** Saudi Arabia
83 J3 **Turana, Khrebet** *mts* Rus. Fed.
54 C1 **Turangi** N.Z.
76 B2 **Turan Lowland** Asia
77 D2 **Turar Ryskulov** Kazakh.
78 A1 **Ţurayf** Saudi Arabia
88 B2 **Turba** Estonia
74 A2 **Turbat** Pak.
150 B2 **Turbo** Col.
110 B1 **Turda** Romania
Turfan China *see* **Turpan**
76 C2 **Turgay** Kazakh.
76 C1 **Turgayskaya Stolovaya Strana** *reg.* Kazakh.
110 C2 **Tŭrgovishte** Bulg.
111 C3 **Turgutlu** Turkey
80 B1 **Turhal** Turkey
107 C2 **Turia** *r.* Spain
108 A1 **Turin** Italy
86 F3 **Turinsk** Rus. Fed.
90 A1 **Turiya** *r.* Ukr.
90 A1 **Turiys'k** Ukr.
90 A2 **Turka** Ukr.
119 D2 **Turkana, Lake** *salt l.* Eth./Kenya
77 C2 **Turkestan** Kazakh.
103 E2 **Túrkeve** Hungary
80 B2 **Turkey** *country* Asia/Europe
50 B1 **Turkey Creek** Austr.
76 C3 **Turkmenabat** Turkm.
76 B2 **Turkmenbashi** Turkm.
76 B2 **Turkmenistan** *country* Asia
Turkmeniya *country* Asia *see* **Turkmenistan**
Turkmenskaya S.S.R. *admin. reg.* Asia *see* **Turkmenistan**
147 C2 **Turks and Caicos Islands** *terr.* West Indies
147 C2 **Turks Islands** Turks and Caicos Is
93 H3 **Turku** Fin.
119 D2 **Turkwel** *watercourse* Kenya
135 B3 **Turlock** U.S.A.
155 D1 **Turmalina** Brazil
54 C2 **Turnagain, Cape** N.Z.
146 B3 **Turneffe Islands** Belize
100 B2 **Turnhout** Belgium
129 D2 **Turnor Lake** Can.
Tŭrnovo Bulg. *see* **Veliko Tŭrnovo**
110 B2 **Turnu Măgurele** Romania
68 B2 **Turpan** China
96 C2 **Turriff** U.K.
64 A3 **Turtle Islands** Phil.
77 D2 **Turugart Pass** China/Kyrg.
82 G2 **Turukhansk** Rus. Fed.
140 C2 **Tuscaloosa** U.S.A.
140 C2 **Tuskegee** U.S.A.
81 C2 **Tutak** Turkey
89 E2 **Tutayev** Rus. Fed.
73 B4 **Tuticorin** India
121 C1 **Tutubu** Tanz.
49 J5 **Tutuila** *i.* American Samoa
120 B3 **Tutume** Botswana
93 H3 **Tuusula** Fin.
49 I4 **Tuvalu** *country* S. Pacific Ocean
78 B2 **Tuwayq, Jabal** *hills* Saudi Arabia
78 B2 **Tuwayq, Jabal** *mts* Saudi Arabia
78 A2 **Tuwwal** Saudi Arabia
144 B2 **Tuxpan** Mex.
145 C2 **Tuxpan** Mex.
145 C3 **Tuxtla Gutiérrez** Mex.
62 B1 **Tuyên Quang** Vietnam
63 B2 **Tuy Hoa** Vietnam
80 B2 **Tuz, Lake** *salt l.* Turkey
Tuz Gölü *salt l.* Turkey *see* **Tuz, Lake**
81 C2 **Tuz Khurmātū** Iraq
109 C2 **Tuzla** Bos.-Herz.
91 E2 **Tuzlov** *r.* Rus. Fed.
89 E2 **Tver'** Rus. Fed.
98 B2 **Tweed** *r.* U.K.
53 D1 **Tweed Heads** Austr.
122 A2 **Twee Rivier** Namibia
135 C4 **Twentynine Palms** U.S.A.
131 E3 **Twillingate** Can.
134 D2 **Twin Falls** U.S.A.
54 B2 **Twizel** *South I.* N.Z.
137 E1 **Two Harbors** U.S.A.
128 C2 **Two Hills** Can.
Tyddewi U.K. *see* **St David's**
143 D2 **Tyler** U.S.A.
83 J3 **Tynda** Rus. Fed.
Tyndinskiy Rus. Fed. *see* **Tynda**
96 B2 **Tyndrum** U.K.
98 C2 **Tyne** *r. England* U.K.
95 C2 **Tyne** *r. Scotland* U.K.
93 F3 **Tynset** Norway
80 B2 **Tyre** Lebanon
69 E1 **Tyrma** Rus. Fed.
111 B3 **Tyrnavos** Greece
52 B3 **Tyrrell, Lake** *dry lake* Austr.
108 B2 **Tyrrhenian Sea** France/Italy
76 B2 **Tyub-Karagan, Mys** *pt* Kazakh.
87 E3 **Tyul'gan** Rus. Fed.
86 F3 **Tyumen'** Rus. Fed.
83 J2 **Tyung** *r.* Rus. Fed.
Tyuratam Kazakh. *see* **Baykonyr**
99 A4 **Tywi** *r.* U.K.
123 D1 **Tzaneen** S. Africa

U

Uaco Congo Angola *see* **Waku-Kungo**
120 B2 **Uamanda** Angola
150 C3 **Uarini** Brazil
150 C3 **Uaupés** Brazil
155 D2 **Ubá** Brazil
155 D1 **Ubaí** Brazil
151 F4 **Ubaitaba** Brazil
118 B3 **Ubangi** *r.* C.A.R./Dem. Rep. Congo
Ubangi-Shari *country* Africa *see* **Central African Republic**
67 B4 **Ube** Japan
106 C2 **Úbeda** Spain
154 C1 **Uberaba** Brazil
154 C1 **Uberlândia** Brazil

Ubombo

123 D2	**Ubombo** S. Africa	
63 B2	**Ubon Ratchathani** Thai.	
119 C3	**Ubundu** Dem. Rep. Congo	
150 B3	**Ucayali** r. Peru	
100 B2	**Uccle** Belgium	
74 B2	**Uch** Pak.	
77 E2	**Ucharal** Kazakh.	
66 D2	**Uchiura-wan** b. Japan	
76 C2	**Uchquduq** Uzbek.	
83 J3	**Uchur** r. Rus. Fed.	
99 D4	**Uckfield** U.K.	
128 B3	**Ucluelet** Can.	
83 I2	**Udachnyy** Rus. Fed.	
74 B2	**Udaipur** India	
91 C1	**Uday** r. Ukr.	
93 F4	**Uddevalla** Sweden	
92 G2	**Uddjaure** l. Sweden	
100 B2	**Uden** Neth.	
74 B1	**Udhampur** Jammu and Kashmir	
108 B1	**Udine** Italy	
89 E2	**Udomlya** Rus. Fed.	
62 B2	**Udon Thani** Thai.	
73 B3	**Udupi** India	
83 K3	**Udyl', Ozero** l. Rus. Fed.	
67 C3	**Ueda** Japan	
61 D2	**Uekuli** Indon.	
118 C2	**Uele** r. Dem. Rep. Congo	
83 N2	**Uelen** Rus. Fed.	
101 E1	**Uelzen** Ger.	
119 C2	**Uere** r. Dem. Rep. Congo	
87 E3	**Ufa** Rus. Fed.	
119 D3	**Ugalla** r. Tanz.	
119 D2	**Uganda** country Africa	
69 F1	**Uglegorsk** Rus. Fed.	
89 E2	**Uglich** Rus. Fed.	
89 D2	**Uglovka** Rus. Fed.	
66 B2	**Uglovoye** Rus. Fed.	
89 D3	**Ugra** Rus. Fed.	
103 D2	**Uherské Hradiště** Czech Rep.	
	Uibhist a' Deas i. U.K. see South Uist	
	Uibhist a' Tuath i. U.K. see North Uist	
101 E2	**Uichteritz** Ger.	
96 A2	**Uig** U.K.	
120 A1	**Uíge** Angola	
65 B2	**Uijŏngbu** S. Korea	
65 A1	**Ŭiju** N. Korea	
135 D2	**Uinta Mountains** U.S.A.	
120 A3	**Uis Mine** Namibia	
65 B2	**Ŭisŏng** S. Korea	
123 C3	**Uitenhage** S. Africa	
100 C1	**Uithuizen** Neth.	
131 D2	**Uivak, Cape** Can.	
	Ujiyamada Japan see Ise	
74 B2	**Ujjain** India	
	Ujung Pandang Indon. see Makassar	
89 F3	**Ukholovo** Rus. Fed.	
	Ukhta Rus. Fed. see Kalevala	
86 E2	**Ukhta** Rus. Fed.	
135 B3	**Ukiah** U.S.A.	
127 I2	**Ukkusissat** Greenland	
88 B2	**Ukmergė** Lith.	
90 C2	**Ukraine** country Europe	
	Ukrainskaya S.S.R. admin. reg. Europe see Ukraine	
	Ulaanbaatar Mongolia see Ulan Bator	
68 C1	**Ulaangom** Mongolia	
59 E3	**Ulamona** P.N.G.	
70 A2	**Ulan** China	
69 D1	**Ulan Bator** Mongolia	
	Ulanhad China see Chifeng	
69 E1	**Ulanhot** China	
87 D4	**Ulan-Khol** Rus. Fed.	
69 D1	**Uliastai** China	
75 D1	**Ulan Ul Hu** l. China	
65 B2	**Ulchin** S. Korea	
	Uleåborg Fin. see Oulu	
88 C2	**Ülenurme** Estonia	
74 B3	**Ulhasnagar** India	
69 D1	**Uliastai** China	
68 C1	**Uliastay** Mongolia	
59 C1	**Ulithi** atoll Micronesia	
53 D3	**Ulladulla** Austr.	
96 B2	**Ullapool** U.K.	
98 B2	**Ullswater** l. U.K.	
65 C2	**Ullŭng-do** i. S. Korea	
102 B2	**Ulm** Ger.	
65 B2	**Ulsan** S. Korea	
96 □	**Ulsta** U.K.	
97 C1	**Ulster** reg. Rep. of Ireland/U.K.	
52 B3	**Ultima** Austr.	
145 D3	**Ulúa** r. Hond.	

111 C3	**Ulubey** Turkey	
111 D3	**Uluborlu** Turkey	
111 C2	**Uludağ** mt. Turkey	
123 D2	**Ulundi** S. Africa	
77 E2	**Ulungur Hu** l. China	
	Uluqsaqtuuq Can. see Holman	
50 C2	**Uluru** hill Austr.	
98 B2	**Ulverston** U.K.	
90 C2	**Ul'yanovka** Ukr.	
87 D3	**Ul'yanovsk** Rus. Fed.	
136 C3	**Ulysses** U.S.A.	
90 C2	**Uman'** Ukr.	
86 C2	**Umba** Rus. Fed.	
59 D3	**Umboi** i. P.N.G.	
59 D3	**Umbukul** P.N.G.	
92 H3	**Umeå** Sweden	
92 H3	**Umeälven** r. Sweden	
123 D2	**Umhlanga Rocks** S. Africa	
127 J2	**Umiiviip Kangertiva** inlet Greenland	
126 E2	**Umingmaktok** Can.	
123 D2	**Umlazi** S. Africa	
78 A2	**Umm al Birak** Saudi Arabia	
79 C2	**Umm as Samīm** salt flat Oman	
116 A3	**Umm Keddada** Sudan	
78 A2	**Umm Lajj** Saudi Arabia	
78 A2	**Umm Mukhbār, Jabal** hill Saudi Arabia	
116 B3	**Umm Ruwaba** Sudan	
115 E1	**Umm Sa'ad** Libya	
134 B2	**Umpqua** r. U.S.A.	
120 A2	**Umpulo** Angola	
	Umtali Zimbabwe see Mutare	
123 C3	**Umtata** S. Africa	
123 D3	**Umtentweni** S. Africa	
154 B2	**Umuarama** Brazil	
123 C3	**Umzimkulu** S. Africa	
109 C1	**Una** r. Bos.-Herz./Croatia	
155 E1	**Una** Brazil	
154 C1	**Unaí** Brazil	
126 B2	**Unalakleet** U.S.A.	
78 B2	**'Unayzah** Saudi Arabia	
136 B3	**Uncompahgre Peak** U.S.A.	
52 B3	**Underbool** Austr.	
136 C1	**Underwood** U.S.A.	
89 D3	**Unecha** Rus. Fed.	
53 C2	**Ungarie** Austr.	
52 A2	**Ungarra** Austr.	
127 H2	**Ungava, Péninsule d'** pen. Can.	
131 D2	**Ungava Bay** Can.	
	Ungeny Moldova see Ungheni	
65 C1	**Unggi** N. Korea	
90 B2	**Ungheni** Moldova	
	Unguja i. Tanz. see Zanzibar Island	
119 E3	**Ungwana Bay** Kenya	
154 B3	**União da Vitória** Brazil	
150 C3	**Unini** r. Brazil	
140 C1	**Union** U.S.A.	
122 C1	**Uniondale** S. Africa	
139 D3	**Uniontown** U.S.A.	
79 C2	**United Arab Emirates** country Asia	
	United Arab Republic country Africa see Egypt	
95 C3	**United Kingdom** country Europe	
	United Provinces state India see Uttar Pradesh	
133 B3	**United States of America** country N. America	
129 D2	**Unity** Can.	
100 C2	**Unna** Ger.	
96 □	**Unst** i. U.K.	
101 E2	**Unstrut** r. Ger.	
89 E3	**Upa** r. Rus. Fed.	
119 C3	**Upemba, Lac** l. Dem. Rep. Congo	
122 B2	**Upington** S. Africa	
74 B2	**Upleta** India	
49 J5	**Upolu** i. Samoa	
134 B2	**Upper Alkali Lake** U.S.A.	
128 C2	**Upper Arrow Lake** Can.	
54 C2	**Upper Hutt** N.Z.	
134 B2	**Upper Klamath Lake** U.S.A.	
128 B1	**Upper Liard** Can.	
97 C1	**Upper Lough Erne** l. U.K.	
137 E1	**Upper Red Lake** U.S.A.	
	Upper Tunguska r. Rus. Fed. see Angara	
	Upper Volta country Africa see Burkina	

93 G4	**Uppsala** Sweden	
78 B2	**'Uqlat aş Şuqūr** Saudi Arabia	
	Urad Qianqi China see Xishanzui	
76 B2	**Ural** r. Kazakh./Rus. Fed.	
53 D2	**Uralla** Austr.	
87 E3	**Ural Mountains** Rus. Fed.	
76 B1	**Ural'sk** Kazakh.	
	Ural'skiy Khrebet mts Rus. Fed. see Ural Mountains	
119 D3	**Urambo** Tanz.	
53 C3	**Urana** Austr.	
129 D2	**Uranium City** Can.	
86 F2	**Uray** Rus. Fed.	
98 C2	**Ure** r. U.K.	
86 D3	**Uren'** Rus. Fed.	
82 G2	**Urengoy** Rus. Fed.	
144 A2	**Ures** Mex.	
	Urfa Turkey see Şanlıurfa	
76 C2	**Urganch** Uzbek.	
100 B1	**Urk** Neth.	
111 C3	**Urla** Turey	
110 C2	**Urlaţi** Romania	
81 C2	**Urmia** Iran	
81 C2	**Urmia, Lake** salt l. Iran	
109 D2	**Uroševac** Serb. and Mont.	
144 B2	**Uruáchic** Mex.	
151 E4	**Uruaçu** Brazil	
144 B3	**Uruapan** Mex.	
150 B4	**Urubamba** r. Peru	
151 D3	**Urucara** Brazil	
151 E3	**Uruçuí** Brazil	
151 E3	**Uruçuí, Serra do** hills Brazil	
151 D3	**Urucurituba** Brazil	
152 C2	**Uruguaiana** Brazil	
153 C3	**Uruguay** country S. America	
	Urumchi China see Ürümqi	
68 B2	**Ürümqi** China	
119 D3	**Urundi** country Africa see Burundi	
53 D2	**Urunga** Austr.	
78 B3	**'Urūq al Awārik** des. Saudi Arabia	
119 D3	**Uruwira** Tanz.	
110 C2	**Urziceni** Romania	
67 B4	**Usa** Japan	
86 E2	**Usa** r. Rus. Fed.	
111 C3	**Uşak** Turkey	
120 A3	**Usakos** Namibia	
88 C2	**Ushachy** Belarus	
82 G1	**Ushakova, Ostrov** i. Rus. Fed.	
77 D2	**Ushtobe** Kazakh.	
	Ush-Tyube Kazakh. see Ushtobe	
153 B5	**Ushuaia** Arg.	
86 E2	**Usinsk** Rus. Fed.	
99 B4	**Usk** r. U.K.	
88 C3	**Uskhodni** Belarus	
89 E3	**Usman'** Rus. Fed.	
86 D2	**Usogorsk** Rus. Fed.	
104 C2	**Ussel** France	
66 C1	**Ussuri** r. China/Rus. Fed.	
66 B2	**Ussuriysk** Rus. Fed.	
	Ust'-Abakanskoye Rus. Fed. see Abakan	
	Ust'-Balyk Rus. Fed. see Nefteyugansk	
91 E2	**Ust'-Donetskiy** Rus. Fed.	
108 B3	**Ustica, Isola di** i. Sicily Italy	
83 H3	**Ust'-Ilimsk** Rus. Fed.	
86 E2	**Ust'-Ilych** Rus. Fed.	
102 C1	**Ústí nad Labem** Czech Rep.	
	Ustinov Rus. Fed. see Izhevsk	
103 D1	**Ustka** Pol.	
83 L3	**Ust'-Kamchatsk** Rus. Fed.	
77 E2	**Ust'-Kamenogorsk** Kazakh.	
86 F2	**Ust'-Kara** Rus. Fed.	
86 E2	**Ust'-Kulom** Rus. Fed.	
83 I3	**Ust'-Kut** Rus. Fed.	
91 D2	**Ust'-Labinsk** Rus. Fed.	
	Ust'-Labinskaya Rus. Fed. see Ust'-Labinsk	
88 C2	**Ust'-Luga** Rus. Fed.	
86 E2	**Ust'-Nem** Rus. Fed.	
83 K2	**Ust'-Nera** Rus. Fed.	
83 K2	**Ust'-Olenek** Rus. Fed.	
83 K2	**Ust'-Omchug** Rus. Fed.	
83 H3	**Ust'-Ordynskiy** Rus. Fed.	
103 E2	**Ustrzyki Dolne** Pol.	
86 E2	**Ust'-Tsil'ma** Rus. Fed.	
86 D2	**Ust'-Ura** Rus. Fed.	

76 B2	**Ustyurt Plateau** Kazakh./Uzbek.	
89 E2	**Ustyuzhna** Rus. Fed.	
146 B3	**Usulután** El Salvador	
	Usumbura Burundi see Bujumbura	
89 D2	**Usvyaty** Rus. Fed.	
135 D3	**Utah** state U.S.A.	
135 D2	**Utah Lake** U.S.A.	
88 C2	**Utena** Lith.	
119 D3	**Utete** Tanz.	
63 B2	**Uthai Thani** Thai.	
74 A2	**Uthal** Pak.	
139 D2	**Utica** U.S.A.	
107 C2	**Utiel** Spain	
128 C2	**Utikuma Lake** Can.	
93 G4	**Utlängan** i. Sweden	
100 B1	**Utrecht** Neth.	
123 D2	**Utrecht** S. Africa	
106 B2	**Utrera** Spain	
92 I2	**Utsjoki** Fin.	
67 C3	**Utsunomiya** Japan	
87 D4	**Utta** Rus. Fed.	
62 B2	**Uttaradit** Thai.	
75 B1	**Uttaranchal** state India	
75 B2	**Uttar Pradesh** state India	
	Uummannaq Greenland see Dundas	
127 I2	**Uummannaq** Greenland	
127 I2	**Uummannaq Fjord** inlet Greenland	
93 H3	**Uusikaupunki** Fin.	
120 A2	**Uutapi** Namibia	
143 D3	**Uvalde** U.S.A.	
81 D1	**Uval Karabaur** hills Uzbek.	
119 D3	**Uvinza** Tanz.	
123 D3	**Uvongo** S. Africa	
68 C1	**Uvs Nuur** salt l. Mongolia	
67 B4	**Uwajima** Japan	
78 A2	**'Uwayriḍ, Ḥarrat al** lava field Saudi Arabia	
116 A2	**Uweinat, Jebel** mt. Sudan	
83 H3	**Uyar** Rus. Fed.	
115 C4	**Uyo** Nigeria	
79 B2	**Uyun** Saudi Arabia	
152 B2	**Uyuni** Bol.	
152 B2	**Uyuni, Salar de** salt flat Bol.	
76 C2	**Uzbekistan** country Asia	
	Uzbekskaya S.S.R. admin. reg. Asia see Uzbekistan	
	Uzbek S.S.R. admin.reg. Asia see Uzbekistan	
104 C2	**Uzerche** France	
105 C3	**Uzès** France	
90 C1	**Uzh** r. Ukr.	
90 A2	**Uzhhorod** Ukr.	
	Uzhorod Ukr. see Uzhhorod	
109 C2	**Užice** Serb. and Mont.	
89 E3	**Uzlovaya** Rus. Fed.	
111 C3	**Üzümlü** Turkey	
111 C2	**Uzunköprü** Turkey	

V

123 B2	**Vaal** r. S. Africa	
92 I3	**Vaala** Fin.	
123 C2	**Vaal Dam** S. Africa	
123 C1	**Vaalwater** S. Africa	
92 H3	**Vaasa** Fin.	
103 D2	**Vác** Hungary	
152 C2	**Vacaria** Brazil	
154 B2	**Vacaria, Serra** hills Brazil	
135 B3	**Vacaville** U.S.A.	
74 B2	**Vadodara** India	
92 I1	**Vadso** Norway	
105 D2	**Vaduz** Liechtenstein	
94 B1	**Vágar** i. Faroe Is	
94 B1	**Vágur** Faroe Is	
103 D2	**Váh** r. Slovakia	
49 I4	**Vaiaku** Tuvalu	
88 B2	**Vaida** Estonia	
136 B3	**Vail** U.S.A.	
77 C3	**Vakhsh** Tajik.	
	Vakhstroy Tajik. see Vakhsh	
79 C2	**Vakīlābād** Iran	
108 B1	**Valdagno** Italy	
	Valdai Hills Rus. Fed. see Valdayskaya Vozvyshennost'	
89 D2	**Valday** Rus. Fed.	
89 D2	**Valdayskaya Vozvyshennost'** hills Rus. Fed.	
106 B2	**Valdecañas, Embalse de** resr Spain	
93 G4	**Valdemarsvik** Sweden	

105 D2 **Val-de-Meuse** France
106 C2 **Valdepeñas** Spain
153 B4 **Valdés, Península** *pen.* Arg.
126 C2 **Valdez** U.S.A.
153 A3 **Valdivia** Chile
130 C3 **Val-d'Or** Can.
141 D2 **Valdosta** U.S.A.
128 C2 **Valemount** Can.
152 E1 **Valença** Brazil
105 C3 **Valence** France
107 C2 **Valencia** Spain
107 C2 **Valencia** *aut. Comm.* Spain
150 C1 **Valencia** Venez.
107 D2 **Valencia, Golfo de** *g.* Spain
106 B1 **Valencia de Don Juan** Spain
97 A3 **Valencia Island** Rep. of Ireland
105 C1 **Valenciennes** France
136 C2 **Valentine** U.S.A.
64 B2 **Valenzuela** Phil.
150 B2 **Valera** Venez.
88 C2 **Valga** Estonia
109 C2 **Valjevo** Serb. and Mont.
88 C2 **Valka** Latvia
93 H3 **Valkeakoski** Fin.
100 B2 **Valkenswaard** Neth.
91 D2 **Valky** Ukr.
55 G2 **Valkyrie Dome** *ice feature* Antarctica
145 D2 **Valladolid** Mex.
106 C1 **Valladolid** Spain
107 C2 **Vall de Uxó** Spain
93 E4 **Valle** Norway
145 C2 **Vallecillos** Mex.
150 C2 **Valle de la Pascua** Venez.
150 B1 **Valledupar** Col.
145 C2 **Valle Hermoso** Mex.
135 B3 **Vallejo** U.S.A.
152 A2 **Vallenar** Chile
84 F5 **Valletta** Malta
137 D1 **Valley City** U.S.A.
134 B2 **Valley Falls** U.S.A.
128 C2 **Valleyview** Can.
107 D1 **Valls** Spain
129 D3 **Val Marie** Can.
88 C2 **Valmiera** Latvia
104 B2 **Valognes** France
88 C3 **Valozhyn** Belarus
154 B2 **Valparaíso** Brazil
153 A3 **Valparaíso** Chile
105 C3 **Valréas** France
59 D3 **Vals, Tanjung** *c.* Indon.
74 B2 **Valsad** India
122 B2 **Valspan** S. Africa
91 D1 **Valuyki** Rus. Fed.
106 B2 **Valverde del Camino** Spain
81 C2 **Van** Turkey
81 C2 **Van, Lake** *salt l.* Turkey
81 C1 **Vanadzor** Armenia
83 H2 **Vanavara** Rus. Fed.
140 B1 **Van Buren** *AR* U.S.A.
139 F1 **Van Buren** *ME* U.S.A.
Van Buren U.S.A. *see* **Kettering**
128 B3 **Vancouver** Can.
134 B1 **Vancouver** U.S.A.
128 B3 **Vancouver Island** Can.
138 B3 **Vandalia** *IL* U.S.A.
138 C3 **Vandalia** *OH* U.S.A.
123 C2 **Vanderbijlpark** S. Africa
128 B2 **Vanderhoof** Can.
122 B3 **Vanderkloof Dam** *resr* S. Africa
50 C1 **Van Diemen Gulf** Austr.
88 C2 **Vändra** Estonia
Väner, Lake Sweden *see* **Vänern**
93 F4 **Vänern** *l.* Sweden
93 F4 **Vänersborg** Sweden
121 □D3 **Vangaindrano** Madag.
Van Gölü *salt l.* Turkey *see* **Van, Lake**
142 C2 **Van Horn** U.S.A.
59 D3 **Vanimo** P.N.G.
83 K3 **Vanino** Rus. Fed.
104 B2 **Vannes** France
Vannovka Kazakh. *see* **Turar Ryskulov**
59 D3 **Van Rees, Pegunungan** *mts* Indon.
122 A3 **Vanrhynsdorp** S. Africa
93 H3 **Vantaa** Fin.
49 I5 **Vanua Levu** *i.* Fiji
48 H5 **Vanuatu** *country* S. Pacific Ocean
138 C2 **Van Wert** U.S.A.
122 B3 **Vanwyksvlei** S. Africa
122 B2 **Van Zylsrus** S. Africa
75 C2 **Varanasi** India
92 I1 **Varangerfjorden** *sea chan.* Norway
92 I1 **Varangerhalvøya** *pen.* Norway
88 C2 **Varapayeva** Belarus
109 C1 **Varaždin** Croatia
93 F4 **Varberg** Sweden
111 B3 **Varda** Greece
111 B2 **Vardar** *r.* Macedonia
93 E4 **Varde** Denmark
92 J1 **Vardø** Norway
101 D1 **Varel** Ger.
88 B3 **Varėna** Lith.
139 E1 **Varennes** Can.
108 A1 **Varese** Italy
155 C2 **Varginha** Brazil
93 I3 **Varkaus** Fin.
110 C2 **Varna** Bulg.
93 F4 **Värnamo** Sweden
155 D1 **Várzea da Palma** Brazil
86 C2 **Varzino** Rus. Fed.
Vasa Fin. *see* **Vaasa**
88 C3 **Vasilyevichy** Belarus
88 C2 **Vasknarva** Estonia
110 C1 **Vaslui** Romania
93 G4 **Västerås** Sweden
93 G3 **Västerdalälven** *r.* Sweden
88 A2 **Västerhaninge** Sweden
93 G4 **Västervik** Sweden
108 B2 **Vasto** Italy
91 D2 **Vasylivka** Ukr.
90 C1 **Vasyl'kiv** Ukr.
91 D2 **Vasyl'kivka** Ukr.
104 C2 **Vatan** France
111 B3 **Vathia** Greece
108 B2 **Vatican City** Europe
92 □B3 **Vatnajökull** *ice cap* Iceland
110 C1 **Vatra Dornei** Romania
Vätter, Lake Sweden *see* **Vättern**
93 F4 **Vättern** *l.* Sweden
142 B2 **Vaughn** U.S.A.
105 C3 **Vauvert** France
121 □D2 **Vavatenina** Madag.
49 J5 **Vava'u Group** *is* Tonga
88 B3 **Vawkavysk** Belarus
93 F4 **Växjö** Sweden
Vayenga Rus. Fed. *see* **Severomorsk**
86 E1 **Vaygach, Ostrov** *i.* Rus. Fed.
154 C1 **Vazante** Brazil
101 D1 **Vechta** Ger.
110 C2 **Vedea** *r.* Romania
100 C1 **Veendam** Neth.
100 B1 **Veenendaal** Neth.
92 F2 **Vega** *i.* Norway
128 C2 **Vegreville** Can.
106 B2 **Vejer de la Frontera** Spain
93 E4 **Vejle** Denmark
110 B2 **Velbŭzhdki Prokhod** *pass* Macedonia
122 A3 **Velddrif** S. Africa
100 B2 **Veldhoven** Neth.
109 B2 **Velebit** *mts* Croatia
100 C2 **Velen** Ger.
109 C1 **Velenje** Slovenia
109 D2 **Veles** Macedonia
106 C2 **Vélez-Málaga** Spain
155 D1 **Velhas** *r.* Brazil
109 D2 **Velika Plana** Serb. and Mont.
88 C2 **Velikaya** *r.* Rus. Fed.
89 D2 **Velikiye Luki** Rus. Fed.
89 D2 **Velikiy Novgorod** Rus. Fed.
86 D2 **Velikiy Ustyug** Rus. Fed.
110 C2 **Veliko Tŭrnovo** Bulg.
108 B2 **Veli Lošinj** Croatia
89 D2 **Velizh** Rus. Fed.
108 B2 **Velletri** Italy
73 B3 **Vellore** India
86 D2 **Vel'sk** Rus. Fed.
101 F1 **Velten** Ger.
91 D1 **Velykyy Burluk** Ukr.
Velykyy Tokmak Ukr. *see* **Tokmak**
159 E4 **Vema Trench** *sea feature* Indian Ocean
108 B2 **Venafro** Italy
154 C2 **Venceslau Bráz** Brazil
104 C2 **Vendôme** France
108 B1 **Veneta, Laguna** *lag.* Italy
89 E3 **Venev** Rus. Fed.
Venezia Italy *see* **Venice**
150 C2 **Venezuela** *country* S. America
150 B1 **Venezuela, Golfo de** *g.* Venez.
108 B1 **Venice** Italy
141 D3 **Venice** U.S.A.
108 B1 **Venice, Gulf of** Europe
100 C2 **Venlo** Neth.
93 E4 **Vennesla** Norway
100 B2 **Venray** Neth.
88 B2 **Venta** *r.* Latvia/Lith.
88 B2 **Venta** Lith.
123 C2 **Ventersburg** S. Africa
123 C3 **Venterstad** S. Africa
108 A2 **Ventimiglia** Italy
99 C4 **Ventnor** U.K.
88 B2 **Ventspils** Latvia
135 C4 **Ventura** U.S.A.
143 C3 **Venustiano Carranza, Presa** *resr* Mex.
107 C2 **Vera** Spain
154 C2 **Vera Cruz** Brazil
145 C3 **Veracruz** Mex.
74 B2 **Veraval** India
108 A1 **Verbania** Italy
108 A1 **Vercelli** Italy
105 D3 **Vercors** *reg.* France
92 F3 **Verdalsøra** Norway
154 B1 **Verde** *r.* Brazil
154 B2 **Verde** *r.* Brazil
144 B2 **Verde** *r.* Mex.
142 A2 **Verde** *r.* U.S.A.
155 D1 **Verde Grande** *r.* Brazil
101 D1 **Verden (Aller)** Ger.
154 B1 **Verdinho, Serra do** *mts* Brazil
105 D3 **Verdon** *r.* France
105 D2 **Verdun** France
123 C2 **Vereeniging** S. Africa
106 B1 **Verín** Spain
91 D3 **Verkhnebakanskiy** Rus. Fed.
89 D3 **Verkhnedneprovskiy** Rus. Fed.
92 J2 **Verkhnetulomskiy** Rus. Fed.
92 J2 **Verkhnetulomskoye Vodokhranilishche** *resr* Rus. Fed.
87 D4 **Verkhniy Baskunchak** Rus. Fed.
91 E1 **Verkhniy Mamon** Rus. Fed.
86 D2 **Verkhnyaya Toyma** Rus. Fed.
89 E3 **Verkhov'ye** Rus. Fed.
90 A2 **Verkhovyna** Ukr.
83 J2 **Verkhoyanskiy Khrebet** *mts* Rus. Fed.
129 C2 **Vermilion** Can.
137 D2 **Vermillion** U.S.A.
130 A3 **Vermillion Bay** Can.
139 E2 **Vermont** *state* U.S.A.
135 E2 **Vernal** U.S.A.
122 B2 **Verneuk Pan** *salt pan* S. Africa
128 C2 **Vernon** Can.
143 D2 **Vernon** U.S.A.
141 D3 **Vero Beach** U.S.A.
111 B2 **Veroia** Greece
108 B1 **Verona** Italy
138 B2 **Verona** U.S.A.
104 C2 **Versailles** France
104 B2 **Vertou** France
123 D2 **Verulam** S. Africa
100 B2 **Verviers** Belgium
105 C2 **Vervins** France
105 D3 **Vescovato** *Corsica* France
87 E3 **Veselaya, Gora** *mt.* Rus. Fed.
91 C2 **Vesele** Ukr.
91 E2 **Veselyy** Rus. Fed.
105 D2 **Vesoul** France
140 C2 **Vestavia Hills** U.S.A.
92 F2 **Vesterålen** *is* Norway
92 F2 **Vestfjorden** *sea chan.* Norway
94 B1 **Vestmanna** Faroe Is
92 □A3 **Vestmannaeyjar** Iceland
92 □A3 **Vestmannaeyjar** *is* Iceland
93 E3 **Vestnes** Norway
Vesuvio *vol.* Italy *see* **Vesuvius**
108 B2 **Vesuvius** *vol.* Italy
89 E2 **Ves'yegonsk** Rus. Fed.
103 D2 **Veszprém** Hungary
93 G4 **Vetlanda** Sweden
86 D3 **Vetluga** Rus. Fed.
86 D3 **Vetluzhskiy** Rus. Fed.
100 A2 **Veurne** Belgium
119 D2 **Veveno** *r.* Sudan
105 D2 **Vevey** Switz.
91 D1 **Veydelevka** Rus. Fed.
80 B1 **Vezirköprü** Turkey
Vialar Alg. *see* **Tissemsilt**
152 C3 **Viamao** Brazil
151 E3 **Viana** Brazil
106 B1 **Viana do Castelo** Port.
Viangchan Laos *see* **Vientiane**
62 B1 **Viangphoukha** Laos
154 C1 **Vianópolis** Brazil
108 B2 **Viareggio** Italy
93 E4 **Viborg** Denmark
Viborg Rus. Fed. *see* **Vyborg**
109 C3 **Vibo Valentia** Italy
107 D1 **Vic** Spain
144 A1 **Vicente Guerrero** Mex.
108 B1 **Vicenza** Italy
89 F2 **Vichuga** Rus. Fed.
105 C2 **Vichy** France
140 B2 **Vicksburg** U.S.A.
155 D2 **Viçosa** Brazil
52 A3 **Victor Harbor** Austr.
50 C1 **Victoria** *r.* Austr.
52 B3 **Victoria** *state* Austr.
Victoria Cameroon *see* **Limbe**
128 B3 **Victoria** Can.
153 A3 **Victoria** Chile
Victoria Malaysia *see* **Labuan**
113 I6 **Victoria** Seychelles
143 D3 **Victoria** U.S.A.
119 D3 **Victoria, Lake** Africa
52 B2 **Victoria, Lake** Austr.
62 A1 **Victoria, Mount** Myanmar
59 D3 **Victoria, Mount** P.N.G.
154 B3 **Victoria, Sierra de la** *hills* Arg.
120 B2 **Victoria Falls** *waterfall* Zambia/Zimbabwe
120 B2 **Victoria Falls** Zimbabwe
126 E2 **Victoria Island** Can.
55 M2 **Victoria Land** *coastal area* Antarctica
50 C1 **Victoria River Downs** Austr.
139 E1 **Victoriaville** Can.
122 B3 **Victoria West** S. Africa
135 C4 **Victorville** U.S.A.
141 D2 **Vidalia** U.S.A.
110 C2 **Videle** Romania
92 □A2 **Víðidalsá** Iceland
110 B2 **Vidin** Bulg.
74 B2 **Vidisha** India
140 B2 **Vidor** U.S.A.
153 B4 **Viedma** Arg.
153 A4 **Viedma, Lago** *l.* Arg.
102 C2 **Viehberg** *mt.* Austria
107 D1 **Vielha** Spain
100 B2 **Vielsalm** Belgium
101 E2 **Vienenburg** Ger.
103 D2 **Vienna** Austria
138 C3 **Vienna** U.S.A.
105 C2 **Vienne** France
104 C2 **Vienne** *r.* France
62 B2 **Vientiane** Laos
100 C2 **Viersen** Ger.
104 C2 **Vierzon** France
144 B2 **Viesca** Mex.
109 C2 **Vieste** Italy
62 B2 **Vietnam** *country* Asia
62 B1 **Việt Tri** Vietnam
64 B2 **Vigan** Phil.
108 A1 **Vigevano** Italy
106 B1 **Vigo** Spain
Viipuri Rus. Fed. *see* **Vyborg**
73 C3 **Vijayawada** India
92 □B3 **Vík** Iceland
111 B2 **Vikhren** *mt.* Bulg.
128 C2 **Viking** Can.
92 F3 **Vikna** *i.* Norway
Vila Alferes Chamusca Moz. *see* **Guija**
Vila Arriaga Angola *see* **Bibala**
Vila Bugaço Angola *see* **Camanongue**
Vila Cabral Moz. *see* **Lichinga**
Vila da Ponte Angola *see* **Kuvango**
Vila de Aljustrel Angola *see* **Cangamba**
Vila de Almoster Angola *see* **Chiange**
Vila de João Belo Moz. *see* **Xai-Xai**

Vila de Trego Morais
Moz. *see* Chókwé
Vila Fontes Moz. *see* Caia
106 B2 Vila Franca de Xira Port.
106 B1 Vilagarcía de Arousa
Spain
123 D1 Vila Gomes da Costa
Moz.
106 B1 Vilalba Spain
Vila Luísa Moz. *see*
Marracuene
Vila Marechal Carmona
Angola *see* Uíge
Vila Miranda Moz. *see*
Macaloge
121 □D2 Vilanandro, Tanjona *pt*
Madag.
88 C2 Viļāni Latvia
106 B1 Vila Nova de Gaia Port.
107 D1 Vilanova i la Geltrú Spain
Vila Paiva de Andrada
Moz. *see* Gorongosa
Vila Pery Moz. *see*
Chimoio
106 B1 Vila Real Port.
106 B1 Vilar Formoso Port.
Vila Salazar Angola *see*
N'dalatando
Vila Salazar Zimbabwe
see Sango
Vila Teixeira de Sousa
Angola *see* Luau
155 D2 Vila Velha Brazil
150 B4 Vilcabamba, Cordillera
mts Peru
82 F1 Vil'cheka, Zemlya *i.*
Rus. Fed.
92 G3 Vilhelmina Sweden
150 C4 Vilhena Brazil
88 C2 Viljandi Estonia
123 C2 Viljoenskroon S. Africa
88 B3 Vilkaviškis Lith.
83 H1 Vil'kitskogo, Proliv *str.*
Rus. Fed.
144 B1 Villa Ahumada Mex.
106 B1 Villablino Spain
102 C2 Villach Austria
Villa Cisneros
Western Sahara *see*
Ad Dakhla
144 B2 Villa de Cos Mex.
152 B3 Villa Dolores Arg.
145 C3 Villa Flores Mex.
153 C3 Villa Gesell Arg.
145 C2 Villagrán Mex.
145 C3 Villahermosa Mex.
144 A2 Villa Insurgentes Mex.
107 C2 Villajoyosa - La Vila
Joiosa Spain
152 B3 Villa María Arg.
153 B3 Villa Mercedes Arg.
152 B2 Villa Montes Bol.
144 B2 Villanueva Mex.
106 B2 Villanueva de la Serena
Spain
106 C2 Villanueva de los
Infantes Spain
152 C2 Villa Ocampo Arg.
142 B3 Villa Ocampo Mex.
108 A3 Villaputzu *Sardinia* Italy
152 C2 Villarrica Para.
106 C2 Villarrobledo Spain
Villasalazar Zimbabwe *see*
Sango
152 B2 Villa Unión Arg.
144 B2 Villa Unión Mex.
144 B2 Villa Unión Mex.
150 B2 Villavicencio Col.
152 B2 Villazón Bol.
104 C3 Villefranche-de-
Rouergue France
105 C2 Villefranche-sur-Saône
France
107 C2 Villena Spain
100 A2 Villeneuve-d'Ascq France
104 C3 Villeneuve-sur-Lot France
140 B2 Ville Platte U.S.A.
100 A3 Villers-Cotterêts France
105 C2 Villeurbanne France
123 C2 Villiers S. Africa
102 B2 Villingen Ger.
137 E2 Villisca U.S.A.
88 C3 Vilnius Lith.
91 C2 Vil'nohirs'k Ukr.
91 D2 Vil'nyans'k Ukr.
100 B2 Vilvoorde Belgium
88 C3 Vilyeyka Belarus
83 J2 Vilyuy *r.* Rus. Fed.
93 G4 Vimmerby Sweden
153 A3 Viña del Mar Chile
107 D1 Vinaròs Spain

138 B3 Vincennes U.S.A.
55 J3 Vincennes Bay Antarctica
139 D3 Vineland U.S.A.
62 B2 Vinh Vietnam
63 B2 Vinh Long Vietnam
143 D1 Vinita U.S.A.
90 B2 Vinnytsya Ukr.
55 R2 Vinson Massif *mt.*
Antarctica
93 E3 Vinstra Norway
108 B1 Vipiteno Italy
64 B2 Virac Phil.
74 B2 Viramgam India
80 B2 Viranşehir Turkey
129 D3 Virden Can.
104 B2 Vire France
120 A2 Virei Angola
155 D1 Virgem da Lapa Brazil
142 A1 Virgin *r.* U.S.A.
123 C2 Virginia S. Africa
137 E1 Virginia U.S.A.
139 D3 Virginia *state* U.S.A.
139 D3 Virginia Beach U.S.A.
135 C3 Virginia City U.S.A.
147 D3 Virgin Islands (U.K.) *terr.*
West Indies
147 D3 Virgin Islands (U.S.A.)
terr. West Indies
63 B2 Viròchey Cambodia
109 C1 Virovitica Croatia
100 B3 Virton Belgium
88 B2 Virtsu Estonia
74 B2 Virudhunagar India
109 C2 Vis *i.* Croatia
88 C2 Visaginas Lith.
135 C3 Visalia U.S.A.
74 B2 Visavadar India
64 B2 Visayan Sea Phil.
93 G4 Visby Sweden
126 E2 Viscount Melville Sound
sea chan. Can.
151 E3 Viseu Brazil
106 B1 Viseu Port.
110 B1 Vişeu de Sus Romania
73 C3 Vishakhapatnam India
88 C2 Viški Latvia
109 C2 Visoko Bos.-Herz.
103 D1 Vistula *r.* Pol.
Vitebsk Belarus *see*
Vitsyebsk
108 B2 Viterbo Italy
49 I5 Viti Levu *i.* Fiji
83 I3 Vitim *r.* Rus. Fed.
155 D2 Vitória Brazil
151 E4 Vitória da Conquista
Brazil
106 C1 Vitoria-Gasteiz Spain
104 B2 Vitré France
105 C2 Vitry-le-François France
89 D2 Vitsyebsk Belarus
105 D2 Vittel France
108 B3 Vittoria *Sicily* Italy
108 B1 Vittorio Veneto Italy
106 B1 Viveiro Spain
136 C2 Vivian U.S.A.
Vizagapatam India *see*
Vishakhapatnam
142 A3 Vizcaíno, Desierto de
des. Mex.
144 A2 Vizcaíno, Sierra *mts* Mex.
111 C2 Vize Turkey
73 C3 Vizianagaram India
100 B2 Vlaardingen Neth.
87 D4 Vladikavkaz Rus. Fed.
89 F2 Vladimir Rus. Fed.
66 B2 Vladivostok Rus. Fed.
109 D2 Vlasotince Serb. and
Mont.
100 B1 Vlieland *i.* Neth.
100 A2 Vlissingen Neth.
109 C2 Vlorë Albania
102 C1 Vltava *r.* Czech Rep.
102 C2 Vöcklabruck Austria
109 C2 Vodice Croatia
Vogelkop Peninsula
Indon. *see* Doberai, Jazirah
101 D2 Vogelsberg *hills* Ger.
Vohémar Madag. *see*
Iharana
Vohibinany Madag. *see*
Ampasimanolotra
Vohimarina Madag. *see*
Iharana
121 □D3 Vohimena, Tanjona *c.*
Madag.
121 □D3 Vohipeno Madag.
119 D3 Voi Kenya
105 D2 Voiron France
131 D2 Voisey Bay Can.
109 C1 Vojvodina *prov.*
Serb. and Mont.

92 J3 Voknavolok Rus. Fed.
Volcano Bay Japan *see*
Uchiura-wan
69 F3 Volcano Islands *is* Japan
Volchansk Ukr. *see*
Vovchans'k
89 E2 Volga Rus. Fed.
89 F2 Volga *r.* Rus. Fed.
87 D4 Volgodonsk Rus. Fed.
87 D4 Volgograd Rus. Fed.
87 D4 Volgogradskoye
Vodokhranilishche *resr*
Rus. Fed.
89 D2 Volkhov Rus. Fed.
89 D1 Volkhov *r.* Rus. Fed.
101 E2 Volkstedt Ger.
91 D2 Volnovakha Ukr.
90 B2 Volochys'k Ukr.
91 D2 Volodars'ke Ukr.
Volodarskoye Kazakh. *see*
Saumalkol'
90 B1 Volodars'k-Volyns'kyy
Ukr.
90 B1 Volodymyrets' Ukr.
90 A1 Volodymyr-Volyns'kyy Ukr.
89 E2 Vologda Rus. Fed.
89 E2 Volokolamsk Rus. Fed.
91 D1 Volokonovka Rus. Fed.
111 B3 Volos Greece
88 C2 Volosovo Rus. Fed.
89 D2 Volot Rus. Fed.
89 E3 Volovo Rus. Fed.
87 D3 Vol'sk Rus. Fed.
114 C4 Volta *r.* Ghana
114 C4 Volta, Lake *resr* Ghana
155 D2 Volta Redonda Brazil
110 C2 Voluntari Romania
87 D4 Volzhskiy Rus. Fed.
92 □C2 Vopnafjörður Iceland
88 C3 Voranava Belarus
160 K3 Voring Plateau *sea feature*
N. Atlantic Ocean
87 E2 Vorkuta Rus. Fed.
88 B2 Vormsi *i.* Estonia
83 G2 Vorogovo Rus. Fed.
89 E3 Voronezh Rus. Fed.
89 E3 Voronezh *r.* Rus. Fed.
91 E1 Vorontsovka Rus. Fed.
Voroshilov Rus. Fed. *see*
Ussuriysk
Voroshilovgrad Ukr. *see*
Luhans'k
Voroshilovsk Rus. Fed. *see*
Stavropol'
Voroshilovsk Ukr. *see*
Alchevs'k
91 C2 Vorskla *r.* Rus. Fed.
88 C2 Võrtsjärv *l.* Estonia
88 C2 Võru Estonia
122 B3 Vosburg S. Africa
105 D2 Vosges *mts* France
89 E2 Voskresensk Rus. Fed.
93 E3 Voss Norway
86 C2 Vostochnaya Litsa
Rus. Fed.
Vostochno-Sibirskoye
More *sea* Rus. Fed. *see*
East Siberian Sea
83 H3 Vostochnyy Sayan *mts*
Rus. Fed.
66 C1 Vostok Rus. Fed.
49 L5 Vostok Island Kiribati
86 E3 Votkinsk Rus. Fed.
Votkinskoye
Vodokhranilishche *resr*
Rus. Fed.
154 C2 Votuporanga Brazil
105 C2 Vouziers France
91 D1 Vovchans'k Ukr.
92 J2 Voynitsa Rus. Fed.
86 E2 Voyvozh Rus. Fed.
92 C2 Voznesens'k Ukr.
76 B2 Vozrozhdenya Island *i.*
Uzbek.
84 B2 Vråjal Norway
90 C2 Vradiyivka Ukr.
66 B2 Vrangel' Rus. Fed.
83 N2 Vrangelya, Ostrov *i.*
Rus. Fed.
109 D2 Vranje Serb. and Mont.
110 C2 Vratnik *pass* Bulg.
110 B2 Vratsa Bulg.
109 C1 Vrbas *r.* Bos.-Herz.
109 C1 Vrbas Serb. and Mont.
122 A3 Vredenburg S. Africa
122 A3 Vredendal S. Africa
100 B3 Vresse Belgium
100 C1 Vriezenveen Neth.
109 D1 Vršac Serb. and Mont.
122 B2 Vryburg S. Africa
123 D2 Vryheid S. Africa

89 D1 Vsevolozhsk Rus. Fed.
109 D2 Vučitrn Serb. and Mont.
109 C1 Vukovar Croatia
86 E2 Vuktyl' Rus. Fed.
123 C2 Vukuzakhe S. Africa
90 B2 Vulcănești Moldova
109 B3 Vulcano, Isola *i.* Italy
Vulkaneshty Moldova *see*
Vulcănești
63 B2 Vung Tau Vietnam
92 H2 Vuollerim Sweden
92 I2 Vuotso Fin.
74 B2 Vyara India
Vyarkhowye Belarus *see*
Ruba
Vyatka Rus. Fed. *see* Kirov
89 D2 Vyaz'ma Rus. Fed.
88 C1 Vyborg Rus. Fed.
88 C1 Vyborgskiy Zaliv *b.*
Rus. Fed.
86 D2 Vychegda *r.* Rus. Fed.
88 C2 Vyerkhnyadzvinsk Belarus
89 D3 Vyetka Belarus
89 D3 Vygonichi Rus. Fed.
86 C2 Vygozero, Ozero *l.*
Rus. Fed.
87 D3 Vyksa Rus. Fed.
90 B2 Vylkove Ukr.
90 A2 Vynohradiv Ukr.
89 D2 Vypolzovo Rus. Fed.
89 D2 Vyritsa Rus. Fed.
91 D2 Vyselki Rus. Fed.
90 C1 Vyshhorod Ukr.
89 D2 Vyshnevolotskaya Gryada
ridge Rus. Fed.
89 D2 Vyshniy-Volochek
Rus. Fed.
103 D2 Vyškov Czech Rep.
89 E2 Vysokovsk Rus. Fed.
86 C2 Vytegra Rus. Fed.

W

114 B3 Wa Ghana
100 B2 Waal *r.* Neth.
100 B2 Waalwijk Neth.
119 D2 Waat Sudan
128 C2 Wabasca *r.* Can.
128 C2 Wabasca-Desmarais Can.
138 B3 Wabash *r.* U.S.A.
117 C4 Wabē Gestro *r.* Eth.
117 C4 Wabē Shebelē Wenz *r.*
Eth.
129 E2 Wabowden Can.
103 D1 Wąbrzeźno Pol.
141 D3 Waccasassa Bay U.S.A.
101 D2 Wächtersbach Ger.
143 D2 Waco U.S.A.
74 A2 Wad Pak.
115 D2 Waddān Libya
Waddeneilanden *is* Neth.
see West Frisian Islands
Wadden Islands Neth. *see*
West Frisian Islands
100 B1 Waddenzee *sea chan.*
Neth.
128 B2 Waddington, Mount Can.
100 B1 Waddinxveen Neth.
129 D2 Wadena Can.
137 D1 Wadena U.S.A.
50 B1 Wadeye Austr.
Wadhwan India *see*
Surendranagar
116 B3 Wadi Halfa Sudan
116 B3 Wad Medani Sudan
122 B3 Waenhuiskrans S. Africa
70 C2 Wafangdian China
100 B2 Wageningen Neth.
127 G2 Wager Bay Can.
53 C3 Wagga Wagga Austr.
137 D2 Wagner U.S.A.
74 B1 Wah Pak.
137 D2 Wahoo U.S.A.
137 D1 Wahpeton U.S.A.
54 B2 Waiau *r.* N.Z.
59 C3 Waigeo *i.* Indon.
61 C2 Waikabubak Indon.
54 C1 Waikaremoana, Lake N.Z.
52 A2 Waikerie Austr.
54 B2 Waimate N.Z.
75 B3 Wainganga *r.* India
61 D2 Waingapu Indon.
129 C2 Wainwright Can.
126 B2 Wainwright U.S.A.
54 C1 Waiouru N.Z.
54 B2 Waipara N.Z.
54 B2 Waipawa N.Z.
54 B2 Wairau *r.* N.Z.
54 C1 Wairoa N.Z.

54 B2 **Waitaki** *r.* N.Z.
54 B1 **Waitara** N.Z.
54 B1 **Waiuku** N.Z.
67 C3 **Wajima** Japan
119 E2 **Wajir** Kenya
67 C3 **Wakasa-wan** *b.* Japan
54 A3 **Wakatipu, Lake** N.Z.
129 D2 **Wakaw** Can.
67 C4 **Wakayama** Japan
136 D3 **WaKeeney** U.S.A.
54 B2 **Wakefield** N.Z.
98 C3 **Wakefield** U.K.
Wakeham Can. *see* **Kangiqsujuaq**
48 H2 **Wake Island** *terr.* N. Pacific Ocean
66 D1 **Wakkanai** Japan
123 D2 **Wakkerstroom** S. Africa
120 A2 **Waku-Kungo** Angola
103 D1 **Wałbrzych** Pol.
53 D2 **Walcha** Austr.
100 C1 **Walchum** Ger.
103 D1 **Wałcz** Pol.
99 B3 **Wales** *admin. div.* U.K.
53 C2 **Walgett** Austr.
119 C3 **Walikale** Dem. Rep. Congo
135 C3 **Walker Lake** U.S.A.
134 C1 **Wallace** *ID* U.S.A.
141 E2 **Wallace** *NC* U.S.A.
52 A2 **Wallaroo** Austr.
98 B3 **Wallasey** U.K.
134 C1 **Walla Walla** U.S.A.
101 D3 **Walldürn** Ger.
122 A3 **Wallekraal** S. Africa
53 C2 **Wallendbeen** Austr.
49 J5 **Wallis, Îles** *is* Wallis and Futuna Is
49 J5 **Wallis and Futuna Islands** *terr.* S. Pacific Ocean
96 □ **Walls** U.K.
98 B2 **Walney, Isle of** *i.* U.K.
99 C3 **Walsall** U.K.
136 C3 **Walsenburg** U.S.A.
101 D1 **Walsrode** Ger.
141 D2 **Walterboro** U.S.A.
120 A3 **Walvis Bay** Namibia
158 F6 **Walvis Ridge** *sea feature* S. Atlantic Ocean
119 C2 **Wamba** Dem. Rep. Congo
52 B1 **Wanaaring** Austr.
54 A2 **Wanaka** N.Z.
54 A2 **Wanaka, Lake** N.Z.
71 B3 **Wan'an** China
130 B3 **Wanapitei Lake** Can.
154 B3 **Wanda** Arg.
66 B1 **Wanda Shan** *mts* China
62 A1 **Wanding** China
Wandingzhen China *see* Wanding
54 C1 **Wanganui** N.Z.
54 B1 **Wanganui** *r.* N.Z.
53 C3 **Wangaratta** Austr.
65 B1 **Wangqing** China
62 A1 **Wan Hsa-la** Myanmar
Wankie Zimbabwe *see* Hwange
71 B4 **Wanning** China
100 B2 **Wanroij** Neth.
99 C4 **Wantage** U.K.
70 A2 **Wanxian** China
70 A2 **Wanyuan** China
117 A4 **Warab** Sudan
73 B3 **Warangal** India
101 D2 **Warburg** Ger.
50 B2 **Warburton** Austr.
52 A1 **Warburton** *watercourse* Austr.
74 B2 **Wardha** India
96 C1 **Ward Hill** U.K.
128 B2 **Ware** Can.
101 F1 **Waren** Ger.
101 C2 **Warendorf** Ger.
53 D1 **Warialda** Austr.
122 A2 **Warmbad** Namibia
135 C3 **Warm Springs** U.S.A.
134 C2 **Warner Lakes** U.S.A.
134 B2 **Warner Mountains** U.S.A.
141 D2 **Warner Robins** U.S.A.
152 B1 **Warnes** Bol.
52 B3 **Warracknabeal** Austr.
53 C3 **Warrandyte** Austr.
53 C2 **Warrego** *r.* Austr.
53 C2 **Warren** Austr.
140 B2 **Warren** *AR* U.S.A.
138 C2 **Warren** *OH* U.S.A.
139 D2 **Warren** *PA* U.S.A.
97 C1 **Warrenpoint** U.K.
137 E3 **Warrensburg** U.S.A.
122 B2 **Warrenton** S. Africa
115 C4 **Warri** Nigeria
98 B3 **Warrington** U.K.
52 B3 **Warrnambool** Austr.
103 E1 **Warsaw** Pol.
138 B2 **Warsaw** U.S.A.
Warszawa Pol. *see* **Warsaw**
103 C1 **Warta** *r.* Pol.
53 D1 **Warwick** Austr.
99 C3 **Warwick** U.K.
139 E2 **Warwick** U.S.A.
134 D3 **Wasatch Range** *mts* U.S.A.
135 C3 **Wasco** U.S.A.
136 C1 **Washburn** U.S.A.
139 D3 **Washington** *DC* U.S.A.
137 E2 **Washington** *IA* U.S.A.
138 B2 **Washington** *IL* U.S.A.
138 B3 **Washington** *IN* U.S.A.
137 E3 **Washington** *MO* U.S.A.
141 E1 **Washington** *NC* U.S.A.
138 C2 **Washington** *PA* U.S.A.
135 D3 **Washington** *UT* U.S.A.
134 B1 **Washington** *state* U.S.A.
139 E2 **Washington, Mount** U.S.A.
138 C3 **Washington Court House** U.S.A.
74 A2 **Washuk** Pak.
130 C2 **Waskaganish** Can.
129 E2 **Waskaiowaka Lake** Can.
122 A2 **Wasser** Namibia
101 D2 **Wasserkuppe** *hill* Ger.
130 C3 **Waswanipi, Lac** *l.* Can.
61 D2 **Watampone** Indon.
Watenstadt-Salzgitter Ger. *see* **Salzgitter**
139 E2 **Waterbury** U.S.A.
129 D2 **Waterbury Lake** Can.
97 C2 **Waterford** Rep. of Ireland
97 C2 **Waterford Harbour** Rep. of Ireland
100 B2 **Waterloo** Belgium
137 E2 **Waterloo** U.S.A.
99 C4 **Waterlooville** U.K.
123 C1 **Waterpoort** S. Africa
139 D2 **Watertown** *NY* U.S.A.
137 D2 **Watertown** *SD* U.S.A.
138 B2 **Watertown** *WI* U.S.A.
97 A3 **Waterville** Rep. of Ireland
139 F2 **Waterville** U.S.A.
99 C4 **Watford** U.K.
136 C1 **Watford City** U.S.A.
129 D2 **Wathaman** *r.* Can.
Watling Island Bahamas *see* **San Salvador**
143 D1 **Watonga** U.S.A.
129 D2 **Watrous** Can.
119 C2 **Watsa** Dem. Rep. Congo
138 B2 **Watseka** U.S.A.
118 C3 **Watsi Kengo** Dem. Rep. Congo
128 B1 **Watson Lake** Can.
135 B3 **Watsonville** U.S.A.
59 C3 **Watubela, Kepulauan** *is* Indon.
59 D3 **Wau** P.N.G.
117 A4 **Wau** Sudan
53 D2 **Wauchope** Austr.
138 B2 **Waukegan** U.S.A.
138 B2 **Waukesha** U.S.A.
143 D2 **Waurika** U.S.A.
138 B2 **Wausau** U.S.A.
99 D3 **Waveney** *r.* U.K.
137 E2 **Waverly** U.S.A.
130 B3 **Wawa** Can.
141 D2 **Waycross** U.S.A.
137 D2 **Wayne** U.S.A.
141 D2 **Waynesboro** *GA* U.S.A.
139 D3 **Waynesboro** *VA* U.S.A.
137 E3 **Waynesville** *MO* U.S.A.
141 D1 **Waynesville** *NC* U.S.A.
74 B1 **Wazirabad** Pak.
60 A1 **We, Pulau** *i.* Indon.
98 C2 **Wear** *r.* U.K.
143 D1 **Weatherford** *OK* U.S.A.
143 D2 **Weatherford** *TX* U.S.A.
134 B2 **Weaverville** U.S.A.
143 D3 **Webb** U.S.A.
130 B2 **Webequie** Can.
117 C4 **Webi Shabeelle** *r.* Somalia
137 D1 **Webster** U.S.A.
137 E2 **Webster City** U.S.A.
55 C3 **Weddell Abyssal Plain** *sea feature* Southern Ocean
55 B3 **Weddell Sea** Antarctica
123 D2 **Weenen** S. Africa
100 B2 **Weert** Neth.
53 C2 **Weethalle** Austr.
53 C2 **Wee Waa** Austr.
100 C2 **Wegberg** Ger.
103 E1 **Węgorzewo** Pol.
103 E1 **Węgrów** Pol.
70 B1 **Weichang** China
101 F3 **Weiden in der Oberpfalz** Ger.
Weidongmen China *see* **Qianjin**
70 B2 **Weifang** China
70 C2 **Weihai** China
70 B2 **Wei He** *r.* China
53 C1 **Weilmoringle** Austr.
101 E2 **Weimar** Ger.
143 D3 **Weimar** U.S.A.
70 A2 **Weinan** China
71 A3 **Weining** China
51 D1 **Weipa** Austr.
53 C1 **Weir** *r.* Austr.
138 C2 **Weirton** U.S.A.
62 B1 **Weishan** China
101 E2 **Weiße Elster** *r.* Ger.
101 E2 **Weißenfels** Ger.
102 C2 **Weißkugel** *mt.* Austria/Italy
71 A3 **Weixin** China
Weizhou China *see* Wenchuan
103 D1 **Wejherowo** Pol.
128 C1 **Wekwetì** Can.
138 C3 **Welch** U.S.A.
117 B3 **Weldiya** Eth.
123 C2 **Welkom** S. Africa
99 C3 **Welland** *r.* U.K.
51 C1 **Wellesley Islands** Austr.
99 C3 **Wellingborough** U.K.
53 C2 **Wellington** Austr.
54 B2 **Wellington** N.Z.
122 A3 **Wellington** S. Africa
136 B2 **Wellington** *CO* U.S.A.
137 D3 **Wellington** *KS* U.S.A.
135 D3 **Wellington** *UT* U.S.A.
153 A4 **Wellington, Isla** *i.* Chile
53 C3 **Wellington, Lake** Austr.
128 B2 **Wells** Can.
99 B4 **Wells** U.K.
134 D2 **Wells** U.S.A.
50 B2 **Wells, Lake** *salt flat* Austr.
54 B1 **Wellsford** N.Z.
99 D3 **Wells-next-the-Sea** U.K.
142 A2 **Wellton** U.S.A.
102 C2 **Wels** Austria
99 B3 **Welshpool** U.K.
Welwitschia Namibia *see* **Khorixas**
123 C2 **Wembesi** S. Africa
130 C2 **Wemindji** Can.
134 B1 **Wenatchee** U.S.A.
71 B4 **Wenchang** China
114 B4 **Wenchi** Ghana
Wenchow China *see* Wenzhou
70 A2 **Wenchuan** China
70 C2 **Wendeng** China
101 E1 **Wendisch Evern** Ger.
117 B4 **Wendo** Eth.
135 D2 **Wendover** U.S.A.
71 B3 **Wengyuan** China
Wenhua China *see* Weishan
Wenlan China *see* **Mengzi**
Wenlin China *see* **Renshou**
71 C3 **Wenling** China
Wenquan China *see* Yingshan
71 A3 **Wenshan** China
52 B2 **Wentworth** Austr.
71 C3 **Wenzhou** China
123 C2 **Wepener** S. Africa
122 B2 **Werda** Botswana
101 F2 **Werdau** Ger.
101 F1 **Werder** Ger.
101 F3 **Wernberg-Köblitz** Ger.
101 E2 **Wernigerode** Ger.
101 D2 **Werra** *r.* Ger.
52 B2 **Werrimull** Austr.
53 D2 **Werris Creek** Austr.
101 D3 **Wertheim** Ger.
100 C2 **Wesel** Ger.
101 E1 **Wesendorf** Ger.
101 D1 **Weser** *r.* Ger.
101 D1 **Weser** *sea chan.* Ger.
51 C1 **Wessel, Cape** Austr.
51 C1 **Wessel Islands** Austr.
123 C2 **Wesselton** S. Africa
55 P2 **West Antarctica** *reg.* Antarctica
156 B7 **West Australian Basin** *sea feature* Indian Ocean
80 B2 **West Bank** *terr.* Asia
138 B2 **West Bend** U.S.A.
75 C2 **West Bengal** *state* India
99 C3 **West Bromwich** U.K.
139 E2 **Westbrook** U.S.A.
137 E2 **West Des Moines** U.S.A.
100 C2 **Westerburg** Ger.
100 C1 **Westerholt** Ger.
139 E2 **Westerly** U.S.A.
50 B2 **Western Australia** *state* Austr.
122 B3 **Western Cape** *prov.* S. Africa
116 A2 **Western Desert** Egypt
Western Dvina *r.* Europe *see* **Zapadnaya Dvina**
73 B3 **Western Ghats** *mts* India
114 A2 **Western Sahara** *terr.* Africa
Western Samoa *country* S. Pacific Ocean *see* Samoa
Western Sayan Mountains *reg.* Rus. Fed. *see* **Zapadnyy Sayan**
100 A2 **Westerschelde** *est.* Neth.
100 C1 **Westerstede** Ger.
101 C2 **Westerwald** *hills* Ger.
153 B5 **West Falkland** *i.* Falkland Is
138 B3 **West Frankfort** U.S.A.
100 B1 **West Frisian Islands** Neth.
96 C2 **Westhill** U.K.
55 I3 **West Ice Shelf** Antarctica
147 D2 **West Indies** *is* Caribbean Sea
100 A2 **Westkapelle** Neth.
96 A1 **West Loch Roag** *b.* U.K.
128 C2 **Westlock** Can.
100 B2 **Westmalle** Belgium
Westman Islands Iceland *see* **Vestmannaeyjar**
53 C1 **Westmar** Austr.
156 C4 **West Mariana Basin** *sea feature* N. Pacific Ocean
140 B1 **West Memphis** U.S.A.
138 C3 **Weston** U.S.A.
99 B4 **Weston-super-Mare** U.K.
141 D3 **West Palm Beach** U.S.A.
137 E3 **West Plains** U.S.A.
137 D2 **West Point** U.S.A.
54 B2 **Westport** N.Z.
97 B2 **Westport** Rep. of Ireland
129 D2 **Westray** Can.
96 C1 **Westray** *i.* U.K.
82 G2 **West Siberian Plain** *plain* Rus. Fed.
100 B1 **West-Terschelling** Neth.
136 A2 **West Thumb** U.S.A.
97 B1 **West Town** Rep. of Ireland
135 D2 **West Valley City** U.S.A.
138 C3 **West Virginia** *state* U.S.A.
53 C2 **West Wyalong** Austr.
134 D2 **West Yellowstone** U.S.A.
59 C3 **Wetar** *i.* Indon.
128 C2 **Wetaskiwin** Can.
119 D3 **Wete** Tanz.
101 D2 **Wetzlar** Ger.
59 D3 **Wewak** P.N.G.
97 C2 **Wexford** Rep. of Ireland
97 C2 **Wexford Harbour** *b.* Rep. of Ireland
129 D2 **Weyakwin** Can.
129 D3 **Weyburn** Can.
101 D1 **Weyhe** Ger.
99 B4 **Weymouth** U.K.
54 C1 **Whakatane** N.Z.
129 E1 **Whale Cove** Can.
96 □ **Whalsay** *i.* U.K.
54 B1 **Whangamomona** N.Z.
54 B1 **Whangaparaoa** N.Z.
54 B1 **Whangarei** N.Z.
98 C3 **Wharfe** *r.* U.K.
143 D3 **Wharton** U.S.A.
128 C1 **Wha Ti** Can.
136 B2 **Wheatland** U.S.A.
138 B2 **Wheaton** U.S.A.
140 C2 **Wheeler Lake** *resr* U.S.A.
142 B1 **Wheeler Peak** *NM* U.S.A.
135 D3 **Wheeler Peak** *NV* U.S.A.
138 C2 **Wheeling** U.S.A.
98 B2 **Whernside** *hill* U.K.
128 B2 **Whistler** Can.
98 C2 **Whitby** U.K.
128 A1 **White** *r.* Can./U.S.A.
140 B2 **White** *r. AR* U.S.A.
138 B3 **White** *r. IN* U.S.A.
50 B2 **White, Lake** *salt flat* Austr.
131 E3 **White Bay** Can.
136 C1 **White Butte** *mt.* U.S.A.
52 B2 **White Cliffs** Austr.
128 C2 **Whitecourt** Can.
134 D1 **Whitefish** U.S.A.
98 B2 **Whitehaven** U.K.

97 D1 **Whitehead** U.K.
128 A1 **Whitehorse** Can.
140 B3 **White Lake** U.S.A.
51 D4 **Whitemark** Austr.
135 C3 **White Mountain Peak** U.S.A.
116 B3 **White Nile** *r.* Sudan/Uganda
White Russia *country* Europe *see* **Belarus**
86 C2 **White Sea** Rus. Fed.
134 D1 **White Sulphur Springs** U.S.A.
141 E2 **Whiteville** U.S.A.
114 B3 **White Volta** *watercourse* Burkina/Ghana
136 B3 **Whitewater** U.S.A.
142 B2 **Whitewater Baldy** *mt.* U.S.A.
130 B2 **Whitewater Lake** Can.
129 D2 **Whitewood** Can.
96 B3 **Whithorn** U.K.
54 C1 **Whitianga** N.Z.
135 C3 **Whitney, Mount** U.S.A.
99 D4 **Whitstable** U.K.
51 D2 **Whitsunday Island** Austr.
53 C3 **Whittlesea** Austr.
52 A2 **Whyalla** Austr.
62 A2 **Wiang Pa Pao** Thai.
100 A2 **Wichelen** Belgium
137 D3 **Wichita** U.S.A.
143 D2 **Wichita Falls** U.S.A.
143 D2 **Wichita Mountains** U.S.A.
96 C1 **Wick** U.K.
142 A2 **Wickenburg** U.S.A.
97 C2 **Wicklow** Rep. of Ireland
97 D2 **Wicklow Head** *hd* Rep. of Ireland
97 C2 **Wicklow Mountains** Rep. of Ireland
98 B3 **Widnes** U.K.
101 D1 **Wiehengebirge** *hills* Ger.
100 C2 **Wiehl** Ger.
103 D1 **Wieluń** Pol.
Wien Austria *see* **Vienna**
103 D2 **Wiener Neustadt** Austria
100 B1 **Wieringerwerf** Neth.
101 D2 **Wiesbaden** Ger.
100 C1 **Wiesmoor** Ger.
103 D1 **Wieżyca** *hill* Pol.
98 B3 **Wigan** U.K.
99 C3 **Wight, Isle of** *i.* U.K.
96 B3 **Wigtown** U.K.
100 B2 **Wijchen** Neth.
130 B3 **Wikwemikong** Can.
52 B2 **Wilcannia** Austr.
Wilczek Land *i.* Rus. Fed. *see* **Vil'cheka, Zemlya**
123 C3 **Wild Coast** S. Africa
101 D1 **Wildeshausen** Ger.
136 C2 **Wild Horse Hill** *mt.* U.S.A.
123 C2 **Wilge** *r.* S. Africa
48 F4 **Wilhelm, Mount** P.N.G.
101 D1 **Wilhelmshaven** Ger.
139 D2 **Wilkes-Barre** U.S.A.
55 K3 **Wilkes Land** *reg.* Antarctica
129 D2 **Wilkie** Can.
134 B1 **Willamette** *r.* U.S.A.
134 B1 **Willapa Bay** U.S.A.
142 B2 **Willcox** U.S.A.
100 B2 **Willebroek** Belgium
147 D3 **Willemstad** Neth. Antilles
52 B3 **William, Mount** Austr.
52 A1 **William Creek** Austr.
142 A1 **Williams** U.S.A.
138 C3 **Williamsburg** *KY* U.S.A.
139 D3 **Williamsburg** *VA* U.S.A.
128 B2 **Williams Lake** Can.
138 C3 **Williamson** U.S.A.
139 D2 **Williamsport** U.S.A.
141 E1 **Williamston** U.S.A.
122 B3 **Williston** S. Africa
136 C1 **Williston** U.S.A.
128 B2 **Williston Lake** Can.
135 B3 **Willits** U.S.A.
137 D1 **Willmar** U.S.A.
122 B3 **Willowmore** S. Africa
135 B3 **Willows** U.S.A.
123 C3 **Willowvale** S. Africa
50 B2 **Wills, Lake** *salt flat* Austr.
52 A3 **Willunga** Austr.
52 A2 **Wilmington** Austr.
139 D3 **Wilmington** *DE* U.S.A.
141 E2 **Wilmington** *NC* U.S.A.
138 C3 **Wilmington** *OH* U.S.A.
141 D2 **Wilmington Island** U.S.A.
Wilno Lith. *see* **Vilnius**
101 D2 **Wilnsdorf** Ger.
101 D1 **Wilseder Berg** *hill* Ger.
141 E1 **Wilson** U.S.A.
53 C3 **Wilson's Promontory** *pen.* Austr.
100 B3 **Wiltz** Lux.
50 B2 **Wiluna** Austr.
99 D4 **Wimereux** France
123 C2 **Winburg** S. Africa
99 B4 **Wincanton** U.K.
99 C4 **Winchester** U.K.
138 C3 **Winchester** *KY* U.S.A.
139 D3 **Winchester** *VA* U.S.A.
98 B2 **Windermere** *l.* U.K.
122 A1 **Windhoek** Namibia
137 D2 **Windom** U.S.A.
51 D2 **Windorah** Austr.
136 B2 **Wind River Range** *mts* U.S.A.
53 D2 **Windsor** Austr.
130 B3 **Windsor** Can.
147 D3 **Windward Islands** Caribbean Sea
147 C3 **Windward Passage** Cuba/Haiti
137 D3 **Winfield** U.S.A.
100 A2 **Wingene** Belgium
53 D2 **Wingham** Austr.
130 B2 **Winisk** Can.
130 B2 **Winisk** *r.* Can.
130 B2 **Winisk Lake** Can.
63 A2 **Winkana** Myanmar
129 E3 **Winkler** Can.
114 B4 **Winneba** Ghana
138 B2 **Winnebago, Lake** U.S.A.
134 C2 **Winnemucca** U.S.A.
136 C2 **Winner** U.S.A.
140 B2 **Winnfield** U.S.A.
137 E1 **Winnibigoshish, Lake** U.S.A.
129 E3 **Winnipeg** Can.
129 E2 **Winnipeg** *r.* Can.
129 E2 **Winnipeg, Lake** Can.
129 D2 **Winnipegosis, Lake** Can.
139 E2 **Winnipesaukee, Lake** U.S.A.
140 B2 **Winnsboro** U.S.A.
137 E2 **Winona** *MN* U.S.A.
140 C2 **Winona** *MS* U.S.A.
100 C1 **Winschoten** Neth.
101 D1 **Winsen (Aller)** Ger.
101 E1 **Winsen (Luhe)** Ger.
142 A1 **Winslow** U.S.A.
141 D1 **Winston-Salem** U.S.A.
101 D2 **Winterberg** Ger.
141 D3 **Winter Haven** U.S.A.
100 C2 **Winterswijk** Neth.
105 D2 **Winterthur** Switz.
51 D2 **Winton** Austr.
54 A3 **Winton** N.Z.
52 A2 **Wirrabara** Austr.
52 A2 **Wirraminna** Austr.
99 D3 **Wisbech** U.K.
138 A2 **Wisconsin** *r.* U.S.A.
138 B2 **Wisconsin** *state* U.S.A.
138 B2 **Wisconsin Rapids** U.S.A.
Wisła *r.* Pol. *see* **Vistula**
101 E1 **Wismar** Ger.
123 C2 **Witbank** S. Africa
122 A2 **Witbooisvlei** Namibia
98 D3 **Witham** *r.* U.K.
98 D3 **Withernsea** U.K.
100 B1 **Witmarsum** Neth.
99 C4 **Witney** U.K.
123 D2 **Witrivier** S. Africa
123 C3 **Witteberg** *mts* S. Africa
101 E1 **Wittenberge** Ger.
101 E1 **Wittenburg** Ger.
50 A2 **Wittenoom** Austr.
101 E1 **Wittingen** Ger.
100 C3 **Wittlich** Ger.
100 C1 **Wittmund** Ger.
101 F1 **Wittstock** Ger.
122 A1 **Witvlei** Namibia
101 D2 **Witzenhausen** Ger.
103 D1 **Władysławowo** Pol.
103 D1 **Włocławek** Pol.
53 C3 **Wodonga** Austr.
59 C3 **Wokam** *i.* Indon.
62 A1 **Wokha** India
99 C4 **Woking** U.K.
101 F2 **Wolfen** Ger.
101 E1 **Wolfenbüttel** Ger.
101 D2 **Wolfhagen** Ger.
136 B1 **Wolf Point** U.S.A.
101 E1 **Wolfsburg** Ger.
100 C3 **Wolfstein** Ger.
131 D3 **Wolfville** Can.
102 C1 **Wolgast** Ger.
102 C1 **Wolin** Pol.
129 D2 **Wollaston Lake** Can.
129 D2 **Wollaston Lake** *l.* Can.
126 E2 **Wollaston Peninsula** Can.
53 D2 **Wollongong** Austr.
101 E2 **Wolmirsleben** Ger.
101 E1 **Wolmirstedt** Ger.
100 C1 **Wolvega** Neth.
99 B3 **Wolverhampton** U.K.
65 B2 **Wŏnju** S. Korea
128 B2 **Wonowon** Can.
65 B2 **Wŏnsan** N. Korea
53 C3 **Wonthaggi** Austr.
52 A2 **Woocalla** Austr.
51 C1 **Woodah, Isle** *i.* Austr.
99 D3 **Woodbridge** U.K.
134 B1 **Woodburn** U.S.A.
136 B3 **Woodland Park** U.S.A.
138 A3 **Wood River** U.S.A.
50 C2 **Woodroffe, Mount** Austr.
51 C1 **Woods, Lake** *salt flat* Austr.
129 E3 **Woods, Lake of the** Can./U.S.A.
53 C3 **Woods Point** Austr.
131 D3 **Woodstock** *N.B.* Can.
138 C2 **Woodstock** *Ont.* Can.
54 C2 **Woodville** N.Z.
143 D1 **Woodward** U.S.A.
98 B2 **Wooler** U.K.
53 D2 **Woolgoolga** Austr.
52 A2 **Woomera** Austr.
138 C2 **Wooster** U.S.A.
122 A3 **Worcester** S. Africa
99 B3 **Worcester** U.K.
139 E2 **Worcester** U.S.A.
102 C2 **Wörgl** Austria
98 B2 **Workington** U.K.
98 C3 **Worksop** U.K.
136 B2 **Worland** U.S.A.
101 D3 **Worms** Ger.
99 A4 **Worms Head** *hd* U.K.
122 A1 **Wortel** Namibia
99 C4 **Worthing** U.K.
137 D2 **Worthington** U.S.A.
61 D2 **Wotu** Indon.
61 D2 **Wowoni** *i.* Indon.
Wrangel Island *see* Vrangelya, Ostrov
128 A2 **Wrangell** U.S.A.
96 B1 **Wrath, Cape** U.K.
136 C2 **Wray** U.S.A.
122 A2 **Wreck Point** S. Africa
Wrecsam U.K. *see* Wrexham
99 B3 **Wrexham** U.K.
136 B2 **Wright** U.S.A.
63 A2 **Wrightmyo** India
142 A2 **Wrightson, Mount** U.S.A.
128 B1 **Wrigley** Can.
103 D1 **Wrocław** Pol.
103 D1 **Września** Pol.
70 B2 **Wu'an** China
Wuchow China *see* Wuzhou
70 A2 **Wudu** China
70 A2 **Wuhai** China
70 B2 **Wuhan** China
70 B2 **Wuhu** China
71 A3 **Wu Jiang** *r.* China
Wujin China *see* Changzhou
115 C4 **Wukari** Nigeria
75 D1 **Wuli** China
62 B1 **Wuliang Shan** *mts* China
59 C3 **Wuliaru** *i.* Indon.
118 B2 **Wum** Cameroon
71 A3 **Wumeng Shan** *mts* China
101 D1 **Wümme** *r.* Ger.
130 B2 **Wunnummin Lake** Can.
101 F2 **Wunsiedel** Ger.
101 D1 **Wunstorf** Ger.
62 A1 **Wuntho** Myanmar
100 C2 **Wuppertal** Ger.
122 A3 **Wuppertal** S. Africa
101 E2 **Wurzbach** Ger.
101 D3 **Würzburg** Ger.
101 F2 **Wurzen** Ger.
101 D2 **Wüstegarten** *hill* Ger.
59 D3 **Wuvulu Island** P.N.G.
70 A2 **Wuwei** China
70 A2 **Wuxi** *Chongqing* China
70 C2 **Wuxi** *Jiangsu* China
Wuxing China *see* Huzhou
71 A3 **Wuxuan** China
Wuyang China *see* Zhenyuan
69 E1 **Wuyiling** China
71 B3 **Wuyishan** China
71 B3 **Wuyi Shan** *mts* China
70 A1 **Wuyuan** China
71 A4 **Wuzhishan** China
70 A2 **Wuzhong** China
71 B3 **Wuzhou** China
51 D2 **Wyandra** Austr.
53 C2 **Wyangala Reservoir** Austr.
52 B3 **Wycheproof** Austr.
99 B4 **Wye** *r.* U.K.
50 B1 **Wyndham** Austr.
52 B3 **Wyndham-Werribee** Austr.
140 B1 **Wynne** U.S.A.
129 D2 **Wynyard** Can.
138 B2 **Wyoming** U.S.A.
136 B2 **Wyoming** *state* U.S.A.
53 D2 **Wyong** Austr.
103 E1 **Wyszków** Pol.
138 C3 **Wytheville** U.S.A.

X

117 D3 **Xaafuun** Somalia
62 B2 **Xaignabouli** Laos
121 C3 **Xai-Xai** Moz.
70 A1 **Xamba** China
62 B1 **Xam Nua** Laos
120 A1 **Xá-Muteba** Angola
120 A2 **Xangongo** Angola
81 C2 **Xankändi** Azer.
111 B2 **Xanthi** Greece
154 B3 **Xanxerê** Brazil
150 C4 **Xapuri** Brazil
107 C2 **Xátiva** Spain
120 B3 **Xhumo** Botswana
Xiaguan China *see* **Dali**
71 B3 **Xiamen** China
70 A2 **Xi'an** China
70 A3 **Xianfeng** China
62 A1 **Xiangcheng** China
70 B2 **Xiangfan** China
62 A1 **Xianggelila** China
Xianghuang Qi China *see* Xin Bulag
Xiangjiang China *see* Huichang
71 B3 **Xiang Jiang** *r.* China
62 B2 **Xiangkhoang** Laos
71 B3 **Xiangtan** China
Xiangyang China *see* Xiangfan
71 B3 **Xiangyin** China
70 B3 **Xianning** China
70 B2 **Xiantao** China
70 A2 **Xianyang** China
70 B2 **Xiaogan** China
69 E1 **Xiao Hinggan Ling** *mts* China
70 C2 **Xiaoshan** China
70 B2 **Xiaowutai Shan** *mt.* China
Xiayingpan China *see* Luzhi
Xibu China *see* **Dongshan**
71 A3 **Xichang** China
145 C2 **Xicohténcatl** Mex.
70 A2 **Xifeng** *Gansu* China
71 A3 **Xifeng** *Guizhou* China
Xifengzhen China *see* Xifeng
75 C2 **Xigazê** China
71 A3 **Xilin** China
69 D2 **Xilinhot** China
68 C2 **Ximiao** China
70 B3 **Xin'anjiang Shuiku** *resr* China
70 B1 **Xin Bulag** China
70 B2 **Xincai** China
Xincun China *see* Dongchuan
Xindi China *see* **Honghu**
71 B3 **Xing'an** China
62 A1 **Xingba** China
68 C2 **Xinghai** China
70 B2 **Xinghua** China
71 B3 **Xingning** China
70 A2 **Xingping** China
70 B2 **Xingtai** China
151 D3 **Xingu** *r.* Brazil
151 D3 **Xinguara** Brazil
71 A3 **Xingyi** China
71 B3 **Xinhua** China
70 A2 **Xining** China
75 C1 **Xinjiang** *aut. reg.* China
Xinjing China *see* **Jingxi**
65 A1 **Xinmin** China
71 B3 **Xinning** China
71 A3 **Xinping** China
Xinshiba China *see* **Ganluo**
70 B2 **Xintai** China
Xinxian China *see* **Xinzhou**
70 B2 **Xinxiang** China
70 B2 **Xinyang** China
71 A4 **Xinying** China
71 B3 **Xinyu** China
77 E2 **Xinyuan** China

69 D2 Xinzhou *Shanxi* China
70 B2 Xinzhou *Shanxi* China
106 B1 Xinzo de Limia Spain
Xiongshan China *see* Zhenghe
Xiongzhou China *see* Nanxiong
70 A2 Xiqing Shan *mts* China
151 E4 Xique Xique Brazil
70 A1 Xishanzui China
71 A3 Xiushan China
Xiushan China *see* Tonghai
71 B3 Xiushui China
71 B3 Xiuying China
70 B2 Xixia China
76 B2 Xo'jayli Uzbek.
63 B2 Xom Dưc Hanh Vietnam
70 B2 Xuancheng China
70 B1 Xuanhua China
71 A3 Xuanwei China
Xuanzhou China *see* Xuancheng
70 B2 Xuchang China
Xucheng China *see* Xuwen
117 C4 Xuddur Somalia
Xuefeng China *see* Mingxi
Xujiang China *see* Guangchang
71 B3 Xun Jiang *r.* China
71 B3 Xunwu China
71 B3 Xuwen China
71 A3 Xuyong China
Xuzhou China *see* Tongshan
111 B3 Xylokastro Greece
70 A2 Ya'an China

Y

117 B4 Yabēlo Eth.
69 D1 Yablonovyy Khrebet *mts* Rus. Fed.
141 D1 Yadkin *r.* U.S.A.
75 C2 Yadong China
70 A1 Yagan China
55 A4 Yaghan Basin *sea feature* S. Atlantic Ocean
89 E2 Yagnitsa Rus. Fed.
83 K2 Yagodnoye Rus. Fed.
118 B1 Yagoua Cameroon
128 C3 Yahk Can.
91 C1 Yahotyn Ukr.
144 B2 Yahualica Mex.
80 B2 Yahyalı Turkey
67 C4 Yaizu Japan
134 B1 Yakima U.S.A.
134 C1 Yakima *r.* U.S.A.
74 A2 Yakmach Pak.
114 B3 Yako Burkina
66 D2 Yakumo Japan
67 B4 Yaku-shima *i.* Japan
126 C3 Yakutat U.S.A.
128 A2 Yakutat Bay U.S.A.
83 J2 Yakutsk Rus. Fed.
91 D2 Yakymivka Ukr.
63 B3 Yala Thai.
118 C2 Yalinga C.A.R.
53 C3 Yallourn Austr.
111 C2 Yalova Turkey
90 B2 Yalpuh, Ozero *l.* Ukr.
91 C3 Yalta Ukr.
65 A1 Yalu Jiang *r.* China/N. Korea
86 F3 Yalutorovsk Rus. Fed.
67 D3 Yamagata Japan
67 B4 Yamaguchi Japan
Yamal, Poluostrov Rus. Fed. *see* Yamal Peninsula
86 F1 Yamal Peninsula *pen.* Rus. Fed.
Yamankhalinka Kazakh. *see* Makhambet
53 D1 Yamba Austr.
150 B2 Yambi, Mesa de *hills* Col.
117 A4 Yambio Sudan
110 C2 Yambol Bulg.
86 G2 Yamburg Rus. Fed.
62 A1 Yamethin Myanmar
88 C2 Yamm Rus. Fed.
51 D2 Yamma Yamma, Lake *salt flat* Austr.
114 B4 Yamoussoukro Côte d'Ivoire
91 C1 Yampil' Ukr.
90 B2 Yampil' Ukr.
75 C2 Yamuna *r.* India
62 A1 Yamzho Yumco *l.* China
83 K2 Yana *r.* Rus. Fed.
70 A2 Yan'an China
150 B4 Yanaoca Peru
78 A2 Yanbu' al Baḩr Saudi Arabia
70 C2 Yancheng China
50 A3 Yanchep Austr.
114 B3 Yanfolila Mali
118 C2 Yangambi Dem. Rep. Congo
70 B2 Yangcheng China
71 B3 Yangchun China
65 B2 Yangdok N. Korea
71 B3 Yangjiang China
Yangôn Myanmar *see* Rangoon
70 B2 Yangquan China
71 B3 Yangshuo China
62 B1 Yangtouyan China
70 C23 Yangtze *r.* China
70 C2 Yangtze, Mouth of the China
Yangtze Kiang *r.* China *see* Yangtze
70 A2 Yangxian China
70 B2 Yangzhou China
65 B1 Yanji China
137 D2 Yankton U.S.A.
83 K2 Yano-Indigirskaya Nizmennost' *lowland* Rus. Fed.
70 B1 Yanqing China
71 A3 Yanshan China
83 K2 Yanskiy Zaliv *g.* Rus. Fed.
53 C1 Yantabulla Austr.
70 C2 Yantai China
118 B2 Yaoundé Cameroon
59 D2 Yap *i.* Micronesia
59 D3 Yapen *i.* Indon.
59 D3 Yapen, Selat *sea chan.* Indon.
144 A2 Yaqui *r.* Mex.
51 D2 Yaraka Austr.
86 D3 Yaransk Rus. Fed.
48 H4 Yaren Nauru
78 B3 Yarīm Yemen
Yarkand China *see* Shache
Yarkant China *see* Shache
77 D3 Yarkant He *r.* China
Yarlung Zangbo *r.* China *see* Brahmaputra
131 D3 Yarmouth Can.
142 A2 Yarnell U.S.A.
86 F2 Yarongo Rus. Fed.
89 E2 Yaroslavl' Rus. Fed.
66 B2 Yaroslavskiy Rus. Fed.
53 C3 Yarra Junction Austr.
53 C3 Yarram Austr.
89 D2 Yartsevo Rus. Fed.
89 E3 Yasnogorsk Rus. Fed.
63 B2 Yasothon Thai.
53 C2 Yass Austr.
81 D2 Yāsūj Iran
111 C3 Yatağan Turkey
119 D3 Yata Plateau Kenya
129 E1 Yathkyed Lake Can.
67 B4 Yatsushiro Japan
150 C3 Yavari *r.* Brazil/Peru
73 B2 Yavatmal India
90 A2 Yavoriv Ukr.
67 B4 Yawatahama Japan
62 A1 Yawng-hwe Myanmar
Yaxian China *see* Sanya
81 D2 Yazd Iran
140 B2 Yazoo *r.* U.S.A.
140 B2 Yazoo City U.S.A.
111 B3 Ydra Greece
111 B3 Ydra *i.* Greece
63 A2 Ye Myanmar
77 D3 Yecheng China
107 C2 Yecla Spain
144 B2 Yécora Mex.
Yedintsy Moldova *see* Edineţ
89 E3 Yefremov Rus. Fed.
91 E2 Yegorlykskaya Rus. Fed.
89 E2 Yegor'yevsk Rus. Fed.
117 B4 Yei Sudan
86 F3 Yekaterinburg Rus. Fed.
Yekaterinodar Rus. Fed. *see* Krasnodar
Yekaterinoslav Ukr. *see* Dnipropetrovs'k
Yekaterinovskaya Rus. Fed. *see* Krylovskaya
Yelenovskiye Kar'yery Ukr. *see* Dokuchayevs'k
89 E3 Yelets Rus. Fed.
89 D2 Yeligovo Rus. Fed.
114 A3 Yélimané Mali
Yelizavetgrad Ukr. *see* Kirovohrad
96 □ Yell *i.* U.K.
128 C1 Yellowknife Can.
53 C2 Yellow Mountain *hill* Austr.
70 B2 Yellow River *r.* China
69 E2 Yellow Sea N. Pacific Ocean
136 C1 Yellowstone *r.* U.S.A.
136 A2 Yellowstone Lake U.S.A.
88 C3 Yel'sk Belarus
78 B3 Yemen *country* Asia
90 B1 Yemil'chyne Ukr.
86 E2 Yemva Rus. Fed.
91 D2 Yenakiyeve Ukr.
62 A1 Yenangyaung Myanmar
62 B1 Yên Bai Vietnam
114 B4 Yendi Ghana
111 C3 Yenice Turkey
111 C3 Yenifoça Turkey
68 C1 Yenisey *r.* Rus. Fed.
Yeotmal India *see* Yavatmal
53 C2 Yeoval Austr.
99 B4 Yeovil U.K.
51 E2 Yeppoon Austr.
Yeraliyev Kazakh. *see* Kuryk
83 I2 Yerbogachen Rus. Fed.
81 C1 Yerevan Armenia
77 D1 Yereymentau Kazakh.
Yermentau Kazakh. *see* Yereymentau
143 C3 Yermo Mex.
135 C4 Yermo U.S.A.
89 D3 Yershichi Rus. Fed.
87 D3 Yershov Rus. Fed.
150 B4 Yerupaja *mt.* Peru
Yerushalayim Israel/West Bank *see* Jerusalem
65 B2 Yesan S. Korea
77 C1 Yesil' Kazakh.
111 C3 Yeşilova Turkey
83 H2 Yessey Rus. Fed.
99 A4 Yes Tor *hill* U.K.
53 D1 Yetman Austr.
62 A1 Ye-U Myanmar
104 B2 Yeu, Île d' *i.* France
87 D4 Yevlax Azer.
91 C2 Yevpatoriya Ukr.
Yexian China *see* Laizhou
91 D2 Yeysk Rus. Fed.
88 C2 Yezyaryshcha Belarus
Y Fenni U.K. *see* Abergavenny
154 A2 Ygatimí Para.
71 A3 Yibin China
70 B2 Yichang China
69 E1 Yichun *Heilong.* China
71 B3 Yichun *Jiangxi* China
Yidu China *see* Qingzhou
66 A1 Yilan China
110 C2 Yıldız Dağları *mts* Turkey
80 B2 Yıldızeli Turkey
Yilong China *see* Shiping
70 A2 Yinchuan China
65 B1 Yingchengzi China
71 B3 Yingde China
70 C1 Yingkou China
70 B2 Yingshan *Hubei* China
70 A2 Yingshan *Sichuan* China
71 B3 Yingtan China
Yining China *see* Xiushui
77 E2 Yining China
62 A1 Yinmabin Myanmar
70 A1 Yin Shan *mts* China
117 B4 Yirga Alem Eth.
119 D2 Yirga Ch'efē Eth.
119 D2 Yirol Sudan
Yishan China *see* Yizhou
70 B2 Yishui China
62 A1 Yi Tu, Nam *r.* Myanmar
68 C2 Yiwu China
70 C1 Yixian China
70 B2 Yixing China
71 B3 Yiyang China
71 B3 Yizhang China
71 A3 Yizhou China
Yizhou China *see* Yixian
92 I2 Yli-Kitka *l.* Fin.
92 H2 Ylitornio Fin.
92 H3 Ylivieska Fin.
93 H3 Ylöjärvi Fin.
83 K2 Ynykchanskiy Rus. Fed.
Ynys Môn *i.* U.K. *see* Anglesey
61 C2 Yogyakarta Indon.
118 B2 Yokadouma Cameroon
118 B2 Yoko Cameroon
67 C3 Yokohama Japan
66 D3 Yokote Japan
115 D4 Yola Nigeria
67 D3 Yonezawa Japan
71 B3 Yong'an China
Yongbei China *see* Yongsheng
71 B3 Yongchun China
70 A2 Yongdeng China
65 B2 Yŏngdŏk S. Korea
65 B2 Yŏnghŭng N. Korea
Yongjing China *see* Xifeng
65 B2 Yŏngju S. Korea
71 C3 Yongkang China
Yongle China *see* Zhen'an
62 B1 Yongren China
62 B1 Yongsheng China
71 B3 Yongzhou China
139 E2 Yonkers U.S.A.
105 C2 Yonne *r.* France
150 B2 Yopal Col.
50 A3 York Austr.
98 C3 York U.K.
140 C2 York *AL* U.S.A.
137 D2 York *NE* U.S.A.
139 D3 York *PA* U.S.A.
51 D1 York, Cape Austr.
52 A3 Yorke Peninsula Austr.
52 A3 Yorketown Austr.
98 C3 Yorkshire Wolds *hills* U.K.
129 D2 Yorkton Can.
87 D3 Yoshkar-Ola Rus. Fed.
97 C3 Youghal Rep. of Ireland
53 C2 Young Austr.
52 A3 Younghusband Peninsula Austr.
138 C2 Youngstown U.S.A.
114 B3 Youvarou Mali
71 A3 Youyang China
77 E2 Youyi Feng *mt.* China/Rus. Fed.
80 B2 Yozgat Turkey
154 A2 Ypé-Jhú Para.
134 B2 Yreka U.S.A.
Yr Wyddfa *mt.* U.K. *see* Snowdon
59 D3 Ysabel Channel P.N.G.
105 C2 Yssingeaux France
93 F4 Ystad Sweden
Ysyk-Köl Kyrg. *see* Balykchy
77 D2 Ysyk-Köl *salt l.* Kyrg.
Y Trallwng U.K. *see* Welshpool
92 □A3 Ytri-Rangá *r.* Iceland
83 J2 Ytyk-Kyuyel' Rus. Fed.
71 A3 Yuanbao Shan *mt.* China
71 A3 Yuanjiang China
62 B1 Yuan Jiang *r.* China
71 B3 Yuanling China
71 A3 Yuanmou China
70 B2 Yuanping China
135 B3 Yuba City U.S.A.
66 D2 Yūbari Japan
145 C3 Yucatán *pen.* Mex.
146 B2 Yucatan Channel Cuba/Mex.
Yuci China *see* Jinzhong
50 C2 Yuendumu Austr.
71 C3 Yueqing China
71 B3 Yueyang China
86 F2 Yugorsk Rus. Fed.
Yugoslavia *country* Europe *see* Serbia and Montenegro
71 B3 Yujiang China
83 L2 Yukagirskoye Ploskogor'ye *plat.* Rus. Fed.
89 E3 Yukhnov Rus. Fed.
126 B2 Yukon *r.* Can./U.S.A.
143 D1 Yukon U.S.A.
128 A1 Yukon Territory *admin. div.* Can.
50 C2 Yulara Austr.
71 B3 Yulin *Guangxi* China
70 A2 Yulin *Shaanxi* China
62 B1 Yulong Xueshan *mt.* China
142 A2 Yuma *AZ* U.S.A.
136 C2 Yuma *CO* U.S.A.
135 D4 Yuma Desert U.S.A.
68 C2 Yumen China
80 B2 Yunak Turkey
70 B2 Yuncheng China
71 B3 Yunfu China
71 A3 Yungui Gaoyuan *plat.* China
Yunjinghong China *see* Jinghong
Yunling China *see* Yunxiao

71 A3 **Yunnan** *prov.* China
52 A2 **Yunta** Austr.
71 B3 **Yunxiao** China
70 B2 **Yunyang** China
71 A3 **Yuping** China
Yuping China *see* **Libo**
82 G3 **Yurga** Rus. Fed.
150 B3 **Yurimaguas** Peru
75 C1 **Yurungkax He** *r.* China
Yuryev Estonia *see* **Tartu**
71 C3 **Yü Shan** *mt.* Taiwan
70 B2 **Yushe** China
68 C2 **Yushu** China
Yushuwan China *see* **Huaihua**
81 C1 **Yusufeli** Turkey
75 C1 **Yutian** China
71 A3 **Yuxi** China
89 F2 **Yuzha** Rus. Fed.
66 D2 **Yuzhno-Kuril'sk** Rus. Fed.
83 K3 **Yuzhno-Sakhalinsk** Rus. Fed.
91 C2 **Yuzhnoukrayinsk** Ukr.
70 B2 **Yuzhou** China
Yuzovka Ukr. *see* **Donets'k**
105 D2 **Yverdon** Switz.
104 C2 **Yvetot** France

Z

100 B1 **Zaandam** Neth.
69 D1 **Zabaykal'sk** Rus. Fed.
119 C2 **Zabia** Dem. Rep. Congo
78 B3 **Zabīd** Yemen
79 D1 **Zābol** Iran
79 D2 **Zābolī** Iran
145 D3 **Zacapa** Guat.
144 B3 **Zacapu** Mex.
144 B2 **Zacatecas** Mex.
145 C3 **Zacatepec** Mex.
145 C3 **Zacatlán** Mex.
111 B3 **Zacharo** Greece
91 D2 **Zachepylivka** Ukr.
144 B2 **Zacoalco** Mex.
145 C2 **Zacualtipán** Mex.
109 C2 **Zadar** Croatia
63 A3 **Zadetkyi Kyun** *i.* Myanmar
89 E3 **Zadonsk** Rus. Fed.
80 B3 **Za'farānah** Egypt
106 B2 **Zafra** Spain
Zagazig Egypt *see* **Az Zaqāzīq**
114 B1 **Zagora** Morocco
Zagorsk Rus. Fed. *see* **Sergiyev Posad**
109 C1 **Zagreb** Croatia
Zagros, Kūhhā-ye Iran *see* **Zagros Mountains**
81 C2 **Zagros Mountains** *mts* Iran
79 D2 **Zāhedān** Iran
80 B2 **Zahlé** Lebanon
78 B3 **Zaḩrān** Saudi Arabia
Zaire *country* Africa *see* **Congo, Democratic Republic of**
109 D2 **Zaječar** Serb. and Mont.
121 C3 **Zaka** Zimbabwe
89 E3 **Zakharovo** Rus. Fed.
81 C2 **Zākhō** Iraq
86 C2 **Zakhrebetnoye** Rus. Fed.
111 B3 **Zakynthos** Greece
111 B3 **Zakynthos** *i.* Greece
103 D2 **Zalaegerszeg** Hungary
110 B1 **Zalău** Romania
78 B2 **Ẓalim** Saudi Arabia
116 A3 **Zalingei** Sudan
90 B2 **Zalishchyky** Ukr.
78 A2 **Zalmā, Jabal aẓ** *mt.* Saudi Arabia
128 C2 **Zama City** Can.
Zambeze *r.* Moz. *see* **Zambezi**
120 B2 **Zambezi** *r.* Africa
120 B2 **Zambezi** Zambia
120 B2 **Zambezi Escarpment** Zambia/Zimbabwe
120 B2 **Zambia** *country* Africa
64 B3 **Zamboanga** Phil.
64 B3 **Zamboanga Peninsula** Phil.
103 E1 **Zambrów** Pol.
106 B1 **Zamora** Spain
144 B3 **Zamora de Hidalgo** Mex.
103 E1 **Zamość** Pol.
Zamost'ye Pol. *see* **Zamość**
75 B1 **Zanda** China
100 B2 **Zandvliet** Belgium
100 B1 **Zandvoort** Neth.
138 C3 **Zanesville** U.S.A.
77 D3 **Zangguy** China
75 C1 **Zangsêr Kangri** *mt.* China
81 C2 **Zanjān** Iran
74 B1 **Zanskar Mountains** India
Zante *i.* Greece *see* **Zakynthos**
119 D3 **Zanzibar** Tanz.
119 D3 **Zanzibar Island** Tanz.
89 E3 **Zaokskiy** Rus. Fed.
115 C2 **Zaouatallaz** Alg.
Zaouet el Kahla Alg. *see* **Bordj Omer Driss**
70 B2 **Zaoyang** China
83 H3 **Zaozernyy** Rus. Fed.
70 B2 **Zaozhuang** China
89 D2 **Zapadnaya Dvina** *r.* Europe
89 D2 **Zapadnaya Dvina** Rus. Fed.
Zapadno-Sibirskaya Ravnina Rus. Fed. *see* **West Siberian Plain**
68 B1 **Zapadnyy Sayan** *reg.* Rus. Fed.
143 D3 **Zapata** U.S.A.
92 J2 **Zapolyarnyy** Rus. Fed.
91 D2 **Zaporizhzhya** Ukr.
101 E2 **Zappendorf** Ger.
81 C1 **Zaqatala** Azer.
Zara China *see* **Zadar**
80 B2 **Zara** Turkey
145 B2 **Zaragoza** Mex.
107 C1 **Zaragoza** Spain
79 C1 **Zarand** Iran
76 C3 **Zaranj** Afgh.
88 C2 **Zarasai** Lith.
89 E3 **Zaraysk** Rus. Fed.
150 C2 **Zaraza** Venez.
115 C3 **Zaria** Nigeria
90 B1 **Zarichne** Ukr.
81 D3 **Zarqān** Iran
66 B2 **Zarubino** Rus. Fed.
103 D1 **Żary** Pol.
115 D1 **Zarzis** Tunisia
88 C3 **Zaslawye** Belarus
123 C3 **Zastron** S. Africa
Zavitaya Rus. Fed. *see* **Zavitinsk**
69 E1 **Zavitinsk** Rus. Fed.
89 F2 **Zavolzhsk** Rus. Fed.
Zavolzh'ye Rus. Fed. *see* **Zavolzhsk**
103 D1 **Zawiercie** Pol.
115 E1 **Zāwiyat Masūs** Libya
77 E2 **Zaysan** Kazakh.
77 E2 **Zaysan, Lake** *l.* Kazakh.
Zaysan, Ozero Kazakh. *see* **Zaysan, Lake**
90 B2 **Zbarazh** Ukr.
90 B1 **Zdolbuniv** Ukr.
93 F4 **Zealand** *i.* Denmark
100 A2 **Zedelgem** Belgium
100 A2 **Zeebrugge** Belgium
123 C2 **Zeerust** S. Africa
101 F1 **Zehdenick** Ger.
50 C2 **Zeil, Mount** Austr.
101 F2 **Zeitz** Ger.
109 C2 **Zelena Gora** *mt.* Bos.-Herz.
87 D3 **Zelenodol'sk** Rus. Fed.
88 C1 **Zelenogorsk** Rus. Fed.
89 E2 **Zelenograd** Rus. Fed.
88 B3 **Zelenogradsk** Rus. Fed.
66 D2 **Zelenyy, Ostrov** *i.* Rus. Fed.
88 B3 **Zel'va** Belarus
119 C2 **Zémio** C.A.R.
107 D2 **Zemmora** Alg.
145 C3 **Zempoaltépetl, Nudo de** *mt.* Mex.
109 D2 **Zemun** Serb. and Mont.
65 B1 **Zengfeng Shan** *mt.* China
109 C2 **Zenica** Bos.-Herz.
107 D2 **Zenzach** Alg.
101 F2 **Zerbst** Ger.
105 D2 **Zermatt** Switz.
91 E2 **Zernograd** Rus. Fed.
Zernovoy Rus. Fed. *see* **Zernograd**
101 E2 **Zeulenroda** Ger.
101 D1 **Zeven** Ger.
100 C2 **Zevenaar** Neth.
100 B2 **Zevenbergen** Neth.
83 J3 **Zeya** Rus. Fed.
79 C2 **Zeydābād** Iran
79 C2 **Zeynalābād** Iran
83 J3 **Zeyskoye Vodokhranilishche** *resr* Rus. Fed.
103 D1 **Zgierz** Pol.
88 B3 **Zhabinka** Belarus
Zhabye Ukr. *see* **Verkhovyna**
Zhaksy Sarysu *watercourse* Kazakh. *see* **Sarysu**
76 A2 **Zhalpaktal** Kazakh.
77 C1 **Zhaltyr** Kazakh.
Zhambyl Kazakh. *see* **Taraz**
76 B2 **Zhanaozen** Kazakh.
Zhangaqazaly Kazakh. *see* **Ayteke Bi**
Zhangde China *see* **Anyang**
Zhangdian China *see* **Zibo**
66 A1 **Zhangguangcai Ling** *mts* China
71 B3 **Zhangjiajie** China
70 B1 **Zhangjiakou** China
71 B3 **Zhangping** China
71 B3 **Zhangshu** China
65 A1 **Zhangwu** China
70 A2 **Zhangxian** China
68 C2 **Zhangye** China
71 B3 **Zhangzhou** China
76 A2 **Zhanibek** Kazakh.
71 B3 **Zhanjiang** China
71 B3 **Zhao'an** China
69 E1 **Zhaodong** China
Zhaoge China *see* **Qixian**
71 B3 **Zhaoqing** China
71 A3 **Zhaotong** China
75 C1 **Zhari Namco** *salt l.* China
77 E2 **Zharkent** Kazakh.
89 D2 **Zharkovskiy** Rus. Fed.
77 E2 **Zharma** Kazakh.
90 C2 **Zhashkiv** Ukr.
Zhaxi China *see* **Weixin**
77 D2 **Zhayrem** Kazakh.
Zhdanov Ukr. *see* **Mariupol'**
71 C3 **Zhejiang** *prov.* China
82 F1 **Zhelaniya, Mys** *c.* Rus. Fed.
Zheleznodorozhnyy Rus. Fed. *see* **Yemva**
Zheleznodorozhnyy Uzbek. *see* **Qo'ng'irot**
89 E3 **Zheleznogorsk** Rus. Fed.
Zheltyye Vody Ukr. *see* **Zhovti Vody**
70 A2 **Zhen'an** China
70 A2 **Zhenba** China
71 A3 **Zheng'an** China
71 B3 **Zhenghe** China
70 B2 **Zhengzhou** China
Zhenjiang China *see* **Dantu**
71 A3 **Zhenyuan** China
91 E1 **Zherdevka** Rus. Fed.
86 D2 **Zheshart** Rus. Fed.
77 C2 **Zhezkazgan** Kazakh.
77 C2 **Zhezkazgan** Kazakh.
83 J2 **Zhigansk** Rus. Fed.
70 B2 **Zhijiang** China
76 C1 **Zhitikara** Kazakh.
89 D3 **Zhizdra** Rus. Fed.
88 D3 **Zhlobin** Belarus
90 B2 **Zhmerynka** Ukr.
74 A1 **Zhob** Pak.
88 C3 **Zhodzina** Belarus
83 L1 **Zhokhova, Ostrov** *i.* Rus. Fed.
Zholkva Ukr. *see* **Zhovkva**
Zhongba China *see* **Jiangyou**
75 C2 **Zhongba** China
Zhongduo China *see* **Youyang**
Zhonghe China *see* **Xiushan**
70 A2 **Zhongning** China
Zhongping China *see* **Huize**
71 B3 **Zhongshan** China
Zhongshan China *see* **Lupanshui**
70 A2 **Zhongwei** China
Zhongxin China *see* **Xianggelila**
70 B2 **Zhoukou** China
70 C2 **Zhoushan** China
90 A1 **Zhovkva** Ukr.
91 C2 **Zhovti Vody** Ukr.
65 A2 **Zhuanghe** China
70 B2 **Zhucheng** China
89 D3 **Zhukovka** Rus. Fed.
89 E2 **Zhukovskiy** Rus. Fed.
70 B2 **Zhumadian** China
Zhuoyang China *see* **Suiping**
71 B3 **Zhuzhou** *Hunan* China
71 B3 **Zhuzhou** *Hunan* China
90 A2 **Zhydachiv** Ukr.
88 C3 **Zhytkavichy** Belarus
90 B1 **Zhytomyr** Ukr.
103 D2 **Žiar nad Hronom** Slovakia
70 B2 **Zibo** China
103 D1 **Zielona Góra** Pol.
100 A2 **Zierikzee** Neth.
62 A1 **Zigaing** Myanmar
115 E2 **Zīghan** Libya
71 A3 **Zigong** China
Zigui China *see* **Guojiaba**
114 A3 **Ziguinchor** Senegal
144 B3 **Zihuatanejo** Mex.
103 D2 **Žilina** Slovakia
115 D2 **Zillah** Libya
83 H3 **Zima** Rus. Fed.
145 C2 **Zimapán** Mex.
121 B2 **Zimbabwe** *country* Africa
114 A4 **Zimmi** Sierra Leone
110 C2 **Zimnicea** Romania
86 C2 **Zimniy Bereg** *coastal area* Rus. Fed.
115 C3 **Zinder** Niger
78 B3 **Zinjibār** Yemen
91 C1 **Zin'kiv** Ukr.
Zinoyevsk Ukr. *see* **Kirovohrad**
150 B2 **Zipaquirá** Col.
103 D2 **Zirc** Hungary
75 D2 **Ziro** India
79 C2 **Zīr Rūd** Iran
103 D2 **Zistersdorf** Austria
145 B3 **Zitácuaro** Mex.
103 C1 **Zittau** Ger.
87 E3 **Zlatoust** Rus. Fed.
103 D2 **Zlín** Czech Rep.
115 D1 **Zlīṭan** Libya
103 D1 **Złotów** Pol.
89 D3 **Zlynka** Rus. Fed.
89 E3 **Zmiyevka** Rus. Fed.
91 D2 **Zmiyiv** Ukr.
89 E3 **Znamenka** Rus. Fed.
91 E1 **Znamenka** Rus. Fed.
91 C2 **Znam"yanka** Ukr.
103 D2 **Znojmo** Czech Rep.
122 B3 **Zoar** S. Africa
70 A2 **Zoigê** China
91 D1 **Zolochiv** Ukr.
90 A2 **Zolochiv** Ukr.
91 C2 **Zolotonosha** Ukr.
89 E3 **Zolotukhino** Rus. Fed.
121 C2 **Zomba** Malawi
118 B2 **Zongo** Dem. Rep. Congo
80 B1 **Zonguldak** Turkey
105 D3 **Zonza** *Corsica* France
114 B3 **Zorgho** Burkina
114 B4 **Zorzor** Liberia
115 D2 **Zouar** Chad
114 A2 **Zouérat** Maur.
109 D1 **Zrenjanin** Serb. and Mont.
89 D2 **Zubtsov** Rus. Fed.
105 D2 **Zug** Switz.
81 C1 **Zugdidi** Georgia
Zuider Zee *l.* Neth. *see* **IJsselmeer**
106 B2 **Zújar** *r.* Spain
100 C2 **Zülpich** Ger.
100 A2 **Zulte** Belgium
121 C2 **Zumbo** Moz.
145 C3 **Zumpango** Mex.
142 B1 **Zuni Mountains** U.S.A.
71 A3 **Zunyi** China
109 C1 **Županja** Croatia
105 D2 **Zürich** Switz.
105 D2 **Zürichsee** *l.* Switz.
100 C1 **Zutphen** Neth.
115 D1 **Zuwārah** Libya
90 C2 **Zvenyhorodka** Ukr.
121 C3 **Zvishavane** Zimbabwe
103 D2 **Zvolen** Slovakia
109 C2 **Zvornik** Bos.-Herz.
114 B4 **Zwedru** Liberia
123 C3 **Zwelitsha** S. Africa
103 D2 **Zwettl** Austria
101 F2 **Zwickau** Ger.
100 C1 **Zwolle** Neth.
83 L2 **Zyryanka** Rus. Fed.
77 E2 **Zyryanovsk** Kazakh.

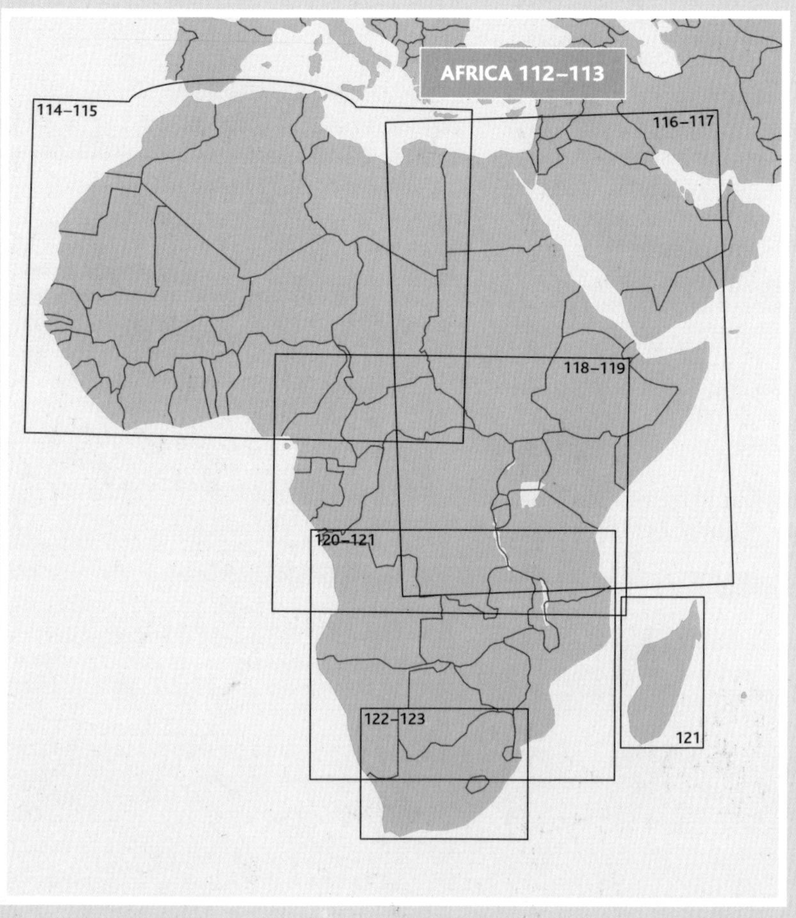

114–115

AFRICA 112–113

116–117

118–119

120–121

122–123

121